The Maastricht Collection (Sixth Edition)

Edited by Sascha Hardt & Nicole Kornet

Volume I: International and European Law

Europa Law Publishing is a publishing company specializing in European Union law, international trade law, public international law, environmental law and comparative national law.
For further information please contact Europa Law Publishing via email: info@europalawpublishing.com or visit our website at: www.europalawpublishing.com.

All rights reserved. No part of this publication may be reproduced or transmitted, in any form or by any means, or stored in any retrieval system of any nature, without the written permission of the publisher. Application for permission for use of copyright material shall be made to the publishers. Full acknowledgement of author, publisher and source must be given.

Voor zover het maken van kopieën uit deze uitgave is toegestaan op grond van artikel 16h t/m 16m Auteurswet 1912 *juncto* het Besluit van 27 november 2002, Stb. 575, dient men de daarvoor wettelijk verschuldigde vergoedingen te voldoen aan de Stichting Reprorecht (Postbus 3060, 2130 KB Hoofddorp). Voor het overnemen van (een) gedeelte(n) uit deze uitgave in bloemlezingen, readers en andere compilatiewerken (artikel 16 Auteurswet 1912) dient men zich tot de uitgever te wenden.

© Europa Law Publishing, S. Hardt, N. Kornet, 2019

Typeset in Scala and Scala Sans, Graphic design by G2K Designers, Groningen/Amsterdam

NUR 828
ISBN 9789089522115 (volumes I-IV)
ISBN 9789089522153 (volume I)
ISBN 9789089522160 (volume II)
ISBN 9789089522177 (volume III)
ISBN 9789089522146 (volume IV)

Preface to the sixth edition

The Faculty of Law of Maastricht University attaches great importance to the study of European and comparative law. Its curriculum includes several internationally oriented Master programmes and the *European Law School* bachelor programme, in which law is taught from a European and comparative perspective from the very first day. These four volumes, *The Maastricht Collection*, are based on the Maastricht Law Faculty's expertise and experience in teaching European, international, and comparative law.

The Maastricht Collection comprises a selection of legal instruments and provisions which have proven to be particularly relevant and useful to students and practitioners of European and comparative law. It includes constitutions, codes and statutory legislation from France, Germany, the Netherlands, and the United Kingdom, international treaties, and instruments of international organisations, as well as legal instruments of the European Union.

The content of the present sixth edition of *The Maastricht Collection* is divided into four volumes, corresponding to different areas of the law. Volume I contains selected international treaties and protocols, important resolutions of international organisations, international and European fundamental rights instruments, as well as the Treaties and selected secondary legislation of the European Union; Volume II contains national instruments from France, Germany, the Netherlands, and the United Kingdom in the areas of constitutional law (where the US constitution is also included as one of the standard points of reference of comparative constitutional law), administrative law, as well as criminal law and procedure; Volume III contains instruments from international and European private law, including international treaties and secondary EU legislation on international business law, private international law, European company law, European private law and civil procedure, as well as tax law; Volume IV contains national legislation from France, Germany, the Netherlands, and the United Kingdom in the area of private law and civil procedure.

Next to a comprehensive update and revision of all the instruments in *The Maastricht Collection*, this sixth edition also contains a number of useful additions, such as legislation relating to Brexit and statutory legislation from France, Germany, the Netherlands, and the United Kingdom in the area of criminal procedure. With these updates and additions, *The Maastricht Collection* now presents itself as an even more comprehensive resource for students of European, international, and comparative law.

While many of the materials included in these four volumes are reproduced in the original English, *The Maastricht Collection* remains true to its original aim of facilitating the study of comparative law by offering fresh translations of legal instruments from different national legal traditions. Many existing translations of written law, including officious translations available on government websites, are significantly out of date and not sufficiently faithful to the original. They often seek to turn old-fashioned or ambiguous original texts into modern and elegant English. Or, instead of translating, they seek to *explain* how certain terms or formulations are interpreted in practice. The translations contained in *The Maastricht Collection* remain true to the content, style, and syntax of the original as far as possible, allowing the reader to appreciate not only the substance but also the authentic form of legal sources.

Formatting styles, such as the use of §§ ('Paragraphs') rather than 'Articles' in most German statutes, and 'Sections' in UK legislation, or the absence of paragraph numbering in French legislation, are preserved. In the interest of consistency of style, the headings of individual articles are suppressed in translated materials. Enactment formulas are omitted; preambles are retained unless indicated otherwise. For easy reference within translated texts, key legal terms and proper names are added in the original language as in-text citations between square brackets.

The idea to create *The Maastricht Collection* came about during a conversation between Philipp Kiiver and Nicole Kornet about the need for English language learning resources for students following a programme on European and comparative law taught entirely in English. Just like students who follow a curriculum oriented on national law, these students also need a compilation of legislation relevant to their studies. Since the publication of the second edition, the editorship of the Maastricht Collection has since been continued by Sascha Hardt and Nicole Kornet. We are more than grateful to Philipp for being such a driving force behind the idea of *The Maastricht Collection*.

We would in particular like to thank Sarah Sørensen, a student of the *European Law School* and assistant to the editors, without whose meticulous hard work and dedication this edition of *The Maastricht Collection* and its publication in keeping with the regular two-year interval would not have been possible.

We would further like to thank the following people for their contributions and input to this and the previous editions: Dr. Bram Akkermans, Prof. Chris Backes, Dr. Anna Berlee, Stephanie Blom, Claire Boost, Caroline Calomme, Sylvain Caris, Prof. Fons Coomans, Merel Dekker, Prof. Mariolina Eliantonio, Prof. Sjef van Erp, Dr. Catalina Goanta, Dr. Franziska Grashof, Dr. Nicola Gundt, Prof. René de Groot, Heike Hauröder, Prof. Aalt-Willem Heringa, Dr. Sander Jansen, Prof. Anselm Kamperman Sanders, Prof. André Klip, Maartje Krabbe, Giesela Kristoferitsch, Prof. Raymond Luja, Prof. Gerrit van Maanen, Prof. Mieke Olaerts, Dr. Christina Peristeridou, Dr. Eveline Ramaekers, Dr. Stephan Rammeloo, Prof. Remco van Rhee, Dr. David Roef, Gereon Roetering, Dr. Kees Saarloos, Dr. René Seerden, Prof. Jan Smits, Prof. Taru Spronken, Dr. Ilse van den Driessche, Dr. Jacob van der Velde, Prof. Luc Verhey, Dr. Remme Verkerk, Yvonne Walhof, Dr. Stefan Weishaar, Dr. Daniëlle Wenders, Rob van de Westelaken, Irene Wieczorek and Prof. Jan Willems.

Maastricht, June 2019,

Dr. Sascha Hardt, Assistant Professor of Comparative Constitutional Law
Dr. Nicole Kornet, Senior Lecturer in Commercial Law and programme coordinator of the *European Law School*

CONTENTS

Preface to the sixth edition
Contents

VOLUME I: INTERNATIONAL AND EUROPEAN LAW

PART I **International Law**

Charter of the United Nations	2
Statute of the International Court of Justice	15
Convention on the Privileges and Immunities of the United Nations	22
United Nations and League of Nations Protocol No. I	26
Convention on the Rights and Duties of States (Montevideo Convention)	27
Draft Articles on Diplomatic Protection	29
Vienna Convention on Diplomatic Relations	32
Optional Protocol concerning the Compulsory Settlement of Disputes	40
United Nations Convention on the Law of the Sea (UNCLOS)	41
Vienna Convention on the Law of Treaties 1969	145
Vienna Convention on the Law of Treaties 1987 (International Organizations)	160
Draft Articles on Responsibility of States for Internationally Wrongful Acts	179
UN General Assembly Resolution A/RES/56/83 on the responsibility of States for internationally wrongful acts	186
Rome Statute of the International Criminal Court	193
Amendments to the Rome Statute of the ICC (Crime of Aggression; Elements of Crimes)	233
Elements of Crimes	237
General Agreement on Tariffs and Trade 1947	259
General Agreement on Tariffs and Trade 1994	296
Agreement Establishing the World Trade Organization	298
UN General Assembly Resolution A/RES/377 (V) "Uniting for Peace",	304
UN General Assembly Resolution A/RES/3314 (XXIX) "Definition of Aggression"	307
UN Security Council Resolution S/RES/660 (1990) "Iraq/Kuwait"	309
UN Security Council Resolution S/RES/661 (1990) "Iraq Sanctions"	310
UN Security Council Resolution S/RES/678 (1990) "Iraq/Kuwait/all necessary means"	312

UN Security Council Resolution S/RES/687 (1991) "Iraq/Kuwait"	313
UN Security Council Resolution S/RES/688 (1991) "Iraq/Kurdish population"	318
UN Security Council Resolution S/RES/794 (1992) "Somalia"	319
UN Security Council Resolution S/RES/836 (1993) "Bosnia Safe Areas"	321
UN Security Council Resolution S/RES/929 (1994) "Rwanda"	323
UN Security Council Resolution S/RES/940 (1994) "Haiti"	325
UN Security Council Resolution S/RES/1199 (1998) "Kosovo"	327
UN Security Council Resolution S/RES/1203 (1998) "Kosovo"	330
UN Security Council Resolution S/RES/1244 (1999) "Kosovo"	332
UN Security Council Resolution S/RES/1325 (2001) "Women and Security"	336
UN Security Council Resolution S/RES/1441 (2002) "Iraq"	338
UN Security Council Resolution S/RES/1540 (2004) "Weapons of Mass Destruction"	343
UN Security Council Resolution S/RES/1851 (2008) "Somalia"	345
UN Security Council Resolution S/RES/1970 (2011) "Peace and Security in Africa"	348
UN Security Council Resolution S/RES/1973 (2011) "Situation in Libya"	354
UN General Assembly Resolution A/RES/68/262 (2014) "Territorial integrity Ukraine"	359
UN Security Council Resolution S/RES/1368 (2001)	360
UN Security Council Resolution S/RES/1373 (2001)	361

PART II Fundamental Rights

Universal Declaration of Human Rights	364
Convention relating to the Status of Refugees	367
Protocol relating to the Status of Refugees	375
International Convention on the Elimination of All Forms of Racial Discrimination (ICERD)	377
International Covenant on Economic, Social and Cultural Rights (ICESCR)	384

Optional Protocol to the (ICESCR)	389
International Covenant on Civil and Political Rights (ICCPR)	394
Optional Protocol to the ICCPR	404
Second Optional Protocol to the ICCPR (Abolition of the Death Penalty)	406
Convention on the Elimination of all Forms of Discrimination against Women (CEDAW)	408
Optional Protocol to the CEDAW	415
Convention against Torture and Other Cruel, Inhuman or Degrading Treatment or Punishment (CAT)	418
Optional Protocol to the CAT	425
Declaration on the Right to Development	432
Convention on the Rights of the Child (CRC)	435
Optional Protocol to the CRC on the sale of children, child prostitution and child pornography	445
UN General Assembly Resolution A/RES/60/251 on the Human Rights Council	450
Human Rights Council Resolution A/HRC/RES/5/1 on Institution-building	453
UN Convention on the Rights of Persons with Disabilities (CRPD)	467
Optional Protocol to the CRPD	481
European Convention for the Protection of Human Rights and Fundamental Freedoms (ECHR)	483
Protocols to the ECHR	491
Rules of Court of the European Court of Human Rights,	496
European Convention for the Prevention of Torture and Inhuman or Degrading Treatment or Punishment (CPT)	512
European Social Charter	516
Additional Protocol to the European Social Charter Providing for a System of Collective Complaints	531
Charter of Fundamental Rights of the European Union	534

PART III European Union

Treaty on European Union	542
Tables of equivalences (TEU)	559
Treaty on the Functioning of the European Union	563
Protocols to the Treaties	635
Annexes to the Treaties	693
Declarations attached to the Treaties	695
Tables of Equivalences (TEU)	708
Rules of Procedure of the Court of Justice	720

Recommendations to National Courts and Tribunals, in
Relation to the Initiation of Preliminary Ruling Proceedings 756
Commission Directive 70/50/EEC 761
Commission practice note on import prohibitions 764
Council Regulation (EC) No 2679/98 766
Council Directive 77/249/EEC 768
Directive 96/71/EC 770
Directive 98/5/EC 776
Council Directive 2003/86/EC 783
Council Directive 2003/109/EC 790
Directive 2004/38/EC 800
Directive 2005/36/EC 813
Directive 2006/123/EC 843
Regulation (EU) No 492/2011 874
Commission Regulation (EU) No 1407/2013 881
Commission Regulation (EU) No 651/2014 888
Commission Decision (EU) 2015/1584 942
Regulation No 17: First Regulation implementing
Articles 85 and 86 of the Treaty 943
Commission Notice 'De Minimis' (2014/C 291/01) 949
Commission Notice on the definition of relevant market
for the purposes of Community competition law
(97/C 372/03) 951
Council Regulation (EC) No 1/2003 959
Council Regulation (EC) No 139/2004 976
Commission Regulation (EC) No 773/2004 995
Commission Regulation (EU) No 330/2010 1001
Commission notice – Guidelines on the effect on trade
concept contained in Articles 81 and 82 of the Treaty
(OJ C 101, 27.4.2004) 1006
Commission Notice on Immunity from fines and
reduction of fines in cartel cases (2006/C 298/11) 1008

International Law

PART I INTERNATIONAL LAW

Charter of the United Nations, San Francisco, 24 June 1945 (entry into force. 24 October 1945), Trb. 1979 Nr. 37

We the peoples of the United Nations determined
to save succeeding generations from the scourge of war, which twice in our lifetime has brought untold sorrow to mankind, and
to reaffirm faith in fundamental human rights, in the dignity and worth of the human person, in the equal rights of men and women and of nations large and small, and
to establish conditions under which justice and respect for the obligations arising from treaties and other sources of international law can be maintained, and
to promote social progress and better standards of life in larger freedom,
And for these ends
to practice tolerance and live together in peace with one another as good neighbours, and
to unite our strength to maintain international peace and security, and
to ensure, by the acceptance of principles and the institution of methods, that armed force shall not be used, save in the common interest, and
to employ international machinery for the promotion of the economic and social advancement of all peoples,
Have resolved to combine our efforts to accomplish these aims.
Accordingly, our respective Governments, through representatives assembled in the city of San Francisco, who have exhibited their full powers found to be in good and due form, have agreed to the present Charter of the United Nations and do hereby establish an international organization to be known as the United Nations.

Chapter I. Purposes and Principles

Article 1. The Purposes of the United Nations are:
(1) To maintain international peace and security, and to that end: to take effective collective measures for the prevention and removal of threats to the peace, and for the suppression of acts of aggression or other breaches of the peace, and to bring about by peaceful means, and in conformity with the principles of justice and international law, adjustment or settlement of international disputes or situations which might lead to a breach of the peace;
(2) To develop friendly relations among nations based on respect for the principle of equal rights and self-determination of peoples, and to take other appropriate measures to strengthen universal peace;
(3) To achieve international co-operation in solving international problems of an economic, social, cultural, or humanitarian character, and in promoting and encouraging respect for human rights and for fundamental freedoms for all without distinction as to race, sex, language, or religion; and
(4) To be a centre for harmonizing the actions of nations in the attainment of these common ends.

Article 2. The Organization and its Members, in pursuit of the Purposes stated in Article 1, shall act in accordance with the following Principles.
(1) The Organization is based on the principle of the sovereign equality of all its Members.
(2) All Members, in order to ensure to all of them the rights and benefits resulting from membership, shall fulfil in good faith the obligations assumed by them in accordance with the present Charter.
(3) All Members shall settle their international disputes by peaceful means in such a manner that international peace and security, and justice, are not endangered.
(4) All Members shall refrain in their international relations from the threat or use of force against the territorial integrity or political independence of any state, or in any other manner inconsistent with the Purposes of the United Nations.
(5) All Members shall give the United Nations every assistance in any action it takes in accordance with the present Charter, and shall refrain from giving assistance to any state against which the United Nations is taking preventive or enforcement action.
(6) The Organization shall ensure that states which are not Members of the United Nations act in accordance with these Principles so far as may be necessary for the maintenance of international peace and security.
(7) Nothing contained in the present Charter shall authorize the United Nations to intervene in matters which are essentially within the domestic jurisdiction of any state or shall require the Members to submit such matters to settlement under the present Charter; but this principle shall not prejudice the application of enforcement measures under Chapter VII.

Chapter II. Membership

Article 3. The original Members of the United Nations shall be the states which, having participated in the United Nations Conference on International Organization at San Francisco, or having previously signed the Declaration by United Nations of 1 January 1942, sign the present Charter and ratify it in accordance with Article 110.

Article 4. (1) Membership in the United Nations is open to all other peace-loving states which accept the obligations contained in the present Charter and, in the judgment of the Organization, are able and willing to carry out these obligations.
(2) The admission of any such state to membership in the United Nations will be effected by a decision of the General Assembly upon the recommendation of the Security Council.

Article 5. A Member of the United Nations against which preventive or enforcement action has been taken by the Security Council may be suspended from the exercise of the rights and privileges of membership by the General Assembly upon the recommendation of the Security Council. The exercise of these rights and privileges may be restored by the Security Council.

Article 6. A Member of the United Nations which has persistently violated the Principles contained in the present Charter may be expelled from the Organization by the General Assembly upon the recommendation of the Security Council.

Chapter III. Organs

Article 7. (1) There are established as principal organs of the United Nations: a General Assembly, a Security Council, an Economic and Social Council, a Trusteeship Council, an International Court of Justice and a Secretariat.
(2) Such subsidiary organs as may be found necessary may be established in accordance with the present Charter.

Article 8. The United Nations shall place no restrictions on the eligibility of men and women to participate in any capacity and under conditions of equality in its principal and subsidiary organs.

Chapter IV. General Assembly

Composition

Article 9. (1) The General Assembly shall consist of all the Members of the United Nations. (2) Each Member shall have not more than five representatives in the General Assembly.

Functions and Powers

Article 10. The General Assembly may discuss any questions or any matters within the scope of the present Charter or relating to the powers and functions of any organs provided for in the present Charter, and, except as provided in Article 12, may make recommendations to the Members of the United Nations or to the Security Council or to both on any such questions or matters.

Article 11. (1) The General Assembly may consider the general principles of co-operation in the maintenance of international peace and security, including the principles governing disarmament and the regulation of armaments, and may make recommendations with regard to such principles to the Members or to the Security Council or to both.
(2) The General Assembly may discuss any questions relating to the maintenance of international peace and security brought before it by any Member of the United Nations, or by the Security Council, or by a state which is not a Member of the United Nations in accordance with Article 35(2), and, except as provided in Article 12, may make recommendations with regard to any such questions to the state or states concerned or to the Security Council or to both. Any such question on which action is necessary shall be referred to the Security Council by the General Assembly either before or after discussion.
(3) The General Assembly may call the attention of the Security Council to situations which are likely to endanger international peace and security.
(4) The powers of the General Assembly set forth in this Article shall not limit the general scope of Article 10.

Article 12. (1) While the Security Council is exercising in respect of any dispute or situation the functions assigned to it in the present Charter, the General Assembly shall not make any recommendation with regard to that dispute or situation unless the Security Council so requests.
(2)The Secretary-General, with the consent of the Security Council, shall notify the General Assem-

bly at each session of any matters relative to the maintenance of international peace and security which are being dealt with by the Security Council and shall similarly notify the General Assembly, or the Members of the United Nations if the General Assembly is not in session, immediately the Security Council ceases to deal with such matters.

Article 13. (1) The General Assembly shall initiate studies and make recommendations for the purpose of:
(a) promoting international co-operation in the political field and encouraging the progressive development of international law and its codification;
(b) promoting international co-operation in the economic, social, cultural, educational, and health fields, and assisting in the realization of human rights and fundamental freedoms for all without distinction as to race, sex, language, or religion.
(c) The further responsibilities, functions and powers of the General Assembly with respect to matters mentioned in paragraph (1) (b) above are set forth in Chapters IX and X.

Article 14. Subject to the provisions of Article 12, the General Assembly may recommend measures for the peaceful adjustment of any situation, regardless of origin, which it deems likely to impair the general welfare or friendly relations among nations, including situations resulting from a violation of the provisions of the present Charter setting forth the Purposes and Principles of the United Nations.

Article 15. (1) The General Assembly shall receive and consider annual and special reports from the Security Council; these reports shall include an account of the measures that the Security Council has decided upon or taken to maintain international peace and security.
(2) The General Assembly shall receive and consider reports from the other organs of the United Nations.

Article 16. The General Assembly shall perform such functions with respect to the international trusteeship system as are assigned to it under Chapters XII and XIII, including the approval of the trusteeship agreements for areas not designated as strategic.

Article 17. (1) The General Assembly shall consider and approve the budget of the Organization.
(2) The expenses of the Organization shall be borne by the Members as apportioned by the General Assembly.
(3) The General Assembly shall consider and approve any financial and budgetary arrangements with specialized agencies referred to in Article 57 and shall examine the administrative budgets of such specialized agencies with a view to making recommendations to the agencies concerned.

Voting

Article 18. (1) Each member of the General Assembly shall have one vote.
(2) Decisions of the General Assembly on important questions shall be made by a two-thirds majority of the members present and voting. These questions shall include: recommendations with respect to the maintenance of international peace and security, the election of the non-permanent members of the Security Council, the election of the members of the Economic and Social Council, the election of members of the Trusteeship Council in accordance with paragraph (1) (c) of Article 86, the admission of new Members to the United Nations, the suspension of the rights and privileges of membership, the expulsion of Members, questions relating to the operation of the trusteeship system, and budgetary questions.
(3)Decisions on other questions, including the determination of additional categories of questions to be decided by a two-thirds majority, shall be made by a majority of the members present and voting.

Article 19. A Member of the United Nations which is in arrears in the payment of its financial contributions to the Organization shall have no vote in the General Assembly if the amount of its arrears equals or exceeds the amount of the contributions due from it for the preceding two full years. The General Assembly may, nevertheless, permit such a Member to vote if it is satisfied that the failure to pay is due to conditions beyond the control of the Member.

Procedure

Article 20. The General Assembly shall meet in regular annual sessions and in such special sessions as occasion may require. Special sessions shall be convoked by the Secretary-General at the request of the Security Council or of a majority of the Members of the United Nations.

Article 21. The General Assembly shall adopt its own rules of procedure. It shall elect its President for each session.

Article 22. The General Assembly may establish such subsidiary organs as it deems necessary for the performance of its functions.

Chapter V. The Security Council

Composition

Article 23. (1) The Security Council shall consist of fifteen Members of the United Nations. The Republic of China, France, the Union of Soviet Socialist Republics, the United Kingdom of Great Britain and Northern Ireland, and the United States of America shall be permanent members of the Security Council. The General Assembly shall elect ten other Members of the United Nations to be non-permanent members of the Security Council, due regard being specially paid, in the first instance to the contribution of Members of the United Nations to the maintenance of international peace and security and to the other purposes of the Organization, and also to equitable geographical distribution.
(2) The non-permanent members of the Security Council shall be elected for a term of two years. In the first election of the non-permanent members after the increase of the membership of the Security Council from eleven to fifteen, two of the four additional members shall be chosen for a term of one year. A retiring member shall not be eligible for immediate re-election.
(3) Each member of the Security Council shall have one representative.

Functions and Powers

Article 24. (1) In order to ensure prompt and effective action by the United Nations, its Members confer on the Security Council primary responsibility for the maintenance of international peace and security, and agree that in carrying out its duties under this responsibility the Security Council acts on their behalf.
(2) In discharging these duties the Security Council shall act in accordance with the Purposes and Principles of the United Nations. The specific powers granted to the Security Council for the discharge of these duties are laid down in Chapters VI, VII, VIII, and XII.
(3) The Security Council shall submit annual and, when necessary, special reports to the General Assembly for its consideration.

Article 25. The Members of the United Nations agree to accept and carry out the decisions of the Security Council in accordance with the present Charter.

Article 26. In order to promote the establishment and maintenance of international peace and security with the least diversion for armaments of the world's human and economic resources, the Security Council shall be responsible for formulating, with the assistance of the Military Staff Committee referred to in Article 47, plans to be submitted to the Members of the United Nations for the establishment of a system for the regulation of armaments.

Voting

Article 27. (1) Each member of the Security Council shall have one vote.
(2) Decisions of the Security Council on procedural matters shall be made by an affirmative vote of nine members.
(3) Decisions of the Security Council on all other matters shall be made by an affirmative vote of nine members including the concurring votes of the permanent members; provided that, in decisions under Chapter VI, and under paragraph (3) of Article 52, a party to a dispute shall abstain from voting.

Procedure

Article 28. (1) The Security Council shall be so organized as to be able to function continuously. Each member of the Security Council shall for this purpose be represented at all times at the seat of the Organization.
(2) The Security Council shall hold periodic meetings at which each of its members may, if it so desires, be represented by a member of the government or by some other specially designated representative.
(3) The Security Council may hold meetings at such places other than the seat of the Organization as in its judgment will best facilitate its work.

Article 29. The Security Council may establish such subsidiary organs as it deems necessary for the performance of its functions.

Article 30. The Security Council shall adopt its own rules of procedure, including the method of selecting its President.

PART I   INTERNATIONAL LAW

Article 31. Any Member of the United Nations which is not a member of the Security Council may participate, without vote, in the discussion of any question brought before the Security Council whenever the latter considers that the interests of that Member are specially affected.

Article 32. Any Member of the United Nations which is not a member of the Security Council or any state which is not a Member of the United Nations, if it is a party to a dispute under consideration by the Security Council, shall be invited to participate, without vote, in the discussion relating to the dispute. The Security Council shall lay down such conditions as it deems just for the participation of a state which is not a Member of the United Nations.

Chapter VI. Pacific settlement of disputes

Article 33. (1) The parties to any dispute, the continuance of which is likely to endanger the maintenance of international peace and security, shall, first of all, seek a solution by negotiation, enquiry, mediation, conciliation, arbitration, judicial settlement, resort to regional agencies or arrangements, or other peaceful means of their own choice.
(2) The Security Council shall, when it deems necessary, call upon the parties to settle their dispute by such means.

Article 34. The Security Council may investigate any dispute, or any situation which might lead to international friction or give rise to a dispute, in order to determine whether the continuance of the dispute or situation is likely to endanger the maintenance of international peace and security.

Article 35. (1) Any Member of the United Nations may bring any dispute, or any situation of the nature referred to in Article 34, to the attention of the Security Council or of the General Assembly.
(2) A state which is not a Member of the United Nations may bring to the attention of the Security Council or of the General Assembly any dispute to which it is a party if it accepts in advance, for the purposes of the dispute, the obligations of pacific settlement provided in the present Charter.
(3) The proceedings of the General Assembly in respect of matters brought to its attention under this Article will be subject to the provisions of Articles 11 and 12.

Article 36. (1) The Security Council may, at any stage of a dispute of the nature referred to in Article 33 or of a situation of like nature, recommend appropriate procedures or methods of adjustment.
(2) The Security Council should take into consideration any procedures for the settlement of the dispute which have already been adopted by the parties.
(3) In making recommendations under this Article the Security Council should also take into consideration that legal disputes should as a general rule be referred by the parties to the International Court of Justice in accordance with the provisions of the Statute of the Court.

Article 37. (1) Should the parties to a dispute of the nature referred to in Article 33 fail to settle it by the means indicated in that Article, they shall refer it to the Security Council.
(2) If the Security Council deems that the continuance of the dispute is in fact likely to endanger the maintenance of international peace and security, it shall decide whether to take action under Article 36 or to recommend such terms of settlement as it may consider appropriate.

Article 38. Without prejudice to the provisions of Articles 33 to 37, the Security Council may, if all the parties to any dispute so request, make recommendations to the parties with a view to a pacific settlement of the dispute.

Chapter VII. Actions with respect to threats to the peace, breaches of the peace and acts of aggression

Article 39. The Security Council shall determine the existence of any threat to the peace, breach of the peace, or act of aggression and shall make recommendations, or decide what measures shall be taken in accordance with Articles 41 and 42, to maintain or restore international peace and security.

Article 40. In order to prevent an aggravation of the situation, the Security Council may, before making the recommendations or deciding upon the measures provided for in Article 39, call upon the parties concerned to comply with such provisional measures as it deems necessary or desirable. Such provisional measures shall be without prejudice to the rights, claims, or position of the parties concerned. The Security Council shall duly take account of failure to comply with such provisional measures.

Article 41. The Security Council may decide what measures not involving the use of armed force are to be employed to give effect to its decisions, and it may call upon the Members of the United

Nations to apply such measures. These may include complete or partial interruption of economic relations and of rail, sea, air, postal, telegraphic, radio, and other means of communication, and the severance of diplomatic relations.

Article 42. Should the Security Council consider that measures provided for in Article 41 would be inadequate or have proved to be inadequate, it may take such action by air, sea, or land forces as may be necessary to maintain or restore international peace and security. Such action may include demonstrations, blockade, and other operations by air, sea, or land forces of Members of the United Nations.

Article 43. (1) All Members of the United Nations, in order to contribute to the maintenance of international peace and security, undertake to make available to the Security Council, on its call and in accordance with a special agreement or agreements, armed forces, assistance, and facilities, including rights of passage, necessary for the purpose of maintaining international peace and security.
(2) Such agreement or agreements shall govern the numbers and types of forces, their degree of readiness and general location, and the nature of the facilities and assistance to be provided.
(3) The agreement or agreements shall be negotiated as soon as possible on the initiative of the Security Council. They shall be concluded between the Security Council and Members or between the Security Council and groups of Members and shall be subject to ratification by the signatory states in accordance with their respective constitutional processes.

Article 44. When the Security Council has decided to use force it shall, before calling upon a Member not represented on it to provide armed forces in fulfilment of the obligations assumed under Article 43, invite that Member, if the Member so desires, to participate in the decisions of the Security Council concerning the employment of contingents of that Member's armed forces.

Article 45. In order to enable the United Nations to take urgent military measures, Members shall hold immediately available national air-force contingents for combined international enforcement action. The strength and degree of readiness of these contingents and plans for their combined action shall be determined within the limits laid down in the special agreement or agreements referred to in Article 43, by the Security Council with the assistance of the Military Staff Committee.

Article 46. Plans for the application of armed force shall be made by the Security Council with the assistance of the Military Staff Committee.

Article 47. (1) There shall be established a Military Staff Committee to advise and assist the Security Council on all questions relating to the Security Council's military requirements for the maintenance of international peace and security, the employment and command of forces placed at its disposal, the regulation of armaments, and possible disarmament.
(2) The Military Staff Committee shall consist of the Chiefs of Staff of the permanent members of the Security Council or their representatives. Any Member of the United Nations not permanently represented on the Committee shall be invited by the Committee to be associated with it when the efficient discharge of the Committee's responsibilities requires the participation of that Member in its work.
(3) The Military Staff Committee shall be responsible under the Security Council for the strategic direction of any armed forces placed at the disposal of the Security Council. Questions relating to the command of such forces shall be worked out subsequently.
(4) The Military Staff Committee, with the authorization of the Security Council and after consultation with appropriate regional agencies, may establish regional sub-committees.

Article 48. (1) The action required to carry out the decisions of the Security Council for the maintenance of international peace and security shall be taken by all the Members of the United Nations or by some of them, as the Security Council may determine.
(2) Such decisions shall be carried out by the Members of the United Nations directly and through their action in the appropriate international agencies of which they are members.

Article 49. The Members of the United Nations shall join in affording mutual assistance in carrying out the measures decided upon by the Security Council.

Article 50. If preventive or enforcement measures against any state are taken by the Security Council, any other state, whether a Member of the United Nations or not, which finds itself confronted with special economic problems arising from the carrying out of those measures shall have the right to consult the Security Council with regard to a solution of those problems.

Article 51. Nothing in the present Charter shall impair the inherent right of individual or collective self-defence if an armed attack occurs against a Member of the United Nations, until the Security

Council has taken measures necessary to maintain international peace and security. Measures taken by Members in the exercise of this right of self-defence shall be immediately reported to the Security Council and shall not in any way affect the authority and responsibility of the Security Council under the present Charter to take at any time such action as it deems necessary in order to maintain or restore international peace and security.

Chapter VIII. Regional arrangements

Article 52. (1) Nothing in the present Charter precludes the existence of regional arrangements or agencies for dealing with such matters relating to the maintenance of international peace and security as are appropriate for regional action provided that such arrangements or agencies and their activities are consistent with the Purposes and Principles of the United Nations.
(2) The Members of the United Nations entering into such arrangements or constituting such agencies shall make every effort to achieve pacific settlement of local disputes through such regional arrangements or by such regional agencies before referring them to the Security Council.
(3) The Security Council shall encourage the development of pacific settlement of local disputes through such regional arrangements or by such regional agencies either on the initiative of the states concerned or by reference from the Security Council.
(4) This Article in no way impairs the application of Articles 34 and 35.

Article 53. (1) The Security Council shall, where appropriate, utilize such regional arrangements or agencies for enforcement action under its authority. But no enforcement action shall be taken under regional arrangements or by regional agencies without the authorization of the Security Council, with the exception of measures against any enemy state, as defined in paragraph (2) of this Article, provided for pursuant to Article 107 or in regional arrangements directed against renewal of aggressive policy on the part of any such state, until such time as the Organization may, on request of the Governments concerned, be charged with the responsibility for preventing further aggression by such a state.
(2) The term enemy state as used in paragraph (1) of this Article applies to any state which during the Second World War has been an enemy of any signatory of the present Charter.

Article 54. The Security Council shall at all times be kept fully informed of activities undertaken or in contemplation under regional arrangements or by regional agencies for the maintenance of international peace and security.

Chapter IX. International economic and social co-operation

Article 55. With a view to the creation of conditions of stability and well-being which are necessary for peaceful and friendly relations among nations based on respect for the principle of equal rights and self-determination of peoples, the United Nations shall promote:
(a) higher standards of living, full employment, and conditions of economic and social progress and development;
(b) solutions of international economic, social, health, and related problems; and international cultural and educational cooperation; and
(c) universal respect for, and observance of, human rights and fundamental freedoms for all without distinction as to race, sex, language, or religion.

Article 56. All Members pledge themselves to take joint and separate action in co-operation with the Organization for the achievement of the purposes set forth in Article 55.

Article 57. (1) The various specialized agencies, established by intergovernmental agreement and having wide international responsibilities, as defined in their basic instruments, in economic, social, cultural, educational, health, and related fields, shall be brought into relationship with the United Nations in accordance with the provisions of Article 63.
(2) Such agencies thus brought into relationship with the United Nations are hereinafter referred to as specialized agencies.

Article 58. The Organization shall make recommendations for the co-ordination of the policies and activities of the specialized agencies.

Article 59. The Organization shall, where appropriate, initiate negotiations among the states concerned for the creation of any new specialized agencies required for the accomplishment of the purposes set forth in Article 55.

Article 60. Responsibility for the discharge of the functions of the Organization set forth in this Chapter shall be vested in the General Assembly and, under the authority of the General Assembly, in the Economic and Social Council, which shall have for this purpose the powers set forth in Chapter X.

Chapter X. The Economic and Social Council

Composition

Article 61. (1) The Economic and Social Council shall consist of fifty-four Members of the United Nations elected by the General Assembly.
(2) Subject to the provisions of paragraph 3, eighteen members of the Economic and Social Council shall be elected each year for a term of three years. A retiring member shall be eligible for immediate re-election.
(3) At the first election after the increase in the membership of the Economic and Social Council from twenty-seven to fifty-four members, in addition to the members elected in place of the nine members whose term of office expires at the end of that year, twenty-seven additional members shall be elected. Of these twenty-seven additional members, the term of office of nine members so elected shall expire at the end of one year, and of nine other members at the end of two years, in accordance with arrangements made by the General Assembly.
(4) Each member of the Economic and Social Council shall have one representative.

Functions and powers

Article 62. (1) The Economic and Social Council may make or initiate studies and reports with respect to international economic, social, cultural, educational, health, and related matters and may make recommendations with respect to any such matters to the General Assembly to the Members of the United Nations, and to the specialized agencies concerned.
(2) It may make recommendations for the purpose of promoting respect for, and observance of, human rights and fundamental freedoms for all.
(3) It may prepare draft conventions for submission to the General Assembly, with respect to matters falling within its competence.
(4) It may call, in accordance with the rules prescribed by the United Nations, international conferences on matters falling within its competence.

Article 63. (1) The Economic and Social Council may enter into agreements with any of the agencies referred to in Article 57, defining the terms on which the agency concerned shall be brought into relationship with the United Nations. Such agreements shall be subject to approval by the General Assembly.
(2) It may co-ordinate the activities of the specialized agencies through consultation with and recommendations to such agencies and through recommendations to the General Assembly and to the Members of the United Nations.

Article 64. (1) The Economic and Social Council may take appropriate steps to obtain regular reports from the specialized agencies. It may make arrangements with the Members of the United Nations and with the specialized agencies to obtain reports on the steps taken to give effect to its own recommendations and to recommendations on matters falling within its competence made by the General Assembly.
(2) It may communicate its observations on these reports to the General Assembly.

Article 65. The Economic and Social Council may furnish information to the Security Council and shall assist the Security Council upon its request.

Article 66. (1) The Economic and Social Council shall perform such functions as fall within its competence in connection with the carrying out of the recommendations of the General Assembly.
(2) It may, with the approval of the General Assembly, perform services at the request of Members of the United Nations and at the request of specialized agencies.
(3) It shall perform such other functions as are specified elsewhere in the present Charter or as may be assigned to it by the General Assembly.

Voting

Article 67. (1) Each member of the Economic and Social Council shall have one vote.
(2) Decisions of the Economic and Social Council shall be made by a majority of the members present and voting.

PART I   INTERNATIONAL LAW

Procedure

Article 68. The Economic and Social Council shall set up commissions in economic and social fields and for the promotion of human rights, and such other commissions as may be required for the performance of its functions.

Article 69. The Economic and Social Council shall invite any Member of the United Nations to participate, without vote, in its deliberations on any matter of particular concern to that Member.

Article 70. The Economic and Social Council may make arrangements for representatives of the specialized agencies to participate, without vote, in its deliberations and in those of the commissions established by it, and for its representatives to participate in the deliberations of the specialized agencies.

Article 71. The Economic and Social Council may make suitable arrangements for consultation with non-governmental organizations which are concerned with matters within its competence. Such arrangements may be made with international organizations and, where appropriate, with national organizations after consultation with the Member of the United Nations concerned.

Article 72. (1) The Economic and Social Council shall adopt its own rules of procedure, including the method of selecting its President.
(2) The Economic and Social Council shall meet as required in accordance with its rules, which shall include provision for the convening of meetings on the request of a majority of its members.

Chapter XI. Declaration regarding non-self-governing territories

Article 73. Members of the United Nations which have or assume responsibilities for the administration of territories whose peoples have not yet attained a full measure of self-government recognize the principle that the interests of the inhabitants of these territories are paramount, and accept as a sacred trust the obligation to promote to the utmost, within the system of international peace and security established by the present Charter, the well-being of the inhabitants of these territories, and, to this end:
(a) to ensure, with due respect for the culture of the peoples concerned, their political, economic, social, and educational advancement, their just treatment, and their protection against abuses;
(b) to develop self-government, to take due account of the political aspirations of the peoples, and to assist them in the progressive development of their free political institutions, according to the particular circumstances of each territory and its peoples and their varying stages of advancement;
(c) to further international peace and security;
(d) to promote constructive measures of development, to encourage research, and to co-operate with one another and, when and where appropriate, with specialized international bodies with a view to the practical achievement of the social, economic, and scientific purposes set forth in this Article; and
(e) to transmit regularly to the Secretary-General for information purposes, subject to such limitation as security and constitutional considerations may require, statistical and other information of a technical nature relating to economic, social, and educational conditions in the territories for which they are respectively responsible other than those territories to which Chapters XII and XIII apply.

Article 74. Members of the United Nations also agree that their policy in respect of the territories to which this Chapter applies, no less than in respect of their metropolitan areas, must be based on the general principle of good-neighbourliness, due account being taken of the interests and well-being of the rest of the world, in social, economic, and commercial matters.

Chapter XII. International trusteeship system

Article 75. The United Nations shall establish under its authority an international trusteeship system for the administration and supervision of such territories as may be placed thereunder by subsequent individual agreements. These territories are hereinafter referred to as trust territories.

Article 76. The basic objectives of the trusteeship system, in accordance with the Purposes of the United Nations laid down in Article 1 of the present Charter, shall be:
(a) to further international peace and security;
(b) to promote the political, economic, social, and educational advancement of the inhabitants of the trust territories, and their progressive development towards self-government or independence as may be appropriate to the particular circumstances of each territory and its peoples and the freely expressed wishes of the peoples concerned, and as may be provided by the terms of each trusteeship agreement;

(c) to encourage respect for human rights and for fundamental freedoms for all without distinction as to race, sex, language, or religion, and to encourage recognition of the interdependence of the peoples of the world; and
(d) to ensure equal treatment in social, economic, and commercial matters for all Members of the United Nations and their nationals, and also equal treatment for the latter in the administration of justice, without prejudice to the attainment of the foregoing objectives and subject to the provisions of Article 80.

Article 77. (1) The trusteeship system shall apply to such territories in the following categories as may be placed thereunder by means of trusteeship agreements:
(a) territories now held under mandate;
(b) territories which may be detached from enemy states as a result of the Second World War; and
(c) territories voluntarily placed under the system by states responsible for their administration.
(2) It will be a matter for subsequent agreement as to which territories in the foregoing categories will be brought under the trusteeship system and upon what terms.

Article 78. The trusteeship system shall not apply to territories which have become Members of the United Nations, relationship among which shall be based on respect for the principle of sovereign equality.

Article 79. The terms of trusteeship for each territory to be placed under the trusteeship system, including any alteration or amendment, shall be agreed upon by the states directly concerned, including the mandatory power in the case of territories held under mandate by a Member of the United Nations, and shall be approved as provided for in Articles 83 and 85.

Article 80. (1) Except as may be agreed upon in individual trusteeship agreements, made under Articles 77, 79, and 81, placing each territory under the trusteeship system, and until such agreements have been concluded, nothing in this Chapter shall be construed in or of itself to alter in any manner the rights whatsoever of any states or any peoples or the terms of existing international instruments to which Members of the United Nations may respectively be parties.
(2) Paragraph (1) of this Article shall not be interpreted as giving grounds for delay or postponement of the negotiation and conclusion of agreements for placing mandated and other territories under the trusteeship system as provided for in Article 77.

Article 81. The trusteeship agreement shall in each case include the terms under which the trust territory will be administered and designate the authority which will exercise the administration of the trust territory. Such authority, hereinafter called the administering authority, may be one or more states or the Organization itself.

Article 82. There may be designated, in any trusteeship agreement, a strategic area or areas which may include part or all of the trust territory to which the agreement applies, without prejudice to any special agreement or agreements made under Article 43.

Article 83. (1) All functions of the United Nations relating to strategic areas, including the approval of the terms of the trusteeship agreements and of their alteration or amendment shall be exercised by the Security Council.
(2) The basic objectives set forth in Article 76 shall be applicable to the people of each strategic area.
(3) The Security Council shall, subject to the provisions of the trusteeship agreements and without prejudice to security considerations, avail itself of the assistance of the Trusteeship Council to perform those functions of the United Nations under the trusteeship system relating to political, economic, social, and educational matters in the strategic areas.

Article 84. It shall be the duty of the administering authority to ensure that the trust territory shall play its part in the maintenance of international peace and security. To this end the administering authority may make use of volunteer forces, facilities, and assistance from the trust territory in carrying out the obligations towards the Security Council undertaken in this regard by the administering authority, as well as for local defence and the maintenance of law and order within the trust territory.

Article 85. (1) The functions of the United Nations with regard to trusteeship agreements for all areas not designated as strategic, including the approval of the terms of the trusteeship agreements and of their alteration or amendment, shall be exercised by the General Assembly.
(2) The Trusteeship Council, operating under the authority of the General Assembly shall assist the General Assembly in carrying out these functions.

PART I INTERNATIONAL LAW

Chapter XIII. The Trusteeship Council

Composition

Article 86. (1) The Trusteeship Council shall consist of the following Members of the United Nations:
(a) those Members administering trust territories;
(b) such of those Members mentioned by name in Article 23 as are not administering trust territories; and
(c) as many other Members elected for three-year terms by the General Assembly as may be necessary to ensure that the total number of members of the Trusteeship Council is equally divided between those Members of the United Nations which administer trust territories and those which do not.
(2) Each member of the Trusteeship Council shall designate one specially qualified person to represent it therein.

Functions and powers

Article 87. The General Assembly and, under its authority, the Trusteeship Council, in carrying out their functions, may:
(a) consider reports submitted by the administering authority;
(b) accept petitions and examine them in consultation with the administering authority;
(c) provide for periodic visits to the respective trust territories at times agreed upon with the administering authority; and
(d) take these and other actions in conformity with the terms of the trusteeship agreements.

Article 88. The Trusteeship Council shall formulate a questionnaire on the political, economic, social, and educational advancement of the inhabitants of each trust territory, and the administering authority for each trust territory within the competence of the General Assembly shall make an annual report to the General Assembly upon the basis of such questionnaire.

Voting

Article 89. (1) Each member of the Trusteeship Council shall have one vote.
(2) Decisions of the Trusteeship Council shall be made by a majority of the members present and voting.

Procedure

Article 90. (1) The Trusteeship Council shall adopt its own rules of procedure, including the method of selecting its President.
(2) The Trusteeship Council shall meet as required in accordance with its rules, which shall include provision for the convening of meetings on the request of a majority of its members.

Article 91. The Trusteeship Council shall, when appropriate, avail itself of the assistance of the Economic and Social Council and of the specialized agencies in regard to matters with which they are respectively concerned.

Chapter XIV. The International Court of Justice

Article 92. The International Court of Justice shall be the principal judicial organ of the United Nations. It shall function in accordance with the annexed Statute, which is based upon the Statute of the Permanent Court of International Justice and forms an integral part of the present Charter.

Article 93. (1) All Members of the United Nations are ipso facto parties to the Statute of the International Court of Justice.
(2) A state which is not a Member of the United Nations may become a party to the Statute of the International Court of Justice on conditions to be determined in each case by the General Assembly upon the recommendation of the Security Council.

Article 94. (1) Each Member of the United Nations undertakes to comply with the decision of the International Court of Justice in any case to which it is a party.
(2) If any party to a case fails to perform the obligations incumbent upon it under a judgment rendered by the Court, the other party may have recourse to the Security Council, which may, if it deems necessary, make recommendations or decide upon measures to be taken to give effect to the judgment.

Article 95. Nothing in the present Charter shall prevent Members of the United Nations from entrusting the solution of their differences to other tribunals by virtue of agreements already in existence or which may be concluded in the future.

Article 96. (1) The General Assembly or the Security Council may request the International Court of Justice to give an advisory opinion on any legal question.
(2) Other organs of the United Nations and specialized agencies, which may at any time be so authorized by the General Assembly, may also request advisory opinions of the Court on legal questions arising within the scope of their activities.

Chapter XV. The Secretariat

Article 97. The Secretariat shall comprise a Secretary-General and such staff as the Organization may require. The Secretary-General shall be appointed by the General Assembly upon the recommendation of the Security Council. He shall be the chief administrative officer of the Organization.

Article 98. The Secretary-General shall act in that capacity in all meetings of the General Assembly, of the Security Council, of the Economic and Social Council, and of the Trusteeship Council, and shall perform such other functions as are entrusted to him by these organs. The Secretary-General shall make an annual report to the General Assembly on the work of the Organization.

Article 99. The Secretary-General may bring to the attention of the Security Council any matter which in his opinion may threaten the maintenance of international peace and security.

Article 100. (1) In the performance of their duties the Secretary-General and the staff shall not seek or receive instructions from any government or from any other authority external to the Organization. They shall refrain from any action which might reflect on their position as international officials responsible only to the Organization.
(2) Each Member of the United Nations undertakes to respect the exclusively international character of the responsibilities of the Secretary-General and the staff and not to seek to influence them in the discharge of their responsibilities.

Article 101. (1) The staff shall be appointed by the Secretary-General under regulations established by the General Assembly.
(2) Appropriate staffs shall be permanently assigned to the Economic and Social Council, the Trusteeship Council, and, as required, to other organs of the United Nations. These staffs shall form a part of the Secretariat.
(3) The paramount consideration in the employment of the staff and in the determination of the conditions of service shall be the necessity of securing the highest standards of efficiency, competence, and integrity. Due regard shall be paid to the importance of recruiting the staff on as wide a geographical basis as possible.

Chapter XVI. Miscellaneous Provisions

Article 102. (1) Every treaty and every international agreement entered into by any Member of the United Nations after the present Charter comes into force shall as soon as possible be registered with the Secretariat and published by it.
(2) No party to any such treaty or international agreement which has not been registered in accordance with the provisions of paragraph (1) of this Article may invoke that treaty or agreement before any organ of the United Nations.

Article 103. In the event of a conflict between the obligations of the Members of the United Nations under the present Charter and their obligations under any other international agreement, their obligations under the present Charter shall prevail.

Article 104. The Organization shall enjoy in the territory of each of its Members such legal capacity as may be necessary for the exercise of its functions and the fulfilment of its purposes.

Article 105. (1) The Organization shall enjoy in the territory of each of its Members such privileges and immunities as are necessary for the fulfilment of its purposes.
(2) Representatives of the Members of the United Nations and officials of the Organization shall similarly enjoy such privileges and immunities as are necessary for the independent exercise of their functions in connexion with the Organization.
(3) The General Assembly may make recommendations with a view to determining the details of the application of paragraphs (1) and (2) of this Article or may propose conventions to the Members of the United Nations for this purpose.

Chapter XVII. Transitional security arrangements

Article 106. Pending the coming into force of such special agreements referred to in Article 43 as in the opinion of the Security Council enable it to begin the exercise of its responsibilities under Article 42, the parties to the Four-Nation Declaration, signed at Moscow, 30 October 1943, and France, shall, in accordance with the provisions of paragraph (5) of that Declaration, consult with one another and as occasion requires with other Members of the United Nations with a view to such joint action on behalf of the Organization as may be necessary for the purpose of maintaining international peace and security.

Article 107. Nothing in the present Charter shall invalidate or preclude action, in relation to any state which during the Second World War has been an enemy of any signatory to the present Charter, taken or authorized as a result of that war by the Governments having responsibility for such action.

Chapter VIII. Amendments

Article 108. Amendments to the present Charter shall come into force for all Members of the United Nations when they have been adopted by a vote of two thirds of the members of the General Assembly and ratified in accordance with their respective constitutional processes by two thirds of the Members of the United Nations, including all the permanent members of the Security Council.

Article 109. (1) A General Conference of the Members of the United Nations for the purpose of reviewing the present Charter may be held at a date and place to be fixed by a two-thirds vote of the members of the General Assembly and by a vote of any nine members of the Security Council. Each Member of the United Nations shall have one vote in the conference.
(2) Any alteration of the present Charter recommended by a two-thirds vote of the conference shall take effect when ratified in accordance with their respective constitutional processes by two thirds of the Members of the United Nations including all the permanent members of the Security Council.
(3) If such a conference has not been held before the tenth annual session of the General Assembly following the coming into force of the present Charter, the proposal to call such a conference shall be placed on the agenda of that session of the General Assembly, and the conference shall be held if so decided by a majority vote of the members of the General Assembly and by a vote of any seven members of the Security Council.

Chapter XIX. Ratification and signature

Article 110. (1) The present Charter shall be ratified by the signatory states in accordance with their respective constitutional processes.
(2) The ratifications shall be deposited with the Government of the United States of America, which shall notify all the signatory states of each deposit as well as the Secretary-General of the Organization when he has been appointed.
(3) The present Charter shall come into force upon the deposit of ratifications by the Republic of China, France, the Union of Soviet Socialist Republics, the United Kingdom of Great Britain and Northern Ireland, and the United States of America, and by a majority of the other signatory states. A protocol of the ratifications deposited shall thereupon be drawn up by the Government of the United States of America which shall communicate copies thereof to all the signatory states.
(4) The states signatory to the present Charter which ratify it after it has come into force will become original Members of the United Nations on the date of the deposit of their respective ratifications.

Article 111. The present Charter, of which the Chinese, French, Russian, English, and Spanish texts are equally authentic, shall remain deposited in the archives of the Government of the United States of America. Duly certified copies thereof shall be transmitted by that Government to the Governments of the other signatory states.

Statute of the International Court of Justice, Trb. 1971 Nr. 55

Article 1. The International Court of Justice established by the Charter of the United Nations as the principal judicial organ of the United Nations shall be constituted and shall function in accordance with the provisions of the present Statute.

Chapter I. Organization of the Court

Article 2. The Court shall be composed of a body of independent judges, elected regardless of their nationality from among persons of high moral character, who possess the qualifications required in their respective countries for appointment to the highest judicial offices, or are jurisconsults of recognized competence in international law.

Article 3. (1) The Court shall consist of fifteen members, no two of whom may be nationals of the same state.
(2) A person who for the purposes of membership in the Court could be regarded as a national of more than one state shall be deemed to be a national of the one in which he ordinarily exercises civil and political rights.

Article 4. (1) The members of the Court shall be elected by the General Assembly and by the Security Council from a list of persons nominated by the national groups in the Permanent Court of Arbitration, in accordance with the following provisions.
(2) In the case of Members of the United Nations not represented in the Permanent Court of Arbitration, candidates shall be nominated by national groups appointed for this purpose by their governments under the same conditions as those prescribed for members of the Permanent Court of Arbitration by Article 44 of the Convention of The Hague of 1907 for the pacific settlement of international disputes.
(3) The conditions under which a state which is a party to the present Statute but is not a Member of the United Nations may participate in electing the members of the Court shall, in the absence of a special agreement, be laid down by the General Assembly upon recommendation of the Security Council.

Article 5. (1) At least three months before the date of the election, the Secretary-General of the United Nations shall address a written request to the members of the Permanent Court of Arbitration belonging to the states which are parties to the present Statute, and to the members of the national groups appointed under Article 4, paragraph (2), inviting them to undertake, within a given time, by national groups, the nomination of persons in a position to accept the duties of a member of the Court.
(2) No group may nominate more than four persons, not more than two of whom shall be of their own nationality. In no case may the number of candidates nominated by a group be more than double the number of seats to be filled.

Article 6. Before making these nominations, each national group is recommended to consult its highest court of justice, its legal faculties and schools of law, and its national academies and national sections of international academies devoted to the study of law.

Article 7. (1) The Secretary-General shall prepare a list in alphabetical order of all the persons thus nominated. Save as provided in Article 12, paragraph (2), these shall be the only persons eligible.
(2) The Secretary-General shall submit this list to the General Assembly and to the Security Council.

Article 8. The General Assembly and the Security Council shall proceed independently of one another to elect the members of the Court.

Article 9. At every election, the electors shall bear in mind not only that the persons to be elected should individually possess the qualifications required, but also that in the body as a whole the representation of the main forms of civilization and of the principal legal systems of the world should be assured.

Article 10. (1) Those candidates who obtain an absolute majority of votes in the General Assembly and in the Security Council shall be considered as elected.
(2) Any vote of the Security Council, whether for the election of judges or for the appointment of members of the conference envisaged in Article 12, shall be taken without any distinction between permanent and non-permanent members of the Security Council.

PART I   INTERNATIONAL LAW

(3) In the event of more than one national of the same state obtaining an absolute majority of the votes both of the General Assembly and of the Security Council, the eldest of these only shall be considered as elected.

Article 11. If, after the first meeting held for the purpose of the election, one or more seats remain to be filled, a second and, if necessary, a third meeting shall take place.

Article 12. (1) If, after the third meeting, one or more seats still remain unfilled, a joint conference consisting of six members, three appointed by the General Assembly and three by the Security Council, may be formed at any time at the request of either the General Assembly or the Security Council, for the purpose of choosing by the vote of an absolute majority one name for each seat still vacant, to submit to the General Assembly and the Security Council for their respective acceptance.
(2) If the joint conference is unanimously agreed upon any person who fulfills the required conditions, he may be included in its list, even though he was not included in the list of nominations referred to in Article 7.
(3) If the joint conference is satisfied that it will not be successful in procuring an election, those members of the Court who have already been elected shall, within a period to be fixed by the Security Council, proceed to fill the vacant seats by selection from among those candidates who have obtained votes either in the General Assembly or in the Security Council.
(4) In the event of an equality of votes among the judges, the eldest judge shall have a casting vote.

Article 13. (1) The members of the Court shall be elected for nine years and may be re-elected; provided, however, that of the judges elected at the first election, the terms of five judges shall expire at the end of three years and the terms of five more judges shall expire at the end of six years.
(2) The judges whose terms are to expire at the end of the above-mentioned initial periods of three and six years shall be chosen by lot to be drawn by the Secretary-General immediately after the first election has been completed.
(3) The members of the Court shall continue to discharge their duties until their places have been filled. Though replaced, they shall finish any cases which they may have begun.
(4) In the case of the resignation of a member of the Court, the resignation shall be addressed to the President of the Court for transmission to the Secretary-General. This last notification makes the place vacant.

Article 14. Vacancies shall be filled by the same method as that laid down for the first election subject to the following provision: the Secretary-General shall, within one month of the occurrence of the vacancy, proceed to issue the invitations provided for in Article 5, and the date of the election shall be fixed by the Security Council.

Article 15. A member of the Court elected to replace a member whose term of office has not expired shall hold office for the remainder of his predecessor's term.

Article 16. (1) No member of the Court may exercise any political or administrative function, or engage in any other occupation of a professional nature.
(2) Any doubt on this point shall be settled by the decision of the Court.

Article 17. (1) No member of the Court may act as agent, counsel, or advocate in any case.
(2) No member may participate in the decision of any case in which he has previously taken part as agent, counsel, or advocate for one of the parties, or as a member of a national or international court, or of a commission of enquiry, or in any other capacity.
(3) Any doubt on this point shall be settled by the decision of the Court.

Article 18. (1) No member of the Court can be dismissed unless, in the unanimous opinion of the other members, he has ceased to fulfil the required conditions.
(2) Formal notification thereof shall be made to the Secretary-General by the Registrar.
(3) This notification makes the place vacant.

Article 19. The members of the Court, when engaged on the business of the Court, shall enjoy diplomatic privileges and immunities.

Article 20. Every member of the Court shall, before taking up his duties, make a solemn declaration in open court that he will exercise his powers impartially and conscientiously.

Article 21. (1) The Court shall elect its President and Vice-President for three years; they may be re-elected.

(2) The Court shall appoint its Registrar and may provide for the appointment of such other officers as may be necessary.

Article 22. (1) The seat of the Court shall be established at The Hague. This, however, shall not prevent the Court from sitting and exercising its functions elsewhere whenever the Court considers it desirable.
(2) The President and the Registrar shall reside at the seat of the Court.

Article 23. (1) The Court shall remain permanently in session, except during the judicial vacations, the dates and duration of which shall be fixed by the Court.
(2) Members of the Court are entitled to periodic leave, the dates and duration of which shall be fixed by the Court, having in mind the distance between The Hague and the home of each judge.
(3) Members of the Court shall be bound, unless they are on leave or prevented from attending by illness or other serious reasons duly explained to the President, to hold themselves permanently at the disposal of the Court.

Article 24. (1) If, for some special reason, a member of the Court considers that he should not take part in the decision of a particular case, he shall so inform the President.
(2) If the President considers that for some special reason one of the members of the Court should not sit in a particular case, he shall give him notice accordingly.
(3) If in any such case the member Court and the President disagree, the matter shall be settled by the decision of the Court.

Article 25. (1) The full Court shall sit except when it is expressly provided otherwise in the present Statute.
(2) Subject to the condition that the number of judges available to constitute the Court is not thereby reduced below eleven, the Rules of the Court may provide for allowing one or more judges, according to circumstances and in rotation, to be dispensed from sitting.
(3) A quorum of nine judges shall suffice to constitute the Court.

Article 26. (1) The Court may from time to time form one or more chambers, composed of three or more judges as the Court may determine, for dealing with particular categories of cases; for example, labour cases and cases relating to transit and communications.
(2) The Court may at any time form a chamber for dealing with a particular case. The number of judges to constitute such a chamber shall be determined by the Court with the approval of the parties.
(3) Cases shall be heard and determined by the chambers provided for in this article if the parties so request.

Article 27. A judgment given by any of the chambers provided for in Articles 26 and 29 shall be considered as rendered by the Court.

Article 28. The chambers provided for in Articles 26 and 29 may, with the consent of the parties, sit and exercise their functions elsewhere than at The Hague.

Article 29. With a view to the speedy dispatch of business, the Court shall form annually a chamber composed of five judges which, at the request of the parties, may hear and determine cases by summary procedure. In addition, two judges shall be selected for the purpose of replacing judges who find it impossible to sit.

Article 30. (1) The Court shall frame rules for carrying out its functions. In particular, it shall lay down rules of procedure.
(2) The Rules of the Court may provide for assessors to sit with the Court or with any of its chambers, without the right to vote.

Article 31 (1) Judges of the nationality of each of the parties shall retain their right to sit in the case before the Court.
(2) If the Court includes upon the Bench a judge of the nationality of one of the parties, any other party may choose a person to sit as judge. Such person shall be chosen preferably from among those persons who have been nominated as candidates as provided in Articles 4 and 5.
(3) If the Court includes upon the Bench no judge of the nationality of the parties, each of these parties may proceed to choose a judge as provided in paragraph (2) of this Article.
(4) The provisions of this Article shall apply to the case of Articles 26 and 29. In such cases, the President shall request one or, if necessary, two of the members of the Court forming the chamber to give place to the members of the Court of the nationality of the parties concerned, and, failing such,

or if they are unable to be present, to the judges specially chosen by the parties.
(5) Should there be several parties in the same interest, they shall, for the purpose of the preceding provisions, be reckoned as one party only. Any doubt upon this point shall be settled by the decision of the Court.
(6) Judges chosen as laid down in paragraphs (2), (3), and (4) of this Article shall fulfil the conditions required by Articles 2, 17 (paragraph (2)), 20, and 24 of the present Statute. They shall take part in the decision on terms of complete equality with their colleagues.

Article 32. (1) Each member of the Court shall receive an annual salary.
(2) The President shall receive a special annual allowance.
(3) The Vice-President shall receive a special allowance for every day on which he acts as President.
(4) The judges chosen under Article 31, other than members of the Court, shall receive compensation for each day on which they exercise their functions.
(5) These salaries, allowances, and compensation shall be fixed by the General Assembly. They may not be decreased during the term of office.
(6) The salary of the Registrar shall be fixed by the General Assembly on the proposal of the Court.
(7) Regulations made by the General Assembly shall fix the conditions under which retirement pensions may be given to members of the Court and to the Registrar, and the conditions under which members of the Court and the Registrar shall have their travelling expenses refunded.
(8) The above salaries, allowances, and compensation shall be free of all taxation.

Article 33. The expenses of the Court shall be borne by the United Nations in such a manner as shall be decided by the General Assembly.

Chapter II. Competence of the Court

Article 34. (1) Only states may be parties in cases before the Court.
(2) The Court, subject to and in conformity with its Rules, may request of public international organizations information relevant to cases before it, and shall receive such information presented by such organizations on their own initiative.
(3) Whenever the construction of the constituent instrument of a public international organization or of an international convention adopted thereunder is in question in a case before the Court, the Registrar shall so notify the public international organization concerned and shall communicate to it copies of all the written proceedings.

Article 35. (1) The Court shall be open to the states parties to the present Statute.
(2) The conditions under which the Court shall be open to other states shall, subject to the special provisions contained in treaties in force, be laid down by the Security Council, but in no case shall such conditions place the parties in a position of inequality before the Court.
(3) When a state which is not a Member of the United Nations is a party to a case, the Court shall fix the amount which that party is to contribute towards the expenses of the Court. This provision shall not apply if such state is bearing a share of the expenses of the Court

Article 36. (1) The jurisdiction of the Court comprises all cases which the parties refer to it and all matters specially provided for in the Charter of the United Nations or in treaties and conventions in force.
(2) The states parties to the present Statute may at any time declare that they recognize as compulsory ipso facto and without special agreement, in relation to any other state accepting the same obligation, the jurisdiction of the Court in all legal disputes concerning:
(a) the interpretation of a treaty;
(b) any question of international law;
(c) the existence of any fact which, if established, would constitute a breach of an international obligation;
(d) the nature or extent of the reparation to be made for the breach of an international obligation.
(3) The declarations referred to above may be made unconditionally or on condition of reciprocity on the part of several or certain states, or for a certain time.
(4) Such declarations shall be deposited with the Secretary-General of the United Nations, who shall transmit copies thereof to the parties to the Statute and to the Registrar of the Court.
(5) Declarations made under Article 36 of the Statute of the Permanent Court of International Justice and which are still in force shall be deemed, as between the parties to the present Statute, to be acceptances of the compulsory jurisdiction of the International Court of Justice for the period which they still have to run and in accordance with their terms.

(6) In the event of a dispute as to whether the Court has jurisdiction, the matter shall be settled by the decision of the Court.

Article 37. Whenever a treaty or convention in force provides for reference of a matter to a tribunal to have been instituted by the League of Nations, or to the Permanent Court of International Justice, the matter shall, as between the parties to the present Statute, be referred to the International Court of Justice.

Article 38. (1) The Court, whose function is to decide in accordance with international law such disputes as are submitted to it, shall apply:
(a) international conventions, whether general or particular, establishing rules expressly recognized by the contesting states;
(b) international custom, as evidence of a general practice accepted as law;
(c) the general principles of law recognized by civilized nations;
(d) subject to the provisions of Article 59, judicial decisions and the teachings of the most highly qualified publicists of the various nations, as subsidiary means for the determination of rules of law.
(2) This provision shall not prejudice the power of the Court to decide a case ex aequo et bono, if the parties agree thereto.

Chapter III. Procedure

Article 39. (1) The official languages of the Court shall be French and English. If the parties agree that the case shall be conducted in French, the judgment shall be delivered in French. If the parties agree that the case shall be conducted in English, the judgment shall be delivered in English.
(2) In the absence of an agreement as to which language shall be employed, each party may, in the pleadings, use the language which it prefers; the decision of the Court shall be given in French and English. In this case the Court shall at the same time determine which of the two texts shall be considered as authoritative.
(3) The Court shall, at the request of any party, authorize a language other than French or English to be used by that party.

Article 40. (1) Cases are brought before the Court, as the case may be, either by the notification of the special agreement or by a written application addressed to the Registrar. In either case the subject of the dispute and the parties shall be indicated.
(2) The Registrar shall forthwith communicate the application to all concerned.
(3) He shall also notify the Members of the United Nations through the Secretary-General, and also any other states entitled to appear before the Court.

Article 41. (1) The Court shall have the power to indicate, if it considers that circumstances so require, any provisional measures which ought to be taken to preserve the respective rights of either party.
(2) Pending the final decision, notice of the measures suggested shall forthwith be given to the parties and to the Security Council

Article 42. (1) The parties shall be represented by agents.
(2) They may have the assistance of counsel or advocates before the Court.
(3) The agents, counsel, and advocates of parties before the Court shall enjoy the privileges and immunities necessary to the independent exercise of their duties.

Article 43. (1) The procedure shall consist of two parts: written and oral.
(2) The written proceedings shall consist of the communication to the Court and to the parties of memorials, counter-memorials and, if necessary, replies; also all papers and documents in support.
(3) These communications shall be made through the Registrar, in the order and within the time fixed by the Court.
(4) A certified copy of every document produced by one party shall be communicated to the other party.
(5) The oral proceedings shall consist of the hearing by the Court of witnesses, experts, agents, counsel, and advocates.

Article 44. (1) For the service of all notices upon persons other than the agents, counsel, and advocates, the Court shall apply direct to the government of the state upon whose territory the notice has to be served.
(2) The same provision shall apply whenever steps are to be taken to procure evidence on the spot.

Article 45. The hearing shall be under the control of the President or, if he is unable to preside, of the Vice-President; if neither is able to preside, the senior judge present shall preside.

Article 46. The hearing in Court shall be public, unless the Court shall decide otherwise, or unless the parties demand that the public be not admitted.

Article 47. (1) Minutes shall be made at each hearing and signed by the Registrar and the President.
(2) These minutes alone shall be authentic.

Article 48. The Court shall make orders for the conduct of the case, shall decide the form and time in which each party must conclude its arguments, and make all arrangements connected with the taking of evidence.

Article 49. The Court may, even before the hearing begins, call upon the agents to produce any document or to supply any explanations. Formal note shall be taken of any refusal.

Article 50. The Court may, at any time, entrust any individual, body, bureau, commission, or other organization that it may select, with the task of carrying out an enquiry or giving an expert opinion.

Article 51. During the hearing any relevant questions are to be put to the witnesses and experts under the conditions laid down by the Court in the rules of procedure referred to in Article 30.

Article 52. After the Court has received the proofs and evidence within the time specified for the purpose, it may refuse to accept any further oral or written evidence that one party may desire to present unless the other side consents.

Article 53. (1) Whenever one of the parties does not appear before the Court, or fails to defend its case, the other party may call upon the Court to decide in favour of its claim.
(2) The Court must, before doing so, satisfy itself, not only that it has jurisdiction in accordance with Articles 36 and 37, but also that the claim is well founded in fact and law.

Article 54. (1) When, subject to the control of the Court, the agents, counsel, and advocates have completed their presentation of the case, the President shall declare the hearing closed.
(2) The Court shall withdraw to consider the judgment.
(3) The deliberations of the Court shall take place in private and remain secret.

Article 55. (1) All questions shall be decided by a majority of the judges present.
(2) In the event of an equality of votes, the President or the judge who acts in his place shall have a casting vote.

Article 57. If the judgment does not represent in whole or in part the unanimous opinion of the judges, any judge shall be entitled to deliver a separate opinion.

Article 58. The judgment shall be signed by the President and by the Registrar. It shall be read in open court, due notice having been given to the agents.

Article 59. The decision of the Court has no binding force except between the parties and in respect of that particular case.

Article 60. The judgment is final and without appeal. In the event of dispute as to the meaning or scope of the judgment, the Court shall construe it upon the request of any party.

Article 61. (1) An application for revision of a judgment may be made only when it is based upon the discovery of some fact of such a nature as to be a decisive factor, which fact was, when the judgment was given, unknown to the Court and also to the party claiming revision, always provided that such ignorance was not due to negligence.
(2) The proceedings for revision shall be opened by a judgment of the Court expressly recording the existence of the new fact, recognizing that it has such a character as to lay the case open to revision, and declaring the application admissible on this ground.
(3) The Court may require previous compliance with the terms of the judgment before it admits proceedings in revision.
(4) The application for revision must be made at latest within six months of the discovery of the new fact.
(5) No application for revision may be made after the lapse of ten years from the date of the judgment.

Article 62. (1) Should a state consider that it has an interest of a legal nature which may be affected by the decision in the case, it may submit a request to the Court to be permitted to intervene.
(2) It shall be for the Court to decide upon this request.

Article 63. (1) Whenever the construction of a convention to which states other than those concerned in the case are parties is in question, the Registrar shall notify all such states forthwith.
(2) Every state so notified has the right to intervene in the proceedings; but if it uses this right, the construction given by the judgment will be equally binding upon it.

Article 64. Unless otherwise decided by the Court, each party shall bear its own costs.

Chapter IV. Advisory Opinions

Article 65. (1) The Court may give an advisory opinion on any legal question at the request of whatever body may be authorized by or in accordance with the Charter of the United Nations to make such a request.
(2) Questions upon which the advisory opinion of the Court is asked shall be laid before the Court by means of a written request containing an exact statement of the question upon which an opinion is required, and accompanied by all documents likely to throw light upon the question.

Article 66. (1) The Registrar shall forthwith give notice of the request for an advisory opinion to all states entitled to appear before the Court.
(2) The Registrar shall also, by means of a special and direct communication, notify any state entitled to appear before the Court or international organization considered by the Court, or, should it not be sitting, by the President, as likely to be able to furnish information on the question, that the Court will be prepared to receive, within a time limit to be fixed by the President, written statements, or to hear, at a public sitting to be held for the purpose, oral statements relating to the question.
(3) Should any such state entitled to appear before the Court have failed to receive the special communication referred to in paragraph (2) of this Article, such state may express a desire to submit a written statement or to be heard; and the Court will decide.
(4) States and organizations having presented written or oral statements or both shall be permitted to comment on the statements made by other states or organizations in the form, to the extent, and within the time limits which the Court, or, should it not be sitting, the President, shall decide in each particular case. Accordingly, the Registrar shall in due time communicate any such written statements to states and organizations having submitted similar statements.

Article 67. The Court shall deliver its advisory opinions in open court, notice having been given to the Secretary-General and to the representatives of Members of the United Nations, of other states and of international organizations immediately concerned.

Article 68. In the exercise of its advisory functions the Court shall further be guided by the provisions of the present Statute which apply in contentious cases to the extent to which it recognizes them to be applicable.

Chapter V. Amendment

Article 69. Amendments to the present Statute shall be effected by the same procedure as is provided by the Charter of the United Nations for amendments to that Charter, subject however to any provisions which the General Assembly upon recommendation of the Security Council may adopt concerning the participation of states which are parties to the present Statute but are not Members of the United Nations.

Article 70. The Court shall have power to propose such amendments to the present Statute as it may deem necessary, through written communications to the Secretary-General, for consideration in conformity with the provisions of Article 69.

PART I INTERNATIONAL LAW

Convention on the Privileges and Immunities of the United Nations
(UN General Assembly, 13 February 1946)

Whereas Article 104 of the Charter of the United Nations provides that the Organization shall enjoy in the territory of each of its Members such legal capacity as may be necessary for the exercise of its functions and the fulfilment of its purposes and
Whereas Article 105 of the Charter of the United Nations provides that the Organization shall enjoy in the territory of each of its Members such privileges and immunities as are necessary for the fulfilment of its purposes and that representatives of the Members of the United Nations and officials of the Organization shall similarly enjoy such privileges ajid immunities as are necessary for the independent exercise of their functions in connection with the Organization.
Consequently the General Assembly by a Resolution adopted on the 13 February 1946, approved the following Convention and proposed it for accession by each Member of the United Nations.

Article I. Juridical personality

Section 1. The United Nations shall possess juridical personality. It shall have the capacity: (a) To contract;
(b) To acquire and dispose of immovable and movable property;
(c) To institute legal proceedings.

Article II. Property, funds and assets

Section 2. The United Nations, its property and assets wherever located and by whomsoever held, shall enjoy immunity from every form of legal process except insofar as in any particular case it has expressly waived its immunity shall extend to any particular case it has expressly waived its immunity. It is, however, understood that no waiver o£ immunity shall ex tend to any measure of execution.

Section 3. The premises of the United Nations shall be inviolable. The property and assets of the United Nations, wherever located and by whomsoever held, shall be immune from search, requisition, confiscation, expropriation and any other form of interference, whether by executive, administrative, judicial or legislative action.

Section 4. The archives of the United Nations, and in general all documents belonging to it or held by it, shall be inviolable wherever located.

Section 5. Without being restricted by financial controls, regulations or moratoria of any kind,
(a) The United Nations may hold funds, gold or currency of any kind and operate accounts in any currency;
(b) The United Nations shall be free to transfer its funds, gold or currency from one country to another or within any country and to convert any currency held by it into any other currency.

Section 6. In exercising its rights under Section 5 above, the United Nations shall pay due regard to any representations made by the Government of any Member insofar as it is considered that effect can be given to such representations without detriment to the interests of the United Nations.

Section 7. The United Nations, its assets, income and other property shall be:
(a) Exempt from all direct taxes; it is understood, however, that the United Nations will not claim exemption from taxes which are, in fact, no more than charges for public utility services;
(b) Exempt from customs duties and prohibitions and restrictions on imports and exports in respect of articles imported or exported by the United Nations for its official use. It is understood, however, that articles imported under such exemption will not be sold in the country into which they were imported except under conditions agreed with the Government of that country;
(c) Exempt from customs duties and prohibitions and restrictions on imports and exports in respect of its publications.

Section 8. While the United Nations will not, as a general rule, claim exemption from excise duties and from taxes on the sale of movable and immovable property which form part of the price to be paid, nevertheless when the United Nations is making important purchases for official use of property on which such duties and taxes have been charged or are charge able, Members will, whenever possible, make appropriate administrative arrangements for the remission or return of the amount of duty or tax.

Article III. Facilitates in respect of Communications

Section 9. The United Nations shall enjoy in the territory of each Member for its official communications treatment not less favourable than that accorded by the Government of that Member to any other Government including its diplomatic mission in the matter of priorities, rates and taxes on mails, cables, telegrams, radiograms, telephotos, telephone and other communications; and press rates for information to the press and radio. No censorship shall be applied to the official correspondence and other official communications of the United Nations.

Section 10. The United Nations shall have the right to use codes and to despatch and receive its correspondence by courier or in bags, which shall have the same immunities and privileges as diplomatic couriers and bags.

Article IV. The representatives of members

Section 11. Representatives of Members to the principal and subsidiary organs of the United Nations and to conferences convened by the United Nations, shall, while exercising their functions and during the journey to and from the place of meeting, enjoy the following privileges and immunities:
(a) Immunity from personal arrest or detention and from seizure of their personal baggage, and, in respect of words spoken or written and all acts done by them in their capacity as representatives, immunity from legal process of every kind;
(b) Inviolability for all papers and documents;
(c) The right to use codes and to receive papers or correspondence by courier or in sealed bags;
(d) Exemption in respect of themselves and their spouses from immigration restrictions, aliens registration or national service obligations in the state they are visiting or through which they are passing in the exercise of their functions;
(e) The same facilities in respect of currency or exchange restrictions as are accorded to representatives of foreign governments on temporary official missions;
(f) The same immunities and facilities in respect of their personal baggage as are accorded to diplomatic envoys, and also;
(g) Such other privileges, immunities and facilities not inconsistent with the foregoing as diplomatic envoys enjoy, except that they shall have no right to claim exemption from customs duties on goods imported (otherwise than as part of their personal baggage) or from excise duties or sales taxes.

Section 12. In order to secure, for the representatives of Members to the principal and subsidiary organs of the United Nations and to conferences convened by the United Nations, complete freedom of speech and independence in the discharge of their duties, the immunity from legal process in respect of words spoken or written and all acts done by them in discharging their duties shall continue to be accorded, notwithstanding that the per sons concerned are no longer the representatives of Members.

Section 13. Where the incidence of any form of taxation depends upon residence, periods during which the representatives of Members to the principal and subsidiary organs of the United Nations and to conferences convened by the United Nations are present in a state for the discharge of their duties shall not be considered as periods of residence.

Section 14. Privileges and immunities are accorded to the representatives of Members not for the personal benefit of the individuals themselves, but in order to safeguard the independent exercise of their functions in connection with the United Nations. Consequently a Member not only has the right but is under a duty to waive the immunity of its representative in any case where in the opinion of the Member the immunity would impede the course of justice, and it can be waived without prejudice to the purpose for which the immunity is accorded.

Section 15. The provisions of Sections n, 12 and 13 are not applicable as between a representative and the authorities o£ the state of which he is a national or of which he is or has been the representative.

Section 16. In this article the expression "representatives" shall be deemed to include all delegates, deputy delegates, advisers, technical experts and secretaries of delegations.

Article V. Officials

Section 17. The Secretary-General will specify the categories of officials to which the provisions of this Article and Article VII shall apply. He shall submit these categories to the General Assembly.

Thereafter these categories shall be communicated to the Governments of all Members. The names of the officials included in these categories shall from time to time be made known to the Governments of Members.

Section 18. Officials of the United Nations shall:
(a) Be immune from legal process in respect of words spoken or written and all acts performed by them in their official capacity;
(b) Be exempt from taxation on the salaries and emoluments paid to them by the United Nations;
(c) Be immune from national service obligations;
(d) Be immune, together with their spouses and relatives dependent on them, from immigration restrictions and alien registration;
(e) Be accorded the same privileges in respect of exchange facilities as are accorded to the officials of comparable ranks forming part of diplomatic missions to the Government concerned;
(f) Be given, together with their spouses and relatives dependent on them, the, same repatriation facilities in time of international crisis as diplomatic envoys;
(g) Have the right to import free of duty their furniture and effects at the time of first taking up their post in the' country in question.

Section 19. In addition to the immunities and privileges specified in Section 18, the Secretary-General and all Assistant Secretaries-General shall be accorded in respect of themselves, their spouses and minor children, privileges and immunities, exemptions and facilities accorded to diplomatic envoys, in accordance with international law.

Section 20. Privileges and immunities are granted to officials in the interests of the United Nations and not for the personal benefit of the individuals themselves. The Secretary-General shall have the right and the duty to waive the immunity of any official in any case where, in his opinion, the immunity would impede the course of justice and can be waived without prejudice to the interests of the United Nations. In the case of the Secretary-General, the Security Council shall have the right to waive immunity.

Section 21. The United Nations shall co-operate at all times with the appropriate authorities of Members to facilitate the proper administration of justice, secure the observance of police regulations and prevent the occurrence of any abuse in connection with the privileges, immunities and facilities mentioned in this Article.

Article VI. Experts on missions for the United Nations

Section 22. Experts (other than officials coming within the scope of Article V) performing missions for the United Nations shall be accorded such privileges and immunities as are necessary for the independent exercise of their functions during the period of their missions, including the time spent on journeys in connection with their missions.
In particular they shall be accorded:
(a) Immunity from personal arrest or detention and from seizure of their personal baggage; (b) In respect of words spoken or written and acts done by them in the course of the performance of their mission, immunity from legal process of every kind. This immunity from legal process shall continue to be accorded notwithstanding that the persons concerned are no longer employed on missions for the United Nations;
(c) Inviolability for all papers and documents;
(d) For the purpose of their communications with the United Nations, the right to use codes and to receive papers or correspondence by courier or in sealed bags;
(e) The Same facilities in respect of currency or exchange restrictions as are accorded to representatives of foreign governments on temporary official missions;
(f) The same immunities and facilities in respect of their personal baggage as are accorded to diplomatic envoys.

Section 23. Privileges and immunities are granted to experts in the interests of the United Nations and not for the personal benefit of the individuals themselves. The Secretary-General shall have the right and the duty to waive the immunity of any expert in any case where, in his opinion, the immunity would impede the course of justice and it can be waived without prejudice to the interests of the United Nations.

Article VII. United Nations laissez-passer

Section 24. The United Nations may issue United Nations laissez-passer to its officials. These laissez-passer shall be recognized and accepted as valid travel documents by the authorities of Members, taking into account the provisions of Section 25.

Section 25. Applications for visas (where required) from the holders of United Nations laissez-passer, when accompanied by a certificate that they are travelling on the business of the United Nations, shall be dealt with as speedily as possible. In addition, such persons shall be granted facilities for speedy travel.

Section 26. Similar facilities to those specified in Section 25 shall be accorded to experts and other persons who, though not the holders of United Nations laissez-passer, have a certificate that they are travelling on the business of the United Nations. SECTION 27. The Secretary-General, Assistant Secretaries General and Directors travelling on United Nations laissez-passer on the business of the United Nations shall be granted the same facilities as are accorded to diplomatic envoys.

Section 28. The provisions of this article may be applied to the com parable officials of specialized agencies if the agreements for relationship made under Article 63 of the Charter so provide.

Article VIII. Settlements of disputes

Section 29. The United Nations shall make provisions for appropriate modes of settlement of: (a) Disputes arising out of contracts or other disputes of a private law character to which the United Nations is a party;
(b) Disputes involving any official of the United Nations who by reason of his official position enjoys immunity, if immunity has not been waived by the Secretary-General.

Section 30. All differences arising out of the interpretation or application of the present convention shall be referred to the International Court of Justice, unless in any case it is agreed by the parties to have recourse to another mode of settlement. If a difference arises between the United Nations on the one hand and a Member on the other hand, a request shall be made for an advisory opinion on any legal question involved in accordance with Article 96 of the Charter and Article 65 of the Statute of the Court. The opinion given by the Court shall be accepted as decisive by the parties.

Final Article

Section 31. This convention is submitted to every Member of the United Nations for accession.

Section 32. Accession shall be affected by deposit of an instrument with the Secretary-General of the United Nations and the convention shall come into force as regards each Member on the date of deposit of each instrument of accession.

Section 33. The Secretary-General shall inform all Members of the United Nations of the deposit of each accession,

Section 34. It is understood that, when an instrument of accession is deposited on behalf of any Member, the Member will be in a position under its own law to give effect to the terms of this convention.

Section 35. This convention shall continue in force as between the United Nations and every Member which has deposited an instrument of accession for so long as that Member remains a Member of the United Nations, or until a revised general convention has been approved by the General Assembly and that Member has become a party to this revised convention.

Section 36. The Secretary-General may conclude with any Member or Members supplementary agreements adjusting the provisions of this convention so far as that Member or those Members are concerned. These supplementary agreements shall in each case be subject to the approval of the General Assembly.

PART I   INTERNATIONAL LAW

United Nations and League of Nations Protocol No. I concerning the execution of various operations in the transfer to the United Nations of certain assets of the League of Nations. Signed at Geneva, on 1 August 1946

Mr. Sean LESTER, Secretary-General of the League of Nations, and Mr. Wlodzimierz MODEROW, Director, Representative of the Secretary General of the United Nations in Geneva:
Note that, in application of the Common Plan, approved by a resolution of the General Assembly of the United Nations, dated 12 February 1946, and by a resolution of the Assembly of the League of Nations, dated 18 April 1946, and of a subsequent Agreement dated 19 July 1946, concerning the execution of the transfer to the United Nations of certain assets of the League of Nations, the following operations were effected on 1 August 1946:

(1) The transfer of rights in respect of the League of Nations buildings and other immovable property was effected on 1 August 1946, and the necessary entries having been made this day in the Land Register of the Republic and Canton of Geneva.

(2) The transfer of the ownership and possession of the movable property was also effected on 1 August 1946.
In accordance with Article 6 of the Agreement of 19 July 1946, the movable objects transferred have been listed in an inventory drawn up by the League of Nations which is in course of being verified by the United Nations. A protocol will be drawn up placing on record the completion of this operation.

(3) A final valuation of the assets will be made in accordance with the terms of the Common Plan. It will be the subject of a special protocol.

Convention on the Rights and Duties of States (Montevideo Convention) 1933

Article 1. The state as a person of international law should possess the following qualifications: a) a permanent population;
b) a defined territory;
c) government; and
d) capacity to enter into relations with other states.

Article 2. The federal state shall constitute a sole person in the eyes of international law.

Article 3. The political existence of the state is independent of recognition by the other states. Even before recognition the state has the right to defend its integrity and independence, to provide for its conservation and prosperity, and consequently to organize itself as it sees fit, to legislate upon its interests, administer its services, and to define the jurisdiction and competence of its courts. The exercise of these rights has no other limitation than the exercise of the rights of other states according to international law.

Article 4. States are juridically equal, enjoy the same rights, and have equal capacity in their exercise. The rights of each one do not depend upon the power which it possesses to assure its exercise, but upon the simple fact of its existence as a person under international law.

Article 5. The fundamental rights of states are not susceptible of being affected in any manner whatsoever.

Article 6. The recognition of a state merely signifies that the state which recognizes it accepts the personality of the other with all the rights and duties determined by international law. Recognition is unconditional and irrevocable.

Article 7. The recognition of a state may be express or tacit. The latter results from any act which implies the intention of recognizing the new state.

Article 8. No state has the right to intervene in the internal or external affairs of another.

Article 9. The jurisdiction of states within the limits of national territory applies to all the inhabitants. Nationals and foreigners are under the same protection of the law and the national authorities and the foreigners may not claim rights other or more extensive than those of the nationals.

Article 10. The primary interest of states is the conservation of peace. Differences of any nature which arise between them should be settled by recognized pacific methods.

Article 11. The contracting states definitely establish as the rule of their conduct the precise obligation not to recognize territorial acquisitions or special advantages which have been obtained by force whether this consists in the employment of arms, in threatening diplomatic representations, or in any other effective coercive measure. The territory of a state is inviolable and may not be the object of military occupation nor of other measures of force imposed by another state directly or indirectly or for any motive whatever even temporarily.

Article 12. The present Convention shall not affect obligations previously entered into by the High Contracting Parties by virtue of international agreements.

Article 13. The present Convention shall be ratified by the High Contracting Parties in conformity with their respective constitutional procedures. The Minister of Foreign Affairs of the Republic of Uruguay shall transmit authentic certified copies to the governments for the aforementioned purpose of ratification. The instrument of ratification shall be deposited in the archives of the Pan American Union in Washington, which shall notify the signatory governments of said deposit. Such notification shall be considered as an exchange of ratifications.

Article 14. The present Convention will enter into force between the High Contracting Parties in the order in which they deposit their respective ratifications.

Article 15. The present Convention shall remain in force indefinitely but may be denounced by means of one year's notice given to the Pan American Union, which shall transmit it to the other signatory governments. After the expiration of this period the Convention shall cease in its effects as regards the party which denounces but shall remain in effect for the remaining High Contracting Parties.

PART I   INTERNATIONAL LAW

Article 16. The present Convention shall be open for the adherence and accession of the States which are not signatories. The corresponding instruments shall be deposited in the archives of the Pan American Union which shall communicate them to the other High Contracting Parties.

Draft Articles on Diplomatic Protection, Text adopted by the International Law Commission at its fifty-eight session, 2006

Part One. General provisions

Article 1. Definition and scope

For the purposes of the present draft articles, diplomatic protection consists of the invocation by a State, through diplomatic action or other means of peaceful settlement, of the responsibility of another State for an injury caused by an internationally wrongful act of that State to a natural or legal person that is a national of the former State with a view to the implementation of such responsibility.

Article 2. Right to exercise diplomatic protection

A State has the right to exercise diplomatic protection in accordance with the present draft articles.

Part Two. Nationality

Chapter I. General principles

Article 3. Protection by the State of nationality

(1) The State entitled to exercise diplomatic protection is the State of nationality.
(2) Notwithstanding paragraph (1), diplomatic protection may be exercised by a State in respect of a person that is not its national in accordance with draft article 8.

Chapter II. Natural persons

Article 4. State of nationality of a natural person

For the purposes of the diplomatic protection of a natural person, a State of nationality means a State whose nationality that person has acquired, in accordance with the law of that State, by birth, descent, naturalization, succession of States or in any other manner, not inconsistent with international law.

Article 5. Continuous nationality of a natural person

(1) A State is entitled to exercise diplomatic protection in respect of a person who was a national of that State continuously from the date of injury to the date of the official presentation of the claim. Continuity is presumed if that nationality existed at both these dates.
(2) Notwithstanding paragraph (1), a State may exercise diplomatic protection in respect of a person who is its national at the date of the official presentation of the claim but was not a national at the date of injury, provided that the person had the nationality of a predecessor State or lost his or her previous nationality and acquired, for a reason unrelated to the bringing of the claim, the nationality of the former State in a manner not inconsistent with international law.
(3) Diplomatic protection shall not be exercised by the present State of nationality in respect of a person against a former State of nationality of that person for an injury caused when that person was a national of the former State of nationality and not of the present State of nationality.
(4) A State is no longer entitled to exercise diplomatic protection in respect of a person who acquires the nationality of the State against which the claim is brought after the date of the official presentation of the claim.

Article 6. Multiple nationality and claim against a third State

(1) Any State of which a dual or multiple national is a national may exercise diplomatic protection in respect of that national against a State of which that person is not a national.
(2) Two or more States of nationality may jointly exercise diplomatic protection in respect of a dual or multiple national.

Article 7. Multiple nationality and claim against a State of nationality

A State of nationality may not exercise diplomatic protection in respect of a person against a State of which that person is also a national unless the nationality of the former State is predominant, both at the date of injury and at the date of the official presentation of the claim.

Article 8. Stateless persons and refugees

(1) A State may exercise diplomatic protection in respect of a stateless person who, at the date of injury and at the date of the official presentation of the claim, is lawfully and habitually resident in that State.
(2) A State may exercise diplomatic protection in respect of a person who is recognized as a refugee by that State, in accordance with internationally accepted standards, when that person, at the date of

injury and at the date of the official presentation of the claim, is lawfully and habitually resident in that State.

(3) Paragraph (2) does not apply in respect of an injury caused by an internationally wrongful act of the State of nationality of the refugee.

Chapter III. Legal persons

Article 9. State of nationality of a corporation

For the purposes of the diplomatic protection of a corporation, the State of nationality means the State under whose law the corporation was incorporated. However, when the corporation is controlled by nationals of another State or States and has no substantial business activities in the State of incorporation, and the seat of management and the financial control of the corporation are both located in another State, that State shall be regarded as the State of nationality.

Article 10. Continuous nationality of a corporation

(1) A State is entitled to exercise diplomatic protection in respect of a corporation that was a national of that State, or its predecessor State, continuously from the date of injury to the date of the official presentation of the claim. Continuity is presumed if that nationality existed at both these dates.

(2) A State is no longer entitled to exercise diplomatic protection in respect of a corporation that acquires the nationality of the State against which the claim is brought after the presentation of the claim.

(3) Notwithstanding paragraph (1), a State continues to be entitled to exercise diplomatic protection in respect of a corporation which was its national at the date of injury and which, as the result of the injury, has ceased to exist according to the law of the State of incorporation.

Article 11. Protection of shareholders

A State of nationality of shareholders in a corporation shall not be entitled to exercise diplomatic protection in respect of such shareholders in the case of an injury to the corporation unless:

(a) the corporation has ceased to exist according to the law of the State of incorporation for a reason unrelated to the injury; or

(b) the corporation had, at the date of injury, the nationality of the State alleged to be responsible for causing the injury, and incorporation in that State was required by it as a precondition for doing business there.

Article 12. Direct injury to shareholders

To the extent that an internationally wrongful act of a State causes direct injury to the rights of shareholders as such, as distinct from those of the corporation itself, the State of nationality of any such shareholders is entitled to exercise diplomatic protection in respect of its nationals.

Article 13. Other legal persons

The principles contained in this chapter shall be applicable, as appropriate, to the diplomatic protection of legal persons other than corporations.

Part Three. Local remedies

Article 14. Exhaustion of local remedies

(1) A State may not present an international claim in respect of an injury to a national or other person referred to in draft article 8 before the injured person has, subject to draft article 15, exhausted all local remedies.

(2) "Local remedies" means legal remedies which are open to an injured person before the judicial or administrative courts or bodies, whether ordinary or special, of the State alleged to be responsible for causing the injury.

(3) Local remedies shall be exhausted where an international claim, or request for a declaratory judgement related to the claim, is brought preponderantly on the basis of an injury to a national or other person referred to in draft article 8.

Article 15. Exceptions to the local remedies rule

Local remedies do not need to be exhausted where:

(a) there are no reasonably available local remedies to provide effective redress, or the local remedies provide no reasonable possibility of such redress;

(b) there is undue delay in the remedial process which is attributable to the State alleged to be responsible;

(c) there was no relevant connection between the injured person and the State alleged to be responsible at the date of injury;

(d) the injured person is manifestly precluded from pursuing local remedies; or
(e) the State alleged to be responsible has waived the requirement that local remedies be exhausted.

Part Four. Miscellaneous provisions

Article 16. Actions or procedures other than diplomatic protection
The rights of States, natural persons, legal persons or other entities to resort under international law to actions or procedures other than diplomatic protection to secure redress for injury suffered as a result of an internationally wrongful act, are not affected by the present draft articles.

Article 17. Special rules of international law
The present draft articles do not apply to the extent that they are inconsistent with special rules of international law, such as treaty provisions for the protection of investments.

Article 18. Protection of ships' crew
The right of the State of nationality of the members of the crew of a ship to exercise diplomatic protection is not affected by the right of the State of nationality of a ship to seek redress on behalf of such crew members, irrespective of their nationality, when they have been injured in connection with an injury to the vessel resulting from an internationally wrongful act.

Article 19. Recommended practice
A State entitled to exercise diplomatic protection according to the present draft articles, should:
(a) give due consideration to the possibility of exercising diplomatic protection, especially when a significant injury has occurred;
(b) take into account, wherever feasible, the views of injured persons with regard to resort to diplomatic protection and the reparation to be sought; and
(c) transfer to the injured person any compensation obtained for the injury from the responsible State subject to any reasonable deductions.

PART I INTERNATIONAL LAW

Vienna Convention on Diplomatic Relations, Vienna 18 April 1961, entry into force 24 April 1964,
Trb. 1962 Nr. 191

The States Parties to the present Convention,
Recalling that peoples of all nations from ancient times have recognized the status of diplomatic agents,
Having in mind the purposes and principles of the Charter of the United Nations concerning the sovereign equality of States, the maintenance of international peace and security, and the promotion of friendly relations among nations,
Believing that an international convention on diplomatic intercourse, privileges and immunities would contribute to the development of friendly relations among nations, irrespective of their differing constitutional and social systems,
Realizing that the purpose of such privileges and immunities is not to benefit individuals but to ensure the efficient performance of the functions of diplomatic missions as representing States,
Affirming that the rules of customary international law should continue to govern questions not expressly regulated by the provisions of the present Convention,
Have agreed as follows:

Article 1. For the purpose of the present Convention, the following expressions shall have the meanings hereunder assigned to them:
(a) The "head of the mission" is the person charged by the sending State with the duty of acting in that capacity;
(b) The "members of the mission" are the head of the mission and the members of the staff of the mission;
(c) The "members of the staff of the mission" are the members of the diplomatic staff, of the administrative and technical staff and of the service staff of the mission;
(d) The "members of the diplomatic staff" are the members of the staff of the mission having diplomatic rank;
(e) A "diplomatic agent" is the head of the mission or a member of the diplomatic staff of the mission;
(f) The "members of the administrative and technical staff" are the members of the staff of the mission employed in the administrative and technical service of the mission;
(g) The "members of the service staff" are the members of the staff of the mission in the domestic service of the mission;
(h) A "private servant" is a person who is in the domestic service of a member of the mission and who is not an employee of the sending State;
(i) The "premises of the mission" are the buildings or parts of buildings and the land ancillary thereto, irrespective of ownership, used for the purposes of the mission including the residence of the head of the mission.

Article 2. The establishment of diplomatic relations between States, and of permanent diplomatic missions, takes place by mutual consent.

Article 3. (1) The functions of a diplomatic mission consist, inter alia, in:
(a) Representing the sending State in the receiving State;
(b) Protecting in the receiving State the interests of the sending State and of its nationals, within the limits permitted by international law;
(c) Negotiating with the Government of the receiving State;
(d) Ascertaining by all lawful means conditions and developments in the receiving State, and reporting thereon to the Government of the sending State;
(e) Promoting friendly relations between the sending State and the receiving State, and developing their economic, cultural and scientific relations.
(2) Nothing in the present Convention shall be construed as preventing the performance of consular functions by a diplomatic mission.

Article 4. (1) The sending State must make certain that the **agrément** of the receiving State has been given for the person it proposes to accredit as head of the mission to that State.

(2) The receiving State is not obliged to give reasons to the sending State for a refusal of **agrément**.

Article 5. (1) The sending State may, after it has given due notification to the receiving States concerned, accredit a head of mission or assign any member of the diplomatic staff, as the case may be, to more than one State, unless there is express objection by any of the receiving States.

(2) If the sending State accredits a head of mission to one or more other States it may establish a diplomatic mission headed by a chargé **d'affaires** ad interim in each State where the head of mission has not his permanent seat.
(3) A head of mission or any member of the diplomatic staff of the mission may act as representative of the sending State to any international organization.

Article 6. Two or more States may accredit the same person as head of mission to another State, unless objection is offered by the receiving State.

Article 7. Subject to the provisions of articles 5, 8, 9 and 11, the sending State may freely appoint the members of the staff of the mission. In the case of military, naval or air attachés, the receiving State may require their names to be submitted beforehand, for its approval.

Article 8. (1) Members of the diplomatic staff of the mission should in principle be of the nationality of the sending State.
(2) Members of the diplomatic staff of the mission may not be appointed from among persons having the nationality of the receiving State, except with the consent of that State which may be withdrawn at any time. 3.The receiving State may reserve the same right with regard to nationals of a third State who are not also nationals of the sending State.

Article 9. (1) The receiving State may at any time and without having to explain its decision, notify the sending State that the head of the mission or any member of the diplomatic staff of the mission is persona non grata or that any other member of the staff of the mission is not acceptable. In any such case, the sending State shall, as appropriate, either recall the person concerned or terminate his functions with the mission. A person may be declared non grata or not acceptable before arriving in the territory of the receiving State.
(2) If the sending State refuses or fails within a reasonable period to carry out its obligations under paragraph (1) of this article, the receiving State may refuse to recognize the person concerned as a member of the mission.

Article 10. (1) The Ministry for Foreign Affairs of the receiving State, or such other ministry as may be agreed, shall be notified of:
(a) The appointment of members of the mission, their arrival and their final departure or the termination of their functions with the mission;
(b) The arrival and final departure of a person belonging to the family of a member of the mission and, where appropriate, the fact that a person becomes or ceases to be a member of the family of a member of the mission;
(c) The arrival and final departure of private servants in the employ of persons referred to in subparagraph (a) of this paragraph and, where appropriate, the fact that they are leaving the employ of such persons;
(d) The engagement and discharge of persons resident in the receiving State as members of the mission or private servants entitled to privileges and immunities. 2.Where possible, prior notification of arrival and final departure shall also be given.

Article 11. (1) In the absence of specific agreement as to the size of the mission, the receiving State may require that the size of a mission be kept within limits considered by it to be reasonable and normal, having regard to circumstances and conditions in the receiving State and to the needs of the particular mission.
(2) The receiving State may equally, within similar bounds and on a non-discriminatory basis, refuse to accept officials of a particular category.

Article 12. The sending State may not, without the prior express consent of the receiving State, establish offices forming part of the mission in localities other than those in which the mission itself is established.

Article 13. (1) The head of the mission is considered as having taken up his functions in the receiving State either when he has presented his credentials or when he has notified his arrival and a true copy of his credentials has been presented to the Ministry for Foreign Affairs of the receiving State, or such other ministry as may be agreed, in accordance with the practice prevailing in the receiving State which shall be applied in a uniform manner. 2.The order of presentation of credentials or of a true copy thereof will be determined by the date and time of the arrival of the head of the mission.

Article 14. (1) Heads of mission are divided into three classes, namely:
(a) That of ambassadors or nuncios accredited to Heads of State, and other heads of mission of equivalent rank;
(b) That of envoys, ministers and internuncios accredited to Heads of State;
(c) That of chargés d'affaires accredited to Ministers for Foreign Affairs.
(2) Except as concerns precedence and etiquette, there shall be no differentiation between heads of mission by reason of their class.

Article 15. The class to which the heads of their missions are to be assigned shall be agreed between States.

Article 16. (1) Heads of mission shall take precedence in their respective classes in the order of the date and time of taking up their functions in accordance with article 13.
(2) Alterations in the credentials of a head of mission not involving any change of class shall not affect his precedence.
(3) This article is without prejudice to any practice accepted by the receiving State regarding the precedence of the representative of the Holy See.

Article 17. The precedence of the members of the diplomatic staff of the mission shall be notified by the head of the mission to the Ministry for Foreign Affairs or such other ministry as may be agreed.

Article 18. The procedure to be observed in each State for the reception of heads of mission shall be uniform in respect of each class.

Article 19. (1) If the post of head of the mission is vacant, or if the head of the mission is unable to perform his functions a chargé d'affaires ad interim shall act provisionally as head of the mission. The name of the chargé d'affaires ad interim shall be notified, either by the head of the mission or, in case he is unable to do so, by the Ministry for Foreign Affairs of the sending State to the Ministry for Foreign Affairs of the receiving State or such other ministry as may be agreed.
(2) In cases where no member of the diplomatic staff of the mission is present in the receiving State, a member of the administrative and technical staff may, with the consent of the receiving State, be designated by the sending State to be in charge of the current administrative affairs of the mission.

Article 20. The mission and its head shall have the right to use the flag and emblem of the sending State on the premises of the mission, including the residence of the head of the mission, and on his means of transport.

Article 21. (1) The receiving State shall either facilitate the acquisition on its territory, in accordance with its laws, by the sending State of premises necessary for its mission or assist the latter in obtaining accommodation in some other way.
(2) It shall also, where necessary, assist missions in obtaining suitable accommodation for their members.

Article 22. (1) The premises of the mission shall be inviolable. The agents of the receiving State may not enter them, except with the consent of the head of the mission.
(2) The receiving State is under a special duty to take all appropriate steps to protect the premises of the mission against any intrusion or damage and to prevent any disturbance of the peace of the mission or impairment of its dignity.
(3) The premises of the mission, their furnishings and other property thereon and the means of transport of the mission shall be immune from search, requisition, attachment or execution.

Article 23. (1)The sending State and the head of the mission shall be exempt from all national, regional or municipal dues and taxes in respect of the premises of the mission, whether owned or leased, other than such as represent payment for specific services rendered.
(2) The exemption from taxation referred to in this article shall not apply to such dues and taxes payable under the law of the receiving State by persons contracting with the sending State or the head of the mission.

Article 24. The archives and documents of the mission shall be inviolable at any time and wherever they may be.

Article 25. The receiving State shall accord full facilities for the performance of the functions of the mission.

Article 26. Subject to its laws and regulations concerning zones entry into which is prohibited or regulated for reasons of national security, the receiving State shall ensure to all members of the mission freedom of movement and travel in its territory.

Article 27. (1) The receiving State shall permit and protect free communication on the part of the mission for all official purposes. In communicating with the Government and the other missions and consulates of the sending State, wherever situated, the mission may employ all appropriate means, including diplomatic couriers and messages in code or cipher. However, the mission may install and use a wireless transmitter only with the consent of the receiving State.
(2) The official correspondence of the mission shall be inviolable. Official correspondence means all correspondence relating to the mission and its functions.
(3) The diplomatic bag shall not be opened or detained.
(4) The packages constituting the diplomatic bag must bear visible external marks of their character and may contain only diplomatic documents or articles intended for official use.
(5) The diplomatic courier, who shall be provided with an official document indicating his status and the number of packages constituting the diplomatic bag, shall be protected by the receiving State in the performance of his functions. He shall enjoy person inviolability and shall not be liable to any form of arrest or detention.
(6) The sending State or the mission may designate diplomatic couriers ad hoc. In such cases the provisions of paragraph (5) of this article shall also apply, except that the immunities therein mentioned shall cease to apply when such a courier has delivered to the consignee the diplomatic bag in his charge.
(7) A diplomatic bag may be entrusted to the captain of a commercial aircraft scheduled to land at an authorized port of entry. He shall be provided with an official document indicating the number of packages constituting the bag but he shall not be considered to be a diplomatic courier. The mission may send one of its members to take possession of the diplomatic bag directly and freely from the captain of the aircraft.

Article 28. The fees and charges levied by the mission in the course of its official duties shall be exempt from all dues and taxes.

Article 29. The person of a diplomatic agent shall be inviolable. He shall not be liable to any form of arrest or detention. The receiving State shall treat him with due respect and shall take all appropriate steps to prevent any attack on his person, freedom or dignity.

Article 30. (1) The private residence of a diplomatic agent shall enjoy the same inviolability and protection as the premises of the mission.
(2) His papers, correspondence and, except as provided in paragraph (3) of article 31, his property, shall likewise enjoy inviolability.

Article 31. (1) A diplomatic agent shall enjoy immunity from the criminal jurisdiction of the receiving State. He shall also enjoy immunity from its civil and administrative jurisdiction, except in the case of:
(a) A real action relating to private immovable property situated in the territory of the receiving State, unless he holds it on behalf of the sending State for the purposes of the mission;
(b) An action relating to succession in which the diplomatic agent is involved as executor, administrator, heir or legatee as a private person and not on behalf of the sending State;
(c) An action relating to any professional or commercial activity exercised by the diplomatic agent in the receiving State outside his official functions.
(2) A diplomatic agent is not obliged to give evidence as a witness.
(3) No measures of execution may be taken in respect of a diplomatic agent except in the cases coming under subparagraphs (a), (b) and (c) of paragraph (1) of this article, and provided that the measures concerned can be taken without infringing the inviolability of his person or of his residence.
(4) The immunity of a diplomatic agent from the jurisdiction of the receiving State does not exempt him from the jurisdiction of the sending State.

Article 32. (1) The immunity from jurisdiction of diplomatic agents and of persons enjoying immunity under article 37 may be waived by the sending State.
(2) Waiver must always be express.
(3) The initiation of proceedings by a diplomatic agent or by a person enjoying immunity from jurisdiction under article 37 shall preclude him from invoking immunity from jurisdiction in respect of any counterclaim directly connected with the principal claim. 4. Waiver of immunity from jurisdiction in respect of civil or administrative proceedings shall not be held to imply waiver of immunity in respect of the execution of the judgement, for which a separate waiver shall be necessary.

Article 33. (1) Subject to the provisions of paragraph (3) of this article, a diplomatic agent shall with respect to services rendered for the sending State be exempt from social security provisions which may be in force in the receiving State.
(2) The exemption provided for in paragraph (1) of this article shall also apply to private servants who are in the sole employ of a diplomatic agent, on condition:
(a) That they are not nationals of or permanently resident in the receiving State; and
(b) That they are covered by the social security provisions which may be in force in the sending State or a third State.
(3) A diplomatic agent who employs persons to whom the exemption provided for in paragraph (2) of this article does not apply shall observe the obligations which the social security provisions of the receiving State impose upon employers.
(4) The exemption provided for in paragraphs (1) and (2) of this article shall not preclude voluntary participation in the social security system of the receiving State provided that such participation is permitted by that State.
(5) The provisions of this article shall not affect bilateral or multilateral agreements concerning social security concluded previously and shall not prevent the conclusion of such agreements in the future.

Article 34. A diplomatic agent shall be exempt from all dues and taxes, personal or real, national, regional or municipal, except:
(a) Indirect taxes of a kind which are normally incorporated in the price of goods or services; (b) Dues and taxes on private immovable property situated in the territory of the receiving State, unless he holds it on behalf of the sending State for the purposes of the mission;
(c) Estate, succession or inheritance duties levied by the receiving State, subject to the provisions of paragraph (4) of article 39;
(d) Dues and taxes on private income having its source in the receiving State and capital taxes on investments made in commercial undertakings in the receiving State;
(e) Charges levied for specific services rendered;
(f) Registration, court or record fees, mortgage dues and stamp duty, with respect to immovable property, subject to the provisions of article 23.

Article 35. The receiving State shall exempt diplomatic agents from all personal services, from all public service of any kind whatsoever, and from military obligations such as those connected with requisitioning, military contributions and billeting.

Article 36. (1) The receiving State shall, in accordance with such laws and regulations as it may adopt, permit entry of and grant exemption from all customs duties, taxes, and related charges other than charges for storage, cartage and similar services, on:
(a) Articles for the official use of the mission;
(b) Articles for the personal use of a diplomatic agent or members of his family forming part of his household, including articles intended for his establishment.
(2) The personal baggage of a diplomatic agent shall be exempt from inspection, unless there are serious grounds for presuming that it contains articles not covered by the exemptions mentioned in paragraph (1) of this article, or articles the import or export of which is prohibited by the law or controlled by the quarantine regulations of the receiving State. Such inspection shall be conducted only in the presence of the diplomatic agent or of his authorized representative.

Article 37. (1) The members of the family of a diplomatic agent forming part of his household shall, if they are not nationals of the receiving State, enjoy the privileges and immunities specified in articles 29 to 36.
(2) Members of the administrative and technical staff of the mission, together with members of their families forming part of their respective households, shall, if they are not nationals of or permanently resident in the receiving State, enjoy the privileges and immunities specified in articles 29 to 35, except that the immunity from civil and administrative jurisdiction of the receiving State specified in paragraph (1) of article 31 shall not extend to acts performed outside the course of their duties. They shall also enjoy the privileges specified in article 36, paragraph (1), in respect of articles imported at the time of first installation.
(3) Members of the service staff of the mission who are not nationals of or permanently resident in the receiving State shall enjoy immunity in respect of acts performed in the course of their duties, exemption from dues and taxes on the emoluments they receive by reason of their employment and the exemption contained in article 33.
(4) Private servants of members of the mission shall, if they are not nationals of or permanently resident in the receiving State, be exempt from dues and taxes on the emoluments they receive by

reason of their employment. In other respects, they may enjoy privileges and immunities only to the extent admitted by the receiving State. However, the receiving State must exercise its jurisdiction over those persons in such a manner as not to interfere unduly with the performance of the functions of the mission.

Article 38. (1) Except insofar as additional privileges and immunities may be granted by the receiving State, a diplomatic agent who is a national of or permanently resident in that State shall enjoy only immunity from jurisdiction, and inviolability, in respect of official acts performed in the exercise of his functions.

(2) Other members of the staff of the mission and private servants who are nationals of or permanently resident in the receiving State shall enjoy privileges and immunities only to the extent admitted by the receiving State. However, the receiving State must exercise its jurisdiction over those persons in such a manner as not to interfere unduly with the performance of the functions of the mission.

Article 39. (1) Every person entitled to privileges and immunities shall enjoy them from the moment he enters the territory of the receiving State on proceeding to take up his post or, if already in its territory, from the moment when his appointment is notified to the Ministry for Foreign Affairs or such other ministry as may be agreed.

(2) When the functions of a person enjoying privileges and immunities have come to an end, such privileges and immunities shall normally cease at the moment when he leaves the country, or on expiry of a reasonable period in which to do so, but shall subsist until that time, even in case of armed conflict. However, with respect to acts performed by such a person in the exercise of his functions as a member of the mission, immunity shall continue to subsist.

(3) In case of the death of a member of the mission, the members of his family shall continue to enjoy the privileges and immunities to which they are entitled until the expiry of a reasonable period in which to leave the country.

(4) In the event of the death of a member of the mission not a national of or permanently resident in the receiving State or a member of his family forming part of his household, the receiving State shall permit the withdrawal of the movable property of the deceased, with the exception of any property acquired in the country the export of which was prohibited at the time of his death. Estate, succession and inheritance duties shall not be levied on movable property the presence of which in the receiving State was due solely to the presence there of the deceased as a member of the mission or as a member of the family of a member of the mission.

Article 40. (1) If a diplomatic agent passes through or is in the territory of a third State, which has granted him a passport visa if such visa was necessary, while proceeding to take up or to return to his post, or when returning to his own country, the third State shall accord him inviolability and such other immunities as may be required to ensure his transit or return. The same shall apply in the case of any members of his family enjoying privileges or immunities who are accompanying the diplomatic agent, or travelling separately to join him or to return to their country.

(2) In circumstances similar to those specified in paragraph (1) of this article, third States shall not hinder the passage of members of the administrative and technical or service staff of a mission, and of members of their families, through their territories.

(3) Third States shall accord to official correspondence and other official communications in transit, including messages in code or cipher, the same freedom and protection as is accorded by the receiving State. They shall accord to diplomatic couriers, who have been granted a passport visa if such visa was necessary, and diplomatic bags in transit, the same inviolability and protection as the receiving State is bound to accord.

(4) The obligations of third States under paragraphs (1), (2) and (3) of this article shall also apply to the persons mentioned respectively in those paragraphs, and to official communications and diplomatic bags, whose presence in the territory of the third State is due to force majeure.

Article 41. (1) Without prejudice to their privileges and immunities, it is the duty of all persons enjoying such privileges and immunities to respect the laws and regulations of the receiving State. They also have a duty not to interfere in the internal affairs of that State.

(2) All official business with the receiving State entrusted to the mission by the sending State shall be conducted with or through the Ministry for Foreign Affairs of the receiving State or such other ministry as may be agreed.

(3) The premises of the mission must not be used in any manner incompatible with the functions of the mission as laid down in the present Convention or by other rules of general international law or by any special agreements in force between the sending and the receiving State.

PART I   INTERNATIONAL LAW

Article 42. A diplomatic agent shall not in the receiving State practise for personal profit any professional or commercial activity.

Article 43. The function of a diplomatic agent comes to an end, inter alia:
(a) On notification by the sending State to the receiving State that the function of the diplomatic agent has come to an end;
(b) On notification by the receiving State to the sending State that, in accordance with paragraph (2) of article 9, it refuses to recognize the diplomatic agent as a member of the mission.

Article 44. The receiving State must, even in case of armed conflict, grant facilities in order to enable persons enjoying privileges and immunities, other than nationals of the receiving State, and members of the families of such persons irrespective of their nationality, to leave at the earliest possible moment. It must, in particular, in case of need, place at their disposal the necessary means of transport for themselves and their property.

Article 45. If diplomatic relations are broken off between two States, or if a mission is permanently or temporarily recalled:
(a) The receiving State must, even in case of armed conflict, respect and protect the premises of the mission, together with its property and archives;
(b) The sending State may entrust the custody of the premises of the mission, together with its property and archives, to a third State acceptable to the receiving State;
(c) The sending State may entrust the protection of its interests and those of its nationals to a third State acceptable to the receiving State.

Article 46. A sending State may with the prior consent of a receiving State, and at the request of a third State not represented in the receiving State, undertake the temporary protection of the interests of the third State and of its nationals.

Article 47. (1) In the application of the provisions of the present Convention, the receiving State shall not discriminate as between States.
(2) However, discrimination shall not be regarded as taking place:
(a) Where the receiving State applies any of the provisions of the present Convention restrictively because of a restrictive application of that provision to its mission in the sending State;
(b) Where by custom or agreement States extend to each other more favourable treatment than is required by the provisions of the present Convention.

Article 48. The present Convention shall be open for signature by all States Members of the United Nations or of any of the specialized agencies Parties to the Statute of the International Court of Justice, and by any other State invited by the General Assembly of the United Nations to become a Party to the Convention, as follows: until 31 October 1961 at the Federal Ministry for Foreign Affairs of Austria and subsequently, until 31 March 1962, at the United Nations Headquarters in New York.

Article 49. The present Convention is subject to ratification. The instruments of ratification shall be deposited with the Secretary-General of the United Nations.

Article 50. The present Convention shall remain open for accession by any State belonging to any of the four categories mentioned in article 48. The instruments of accession shall be deposited with the Secretary General of the United Nations.

Article 51. (1) The present Convention shall enter into force on the thirtieth day following the date of deposit of the twenty-second instrument of ratification or accession with the Secretary-General of the United Nations.
(2) For each State ratifying or acceding to the Convention after the deposit of the twenty-second instrument of ratification or accession, the Convention shall enter into force on the thirtieth day after deposit by such State of its instrument of ratification or accession.

Article 52. The Secretary-General of the United Nations shall inform all States belonging to any of the four categories mentioned in article 48:
(a) Of signatures to the present Convention and of the deposit of instruments of ratification or accession, in accordance with articles 48, 49 and 50;
(b) Of the date on which the present Convention will enter into force, in accordance with article 51.

Article 53. The original of the present Convention, of which the Chinese, English, French, Russian and Spanish texts are equally authentic, shall be deposited with the Secretary-General of the United

VIENNA CONVENTION ON DIPLOMATIC RELATIONS

Nations, who shall send certified copies thereof to all States belonging to any of the four categories mentioned in article 48.

PART I   INTERNATIONAL LAW

Optional Protocol concerning the Compulsory Settlement of Disputes
Vienna 24 April 1963, entry into Force 19 March 1967

The States Parties to the present Protocol and to the Vienna Convention on Consular Relations, hereinafter referred to as "the Convention", adopted by the United Nations Conference held at Vienna from 4 March to 22 April 1963,
Expressing their wish to resort in all matters concerning them in respect of any dispute arising out of the interpretation or application of the Convention to the compulsory jurisdiction of the International Court of Justice, unless some other form of settlement has been agreed upon by the parties within a reasonable period.
Have agreed as follows:

Article I. Disputes arising out of the interpretation or application of the Convention shall lie within the compulsory jurisdiction of the International Court of Justice and may accordingly be brought before the Court by an application made by any party to the dispute being a Party to the present Protocol.

Article II. The parties may agree, within a period of two months after one party has notified its opinion to the other that a dispute exists, to resort not to the International Court of Justice but to an arbitral tribunal. After the expiry of the said period, either party may bring the dispute before the Court by an application.

Article III. (1) Within the same period of two months, the parties may agree to adopt a conciliation procedure before resorting to the International Court of Justice.
(2) The conciliation commission shall make its recommendations within five months after its appointment. If its recommendations are not accepted by the parties to the dispute within two months after they have been delivered, either party may bring the dispute before the Court by an application.

Article IV. States Parties to the Convention, to the Optional Protocol concerning Acquisition of Nationality, and to the present Protocol may at any time declare that they will extend the provisions of the present Protocol to disputes arising out of the interpretation or application of the Optional Protocol concerning Acquisition of Nationality. Such declarations shall be notified to the Secretary-General of the United Nations.

Article V. The present Protocol shall be open for signature by all States which may become Parties to the Convention as follows: until 31 October 1963 at the Federal Ministry for Foreign Affairs of the Republic of Austria and, subsequently, until 31 March 1964, at the United Nations Headquarters in New York.

Article VI. The present Protocol is subject to ratification. The instruments of ratification shall be deposited with the Secretary-General of the United Nations. Article VII The present Protocol shall remain open for accession by all States which may become Parties to the Convention. The instruments of accession shall be deposited with the Secretary-General of the United Nations.

Article VIII. (1) The present Protocol shall enter into force on the same day as the Convention or on the thirtieth day following the date of deposit of the second instrument of ratification or accession to the Protocol with the Secretary-General of the United Nations, whichever date is the later. (2) For each State ratifying or acceding to the present Protocol after its entry into force in accordance with paragraph (1) of this article, the Protocol shall enter into force on the thirtieth day after deposit by such State of its instrument of ratification or accession.

Article IX. The Secretary-General of the United Nations shall inform all States which may become Parties to the Convention:
(a) of signatures to the present Protocol and of the deposit of instruments of ratification or accession, in accordance with articles V, VI and VII;
(b) of declarations made in accordance with article IV of the present Protocol;
(c) of the date on which the present Protocol will enter into force, in accordance with article VIII.

Article X. The original of the present Protocol, of which the Chinese, English, French, Russian and Spanish texts are equally authentic, shall be deposited with the Secretary-General of the United Nations, who shall send certified copies thereof to all States referred to in article V.

United Nations Convention on the Law of the Sea (UNCLOS), Montego Bay 10 December1982, Trb. 1983 Nr. 83

The States Parties to this Convention,
Prompted by the desire to settle, in a spirit of mutual understanding and cooperation, all issues relating to the law of the sea and aware of the historic significance of this Convention as an important contribution to the maintenance of peace, justice and progress for all peoples of the world,
Noting that developments since the United Nations Conferences on the Law of the Sea held at Geneva in 1958 and 1960 have accentuated the need for a new and generally acceptable Convention on the law of the sea,
Conscious that the problems of ocean space are closely interrelated and need to be considered as a whole,
Recognizing the desirability of establishing through this Convention, with due regard for the sovereignty of all States, a legal order for the seas and oceans which will facilitate international communication, and will promote the peaceful uses of the seas and oceans, the equitable and efficient utilization of their resources, the conservation of their living resources, and the study, protection and preservation of the marine environment,
Bearing in mind that the achievement of these goals will contribute to the realization of a just and equitable international economic order which takes into account the interests and needs of mankind as a whole and, in particular, the special interests and needs of developing countries, whether coastal or land-locked,
Desiring by this Convention to develop the principles embodied in resolution 2749 (XXV) of 17 December 1970 in which the General Assembly of the United Nations solemnly declared inter alia that the area of the seabed and ocean floor and the subsoil thereof, beyond the limits of national jurisdiction, as well as its resources, are the common heritage of mankind, the exploration and exploitation of which shall be carried out for the benefit of mankind as a whole, irrespective of the geographical location of States,
Believing that the codification and progressive development of the law of the sea achieved in this Convention will contribute to the strengthening of peace, security, cooperation and friendly relations among all nations in conformity with the principles of justice and equal rights and will promote the economic and social advancement of all peoples of the world, in accordance with the Purposes and Principles of the United Nations as set forth in the Charter,
Affirming that matters not regulated by this Convention continue to be governed by the rules and principles of general international law,
Have agreed as follows:

Part I. Introduction

Article 1. Use of terms and scope
(1) For the purposes of this Convention:
(1) "Area" means the seabed and ocean floor and subsoil thereof, beyond the limits of national jurisdiction;
(2) "Authority" means the International Seabed Authority;
(3) "activities in the Area" means all activities of exploration for, and exploitation of, the resources of the Area;
(4) "pollution of the marine environment" means the introduction by man, directly or indirectly, of substances or energy into the marine environment, including estuaries, which results or is likely to result in such deleterious effects as harm to living resources and marine life, hazards to human health, hindrance to marine activities, including fishing and other legitimate uses of the sea, impairment of quality for use of sea water and reduction of amenities;
(5) (a) "dumping" means:
(i) any deliberate disposal of wastes or other matter from vessels, aircraft, platforms or other man-made structures at sea;
(ii) any deliberate disposal of vessels, aircraft, platforms or other man-made structures at sea; (b) "dumping" does not include:
(i) the disposal of wastes or other matter incidental to, or derived from the normal operations of vessels, aircraft, platforms or other man-made structures at sea and their equipment, other than wastes or other matter transported by or to vessels, aircraft, platforms or other man-made structures at sea, operating for the purpose of disposal of such matter or derived from the treatment of such wastes or other matter on such vessels, aircraft, platforms or structures; (ii) placement of matter for a purpose other than the mere disposal thereof, provided that such placement is not contrary to the aims of this Convention.

(2) (1) "States Parties" means States which have consented to be bound by this Convention and for which this Convention is in force.
(2) This Convention applies *mutatis mutandis* to the entities referred to in article 305, paragraph (1) (b), (c), (d), (e) and (f), which become Parties to this Convention in accordance with the conditions relevant to each, and to that extent "States Parties" refers to those entities.

Part II. Territorial sea and contiguous zone

Section 1. General provisions

Article 2. Legal status of the territorial sea, of the air space over the territorial sea and of its bed and subsoil

(1) The sovereignty of a coastal State extends, beyond its land territory and internal waters and, in the case of an archipelagic State, its archipelagic waters, to an adjacent belt of sea, described as the territorial sea.
(2) This sovereignty extends to the air space over the territorial sea as well as to its bed and subsoil.
(3) The sovereignty over the territorial sea is exercised subject to this Convention and to other rules of international law.

Section 2. Limits of the territorial sea

Article 3. Breadth of the territorial sea
Every State has the right to establish the breadth of its territorial sea up to a limit not exceeding 12 nautical miles, measured from baselines determined in accordance with this Convention.

Article 4. Outer limit of the territorial sea
The outer limit of the territorial sea is the line every point of which is at a distance from the nearest point of the baseline equal to the breadth of the territorial sea.

Article 5. Normal baseline
Except where otherwise provided in this Convention, the normal baseline for measuring the breadth of the territorial sea is the low-water line along the coast as marked on large-scale charts officially recognized by the coastal State.

Article 6. Reefs
In the case of islands situated on atolls or of islands having fringing reefs, the baseline for measuring the breadth of the territorial sea is the seaward low-water line of the reef, as shown by the appropriate symbol on charts officially recognized by the coastal State.

Article 7. Straight baselines
(1) In localities where the coastline is deeply indented and cut into, or if there is a fringe of islands along the coast in its immediate vicinity, the method of straight baselines joining appropriate points may be employed in drawing the baseline from which the breadth of the territorial sea is measured.
(2) Where because of the presence of a delta and other natural conditions the coastline is highly unstable, the appropriate points may be selected along the furthest seaward extent of the low-water line and, notwithstanding subsequent regression of the low-water line, the straight baselines shall remain effective until changed by the coastal State in accordance with this Convention.
(3) The drawing of straight baselines must not depart to any appreciable extent from the general direction of the coast, and the sea areas lying within the lines must be sufficiently closely linked to the land domain to be subject to the regime of internal waters.
(4) Straight baselines shall not be drawn to and from low-tide elevations, unless lighthouses or similar installations which are permanently above sea level have been built on them or except in instances where the drawing of baselines to and from such elevations has received general international recognition.
(5) Where the method of straight baselines is applicable under paragraph (1), account may be taken, in determining particular baselines, of economic interests peculiar to the region concerned, the reality and the importance of which are clearly evidenced by long usage.
(6) The system of straight baselines may not be applied by a State in such a manner as to cut off the territorial sea of another State from the high seas or an exclusive economic zone.

Article 8. Internal waters
(1) Except as provided in Part IV, waters on the landward side of the baseline of the territorial sea form part of the internal waters of the State.
(2) Where the establishment of a straight baseline in accordance with the method set forth in article 7

has the effect of enclosing as internal waters areas which had not previously been considered as such, a right of innocent passage as provided in this Convention shall exist in those waters.

Article 9. Mouths of rivers
If a river flows directly into the sea, the baseline shall be a straight line across the mouth of the river between points on the low-water line of its banks.

Article 10. Bays
(1) This article relates only to bays the coasts of which belong to a single State.
(2) For the purposes of this Convention, a bay is a well-marked indentation whose penetration is in such proportion to the width of its mouth as to contain land-locked waters and constitute more than a mere curvature of the coast. An indentation shall not, however, be regarded as a bay unless its area is as large as, or larger than, that of the semi-circle whose diameter is a line drawn across the mouth of that indentation.
(3) For the purpose of measurement, the area of an indentation is that lying between the low-water mark around the shore of the indentation and a line joining the low-water mark of its natural entrance points. Where, because of the presence of islands, an indentation has more than one mouth, the semi-circle shall be drawn on a line as long as the sum total of the lengths of the lines across the different mouths. Islands within an indentation shall be included as if they were part of the water area of the indentation.
(4) If the distance between the low-water marks of the natural entrance points of a bay does not exceed 24 nautical miles, a closing line may be drawn between these two low-water marks, and the waters enclosed thereby shall be considered as internal waters. 5. Where the distance between the low-water marks of the natural entrance points of a bay exceeds 24 nautical miles, a straight baseline of 24 nautical miles shall be drawn within the bay in such a manner as to enclose the maximum area of water that is possible with a line of that length. 6. The foregoing provisions do not apply to so-called "historic" bays, or in any case where the system of straight baselines provided for in article 7 is applied.

Article 11. Ports
For the purpose of delimiting the territorial sea, the outermost permanent harbour works which form an integral part of the harbour system are regarded as forming part of the coast. Off-shore installations and artificial islands shall not be considered as permanent harbour works.

Article 12. Roadsteads
Roadsteads which are normally used for the loading, unloading and anchoring of ships, and which would otherwise be situated wholly or partly outside the outer limit of the territorial sea, are included in the territorial sea.

Article 13. Low-tide elevations
(1) A low-tide elevation is a naturally formed area of land which is surrounded by and above water at low tide but submerged at high tide. Where a low-tide elevation is situated wholly or partly at a distance not exceeding the breadth of the territorial sea from the mainland or an island, the low-water line on that elevation may be used as the baseline for measuring the breadth of the territorial sea.
(2) Where a low-tide elevation is wholly situated at a distance exceeding the breadth of the territorial sea from the mainland or an island, it has no territorial sea of its own.

Article 14. Combination of methods for determining baselines
The coastal State may determine baselines in turn by any of the methods provided for in the foregoing articles to suit different conditions.

Article 15. Delimitation of the territorial sea between States with opposite or adjacent coasts
Where the coasts of two States are opposite or adjacent to each other, neither of the two States is entitled, failing agreement between them to the contrary, to extend its territorial sea beyond the median line every point of which is equidistant from the nearest points on the baselines from which the breadth of the territorial seas of each of the two States is measured. The above provision does not apply, however, where it is necessary by reason of historic title or other special circumstances to delimit the territorial seas of the two States in a way which is at variance therewith.

Article 16. Charts and lists of geographical coordinates
(1) The baselines for measuring the breadth of the territorial sea determined in accordance with articles 7, 9 and 10, or the limits derived therefrom, and the lines of delimitation drawn in accordance with articles 12 and 15 shall be shown on charts of a scale or scales adequate for ascertaining their

PART I INTERNATIONAL LAW

position. Alternatively, a list of geographical coordinates of points, specifying the geodetic datum, may be substituted.

(2) The coastal State shall give due publicity to such charts or lists of geographical coordinates and shall deposit a copy of each such chart or list with the Secretary-General of the United Nations.

Section 3. Innocent passage in the territorial sea

Subsection A. Rules applicable to all ships

Article 17. Right of innocent passage

Subject to this Convention, ships of all States, whether coastal or land-locked, enjoy the right of innocent passage through the territorial sea.

Article 18. Meaning of passage

(1) Passage means navigation through the territorial sea for the purpose of:
(a) traversing that sea without entering internal waters or calling at a roadstead or port facility outside internal waters; or
(b) proceeding to or from internal waters or a call at such roadstead or port facility.
(2) Passage shall be continuous and expeditious. However, passage includes stopping and anchoring, but only in so far as the same are incidental 31 to ordinary navigation or are rendered necessary by force majeure or distress or for the purpose of rendering assistance to persons, ships or aircraft in danger or distress.

Article 19. Meaning of innocent passage

(1) Passage is innocent so long as it is not prejudicial to the peace, good order or security of the coastal State. Such passage shall take place in conformity with this Convention and with other rules of international law.
(2) Passage of a foreign ship shall be considered to be prejudicial to the peace, good order or security of the coastal State if in the territorial sea it engages in any of the following activities:
(a) any threat or use of force against the sovereignty, territorial integrity or political independence of the coastal State, or in any other manner in violation of the principles of international law embodied in the Charter of the United Nations;
(b) any exercise or practice with weapons of any kind;
(c) any act aimed at collecting information to the prejudice of the defence or security of the coastal State;
(d) any act of propaganda aimed at affecting the defence or security of the coastal State;
(e) the launching, landing or taking on board of any aircraft;
(f) the launching, landing or taking on board of any military device;
(g) the loading or unloading of any commodity, currency or person contrary to the customs, fiscal, immigration or sanitary laws and regulations of the coastal State;
(h) any act of wilful and serious pollution contrary to this Convention;
(i) any fishing activities;
(j) the carrying out of research or survey activities;
(k) any act aimed at interfering with any systems of communication or any other facilities or installations of the coastal State;
(l) any other activity not having a direct bearing on passage.

Article 20. Submarines and other underwater vehicles

In the territorial sea, submarines and other underwater vehicles are required to navigate on the surface and to show their flag.

Article 21. Laws and regulations of the coastal State relating to innocent passage

(1) The coastal State may adopt laws and regulations, in conformity with the provisions of this Convention and other rules of international law, relating to innocent passage through the territorial sea, in respect of all or any of the following:
(a) the safety of navigation and the regulation of maritime traffic;
(b) the protection of navigational aids and facilities and other facilities or installations;
(c) the protection of cables and pipelines;
(d) the conservation of the living resources of the sea;
(e) the prevention of infringement of the fisheries laws and regulations of the coastal State; (f) the preservation of the environment of the coastal State and the prevention, reduction and control of pollution thereof;
(g) marine scientific research and hydrographic surveys;

(h) the prevention of infringement of the customs, fiscal, immigration or sanitary laws and regulations of the coastal State.
(2) Such laws and regulations shall not apply to the design, construction, manning or equipment of foreign ships unless they are giving effect to generally accepted international rules or standards.
(3) The coastal State shall give due publicity to all such laws and regulations.
(4) Foreign ships exercising the right of innocent passage through the territorial sea shall comply with all such laws and regulations and all generally accepted international regulations relating to the prevention of collisions at sea.

Article 22. Sea lanes and traffic separation schemes in the territorial sea
(1) The coastal State may, where necessary having regard to the safety of navigation, require foreign ships exercising the right of innocent passage through its territorial sea to use such sea lanes and traffic separation schemes as it may designate or prescribe for the regulation of the passage of ships.
(2) In particular, tankers, nuclear-powered ships and ships carrying nuclear or other inherently dangerous or noxious substances or materials may be required to confine their passage to such sea lanes.
(3) In the designation of sea lanes and the prescription of traffic separation schemes under this article, the coastal State shall take into account:
(a) the recommendations of the competent international organization;
(b) any channels customarily used for international navigation;
(c) the special characteristics of particular ships and channels; and
(d) the density of traffic.
(4) The coastal State shall clearly indicate such sea lanes and traffic separation schemes on charts to which due publicity shall be given.

Article 23. Foreign nuclear-powered ships and ships carrying nuclear or other inherently dangerous or noxious substances
Foreign nuclear-powered ships and ships carrying nuclear or other inherently dangerous or noxious substances shall, when exercising the right of innocent passage through the territorial sea, carry documents and observe special precautionary measures established for such ships by international agreements.

Article 24. Duties of the coastal State
(1) The coastal State shall not hamper the innocent passage of foreign ships through the territorial sea except in accordance with this Convention. In particular, in the application of this Convention or of any laws or regulations adopted in conformity with this Convention, the coastal State shall not:
(a) impose requirements on foreign ships which have the practical effect of denying or impairing the right of innocent passage; or
(b) discriminate in form or in fact against the ships of any State or against ships carrying cargoes to, from or on behalf of any State.
(2) The coastal State shall give appropriate publicity to any danger to navigation, of which it has knowledge, within its territorial sea.

Article 25. Rights of protection of the coastal State
(1) The coastal State may take the necessary steps in its territorial sea to prevent passage which is not innocent.
(2) In the case of ships proceeding to internal waters or a call at a port facility outside internal waters, the coastal State also has the right to take the necessary steps to prevent any breach of the conditions to which admission of those ships to internal waters or such a call is subject.
(3) The coastal State may, without discrimination in form or in fact among foreign ships, suspend temporarily in specified areas of its territorial sea the innocent passage of foreign ships if such suspension is essential for the protection of its security, including weapons exercises. Such suspension shall take effect only after having been duly published.

Article 26. Charges which may be levied upon foreign ships
(1) No charge may be levied upon foreign ships by reason only of their passage through the territorial sea.
(2) Charges may be levied upon a foreign ship passing through the territorial sea as payment only for specific services rendered to the ship. These charges shall be levied without discrimination.

Subsection B. Rules applicable to merchant ships and government ships operated for commercial purposes

PART I INTERNATIONAL LAW

Article 27. Criminal jurisdiction on board a foreign ship

(1) The criminal jurisdiction of the coastal State should not be exercised on board a foreign ship passing through the territorial sea to arrest any person or to conduct any investigation in connection with any crime committed on board the ship during its passage, save only in the following cases:
(a) if the consequences of the crime extend to the coastal State;
(b) if the crime is of a kind to disturb the peace of the country or the good order of the territorial sea;
(c) if the assistance of the local authorities has been requested by the master of the ship or by a diplomatic agent or consular officer of the flag State; or
(d) if such measures are necessary for the suppression of illicit traffic in narcotic drugs or psychotropic substances.
(2) The above provisions do not affect the right of the coastal State to take any steps authorized by its laws for the purpose of an arrest or investigation on board a foreign ship passing through the territorial sea after leaving internal waters.
(3) In the cases provided for in paragraphs (1) and (2), the coastal State shall, if the master so requests, notify a diplomatic agent or consular officer of the flag State before taking any steps, and shall facilitate contact between such agent or officer and the ship's crew. In cases of emergency this notification may be communicated while the measures are being taken.
(4) In considering whether or in what manner an arrest should be made, the local authorities shall have due regard to the interests of navigation.
(5) Except as provided in Part XII or with respect to violations of laws and regulations adopted in accordance with Part V, the coastal State may not take any steps on board a foreign ship passing through the territorial sea to arrest any person or to conduct any investigation in connection with any crime committed before the ship entered the territorial sea, if the ship, proceeding from a foreign port, is only passing through the territorial sea without entering internal waters.

Article 28. Civil jurisdiction in relation to foreign ships

(1) The coastal State should not stop or divert a foreign ship passing through the territorial sea for the purpose of exercising civil jurisdiction in relation to a person on board the ship.
(2) The coastal State may not levy execution against or arrest the ship for the purpose of any civil proceedings, save only in respect of obligations or liabilities assumed or incurred by the ship itself in the course or for the purpose of its voyage through the waters of the coastal State.
(3) Paragraph (2) is without prejudice to the right of the coastal State, in accordance with its laws, to levy execution against or to arrest, for the purpose of any civil proceedings, a foreign ship lying in the territorial sea, or passing through the territorial sea after leaving internal waters.

Subsection C. Rules applicable to warships and other government ships operated for non-commercial purposes

Article 29. Definition of warships

For the purposes of this Convention, "warship" means a ship belonging to the armed forces of a State bearing the external marks distinguishing such ships of its nationality, under the command of an officer duly commissioned by the government of the State and whose name appears in the appropriate service list or its equivalent, and manned by a crew which is under regular armed forces discipline.

Article 30. Non-compliance by warships with the laws and regulations of the coastal State

If any warship does not comply with the laws and regulations of the coastal State concerning passage through the territorial sea and disregards any request for compliance therewith which is made to it, the coastal State may require it to leave the territorial sea immediately.

Article 31. Responsibility of the flag State for damage caused by a warship or other government ship operated for non-commercial purposes

The flag State shall bear international responsibility for any loss or damage to the coastal State resulting from the non-compliance by a warship or other government ship operated for non-commercial purposes with the laws and regulations of the coastal State concerning passage through the territorial sea or with the provisions of this Convention or other rules of international law.

Article 32. Immunities of warships and other government ships operated for non-commercial purposes

With such exceptions as are contained in subsection A and in articles 30 and 31, nothing in this Convention affects the immunities of warships and other government ships operated for non-commercial purposes.

Section 4. Contiguous zone

Article 33. Contiguous zone
(1) In a zone contiguous to its territorial sea, described as the contiguous zone, the coastal State may exercise the control necessary to:
(a) prevent infringement of its customs, fiscal, immigration or sanitary laws and regulations within its territory or territorial sea;
(b) punish infringement of the above laws and regulations committed within its territory or territorial sea.
(2) The contiguous zone may not extend beyond 24 nautical miles from the baselines from which the breadth of the territorial sea is measured.

Part III. Straits used for international navigation

Section 1. General provisions

Article 34. Legal status of waters forming straits used for international navigation
(1) The regime of passage through straits used for international navigation established in this Part shall not in other respects affect the legal status of the waters forming such straits or the exercise by the States bordering the straits of their sovereignty or jurisdiction over such waters and their air space, bed and subsoil.
(2) The sovereignty or jurisdiction of the States bordering the straits is exercised subject to this Part and to other rules of international law.

Article 35. Scope of this Part
Nothing in this Part affects:
(a) any areas of internal waters within a strait, except where the establishment of a straight baseline in accordance with the method set forth in article 7 has the effect of enclosing as internal waters areas which had not previously been considered as such;
(b) the legal status of the waters beyond the territorial seas of States bordering straits as exclusive economic zones or high seas; or
(c) the legal regime in straits in which passage is regulated in whole or in part by long-standing international conventions in force specifically relating to such straits.

Article 36. High seas routes or routes through exclusive economic zones through straits used for international navigation
This Part does not apply to a strait used for international navigation if there exists through the strait a route through the high seas or through an exclusive economic zone of similar convenience with respect to navigational and hydrographical characteristics; in such routes, the other relevant Parts of this Convention, including the provisions regarding the freedoms of navigation and overflight, apply.

Section 2. Transit passage

Article 37. Scope of this section
This section applies to straits which are used for international navigation between one part of the high seas or an exclusive economic zone and another part of the high seas or an exclusive economic zone.

Article 38. Right of transit passage
(1) In straits referred to in article 37, all ships and aircraft enjoy the right of transit passage, which shall not be impeded; except that, if the strait is formed by an island of a State bordering the strait and its mainland, transit passage shall not apply if there exists seaward of the island a route through the high seas or through an exclusive economic zone of similar convenience with respect to navigational and hydrographical characteristics.
(2) Transit passage means the exercise in accordance with this Part of the freedom of navigation and overflight solely for the purpose of continuous and expeditious transit of the strait between one part of the high seas or an exclusive economic zone and another part of the high seas or an exclusive economic zone. However, the requirement of continuous and expeditious transit does not preclude passage through the strait for the purpose of entering, leaving or returning from a State bordering the strait, subject to the conditions of entry to that State.
(3) Any activity which is not an exercise of the right of transit passage through a strait remains subject to the other applicable provisions of this Convention.

Article 39. Duties of ships and aircraft during transit passage
(1) Ships and aircraft, while exercising the right of transit passage, shall:
(a) proceed without delay through or over the strait;

PART I   INTERNATIONAL LAW

(b) refrain from any threat or use of force against the sovereignty, territorial integrity or political independence of States bordering the strait, or in any other manner in violation of the principles of international law embodied in the Charter of the United Nations;
(c) refrain from any activities other than those incident to their normal
modes of continuous and expeditious transit unless rendered necessary by force majeure or by distress;
(d) comply with other relevant provisions of this Part.
(2) Ships in transit passage shall:
(a) comply with generally accepted international regulations, procedures and practices for safety at sea, including the International Regulations for Preventing Collisions at Sea;
(b) comply with generally accepted international regulations, procedures and practices for the prevention, reduction and control of pollution from ships.
(3) Aircraft in transit passage shall:
(a) observe the Rules of the Air established by the International Civil Aviation Organization as they apply to civil aircraft; state aircraft will normally comply with such safety measures and will at all times operate with due regard for the safety of navigation;
(b) at all times monitor the radio frequency assigned by the competent internationally designated air traffic control authority or the appropriate international distress radio frequency.

Article 40. Research and survey activities
During transit passage, foreign ships, including marine scientific research and hydrographic survey ships, may not carry out any research or survey activities without the prior authorization of the States bordering straits.

Article 41. Sea lanes and traffic separation schemes in straits used for international navigation
(1) In conformity with this Part, States bordering straits may designate sea lanes and prescribe traffic separation schemes for navigation in straits where necessary to promote the safe passage of ships.
(2) Such States may, when circumstances require, and after giving due publicity thereto, substitute other sea lanes or traffic separation schemes for any sea lanes or traffic separation schemes previously designated or prescribed by them.
(3) Such sea lanes and traffic separation schemes shall conform to generally accepted international regulations.
(4) Before designating or substituting sea lanes or prescribing or substituting traffic separation schemes, States bordering straits shall refer proposals to the competent international organization with a view to their adoption. The organization may adopt only such sea lanes and traffic separation schemes as may be agreed with the States bordering the straits, after which the States may designate, prescribe or substitute them.
(5) In respect of a strait where sea lanes or traffic separation schemes through the waters of two or more States bordering the strait are being proposed, the States concerned shall cooperate in formulating proposals in consultation with the competent international organization.
(6) States bordering straits shall clearly indicate all sea lanes and traffic separation schemes designated or prescribed by them on charts to which due publicity shall be given. 7. Ships in transit passage shall respect applicable sea lanes and traffic separation schemes established in accordance with this article.

Article 42. Laws and regulations of States bordering straits relating to transit passage
(1) Subject to the provisions of this section, States bordering straits may adopt laws and regulations relating to transit passage through straits, in respect of all or any of the following: (a) the safety of navigation and the regulation of maritime traffic, as provided in article 41; (b) the prevention, reduction and control of pollution, by giving effect to applicable international regulations regarding the discharge of oil, oily wastes and other noxious substances in the strait;
(c) with respect to fishing vessels, the prevention of fishing, including the stowage of fishing gear; 39
(d) the loading or unloading of any commodity, currency or person in contravention of the customs, fiscal, immigration or sanitary laws and regulations of States bordering straits. 2. Such laws and regulations shall not discriminate in form or in fact among foreign ships or in their application have the practical effect of denying, hampering or impairing the right of transit passage as defined in this section.
(3) States bordering straits shall give due publicity to all such laws and regulations.
(4) Foreign ships exercising the right of transit passage shall comply with such laws and regulations.
(5) The flag State of a ship or the State of registry of an aircraft entitled to sovereign immunity which acts in a manner contrary to such laws and regulations or other provisions of this Part shall bear international responsibility for any loss or damage which results to States bordering straits.

Article 43. Navigational and safety aids and other improvements and the prevention, reduction and control of pollution

User States and States bordering a strait should by agreement cooperate:
(a) in the establishment and maintenance in a strait of necessary navigational and safety aids or other improvements in aid of international navigation; and
(b) for the prevention, reduction and control of pollution from ships.

Article 44. Duties of States bordering straits

States bordering straits shall not hamper transit passage and shall give appropriate publicity to any danger to navigation or overflight within or over the strait of which they have knowledge. There shall be no suspension of transit passage.

Section 3. Innocent passage

Article 45. Innocent passage

(1) The regime of innocent passage, in accordance with Part II, section 3, shall apply in straits used for international navigation:
(a) excluded from the application of the regime of transit passage under article 38, paragraph (1); or
(b) between a part of the high seas or an exclusive economic zone and the territorial sea of a foreign State.
(2) There shall be no suspension of innocent passage through such straits.

Part IV. Archipelagic states

Article 46. Use of terms

For the purposes of this Convention:
(a) "archipelagic State" means a State constituted wholly by one or more archipelagos and may include other islands;
(b) "archipelago" means a group of islands, including parts of islands, interconnecting waters and other natural features which are so closely interrelated that such islands, waters and other natural features form an intrinsic geographical, economic and political entity, or which historically have been regarded as such.

Article 47. Archipelagic baselines

(1) An archipelagic State may draw straight archipelagic baselines joining the outermost points of the outermost islands and drying reefs of the archipelago provided that within such baselines are included the main islands and an area in which the ratio of the area of the water to the area of the land, including atolls, is between 1 to 1 and 9 to 1.
(2) The length of such baselines shall not exceed 100 nautical miles, except that up to 3 per cent of the total number of baselines enclosing any archipelago may exceed that length, up to a maximum length of 125 nautical miles.
(3) The drawing of such baselines shall not depart to any appreciable extent from the general configuration of the archipelago.
(4) Such baselines shall not be drawn to and from low-tide elevations, unless lighthouses or similar installations which are permanently above sea level have been built on them or where a low-tide elevation is situated wholly or partly at a distance not exceeding the breadth of the territorial sea from the nearest island.
(5) The system of such baselines shall not be applied by an archipelagic State in such a manner as to cut off from the high seas or the exclusive economic zone the territorial sea of another State.
(6) If a part of the archipelagic waters of an archipelagic State lies between two parts of an immediately adjacent neighbouring State, existing rights and all other legitimate interests which the latter State has traditionally exercised in such waters and all rights stipulated by agreement between those States shall continue and be respected.
(7) For the purpose of computing the ratio of water to land under paragraph (1), land areas may include waters lying within the fringing reefs of islands and atolls, including that part of a steep-sided oceanic plateau which is enclosed or nearly enclosed by a chain of limestone islands and drying reefs lying on the perimeter of the plateau.
(8) The baselines drawn in accordance with this article shall be shown on charts of a scale or scales adequate for ascertaining their position. Alternatively, lists of geographical coordinates of points, specifying the geodetic datum, may be substituted.
(9) The archipelagic State shall give due publicity to such charts or lists of geographical coordinates and shall deposit a copy of each such chart or list with the Secretary-General of the United Nations.

PART I   INTERNATIONAL LAW

Article 48. Measurement of the breadth of the territorial sea, the contiguous zone, the exclusive economic zone and the continental shelf
The breadth of the territorial sea, the contiguous zone, the exclusive economic zone and the continental shelf shall be measured from archipelagic baselines drawn in accordance with article 47.

Article 49. Legal status of archipelagic waters, of the air space over archipelagic waters and of their bed and subsoil
(1) The sovereignty of an archipelagic State extends to the waters enclosed by the archipelagic baselines drawn in accordance with article 47, described as archipelagic waters, regardless of their depth or distance from the coast.
(2) This sovereignty extends to the air space over the archipelagic waters, as well as to their bed and subsoil, and the resources contained therein.
(3) This sovereignty is exercised subject to this Part.
(4) The regime of archipelagic sea lanes passage established in this Part shall not in other respects affect the status of the archipelagic waters, including the sea lanes, or the exercise by the archipelagic State of its sovereignty over such waters and their air space, bed and subsoil, and the resources contained therein.

Article 50. Delimitation of internal waters
Within its archipelagic waters, the archipelagic State may draw closing lines for the delimitation of internal waters, in accordance with articles 9, 10 and 11.

Article 51. Existing agreements, traditional fishing rights and existing submarine cables
(1) Without prejudice to article 49, an archipelagic State shall respect existing agreements with other States and shall recognize traditional fishing rights and other legitimate activities of the immediately adjacent neighbouring States in certain areas falling within archipelagic waters. The terms and conditions for the exercise of such rights and activities, including the nature, the extent and the areas to which they apply, shall, at the request of any of the States concerned, be regulated by bilateral agreements between them. Such rights shall not be transferred to or shared with third States or their nationals.
(2) An archipelagic State shall respect existing submarine cables laid by other States and passing through its waters without making a landfall. An archipelagic State shall permit the maintenance and replacement of such 42 cables upon receiving due notice of their location and the intention to repair or replace them.

Article 52. Right of innocent passage
(1) Subject to article 53 and without prejudice to article 50, ships of all States enjoy the right of innocent passage through archipelagic waters, in accordance with Part II, section 3.
(2) The archipelagic State may, without discrimination in form or in fact among foreign ships, suspend temporarily in specified areas of its archipelagic waters the innocent passage of foreign ships if such suspension is essential for the protection of its security. Such suspension shall take effect only after having been duly published.

Article 53. Right of archipelagic sea lanes passage
(1) An archipelagic State may designate sea lanes and air routes thereabove, suitable for the continuous and expeditious passage of foreign ships and aircraft through or over its archipelagic waters and the adjacent territorial sea.
(2) All ships and aircraft enjoy the right of archipelagic sea lanes passage in such sea lanes and air routes.
(3) Archipelagic sea lanes passage means the exercise in accordance with this Convention of the rights of navigation and overflight in the normal mode solely for the purpose of continuous, expeditious and unobstructed transit between one part of the high seas or an exclusive economic zone and another part of the high seas or an exclusive economic zone.
(4) Such sea lanes and air routes shall traverse the archipelagic waters and the adjacent territorial sea and shall include all normal passage routes used as routes for international navigation or overflight through or over archipelagic waters and, within such routes, so far as ships are concerned, all normal navigational channels, provided that duplication of routes of similar convenience between the same entry and exit points shall not be necessary.
(5) Such sea lanes and air routes shall be defined by a series of continuous axis lines from the entry points of passage routes to the exit points. Ships and aircraft in archipelagic sea lanes passage shall not deviate more than 25 nautical miles to either side of such axis lines during passage, provided that such ships and aircraft shall not navigate closer to the coasts than 10 per cent of the distance between

the nearest points on islands bordering the sea lane.
(6) An archipelagic State which designates sea lanes under this article may also prescribe traffic separation schemes for the safe passage of ships through narrow channels in such sea lanes.
(7) An archipelagic State may, when circumstances require, after giving due publicity thereto, substitute other sea lanes or traffic separation schemes for any sea lanes or traffic separation schemes previously designated or prescribed by it.
(8) Such sea lanes and traffic separation schemes shall conform to generally accepted international regulations.
(9) In designating or substituting sea lanes or prescribing or substituting traffic separation schemes, an archipelagic State shall refer proposals to the 43 competent international organization with a view to their adoption. The organization may adopt only such sea lanes and traffic separation schemes as may be agreed with the archipelagic State, after which the archipelagic State may designate, prescribe or substitute them.
(10) The archipelagic State shall clearly indicate the axis of the sea lanes and the traffic separation schemes designated or prescribed by it on charts to which due publicity shall be given.
(11) Ships in archipelagic sea lanes passage shall respect applicable sea lanes and traffic separation schemes established in accordance with this article.
(12) If an archipelagic State does not designate sea lanes or air routes, the right of archipelagic sea lanes passage may be exercised through the routes normally used for international navigation.

Article 54. Duties of ships and aircraft during their passage, research and survey activities, duties of the archipelagic State and laws and regulations of the archipelagic State relating to archipelagic sea lanes passage
Articles 39, 40, 42 and 44 apply *mutatis mutandis* to archipelagic sea lanes passage.

Part V. Exclusive Economic Zone

Article 55. Specific legal regime of the exclusive economic zone
The exclusive economic zone is an area beyond and adjacent to the territorial sea, subject to the specific legal regime established in this Part, under which the rights and jurisdiction of the coastal State and the rights and freedoms of other States are governed by the relevant provisions of this Convention.

Article 56. Rights, jurisdiction and duties of the coastal State in the exclusive economic zone
(1) In the exclusive economic zone, the coastal State has:
(a) sovereign rights for the purpose of exploring and exploiting, conserving and managing the natural resources, whether living or non-living, of the waters superjacent to the seabed and of the seabed and its subsoil, and with regard to other activities for the economic exploitation and exploration of the zone, such as the production of energy from the water, currents and winds;
(b) jurisdiction as provided for in the relevant provisions of this Convention with regard to: (i) the establishment and use of artificial islands, installations and structures;
(ii) marine scientific research;
(iii) the protection and preservation of the marine environment;
(c) other rights and duties provided for in this Convention.
(2) In exercising its rights and performing its duties under this Convention in the exclusive economic zone, the coastal State shall have due regard to the rights and duties of other States and shall act in a manner compatible with the provisions of this Convention.
(3) The rights set out in this article with respect to the seabed and subsoil shall be exercised in accordance with Part VI.

Article 57. Breadth of the exclusive economic zone
The exclusive economic zone shall not extend beyond 200 nautical miles from the baselines from which the breadth of the territorial sea is measured.

Article 58. Rights and duties of other States in the exclusive economic zone
(1) In the exclusive economic zone, all States, whether coastal or land-locked, enjoy, subject to the relevant provisions of this Convention, the freedoms referred to in article 87 of navigation and overflight and of the laying of submarine cables and pipelines, and other internationally lawful uses of the sea related to these freedoms, such as those associated with the operation of ships, aircraft and submarine cables and pipelines, and compatible with the other provisions of this Convention.
(2) Articles 88 to 115 and other pertinent rules of international law apply to the exclusive economic zone in so far as they are not incompatible with this Part.

PART I   INTERNATIONAL LAW

(3) In exercising their rights and performing their duties under this Convention in the exclusive economic zone, States shall have due regard to the rights and duties of the coastal State and shall comply with the laws and regulations adopted by the coastal State in accordance with the provisions of this Convention and other rules of international law in so far as they are not incompatible with this Part.

Article 59. Basis for the resolution of conflicts regarding the attribution of rights and jurisdiction in the exclusive economic zone
In cases where this Convention does not attribute rights or jurisdiction to the coastal State or to other States within the exclusive economic zone, and a conflict arises between the interests of the coastal State and any other State or States, the conflict should be resolved on the basis of equity and in the light of all the relevant circumstances, taking into account the respective importance of the interests involved to the parties as well as to the international community as a whole.

Article 60. Artificial islands, installations and structures in the exclusive economic zone
(1) In the exclusive economic zone, the coastal State shall have the exclusive right to construct and to authorize and regulate the construction, operation and use of:
(a) artificial islands;
(b) installations and structures for the purposes provided for in article 56 and other economic purposes;
(c) installations and structures which may interfere with the exercise of the rights of the coastal State in the zone.
(2) The coastal State shall have exclusive jurisdiction over such artificial islands, installations and structures, including jurisdiction with regard to customs, fiscal, health, safety and immigration laws and regulations.
(3) Due notice must be given of the construction of such artificial islands, installations or structures, and permanent means for giving warning of their presence must be maintained. Any installations or structures which are abandoned or disused shall be removed to ensure safety of navigation, taking into account any generally accepted international standards established in this regard by the competent international organization. Such removal shall also have due regard to fishing, the protection of the marine environment and the rights and duties of other States. Appropriate publicity shall be given to the depth, position and dimensions of any installations or structures not entirely removed.
(4) The coastal State may, where necessary, establish reasonable safety zones around such artificial islands, installations and structures in which it may take appropriate measures to ensure the safety both of navigation and of the artificial islands, installations and structures. (5) The breadth of the safety zones shall be determined by the coastal State, taking into account applicable international standards. Such zones shall be designed to ensure that they are reasonably related to the nature and function of the artificial islands, installations or structures, and shall not exceed a distance of 500 metres around them, measured from each point of their outer edge, except as authorized by generally accepted international standards or as recommended by the competent international organization. Due notice shall be given of the extent of safety zones.
(6) All ships must respect these safety zones and shall comply with generally accepted international standards regarding navigation in the vicinity of artificial islands, installations, structures and safety zones.
(7) Artificial islands, installations and structures and the safety zones around them may not be established where interference may be caused to the use of recognized sea lanes essential to international navigation.
(8) Artificial islands, installations and structures do not possess the status of islands. They have no territorial sea of their own, and their presence does not affect the delimitation of the territorial sea, the exclusive economic zone or the continental shelf.

Article 61. Conservation of the living resources
(1) The coastal State shall determine the allowable catch of the living resources in its exclusive economic zone.
(2) The coastal State, taking into account the best scientific evidence available to it, shall ensure through proper conservation and management measures that the maintenance of the living resources in the exclusive economic zone is not endangered by over-exploitation. As appropriate, the coastal State and competent international organizations, whether subregional, regional or global, shall cooperate to this end.
(3) Such measures shall also be designed to maintain or restore populations of harvested species at levels which can produce the maximum sustainable yield, as qualified by relevant environmental and economic factors, including the economic needs of coastal fishing communities and the special

requirements of developing States, and taking into account fishing patterns, the interdependence of stocks and any generally recommended international minimum standards, whether subregional, regional or global.
(4) In taking such measures the coastal State shall take into consideration the effects on species associated with or dependent upon harvested species with a view to maintaining or restoring populations of such associated or dependent species above levels at which their reproduction may become seriously threatened.
(5) Available scientific information, catch and fishing effort statistics, and other data relevant to the conservation of fish stocks shall be contributed and exchanged on a regular basis through competent international organizations, whether subregional, regional or global, where appropriate and with participation by all States concerned, including States whose nationals are allowed to fish in the exclusive economic zone.

Article 62. Utilization of the living resources
(1) The coastal State shall promote the objective of optimum utilization of the living resources in the exclusive economic zone without prejudice to article 61.
(2) The coastal State shall determine its capacity to harvest the living resources of the exclusive economic zone. Where the coastal State does not have the capacity to harvest the entire allowable catch, it shall, through agreements or other arrangements and pursuant to the terms, conditions, laws and regulations referred to in paragraph (4), give other States access to the surplus of the allowable catch, having particular regard to the provisions of articles 69 and 70, especially in relation to the developing States mentioned therein.
(3) In giving access to other States to its exclusive economic zone under this article, the coastal State shall take into account all relevant factors, including, inter alia, the significance of the living resources of the area to the economy of the coastal State concerned and its other national interests, the provisions of articles 69 and 70, the requirements of developing States in the subregion or region in harvesting part of the surplus and the need to minimize economic dislocation in States whose nationals have habitually fished in the zone or which have made substantial efforts in research and identification of stocks.
(4) Nationals of other States fishing in the exclusive economic zone shall comply with the conservation measures and with the other terms and conditions established in the laws and regulations of the coastal State. These laws and regulations shall be consistent with this Convention and may relate, inter alia, to the following:
(a) licensing of fishermen, fishing vessels and equipment, including payment of fees and other forms of remuneration, which, in the case of developing coastal States, may consist of adequate compensation in the field of financing, equipment and technology relating to the fishing industry;
(b) determining the species which may be caught, and fixing quotas of catch, whether in relation to particular stocks or groups of stocks or catch per vessel over a period of time or to the catch by nationals of any State during a specified period;
(c) regulating seasons and areas of fishing, the types, sizes and amount of gear, and the types, sizes and number of fishing vessels that may be used;
(d) fixing the age and size of fish and other species that may be caught;
(e) specifying information required of fishing vessels, including catch and effort statistics and vessel position reports;
(f) requiring, under the authorization and control of the coastal State, the conduct of specified fisheries research programmes and regulating the conduct of such research, including the sampling of catches, disposition of samples and reporting of associated scientific data;
(g) the placing of observers or trainees on board such vessels by the coastal State;
(h) the landing of all or any part of the catch by such vessels in the ports of the coastal State; (i) terms and conditions relating to joint ventures or other cooperative arrangements;
(j) requirements for the training of personnel and the transfer of fisheries technology, including enhancement of the coastal State's capability of undertaking fisheries research;
(k) enforcement procedures.
(5) Coastal States shall give due notice of conservation and management laws and regulations.

Article 63. Stocks occurring within the exclusive economic zones of two or more coastal States or both within the exclusive economic zone and in an area beyond and adjacent to it
(1) Where the same stock or stocks of associated species occur within the exclusive economic zones of two or more coastal States, these States shall seek, either directly or through appropriate subregional or regional organizations, to agree upon the measures necessary to coordinate and ensure the conservation and development of such stocks without prejudice to the other provisions of this Part.

(2) Where the same stock or stocks of associated species occur both within the exclusive economic zone and in an area beyond and adjacent to the zone, the coastal State and the States fishing for such stocks in the adjacent area shall seek, either directly or through appropriate subregional or regional organizations, to agree upon the measures necessary for the conservation of these stocks in the adjacent area.

Article 64. Highly migratory species

(1) The coastal State and other States whose nationals fish in the region for the highly migratory species listed in Annex I shall cooperate directly or through appropriate international organizations with a view to ensuring conservation and promoting the objective of optimum utilization of such species throughout the region, both within and beyond the exclusive economic zone. In regions for which no appropriate international organization exists, the coastal State and other States whose nationals harvest these species in the region shall cooperate to establish such an organization and participate in its work.
(2) The provisions of paragraph (1) apply in addition to the other provisions of this Part. Article 65 Marine mammals Nothing in this Part restricts the right of a coastal State or the competence of an international organization, as appropriate, to prohibit, limit or regulate the exploitation of marine mammals more strictly than provided for in this Part. States shall cooperate with a view to the conservation of marine mammals and in the case of cetaceans shall in particular work through the appropriate international organizations for their conservation, management and study.

Article 66. Anadromous stocks

(1) States in whose rivers anadromous stocks originate shall have the primary interest in and responsibility for such stocks.
(2) The State of origin of anadromous stocks shall ensure their conservation by the establishment of appropriate regulatory measures for fishing in all waters landward of the outer limits of its exclusive economic zone and for fishing provided for in paragraph (3)(b). The State of origin may, after consultations with the other States referred to in paragraphs (3) and (4) fishing these stocks, establish total allowable catches for stocks originating in its rivers.
(3)(a) Fisheries for anadromous stocks shall be conducted only in waters landward of the outer limits of exclusive economic zones, except in cases where this provision would result in economic dislocation for a State other than the State of origin. With respect to such fishing beyond the outer limits of the exclusive economic zone, States concerned shall maintain consultations with a view to achieving agreement on terms and conditions of such fishing giving due regard to the conservation requirements and the needs of the State of origin in respect of these stocks.
(b) The State of origin shall cooperate in minimizing economic dislocation in such other States fishing these stocks, taking into account the normal catch and the mode of operations of such States, and all the areas in which such fishing has occurred.
(c) States referred to in subparagraph (b), participating by agreement with the State of origin in measures to renew anadromous stocks, particularly by expenditures for that purpose, shall be given special consideration by the State of origin in the harvesting of stocks originating in its rivers.
(d) Enforcement of regulations regarding anadromous stocks beyond the exclusive economic zone shall be by agreement between the State of origin and the other States concerned.
(4) In cases where anadromous stocks migrate into or through the waters landward of the outer limits of the exclusive economic zone of a State other than the State of origin, such State shall cooperate with the State of origin with regard to the conservation and management of such stocks.
(5) The State of origin of anadromous stocks and other States fishing these stocks shall make arrangements for the implementation of the provisions of this article, where appropriate, through regional organizations.

Article 67. Catadromous species

(1) A coastal State in whose waters catadromous species spend the greater part of their life cycle shall have responsibility for the management of these species and shall ensure the ingress and egress of migrating fish.
(2) Harvesting of catadromous species shall be conducted only in waters landward of the outer limits of exclusive economic zones. When conducted in exclusive economic zones, harvesting shall be subject to this article and the other provisions of this Convention concerning fishing in these zones.
(3) In cases where catadromous fish migrate through the exclusive economic zone of another State, whether as juvenile or maturing fish, the management, including harvesting, of such fish shall be regulated by agreement between the State mentioned in paragraph (1) and the other State concerned. Such agreement shall ensure the rational management of the species and take into account the responsibilities of the State mentioned in paragraph (1) for the maintenance of these species.

Article 68. Sedentary species
This Part does not apply to sedentary species as defined in article 77, paragraph (4).

Article 69. Right of land-locked States
(1) Land-locked States shall have the right to participate, on an equitable basis, in the exploitation of an appropriate part of the surplus of the living resources of the exclusive economic zones of coastal States of the same subregion or region, taking into account the relevant economic and geographical circumstances of all the States concerned and in conformity with the provisions of this article and of articles 61 and 62.
(2) The terms and modalities of such participation shall be established by the States concerned through bilateral, subregional or regional agreements taking into account, inter alia:
(a) the need to avoid effects detrimental to fishing communities or fishing industries of the coastal State;
(b) the extent to which the land-locked State, in accordance with the provisions of this article, is participating or is entitled to participate under existing bilateral, subregional or regional agreements in the exploitation of living resources of the exclusive economic zones of other coastal States;
(c) the extent to which other land-locked States and geographically disadvantaged States are participating in the exploitation of the living resources of the exclusive economic zone of the coastal State and the consequent need to avoid a particular burden for any single coastal State or a part of it;
(d) the nutritional needs of the populations of the respective States.
(3) When the harvesting capacity of a coastal State approaches a point which would enable it to harvest the entire allowable catch of the living resources in its exclusive economic zone, the coastal State and other States concerned shall cooperate in the establishment of equitable arrangements on a bilateral, subregional or regional basis to allow for participation of developing land-locked States of the same subregion or region in the exploitation of the living resources of the exclusive economic zones of coastal States of the subregion or region, as may be appropriate in the circumstances and on terms satisfactory to all parties. In the implementation of this provision the factors mentioned in paragraph (2) shall also be taken into account.
(4) Developed land-locked States shall, under the provisions of this article, be entitled to participate in the exploitation of living resources only in the exclusive economic zones of developed coastal States of the same subregion or region having regard to the extent to which the coastal State, in giving access to other States to the living resources of its exclusive economic zone, has taken into account the need to minimize detrimental effects on fishing communities and economic dislocation in States whose nationals have habitually fished in the zone.
(5) The above provisions are without prejudice to arrangements agreed upon in subregions or regions where the coastal States may grant to land-locked States of the same subregion or region equal or preferential rights for the exploitation of the living resources in the exclusive economic zones.

Article 70. Right of geographically disadvantaged States
(1) Geographically disadvantaged States shall have the right to participate, on an equitable basis, in the exploitation of an appropriate part of the surplus of the living resources of the exclusive economic zones of coastal States of the same subregion or region, taking into account the relevant economic and geographical circumstances of all the States concerned and in conformity with the provisions of this article and of articles 61 and 62.
(2) For the purposes of this Part, "geographically disadvantaged States" means coastal States, including States bordering enclosed or semi-enclosed seas, whose geographical situation makes them dependent upon the exploitation of the living resources of the exclusive economic zones of other States in the subregion or region for adequate supplies of fish for the nutritional purposes of their populations or parts thereof, and coastal States which can claim no exclusive economic zones of their own.
(3) The terms and modalities of such participation shall be established by the States concerned through bilateral, subregional or regional agreements taking into account, inter alia:
(a) the need to avoid effects detrimental to fishing communities or fishing industries of the coastal State;
(b) the extent to which the geographically disadvantaged State, in accordance with the provisions of this article, is participating or is entitled to participate under existing bilateral, subregional or regional agreements in the exploitation of living resources of the exclusive economic zones of other coastal States;
(c) the extent to which other geographically disadvantaged States and land-locked States are participating in the exploitation of the living resources of the exclusive economic zone of the coastal State and the consequent need to avoid a particular burden for any single coastal State or a part of it;

PART I   INTERNATIONAL LAW

(d) the nutritional needs of the populations of the respective States.
(4) When the harvesting capacity of a coastal State approaches a point which would enable it to harvest the entire allowable catch of the living resources in its exclusive economic zone, the coastal State and other States concerned shall cooperate in the establishment of equitable arrangements on a bilateral, subregional or regional basis to allow for participation of developing geographically disadvantaged States of the same subregion or region in the exploitation of the living resources of the exclusive economic zones of coastal States of the subregion or region, as may be appropriate in the circumstances and on terms satisfactory to all parties. In the implementation of this provision the factors mentioned in paragraph (3) shall also be taken into account.
(5) Developed geographically disadvantaged States shall, under the provisions of this article, be entitled to participate in the exploitation of living resources only in the exclusive economic zones of developed coastal States of the same subregion or region having regard to the extent to which the coastal State, in giving access to other States to the living resources of its exclusive economic zone, has taken into account the need to minimize detrimental effects on fishing communities and economic dislocation in States whose nationals have habitually fished in the zone.
(6) The above provisions are without prejudice to arrangements agreed upon in subregions or regions where the coastal States may grant to geographically disadvantaged States of the same subregion or region equal or preferential rights for the exploitation of the living resources in the exclusive economic zones.

Article 71. Non-applicability of articles 69 and 70
The provisions of articles 69 and 70 do not apply in the case of a coastal State whose economy is overwhelmingly dependent on the exploitation of the living resources of its exclusive economic zone.
Article 72 Restrictions on transfer of rights
(1) Rights provided under articles 69 and 70 to exploit living resources shall not be directly or indirectly transferred to third States or their nationals 52 by lease or licence, by establishing joint ventures or in any other manner which has the effect of such transfer unless otherwise agreed by the States concerned.
(2) The foregoing provision does not preclude the States concerned from obtaining technical or financial assistance from third States or international organizations in order to facilitate the exercise of the rights pursuant to articles 69 and 70, provided that it does not have the effect referred to in paragraph (1).

Article 73. Enforcement of laws and regulations of the coastal State
(1) The coastal State may, in the exercise of its sovereign rights to explore, exploit, conserve and manage the living resources in the exclusive economic zone, take such measures, including boarding, inspection, arrest and judicial proceedings, as may be necessary to ensure compliance with the laws and regulations adopted by it in conformity with this Convention. (2) Arrested vessels and their crews shall be promptly released upon the posting of reasonable bond or other security.
(3) Coastal State penalties for violations of fisheries laws and regulations in the exclusive economic zone may not include imprisonment, in the absence of agreements to the contrary by the States concerned, or any other form of corporal punishment.
(4) In cases of arrest or detention of foreign vessels the coastal State shall promptly notify the flag State, through appropriate channels, of the action taken and of any penalties subsequently imposed.

Article 74. Delimitation of the exclusive economic zone between States with opposite or adjacent coasts
(1) The delimitation of the exclusive economic zone between States with opposite or adjacent coasts shall be effected by agreement on the basis of international law, as referred to in Article 38 of the Statute of the International Court of Justice, in order to achieve an equitable solution.
(2) If no agreement can be reached within a reasonable period of time, the States concerned shall resort to the procedures provided for in Part XV.
(3) Pending agreement as provided for in paragraph (1), the States concerned, in a spirit of understanding and cooperation, shall make every effort to enter into provisional arrangements of a practical nature and, during this transitional period, not to jeopardize or hamper the reaching of the final agreement. Such arrangements shall be without prejudice to the final delimitation.
(4) Where there is an agreement in force between the States concerned, questions relating to the delimitation of the exclusive economic zone shall be determined in accordance with the provisions of that agreement.

Article 75. Charts and lists of geographical coordinates
(1) Subject to this Part, the outer limit lines of the exclusive economic zone and the lines of delimita-

tion drawn in accordance with article 74 shall be shown on charts of a scale or scales adequate for ascertaining their 53 position. Where appropriate, lists of geographical coordinates of points, specifying the geodetic datum, may be substituted for such outer limit lines or lines of delimitation.
(2) The coastal State shall give due publicity to such charts or lists of geographical coordinates and shall deposit a copy of each such chart or list with the Secretary-General of the United Nations.

Part VI. Continental shelf

Article 76. Definition of the continental shelf
(1) The continental shelf of a coastal State comprises the seabed and subsoil of the submarine areas that extend beyond its territorial sea throughout the natural prolongation of its land territory to the outer edge of the continental margin, or to a distance of 200 nautical miles from the baselines from which the breadth of the territorial sea is measured where the outer edge of the continental margin does not extend up to that distance.
(2) The continental shelf of a coastal State shall not extend beyond the limits provided for in paragraphs (4) to (6).
(3) The continental margin comprises the submerged prolongation of the land mass of the coastal State, and consists of the seabed and subsoil of the shelf, the slope and the rise. It does not include the deep ocean floor with its oceanic ridges or the subsoil thereof.
(4)(a) For the purposes of this Convention, the coastal State shall establish the outer edge of the continental margin wherever the margin extends beyond 200 nautical miles from the baselines from which the breadth of the territorial sea is measured, by either:
(i) a line delineated in accordance with paragraph (7) by reference to the outermost fixed points at each of which the thickness of sedimentary rocks is at least 1 per cent of the shortest distance from such point to the foot of the continental slope; or
(ii) a line delineated in accordance with paragraph (7) by reference to fixed points not more than 60 nautical miles from the foot of the continental slope.
(b) In the absence of evidence to the contrary, the foot of the continental slope shall be determined as the point of maximum change in the gradient at its base.
(5) The fixed points comprising the line of the outer limits of the continental shelf on the seabed, drawn in accordance with paragraph (4)(a)(i) and (ii), either shall not exceed 350 nautical miles from the baselines from which the breadth of the territorial sea is measured or shall not exceed 100 nautical miles from the 2,500 metre isobath, which is a line connecting the depth of 2,500 metres.
(6) Notwithstanding the provisions of paragraph (5), on submarine ridges, the outer limit of the continental shelf shall not exceed 350 nautical miles from the baselines from which the breadth of the territorial sea is measured. This paragraph does not apply to submarine elevations that are natural 54 components of the continental margin, such as its plateaux, rises, caps, banks and spurs.
(7) The coastal State shall delineate the outer limits of its continental shelf, where that shelf extends beyond 200 nautical miles from the baselines from which the breadth of the territorial sea is measured, by straight lines not exceeding 60 nautical miles in length, connecting fixed points, defined by coordinates of latitude and longitude.
(8) Information on the limits of the continental shelf beyond 200 nautical miles from the baselines from which the breadth of the territorial sea is measured shall be submitted by the coastal State to the Commission on the Limits of the Continental Shelf set up under Annex II on the basis of equitable geographical representation. The Commission shall make recommendations to coastal States on matters related to the establishment of the outer limits of their continental shelf. The limits of the shelf established by a coastal State on the basis of these recommendations shall be final and binding.
(9) The coastal State shall deposit with the Secretary-General of the United Nations charts and relevant information, including geodetic data, permanently describing the outer limits of its continental shelf. The Secretary-General shall give due publicity thereto.
(10) The provisions of this article are without prejudice to the question of delimitation of the continental shelf between States with opposite or adjacent coasts.

Article 77. Rights of the coastal State over the continental shelf
(1) The coastal State exercises over the continental shelf sovereign rights for the purpose of exploring it and exploiting its natural resources.
(2) The rights referred to in paragraph (1) are exclusive in the sense that if the coastal State does not explore the continental shelf or exploit its natural resources, no one may undertake these activities without the express consent of the coastal State.
(3) The rights of the coastal State over the continental shelf do not depend on occupation, effective or notional, or on any express proclamation.

(4) The natural resources referred to in this Part consist of the mineral and other non-living resources of the seabed and subsoil together with living organisms belonging to sedentary species, that is to say, organisms which, at the harvestable stage, either are immobile on or under the seabed or are unable to move except in constant physical contact with the seabed or the subsoil.

Article 78. Legal status of the superjacent waters and air space and the rights and freedoms of other States
(1) The rights of the coastal State over the continental shelf do not affect the legal status of the superjacent waters or of the air space above those waters.
(2) The exercise of the rights of the coastal State over the continental shelf must not infringe or result in any unjustifiable interference with navigation and other rights and freedoms of other States as provided for in this Convention.

Article 79. Submarine cables and pipelines on the continental shelf
(1) All States are entitled to lay submarine cables and pipelines on the continental shelf, in accordance with the provisions of this article.
(2) Subject to its right to take reasonable measures for the exploration of the continental shelf, the exploitation of its natural resources and the prevention, reduction and control of pollution from pipelines, the coastal State may not impede the laying or maintenance of such cables or pipelines.
(3) The delineation of the course for the laying of such pipelines on the continental shelf is subject to the consent of the coastal State.
(4) Nothing in this Part affects the right of the coastal State to establish conditions for cables or pipelines entering its territory or territorial sea, or its jurisdiction over cables and pipelines constructed or used in connection with the exploration of its continental shelf or exploitation of its resources or the operations of artificial islands, installations and structures under its jurisdiction.
(5) When laying submarine cables or pipelines, States shall have due regard to cables or pipelines already in position. In particular, possibilities of repairing existing cables or pipelines shall not be prejudiced.

Article 80. Artificial islands, installations and structures on the continental shelf
Article 60 applies *mutatis mutandis* to artificial islands, installations and structures on the continental shelf.

Article 81. Drilling on the continental shelf
The coastal State shall have the exclusive right to authorize and regulate drilling on the continental shelf for all purposes.

Article 82. Payments and contributions with respect to the exploitation of the continental shelf beyond 200 nautical miles
(1) The coastal State shall make payments or contributions in kind in respect of the exploitation of the non-living resources of the continental shelf beyond 200 nautical miles from the baselines from which the breadth of the territorial sea is measured.
(2) The payments and contributions shall be made annually with respect to all production at a site after the first five years of production at that site. For the sixth year, the rate of payment or contribution shall be 1 per cent of the value or volume of production at the site. The rate shall increase by 1 per cent for each subsequent year until the twelfth year and shall remain
at 7 per cent thereafter. Production does not include resources used in connection with exploitation.
(3) A developing State which is a net importer of a mineral resource produced from its continental shelf is exempt from making such payments or contributions in respect of that mineral resource.
(4) The payments or contributions shall be made through the Authority, which shall distribute them to States Parties to this Convention, on the basis of equitable sharing criteria, taking into account the interests and needs of developing States, particularly the least developed and the land-locked among them.

Article 83. Delimitation of the continental shelf between States with opposite or adjacent coasts
(1) The delimitation of the continental shelf between States with opposite or adjacent coasts shall be effected by agreement on the basis of international law, as referred to in Article 38 of the Statute of the International Court of Justice, in order to achieve an equitable solution.
(2) If no agreement can be reached within a reasonable period of time, the States concerned shall resort to the procedures provided for in Part XV.
(3) Pending agreement as provided for in paragraph (1), the States concerned, in a spirit of understanding and cooperation, shall make every effort to enter into provisional arrangements of a practical

nature and, during this transitional period, not to jeopardize or hamper the reaching of the final agreement. Such arrangements shall be without prejudice to the final delimitation.
(4) Where there is an agreement in force between the States concerned, questions relating to the delimitation of the continental shelf shall be determined in accordance with the provisions of that agreement.

Article 84. Charts and lists of geographical coordinates
(1) Subject to this Part, the outer limit lines of the continental shelf and the lines of delimitation drawn in accordance with article 83 shall be shown on charts of a scale or scales adequate for ascertaining their position. Where appropriate, lists of geographical coordinates of points, specifying the geodetic datum, may be substituted for such outer limit lines or lines of delimitation.
(2) The coastal State shall give due publicity to such charts or lists of geographical coordinates and shall deposit a copy of each such chart or list with the Secretary-General of the United Nations and, in the case of those showing the outer limit lines of the continental shelf, with the Secretary-General of the Authority.

Article 85. Tunnelling
This Part does not prejudice the right of the coastal State to exploit the subsoil by means of tunnelling, irrespective of the depth of water above the subsoil.

Part VII. High Seas

Section 1. General provisions

Article 86. Application of the provisions of this Part
The provisions of this Part apply to all parts of the sea that are not included in the exclusive economic zone, in the territorial sea or in the internal waters of a State, or in the archipelagic waters of an archipelagic State. This article does not entail any abridgement of the freedoms enjoyed by all States in the exclusive economic zone in accordance with article 58.

Article 87. Freedom of the high seas
(1) The high seas are open to all States, whether coastal or land-locked. Freedom of the high seas is exercised under the conditions laid down by this Convention and by other rules of international law. It comprises, inter alia, both for coastal and land-locked States:
(a) freedom of navigation;
(b) freedom of overflight;
(c) freedom to lay submarine cables and pipelines, subject to Part VI;
(d) freedom to construct artificial islands and other installations permitted under international law, subject to Part VI;
(e) freedom of fishing, subject to the conditions laid down in section 2;
(f) freedom of scientific research, subject to Parts VI and XIII. 2. These freedoms shall be exercised by all States with due regard for the interests of other States in their exercise of the freedom of the high seas, and also with due regard for the rights under this Convention with respect to activities in the Area.

Article 88. Reservation of the high seas for peaceful purposes
The high seas shall be reserved for peaceful purposes.

Article 89. Invalidity of claims of sovereignty over the high seas
No State may validly purport to subject any part of the high seas to its sovereignty.

Article 90. Right of navigation
Every State, whether coastal or land-locked, has the right to sail ships flying its flag on the high seas.

Article 91. Nationality of ships
(1) Every State shall fix the conditions for the grant of its nationality to ships, for the registration of ships in its territory, and for the right to fly its flag. Ships have the nationality of the State whose flag they are entitled to fly. There must exist a genuine link between the State and the ship.
(2) Every State shall issue to ships to which it has granted the right to fly its flag documents to that effect.

Article 92. Status of ships
(1) Ships shall sail under the flag of one State only and, save in exceptional cases expressly provided for in international treaties or in this Convention, shall be subject to its exclusive jurisdiction on the high seas. A ship may not change its flag during a voyage or while in a port of call, save in the case of

a real transfer of ownership or change of registry.
(2) A ship which sails under the flags of two or more States, using them according to convenience, may not claim any of the nationalities in question with respect to any other State, and may be assimilated to a ship without nationality.

Article 93. Ships flying the flag of the United Nations, its specialized agencies and the International Atomic Energy Agency

The preceding articles do not prejudice the question of ships employed on the official service of the United Nations, its specialized agencies or the International Atomic Energy Agency, flying the flag of the organization.

Article 94. Duties of the flag State

(1) Every State shall effectively exercise its jurisdiction and control in administrative, technical and social matters over ships flying its flag.
(2) In particular every State shall:
(a) maintain a register of ships containing the names and particulars of ships flying its flag, except those which are excluded from generally accepted international regulations on account of their small size; and
(b) assume jurisdiction under its internal law over each ship flying its flag and its master, officers and crew in respect of administrative, technical and social matters concerning the ship.
(3) Every State shall take such measures for ships flying its flag as are necessary to ensure safety at sea with regard, inter alia, to:
(a) the construction, equipment and seaworthiness of ships;
(b) the manning of ships, labour conditions and the training of crews, taking into account the applicable international instruments;
(c) the use of signals, the maintenance of communications and the prevention of collisions.
(4) Such measures shall include those necessary to ensure:
(a) that each ship, before registration and thereafter at appropriate intervals, is surveyed by a qualified surveyor of ships, and has on board such charts, nautical publications and navigational equipment and instruments as are appropriate for the safe navigation of the ship;
(b) that each ship is in the charge of a master and officers who possess appropriate qualifications, in particular in seamanship, navigation, communications and marine engineering, and that the crew is appropriate in qualification and numbers for the type, size, machinery and equipment of the ship;
(c) that the master, officers and, to the extent appropriate, the crew are fully conversant with and required to observe the applicable international regulations concerning the safety of life at sea, the prevention of collisions, the prevention, reduction and control of marine pollution, and the maintenance of communications by radio.
(5) In taking the measures called for in paragraphs (3) and (4) each State is required to conform to generally accepted international regulations, procedures and practices and to take any steps which may be necessary to secure their observance.
(6) A State which has clear grounds to believe that proper jurisdiction and control with respect to a ship have not been exercised may report the facts to the flag State. Upon receiving such a report, the flag State shall investigate the matter and, if appropriate, take any action necessary to remedy the situation.
(7) Each State shall cause an inquiry to be held by or before a suitably qualified person or persons into every marine casualty or incident of navigation on the high seas involving a ship flying its flag and causing loss of life or serious injury to nationals of another State or serious damage to ships or installations of another State or to the marine environment. The flag State and the other State shall cooperate in the conduct of any inquiry held by that other State into any such marine casualty or incident of navigation.

Article 95. Immunity of warships on the high seas

Warships on the high seas have complete immunity from the jurisdiction of any State other than the flag State.

Article 96. Immunity of ships used only on government non-commercial service

Ships owned or operated by a State and used only on government non-commercial service shall, on the high seas, have complete immunity from the jurisdiction of any State other than the flag State.

Article 97. Penal jurisdiction in matters of collision or any other incident of navigation

(1) In the event of a collision or any other incident of navigation concerning a ship on the high seas, involving the penal or disciplinary responsibility of the master or of any other person in the service of

the ship, no penal or disciplinary proceedings may be instituted against such person except before the judicial or administrative authorities either of the flag State or of the State of which such person is a national.
(2) In disciplinary matters, the State which has issued a master's certificate or a certificate of competence or licence shall alone be competent, after due legal process, to pronounce the withdrawal of such certificates, even if the holder is not a national of the State which issued them.
(3) No arrest or detention of the ship, even as a measure of investigation, shall be ordered by any authorities other than those of the flag State.

Article 98. Duty to render assistance
(1) Every State shall require the master of a ship flying its flag, in so far as he can do so without serious danger to the ship, the crew or the passengers:
(a) to render assistance to any person found at sea in danger of being lost;
(b) to proceed with all possible speed to the rescue of persons in distress, if informed of their need of assistance, in so far as such action may reasonably be expected of him;
(c) after a collision, to render assistance to the other ship, its crew and its passengers and, where possible, to inform the other ship of the name of his own ship, its port of registry and the nearest port at which it will call.
(2) Every coastal State shall promote the establishment, operation and maintenance of an adequate and effective search and rescue service regarding safety on and over the sea and, where circumstances so require, by way of mutual regional arrangements cooperate with neighbouring States for this purpose.

Article 99. Prohibition of the transport of slaves
Every State shall take effective measures to prevent and punish the transport of slaves in ships authorized to fly its flag and to prevent the unlawful use of its flag for that purpose. Any slave taking refuge on board any ship, whatever its flag, shall ipso facto be free.

Article 100. Duty to cooperate in the repression of piracy
All States shall cooperate to the fullest possible extent in the repression of piracy on the high seas or in any other place outside the jurisdiction of any State.

Article 101. Definition of piracy
Piracy consists of any of the following acts:
(a) any illegal acts of violence or detention, or any act of depredation, committed for private ends by the crew or the passengers of a private ship or a private aircraft, and directed:
(i) on the high seas, against another ship or aircraft, or against persons or property on board such ship or aircraft;
(ii) against a ship, aircraft, persons or property in a place outside the jurisdiction of any State; (b) any act of voluntary participation in the operation of a ship or of an aircraft with knowledge of facts making it a pirate ship or aircraft;
(c) any act of inciting or of intentionally facilitating an act described in
subparagraph (a) or (b).

Article 102. Piracy by a warship, government ship or government aircraft whose crew has mutinied
The acts of piracy, as defined in article 101, committed by a warship, government ship or government aircraft whose crew has mutinied and taken control of the ship or aircraft are assimilated to acts committed by a private ship or aircraft.

Article 103. Definition of a pirate ship or aircraft
A ship or aircraft is considered a pirate ship or aircraft if it is intended by the persons in dominant control to be used for the purpose of committing one of the acts referred to in article 101. The same applies if the ship or aircraft has been used to commit any such act, so long as it remains under the control of the persons guilty of that act.

Article 104. Retention or loss of the nationality of a pirate ship or aircraft
A ship or aircraft may retain its nationality although it has become a pirate ship or aircraft. The retention or loss of nationality is determined by the law of the State from which such nationality was derived.

Article 105. Seizure of a pirate ship or aircraft
On the high seas, or in any other place outside the jurisdiction of any State, every State may seize a

pirate ship or aircraft, or a ship or aircraft taken by piracy and under the control of pirates, and arrest the persons and seize the property on board. The courts of the State which carried out the seizure may decide upon the penalties to be imposed, and may also determine the action to be taken with regard to the ships, aircraft or property, subject to the rights of third parties acting in good faith.

Article 106. Liability for seizure without adequate grounds

Where the seizure of a ship or aircraft on suspicion of piracy has been effected without adequate grounds, the State making the seizure shall be liable to the State the nationality of which is possessed by the ship or aircraft for any loss or damage caused by the seizure.

Article 107. Ships and aircraft which are entitled to seize on account of piracy

A seizure on account of piracy may be carried out only by warships or military aircraft, or other ships or aircraft clearly marked and identifiable as being on government service and authorized to that effect.

Article 108. Illicit traffic in narcotic drugs or psychotropic substances

(1) All States shall cooperate in the suppression of illicit traffic in narcotic drugs and psychotropic substances engaged in by ships on the high seas contrary to international conventions.
(2) Any State which has reasonable grounds for believing that a ship flying its flag is engaged in illicit traffic in narcotic drugs or psychotropic substances may request the cooperation of other States to suppress such traffic.

Article 109. Unauthorized broadcasting from the high seas

(1) All States shall cooperate in the suppression of unauthorized broadcasting from the high seas.
(2) For the purposes of this Convention, "unauthorized broadcasting" means the transmission of sound radio or television broadcasts from a ship or installation on the high seas intended for reception by the general public contrary to international regulations, but excluding the transmission of distress calls.
(3) Any person engaged in unauthorized broadcasting may be prosecuted before the court of: (a) the flag State of the ship;
(b) the State of registry of the installation;
(c) the State of which the person is a national;
(d) any State where the transmissions can be received; or
(e) any State where authorized radio communication is suffering interference.
(4) On the high seas, a State having jurisdiction in accordance with paragraph (3) may, in conformity with article 110, arrest any person or ship engaged in unauthorized broadcasting and seize the broadcasting apparatus.

Article 110. Right of visit

(1) Except where acts of interference derive from powers conferred by treaty, a warship which encounters on the high seas a foreign ship, other than a ship entitled to complete immunity in accordance with articles 95 and 96, is not justified in boarding it unless there is reasonable ground for suspecting that:
(a) the ship is engaged in piracy;
(b) the ship is engaged in the slave trade;
(c) the ship is engaged in unauthorized broadcasting and the flag State of the warship has jurisdiction under article 109;
(d) the ship is without nationality; or
(e) though flying a foreign flag or refusing to show its flag, the ship is, in reality, of the same nationality as the warship.
(2) In the cases provided for in paragraph (1), the warship may proceed to verify the ship's right to fly its flag. To this end, it may send a boat under the command of an officer to the suspected ship. If suspicion remains after the documents have been checked, it may proceed to a further examination on board the ship, which must be carried out with all possible consideration.
(3) If the suspicions prove to be unfounded, and provided that the ship boarded has not committed any act justifying them, it shall be compensated for any loss or damage that may have been sustained.
(4) These provisions apply *mutatis mutandis* to military aircraft.
(5) These provisions also apply to any other duly authorized ships or aircraft clearly marked and identifiable as being on government service.

Article 111. Right of hot pursuit

(1) The hot pursuit of a foreign ship may be undertaken when the competent authorities of the coastal

State have good reason to believe that the ship has violated the laws and regulations of that State. Such pursuit must be commenced when the foreign ship or one of its boats is within the internal waters, the archipelagic waters, the territorial sea or the contiguous zone of the pursuing State, and may only be continued outside the territorial sea or the contiguous zone if the pursuit has not been interrupted. It is not necessary that, at the time when the foreign ship within the territorial sea or the contiguous zone receives the order to stop, the ship giving the order should likewise be within the territorial sea or the contiguous zone. If the foreign ship is within a contiguous zone, as defined in article 33, the pursuit may only be undertaken if there has been a violation of the rights for the protection of which the zone was established.

(2) The right of hot pursuit shall apply *mutatis mutandis* to violations in the exclusive economic zone or on the continental shelf, including safety zones around continental shelf installations, of the laws and regulations of the coastal State applicable in accordance with this Convention to the exclusive economic zone or the continental shelf, including such safety zones.

(3) The right of hot pursuit ceases as soon as the ship pursued enters the territorial sea of its own State or of a third State.

(4) Hot pursuit is not deemed to have begun unless the pursuing ship has satisfied itself by such practicable means as may be available that the ship pursued or one of its boats or other craft working as a team and using the ship pursued as a mother ship is within the limits of the territorial sea, or, as the case may be, within the contiguous zone or the exclusive economic zone or above the continental shelf. The pursuit may only be commenced after a visual or auditory signal to stop has been given at a distance which enables it to be seen or heard by the foreign ship.

(5) The right of hot pursuit may be exercised only by warships or military aircraft, or other ships or aircraft clearly marked and identifiable as being on government service and authorized to that effect.

(6) Where hot pursuit is effected by an aircraft:

(a) the provisions of paragraphs (1) to (4) shall apply *mutatis mutandis*;

(b) the aircraft giving the order to stop must itself actively pursue the ship until a ship or another aircraft of the coastal State, summoned by the aircraft, arrives to take over the pursuit, unless the aircraft is itself able to arrest the ship. It does not suffice to justify an arrest outside the territorial sea that the ship was merely sighted by the aircraft as an offender or suspected offender, if it was not both ordered to stop and pursued by the aircraft itself or other aircraft or ships which continue the pursuit without interruption.

(7) The release of a ship arrested within the jurisdiction of a State and escorted to a port of that State for the purposes of an inquiry before the competent authorities may not be claimed solely on the ground that the ship, in the course of its voyage, was escorted across a portion of the exclusive economic zone or the high seas, if the circumstances rendered this necessary. (8) Where a ship has been stopped or arrested outside the territorial sea in circumstances which do not justify the exercise of the right of hot pursuit, it shall be compensated for any loss or damage that may have been thereby sustained.

Article 112. Right to lay submarine cables and pipelines

(1) All States are entitled to lay submarine cables and pipelines on the bed of the high seas beyond the continental shelf.

(2) Article 79, paragraph (5), applies to such cables and pipelines.

Article 113. Breaking or injury of a submarine cable or pipeline

Every State shall adopt the laws and regulations necessary to provide that the breaking or injury by a ship flying its flag or by a person subject to its jurisdiction of a submarine cable beneath the high seas done wilfully or through culpable negligence, in such a manner as to be liable to interrupt or obstruct telegraphic or telephonic communications, and similarly the breaking or injury of a submarine pipeline or high-voltage power cable, shall be a punishable offence. This provision shall apply also to conduct calculated or likely to result in such breaking or injury. However, it shall not apply to any break or injury caused by persons who acted merely with the legitimate object of saving their lives or their ships, after having taken all necessary precautions to avoid such break or injury.

Article 114. Breaking or injury by owners of a submarine cable or pipeline of another submarine cable or pipeline

Every State shall adopt the laws and regulations necessary to provide that, if persons subject to its jurisdiction who are the owners of a submarine cable or pipeline beneath the high seas, in laying or repairing that cable or pipeline, cause a break in or injury to another cable or pipeline, they shall bear the cost of the repairs.

Article 115. Indemnity for loss incurred in avoiding injury to a submarine cable or pipeline

PART I   INTERNATIONAL LAW

Every State shall adopt the laws and regulations necessary to ensure that the owners of ships who can prove that they have sacrificed an anchor, a net or any other fishing gear, in order to avoid injuring a submarine cable or pipeline, shall be indemnified by the owner of the cable or pipeline, provided that the owner of the ship has taken all reasonable precautionary measures beforehand.

Section 2. Conservation and management of the living resources of the high seas

Article 116. Right to fish on the high seas
All States have the right for their nationals to engage in fishing on the high seas subject to:
(a) their treaty obligations;
(b) the rights and duties as well as the interests of coastal States provided for, inter alia, in article 63, paragraph (2), and articles 64 to 67; and
(c) the provisions of this section.

Article 117. Duty of States to adopt with respect to their nationals measures for the conservation of the living resources of the high seas
All States have the duty to take, or to cooperate with other States in taking, such measures for their respective nationals as may be necessary for the conservation of the living resources of the high seas.

Article 118. Cooperation of States in the conservation and management of living resources
States shall cooperate with each other in the conservation and management of living resources in the areas of the high seas. States whose nationals exploit identical living resources, or different living resources in the same area, shall enter into negotiations with a view to taking the measures necessary for the conservation of the living resources concerned. They shall, as appropriate, cooperate to establish subregional or regional fisheries organizations to this end.

Article 119. Conservation of the living resources of the high seas
(1) In determining the allowable catch and establishing other conservation measures for the living resources in the high seas, States shall:
(a) take measures which are designed, on the best scientific evidence available to the States concerned, to maintain or restore populations of harvested species at levels which can produce the maximum sustainable yield, as qualified by relevant environmental and economic factors, including the special requirements of developing States, and taking into account fishing patterns, the interdependence of stocks and any generally recommended international minimum standards, whether subregional, regional or global;
(b) take into consideration the effects on species associated with or dependent upon harvested species with a view to maintaining or restoring populations of such associated or dependent species above levels at which their reproduction may become seriously threatened.
(2) Available scientific information, catch and fishing effort statistics, and other data relevant to the conservation of fish stocks shall be contributed and exchanged on a regular basis through competent international organizations, whether subregional, regional or global, where appropriate and with participation by all States concerned.
(3) States concerned shall ensure that conservation measures and their implementation do not discriminate in form or in fact against the fishermen of any State.

Article 120. Marine mammals
Article 65 also applies to the conservation and management of marine mammals in the high seas.

Part VIII. Regime of islands

Article 121. Regime of islands
(1) An island is a naturally formed area of land, surrounded by water, which is above water at high tide.
(2) Except as provided for in paragraph (3), the territorial sea, the contiguous zone, the exclusive economic zone and the continental shelf of an island are determined in accordance with the provisions of this Convention applicable to other land territory.
(3) Rocks which cannot sustain human habitation or economic life of their own shall have no exclusive economic zone or continental shelf.

Part IX. Enclosed or semi-enclosed seas

Article 122. Definition
For the purposes of this Convention, "enclosed or semi-enclosed sea" means a gulf, basin or sea surrounded by two or more States and connected to another sea or the ocean by a narrow outlet or

consisting entirely or primarily of the territorial seas and exclusive economic zones of two or more coastal States.

Article 123. Cooperation of States bordering enclosed or semi-enclosed seas
States bordering an enclosed or semi-enclosed sea should cooperate with each other in the exercise of their rights and in the performance of their duties under this Convention.
To this end they shall endeavour, directly or through an appropriate regional organization:
(a) to coordinate the management, conservation, exploration and exploitation of the living resources of the sea;
(b) to coordinate the implementation of their rights and duties with respect to the protection and preservation of the marine environment;
(c) to coordinate their scientific research policies and undertake where appropriate joint programmes of scientific research in the area;
(d) to invite, as appropriate, other interested States or international organizations to cooperate with them in furtherance of the provisions of this article.

Part X Right of access of land-locked states to and from the sea and freedom of transit

Article 124. Use of terms
(1) For the purposes of this Convention:
(a) "land-locked State" means a State which has no sea-coast;
(b) "transit State" means a State, with or without a sea-coast, situated between a land-locked State and the sea, through whose territory traffic in transit passes;
(c) "traffic in transit" means transit of persons, baggage, goods and means of transport across the territory of one or more transit States, when the passage across such territory, with or without trans-shipment, warehousing, breaking bulk or change in the mode of transport, is only a portion of a complete journey which begins or terminates within the territory of the land-locked State;
(d) "means of transport" means:
(i) railway rolling stock, sea, lake and river craft and road vehicles;
(ii) where local conditions so require, porters and pack animals.
(2) Land-locked States and transit States may, by agreement between them, include as means of transport pipelines and gas lines and means of transport other than those included in paragraph (1).

Article 125. Right of access to and from the sea and freedom of transit
(1) Land-locked States shall have the right of access to and from the sea for the purpose of exercising the rights provided for in this Convention including those relating to the freedom of the high seas and the common heritage of mankind. To this end, land-locked States shall enjoy freedom of transit through the territory of transit States by all means of transport.
(2) The terms and modalities for exercising freedom of transit shall be agreed between the land-locked States and transit States concerned through bilateral, subregional or regional agreements.
(3) Transit States, in the exercise of their full sovereignty over their territory, shall have the right to take all measures necessary to ensure that the rights and facilities provided for in this Part for land-locked States shall in no way infringe their legitimate interests.

Article 126. Exclusion of application of the most-favoured-nation clause
The provisions of this Convention, as well as special agreements relating to the exercise of the right of access to and from the sea, establishing rights and facilities on account of the special geographical position of land-locked States, are excluded from the application of the most-favoured-nation clause.

Article 127. Customs duties, taxes and other charges
(1) Traffic in transit shall not be subject to any customs duties, taxes or other charges except charges levied for specific services rendered in connection with such traffic.
(2) Means of transport in transit and other facilities provided for and used by land-locked States shall not be subject to taxes or charges higher than those levied for the use of means of transport of the transit State.

Article 128. Free zones and other customs facilities
For the convenience of traffic in transit, free zones or other customs facilities may be provided at the ports of entry and exit in the transit States, by agreement between those States and the land-locked States.

Article 129. Cooperation in the construction and improvement of means of transport
Where there are no means of transport in transit States to give effect to the freedom of transit or

where the existing means, including the port installations and equipment, are inadequate in any respect, the transit States and land-locked States concerned may cooperate in constructing or improving them.

Article 130. Measures to avoid or eliminate delays or other difficulties of a technical nature in traffic in transit

(1) Transit States shall take all appropriate measures to avoid delays or other difficulties of a technical nature in traffic in transit.
(2) Should such delays or difficulties occur, the competent authorities of the transit States and land-locked States concerned shall cooperate towards their expeditious elimination.

Article 131. Equal treatment in maritime ports

Ships flying the flag of land-locked States shall enjoy treatment equal to that accorded to other foreign ships in maritime ports.

Article 132. Grant of greater transit facilities

This Convention does not entail in any way the withdrawal of transit facilities which are greater than those provided for in this Convention and which are agreed between States Parties to this Convention or granted by a State Party. This Convention also does not preclude such grant of greater facilities in the future.

Part XI. The area

Section 1. General provisions

Article 133. Use of terms

For the purposes of this Part:
(a) "resources" means all solid, liquid or gaseous mineral resources in situ in the Area at or beneath the seabed, including polymetallic nodules;
(b) resources, when recovered from the Area, are referred to as "minerals".

Article 134. Scope of this Part

(1) This Part applies to the Area.
(2) Activities in the Area shall be governed by the provisions of this Part.
(3) The requirements concerning deposit of, and publicity to be given to, the charts or lists of geographical coordinates showing the limits referred to in article l, paragraph (l)(1), are set forth in Part VI.
(4) Nothing in this article affects the establishment of the outer limits of the continental shelf in accordance with Part VI or the validity of agreements relating to delimitation between States with opposite or adjacent coasts.

Article 135. Legal status of the superjacent waters and air space

Neither this Part nor any rights granted or exercised pursuant thereto shall affect the legal status of the waters superjacent to the Area or that of the air space above those waters.

Section 2. Principles governing the area

Article 136. Common heritage of mankind

The Area and its resources are the common heritage of mankind.

Article 137. Legal status of the Area and its resources

(1) No State shall claim or exercise sovereignty or sovereign rights over any part of the Area or its resources, nor shall any State or natural or juridical person appropriate any part thereof. No such claim or exercise of sovereignty or sovereign rights nor such appropriation shall be recognized.
(2) All rights in the resources of the Area are vested in mankind as a whole, on whose behalf the Authority shall act. These resources are not subject to alienation. The minerals recovered from the Area, however, may only be alienated in accordance with this Part and the rules, regulations and procedures of the Authority.
(3) No State or natural or juridical person shall claim, acquire or exercise rights with respect to the minerals recovered from the Area except in accordance with this Part. Otherwise, no such claim, acquisition or exercise of such rights shall be recognized.

Article 138. General conduct of States in relation to the Area

The general conduct of States in relation to the Area shall be in accordance with the provisions of this Part, the principles embodied in the Charter of the United Nations and other rules of international law in the interests of maintaining peace and security and promoting international cooperation and mutual understanding.

Article 139. Responsibility to ensure compliance and liability for damage

(1) States Parties shall have the responsibility to ensure that activities in the Area, whether carried out by States Parties, or state enterprises or natural or juridical persons which possess the nationality of States Parties or are effectively controlled by them or their nationals, shall be carried out in conformity with this Part. The same responsibility applies to international organizations for activities in the Area carried out by such organizations.

(2) Without prejudice to the rules of international law and Annex III, article 22, damage caused by the failure of a State Party or international organization to carry out its responsibilities under this Part shall entail liability; States Parties or international organizations acting together shall bear joint and several liability. A State Party shall not however be liable for damage caused by any failure to comply with this Part by a person whom it has sponsored under article 153, paragraph (2)(b), if the State Party has taken all necessary and appropriate measures to secure effective compliance under article 153, paragraph (4), and Annex III, article 4, paragraph (4).

(3) States Parties that are members of international organizations shall take appropriate measures to ensure the implementation of this article with respect to such organizations.

Article 140. Benefit of mankind

(1) Activities in the Area shall, as specifically provided for in this Part, be carried out for the benefit of mankind as a whole, irrespective of the geographical location of States, whether coastal or land-locked, and taking into particular consideration the interests and needs of developing States and of peoples who have not attained full independence or other self-governing status recognized by the United Nations in accordance with General Assembly resolution 1514 (XV) and other relevant General Assembly resolutions.

(2) The Authority shall provide for the equitable sharing of financial and other economic benefits derived from activities in the Area through any appropriate mechanism, on a non-discriminatory basis, in accordance with article 160, paragraph (2)(f)(i).

Article 141. Use of the Area exclusively for peaceful purposes

The Area shall be open to use exclusively for peaceful purposes by all States, whether coastal or land-locked, without discrimination and without prejudice to the other provisions of this Part.

Article 142. Rights and legitimate interests of coastal States

(1) Activities in the Area, with respect to resource deposits in the Area which lie across limits of national jurisdiction, shall be conducted with due regard to the rights and legitimate interests of any coastal State across whose jurisdiction such deposits lie.

(2) Consultations, including a system of prior notification, shall be maintained with the State concerned, with a view to avoiding infringement of such rights and interests. In cases where activities in the Area may result in the exploitation of resources lying within national jurisdiction, the prior consent of the coastal State concerned shall be required.

(3) Neither this Part nor any rights granted or exercised pursuant thereto shall affect the rights of coastal States to take such measures consistent with the relevant provisions of Part XII as may be necessary to prevent, mitigate or eliminate grave and imminent danger to their coastline, or related interests from pollution or threat thereof or from other hazardous occurrences resulting from or caused by any activities in the Area.

Article 143. Marine scientific research

(1) Marine scientific research in the Area shall be carried out exclusively for peaceful purposes and for the benefit of mankind as a whole, in accordance with Part XIII.

(2) The Authority may carry out marine scientific research concerning the Area and its resources, and may enter into contracts for that purpose. The Authority shall promote and encourage the conduct of marine scientific research in the Area, and shall coordinate and disseminate the results of such research and analysis when available.

(3) States Parties may carry out marine scientific research in the Area. States Parties shall promote international cooperation in marine scientific research in the Area by:

(a) participating in international programmes and encouraging cooperation in marine scientific research by personnel of different countries and of the Authority;

(b) ensuring that programmes are developed through the Authority or other international organizations as appropriate for the benefit of developing States and technologically less developed States

with a view to:
(i) strengthening their research capabilities;
(ii) training their personnel and the personnel of the Authority in the techniques and applications of research;
(iii) fostering the employment of their qualified personnel in research in the Area;
(c) effectively disseminating the results of research and analysis when available, through the Authority or other international channels when appropriate.

Article 144. Transfer of technology

(1) The Authority shall take measures in accordance with this Convention:
(a) to acquire technology and scientific knowledge relating to activities in the Area; and
(b) to promote and encourage the transfer to developing States of such technology and scientific knowledge so that all States Parties benefit therefrom.
(2) To this end the Authority and States Parties shall cooperate in promoting the transfer of technology and scientific knowledge relating to activities in the Area so that the Enterprise and all States Parties may benefit therefrom.
In particular they shall initiate and promote:
(a) programmes for the transfer of technology to the Enterprise and to developing States with regard to activities in the Area, including, inter alia, facilitating the access of the Enterprise and of developing States to the relevant technology, under fair and reasonable terms and conditions;
(b) measures directed towards the advancement of the technology of the Enterprise and the domestic technology of developing States, particularly by providing opportunities to personnel from the Enterprise and from developing States for training in marine science and technology and for their full participation in activities in the Area.

Article 145. Protection of the marine environment

Necessary measures shall be taken in accordance with this Convention with respect to activities in the Area to ensure effective protection for the marine environment from harmful effects which may arise from such activities.
To this end the Authority shall adopt appropriate rules, regulations and procedures for inter alia:
(a) the prevention, reduction and control of pollution and other hazards to the marine environment, including the coastline, and of interference with the ecological balance of the marine environment, particular attention being paid to the need for protection from harmful effects of such activities as drilling, dredging, excavation, disposal of waste, construction and operation or maintenance of installations, pipelines and other devices related to such activities;
(b) the protection and conservation of the natural resources of the Area and the prevention of damage to the flora and fauna of the marine environment. Article 146 Protection of human life with respect to activities in the Area, necessary measures shall be taken to ensure effective protection of human life. To this end the Authority shall adopt appropriate rules, regulations and procedures to supplement existing international law as embodied in relevant treaties.

Article 147. Accommodation of activities in the Area and in the marine environment

(1) Activities in the Area shall be carried out with reasonable regard for other activities in the marine environment.
(2) Installations used for carrying out activities in the Area shall be subject to the following conditions:
(a) such installations shall be erected, emplaced and removed solely in accordance with this Part and subject to the rules, regulations and procedures of the Authority. Due notice must 74 be given of the erection, emplacement and removal of such installations, and permanent means for giving warning of their presence must be maintained;
(b) such installations may not be established where interference may be caused to the use of recognized sea lanes essential to international navigation or in areas of intense fishing activity;
(c) safety zones shall be established around such installations with appropriate markings to ensure the safety of both navigation and the installations. The configuration and location of such safety zones shall not be such as to form a belt impeding the lawful access of shipping to particular maritime zones or navigation along international sea lanes;
(d) such installations shall be used exclusively for peaceful purposes;
(e) such installations do not possess the status of islands. They have no territorial sea of their own, and their presence does not affect the delimitation of the territorial sea, the exclusive economic zone or the continental shelf.
(3) Other activities in the marine environment shall be conducted with reasonable regard for activities in the Area.

Article 148. Participation of developing States in activities in the Area
The effective participation of developing States in activities in the Area shall be promoted as specifically provided for in this Part, having due regard to their special interests and needs, and in particular to the special need of the land-locked and geographically disadvantaged among them to overcome obstacles arising from their disadvantaged location, including remoteness from the Area and difficulty of access to and from it.

Article 149. Archaeological and historical objects
All objects of an archaeological and historical nature found in the Area shall be preserved or disposed of for the benefit of mankind as a whole, particular regard being paid to the preferential rights of the State or country of origin, or the State of cultural origin, or the State of historical and archaeological origin.

Section 3. Development of resources of the area

Article 150. Policies relating to activities in the Area
Activities in the Area shall, as specifically provided for in this Part, be carried out in such a manner as to foster healthy development of the world economy and balanced growth of international trade, and to promote international cooperation for the over-all development of all countries, especially developing States, and with a view to ensuring:
(a) the development of the resources of the Area;
(b) orderly, safe and rational management of the resources of the Area, including the efficient conduct of activities in the Area and, in accordance with sound principles of conservation, the avoidance of unnecessary waste;
(c) the expansion of opportunities for participation in such activities consistent in particular with articles 144 and 148;
(d) participation in revenues by the Authority and the transfer of technology to the Enterprise and developing States as provided for in this Convention;
(e) increased availability of the minerals derived from the Area as needed in conjunction with minerals derived from other sources, to ensure supplies to consumers of such minerals;
(f) the promotion of just and stable prices remunerative to producers and fair to consumers for minerals derived both from the Area and from other sources, and the promotion of long-term equilibrium between supply and demand;
(g) the enhancement of opportunities for all States Parties, irrespective of their social and economic systems or geographical location, to participate in the development of the resources of the Area and the prevention of monopolization of activities in the Area;
(h) the protection of developing countries from adverse effects on their economies or on their export earnings resulting from a reduction in the price of an affected mineral, or in the volume of exports of that mineral, to the extent that such reduction is caused by activities in the Area, as provided in article 151;
(i) the development of the common heritage for the benefit of mankind as a whole; and
(j) conditions of access to markets for the imports of minerals produced from the resources of the Area and for imports of commodities produced from such minerals shall not be more favourable than the most favourable applied to imports from other sources.

Article 151. Production policies
(1)(a) Without prejudice to the objectives set forth in article 150 and for the purpose of implementing subparagraph (h) of that article, the Authority, acting through existing forums or such new arrangements or agreements as may be appropriate, in which all interested parties, including both producers and consumers, participate, shall take measures necessary to promote the growth, efficiency and stability of markets for those commodities produced from the minerals derived from the Area, at prices remunerative to producers and fair to consumers. All States Parties shall cooperate to this end.
(b) The Authority shall have the right to participate in any commodity conference dealing with those commodities and in which all interested parties including both producers and consumers participate. The Authority shall have the right to become a party to any arrangement or agreement resulting from such conferences. Participation of the Authority in any organs established under those arrangements or agreements shall be in respect of production in the Area and in accordance with the relevant rules of those organs.
(c) The Authority shall carry out its obligations under the arrangements or agreements referred to in this paragraph in a manner which assures a uniform and non-discriminatory implementation in respect of all production in the Area of the minerals concerned. In doing so, the Authority shall act in a manner consistent with the terms of existing contracts and approved plans of work of the Enterprise.

PART I INTERNATIONAL LAW

(2)(a) During the interim period specified in paragraph (3), commercial production shall not be undertaken pursuant to an approved plan of work until the operator has applied for and has been issued a production authorization by the Authority. Such production authorizations may not be applied for or issued more than five years prior to the planned commencement of commercial production under the plan of work unless, having regard to the nature and timing of project development, the rules, regulations and procedures of the Authority prescribe another period.

(b) In the application for the production authorization, the operator shall specify the annual quantity of nickel expected to be recovered under the approved plan of work. The application shall include a schedule of expenditures to be made by the operator after he has received the authorization which are reasonably calculated to allow him to begin commercial production on the date planned.

(c) For the purposes of subparagraphs (a) and (b), the Authority shall establish appropriate performance requirements in accordance with Annex III, article 17.

(d) The Authority shall issue a production authorization for the level of production applied for unless the sum of that level and the levels already authorized exceeds the nickel production ceiling, as calculated pursuant to paragraph (4) in the year of issuance of the authorization, during any year of planned production falling within the interim period.

(e) When issued, the production authorization and approved application shall become a part of the approved plan of work.

(f) If the operator's application for a production authorization is denied pursuant to subparagraph (d), the operator may apply again to the Authority at any time.

(3) The interim period shall begin five years prior to 1 January of the year in which the earliest commercial production is planned to commence under an approved plan of work. If the earliest commercial production is delayed beyond the year originally planned, the beginning of the interim period and the production ceiling originally calculated shall be adjusted accordingly. The interim period shall last 25 years or until the end of the Review Conference referred to in article 155 or until the day when such new arrangements or agreements as are referred to in paragraph (1) enter into force, whichever is earliest. The Authority shall resume the power provided in this article for the remainder of the interim period if the said arrangements or agreements should lapse or become ineffective for any reason whatsoever.

(4)(a) The production ceiling for any year of the interim period shall be the sum of:
(i) the difference between the trend line values for nickel consumption, as calculated pursuant to subparagraph (b), 77 for the year immediately prior to the year of the earliest commercial production and the year immediately prior to the commencement of the interim period; and (ii) sixty per cent of the difference between the trend line values for nickel consumption, as calculated pursuant to subparagraph (b), for the year for which the production authorization is being applied for and the year immediately prior to the year of the earliest commercial production.

(b) For the purposes of subparagraph (a):
(i) trend line values used for computing the nickel production ceiling shall be those annual nickel consumption values on a trend line computed during the year in which a production authorization is issued. The trend line shall be derived from a linear regression of the logarithms of actual nickel consumption for the most recent 15-year period for which such data are available, time being the independent variable. This trend line shall be referred to as the original trend line;
(ii) if the annual rate of increase of the original trend line is less than 3 per cent, then the trend line used to determine the quantities referred to in subparagraph (a) shall instead be one passing through the original trend line at the value for the first year of the relevant 15-year period, and increasing at 3 per cent annually; provided however that the production ceiling established for any year of the interim period may not in any case exceed the difference between the original trend line value for that year and the original trend line value for the year immediately prior to the commencement of the interim period.

(5) The Authority shall reserve to the Enterprise for its initial production a quantity of 38,000 metric tonnes of nickel from the available production ceiling calculated pursuant to paragraph (4).

(6)(a) An operator may in any year produce less than or up to 8 per cent more than the level of annual production of minerals from polymetallic nodules specified in his production authorization, provided that the over-all amount of production shall not exceed that specified in the authorization. Any excess over 8 per cent and up to 20 per cent in any year, or any excess in the first and subsequent years following two consecutive years in which excesses occur, shall be negotiated with the Authority, which may require the operator to obtain a supplementary production authorization to cover additional production.

(b) Applications for such supplementary production authorizations shall be considered by the Authority only after all pending applications by operators who have not yet received production authorizations have been acted upon and due account has been taken of other likely applicants. The Authority shall be guided by the principle of not exceeding the total production allowed under the production ceiling in any year of the interim period. It shall not authorize the production under any plan of work of a quantity in excess of 46,500 metric tonnes of nickel per year.

(7) The levels of production of other metals such as copper, cobalt and manganese extracted from the polymetallic nodules that are recovered pursuant to a production authorization should not be higher than those which would have been produced had the operator produced the maximum level of nickel from those nodules pursuant to this article. The Authority shall establish rules, regulations and procedures pursuant to Annex III, article 17, to implement this paragraph.

(8) Rights and obligations relating to unfair economic practices under relevant multilateral trade agreements shall apply to the exploration for and exploitation of minerals from the Area. In the settlement of disputes arising under this provision, States Parties which are Parties to such multilateral trade agreements shall have recourse to the dispute settlement procedures of such agreements.

(9) The Authority shall have the power to limit the level of production of minerals from the Area, other than minerals from polymetallic nodules, under such conditions and applying such methods as may be appropriate by adopting regulations in accordance with article 161, paragraph (8).

(10) Upon the recommendation of the Council on the basis of advice from the Economic Planning Commission, the Assembly shall establish a system of compensation or take other measures of economic adjustment assistance including cooperation with specialized agencies and other international organizations to assist developing countries which suffer serious adverse effects on their export earnings or economies resulting from a reduction in the price of an affected mineral or in the volume of exports of that mineral, to the extent that such reduction is caused by activities in the Area. The Authority on request shall initiate studies on the problems of those States which are likely to be most seriously affected with a view to minimizing their difficulties and assisting them in their economic adjustment.

Article 152. Exercise of powers and functions by the Authority

(1) The Authority shall avoid discrimination in the exercise of its powers and functions, including the granting of opportunities for activities in the Area.

(2) Nevertheless, special consideration for developing States, including particular consideration for the land-locked and geographically disadvantaged among them, specifically provided for in this Part shall be permitted.

Article 153. System of exploration and exploitation

(1) Activities in the Area shall be organized, carried out and controlled by the Authority on behalf of mankind as a whole in accordance with this article as well as other relevant provisions of this Part and the relevant Annexes, and the rules, regulations and procedures of the Authority.

(2) Activities in the Area shall be carried out as prescribed in paragraph (3):
(a) by the Enterprise, and
(b) in association with the Authority by States Parties, or state enterprises or natural or juridical persons which possess the nationality of States Parties or are effectively controlled by them or their nationals, when sponsored by such States, or any group of the foregoing which meets the requirements provided in this Part and in Annex III.

(3) Activities in the Area shall be carried out in accordance with a formal written plan of work drawn up in accordance with Annex III and approved by the Council after review by the Legal and Technical Commission. In the case of activities in the Area carried out as authorized by the Authority by the entities specified in paragraph (2)(b), the plan of work shall, in accordance with Annex III, article 3, be in the form of a contract. Such contracts may provide for joint arrangements in accordance with Annex III, article 11.

(4) The Authority shall exercise such control over activities in the Area as is necessary for the purpose of securing compliance with the relevant provisions of this Part and the Annexes relating thereto, and the rules, regulations and procedures of the Authority, and the plans of work approved in accordance with paragraph (3). States Parties shall assist the Authority by taking all measures necessary to ensure such compliance in accordance with article 139.

(5) The Authority shall have the right to take at any time any measures provided for under this Part to ensure compliance with its provisions and the exercise of the functions of control and regulation assigned to it thereunder or under any contract.
The Authority shall have the right to inspect all installations in the Area used in connection with activities in the Area.

(6) A contract under paragraph (3) shall provide for security of tenure. Accordingly, the contract shall not be revised, suspended or terminated except in accordance with Annex III, articles 18 and 19.

Article 154. Periodic review

Every five years from the entry into force of this Convention, the Assembly shall undertake a general and systematic review of the manner in which the international regime of the Area established in this Convention has operated in practice. In the light of this review the Assembly may take, or recommend that other organs take, measures in accordance with the provisions and procedures of this Part and the Annexes relating thereto which will lead to the improvement of the operation of the regime.

Article 155. The Review Conference

(1) Fifteen years from 1 January of the year in which the earliest commercial production commences under an approved plan of work, the Assembly shall convene a conference for the review of those provisions of this Part and the relevant Annexes which govern the system of exploration and exploitation of the resources of the Area.

The Review Conference shall consider in detail, in the light of the experience acquired during that period:

(a) whether the provisions of this Part which govern the system of exploration and exploitation of the resources of the Area have achieved their aims in all respects, including whether they have benefited mankind as a whole;

(b) whether, during the 15-year period, reserved areas have been exploited in an effective and balanced manner in comparison with non-reserved areas;

(c) whether the development and use of the Area and its resources have been undertaken in such a manner as to foster healthy development of the world economy and balanced growth of international trade;

(d) whether monopolization of activities in the Area has been prevented;

(e) whether the policies set forth in articles 150 and 151 have been fulfilled; and

(f) whether the system has resulted in the equitable sharing of benefits derived from activities in the Area, taking into particular consideration the interests and needs of the developing States.

(2) The Review Conference shall ensure the maintenance of the principle of the common heritage of mankind, the international regime designed to ensure equitable exploitation of the resources of the Area for the benefit of all countries, especially the developing States, and an Authority to organize, conduct and control activities in the Area. It shall also ensure the maintenance of the principles laid down in this Part with regard to the exclusion of claims or exercise of sovereignty over any part of the Area, the rights of States and their general conduct in relation to the Area, and their participation in activities in the Area in conformity with this Convention, the prevention of monopolization of activities in the Area, the use of the Area exclusively for peaceful purposes, economic aspects of activities in the Area, marine scientific research, transfer of technology, protection of the marine environment, protection of human life, rights of coastal States, the legal status of the waters superjacent to the Area and that of the air space above those waters and accommodation between activities in the Area and other activities in the marine environment.

(3) The decision-making procedure applicable at the Review Conference shall be the same as that applicable at the Third United Nations Conference on the Law of the Sea. The Conference shall make every effort to reach agreement on any amendments by way of consensus and there should be no voting on such matters until all efforts at achieving consensus have been exhausted.

(4) If, five years after its commencement, the Review Conference has not reached agreement on the system of exploration and exploitation of the resources of the Area, it may decide during the ensuing 12 months, by a three-fourths majority of the States Parties, to adopt and submit to the States Parties for ratification or accession such amendments changing or modifying the system as it determines necessary and appropriate. Such amendments shall enter into force for all States Parties 12 months after the deposit of instruments of ratification or accession by three fourths of the States Parties.

(5) Amendments adopted by the Review Conference pursuant to this article shall not affect rights acquired under existing contracts.

Section 4. The Authority

Subsection A. General provisions

Article 156. Establishment of the Authority

(1) There is hereby established the International Seabed Authority, which shall function in accordance with this Part.

(2) All States Parties are ipso facto members of the Authority.

(3) Observers at the Third United Nations Conference on the Law of the Sea who have signed the Final Act and who are not referred to in article 305, paragraph (1)(c), (d), (e) or (f), shall have the right to participate in the Authority as observers, in accordance with its rules, regulations and procedures.

(4) The seat of the Authority shall be in Jamaica.
(5) The Authority may establish such regional centres or offices as it deems necessary for the exercise of its functions.

Article 157. Nature and fundamental principles of the Authority
(1) The Authority is the organization through which States Parties shall, in accordance with this Part, organize and control activities in the Area, particularly with a view to administering the resources of the Area.
(2) The powers and functions of the Authority shall be those expressly conferred upon it by this Convention. The Authority shall have such incidental powers, consistent with this Convention, as are implicit in and necessary for the exercise of those powers and functions with respect to activities in the Area.
(3) The Authority is based on the principle of the sovereign equality of all its members.
(4) All members of the Authority shall fulfil in good faith the obligations assumed by them in accordance with this Part in order to ensure to all of them the rights and benefits resulting from membership.

Article 158. Organs of the Authority
(1) There are hereby established, as the principal organs of the Authority, an Assembly, a Council and a Secretariat.
(2) There is hereby established the Enterprise, the organ through which the Authority shall carry out the functions referred to in article 170, paragraph (1).
(3) Such subsidiary organs as may be found necessary may be established in accordance with this Part. 4. Each principal organ of the Authority and the Enterprise shall be responsible for exercising those powers and functions which are conferred upon it. In exercising such powers and functions each organ shall avoid taking any action which may derogate from or impede the exercise of specific powers and functions conferred upon another organ.

Subsection B. The Assembly

Article 159. Composition, procedure and voting
(1) The Assembly shall consist of all the members of the Authority. Each member shall have one representative in the Assembly, who may be accompanied by alternates and advisers.
(2) The Assembly shall meet in regular annual sessions and in such special sessions as may be decided by the Assembly, or convened by the Secretary-General at the request of the Council or of a majority of the members of the Authority.
(3) Sessions shall take place at the seat of the Authority unless otherwise decided by the Assembly.
(4) The Assembly shall adopt its rules of procedure. At the beginning of each regular session, it shall elect its President and such other officers as may be required. They shall hold office until a new President and other officers are elected at the next regular session.
(5) A majority of the members of the Assembly shall constitute a quorum.
(6) Each member of the Assembly shall have one vote.
(7) Decisions on questions of procedure, including decisions to convene special sessions of the Assembly, shall be taken by a majority of the members present and voting.
(8) Decisions on questions of substance shall be taken by a two-thirds majority of the members present and voting, provided that such majority includes a majority of the members participating in the session. When the issue arises as to whether a question is one of substance or not, that question shall be treated as one of substance unless otherwise decided by the Assembly by the majority required for decisions on questions of substance.
(9) When a question of substance comes up for voting for the first time, the President may, and shall, if requested by at least one fifth of the members of the Assembly, defer the issue of taking a vote on that question for a period not exceeding five calendar days. This rule may be applied only once to any question, and shall not be applied so as to defer the question beyond the end of the session.
(10) Upon a written request addressed to the President and sponsored by at least one fourth of the members of the Authority for an advisory opinion on the conformity with this Convention of a proposal before the Assembly on any matter, the Assembly shall request the Seabed Disputes Chamber of the International Tribunal for the Law of the Sea to give an advisory opinion thereon and shall defer voting on that proposal pending receipt of the advisory opinion by the Chamber. If the advisory opinion is not received before the final week of the session in which it is requested, the Assembly shall decide when it will meet to vote upon the deferred proposal.

Article 160. Powers and functions
(1) The Assembly, as the sole organ of the Authority consisting of all the members, shall be consid-

ered the supreme organ of the Authority to which the other principal organs shall be accountable as specifically provided for in this Convention. The Assembly shall have the power to establish general policies in conformity with the relevant provisions of this Convention on any question or matter within the competence of the Authority.

(2) In addition, the powers and functions of the Assembly shall be:

(a) to elect the members of the Council in accordance with article 161;

(b) to elect the Secretary-General from among the candidates proposed by the Council;

(c) to elect, upon the recommendation of the Council, the members of the Governing Board of the Enterprise and the Director-General of the Enterprise;

(d) to establish such subsidiary organs as it finds necessary for the exercise of its functions in accordance with this Part. In the composition of these subsidiary organs due account shall be taken of the principle of equitable geographical distribution and of special interests and the need for members qualified and competent in the relevant technical questions dealt with by such organs;

(e) to assess the contributions of members to the administrative budget of the Authority in accordance with an agreed scale of assessment based upon the scale used for the regular budget of the United Nations until the Authority shall have sufficient income from other sources to meet its administrative expenses;

(f) (i) to consider and approve, upon the recommendation of the Council, the rules, regulations and procedures on the equitable sharing of financial and other economic benefits derived from activities in the Area and the payments and contributions made pursuant to article 82, taking into particular consideration the interests and needs of developing States and peoples who have not attained full independence or other self-governing status. If the Assembly does not approve the recommendations of the Council, the Assembly shall return them to the Council for reconsideration in the light of the views expressed by the Assembly; (ii) to consider and approve the rules, regulations and procedures of the Authority, and any amendments thereto, provisionally adopted by the Council pursuant to article 162,

paragraph (2)(o)(ii). These rules, regulations and procedures shall relate to prospecting, exploration and exploitation in the Area, the financial management and internal administration of the Authority, and, upon the recommendation of the Governing Board of the Enterprise, to the transfer of funds from the Enterprise to the Authority;

(g) to decide upon the equitable sharing of financial and other economic benefits derived from activities in the Area, consistent with this Convention and the rules, regulations and procedures of the Authority;

(h) to consider and approve the proposed annual budget of the Authority submitted by the Council;

(i) to examine periodic reports from the Council and from the Enterprise and special reports requested from the Council or any other organ of the Authority;

(j) to initiate studies and make recommendations for the purpose of promoting international cooperation concerning activities in the Area and encouraging the progressive development of international law relating thereto and its codification;

(k) to consider problems of a general nature in connection with activities in the Area arising in particular for developing States, as well as those problems for States in connection with activities in the Area that are due to their geographical location, particularly for land-locked and geographically disadvantaged States;

(l) to establish, upon the recommendation of the Council, on the basis of advice from the Economic Planning Commission, a system of compensation or other measures of economic adjustment assistance as provided in article 151, paragraph (10);

(m) to suspend the exercise of rights and privileges of membership pursuant to article 185; (n) to discuss any question or matter within the competence of the Authority and to decide as to which organ of the Authority shall deal with any such question or matter not specifically entrusted to a particular organ, consistent with the distribution of powers and functions among the organs of the Authority.

Subsection C. The Council

Article 161. Composition, procedure and voting

(1) The Council shall consist of 36 members of the Authority elected by the Assembly in the following order:

(a) four members from among those States Parties which, during the last five years for which statistics are available, have either consumed more than 2 per cent of total world consumption or have had net imports of more than 2 per cent of total world imports of the commodities produced from the categories of minerals to be derived from the Area, and in any case one State from the Eastern European (Socialist) region, as well as the largest consumer;

(b) four members from among the eight States Parties which have the largest investments in preparation for and in the conduct of activities in the Area, either directly or through their nationals, including at least one State from the Eastern European (Socialist) region;
(c) four members from among States Parties which on the basis of production in areas under their jurisdiction are major net exporters of the categories of minerals to be derived from the Area, including at least two developing States whose exports of such minerals have a substantial bearing upon their economies;
(d) six members from among developing States Parties, representing special interests. The special interests to be represented shall include those of States with large populations, States which are land-locked or geographically disadvantaged, States which are major importers of the categories of minerals to be derived from the Area, States which are potential producers of such minerals, and least developed States;
(e) eighteen members elected according to the principle of ensuring an equitable geographical distribution of seats in the Council as a whole, provided that each geographical region shall have at least one member elected under this subparagraph. For this purpose, the geographical regions shall be Africa, Asia, Eastern European (Socialist), Latin America and Western European and Others.
(2) In electing the members of the Council in accordance with paragraph (1), the Assembly shall ensure that:
(a) land-locked and geographically disadvantaged States are represented to a degree which is reasonably proportionate to their representation in the Assembly;
(b) coastal States, especially developing States, which do not qualify under
paragraph (1)(a), (b), (c) or (d) are represented to a degree which is reasonably proportionate to their representation in the Assembly; (c) each group of States Parties to be represented on the Council is represented by those members, if any, which are nominated by that group.
(3) Elections shall take place at regular sessions of the Assembly. Each member of the Council shall be elected for four years. At the first election, however, the term of one half of the members of each group referred to in paragraph 1 shall be two years.
(4) Members of the Council shall be eligible for re-election, but due regard should be paid to the desirability of rotation of membership.
(5) The Council shall function at the seat of the Authority, and shall meet as often as the business of the Authority may require, but not less than three times a year.
(6) A majority of the members of the Council shall constitute a quorum.
(7) Each member of the Council shall have one vote.
(8) (a) Decisions on questions of procedure shall be taken by a majority of the members present and voting.
(b) Decisions on questions of substance arising under the following provisions shall be taken by a two-thirds majority of the members present and voting, provided that such majority includes a majority of the members of the Council: article 162, paragraph (2),
subparagraphs (f); (g); (h); (i); (n); (p); (v); article 191. (c) Decisions on questions of substance arising under the following provisions shall be taken by a three-fourths majority of the members present and voting, provided that such majority includes a majority of the members of the Council: article 162, paragraph (1); article 162, paragraph (2),
subparagraphs (a); (b); (c); (d); (e); (l); (q); (r); (s); (t); (u) in cases of non-compliance by a contractor or a sponsor; (w) provided that orders issued thereunder may be binding for not more than 30 days unless confirmed by a decision taken in accordance with subparagraph (d); article 162, paragraph (2), subparagraphs (x); (y); (z); article 163, paragraph (2); article 174, paragraph (3); Annex IV, article 11.
(d) Decisions on questions of substance arising under the following provisions shall be taken by consensus: article 162, paragraph (2)(m) and (o); adoption of amendments to Part XI.
(e) For the purposes of subparagraphs (d), (f) and (g), "consensus" means the absence of any formal objection. Within 14 days of the submission of a proposal to the Council, the President of the Council shall determine whether there would be a formal objection to the adoption of the proposal. If the President determines that there would be such an objection, the President shall establish and convene, within three days following such determination, a conciliation committee consisting of not more than nine members of the Council, with the President as chairman, for the purpose of reconciling the differences and producing a proposal which can be adopted by consensus.
The committee shall work expeditiously and report to the Council within 14 days following its establishment. If the committee is unable to recommend a proposal which can be adopted by consensus, it shall set out in its report the grounds on which the proposal is being opposed. (f) Decisions on questions not listed above which the Council is authorized to take by the rules, regulations and procedures of the Authority or otherwise shall be taken pursuant to the subparagraphs of this paragraph specified

PART I   INTERNATIONAL LAW

in the rules, regulations and procedures or, if not specified therein, then pursuant to the subparagraph determined by the Council if possible in advance, by consensus.

(g) When the issue arises as to whether a question is within subparagraph (a), (b), (c) or (d), the question shall be treated as being within the subparagraph requiring the higher or highest majority or consensus as the case may be, unless otherwise decided by the Council by the said majority or by consensus.

(9) The Council shall establish a procedure whereby a member of the Authority not represented on the Council may send a representative to attend a meeting of the Council when a request is made by such member, or a matter particularly affecting it is under consideration. Such a representative shall be entitled to participate in the deliberations but not to vote.

Article 162. Powers and functions

(1) The Council is the executive organ of the Authority. The Council shall have the power to establish, in conformity with this Convention and the general policies established by the Assembly, the specific policies to be pursued by the Authority on any question or matter within the competence of the Authority.

(2) In addition, the Council shall:

(a) supervise and coordinate the implementation of the provisions of this Part on all questions and matters within the competence of the Authority and invite the attention of the Assembly to cases of non-compliance;

(b) propose to the Assembly a list of candidates for the election of the Secretary-General;

(c) recommend to the Assembly candidates for the election of the members of the Governing Board of the Enterprise and the Director-General of the Enterprise;

(d) establish, as appropriate, and with due regard to economy and efficiency, such subsidiary organs as it finds necessary for the exercise of its functions in accordance with this Part. In the composition of subsidiary organs, emphasis shall be placed on the need for members qualified and competent in relevant technical matters dealt with by those organs provided that due account shall be taken of the principle of equitable geographical distribution and of special interests;

(e) adopt its rules of procedure including the method of selecting its president;

(f) enter into agreements with the United Nations or other international organizations on behalf of the Authority and within its competence, subject to approval by the Assembly;

(g) consider the reports of the Enterprise and transmit them to the Assembly with its recommendations;

(h) present to the Assembly annual reports and such special reports as the Assembly may request;

(i) issue directives to the Enterprise in accordance with article 170;

(j) approve plans of work in accordance with Annex III, article 6.

The Council shall act upon each plan of work within 60 days of its submission by the Legal and Technical Commission at a session of the Council in accordance with the following procedures:

(i) if the Commission recommends the approval of a plan of work, it shall be deemed to have been approved by the Council if no member of the Council submits in writing to the President within 14 days a specific objection alleging non-compliance with the requirements of Annex III, article 6. If there is an objection, the conciliation procedure set forth in

article 161, paragraph (8)(e), shall apply. If, at the end of the conciliation procedure, the objection is still maintained, the plan of work shall be deemed to have been approved by the Council unless the Council disapproves it by consensus among its members excluding any State or States making the application or sponsoring the applicant;

(ii) if the Commission recommends the disapproval of a plan of work or does not make a recommendation, the Council may approve the plan of work by a three-fourths majority of the members present and voting, provided that such majority includes a majority of the members participating in the session;

(k) approve plans of work submitted by the Enterprise in accordance with Annex IV, article 12, applying, *mutatis mutandis*, the procedures set forth in subparagraph (j);

(l) exercise control over activities in the Area in accordance with article 153, paragraph (4), and the rules, regulations and procedures of the Authority;

(m) take, upon the recommendation of the Economic Planning Commission, necessary and appropriate measures in accordance 88 with article 150, subparagraph (h), to provide protection from the adverse economic effects specified therein;

(n) make recommendations to the Assembly, on the basis of advice from the Economic Planning Commission, for a system of compensation or other measures of economic adjustment assistance as provided in article 151, paragraph (10);

(o) (i) recommend to the Assembly rules, regulations and procedures on the equitable sharing of financial and other economic benefits derived from activities in the Area and the payments and contributions made pursuant to article 82, taking into particular consideration the interests and needs of the developing States and peoples who have not attained full independence or other self-governing status;
(ii) adopt and apply provisionally, pending approval by the Assembly, the rules, regulations and procedures of the Authority, and any amendments thereto, taking into account the recommendations of the Legal and Technical Commission or other subordinate organ concerned. These rules, regulations and procedures shall relate to prospecting, exploration and exploitation in the Area and the financial management and internal administration of the Authority. Priority shall be given to the adoption of rules, regulations and procedures for the exploration for and exploitation of polymetallic nodules. Rules, regulations and procedures for the exploration for and exploitation of any resource other than polymetallic nodules shall be adopted within three years from the date of a request to the Authority by any of its members to adopt such rules, regulations and procedures in respect of such resource. All rules, regulations and procedures shall remain in effect on a provisional basis until approved by the Assembly or until amended by the Council in the light of any views expressed by the Assembly;
(p) review the collection of all payments to be made by or to the Authority in connection with operations pursuant to this Part;
(q) make the selection from among applicants for production authorizations pursuant to Annex III, article 7, where such selection is required by that provision;
(r) submit the proposed annual budget of the Authority to the Assembly for its approval;
(s) make recommendations to the Assembly concerning policies on any question or matter within the competence of the Authority;
(t) make recommendations to the Assembly concerning suspension of the exercise of the rights and privileges of membership pursuant to article 185;
(u) institute proceedings on behalf of the Authority before the Seabed Disputes Chamber in cases of non-compliance;
(v) notify the Assembly upon a decision by the Seabed Disputes Chamber in proceedings instituted under subparagraph (u), and make any recommendations which it may find appropriate with respect to measures to be taken;
(w) issue emergency orders, which may include orders for the suspension or adjustment of operations, to prevent serious harm to the marine environment arising out of activities in the Area;
(x) disapprove areas for exploitation by contractors or the Enterprise in cases where substantial evidence indicates the risk of serious harm to the marine environment;
(y) establish a subsidiary organ for the elaboration of draft financial rules, regulations and procedures relating to: (i) financial management in accordance with articles 171 to 175; and (ii) financial arrangements in accordance with Annex III, article 13 and article 17,
paragraph (1)(c);
(z) establish appropriate mechanisms for directing and supervising a staff of inspectors who shall inspect activities in the Area to determine whether this Part, the rules, regulations and procedures of the Authority, and the terms and conditions of any contract with the Authority are being complied with.

Article 163. Organs of the Council
(1) There are hereby established the following organs of the Council:
(a) an Economic Planning Commission;
(b) a Legal and Technical Commission.
(2) Each Commission shall be composed of 15 members, elected by the Council from among the candidates nominated by the States Parties. However, if necessary, the Council may decide to increase the size of either Commission having due regard to economy and efficiency.
(3) Members of a Commission shall have appropriate qualifications in the area of competence of that Commission. States Parties shall nominate candidates of the highest standards of competence and integrity with qualifications in relevant fields so as to ensure the effective exercise of the functions of the Commissions.
(4) In the election of members of the Commissions, due account shall be taken of the need for equitable geographical distribution and the representation of special interests.
(5) No State Party may nominate more than one candidate for the same Commission. No person shall be elected to serve on more than one Commission.
(6) Members of the Commissions shall hold office for a term of five years. They shall be eligible for re-election for a further term.
(7) In the event of the death, incapacity or resignation of a member of a Commission prior to the

expiration of the term of office, the Council shall elect for the remainder of the term, a member from the same geographical region or area of interest.

(8) Members of Commissions shall have no financial interest in any activity relating to exploration and exploitation in the Area. Subject to their responsibilities to the Commissions upon which they serve, they shall not disclose, even after the termination of their functions, any industrial secret, proprietary data which are transferred to the Authority in accordance with Annex III, article 14, or any other confidential information coming to their knowledge by reason of their duties for the Authority.

(9) Each Commission shall exercise its functions in accordance with such guidelines and directives as the Council may adopt.

(10) Each Commission shall formulate and submit to the Council for approval such rules and regulations as may be necessary for the efficient conduct of the Commission's functions.

(11) The decision-making procedures of the Commissions shall be established by the rules, regulations and procedures of the Authority. Recommendations to the Council shall, where necessary, be accompanied by a summary on the divergencies of opinion in the Commission. (12) Each Commission shall normally function at the seat of the Authority and shall meet as often as is required for the efficient exercise of its functions.

(13) In the exercise of its functions, each Commission may, where appropriate, consult another commission, any competent organ of the United Nations or of its specialized agencies or any international organizations with competence in the subject-matter of such consultation.

Article 164. The Economic Planning Commission

(1) Members of the Economic Planning Commission shall have appropriate qualifications such as those relevant to mining, management of mineral resource activities, international trade or international economics. The Council shall endeavour to ensure that the membership of the Commission reflects all appropriate qualifications. The Commission shall include at least two members from developing States whose exports of the categories of minerals to be derived from the Area have a substantial bearing upon their economies.

(2) The Commission shall:

(a) propose, upon the request of the Council, measures to implement decisions relating to activities in the Area taken in accordance with this Convention;

(b) review the trends of and the factors affecting supply, demand and prices of minerals which may be derived from the Area, bearing in mind the interests of both importing and exporting countries, and in particular of the developing States among them;

(c) examine any situation likely to lead to the adverse effects referred to in article 150, subparagraph (h), brought to its attention by the State Party or States Parties concerned, and make appropriate recommendations to the Council;

(d) propose to the Council for submission to the Assembly, as provided in article 151, paragraph (10), a system of compensation or other measures of economic adjustment assistance for developing States which suffer adverse effects caused by activities in the Area. The Commission shall make the recommendations to the Council that are necessary for the application of the system or other measures adopted by the Assembly in specific cases.

Article 165. The Legal and Technical Commission

(1) Members of the Legal and Technical Commission shall have appropriate qualifications such as those relevant to exploration for and exploitation and processing of mineral resources, oceanology, protection of the marine environment, or economic or legal matters relating to ocean mining and related fields of expertise. The Council shall endeavour to ensure that the membership of the Commission reflects all appropriate qualifications.

(2) The Commission shall:

(a) make recommendations with regard to the exercise of the Authority's functions upon the request of the Council;

(b) review formal written plans of work for activities in the Area in accordance with article 153, paragraph (3), and submit appropriate recommendations to the Council. The Commission shall base its recommendations solely on the grounds stated in Annex III and shall report fully thereon to the Council;

(c) supervise, upon the request of the Council, activities in the Area, where appropriate, in consultation and collaboration with any entity carrying out such activities or State or States concerned and report to the Council;

(d) prepare assessments of the environmental implications of activities in the Area;

(e) make recommendations to the Council on the protection of the marine environment, taking into account the views of recognized experts in that field;

(f) formulate and submit to the Council the rules, regulations and procedures referred to in article

162, paragraph (2)(o), taking into account all relevant factors including assessments of the environmental implications of activities in the Area;

(g) keep such rules, regulations and procedures under review and recommend to the Council from time to time such amendments thereto as it may deem necessary or desirable;

(h) make recommendations to the Council regarding the establishment of a monitoring programme to observe, measure, evaluate and analyse, by recognized scientific methods, on a regular basis, the risks or effects of pollution of the marine environment resulting from activities in the Area, ensure that existing regulations are adequate and are complied with and coordinate the implementation of the monitoring programme approved by the Council;

(i) recommend to the Council that proceedings be instituted on behalf of the Authority before the Seabed Disputes Chamber, in accordance with this Part and the relevant Annexes taking into account particularly article 187;

(j) make recommendations to the Council with respect to measures to be taken, upon a decision by the Seabed Disputes Chamber in proceedings instituted in accordance with subparagraph (i);

(k) make recommendations to the Council to issue emergency orders, which may include orders for the suspension or adjustment of operations, to prevent serious harm to the marine environment arising out of activities in the Area. Such 92 recommendations shall be taken up by the Council on a priority basis;

(l) make recommendations to the Council to disapprove areas for exploitation by contractors or the Enterprise in cases where substantial evidence indicates the risk of serious harm to the marine environment;

(m) make recommendations to the Council regarding the direction and supervision of a staff of inspectors who shall inspect activities in the Area to determine whether the provisions of this Part, the rules, regulations and procedures of the Authority, and the terms and conditions of any contract with the Authority are being complied with;

(n) calculate the production ceiling and issue production authorizations on behalf of the Authority pursuant to article 151, paragraphs (2) to (7), following any necessary selection among applicants for production authorizations by the Council in accordance with Annex III, article 7.

(3) The members of the Commission shall, upon request by any State Party or other party concerned, be accompanied by a representative of such State or other party concerned when carrying out their function of supervision and inspection.

Subsection D. The Secretariat

Article 166. The Secretariat
(1) The Secretariat of the Authority shall comprise a Secretary-General and such staff as the Authority may require.
(2) The Secretary-General shall be elected for four years by the Assembly from among the candidates proposed by the Council and may be re-elected.
(3) The Secretary-General shall be the chief administrative officer of the Authority, and shall act in that capacity in all meetings of the Assembly, of the Council and of any subsidiary organ, and shall perform such other administrative functions as are entrusted to the Secretary-General by these organs.
(4) The Secretary-General shall make an annual report to the Assembly on the work of the Authority.

Article 167. The staff of the Authority
(1) The staff of the Authority shall consist of such qualified scientific and technical and other personnel as may be required to fulfil the administrative functions of the Authority.
(2) The paramount consideration in the recruitment and employment of the staff and in the determination of their conditions of service shall be the necessity of securing the highest standards of efficiency, competence and integrity. Subject to this consideration, due regard shall be paid to the importance of recruiting the staff on as wide a geographical basis as possible.
(3) The staff shall be appointed by the Secretary-General. The terms and conditions on which they shall be appointed, remunerated and dismissed shall be in accordance with the rules, regulations and procedures of the Authority.

Article 168. International character of the Secretariat
(1) In the performance of their duties the Secretary-General and the staff shall not seek or receive instructions from any government or from any other source external to the Authority. They shall refrain from any action which might reflect on their position as international officials responsible only to the Authority. Each State Party undertakes to respect the exclusively international character of the responsibilities of the Secretary-General and the staff and not to seek to influence them in the

discharge of their responsibilities. Any violation of responsibilities by a staff member shall be submitted to the appropriate administrative tribunal as provided in the rules, regulations and procedures of the Authority.

(2) The Secretary-General and the staff shall have no financial interest in any activity relating to exploration and exploitation in the Area. Subject to their responsibilities to the Authority, they shall not disclose, even after the termination of their functions, any industrial secret, proprietary data which are transferred to the Authority in accordance with Annex III, article 14, or any other confidential information coming to their knowledge by reason of their employment with the Authority.

(3) Violations of the obligations of a staff member of the Authority set forth in paragraph (2) shall, on the request of a State Party affected by such violation, or a natural or juridical person, sponsored by a State Party as provided in article 153, paragraph (2)(b), and affected by such violation, be submitted by the Authority against the staff member concerned to a tribunal designated by the rules, regulations and procedures of the Authority. The Party affected shall have the right to take part in the proceedings. If the tribunal so recommends, the Secretary-General shall dismiss the staff member concerned.

(4) The rules, regulations and procedures of the Authority shall contain such provisions as are necessary to implement this article.

Article 169. Consultation and cooperation with international and non-governmental organizations

(1) The Secretary-General shall, on matters within the competence of the Authority, make suitable arrangements, with the approval of the Council, for consultation and cooperation with international and non-governmental organizations recognized by the Economic and Social Council of the United Nations.

(2) Any organization with which the Secretary-General has entered into an arrangement under paragraph (1) may designate representatives to attend meetings of the organs of the Authority as observers in accordance with the rules of procedure of these organs. Procedures shall be established for obtaining the views of such organizations in appropriate cases.

(3) The Secretary-General may distribute to States Parties written reports submitted by the non-governmental organizations referred to in paragraph (l) on subjects in which they have special competence and which are related to the work of the Authority.

Subsection E. The Enterprise

Article 170. The Enterprise

(1) The Enterprise shall be the organ of the Authority which shall carry out activities in the Area directly, pursuant to article 153, paragraph (2)(a), as well as the transporting, processing and marketing of minerals recovered from the Area.

(2) The Enterprise shall, within the framework of the international legal personality of the Authority, have such legal capacity as is provided for in the Statute set forth in Annex IV. The Enterprise shall act in accordance with this Convention and the rules, regulations and procedures of the Authority, as well as the general policies established by the Assembly, and shall be subject to the directives and control of the Council.

(3) The Enterprise shall have its principal place of business at the seat of the Authority.

(4) The Enterprise shall, in accordance with article 173, paragraph (2), and Annex IV, article 11, be provided with such funds as it may require to carry out its functions, and shall receive technology as provided in article 144 and other relevant provisions of this Convention.

Subsection F. Financial arrangements of the authority

Article 171. Funds of the Authority

The funds of the Authority shall include:
(a) assessed contributions made by members of the Authority in accordance with article 160, paragraph (2)(e);
(b) funds received by the Authority pursuant to Annex III, article 13, in connection with activities in the Area;
(c) funds transferred from the Enterprise in accordance with Annex IV, article 10;
(d) funds borrowed pursuant to article 174;
(e) voluntary contributions made by members or other entities; and
(f) payments to a compensation fund, in accordance with article 151, paragraph (10), whose sources are to be recommended by the Economic Planning Commission.

Article 172. Annual budget of the Authority
The Secretary-General shall draft the proposed annual budget of the Authority and submit it to the Council. The Council shall consider the proposed annual budget and submit it to the Assembly, together with any recommendations thereon. The Assembly shall consider and approve the proposed annual budget in accordance with article 160, paragraph (2)(h). 95

Article 173. Expenses of the Authority
(1) The contributions referred to in article 171, subparagraph (a), shall be paid into a special account to meet the administrative expenses of the Authority until the Authority has sufficient funds from other sources to meet those expenses.
(2) The administrative expenses of the Authority shall be a first call upon the funds of the Authority. Except for the assessed contributions referred to in article 171, subparagraph (a), the funds which remain after payment of administrative expenses may, inter alia:
(a) be shared in accordance with article 140 and article 160, paragraph (2)(g);
(b) be used to provide the Enterprise with funds in accordance with article 170, paragraph (4); (c) be used to compensate developing States in accordance with article 151, paragraph (10), and article 160, paragraph 2(l).

Article 174. Borrowing power of the Authority
(1) The Authority shall have the power to borrow funds.
(2) The Assembly shall prescribe the limits on the borrowing power of the Authority in the financial regulations adopted pursuant to article 160, paragraph (2)(f).
(3) The Council shall exercise the borrowing power of the Authority.
(4) States Parties shall not be liable for the debts of the Authority.

Article 175. Annual audit
The records, books and accounts of the Authority, including its annual financial statements, shall be audited annually by an independent auditor appointed by the Assembly.

Subsection G. Legal status, privileges and immunities

Article 176. Legal status
The Authority shall have international legal personality and such legal capacity as may be necessary for the exercise of its functions and the fulfilment of its purposes.

Article 177. Privileges and immunities
To enable the Authority to exercise its functions, it shall enjoy in the territory of each State Party the privileges and immunities set forth in this subsection.
The privileges and immunities relating to the Enterprise shall be those set forth in Annex IV, article 13.

Article 178. Immunity from legal process
The Authority, its property and assets, shall enjoy immunity from legal process except to the extent that the Authority expressly waives this immunity in a particular case.

Article 179. Immunity from search and any form of seizure
The property and assets of the Authority, wherever located and by whomsoever held, shall be immune from search, requisition, confiscation, expropriation or any other form of seizure by executive or legislative action.

Article 180. Exemption from restrictions, regulations, controls and moratoria
The property and assets of the Authority shall be exempt from restrictions, regulations, controls and moratoria of any nature.

Article 181. Archives and official communications of the Authority
(1) The archives of the Authority, wherever located, shall be inviolable.
(2) Proprietary data, industrial secrets or similar information and personnel records shall not be placed in archives which are open to public inspection.
(3) With regard to its official communications, the Authority shall be accorded by each State Party treatment no less favourable than that accorded by that State to other international organizations.

Article 182. Privileges and immunities of certain persons connected with the Authority
Representatives of States Parties attending meetings of the Assembly, the Council or organs of the Assembly or the Council, and the Secretary-General and staff of the Authority, shall enjoy in the territory of each State Party:

(a) immunity from legal process with respect to acts performed by them in the exercise of their functions, except to the extent that the State which they represent or the Authority, as appropriate, expressly waives this immunity in a particular case;
(b) if they are not nationals of that State Party, the same exemptions from immigration restrictions, alien registration requirements and national service obligations, the same facilities as regards exchange restrictions and the same treatment in respect of travelling facilities as are accorded by that State to the representatives, officials and employees of comparable rank of other States Parties.

Article 183. Exemption from taxes and customs duties
(1) Within the scope of its official activities, the Authority, its assets and property, its income, and its operations and transactions, authorized by this Convention, shall be exempt from all direct taxation and goods imported or exported for its official use shall be exempt from all customs duties.
The Authority shall not claim exemption from taxes which are no more than charges for services rendered.
(2) When purchases of goods or services of substantial value necessary for the official activities of the Authority are made by or on behalf of the Authority, and when the price of such goods or services includes taxes or duties, appropriate measures shall, to the extent practicable, be taken by States Parties to grant exemption from such taxes or duties or provide for their reimbursement. Goods imported or purchased under an exemption provided for in this article shall not be sold or otherwise disposed of in the territory of the State Party which granted the exemption, except under conditions agreed with that State Party.
(3) No tax shall be levied by States Parties on or in respect of salaries and emoluments paid or any other form of payment made by the Authority to the Secretary-General and staff of the Authority, as well as experts performing missions for the Authority, who are not their nationals.

Subsection H. Suspension of the exercise of rights and privileges of members

Article 184. Suspension of the exercise of voting rights
A State Party which is in arrears in the payment of its financial contributions to the Authority shall have no vote if the amount of its arrears equals or exceeds the amount of the contributions due from it for the preceding two full years.
The Assembly may, nevertheless, permit such a member to vote if it is satisfied that the failure to pay is due to conditions beyond the control of the member.

Article 185. Suspension of exercise of rights and privileges of membership
(1) A State Party which has grossly and persistently violated the provisions of this Part may be suspended from the exercise of the rights and privileges of membership by the Assembly upon the recommendation of the Council.
(2) No action may be taken under paragraph (1) until the Seabed Disputes Chamber has found that a State Party has grossly and persistently violated the provisions of this Part.

Section 5. Settlement of disputes and advisory opinions

Article 186. Seabed Disputes Chamber of the International Tribunal for the Law of the Sea The establishment of the Seabed Disputes Chamber and the manner in which it shall exercise its jurisdiction shall be governed by the provisions of this section, of Part XV and of
Annex VI. 98

Article 187. Jurisdiction of the Seabed Disputes Chamber
The Seabed Disputes Chamber shall have jurisdiction under this Part and the Annexes relating thereto in disputes with respect to activities in the Area falling within the following categories:
(a) disputes between States Parties concerning the interpretation or application of this Part and the Annexes relating thereto;
(b) disputes between a State Party and the Authority concerning:
(i) acts or omissions of the Authority or of a State Party alleged to be in violation of this Part or the Annexes relating thereto or of rules, regulations and procedures of the Authority adopted in accordance therewith; or
(ii) acts of the Authority alleged to be in excess of jurisdiction or a misuse of power;
(c) disputes between parties to a contract, being States Parties, the Authority or the Enterprise, state enterprises and natural or juridical persons referred to in article 153, paragraph (2)(b), concerning:
(i) the interpretation or application of a relevant contract or a plan of work; or
(ii) acts or omissions of a party to the contract relating to activities in the Area and directed to the other party or directly affecting its legitimate interests;
(d) disputes between the Authority and a prospective contractor who has been sponsored by a State

as provided in article 153, paragraph (2)(b), and has duly fulfilled the conditions referred to in Annex III, article 4, paragraph (6), and article 13, paragraph (2), concerning the refusal of a contract or a legal issue arising in the negotiation of the contract;
(e) disputes between the Authority and a State Party, a state enterprise or a natural or juridical person sponsored by a State Party as provided for in article 153, paragraph (2)(b), where it is alleged that the Authority has incurred liability as provided in Annex III, article 22;
(f) any other disputes for which the jurisdiction of the Chamber is specifically provided in this Convention.

Article 188. Submission of disputes to a special chamber of the International Tribunal for the Law of the Sea or an ad hoc chamber of the Seabed Disputes Chamber or to binding commercial arbitration
(1) Disputes between States Parties referred to in article 187, subparagraph (a), may be submitted:
(a) at the request of the parties to the dispute, to a special chamber of the International Tribunal for the Law of the Sea to be formed in accordance with Annex VI, articles 15 and 17; or
(b) at the request of any party to the dispute, to an ad hoc chamber of the Seabed Disputes Chamber to be formed in accordance with Annex VI, article 36.
(2) (a) Disputes concerning the interpretation or application of a contract referred to in
article 187, subparagraph (c)(i), shall be submitted, at the request of any party to the dispute, to binding commercial arbitration, unless the parties otherwise agree.
A commercial arbitral tribunal to which the dispute is submitted shall have no jurisdiction to decide any question of interpretation of this Convention. When the dispute also involves a question of the interpretation of Part XI and the Annexes relating thereto, with respect to activities in the Area, that question shall be referred to the Seabed Disputes Chamber for a ruling.
(b) If, at the commencement of or in the course of such arbitration, the arbitral tribunal determines, either at the request of any party to the dispute or proprio motu, that its decision depends upon a ruling of the Seabed Disputes Chamber, the arbitral tribunal shall refer such question to the Seabed Disputes Chamber for such ruling. The arbitral tribunal shall then proceed to render its award in conformity with the ruling of the Seabed Disputes Chamber. (c) In the absence of a provision in the contract on the arbitration procedure to be applied in the dispute, the arbitration shall be conducted in accordance with the UNCITRAL Arbitration Rules or such other arbitration rules as may be prescribed in the rules, regulations and procedures of the Authority, unless the parties to the dispute otherwise agree.
Article 189 Limitation on jurisdiction with regard to decisions of the Authority
The Seabed Disputes Chamber shall have no jurisdiction with regard to the exercise by the Authority of its discretionary powers in accordance with this Part; in no case shall it substitute its discretion for that of the Authority. Without prejudice to article 191, in exercising its jurisdiction pursuant to article 187, the Seabed Disputes Chamber shall not pronounce itself on the question of whether any rules, regulations and procedures of the Authority are in conformity with this Convention, nor declare invalid any such rules, regulations and procedures. Its jurisdiction in this regard shall be confined to deciding claims that the application of any rules, regulations and procedures of the Authority in individual cases would be in conflict with the contractual obligations of the parties to the dispute or their obligations under this Convention, claims concerning excess of jurisdiction or misuse of power, and to claims for damages to be paid or other remedy to be given to the party concerned for the failure of the other party to comply with its contractual obligations or its obligations under this Convention.

Article 190. Participation and appearance of sponsoring States Parties in proceedings
(1) If a natural or juridical person is a party to a dispute referred to in article 187, the sponsoring State shall be given notice thereof and shall have the right to participate in the proceedings by submitting written or oral statements.
(2) If an action is brought against a State Party by a natural or juridical person sponsored by another State Party in a dispute referred to in article 187, subparagraph (c), the respondent State may request the State sponsoring that person to appear in the proceedings on behalf of that person. Failing such appearance, the respondent State may arrange to be represented by a juridical person of its nationality.

Article 191. Advisory opinions
The Seabed Disputes Chamber shall give advisory opinions at the request of the Assembly or the Council on legal questions arising within the scope of their activities. Such opinions shall be given as a matter of urgency.

Part XII. Protection and preservation of the marine environment

Section 1. General provisions

Article 192. General obligation

States have the obligation to protect and preserve the marine environment.

Article 193. Sovereign right of States to exploit their natural resources

States have the sovereign right to exploit their natural resources pursuant to their environmental policies and in accordance with their duty to protect and preserve the marine environment.

Article 194. Measures to prevent, reduce and control pollution of the marine environment

(1) States shall take, individually or jointly as appropriate, all measures consistent with this Convention that are necessary to prevent, reduce and control pollution of the marine environment from any source, using for this purpose the best practicable means at their disposal and in accordance with their capabilities, and they shall endeavour to harmonize their policies in this connection.

(2) States shall take all measures necessary to ensure that activities under their jurisdiction or control are so conducted as not to cause damage by pollution to other States and their environment, and that pollution arising from incidents or activities under their jurisdiction or control does not spread beyond the areas where they exercise sovereign rights in accordance with this Convention.

(3) The measures taken pursuant to this Part shall deal with all sources of pollution of the marine environment. These measures shall include, inter alia, those designed to minimize to the fullest possible extent:

(a) the release of toxic, harmful or noxious substances, especially those which are persistent, from land-based sources, from or through the atmosphere or by dumping;

(b) pollution from vessels, in particular measures for preventing accidents and dealing with emergencies, ensuring the safety of operations at sea, preventing intentional and unintentional discharges, and regulating the design, construction, equipment, operation and manning of vessels;

(c) pollution from installations and devices used in exploration or exploitation of the natural resources of the seabed and subsoil, in particular measures for preventing accidents and dealing with emergencies, ensuring the safety of operations at sea, and regulating the design, construction, equipment, operation and manning of such installations or devices;

(d) pollution from other installations and devices operating in the marine environment, in particular measures for preventing accidents and dealing with emergencies, ensuring the safety of operations at sea, and regulating the design, construction, equipment, operation and manning of such installations or devices.

(4) In taking measures to prevent, reduce or control pollution of the marine environment, States shall refrain from unjustifiable interference with activities carried out by other States in the exercise of their rights and in pursuance of their duties in conformity with this Convention.

(5) The measures taken in accordance with this Part shall include those necessary to protect and preserve rare or fragile ecosystems as well as the habitat of depleted, threatened or endangered species and other forms of marine life.

Article 195. Duty not to transfer damage or hazards or transform one type of pollution into another

In taking measures to prevent, reduce and control pollution of the marine environment, States shall act so as not to transfer, directly or indirectly, damage or hazards from one area to another or transform one type of pollution into another.

Article 196. Use of technologies or introduction of alien or new species

(1) States shall take all measures necessary to prevent, reduce and control pollution of the marine environment resulting from the use of technologies under their jurisdiction or control, or the intentional or accidental introduction of species, alien or new, to a particular part of the marine environment, which may cause significant and harmful changes thereto.

(2) This article does not affect the application of this Convention regarding the prevention, reduction and control of pollution of the marine environment.

Section 2. Global and regional cooperation

Article 197. Cooperation on a global or regional basis

States shall cooperate on a global basis and, as appropriate, on a regional basis, directly or through competent international organizations, in formulating and elaborating international rules, standards and recommended practices and procedures consistent with this Convention, for the protection and preservation of the marine environment, taking into account characteristic regional features.

Article 198. Notification of imminent or actual damage
When a State becomes aware of cases in which the marine environment is in imminent danger of being damaged or has been damaged by pollution, it shall immediately notify other States it deems likely to be affected by such damage, as well as the competent international organizations.

Article 199. Contingency plans against pollution
In the cases referred to in article 198, States in the area affected, in accordance with their capabilities, and the competent international organizations shall cooperate, to the extent possible, in eliminating the effects of pollution and preventing or minimizing the damage. To this end, States shall jointly develop and promote contingency plans for responding to pollution incidents in the marine environment.

Article 200. Studies, research programmes and exchange of information and data
States shall cooperate, directly or through competent international organizations, for the purpose of promoting studies, undertaking programmes of scientific research and encouraging the exchange of information and data acquired about pollution of the marine environment. They shall endeavour to participate actively in regional and global programmes to acquire knowledge for the assessment of the nature and extent of pollution, exposure to it, and its pathways, risks and remedies.

Article 201. Scientific criteria for regulations
In the light of the information and data acquired pursuant to article 200, States shall cooperate, directly or through competent international organizations, in establishing appropriate scientific criteria for the formulation and elaboration of rules, standards and recommended practices and procedures for the prevention, reduction and control of pollution of the marine environment.

Section 3. Technical assistance

Article 202. Scientific and technical assistance to developing States
States shall, directly or through competent international organizations:
(a) promote programmes of scientific, educational, technical and other assistance to developing States for the protection and preservation of the marine environment and the prevention, reduction and control of marine pollution. Such assistance shall include, inter alia:
(i) training of their scientific and technical personnel;
(ii) facilitating their participation in relevant international programmes;
(iii) supplying them with necessary equipment and facilities;
(iv) enhancing their capacity to manufacture such equipment;
(v) advice on and developing facilities for research, monitoring, educational and other programmes;
(b) provide appropriate assistance, especially to developing States, for the minimization of the effects of major incidents which may cause serious pollution of the marine environment; (c) provide appropriate assistance, especially to developing States, concerning the preparation of environmental assessments.

Article 203. Preferential treatment for developing States
Developing States shall, for the purposes of prevention, reduction and control of pollution of the marine environment or minimization of its effects, be granted preference by international organizations in:
(a) the allocation of appropriate funds and technical assistance; and
(b) the utilization of their specialized services.

Section 4. Monitoring and environmental assessment

Article 204. Monitoring of the risks or effects of pollution
(1) States shall, consistent with the rights of other States, endeavour, as far as practicable, directly or through the competent international organizations, to observe, measure, evaluate and analyse, by recognized scientific methods, the risks or effects of pollution of the marine environment.
(2) In particular, States shall keep under surveillance the effects of any activities which they permit or in which they engage in order to determine whether these activities are likely to pollute the marine environment.

Article 205. Publication of reports
States shall publish reports of the results obtained pursuant to article 204 or provide such reports at appropriate intervals to the competent international organizations, which should make them available to all States.

Article 206. Assessment of potential effects of activities

When States have reasonable grounds for believing that planned activities under their jurisdiction or control may cause substantial pollution of or significant and harmful changes to the marine environment, they shall, as far as practicable, assess the potential effects of such activities on the marine environment and shall communicate reports of the results of such assessments in the manner provided in article 205.

Section 5. International rules and national legislation to prevent, reduce and control pollution of the marine environment

Article 207. Pollution from land-based sources

(1) States shall adopt laws and regulations to prevent, reduce and control pollution of the marine environment from land-based sources, including rivers, estuaries, pipelines and outfall structures, taking into account internationally agreed rules, standards and recommended practices and procedures.

(2) States shall take other measures as may be necessary to prevent, reduce and control such pollution.

(3) States shall endeavour to harmonize their policies in this connection at the appropriate regional level.

(4) States, acting especially through competent international organizations or diplomatic conference, shall endeavour to establish global and regional rules, standards and recommended practices and procedures to prevent, reduce and control pollution of the marine environment from land-based sources, taking into account characteristic regional features, the economic capacity of developing States and their need for economic development. Such rules, standards and recommended practices and procedures shall be re-examined from time to time as necessary.

(5) Laws, regulations, measures, rules, standards and recommended practices and procedures referred to in paragraphs (1), (2) and (4) shall include those designed to minimize, to the fullest extent possible, the release of toxic, harmful or noxious substances, especially those which are persistent, into the marine environment.

Article 208. Pollution from seabed activities subject to national jurisdiction

(1) Coastal States shall adopt laws and regulations to prevent, reduce and control pollution of the marine environment arising from or in connection with seabed activities subject to their jurisdiction and from artificial islands, installations and structures under their jurisdiction, pursuant to articles 60 and 80.

(2) States shall take other measures as may be necessary to prevent, reduce and control such pollution.

(3) Such laws, regulations and measures shall be no less effective than international rules, standards and recommended practices and procedures.

(4) States shall endeavour to harmonize their policies in this connection at the appropriate regional level.

(5) States, acting especially through competent international organizations or diplomatic conference, shall establish global and regional rules, standards and recommended practices and procedures to prevent, reduce and control pollution of the marine environment referred to in paragraph (l). Such rules, standards and recommended practices and procedures shall be re-examined from time to time as necessary.

Article 209. Pollution from activities in the Area

(1) International rules, regulations and procedures shall be established in accordance
with Part XI to prevent, reduce and control pollution of the marine environment from activities in the Area. Such rules, regulations and procedures shall be re-examined from time to time as necessary.

(2) Subject to the relevant provisions of this section, States shall adopt laws and regulations to prevent, reduce and control pollution of the marine environment from activities in the Area undertaken by vessels, installations, structures and other devices flying their flag or of their registry or operating under their authority, as the case may be.
The requirements of such laws and regulations shall be no less effective than the international rules, regulations and procedures referred to in paragraph (1).

Article 210. Pollution by dumping

(1) States shall adopt laws and regulations to prevent, reduce and control pollution of the marine environment by dumping.

(2) States shall take other measures as may be necessary to prevent, reduce and control such pollution.

(3) Such laws, regulations and measures shall ensure that dumping is not carried out without the permission of the competent authorities of States.
(4) States, acting especially through competent international organizations or diplomatic conference, shall endeavour to establish global and regional rules, standards and recommended practices and procedures to prevent, reduce and control such pollution. Such rules, standards and recommended practices and procedures shall be re-examined from time to time as necessary.
(5) Dumping within the territorial sea and the exclusive economic zone or onto the continental shelf shall not be carried out without the express prior approval of the coastal State, which has the right to permit, regulate and control such dumping after due consideration of the matter with other States which by reason of their geographical situation may be adversely affected thereby.
(6) National laws, regulations and measures shall be no less effective in preventing, reducing and controlling such pollution than the global rules and standards.

Article 211. Pollution from vessels
(1) States, acting through the competent international organization or general diplomatic conference, shall establish international rules and standards to prevent, reduce and control pollution of the marine environment from vessels and promote the adoption, in the same manner, wherever appropriate, of routeing systems designed to minimize the threat of accidents which might cause pollution of the marine environment, including the coastline, and pollution damage to the related interests of coastal States. Such rules and standards shall, in the same manner, be re-examined from time to time as necessary.
(2) States shall adopt laws and regulations for the prevention, reduction and control of pollution of the marine environment from vessels flying their flag or of their registry. Such laws and regulations shall at least have the same effect as that of generally accepted international rules and standards established through the competent international organization or general diplomatic conference.
(3) States which establish particular requirements for the prevention, reduction and control of pollution of the marine environment as a condition for the entry of foreign vessels into their ports or internal waters or for a call at their off-shore terminals shall give due publicity to such requirements and shall communicate them to the competent international organization. Whenever such requirements are established in identical form by two or more coastal States in an endeavour to harmonize policy, the communication shall indicate which States are participating in such cooperative arrangements. Every State shall require the master of a vessel flying its flag or of its registry, when navigating within the territorial sea of a State participating in such cooperative arrangements, to furnish, upon the request of that State, information as to whether it is proceeding to a State of the same region participating in such cooperative arrangements and, if so, to indicate whether it complies with the port entry requirements of that State. This article is without prejudice to the continued exercise by a vessel of its right of innocent passage or to the application of article 25, paragraph (2).
(4) Coastal States may, in the exercise of their sovereignty within their territorial sea, adopt laws and regulations for the prevention, reduction and control of marine pollution from foreign vessels, including vessels exercising the right of innocent passage. Such laws and regulations shall, in accordance with Part II, section 3, not hamper innocent passage of foreign vessels.
(5) Coastal States, for the purpose of enforcement as provided for in section 6, may in respect of their exclusive economic zones adopt laws and regulations for the prevention, reduction and control of pollution from vessels conforming to and giving effect to generally accepted international rules and standards established through the competent international organization or general diplomatic conference.
(6) (a) Where the international rules and standards referred to in paragraph (1) are inadequate to meet special circumstances and coastal States have reasonable grounds for believing that a particular, clearly defined area of their respective exclusive economic zones is an area where the adoption of special mandatory measures for the prevention of pollution from vessels is required for recognized technical reasons in relation to its oceanographical and ecological conditions, as well as its utilization or the protection of its resources and the particular character of its traffic, the coastal States, after appropriate consultations through the competent international organization with any other States concerned, may, for that area, direct a communication to that organization, submitting scientific and technical evidence in support and information on necessary reception facilities. Within 12 months after receiving such a communication, the organization shall determine whether the conditions in that area correspond to the requirements set out above. If the organization so determines, the coastal States may, for that area, adopt laws and regulations for the prevention, reduction and control of pollution from vessels implementing such international rules and standards or navigational practices as are made applicable, through the organization, for special areas. These laws and regulations shall not

become applicable to foreign vessels until 15 months after the submission of the communication to the organization.
(b) The coastal States shall publish the limits of any such particular, clearly defined area.
(c) If the coastal States intend to adopt additional laws and regulations for the same area for the prevention, reduction and control of pollution from vessels, they shall, when submitting the aforesaid communication, at the same time notify the organization thereof. Such additional laws and regulations may relate to discharges or navigational practices but shall not require foreign vessels to observe design, construction, manning or equipment standards other than generally accepted international rules and standards; they shall become applicable to foreign vessels 15 months after the submission of the communication to the organization, provided that the organization agrees within 12 months after the submission of the communication.
(7) The international rules and standards referred to in this article should include inter alia those relating to prompt notification to coastal States, whose coastline or related interests may be affected by incidents, including maritime casualties, which involve discharges or probability of discharges.

Article 212. Pollution from or through the atmosphere
(1) States shall adopt laws and regulations to prevent, reduce and control pollution of the marine environment from or through the atmosphere, applicable to the air space under their sovereignty and to vessels flying their flag or vessels or aircraft of their registry, taking into account internationally agreed rules, standards and recommended practices and procedures and the safety of air navigation.
(2) States shall take other measures as may be necessary to prevent, reduce and control such pollution.
(3) States, acting especially through competent international organizations or diplomatic conference, shall endeavour to establish global and regional rules, standards and recommended practices and procedures to prevent, reduce and control such pollution.

Section 6. Enforcement

Article 213. Enforcement with respect to pollution from land-based sources
States shall enforce their laws and regulations adopted in accordance with article 207 and shall adopt laws and regulations and take other measures necessary to implement applicable international rules and standards established through competent international organizations or diplomatic conference to prevent, reduce and control pollution of the marine environment from land-based sources.

Article 214. Enforcement with respect to pollution from seabed activities
States shall enforce their laws and regulations adopted in accordance with article 208 and shall adopt laws and regulations and take other measures necessary to implement applicable international rules and standards established through competent international organizations or diplomatic conference to prevent, reduce and control pollution of the marine environment arising from or in connection with seabed activities subject to their jurisdiction and from artificial islands, installations and structures under their jurisdiction, pursuant to articles 60 and 80.

Article 215. Enforcement with respect to pollution from activities in the Area
Enforcement of international rules, regulations and procedures established in accordance with Part XI to prevent, reduce and control pollution of the marine environment from activities in the Area shall be governed by that Part.

Article 216. Enforcement with respect to pollution by dumping
(1) Laws and regulations adopted in accordance with this Convention and applicable international rules and standards established through competent international organizations or diplomatic conference for the prevention, reduction and control of pollution of the marine environment by dumping shall be enforced:
(a) by the coastal State with regard to dumping within its territorial sea or its exclusive economic zone or onto its continental shelf;
(b) by the flag State with regard to vessels flying its flag or vessels or aircraft of its registry; (c) by any State with regard to acts of loading of wastes or other matter occurring within its territory or at its off-shore terminals.
(2) No State shall be obliged by virtue of this article to institute proceedings when another State has already instituted proceedings in accordance with this article.

Article 217. Enforcement by flag States
(1) States shall ensure compliance by vessels flying their flag or of their registry with applicable international rules and standards, established through the competent international organization or

general diplomatic conference, and with their laws and regulations adopted in accordance with this Convention for the prevention, reduction and control of pollution of the marine environment from vessels and shall accordingly adopt laws and regulations and take other measures necessary for their implementation. Flag States shall provide for the effective enforcement of such rules, standards, laws and regulations, irrespective of where a violation occurs.

(2) States shall, in particular, take appropriate measures in order to ensure that vessels flying their flag or of their registry are prohibited from sailing, until they can proceed to sea in compliance with the requirements of the international rules and standards referred to in paragraph (1), including requirements in respect of design, construction, equipment and manning of vessels.

(3) States shall ensure that vessels flying their flag or of their registry carry on board certificates required by and issued pursuant to international rules and standards referred to in paragraph (1). States shall ensure that vessels flying their flag are periodically inspected in order to verify that such certificates are in conformity with the actual condition of the vessels. These certificates shall be accepted by other States as evidence of the condition of the vessels and shall be regarded as having the same force as certificates issued by them, unless there are clear grounds for believing that the condition of the vessel does not correspond substantially with the particulars of the certificates.

(4) If a vessel commits a violation of rules and standards established through the competent international organization or general diplomatic conference, the flag State, without prejudice to articles 218, 220 and 228, shall provide for immediate investigation and where appropriate institute proceedings in respect of the alleged violation irrespective of where the violation occurred or where the pollution caused by such violation has occurred or has been spotted.

(5) Flag States conducting an investigation of the violation may request the assistance of any other State whose cooperation could be useful in clarifying the circumstances of the case. States shall endeavour to meet appropriate requests of flag States.

(6) States shall, at the written request of any State, investigate any violation alleged to have been committed by vessels flying their flag. If satisfied that sufficient evidence is available to enable proceedings to be brought in respect of the alleged violation, flag States shall without delay institute such proceedings in accordance with their laws.

(7) Flag States shall promptly inform the requesting State and the competent international organization of the action taken and its outcome. Such information shall be available to all States.

(8) Penalties provided for by the laws and regulations of States for vessels flying their flag shall be adequate in severity to discourage violations wherever they occur.

Article 218. Enforcement by port States

(1) When a vessel is voluntarily within a port or at an off-shore terminal of a State, that State may undertake investigations and, where the evidence so warrants, institute proceedings in respect of any discharge from that vessel outside the internal waters, territorial sea or exclusive economic zone of that State in violation of applicable international rules and standards established through the competent international organization or general diplomatic conference.

(2) No proceedings pursuant to paragraph (1) shall be instituted in respect of a discharge violation in the internal waters, territorial sea or exclusive economic zone of another State unless requested by that State, the flag State, or a State damaged or threatened by the discharge violation, or unless the violation has caused or is likely to cause pollution in the internal waters, territorial sea or exclusive economic zone of the State instituting the proceedings.

(3) When a vessel is voluntarily within a port or at an off-shore terminal of a State, that State shall, as far as practicable, comply with requests from any State for investigation of a discharge violation referred to in paragraph (1), believed to have occurred in, caused, or threatened damage to the internal waters, territorial sea or exclusive economic zone of the requesting State. It shall likewise, as far as practicable, comply with requests from the flag State for investigation of such a violation, irrespective of where the violation occurred.

(4) The records of the investigation carried out by a port State pursuant to this article shall be transmitted upon request to the flag State or to the coastal State. Any proceedings instituted by the port State on the basis of such an investigation may, subject to section 7, be suspended at the request of the coastal State when the violation has occurred within its internal waters, territorial sea or exclusive economic zone. The evidence and records of the case, together with any bond or other financial security posted with the authorities of the port State, shall in that event be transmitted to the coastal State. Such transmittal shall preclude the continuation of proceedings in the port State.

Article 219. Measures relating to seaworthiness of vessels to avoid pollution

Subject to section 7, States which, upon request or on their own initiative, have ascertained that a vessel within one of their ports or at one of their off-shore terminals is in violation of applicable international rules and standards relating to seaworthiness of vessels and thereby threatens damage to the marine environment shall, as far as practicable, take administrative measures to prevent the vessel from sailing. Such States may permit the vessel to proceed only to the nearest appropriate repair yard and, upon removal of the causes of the violation, shall permit the vessel to continue immediately.

Article 220. Enforcement by coastal States
(1) When a vessel is voluntarily within a port or at an off-shore terminal of a State, that State may, subject to section 7, institute proceedings in respect of any violation of its laws and regulations adopted in accordance with this Convention or applicable international rules and standards for the prevention, reduction and control of pollution from vessels when the violation has occurred within the territorial sea or the exclusive economic zone of that State. (2) Where there are clear grounds for believing that a vessel navigating in the territorial sea of a State has, during its passage therein, violated laws and regulations of that State adopted in accordance with this Convention or applicable international rules and standards for the prevention, reduction and control of pollution from vessels, that State, without prejudice to the application of the relevant provisions of Part II, section 3, may undertake physical inspection of the vessel relating to the violation and may, where the evidence so warrants, institute proceedings, including detention of the vessel, in accordance with its laws, subject to the provisions of section 7.
(3) Where there are clear grounds for believing that a vessel navigating in the exclusive economic zone or the territorial sea of a State has, in the exclusive economic zone, committed a violation of applicable international rules and standards for the prevention, reduction and control of pollution from vessels or laws and regulations of that State conforming and giving effect to such rules and standards, that State may require the vessel to give information regarding its identity and port of registry, its last and its next port of call and other relevant information required to establish whether a violation has occurred.
(4) States shall adopt laws and regulations and take other measures so that vessels flying their flag comply with requests for information pursuant to paragraph (3).
(5) Where there are clear grounds for believing that a vessel navigating in the exclusive economic zone or the territorial sea of a State has, in the exclusive economic zone, committed a violation referred to in paragraph (3) resulting in a substantial discharge causing or threatening significant pollution of the marine environment, that State may undertake physical inspection of the vessel for matters relating to the violation if the vessel has refused to give information or if the information supplied by the vessel is manifestly at variance with the evident factual situation and if the circumstances of the case justify such inspection.
(6) Where there is clear objective evidence that a vessel navigating in the exclusive economic zone or the territorial sea of a State has, in the exclusive economic zone, committed a violation referred to in paragraph (3) resulting in a discharge causing major damage or threat of major damage to the coastline or related interests of the coastal State, or to any resources of its territorial sea or exclusive economic zone, that State may, subject to section 7, provided that the evidence so warrants, institute proceedings, including detention of the vessel, in accordance with its laws.
(7) Notwithstanding the provisions of paragraph (6), whenever appropriate procedures have been established, either through the competent international organization or as otherwise agreed, whereby compliance with requirements for bonding or other appropriate financial security has been assured, the coastal State if bound by such procedures shall allow the vessel to proceed.
(8) The provisions of paragraphs (3), (4), (5), (6) and (7) also apply in respect of national laws and regulations adopted pursuant to article 211, paragraph (6).

Article 221. Measures to avoid pollution arising from maritime casualties
(1) Nothing in this Part shall prejudice the right of States, pursuant to international law, both customary and conventional, to take and enforce measures beyond the territorial sea proportionate to the actual or threatened damage to protect their coastline or related interests, including fishing, from pollution or threat of pollution following upon a maritime casualty or acts relating to such a casualty, which may reasonably be expected to result in major harmful consequences.
(2) For the purposes of this article, "maritime casualty" means a collision of vessels, stranding or other incident of navigation, or other occurrence on board a vessel or external to it resulting in material damage or imminent threat of material damage to a vessel or cargo. Article 222 Enforcement with respect to pollution from or through the atmosphere States shall enforce, within the air space under their sovereignty or with regard to vessels flying their flag or vessels or aircraft of their registry, their laws and regulations adopted in accordance with article 212, paragraph (1), and with other provisions of this Convention and shall adopt laws and regulations and take other measures necessary to implement applicable international rules and standards established through competent international organi-

zations or diplomatic conference to prevent, reduce and control pollution of the marine environment from or through the atmosphere, in conformity with all relevant international rules and standards concerning the safety of air navigation.

Section 7. Safeguards

Article 223. Measures to facilitate proceedings

In proceedings instituted pursuant to this Part, States shall take measures to facilitate the hearing of witnesses and the admission of evidence submitted by authorities of another State, or by the competent international organization, and shall facilitate the attendance at such proceedings of official representatives of the competent international organization, the flag State and any State affected by pollution arising out of any violation. The official representatives attending such proceedings shall have such rights and duties as may be provided under national laws and regulations or international law.

Article 224. Exercise of powers of enforcement

The powers of enforcement against foreign vessels under this Part may only be exercised by officials or by warships, military aircraft, or other ships or aircraft clearly marked and identifiable as being on government service and authorized to that effect.

Article 225. Duty to avoid adverse consequences in the exercise of the powers of enforcement

In the exercise under this Convention of their powers of enforcement against foreign vessels, States shall not endanger the safety of navigation or otherwise create any hazard to a vessel, or bring it to an unsafe port or anchorage, or expose the marine environment to an unreasonable risk.

Article 226. Investigation of foreign vessels

(1)(a) States shall not delay a foreign vessel longer than is essential for purposes of the investigations provided for in articles 216, 218 and 220. Any physical inspection of a foreign vessel shall be limited to an examination of such certificates, records or other documents as the vessel is required to carry by generally accepted international rules and standards or of any similar documents which it is carrying; further physical inspection of the vessel may be undertaken only after such an examination and only when:
(i) there are clear grounds for believing that the condition of the vessel or its equipment does not correspond substantially with the particulars of those documents;
(ii) the contents of such documents are not sufficient to confirm or verify a suspected violation; or
(iii) the vessel is not carrying valid certificates and records.
(b) If the investigation indicates a violation of applicable laws and regulations or international rules and standards for the protection and preservation of the marine environment, release shall be made promptly subject to reasonable procedures such as bonding or other appropriate financial security.
(c) Without prejudice to applicable international rules and standards relating to the seaworthiness of vessels, the release of a vessel may, whenever it would present an unreasonable threat of damage to the marine environment, be refused or made conditional upon proceeding to the nearest appropriate repair yard. Where release has been refused or made conditional, the flag State of the vessel must be promptly notified, and may seek release of the vessel in accordance with Part XV.
(2) States shall cooperate to develop procedures for the avoidance of unnecessary physical inspection of vessels at sea.

Article 227. Non-discrimination with respect to foreign vessels

In exercising their rights and performing their duties under this Part, States shall not discriminate in form or in fact against vessels of any other State.

Article 228. Suspension and restrictions on institution of *proceedings*

(1) Proceedings to impose penalties in respect of any violation of applicable laws and regulations or international rules and standards relating to the prevention, reduction and control of pollution from vessels committed by a foreign vessel beyond the territorial sea of the State instituting proceedings shall be suspended upon the taking of proceedings to impose penalties in respect of corresponding charges by the flag State within six months of the date on which proceedings were first instituted, unless those proceedings relate to a case of major damage to the coastal State or the flag State in question has repeatedly disregarded its obligation to enforce effectively the applicable international rules and standards in respect of violations committed by its vessels.
The flag State shall in due course make available to the State previously instituting proceedings a full dossier of the case and the records of the proceedings, whenever the flag State has requested the suspension of proceedings in accordance with this article. When proceedings instituted by the flag State

PART I INTERNATIONAL LAW

have been brought to a conclusion, the suspended proceedings shall be terminated. Upon payment of costs incurred in respect of such proceedings, any bond posted or other financial security provided in connection with the suspended proceedings shall be released by the coastal State.

(2) Proceedings to impose penalties on foreign vessels shall not be instituted after the expiry of three years from the date on which the violation was committed, and shall not be taken by any State in the event of proceedings having been instituted by another State subject to the provisions set out in paragraph (1).

(3) The provisions of this article are without prejudice to the right of the flag State to take any measures, including proceedings to impose penalties, according to its laws irrespective of prior proceedings by another State.

Article 229. Institution of civil proceedings

Nothing in this Convention affects the institution of civil proceedings in respect of any claim for loss or damage resulting from pollution of the marine environment.

Article 230. Monetary penalties and the observance of recognized rights of the accused

(1) Monetary penalties only may be imposed with respect to violations of national laws and regulations or applicable international rules and standards for the prevention, reduction and control of pollution of the marine environment, committed by foreign vessels beyond the territorial sea.

(2) Monetary penalties only may be imposed with respect to violations of national laws and regulations or applicable international rules and standards for the prevention, reduction and control of pollution of the marine environment, committed by foreign vessels in the territorial sea, except in the case of a wilful and serious act of pollution in the territorial sea.

(3) In the conduct of proceedings in respect of such violations committed by a foreign vessel which may result in the imposition of penalties, recognized rights of the accused shall be observed.

Article 231. Notification to the flag State and other States concerned

States shall promptly notify the flag State and any other State concerned of any measures taken pursuant to section 6 against foreign vessels, and shall submit to the flag State all official reports concerning such measures.

However, with respect to violations committed in the territorial sea, the foregoing obligations of the coastal State apply only to such measures as are taken in proceedings. The diplomatic agents or consular officers and where possible the maritime authority of the flag State, shall be immediately informed of any such measures taken pursuant to section 6 against foreign vessels.

Article 232. Liability of States arising from enforcement measures

States shall be liable for damage or loss attributable to them arising from measures taken pursuant to section 6 when such measures are unlawful or exceed those reasonably required in the light of available information.

States shall provide for recourse in their courts for actions in respect of such damage or loss.

Article 233. Safeguards with respect to straits used for international navigation

Nothing in sections 5, 6 and 7 affects the legal regime of straits used for international navigation. However, if a foreign ship other than those referred to in section 10 has committed a violation of the laws and regulations referred to in article 42, paragraph (1)(a) and (b), causing or threatening major damage to the marine environment of the straits, the States bordering the straits may take appropriate enforcement measures and if so shall respect *mutatis mutandis* the provisions of this section.

Section 8. Ice-covered areas

Article 234. Ice-covered areas

Coastal States have the right to adopt and enforce non-discriminatory laws and regulations for the prevention, reduction and control of marine pollution from vessels in ice-covered areas within the limits of the exclusive economic zone, where particularly severe climatic conditions and the presence of ice covering such areas for most of the year create obstructions or exceptional hazards to navigation, and pollution of the marine environment could cause major harm to or irreversible disturbance of the ecological balance. Such laws and regulations shall have due regard to navigation and the protection and preservation of the marine environment based on the best available scientific evidence.

Section 9. Responsibility and liability

Article 235. Responsibility and liability

(1) States are responsible for the fulfilment of their international obligations concerning the protection and preservation of the marine environment. They shall be liable in accordance with international law.

(2) States shall ensure that recourse is available in accordance with their legal systems for prompt and adequate compensation or other relief in respect of damage caused by pollution of the marine environment by natural or juridical persons under their jurisdiction.
(3) With the objective of assuring prompt and adequate compensation in respect of all damage caused by pollution of the marine environment, States shall cooperate in the implementation of existing international law and the further development of international law relating to responsibility and liability for the assessment of and compensation for damage and the settlement of related disputes, as well as, where appropriate, development of criteria and procedures for payment of adequate compensation, such as compulsory insurance or compensation funds.

Section 10. Sovereign immunity

Article 236. Sovereign immunity
The provisions of this Convention regarding the protection and preservation of the marine environment do not apply to any warship, naval auxiliary, other vessels or aircraft owned or operated by a State and used, for the time being, only on government non-commercial service. However, each State shall ensure, by the adoption of appropriate measures not impairing operations or operational capabilities of such vessels or aircraft owned or operated by it, that such vessels or aircraft act in a manner consistent, so far as is reasonable and practicable, with this Convention.

Section 11. Obligations under other conventions on the protection and preservation of the marine environment

Article 237. Obligations under other conventions on the protection and preservation of the marine environment
(1) The provisions of this Part are without prejudice to the specific obligations assumed by States under special conventions and agreements concluded previously which relate to the protection and preservation of the marine environment and to agreements which may be concluded in furtherance of the general principles set forth in this Convention.
(2) Specific obligations assumed by States under special conventions, with respect to the protection and preservation of the marine environment, should be carried out in a manner consistent with the general principles and objectives of this Convention.

Part XIII. Marine scientific research

Section 1. General provisions

Article 238. Right to conduct marine scientific research
All States, irrespective of their geographical location, and competent international organizations have the right to conduct marine scientific research subject to the rights and duties of other States as provided for in this Convention.

Article 239. Promotion of marine scientific research
States and competent international organizations shall promote and facilitate the development and conduct of marine scientific research in accordance with this Convention.

Article 240. General principles for the conduct of marine scientific research
In the conduct of marine scientific research the following principles shall apply:
(a) marine scientific research shall be conducted exclusively for peaceful purposes;
(b) marine scientific research shall be conducted with appropriate scientific methods and means compatible with this Convention;
(c) marine scientific research shall not unjustifiably interfere with other legitimate uses of the sea compatible with this Convention and shall be duly respected in the course of such uses; (d) marine scientific research shall be conducted in compliance with all relevant regulations adopted in conformity with this Convention including those for the protection and preservation of the marine environment.

Article 241. Non-recognition of marine scientific research activities as the legal basis for claims
Marine scientific research activities shall not constitute the legal basis for any claim to any part of the marine environment or its resources.

Section 2. International cooperation

Article 242. Promotion of international cooperation
(1) States and competent international organizations shall, in accordance with the principle of respect

for sovereignty and jurisdiction and on the basis of mutual benefit, promote international cooperation in marine scientific research for peaceful purposes.
(2) In this context, without prejudice to the rights and duties of States under this Convention, a State, in the application of this Part, shall provide, as appropriate, other States with a reasonable opportunity to obtain from it, or with its cooperation, information necessary to prevent and control damage to the health and safety of persons and to the marine environment.

Article 243. Creation of favourable conditions States and competent international organizations shall cooperate, through the conclusion of bilateral and multilateral agreements, to create favourable conditions for the conduct of marine scientific research in the marine environment and to integrate the efforts of scientists in studying the essence of phenomena and processes occurring in the marine environment and the interrelations between them.

Article 244. Publication and dissemination of information and knowledge
(1) States and competent international organizations shall, in accordance with this Convention, make available by publication and dissemination through appropriate channels information on proposed major programmes and their objectives as well as knowledge resulting from marine scientific research.
(2) For this purpose, States, both individually and in cooperation with other States and with competent international organizations, shall actively promote the flow of scientific data and information and the transfer of knowledge resulting from marine scientific research, especially to developing States, as well as the strengthening of the autonomous marine scientific research capabilities of developing States through, inter alia, programmes to provide adequate education and training of their technical and scientific personnel.

Section 3. Conduct and promotion of marine scientific research

Article 245. Marine scientific research in the territorial sea
Coastal States, in the exercise of their sovereignty, have the exclusive right to regulate, authorize and conduct marine scientific research in their territorial sea. Marine scientific research therein shall be conducted only with the express consent of and under the conditions set forth by the coastal State.

Article 246. Marine scientific research in the exclusive economic zone and on the continental shelf
(1) Coastal States, in the exercise of their jurisdiction, have the right to regulate, authorize and conduct marine scientific research in their exclusive economic zone and on their continental shelf in accordance with the relevant provisions of this Convention.
(2) Marine scientific research in the exclusive economic zone and on the continental shelf shall be conducted with the consent of the coastal State.
(3) Coastal States shall, in normal circumstances, grant their consent for marine scientific research projects by other States or competent international organizations in their exclusive economic zone or on their continental shelf to be carried out in accordance with this Convention exclusively for peaceful purposes and in order to increase scientific knowledge of the marine environment for the benefit of all mankind. To this end, coastal States shall establish rules and procedures ensuring that such consent will not be delayed or denied unreasonably.
(4) For the purposes of applying paragraph (3), normal circumstances may exist in spite of the absence of diplomatic relations between the coastal State and the researching State.
(5) Coastal States may however in their discretion withhold their consent to the conduct of a marine scientific research project of another State or competent international organization in the exclusive economic zone or on the continental shelf of the coastal State if that project:
(a) is of direct significance for the exploration and exploitation of natural resources, whether living or non-living;
(b) involves drilling into the continental shelf, the use of explosives or the introduction of harmful substances into the marine environment;
(c) involves the construction, operation or use of artificial islands, installations and structures referred to in articles 60 and 80;
(d) contains information communicated pursuant to article 248 regarding the nature and objectives of the project which is inaccurate or if the researching State or competent international organization has outstanding obligations to the coastal State from a prior research project.
(6) Notwithstanding the provisions of paragraph (5), coastal States may not exercise their discretion to withhold consent under subparagraph (a) of that paragraph in respect of marine scientific research projects to be undertaken in accordance with the provisions of this Part on the continental shelf,

beyond 200 nautical miles from the baselines from which the breadth of the territorial sea is measured, outside those specific areas which coastal States may at any time publicly designate as areas in which exploitation or detailed exploratory operations focused on those areas are occurring or will occur within a reasonable period of time. Coastal States shall give reasonable notice of the designation of such areas, as well as any modifications thereto, but shall not be obliged to give details of the operations therein.

(7) The provisions of paragraph (6) are without prejudice to the rights of coastal States over the continental shelf as established in article 77.

(8) Marine scientific research activities referred to in this article shall not unjustifiably interfere with activities undertaken by coastal States in the exercise of their sovereign rights and jurisdiction provided for in this Convention.

Article 247. Marine scientific research projects undertaken by or under the auspices of international organizations

A coastal State which is a member of or has a bilateral agreement with an international organization, and in whose exclusive economic zone or on whose continental shelf that organization wants to carry out a marine scientific research project, directly or under its auspices, shall be deemed to have authorized the project to be carried out in conformity with the agreed specifications if that State approved the detailed project when the decision was made by the organization for the undertaking of the project, or is willing to participate in it, and has not expressed any objection within four months of notification of the project by the organization to the coastal State.

Article 248. Duty to provide information to the coastal State

States and competent international organizations which intend to undertake marine scientific research in the exclusive economic zone or on the continental shelf of a coastal State shall, not less than six months in advance of the expected starting date of the marine scientific research project, provide that State with a full description of:

(a) the nature and objectives of the project;
(b) the method and means to be used, including name, tonnage, type and class of vessels and a description of scientific equipment;
(c) the precise geographical areas in which the project is to be conducted;
(d) the expected date of first appearance and final departure of the research vessels, or deployment of the equipment and its removal, as appropriate;
(e) the name of the sponsoring institution, its director, and the person in charge of the project; and
(f) the extent to which it is considered that the coastal State should be able to participate or to be represented in the project.

Article 249. Duty to comply with certain conditions

(1) States and competent international organizations when undertaking marine scientific research in the exclusive economic zone or on the continental shelf of a coastal State shall comply with the following conditions:

(a) ensure the right of the coastal State, if it so desires, to participate or be represented in the marine scientific research project, especially on board research vessels and other craft or scientific research installations, when practicable, without payment of any remuneration to the scientists of the coastal State and without obligation to contribute towards the costs of the project;
(b) provide the coastal State, at its request, with preliminary reports, as soon as practicable, and with the final results and conclusions after the completion of the research;
(c) undertake to provide access for the coastal State, at its request, to all data and samples derived from the marine scientific research project and likewise to furnish it with data which may be copied and samples which may be divided without detriment to their scientific value; (d) if requested, provide the coastal State with an assessment of such data, samples and research results or provide assistance in their assessment or interpretation;
(e) ensure, subject to paragraph (2), that the research results are made internationally available through appropriate national or international channels, as soon as practicable;
(f) inform the coastal State immediately of any major change in the research programme;
(g) unless otherwise agreed, remove the scientific research installations or equipment once the research is completed.

(2) This article is without prejudice to the conditions established by the laws and regulations of the coastal State for the exercise of its discretion to grant or withhold consent pursuant to article 246, paragraph (5), including requiring prior agreement for making internationally available the research results of a project of direct significance for the exploration and exploitation of natural resources.

PART I   INTERNATIONAL LAW

Article 250. Communications concerning marine scientific research projects Communications concerning the marine scientific research projects shall be made through appropriate official channels, unless otherwise agreed.

Article 251. General criteria and guidelines
States shall seek to promote through competent international organizations the establishment of general criteria and guidelines to assist States in ascertaining the nature and implications of marine scientific research.

Article 252. Implied consent
States or competent international organizations may proceed with a marine scientific research project six months after the date upon which the information required pursuant to article 248 was provided to the coastal State unless within four months of the receipt of the communication containing such information the coastal State has informed the State or organization conducting the research that:
(a) it has withheld its consent under the provisions of article 246; or
(b) the information given by that State or competent international organization regarding the nature or objectives of the project does not conform to the manifestly evident facts; or
(c) it requires supplementary information relevant to conditions and the information provided for under articles 248 and 249; or
(d) outstanding obligations exist with respect to a previous marine scientific research project carried out by that State or organization, with regard to conditions established in article 249.

Article 253. Suspension or cessation of marine scientific research activities
(1) A coastal State shall have the right to require the suspension of any marine scientific research activities in progress within its exclusive economic zone or on its continental shelf if:
(a) the research activities are not being conducted in accordance with the information communicated as provided under article 248 upon which the consent of the coastal State was based; or
(b) the State or competent international organization conducting the research activities fails to comply with the provisions of article 249 concerning the rights of the coastal State with respect to the marine scientific research project.
(2) A coastal State shall have the right to require the cessation of any marine scientific research activities in case of any non-compliance with the provisions of article 248 which amounts to a major change in the research project or the research activities.
(3) A coastal State may also require cessation of marine scientific research activities if any of the situations contemplated in paragraph (1) are not rectified within a reasonable period of time.
(4) Following notification by the coastal State of its decision to order suspension or cessation, States or competent international organizations authorized to conduct marine scientific research activities shall terminate the research activities that are the subject of such a notification.
(5) An order of suspension under paragraph (1) shall be lifted by the coastal State and the marine scientific research activities allowed to continue once the researching State or competent international organization has complied with the conditions required under
articles 248 and 249.

Article 254. Rights of neighbouring land-locked and geographically disadvantaged States
(1) States and competent international organizations which have submitted to a coastal State a project to undertake marine scientific research referred to in article 246, paragraph (3), shall give notice to the neighbouring land-locked and geographically disadvantaged States of the proposed research project, and shall notify the coastal State thereof.
(2) After the consent has been given for the proposed marine scientific research project by the coastal State concerned, in accordance with article 246 and other relevant provisions of this Convention, States and competent international organizations undertaking such a project shall provide to the neighbouring land-locked and geographically disadvantaged States, at their request and when appropriate, relevant information as specified in article 248 and article 249, paragraph (1)(f).
(3) The neighbouring land-locked and geographically disadvantaged States referred to above shall, at their request, be given the opportunity to participate, whenever feasible, in the proposed marine scientific research project through qualified experts appointed by them and not objected to by the coastal State, in accordance with the conditions agreed for the project, in conformity with the provisions of this Convention, between the coastal State concerned and the State or competent international organizations conducting the marine scientific research.
(4) States and competent international organizations referred to in paragraph (1) shall provide to the above-mentioned land-locked and geographically disadvantaged States, at their request, the information and assistance specified in article 249, paragraph (1)(d), subject to the provisions of article 249, paragraph (2).

Article 255. Measures to facilitate marine scientific research and assist research vessels
States shall endeavour to adopt reasonable rules, regulations and procedures to promote and facilitate marine scientific research conducted in accordance with this Convention beyond their territorial sea and, as appropriate, to facilitate, subject to the provisions of their laws and regulations, access to their harbours and promote assistance for marine scientific research vessels which comply with the relevant provisions of this Part.

Article 256. Marine scientific research in the Area
All States, irrespective of their geographical location, and competent international organizations have the right, in conformity with the provisions of Part XI, to conduct marine scientific research in the Area.

Article 257. Marine scientific research in the water column beyond the exclusive economic zone
All States, irrespective of their geographical location, and competent international organizations have the right, in conformity with this Convention, to conduct marine scientific research in the water column beyond the limits of the exclusive economic zone.

Section 4. Scientific research installations or equipment in the marine environment

Article 258. Deployment and use
The deployment and use of any type of scientific research installations or equipment in any area of the marine environment shall be subject to the same conditions as are prescribed in this Convention for the conduct of marine scientific research in any such area.

Article 259. Legal status
The installations or equipment referred to in this section do not possess the status of islands. They have no territorial sea of their own, and their presence does not affect the delimitation of the territorial sea, the exclusive economic zone or the continental shelf.

Article 260. Safety zones
Safety zones of a reasonable breadth not exceeding a distance of 500 metres may be created around scientific research installations in accordance with the relevant provisions of this Convention. All States shall ensure that such safety zones are respected by their vessels.

Article 261. Non-interference with shipping routes
The deployment and use of any type of scientific research installations or equipment shall not constitute an obstacle to established international shipping routes.

Article 262. Identification markings and warning signals
Installations or equipment referred to in this section shall bear identification markings indicating the State of registry or the international organization to which they belong and shall have adequate internationally agreed warning signals to ensure safety at sea and the safety of air navigation, taking into account rules and standards established by competent international organizations.

Section 5. Responsibility and liability

Article 263. Responsibility and liability
(1) States and competent international organizations shall be responsible for ensuring that marine scientific research, whether undertaken by them or on their behalf, is conducted in accordance with this Convention.
(2) States and competent international organizations shall be responsible and liable for the measures they take in contravention of this Convention in respect of marine scientific research conducted by other States, their natural or juridical persons or by competent international organizations, and shall provide compensation for damage resulting from such measures.
(3) States and competent international organizations shall be responsible and liable pursuant to article 235 for damage caused by pollution of the marine environment arising out of marine scientific research undertaken by them or on their behalf.

Section 6. Settlement of disputes and interim measures

Article 264. Settlement of disputes
Disputes concerning the interpretation or application of the provisions of this Convention with regard to marine scientific research shall be settled in accordance with Part XV, sections 2 and 3.

Article 265. Interim measures
Pending settlement of a dispute in accordance with Part XV, sections 2 and 3, the State or compe-

tent international organization authorized to conduct a marine scientific research project shall not allow research activities to commence or continue without the express consent of the coastal State concerned.

Part XIV. Development and transfer of marine technology

Section 1. General provisions

Article 266. Promotion of the development and transfer of marine technology

(1) States, directly or through competent international organizations, shall cooperate in accordance with their capabilities to promote actively the development and transfer of marine science and marine technology on fair and reasonable terms and conditions.

(2) States shall promote the development of the marine scientific and technological capacity of States which may need and request technical assistance in this field, particularly developing States, including land-locked and geographically disadvantaged States, with regard to the exploration, exploitation, conservation and management of marine resources, the protection and preservation of the marine environment, marine scientific research and other activities in the marine environment compatible with this Convention, with a view to accelerating the social and economic development of the developing States.

(3) States shall endeavour to foster favourable economic and legal conditions for the transfer of marine technology for the benefit of all parties concerned on an equitable basis.

Article 267. Protection of legitimate interests

States, in promoting cooperation pursuant to article 266, shall have due regard for all legitimate interests including, inter alia, the rights and duties of holders, suppliers and recipients of marine technology.

Article 268. Basic objectives

States, directly or through competent international organizations, shall promote:
(a) the acquisition, evaluation and dissemination of marine technological knowledge and facilitate access to such information and data;
(b) the development of appropriate marine technology;
(c) the development of the necessary technological infrastructure to facilitate the transfer of marine technology;
(d) the development of human resources through training and education of nationals of developing States and countries and especially the nationals of the least developed among them;
(e) international cooperation at all levels, particularly at the regional, subregional and bilateral levels.

Article 269. Measures to achieve the basic objectives

In order to achieve the objectives referred to in article 268, States, directly or through competent international organizations, shall endeavour, inter alia, to:
(a) establish programmes of technical cooperation for the effective transfer of all kinds of marine technology to States which may need and request technical assistance in this field, particularly the developing land-locked and geographically disadvantaged States, as well as other developing States which have not been able either to establish or develop their own technological capacity in marine science and in the exploration and exploitation of marine resources or to develop the infrastructure of such technology;
(b) promote favourable conditions for the conclusion of agreements, contracts and other similar arrangements, under equitable and reasonable conditions;
(c) hold conferences, seminars and symposia on scientific and technological subjects, in particular on policies and methods for the transfer of marine technology;
(d) promote the exchange of scientists and of technological and other experts;
(e) undertake projects and promote joint ventures and other forms of bilateral and multilateral cooperation.

Section 2. International cooperation

Article 270. Ways and means of international cooperation

International cooperation for the development and transfer of marine technology shall be carried out, where feasible and appropriate, through existing bilateral, regional or multilateral programmes, and also through expanded and new programmes in order to facilitate marine scientific research, the transfer of marine technology, particularly in new fields, and appropriate international funding for ocean research and development.

Article 271. Guidelines, criteria and standards
States, directly or through competent international organizations, shall promote the establishment of generally accepted guidelines, criteria and standards for the transfer of marine technology on a bilateral basis or within the framework of international organizations and other fora, taking into account, in particular, the interests and needs of developing States.

Article 272. Coordination of international programmes
In the field of transfer of marine technology, States shall endeavour to ensure that competent international organizations coordinate their activities, including any regional or global programmes, taking into account the interests and needs of developing States, particularly land-locked and geographically disadvantaged States.

Article 273. Cooperation with international organizations and the Authority
States shall cooperate actively with competent international organizations and the Authority to encourage and facilitate the transfer to developing States, their nationals and the Enterprise of skills and marine technology with regard to activities in the Area.

Article 274. Objectives of the Authority
Subject to all legitimate interests including, inter alia, the rights and duties of holders, suppliers and recipients of technology, the Authority, with regard to activities in the Area, shall ensure that:
(a) on the basis of the principle of equitable geographical distribution, nationals of developing States, whether coastal, land-locked or geographically disadvantaged, shall be taken on for the purposes of training as members of the managerial, research and technical staff constituted for its undertakings;
(b) the technical documentation on the relevant equipment, machinery, devices and processes is made available to all States, in particular developing States which may need and request technical assistance in this field;
(c) adequate provision is made by the Authority to facilitate the acquisition of technical assistance in the field of marine technology by States which may need and request it, in particular developing States, and the acquisition by their nationals of the necessary skills and know-how, including professional training;
(d) States which may need and request technical assistance in this field, in particular developing States, are assisted in the acquisition of necessary equipment, processes, plant and other technical know-how through any financial arrangements provided for in this Convention.

Section 3. National and regional marine scientific and technological centres

Article 275. Establishment of national centres
(1) States, directly or through competent international organizations and the Authority, shall promote the establishment, particularly in developing coastal States, of national marine scientific and technological research centres and the strengthening of existing national centres, in order to stimulate and advance the conduct of marine scientific research by developing coastal States and to enhance their national capabilities to utilize and preserve their marine resources for their economic benefit.
(2) States, through competent international organizations and the Authority, shall give adequate support to facilitate the establishment and strengthening of such national centres so as to provide for advanced training facilities and necessary equipment, skills and know-how as well as technical experts to such States which may need and request such assistance.

Article 276. Establishment of regional centres
(1) States, in coordination with the competent international organizations, the Authority and national marine scientific and technological research institutions, shall promote the establishment of regional marine scientific and technological research centres, particularly in developing States, in order to stimulate and advance the conduct of marine scientific research by developing States and foster the transfer of marine technology.
(2) All States of a region shall cooperate with the regional centres therein to ensure the more effective achievement of their objectives.

Article 277. Functions of regional centres
The functions of such regional centres shall include, inter alia:
(a) training and educational programmes at all levels on various aspects of marine scientific and technological research, particularly marine biology, including conservation and management of living resources, oceanography, hydrography, engineering, geological exploration of the seabed, mining and desalination technologies;
(b) management studies;

(c) study programmes related to the protection and preservation of the marine environment and the prevention, reduction and control of pollution;
(d) organization of regional conferences, seminars and symposia;
(e) acquisition and processing of marine scientific and technological data and information;
(f) prompt dissemination of results of marine scientific and technological research in readily available publications;
(g) publicizing national policies with regard to the transfer of marine technology and systematic comparative study of those policies;
(h) compilation and systematization of information on the marketing of technology and on contracts and other arrangements concerning patents;
(i) technical cooperation with other States of the region.

Section 4. Cooperation among international organization

Article 278. Cooperation among international organizations

The competent international organizations referred to in this Part and in Part XIII shall take all appropriate measures to ensure, either directly or in close cooperation among themselves, the effective discharge of their functions and responsibilities under this Part.

Part XV. Settlement of disputes

Section 1. General provisions

Article 279. Obligation to settle disputes by peaceful means

States Parties shall settle any dispute between them concerning the interpretation or application of this Convention by peaceful means in accordance with Article 2, paragraph (3), of the Charter of the United Nations and, to this end, shall seek a solution by the means indicated in Article 33, paragraph (1), of the Charter.

Article 280. Settlement of disputes by any peaceful means chosen by the parties

Nothing in this Part impairs the right of any States Parties to agree at any time to settle a dispute between them concerning the interpretation or application of this Convention by any peaceful means of their own choice.

Article 281. Procedure where no settlement has been reached by the parties

(1) If the States Parties which are parties to a dispute concerning the interpretation or application of this Convention have agreed to seek settlement of the dispute by a peaceful means of their own choice, the procedures provided for in this Part apply only where no settlement has been reached by recourse to such means and the agreement between the parties does not exclude any further procedure.

(2) If the parties have also agreed on a time-limit, paragraph (1) applies only upon the expiration of that time-limit.

Article 282. Obligations under general, regional or bilateral agreements

If the States Parties which are parties to a dispute concerning the interpretation or application of this Convention have agreed, through a general, regional or bilateral agreement or otherwise, that such dispute shall, at the request of any party to the dispute, be submitted to a procedure that entails a binding decision, that procedure shall apply in lieu of the procedures provided for in this Part, unless the parties to the dispute otherwise agree.

Article 283. Obligation to exchange views

(1) When a dispute arises between States Parties concerning the interpretation or application of this Convention, the parties to the dispute shall proceed expeditiously to an exchange of views regarding its settlement by negotiation or other peaceful means.

(2) The parties shall also proceed expeditiously to an exchange of views where a procedure for the settlement of such a dispute has been terminated without a settlement or where a settlement has been reached and the circumstances require consultation regarding the manner of implementing the settlement.

Article 284. Conciliation

(1) A State Party which is a party to a dispute concerning the interpretation or application of this Convention may invite the other party or parties to submit the dispute to conciliation in accordance with the procedure under Annex V, section 1, or another conciliation procedure. (2) If the invitation is accepted and if the parties agree upon the conciliation procedure to be applied, any party may submit

the dispute to that procedure.
(3) If the invitation is not accepted or the parties do not agree upon the procedure, the conciliation proceedings shall be deemed to be terminated.
(4) Unless the parties otherwise agree, when a dispute has been submitted to conciliation, the proceedings may be terminated only in accordance with the agreed conciliation procedure.

Article 285. Application of this section to disputes submitted pursuant to Part XI
This section applies to any dispute which pursuant to Part XI, section 5, is to be settled in accordance with procedures provided for in this Part. If an entity other than a State Party is a party to such a dispute, this section applies *mutatis mutandis*.

Section 2. Compulsory procedures entailing binding decisions

Article 286. Application of procedures under this section
Subject to section 3, any dispute concerning the interpretation or application of this Convention shall, where no settlement has been reached by recourse to section 1, be submitted at the request of any party to the dispute to the court or tribunal having jurisdiction under this section.

Article 287. Choice of procedure
(1) When signing, ratifying or acceding to this Convention or at any time thereafter, a State shall be free to choose, by means of a written declaration, one or more of the following means for the settlement of disputes concerning the interpretation or application of this Convention:
(a) the International Tribunal for the Law of the Sea established in accordance with Annex VI;
(b) the International Court of Justice;
(c) an arbitral tribunal constituted in accordance with Annex VII;
(d) a special arbitral tribunal constituted in accordance with Annex VIII for one or more of the categories of disputes specified therein.
(2) A declaration made under paragraph (1) shall not affect or be affected by the obligation of a State Party to accept the jurisdiction of the Seabed Disputes Chamber of the International Tribunal for the Law of the Sea to the extent and in the manner provided for in Part XI, section 5.
(3) A State Party, which is a party to a dispute not covered by a declaration in force, shall be deemed to have accepted arbitration in accordance with Annex VII.
(4) If the parties to a dispute have accepted the same procedure for the settlement of the dispute, it may be submitted only to that procedure, unless the parties otherwise agree.
(5) If the parties to a dispute have not accepted the same procedure for the settlement of the dispute, it may be submitted only to arbitration in accordance with Annex VII, unless the parties otherwise agree.
(6) A declaration made under paragraph (1) shall remain in force until three months after notice of revocation has been deposited with the Secretary-General of the United Nations.
(7) A new declaration, a notice of revocation or the expiry of a declaration does not in any way affect proceedings pending before a court or tribunal having jurisdiction under this article, unless the parties otherwise agree.
(8) Declarations and notices referred to in this article shall be deposited with the Secretary-General of the United Nations, who shall transmit copies thereof to the States Parties.

Article 288. Jurisdiction
(1) A court or tribunal referred to in article 287 shall have jurisdiction over any dispute concerning the interpretation or application of this Convention which is submitted to it in accordance with this Part.
(2) A court or tribunal referred to in article 287 shall also have jurisdiction over any dispute concerning the interpretation or application of an international agreement related to the purposes of this Convention, which is submitted to it in accordance with the agreement.
(3) The Seabed Disputes Chamber of the International Tribunal for the Law of the Sea established in accordance with Annex VI, and any other chamber or arbitral tribunal referred to in Part XI, section 5, shall have jurisdiction in any matter which is submitted to it in accordance therewith.
(4) In the event of a dispute as to whether a court or tribunal has jurisdiction, the matter shall be settled by decision of that court or tribunal.

Article 289. Experts
In any dispute involving scientific or technical matters, a court or tribunal exercising jurisdiction under this section may, at the request of a party or proprio motu, select in consultation with the par-

ties no fewer than two scientific or technical experts chosen preferably from the relevant list prepared in accordance with Annex VIII, article 2, to sit with the court or tribunal but without the right to vote.

Article 290. Provisional measures

(1) If a dispute has been duly submitted to a court or tribunal which considers that prima facie it has jurisdiction under this Part or Part XI, section 5, the court or tribunal may prescribe any provisional measures which it considers appropriate under the circumstances to preserve the respective rights of the parties to the dispute or to prevent serious harm to the marine environment, pending the final decision.

(2) Provisional measures may be modified or revoked as soon as the circumstances justifying them have changed or ceased to exist.

(3) Provisional measures may be prescribed, modified or revoked under this article only at the request of a party to the dispute and after the parties have been given an opportunity to be heard.

(4) The court or tribunal shall forthwith give notice to the parties to the dispute, and to such other States Parties as it considers appropriate, of the prescription, modification or revocation of provisional measures.

(5) Pending the constitution of an arbitral tribunal to which a dispute is being submitted under this section, any court or tribunal agreed upon by the parties or, failing such agreement within two weeks from the date of the request for provisional measures, the International Tribunal for the Law of the Sea or, with respect to activities in the Area, the Seabed Disputes Chamber, may prescribe, modify or revoke provisional measures in accordance with this article if it considers that prima facie the tribunal which is to be constituted would have jurisdiction and that the urgency of the situation so requires. Once constituted, the tribunal to which the dispute has been submitted may modify, revoke or affirm those provisional measures, acting in conformity with paragraphs (1) to (4).

(6) The parties to the dispute shall comply promptly with any provisional measures prescribed under this article.

Article 291. Access

(1) All the dispute settlement procedures specified in this Part shall be open to States Parties. (2) The dispute settlement procedures specified in this Part shall be open to entities other than States Parties only as specifically provided for in this Convention.

Article 292. Prompt release of vessels and crews

(1) Where the authorities of a State Party have detained a vessel flying the flag of another State Party and it is alleged that the detaining State has not complied with the provisions of this Convention for the prompt release of the vessel or its crew upon the posting of a reasonable bond or other financial security, the question of release from detention may be submitted to any court or tribunal agreed upon by the parties or, failing such agreement within 10 days from the time of detention, to a court or tribunal accepted by the detaining State under article 287 or to the International Tribunal for the Law of the Sea, unless the parties otherwise agree.

(2) The application for release may be made only by or on behalf of the flag State of the vessel.

(3) The court or tribunal shall deal without delay with the application for release and shall deal only with the question of release, without prejudice to the merits of any case before the appropriate domestic forum against the vessel, its owner or its crew. The authorities of the detaining State remain competent to release the vessel or its crew at any time.

(4) Upon the posting of the bond or other financial security determined by the court or tribunal, the authorities of the detaining State shall comply promptly with the decision of the court or tribunal concerning the release of the vessel or its crew.

Article 293. Applicable law

(1) A court or tribunal having jurisdiction under this section shall apply this Convention and other rules of international law not incompatible with this Convention.

(2) Paragraph (l) does not prejudice the power of the court or tribunal having jurisdiction under this section to decide a case *ex aequo et bono*, if the parties so agree.

Article 294. Preliminary proceedings

(1) A court or tribunal provided for in article 287 to which an application is made in respect of a dispute referred to in article 297 shall 134 determine at the request of a party, or may determine *proprio motu*, whether the claim constitutes an abuse of legal process or whether prima facie it is well founded. If the court or tribunal determines that the claim constitutes an abuse of legal process or is prima facie unfounded, it shall take no further action in the case. (2) Upon receipt of the application, the court or tribunal shall immediately notify the other party or parties of the application, and shall fix

a reasonable time-limit within which they may request it to make a determination in accordance with paragraph (1).
(3) Nothing in this article affects the right of any party to a dispute to make preliminary objections in accordance with the applicable rules of procedure.

Article 295. Exhaustion of local remedies
Any dispute between States Parties concerning the interpretation or application of this Convention may be submitted to the procedures provided for in this section only after local remedies have been exhausted where this is required by international law.

Article 296. Finality and binding force of decisions
(1) Any decision rendered by a court or tribunal having jurisdiction under this section shall be final and shall be complied with by all the parties to the dispute.
(2) Any such decision shall have no binding force except between the parties and in respect of that particular dispute.

Section 3. Limitations and exceptions to applicability of Section 2

Article 297. Limitations on applicability of section 2
(1) Disputes concerning the interpretation or application of this Convention with regard to the exercise by a coastal State of its sovereign rights or jurisdiction provided for in this Convention shall be subject to the procedures provided for in section 2 in the following cases: (a) when it is alleged that a coastal State has acted in contravention of the provisions of this Convention in regard to the freedoms and rights of navigation, overflight or the laying of submarine cables and pipelines, or in regard to other internationally lawful uses of the sea specified in article 58;
(b) when it is alleged that a State in exercising the aforementioned freedoms, rights or uses has acted in contravention of this Convention or of laws or regulations adopted by the coastal State in conformity with this Convention and other rules of international law not incompatible with this Convention; or
(c) when it is alleged that a coastal State has acted in contravention of specified international rules and standards for the protection and preservation of the marine environment which are 135 applicable to the coastal State and which have been established by this Convention or through a competent international organization or diplomatic conference in accordance with this Convention.
(2) (a) Disputes concerning the interpretation or application of the provisions of this Convention with regard to marine scientific research shall be settled in accordance with section 2, except that the coastal State shall not be obliged to accept the submission to such settlement of any dispute arising out of:
(i) the exercise by the coastal State of a right or discretion in accordance with article 246; or (ii) a decision by the coastal State to order suspension or cessation of a research project in accordance with article 253.
(b) A dispute arising from an allegation by the researching State that with respect to a specific project the coastal State is not exercising its rights under articles 246 and 253 in a manner compatible with this Convention shall be submitted, at the request of either party, to conciliation under Annex V, section 2, provided that the conciliation commission shall not call in question the exercise by the coastal State of its discretion to designate specific areas as referred to in article 246, paragraph (6), or of its discretion to withhold consent in accordance with article 246, paragraph (5).
(3) (a) Disputes concerning the interpretation or application of the provisions of this Convention with regard to fisheries shall be settled in accordance with section 2, except that the coastal State shall not be obliged to accept the submission to such settlement of any dispute relating to its sovereign rights with respect to the living resources in the exclusive economic zone or their exercise, including its discretionary powers for determining the allowable catch, its harvesting capacity, the allocation of surpluses to other States and the terms and conditions established in its conservation and management laws and regulations. (b) Where no settlement has been reached by recourse to section 1 of this Part, a dispute shall be submitted to conciliation under Annex V, section 2, at the request of any party to the dispute, when it is alleged that:
(i) a coastal State has manifestly failed to comply with its obligations to ensure through proper conservation and management measures that the maintenance of the living resources in the exclusive economic zone is not seriously endangered;
(ii) a coastal State has arbitrarily refused to determine, at the request of another State, the allowable catch and its capacity to harvest living resources with respect to stocks which that other State is interested in fishing; or
(iii) a coastal State has arbitrarily refused to allocate to any State, under articles 62, 69 and 70 and

under the terms and conditions established by the coastal State consistent with this Convention, the whole or part of the surplus it has declared to exist.
(c) In no case shall the conciliation commission substitute its discretion for that of the coastal State.
(d) The report of the conciliation commission shall be communicated to the appropriate international organizations.
(e) In negotiating agreements pursuant to articles 69 and 70, States Parties, unless they otherwise agree, shall include a clause on measures which they shall take in order to minimize the possibility of a disagreement concerning the interpretation or application of the agreement, and on how they should proceed if a disagreement nevertheless arises.

Article 298. Optional exceptions to applicability of section 2

(1) When signing, ratifying or acceding to this Convention or at any time thereafter, a State may, without prejudice to the obligations arising under section 1, declare in writing that it does not accept any one or more of the procedures provided for in section 2 with respect to one or more of the following categories of disputes:
(a) (i) disputes concerning the interpretation or application of articles 15, 74 and 83 relating to sea boundary delimitations, or those involving historic bays or titles, provided that a State having made such a declaration shall, when such a dispute arises subsequent to the entry into force of this Convention and where no agreement within a reasonable period of time is reached in negotiations between the parties, at the request of any party to the dispute, accept submission of the matter to conciliation under Annex V, section 2; and provided further that any dispute that necessarily involves the concurrent consideration of any unsettled dispute concerning sovereignty or other rights over continental or insular land territory shall be excluded from such submission;
(ii) after the conciliation commission has presented its report, which shall state the reasons on which it is based, the parties shall negotiate an agreement on the basis of that report; if these negotiations do not result in an agreement, the parties shall, by mutual consent, submit the question to one of the procedures provided for in section 2, unless the parties otherwise agree;
(iii) this subparagraph does not apply to any sea boundary dispute finally settled by an arrangement between the parties, or to any such dispute which is to be settled in accordance with a bilateral or multilateral agreement binding upon those parties;
(b) disputes concerning military activities, including military activities by government vessels and aircraft engaged in non-commercial service, and disputes concerning law enforcement activities in regard to the exercise of sovereign rights or jurisdiction excluded from the jurisdiction of a court or tribunal under article 297, paragraph (2) or (3);
(c) disputes in respect of which the Security Council of the United Nations is exercising the functions assigned to it by the Charter of the United Nations, unless the Security Council decides to remove the matter from its agenda or calls upon the parties to settle it by the means provided for in this Convention.
(2) A State Party which has made a declaration under paragraph (1) may at any time withdraw it, or agree to submit a dispute excluded by such declaration to any procedure specified in this Convention.
(3) A State Party which has made a declaration under paragraph (1) shall not be entitled to submit any dispute falling within the excepted category of disputes to any procedure in this Convention as against another State Party, without the consent of that party.
(4) If one of the States Parties has made a declaration under paragraph (1)(a), any other State Party may submit any dispute falling within an excepted category against the declarant party to the procedure specified in such declaration.
(5) A new declaration, or the withdrawal of a declaration, does not in any way affect proceedings pending before a court or tribunal in accordance with this article, unless the parties otherwise agree.
(6) Declarations and notices of withdrawal of declarations under this article shall be deposited with the Secretary-General of the United Nations, who shall transmit copies thereof to the States Parties.

Article 299. Right of the parties to agree upon a procedure

(1) A dispute excluded under article 297 or excepted by a declaration made under article 298 from the dispute settlement procedures provided for in section 2 may be submitted to such procedures only by agreement of the parties to the dispute.
(2) Nothing in this section impairs the right of the parties to the dispute to agree to some other procedure for the settlement of such dispute or to reach an amicable settlement.

Part XVI. General provisions

Article 300. Good faith and abuse of rights

States Parties shall fulfil in good faith the obligations assumed under this Convention and shall exercise the rights, jurisdiction and freedoms recognized in this Convention in a manner which would not constitute an abuse of right.

Article 301. Peaceful uses of the seas
In exercising their rights and performing their duties under this Convention, States Parties shall refrain from any threat or use of force against the territorial integrity or political independence of any State, or in any other manner inconsistent with the principles of international law embodied in the Charter of the United Nations.

Article 302. Disclosure of information
Without prejudice to the right of a State Party to resort to the procedures for the settlement of disputes provided for in this Convention, nothing in this Convention shall be deemed to require a State Party, in the fulfilment of its obligations under this Convention, to supply information the disclosure of which is contrary to the essential interests of its security.

Article 303. Archaeological and historical objects found at sea
(1) States have the duty to protect objects of an archaeological and historical nature found at sea and shall cooperate for this purpose.
(2) In order to control traffic in such objects, the coastal State may, in applying article 33, presume that their removal from the seabed in the zone referred to in that article without its approval would result in an infringement within its territory or territorial sea of the laws and regulations referred to in that article.
(3) Nothing in this article affects the rights of identifiable owners, the law of salvage or other rules of admiralty, or laws and practices with respect to cultural exchanges.
(4) This article is without prejudice to other international agreements and rules of international law regarding the protection of objects of an archaeological and historical nature. Article 304 Responsibility and liability for damage
The provisions of this Convention regarding responsibility and liability for damage are without prejudice to the application of existing rules and the development of further rules regarding responsibility and liability under international law.

Part XVII. Final provisions

Article 305. Signature
(1) This Convention shall be open for signature by:
(a) all States;
(b) Namibia, represented by the United Nations Council for Namibia;
(c) all self-governing associated States which have chosen that status in an act of self-determination supervised and approved by the United Nations in accordance with General Assembly resolution 1514 (XV) and which have competence over the matters governed by this Convention, including the competence to enter into treaties in respect of those matters; (d) all self-governing associated States which, in accordance with their respective instruments of association, have competence over the matters governed by this Convention, including the competence to enter into treaties in respect of those matters;
(e) all territories which enjoy full internal self-government, recognized as such by the United Nations, but have not attained full independence in accordance with General Assembly resolution 1514 (XV) and which have competence over the matters governed by this Convention, including the competence to enter into treaties in respect of those matters;
(f) international organizations, in accordance with Annex IX. 2.
This Convention shall remain open for signature until 9 December 1984 at the Ministry of Foreign Affairs of Jamaica and also, from 1 July 1983 until 9 December 1984, at United Nations Headquarters in New York.

Article 306. Ratification and formal confirmation
This Convention is subject to ratification by States and the other entities referred to in
article 305, paragraph (l)(b), (c), (d) and (e), and to formal confirmation, in accordance with Annex IX, by the entities referred to in article 305, paragraph (l)(f). The instruments of ratification and of formal confirmation shall be deposited with the Secretary-General of the United Nations.

Article 307. Accession
This Convention shall remain open for accession by States and the other entities referred to in article 305. Accession by the entities referred to in article 305, paragraph (l)(f), shall be in accordance with Annex IX. The instruments of accession shall be deposited with the Secretary-General of the United Nations.

Article 308. Entry into force

(1) This Convention shall enter into force 12 months after the date of deposit of the sixtieth instrument of ratification or accession.

(2) For each State ratifying or acceding to this Convention after the deposit of the sixtieth instrument of ratification or accession, the Convention shall enter into force on the thirtieth day following the deposit of its instrument of ratification or accession, subject to paragraph (1).

(3) The Assembly of the Authority shall meet on the date of entry into force of this Convention and shall elect the Council of the Authority. The first Council shall be constituted in a manner consistent with the purpose of article 161 if the provisions of that article cannot be strictly applied.

(4) The rules, regulations and procedures drafted by the Preparatory Commission shall apply provisionally pending their formal adoption by the Authority in accordance with Part XI.

(5) The Authority and its organs shall act in accordance with resolution II of the Third United Nations Conference on the Law of the Sea relating to preparatory investment and with decisions of the Preparatory Commission taken pursuant to that resolution.

Article 309. Reservations and exceptions

No reservations or exceptions may be made to this Convention unless expressly permitted by other articles of this Convention.

Article 310. Declarations and statements

Article 309 does not preclude a State, when signing, ratifying or acceding to this Convention, from making declarations or statements, however phrased or named, with a view, inter alia, to the harmonization of its laws and regulations with the provisions of this Convention, provided that such declarations or statements do not purport to exclude or to modify the legal effect of the provisions of this Convention in their application to that State.

Article 311. Relation to other conventions and international agreements

(1) This Convention shall prevail, as between States Parties, over the Geneva Conventions on the Law of the Sea of 29 April 1958.

(2) This Convention shall not alter the rights and obligations of States Parties which arise from other agreements compatible with this Convention and which do not affect the enjoyment by other States Parties of their rights or the performance of their obligations under this Convention.

(3) Two or more States Parties may conclude agreements modifying or suspending the operation of provisions of this Convention, applicable solely to the relations between them, provided that such agreements do not relate to a provision derogation from which is incompatible with the effective execution of the object and purpose of this Convention, and provided further that such agreements shall not affect the application of the basic principles embodied herein, and that the provisions of such agreements do not affect the enjoyment by other States Parties of their rights or the performance of their obligations under this Convention.

(4) States Parties intending to conclude an agreement referred to in paragraph (3) shall notify the other States Parties through the depositary of this Convention of their intention to conclude the agreement and of the modification or suspension for which it provides.

(5) This article does not affect international agreements expressly permitted or preserved by other articles of this Convention.

(6) States Parties agree that there shall be no amendments to the basic principle relating to the common heritage of mankind set forth in article 136 and that they shall not be party to any agreement in derogation thereof.

Article 312. Amendment

(1) After the expiry of a period of 10 years from the date of entry into force of this Convention, a State Party may, by written communication addressed to the Secretary-General of the United Nations, propose specific amendments to this Convention, other than those relating to activities in the Area, and request the convening of a conference to consider such proposed amendments. The Secretary-General shall circulate such communication to all States Parties. If, within 12 months from the date of the circulation of the communication, not less than one half of the States Parties reply favourably to the request, the Secretary-General shall convene the conference.

(2) The decision-making procedure applicable at the amendment conference shall be the same as that applicable at the Third United Nations Conference on the Law of the Sea unless otherwise decided by the conference. The conference should make every effort to reach agreement on any amendments by way of consensus and there should be no voting on them until all efforts at consensus have been exhausted.

Article 313. Amendment by simplified procedure

(1) A State Party may, by written communication addressed to the Secretary-General of the United Nations, propose an amendment to this Convention, other than an amendment relating to activities in the Area, to be adopted by the simplified procedure set forth in this article without convening a conference. The Secretary-General shall circulate the communication to all States Parties.

(2) If, within a period of 12 months from the date of the circulation of the communication, a State Party objects to the proposed amendment or to the proposal for its adoption by the simplified procedure, the amendment shall be considered rejected. The Secretary-General shall immediately notify all States Parties accordingly.

(3) If, 12 months from the date of the circulation of the communication, no State Party has objected to the proposed amendment or to the proposal for its adoption by the simplified procedure, the proposed amendment shall be considered adopted. The Secretary-General shall notify all States Parties that the proposed amendment has been adopted.

Article 314. Amendments to the provisions of this Convention relating exclusively to activities in the Area

(1) A State Party may, by written communication addressed to the Secretary-General of the Authority, propose an amendment to the provisions of this Convention relating exclusively to activities in the Area, including Annex VI, section 4. The Secretary-General shall circulate such communication to all States Parties. The proposed amendment shall be subject to approval by the Assembly following its approval by the Council. Representatives of States Parties in those organs shall have full powers to consider and approve the proposed amendment. The proposed amendment as approved by the Council and the Assembly shall be considered adopted.

(2) Before approving any amendment under paragraph (1), the Council and the Assembly shall ensure that it does not prejudice the system of exploration for and exploitation of the resources of the Area, pending the Review Conference in accordance with article 155.

Article 315. Signature, ratification of, accession to and authentic texts of amendments

(1) Once adopted, amendments to this Convention shall be open for signature by States Parties for 12 months from the date of adoption, at United Nations Headquarters in New York, unless otherwise provided in the amendment itself.

(2) Articles 306, 307 and 320 apply to all amendments to this Convention.

Article 316. Entry into force of amendments

(1) Amendments to this Convention, other than those referred to in paragraph (5), shall enter into force for the States Parties ratifying or acceding to them on the thirtieth day following the deposit of instruments of ratification or accession by two thirds of the States Parties or by States Parties, whichever is greater. Such amendments shall not affect the enjoyment by other States Parties of their rights or the performance of their obligations under this Convention.

(2) An amendment may provide that a larger number of ratifications or accessions shall be required for its entry into force than are required by this article.

(3) For each State Party ratifying or acceding to an amendment referred to in paragraph (1) after the deposit of the required number of instruments of ratification or accession, the amendment shall enter into force on the thirtieth day following the deposit of its instrument of ratification or accession.

(4) A State which becomes a Party to this Convention after the entry into force of an amendment in accordance with paragraph (1) shall, failing an expression of a different intention by that State:
(a) be considered as a Party to this Convention as so amended; and
(b) be considered as a Party to the unamended Convention in relation to any State Party not bound by the amendment.

(5) Any amendment relating exclusively to activities in the Area and any amendment to Annex VI shall enter into force for all States Parties one year following the deposit of instruments of ratification or accession by three fourths of the States Parties.

(6) A State which becomes a Party to this Convention after the entry into force of amendments in accordance with paragraph (5) shall be considered as a Party to this Convention as so amended.

Article 317. Denunciation

(1) A State Party may, by written notification addressed to the Secretary-General of the United Nations, denounce this Convention and may indicate its reasons. Failure to indicate reasons shall not affect the validity of the denunciation. The denunciation shall take effect one year after the date of receipt of the notification, unless the notification specifies a later date.

(2) A State shall not be discharged by reason of the denunciation from the financial and contractual obligations which accrued while it was a Party to this Convention, nor shall the denunciation affect

PART I INTERNATIONAL LAW

any right, obligation or legal situation of that State created through the execution of this Convention prior to its termination for that State.

(3) The denunciation shall not in any way affect the duty of any State Party to fulfil any obligation embodied in this Convention to which it would be subject under international law independently of this Convention.

Article 318. Status of Annexes

The Annexes form an integral part of this Convention and, unless expressly provided otherwise, a reference to this Convention or to one of its Parts includes a reference to the Annexes relating thereto.

Article 319. Depositary

(1) The Secretary-General of the United Nations shall be the depositary of this Convention and amendments thereto.

(2) In addition to his functions as depositary, the Secretary-General shall:

(a) report to all States Parties, the Authority and competent international organizations on issues of a general nature that have arisen with respect to this Convention;

(b) notify the Authority of ratifications and formal confirmations of and accessions to this Convention and amendments thereto, as well as of denunciations of this Convention;

(c) notify States Parties of agreements in accordance with article 311, paragraph (4);

(d) circulate amendments adopted in accordance with this Convention to States Parties for ratification or accession;

(e) convene necessary meetings of States Parties in accordance with this Convention.

(3)(a) The Secretary-General shall also transmit to the observers referred to in
article 156: (i) reports referred to in paragraph 2(a); (ii) notifications referred to in
paragraph (2)(b) and (c); and (iii) texts of amendments referred to in paragraph 2(d), for their information.

(b) The Secretary-General shall also invite those observers to participate as observers at meetings of States Parties referred to in paragraph (2)(e).

Article 320. Authentic texts

The original of this Convention, of which the Arabic, Chinese, English, French, Russian and Spanish texts are equally authentic, shall, subject to article 305, paragraph (2), be deposited with the Secretary-General of the United Nations.

Annex I. Highly migratory species

(1) Albacore tuna: Thunnus alalunga.
(2) Bluefin tuna: Thunnus thynnus.
(3) Bigeye tuna: Thunnus obesus.
(4) Skipjack tuna: Katsuwonus pelamis.
(5) Yellowfin tuna: Thunnus albacares.
(6) Blackfin tuna: Thunnus atlanticus.
(7) Little tuna: Euthynnus alletteratus; Euthynnus affinis.
(8) Southern bluefin tuna: Thunnus maccoyii.
(9) Frigate mackerel: Auxis thazard; Auxis rochei.
(10) Pomfrets: Family Bramidae.
(11) Marlins: Tetrapturus angustirostris; Tetrapturus belone; Tetrapturus pfluegeri; Tetrapturus albidus; Tetrapturus audax; Tetrapturus georgei; Makaira mazara; Makaira indica; Makaira nigricans.
(12) Sail-fishes: Istiophorus platypterus; Istiophorus albicans.
(13) Swordfish: Xiphias gladius.
(14) Sauries: Scomberesox saurus; Cololabis saira; Cololabis adocetus; Scomberesox saurus scombroides.
(15) Dolphin: Coryphaena hippurus; Coryphaena equiselis.
(16) Oceanic sharks: Hexanchus griseus; Cetorhinus maximus; Family Alopiidae; Rhincodon typus; Family Carcharhinidae; Family Sphyrnidae; Family Isurida.
(17) Cetaceans: Family Physeteridae; Family Balaenopteridae; Family Balaenidae; Family Eschrichtiidae; Family Monodontidae; Family Ziphiidae; Family Delphinidae.

Annex II. Commission on the limits of the continental shelf

Article 1. In accordance with the provisions of article 76, a Commission on the Limits of the Continental Shelf beyond 200 nautical miles shall be established in conformity with the following articles.

Article 2. (1) The Commission shall consist of 21 members who shall be experts in the field of geology, geophysics or hydrography, elected by States Parties to this Convention from among their nationals, having due regard to the need to ensure equitable geographical representation, who shall serve in their personal capacities.
(2) The initial election shall be held as soon as possible but in any case within 18 months after the date of entry into force of this Convention. At least three months before the date of each election, the Secretary-General of the United Nations shall address a letter to the States Parties, inviting the submission of nominations, after appropriate regional consultations, within three months. The Secretary-General shall prepare a list in alphabetical order of all persons thus nominated and shall submit it to all the States Parties.
(3) Elections of the members of the Commission shall be held at a meeting of States Parties convened by the Secretary-General at United 146 Nations Headquarters. At that meeting, for which two thirds of the States Parties shall constitute a quorum, the persons elected to the Commission shall be those nominees who obtain a two-thirds majority of the votes of the representatives of States Parties present and voting. Not less than three members shall be elected from each geographical region.
(4) The members of the Commission shall be elected for a term of five years. They shall be eligible for re-election.
(5) The State Party which submitted the nomination of a member of the Commission shall defray the expenses of that member while in performance of Commission duties. The coastal State concerned shall defray the expenses incurred in respect of the advice referred to in article 3, paragraph (1)(b), of this Annex. The secretariat of the Commission shall be provided by the Secretary-General of the United Nations.

Article 3. (1) The functions of the Commission shall be:
(a) to consider the data and other material submitted by coastal States concerning the outer limits of the continental shelf in areas where those limits extend beyond 200 nautical miles, and to make recommendations in accordance with article 76 and the Statement of Understanding adopted on 29 August 1980 by the Third United Nations Conference on the Law of the Sea;
(b) to provide scientific and technical advice, if requested by the coastal State concerned during the preparation of the data referred to in subparagraph (a).
(2) The Commission may cooperate, to the extent considered necessary and useful, with the Intergovernmental Oceanographic Commission of UNESCO, the International Hydrographic Organization and other competent international organizations with a view to exchanging scientific and technical information which might be of assistance in discharging the Commission's responsibilities.

Article 4. Where a coastal State intends to establish, in accordance with article 76, the outer limits of its continental shelf beyond 200 nautical miles, it shall submit particulars of such limits to the Commission along with supporting scientific and technical data as soon as possible but in any case within 10 years of the entry into force of this Convention for that State. The coastal State shall at the same time give the names of any Commission members who have provided it with scientific and technical advice.

Article 5. Unless the Commission decides otherwise, the Commission shall function by way of sub-commissions composed of seven members, appointed in a balanced manner taking into account the specific elements of each submission by a coastal State. Nationals of the coastal State making the submission who are members of the Commission and any Commission member who has assisted a coastal State by providing scientific and technical advice with respect to the delineation shall not be a member of the sub-commission dealing with that submission but has the right to participate as a member in the proceedings of the Commission concerning the said submission. The coastal State which has made a submission to the Commission may send its representatives to participate in the relevant proceedings without the right to vote.

Article 6. (1) The sub-commission shall submit its recommendations to the Commission.
(2) Approval by the Commission of the recommendations of the sub-commission shall be by a majority of two thirds of Commission members present and voting.
(3) The recommendations of the Commission shall be submitted in writing to the coastal State which made the submission and to the Secretary-General of the United Nations.

Article 7. Coastal States shall establish the outer limits of the continental shelf in conformity with the provisions of article 76, paragraph (8), and in accordance with the appropriate national procedures.

Article 8. In the case of disagreement by the coastal State with the recommendations of the Commission, the coastal State shall, within a reasonable time, make a revised or new submission to the Commission.

Article 9. The actions of the Commission shall not prejudice matters relating to delimitation of boundaries between States with opposite or adjacent coasts.

Annex III. Basic conditions of prospecting, exploration and exploitation

Article 1. Title to minerals
Title to minerals shall pass upon recovery in accordance with this Convention.

Article 2. Prospecting
(1)(a) The Authority shall encourage prospecting in the Area.
(b) Prospecting shall be conducted only after the Authority has received a satisfactory written undertaking that the proposed prospector will comply with this Convention and the relevant rules, regulations and procedures of the Authority concerning cooperation in the training programmes referred to in articles 143 and 144 and the protection of the marine environment, and will accept verification by the Authority of 148 compliance therewith. The proposed prospector shall, at the same time, notify the Authority of the approximate area or areas in which prospecting is to be conducted.
(c) Prospecting may be conducted simultaneously by more than one prospector in the same area or areas.
(2) Prospecting shall not confer on the prospector any rights with respect to resources. A prospector may, however, recover a reasonable quantity of minerals to be used for testing.

Article 3. Exploration and exploitation
(1) The Enterprise, States Parties, and the other entities referred to in article 153,
paragraph (2)(b), may apply to the Authority for approval of plans of work for activities in the Area.
(2) The Enterprise may apply with respect to any part of the Area, but applications by others with respect to reserved areas are subject to the additional requirements of article 9 of this Annex.
(3) Exploration and exploitation shall be carried out only in areas specified in plans of work referred to in article 153, paragraph (3), and approved by the Authority in accordance with this Convention and the relevant rules, regulations and procedures of the Authority.
(4) Every approved plan of work shall:
(a) be in conformity with this Convention and the rules, regulations and procedures of the Authority;
(b) provide for control by the Authority of activities in the Area in accordance with
article 153, paragraph (4);
(c) confer on the operator, in accordance with the rules, regulations and procedures of the Authority, the exclusive right to explore for and exploit the specified categories of resources in the area covered by the plan of work. If, however, the applicant presents for approval a plan of work covering only the stage of exploration or the stage of exploitation, the approved plan of work shall confer such exclusive right with respect to that stage only.
(5) Upon its approval by the Authority, every plan of work, except those presented by the Enterprise, shall be in the form of a contract concluded between the Authority and the applicant or applicants.

Article 4. Qualifications of applicants
(1) Applicants, other than the Enterprise, shall be qualified if they have the nationality or control and sponsorship required by article 153, paragraph (2)(b), and if they follow the procedures and meet the qualification standards set forth in the rules, regulations and procedures of the Authority.
(2) Except as provided in paragraph (6), such qualification standards shall relate to the financial and technical capabilities of the applicant and his performance under any previous contracts with the Authority.
(3) Each applicant shall be sponsored by the State Party of which it is a national unless the applicant has more than one nationality, as in the case of a partnership or consortium of entities from several States, in which event all States Parties involved shall sponsor the application, or unless the applicant is effectively controlled by another State Party or its nationals, in which event both States Parties shall sponsor the application. The criteria and procedures for implementation of the sponsorship requirements shall be set forth in the rules, regulations and procedures of the Authority.
(4) The sponsoring State or States shall, pursuant to article 139, have the responsibility to ensure, within their legal systems, that a contractor so sponsored shall carry out activities in the Area in conformity with the terms of its contract and its obligations under this Convention. A sponsoring State shall not, however, be liable for damage caused by any failure of a contractor sponsored by it to

comply with its obligations if that State Party has adopted laws and regulations and taken administrative measures which are, within the framework of its legal system, reasonably appropriate for securing compliance by persons under its jurisdiction.
(5) The procedures for assessing the qualifications of States Parties which are applicants shall take into account their character as States.
(6) The qualification standards shall require that every applicant, without exception, shall as part of his application undertake:
(a) to accept as enforceable and comply with the applicable obligations created by the provisions of Part XI, the rules, regulations and procedures of the Authority, the decisions of the organs of the Authority and terms of his contracts with the Authority;
(b) to accept control by the Authority of activities in the Area, as authorized by this Convention;
(c) to provide the Authority with a written assurance that his obligations under the contract will be fulfilled in good faith;
(d) to comply with the provisions on the transfer of technology set forth in article 5 of this Annex.

Article 5. Transfer of technology
(1) When submitting a plan of work, every applicant shall make available to the Authority a general description of the equipment and methods to be used in carrying out activities in the Area, and other relevant non-proprietary information about the characteristics of such technology and information as to where such technology is available.
(2) Every operator shall inform the Authority of revisions in the description and information made available pursuant to paragraph (1) whenever a substantial technological change or innovation is introduced.
(3) Every contract for carrying out activities in the Area shall contain the following undertakings by the contractor:
(a) to make available to the Enterprise on fair and reasonable commercial terms and conditions, whenever the Authority so requests, the technology which he uses in carrying out activities in the Area under the contract, which the contractor is legally entitled to transfer. This shall be done by means of licences or other appropriate arrangements which the contractor shall negotiate with the Enterprise and which shall be set forth in a specific agreement supplementary to the contract. This undertaking may be invoked only if the Enterprise finds that it is unable to obtain the same or equally efficient and useful 150 technology on the open market on fair and reasonable commercial terms and conditions;
(b) to obtain a written assurance from the owner of any technology used in carrying out activities in the Area under the contract, which is not generally available on the open market and which is not covered by subparagraph (a), that the owner will, whenever the Authority so requests, make that technology available to the Enterprise under licence or other appropriate arrangements and on fair and reasonable commercial terms and conditions, to the same extent as made available to the contractor. If this assurance is not obtained, the technology in question shall not be used by the contractor in carrying out activities in the Area;
(c) to acquire from the owner by means of an enforceable contract, upon the request of the Enterprise and if it is possible to do so without substantial cost to the contractor, the legal right to transfer to the Enterprise any technology used by the contractor, in carrying out activities in the Area under the contract, which the contractor is otherwise not legally entitled to transfer and which is not generally available on the open market. In cases where there is a substantial corporate relationship between the contractor and the owner of the technology, the closeness of this relationship and the degree of control or influence shall be relevant to the determination whether all feasible measures have been taken to acquire such a right. In cases where the contractor exercises effective control over the owner, failure to acquire from the owner the legal right shall be considered relevant to the contractor's qualification for any subsequent application for approval of a plan of work;
(d) to facilitate, upon the request of the Enterprise, the acquisition by the Enterprise of any technology covered by subparagraph (b), under licence or other appropriate arrangements and on fair and reasonable commercial terms and conditions, if the Enterprise decides to negotiate directly with the owner of the technology;
(e) to take the same measures as are prescribed in subparagraphs (a), (b), (c) and (d) for the benefit of a developing State or group of developing States which has applied for a contract under article 9 of this Annex, provided that these measures shall be limited to the exploitation of the part of the area proposed by the contractor which has been reserved pursuant to article 8 of this Annex and provided that activities under the contract sought by the developing State or group of developing States would not involve transfer of technology to a third State or the nationals of a third State. The obligation

under this provision shall only apply with respect to any given contractor where technology has not been requested by the Enterprise or transferred by that contractor to the Enterprise.
(4) Disputes concerning undertakings required by paragraph (3), like other provisions of the contracts, shall be subject to compulsory settlement in accordance with Part XI and, in cases of violation of these undertakings, suspension or termination of the contract or monetary penalties may be 151 ordered in accordance with article 18 of this Annex. Disputes as to whether offers made by the contractor are within the range of fair and reasonable commercial terms and conditions may be submitted by either party to binding commercial arbitration in accordance with the UNCITRAL Arbitration Rules or such other arbitration rules as may be prescribed in the rules, regulations and procedures of the Authority. If the finding is that the offer made by the contractor is not within the range of fair and reasonable commercial terms and conditions, the contractor shall be given 45 days to revise his offer to bring it within that range before the Authority takes any action in accordance with article 18 of this Annex.
(5) If the Enterprise is unable to obtain on fair and reasonable commercial terms and conditions appropriate technology to enable it to commence in a timely manner the recovery and processing of minerals from the Area, either the Council or the Assembly may convene a group of States Parties composed of those which are engaged in activities in the Area, those which have sponsored entities which are engaged in activities in the Area and other States Parties having access to such technology. This group shall consult together and shall take effective measures to ensure that such technology is made available to the Enterprise on fair and reasonable commercial terms and conditions. Each such State Party shall take all feasible measures to this end within its own legal system.
(6) In the case of joint ventures with the Enterprise, transfer of technology will be in accordance with the terms of the joint venture agreement.
(7) The undertakings required by paragraph (3) shall be included in each contract for the carrying out of activities in the Area until 10 years after the commencement of commercial production by the Enterprise, and may be invoked during that period.
(8) For the purposes of this article, "technology" means the specialized equipment and technical know-how, including manuals, designs, operating instructions, training and technical advice and assistance, necessary to assemble, maintain and operate a viable system and the legal right to use these items for that purpose on a non-exclusive basis.

Article 6. Approval of plans of work
(1) Six months after the entry into force of this Convention, and thereafter each fourth month, the Authority shall take up for consideration proposed plans of work.
(2) When considering an application for approval of a plan of work in the form of a contract, the Authority shall first ascertain whether:
(a) the applicant has complied with the procedures established for applications in accordance with article 4 of this Annex and has given the Authority the undertakings and assurances required by that article. In cases of non-compliance with these procedures or in the absence of any of these undertakings and assurances, the applicant shall be given 45 days to remedy these defects;
(b) the applicant possesses the requisite qualifications provided for in article 4 of this Annex. (3) All proposed plans of work shall be taken up in the order in which they are received. The proposed plans of work shall comply with and be governed by the relevant provisions of this Convention and the rules, regulations and procedures of the Authority, including those on operational requirements, financial contributions and the undertakings concerning the transfer of technology. If the proposed plans of work conform to these requirements, the Authority shall approve them provided that they are in accordance with the uniform and non-discriminatory requirements set forth in the rules, regulations and procedures of the Authority, unless:
(a) part or all of the area covered by the proposed plan of work is included in an approved plan of work or a previously submitted proposed plan of work which has not yet been finally acted on by the Authority;
(b) part or all of the area covered by the proposed plan of work is disapproved by the Authority pursuant to article 162, paragraph (2)(x); or (c) the proposed plan of work has been submitted or sponsored by a State Party which already holds:
(i) plans of work for exploration and exploitation of polymetallic nodules in non-reserved areas that, together with either part of the area covered by the application for a plan of work, exceed in size 30 per cent of a circular area of 400,000 square kilometres surrounding the centre of either part of the area covered by the proposed plan of work;
(ii) plans of work for the exploration and exploitation of polymetallic nodules in non-reserved areas which, taken together, constitute 2 per cent of the total seabed area which is not reserved or disapproved for exploitation pursuant to article 162, paragraph (2)(x).

(4) For the purpose of the standard set forth in paragraph (3)(c), a plan of work submitted by a partnership or consortium shall be counted on a pro rata basis among the sponsoring States Parties involved in accordance with article 4, paragraph (3), of this Annex. The Authority may approve plans of work covered by paragraph (3)(c) if it determines that such approval would not permit a State Party or entities sponsored by it to monopolize the conduct of activities in the Area or to preclude other States Parties from activities in the Area.
(5) Notwithstanding paragraph (3)(a), after the end of the interim period specified in article 151, paragraph (3), the Authority may adopt by means of rules, regulations and procedures other procedures and criteria consistent with this Convention for deciding which applicants shall have plans of work approved in cases of selection among applicants for a proposed area. These procedures and criteria shall ensure approval of plans of work on an equitable and non-discriminatory basis.

Article 7. Selection among applicants for production authorizations

(1) Six months after the entry into force of this Convention, and thereafter each fourth month, the Authority shall take up for consideration applications for production authorizations submitted during the immediately preceding period. The Authority shall issue the authorizations applied for if all such applications can be approved without exceeding the production limitation or contravening the obligations of the Authority under a commodity agreement or arrangement to which it has become a party, as provided in article 151.
(2) When a selection must be made among applicants for production authorizations because of the production limitation set forth in article 151, paragraphs (2) to (7), or because of the obligations of the Authority under a commodity agreement or arrangement to which it has become a party, as provided for in article 151, paragraph (1), the Authority shall make the selection on the basis of objective and non-discriminatory standards set forth in its rules, regulations and procedures.
(3) In the application of paragraph (2), the Authority shall give priority to those applicants which:
(a) give better assurance of performance, taking into account their financial and technical qualifications and their performance, if any, under previously approved plans of work;
(b) provide earlier prospective financial benefits to the Authority, taking into account when commercial production is scheduled to begin;
(c) have already invested the most resources and effort in prospecting or exploration.
(4) Applicants which are not selected in any period shall have priority in subsequent periods until they receive a production authorization.
(5) Selection shall be made taking into account the need to enhance opportunities for all States Parties, irrespective of their social and economic systems or geographical locations so as to avoid discrimination against any State or system, to participate in activities in the Area and to prevent monopolization of those activities.
(6) Whenever fewer reserved areas than non-reserved areas are under exploitation, applications for production authorizations with respect to reserved areas shall have priority. (7) The decisions referred to in this article shall be taken as soon as possible after the close of each period.

Article 8. Reservation of areas

Each application, other than those submitted by the Enterprise or by any other entities for reserved areas, shall cover a total area, which need not be a single continuous area, sufficiently large and of sufficient estimated commercial value to allow two mining operations. The applicant shall indicate the coordinates dividing the area into two parts of equal estimated commercial value and submit all the data obtained by him with respect to both parts. Without prejudice to the powers of the Authority pursuant to article 17 of this Annex, the data to be submitted concerning polymetallic nodules shall relate to mapping, sampling, the abundance of nodules, and their metal content.
Within 45 days of receiving such data, the Authority shall designate which part is to be reserved solely for the conduct of activities by the Authority through the Enterprise or in association with developing States. This designation may be deferred for a further period of 45 days if the Authority requests an independent expert to assess whether all data required by this article has been submitted. The area designated shall become a reserved area as soon as the plan of work for the non-reserved area is approved and the contract is signed.

Article 9. Activities in reserved areas

(1) The Enterprise shall be given an opportunity to decide whether it intends to carry out activities in each reserved area. This decision may be taken at any time, unless a notification pursuant to paragraph (4) is received by the Authority, in which event the Enterprise shall take its decision within a reasonable time. The Enterprise may decide to exploit such areas in joint ventures with the interested State or entity.

(2) The Enterprise may conclude contracts for the execution of part of its activities in accordance with Annex IV, article 12. It may also enter into joint ventures for the conduct of such activities with any entities which are eligible to carry out activities in the Area pursuant to article 153, paragraph (2)(b). When considering such joint ventures, the Enterprise shall offer to States Parties which are developing States and their nationals the opportunity of effective participation.

(3) The Authority may prescribe, in its rules, regulations and procedures, substantive and procedural requirements and conditions with respect to such contracts and joint ventures.

(4) Any State Party which is a developing State or any natural or juridical person sponsored by it and effectively controlled by it or by other developing State which is a qualified applicant, or any group of the foregoing, may notify the Authority that it wishes to submit a plan of work pursuant to article 6 of this Annex with respect to a reserved area. The plan of work shall be considered if the Enterprise decides, pursuant to paragraph (1), that it does not intend to carry out activities in that area.

Article 10. Preference and priority among applicants

An operator who has an approved plan of work for exploration only, as provided in article 3, paragraph 4(c), of this Annex shall have a preference and a priority among applicants for a plan of work covering exploitation of the same area and resources. However, such preference or priority may be withdrawn if the operator's performance has not been satisfactory.

Article 11. Joint arrangements

(1) Contracts may provide for joint arrangements between the contractor and the Authority through the Enterprise, in the form of joint ventures or production sharing, as well as any other form of joint arrangement, which shall have the same protection against revision, suspension or termination as contracts with the Authority.

(2) Contractors entering into such joint arrangements with the Enterprise may receive financial incentives as provided for in article 13 of this Annex.

(3) Partners in joint ventures with the Enterprise shall be liable for the payments required by article 13 of this Annex to the extent of their share in the joint ventures, subject to financial incentives as provided for in that article.

Article 12. Activities carried out by the Enterprise

(1) Activities in the Area carried out by the Enterprise pursuant to article 153,
paragraph (2)(a), shall be governed by Part XI, the rules, regulations and procedures of the Authority and its relevant decisions.

(2) Any plan of work submitted by the Enterprise shall be accompanied by evidence supporting its financial and technical capabilities.

Article 13. Financial terms of contracts

(1) In adopting rules, regulations and procedures concerning the financial terms of a contract between the Authority and the entities referred to in article 153, paragraph (2)(b), and in negotiating those financial terms in accordance with Part XI and those rules, regulations and procedures, the Authority shall be guided by the following objectives:

(a) to ensure optimum revenues for the Authority from the proceeds of commercial production;
(b) to attract investments and technology to the exploration and exploitation of the Area;
(c) to ensure equality of financial treatment and comparable financial obligations for contractors;
(d) to provide incentives on a uniform and non-discriminatory basis for contractors to undertake joint arrangements with the Enterprise and developing States or their nationals, to stimulate the transfer of technology thereto, and to train the personnel of the Authority and of developing States;
(e) to enable the Enterprise to engage in seabed mining effectively at the same time as the entities referred to in article 153, paragraph (2)(b); and
(f) to ensure that, as a result of the financial incentives provided to contractors under paragraph (14), under the terms of contracts reviewed in accordance with article 19 of this Annex or under the provisions of article 11 of this Annex with respect to joint ventures, contractors are not subsidized so as to be given an artificial competitive advantage with respect to land-based miners.

(2) A fee shall be levied for the administrative cost of processing an application for approval of a plan of work in the form of a contract and shall be fixed at an amount of $US 500,000 per application. The amount of the fee shall be reviewed from time to time by the Council in order to ensure that it covers the administrative cost incurred. If such administrative cost incurred by the Authority in processing an application is less than the fixed amount, the Authority shall refund the difference to the applicant.

(3) A contractor shall pay an annual fixed fee of $US 1 million from the date of entry into force of the contract. If the approved date of commencement of commercial production is postponed because of a delay in issuing the production authorization, in accordance with article 151, the annual fixed

fee shall be waived for the period of postponement. From the date of commencement of commercial production, the contractor shall pay either the production charge or the annual fixed fee, whichever is greater.

(4) Within a year of the date of commencement of commercial production, in conformity with paragraph (3), a contractor shall choose to make his financial contribution to the Authority by either:
(a) paying a production charge only; or
(b) paying a combination of a production charge and a share of net proceeds.

(5) (a) If a contractor chooses to make his financial contribution to the Authority by paying a production charge only, it shall be fixed at a percentage of the market value of the processed metals produced from the polymetallic nodules recovered from the area covered by the contract. This percentage shall be fixed as follows:
(i) years 1-10 of commercial production 5 per cent
(ii) years 11 to the end of commercial production 12 per cent
(b) The said market value shall be the product of the quantity of the processed metals produced from the polymetallic nodules extracted from the area covered by the contract and the average price for those metals during the relevant accounting year, as defined in paragraphs (7) and (8).

(6) If a contractor chooses to make his financial contribution to the Authority by paying a combination of a production charge and a share of net proceeds, such payments shall be determined as follows:
(a) The production charge shall be fixed at a percentage of the market value, determined in accordance with subpara-graph (b), of the processed metals produced from the polymetallic nodules recovered from the area covered by the contract. This percentage shall be fixed as follows:
(i) first period of commercial production 2 per cent
(ii) second period of commercial production 4 per cent If, in the second period of commercial production, as defined in subparagraph (d), the return on investment in any accounting year as defined in subparagraph (m) falls below 15 per cent as a result of the payment of the production charge at 4 per cent, the production charge shall be 2 per cent instead of 4 per cent in that accounting year.
(b) The said market value shall be the product of the quantity of the processed metals produced from the polymetallic nodules recovered from the area covered by the contract and the average price for those metals during the relevant accounting year as defined in paragraphs (7) and (8).
(c) (i) The Authority's share of net proceeds shall be taken out of that portion of the contractor's net proceeds which is attributable to the mining of the resources of the area covered by the contract, referred to hereinafter as attributable net proceeds.
(ii) The Authority's share of attributable net proceeds shall be determined in accordance with the following incremental schedule:

Portion of attributable net proceeds	Share of the Authority	
	First period of commercial production	Second period of commercial production
That portion representing a return on investment which is greater than 0 per cent, but less than 10 per cent	35 per cent	40 per cent
That portion representing a return on investment which is 10 per cent or greater, but less than 20 per cent	42.5 per cent	50 per cent
That portion representing a return on investment which is 20 per cent or greater	50 per cent	70 per cent

(d) (i) The first period of commercial production referred to in subparagraphs (a) and (c) shall commence in the first accounting year of commercial production and terminate in the accounting year in which the contractor's development costs with interest on the unrecovered portion thereof are fully recovered by his cash surplus, as follows: In the first accounting year during which development costs are incurred, unrecovered development costs shall equal the development costs less cash surplus in that year. In each subsequent accounting year, unrecovered development costs shall equal the unrecovered development costs at the end of the preceding accounting year, plus interest thereon at the rate of 10 per cent per annum, plus development costs incurred in the current accounting year and less contractor's cash surplus in the current accounting year.

The accounting year in which unrecovered development costs become zero for the first time shall be the accounting year in which the contractor's development costs with interest on the unrecovered portion thereof are fully recovered by his cash surplus. The contractor's cash surplus in any accounting year shall be his gross proceeds less his operating costs and less his payments to the Authority under subparagraph (c).

(ii) The second period of commercial production shall commence in the accounting year following the termination of the first period of commercial production and shall continue until the end of the contract.

(e) "Attributable net proceeds" means the product of the contractor's net proceeds and the ratio of the development costs in the mining sector to the contractor's development costs. If the contractor engages in mining, transporting polymetallic nodules and production primarily of three processed metals, 158 namely, cobalt, copper and nickel, the amount of attributable net proceeds shall not be less than 25 per cent of the contractor's net proceeds. Subject to subparagraph (n), in all other cases, including those where the contractor engages in mining, transporting polymetallic nodules, and production primarily of four processed metals, namely, cobalt, copper, manganese and nickel, the Authority may, in its rules, regulations and procedures, prescribe appropriate floors which shall bear the same relationship to each case as the 25 per cent floor does to the three-metal case.

(f) "Contractor's net proceeds" means the contractor's gross proceeds less his operating costs and less the recovery of his development costs as set out in subparagraph (j).

(g) (i) If the contractor engages in mining, transporting polymetallic nodules and production of processed metals, "contractor's gross proceeds" means the gross revenues from the sale of the processed metals and any other monies deemed reasonably attributable to operations under the contract in accordance with the financial rules, regulations and procedures of the Authority.

(ii) In all cases other than those specified in subparagraphs (g)(i) and (n)(iii), "contractor's gross proceeds" means the gross revenues from the sale of the semi-processed metals from the polymetallic nodules recovered from the area covered by the contract, and any other monies deemed reasonably attributable to operations under the contract in accordance with the financial rules, regulations and procedures of the Authority.

(h) "Contractor's development costs" means:

(i) all expenditures incurred prior to the commencement of commercial production which are directly related to the development of the productive capacity of the area covered by the contract and the activities related thereto for operations under the contract in all cases other than that specified in subparagraph (n), in conformity with generally recognized accounting principles, including, inter alia, costs of machinery, equipment, ships, processing plant, construction, buildings, land, roads, prospecting and exploration of the area covered by the contract, research and development, interest, required leases, licences and fees; and

(ii) expenditures similar to those set forth in (i) above incurred subsequent to the commencement of commercial production and necessary to carry out the plan of work, except those chargeable to operating costs. (i) The proceeds from the disposal of capital assets and the market value of those capital assets which are no longer required for operations under the contract and which are not sold shall be deducted from the contractor's development costs during the relevant accounting year. When these deductions exceed the contractor's development costs the excess shall be added to the contractor's gross proceeds.

(j) The contractor's development costs incurred prior to the commencement of commercial production referred to in subparagraphs (h)(i) and (n)(iv) shall be recovered in 10 equal annual instalments from the date of commencement of commercial production. The contractor's development costs incurred subsequent to the commencement of commercial production referred to in subparagraphs (h)(ii) and (n)(iv) shall be recovered in 10 or fewer equal annual instalments so as to ensure their complete recovery by the end of the contract. (k) "Contractor's operating costs" means all expenditures incurred after the commencement of commercial production in the operation of the productive capacity of the area covered by the contract and the activities related thereto for operations under the contract, in conformity with generally recognized accounting principles, including, inter alia, the annual fixed fee or the production charge, whichever is greater, expenditures for wages, salaries, employee benefits, materials, services, transporting, processing and marketing costs, interest, utilities, preservation of the marine environment, overhead and administrative costs specifically related to operations under the contract, and any net operating losses carried forward or backward as specified herein. Net operating losses may be carried forward for two consecutive years except in the last two

years of the contract in which case they may be carried backward to the two preceding years.
(l) If the contractor engages in mining, transporting of polymetallic nodules, and production of processed and semi-processed metals, "development costs of the mining sector" means the portion of the contractor's development costs which is directly related to the mining of the resources of the area covered by the contract, in conformity with generally recognized accounting principles, and the financial rules, regulations and procedures of the Authority, including, inter alia, application fee, annual fixed fee and, where applicable, costs of prospecting and exploration of the area covered by the contract, and a portion of research and development costs.
(m) "Return on investment" in any accounting year means the ratio of attributable net proceeds in that year to the development costs of the mining sector. For the purpose of computing this ratio the development costs of the mining sector shall include expenditures on new or replacement equipment in the mining sector less the original cost of the equipment replaced.
(n) If the contractor engages in mining only:
(i) "attributable net proceeds" means the whole of the contractor's net proceeds;
(ii) "contractor's net proceeds" shall be as defined in subparagraph (f);
(iii) "contractor's gross proceeds" means the gross revenues from the sale of the polymetallic nodules, and any other monies deemed reasonably attributable to operations under the contract in accordance with the financial rules, regulations and procedures of the Authority; (iv) "contractor's development costs" means all expenditures incurred prior to the commencement of commercial production as set forth in subparagraph (h)(i), and all expenditures incurred subsequent to the commencement of commercial production as set forth in subparagraph (h)(ii), which are directly related to the mining of the resources of
the area covered by the contract, in conformity with generally recognized accounting principles;
(v) "contractor's operating costs" means the contractor's operating costs as in
subparagraph (k) which are directly related to the mining of the resources of the area covered by the contract in conformity with generally recognized accounting principles;
(vi) "return on investment" in any accounting year means the ratio of the contractor's net proceeds in that year to the contractor's development costs. For the purpose of computing this ratio, the contractor's development costs shall include expenditures on new or replacement equipment less the original cost of the equipment replaced.
(o) The costs referred to in subparagraphs (h), (k), (l) and (n) in respect of interest paid by the contractor shall be allowed to the extent that, in all the circumstances, the Authority approves, pursuant to article 4, paragraph (1), of this Annex, the debt-equity ratio and the rates of interest as reasonable, having regard to existing commercial practice.
(p) The costs referred to in this paragraph shall not be interpreted as including payments of corporate income taxes or similar charges levied by States in respect of the operations of the contractor.
(7) (a) "Processed metals", referred to in paragraphs (5) and (6), means the metals in the most basic form in which they are customarily traded on international terminal markets. For this purpose, the Authority shall specify, in its financial rules, regulations and procedures, the relevant international terminal market. For the metals which are not traded on such markets, "processed metals" means the metals in the most basic form in which they are customarily traded in representative arm's length transactions.
(b) If the Authority cannot otherwise determine the quantity of the processed metals produced from the polymetallic nodules recovered from the area covered by the contract referred to in paragraphs (5)(b) and (6)(b), the quantity shall be determined on the basis of the metal content of the nodules, processing recovery efficiency and other relevant factors, in accordance with the rules, regulations and procedures of the Authority and in conformity with generally recognized accounting principles.
(8) If an international terminal market provides a representative pricing mechanism for processed metals, polymetallic nodules and semi-processed metals from the nodules, the average price on that market shall be used. In all other cases, the Authority shall, after consulting the contractor, determine a fair price for the said products in accordance with paragraph (9).
(9) (a) All costs, expenditures, proceeds and revenues and all determinations of price and value referred to in this article shall be the result of free market or arm's length transactions. In the absence thereof, they shall be determined by the Authority, after consulting the contractor, as though they were the result of free market or arm's length transactions, taking into account relevant transactions in other markets.
(b) In order to ensure compliance with and enforcement of the provisions of this paragraph, the Authority shall be guided by the principles adopted for, and the interpretation given to, arm's length transactions by the Commission on Transnational Corporations of the United Nations, the Group of Experts on Tax Treaties between Developing and Developed Countries and other international

organizations, and shall, in its rules, regulations and procedures, specify uniform and internationally acceptable accounting rules and procedures, and the means of selection by the contractor of certified independent accountants acceptable to the Authority for the purpose of carrying out auditing in compliance with those rules, regulations and procedures.
(10) The contractor shall make available to the accountants, in accordance with the financial rules, regulations and procedures of the Authority, such financial data as are required to determine compliance with this article.
(11) All costs, expenditures, proceeds and revenues, and all prices and values referred to in this article, shall be determined in accordance with generally recognized accounting principles and the financial rules, regulations and procedures of the Authority.
(12) Payments to the Authority under paragraphs (5) and (6) shall be made in freely usable currencies or currencies which are freely available and effectively usable on the major foreign exchange markets or, at the contractor's option, in the equivalents of processed metals at market value. The market value shall be determined in accordance with paragraph (5)(b). The freely usable currencies and currencies which are freely available and effectively usable on the major foreign exchange markets shall be defined in the rules, regulations and procedures of the Authority in accordance with prevailing international monetary practice. (13) All financial obligations of the contractor to the Authority, as well as all his fees, costs, expenditures, proceeds and revenues referred to in this article, shall be adjusted by expressing them in constant terms relative to a base year.
(14) The Authority may, taking into account any recommendations of the Economic Planning Commission and the Legal and Technical Commission, adopt rules, regulations and procedures that provide for incentives, on a uniform and non-discriminatory basis, to contractors to further the objectives set out in paragraph (1).
(15) In the event of a dispute between the Authority and a contractor over the interpretation or application of the financial terms of a contract, either party may submit the dispute to binding commercial arbitration, unless both parties agree to settle the dispute by other means, in accordance with article 188, paragraph (2).

Article 14. Transfer of data
(1) The operator shall transfer to the Authority, in accordance with its rules, regulations and procedures and the terms and conditions of the plan of work, at time intervals determined by the Authority all data which are both necessary for and relevant to the effective exercise of the powers and functions of the principal organs of the Authority in respect of the area covered by the plan of work.
(2) Transferred data in respect of the area covered by the plan of work, deemed proprietary, may only be used for the purposes set forth in this article. Data necessary for the formulation by the Authority of rules, regulations and procedures concerning protection of the marine environment and safety, other than equipment design data, shall not be deemed proprietary.
(3) Data transferred to the Authority by prospectors, applicants for contracts or contractors, deemed proprietary, shall not be disclosed by the Authority to the Enterprise or to anyone external to the Authority, but data on the reserved areas may be disclosed to the Enterprise. Such data transferred by such persons to the Enterprise shall not be disclosed by the Enterprise to the Authority or to anyone external to the Authority.

Article 15. Training programmes
The contractor shall draw up practical programmes for the training of personnel of the Authority and developing States, including the participation of such personnel in all activities in the Area which are covered by the contract, in accordance with article 144, paragraph (2).

Article 16. Exclusive right to explore and exploit
The Authority shall, pursuant to Part XI and its rules, regulations and procedures, accord the operator the exclusive right to explore and exploit the area covered by the plan of work in respect of a specified category of resources and shall ensure that no other entity operates in the same area for a different category of resources in a manner which might interfere with the operations of the operator. The operator shall have security of tenure in accordance with article 153, paragraph (6).

Article 17. Rules, regulations and procedures of the Authority
(1) The Authority shall adopt and uniformly apply rules, regulations and procedures in accordance with article 160, paragraph (2)(f)(ii), and article 162, paragraph (2)(o)(ii), for the exercise of its functions as set forth in Part XI on, inter alia, the following matters:
(a) administrative procedures relating to prospecting, exploration and exploitation in the Area;
(b) operations:
(i) size of area;

(ii) duration of operations;
(iii) performance requirements including assurances pursuant to article 4, paragraph (6)(c), of this Annex;
(iv) categories of resources;
(v) renunciation of areas;
(vi) progress reports;
(vii) submission of data;
(viii) inspection and supervision of operations;
(ix) prevention of interference with other activities in the marine environment;
(x) transfer of rights and obligations by a contractor;
(xi) procedures for transfer of technology to developing States in accordance with article 144 and for their direct participation;
(xii) mining standards and practices, including those relating to operational safety, conservation of the resources and the protection of the marine environment;
(xiii) definition of commercial production;
(xiv) qualification standards for applicants;
(c) financial matters:
(i) establishment of uniform and non-discriminatory costing and accounting rules and the method of selection of auditors;
(ii) apportionment of proceeds of operations;
(iii) the incentives referred to in article 13 of this Annex;
(d) implementation of decisions taken pursuant to article 151, paragraph (10), and article 164, paragraph 2(d).
(2) Rules, regulations and procedures on the following items shall fully reflect the objective criteria set out below:
(a) Size of areas: The Authority shall determine the appropriate size of areas for exploration which may be up to twice as large as those for exploitation in order to permit intensive exploration operations. The size of area shall be calculated to satisfy the requirements of article 8 of this Annex on reservation of areas as well as stated production requirements consistent with article 151 in accordance with the terms of the contract taking into account the state of the art of technology then available for seabed mining and the relevant physical characteristics of the areas. Areas shall be neither smaller nor larger than are necessary to satisfy this objective.
(b) Duration of operations:
(i) Prospecting shall be without time-limit;
(ii) Exploration should be of sufficient duration to permit a thorough survey of the specific area, the design and construction of mining equipment for the area and the design and construction of small and medium-size processing plants for the purpose of testing mining and processing systems;
(iii) The duration of exploitation should be related to the economic life of the mining project, taking into consideration such factors as the depletion of the ore, the useful life of mining equipment and processing facilities and commercial viability. Exploitation should be of 164 sufficient duration to permit commercial extraction of minerals of the area and should include a reasonable time period for construction of commercial-scale mining and processing systems, during which period commercial production should not be required. The total duration of exploitation, however, should also be short enough to give the Authority an opportunity to amend the terms and conditions of the plan of work at the time it considers renewal in accordance with rules, regulations and procedures which it has adopted subsequent to approving the plan of work.
(c) Performance requirements: The Authority shall require that during the exploration stage periodic expenditures be made by the operator which are reasonably related to the size of the area covered by the plan of work and the expenditures which would be expected of a bona fide operator who intended to bring the area into commercial production within the time-limits established by the Authority. The required expenditures should not be established at a level which would discourage prospective operators with less costly technology than is prevalently in use. The Authority shall establish a maximum time interval, after the exploration stage is completed and the exploitation stage begins, to achieve commercial production. To determine this interval, the Authority should take into consideration that construction of large-scale mining and processing systems cannot be initiated until after the termination of the exploration stage and the commencement of the exploitation stage. Accordingly, the interval to bring an area into commercial production should take into account the time necessary for this construction after the completion of the exploration stage and reasonable allowance should be made for unavoidable delays in the construction schedule. Once commercial production is achieved, the Authority shall within reasonable limits and taking into consideration all relevant factors require

the operator to maintain commercial production throughout the period of the plan of work.
(d) Categories of resources: In determining the category of resources in respect of which a plan of work may be approved, the Authority shall give emphasis inter alia to the following characteristics:
(i) that certain resources require the use of similar mining methods; and
(ii) that some resources can be developed simultaneously without undue interference between operators developing different resources in the same area. Nothing in this subparagraph shall preclude the Authority from approving a plan of work with respect to more than one category of resources in the same area to the same applicant.
(e) Renunciation of areas: The operator shall have the right at any time to renounce without penalty the whole or part of his rights in the area covered by a plan of work.
(f) Protection of the marine environment: Rules, regulations and procedures shall be drawn up in order to secure effective protection of the marine environment from harmful effects directly resulting from activities in the Area or from shipboard processing immediately above a mine site of minerals derived from that mine site, taking into account the extent to which such harmful effects may directly result from drilling, dredging, coring and excavation and from disposal, dumping and discharge into the marine environment of sediment, wastes or other effluents.
(g) Commercial production: Commercial production shall be deemed to have begun if an operator engages in sustained large-scale recovery operations which yield a quantity of materials sufficient to indicate clearly that the principal purpose is large-scale production rather than production intended for information gathering, analysis or the testing of equipment or plant.

Article 18. Penalties
(1) A contractor's rights under the contract may be suspended or terminated only in the following cases:
(a) if, in spite of warnings by the Authority, the contractor has conducted his activities in such a way as to result in serious, persistent and wilful violations of the fundamental terms of the contract, Part XI and the rules, regulations and procedures of the Authority; or
(b) if the contractor has failed to comply with a final binding decision of the dispute settlement body applicable to him.
(2) In the case of any violation of the contract not covered by paragraph (1)(a), or in lieu of suspension or termination under paragraph (1)(a), the Authority may impose upon the contractor monetary penalties proportionate to the seriousness of the violation.
(3) Except for emergency orders under article 162, paragraph (2)(w), the Authority may not execute a decision involving monetary penalties, suspension or termination until the contractor has been accorded a reasonable opportunity to exhaust the judicial remedies available to him pursuant to Part XI, section 5.

Article 19. Revision of contract
(1) When circumstances have arisen or are likely to arise which, in the opinion of either party, would render the contract inequitable or make it impracticable or impossible to achieve the objectives set out in the contract or in Part XI, the parties shall enter into negotiations to revise it accordingly.
(2) Any contract entered into in accordance with article 153, paragraph (3), may be revised only with the consent of the parties.

Article 20. Transfer of rights and obligations
The rights and obligations arising under a contract may be transferred only with the consent of the Authority, and in accordance with its rules, regulations and procedures. The Authority shall not unreasonably withhold consent to the transfer if the proposed transferee is in all respects a qualified applicant and assumes all of the obligations of the transferor and if the transfer does not confer to the transferee a plan of work, the approval of which would be forbidden by article 6, paragraph (3)(c), of this Annex.

Article 21. Applicable law
(1) The contract shall be governed by the terms of the contract, the rules, regulations and procedures of the Authority, Part XI and other rules of international law not incompatible with this Convention.
(2) Any final decision rendered by a court or tribunal having jurisdiction under this Convention relating to the rights and obligations of the Authority and of the contractor shall be enforceable in the territory of each State Party.
(3) No State Party may impose conditions on a contractor that are inconsistent with Part XI. However, the application by a State Party to contractors sponsored by it, or to ships flying its flag, of environmental or other laws and regulations more stringent than those in the rules, regulations and procedures of the Authority adopted pursuant to article 17, paragraph (2)(f), of this Annex shall not be deemed inconsistent with Part XI.

Article 22. Responsibility

The contractor shall have responsibility or liability for any damage arising out of wrongful acts in the conduct of its operations, account being taken of contributory acts or omissions by the Authority. Similarly, the Authority shall have responsibility or liability for any damage arising out of wrongful acts in the exercise of its powers and functions, including violations under article 168, paragraph (2), account being taken of contributory acts or omissions by the contractor. Liability in every case shall be for the actual amount of damage.

Annex IV. Statute of the Enterprise

Article 1. Purposes

(1) The Enterprise is the organ of the Authority which shall carry out activities in the Area directly, pursuant to article 153, paragraph (2)(a), as well as the transporting, processing and marketing of minerals recovered from the Area.
(2) In carrying out its purposes and in the exercise of its functions, the Enterprise shall act in accordance with this Convention and the rules, regulations and procedures of the Authority. (3) In developing the resources of the Area pursuant to paragraph (1), the Enterprise shall, subject to this Convention, operate in accordance with sound commercial principles.

Article 2. Relationship to the Authority

(1) Pursuant to article 170, the Enterprise shall act in accordance with the general policies of the Assembly and the directives of the Council.
2. Subject to paragraph (l), the Enterprise shall enjoy autonomy in the conduct of its operations.
3. Nothing in this Convention shall make the Enterprise liable for the acts or obligations of the Authority, or make the Authority liable for the acts or obligations of the Enterprise.

Article 3. Limitation of liability

Without prejudice to article 11, paragraph (3), of this Annex, no member of the Authority shall be liable by reason only of its membership for the acts or obligations of the Enterprise.

Article 4. Structure

The Enterprise shall have a Governing Board, a Director-General and the staff necessary for the exercise of its functions.

Article 5. Governing Board

(1) The Governing Board shall be composed of 15 members elected by the Assembly in accordance with article 160, paragraph (2)(c). In the election of the members of the Board, due regard shall be paid to the principle of equitable geographical distribution. In submitting nominations of candidates for election to the Board, members of the Authority shall bear in mind the need to nominate candidates of the highest standard of competence, with qualifications in relevant fields, so as to ensure the viability and success of the Enterprise.
(2) Members of the Board shall be elected for four years and may be re-elected; and due regard shall be paid to the principle of rotation of membership.
(3) Members of the Board shall continue in office until their successors are elected. If the office of a member of the Board becomes vacant, the Assembly shall, in accordance with article 160, paragraph (2)(c), elect a new member for the remainder of his predecessor's term. (4) Members of the Board shall act in their personal capacity. In the performance of their duties they shall not seek or receive instructions from any government or from any other source. Each member of the Authority shall respect the independent character of the members of the Board and shall refrain from all attempts to influence any of them in the discharge of their duties.
(5) Each member of the Board shall receive remuneration to be paid out of the funds of the Enterprise. The amount of remuneration shall be fixed by the Assembly, upon the recommendation of the Council.
(6) The Board shall normally function at the principal office of the Enterprise and shall meet as often as the business of the Enterprise may require.
(7) Two thirds of the members of the Board shall constitute a quorum.
(8) Each member of the Board shall have one vote. All matters before the Board shall be decided by a majority of its members. If a member has a conflict of interest on a matter before the Board he shall refrain from voting on that matter.
(9) Any member of the Authority may ask the Board for information in respect of its operations which particularly affect that member. The Board shall endeavour to provide such information.

Article 6. Powers and functions of the Governing Board

The Governing Board shall direct the operations of the Enterprise. Subject to this Convention, the Governing Board shall exercise the powers necessary to fulfil the purposes of the Enterprise, including powers:

(a) to elect a Chairman from among its members;
(b) to adopt its rules of procedure;
(c) to draw up and submit formal written plans of work to the Council in accordance with article 153, paragraph (3), and article 162, paragraph (2)(j);
(d) to develop plans of work and programmes for carrying out the activities specified in article 170;
(e) to prepare and submit to the Council applications for production authorizations in accordance with article 151, paragraphs (2) to (7);
(f) to authorize negotiations concerning the acquisition of technology, including those provided for in Annex III, article 5, paragraph (3)(a), (c) and (d), and to approve the results of those negotiations;
(g) to establish terms and conditions, and to authorize negotiations, concerning joint ventures and other forms of joint arrangements referred to in Annex III, articles 9 and 11, and to approve the results of such negotiations;
(h) to recommend to the Assembly what portion of the net income of the Enterprise should be retained as its reserves in accordance with article 160, paragraph (2)(f), and article 10 of this Annex;
(i) to approve the annual budget of the Enterprise;
(j) to authorize the procurement of goods and services in accordance with article 12, paragraph (3), of this Annex;
(k) to submit an annual report to the Council in accordance with article 9 of this Annex;
(l) to submit to the Council for the approval of the Assembly draft rules in respect of the organization, management, appointment and dismissal of the staff of the Enterprise and to adopt regulations to give effect to such rules;
(m) to borrow funds and to furnish such collateral or other security as it may determine in accordance with article 11, paragraph (2), of this Annex;
(n) to enter into any legal proceedings, agreements and transactions and to take any other actions in accordance with article 13 of this Annex;
(o) to delegate, subject to the approval of the Council, any non-discretionary powers to the Director-General and to its committees.

Article 7. Director-General and staff of the Enterprise

(1) The Assembly shall, upon the recommendation of the Council and the nomination of the Governing Board, elect the Director-General of the Enterprise who shall not be a member of the Board. The Director-General shall hold office for a fixed term, not exceeding five years, and may be re-elected for further terms.

(2) The Director-General shall be the legal representative and chief executive of the Enterprise and shall be directly responsible to the Board for the conduct of the operations of the Enterprise. He shall be responsible for the organization, management, appointment and dismissal of the staff of the Enterprise in accordance with the rules and regulations referred to in article 6, subparagraph (l), of this Annex. He shall participate, without the right to vote, in the meetings of the Board and may participate, without the right to vote, in the meetings of the Assembly and the Council when these organs are dealing with matters concerning the Enterprise.

(3) The paramount consideration in the recruitment and employment of the staff and in the determination of their conditions of service shall be the necessity of securing the highest standards of efficiency and of technical competence. Subject to this consideration, due regard shall be paid to the importance of recruiting the staff on an equitable geographical basis.

(4) In the performance of their duties the Director-General and the staff shall not seek or receive instructions from any government or from any other source external to the Enterprise. They shall refrain from any action which might reflect on their position as international officials of the Enterprise responsible only to the Enterprise. Each State Party undertakes to respect the exclusively international character of the responsibilities of the Director-General and the staff and not to seek to influence them in the discharge of their responsibilities.

(5) The responsibilities set forth in article 168, paragraph (2), are equally applicable to the staff of the Enterprise.

Article 8. Location

The Enterprise shall have its principal office at the seat of the Authority. The Enterprise may establish other offices and facilities in the territory of any State Party with the consent of that State Party.

Article 9. Reports and financial statements

(1) The Enterprise shall, not later than three months after the end of each financial year, submit to the Council for its consideration an annual report containing an audited statement of its accounts and shall transmit to the Council at appropriate intervals a summary statement of its financial position and a profit and loss statement showing the results of its operations. (2) The Enterprise shall publish its annual report and such other reports as it finds appropriate.

(3) All reports and financial statements referred to in this article shall be distributed to the members of the Authority.

Article 10. Allocation of net income

(1) Subject to paragraph (3), the Enterprise shall make payments to the Authority under Annex III, article 13, or their equivalent.

(2) The Assembly shall, upon the recommendation of the Governing Board, determine what portion of the net income of the Enterprise shall be retained as reserves of the Enterprise. The remainder shall be transferred to the Authority.

(3) During an initial period required for the Enterprise to become self-supporting, which shall not exceed 10 years from the commencement of commercial production by it, the Assembly shall exempt the Enterprise from the payments referred to in paragraph (1), and shall leave all of the net income of the Enterprise in its reserves.

Article 11. Finances

(1) The funds of the Enterprise shall include:
(a) amounts received from the Authority in accordance with article 173, paragraph (2)(b);
(b) voluntary contributions made by States Parties for the purpose of financing activities of the Enterprise;
(c) amounts borrowed by the Enterprise in accordance with paragraphs (2) and (3);
(d) income of the Enterprise from its operations;
(e) other funds made available to the Enterprise to enable it to commence operations as soon as possible and to carry out its functions.
(2) (a) The Enterprise shall have the power to borrow funds and to furnish such collateral or other security as it may determine. Before making a public sale of its obligations in the financial markets or currency of a State Party, the Enterprise shall obtain the approval of that State Party. The total amount of borrowings shall be approved by the Council upon the recommendation of the Governing Board.
(b) States Parties shall make every reasonable effort to support applications by the Enterprise for loans on capital markets and from international financial institutions.
(3) (a) The Enterprise shall be provided with the funds necessary to explore and exploit one mine site, and to transport, process and market the minerals recovered therefrom and the nickel, copper, cobalt and manganese obtained, and to meet its initial administrative expenses. The amount of the said funds, and the criteria and factors for its adjustment, shall be included by the Preparatory Commission in the draft rules, regulations and procedures of the Authority.
(b) All States Parties shall make available to the Enterprise an amount equivalent to one half of the funds referred to in subparagraph (a) by way of long-term interest-free loans in accordance with the scale of assessments for the United Nations regular budget in force at the time when the assessments are made, adjusted to take into account the States which are not members of the United Nations. Debts incurred by the Enterprise in raising the other half of the funds shall be guaranteed by all States Parties in accordance with the same scale.
(c) If the sum of the financial contributions of States Parties is less than the funds to be provided to the Enterprise under subparagraph (a), the Assembly shall, at its first session, consider the extent of the shortfall and adopt by consensus measures for dealing with this shortfall, taking into account the obligation of States Parties under subparagraphs (a) and (b) and any recommendations of the Preparatory Commission.
(d) (i) Each State Party shall, within 60 days after the entry into force of this Convention, or within 30 days after the deposit of its instrument of ratification or accession, whichever is later, deposit with the Enterprise irrevocable, non-negotiable, non-interest-bearing promissory notes in the amount of the share of such State Party of interest-free loans pursuant to subparagraph (b).
(ii) The Board shall prepare, at the earliest practicable date after this Convention enters into force, and thereafter at annual or other appropriate intervals, a schedule of the magnitude and timing of its requirements for the funding of its administrative expenses and for activities carried out by the Enterprise in accordance with article 170 and article 12 of this Annex.
(iii) The States Parties shall, thereupon, be notified by the Enterprise, through the Authority, of their respective shares of the funds in accordance with subparagraph (b), required for such expenses.

PART I   INTERNATIONAL LAW

The Enterprise shall encash such amounts of the promissory notes as may be required to meet the expenditure referred to in the schedule with respect to interest-free loans. (iv) States Parties shall, upon receipt of the notification, make available their respective shares of debt guarantees for the Enterprise in accordance with subparagraph (b).

(e) (i) If the Enterprise so requests, State Parties may provide debt guarantees in addition to those provided in accordance with the scale referred to in subparagraph (b).

(ii) In lieu of debt guarantees, a State Party may make a voluntary contribution to the Enterprise in an amount equivalent to that portion of the debts which it would otherwise be liable to guarantee.

(f) Repayment of the interest-bearing loans shall have priority over the repayment of the interest-free loans. Repayment of interest-free loans shall be in accordance with a schedule adopted by the Assembly, upon the recommendation of the Council and the advice of the Board. In the exercise of this function the Board shall be guided by the relevant provisions of the rules, regulations and procedures of the Authority, which shall take into account the paramount importance of ensuring the effective functioning of the Enterprise and, in particular, ensuring its financial independence.

(g) Funds made available to the Enterprise shall be in freely usable currencies or currencies which are freely available and effectively usable in the major foreign exchange markets. These currencies shall be defined in the rules, regulations and procedures of the Authority in accordance with prevailing international monetary practice. Except as provided in
paragraph (2), no State Party shall maintain or impose restrictions on the holding, use or exchange by the Enterprise of these funds.

(h) "Debt guarantee" means a promise of a State Party to creditors of the Enterprise to pay, pro rata in accordance with the appropriate scale, the financial obligations of the Enterprise covered by the guarantee following notice by the creditors to the State Party of a default by the Enterprise. Procedures for the payment of those obligations shall be in conformity with the rules, regulations and procedures of the Authority.

(4) The funds, assets and expenses of the Enterprise shall be kept separate from those of the Authority. This article shall not prevent the Enterprise from making arrangements with the Authority regarding facilities, personnel and services and arrangements for reimbursement of administrative expenses paid by either on behalf of the other.

(5) The records, books and accounts of the Enterprise, including its annual financial statements, shall be audited annually by an independent auditor appointed by the Council.

Article 12. Operations

(1) The Enterprise shall propose to the Council projects for carrying out activities in accordance with article 170. Such proposals shall include a formal written plan of work for activities in the Area in accordance with article 153, paragraph (3), and all such other information and data as may be required from time to time for its appraisal by the Legal and Technical Commission and approval by the Council.

(2) Upon approval by the Council, the Enterprise shall execute the project on the basis of the formal written plan of work referred to in paragraph (1).

(3) (a) If the Enterprise does not possess the goods and services required for its operations it may procure them. For that purpose, it shall issue invitations to tender and award contracts to bidders offering the best combination of quality, price and delivery time.

(b) If there is more than one bid offering such a combination, the contract shall be awarded in accordance with:

(i) the principle of non-discrimination on the basis of political or other considerations not relevant to the carrying out of operations with due diligence and efficiency; and

(ii) guidelines approved by the Council with regard to the preferences to be accorded to goods and services originating in developing States, including the land-locked and geographically disadvantaged among them.

(c) The Governing Board may adopt rules determining the special circumstances in which the requirement of invitations to bid may, in the best interests of the Enterprise, be dispensed with.

(4) The Enterprise shall have title to all minerals and processed substances produced by it.

(5) The Enterprise shall sell its products on a non-discriminatory basis. It shall not give non-commercial discounts.

(6) Without prejudice to any general or special power conferred on the Enterprise under any other provision of this Convention, the Enterprise shall exercise such powers incidental to its business as shall be necessary.

(7) The Enterprise shall not interfere in the political affairs of any State Party; nor shall it be influenced in its decisions by the political character of the State Party concerned. Only commercial

considerations shall be relevant to its decisions, and these considerations shall be weighed impartially in order to carry out the purposes specified in article 1 of this Annex.

Article 13. Legal status, privileges and immunities

(1) To enable the Enterprise to exercise its functions, the status, privileges and immunities set forth in this article shall be accorded to the Enterprise in the territories of States Parties. To give effect to this principle the Enterprise and States Parties may, where necessary, enter into special agreements.

(2) The Enterprise shall have such legal capacity as is necessary for the exercise of its functions and the fulfilment of its purposes and, in particular, the capacity:

(a) to enter into contracts, joint arrangements or other arrangements, including agreements with States and international organizations;

(b) to acquire, lease, hold and dispose of immovable and movable property;

(c) to be a party to legal proceedings.

(3) (a) Actions may be brought against the Enterprise only in a court of competent jurisdiction in the territory of a State Party in which the Enterprise:

(i) has an office or facility;

(ii) has appointed an agent for the purpose of accepting service or notice of process;

(iii) has entered into a contract for goods or services;

(iv) has issued securities; or

(v) is otherwise engaged in commercial activity.

(b) The property and assets of the Enterprise, wherever located and by whomsoever held, shall be immune from all forms of seizure, attachment or execution before the delivery of final judgment against the Enterprise.

(4) (a) The property and assets of the Enterprise, wherever located and by whomsoever held, shall be immune from requisition, confiscation, expropriation or any other form of seizure by executive or legislative action.

(b) The property and assets of the Enterprise, wherever located and by whomsoever held, shall be free from discriminatory restrictions, regulations, controls and moratoria of any nature.

(c) The Enterprise and its employees shall respect local laws and regulations in any State or territory in which the Enterprise or its employees may do business or otherwise act.

(d) States Parties shall ensure that the Enterprise enjoys all rights, privileges and immunities accorded by them to entities conducting commercial activities in their territories. These rights, privileges and immunities shall be accorded to the Enterprise on no less favourable a basis than that on which they are accorded to entities engaged in similar commercial activities. If special privileges are provided by States Parties for developing States or their commercial entities, the Enterprise shall enjoy those privileges on a similarly preferential basis.

(e) States Parties may provide special incentives, rights, privileges and immunities to the Enterprise without the obligation to provide such incentives, rights, privileges and immunities to other commercial entities.

(5) The Enterprise shall negotiate with the host countries in which its offices and facilities are located for exemption from direct and indirect taxation.

(6) Each State Party shall take such action as is necessary for giving effect in terms of its own law to the principles set forth in this Annex and shall inform the Enterprise of the specific action which it has taken.

(7) The Enterprise may waive any of the privileges and immunities conferred under this article or in the special agreements referred to in paragraph (1) to such extent and upon such conditions as it may determine.

Annex V. Conciliation

Section 1. Conciliation procedure pursuant to Section 1 of Part XV

Article 1. Institution of proceedings

If the parties to a dispute have agreed, in accordance with article 284, to submit it to conciliation under this section, any such party may institute the proceedings by written notification addressed to the other party or parties to the dispute.

Article 2. List of conciliators

A list of conciliators shall be drawn up and maintained by the Secretary-General of the United Nations. Every State Party shall be entitled to nominate four conciliators, each of whom shall be a person enjoying the highest reputation for fairness, competence and integrity. The names of the persons so nominated shall constitute the list. If at any time the conciliators nominated by a State Party in the list so constituted shall be fewer than four, that State Party shall be entitled to make further nominations as necessary. The name of a conciliator shall remain on the list until withdrawn by the State Party which made the nomination, provided that such conciliator shall continue to serve on any conciliation commission to which that conciliator has been appointed until the completion of the proceedings before that commission.

Article 3. Constitution of conciliation commission
The conciliation commission shall, unless the parties otherwise agree, be constituted as follows:
(a) Subject to subparagraph (g), the conciliation commission shall consist of five members. (b) The party instituting the proceedings shall appoint two conciliators to be chosen preferably from the list referred to in article 2 of this Annex, one of whom may be its national, unless the parties otherwise agree. Such appointments shall be included in the notification referred to in article 1 of this Annex.
(c) The other party to the dispute shall appoint two conciliators in the manner set forth in subparagraph (b) within 21 days of receipt of the notification referred to in article 1 of this Annex. If the appointments are not made within that period, the party instituting the proceedings may, within one week of the expiration of that period, either terminate the proceedings by notification addressed to the other party or request the Secretary-General of the United Nations to make the appointments in accordance with subparagraph (e).
(d) Within 30 days after all four conciliators have been appointed, they shall appoint a fifth conciliator chosen from the list referred to in article 2 of this Annex, who shall be chairman. If the appointment is not made within that period, either party may, within one week of the expiration of that period, request the Secretary-General of the United Nations to make the appointment in accordance with subparagraph (e).
(e) Within 30 days of the receipt of a request under subparagraph (c) or (d), the Secretary-General of the United Nations shall make the necessary appointments from the list referred to in article 2 of this Annex in consultation with the parties to the dispute.
(f) Any vacancy shall be filled in the manner prescribed for the initial appointment.
(g) Two or more parties which determine by agreement that they are in the same interest shall appoint two conciliators jointly. Where two or more parties have separate interests or there is a disagreement as to whether they are of the same interest, they shall appoint conciliators separately.
(h) In disputes involving more than two parties having separate interests, or where there is disagreement as to whether they are of the same interest, the parties shall apply subparagraphs (a) to (f) in so far as possible.

Article 4. Procedure
The conciliation commission shall, unless the parties otherwise agree, determine its own procedure. The commission may, with the consent of the parties to the dispute, invite any State Party to submit to it its views orally or in writing. Decisions of the commission regarding procedural matters, the report and recommendations shall be made by a majority vote of its members.

Article 5. Amicable settlement
The commission may draw the attention of the parties to any measures which might facilitate an amicable settlement of the dispute.

Article 6. Functions of the commission
The commission shall hear the parties, examine their claims and objections, and make proposals to the parties with a view to reaching an amicable settlement.

Article 7. Report
(1) The commission shall report within 12 months of its constitution. Its report shall record any agreements reached and, failing agreement, its conclusions on all questions of fact or law relevant to the matter in dispute and such recommendations as the commission may deem appropriate for an amicable settlement. The report shall be deposited with the Secretary-General of the United Nations and shall immediately be transmitted by him to the parties to the dispute.
(2) The report of the commission, including its conclusions or recommendations, shall not be binding upon the parties. Article 8 Termination The conciliation proceedings are terminated when a settlement has been reached, when the parties have accepted or one party has rejected the recommendations of the report by written notification addressed to the Secretary-General of the United Nations, or when a period of three months has expired from the date of transmission of the report to the parties.

Article 9. Fees and expenses
The fees and expenses of the commission shall be borne by the parties to the dispute.

Article 10. Right of parties to modify procedure
The parties to the dispute may by agreement applicable solely to that dispute modify any provision of this Annex.

Section 2. Compulsory submission to conciliation procedure pursuant to Section 3 of Part XV

Article 11. Institution of proceedings
1. Any party to a dispute which, in accordance with Part XV, section 3, may be submitted to conciliation under this section, may institute the proceedings by written notification addressed to the other party or parties to the dispute.
2. Any party to the dispute, notified under paragraph (1), shall be obliged to submit to such proceedings.

Article 12. Failure to reply or to submit to conciliation
The failure of a party or parties to the dispute to reply to notification of institution of proceedings or to submit to such proceedings shall not constitute a bar to the proceedings.

Article 13. Competence
A disagreement as to whether a conciliation commission acting under this section has competence shall be decided by the commission.

Article 14. Application of section 1
Articles 2 to 10 of section 1 of this Annex apply subject to this section.

Annex VI. Statute of the International Tribunal for the Law of the Sea

Article 1. General provisions
(1) The International Tribunal for the Law of the Sea is constituted and shall function in accordance with the provisions of this Convention and this Statute.
(2) The seat of the Tribunal shall be in the Free and Hanseatic City of Hamburg in the Federal Republic of Germany.
(3) The Tribunal may sit and exercise its functions elsewhere whenever it considers this desirable.
(4) A reference of a dispute to the Tribunal shall be governed by the provisions of Parts XI and XV.

Section 1. Organization of the tribunal

Article 2. Composition
(1) The Tribunal shall be composed of a body of 21 independent members, elected from among persons enjoying the highest reputation for fairness and integrity and of recognized competence in the field of the law of the sea.
(2) In the Tribunal as a whole the representation of the principal legal systems of the world and equitable geographical distribution shall be assured.

Article 3. Membership
(1) No two members of the Tribunal may be nationals of the same State. A person who for the purposes of membership in the Tribunal could be regarded as a national of more than one State shall be deemed to be a national of the one in which he ordinarily exercises civil and political rights.
(2) There shall be no fewer than three members from each geographical group as established by the General Assembly of the United Nations.

Article 4. Nominations and elections
(1) Each State Party may nominate not more than two persons having the qualifications prescribed in article 2 of this Annex. The members of the Tribunal shall be elected from the list of persons thus nominated.
(2) At least three months before the date of the election, the Secretary-General of the United Nations in the case of the first election and the Registrar of the Tribunal in the case of subsequent elections shall address a written invitation to the States Parties to submit their nominations for members of the Tribunal within two months. He shall prepare a list in alphabetical order of all the persons thus nominated, with an indication of the States Parties which have nominated them, and shall submit it to the States Parties before the seventh day of the last month before the date of each election.
(3) The first election shall be held within six months of the date of entry into force of this Convention.
(4) The members of the Tribunal shall be elected by secret ballot. Elections shall be held at a meet-

ing of the States Parties convened by the Secretary-General of the United Nations in the case of the first election and by a procedure agreed to by the States Parties in the case of subsequent elections. Two thirds of the States Parties shall constitute a quorum at that meeting. The persons elected to the Tribunal shall be those nominees who obtain the largest number of votes and a two-thirds majority of the States Parties present and voting, provided that such majority includes a majority of the States Parties.

Article 5. Term of office
(1) The members of the Tribunal shall be elected for nine years and may be re-elected; provided, however, that of the members elected at the first election, the terms of seven members shall expire at the end of three years and the terms of seven more members shall expire at the end of six years.
(2) The members of the Tribunal whose terms are to expire at the end of the above-mentioned initial periods of three and six years shall be chosen by lot to be drawn by the Secretary-General of the United Nations immediately after the first election.
(3) The members of the Tribunal shall continue to discharge their duties until their places have been filled. Though replaced, they shall finish any proceedings which they may have begun before the date of their replacement.
(4) In the case of the resignation of a member of the Tribunal, the letter of resignation shall be addressed to the President of the Tribunal. The place becomes vacant on the receipt of that letter.

Article 6. Vacancies
(1) Vacancies shall be filled by the same method as that laid down for the first election, subject to the following provision: the Registrar shall, within one month of the occurrence of the vacancy, proceed to issue the invitations provided for in article 4 of this Annex, and the date of the election shall be fixed by the President of the Tribunal after consultation with the States Parties.
(2) A member of the Tribunal elected to replace a member whose term of office has not expired shall hold office for the remainder of his predecessor's term.

Article 7. Incompatible activities
(1) No member of the Tribunal may exercise any political or administrative function, or associate actively with or be financially interested in any of the operations of any enterprise concerned with the exploration for or exploitation of the resources of the sea or the seabed or other commercial use of the sea or the seabed.
(2) No member of the Tribunal may act as agent, counsel or advocate in any case.
(3) Any doubt on these points shall be resolved by decision of the majority of the other members of the Tribunal present.

Article 8. Conditions relating to participation of members in a particular case
(1) No member of the Tribunal may participate in the decision of any case in which he has previously taken part as agent, counsel or advocate for one of the parties, or as a member of a national or international court or tribunal, or in any other capacity.
(2) If, for some special reason, a member of the Tribunal considers that he should not take part in the decision of a particular case, he shall so inform the President of the Tribunal.
(3) If the President considers that for some special reason one of the members of the Tribunal should not sit in a particular case, he shall give him notice accordingly.
(4) Any doubt on these points shall be resolved by decision of the majority of the other members of the Tribunal present.

Article 9. Consequence of ceasing to fulfil required conditions
If, in the unanimous opinion of the other members of the Tribunal, a member has ceased to fulfil the required conditions, the President of the Tribunal shall declare the seat vacant.

Article 10. Privileges and immunities
The members of the Tribunal, when engaged on the business of the Tribunal, shall enjoy diplomatic privileges and immunities.

Article 11. Solemn declaration by members
Every member of the Tribunal shall, before taking up his duties, make a solemn declaration in open session that he will exercise his powers impartially and conscientiously.

Article 12. President, Vice-President and Registrar
(1) The Tribunal shall elect its President and Vice-President for three years; they may be re-elected.
(2) The Tribunal shall appoint its Registrar and may provide for the appointment of such other officers as may be necessary.

(3) The President and the Registrar shall reside at the seat of the Tribunal.

Article 13. Quorum
(1) All available members of the Tribunal shall sit; a quorum of 11 elected members shall be required to constitute the Tribunal.
(2) Subject to article 17 of this Annex, the Tribunal shall determine which members are available to constitute the Tribunal for the consideration of a particular dispute, having regard to the effective functioning of the chambers as provided for in articles 14 and 15 of this Annex.
(3) All disputes and applications submitted to the Tribunal shall be heard and determined by the Tribunal, unless article 14 of this Annex applies, or the parties request that it shall be dealt with in accordance with article 15 of this Annex.

Article 14. Seabed Disputes Chamber
A Seabed Disputes Chamber shall be established in accordance with the provisions of section 4 of this Annex. Its jurisdiction, powers and functions shall be as provided for in Part XI, section 5.

Article 15. Special chambers
(1) The Tribunal may form such chambers, composed of three or more of its elected members, as it considers necessary for dealing with particular categories of disputes.
(2) The Tribunal shall form a chamber for dealing with a particular dispute submitted to it if the parties so request. The composition of such a chamber shall be determined by the Tribunal with the approval of the parties.
(3) With a view to the speedy dispatch of business, the Tribunal shall form annually a chamber composed of five of its elected members which may hear and determine disputes by summary procedure. Two alternative members shall be selected for the purpose of replacing members who are unable to participate in a particular proceeding.
(4) Disputes shall be heard and determined by the chambers provided for in this article if the parties so request.
(5) A judgment given by any of the chambers provided for in this article and in article 14 of this Annex shall be considered as rendered by the Tribunal.

Article 16. Rules of the Tribunal
The Tribunal shall frame rules for carrying out its functions. In particular it shall lay down rules of procedure.

Article 17. Nationality of members
(1) Members of the Tribunal of the nationality of any of the parties to a dispute shall retain their right to participate as members of the Tribunal.
(2) If the Tribunal, when hearing a dispute, includes upon the bench a member of the nationality of one of the parties, any other party may choose a person to participate as a member of the Tribunal.
(3) If the Tribunal, when hearing a dispute, does not include upon the bench a member of the nationality of the parties, each of those parties may choose a person to participate as a member of the Tribunal.
(4) This article applies to the chambers referred to in articles 14 and 15 of this Annex. In such cases, the President, in consultation with the parties, shall request specified members of the Tribunal forming the chamber, as many as necessary, to give place to the members of the Tribunal of the nationality of the parties concerned, and, failing such, or if they are unable to be present, to the members specially chosen by the parties.
(5) Should there be several parties in the same interest, they shall, for the purpose of the preceding provisions, be considered as one party only. Any doubt on this point shall be settled by the decision of the Tribunal.
(6) Members chosen in accordance with paragraphs (2), (3) and (4) shall fulfil the conditions required by articles 2, 8 and 11 of this Annex. They shall participate in the decision on terms of complete equality with their colleagues.

Article 18. Remuneration of members
(1) Each elected member of the Tribunal shall receive an annual allowance and, for each day on which he exercises his functions, a special allowance, provided that in any year the total sum payable to any member as special allowance shall not exceed the amount of the annual allowance.
(2) The President shall receive a special annual allowance.
(3) The Vice-President shall receive a special allowance for each day on which he acts as President.
(4) The members chosen under article 17 of this Annex, other than elected members of the Tribunal,

shall receive compensation for each day on which they exercise their functions.
(5) The salaries, allowances and compensation shall be determined from time to time at meetings of the States Parties, taking into account the workload of the Tribunal. They may not be decreased during the term of office.
(6) The salary of the Registrar shall be determined at meetings of the States Parties, on the proposal of the Tribunal.
(7) Regulations adopted at meetings of the States Parties shall determine the conditions under which retirement pensions may be given to members of the Tribunal and to the Registrar, and the conditions under which members of the Tribunal and Registrar shall have their travelling expenses refunded.
(8) The salaries, allowances, and compensation shall be free of all taxation.

Article 19. Expenses of the Tribunal
(1) The expenses of the Tribunal shall be borne by the States Parties and by the Authority on such terms and in such a manner as shall be decided at meetings of the States Parties.
(2) When an entity other than a State Party or the Authority is a party to a case submitted to it, the Tribunal shall fix the amount which that party is to contribute towards the expenses of the Tribunal.

Section 2. Competence

Article 20. Access to the Tribunal
(1) The Tribunal shall be open to States Parties.
(2) The Tribunal shall be open to entities other than States Parties in any case expressly provided for in Part XI or in any case submitted pursuant to any other agreement conferring jurisdiction on the Tribunal which is accepted by all the parties to that case.

Article 21. Jurisdiction
The jurisdiction of the Tribunal comprises all disputes and all applications submitted to it in accordance with this Convention and all matters specifically provided for in any other agreement which confers jurisdiction on the Tribunal.

Article 22. Reference of disputes subject to other agreements
If all the parties to a treaty or convention already in force and concerning the subject-matter covered by this Convention so agree, any disputes concerning the interpretation or application of such treaty or convention may, in accordance with such agreement, be submitted to the Tribunal.

Article 23. Applicable law
The Tribunal shall decide all disputes and applications in accordance with article 293.

Section 3. Procedure

Article 24. Institution of proceedings
(1) Disputes are submitted to the Tribunal, as the case may be, either by notification of a special agreement or by written application, addressed to the Registrar. In either case, the subject of the dispute and the parties shall be indicated.
(2) The Registrar shall forthwith notify the special agreement or the application to all concerned.
(3) The Registrar shall also notify all States Parties.

Article 25. Provisional measures
(1) In accordance with article 290, the Tribunal and its Seabed Disputes Chamber shall have the power to prescribe provisional measures.
(2) If the Tribunal is not in session or a sufficient number of members is not available to constitute a quorum, the provisional measures shall be prescribed by the chamber of summary procedure formed under article 15, paragraph (3), of this Annex. Notwithstanding article 15, paragraph (4), of this Annex, such provisional measures may be adopted at the request of any party to the dispute. They shall be subject to review and revision by the Tribunal.

Article 26. Hearing
(1) The hearing shall be under the control of the President or, if he is unable to preside, of the Vice-President. If neither is able to preside, the senior judge present of the Tribunal shall preside.
(2) The hearing shall be public, unless the Tribunal decides otherwise or unless the parties demand that the public be not admitted.

Article 27. Conduct of case
The Tribunal shall make orders for the conduct of the case, decide the form and time in which each party must conclude its arguments, and make all arrangements connected with the taking of evidence.

Article 28. Default
When one of the parties does not appear before the Tribunal or fails to defend its case, the other party may request the Tribunal to continue the proceedings and make its decision. Absence of a party or failure of a party to defend its case shall not constitute a bar to the proceedings. Before making its decision, the Tribunal must satisfy itself not only that it has jurisdiction over the dispute, but also that the claim is well founded in fact and law.

Article 29. Majority for decision
(1) All questions shall be decided by a majority of the members of the Tribunal who are present.
(2) In the event of an equality of votes, the President or the member of the Tribunal who acts in his place shall have a casting vote.

Article 30. Judgment
(1) The judgment shall state the reasons on which it is based.
(2) It shall contain the names of the members of the Tribunal who have taken part in the decision.
(3) If the judgment does not represent in whole or in part the unanimous opinion of the members of the Tribunal, any member shall be entitled to deliver a separate opinion.
(4) The judgment shall be signed by the President and by the Registrar. It shall be read in open court, due notice having been given to the parties to the dispute.

Article 3l. Request to intervene
(1) Should a State Party consider that it has an interest of a legal nature which may be affected by the decision in any dispute, it may submit a request to the Tribunal to be permitted to intervene.
(2) It shall be for the Tribunal to decide upon this request.
(3) If a request to intervene is granted, the decision of the Tribunal in respect of the dispute shall be binding upon the intervening State Party in so far as it relates to matters in respect of which that State Party intervened.

Article 32. Right to intervene in cases of interpretation or application
(1) Whenever the interpretation or application of this Convention is in question, the Registrar shall notify all States Parties forthwith.
(2) Whenever pursuant to article 21 or 22 of this Annex the interpretation or application of an international agreement is in question, the Registrar shall notify all the parties to the agreement.
(3) Every party referred to in paragraphs (1) and (2) has the right to intervene in the proceedings; if it uses this right, the interpretation given by the judgment will be equally binding upon it.

Article 33. Finality and binding force of decisions
(1) The decision of the Tribunal is final and shall be complied with by all the parties to the dispute.
(2) The decision shall have no binding force except between the parties in respect of that particular dispute.
(3) In the event of dispute as to the meaning or scope of the decision, the Tribunal shall construe it upon the request of any party.

Article 34. Costs
Unless otherwise decided by the Tribunal, each party shall bear its own costs.

Section 4. Seabed Disputes Chamber

Article 35. Composition
(1) The Seabed Disputes Chamber referred to in article 14 of this Annex shall be composed of 11 members, selected by a majority of the elected members of the Tribunal from among them.
(2) In the selection of the members of the Chamber, the representation of the principal legal systems of the world and equitable geographical distribution shall be assured. The Assembly of the Authority may adopt recommendations of a general nature relating to such representation and distribution.
(3) The members of the Chamber shall be selected every three years and may be selected for a second term.
(4) The Chamber shall elect its President from among its members, who shall serve for the term for which the Chamber has been selected.
(5) If any proceedings are still pending at the end of any three-year period for which the Chamber has been selected, the Chamber shall complete the proceedings in its original composition.
(6) If a vacancy occurs in the Chamber, the Tribunal shall select a successor from among its elected members, who shall hold office for the remainder of his predecessor's term.
(7) A quorum of seven of the members selected by the Tribunal shall be required to constitute the Chamber.

Article 36. Ad hoc chambers

(1) The Seabed Disputes Chamber shall form an ad hoc chamber, composed of three of its members, for dealing with a particular dispute submitted to it in accordance with article 188, paragraph (1)(b). The composition of such a chamber shall be determined by the Seabed Disputes Chamber with the approval of the parties.

(2) If the parties do not agree on the composition of an ad hoc chamber, each party to the dispute shall appoint one member, and the third member shall be appointed by them in agreement. If they disagree, or if any party fails to make an appointment, the President of the Seabed Disputes Chamber shall promptly make the appointment or appointments from among its members, after consultation with the parties.

(3) Members of the ad hoc chamber must not be in the service of, or nationals of, any of the parties to the dispute.

Article 37. Access

The Chamber shall be open to the States Parties, the Authority and the other entities referred to in Part XI, section 5.

Article 38. Applicable law

In addition to the provisions of article 293, the Chamber shall apply:

(a) the rules, regulations and procedures of the Authority adopted in accordance with this Convention; and

(b) the terms of contracts concerning activities in the Area in matters relating to those contracts.

Article 39. Enforcement of decisions of the Chamber

The decisions of the Chamber shall be enforceable in the territories of the States Parties in the same manner as judgments or orders of the highest court of the State Party in whose territory the enforcement is sought.

Article 40. Applicability of other sections of this Annex

(1) The other sections of this Annex which are not incompatible with this section apply to the Chamber.

(2) In the exercise of its functions relating to advisory opinions, the Chamber shall be guided by the provisions of this Annex relating to procedure before the Tribunal to the extent to which it recognizes them to be applicable.

Section 5. Amendments

Article 41. Amendments

(1) Amendments to this Annex, other than amendments to section 4, may be adopted only in accordance with article 313 or by consensus at a conference convened in accordance with this Convention.

(2) Amendments to section 4 may be adopted only in accordance with article 314.

(3) The Tribunal may propose such amendments to this Statute as it may consider necessary, by written communications to the States Parties for their consideration in conformity with paragraphs (1) and (2).

Annex VII. Arbitration

Article 1. Institution of proceedings

Subject to the provisions of Part XV, any party to a dispute may submit the dispute to the arbitral procedure provided for in this Annex by written notification addressed to the other party or parties to the dispute. The notification shall be accompanied by a statement of the claim and the grounds on which it is based.

Article 2. List of arbitrators

(1) A list of arbitrators shall be drawn up and maintained by the Secretary-General of the United Nations. Every State Party shall be entitled to nominate four arbitrators, each of whom shall be a person experienced in maritime affairs and enjoying the highest reputation for fairness, competence and integrity. The names of the persons so nominated shall constitute the list.

(2) If at any time the arbitrators nominated by a State Party in the list so constituted shall be fewer than four, that State Party shall be entitled to make further nominations as necessary.

(3) The name of an arbitrator shall remain on the list until withdrawn by the State Party which made the nomination, provided that such arbitrator shall continue to serve on any arbitral tribunal to which that arbitrator has been appointed until the completion of the proceedings before that arbitral tribunal.

Article 3. Constitution of arbitral tribunal

For the purpose of proceedings under this Annex, the arbitral tribunal shall, unless the parties otherwise agree, be constituted as follows:

(a) Subject to subparagraph (g), the arbitral tribunal shall consist of five members.

(b) The party instituting the proceedings shall appoint one member to be chosen preferably from the list referred to in article 2 of this Annex, who may be its national. The appointment shall be included in the notification referred to in article 1 of this Annex.

(c) The other party to the dispute shall, within 30 days of receipt of the notification referred to in article 1 of this Annex, appoint one member to be chosen preferably from the list, who may be its national. If the appointment is not made within that period, the party instituting the proceedings may, within two weeks of the expiration of that period, request that the appointment be made in accordance with subparagraph (e).

(d) The other three members shall be appointed by agreement between the parties. They shall be chosen preferably from the list and shall be nationals of third States unless the parties otherwise agree. The parties to the dispute shall appoint the President of the arbitral tribunal from among those three members. If, within 60 days of receipt of the notification referred to in article 1 of this Annex, the parties are unable to reach agreement on the appointment of one or more of the members of the tribunal to be appointed by agreement, or on the appointment of the President, the remaining appointment or appointments shall be made in accordance with subparagraph (e), at the request of a party to the dispute. Such request shall be made within two weeks of the expiration of the aforementioned 60-day period.

(e) Unless the parties agree that any appointment under subparagraphs (c) and (d) be made by a person or a third State chosen by the parties, the President of the International Tribunal for the Law of the Sea shall make the necessary appointments. If the President is unable to act under this subparagraph or is a national of one of the parties to the dispute, the appointment shall be made by the next senior member of the International Tribunal for the Law of the Sea who is available and is not a national of one of the parties. The appointments referred to in this subparagraph shall be made from the list referred to in article 2 of this Annex within a period of 30 days of the receipt of the request and in consultation with the parties. The members so appointed shall be of different nationalities and may not be in the service of, ordinarily resident in the territory of, or nationals of, any of the parties to the dispute.

(f) Any vacancy shall be filled in the manner prescribed for the initial appointment.

(g) Parties in the same interest shall appoint one member of the tribunal jointly by agreement. Where there are several parties having separate interests or where there is disagreement as to whether they are of the same interest, each of them shall appoint one member of the tribunal. The number of members of the tribunal appointed separately by the parties shall always be smaller by one than the number of members of the tribunal to be appointed jointly by the parties.

(h) In disputes involving more than two parties, the provisions of subparagraphs (a) to (f) shall apply to the maximum extent possible. Article 4 Functions of arbitral tribunal An arbitral tribunal constituted under article 3 of this Annex shall function in accordance with this Annex and the other provisions of this Convention. 189 Article 5 Procedure Unless the parties to the dispute otherwise agree, the arbitral tribunal shall determine its own procedure, assuring to each party a full opportunity to be heard and to present its case.

Article 6. Duties of parties to a dispute

The parties to the dispute shall facilitate the work of the arbitral tribunal and, in particular, in accordance with their law and using all means at their disposal, shall:

(a) provide it with all relevant documents, facilities and information; and

(b) enable it when necessary to call witnesses or experts and receive their evidence and to visit the localities to which the case relates.

Article 7. Expenses

Unless the arbitral tribunal decides otherwise because of the particular circumstances of the case, the expenses of the tribunal, including the remuneration of its members, shall be borne by the parties to the dispute in equal shares.

Article 8. Required majority for decisions

Decisions of the arbitral tribunal shall be taken by a majority vote of its members. The absence or abstention of less than half of the members shall not constitute a bar to the tribunal reaching a decision. In the event of an equality of votes, the President shall have a casting vote.

Article 9. Default of appearance

PART I INTERNATIONAL LAW

If one of the parties to the dispute does not appear before the arbitral tribunal or fails to defend its case, the other party may request the tribunal to continue the proceedings and to make its award. Absence of a party or failure of a party to defend its case shall not constitute a bar to the proceedings. Before making its award, the arbitral tribunal must satisfy itself not only that it has jurisdiction over the dispute but also that the claim is well founded in fact and law.

Article 10. Award
The award of the arbitral tribunal shall be confined to the subject-matter of the dispute and state the reasons on which it is based. It shall contain the names of the members who have participated and the date of the award. Any member of the tribunal may attach a separate or dissenting opinion to the award.

Article 11. Finality of award
The award shall be final and without appeal, unless the parties to the dispute have agreed in advance to an appellate procedure. It shall be complied with by the parties to the dispute.

Article 12 Interpretation or implementation of award

(1) Any controversy which may arise between the parties to the dispute as regards the interpretation or manner of implementation of the award may be submitted by either party for decision to the arbitral tribunal which made the award. For this purpose, any vacancy in the tribunal shall be filled in the manner provided for in the original appointments of the members of the tribunal.

(2) Any such controversy may be submitted to another court or tribunal under article 287 by agreement of all the parties to the dispute.

Article 13. Application to entities other than States Parties
The provisions of this Annex shall apply *mutatis mutandis* to any dispute involving entities other than States Parties.

Annex VIII. Special arbitration

Article 1. Institution of proceedings
Subject to Part XV, any party to a dispute concerning the interpretation or application of the articles of this Convention relating to (1) fisheries, (2) protection and preservation of the marine environment, (3) marine scientific research, or (4) navigation, including pollution from vessels and by dumping, may submit the dispute to the special arbitral procedure provided for in this Annex by written notification addressed to the other party or parties to the dispute. The notification shall be accompanied by a statement of the claim and the grounds on which it is based.

Article 2. Lists of experts
(1) A list of experts shall be established and maintained in respect of each of the fields of (1) fisheries, (2) protection and preservation of the marine environment, (3) marine scientific research, and (4) navigation, including pollution from vessels and by dumping.

(2) The lists of experts shall be drawn up and maintained, in the field of fisheries by the Food and Agriculture Organization of the United Nations, in the field of protection and preservation of the marine environment by the United Nations Environment Programme, in the field of marine scientific research by the Intergovernmental Oceanographic Commission, in the field of navigation, including pollution from vessels and by dumping, by the International Maritime Organization, or in each case by the appropriate subsidiary body concerned to which such organization, programme or commission has delegated this function.

(3) Every State Party shall be entitled to nominate two experts in each field whose competence in the legal, scientific or technical aspects of such field is established and generally recognized and who enjoy the highest reputation for fairness and integrity. The names of the persons so nominated in each field shall constitute the appropriate list. 4. If at any time the experts nominated by a State Party in the list so constituted shall be fewer than two, that State Party shall be entitled to make further nominations as necessary. 5. The name of an expert shall remain on the list until withdrawn by the State Party which made the nomination, provided that such expert shall continue to serve on any special arbitral tribunal to which that expert has been appointed until the completion of the proceedings before that special arbitral tribunal.

Article 3. Constitution of special arbitral tribunal
For the purpose of proceedings under this Annex, the special arbitral tribunal shall, unless the parties otherwise agree, be constituted as follows:

(a) Subject to subparagraph (g), the special arbitral tribunal shall consist of five members.

(b) The party instituting the proceedings shall appoint two members to be chosen preferably from the appropriate list or lists referred to in article 2 of this Annex relating to the matters in dispute, one of whom may be its national. The appointments shall be included in the notification referred to in article 1 of this Annex.
(c) The other party to the dispute shall, within 30 days of receipt of the notification referred to in article 1 of this Annex, appoint two members to be chosen preferably from the appropriate list or lists relating to the matters in dispute, one of whom may be its national. If the appointments are not made within that period, the party instituting the proceedings may, within two weeks of the expiration of that period, request that the appointments be made in accordance with subparagraph (e).
(d) The parties to the dispute shall by agreement appoint the President of the special arbitral tribunal, chosen preferably from the appropriate list, who shall be a national of a third State, unless the parties otherwise agree. If, within 30 days of receipt of the notification referred to in article 1 of this Annex, the parties are unable to reach agreement on the appointment of the President, the appointment shall be made in accordance with subparagraph (e), at the request of a party to the dispute. Such request shall be made within two weeks of the expiration of the aforementioned 30-day period.
(e) Unless the parties agree that the appointment be made by a person or a third State chosen by the parties, the Secretary-General of the United Nations shall make the necessary appointments within 30 days of receipt of a request under subparagraphs (c) and (d). The appointments referred to in this subparagraph shall be made from the appropriate list or lists of experts referred to in article 2 of this Annex and in consultation with the parties to the dispute and the 192 appropriate international organization. The members so appointed shall be of different nationalities and may not be in the service of, ordinarily resident in the territory of, or nationals of, any of the parties to the dispute.
(f) Any vacancy shall be filled in the manner prescribed for the initial appointment.
(g) Parties in the same interest shall appoint two members of the tribunal jointly by agreement. Where there are several parties having separate interests or where there is disagreement as to whether they are of the same interest, each of them shall appoint one member of the tribunal.
(h) In disputes involving more than two parties, the provisions of subparagraphs (a) to (f) shall apply to the maximum extent possible.

Article 4. General provisions
Annex VII, articles 4 to 13, apply *mutatis mutandis* to the special arbitration proceedings in accordance with this Annex.

Article 5. Fact finding
1. The parties to a dispute concerning the interpretation or application of the provisions of this Convention relating to (1) fisheries, (2) protection and preservation of the marine environment, (3) marine scientific research, or (4) navigation, including pollution from vessels and by dumping, may at any time agree to request a special arbitral tribunal constituted in accordance with article 3 of this Annex to carry out an inquiry and establish the facts giving rise to the dispute.
2. Unless the parties otherwise agree, the findings of fact of the special arbitral tribunal acting in accordance with paragraph (1), shall be considered as conclusive as between the parties.
3. If all the parties to the dispute so request, the special arbitral tribunal may formulate recommendations which, without having the force of a decision, shall only constitute the basis for a review by the parties of the questions giving rise to the dispute.
4. Subject to paragraph (2), the special arbitral tribunal shall act in accordance with the provisions of this Annex, unless the parties otherwise agree.

Annex IX. Participation by international organizations

Article 1. Use of terms
For the purposes of article 305 and of this Annex, "international organization" means an intergovernmental organization constituted by States to which its member States have transferred competence over matters governed by this Convention, including the competence to enter into treaties in respect of those matters.

Article 2. Signature
An international organization may sign this Convention if a majority of its member States are signatories of this Convention. At the time of signature an international organization shall make a declaration specifying the matters governed by this Convention in respect of which competence has been transferred to that organization by its member States which are signatories, and the nature and extent of that competence.

PART I   INTERNATIONAL LAW

Article 3. Formal confirmation and accession

(1) An international organization may deposit its instrument of formal confirmation or of accession if a majority of its member States deposit or have deposited their instruments of ratification or accession.

(2) The instruments deposited by the international organization shall contain the undertakings and declarations required by articles 4 and 5 of this Annex.

Article 4. Extent of participation and rights and obligations

(1) The instrument of formal confirmation or of accession of an international organization shall contain an undertaking to accept the rights and obligations of States under this Convention in respect of matters relating to which competence has been transferred to it by its member States which are Parties to this Convention.

(2) An international organization shall be a Party to this Convention to the extent that it has competence in accordance with the declarations, communications of information or notifications referred to in article 5 of this Annex.

(3) Such an international organization shall exercise the rights and perform the obligations which its member States which are Parties would otherwise have under this Convention, on matters relating to which competence has been transferred to it by those member States. The member States of that international organization shall not exercise competence which they have transferred to it.

(4) Participation of such an international organization shall in no case entail an increase of the representation to which its member States which are States Parties would otherwise be entitled, including rights in decision-making.

(5) Participation of such an international organization shall in no case confer any rights under this Convention on member States of the organization which are not States Parties to this Convention.

(6) In the event of a conflict between the obligations of an international organization under this Convention and its obligations under the agreement establishing the organization or any acts relating to it, the obligations under this Convention shall prevail.

Article 5. Declarations, notifications and communications

(1) The instrument of formal confirmation or of accession of an international organization shall contain a declaration specifying the matters governed by this Convention in respect of which competence has been transferred to the organization by its member States which are Parties to this Convention.

(2) A member State of an international organization shall, at the time it ratifies or accedes to this Convention or at the time when the organization deposits its instrument of formal confirmation or of accession, whichever is later, make a declaration specifying the matters governed by this Convention in respect of which it has transferred competence to the organization.

(3) States Parties which are member States of an international organization which is a Party to this Convention shall be presumed to have competence over all matters governed by this Convention in respect of which transfers of competence to the organization have not been specifically declared, notified or communicated by those States under this article.

(4) The international organization and its member States which are States Parties shall promptly notify the depositary of this Convention of any changes to the distribution of competence, including new transfers of competence, specified in the declarations under paragraphs (1) and (2).

(5) Any State Party may request an international organization and its member States which are States Parties to provide information as to which, as between the organization and its member States, has competence in respect of any specific question which has arisen. The organization and the member States concerned shall provide this information within a reasonable time. The international organization and the member States may also, on their own initiative, provide this information.

(6) Declarations, notifications and communications of information under this article shall specify the nature and extent of the competence transferred.

Article 6. Responsibility and liability

(1) Parties which have competence under article 5 of this Annex shall have responsibility for failure to comply with obligations or for any other violation of this Convention.

(2) Any State Party may request an international organization or its member States which are States Parties for information as to who has responsibility in respect of any specific matter. The organization and the member States concerned shall provide this information. Failure to provide this information within a reasonable time or the provision of contradictory information shall result in joint and several liability.

Article 7. Settlement of disputes

(1) At the time of deposit of its instrument of formal confirmation or of accession, or at any time thereafter, an international organization shall be free to choose, by means of a written declaration, one

or more of the means for the settlement of disputes concerning the interpretation or application of this Convention, referred to in article 287, paragraph (1)(a), (c) or (d).
(2) Part XV applies *mutatis mutandis* to any dispute between Parties to this Convention, one or more of which are international organizations.
(3) When an international organization and one or more of its member States are joint parties to a dispute, or parties in the same interest, the organization shall be deemed to have accepted the same procedures for the settlement of disputes as the member States; when, however, a member State has chosen only the International Court of Justice under article 287, the organization and the member State concerned shall be deemed to have accepted arbitration in accordance with Annex VII, unless the parties to the dispute otherwise agree. Article 8 Applicability of Part XVII Part XVII applies *mutatis mutandis* to an international organization, except in respect of the following:
(a) the instrument of formal confirmation or of accession of an international organization shall not be taken into account in the application of article 308, paragraph (l);
(b) (i) an international organization shall have exclusive capacity with respect to the application of articles 312 to 315, to the extent that it has competence under article 5 of this Annex over the entire subject-matter of the amendment;
(ii) the instrument of formal confirmation or of accession of an international organization to an amendment, the entire subject-matter over which the international organization has competence under article 5 of this Annex, shall be considered to be the instrument of ratification or accession of each of the member States which are States Parties, for the purposes of applying article 316, paragraphs (1), (2) and (3);
(iii) the instrument of formal confirmation or of accession of the international organization shall not be taken into account in the application of article 316, paragraphs (1) and (2), with regard to all other amendments;
(c) (i) an international organization may not denounce this Convention in accordance with article 317 if any of its member States is a State Party and if it continues to fulfil the qualifications specified in article 1 of this Annex;
(ii) an international organization shall denounce this Convention when none of its member States is a State Party or if the international organization no longer fulfils the qualifications specified in article 1 of this Annex. Such denunciation shall take effect immediately.

Final Act of the Third United Nations Conference on the Law of the Sea (excerpts)

Annex I Resolution I Establishment of the Preparatory Commission for the International Seabed Authority and for the International Tribunal for the Law of the Sea

The Third United Nations Conference on the Law of the Sea,
Having adopted the Convention on the Law of the Sea which provides for the establishment of the International Seabed Authority and the International Tribunal for the Law of the Sea,
Having decided to take all possible measures to ensure the entry into effective operation without undue delay of the Authority and the Tribunal and to make the necessary arrangements for the commencement of their functions,
Having decided that a Preparatory Commission should be established for the fulfilment of these purposes,
Decides as follows:

(l) There is hereby established the Preparatory Commission for the International Seabed Authority and for the International Tribunal for the Law of the Sea. Upon signature of or accession to the Convention by 50 States, the Secretary-General of the United Nations shall convene the Commission, and it shall meet no sooner than 60 days and no later than 90 days thereafter.
(2) The Commission shall consist of the representatives of States and of Namibia, represented by the United Nations Council for Namibia, which have signed the Convention or acceded to it. The representatives of signatories of the Final Act may participate fully in the deliberations of the Commission as observers but shall not be entitled to participate in the taking of decisions.
(3) The Commission shall elect its Chairman and other officers.
(4) The Rules of Procedure of the Third United Nations Conference on the Law of the Sea shall apply *mutatis mutandis* to the adoption of the rules of procedure of the Commission.
(5) The Commission shall:
(a) prepare the provisional agenda for the first session of the Assembly and of the Council and, as appropriate, make recommendations relating to items thereon;

PART I INTERNATIONAL LAW

(b) prepare draft rules of procedure of the Assembly and of the Council;
(c) make recommendations concerning the budget for the first financial period of the Authority;
(d) make recommendations concerning the relationship between the Authority and the United Nations and other international organizations;
(e) make recommendations concerning the Secretariat of the Authority in accordance with the relevant provisions of the Convention;
(f) undertake studies, as necessary, concerning the establishment of the headquarters of the Authority, and make recommendations relating thereto;
(g) prepare draft rules, regulations and procedures, as necessary, to enable the Authority to commence its functions, including draft regulations concerning the financial management and the internal administration of the Authority;
(h) exercise the powers and functions assigned to it by resolution II of the Third United Nations Conference on the Law of the Sea relating to preparatory investment;
(i) undertake studies on the problems which would be encountered by developing land-based producer States likely to be most seriously affected by the production of minerals derived from the Area with a view to minimizing their difficulties and helping them to make the necessary economic adjustment, including studies on the establishment of a compensation fund, and submit recommendations to the Authority thereon.
(6) The Commission shall have such legal capacity as may be necessary for the exercise of its functions and the fulfilment of its purposes as set forth in this resolution.
(7) The Commission may establish such subsidiary bodies as are necessary for the exercise of its functions and shall determine their functions and rules of procedure. It may also make use, as appropriate, of outside sources of expertise in accordance with United Nations practice to facilitate the work of bodies so established.
(8) The Commission shall establish a special commission for the Enterprise and entrust to it the functions referred to in paragraph (12) of resolution II of the Third United Nations Conference on the Law of the Sea relating to preparatory investment. The special commission shall take all measures necessary for the early entry into effective operation of the Enterprise.
(9) The Commission shall establish a special commission on the problems which would be encountered by developing land-based producer States likely to be most seriously affected by the production of minerals derived from the Area and entrust to it the functions referred to in paragraph (5)(i).
(10) The Commission shall prepare a report containing recommendations for submission to the meeting of the States Parties to be convened in accordance with Annex VI, article 4, of the Convention regarding practical arrangements for the establishment of the International Tribunal for the Law of the Sea.
(11) The Commission shall prepare a final report on all matters within its mandate, except as provided in paragraph (10), for the presentation to the Assembly at its first session. Any action which may be taken on the basis of the report must be in conformity with the provisions of the Convention concerning the powers and functions entrusted to the respective organs of the Authority.
(12) The Commission shall meet at the seat of the Authority if facilities are available; it shall meet as often as necessary for the expeditious exercise of its functions.
(13) The Commission shall remain in existence until the conclusion of the first session of the Assembly, at which time its property and records shall be transferred to the Authority.
(14) The expenses of the Commission shall be met from the regular budget of the United Nations, subject to the approval of the General Assembly of the United Nations.
(15) The Secretary-General of the United Nations shall make available to the Commission such secretariat services as may be required.
(16) The Secretary-General of the United Nations shall bring this resolution, in particular paragraphs (14) and (15), to the attention of the General Assembly for necessary action.

Resolution II Governing preparatory investment in pioneer activities relating to polymetallic nodules

The Third United Nations Conference on the Law of the Sea,
Having adopted the Convention on the Law of the Sea (the "Convention"),
Having established by resolution I the Preparatory Commission for the International Seabed Authority and for the International Tribunal for the Law of the Sea (the "Commission") and directed it to prepare draft rules, regulations and procedures, as necessary to enable the Authority to commence its functions, as well as to make recommendations for the early entry into effective operation of the Enterprise,

Desirous of making provision for investments by States and other entities made in a manner compatible with the international regime set forth in Part XI of the Convention and the Annexes relating thereto, before the entry into force of the Convention,
Recognizing the need to ensure that the Enterprise will be provided with the funds, technology and expertise necessary to enable it to keep pace with the States and other entities referred to in the preceding paragraph with respect to activities in the Area,
Decides as follows:

(1) For the purposes of this resolution:
(a) "pioneer investor" refers to:
(i) France, India, Japan and the Union of Soviet Socialist Republics, or a state enterprise of each of those States or one natural or juridical person which possesses the nationality of or is effectively controlled by each of those States, or their nationals, provided that the State concerned signs the Convention and the State or state enterprise or natural or juridical person has expended, before 1 January 1983, an amount equivalent to at least $US 30 million (United States dollars calculated in constant dollars relative to 1982) in pioneer activities and has expended no less than 10 per cent of that amount in the location, survey and evaluation of the area referred to in paragraph (3)(a);
(ii) four entities, whose components being natural or juridical persons 1 possess the nationality of one or more of the following States, or are effectively controlled by one or more of them or their nationals: Belgium, Canada, the Federal Republic of Germany, Italy, Japan, the Netherlands, the United Kingdom of Great Britain and Northern Ireland, and the United States of America, provided that the certifying State or States sign the Convention and the entity concerned has expended, before 1 January 1983, the levels of expenditure for the purpose stated in subparagraph (i);
(iii) any developing State which signs the Convention or any state enterprise or natural or juridical person which possesses the nationality of such State or is effectively controlled by it or its nationals, or any group of the foregoing, which, before 1 January 1985, has expended the levels of expenditure for the purpose stated in subparagraph (i); The rights of the pioneer investor may devolve upon its successor in interest.
(b) "pioneer activities" means undertakings, commitments of financial and other assets, investigations, findings, research, engineering development and other activities relevant to the identification, discovery, and systematic analysis and evaluation of polymetallic nodules and to the determination of the technical and economic feasibility of exploitation. Pioneer activities include:
(i) any at-sea observation and evaluation activity which has as its objective the establishment and documentation of the nature, shape, concentration, location and grade of polymetallic nodules and of the environmental, technical and other appropriate factors which must be taken into account before exploitation;
(ii) the recovery from the Area of polymetallic nodules with a view to the designing, fabricating and testing of equipment which is intended to be used in the exploitation of polymetallic nodules;
(c) "certifying State" means a State which signs the Convention, standing in the same relation to a pioneer investor as would a sponsoring State pursuant to Annex III, article 4, of the Convention and which certifies the levels of expenditure specified in subparagraph (a);
(d) "polymetallic nodules" means one of the resources of the Area consisting of any deposit or accretion of nodules, on or just below the surface of the deep seabed, which contain manganese, nickel, cobalt and copper;
(e) "pioneer area" means an area allocated by the Commission to a pioneer investor for pioneer activities pursuant to this resolution. A pioneer area shall not exceed 150,000 square kilometres. The pioneer investor shall relinquish portions of the pioneer area to revert to the Area, in accordance with the following schedule:
(i) 20 per cent of the area allocated by the end of the third year from the date of the allocation;
(ii) an additional 10 per cent of the area allocated by the end of the fifth year from the date of the allocation;
(iii) an additional 20 per cent of the area allocated or such larger amount as would exceed the exploitation area decided upon by the Authority in its rules, regulations and procedures, after eight years from the date of the allocation of the area or the date of the award of a production authorization, whichever is earlier;
(f) "Area", "Authority", "activities in the Area" and "resources" have the meanings assigned to those terms in the Convention.
(2) As soon as the Commission begins to function, any State which has signed the Convention may apply to the Commission on its behalf or on behalf of any state enterprise or entity or natural or juridical person specified in paragraph (1)(a) for registration as a pioneer investor. The Commission shall register the applicant as a pioneer investor if the application:
(a) is accompanied, in the case of a State which has signed the Convention, by a statement certifying

the level of expenditure made in accordance with paragraph (1)(a), and, in all other cases, a certificate concerning such level of expenditure issued by a certifying State or States; and
(b) is in conformity with the other provisions of this resolution, including paragraph (5).
(3) (a) Every application shall cover a total area which need not be a single continuous area, sufficiently large and of sufficient estimated commercial value to allow two mining operations. The application shall indicate the coordinates of the area defining the total area and dividing it into two parts of equal estimated commercial value and shall contain all the data available to the applicant with respect to both parts of the area. Such data shall include, inter alia, information relating to mapping, testing, the density of polymetallic nodules and their metal content. In dealing with such data, the Commission and its staff shall act in accordance with the relevant provisions of the Convention and its Annexes concerning the confidentiality of data.
(b) Within 45 days of receiving the data required by subparagraph (a), the Commission shall designate the part of the area which is to be reserved in accordance with the 201 Convention for the conduct of activities in the Area by the Authority through the Enterprise or in association with developing States. The other part of the area shall be allocated to the pioneer investor as a pioneer area.
(4) No pioneer investor may be registered in respect of more than one pioneer area. In the case of a pioneer investor which is made up of two or more components, none of such components may apply to be registered as a pioneer investor in its own right or under paragraph (1)(a)(iii).
(5) (a) Any State which has signed the Convention and which is a prospective certifying State shall ensure, before making applications to the Commission under paragraph (2), that areas in respect of which applications are made do not overlap one another or areas previously allocated as pioneer areas. The States concerned shall keep the Commission currently and fully informed of any efforts to resolve conflicts with respect to overlapping claims and of the results thereof.
(b) Certifying States shall ensure, before the entry into force of the Convention, that pioneer activities are conducted in a manner compatible with it.
(c) The prospective certifying States, including all potential claimants, shall resolve their conflicts as required under subparagraph (a) by negotiations within a reasonable period. If such conflicts have not been resolved by 1 March 1983, the prospective certifying States shall arrange for the submission of all such claims to binding arbitration in accordance with UNCITRAL Arbitration Rules to commence not later than 1 May 1983 and to be completed by 1 December 1984. If one of the States concerned does not wish to participate in the arbitration, it shall arrange for a juridical person of its nationality to represent it in the arbitration. The arbitral tribunal may, for good cause, extend the deadline for the making of the award for one or more 30-day periods.
(d) In determining the issue as to which applicant involved in a conflict shall be awarded all or part of each area in conflict, the arbitral tribunal shall find a solution which is fair and equitable, having regard, with respect to each applicant involved in the conflict, to the following factors:
(i) the deposit of the list of relevant coordinates with the prospective certifying State or States not later than the date of adoption of the Final Act or 1 January 1983, whichever is earlier; (ii) the continuity and extent of past activities relevant to each area in conflict and to the application area of which it is a part;
(iii) the date on which each pioneer investor concerned or predecessor in interest or component organization thereof commenced activities at sea in the application area;
(iv) the financial cost of activities measured in constant United States dollars relevant to each area in conflict and to the application area of which it is a part; and
(v) the time when those activities were carried out and the quality of activities.
(6) A pioneer investor registered pursuant to this resolution shall, from the date of registration, have the exclusive right to carry out pioneer activities in the pioneer area allocated to it.
(7) (a) Every applicant for registration as a pioneer investor shall pay to the Commission a fee of $US 250,000. When the pioneer investor applies to the Authority for a plan of work for exploration and exploitation the fee referred to in Annex III, article 13, paragraph (2), of the Convention shall be $US 250,000.
(b) Every registered pioneer investor shall pay an annual fixed fee of $US 1 million commencing from the date of the allocation of the pioneer area. The payments shall be made by the pioneer investor to the Authority upon the approval of its plan of work for exploration and exploitation. The financial arrangements undertaken pursuant to such plan of work shall be adjusted to take account of the payments made pursuant to this paragraph.
(c) Every registered pioneer investor shall agree to incur periodic expenditures, with respect to the pioneer area allocated to it, until approval of its plan of work pursuant to paragraph (8), of an amount to be determined by the Commission. The amount should be reasonably related to the size of the

pioneer area and the expenditures which would be expected of a bona fide operator who intends to bring that area into commercial production within a reasonable time.

(8) (a) Within six months of the entry into force of the Convention and certification by the Commission in accordance with paragraph (11), of compliance with this resolution, the pioneer investor so registered shall apply to the Authority for approval of a plan of work for exploration and exploitation, in accordance with the Convention. The plan of work in respect of such application shall comply with and be governed by the relevant provisions of the Convention and the rules, regulations and procedures of the Authority, including those on the operational requirements, the financial requirements and the undertakings concerning the transfer of technology. Accordingly, the Authority shall approve such application.

(b) When an application for approval of a plan of work is submitted by an entity other than a State, pursuant to subparagraph (a), the certifying State or States shall be deemed to be the sponsoring State for the purposes of Annex III, article 4, of the Convention, and shall thereupon assume such obligations.

(c) No plan of work for exploration and exploitation shall be approved unless the certifying State is a Party to the Convention. In the case of the entities referred to in paragraph (1)(a)(ii), the plan of work for exploration and exploitation shall not be approved unless all the States whose natural or juridical persons comprise those entities are Parties to the Convention. If any such State fails to ratify the Convention within six months after it has received a notification from the Authority that an application by it, or sponsored by it, is pending, its status as a pioneer investor or certifying State, as the case may be, shall terminate, unless the Council, by a majority of three fourths of its members present and voting, decides to postpone the terminal date for a period not exceeding six months.

(9) (a) In the allocation of production authorizations, in accordance with article 151 and Annex III, article 7, of the Convention, the pioneer investors who have obtained approval of plans of work for exploration and exploitation shall have priority over all applicants other than the Enterprise which shall be entitled to production authorizations for two mine sites including that referred to in article 151, paragraph (5), of the Convention. After each of the pioneer investors has obtained production authorization for its first mine site, the priority for the Enterprise contained in Annex III, article 7, paragraph (6), of the Convention shall apply. (b) Production authorizations shall be issued to each pioneer investor within 30 days of the date on which that pioneer investor notifies the Authority that it will commence commercial production within five years. If a pioneer investor is unable to begin production within the period of five years for reasons beyond its control, it shall apply to the Legal and Technical Commission for an extension of time. That Commission shall grant the extension of time, for a period not exceeding five years and not subject to further extension, if it is satisfied that the pioneer investor cannot begin on an economically viable basis at the time originally planned. Nothing in this subparagraph shall prevent the Enterprise or any other pioneer applicant, who has notified the Authority that it will commence commercial production within five years, from being given a priority over any applicant who has obtained an extension of time under this subparagraph.

(c) If the Authority, upon being given notice, pursuant to subparagraph (b), determines that the commencement of commercial production within five years would exceed the production ceiling in article 151, paragraphs (2) to (7), of the Convention, the applicant shall hold a priority over any other applicant for the award of the next production authorization allowed by the production ceiling.

(d) If two or more pioneer investors apply for production authorizations to begin commercial production at the same time and article 151, paragraphs (2) to (7), of the Convention, would not permit all such production to commence simultaneously, the Authority shall notify the pioneer investors concerned. Within three months of such notification, they shall decide whether and, if so, to what extent they wish to apportion the allowable tonnage among themselves.

(e) If, pursuant to subparagraph (d), the pioneer investors concerned decide not to apportion the available production among themselves they shall agree on an order of priority for production authorizations and all subsequent applications for production authorizations will be granted after those referred to in this subparagraph have been approved.

(f) If, pursuant to subparagraph (d), the pioneer investors concerned decide to apportion the available production among themselves, the Authority shall award each of them a production authorization for such lesser quantity as they have agreed. In each case the stated production requirements of the applicant will be approved and their full production will be allowed as soon as the production ceiling admits of additional capacity sufficient for the applicants involved in the competition. All subsequent applications for production authorizations will only be granted after the requirements of this subparagraph have been met and the applicant is no longer subject to the reduction of production provided for in this subparagraph.

(g) If the parties fail to reach agreement within the stated time period, the matter shall be decided

PART I INTERNATIONAL LAW

immediately by the means provided for in paragraph (5)(c) in accordance with the criteria set forth in Annex III, article 7, paragraphs (3) and (5), of the Convention.

(10) (a) Any rights acquired by entities or natural or juridical persons which possess the nationality of or are effectively controlled by a State or States whose status as certifying State has been terminated, shall lapse unless the pioneer investor changes its nationality and sponsorship within six months of the date of such termination, as provided for in subparagraph (b).

(b) A pioneer investor may change its nationality and sponsorship from that existing at the time of its registration as a pioneer investor to that of any State Party to the Convention which has effective control over the pioneer investor in terms of paragraph l(a).

(c) Changes of nationality and sponsorship pursuant to this paragraph shall not affect any right or priority conferred on a pioneer investor pursuant to paragraphs (6) and (8).

(11) The Commission shall:

(a) provide each pioneer investor with the certificate of compliance with the provisions of this resolution referred to in paragraph 8; and

(b) include in its final report required by paragraph (11) of resolution I of the Conference details of all registrations of pioneer investors and allocations of pioneer areas pursuant to this resolution.

(12) In order to ensure that the Enterprise is able to carry out activities in the Area in such a manner as to keep pace with States and other entities:

(a) every registered pioneer investor shall:

(i) carry out exploration, at the request of the Commission, in the area reserved, pursuant to paragraph (3) in connection with its application, for activities in the Area by the Authority through the Enterprise or in association with developing States, on the basis that the costs so incurred plus interest thereon at the rate of 10 per cent per annum shall be reimbursed;

(ii) provide training at all levels for personnel designated by the Commission;

(iii) undertake before the entry into force of the Convention, to perform the obligations prescribed in the Convention relating to transfer of technology;

(b) every certifying State shall:

(i) ensure that the necessary funds are made available to the Enterprise in a timely manner in accordance with the Convention, upon its entry into force; and

(ii) report periodically to the Commission on the activities carried out by it, by its entities or natural or juridical persons.

(13) The Authority and its organs shall recognize and honour the rights and obligations arising from this resolution and the decisions of the Commission taken pursuant to it.

(14) Without prejudice to paragraph (13), this resolution shall have effect until the entry into force of the Convention.

(15) Nothing in this resolution shall derogate from Annex III, article 6, paragraph (3)(c), of the Convention.

Resolution III

The Third United Nations Conference on the Law of the Sea,
Having regard to the Convention on the Law of the Sea, Bearing in mind the Charter of the United Nations, in particular Article 73, (1) Declares that:

(1) (a) In the case of a territory whose people have not attained full independence or other self-governing status recognized by the United Nations, or a territory under colonial domination, provisions concerning rights and interests under the Convention shall be implemented for the benefit of the people of the territory with a view to promoting their well-being and development.

(b) Where a dispute exists between States over the sovereignty of a territory to which this resolution applies, in respect of which the United Nations has recommended specific means of settlement, there shall be consultations between the parties to that dispute regarding the exercise of the rights referred to in subparagraph (a). In such consultations the interests of the people of the territory concerned shall be a fundamental consideration. Any exercise of those rights shall take into account the relevant resolutions of the United Nations and shall be without prejudice to the position of any party to the dispute. The States concerned shall make every effort to enter into provisional arrangements of a practical nature and shall not jeopardize or hamper the reaching of a final settlement of the dispute.

(2) Requests the Secretary-General of the United Nations to bring this resolution to the attention of all Members of the United Nations and the other participants in the Conference, as well as the principal organs of the United Nations, and to request their compliance with it.

UN CONVENTION ON THE LAW OF THE SEA

Resolution IV

The Third United Nations Conference on the Law of the Sea,
Bearing in mind that national liberation movements have been invited to participate in the Conference as observers in accordance with rule 62 of its rules of procedure,
Decides that the national liberation movements, which have been participating in the Third United Nations Conference on the Law of the Sea, shall be entitled to sign the Final Act of the Conference, in their capacity as observers.

Annex II Statement of understanding concerning a specific method to be used in establishing the outer edge of the continental margin

The Third United Nations Conference on the Law of the Sea,
Considering the special characteristics of a State's continental margin where:

(1) the average distance at which the 200 metre isobath occurs is not more than 20 nautical miles;
(2) the greater proportion of the sedimentary rock of the continental margin lies beneath the rise; and
Taking into account the inequity that would result to that State from the application to its continental margin of article 76 of the Convention, in that, the mathematical average of the thickness of sedimentary rock along a line established at the maximum distance permissible in accordance with the provisions of paragraph (4)(a)(i) and (ii) of that article as representing the entire outer edge of the continental margin would not be less than 3.5 kilometres; and that more than half of the margin would be excluded thereby; Recognizes that such State may, notwithstanding the provisions of article 76, establish the outer edge of its continental margin by straight lines not exceeding 60 nautical miles in length connecting fixed points, defined by latitude and longitude, at each of which the thickness of sedimentary rock is not less than 1 kilometre, Where a State establishes the outer edge of its continental margin by applying the method set forth in the preceding paragraph of this statement, this method may also be utilized by a neighbouring State for delineating the outer edge of its continental margin on a common geological feature, where its outer edge would lie on such feature on a line established at the maximum distance permissible in accordance with article 76, paragraph (4)(a)(i) and (ii), along which the mathematical average of the thickness of sedimentary rock is not less than 3.5 kilometres,
The Conference requests the Commission on the Limits of the Continental Shelf set up pursuant to Annex II of the Convention, to be governed by the terms of this Statement when making its recommendations on matters related to the establishment of the outer edge of the continental margins of these States in the southern part of the Bay of Bengal.

Annex VI Resolution on development of national marine science, technology and ocean service infrastructures

The Third United Nations Conference on the Law of the Sea,
Recognizing that the Convention on the Law of the Sea is intended to establish a new regime for the seas and oceans which will contribute to the realization of a just and equitable international economic order through making provision for the peaceful use of ocean space, the equitable and efficient management and utilization of its resources, and the study, protection and preservation of the marine environment,
Bearing in mind that the new regime must take into account, in particular, the special needs and interests of the developing countries, whether coastal, land-locked, or geographically disadvantaged,
Aware of the rapid advances being made in the field of marine science and technology, and the need for the developing countries, whether coastal, land-locked, or geographically disadvantaged, to share in these achievements if the aforementioned goals are to be met,
Convinced that, unless urgent measures are taken, the marine scientific and technological gap between the developed and the developing countries will widen further and thus endanger the very foundations of the new regime,
Believing that optimum utilization of the new opportunities for social and economic development offered by the new regime will be facilitated through action at the national and international level aimed at strengthening national capabilities in marine science, technology and ocean services, particularly in the developing countries, with a view to ensuring the rapid absorption and efficient application of technology and scientific knowledge available to them,

PART I   INTERNATIONAL LAW

Considering that national and regional marine scientific and technological centres would be the principal institutions through which States and, in particular, the developing countries, foster and conduct marine scientific research, and receive and disseminate marine technology,
Recognizing the special role of the competent international organizations envisaged by the Convention on the Law of the Sea, especially in relation to the establishment and development of national and regional marine scientific and technological centres,
Noting that present efforts undertaken within the United Nations system in training, education and assistance in the field of marine science and technology and ocean services are far below current requirements and would be particularly inadequate to meet the demands generated through operation of the Convention on the Law of the Sea,
Welcoming recent initiatives within international organizations to promote and coordinate their major international assistance programmes aimed at strengthening marine science infrastructures in developing countries,

(1) Calls upon all Member States to determine appropriate priorities in their development plans for the strengthening of their marine science, technology and ocean services;
(2) Calls upon the developing countries to establish programmes for the promotion of technical cooperation among themselves in the field of marine science, technology and ocean service development;
(3) Urges the industrialized countries to assist the developing countries in the preparation and implementation of their marine science, technology and ocean service development programmes;
(4) Recommends that the World Bank, the regional banks, the United Nations Development Programme, the United Nations Financing System for Science and Technology and other multilateral funding agencies augment and coordinate their operations for the provision of funds to developing countries for the preparation and implementation of major programmes of assistance in strengthening their marine science, technology and ocean services;
(5) Recommends that all competent international organizations within the United Nations system expand programmes within their respective fields of competence for assistance to developing countries in the field of marine science, technology and ocean services and coordinate their efforts on a system-wide basis in the implementation of such programmes, paying particular attention to the special needs of the developing countries, whether coastal, land-locked or geographically disadvantaged;
(6) Requests the Secretary-General of the United Nations to transmit this resolution to the General Assembly at its thirty-seventh session.

VIENNA CONVENTION ON THE LAW OF TREATIES 1969

Vienna Convention on the Law of Treaties 1969 with Annex, Vienna 23 May 1969, Entry into Force 27 January 1980,
Trb 1972 Nr. 51

The States Parties to the present Convention,
Considering the fundamental role of treaties in the history of international relations,
Recognizing the ever-increasing importance of treaties as a source of international law and as a means of developing peaceful cooperation among nations, whatever their constitutional and social systems,
Noting that the principles of free consent and of good faith and the pacta sunt servanda rule are universally recognized,
Affirming that disputes concerning treaties, like other international disputes, should be settled by peaceful means and in conformity with the principles of justice and international law,
Recalling the determination of the peoples of the United Nations to establish conditions under which justice and respect for the obligations arising from treaties can be maintained,
Having in mind the principles of international law embodied in the Charter of the United Nations, such as the principles of the equal rights and self-determination of peoples, of the sovereign equality and independence of all States, of non-interference in the domestic affairs of States, of the prohibition of the threat or use of force and of universal respect for, and observance of, human rights and fundamental freedoms for all,
Believing that the codification and progressive development of the law of treaties achieved in the present Convention will promote the purposes of the United Nations set forth in the Charter, namely, the maintenance of international peace and security, the development of friendly relations and the achievement of cooperation among nations,
Affirming that the rules of customary international law will continue to govern questions not regulated by the provisions of the present Convention,
Have agreed as follows:

Part I. Introduction

Article 1. Scope of the present Convention
The present Convention applies to treaties between States.

Article 2. Use of terms
(1) For the purposes of the present Convention:
(a) "treaty" means an international agreement concluded between States in written form and governed by international law, whether embodied in a single instrument or in two or more related instruments and whatever its particular designation;
(b) "ratification", "acceptance", "approval" and "accession" mean in each case the international act so named whereby a State establishes on the international plane its consent to be bound by a treaty;
(c) "full powers" means a document emanating from the competent authority of a State designating a person or persons to represent the State for negotiating, adopting or authenticating the text of a treaty, for expressing the consent of the State to be bound by a treaty, or for accomplishing any other act with respect to a treaty;
(d) "reservation" means a unilateral statement, however phrased or named, made by a State, when signing, ratifying, accepting, approving or acceding to a treaty, whereby it purports to exclude or to modify the legal effect of certain provisions of the treaty in their application to that State;
(e) "negotiating State" means a State which took part in the drawing up and adoption of the text of the treaty;
(f) "contracting State" means a State which has consented to be bound by the treaty, whether or not the treaty has entered into force;
(g) "party" means a State which has consented to be bound by the treaty and for which the treaty is in force;
(h) "third State" means a State not a party to the treaty;
(i) "international organization" means an intergovernmental organization.
(2) The provisions of paragraph (1) regarding the use of terms in the present Convention are without prejudice to the use of those terms or to the meanings which may be given to them in the internal law of any State.

Article 3. International agreements not within the scope of the present Convention
The fact that the present Convention does not apply to international agreements concluded between States and other subjects of international law or between such other subjects of international law, or to international agreements not in written form, shall not affect:

(a) the legal force of such agreements;
(b) the application to them of any of the rules set forth in the present Convention to which they would be subject under international law independently of the Convention;
(c) the application of the Convention to the relations of States as between themselves under international agreements to which other subjects of international law are also parties.

Article 4. Non-retroactivity of the present Convention
Without prejudice to the application of any rules set forth in the present Convention to which treaties would be subject under international law independently of the Convention, the Convention applies only to treaties which are concluded by States after the entry into force of the present Convention with regard to such States.

Article 5. Treaties constituting international organizations and treaties adopted within an international organization
The present Convention applies to any treaty which is the constituent instrument of an international organization and to any treaty adopted within an international organization without prejudice to any relevant rules of the organization.

Part II. Conclusion and entry into force of treaties

Section 1. Conclusion of treaties

Article 6. Capacity of States to conclude treaties
Every State possesses capacity to conclude treaties.

Article 7. Full powers
1. A person is considered as representing a State for the purpose of adopting or authenticating the text of a treaty or for the purpose of expressing the consent of the State to be bound by a treaty if:
(a) he produces appropriate full powers; or
(b) it appears from the practice of the States concerned or from other circumstances that their intention was to consider that person as representing the State for such purposes and to dispense with full powers.
(2) In virtue of their functions and without having to produce full powers, the following are considered as representing their State:
(a) Heads of State, Heads of Government and Ministers for Foreign Affairs, for the purpose of performing all acts relating to the conclusion of a treaty;
(b) heads of diplomatic missions, for the purpose of adopting the text of a treaty between the accrediting State and the State to which they are accredited;
(c) representatives accredited by States to an international conference or to an international organization or one of its organs, for the purpose of adopting the text of a treaty in that conference, organization or organ.

Article 8. Subsequent confirmation of an act performed without authorization
An act relating to the conclusion of a treaty performed by a person who cannot be considered under article 7 as authorized to represent a State for that purpose is without legal effect unless afterwards confirmed by that State.

Article 9. Adoption of the text
(1) The adoption of the text of a treaty takes place by the consent of all the States participating in its drawing up except as provided in paragraph (2).
(2) The adoption of the text of a treaty at an international conference takes place by the vote of two thirds of the States present and voting, unless by the same majority they shall decide to apply a different rule.

Article 10. Authentication of the text
The text of a treaty is established as authentic and definitive:
(a) by such procedure as may be provided for in the text or agreed upon by the States participating in its drawing up; or
(b) failing such procedure, by the signature, signature ad referendum or initialling by the representatives of those States of the text of the treaty or of the Final Act of a conference incorporating the text.

Article 11. Means of expressing consent to be bound by a treaty
The consent of a State to be bound by a treaty may be expressed by signature, exchange of instruments constituting a treaty, ratification, acceptance, approval or accession, or by any other means if so agreed.

Article 12. Consent to be bound by a treaty expressed by signature

(1) The consent of a State to be bound by a treaty is expressed by the signature of its representative when:
(a) the treaty provides that signature shall have that effect;
(b) it is otherwise established that the negotiating States were agreed that signature should have that effect; or
(c) the intention of the State to give that effect to the signature appears from the full powers of its representative or was expressed during the negotiation.
(2) For the purposes of paragraph (1):
(a) the initialling of a text constitutes a signature of the treaty when it is established that the negotiating States so agreed;
(b) the signature ad referendum of a treaty by a representative, if confirmed by his State, constitutes a full signature of the treaty.

Article 13. Consent to be bound by a treaty expressed by an exchange of instruments constituting a treaty

The consent of States to be bound by a treaty constituted by instruments exchanged between them is expressed by that exchange when:
(a) the instruments provide that their exchange shall have that effect; or
(b) it is otherwise established that those States were agreed that the exchange of instruments should have that effect.

Article 14. Consent to be bound by a treaty expressed by ratification, acceptance or approval

(1) The consent of a State to be bound by a treaty is expressed by ratification when:
(a) the treaty provides for such consent to be expressed by means of ratification;
(b) it is otherwise established that the negotiating States were agreed that ratification should be required;
(c) the representative of the State has signed the treaty subject to ratification; or
(d) the intention of the State to sign the treaty subject to ratification appears from the full powers of its representative or was expressed during the negotiation.
(2) The consent of a State to be bound by a treaty is expressed by acceptance or approval under conditions similar to those which apply to ratification.

Article 15. Consent to be bound by a treaty expressed by accession

The consent of a State to be bound by a treaty is expressed by accession when:
(a) the treaty provides that such consent may be expressed by that State by means of accession;
(b) it is otherwise established that the negotiating States were agreed that such consent may be expressed by that State by means of accession; or
(c) all the parties have subsequently agreed that such consent may be expressed by that State by means of accession.

Article 16. Exchange or deposit of instruments of ratification, acceptance, approval or accession

Unless the treaty otherwise provides, instruments of ratification, acceptance, approval or accession establish the consent of a State to be bound by a treaty upon:
(a) their exchange between the contracting States;
(b) their deposit with the depositary; or
(c) their notification to the contracting States or to the depositary, if so agreed.

Article 17. Consent to be bound by part of a treaty and choice of differing provisions

(1) Without prejudice to articles 19 to 23, the consent of a State to be bound by part of a treaty is effective only if the treaty so permits or the other contracting States so agree.
(2) The consent of a State to be bound by a treaty which permits a choice between differing provisions is effective only if it is made clear to which of the provisions the consent relates.

Article 18. Obligation not to defeat the object and purpose of a treaty prior to its entry into force

A State is obliged to refrain from acts which would defeat the object and purpose of a treaty when:
(a) it has signed the treaty or has exchanged instruments constituting the treaty subject to ratification, acceptance or approval, until it shall have made its intention clear not to become a party to the treaty; or
(b) it has expressed its consent to be bound by the treaty, pending the entry into force of the treaty and provided that such entry into force is not unduly delayed.

PART I   INTERNATIONAL LAW

Section 2. Reservations

Article 19. Formulation of reservations

A State may, when signing, ratifying, accepting, approving or acceding to a treaty, formulate a reservation unless:
(a) the reservation is prohibited by the treaty;
(b) the treaty provides that only specified reservations, which do not include the reservation in question, may be made; or
(c) in cases not failing under subparagraphs (a) and (b), the reservation is incompatible with the object and purpose of the treaty.

Article 20. Acceptance of and objection to reservations

(1) A reservation expressly authorized by a treaty does not require any subsequent acceptance by the other contracting States unless the treaty so provides.
(2) When it appears from the limited number of the negotiating States and the object and purpose of a treaty that the application of the treaty in its entirety between all the parties is an essential condition of the consent of each one to be bound by the treaty, a reservation requires acceptance by all the parties.
(3) When a treaty is a constituent instrument of an international organization and unless it otherwise provides, a reservation requires the acceptance of the competent organ of that organization.
(4) In cases not falling under the preceding paragraphs and unless the treaty otherwise provides:
(a) acceptance by another contracting State of a reservation constitutes the reserving State a party to the treaty in relation to that other State if or when the treaty is in force for those States;
(b) an objection by another contracting State to a reservation does not preclude the entry into force of the treaty as between the objecting and reserving States unless a contrary intention is definitely expressed by the objecting State;
(c) an act expressing a State's consent to be bound by the treaty and containing a reservation is effective as soon as at least one other contracting State has accepted the reservation. 5. For the purposes of paragraphs (2) and (4) and unless the treaty otherwise provides, a reservation is considered to have been accepted by a State if it shall have raised no objection to the reservation by the end of a period of twelve months after it was notified of the reservation or by the date on which it expressed its consent to be bound by the treaty, whichever is later.

Article 21. Legal effects of reservations and of objections to reservations

(1) A reservation established with regard to another party in accordance with articles 19, 20 and 23:
(a) modifies for the reserving State in its relations with that other party the provisions of the treaty to which the reservation relates to the extent of the reservation; and
(b) modifies those provisions to the same extent for that other party in its relations with the reserving State.
(2) The reservation does not modify the provisions of the treaty for the other parties to the treaty inter se.
(3) When a State objecting to a reservation has not opposed the entry into force of the treaty between itself and the reserving State, the provisions to which the reservation relates do not apply as between the two States to the extent of the reservation.

Article 22. Withdrawal of reservations and of objections to reservations

(1) Unless the treaty otherwise provides, a reservation may be withdrawn at any time and the consent of a State which has accepted the reservation is not required for its withdrawal.
(2) Unless the treaty otherwise provides, an objection to a reservation may be withdrawn at any time.
(3) Unless the treaty otherwise provides, or it is otherwise agreed:
(a) the withdrawal of a reservation becomes operative in relation to another contracting State only when notice of it has been received by that State;
(b) the withdrawal of an objection to a reservation becomes operative only when notice of it has been received by the State which formulated the reservation.

Article 23. Procedure regarding reservations

(1) A reservation, an express acceptance of a reservation and an objection to a reservation must be formulated in writing and communicated to the contracting States and other States entitled to become parties to the treaty.
(2) If formulated when signing the treaty subject to ratification, acceptance or approval, a reservation must be formally confirmed by the reserving State when expressing its consent to be bound by the treaty. In such a case the reservation shall be considered as having been made on the date of its confirmation.

(3) An express acceptance of, or an objection to, a reservation made previously to confirmation of the reservation does not itself require confirmation.
(4) The withdrawal of a reservation or of an objection to a reservation must be formulated in writing.

Section 3. Entry into force and provisional, application of treaties

Article 24. Entry into force
(1) A treaty enters into force in such manner and upon such date as it may provide or as the negotiating States may agree.
(2) Failing any such provision or agreement, a treaty enters into force as soon as consent to be bound by the treaty has been established for all the negotiating States.
(3) When the consent of a State to be bound by a treaty is established on a date after the treaty has come into force, the treaty enters into force for that State on that date, unless the treaty otherwise provides.
(4) The provisions of a treaty regulating the authentication of its text, the establishment of the consent of States to be bound by the treaty, the manner or date of its entry into force, reservations, the functions of the depositary and other matters arising necessarily before the entry into force of the treaty apply from the time of the adoption of its text. 10

Article 25. Provisional application
(1) A treaty or a part of a treaty is applied provisionally pending its entry into force if:
(a) the treaty itself so provides; or
(b) the negotiating States have in some other manner so agreed.
(2) Unless the treaty otherwise provides or the negotiating States have otherwise agreed, the provisional application of a treaty or a part of a treaty with respect to a State shall be terminated if that State notifies the other States between which the treaty is being applied provisionally of its intention not to become a party to the treaty.

Part III. Observance, application and interpretation of treaties

Section 1. Observance of treaties

Article 26. *"Pacta sunt servanda"*
Every treaty in force is binding upon the parties to it and must be performed by them in good faith.

Article 27. Internal law and observance of treaties
A party may not invoke the provisions of its internal law as justification for its failure to perform a treaty. This rule is without prejudice to article 46.

Section 2. Application of treaties

Article 28. Non-retroactivity of treaties
Unless a different intention appears from the treaty or is otherwise established, its provisions do not bind a party in relation to any act or fact which took place or any situation which ceased to exist before the date of the entry into force of the treaty with respect to that party.

Article 29. Territorial scope of treaties
Unless a different intention appears from the treaty or is otherwise established, a treaty is binding upon each party in respect of its entire territory.

Article 30. Application of successive treaties relating to the same subject matter
(1) Subject to Article 103 of the Charter of the United Nations, the rights and obligations of States Parties to successive treaties relating to the same subject matter shall be determined in accordance with the following paragraphs.
(2) When a treaty specifies that it is subject to, or that it is not to be considered as incompatible with, an earlier or later treaty, the provisions of that other treaty prevail.
(3) When all the parties to the earlier treaty are parties also to the later treaty but the earlier treaty is not terminated or suspended in operation under article 59, the earlier treaty applies only to the extent that its provisions are compatible with those of the later treaty.
(4) When the parties to the later treaty do not include all the parties to the earlier one: (a) as between States Parties to both treaties the same rule applies as in paragraph (3); (b) as between a State party to both treaties and a State party to only one of the treaties, the treaty to which both States are parties governs their mutual rights and obligations.
(5) Paragraph (4) is without prejudice to article 41, or to any question of the termination or suspen-

sion of the operation of a treaty under article 60 or to any question of responsibility which may arise for a State from the conclusion or application of a treaty the provisions of which are incompatible with its obligations towards another State under another treaty.

Section 3. Interpretation of treaties

Article 31. General rule of interpretation

(1) A treaty shall be interpreted in good faith in accordance with the ordinary meaning to be given to the terms of the treaty in their context and in the light of its object and purpose.

(2) The context for the purpose of the interpretation of a treaty shall comprise, in addition to the text, including its preamble and annexes:

(a) any agreement relating to the treaty which was made between all the parties in connection with the conclusion of the treaty;

(b) any instrument which was made by one or more parties in connection with the conclusion of the treaty and accepted by the other parties as an instrument related to the treaty.

(3) There shall be taken into account, together with the context:

(a) any subsequent agreement between the parties regarding the interpretation of the treaty or the application of its provisions;

(b) any subsequent practice in the application of the treaty which establishes the agreement of the parties regarding its interpretation;

(c) any relevant rules of international law applicable in the relations between the parties.

(4) A special meaning shall be given to a term if it is established that the parties so intended.

Article 32. Supplementary means of interpretation

Recourse may be had to supplementary means of interpretation, including the preparatory work of the treaty and the circumstances of its conclusion, in order to confirm the meaning resulting from the application of article 31, or to determine the meaning when the interpretation according to article 31:

(a) leaves the meaning ambiguous or obscure; or

(b) leads to a result which is manifestly absurd or unreasonable.

Article 33. Interpretation of treaties authenticated in two or more languages

(1) When a treaty has been authenticated in two or more languages, the text is equally authoritative in each language, unless the treaty provides or the parties agree that, in case of divergence, a particular text shall prevail.

(2) A version of the treaty in a language other than one of those in which the text was authenticated shall be considered an authentic text only if the treaty so provides or the parties so agree.

(3) The terms of the treaty are presumed to have the same meaning in each authentic text.

(4) Except where a particular text prevails in accordance with paragraph (1), when a comparison of the authentic texts discloses a difference of meaning which the application of articles 31 and 32 does not remove, the meaning which best reconciles the texts, having regard to the object and purpose of the treaty, shall be adopted.

Section 4. Treaties and third states

Article 34. General rule regarding third States

A treaty does not create either obligations or rights for a third State without its consent.

Article 35. Treaties providing for obligations for third States

An obligation arises for a third State from a provision of a treaty if the parties to the treaty intend the provision to be the means of establishing the obligation and the third State expressly accepts that obligation in writing.

Article 36. Treaties providing for rights for third States

(1) A right arises for a third State from a provision of a treaty if the parties to the treaty intend the provision to accord that right either to the third State, or to a group of States to which it belongs, or to all States, and the third State assents thereto. Its assent shall be presumed so long as the contrary is not indicated, unless the treaty otherwise provides.

(2) A State exercising a right in accordance with paragraph (1) shall comply with the conditions for its exercise provided for in the treaty or established in conformity with the treaty.

Article 37. Revocation or modification of obligations or rights of third States

(1) When an obligation has arisen for a third State in conformity with article 35, the obligation may be revoked or modified only with the consent of the parties to the treaty and of the third State, unless it is established that they had otherwise agreed.

(2) When a right has arisen for a third State in conformity with article 36, the right may not be revoked or modified by the parties if it is established that the right was intended not to be revocable or subject to modification without the consent of the third State.

Article 38. Rules in a treaty becoming binding on third States through international custom
Nothing in articles 34 to 37 precludes a rule set forth in a treaty from becoming binding upon a third State as a customary rule of international law, recognized as such.

Part IV. Amendment and modification of treaties

Article 39. General rule regarding the amendment of treaties
A treaty may be amended by agreement between the parties. The rules laid down in Part II apply to such an agreement except insofar as the treaty may otherwise provide.

Article 40. Amendment of multilateral treaties
(1) Unless the treaty otherwise provides, the amendment of multilateral treaties shall be governed by the following paragraphs.
(2) Any proposal to amend a multilateral treaty as between all the parties must be notified to all the contracting States, each one of which shall have the right to take part in:
(a) the decision as to the action to be taken in regard to such proposal;
(b) the negotiation and conclusion of any agreement for the amendment of the treaty.
(3) Every State entitled to become a party to the treaty shall also be entitled to become a party to the treaty as amended.
(4) The amending agreement does not bind any State already a party to the treaty which does not become a party to the amending agreement; article 30, paragraph (4) (b), applies in relation to such State.
(5) Any State which becomes a party to the treaty after the entry into force of the amending agreement shall, failing an expression of a different intention by that State:
(a) be considered as a party to the treaty as amended; and
(b) be considered as a party to the unamended treaty in relation to any party to the treaty not bound by the amending agreement.

Article 41. Agreements to modify multilateral treaties between certain of the parties only
(1) Two or more of the parties to a multilateral treaty may conclude an agreement to modify the treaty as between themselves alone if:
(a) the possibility of such a modification is provided for by the treaty; or
(b) the modification in question is not prohibited by the treaty and:
(i) does not affect the enjoyment by the other parties of their rights under the treaty or the performance of their obligations;
(ii) does not relate to a provision, derogation from which is incompatible with the effective execution of the object and purpose of the treaty as a whole.
(2) Unless in a case falling under paragraph (1)
(a) the treaty otherwise provides, the parties in question shall notify the other parties of their intention to conclude the agreement and of the modification to the treaty for which it provides.

Part V. Invalidity, termination and suspension of the operation of treaties

Section 1. General provisions

Article 42. Validity and continuance in force of treaties
(1) The validity of a treaty or of the consent of a State to be bound by a treaty may be impeached only through the application of the present Convention.
(2) The termination of a treaty, its denunciation or the withdrawal of a party, may take place only as a result of the application of the provisions of the treaty or of the present Convention. The same rule applies to suspension of the operation of a treaty.

Article 43. Obligations imposed by international law independently of a treaty
The invalidity, termination or denunciation of a treaty, the withdrawal of a party from it, or the suspension of its operation, as a result of the application of the present Convention or of the provisions of the treaty, shall not in any way impair the duty of any State to fulfil any obligation embodied in the treaty to which it would be subject under international law independently of the treaty.

Article 44. Separability of treaty provisions
(1) A right of a party, provided for in a treaty or arising under article 56, to denounce, withdraw from

or suspend the operation of the treaty may be exercised only with respect to the whole treaty unless the treaty otherwise provides or the parties otherwise agree.
(2.) A ground for invalidating, terminating, withdrawing from or suspending the operation of a treaty recognized in the present Convention may be invoked only with respect to the whole treaty except as provided in the following paragraphs or in article 60.
(3) If the ground relates solely to particular clauses, it may be invoked only with respect to those clauses where:
(a) the said clauses are separable from the remainder of the treaty with regard to their application;
(b) it appears from the treaty or is otherwise established that acceptance of those clauses was not an essential basis of the consent of the other party or parties to be bound by the treaty as a whole; and
(c) continued performance of the remainder of the treaty would not be unjust.
(4) In cases falling under articles 49 and 50, the State entitled to invoke the fraud or corruption may do so with respect either to the whole treaty or, subject to paragraph (3), to the particular clauses alone. 16 5. In cases falling under articles 51, 52 and 53, no separation of the provisions of the treaty is permitted.

Article 45. Loss of a right to invoke a ground for invalidating, terminating, withdrawing from or suspending the operation of a treaty

A State may no longer invoke a ground for invalidating, terminating, withdrawing from or suspending the operation of a treaty under articles 46 to 50 or articles 60 and 62 if, after becoming aware of the facts:
(a) it shall have expressly agreed that the treaty is valid or remains in force or continues in operation, as the case may be; or
(b) it must by reason of its conduct be considered as having acquiesced in the validity of the treaty or in its maintenance in force or in operation, as the case may be.

Section 2. Invalidity of treaties

Article 46. Provisions of internal law regarding competence to conclude treaties

(1) A State may not invoke the fact that its consent to be bound by a treaty has been expressed in violation of a provision of its internal law regarding competence to conclude treaties as invalidating its consent unless that violation was manifest and concerned a rule of its internal law of fundamental importance.
(2) A violation is manifest if it would be objectively evident to any State conducting itself in the matter in accordance with normal practice and in good faith. Article 47 Specific restrictions on authority to express the consent of a State If the authority of a representative to express the consent of a State to be bound by a particular treaty has been made subject to a specific restriction, his omission to observe that restriction may not be invoked as invalidating the consent expressed by him unless the restriction was notified to the other negotiating States prior to his expressing such consent.

Article 48. Error

(1) A State may invoke an error in a treaty as invalidating its consent to be bound by the treaty if the error relates to a fact or situation which was assumed by that State to exist at the time when the treaty was concluded and formed an essential basis of its consent to be bound by the treaty.
(2) Paragraph (1) shall not apply if the State in question contributed by its own conduct to the error or if the circumstances were such as to put that State on notice of a possible error. 3. An error relating only to the wording of the text of a treaty does not affect its validity; article 79 then applies.

Article 49. Fraud

If a State has been induced to conclude a treaty by the fraudulent conduct of another negotiating State, the State may invoke the fraud as invalidating its consent to be bound by the treaty.

Article 50. Corruption of a representative of a State

If the expression of a State's consent to be bound by a treaty has been procured through the corruption of its representative directly or indirectly by another negotiating State, the State may invoke such corruption as invalidating its consent to be bound by the treaty.

Article 51. Coercion of a representative of a State

The expression of a State's consent to be bound by a treaty which has been procured by the coercion of its representative through acts or threats directed against him shall be without any legal effect.

Article 52. Coercion of a State by the threat or use of force

A treaty is void if its conclusion has been procured by the threat or use of force in violation of the principles of international law embodied in the Charter of the United Nations.

Article 53. Treaties conflicting with a peremptory norm of general international law (jus cogens)

A treaty is void if, at the time of its conclusion, it conflicts with a peremptory norm of general international law. For the purposes of the present Convention, a peremptory norm of general international law is a norm accepted and recognized by the international community of States as a whole as a norm from which no derogation is permitted and which can be modified only by a subsequent norm of general international law having the same character.

Section 3. Termination and suspension of the operation of treaties

Article 54. Termination of or withdrawal from a treaty under its provisions or by consent of the parties

The termination of a treaty or the withdrawal of a party may take place:
(a) in conformity with the provisions of the treaty; or
(b) at any time by consent of all the parties after consultation with the other contracting States. Article 55 Reduction of the parties to a multilateral treaty below the number necessary for its entry into force Unless the treaty otherwise provides, a multilateral treaty does not terminate by reason only of the fact that the number of the parties falls below the number necessary for its entry into force.

Article 56. Denunciation of or withdrawal from a treaty containing no provision regarding termination, denunciation or withdrawal

(1) A treaty which contains no provision regarding its termination and which does not provide for denunciation or withdrawal is not subject to denunciation or withdrawal unless: (a) it is established that the parties intended to admit the possibility of denunciation or withdrawal; or
(b) a right of denunciation or withdrawal may be implied by the nature of the treaty.
(2) A party shall give not less than twelve months' notice of its intention to denounce or withdraw from a treaty under paragraph (1).

Article 57. Suspension of the operation of a treaty under its provisions or by consent of the parties

The operation of a treaty in regard to all the parties or to a particular party may be suspended: (a) in conformity with the provisions of the treaty; or
(b) at any time by consent of all the parties after consultation with the other contracting States.

Article 58 Suspension of the operation of a multilateral treaty by agreement between certain of the parties only

(1) Two or more parties to a multilateral treaty may conclude an agreement to suspend the operation of provisions of the treaty, temporarily and as between themselves alone, if:
(a) the possibility of such a suspension is provided for by the treaty; or
(b) the suspension in question is not prohibited by the treaty and:
(i) does not affect the enjoyment by the other parties of their rights under the treaty or the performance of their obligations;
(ii) is not incompatible with the object and purpose of the treaty.
(2) Unless in a case falling under paragraph (1)
(a) the treaty otherwise provides, the parties in question shall notify the other parties of their intention to conclude the agreement and of those provisions of the treaty the operation of which they intend to suspend.

Article 59. Termination or suspension of the operation of a treaty implied by conclusion of a later treaty

(1) A treaty shall be considered as terminated if all the parties to it conclude a later treaty relating to the same subject matter and:
(a) it appears from the later treaty or is otherwise established that the parties intended that the matter should be governed by that treaty; or
(b) the provisions of the later treaty are so far incompatible with those of the earlier one that the two treaties are not capable of being applied at the same time.
(2) The earlier treaty shall be considered as only suspended in operation if it appears from the later treaty or is otherwise established that such was the intention of the parties.

Article 60. Termination or suspension of the operation of a treaty as a consequence of its breach

(1) A material breach of a bilateral treaty by one of the parties entitles the other to invoke the breach as a ground for terminating the treaty or suspending its operation in whole or in part. (2) A material breach of a multilateral treaty by one of the parties entitles:
(a) the other parties by unanimous agreement to suspend the operation of the treaty in whole or in part or to terminate it either:

(i) in the relations between themselves and the defaulting State; or
(ii) as between all the parties;
(b) a party specially affected by the breach to invoke it as a ground for suspending the operation of the treaty in whole or in part in the relations between itself and the defaulting State;
(c) any party other than the defaulting State to invoke the breach as a ground for suspending the operation of the treaty in whole or in part with respect to itself if the treaty is of such a character that a material breach of its provisions by one party radically changes the position of every party with respect to the further performance of its obligations under the treaty.
(3) A material breach of a treaty, for the purposes of this article, consists in:
(a) a repudiation of the treaty not sanctioned by the present Convention; or
(b) the violation of a provision essential to the accomplishment of the object or purpose of the treaty.
(4) The foregoing paragraphs are without prejudice to any provision in the treaty applicable in the event of a breach.
(5) Paragraphs (1) to (3) do not apply to provisions relating to the protection of the human person contained in treaties of a humanitarian character, in particular to provisions prohibiting any form of reprisals against persons protected by such treaties.

Article 61. Supervening impossibility of performance

(1) A party may invoke the impossibility of performing a treaty as a ground for terminating or withdrawing from it if the impossibility results from the permanent disappearance or destruction of an object indispensable for the execution of the treaty. If the impossibility is temporary, it may be invoked only as a ground for suspending the operation of the treaty.
(2) Impossibility of performance may not be invoked by a party as a ground for terminating, withdrawing from or suspending the operation of a treaty if the impossibility is the result of a breach by that party either of an obligation under the treaty or of any other international obligation owed to any other party to the treaty.

Article 62. Fundamental change of circumstances

(1) A fundamental change of circumstances which has occurred with regard to those existing at the time of the conclusion of a treaty, and which was not foreseen by the parties, may not be invoked as a ground for terminating or withdrawing from the treaty unless:
(a) the existence of those circumstances constituted an essential basis of the consent of the parties to be bound by the treaty; and
(b) the effect of the change is radically to transform the extent of obligations still to be performed under the treaty.
(2) A fundamental change of circumstances may not be invoked as a ground for terminating or withdrawing from a treaty:
(a) if the treaty establishes a boundary; or
(b) if the fundamental change is the result of a breach by the party invoking it either of an obligation under the treaty or of any other international obligation owed to any other party to the treaty.
(3) If, under the foregoing paragraphs, a party may invoke a fundamental change of circumstances as a ground for terminating or withdrawing from a treaty it may also invoke the change as a ground for suspending the operation of the treaty.

Article 63. Severance of diplomatic or consular relations

The severance of diplomatic or consular relations between parties to a treaty does not affect the legal relations established between them by the treaty except insofar as the existence of diplomatic or consular relations is indispensable for the application of the treaty.

Article 64. Emergence of a new peremptory norm of general international law *("jus cogens")* If a new peremptory norm of general international law emerges, any existing treaty which is in conflict with that norm becomes void and terminates.

Section 4. Procedure

Article 65. Procedure to be followed with respect to invalidity, termination, withdrawal from or suspension of the operation of a treaty

(1) A party which, under the provisions of the present Convention, invokes either a defect in its consent to be bound by a treaty or a ground for impeaching the validity of a treaty, terminating it, withdrawing from it or suspending its operation, must notify the other parties of its claim. The notification shall indicate the measure proposed to be taken with respect to the treaty and the reasons therefor.
(2) If, after the expiry of a period which, except in cases of special urgency, shall not be less than

three months after the receipt of the notification, no party has raised any objection, the party making the notification may carry out in the manner provided in article 67 the measure which it has proposed.
(3) If, however, objection has been raised by any other party, the parties shall seek a solution through the means indicated in Article 33 of the Charter of the United Nations.
(4) Nothing in the foregoing paragraphs shall affect the rights or obligations of the parties under any provisions in force binding the parties with regard to the settlement of disputes.
(5) Without prejudice to article 45, the fact that a State has not previously made the notification prescribed in paragraph (1) shall not prevent it from making such notification in answer to another party claiming performance of the treaty or alleging its violation.

Article 66. Procedures for judicial settlement, arbitration and conciliation
If, under paragraph (3) of article 65, no solution has been reached within a period of 12 months following the date on which the objection was raised, the following procedures shall be followed:
(a) any one of the parties to a dispute concerning the application or the interpretation of article 53 or 64 may, by a written application, submit it to the International Court of Justice for a decision unless the parties by common consent agree to submit the dispute to arbitration;
(b) any one of the parties to a dispute concerning the application or the interpretation of any of the other articles in part V of the present Convention may set in motion the procedure specified in the Annex to the Convention by submitting a request to that effect to the Secretary-General of the United Nations.

Article 67. Instruments for declaring invalid, terminating, withdrawing from or suspending the operation of a treaty
(1) The notification provided for under article 65, paragraph (1), must be made in writing.
(2) Any act of declaring invalid, terminating, withdrawing from or suspending the operation of a treaty pursuant to the provisions of the treaty or of paragraphs (2) or (3) of article 65 shall be carried out through an instrument communicated to the other parties. If the instrument is not signed by the Head of State, Head of Government or Minister for Foreign Affairs, the representative of the State communicating it may be called upon to produce full powers.

Article 68. Revocation of notifications and instruments provided for in articles 65 and 67
A notification or instrument provided for in article 65 or 67 may be revoked at any time before it takes effect.

Section 5. Consequences of the invalidity, termination or suspension of the operation of a treaty

Article 69. Consequences of the invalidity of a treaty
(1) A treaty the invalidity of which is established under the present Convention is void. The provisions of a void treaty have no legal force.
(2) If acts have nevertheless been performed in reliance on such a treaty:
(a) each party may require any other party to establish as far as possible in their mutual relations the position that would have existed if the acts had not been performed;
(b) acts performed in good faith before the invalidity was invoked are not rendered unlawful by reason only of the invalidity of the treaty.
(3) In cases falling under article 49, 50, 51 or 52, paragraph (2) does not apply with respect to the party to which the fraud, the act of corruption or the coercion is imputable. 4. In the case of the invalidity of a particular State's consent to be bound by a multilateral treaty, the foregoing rules apply in the relations between that State and the parties to the treaty.

Article 70. Consequences of the termination of a treaty
(1) Unless the treaty otherwise provides or the parties otherwise agree, the termination of a treaty under its provisions or in accordance with the present Convention:
(a) releases the parties from any obligation further to perform the treaty;
(b) does not affect any right, obligation or legal situation of the parties created through the execution of the treaty prior to its termination.
(2) If a State denounces or withdraws from a multilateral treaty, paragraph (1) applies in the relations between that State and each of the other parties to the treaty from the date when such denunciation or withdrawal takes effect.

Article 71. Consequences of the invalidity of a treaty which conflicts with a peremptory norm of general international law
(1) In the case of a treaty which is void under article 53 the parties shall:
(a) eliminate as far as possible the consequences of any act performed in reliance on any provision

which conflicts with the peremptory norm of general international law; and
(b) bring their mutual relations into conformity with the peremptory norm of general international law.
(2) In the case of a treaty which becomes void and terminates under article 64, the termination of the treaty:
(a) releases the parties from any obligation further to perform the treaty;
(b) does not affect any right, obligation or legal situation of the parties created through the execution of the treaty prior to its termination, provided that those rights, obligations or situations may thereafter be maintained only to the extent that their maintenance is not in itself in conflict with the new peremptory norm of general international law.

Article 72. Consequences of the suspension of the operation of a treaty
(1) Unless the treaty otherwise provides or the parties otherwise agree, the suspension of the operation of a treaty under its provisions or in accordance with the present Convention:
(a) releases the parties between which the operation of the treaty is suspended from the obligation to perform the treaty in their mutual relations during the period of the suspension; (b) does not otherwise affect the legal relations between the parties established by the treaty. (2) During the period of the suspension the parties shall refrain from acts tending to obstruct the resumption of the operation of the treaty.

Part VI. Miscellaneous provisions

Article 73. Cases of State succession, State responsibility and outbreak of hostilities
The provisions of the present Convention shall not prejudge any question that may arise in regard to a treaty from a succession of States or from the international responsibility of a State or from the outbreak of hostilities between States.

Article 74. Diplomatic and consular relations and the conclusion of treaties
The severance or absence of diplomatic or consular relations between two or more States does not prevent the conclusion of treaties between those States. The conclusion of a treaty does not in itself affect the situation in regard to diplomatic or consular relations.

Article 75. Case of an aggressor State
The provisions of the present Convention are without prejudice to any obligation in relation to a treaty which may arise for an aggressor State in consequence of measures taken in conformity with the Charter of the United Nations with reference to that State's aggression.

Part VII. Depositaries, notifications, corrections and registration

Article 76. Depositaries of treaties
(1) The designation of the depositary of a treaty may be made by the negotiating States, either in the treaty itself or in some other manner. The depositary may be one or more States, an international organization or the chief administrative officer of the organization.
(2) The functions of the depositary of a treaty are international in character and the depositary is under an obligation to act impartially in their performance. In particular, the fact that a treaty has not entered into force between certain of the parties or that a difference has appeared between a State and a depositary with regard to the performance of the latter's functions shall not affect that obligation.

Article 77. Functions of depositaries
(1) The functions of a depositary, unless otherwise provided in the treaty or agreed by the contracting States, comprise in particular:
(a) keeping custody of the original text of the treaty and of any full powers delivered to the depositary;
(b) preparing certified copies of the original text and preparing any further text of the treaty in such additional languages as may be required by the treaty and transmitting them to the parties and to the States entitled to become parties to the treaty;
(c) receiving any signatures to the treaty and receiving and keeping custody of any instruments, notifications and communications relating to it;
(d) examining whether the signature or any instrument, notification or communication relating to the treaty is in due and proper form and, if need be, bringing the matter to the attention of the State in question;
(e) informing the parties and the States entitled to become parties to the treaty of acts, notifications and communications relating to the treaty;

(f) informing the States entitled to become parties to the treaty when the number of signatures or of instruments of ratification, acceptance, approval or accession required for the entry into force of the treaty has been received or deposited;
(g) registering the treaty with the Secretariat of the United Nations;
(h) performing the functions specified in other provisions of the present Convention.
(2) In the event of any difference appearing between a State and the depositary as to the performance of the latter's functions, the depositary shall bring the question to the attention of the signatory States and the contracting States or, where appropriate, of the competent organ of the international organization concerned.

Article 78. Notifications and communications
Except as the treaty or the present Convention otherwise provide, any notification or communication to be made by any State under the present Convention shall:
(a) if there is no depositary, be transmitted direct to the States for which it is intended, or if there is a depositary, to the latter;
(b) be considered as having been made by the State in question only upon its receipt by the State to which it was transmitted or, as the case may be, upon its receipt by the depositary;
(c) if transmitted to a depositary, be considered as received by the State for which it was intended only when the latter State has been informed by the depositary in accordance with article 77, paragraph (1) (e).

Article 79. Correction of errors in texts or in certified copies of treaties
(1) Where, after the authentication of the text of a treaty, the signatory States and the contracting States are agreed that it contains an error, the error shall, unless they decide upon some other means of correction, be corrected:
(a) by having the appropriate correction made in the text and causing the correction to be initialled by duly authorized representatives;
(b) by executing or exchanging an instrument or instruments setting out the correction which it has been agreed to make; or
(c) by executing a corrected text of the whole treaty by the same procedure as in the case of the original text.
(2) Where the treaty is one for which there is a depositary, the latter shall notify the signatory States and the contracting States of the error and of the proposal to correct it and shall specify an appropriate time-limit within which objection to the proposed correction may be raised. If, on the expiry of the time-limit:
(a) no objection has been raised, the depositary shall make and initial the correction in the text and shall execute a procès-verbal of the rectification of the text and communicate a copy of it to the parties and to the States entitled to become parties to the treaty;
(b) an objection has been raised, the depositary shall communicate the objection to the signatory States and to the contracting States.
(3) The rules in paragraphs (I) and (2) apply also where the text has been authenticated in two or more languages and it appears that there is a lack of concordance which the signatory States and the contracting States agree should be corrected.
(4) The corrected text replaces the defective text ab initio, unless the signatory States and the contracting States otherwise decide.
(5) The correction of the text of a treaty that has been registered shall be notified to the Secretariat of the United Nations.
(6) Where an error is discovered in a certified copy of a treaty, the depositary shall execute a procès-verbal specifying the rectification and communicate a copy of it to the signatory States and to the contracting States.

Article 80. Registration and publication of treaties
(1) Treaties shall, after their entry into force, be transmitted to the Secretariat of the United Nations for registration or filing and recording, as the case may be, and for publication.
(2) The designation of a depositary shall constitute authorization for it to perform the acts specified in the preceding paragraph.

Part VIII. Final provisions

Article 81. Signature
The present Convention shall be open for signature by all States Members of the United Nations or of any of the specialized agencies or of the International Atomic Energy Agency or parties to the Statute

PART I   INTERNATIONAL LAW

of the International Court of Justice, and by any other State invited by the General Assembly of the United Nations to become a party to the Convention, as follows: until 30 November 1969, at the 28 Federal Ministry for Foreign Affairs of the Republic of Austria, and subsequently, until 30 April 1970, at United Nations Headquarters, New York.

Article 82. Ratification
The present Convention is subject to ratification. The instruments of ratification shall be deposited with the Secretary-General of the United Nations.

Article 83. Accession
The present Convention shall remain open for accession by any State belonging to any of the categories mentioned in article 81. The instruments of accession shall be deposited with the Secretary General of the United Nations.

Article 84. Entry into force
(1) The present Convention shall enter into force on the thirtieth day following the date of deposit of the thirty-fifth instrument of ratification or accession.
(2) For each State ratifying or acceding to the Convention after the deposit of the thirty-fifth instrument of ratification or accession, the Convention shall enter into force on the thirtieth day after deposit by such State of its instrument of ratification or accession.

Article 85. Authentic texts
The original of the present Convention, of which the Chinese, English, French, Russian and Spanish texts are equally authentic, shall be deposited with the Secretary-General of the United Nations.

Annex
(1) A list of conciliators consisting of qualified jurists shall be drawn up and maintained by the Secretary-General of the United Nations. To this end, every State which is a Member of the United Nations or a party to the present Convention shall be invited to nominate two conciliators, and the names of the persons so nominated shall constitute the list. The term of a conciliator, including that of any conciliator nominated to fill a casual vacancy, shall be five years and may be renewed. A conciliator whose term expires shall continue to fulfil any function for which he shall have been chosen under the following paragraph.
(2) When a request has been made to the Secretary-General under article 66, the Secretary-General shall bring the dispute before a conciliation commission constituted as follows: The State or States constituting one of the parties to the dispute shall appoint:
(a) one conciliator of the nationality of that State or of one of those States, who may or may not be chosen from the list referred to in paragraph (1); and
(b) one conciliator not of the nationality of that State or of any of those States, who shall be chosen from the list. The State or States constituting the other party to the dispute shall appoint two conciliators in the same way. The four conciliators chosen by the parties shall be appointed within sixty days following the date on which the Secretary-General receives the request. The four conciliators shall, within sixty days following the date of the last of their own appointments, appoint a fifth conciliator chosen from the list, who shall be chairman. If the appointment of the chairman or of any of the other conciliators has not been made within the period prescribed above for such appointment, it shall be made by the Secretary-General within sixty days following the expiry of that period. The appointment of the chairman may be made by the Secretary-General either from the list or from the membership of the International Law Commission. Any of the periods within which appointments must be made may be extended by agreement between the parties to the dispute. Any vacancy shall be filled in the manner prescribed for the initial appointment.
(3) The Conciliation Commission shall decide its own procedure. The Commission, with the consent of the parties to the dispute, may invite any party to the treaty to submit to it its views orally or in writing. Decisions and recommendations of the Commission shall be made by a majority vote of the five members.
(4) The Commission may draw the attention of the parties to the dispute to any measures which might facilitate an amicable settlement.
(5) The Commission shall hear the parties, examine the claims and objections, and make proposals to the parties with a view to reaching an amicable settlement of the dispute.
(6) The Commission shall report within twelve months of its constitution. Its report shall be deposited with the Secretary-General and transmitted to the parties to the dispute. The report of the Commission, including any conclusions stated therein regarding the facts or questions of law, shall not be binding upon the parties and it shall have no other character than that of recommendations submitted

for the consideration of the parties in order to facilitate an amicable settlement of the dispute.
(7) The Secretary-General shall provide the Commission with such assistance and facilities as it may require. The expenses of the Commission shall be borne by the United Nations.

PART I INTERNATIONAL LAW

Vienna Convention on the Law of Treaties 1987 (International Organizations)

Vienna Convention on the Law of Treaties between States and International Organizations or between International Organizations, Vienna 21 March 1986, Trb. 1987, 136

The Parties to the present Convention,
Considering the fundamental role of treaties in the history of international relations,
Recognizing the consensual nature of treaties and their ever-increasing importance as a source of international law,
Noting that the principles of free consent and of good faith and the pacta sunt servanda rule are universally recognized,
Affirming the importance of enhancing the process of codification and progressive development of international law at a universal level,
Believing that the codification and progressive development of the rules relating to treaties between States and international organizations or between international organizations are means of enhancing legal order in international relations and of serving the purposes of the United Nations,
Having in mind the principles of international law embodied in the Charter of the United Nations, such as the principles of the equal rights and self-determination of peoples, of the sovereign equality and independence of all States, of non-interference in the domestic affairs of States, of the prohibition of the threat or use of force and of universal respect for, and observance of, human rights and fundamental freedoms for all,
Bearing in mind the provisions of the Vienna Convention on the Law of Treaties of 1969,
Recognizing the relationship between the law of treaties between States and the law of treaties between States and international organizations or between international organizations,
Considering the importance of treaties between States and international organizations or between international organizations as a useful means of developing international relations and ensuring conditions for peaceful cooperation among nations, whatever their constitutional and social systems,
Having in mind the specific features of treaties to which international organizations are parties as subjects of international law distinct from States,
Noting that international organizations possess the capacity to conclude treaties, which is necessary for the exercise of their functions and the fulfilment of their purposes,
Recognizing that the practice of international organizations in concluding treaties with States or between themselves should be in accordance with their constituent instruments,
Affirming that nothing in the present Convention should be interpreted as affecting those relations between an international organization and its members which are regulated by the rules of the organization,
Affirming also that disputes concerning treaties, like other international disputes, should be settled, in conformity with the Charter of the United Nations, by peaceful means and in conformity with the principles of justice and international law,
Affirming also that the rules of customary international law will continue to govern questions not regulated by the provisions of the present Convention,
Have agreed as follows:

Part I. Introduction

Article 1. Scope of the present Convention
The present Convention applies to:
(a) treaties between one or more States and one or more international organizations, and
(b) treaties between international organizations.

Article 2. Use of terms
(1) For the purposes of the present Convention:
(a) "treaty" means an international agreement governed by international law and concluded in written form:
(i) between one or more States and one or more international organizations; or
(ii) between international organizations, whether that agreement is embodied in a single instrument or in two or more related instruments and whatever its particular designation;
(b) "ratification" means the international act so named whereby a State establishes on the international plane its consent to be bound by a treaty;
(b bis) "act of formal confirmation" means an international act corresponding to that of ratification by a State, whereby an international organization establishes on the international plane its consent to be bound by a treaty;

(b ter) "acceptance", "approval" and "accession" mean in each case the international act so named whereby a State or an international organization establishes on the international plane its consent to be bound by a treaty;
(c) "full powers" means a document emanating from the competent authority of a State or from the competent organ of an international organization designating a person or persons to represent the State or the organization for negotiating, adopting or authenticating the text of a treaty, for expressing the consent of the State or of the organization to be bound by a treaty, or for accomplishing any other act with respect to a treaty;
(d) "reservation" means a unilateral statement, however phrased or named, made by a State or by an international organization when signing, ratifying, formally confirming, accepting, approving or acceding to a treaty, whereby it purports to exclude or to modify the legal effect of certain provisions of the treaty in their application to that State or to that organization;
(e) "negotiating State" and "negotiating organization" mean respectively:
(i) a State, or
(ii) an international organization, which took part in the drawing up and adoption of the text of the treaty;
(f) "contracting State" and "contracting organization" mean respectively:
(i) a State, or
(ii) an international organization, which has consented to be bound by the treaty, whether or not the treaty has entered into force;
(g) "party" means a State or an international organization which has consented to be bound by the treaty and for which the treaty is in force;
(h) "third State" and "third organization" mean respectively:
(i) a State, or
(ii) an international organization, not a party to the treaty;
(i) "international organization" means an intergovernmental organization;
(j) "rules of the organization" means, in particular, the constituent instruments, decisions and resolutions adopted in accordance with them, and established practice of the organization.
(2) The provisions of paragraph (1) regarding the use of terms in the present Convention are without prejudice to the use of those terms or to the meanings which may be given to them in the internal law of any State or in the rules of any international organization.

Article 3. International agreements not within the scope of the present Convention
The fact that the present Convention does not apply:
(i) to international agreements to which one or more States, one or more international organizations and one or more subjects of international law other than States or organizations are parties;
(ii) to international agreements to which one or more international organizations and one or more subjects of international law other than States or organizations are parties;
(iii) to international agreements not in written form between one or more States and one or more international organizations, or between international organizations; or
(iv) to international agreements between subjects of international law other than States or international organizations;
shall not affect:
(a) the legal force of such agreements;
(b) the application to them of any of the rules set forth in the present Convention to which they would be subject under international law independently of the Convention;
(c) the application of the Convention to the relations between States and international organizations or to the relations of organizations as between themselves, when those relations are governed by international agreements to which other subjects of international law are also parties.

Article 4. Non-retroactivity of the present Convention
Without prejudice to the application of any rules set forth in the present Convention to which treaties between one or more States and one or more international organizations or between international organizations would be subject under international law independently of the Convention, the Convention applies only to such treaties concluded after the entry into force of the present Convention with regard to those States and those organizations.

Article 5. Treaties constituting international organizations and treaties adopted within an international organization
The present Convention applies to any treaty between one or more States and one or more international organizations which is the constituent instrument of an international organization and to any

PART I INTERNATIONAL LAW

treaty adopted within an international organization, without prejudice to any relevant rules of the organization.

Part II. Conclusion and entry into force of treaties

Section 1 Conclusion of treaties

Article 6. Capacity of international organizations to conclude treaties

The capacity of an international organization to conclude treaties is governed by the rules of that organization.

Article 7. Full powers

(1) A person is considered as representing a State for the purpose of adopting or authenticating the text of a treaty or for the purpose of expressing the consent of the State to be bound by a treaty if:
(a) that person produces appropriate full powers; or
(b) it appears from practice or from other circumstances that it was the intention of the States and international organizations concerned to consider that person as representing the State for such purposes without having to produce full powers.
(2) In virtue of their functions and without having to produce full powers, the following are considered as representing their State:
(a) Heads of State, Heads of Government and Ministers for Foreign Affairs, for the purpose of performing all acts relating to the conclusion of a treaty between one or more States and one or more international organizations;
(b) representatives accredited by States to an international conference, for the purpose of adopting the text of a treaty between States and international organizations;
(c) representatives accredited by States to an international organization or one of its organs, for the purpose of adopting the text of a treaty in that organization or organ;
(d) heads of permanent missions to an international organization, for the purpose of adopting the text of a treaty between the accrediting States and that organization.
(3) A person is considered as representing an international organization for the purpose of adopting or authenticating the text of a treaty, or expressing the consent of that organization to be bound by a treaty, if:
(a) that person produces appropriate full powers; or
(b) it appears from the circumstances that it was the intention of the States and international organizations concerned to consider that person as representing the organization for such purposes, in accordance with the rules of the organization, without having to produce full powers.

Article 8. Subsequent confirmation of an act performed without authorization

An act relating to the conclusion of a treaty performed by a person who cannot be considered under article 7 as authorized to represent a State or an international organization for that purpose is without legal effect unless afterwards confirmed by that State or that organization.

Article 9. Adoption of the text

(1) The adoption of the text of a treaty takes place by the consent of all the States and international organizations or, as the case may be, all the organizations participating in its drawing up except as provided in paragraph (2).
(2) The adoption of the text of a treaty at an international conference takes place in accordance with the procedure agreed upon by the participants in that conference. If, however, no agreement is reached on any such procedure, the adoption of the text shall take place by the vote of two thirds of the participants present and voting unless by the same majority they shall decide to apply a different rule.

Article 10. Authentication of the text

(1) The text of a treaty between one or more States and one or more international organizations is established as authentic and definitive:
(a) by such procedure as may be provided for in the text or agreed upon by the States and organizations participating in its drawing up; or
(b) failing such procedure, by the signature, signature ad referendum or initialling by the representatives of those States and those organizations of the text of the treaty or of the Final Act of a conference incorporating the text.
(2) The text of a treaty between international organizations is established as authentic and definitive:
(a) by such procedure as may be provided for in the text or agreed upon by the organizations participating in its drawing up; or

(b) failing such procedure, by the signature, signature ad referendum or initialling by the representatives of those States and those organizations of the text of the treaty or of the Final Act of a conference incorporating the text.

Article 11. Means of expressing consent to be bound by a treaty

(1) The consent of a State to be bound by a treaty may be expressed by signature, exchange of instruments constituting a treaty, ratification, acceptance, approval or accession, or by any other means if so agreed.
(2) The consent of an international organization to be bound by a treaty may be expressed by signature, exchange of instruments constituting a treaty, act of formal confirmation, acceptance, approval or accession, or by any other means if so agreed.

Article 12. Consent to be bound by a treaty expressed by signature

(1) The consent of a State or of an international organization to be bound by a treaty is expressed by the signature of the representative of that State or of that organization when:
(a) the treaty provides that signature shall have that effect;
(b) it is otherwise established that the negotiating States and negotiating organizations or, as the case may be, the negotiating organizations were agreed that signature should have that effect; or
(c) the intention of the State or organization to give that effect to the signature appears from the full powers of its representative or was expressed during the negotiation.
(2) For the purposes of paragraph (1):
(a) the initialling of a text constitutes a signature of the treaty when it is established that the negotiating States and negotiating organizations or, as the case may be, the negotiating organizations so agreed;
(b) the signature ad referendum of a treaty by the representative of a State or an international organization, if confirmed by his State or organization, constitutes a full signature of the treaty.

Article 13. Consent to be bound by a treaty expressed by an exchange of instruments constituting a treaty

The consent of States or of international organizations to be bound by a treaty constituted by instruments exchanged between them is expressed by that exchange when:
(a) the instruments provide that their exchange shall have that effect; or
(b) it is otherwise established that those States and those organizations or, as the case may be, those organizations were agreed that the exchange of instruments should have that effect.

Article 14. Consent to be bound by a treaty expressed by ratification, act of formal confirmation, acceptance or approval

(1) The consent of a State to be bound by a treaty is expressed by ratification when:
(a) the treaty provides for such consent to be expressed by means of ratification;
(b) it is otherwise established that the negotiating States and negotiating organizations were agreed that ratification should be required;
(c) the representative of the State has signed the treaty subject to ratification; or
(d) the intention of the State to sign the treaty subject to ratification appears from the full powers of its representative or was expressed during the negotiation.
(2) The consent of an international organization to be bound by a treaty is expressed by an act of formal confirmation when:
(a) the treaty provides for such consent to be expressed by means of an act of formal confirmation;
(b) it is otherwise established that the negotiating States and negotiating organizations or, as the case may be, the negotiating organizations were agreed that an act of formal confirmation should be required;
(c) the representative of the organization has signed the treaty subject to an act of formal confirmation; or
(d) the intention of the organization to sign the treaty subject to an act of formal confirmation appears from the full powers of its representative or was expressed during the negotiation. (3)The consent of a State or of an international organization to be bound by a treaty is expressed by acceptance or approval under conditions similar to those which apply to ratification or, as the case may be, to an act of formal confirmation.

Article 15. Consent to be bound by a treaty expressed by accession

The consent of a State or of an international organization to be bound by a treaty is expressed by accession when:
(a) the treaty provides that such consent may be expressed by that State or that organization by means of accession;

(b) it is otherwise established that the negotiating States and negotiating organizations or, as the case may be, the negotiating organizations were agreed that such consent may be expressed by that State or that organization by means of accession; or
(c) all the parties have subsequently agreed that such consent may be expressed by that State or that organization by means of accession.

Article 16. Exchange or deposit of instruments of ratification, formal confirmation, acceptance, approval or accession

(1) Unless the treaty otherwise provides, instruments of ratification, instruments relating to an act of formal confirmation or instruments of acceptance, approval or accession establish the consent of a State or of an international organization to be bound by a treaty between one or more States and one or more international organizations upon:
(a) their exchange between the contracting States and contracting organizations;
(b) their deposit with the depositary; or
(c) their notification to the contracting States and to the contracting organizations or to the depositary, if so agreed.
(2) Unless the treaty otherwise provides, instruments relating to an act of formal confirmation or instruments of acceptance, approval or accession establish the consent of an international organization to be bound by a treaty between international organizations upon:
(a) their exchange between the contracting organizations;
(b) their deposit with the depositary; or
(c) their notification to the contracting organizations or to the depositary, if so agreed.

Article 17. Consent to be bound by part of a treaty and choice of differing provisions

(1) Without prejudice to articles 19 to 23, the consent of a State or of an international organization to be bound by part of a treaty is effective only if the treaty so permits, or if the contracting States and contracting organizations or, as the case may be, the contracting organizations so agree.
(2) The consent of a State or of an international organization to be bound by a treaty which permits a choice between differing provisions is effective only if it is made clear to which of the provisions the consent relates.

Article 18. Obligation not to defeat the object and purpose of a treaty prior to its entry into force

A State or an international organization is obliged to refrain from acts which would defeat the object and purpose of a treaty when:
(a) that State or that organization has signed the treaty or has exchanged instruments constituting the treaty subject to ratification, act of formal confirmation, acceptance or approval, until that State or that organization shall have made its intention clear not to become a party to the treaty; or
(b) that State or that organization has expressed its consent to be bound by the treaty, pending the entry into force of the treaty and provided that such entry into force is not unduly delayed.

Section 2. Reservations

Article 19. Formulation of reservations

A State or an international organization may, when signing, ratifying, formally confirming, accepting, approving or acceding to a treaty, formulate a reservation unless:
(a) the reservation is prohibited by the treaty;
(b) the treaty provides that only specified reservations, which do not include the reservation in question, may be made; or
(c) in cases not falling under subparagraphs (a) and (b), the reservation is incompatible with the object and purpose of the treaty.

Article 20. Acceptance of and objection to reservations

(1) A reservation expressly authorized by a treaty does not require any subsequent acceptance by the contracting States and contracting organizations or, as the case may be, by the contracting organizations unless the treaty so provides.
(2) When it appears from the limited number of the negotiating States and negotiating organizations or, as the case may be, of the negotiating organizations and the object and purpose of a treaty that the application of the treaty in its entirety between all the parties is an essential condition of the consent of each one to be bound by the treaty, a reservation requires acceptance by all the parties.
(3) When a treaty is a constituent instrument of an international organization and unless it otherwise provides, a reservation requires the acceptance of the competent organ of that organization.

VIENNA CONVENTION ON THE LAW OF TREATIES 1987 (INT. ORGANISATIONS)

(4) In cases not falling under the preceding paragraphs and unless the treaty otherwise provides:
(a) acceptance of a reservation by a contracting State or by a contracting organization constitutes the reserving State or international organization a party to the treaty in relation to the accepting State or organization if or when the treaty is in force for the reserving State or organization and for the accepting State or organization;
(b) an objection by a contracting State or by a contracting organization to a reservation does not preclude the entry into force of the treaty as between the objecting State or international organization and the reserving State or organization unless a contrary intention is definitely expressed by the objecting State or organization;
(c) an act expressing the consent of a State or of an international organization to be bound by the treaty and containing a reservation is effective as soon as at least one contracting State or one contracting organization has accepted the reservation.
(5) For the purposes of paragraphs (2) and (4), and unless the treaty otherwise provides, a reservation is considered to have been accepted by a State or an international organization if it shall have raised no objection to the reservation by the end of a period of twelve months after it was notified of the reservation or by the date on which it expressed its consent to be bound by the treaty, whichever is later.

Article 21. Legal effects of reservations and of objections to reservations
(1) A reservation established with regard to another party in accordance with articles 19, 20 and 23:
(a) modifies for the reserving State or international organization in its relations with that other party the provisions of the treaty to which the reservation relates to the extent of the reservation; and
(b) modifies those provisions to the same extent for that other party in its relations with the reserving State or international organization.
(2) The reservation does not modify the provisions of the treaty for the other parties to the treaty inter se.
(3) When a State or an international organization objecting to a reservation has not opposed the entry into force of the treaty between itself and the reserving State or organization, the provisions to which the reservation relates do not apply as between the reserving State or organization and the objecting State or organization to the extent of the reservation.

Article 22. Withdrawal of reservations and of objections to reservations
(1) Unless the treaty otherwise provides, a reservation may be withdrawn at any time and the consent of a State or of an international organization which has accepted the reservation is not required for its withdrawal.
(2) Unless the treaty otherwise provides, an objection to a reservation may be withdrawn at any time.
(3) Unless the treaty otherwise provides, or it is otherwise agreed:
(a) the withdrawal of a reservation becomes operative in relation to a contracting State or a contracting organization only when notice of it has been received by that State or that organization;
(b) the withdrawal of an objection to a reservation becomes operative only when notice of it has been received by the State or international organization which formulated the reservation.

Article 23. Procedure regarding reservations
(1) A reservation, an express acceptance of a reservation and an objection to a reservation must be formulated in writing and communicated to the contracting States and contracting organizations and other States and international organizations entitled to become parties to the treaty.
(2) If formulated when signing the treaty subject to ratification, act of formal confirmation, acceptance or approval, a reservation must be formally confirmed by the reserving State or international organization when expressing its consent to be bound by the treaty. In such a case the reservation shall be considered as having been made on the date of its confirmation. (3) An express acceptance of, or an objection to, a reservation made previously to confirmation of the reservation does not itself require confirmation.
(4) The withdrawal of a reservation or of an objection to a reservation must be formulated in writing.

Section 3. Entry into force and provisional application of treaties

Article 24. Entry into force
(1) A treaty enters into force in such manner and upon such date as it may provide or as the negotiating States and negotiating organizations or, as the case may be, the negotiating organizations may agree.
(2) Failing any such provision or agreement, a treaty enters into force as soon as consent to be bound by the treaty has been established for all the negotiating States and negotiating organizations or, as the case may be, all the negotiating organizations.

(3) When the consent of a State or of an international organization to be bound by a treaty is established on a date after the treaty has come into force, the treaty enters into force for that State or that organization on that date, unless the treaty otherwise provides.
(4) The provisions of a treaty regulating the authentication of its text, the establishment of consent to be bound by the treaty, the manner or date of its entry into force, reservations, the functions of the depositary and other matters arising necessarily before the entry into force of the treaty apply from the time of the adoption of its text.

Article 25. Provisional application
(1) A treaty or a part of a treaty is applied provisionally pending its entry into force if:
(a) the treaty itself so provides; or
(b) the negotiating States and negotiating organizations or, as the case may be, the negotiating organizations have in some other manner so agreed.
(2) Unless the treaty otherwise provides or the negotiating States and negotiating organizations or, as the case may be, the negotiating organizations have otherwise agreed, the provisional application of a treaty or a part of a treaty with respect to a State or an international organization shall be terminated if that State or that organization notifies the States and organizations with regard to which the treaty is being applied provisionally of its intention not to become a party to the treaty.

Part III. Observance, application and interpretation of treaties

Section 1. Observance of treaties

Article 26. Pacta sunt servanda
Every treaty in force is binding upon the parties to it and must be performed by them in good faith.

Article 27. Internal law of States, rules of international organizations and observance of treaties
(1) A State party to a treaty may not invoke the provisions of its internal law as justification for its failure to perform the treaty.
(2) An international organization party to a treaty may not invoke the rules of the organization as justification for its failure to perform the treaty.
(3) The rules contained in the preceding paragraphs are without prejudice to article 46.

Section 2. Application of treaties

Article 28. Non-retroactivity of treaties
Unless a different intention appears from the treaty or is otherwise established, its provisions do not bind a party in relation to any act or fact which took place or any situation which ceased to exist before the date of the entry into force of the treaty with respect to that party.

Article 29. Territorial scope of treaties
Unless a different intention appears from the treaty or is otherwise established, a treaty between one or more States and one or more international organizations is binding upon each State party in respect of its entire territory.

Article 30. Application of successive treaties relating to the same subject matter
(1) The rights and obligations of States and international organizations parties to successive treaties relating to the same subject matter shall be determined in accordance with the following paragraphs.
(2) When a treaty specifies that it is subject to, or that it is not to be considered as incompatible with, an earlier or later treaty, the provisions of that other treaty prevail.
(3) When all the parties to the earlier treaty are parties also to the later treaty but the earlier treaty is not terminated or suspended in operation under article 59, the earlier treaty applies to the extent that its provisions are compatible with those of the later treaty.
4. When the parties to the later treaty do not include all the parties to the earlier one:
(a) as between two parties, each of which is a party to both treaties, the same rule applies as in paragraph (3);
(b) as between a party to both treaties and a party to only one of the treaties, the treaty to which both are parties governs their mutual rights and obligations.
(5) Paragraph (4) is without prejudice to article 41, or to any question of the termination or suspension of the operation of a treaty under article 60 or to any question of responsibility which may arise for a State or for an international organization from the conclusion or application of a treaty the provisions of which are incompatible with its obligations towards a State or an organization under another treaty.
(6) The preceding paragraphs are without prejudice to the fact that, in the event of a conflict between

obligations under the Charter of the United Nations and obligations under a treaty, the obligations under the Charter shall prevail.

Section 3. Interpretation of treaties

Article 31. General rule of interpretation
(1) A treaty shall be interpreted in good faith in accordance with the ordinary meaning to be given to the terms of the treaty in their context and in the light of its object and purpose.
(2) The context for the purpose of the interpretation of a treaty shall comprise, in addition to the text, including its preamble and annexes:
(a) any agreement relating to the treaty which was made between all the parties in connection with the conclusion of the treaty;
(b) any instrument which was made by one or more parties in connection with the conclusion of the treaty and accepted by the other parties as an instrument related to the treaty.
(3) There shall be taken into account, together with the context:
(a) any subsequent agreement between the parties regarding the interpretation of the treaty or the application of its provisions;
(b) any subsequent practice in the application of the treaty which establishes the agreement of the parties regarding its interpretation;
(c) any relevant rules of international law applicable in the relations between the parties.
(4) A special meaning shall be given to a term if it is established that the parties so intended.

Article 32. Supplementary means of interpretation
Recourse may be had to supplementary means of interpretation, including the preparatory work of the treaty and the circumstances of its conclusion, in order to confirm the meaning resulting from the application of article 31, or to determine the meaning when the interpretation according to article 31:
(a) leaves the meaning ambiguous or obscure; or
(b) leads to a result which is manifestly absurd or unreasonable.

Article 33. Interpretation of treaties authenticated in two or more languages
(1) When a treaty has been authenticated in two or more languages, the text is equally authoritative in each language, unless the treaty provides or the parties agree that, in case of divergence, a particular text shall prevail.
(2) A version of the treaty in a language other than one of those in which the text was authenticated shall be considered an authentic text only if the treaty so provides or the parties so agree.
(3) The terms of a treaty are presumed to have the same meaning in each authentic text.
(4) Except where a particular text prevails in accordance with paragraph (1), when a comparison of the authentic texts discloses a difference of meaning which the application of articles 31 and 32 does not remove, the meaning which best reconciles the texts, having regard to the object and purpose of the treaty, shall be adopted.

Section 4. Treaties and third states or third organizations

Article 34. General rule regarding third States and third organizations
A treaty does not create either obligations or rights for a third State or a third organization without the consent of that State or that organization.

Article 35. Treaties providing for obligations for third States or third organizations
An obligation arises for a third State or a third organization from a provision of a treaty if the parties to the treaty intend the provision to be the means of establishing the obligation and the third State or the third organization expressly accepts that obligation in writing. Acceptance by the third organization of such an obligation shall be governed by the rules of that organization.

Article 36. Treaties providing for rights for third States or third organizations
(1) A right arises for a third State from a provision of a treaty if the parties to the treaty intend the provision to accord that right either to the third State, or to a group of States to which it belongs, or to all States, and the third State assents thereto. Its assent shall be presumed so long as the contrary is not indicated, unless the treaty otherwise provides.
(2) A right arises for a third organization from a provision of a treaty if the parties to the treaty intend the provision to accord that right either to the third organization, or to a group of international organizations to which it belongs, or to all organizations, and the third organization assents thereto. Its assent shall be governed by the rules of the organization.
(3) A State or an international organization exercising a right in accordance with paragraph (1) or 2

shall comply with the conditions for its exercise provided for in the treaty or established in conformity with the treaty.

Article 37. Revocation or modification of obligations or rights of third States or third organizations

(1) When an obligation has arisen for a third State or a third organization in conformity with article 35, the obligation may be revoked or modified only with the consent of the parties to the treaty and of the third State or the third organization, unless it is established that they had otherwise agreed.

(2) When a right has arisen for a third State or a third organization in conformity with article 36, the right may not be revoked or modified by the parties if it is established that the right was intended not to be revocable or subject to modification without the consent of the third State or the third organization.

(3) The consent of an international organization party to the treaty or of a third organization, as provided for in the foregoing paragraphs, shall be governed by the rules of that organization.

Article 38. Rules in a treaty becoming binding on third States or third organizations through international custom

Nothing in articles 34 to 37 precludes a rule set forth in a treaty from becoming binding upon a third State or a third organization as a customary rule of international law, recognized as such.

Part IV. Amendment and modifications of treaties

Article 39. General rule regarding the amendment of treaties

(1) A treaty may be amended by agreement between the parties. The rules laid down in Part II apply to such an agreement except insofar as the treaty may otherwise provide.

(2) The consent of an international organization to an agreement provided for in paragraph (1) shall be governed by the rules of that organization.

Article 40. Amendment of multilateral treaties

(1) Unless the treaty otherwise provides, the amendment of multilateral treaties shall be governed by the following paragraphs.

(2) Any proposal to amend a multilateral treaty as between all the parties must be notified to all the contracting States and all the contracting organizations, each one of which shall have the right to take part in:

(a) the decision as to the action to be taken in regard to such proposal;

(b) the negotiation and conclusion of any agreement for the amendment of the treaty. 3.Every State or international organization entitled to become a party to the treaty shall also be entitled to become a party to the treaty as amended.

(4) The amending agreement does not bind any State or international organization already a party to the treaty which does not become a party to the amending agreement; article 30, paragraph (4)(b), applies in relation to such State or organization.

(5) Any State or international organization which becomes a party to the treaty after the entry into force of the amending agreement shall, failing an expression of a different intention by that State or that organization:

(a) be considered as a party to the treaty as amended; and 20

(b) be considered as a party to the unamended treaty in relation to any party to the treaty not bound by the amending agreement.

Article 41. Agreements to modify multilateral treaties between certain of the parties only

(1) Two or more of the parties to a multilateral treaty may conclude an agreement to modify the treaty as between themselves alone if:

(a) the possibility of such a modification is provided for by the treaty; or

(b) the modification in question is not prohibited by the treaty and:

(i) does not affect the enjoyment by the other parties of their rights under the treaty or the performance of their obligations;

(ii) does not relate to a provision, derogation from which is incompatible with the effective execution of the object and purpose of the treaty as a whole.

(2) Unless in a case falling under paragraph (1)(a) the treaty otherwise provides, the parties in question shall notify the other parties of their intention to conclude the agreement and of the modification to the treaty for which it provides.

Part V. Invalidity, termination and suspension of the operation of treaties

VIENNA CONVENTION ON THE LAW OF TREATIES 1987 (INT. ORGANISATIONS)

Section 1. General provisions

Article 42. Validity and continuance in force of treaties
(1) The validity of a treaty or of the consent of a State or an international organization to be bound by a treaty may be impeached only through the application of the present Convention. (2) The termination of a treaty, its denunciation or the withdrawal of a party, may take place only as a result of the application of the provisions of the treaty or of the present Convention. The same rule applies to suspension of the operation of a treaty.

Article 43. Obligations imposed by international law independently of a treaty
The invalidity, termination or denunciation of a treaty, the withdrawal of a party from it, or the suspension of its operation, as a result of the application of the present Convention or of the provisions of the treaty, shall not in any way impair the duty of any State or of any international organization to 21 fulfil any obligation embodied in the treaty to which that State or that organization would be subject under international law independently of the treaty.

Article 44. Separability of treaty provisions
(1) A right of a party, provided for in a treaty or arising under article 56, to denounce, withdraw from or suspend the operation of the treaty may be exercised only with respect to the whole treaty unless the treaty otherwise provides or the parties otherwise agree.
(2) A ground for invalidating, terminating, withdrawing from or suspending the operation of a treaty recognized in the present Convention may be invoked only with respect to the whole treaty except as provided in the following paragraphs or in article 60.
(3) If the ground relates solely to particular clauses, it may be invoked only with respect to those clauses where:
(a) the said clauses are separable from the remainder of the treaty with regard to their application;
(b) it appears from the treaty or is otherwise established that acceptance of those clauses was not an essential basis of the consent of the other party or parties to be bound by the treaty as a whole; and
(c) continued performance of the remainder of the treaty would not be unjust.
(4) In cases falling under articles 49 and 50, the State or international organization entitled to invoke the fraud or corruption may do so with respect either to the whole treaty or, subject to paragraph (3), to the particular clauses alone. 5.In cases falling under articles 51, 52 and 53, no separation of the provisions of the treaty is permitted.

Article 45. Loss of a right to invoke a ground for invalidating, terminating, withdrawing from or suspending the operation of a treaty
(1) A State may no longer invoke a ground for invalidating, terminating, withdrawing from or suspending the operation of a treaty under articles 46 to 50 or articles 60 and 62 if, after becoming aware of the facts:
(a) it shall have expressly agreed that the treaty is valid or remains in force or continues in operation, as the case may be; or
(b) it must by reason of its conduct be considered as having acquiesced in the validity of the treaty or in its maintenance in force or in operation, as the case may be.
(2) An international organization may no longer invoke a ground for invalidating, terminating, withdrawing from or suspending the operation of a treaty under articles 46 to 50 or articles 60 and 62 if, after becoming aware of the facts:
(a) it shall have expressly agreed that the treaty is valid or remains in force or continues in operation, as the case may be; or
(b) it must by reason of the conduct of the competent organ be considered as having renounced the right to invoke that ground.

Section 2. Invalidity of treaties

Article 46. Provisions of internal law of a State and rules of an international organization regarding competence to conclude treaties
(1) A State may not invoke the fact that its consent to be bound by a treaty has been expressed in violation of a provision of its internal law regarding competence to conclude treaties as invalidating its consent unless that violation was manifest and concerned a rule of its internal law of fundamental importance.
(2) An international organization may not invoke the fact that its consent to be bound by a treaty has been expressed in violation of the rules of the organization regarding competence to conclude treaties as invalidating its consent unless that violation was manifest and concerned a rule of fundamental importance.

(3) A violation is manifest if it would be objectively evident to any State or any international organization conducting itself in the matter in accordance with the normal practice of States and, where appropriate, of international organizations and in good faith.

Article 47. Specific restrictions on authority to express the consent of a State or an international organization

If the authority of a representative to express the consent of a State or of an international organization to be bound by a particular treaty has been made subject to a specific restriction, his omission to observe that restriction may not be invoked as invalidating the consent expressed by him unless the restriction was notified to the negotiating States and negotiating organizations prior to his expressing such consent.

Article 48. Error

(1) A State or an international organization may invoke an error in a treaty as invalidating its consent to be bound by the treaty if the error relates to a fact or situation which was assumed by that 23 State or that organization to exist at the time when the treaty was concluded and formed an essential basis of the consent of that State or that organization to be bound by the treaty.

(2) Paragraph (1) shall not apply if the State or international organization in question contributed by its own conduct to the error or if the circumstances were such as to put that State or that organization on notice of a possible error.

(3) An error relating only to the wording of the text of a treaty does not affect its validity; article 80 then applies.

Article 49. Fraud

A State or an international organization induced to conclude a treaty by the fraudulent conduct of a negotiating State or a negotiating organization may invoke the fraud as invalidating its consent to be bound by the treaty.

Article 50. Corruption of a representative of a State or of an international organization

A State or an international organization the expression of whose consent to be bound by a treaty has been procured through the corruption of its representative directly or indirectly by a negotiating State or a negotiating organization may invoke such corruption as invalidating its consent to be bound by the treaty.

Article 51. Coercion of a representative of a State or of an international organization

The expression by a State or an international organization of consent to be bound by a treaty which has been procured by the coercion of the representative of that State or that organization through acts or threats directed against him shall be without any legal effect.

Article 52. Coercion of a State or of an international organization by the threat or use of force

A treaty is void if its conclusion has been procured by the threat or use of force in violation of the principles of international law embodied in the Chatter of the United Nations.

Article 53. Treaties conflicting with a peremptory norm of general international law (jus cogens)

A treaty is void if, at the time of its conclusion, it conflicts with a peremptory norm of general international law. For the purposes of the present Convention, a peremptory norm of general 24 international law is a norm accepted and recognized by the international community of States as a whole as a norm from which no derogation is permitted and which can be modified only by a subsequent norm of general international law having the same character.

Section 3. Termination and suspension of the operation of treaties

Article 54. Termination of or withdrawal from a treaty under its provisions or by consent of the parties

The termination of a treaty or the withdrawal of a party may take place: (a) in conformity with the provisions of the treaty; or (b) at any time by consent of all the parties after consultation with the contracting States and contracting organizations.

Article 55. Reduction of the parties to a multilateral treaty below the number necessary for its entry into force

Unless the treaty otherwise provides, a multilateral treaty does not terminate by reason only of the fact that the number of the parties falls below the number necessary for its entry into force.

Article 56. Denunciation of or withdrawal from a treaty containing no provision regarding termination, denunciation or withdrawal

(1) A treaty which contains no provision regarding its termination and which does not provide for denunciation or withdrawal is not subject to denunciation or withdrawal unless:
(a) it is established that the parties intended to admit the possibility of denunciation or withdrawal; or
(b) a right of denunciation or withdrawal may be implied by the nature of the treaty.
(2) A party shall give not less than twelve months' notice of its intention to denounce or withdraw from a treaty under paragraph (1).

Article 57. Suspension of the operation of a treaty under its provisions or by consent of the parties

The operation of a treaty in regard to all the parties or to a particular party may be suspended: (a) in conformity with the provisions of the treaty; or
(b) at any time by consent of all the parties after consultation with the contracting States and contracting organizations.

Article 58. Suspension of the operation of a multilateral treaty by agreement between certain of the parties only

(1) Two or more parties to a multilateral treaty may conclude an agreement to suspend the operation of provisions of the treaty, temporarily and as between themselves alone, if:
(a) the possibility of such a suspension is provided for by the treaty; or
(b) the suspension in question is not prohibited by the treaty and:
(i) does not affect the enjoyment by the other parties of their rights under the treaty or the performance of their obligations;
(ii) is not incompatible with the object and purpose of the treaty.
(2) Unless in a case falling under paragraph (1)(a) the treaty otherwise provides, the parties in question shall notify the other parties of their intention to conclude the agreement and of those provisions of the treaty the operation of which they intend to suspend.

Article 59. Termination or suspension of the operation of a treaty implied by conclusion of a later treaty

(1) A treaty shall be considered as terminated if all the parties to it conclude a later treaty relating to the same subject matter and:
(a) it appears from the later treaty or is otherwise established that the parties intended that the matter should be governed by that treaty; or
(b) the provisions of the later treaty are so far incompatible with those of the earlier one that the two treaties are not capable of being applied at the same time.
(2) The earlier treaty shall be considered as only suspended in operation if it appears from the later treaty or is otherwise established that such was the intention of the parties.

Article 60. Termination or suspension of the operation of a treaty as a consequence of its breach

(1) A material breach of a bilateral treaty by one of the parties entitles the other to invoke the breach as a ground for terminating the treaty or suspending its operation in whole or in part. 2.A material breach of a multilateral treaty by one of the parties entitles:
(a) the other parties by unanimous agreement to suspend the operation of the treaty in whole or in part or to terminate it either:
(i) in the relations between themselves and the defaulting State or international organization; or
(ii) as between all the parties;
(b) a party specially affected by the breach to invoke it as a ground for suspending the operation of the treaty in whole or in part in the relations between itself and the defaulting State or international organization;
(c) any party other than the defaulting State or international organization to invoke the breach as a ground for suspending the operation of the treaty in whole or in part with respect to itself if the treaty is of such a character that a material breach of its provisions by one party radically changes the position of every party with respect to the further performance of its obligations under the treaty.
(3) A material breach of a treaty, for the purposes of this article, consists in:
(a) a repudiation of the treaty not sanctioned by the present Convention; or
(b) the violation of a provision essential to the accomplishment of the object or purpose of the treaty.
(4) The foregoing paragraphs are without prejudice to any provision in the treaty applicable in the event of a breach.
(5) Paragraphs (1) to (3) do not apply to provisions relating to the protection of the human person contained in treaties of a humanitarian character, in particular to provisions prohibiting any form of reprisals against persons protected by such treaties.

Article 61. Supervening impossibility of performance

(1) A party may invoke the impossibility of performing a treaty as a ground for terminating or withdrawing from it if the impossibility results from the permanent disappearance or destruction of an object indispensable for the execution of the treaty. If the impossibility is temporary, it may be invoked only as a ground for suspending the operation of the treaty.

(2) Impossibility of performance may not be invoked by a party as a ground for terminating, withdrawing from or suspending the operation of a treaty if the impossibility is the result of a breach by that party either of an obligation under the treaty or of any other international obligation owed to any other party to the treaty.

Article 62. Fundamental change of circumstances

(1) A fundamental change of circumstances which has occurred with regard to those existing at the time of the conclusion of a treaty, and which was not foreseen by the parties, may not be invoked as a ground for terminating or withdrawing from the treaty unless:

(a) the existence of those circumstances constituted an essential basis of the consent of the parties to be bound by the treaty; and

(b) the effect of the change is radically to transform the extent of obligations still to be performed under the treaty.

(2) A fundamental change of circumstances may not be invoked as a ground for terminating or withdrawing from a treaty between two or more States and one or more international organizations if the treaty establishes a boundary.

(3) A fundamental change of circumstances may not be invoked as a ground for terminating or withdrawing from a treaty if the fundamental change is the result of a breach by the party invoking it either of an obligation under the treaty or of any other international obligation owed to any other party to the treaty.

(4) If, under the foregoing paragraphs, a party may invoke a fundamental change of circumstances as a ground for terminating or withdrawing from a treaty it may also invoke the change as a ground for suspending the operation of the treaty.

Article 63. Severance of diplomatic or consular relations

The severance of diplomatic or consular relations between States Parties to a treaty between two or more States and one or more international organizations does not affect the legal relations established between those States by the treaty except insofar as the existence of diplomatic or consular relations is indispensable for the application of the treaty.

Article 64. Emergence of a new peremptory norm of general international law *(*jus cogens*)*

If a new peremptory norm of general international law emerges, any existing treaty which is in conflict with that norm becomes void and terminates.

Section 4. Procedure

Article 65. Procedure to be followed with respect to invalidity, termination, withdrawal from or suspension of the operation of a treaty

(1) A party which, under the provisions of the present Convention, invokes either a defect in its consent to be bound by a treaty or a ground for impeaching the validity of a treaty, terminating it, withdrawing from it or suspending its operation, must notify the other parties of its claim. The notification shall indicate the measure proposed to be taken with respect to the treaty and the reasons therefor.

(2) If, after the expiry of a period which, except in cases of special urgency, shall not be less than three months after the receipt of the notification, no party has raised any objection, the party making the notification may carry out in the manner provided in article 67 the measure which it has proposed.

(3) If, however, objection has been raised by any other party, the parties shall seek a solution through the means indicated in Article 33 of the Charter of the United Nations.

(4) The notification or objection made by an international organization shall be governed by the rules of that organization.

(5) Nothing in the foregoing paragraphs shall affect the rights or obligations of the parties under any provisions in force binding the parties with regard to the settlement of disputes.

(6) Without prejudice to article 45, the fact that a State or an international organization has not previously made the notification prescribed in paragraph (1) shall not prevent it from making such notification in answer to another party claiming performance of the treaty or alleging its violation.

Article 66. Procedures for judicial settlement, arbitration and conciliation

(1) If, under paragraph (3) of article 65, no solution has been reached within a period of twelve

months following the date on which the objection was raised, the procedures specified in the following paragraphs shall be followed.
(2) With respect to a dispute concerning the application or the interpretation of article 53 or 64:
(a) if a State is a party to the dispute with one or more States, it may, by a written application, submit the dispute to the International Court of Justice for a decision;
(b) if a State is a party to the dispute to which one or more international organizations are parties, the State may, through a Member State of the United Nations if necessary, request the General Assembly or the Security Council or, where appropriate, the competent organ of an international organization which is a party to the dispute and is authorized in accordance with Article 96 of the Charter of the United Nations, to request an advisory opinion of the International Court of Justice in accordance with Article 65 of the Statute of the Court; 29
(c) if the United Nations or an international organization that is authorized in accordance with Article 96 of the Charter of the United Nations is a party to the dispute, it may request an advisory opinion of the International Court of Justice in accordance with Article 65 of the Statute of the Court;
(d) if an international organization other than those referred to in subparagraph (c) is a party to the dispute, it may, through a Member State of the United Nations, follow the procedure specified in subparagraph (b);
(e) the advisory opinion given pursuant to subparagraph (b), (c) or (d) shall be accepted as decisive by all the parties to the dispute concerned;
(f) if the request under subparagraph (b), (c) or (d) for an advisory opinion of the Court is not granted, any one of the parties to the dispute may, by written notification to the other party or parties, submit it to arbitration in accordance with the provisions of the Annex to the present Convention.
(3) The provisions of paragraph (2) apply unless all the parties to a dispute referred to in that paragraph by common consent agree to submit the dispute to an arbitration procedure, including the one specified in the Annex to the present Convention.
(4) With respect to a dispute concerning the application or the interpretation of any of the articles in Part V, other than articles 53 and 64, of the present Convention, any one of the parties to the dispute may set in motion the conciliation procedure specified in the Annex to the Convention by submitting a request to that effect to the Secretary-General of the United Nations.

Article 67. Instruments for declaring invalid, terminating, withdrawing from or suspending the operation of a treaty

The notification provided for under article 65, paragraph (1), must be made in writing. 2.Any act declaring invalid, terminating, withdrawing from or suspending the operation of a treaty pursuant to the provisions of the treaty or of paragraphs (2) or (3) of article 65 shall be carried out through an instrument communicated to the other parties. If the instrument emanating from a State is not signed by the Head of State, Head of Government or Minister for Foreign Affairs, the representative of the State communicating it may be called upon to produce full powers. If the instrument emanates from an international organization, the representative of the organization communicating it may be called upon to produce full powers.

Article 68. Revocation of notifications and instruments provided for in articles 65 and 67

A notification or instrument provided for in articles 65 or 67 may be revoked at any time before it takes effect.

Section 5. Consequences of the invalidity, termination or suspension of the operation of a treaty

Article 69. Consequences of the invalidity of a treaty

(1) A treaty the invalidity of which is established under the present Convention is void. The provisions of a void treaty have no legal force.
(2) If acts have nevertheless been performed in reliance on such a treaty:
(a) each party may require any other party to establish as far as possible in their mutual relations the position that would have existed if the acts had not been performed;
(b) acts performed in good faith before the invalidity was invoked are not rendered unlawful by reason only of the invalidity of the treaty.
(3) In cases falling under articles 49, 50, 51 or 52, paragraph (2) does not apply with respect to the party to which the fraud, the act of corruption or the coercion is imputable.
(4) In the case of the invalidity of the consent of a particular State or a particular international organization to be bound by a multilateral treaty, the foregoing rules apply in the relations between that State or that organization and the parties to the treaty.

PART I   INTERNATIONAL LAW

Article 70. Consequences of the termination of a treaty
(1) Unless the treaty otherwise provides or the parties otherwise agree, the termination of a treaty under its provisions or in accordance with the present Convention:
(a) releases the parties from any obligation further to perform the treaty;
(b) does not affect any right, obligation or legal situation of the parties created through the execution of the treaty prior to its termination.
(2) If a State or an international organization denounces or withdraws from a multilateral treaty, paragraph (1) applies in the relations between that State or that organization and each of the other parties to the treaty from the date when such denunciation or withdrawal takes effect.

Article 71. Consequences of the invalidity of a treaty which conflicts with a peremptory norm of general international law
(1) In the case of a treaty which is void under article 53 the parties shall:
(a) eliminate as far as possible the consequences of any act performed in reliance on any provision which conflicts with the peremptory norm of general international law; and
(b) bring their mutual relations into conformity with the peremptory norm of general international law.
(2) In the case of a treaty which becomes void and terminates under article 64, the termination of the treaty:
(a) releases the parties from any obligation further to perform the treaty;
(b) does not affect any right, obligation or legal situation of the parties created through the execution of the treaty prior to its termination; provided that those rights, obligations or situations may thereafter be maintained only to the extent that their maintenance is not in itself in conflict with the new peremptory norm of general international law.

Article 72. Consequences of the suspension of the operation of a treaty
(1) Unless the treaty otherwise provides or the parties otherwise agree, the suspension of the operation of a treaty under its provisions or in accordance with the present Convention:
(a) releases the parties between which the operation of the treaty is suspended from the obligation to perform the treaty in their mutual relations during the period of the suspension; (b) does not otherwise affect the legal relations between the parties established by the treaty. (2) During the period of the suspension the parties shall refrain from acts tending to obstruct the resumption of the operation of the treaty.

Part VI. Miscellaneous provisions

Article 73. Relationship to the Vienna Convention on the Law of Treaties
As between States Parties to the Vienna Convention on the Law of Treaties of 1969, the relations of those States under a treaty between two or more States and one or more international organizations shall be governed by that Convention.

Article 74. Questions not prejudged by the present Convention
(1) The provisions of the present Convention shall not prejudge any question that may arise in regard to a treaty between one or more States and one or more international organizations from a 32 succession of States or from the international responsibility of a State or from the outbreak of hostilities between States.
(2) The provisions of the present Convention shall not prejudge any question that may arise in regard to a treaty from the international responsibility of an international organization, from the termination of the existence of the organization or from the termination of participation by a State in the membership of the organization.
(3) The provisions of the present Convention shall not prejudge any question that may arise in regard to the establishment of obligations and rights for States members of an international organization under a treaty to which that organization is a party.

Article 75. Diplomatic and consular relations and the conclusion of treaties
The severance or absence of diplomatic or consular relations between two or more States does not prevent the conclusion of treaties between two or more of those States and one or more international organizations. The conclusion of such a treaty does not in itself affect the situation in regard to diplomatic or consular relations.

Article 76. Case of an aggressor State
The provisions of the present Convention are without prejudice to any obligation in relation to a treaty between one or more States and one or more international organizations which may arise for

an aggressor State in consequence of measures taken in conformity with the Charter of the United Nations with reference to that State's aggression.

Part VII. Depositaries, notifications, corrections and registration

Article 77. Depositaries of treaties
(1) The designation of the depositary of a treaty may be made by the negotiating States and negotiating organizations or, as the case may be, the negotiating organizations, either in the treaty itself or in some other manner. The depositary may be one or more States, an international organization or the chief administrative officer of the organization.
(2) The functions of the depositary of a treaty are international in character and the depositary is under an obligation to act impartially in their performance. In particular, the fact that a treaty has not entered into force between certain of the parties or that a difference has appeared between a State or an international organization and a depositary with regard to the performance of the latter's functions shall not affect that obligation.

Article 78. Functions of depositaries
(1) The functions of a depositary, unless otherwise provided in the treaty or agreed by the contracting States and contracting organizations or, as the case may be, by the contracting organizations, comprise in particular:
(a) keeping custody of the original text of the treaty and of any full powers delivered to the depositary;
(b) preparing certified copies of the original text and preparing any further text of the treaty in such additional languages as may be required by the treaty and transmitting them to the parties and to the States and international organizations entitled to become parties to the treaty;
(c) receiving any signatures to the treaty and receiving and keeping custody of any instruments, notifications and communications relating to it;
(d) examining whether the signature or any instrument, notification or communication relating to the treaty is in due and proper form and, if need be, bringing the matter to the attention of the State or international organization in question;
(e) informing the parties and the States and international organizations entitled to become parties to the treaty of acts, notifications and communications relating to the treaty;
(f) informing the States and international organizations entitled to become parties to the treaty when the number of signatures or of instruments of ratification, instruments relating to an act of formal confirmation, or of instruments of acceptance, approval or accession required for the entry into force of the treaty has been received or deposited;
(g) registering the treaty with the Secretariat of the United Nations;
(h) performing the functions specified in other provisions of the present Convention.
(2) In the event of any difference appearing between a State or an international organization and the depositary as to the performance of the latter's functions, the depositary shall bring the question to the attention of:
(a) the signatory States and organizations and the contracting States and contracting organizations; or
(b) where appropriate, the competent organ of the international organization concerned.

Article 79. Notifications and communications
Except as the treaty or the present Convention otherwise provide, any notification or communication to be made by any State or any international organization under the present Convention shall:
(a) if there is no depositary, be transmitted direct to the States and organizations for which it is intended, or if there is a depositary, to the latter;
(b) be considered as having been made by the State or organization in question only upon its receipt by the State or organization to which it was transmitted or, as the case may be, upon its receipt by the depositary;
(c) if transmitted to a depositary, be considered as received by the State or organization for which it was intended only when the latter State or organization has been informed by the depositary in accordance with article 78, paragraph (l)(e).

Article 80. Correction of errors in texts or in certified copies of treaties
(1) Where, after the authentication of the text of a treaty, the signatory States and international organizations and the contracting States and contracting organizations are agreed that it contains an error, the error shall, unless those States and organizations decide upon some other means of correction, be corrected:
(a) by having the appropriate correction made in the text and causing the correction to be initialled by duly authorized representatives;

(b) by executing or exchanging an instrument or instruments setting out the correction which it has been agreed to make; or
(c) by executing a corrected text of the whole treaty by the same procedure as in the case of the original text.
(2) Where the treaty is one for which there is a depositary, the latter shall notify the signatory States and international organizations and the contracting States and contracting organizations of the error and of the proposal to correct it and shall specify an appropriate time limit within which objection to the proposed correction may be raised. If, on the expiry of the time limit:
(a) no objection has been raised, the depositary shall make and initial the correction in the text and shall execute a procés-verbal of the rectification of the text and communicate a copy of it to the parties and to the States and organizations entitled to become parties to the treaty; (b) an objection has been raised, the depositary shall communicate the objection to the signatory States and organizations and to the contracting States and contracting organizations.
(3) The rules in paragraphs (1) and (2) apply also where the text has been authenticated in two or more languages and it appears that there is a lack of concordance which the signatory States and international organizations and the contracting States and contracting organizations agree should be corrected.
(4) The corrected text replaces the defective text ab initio, unless the signatory States and international organizations and the contracting States and contracting organizations otherwise decide.
(5) The correction of the text of a treaty that has been registered shall be notified to the Secretariat of the United Nations.
(6) Where an error is discovered in a certified copy of a treaty, the depositary shall execute a procés-verbal specifying the rectification and communicate a copy of it to the signatory States and international organizations and to the contracting States and contracting organizations.

Article 81. Registration and publication of treaties
(1) Treaties shall, after their entry into force, be transmitted to the Secretariat of the United Nations for registration or filing and recording, as the case may be, and for publication.
(2) The designation of a depositary shall constitute authorization for it to perform the acts specified in the preceding paragraph.

Part VIII. Final provisions

Article 82. Signature
The present Convention shall be open for signature until 31 December 1986 at the Federal Ministry for Foreign Affairs of the Republic of Austria, and subsequently, until 30 June 1987, at United Nations Headquarters, New York by:
(a) all States;
(b) Namibia, represented by the United Nations Council for Namibia;
(c) international organizations invited to participate in the United Nations Conference on the Law of Treaties between States and International Organizations or between International Organizations.

Article 83. Ratification or act of formal confirmation
The present Convention is subject to ratification by States and by Namibia, represented by the United Nations Council for Namibia, and to acts of formal confirmation by international organizations. The instruments of ratification and those relating to acts of formal confirmation shall be deposited with the Secretary-General of the United Nations.

Article 84. Accession
(1) The present Convention shall remain open for accession by any State, by Namibia, represented by the United Nations Council for Namibia, and by any international organization which has the capacity to conclude treaties.
(2) An instrument of accession of an international organization shall contain a declaration that it has the capacity to conclude treaties.
(3) The instruments of accession shall be deposited with the Secretary-General of the United Nations.

Article 85. Entry into force
(1) The present Convention shall enter into force on the thirtieth day following the date of deposit of the thirty-fifth instrument of ratification or accession by States or by Namibia, represented by the United Nations Council for Namibia.
(2) For each State or for Namibia, represented by the United Nations Council for Namibia, ratifying or acceding to the Convention after the condition specified in paragraph (1) has been fulfilled, the

Convention shall enter into force on the thirtieth day after deposit by such State or by Namibia of its instrument of ratification or accession.

(3) For each international organization depositing an instrument relating to an act of formal confirmation or an instrument of accession, the Convention shall enter into force on the thirtieth day after such deposit, or at the date the Convention enters into force pursuant to paragraph (1), whichever is later.

Article 86. Authentic texts

The original of the present Convention, of which the Arabic, Chinese, English, French, Russian and Spanish texts are equally authentic, shall be deposited with the Secretary-General of the United Nations.

IN WITNESS WHEREOF the undersigned Plenipotentiaries, being duly authorized by their respective Governments, and duly authorized representatives of the United Nations Council for Namibia and of international organizations have signed the present Convention.

Done at Vienna, this twenty-first day of March one thousand nine hundred and eighty-six.

Annex arbitration and conciliation procedures established in application of Article 66

I. Establishment of the arbitral tribunal or conciliation commission

(1) A list consisting of qualified jurists, from which the parties to a dispute may choose the persons who are to constitute an arbitral tribunal or, as the case may be, a conciliation commission, shall be drawn up and maintained by the Secretary-General of the United Nations. To this end, every State which is a Member of the United Nations and every Party to the present Convention shall be invited to nominate two persons, and the names of the persons so nominated shall constitute the list, a copy of which shall be transmitted to the President of the International Court of Justice. The term of office of a person on the list, including that of any person nominated to fill a casual vacancy, shall be five years and may be renewed. A person whose term expires shall continue to fulfil any function for which he shall have been chosen under the following paragraphs.

(2) When notification has been made under article 66, paragraph (2), subparagraph (f), or agreement on the procedure in the present Annex has been reached under paragraph (3), the dispute shall be brought before an arbitral tribunal. When a request has been made to the Secretary-General under article 66, paragraph (4), the Secretary-General shall bring the dispute before a conciliation commission. Both the arbitral tribunal and the conciliation commission shall be constituted as follows: The States, international organizations or, as the case may be, the States and organizations which constitute one of the parties to the dispute shall appoint by common consent:

(a) one arbitrator or, as the case may be, one conciliator, who may or may not be chosen from the list referred to in paragraph (1); and

(b) one arbitrator or, as the case may be, one conciliator, who shall be chosen from among those included in the list and shall not be of the nationality of any of the States or nominated by any of the organizations which constitute that party to the dispute, provided that a dispute between two international organizations is not considered by nationals of one and the same State. The States, international organizations or, as the case may be, the States and organizations which constitute the other party to the dispute shall appoint two arbitrators or, as the case may be, two conciliators, in the same way. The four persons chosen by the parties shall be appointed within sixty days following the date on which the other party to the dispute receives notification under article 66, paragraph (2), subparagraph (f), or on which the agreement on the procedure in the present Annex under paragraph (3) is reached, or on which the Secretary-General receives the request for conciliation. The four persons so chosen shall, within sixty days following the date of the last of their own appointments, appoint from the list a fifth arbitrator or, as the case may be, conciliator, who shall be chairman. 38 If the appointment of the chairman, or any of the arbitrators or, as the case may be, conciliators, has not been made within the period prescribed above for such appointment, it shall be made by the SecretaryGeneral of the United Nations within sixty days following the expiry of that period. The appointment of the chairman may be made by the Secretary-General either from the list or from the membership of the International Law Commission. Any of the periods within which appointments must be made may be extended by agreement between the parties to the dispute. If the United Nations is a party or is included in one of the parties to the dispute, the Secretary-General shall transmit the above-mentioned request to the President of the International Court of Justice, who shall perform the functions conferred upon the Secretary-General under this subparagraph. Any vacancy shall be filled in the manner prescribed for the initial appointment. The appointment of arbitrators or conciliators by an international organization provided for in paragraphs (1) and (2) shall be governed by the rules of that organization.

PART I   INTERNATIONAL LAW

II. Functioning of the arbitral tribunal

(3) Unless the parties to the dispute otherwise agree, the Arbitral Tribunal shall decide its own procedure, assuring to each party to the dispute a full opportunity to be heard and to present its case.

(4) The Arbitral Tribunal, with the consent of the parties to the dispute, may invite any interested State or international organization to submit to it its views orally or in writing.

(5) Decisions of the Arbitral Tribunal shall be adopted by a majority vote of the members. In the event of an equality of votes, the vote of the Chairman shall be decisive.

(6) When one of the parties to the dispute does not appear before the Tribunal or fails to defend its case, the other party may request the Tribunal to continue the proceedings and to make its award. Before making its award, the Tribunal must satisfy itself not only that it has jurisdiction over the dispute but also that the claim is well founded in fact and law.

(7) The award of the Arbitral Tribunal shall be confined to the subject matter of the dispute and state the reasons on which it is based. Any member of the Tribunal may attach a separate or dissenting opinion to the award.

(8) The award shall be final and without appeal. It shall be complied with by all parties to the dispute.

(9) The Secretary-General shall provide the Tribunal with such assistance and facilities as it may require. The expenses of the Tribunal shall be borne by the United Nations. III.

Functioning of the conciliation commission

(10) The Conciliation Commission shall decide its own procedure. The Commission, with the consent of the parties to the dispute, may invite any party to the treaty to submit to it its views orally or 39 in writing. Decisions and recommendations of the Commission shall be made by a majority vote of the five members.

(11) The Commission may draw the attention of the parties to the dispute to any measures which might facilitate an amicable settlement.

(12) The Commission shall hear the parties, examine the claims and objections, and make proposals to the parties with a view to reaching an amicable settlement of the dispute.

(13) The Commission shall report within twelve months of its constitution. Its report shall be deposited with the Secretary-General and transmitted to the parties to the dispute. The report of the Commission, including any conclusions stated therein regarding the facts or questions of law, shall not be binding upon the parties and it shall have no other character than that of recommendations submitted for the consideration of the parties in order to facilitate an amicable settlement of the dispute.

(14) The Secretary-General shall provide the Commission with such assistance and facilities as it may require. The expenses of the Commission shall be borne by the United Nations.

Draft Articles on Responsibility of States for Internationally Wrongful Acts, Text adopted by the International Law Commission in 2001. Text reproduced as it appears in the annex to General Assembly resolution 56/83 of 12 December 2001

Part One. The internationally wrongful act of a state

Chapter I. General principles

Article l. Responsibility of a State for its internationally wrongful acts
Every internationally wrongful act of a State entails the international responsibility of that State.

Article 2. Elements of an internationally wrongful act of a State
There is an internationally wrongful act of a State when conduct consisting of an action or omission:
(a) Is attributable to the State under international law; and
(b) Constitutes a breach of an international obligation of the State.

Article 3. Characterization of an act of a State as internationally wrongful
The characterization of an act of a State as internationally wrongful is governed by international law. Such characterization is not affected by the characterization of the same act as lawful by internal law.

Chapter II. Attribution of conduct to a state

Article 4. Conduct of organs of a State
(1) The conduct of any State organ shall be considered an act of that State under international law, whether the organ exercises legislative, executive, judicial or any other functions, whatever position it holds in the organization of the State, and whatever its character as an organ of the central Government or of a territorial unit of the State.
(2) An organ includes any person or entity which has that status in accordance with the internal law of the State.

Article 5. Conduct of persons or entities exercising elements of governmental authority
The conduct of a person or entity which is not an organ of the State under article 4 but which is empowered by the law of that State to exercise elements of the governmental authority shall be considered an act of the State under international law, provided the person or entity is acting in that capacity in the particular instance.

Article 6. Conduct of organs placed at the disposal of a State by another State
The conduct of an organ placed at the disposal of a State by another State shall be considered an act of the former State under international law if the organ is acting in the exercise of elements of the governmental authority of the State at whose disposal it is placed.

Article 7. Excess of authority or contravention of instructions
The conduct of an organ of a State or of a person or entity empowered to exercise elements of the governmental authority shall be considered an act of the State under international law if the organ, person or entity acts in that capacity, even if it exceeds its authority or contravenes instructions.

Article 8. Conduct directed or controlled by a State
The conduct of a person or group of persons shall be considered an act of a State under international law if the person or group of persons is in fact acting on the instructions of, or under the direction or control of, that State in carrying out the conduct.

Article 9. Conduct carried out in the absence or default of the official authorities
The conduct of a person or group of persons shall be considered an act of a State under international law if the person or group of persons is in fact exercising elements of the governmental authority in the absence or default of the official authorities and in circumstances such as to call for the exercise of those elements of authority.

Article 10. Conduct of an insurrectional or other movement
(1) The conduct of an insurrectional movement which becomes the new Government of a State shall be considered an act of that State under international law.
(2) The conduct of a movement, insurrectional or other, which succeeds in establishing a new State in part of the territory of a pre-existing State or in a territory under its administration shall be considered an act of the new State under international law.
(3) This article is without prejudice to the attribution to a State of any conduct, however related to

that of the movement concerned, which is to be considered an act of that State by virtue of articles 4 to 9.

Article 11. Conduct acknowledged and adopted by a State as its own
Conduct which is not attributable to a State under the preceding articles shall nevertheless be considered an act of that State under international law if and to the extent that the State acknowledges and adopts the conduct in question as its own.

Chapter III. Breach of an international obligation

Article 12. Existence of a breach of an international obligation
There is a breach of an international obligation by a State when an act of that State is not in conformity with what is required of it by that obligation, regardless of its origin or character.

Article 13. International obligation in force for a State
An act of a State does not constitute a breach of an international obligation unless the State is bound by the obligation in question at the time the act occurs.

Article 14. Extension in time of the breach of an international obligation
(1) The breach of an international obligation by an act of a State not having a continuing character occurs at the moment when the act is performed, even if its effects continue.
(2) The breach of an international obligation by an act of a State having a continuing character extends over the entire period during which the act continues and remains not in conformity with the international obligation.
(3) The breach of an international obligation requiring a State to prevent a given event occurs when the event occurs and extends over the entire period during which the event continues and remains not in conformity with that obligation.

Article 15. Breach consisting of a composite act
(1) The breach of an international obligation by a State through a series of actions or omissions defined in aggregate as wrongful occurs when the action or omission occurs which, taken with the other actions or omissions, is sufficient to constitute the wrongful act.
(2) In such a case, the breach extends over the entire period starting with the first of the actions or omissions of the series and lasts for as long as these actions or omissions are repeated and remain not in conformity with the international obligation.

Chapter IV. Responsibility of a state in connection with the act of another state

Article 16. Aid or assistance in the commission of an internationally wrongful act
A State which aids or assists another State in the commission of an internationally wrongful act by the latter is internationally responsible for doing so if:
(a) That State does so with knowledge of the circumstances of the internationally wrongful act; and
(b) The act would be internationally wrongful if committed by that State.

Article 17. Direction and control exercised over the commission of an internationally wrongful act
A State which directs and controls another State in the commission of an internationally wrongful act by the latter is internationally responsible for that act if:
(a) That State does so with knowledge of the circumstances of the internationally wrongful act; and
(b) The act would be internationally wrongful if committed by that State.

Article 18. Coercion of another State
A State which coerces another State to commit an act is internationally responsible for that act if:
(a) The act would, but for the coercion, be an internationally wrongful act of the coerced State; and
(b) The coercing State does so with knowledge of the circumstances of the act.

Article 19. Effect of this chapter
This chapter is without prejudice to the international responsibility, under other provisions of these articles, of the State which commits the act in question, or of any other State.

Chapter V. Circumstances precluding wrongfulness

Article 20. Consent
Valid consent by a State to the commission of a given act by another State precludes the wrongfulness of that act in relation to the former State to the extent that the act remains within the limits of that consent.

Article 21. Self-defence

The wrongfulness of an act of a State is precluded if the act constitutes a lawful measure of self-defence taken in conformity with the Charter of the United Nations.

Article 22. Countermeasures in respect of an internationally wrongful act

The wrongfulness of an act of a State not in conformity with an international obligation towards another State is precluded if and to the extent that the act constitutes a countermeasure taken against the latter State in accordance with chapter II of part three.

Article 23. Force majeure

(1) The wrongfulness of an act of a State not in conformity with an international obligation of that State is precluded if the act is due to force majeure, that is the occurrence of an irresistible force or of an unforeseen event, beyond the control of the State, making it materially impossible in the circumstances to perform the obligation.
(2) Paragraph (1) does not apply if:
(a) The situation of force majeure is due, either alone or in combination with other factors, to the conduct of the State invoking it; or
(b) The State has assumed the risk of that situation occurring.

Article 24. Distress

(1) The wrongfulness of an act of a State not in conformity with an international obligation of that State is precluded if the author of the act in question has no other reasonable way, in a situation of distress, of saving the author's life or the lives of other persons entrusted to the author's care.
(2) Paragraph (1) does not apply if:
(a) The situation of distress is due, either alone or in combination with other factors, to the conduct of the State invoking it; or
(b) The act in question is likely to create a comparable or greater peril.

Article 25. Necessity

(1) Necessity may not be invoked by a State as a ground for precluding the wrongfulness of an act not in conformity with an international obligation of that State unless the act:
(a) Is the only way for the State to safeguard an essential interest against a grave and imminent peril; and
(b) Does not seriously impair an essential interest of the State or States towards which the obligation exists, or of the international community as a whole.
(2) In any case, necessity may not be invoked by a State as a ground for precluding wrongfulness if:
(a) The international obligation in question excludes the possibility of invoking necessity; or
(b) The State has contributed to the situation of necessity.

Article 26. Compliance with peremptory norms

Nothing in this chapter precludes the wrongfulness of any act of a State which is not in conformity with an obligation arising under a peremptory norm of general international law.

Article 27. Consequences of invoking a circumstance precluding wrongfulness

The invocation of a circumstance precluding wrongfulness in accordance with this chapter is without prejudice to:
(a) Compliance with the obligation in question, if and to the extent that the circumstance precluding wrongfulness no longer exists;
(b) The question of compensation for any material loss caused by the act in question.

Part Two. Content of the international responsibility of a state

Chapter I. General principles

Article 28. Legal consequences of an internationally wrongful act

The international responsibility of a State which is entailed by an internationally wrongful act in accordance with the provisions of part one involves legal consequences as set out in this part.

Article 29. Continued duty of performance

The legal consequences of an internationally wrongful act under this part do not affect the continued duty of the responsible State to perform the obligation breached.

Article 30. Cessation and non-repetition

The State responsible for the internationally wrongful act is under an obligation:

(a) To cease that act, if it is continuing;
(b) To offer appropriate assurances and guarantees of non-repetition, if circumstances so require.

Article 31. Reparation
(1) The responsible State is under an obligation to make full reparation for the injury caused by the internationally wrongful act.
(2) Injury includes any damage, whether material or moral, caused by the internationally wrongful act of a State.

Article 32. Irrelevance of internal law
The responsible State may not rely on the provisions of its internal law as justification for failure to comply with its obligations under this part.

Article 33. Scope of international obligations set out in this part
(1) The obligations of the responsible State set out in this part may be owed to another State, to several States, or to the international community as a whole, depending in particular on the character and content of the international obligation and on the circumstances of the breach.
(2) This part is without prejudice to any right, arising from the international responsibility of a State, which may accrue directly to any person or entity other than a State.

Chapter II. Reparation for injury

Article 34. Forms of reparation
Full reparation for the injury caused by the internationally wrongful act shall take the form of restitution, compensation and satisfaction, either singly or in combination, in accordance with the provisions of this chapter.

Article 35. Restitution
A State responsible for an internationally wrongful act is under an obligation to make restitution, that is, to re-establish the situation which existed before the wrongful act was committed, provided and to the extent that restitution:
(a) Is not materially impossible;
(b) Does not involve a burden out of all proportion to the benefit deriving from restitution instead of compensation.

Article 36. Compensation
(1) The State responsible for an internationally wrongful act is under an obligation to compensate for the damage caused thereby, insofar as such damage is not made good by restitution.
(2) The compensation shall cover any financially assessable damage including loss of profits insofar as it is established.

Article 37. Satisfaction
(1) The State responsible for an internationally wrongful act is under an obligation to give satisfaction for the injury caused by that act insofar as it cannot be made good by restitution or compensation.
(2) Satisfaction may consist in an acknowledgement of the breach, an expression of regret, a formal apology or another appropriate modality.
(3) Satisfaction shall not be out of proportion to the injury and may not take a form humiliating to the responsible State.

Article 38. Interest
(1) Interest on any principal sum due under this chapter shall be payable when necessary in order to ensure full reparation. The interest rate and mode of calculation shall be set so as to achieve that result.
(2) Interest runs from the date when the principal sum should have been paid until the date the obligation to pay is fulfilled.

Article 39. Contribution to the injury
In the determination of reparation, account shall be taken of the contribution to the injury by wilful or negligent action or omission of the injured State or any person or entity in relation to whom reparation is sought.

Chapter III. Serious breaches of obligations under peremptory norms of general international law

Article 40. Application of this chapter
(1) This chapter applies to the international responsibility which is entailed by a serious breach by a State of an obligation arising under a peremptory norm of general international law.
(2) A breach of such an obligation is serious if it involves a gross or systematic failure by the responsible State to fulfil the obligation.

Article 41. Particular consequences of a serious breach of an obligation under this chapter
(1) States shall cooperate to bring to an end through lawful means any serious breach within the meaning of article 40.
(2) No State shall recognize as lawful a situation created by a serious breach within the meaning of article 40, nor render aid or assistance in maintaining that situation.
(3) This article is without prejudice to the other consequences referred to in this part and to such further consequences that a breach to which this chapter applies may entail under international law.

Part Three. The implementation of the international responsibility of a state

Chapter I. Invocation of the responsibility of a state

Article 42. Invocation of responsibility by an injured State
A State is entitled as an injured State to invoke the responsibility of another State if the obligation breached is owed to:
(a) That State individually; or
(b) A group of States including that State, or the international community as a whole, and the breach of the obligation:
(i) Specifically affects that State; or
(ii) Is of such a character as radically to change the position of all the other States to which the obligation is owed with respect to the further performance of the obligation.

Article 43. Notice of claim by an injured State
(1) An injured State which invokes the responsibility of another State shall give notice of its claim to that State.
(2) The injured State may specify in particular:
(a) The conduct that the responsible State should take in order to cease the wrongful act, if it is continuing;
(b) What form reparation should take in accordance with the provisions of part two.

Article 44. Admissibility of claims
The responsibility of a State may not be invoked if:
(a) The claim is not brought in accordance with any applicable rule relating to the nationality of claims;
(b) The claim is one to which the rule of exhaustion of local remedies applies and any available and effective local remedy has not been exhausted.

Article 45. Loss of the right to invoke responsibility
The responsibility of a State may not be invoked if:
(a) The injured State has validly waived the claim;
(b) The injured State is to be considered as having, by reason of its conduct, validly acquiesced in the lapse of the claim.

Article 46. Plurality of injured States
Where several States are injured by the same internationally wrongful act, each injured State may separately invoke the responsibility of the State which has committed the internationally wrongful act.

Article 47. Plurality of responsible States
(1) Where several States are responsible for the same internationally wrongful act, the responsibility of each State may be invoked in relation to that act.
(2) Paragraph (1):
(a) Does not permit any injured State to recover, by way of compensation, more than the damage it has suffered;
(b) Is without prejudice to any right of recourse against the other responsible States.

Article 48. Invocation of responsibility by a State other than an injured State
(1) Any State other than an injured State is entitled to invoke the responsibility of another State in accordance with paragraph (2) if:

PART I INTERNATIONAL LAW

(a) The obligation breached is owed to a group of States including that State, and is established for the protection of a collective interest of the group; or

(b) The obligation breached is owed to the international community as a whole.

(2) Any State entitled to invoke responsibility under paragraph (1) may claim from the responsible State:

(a) Cessation of the internationally wrongful act, and assurances and guarantees of non-repetition in accordance with article 30; and

(b) Performance of the obligation of reparation in accordance with the preceding articles, in the interest of the injured State or of the beneficiaries of the obligation breached.

(3) The requirements for the invocation of responsibility by an injured State under articles 43, 44 and 45 apply to an invocation of responsibility by a State entitled to do so under paragraph (1).

Chapter II. Countermeasures

Article 49. Object and limits of countermeasures

(1) An injured State may only take countermeasures against a State which is responsible for an internationally wrongful act in order to induce that State to comply with its obligations under part two.

(2) Countermeasures are limited to the non-performance for the time being of international obligations of the State taking the measures towards the responsible State.

(3) Countermeasures shall, as far as possible, be taken in such a way as to permit the resumption of performance of the obligations in question.

Article 50. Obligations not affected by countermeasures

(1) Countermeasures shall not affect:

(a) The obligation to refrain from the threat or use of force as embodied in the Charter of the United Nations;

(b) Obligations for the protection of fundamental human rights;

(c) Obligations of a humanitarian character prohibiting reprisals;

(d) Other obligations under peremptory norms of general international law.

(2) A State taking countermeasures is not relieved from fulfilling its obligations:

(a) Under any dispute settlement procedure applicable between it and the responsible State;

(b) To respect the inviolability of diplomatic or consular agents, premises, archives and documents.

Article 51. Proportionality

Countermeasures must be commensurate with the injury suffered, taking into account the gravity of the internationally wrongful act and the rights in question.

Article 52. Conditions relating to resort to countermeasures

(1) Before taking countermeasures, an injured State shall:

(a) Call upon the responsible State, in accordance with article 43, to fulfil its obligations under part two;

(b) Notify the responsible State of any decision to take countermeasures and offer to negotiate with that State.

(2) Notwithstanding paragraph (1) (b), the injured State may take such urgent countermeasures as are necessary to preserve its rights.

(3) Countermeasures may not be taken, and if already taken must be suspended without undue delay if:

(a) The internationally wrongful act has ceased; and

(b) The dispute is pending before a court or tribunal which has the authority to make decisions binding on the parties.

(4) Paragraph (3) does not apply if the responsible State fails to implement the dispute settlement procedures in good faith.

Article 53. Termination of countermeasures

Countermeasures shall be terminated as soon as the responsible State has complied with its obligations under part two in relation to the internationally wrongful act.

Article 54. Measures taken by States other than an injured State

This chapter does not prejudice the right of any State, entitled under article 48, paragraph (1), to invoke the responsibility of another State, to take lawful measures against that State to ensure cessation of the breach and reparation in the interest of the injured State or of the beneficiaries of the obligation breached.

RESPONSIBILITIES FOR INTERNATIONALLY WRONGFUL ACTS

Part Four. General provisions

Article 55. Lex specialis

These articles do not apply where and to the extent that the conditions for the existence of an internationally wrongful act or the content or implementation of the international responsibility of a State are governed by special rules of international law.

Article 56. Questions of State responsibility not regulated by these articles

The applicable rules of international law continue to govern questions concerning the responsibility of a State for an internationally wrongful act to the extent that they are not regulated by these articles.

Article 57. Responsibility of an international organization

These articles are without prejudice to any question of the responsibility under international law of an international organization, or of any State for the conduct of an international organization.

Article 58. Individual responsibility

These articles are without prejudice to any question of the individual responsibility under international law of any person acting on behalf of a State.

Article 59. Charter of the United Nations

These articles are without prejudice to the Charter of the United Nations.

PART I INTERNATIONAL LAW

UN General Assembly Resolution A/RES/56/83 on the responsibility of States for internationally wrongful acts; adopted by the General Assembly [on the report of the Sixth Committee (A/56/589 and Corr.1)], 12 December 2001

The General Assembly,
Having considered chapter IV of the report of the International Law Commission on the work of its fifty-third session, which contains the draft articles on responsibility of States for internationally wrongful acts,
Noting that the International Law Commission decided to recommend to the General Assembly that it should take note of the draft articles on responsibility of States for internationally wrongful acts in a resolution and annex the draft articles to that resolution, and that it should consider at a later stage, in the light of the
importance of the topic, the possibility of convening an international conference of plenipotentiaries to examine the draft articles with a view to concluding a convention on the topic,
Emphasizing the continuing importance of the codification and progressive development of international law, as referred to in Article 13, paragraph 1 (a), of the Charter of the United Nations,
Noting that the subject of responsibility of States for internationally wrongful acts is of major importance in the relations of States,
(1) Welcomes the conclusion of the work of the International Law Commission on responsibility of States for internationally wrongful acts and its adoption of the draft articles and a detailed commentary on the subject;
(2) Expresses its appreciation to the International Law Commission for its continuing contribution to the codification and progressive development of international law;
(3) Takes note of the articles on responsibility of States for internationally wrongful acts, presented by the International Law Commission, the text of which is annexed to the present resolution, and commends them to the attention of Governments without prejudice to the question of their future adoption or other appropriate action;
(4) Decides to include in the provisional agenda of its fifty-ninth session an item entitled "Responsibility of States for internationally wrongful acts".

85th plenary meeting

12 December 2001

Annex. Responsibility of States for internationally wrongful acts

Part One. The internationally wrongful acts of a state

Chapter I. General principles

Article 1. Responsibility of a State for its internationally wrongful acts
Every internationally wrongful act of a State entails the international responsibility of that State.

Article 2. Elements of an internationally wrongful act of a State
There is an internationally wrongful act of a State when conduct consisting of an action or omission:
(a) Is attributable to the State under international law; and
(b) Constitutes a breach of an international obligation of the State.

Article 3. Characterization of an act of a State as internationally wrongful
The characterization of an act of a State as internationally wrongful is governed by international law. Such characterization is not affected by the characterization of the same act as lawful by internal law.

Chapter II. Attribution of conduct to a State

Article 4. Conduct of organs of a State
(1) The conduct of any State organ shall be considered an act of that State under international law, whether the organ exercises legislative, executive, judicial or any other functions, whatever position it holds in the organization of the State, and whatever its character as an organ of the central government or of a territorial unit of the State.
(2) An organ includes any person or entity which has that status in accordance with the internal law of the State.

Article 5. Conduct of persons or entities exercising elements of governmental authority
The conduct of a person or entity which is not an organ of the State under article 4 but which is

empowered by the law of that State to exercise elements of the governmental authority shall be considered an act of the State under international law, provided the person or entity is acting in that capacity in the particular instance.

Article 6. Conduct of organs placed at the disposal of a State by another State
The conduct of an organ placed at the disposal of a State by another State shall be considered an act of the former State under international law if the organ is acting in the exercise of elements of the governmental authority of the State at whose disposal it is placed.

Article 7. Excess of authority or contravention of instructions
The conduct of an organ of a State or of a person or entity empowered to exercise elements of the governmental authority shall be considered an act of the State under international law if the organ, person or entity acts in that capacity, even if it exceeds its authority or contravenes instructions.

Article 8. Conduct directed or controlled by a State
The conduct of a person or group of persons shall be considered an act of a State under international law if the person or group of persons is in fact acting on the instructions of, or under the direction or control of, that State in carrying out the conduct.

Article 9. Conduct carried out in the absence or default of the official authorities
The conduct of a person or group of persons shall be considered an act of a State under international law if the person or group of persons is in fact exercising elements of the governmental authority in the absence or default of the official authorities and in circumstances such as to call for the exercise of those elements of authority.

Article 10. Conduct of an insurrectional or other movement
(1) The conduct of an insurrectional movement which becomes the new government of a State shall be considered an act of that State under international law.
(2) The conduct of a movement, insurrectional or other, which succeeds in establishing a new State in part of the territory of a pre-existing State or in a territory under its administration shall be considered an act of the new State under international law.
(3) This article is without prejudice to the attribution to a State of any conduct, however related to that of the movement concerned, which is to be considered an act of that State by virtue of articles 4 to 9.

Article 11. Conduct acknowledged and adopted by a State as its own
Conduct which is not attributable to a State under the preceding articles shall nevertheless be considered an act of that State under international law if and to the extent that the State acknowledges and adopts the conduct in question as its own.

Chapter III. Breach of an international obligation

Article 12. Existence of a breach of an international obligation
There is a breach of an international obligation by a State when an act of that State is not in conformity with what is required of it by that obligation, regardless of its origin or character.

Article 13. International obligation in force for a State
An act of a State does not constitute a breach of an international obligation unless the State is bound by the obligation in question at the time the act occurs.

Article 14. Extension in time of the breach of an international obligation
(1) The breach of an international obligation by an act of a State not having a continuing character occurs at the moment when the act is performed, even if its effects continue.
(2) The breach of an international obligation by an act of a State having a continuing character extends over the entire period during which the act continues and remains not in conformity with the international obligation.
(3) The breach of an international obligation requiring a State to prevent a given event occurs when the event occurs and extends over the entire period during which the event continues and remains not in conformity with that obligation.

Article 15. Breach consisting of a composite act
(1) The breach of an international obligation by a State through a series of actions or omissions defined in aggregate as wrongful occurs when the action or omission occurs which, taken with the other actions or omissions, is sufficient to constitute the wrongful act.

(2) In such a case, the breach extends over the entire period starting with the first of the actions or omissions of the series and lasts for as long as these actions or omissions are repeated and remain not in conformity with the international obligation.

Chapter IV. Responsibility of a State in connection with the act of another State

Article 16. Aid or assistance in the commission of an internationally wrongful act

A State which aids or assists another State in the commission of an internationally wrongful act by the latter is internationally responsible for doing so if:
(a) That State does so with knowledge of the circumstances of the internationally wrongful act; and
(b) The act would be internationally wrongful if committed by that State.

Article 17. Direction and control exercised over the commission of an internationally wrongful act

A State which directs and controls another State in the commission of an internationally wrongful act by the latter is internationally responsible for that act if:
(a) That State does so with knowledge of the circumstances of the internationally wrongful act; and
(b) The act would be internationally wrongful if committed by that State.

Article 18. Coercion of another State

A State which coerces another State to commit an act is internationally responsible for that act if:
(a) The act would, but for the coercion, be an internationally wrongful act of the coerced State; and
(b) The coercing State does so with knowledge of the circumstances of the act.

Article 19. Effect of this chapter

This chapter is without prejudice to the international responsibility, under other provisions of these articles, of the State which commits the act in question, or of any other State.

Chapter V. Circumstances precluding wrongfulness

Article 20. Consent

Valid consent by a State to the commission of a given act by another State precludes the wrongfulness of that act in relation to the former State to the extent that the act remains within the limits of that consent.

Article 21. Self-defence

The wrongfulness of an act of a State is precluded if the act constitutes a lawful measure of self-defence taken in conformity with the Charter of the United Nations.

Article 22. Countermeasures in respect of an internationally wrongful act

The wrongfulness of an act of a State not in conformity with an international obligation towards another State is precluded if and to the extent that the act constitutes a countermeasure taken against the latter State in accordance with chapter II of part three.

Article 23. Force majeure

(1) The wrongfulness of an act of a State not in conformity with an international obligation of that State is precluded if the act is due to force majeure, that is the occurrence of an irresistible force or of an unforeseen event, beyond the control of the State, making it materially impossible in the circumstances to perform the obligation.
(2) Paragraph (1) does not apply if:
(a) The situation of force majeure is due, either alone or in combination with other factors, to the conduct of the State invoking it; or
(b) The State has assumed the risk of that situation occurring.

Article 24. Distress

(1) The wrongfulness of an act of a State not in conformity with an international obligation of that State is precluded if the author of the act in question has no other reasonable way, in a situation of distress, of saving the author's life or the lives of other persons entrusted to the author's care.
(2) Paragraph (1) does not apply if:
(a) The situation of distress is due, either alone or in combination with other
factors, to the conduct of the State invoking it; or
(b) The act in question is likely to create a comparable or greater peril.

Article 25. Necessity

(1) Necessity may not be invoked by a State as a ground for precluding the wrongfulness of an act

not in conformity with an international obligation of that State unless the act:
(a) Is the only way for the State to safeguard an essential interest against a grave and imminent peril; and
(b) Does not seriously impair an essential interest of the State or States towards which the obligation exists, or of the international community as a whole.
(2) In any case, necessity may not be invoked by a State as a ground for precluding wrongfulness if:
(a) The international obligation in question excludes the possibility of invoking necessity; or
(b) The State has contributed to the situation of necessity.

Article 26. Compliance with peremptory norms
Nothing in this chapter precludes the wrongfulness of any act of a State which is not in conformity with an obligation arising under a peremptory norm of general international law.

Article 27. Consequences of invoking a circumstance precluding wrongfulness
The invocation of a circumstance precluding wrongfulness in accordance with this chapter is without prejudice to:
(a) Compliance with the obligation in question, if and to the extent that the circumstance precluding wrongfulness no longer exists;
(b) The question of compensation for any material loss caused by the act in question.

Part Two. Content of the international responsibility of a state

Chapter I. General principles

Article 28. Legal consequences of an internationally wrongful act
The international responsibility of a State which is entailed by an internationally wrongful act in accordance with the provisions of part one involves legal consequences as set out in this part.

Article 29. Continued duty of performance
The legal consequences of an internationally wrongful act under this part do not affect the continued duty of the responsible State to perform the obligation breached.

Article 30. Cessation and non-repetition
The State responsible for the internationally wrongful act is under an obligation:
(a) To cease that act, if it is continuing;
(b) To offer appropriate assurances and guarantees of non-repetition, if circumstances so require.

Article 31. Reparation
(1) The responsible State is under an obligation to make full reparation for the injury caused by the internationally wrongful act.
(2) Injury includes any damage, whether material or moral, caused by the internationally wrongful act of a State.

Article 32. Irrelevance of internal law
The responsible State may not rely on the provisions of its internal law as justification for failure to comply with its obligations under this part.

Article 33. Scope of international obligations set out in this part
(1) The obligations of the responsible State set out in this part may be owed to another State, to several States, or to the international community as a whole, depending in particular on the character and content of the international obligation and on the circumstances of the breach.
(2) This part is without prejudice to any right, arising from the international responsibility of a State, which may accrue directly to any person or entity other than a State.

Chapter II. Reparation for injury

Article 34. Forms of reparation
Full reparation for the injury caused by the internationally wrongful act shall take the form of restitution, compensation and satisfaction, either singly or in combination, in accordance with the provisions of this chapter.

Article 35. Restitution
A State responsible for an internationally wrongful act is under an obligation to make restitution, that is, to re-establish the situation which existed before the wrongful act was committed, provided and to the extent that restitution:

(a) Is not materially impossible;
(b) Does not involve a burden out of all proportion to the benefit deriving from restitution instead of compensation.

Article 36. Compensation
(1) The State responsible for an internationally wrongful act is under an obligation to compensate for the damage caused thereby, insofar as such damage is not made good by restitution.
(2) The compensation shall cover any financially assessable damage including loss of profits insofar as it is established.

Article 37. Satisfaction
(1) The State responsible for an internationally wrongful act is under an obligation to give satisfaction for the injury caused by that act insofar as it cannot be made good by restitution or compensation.
(2) Satisfaction may consist in an acknowledgement of the breach, an expression of regret, a formal apology or another appropriate modality.
(3) Satisfaction shall not be out of proportion to the injury and may not take a form humiliating to the responsible State.

Article 38. Interest
(1) Interest on any principal sum due under this chapter shall be payable when necessary in order to ensure full reparation. The interest rate and mode of calculation shall be set so as to achieve that result.
(2) Interest runs from the date when the principal sum should have been paid until the date the obligation to pay is fulfilled.

Article 39. Contribution to the injury
In the determination of reparation, account shall be taken of the contribution to the injury by wilful or negligent action or omission of the injured State or any person or entity in relation to whom reparation is sought.

Chapter III. Serious breaches of obligations under peremptory norms of general international law

Article 40. Application of this chapter
(1) This chapter applies to the international responsibility which is entailed by a serious breach by a State of an obligation arising under a peremptory norm of general international law.
(2) A breach of such an obligation is serious if it involves a gross or systematic failure by the responsible State to fulfil the obligation.

Article 41. Particular consequences of a serious breach of an obligation under this chapter
(1) States shall cooperate to bring to an end through lawful means any serious breach within the meaning of article 40.
(2) No State shall recognize as lawful a situation created by a serious breach within the meaning of article 40, nor render aid or assistance in maintaining that situation.
(3) This article is without prejudice to the other consequences referred to in this part and to such further consequences that a breach to which this chapter applies may entail under international law.

Part Three. The implementation of the international responsibility of a state

Chapter I. Invocation of the responsibility of a State

Article 42. Invocation of responsibility by an injured State
A State is entitled as an injured State to invoke the responsibility of another State if the obligation breached is owed to:
(a) That State individually; or
(b) A group of States including that State, or the international community as a whole, and the breach of the obligation:
(i) Specifically affects that State; or
(ii) Is of such a character as radically to change the position of all the other States to which the obligation is owed with respect to the further performance of the obligation.

Article 43. Notice of claim by an injured State
(1) An injured State which invokes the responsibility of another State shall give notice of its claim to that State.

(2) The injured State may specify in particular:
(a) The conduct that the responsible State should take in order to cease the wrongful act, if it is continuing;
(b) What form reparation should take in accordance with the provisions of part two.

Article 44. Admissibility of claims
The responsibility of a State may not be invoked if:
(a) The claim is not brought in accordance with any applicable rule relating to the nationality of claims;
(b) The claim is one to which the rule of exhaustion of local remedies applies and any available and effective local remedy has not been exhausted.

Article 45. Loss of the right to invoke responsibility
The responsibility of a State may not be invoked if:
(a) The injured State has validly waived the claim;
(b) The injured State is to be considered as having, by reason of its conduct, validly acquiesced in the lapse of the claim.

Article 46. Plurality of injured States
Where several States are injured by the same internationally wrongful act, each injured State may separately invoke the responsibility of the State which has committed the internationally wrongful act.

Article 47. Plurality of responsible States
(1) Where several States are responsible for the same internationally wrongful act, the responsibility of each State may be invoked in relation to that act.
(2) Paragraph (1):
(a) Does not permit any injured State to recover, by way of compensation, more than the damage it has suffered;
(b) Is without prejudice to any right of recourse against the other responsible States.

Article 48. Invocation of responsibility by a State other than an injured State
(1) Any State other than an injured State is entitled to invoke the responsibility of another State in accordance with paragraph (2) if:
(a) The obligation breached is owed to a group of States including that State, and is established for the protection of a collective interest of the group; or
(b) The obligation breached is owed to the international community as a whole.
(2) Any State entitled to invoke responsibility under paragraph (1) may claim from the responsible State:
(a) Cessation of the internationally wrongful act, and assurances and guarantees of non-repetition in accordance with article 30; and
(b) Performance of the obligation of reparation in accordance with the preceding articles, in the interest of the injured State or of the beneficiaries of the obligation breached.
(3) The requirements for the invocation of responsibility by an injured State under articles 43, 44 and 45 apply to an invocation of responsibility by a State entitled to do so under paragraph (1).

Chapter II. Countermeasures

Article 49. Object and limits of countermeasures
(1) An injured State may only take countermeasures against a State which is responsible for an internationally wrongful act in order to induce that State to comply with its obligations under part two.
(2) Countermeasures are limited to the non-performance for the time being of international obligations of the State taking the measures towards the responsible State.
(3) Countermeasures shall, as far as possible, be taken in such a way as to permit the resumption of performance of the obligations in question.

Article 50. Obligations not affected by countermeasures
(1) Countermeasures shall not affect:
(a) The obligation to refrain from the threat or use of force as embodied in the Charter of the United Nations;
(b) Obligations for the protection of fundamental human rights;
(c) Obligations of a humanitarian character prohibiting reprisals;
(d) Other obligations under peremptory norms of general international law.

(2) A State taking countermeasures is not relieved from fulfilling its obligations:
(a) Under any dispute settlement procedure applicable between it and the responsible State;
(b) To respect the inviolability of diplomatic or consular agents, premises, archives and documents.

Article 51. Proportionality

Countermeasures must be commensurate with the injury suffered, taking into account the gravity of the internationally wrongful act and the rights in question.

Article 52. Conditions relating to resort to countermeasures

(1) Before taking countermeasures, an injured State shall:
(a) Call upon the responsible State, in accordance with article 43, to fulfil its obligations under part two;
(b) Notify the responsible State of any decision to take countermeasures and offer to negotiate with that State.
(2) Notwithstanding paragraph (1) (b), the injured State may take such urgent countermeasures as are necessary to preserve its rights.
(3) Countermeasures may not be taken, and if already taken must be suspended without undue delay if:
(a) The internationally wrongful act has ceased; and
(b) The dispute is pending before a court or tribunal which has the authority to make decisions binding on the parties.
(4) Paragraph (3) does not apply if the responsible State fails to implement the dispute settlement procedures in good faith.

Article 53. Termination of countermeasures

Countermeasures shall be terminated as soon as the responsible State has complied with its obligations under part two in relation to the internationally wrongful act.

Article 54. Measures taken by States other than an injured State

This chapter does not prejudice the right of any State, entitled under article 48, paragraph (1), to invoke the responsibility of another State, to take lawful measures against that State to ensure cessation of the breach and reparation in the interest of the injured State or of the beneficiaries of the obligation breached.

Part Four. General Provisions

Article 55. Lex specialis

These articles do not apply where and to the extent that the conditions for the existence of an internationally wrongful act or the content or implementation of the international responsibility of a State are governed by special rules of international law.

Article 56. Questions of State responsibility not regulated by these articles

The applicable rules of international law continue to govern questions concerning the responsibility of a State for an internationally wrongful act to the extent that they are not regulated by these articles.

Article 57. Responsibility of an international organization

These articles are without prejudice to any question of the responsibility under international law of an international organization, or of any State for the conduct of an international organization.

Article 58. Individual responsibility

These articles are without prejudice to any question of the individual responsibility under international law of any person acting on behalf of a State.

Article 59. Charter of the United Nations

These articles are without prejudice to the Charter of the United Nations.

Rome Statute of the International Criminal Court, Rome 17 July 1998

The States Parties to this Statute,
Conscious that all peoples are united by common bonds, their cultures pieced together in a shared heritage, and concerned that this delicate mosaic may be shattered at any time,
Mindful that during this century millions of children, women and men have been victims of unimaginable atrocities that deeply shock the conscience of humanity,
Recognizing that such grave crimes threaten the peace, security and well-being of the world,
Affirming that the most serious crimes of concern to the international community as a whole must not go unpunished and that their effective prosecution must be ensured by taking measures at the national level and by enhancing international cooperation,
Determined to put an end to impunity for the perpetrators of these crimes and thus to contribute to the prevention of such crimes,
Recalling that it is the duty of every State to exercise its criminal jurisdiction over those responsible for international crimes,
Reaffirming the Purposes and Principles of the Charter of the United Nations, and in particular that all States shall refrain from the threat or use of force against the territorial integrity or political independence of any State, or in any other manner inconsistent with the Purposes of the United Nations,
Emphasizing in this connection that nothing in this Statute shall be taken as authorizing any State Party to intervene in an armed conflict or in the internal affairs of any State,
Determined to these ends and for the sake of present and future generations, to establish an independent permanent International Criminal Court in relationship with the United Nations system, with jurisdiction over the most serious crimes of concern to the international community as a whole,
Emphasizing that the International Criminal Court established under this Statute shall be complementary to national criminal jurisdictions,
Resolved to guarantee lasting respect for and the enforcement of international justice,
Have agreed as follows:

Part I. Establishment of the Court

Article 1. The Court

An International Criminal Court ('the Court') is hereby established. It shall be a permanent institution and shall have the power to exercise its jurisdiction over persons for the most serious crimes of international concern, as referred to in this Statute, and shall be complementary to national criminal jurisdictions. The jurisdiction and functioning of the Court shall be governed by the provisions of this Statute.

Article 2. Relationship of the Court with the United Nations

The Court shall be brought into relationship with the United Nations through an agreement to be approved by the Assembly of States Parties to this Statute and thereafter concluded by the President of the Court on its behalf.

Article 3. Seat of the Court

(1) The seat of the Court shall be established at The Hague in the Netherlands ('the host State').
(2) The Court shall enter into a headquarters agreement with the host State, to be approved by the Assembly of States Parties and thereafter concluded by the President of the Court on its behalf.
(3) The Court may sit elsewhere, whenever it considers it desirable, as provided in this Statute.

Article 4. Legal status and powers of the Court

(1) The Court shall have international legal personality. It shall also have such legal capacity as may be necessary for the exercise of its functions and the fulfilment of its purposes.
(2) The Court may exercise its functions and powers, as provided in this Statute, on the territory of any State Party and, by special agreement, on the territory of any other State.

Part II. Jurisdiction, admissibility and applicable law

Article 5. Crimes within the jurisdiction of the Court

(1) The jurisdiction of the Court shall be limited to the most serious crimes of concern to the international community as a whole. The Court has jurisdiction in accordance with this Statute with respect to the following crimes:
(a) The crime of genocide;
(b) Crimes against humanity;

(c) War crimes;
(d) The crime of aggression.
(2) The Court shall exercise jurisdiction over the crime of aggression once a provision is adopted in accordance with articles 121 and 123 defining the crime and setting out the conditions under which the Court shall exercise jurisdiction with respect to this crime. Such a provision shall be consistent with the relevant provisions of the

Article 6. Genocide
For the purpose of this Statute, 'genocide' means any of the following acts committed with intent to destroy, in whole or in part, a national, ethnical, racial or religious group, as such:
(a) Killing members of the group;
(b) Causing serious bodily or mental harm to members of the group;
(c) Deliberately inflicting on the group conditions of life calculated to bring about its physical destruction in whole or in part;
(d) Imposing measures intended to prevent births within the group;
(e) Forcibly transferring children of the group to another group.

Article 7. Crimes against humanity
(1) For the purpose of this Statute, 'crime against humanity' means any of the following acts when committed as part of a widespread or systematic attack directed against any civilian population, with knowledge of the attack:
(a) Murder;
(b) Extermination;
(c) Enslavement;
(d) Deportation or forcible transfer of population;
(e) Imprisonment or other severe deprivation of physical liberty in violation of fundamental rules of international law;
(f) Torture;
(g) Rape, sexual slavery, enforced prostitution, forced pregnancy, enforced sterilization, or any other form of sexual violence of comparable gravity;
(h) Persecution against any identifiable group or collectivity on political, racial, national, ethnic, cultural, religious, gender as defined in paragraph (3), or other grounds that are universally recognized as impermissible under international law, in connection with any act referred to in this paragraph or any crime within the jurisdiction of the Court;
(i) Enforced disappearance of persons;
(j) The crime of apartheid;
(k) Other inhumane acts of a similar character intentionally causing great suffering, or serious injury to body or to mental or physical health.
(2) For the purpose of paragraph (1):
(a) 'Attack directed against any civilian population' means a course of conduct involving the multiple commission of acts referred to in paragraph (1) against any civilian population, pursuant to or in furtherance of a State or organizational policy to commit such attack;
(b) 'Extermination' includes the intentional infliction of conditions of life, inter alia the deprivation of access to food and medicine, calculated to bring about the destruction of part of a population;
(c) 'Enslavement' means the exercise of any or all of the powers attaching to the right of ownership over a person and includes the exercise of such power in the course of trafficking in persons, in particular women and children;
(d) 'Deportation or forcible transfer of population' means forced displacement of the persons concerned by expulsion or other coercive acts from the area in which they are lawfully present, without grounds permitted under international law;
(e) 'Torture' means the intentional infliction of severe pain or suffering, whether physical or mental, upon a person in the custody or under thecontrol of the accused; except that torture shall not include pain orsuffering arising only from, inherent in or incidental to, lawful sanctions;
(f) 'Forced pregnancy' means the unlawful confinement of a woman forcibly made pregnant, with the intent of affecting the ethnic composition of any population or carrying out other grave violations of international law. This definition shall not in any way be interpreted as affecting national laws relating to pregnancy;
(g) 'Persecution' means the intentional and severe deprivation of fundamental rights contrary to international law by reason of the identity of the group or collectivity;
(h) 'The crime of apartheid' means inhumane acts of a character similar to those referred to in paragraph (1), committed in the context of an institutionalized regime of systematic oppression and

domination by one racial group over any other racial group or groups and committed with the intention of maintaining that regime;
(i) 'Enforced disappearance of persons' means the arrest, detention or abduction of persons by, or with the authorization, support or acquiescence of, a State or a political organization, followed by a refusal to acknowledge that deprivation of freedom or to give information on the fate or whereabouts of those persons, with the intention of removing them from the protection of the law for a prolonged period of time.
(3) For the purpose of this Statute, it is understood that the term 'gender' refers to the two sexes, male and female, within the context of society. The term 'gender' does not indicate any meaning different from the above.

Article 8. War crimes
(1) The Court shall have jurisdiction in respect of war crimes in particular when committed as part of a plan or policy or as part of a large-scale commission of such crimes.
(2) For the purpose of this Statute, 'war crimes' means:
(a) Grave breaches of the Geneva Conventions of 12 August 1949, namely, any of the following acts against persons or property protected under the provisions of the relevant Geneva Convention:
(i) Wilful killing;
(ii) Torture or inhuman treatment, including biological experiments;
(iii) Wilfully causing great suffering, or serious injury to body or health;
(iv) Extensive destruction and appropriation of property, not justified by military necessity and carried out unlawfully and wantonly;
(v) Compelling a prisoner of war or other protected person to serve in the forces of a hostile Power;
(vi) Wilfully depriving a prisoner of war or other protected person of the
rights of fair and regular trial;
(vii) Unlawful deportation or transfer or unlawful confinement;
(viii) Taking of hostages.
(b) Other serious violations of the laws and customs applicable in international armed conflict, within the established framework of international law, namely, any of the following acts:
(i) Intentionally directing attacks against the civilian population as such or against individual civilians not taking direct part in hostilities;
(ii) Intentionally directing attacks against civilian objects, that is, objects which are not military objectives;
(iii) Intentionally directing attacks against personnel, installations, material, units or vehicles involved in a humanitarian assistance or peacekeeping mission in accordance with the Charter of the United Nations, as long as they are entitled to the protection given to civilians or civilian objects under the international law of armed conflict;
(iv) Intentionally launching an attack in the knowledge that such attack will cause incidental loss of life or injury to civilians or damage to civilian objects or widespread, long-term and severe damage to the natural environment which would be clearly excessive in relation to the concrete and direct overall military advantage anticipated;
(v) Attacking or bombarding, by whatever means, towns, villages, dwellings or buildings which are undefended and which are not military objectives;
(vi) Killing or wounding a combatant who, having laid down his arms or having no longer means of defence, has surrendered at discretion;
(vii) Making improper use of a flag of truce, of the flag or of the military insignia and uniform of the enemy or of the United Nations, as well as of the distinctive emblems of the Geneva Conventions, resulting in death or serious personal injury;
(viii) The transfer, directly or indirectly, by the Occupying Power of parts of its own civilian population into the territory it occupies, or the deportation or transfer of all or parts of the population of the occupied territory within or outside this territory;
(ix) Intentionally directing attacks against buildings dedicated to religion, education, art, science or charitable purposes, historic monuments, hospitals and places where the sick and wounded are collected, provided they are not military objectives;
(x) Subjecting persons who are in the power of an adverse party to physical mutilation or to medical or scientific experiments of any kind which are neither justified by the medical, dental or hospital treatment of the person concerned nor carried out in his or her interest, and which cause death to or seriously endanger the health of such person or persons;
(xi) Killing or wounding treacherously individuals belonging to the hostile nation or army;
(xii) Declaring that no quarter will be given;

PART I INTERNATIONAL LAW

(xiii) Destroying or seizing the enemy's property unless such destruction or seizure be imperatively demanded by the necessities of war;
(xiv) Declaring abolished, suspended or inadmissible in a court of law the rights and actions of the nationals of the hostile party;
(xv) Compelling the nationals of the hostile party to take part in the operations of war directed against their own country, even if they were in the belligerent's service before the commencement of the war;
(xvi) Pillaging a town or place, even when taken by assault;
(xvii) Employing poison or poisoned weapons;
(xviii) Employing asphyxiating, poisonous or other gases, and all analogous liquids, materials or devices;
(xix) Employing bullets which expand or flatten easily in the human body, such as bullets with a hard envelope which does not entirely cover the core or is pierced with incisions;
(xx) Employing weapons, projectiles and material and methods of warfare which are of a nature to cause superfluous injury or unnecessary suffering or which are inherently indiscriminate in violation of the international law of armed conflict, provided that such weapons, projectiles and material and methods of warfare are the subject of a comprehensive prohibition and are included in an annex to this Statute, by an amendment in accordance with the relevant provisions set forth in articles 121 and 123;
(xxi) Committing outrages upon personal dignity, in particular humiliating and degrading treatment;
(xxii) Committing rape, sexual slavery, enforced prostitution, forced pregnancy, as defined in article 7, paragraph (2)(f), enforced sterilization, or any other form of sexual violence also constituting a grave breach of the Geneva Conventions;
(xxiii) Utilizing the presence of a civilian or other protected person to render certain points, areas or military forces immune from military operations;
(xxiv) Intentionally directing attacks against buildings, material, medical units and transport, and personnel using the distinctive emblems of the Geneva Conventions in conformity with international law;
(xxv) Intentionally using starvation of civilians as a method of warfare by depriving them of objects indispensable to their survival, including wilfully impeding relief supplies as provided for under the Geneva Conventions;
(xxvi) Conscripting or enlisting children under the age of fifteen years into the national armed forces or using them to participate actively in hostilities.
(c) In the case of an armed conflict not of an international character, serious violations of article 3 common to the four Geneva Conventions of 12 August 1949, namely, any of the following acts committed against persons taking no active part in the hostilities, including members of armed forces who have laid down their arms and those placed hors de combat by sickness, wounds, detention or any other cause:
(i) Violence to life and person, in particular murder of all kinds, mutilation, cruel treatment and torture;
(ii) Committing outrages upon personal dignity, in particular humiliating and degrading treatment;
(iii) Taking of hostages;
(iv) The passing of sentences and the carrying out of executions without previous judgement pronounced by a regularly constituted court, affording all judicial guarantees which are generally recognized as indispensable.
(d) Paragraph (2)(c) applies to armed conflicts not of an international character and thus does not apply to situations of internal disturbances and tensions, such as riots, isolated and sporadic acts of violence or other acts of a similar nature.
(e) Other serious violations of the laws and customs applicable in armed conflicts not of an international character, within the established framework of international law, namely, any of the following acts:
(i) Intentionally directing attacks against the civilian population as such or against individual civilians not taking direct part in hostilities;
(ii) Intentionally directing attacks against buildings, material, medical units and transport, and personnel using the distinctive emblems of the Geneva Conventions in conformity with international law;
(iii) Intentionally directing attacks against personnel, installations, material, units or vehicles involved in a humanitarian assistance or peacekeeping mission in accordance with the Charter of the United Nations, as long as they are entitled to the protection given to civilians or civilian objects under the international law of armed conflict;

(iv) Intentionally directing attacks against buildings dedicated to religion, education, art, science or charitable purposes, historic monuments, hospitals and places where the sick and wounded are collected, provided they are not military objectives;
(v) Pillaging a town or place, even when taken by assault;
(vi) Committing rape, sexual slavery, enforced prostitution, forced pregnancy, as defined in article 7, paragraph (2)(f), enforced sterilization, and any other form of sexual violence also constituting a serious violation of article 3 common to the four Geneva Conventions;
(vii) Conscripting or enlisting children under the age of fifteen years into armed forces or groups or using them to participate actively in hostilities;
(viii) Ordering the displacement of the civilian population for reasons related to the conflict, unless the security of the civilians involved or imperative military reasons so demand;
(ix) Killing or wounding treacherously a combatant adversary;
(x) Declaring that no quarter will be given;
(xi) Subjecting persons who are in the power of another party to the conflict to physical mutilation or to medical or scientific experiments of any kind which are neither justified by the medical, dental or hospital treatment of the person concerned nor carried out in his or
her interest, and which cause death to or seriously endanger the health of such person or persons;
(xii) Destroying or seizing the property of an adversary unless such destruction or seizure be imperatively demanded by the necessities of the conflict;
(f) Paragraph (2)(e) applies to armed conflicts not of an international character and thus does not apply to situations of internal disturbances and tensions, such as riots, isolated and sporadic acts of violence or other acts of a similar nature. It applies to armed conflicts that take place in the territory of a State when there is protracted armed conflict between
governmental authorities and organized armed groups or between such groups.
(3) Nothing in paragraph (2)(c) and (e) shall affect the responsibility of a Government to maintain or re-establish law and order in the State or to defend the unity and territorial integrity of the State, by all legitimate means.

Article 9. Elements of Crimes
(1) Elements of Crimes shall assist the Court in the interpretation and application of articles 6, 7 and 8. They shall be adopted by a two-thirds majority of the members of the Assembly of States Parties.
(2) Amendments to the Elements of Crimes may be proposed by:
(a) Any State Party;
(b) The judges acting by an absolute majority;
(c) The Prosecutor.
Such amendments shall be adopted by a two-thirds majority of the members of
the Assembly of States Parties.
(3) The Elements of Crimes and amendments thereto shall be consistent with this
Statute.

Article 10.
Nothing in this Part shall be interpreted as limiting or prejudicing in any way existing or developing rules of international law for purposes other than this Statute.

Article 11. Jurisdiction ratione temporis
(1) The Court has jurisdiction only with respect to crimes committed after the entry into force of this Statute.
(2) If a State becomes a Party to this Statute after its entry into force, the Court may exercise its jurisdiction only with respect to crimes committed after the entry into force of this Statute for that State, unless that State has made a declaration under article 12, paragraph (3).

Article 12. Preconditions to the exercise of jurisdiction
(1) A State which becomes a Party to this Statute thereby accepts the jurisdiction of the Court with respect to the crimes referred to in article 5.
(2) In the case of article 13, paragraph (a) or (c), the Court may exercise its jurisdiction if one or more of the following States are Parties to this Statute or have accepted the jurisdiction of the Court in accordance with paragraph (3):
(a) The State on the territory of which the conduct in question occurred or, if the crime was committed on board a vessel or aircraft, the State of registration of that vessel or aircraft;
(b) The State of which the person accused of the crime is a national.
(3) If the acceptance of a State which is not a Party to this Statute is required under paragraph (2),

PART I INTERNATIONAL LAW

that State may, by declaration lodged with the Registrar, accept the exercise of jurisdiction by the Court with respect to the crime in question. The accepting State shall cooperate with the Court without any delay or exception in accordance with Part 9.

Article 13. Exercise of jurisdiction
The Court may exercise its jurisdiction with respect to a crime referred to in article 5 in accordance with the provisions of this Statute if:
(a) A situation in which one or more of such crimes appears to have been committed is referred to the Prosecutor by a State Party in accordance with article 14;
(b) A situation in which one or more of such crimes appears to have been committed is referred to the Prosecutor by the Security Council acting under Chapter VII of the Charter of the United Nations; or
(c) The Prosecutor has initiated an investigation in respect of such a crime in accordance with article 15.

Article 14. Referral of a situation by a State Party
(1) A State Party may refer to the Prosecutor a situation in which one or more crimes within the jurisdiction of the Court appear to have been committed requesting the Prosecutor to investigate the situation for the purpose of determining whether one or more specific persons should be charged with the commission of such crimes.
(2) As far as possible, a referral shall specify the relevant circumstances and be accompanied by such supporting documentation as is available to the State referring the situation.

Article 15. Prosecutor
(1) The Prosecutor may initiate investigations *proprio motu* on the basis of information on crimes within the jurisdiction of the Court.
(2) The Prosecutor shall analyse the seriousness of the information received. For this purpose, he or she may seek additional information from States, organs of the United Nations, intergovernmental or non-governmental organizations, or other reliable sources that he or she deems appropriate, and may receive written or oral testimony at the seat of the Court.
(3) If the Prosecutor concludes that there is a reasonable basis to proceed with an investigation, he or she shall submit to the Pre-Trial Chamber a request for authorization of an investigation, together with any supporting material collected. Victims may make representations to the Pre-Trial Chamber, in accordance with the Rules of Procedure and Evidence.
(4) If the Pre-Trial Chamber, upon examination of the request and the supporting material, considers that there is a reasonable basis to proceed with an investigation, and that the case appears to fall within the jurisdiction of the Court, it shall authorize the commencement of the investigation, without prejudice to subsequent determinations by the Court with regard to the jurisdiction and admissibility of a case.
(5) The refusal of the Pre-Trial Chamber to authorize the investigation shall not preclude the presentation of a subsequent request by the Prosecutor based on new
facts or evidence regarding the same situation.
(6) If, after the preliminary examination referred to in paragraphs (1) and (2), the Prosecutor concludes that the information provided does not constitute a reasonable basis for an investigation, he or she shall inform those who provided the information. This shall not preclude the Prosecutor from considering further information submitted to him or her regarding the same situation in the light of new facts or evidence.

Article 16. Deferral of investigation or prosecution
No investigation or prosecution may be commenced or proceeded with under this Statute for a period of 12 months after the Security Council, in a resolution adopted under Chapter VII of the Charter of the United Nations, has requested the Court to that effect; that request may be renewed by the Council under the same conditions.

Article 17. Issues of admissibility
(1) Having regard to paragraph (10) of the Preamble and article 1, the Court shall determine that a case is inadmissible where:
(a) The case is being investigated or prosecuted by a State which has jurisdiction over it, unless the State is unwilling or unable genuinely to carry out the investigation or prosecution;
(b) The case has been investigated by a State which has jurisdiction over it and the State has decided not to prosecute the person concerned, unless the decision resulted from the unwillingness or inability of the State genuinely to prosecute;
(c) The person concerned has already been tried for conduct which is the subject of the complaint,

and a trial by the Court is not permitted under article 20, paragraph (3);
(d) The case is not of sufficient gravity to justify further action by the Court.
(2) In order to determine unwillingness in a particular case, the Court shall consider, having regard to the principles of due process recognized by international law, whether one or more of the following exist, as applicable:
(a) The proceedings were or are being undertaken or the national decision was made for the purpose of shielding the person concerned from criminal responsibility for crimes within the jurisdiction of the Court referred to in article 5;
(b) There has been an unjustified delay in the proceedings which in the circumstances is inconsistent with an intent to bring the person concerned to justice;
(c) The proceedings were not or are not being conducted independently or impartially, and they were or are being conducted in a manner which, in the circumstances, is inconsistent with an intent to bring the person concerned to justice.
(3) In order to determine inability in a particular case, the Court shall consider whether, due to a total or substantial collapse or unavailability of its national judicial system, the State is unable to obtain the accused or the necessary evidence and testimony or otherwise unable to carry out its proceedings.

Article 18. Preliminary rulings regarding admissibility
(1) When a situation has been referred to the Court pursuant to article 13 (a) and the Prosecutor has determined that there would be a reasonable basis to commence an investigation, or the Prosecutor initiates an investigation pursuant to articles 13 (c) and 15, the Prosecutor shall notify all States Parties and those States which, taking into account the information available, would normally exercise jurisdiction over the crimes concerned. The Prosecutor may notify such States on a confidential basis and, where the Prosecutor believes it necessary to protect persons, prevent destruction of evidence or prevent the absconding of persons, may limit the scope
of the information provided to States.
(2) Within one month of receipt of that notification, a State may inform the Court that it is investigating or has investigated its nationals or others within its jurisdiction with respect to criminal acts which may constitute crimes referred to in article 5 and which relate to the information provided in the notification to States. At the
request of that State, the Prosecutor shall defer to the State's investigation of those persons unless the Pre-Trial Chamber, on the application of the Prosecutor, decides to authorize the investigation.
(3) The Prosecutor's deferral to a State's investigation shall be open to review by the Prosecutor six months after the date of deferral or at any time when there has been a significant change of circumstances based on the State's unwillingness or inability genuinely to carry out the investigation.
(4) The State concerned or the Prosecutor may appeal to the Appeals Chamber against a ruling of the Pre-Trial Chamber, in accordance with article 82. The appeal may be heard on an expedited basis.
(5) When the Prosecutor has deferred an investigation in accordance with paragraph (2), the Prosecutor may request that the State concerned periodically inform the Prosecutor of the progress of its investigations and any subsequent prosecutions. States Parties shall respond to such requests without undue delay.
(6) Pending a ruling by the Pre-Trial Chamber, or at any time when the Prosecutor has deferred an investigation under this article, the Prosecutor may, on an exceptional basis, seek authority from the Pre-Trial Chamber to pursue necessary investigative steps for the purpose of preserving evidence where there is a unique opportunity to obtain important evidence or there is a significant risk that such evidence may not be subsequently available.
(7) A State which has challenged a ruling of the Pre-Trial Chamber under this article may challenge the admissibility of a case under article 19 on the grounds of additional significant facts or significant change of circumstances.

Article 19. Challenges to the jurisdiction of the Court or the admissibility of a case
(1) The Court shall satisfy itself that it has jurisdiction in any case brought before it. The Court may, on its own motion, determine the admissibility of a case in accordance with article 17.
(2) Challenges to the admissibility of a case on the grounds referred to in article 17 or challenges to the jurisdiction of the Court may be made by:
(a) An accused or a person for whom a warrant of arrest or a summons to appear has been issued under article 58;
(b) A State which has jurisdiction over a case, on the ground that it is investigating or prosecuting the case or has investigated or prosecuted; or
(c) A State from which acceptance of jurisdiction is required under article 12.
(3) The Prosecutor may seek a ruling from the Court regarding a question of jurisdiction or admis-

sibility. In proceedings with respect to jurisdiction or admissibility, those who have referred the situation under article 13, as well as victims, may also submit observations to the Court.

(4) The admissibility of a case or the jurisdiction of the Court may be challenged only once by any person or State referred to in paragraph (2). The challenge shall take place prior to or at the commencement of the trial. In exceptional circumstances, the Court may grant leave for a challenge to be brought more than once or at a

time later than the commencement of the trial. Challenges to the admissibility of a case, at the commencement of a trial, or subsequently with the leave of the Court, may be based only on article 17, paragraph (1)(c).

(5) A State referred to in paragraph (2)(b) and (c) shall make a challenge at the earliest opportunity.

(6) Prior to the confirmation of the charges, challenges to the admissibility of a case or challenges to the jurisdiction of the Court shall be referred to the Pre-Trial Chamber. After confirmation of the charges, they shall be referred to the Trial Chamber. Decisions with respect to jurisdiction or admissibility may be appealed to the Appeals Chamber in accordance with article 82.

(7) If a challenge is made by a State referred to in paragraph (2) (b) or (c), the Prosecutor shall suspend the investigation until such time as the Court makes a determination in accordance with article 17.

(8) Pending a ruling by the Court, the Prosecutor may seek authority from the Court:
(a) To pursue necessary investigative steps of the kind referred to in article 18, paragraph (6);
(b) To take a statement or testimony from a witness or complete the collection and examination of evidence which had begun prior to the making of the challenge; and
(c) In cooperation with the relevant States, to prevent the absconding of persons in respect of whom the Prosecutor has already requested a warrant of arrest under article 58.

(9) The making of a challenge shall not affect the validity of any act performed by the Prosecutor or any order or warrant issued by the Court prior to the making of the challenge.

(10) If the Court has decided that a case is inadmissible under article 17, the Prosecutor may submit a request for a review of the decision when he or she is fully satisfied that new facts have arisen which negate the basis on which the case had previously been found inadmissible under article 17.

(11) If the Prosecutor, having regard to the matters referred to in article 17, defers an investigation, the Prosecutor may request that the relevant State make available to the Prosecutor information on the proceedings. That information shall, at the request of the State concerned, be confidential. If the Prosecutor thereafter decides

to proceed with an investigation, he or she shall notify the State to which deferral of the proceedings has taken place.

Article 20. Ne bis in idem

(1) Except as provided in this Statute, no person shall be tried before the Court with respect to conduct which formed the basis of crimes for which the person has been convicted or acquitted by the Court.

(2) No person shall be tried by another court for a crime referred to in article 5 for which that person has already been convicted or acquitted by the Court.

(3) No person who has been tried by another court for conduct also proscribed under article 6, 7 or 8 shall be tried by the Court with respect to the same conduct unless the proceedings in the other court:
(a) Were for the purpose of shielding the person concerned from criminal responsibility for crimes within the jurisdiction of the Court; or
(b) Otherwise were not conducted independently or impartially in accordance with the norms of due process recognized by international law and were conducted in a manner which, in the circumstances, was inconsistent with an intent to bring the person concerned to justice.

Article 21. Applicable law

(1) The Court shall apply:
(a) In the first place, this Statute, Elements of Crimes and its Rules of Procedure and Evidence;
(b) In the second place, where appropriate, applicable treaties and the principles and rules of international law, including the established principles of the international law of armed conflict;
(c) Failing that, general principles of law derived by the Court from national laws of legal systems of the world including, as appropriate, the national laws of States that would normally exercise jurisdiction over the crime,

provided that those principles are not inconsistent with this Statute and with international law and internationally recognized norms and standards.

(2) The Court may apply principles and rules of law as interpreted in its previous decisions.

(3) The application and interpretation of law pursuant to this article must be consistent with internationally recognized human rights, and be without any adverse distinction founded on grounds such as gender as defined in article 7, paragraph (3), age, race, colour, language, religion or belief, political or other opinion, national, ethnic or social origin, wealth, birth or other status.

Part III. General principles of Criminal Law

Article 22. Nullum crimen sine lege

(1) A person shall not be criminally responsible under this Statute unless the conduct in question constitutes, at the time it takes place, a crime within the jurisdiction of the Court.
(2) The definition of a crime shall be strictly construed and shall not be extended by analogy. In case of ambiguity, the definition shall be interpreted in favour of the person being investigated, prosecuted or convicted.
(3) This article shall not affect the characterization of any conduct as criminal under international law independently of this Statute.

Article 23. Nulla poena sine lege

A person convicted by the Court may be punished only in accordance with this Statute.

Article 24. Non-retroactivity ratione personae

(1) No person shall be criminally responsible under this Statute for conduct prior to the entry into force of the Statute.
(2) In the event of a change in the law applicable to a given case prior to a final judgement, the law more favourable to the person being investigated, prosecuted or convicted shall apply.

Article 25. Individual criminal responsibility

(1) The Court shall have jurisdiction over natural persons pursuant to this Statute.
(2) A person who commits a crime within the jurisdiction of the Court shall be individually responsible and liable for punishment in accordance with this Statute.
(3) In accordance with this Statute, a person shall be criminally responsible and liable for punishment for a crime within the jurisdiction of the Court if that person:
(a) Commits such a crime, whether as an individual, jointly with another or through another person, regardless of whether that other person is criminally responsible;
(b) Orders, solicits or induces the commission of such a crime which in fact occurs or is attempted;
(c) For the purpose of facilitating the commission of such a crime, aids, abets or otherwise assists in its commission or its attempted commission, including providing the means for its commission;
(d) In any other way contributes to the commission or attempted commission of such a crime by a group of persons acting with a common purpose. Such contribution shall be intentional and shall either:
(i) Be made with the aim of furthering the criminal activity or criminal purpose of the group, where such activity or purpose involves the commission of a crime within the jurisdiction of the Court; or
(ii) Be made in the knowledge of the intention of the group to commit the crime;
(e) In respect of the crime of genocide, directly and publicly incites others to commit genocide;
(f) Attempts to commit such a crime by taking action that commences its execution by means of a substantial step, but the crime does not occur because of circumstances independent of the person's intentions.
However, a person who abandons the effort to commit the crime or otherwise prevents the completion of the crime shall not be liable for punishment under this Statute for the attempt to commit that crime if that person completely and voluntarily gave up the criminal purpose.
(4) No provision in this Statute relating to individual criminal responsibility shall affect the responsibility of States under international law.

Article 26. Exclusion of jurisdiction over persons under eighteen

The Court shall have no jurisdiction over any person who was under the age of 18 at the time of the alleged commission of a crime.

Article 27. Irrelevance of official capacity

(1) This Statute shall apply equally to all persons without any distinction based on official capacity. In particular, official capacity as a Head of State or Government, a member of a Government or parliament, an elected representative or a government official shall in no case exempt a person from criminal responsibility under this Statute, nor shall it, in and of itself, constitute a ground for reduction of sentence.

(2) Immunities or special procedural rules which may attach to the official capacity of a person, whether under national or international law, shall not bar the Court from exercising its jurisdiction over such a person.

Article 28. Responsibility of commanders and other superiors

In addition to other grounds of criminal responsibility under this Statute for crimes within the jurisdiction of the Court:

(a) A military commander or person effectively acting as a military commander shall be criminally responsible for crimes within the jurisdiction of the Court committed by forces under his or her effective command and control, or effective authority and control as the case may be, as a result of his or her failure to exercise control properly over such forces, where:

(i) That military commander or person either knew or, owing to the circumstances at the time, should have known that the forces were committing or about to commit such crimes; and

(ii) That military commander or person failed to take all necessary and reasonable measures within his or her power to prevent or repress their commission or to submit the matter to the competent authorities for investigation and prosecution.

(b) With respect to superior and subordinate relationships not described in paragraph (a), a superior shall be criminally responsible for crimes within the jurisdiction of the Court committed by subordinates under his or her effective authority and control, as a result of his or her failure to exercise control properly over such subordinates, where:

(i) The superior either knew, or consciously disregarded information which clearly indicated, that the subordinates were committing or about to commit such crimes;

(ii) The crimes concerned activities that were within the effective responsibility and control of the superior; and

(iii) The superior failed to take all necessary and reasonable measures within his or her power to prevent or repress their commission or to submit the matter to the competent authorities for investigation and prosecution.

Article 29. Non-applicability of statute of limitations

The crimes within the jurisdiction of the Court shall not be subject to any statute of limitations.

Article 30. Mental element

(1) Unless otherwise provided, a person shall be criminally responsible and liable for punishment for a crime within the jurisdiction of the Court only if the material elements are committed with intent and knowledge.

(2) For the purposes of this article, a person has intent where:

(a) In relation to conduct, that person means to engage in the conduct;

(b) In relation to a consequence, that person means to cause that consequence or is aware that it will occur in the ordinary course of events.

(3) For the purposes of this article, 'knowledge' means awareness that a circumstance exists or a consequence will occur in the ordinary course of events. 'Know' and 'knowingly' shall be construed accordingly.

Article 31. Grounds for excluding criminal responsibility

(1) In addition to other grounds for excluding criminal responsibility provided for in this Statute, a person shall not be criminally responsible if, at the time of that person's conduct:

(a) The person suffers from a mental disease or defect that destroys that person's capacity to appreciate the unlawfulness or nature of his or her conduct, or capacity to control his or her conduct to conform to the requirements of law;

(b) The person is in a state of intoxication that destroys that person's capacity to appreciate the unlawfulness or nature of his or her conduct, or capacity to control his or her conduct to conform to the requirements of law, unless the person has become voluntarily intoxicated under such circumstances that the person knew, or disregarded the risk, that, as a result of the intoxication, he or she was likely to engage in conduct constituting a crime within the jurisdiction of the Court;

(c) The person acts reasonably to defend himself or herself or another person or, in the case of war crimes, property which is essential for the survival of the person or another person or property which is essential for accomplishing a military mission, against an imminent and unlawful use of force in a manner proportionate to the degree of danger to the person or the other person or property protected. The fact that the person was involved in a defensive operation conducted by forces shall not in itself constitute a ground for excluding criminal responsibility under this subparagraph;

(d) The conduct which is alleged to constitute a crime within the jurisdiction of the Court has been caused by duress resulting from a threat of imminent death or of continuing or imminent serious

bodily harm against that person or another person, and the person acts necessarily and reasonably to avoid this threat, provided that the person does not intend to cause a greater harm than the one sought to be avoided. Such a threat may either be:
(i) Made by other persons; or
(ii) Constituted by other circumstances beyond that person's control.
(2) The Court shall determine the applicability of the grounds for excluding criminal responsibility provided for in this Statute to the case before it.
(3) At trial, the Court may consider a ground for excluding criminal responsibility other than those referred to in paragraph (1) where such a ground is derived from applicable law as set forth in article 21. The procedures relating to the consideration of such a ground shall be provided for in the Rules of Procedure and Evidence.

Article 32. Mistake of fact or mistake of law
(1) A mistake of fact shall be a ground for excluding criminal responsibility only if it negates the mental element required by the crime.
(2) A mistake of law as to whether a particular type of conduct is a crime within the jurisdiction of the Court shall not be a ground for excluding criminal responsibility. A mistake of law may, however, be a ground for excluding criminal responsibility if it negates the mental element required by such a crime, or as provided for in article 33.

Article 33. Superior orders and prescription of law
(1) The fact that a crime within the jurisdiction of the Court has been committed by a person pursuant to an order of a Government or of a superior, whether military or civilian, shall not relieve that person of criminal responsibility unless:
(a) The person was under a legal obligation to obey orders of the Government or the superior in question;
(b) The person did not know that the order was unlawful; and
(c) The order was not manifestly unlawful.
(2) For the purposes of this article, orders to commit genocide or crimes against humanity are manifestly unlawful.

Part IV. Composition and administration of the Court

Article 34. Organs of the Court
The Court shall be composed of the following organs:
(a) The Presidency;
(b) An Appeals Division, a Trial Division and a Pre-Trial Division;
(c) The Office of the Prosecutor;
(d) The Registry.

Article 35. Service of judges
(1) All judges shall be elected as full-time members of the Court and shall be available to serve on that basis from the commencement of their terms of office.
(2) The judges composing the Presidency shall serve on a full-time basis as soon as they are elected.
(3) The Presidency may, on the basis of the workload of the Court and in consultation with its members, decide from time to time to what extent the remaining judges shall be required to serve on a full-time basis. Any such arrangement shall be without prejudice to the provisions of article 40.
(4) The financial arrangements for judges not required to serve on a full-time basis shall be made in accordance with article 49.

Article 36. Qualifications, nomination and election of judges
(1) Subject to the provisions of paragraph (2), there shall be 18 judges of the Court.
(2) (a) The Presidency, acting on behalf of the Court, may propose an increase in the number of judges specified in paragraph (1), indicating the reasons why this is considered necessary and appropriate. The Registrar shall promptly circulate any such proposal to all States Parties.
(b) Any such proposal shall then be considered at a meeting of the Assembly
of States Parties to be convened in accordance with article 112. The proposal shall be considered adopted if approved at the meeting by a vote of two thirds of the members of the Assembly of States Parties and shall enter into force at such time as decided by the Assembly of States Parties.
(c) (i) Once a proposal for an increase in the number of judges has been adopted under subparagraph (b), the election of the additional judges shall take place at the next session of the Assembly of States Parties in accordance with paragraphs (3) to (8), and article 37, paragraph (2);

PART I INTERNATIONAL LAW

(ii) Once a proposal for an increase in the number of judges has been adopted and brought into effect under subparagraphs (b) and (c) (i), it shall be open to the Presidency at any time thereafter, if the workload of the Court justifies it, to propose a reduction in the number of judges, provided that the number of judges shall not be reduced below that specified in paragraph (1). The proposal shall be dealt with in accordance with the procedure laid down in subparagraphs (a) and (b). In the event that the proposal is adopted, the number of judges shall be progressively decreased as the terms of office of serving judges expire, until the necessary number has been reached.

(3) (a) The judges shall be chosen from among persons of high moral character, impartiality and integrity who possess the qualifications required in their respective States for appointment to the highest judicial offices.

(b) Every candidate for election to the Court shall:

(i) Have established competence in criminal law and procedure, and the necessary relevant experience, whether as judge, prosecutor, advocate or in other similar capacity, in criminal proceedings; or

(ii) Have established competence in relevant areas of international law such as international humanitarian law and the law of human rights, and extensive experience in a professional legal capacity which is of relevance to the judicial work of the Court;

(c) Every candidate for election to the Court shall have an excellent knowledge of and be fluent in at least one of the working languages of the Court.

(4) (a) Nominations of candidates for election to the Court may be made by any State Party to this Statute, and shall be made either:

(i) By the procedure for the nomination of candidates for appointment to the highest judicial offices in the State in question; or

(ii) By the procedure provided for the nomination of candidates for the International Court of Justice in the Statute of that Court.

Nominations shall be accompanied by a statement in the necessary detail specifying how the candidate fulfils the requirements of paragraph (3).

(b) Each State Party may put forward one candidate for any given election who need not necessarily be a national of that State Party but shall in any case be a national of a State Party.

(c) The Assembly of States Parties may decide to establish, if appropriate, an Advisory Committee on nominations. In that event, the Committee's composition and mandate shall be established by the Assembly of States Parties.

(5) For the purposes of the election, there shall be two lists of candidates:

List A containing the names of candidates with the qualifications specified in paragraph (3) (b) (i); and List B containing the names of candidates with the qualifications specified in paragraph (3)(b) (ii).

A candidate with sufficient qualifications for both lists may choose on which list to appear. At the first election to the Court, at least nine judges shall be elected from list A and at least five judges from list B. Subsequent elections shall be so organized as to maintain the equivalent proportion on the Court of judges qualified on the two lists.

(6) (a) The judges shall be elected by secret ballot at a meeting of the Assembly of States Parties convened for that purpose under article 112. Subject to paragraph (7), the persons elected to the Court shall be the 18 candidates who obtain the highest number of votes and a two-thirds majority of the States Parties present and voting.

(b) In the event that a sufficient number of judges is not elected on the first ballot, successive ballots shall be held in accordance with the procedures laid down in subparagraph (a) until the remaining places have been filled.

(7) No two judges may be nationals of the same State. A person who, for the purposes
of membership of the Court, could be regarded as a national of more than one State shall be deemed to be a national of the State in which that person ordinarily exercises civil and political rights.

(8)(a) The States Parties shall, in the selection of judges, take into account the need, within the membership of the Court, for:

(i) The representation of the principal legal systems of the world;

(ii) Equitable geographical representation; and

(iii) A fair representation of female and male judges.

(b) States Parties shall also take into account the need to include judges with legal expertise on specific issues, including, but not limited to, violence against women or children.

(9) (a) Subject to subparagraph (b), judges shall hold office for a term of nine years and, subject to subparagraph (c) and to article 37, paragraph (2), shall not be eligible for re-election.

(b) At the first election, one third of the judges elected shall be selected by lot to serve for a term of three years; one third of the judges elected shall be selected by lot to serve for a term of six years; and

the remainder shall serve for a term of nine years.
(c) A judge who is selected to serve for a term of three years under subparagraph (b) shall be eligible for re-election for a full term.
(10) Notwithstanding paragraph (9), a judge assigned to a Trial or Appeals Chamber in accordance with article 39 shall continue in office to complete any trial or appeal the hearing of which has already commenced before that Chamber.

Article 37. Judicial vacancies
(1) In the event of a vacancy, an election shall be held in accordance with article 36 to fill the vacancy.
(2) A judge elected to fill a vacancy shall serve for the remainder of the predecessor's term and, if that period is three years or less, shall be eligible for re-election for a full term under article 36.

Article 38. The Presidency
(1) The President and the First and Second Vice-Presidents shall be elected by an absolute majority of the judges. They shall each serve for a term of three years or until the end of their respective terms of office as judges, whichever expires earlier. They shall be eligible for re-election once.
(2) The First Vice-President shall act in place of the President in the event that the President is unavailable or disqualified. The Second Vice-President shall act in place of the President in the event that both the President and the First Vice-President are unavailable or disqualified.
(3) The President, together with the First and Second Vice-Presidents, shall constitute the Presidency, which shall be responsible for:
(a) The proper administration of the Court, with the exception of the Office of the Prosecutor; and
(b) The other functions conferred upon it in accordance with this Statute.
(4) In discharging its responsibility under paragraph 3 (a), the Presidency shall coordinate with and seek the concurrence of the Prosecutor on all matters of mutual concern.

Article 39. Chambers
(1) As soon as possible after the election of the judges, the Court shall organize itself into the divisions specified in article 34, paragraph (b). The Appeals Division shall be composed of the President and four other judges, the Trial Division of not less than six judges and the Pre-Trial Division of not less than six judges. The
assignment of judges to divisions shall be based on the nature of the functions to be performed by each division and the qualifications and experience of the judges elected to the Court, in such a way that each division shall contain an appropriate combination of expertise in criminal law and procedure and in international law.
The Trial and Pre-Trial Divisions shall be composed predominantly of judges with criminal trial experience.
(2) (a) The judicial functions of the Court shall be carried out in each division by Chambers.
(b) (i) The Appeals Chamber shall be composed of all the judges of the Appeals Division;
(ii) The functions of the Trial Chamber shall be carried out by three judges of the Trial Division;
(iii) The functions of the Pre-Trial Chamber shall be carried out either by three judges of the Pre-Trial Division or by a single judge of that division in accordance with this Statute and the Rules of Procedure and Evidence;
(c) Nothing in this paragraph shall preclude the simultaneous constitution of more than one Trial Chamber or Pre-Trial Chamber when the efficient management of the Court's workload so requires.
(3) (a) Judges assigned to the Trial and Pre-Trial Divisions shall serve in those divisions for a period of three years, and thereafter until the completion of any case the hearing of which has already commenced in the division concerned.
(b) Judges assigned to the Appeals Division shall serve in that division
for their entire term of office.
(4) Judges assigned to the Appeals Division shall serve only in that division. Nothing
in this article shall, however, preclude the temporary attachment of judges from the Trial Division to the Pre-Trial Division or vice versa, if the Presidency considers that the efficient management of the Court's workload so requires, provided that under no circumstances shall a judge who has participated in the pre-trial phase of a case be eligible to sit on the Trial Chamber hearing that case.

Article 40. Independence of the judges
(1) The judges shall be independent in the performance of their functions.
(2) Judges shall not engage in any activity which is likely to interfere with their judicial functions or to affect confidence in their independence.
(3) Judges required to serve on a full-time basis at the seat of the Court shall not engage in any other

PART I INTERNATIONAL LAW

occupation of a professional nature.

(4) Any question regarding the application of paragraphs (2) and (3) shall be decided by an absolute majority of the judges. Where any such question concerns an individual judge, that judge shall not take part in the decision.

Article 41. Excusing and disqualification of judges

(1) The Presidency may, at the request of a judge, excuse that judge from the exercise of a function under this Statute, in accordance with the Rules of Procedure and Evidence.

(2) (a) A judge shall not participate in any case in which his or her impartiality might reasonably be doubted on any ground. A judge shall be disqualified from a case in accordance with this paragraph if, inter alia, that judge has previously been involved in any capacity in that case before the Court or in a related criminal case at the national level involving the person being investigated or prosecuted. A judge shall also be disqualified on such other grounds as may be provided for in the Rules of Procedure and Evidence.

(b) The Prosecutor or the person being investigated or prosecuted may request the disqualification of a judge under this paragraph.

(c) Any question as to the disqualification of a judge shall be decided by an absolute majority of the judges. The challenged judge shall be entitled to present his or her comments on the matter, but shall not take part in the decision.

Article 42. The Office of the Prosecutor

(1) The Office of the Prosecutor shall act independently as a separate organ of the Court. It shall be responsible for receiving referrals and any substantiated information on crimes within the jurisdiction of the Court, for examining them and for conducting investigations and prosecutions before the Court. A member of the Office shall not seek or act on instructions from any external source.

(2) The Office shall be headed by the Prosecutor. The Prosecutor shall have full authority over the management and administration of the Office, including the staff, facilities and other resources thereof. The Prosecutor shall be assisted by one or more Deputy Prosecutors, who shall be entitled to carry out any of the acts required of the Prosecutor under this Statute. The Prosecutor and the Deputy Prosecutors shall be of different nationalities. They shall serve on a full-time basis.

(3) The Prosecutor and the Deputy Prosecutors shall be persons of high moral character, be highly competent in and have extensive practical experience in the prosecution or trial of criminal cases. They shall have an excellent knowledge of and be fluent in at least one of the working languages of the Court.

(4) The Prosecutor shall be elected by secret ballot by an absolute majority of the members of the Assembly of States Parties. The Deputy Prosecutors shall be elected in the same way from a list of candidates provided by the Prosecutor. The Prosecutor shall nominate three candidates for each position of Deputy Prosecutor to be filled. Unless a shorter term is decided upon at the time of their election, the Prosecutor and the Deputy Prosecutors shall hold office for a term of nine years and shall not be eligible for re-election.

(5) Neither the Prosecutor nor a Deputy Prosecutor shall engage in any activity which is likely to interfere with his or her prosecutorial functions or to affect confidence in his or her independence. They shall not engage in any other occupation of a professional nature.

(6) The Presidency may excuse the Prosecutor or a Deputy Prosecutor, at his or her request, from acting in a particular case.

(7) Neither the Prosecutor nor a Deputy Prosecutor shall participate in any matter in which their impartiality might reasonably be doubted on any ground. They shall be disqualified from a case in accordance with this paragraph if, inter alia, they have previously been involved in any capacity in that case before the Court or in a related criminal case at the national level involving the person being investigated or prosecuted.

(8) Any question as to the disqualification of the Prosecutor or a Deputy Prosecutor shall be decided by the Appeals Chamber.

(a) The person being investigated or prosecuted may at any time request the disqualification of the Prosecutor or a Deputy Prosecutor on the grounds set out in this article;

(b) The Prosecutor or the Deputy Prosecutor, as appropriate, shall be entitled to present his or her comments on the matter.

(9) The Prosecutor shall appoint advisers with legal expertise on specific issues, including, but not limited to, sexual and gender violence and violence against children.

Article 43. The Registry

(1) The Registry shall be responsible for the non-judicial aspects of the administration

and servicing of the Court, without prejudice to the functions and powers of the Prosecutor in accordance with article 42.
(2) The Registry shall be headed by the Registrar, who shall be the principal administrative officer of the Court. The Registrar shall exercise his or her functions under the authority of the President of the Court.
(3) The Registrar and the Deputy Registrar shall be persons of high moral character, be highly competent and have an excellent knowledge of and be fluent in at least one of the working languages of the Court.
(4) The judges shall elect the Registrar by an absolute majority by secret ballot, taking into account any recommendation by the Assembly of States Parties. If the need arises and upon the recommendation of the Registrar, the judges shall elect, in the same manner, a Deputy Registrar.
(5) The Registrar shall hold office for a term of five years, shall be eligible for re-election once and shall serve on a full-time basis. The Deputy Registrar shall hold office for a term of five years or such shorter term as may be decided upon by an absolute majority of the judges, and may be elected on the basis that the Deputy Registrar shall be called upon to serve as required.
(6) The Registrar shall set up a Victims and Witnesses Unit within the Registry. This Unit shall provide, in consultation with the Office of the Prosecutor, protective measures and security arrangements, counselling and other appropriate assistance for witnesses, victims who appear before the Court, and others who are at risk on
account of testimony given by such witnesses. The Unit shall include staff with expertise in trauma, including trauma related to crimes of sexual violence.

Article 44. Staff
(1) The Prosecutor and the Registrar shall appoint such qualified staff as may be required to their respective offices. In the case of the Prosecutor, this shall include the appointment of investigators.
(2) In the employment of staff, the Prosecutor and the Registrar shall ensure the highest standards of efficiency, competency and integrity, and shall have regard, *mutatis mutandis*, to the criteria set forth in article 36, paragraph (8).
(3) The Registrar, with the agreement of the Presidency and the Prosecutor, shall propose Staff Regulations which include the terms and conditions upon which the staff of the Court shall be appointed, remunerated and dismissed. The Staff Regulations shall be approved by the Assembly of States Parties.
(4) The Court may, in exceptional circumstances, employ the expertise of gratis personnel offered by States Parties, intergovernmental organizations or nongovernmental organizations to assist with the work of any of the organs of the Court. The Prosecutor may accept any such offer on behalf of the Office of the Prosecutor. Such gratis personnel shall be employed in accordance with guidelines to be established by the Assembly of States Parties.

Article 45. Solemn undertaking
Before taking up their respective duties under this Statute, the judges, the Prosecutor, the Deputy Prosecutors, the Registrar and the Deputy Registrar shall each make a solemn undertaking in open court to exercise his or her respective functions impartially and conscientiously.

Article 46. Removal from office
(1) A judge, the Prosecutor, a Deputy Prosecutor, the Registrar or the Deputy Registrar shall be removed from office if a decision to this effect is made in accordance with paragraph (2), in cases where that person:
(a) Is found to have committed serious misconduct or a serious breach of his or her duties under this Statute, as provided for in the Rules of Procedure and Evidence; or
(b) Is unable to exercise the functions required by this Statute.
(2) A decision as to the removal from office of a judge, the Prosecutor or a Deputy Prosecutor under paragraph (1) shall be made by the Assembly of States Parties, by secret ballot:
(a) In the case of a judge, by a two-thirds majority of the States Parties upon a recommendation adopted by a two-thirds majority of the other judges;
(b) In the case of the Prosecutor, by an absolute majority of the States Parties;
(c) In the case of a Deputy Prosecutor, by an absolute majority of the States Parties upon the recommendation of the Prosecutor.
(3) A decision as to the removal from office of the Registrar or Deputy Registrar shall be made by an absolute majority of the judges.
(4) A judge, Prosecutor, Deputy Prosecutor, Registrar or Deputy Registrar whose conduct or ability to exercise the functions of the office as required by this Statute is challenged under this article shall

have full opportunity to present and receive evidence and to make submissions in accordance with the Rules of Procedure and Evidence. The person in question shall not otherwise participate in the consideration of the matter.

Article 47. Disciplinary measures
A judge, Prosecutor, Deputy Prosecutor, Registrar or Deputy Registrar who has committed misconduct of a less serious nature than that set out in article 46, paragraph (1), shall be subject to disciplinary measures, in accordance with the Rules of Procedure and Evidence.

Article 48. Privileges and immunities
(1) The Court shall enjoy in the territory of each State Party such privileges and immunities as are necessary for the fulfilment of its purposes.
(2) The judges, the Prosecutor, the Deputy Prosecutors and the Registrar shall, when engaged on or with respect to the business of the Court, enjoy the same privileges and immunities as are accorded to heads of diplomatic missions and shall, after the expiry of their terms of office, continue to be accorded immunity from legal
process of every kind in respect of words spoken or written and acts performed by them in their official capacity.
(3) The Deputy Registrar, the staff of the Office of the Prosecutor and the staff of the Registry shall enjoy the privileges and immunities and facilities necessary for the performance of their functions, in accordance with the agreement on the privileges and immunities of the Court.
(4) Counsel, experts, witnesses or any other person required to be present at the seat of the Court shall be accorded such treatment as is necessary for the proper functioning of the Court, in accordance with the agreement on the privileges and immunities of the Court.
(5) The privileges and immunities of:
(a) A judge or the Prosecutor may be waived by an absolute majority of the judges;
(b) The Registrar may be waived by the Presidency;
(c) The Deputy Prosecutors and staff of the Office of the Prosecutor may be waived by the Prosecutor;
(d) The Deputy Registrar and staff of the Registry may be waived by the Registrar.

Article 49. Salaries, allowances and expenses
The judges, the Prosecutor, the Deputy Prosecutors, the Registrar and the Deputy Registrar shall receive such salaries, allowances and expenses as may be decided upon by the Assembly of States Parties. These salaries and allowances shall not be reduced during their terms of office.

Article 50. Official and working languages
(1) The official languages of the Court shall be Arabic, Chinese, English, French, Russian and Spanish. The judgements of the Court, as well as other decisions resolving fundamental issues before the Court, shall be published in the official languages. The Presidency shall, in accordance with the criteria established by the Rules of Procedure and Evidence, determine which decisions may be considered as resolving fundamental issues for the purposes of this paragraph.
(2) The working languages of the Court shall be English and French. The Rules of Procedure and Evidence shall determine the cases in which other official languages may be used as working languages.
(3) At the request of any party to a proceeding or a State allowed to intervene in a proceeding, the Court shall authorize a language other than English or French to be used by such a party or State, provided that the Court considers such authorization to be adequately justified.

Article 51. Rules of Procedure and Evidence
(1) The Rules of Procedure and Evidence shall enter into force upon adoption by a two-thirds majority of the members of the Assembly of States Parties.
(2) Amendments to the Rules of Procedure and Evidence may be proposed by:
(a) Any State Party;
(b) The judges acting by an absolute majority; or
(c) The Prosecutor.
Such amendments shall enter into force upon adoption by a two-thirds majority of the members of the Assembly of States Parties.
(3) After the adoption of the Rules of Procedure and Evidence, in urgent cases where the Rules do not provide for a specific situation before the Court, the judges may, by a two-thirds majority, draw up provisional Rules to be applied until adopted, amended or rejected at the next ordinary or special session of the Assembly of States Parties.

(4) The Rules of Procedure and Evidence, amendments thereto and any provisional Rule shall be consistent with this Statute. Amendments to the Rules of Procedure and Evidence as well as provisional Rules shall not be applied retroactively to the detriment of the person who is being investigated or prosecuted or who has been convicted.
(5) In the event of conflict between the Statute and the Rules of Procedure and Evidence, the Statute shall prevail.

Article 52. Regulations of the Court
(1) The judges shall, in accordance with this Statute and the Rules of Procedure and Evidence, adopt, by an absolute majority, the Regulations of the Court necessary for its routine functioning.
(2) The Prosecutor and the Registrar shall be consulted in the elaboration of the Regulations and any amendments thereto.
(3) The Regulations and any amendments thereto shall take effect upon adoption unless otherwise decided by the judges. Immediately upon adoption, they shall be circulated to States Parties for comments. If within six months there are no objections from a majority of States Parties, they shall remain in force.

Part V. Investigation and prosecution

Article 53. Initiation of an investigation
(1) The Prosecutor shall, having evaluated the information made available to him or her, initiate an investigation unless he or she determines that there is no reasonable basis to proceed under this Statute. In deciding whether to initiate an investigation, the Prosecutor shall consider whether:
(a) The information available to the Prosecutor provides a reasonable basis to believe that a crime within the jurisdiction of the Court has been or is being committed;
(b) The case is or would be admissible under article 17; and
(c) Taking into account the gravity of the crime and the interests of victims, there are nonetheless substantial reasons to believe that an investigation would not serve the interests of justice. If the Prosecutor determines that there is no reasonable basis to proceed and his or her determination is based solely on subparagraph (c) above, he or she shall inform the Pre-Trial Chamber.
(2) If, upon investigation, the Prosecutor concludes that there is not a sufficient basis for a prosecution because:
(a) There is not a sufficient legal or factual basis to seek a warrant or summons under article 58;
(b) The case is inadmissible under article 17; or
(c) A prosecution is not in the interests of justice, taking into account all the circumstances, including the gravity of the crime, the interests of victims and the age or infirmity of the alleged perpetrator, and his or her role in the alleged crime; the Prosecutor shall inform the Pre-Trial Chamber and the State making a referral under
article 14 or the Security Council in a case under article 13, paragraph (b), of his or her conclusion and the reasons for the conclusion.
(3) (a) At the request of the State making a referral under article 14 or the Security Council under article 13, paragraph (b), the Pre-Trial Chamber may review a decision of the Prosecutor under paragraph (1) or (2) not to proceed and may request the Prosecutor to reconsider that decision.
(b) In addition, the Pre-Trial Chamber may, on its own initiative, review a decision of the Prosecutor not to proceed if it is based solely on paragraph (1) (c) or (2) (c). In such a case, the decision of the Prosecutor shall be effective only if confirmed by the Pre-Trial Chamber.
(4) The Prosecutor may, at any time, reconsider a decision whether to initiate an investigation or prosecution based on new facts or information.

Article 54. Duties and powers of the Prosecutor with respect to investigations
(1) The Prosecutor shall:
(a) In order to establish the truth, extend the investigation to cover all facts and evidence relevant to an assessment of whether there is criminal responsibility under this Statute, and, in doing so, investigate incriminating and exonerating circumstances equally;
(b) Take appropriate measures to ensure the effective investigation and prosecution of crimes within the jurisdiction of the Court, and in doing so, respect the interests and personal circumstances of victims and witnesses, including age, gender as defined in article 7, paragraph (3), and health, and take into account the nature of the crime, in particular where it involves sexual violence, gender violence or violence against children; and
(c) Fully respect the rights of persons arising under this Statute.
(2) The Prosecutor may conduct investigations on the territory of a State:
(a) In accordance with the provisions of Part 9; or

(b) As authorized by the Pre-Trial Chamber under article 57, paragraph (3) (d).
(3) The Prosecutor may:
(a) Collect and examine evidence;
(b) Request the presence of and question persons being investigated, victims and witnesses;
(c) Seek the cooperation of any State or intergovernmental organization or arrangement in accordance with its respective competence and/or mandate;
(d) Enter into such arrangements or agreements, not inconsistent with this Statute, as may be necessary to facilitate the cooperation of a State, intergovernmental organization or person;
(e) Agree not to disclose, at any stage of the proceedings, documents or information that the Prosecutor obtains on the condition of confidentiality and solely for the purpose of generating new evidence, unless the provider of the information consents; and
(f) Take necessary measures, or request that necessary measures be taken, to ensure the confidentiality of information, the protection of any person or the preservation of evidence.

Article 55. Rights of persons during an investigation
(1) In respect of an investigation under this Statute, a person:
(a) Shall not be compelled to incriminate himself or herself or to confess guilt;
(b) Shall not be subjected to any form of coercion, duress or threat, to torture or to any other form of cruel, inhuman or degrading treatment or punishment;
(c) Shall, if questioned in a language other than a language the person fully understands and speaks, have, free of any cost, the assistance of a competent interpreter and such translations as are necessary to meet the requirements of fairness; and
(d) Shall not be subjected to arbitrary arrest or detention, and shall not be deprived of his or her liberty except on such grounds and in accordance with such procedures as are established in this Statute.
(2) Where there are grounds to believe that a person has committed a crime within the jurisdiction of the Court and that person is about to be questioned either by the Prosecutor, or by national authorities pursuant to a request made under Part 9, that person shall also have the following rights of which he or she shall be informed prior to being questioned:
(a) To be informed, prior to being questioned, that there are grounds to believe that he or she has committed a crime within the jurisdiction of the Court;
(b) To remain silent, without such silence being a consideration in the determination of guilt or innocence;
(c) To have legal assistance of the person's choosing, or, if the person does not have legal assistance, to have legal assistance assigned to him or her, in any case where the interests of justice so require, and without payment by the person in any such case if the person does not have sufficient means to pay for it; and
(d) To be questioned in the presence of counsel unless the person has voluntarily waived his or her right to counsel.

Article 56. Role of the Pre-Trial Chamber in relation to a unique investigative opportunity
(1) (a) Where the Prosecutor considers an investigation to present a unique opportunity to take testimony or a statement from a witness or to examine, collect or test evidence, which may not be available subsequently for the purposes of a trial, the Prosecutor shall so inform the Pre-Trial Chamber.
(b) In that case, the Pre-Trial Chamber may, upon request of the Prosecutor, take such measures as may be necessary to ensure the efficiency and integrity of the proceedings and, in particular, to protect the rights of the defence.
(c) Unless the Pre-Trial Chamber orders otherwise, the Prosecutor shall provide the relevant information to the person who has been arrested or appeared in response to a summons in connection with the investigation
referred to in subparagraph (a), in order that he or she may be heard on the matter.
(2) The measures referred to in paragraph (1) (b) may include:
(a) Making recommendations or orders regarding procedures to be followed;
(b) Directing that a record be made of the proceedings;
(c) Appointing an expert to assist;
(d) Authorizing counsel for a person who has been arrested, or appeared before the Court in response to a summons, to participate, or where there has not yet been such an arrest or appearance or counsel has not been designated, appointing another counsel to attend and represent the interests of the defence;
(e) Naming one of its members or, if necessary, another available judge of the Pre-Trial or Trial Division to observe and make recommendations or orders regarding the collection and preservation of evidence and the questioning of persons;

(f) Taking such other action as may be necessary to collect or preserve evidence.
(3) (a) Where the Prosecutor has not sought measures pursuant to this article but the Pre-Trial Chamber considers that such measures are required to preserve evidence that it deems would be essential for the defence at trial, it shall consult with the Prosecutor as to whether there is good reason for the Prosecutor's failure to request the measures. If upon consultation, the Pre-Trial Chamber concludes that the Prosecutor's failure to request such measures is unjustified, the Pre-Trial Chamber may take such measures on its own initiative.
(b) A decision of the Pre-Trial Chamber to act on its own initiative under this paragraph may be appealed by the Prosecutor. The appeal shall be heard on an expedited basis.
(4) The admissibility of evidence preserved or collected for trial pursuant to this article, or the record thereof, shall be governed at trial by article 69, and given such weight as determined by the Trial Chamber.

Article 57. Functions and powers of the Pre-Trial Chamber
(1) Unless otherwise provided in this Statute, the Pre-Trial Chamber shall exercise its functions in accordance with the provisions of this article.
(2) (a) Orders or rulings of the Pre-Trial Chamber issued under articles 15, 18, 19, 54, paragraph (2), (61), paragraph (7), and (72) must be concurred in by a majority of its judges.
(b) In all other cases, a single judge of the Pre-Trial Chamber may exercise the functions provided for in this Statute, unless otherwise provided for in the Rules of Procedure and Evidence or by a majority of the Pre-Trial Chamber.
(3) In addition to its other functions under this Statute, the Pre-Trial Chamber may:
(a) At the request of the Prosecutor, issue such orders and warrants as may be required for the purposes of an investigation;
(b) Upon the request of a person who has been arrested or has appeared pursuant to a summons under article 58, issue such orders, including measures such as those described in article 56, or seek such cooperation pursuant to Part 9 as may be necessary to assist the person in the preparation of his or her defence;
(c) Where necessary, provide for the protection and privacy of victims and witnesses, the preservation of evidence, the protection of persons who have been arrested or appeared in response to a summons, and the protection of national security information;
(d) Authorize the Prosecutor to take specific investigative steps within the territory of a State Party without having secured the cooperation of that State under Part 9 if, whenever possible having regard to the views of the State concerned, the Pre-Trial Chamber has determined in that case that the State is clearly unable to execute a request for cooperation due to the
unavailability of any authority or any component of its judicial system competent to execute the request for cooperation under Part 9;
(e) Where a warrant of arrest or a summons has been issued under article 58, and having due regard to the strength of the evidence and the rights of the parties concerned, as provided for in this Statute and the Rules of Procedure and Evidence, seek the cooperation of States pursuant to article 93, paragraph (1) (k), to take protective measures for the purpose of forfeiture, in particular for the ultimate benefit of victims.

Article 58. Issuance by the Pre-Trial Chamber of a warrant of arrest or a summons to appear
(1) At any time after the initiation of an investigation, the Pre-Trial Chamber shall, on the application of the Prosecutor, issue a warrant of arrest of a person if, having examined the application and the evidence or other information submitted by the Prosecutor, it is satisfied that:
(a) There are reasonable grounds to believe that the person has committed a crime within the jurisdiction of the Court; and
(b) The arrest of the person appears necessary:
(i) To ensure the person's appearance at trial;
(ii) To ensure that the person does not obstruct or endanger the investigation or the court proceedings; or
(iii) Where applicable, to prevent the person from continuing with the commission of that crime or a related crime which is within the jurisdiction of the Court and which arises out of the same circumstances.
(2) The application of the Prosecutor shall contain:
(a) The name of the person and any other relevant identifying information;
(b) A specific reference to the crimes within the jurisdiction of the Court which the person is alleged to have committed;
(c) A concise statement of the facts which are alleged to constitute those crimes;

(d) A summary of the evidence and any other information which establish reasonable grounds to believe that the person committed those crimes; and
(e) The reason why the Prosecutor believes that the arrest of the person is necessary.
(3) The warrant of arrest shall contain:
(a) The name of the person and any other relevant identifying information;
(b) A specific reference to the crimes within the jurisdiction of the Court for which the person's arrest is sought; and
(c) A concise statement of the facts which are alleged to constitute those crimes.
(4) The warrant of arrest shall remain in effect until otherwise ordered by the Court.
(5) On the basis of the warrant of arrest, the Court may request the provisional arrest or the arrest and surrender of the person under Part 9.
(6) The Prosecutor may request the Pre-Trial Chamber to amend the warrant of arrest by modifying or adding to the crimes specified therein. The Pre-Trial Chamber shall so amend the warrant if it is satisfied that there are reasonable grounds to believe that the person committed the modified or additional crimes.
(7) As an alternative to seeking a warrant of arrest, the Prosecutor may submit an application requesting that the Pre-Trial Chamber issue a summons for the person to appear. If the Pre-Trial Chamber is satisfied that there are reasonable grounds to believe that the person committed the crime alleged and that a summons is sufficient to ensure the person's appearance, it shall issue the summons, with or without conditions restricting liberty (other than detention) if provided for by national law, for the person to appear. The summons shall contain:
(a) The name of the person and any other relevant identifying information;
(b) The specified date on which the person is to appear;
(c) A specific reference to the crimes within the jurisdiction of the Court which the person is alleged to have committed; and
(d) A concise statement of the facts which are alleged to constitute the crime.
The summons shall be served on the person.

Article 59. Arrest proceedings in the custodial State
(1) A State Party which has received a request for provisional arrest or for arrest and surrender shall immediately take steps to arrest the person in question in accordance with its laws and the provisions of Part 9.
(2) A person arrested shall be brought promptly before the competent judicial authority in the custodial State which shall determine, in accordance with the law of that State, that:
(a) The warrant applies to that person;
(b) The person has been arrested in accordance with the proper process; and
(c) The person's rights have been respected.
(3) The person arrested shall have the right to apply to the competent authority in the custodial State for interim release pending surrender.
(4) In reaching a decision on any such application, the competent authority in the custodial State shall consider whether, given the gravity of the alleged crimes, there are urgent and exceptional circumstances to justify interim release and whether necessary safeguards exist to ensure that the custodial State can fulfil its duty to surrender the person to the Court. It shall not be open to the competent authority of the custodial State to consider whether the warrant of arrest was properly issued in accordance with article 58, paragraph (1) (a) and (b).
(5) The Pre-Trial Chamber shall be notified of any request for interim release and shall make recommendations to the competent authority in the custodial State. The competent authority in the custodial State shall give full consideration to such recommendations, including any recommendations on measures to prevent the escape of the person, before rendering its decision.
(6) If the person is granted interim release, the Pre-Trial Chamber may request periodic reports on the status of the interim release.
(7) Once ordered to be surrendered by the custodial State, the person shall be delivered to the Court as soon as possible.

Article 60. Initial proceedings before the Court
(1) Upon the surrender of the person to the Court, or the person's appearance before the Court voluntarily or pursuant to a summons, the Pre-Trial Chamber shall satisfy itself that the person has been informed of the crimes which he or she is alleged to have committed, and of his or her rights under this Statute, including the right to apply for interim release pending trial.
(2) A person subject to a warrant of arrest may apply for interim release pending trial. If the Pre-Trial

Chamber is satisfied that the conditions set forth in article 58, paragraph (1), are met, the person shall continue to be detained. If it is not so satisfied, the Pre-Trial Chamber shall release the person, with or without conditions.

(3) The Pre-Trial Chamber shall periodically review its ruling on the release or detention of the person, and may do so at any time on the request of the Prosecutor or the person. Upon such review, it may modify its ruling as to detention, release or conditions of release, if it is satisfied that changed circumstances so require.

(4) The Pre-Trial Chamber shall ensure that a person is not detained for an unreasonable period prior to trial due to inexcusable delay by the Prosecutor. If such delay occurs, the Court shall consider releasing the person, with or without conditions.

(5) If necessary, the Pre-Trial Chamber may issue a warrant of arrest to secure the presence of a person who has been released.

Article 61. Confirmation of the charges before trial

(1) Subject to the provisions of paragraph (2), within a reasonable time after the person's surrender or voluntary appearance before the Court, the Pre-Trial Chamber shall hold a hearing to confirm the charges on which the Prosecutor intends to seek trial. The hearing shall be held in the presence of the Prosecutor and the person charged, as well as his or her counsel.

(2) The Pre-Trial Chamber may, upon request of the Prosecutor or on its own motion, hold a hearing in the absence of the person charged to confirm the charges on which the Prosecutor intends to seek trial when the person has:

(a) Waived his or her right to be present; or

(b) Fled or cannot be found and all reasonable steps have been taken to secure his or her appearance before the Court and to inform the person of the charges and that a hearing to confirm those charges will be held.

In that case, the person shall be represented by counsel where the Pre-Trial Chamber determines that it is in the interests of justice.

(3) Within a reasonable time before the hearing, the person shall:

(a) Be provided with a copy of the document containing the charges on which the Prosecutor intends to bring the person to trial; and

(b) Be informed of the evidence on which the Prosecutor intends to rely at the hearing.

The Pre-Trial Chamber may issue orders regarding the disclosure of information for the purposes of the hearing.

(4) Before the hearing, the Prosecutor may continue the investigation and may amend or withdraw any charges. The person shall be given reasonable notice before the hearing of any amendment to or withdrawal of charges. In case of a withdrawal of charges, the Prosecutor shall notify the Pre-Trial Chamber of the reasons for the withdrawal.

(5) At the hearing, the Prosecutor shall support each charge with sufficient evidence to establish substantial grounds to believe that the person committed the crime charged. The Prosecutor may rely on documentary or summary evidence and need not call the witnesses expected to testify at the trial.

(6) At the hearing, the person may:

(a) Object to the charges;

(b) Challenge the evidence presented by the Prosecutor; and

(c) Present evidence.

(7) The Pre-Trial Chamber shall, on the basis of the hearing, determine whether there is sufficient evidence to establish substantial grounds to believe that the person committed each of the crimes charged. Based on its determination, the Pre-Trial Chamber shall:

(a) Confirm those charges in relation to which it has determined that there is sufficient evidence, and commit the person to a Trial Chamber for trial on the charges as confirmed;

(b) Decline to confirm those charges in relation to which it has determined that there is insufficient evidence;

(c) Adjourn the hearing and request the Prosecutor to consider:

(i) Providing further evidence or conducting further investigation with respect to a particular charge; or

(ii) Amending a charge because the evidence submitted appears to establish a different crime within the jurisdiction of the Court.

(8) Where the Pre-Trial Chamber declines to confirm a charge, the Prosecutor shall not be precluded from subsequently requesting its confirmation if the request is supported by additional evidence.

(9) After the charges are confirmed and before the trial has begun, the Prosecutor may, with the per-

mission of the Pre-Trial Chamber and after notice to the accused, amend the charges. If the Prosecutor seeks to add additional charges or to substitute more serious charges, a hearing under this article to confirm those charges must be held. After commencement of the trial, the Prosecutor may, with the permission of the Trial Chamber, withdraw the charges.

(10) Any warrant previously issued shall cease to have effect with respect to any charges which have not been confirmed by the Pre-Trial Chamber or which have been withdrawn by the Prosecutor.

(11) Once the charges have been confirmed in accordance with this article, the Presidency shall constitute a Trial Chamber which, subject to paragraph (9) and to article 64, paragraph (4), shall be responsible for the conduct of subsequent proceedings and may exercise any function of the Pre-Trial Chamber that is relevant and capable of application in those proceedings.

Part VI. The trial

Article 62. Place of trial
Unless otherwise decided, the place of the trial shall be the seat of the Court.

Article 63. Trial in the presence of the accused
(1) The accused shall be present during the trial.
(2) If the accused, being present before the Court, continues to disrupt the trial, the Trial Chamber may remove the accused and shall make provision for him or her to observe the trial and instruct counsel from outside the courtroom, through the use of communications technology, if required. Such measures shall be taken only in exceptional circumstances after other reasonable alternatives have proved inadequate, and only for such duration as is strictly required.

Article 64. Functions and powers of the Trial Chamber
(1) The functions and powers of the Trial Chamber set out in this article shall be exercised in accordance with this Statute and the Rules of Procedure and Evidence.
(2) The Trial Chamber shall ensure that a trial is fair and expeditious and is conducted with full respect for the rights of the accused and due regard for the protection of victims and witnesses.
(3) Upon assignment of a case for trial in accordance with this Statute, the Trial Chamber assigned to deal with the case shall:
(a) Confer with the parties and adopt such procedures as are necessary to facilitate the fair and expeditious conduct of the proceedings;
(b) Determine the language or languages to be used at trial; and
(c) Subject to any other relevant provisions of this Statute, provide for disclosure of documents or information not previously disclosed, sufficiently in advance of the commencement of the trial to enable adequate preparation for trial.
(4) The Trial Chamber may, if necessary for its effective and fair functioning, refer preliminary issues to the Pre-Trial Chamber or, if necessary, to another available judge of the Pre-Trial Division.
(5) Upon notice to the parties, the Trial Chamber may, as appropriate, direct that there be joinder or severance in respect of charges against more than one accused.
(6) In performing its functions prior to trial or during the course of a trial, the Trial Chamber may, as necessary:
(a) Exercise any functions of the Pre-Trial Chamber referred to in article 61, paragraph (11);
(b) Require the attendance and testimony of witnesses and production of documents and other evidence by obtaining, if necessary, the assistance of States as provided in this Statute;
(c) Provide for the protection of confidential information;
(d) Order the production of evidence in addition to that already collected prior to the trial or presented during the trial by the parties;
(e) Provide for the protection of the accused, witnesses and victims; and
(f) Rule on any other relevant matters.
(7) The trial shall be held in public. The Trial Chamber may, however, determine that special circumstances require that certain proceedings be in closed session for the purposes set forth in article 68, or to protect confidential or sensitive information to be given in evidence.
(8) (a) At the commencement of the trial, the Trial Chamber shall have read to the accused the charges previously confirmed by the Pre-Trial Chamber. The Trial Chamber shall satisfy itself that the accused understands the nature of the charges. It shall afford him or her the opportunity to make an admission of guilt in accordance with article 65 or to plead not guilty.
(b) At the trial, the presiding judge may give directions for the conduct of proceedings, including to ensure that they are conducted in a fair and impartial manner. Subject to any directions of the presiding judge, the parties may submit evidence in accordance with the provisions of this Statute.
(9) The Trial Chamber shall have, inter alia, the power on application of a party or on its own motion to:

(a) Rule on the admissibility or relevance of evidence; and
(b) Take all necessary steps to maintain order in the course of a hearing.
(10) The Trial Chamber shall ensure that a complete record of the trial, which accurately reflects the proceedings, is made and that it is maintained and preserved by the Registrar.

Article 65. Proceedings on an admission of guilt
(1) Where the accused makes an admission of guilt pursuant to article 64, paragraph (8) (a), the Trial Chamber shall determine whether:
(a) The accused understands the nature and consequences of the admission of guilt;
(b) The admission is voluntarily made by the accused after sufficient consultation with defence counsel; and
(c) The admission of guilt is supported by the facts of the case that are contained in:
(i) The charges brought by the Prosecutor and admitted by the accused;
(ii) Any materials presented by the Prosecutor which supplement the charges and which the accused accepts; and
(iii) Any other evidence, such as the testimony of witnesses, presented by the Prosecutor or the accused.
(2) Where the Trial Chamber is satisfied that the matters referred to in paragraph (1) are established, it shall consider the admission of guilt, together with any additional evidence presented, as establishing all the essential facts that are required to prove the crime to which the admission of guilt relates, and may convict the accused of that crime.
(3) Where the Trial Chamber is not satisfied that the matters referred to in paragraph (1) are established, it shall consider the admission of guilt as not having been made, in which case it shall order that the trial be continued under the ordinary trial procedures provided by this Statute and may remit the case to another Trial Chamber.
(4) Where the Trial Chamber is of the opinion that a more complete presentation of the facts of the case is required in the interests of justice, in particular the interests of the victims, the Trial Chamber may:
(a) Request the Prosecutor to present additional evidence, including the testimony of witnesses; or
(b) Order that the trial be continued under the ordinary trial procedures provided by this Statute, in which case it shall consider the admission of guilt as not having been made and may remit the case to another Trial Chamber.
(5) Any discussions between the Prosecutor and the defence regarding modification of the charges, the admission of guilt or the penalty to be imposed shall not be binding on the Court.

Article 66. Presumption of innocence
(1) Everyone shall be presumed innocent until proved guilty before the Court in accordance with the applicable law.
(2) The onus is on the Prosecutor to prove the guilt of the accused.
(3) In order to convict the accused, the Court must be convinced of the guilt of the accused beyond reasonable doubt.

Article 67. Rights of the accused
(1) In the determination of any charge, the accused shall be entitled to a public hearing, having regard to the provisions of this Statute, to a fair hearing conducted impartially, and to the following minimum guarantees, in full equality:
(a) To be informed promptly and in detail of the nature, cause and content of the charge, in a language which the accused fully understands and speaks;
(b) To have adequate time and facilities for the preparation of the defence and to communicate freely with counsel of the accused's choosing in confidence;
(c) To be tried without undue delay;
(d) Subject to article 63, paragraph (2), to be present at the trial, to conduct the defence in person or through legal assistance of the accused's choosing, to be informed, if the accused does not have legal assistance, of this right and to have legal assistance assigned by the Court in any case where the interests of justice so require, and without payment if the accused lacks sufficient means to pay for it;
(e) To examine, or have examined, the witnesses against him or her and to obtain the attendance and examination of witnesses on his or her behalf under the same conditions as witnesses against him or her. The accused shall also be entitled to raise defences and to present other evidence admissible under this Statute;
(f) To have, free of any cost, the assistance of a competent interpreter and such translations as are necessary to meet the requirements of fairness, if any of the proceedings of or documents presented

to the Court are not in a language which the accused fully understands and speaks;

(g) Not to be compelled to testify or to confess guilt and to remain silent, without such silence being a consideration in the determination of guilt or innocence;

(h) To make an unsworn oral or written statement in his or her defence; and

(i) Not to have imposed on him or her any reversal of the burden of proof or any onus of rebuttal.

(2) In addition to any other disclosure provided for in this Statute, the Prosecutor shall, as soon as practicable, disclose to the defence evidence in the Prosecutor's possession or control which he or she believes shows or tends to show the innocence of the accused, or to mitigate the guilt of the accused, or which may affect the credibility of prosecution evidence. In case of doubt as to the application of this paragraph, the Court shall decide.

Article 68. Protection of the victims and witnesses and their participation in the proceedings

(1) The Court shall take appropriate measures to protect the safety, physical and psychological well-being, dignity and privacy of victims and witnesses. In so doing, the Court shall have regard to all relevant factors, including age, gender as defined in article 7, paragraph (3), and health, and the nature of the crime, in particular, but not limited to, where the crime involves sexual or gender violence or violence against children. The Prosecutor shall take such measures particularly during the investigation and prosecution of such crimes. These measures shall not be prejudicial to or inconsistent with the rights of the accused and a fair and impartial trial.

(2) As an exception to the principle of public hearings provided for in article 67, the Chambers of the Court may, to protect victims and witnesses or an accused, conduct any part of the proceedings in camera or allow the presentation of evidence by electronic or other special means. In particular, such measures shall be implemented in the case of a victim of sexual violence or a child who is a victim or a witness, unless otherwise ordered by the Court, having regard to all the circumstances, particularly the views of the victim or witness.

(3) Where the personal interests of the victims are affected, the Court shall permit their views and concerns to be presented and considered at stages of the proceedings determined to be appropriate by the Court and in a manner which is not prejudicial to or inconsistent with the rights of the accused and a fair and impartial trial. Such views and concerns may be presented by the legal representatives of the victims where the Court considers it appropriate, in accordance with the Rules of Procedure and Evidence.

(4) The Victims and Witnesses Unit may advise the Prosecutor and the Court on appropriate protective measures, security arrangements, counselling and assistance as referred to in article 43, paragraph (6).

(5) Where the disclosure of evidence or information pursuant to this Statute may lead to the grave endangerment of the security of a witness or his or her family, the Prosecutor may, for the purposes of any proceedings conducted prior to the commencement of the trial, withhold such evidence or information and instead

submit a summary thereof. Such measures shall be exercised in a manner which is not prejudicial to or inconsistent with the rights of the accused and a fair and impartial trial.

(6) A State may make an application for necessary measures to be taken in respect of the protection of its servants or agents and the protection of confidential or sensitive information.

Article 69. Evidence

(1) Before testifying, each witness shall, in accordance with the Rules of Procedure and Evidence, give an undertaking as to the truthfulness of the evidence to be given by that witness.

(2) The testimony of a witness at trial shall be given in person, except to the extent provided by the measures set forth in article 68 or in the Rules of Procedure and Evidence. The Court may also permit the giving of viva voce (oral) or recorded testimony of a witness by means of video or audio technology, as well as the introduction of documents or written transcripts, subject to this Statute and in accordance with the Rules of Procedure and Evidence. These measures shall not be prejudicial to or inconsistent with the rights of the accused.

(3) The parties may submit evidence relevant to the case, in accordance with article 64. The Court shall have the authority to request the submission of all evidence that it considers necessary for the determination of the truth.

(4) The Court may rule on the relevance or admissibility of any evidence, taking into account, inter alia, the probative value of the evidence and any prejudice that such evidence may cause to a fair trial or to a fair evaluation of the testimony of a witness, in accordance with the Rules of Procedure and Evidence.

(5) The Court shall respect and observe privileges on confidentiality as provided for in the Rules of Procedure and Evidence.

(6) The Court shall not require proof of facts of common knowledge but may take judicial notice of them.
(7) Evidence obtained by means of a violation of this Statute or internationally recognized human rights shall not be admissible if:
(a) The violation casts substantial doubt on the reliability of the evidence; or
(b) The admission of the evidence would be antithetical to and would seriously damage the integrity of the proceedings.
(8) When deciding on the relevance or admissibility of evidence collected by a State, the Court shall not rule on the application of the State's national law.

Article 70. Offences against the administration of justice

(1) The Court shall have jurisdiction over the following offences against its administration of justice when committed intentionally:
(a) Giving false testimony when under an obligation pursuant to article 69, paragraph (1), to tell the truth;
(b) Presenting evidence that the party knows is false or forged;
(c) Corruptly influencing a witness, obstructing or interfering with the attendance or testimony of a witness, retaliating against a witness for giving testimony or destroying, tampering with or interfering with the collection of evidence;
(d) Impeding, intimidating or corruptly influencing an official of the Court for the purpose of forcing or persuading the official not to perform, or to perform improperly, his or her duties;
(e) Retaliating against an official of the Court on account of duties performed by that or another official;
(f) Soliciting or accepting a bribe as an official of the Court in connection with his or her official duties.
(2) The principles and procedures governing the Court's exercise of jurisdiction over offences under this article shall be those provided for in the Rules of Procedure and Evidence. The conditions for providing international cooperation to the Court with respect to its proceedings under this article shall be governed by the domestic laws of the requested State.
(3) In the event of conviction, the Court may impose a term of imprisonment not exceeding five years, or a fine in accordance with the Rules of Procedure and Evidence, or both.
(4) (a) Each State Party shall extend its criminal laws penalizing offences against the integrity of its own investigative or judicial process to offences against the administration of justice referred to in this article, committed on its territory, or by one of its nationals;
(b) Upon request by the Court, whenever it deems it proper, the State Party shall submit the case to its competent authorities for the purpose of prosecution. Those authorities shall treat such cases with diligence and devote sufficient resources to enable them to be conducted effectively.

Article 71. Sanctions for misconduct before the Court

(1) The Court may sanction persons present before it who commit misconduct, including disruption of its proceedings or deliberate refusal to comply with its directions, by administrative measures other than imprisonment, such as temporary or permanent removal from the courtroom, a fine or other similar measures provided for in the Rules of Procedure and Evidence.
(2) The procedures governing the imposition of the measures set forth in paragraph (1) shall be those provided for in the Rules of Procedure and Evidence.

Article 72. Protection of national security information

(1) This article applies in any case where the disclosure of the information or documents of a State would, in the opinion of that State, prejudice its national security interests. Such cases include those falling within the scope of article 56, paragraphs (2) and (3), article 61, paragraph (3), article 64, paragraph (3), article 67, paragraph (2), article 68, paragraph (6), article 87, paragraph (6) and article 93, as well as cases arising at any other stage of the proceedings where such disclosure may be at issue.
(2) This article shall also apply when a person who has been requested to give information or evidence has refused to do so or has referred the matter to the State on the ground that disclosure would prejudice the national security interests of a State and the State concerned confirms that it is of the opinion that disclosure would prejudice its national security interests.
(3) Nothing in this article shall prejudice the requirements of confidentiality applicable under article 54, paragraph (3) (e) and (f), or the application of article 73.
(4) If a State learns that information or documents of the State are being, or are likely to be, disclosed at any stage of the proceedings, and it is of the opinion that disclosure would prejudice its national

security interests, that State shall have the right to intervene in order to obtain resolution of the issue in accordance with this article.

(5) If, in the opinion of a State, disclosure of information would prejudice its national security interests, all reasonable steps will be taken by the State, acting in conjunction with the Prosecutor, the defence or the Pre-Trial Chamber or Trial Chamber, as the case may be, to seek to resolve the matter by cooperative means.

Such steps may include:

(a) Modification or clarification of the request;

(b) A determination by the Court regarding the relevance of the information or evidence sought, or a determination as to whether the evidence, though relevant, could be or has been obtained from a source other than the requested State;

(c) Obtaining the information or evidence from a different source or in a different form; or

(d) Agreement on conditions under which the assistance could be provided including, among other things, providing summaries or redactions, limitations on disclosure, use of in camera or ex parte proceedings, or other

protective measures permissible under the Statute and the Rules of Procedure and Evidence.

(6) Once all reasonable steps have been taken to resolve the matter through cooperative means, and if the State considers that there are no means or conditions under which the information or documents could be provided or disclosed without prejudice to its national security interests, it shall so notify the Prosecutor or the Court of the specific reasons for its decision, unless a specific description of the reasons would itself necessarily result in such prejudice to the State's national security interests.

(7) Thereafter, if the Court determines that the evidence is relevant and necessary for the establishment of the guilt or innocence of the accused, the Court may undertake the following actions:

(a) Where disclosure of the information or document is sought pursuant to a request for cooperation under Part 9 or the circumstances described in paragraph (2), and the State has invoked the ground for refusal referred to in article 93, paragraph (4):

(i) The Court may, before making any conclusion referred to in subparagraph (7) (a) (ii), request further consultations for the purpose of considering the State's representations, which may include, as appropriate, hearings in camera and ex parte;

(ii) If the Court concludes that, by invoking the ground for refusal under article 93, paragraph (4), in the circumstances of the case, the requested State is not acting in accordance with its obligations under this Statute, the Court may refer the matter in accordance with article 87, paragraph (7), specifying the reasons for its conclusion; and

(iii) The Court may make such inference in the trial of the accused as to the existence or non-existence of a fact, as may be appropriate in the circumstances; or

(b) In all other circumstances:

(i) Order disclosure; or

(ii) To the extent it does not order disclosure, make such inference in the trial of the accused as to the existence or non-existence of a fact, as may be appropriate in the circumstances.

Article 73. Third-party information or documents

If a State Party is requested by the Court to provide a document or information in its custody, possession or control, which was disclosed to it in confidence by a State, intergovernmental organization or international organization, it shall seek the consent of the originator to disclose that document or information. If the originator is a State Party, it shall either consent to disclosure of the information or document or undertake to resolve the issue of disclosure with the Court, subject to the provisions of article 72. If the originator is not a State Party and refuses to consent to disclosure, the requested State shall inform the Court that it is unable to provide the document or information because of a pre-existing obligation of confidentiality to the originator.

Article 74. Requirements for the decision

(1) All the judges of the Trial Chamber shall be present at each stage of the trial and throughout their deliberations. The Presidency may, on a case-by-case basis, designate, as available, one or more alternate judges to be present at each stage of the trial and to replace a member of the Trial Chamber if that member is unable to continue attending.

(2) The Trial Chamber's decision shall be based on its evaluation of the evidence and the entire proceedings. The decision shall not exceed the facts and circumstances described in the charges and any amendments to the charges. The Court may base its decision only on evidence submitted and discussed before it at the trial.

(3) The judges shall attempt to achieve unanimity in their decision, failing which the decision shall be

taken by a majority of the judges.
(4) The deliberations of the Trial Chamber shall remain secret.
(5) The decision shall be in writing and shall contain a full and reasoned statement of the Trial Chamber's findings on the evidence and conclusions. The Trial Chamber shall issue one decision. When there is no unanimity, the Trial Chamber's decision shall contain the views of the majority and the minority. The decision or a summary thereof shall be delivered in open court.

Article 75. Reparations to victims

(1) The Court shall establish principles relating to reparations to, or in respect of, victims, including restitution, compensation and rehabilitation. On this basis, in its decision the Court may, either upon request or on its own motion in exceptional circumstances, determine the scope and extent of any damage, loss and injury to, or in respect of, victims and will state the principles on which it is acting.
(2) The Court may make an order directly against a convicted person specifying appropriate reparations to, or in respect of, victims, including restitution, compensation and rehabilitation. Where appropriate, the Court may order that the award for reparations be made through the Trust Fund provided for in article 79.
(3) Before making an order under this article, the Court may invite and shall take account of representations from or on behalf of the convicted person, victims, other interested persons or interested States.
(4) In exercising its power under this article, the Court may, after a person is convicted of a crime within the jurisdiction of the Court, determine whether, in order to give effect to an order which it may make under this article, it is necessary to seek measures under article 93, paragraph (1).
(5) A State Party shall give effect to a decision under this article as if the provisions of article 109 were applicable to this article.
(6) Nothing in this article shall be interpreted as prejudicing the rights of victims under national or international law.

Article 76. Sentencing

(1) In the event of a conviction, the Trial Chamber shall consider the appropriate sentence to be imposed and shall take into account the evidence presented and submissions made during the trial that are relevant to the sentence.
(2) Except where article 65 applies and before the completion of the trial, the Trial Chamber may on its own motion and shall, at the request of the Prosecutor or the accused, hold a further hearing to hear any additional evidence or submissions relevant to the sentence, in accordance with the Rules of Procedure and Evidence.
(3) Where paragraph (2) applies, any representations under article 75 shall be heard during the further hearing referred to in paragraph (2) and, if necessary, during any additional hearing.
(4) The sentence shall be pronounced in public and, wherever possible, in the presence of the accused.

Part VII. Penalties

Article 77. Applicable penalties

(1) Subject to article 110, the Court may impose one of the following penalties on a person convicted of a crime referred to in article 5 of this Statute:
(a) Imprisonment for a specified number of years, which may not exceed a maximum of 30 years; or
(b) A term of life imprisonment when justified by the extreme gravity of the crime and the individual circumstances of the convicted person.
(2) In addition to imprisonment, the Court may order:
(a) A fine under the criteria provided for in the Rules of Procedure and Evidence;
(b) A forfeiture of proceeds, property and assets derived directly or indirectly from that crime, without prejudice to the rights of bona fide third parties.

Article 78. Determination of the sentence

(1) In determining the sentence, the Court shall, in accordance with the Rules of Procedure and Evidence, take into account such factors as the gravity of the crime and the individual circumstances of the convicted person.
(2) In imposing a sentence of imprisonment, the Court shall deduct the time, if any, previously spent in detention in accordance with an order of the Court. The Court may deduct any time otherwise spent in detention in connection with conduct underlying the crime.
(3) When a person has been convicted of more than one crime, the Court shall pronounce a sentence for each crime and a joint sentence specifying the total period of imprisonment. This period shall be

PART I   INTERNATIONAL LAW

no less than the highest individual sentence pronounced and shall not exceed 30 years imprisonment or a sentence of life imprisonment in conformity with article 77, paragraph (1)(b).

Article 79. Trust Fund
(1) A Trust Fund shall be established by decision of the Assembly of States Parties for the benefit of victims of crimes within the jurisdiction of the Court, and of the families of such victims.
(2) The Court may order money and other property collected through fines or forfeiture to be transferred, by order of the Court, to the Trust Fund.
(3) The Trust Fund shall be managed according to criteria to be determined by the Assembly of States Parties.

Article 80. Non-prejudice to national application of penalties and national laws
Nothing in this Part affects the application by States of penalties prescribed by their national law, nor the law of States which do not provide for penalties prescribed in this Part.

Part VIII. Appeal and Revision

Article 81. Appeal against decision of acquittal or conviction or against sentence
(1) A decision under article 74 may be appealed in accordance with the Rules of Procedure and Evidence as follows:
(a) The Prosecutor may make an appeal on any of the following grounds:
(i) Procedural error,
(ii) Error of fact, or
(iii) Error of law;
(b) The convicted person, or the Prosecutor on that person's behalf, may make an appeal on any of the following grounds:
(i) Procedural error,
(ii) Error of fact,
(iii) Error of law, or
(iv) Any other ground that affects the fairness or reliability of the proceedings or decision.
(2) (a) A sentence may be appealed, in accordance with the Rules of Procedure and Evidence, by the Prosecutor or the convicted person on the ground of disproportion between the crime and the sentence;
(b) If on an appeal against sentence the Court considers that there are grounds on which the conviction might be set aside, wholly or in part, it may invite the Prosecutor and the convicted person to submit grounds under article 81, paragraph (1) (a) or (b), and may render a decision on conviction in accordance with article 83;
(c) The same procedure applies when the Court, on an appeal against conviction only, considers that there are grounds to reduce the sentence under paragraph (2)(a).
(3)(a) Unless the Trial Chamber orders otherwise, a convicted person shall remain in custody pending an appeal;
(b) When a convicted person's time in custody exceeds the sentence of imprisonment imposed, that person shall be released, except that if the Prosecutor is also appealing, the release may be subject to the conditions under subparagraph (c) below;
(c) In case of an acquittal, the accused shall be released immediately, subject to the following:
(i) Under exceptional circumstances, and having regard, inter alia, to the concrete risk of flight, the seriousness of the offence charged and the probability of success on appeal, the Trial Chamber, at the request of the Prosecutor, may maintain the detention of the person pending appeal;
(ii) A decision by the Trial Chamber under subparagraph (c) (i) may be appealed in accordance with the Rules of Procedure and Evidence.
(4) Subject to the provisions of paragraph (3) (a) and (b), execution of the decision or sentence shall be suspended during the period allowed for appeal and for the duration of the appeal proceedings.

Article 82. Appeal against other decisions
(1) Either party may appeal any of the following decisions in accordance with the Rules of Procedure and Evidence:
(a) A decision with respect to jurisdiction or admissibility;
(b) A decision granting or denying release of the person being investigated or prosecuted;
(c) A decision of the Pre-Trial Chamber to act on its own initiative under article 56, paragraph (3);
(d) A decision that involves an issue that would significantly affect the fair and expeditious conduct of the proceedings or the outcome of the trial, and for which, in the opinion of the Pre-Trial or Trial Chamber, an immediate resolution by the Appeals Chamber may materially advance the proceedings.

(2) A decision of the Pre-Trial Chamber under article 57, paragraph (3) (d), may be appealed against by the State concerned or by the Prosecutor, with the leave of the Pre-Trial Chamber. The appeal shall be heard on an expedited basis.
(3) An appeal shall not of itself have suspensive effect unless the Appeals Chamber so orders, upon request, in accordance with the Rules of Procedure and Evidence.
(4) A legal representative of the victims, the convicted person or a bona fide owner of property adversely affected by an order under article 75 may appeal against the order for reparations, as provided in the Rules of Procedure and Evidence.

Article 83. Proceedings on appeal
(1) For the purposes of proceedings under article 81 and this article, the Appeals Chamber shall have all the powers of the Trial Chamber.
(2) If the Appeals Chamber finds that the proceedings appealed from were unfair in a way that affected the reliability of the decision or sentence, or that the decision or sentence appealed from was materially affected by error of fact or law or procedural error, it may:
(a) Reverse or amend the decision or sentence; or
(b) Order a new trial before a different Trial Chamber.
For these purposes, the Appeals Chamber may remand a factual issue to the original Trial Chamber for it to determine the issue and to report back accordingly, or may itself call evidence to determine the issue. When the decision or sentence has been appealed only by the person convicted, or the Prosecutor on that person's behalf, it cannot be amended to his or her detriment.
(3) If in an appeal against sentence the Appeals Chamber finds that the sentence is disproportionate to the crime, it may vary the sentence in accordance with Part 7.
(4) The judgement of the Appeals Chamber shall be taken by a majority of the judges and shall be delivered in open court. The judgement shall state the reasons on which it is based. When there is no unanimity, the judgement of the Appeals Chamber shall contain the views of the majority and the minority, but a judge may deliver a separate or dissenting opinion on a question of law.
(5) The Appeals Chamber may deliver its judgement in the absence of the person acquitted or convicted.

Article 84. Revision of conviction or sentence
(1) The convicted person or, after death, spouses, children, parents or one person alive at the time of the accused's death who has been given express written instructions from the accused to bring such a claim, or the Prosecutor on the person's behalf, may apply to the Appeals Chamber to revise the final judgement of conviction or sentence on the grounds that:
(a) New evidence has been discovered that:
(i) Was not available at the time of trial, and such unavailability was not wholly or partially attributable to the party making application; and
(ii) Is sufficiently important that had it been proved at trial it would have been likely to have resulted in a different verdict;
(b) It has been newly discovered that decisive evidence, taken into account at trial and upon which the conviction depends, was false, forged or falsified;
(c) One or more of the judges who participated in conviction or confirmation of the charges has committed, in that case, an act of serious misconduct or serious breach of duty of sufficient gravity to justify the removal of that judge or those judges from office under article 46.
(2) The Appeals Chamber shall reject the application if it considers it to be unfounded. If it determines that the application is meritorious, it may, as appropriate:
(a) Reconvene the original Trial Chamber;
(b) Constitute a new Trial Chamber; or
(c) Retain jurisdiction over the matter,
with a view to, after hearing the parties in the manner set forth in the Rules of Procedure and Evidence, arriving at a determination on whether the judgement should be revised.

Article 85. Compensation to an arrested or convicted person
(1) Anyone who has been the victim of unlawful arrest or detention shall have an enforceable right to compensation.
(2) When a person has by a final decision been convicted of a criminal offence, and when subsequently his or her conviction has been reversed on the ground that a new or newly discovered fact shows conclusively that there has been a miscarriage of justice, the person who has suffered punishment as a result of such conviction
shall be compensated according to law, unless it is proved that the non-disclosure of the unknown

fact in time is wholly or partly attributable to him or her.

(3) In exceptional circumstances, where the Court finds conclusive facts showing that there has been a grave and manifest miscarriage of justice, it may in its discretion award compensation, according to the criteria provided in the Rules of Procedure and Evidence, to a person who has been released from detention following a final decision of acquittal or a termination of the proceedings for that reason.

Part IX. International cooperation and judicial assistance

Article 86. General obligation to cooperate

States Parties shall, in accordance with the provisions of this Statute, cooperate fully with the Court in its investigation and prosecution of crimes within the jurisdiction of the Court.

Article 87. Requests for cooperation: general provisions

(1) (a) The Court shall have the authority to make requests to States Parties for cooperation. The requests shall be transmitted through the diplomatic channel or any other appropriate channel as may be designated by each State Party upon ratification, acceptance, approval or accession. Subsequent changes to the designation shall be made by each State Party in accordance with the Rules of Procedure and Evidence.

(b) When appropriate, without prejudice to the provisions of subparagraph (a), requests may also be transmitted through the International Criminal Police Organization or any appropriate regional organization.

(2) Requests for cooperation and any documents supporting the request shall either be in or be accompanied by a translation into an official language of the requested State or one of the working languages of the Court, in accordance with the choice made by that State upon ratification, acceptance, approval or accession. Subsequent changes to this choice shall be made in accordance with the Rules of Procedure and Evidence.

(3) The requested State shall keep confidential a request for cooperation and any documents supporting the request, except to the extent that the disclosure is necessary for execution of the request.

(4) In relation to any request for assistance presented under this Part, the Court may take such measures, including measures related to the protection of information, as may be necessary to ensure the safety or physical or psychological well-being of any victims, potential witnesses and their families. The Court may request that any information that is made available under this Part shall be provided and handled in a manner that protects the safety and physical or psychological well-being of any victims, potential witnesses and their families.

(5) (a) The Court may invite any State not party to this Statute to provide assistance under this Part on the basis of an ad hoc arrangement, an agreement with such State or any other appropriate basis.

(b) Where a State not party to this Statute, which has entered into an ad hoc arrangement or an agreement with the Court, fails to cooperate with requests pursuant to any such arrangement or agreement, the Court may so inform the Assembly of States Parties or, where the Security Council referred the matter to the Court, the Security Council.

(6) The Court may ask any intergovernmental organization to provide information or documents. The Court may also ask for other forms of cooperation and assistance which may be agreed upon with such an organization and which are in accordance with its competence or mandate.

(7) Where a State Party fails to comply with a request to cooperate by the Court contrary to the provisions of this Statute, thereby preventing the Court from exercising its functions and powers under this Statute, the Court may make a finding to that effect and refer the matter to the Assembly of States Parties or,

where the Security Council referred the matter to the Court, to the Security Council.

Article 88. Availability of procedures under national law

States Parties shall ensure that there are procedures available under their national law for all of the forms of cooperation which are specified under this Part.

Article 89. Surrender of persons to the Court

(1) The Court may transmit a request for the arrest and surrender of a person, together with the material supporting the request outlined in article 91, to any State on the territory of which that person may be found and shall request the cooperation of that State in the arrest and surrender of such a person. States Parties shall, in accordance with the provisions of this Part and the procedure under their national law, comply with requests for arrest and surrender.

(2) Where the person sought for surrender brings a challenge before a national court on the basis of the principle of ne bis in idem as provided in article 20, the requested State shall immediately consult with the Court to determine if there has been a relevant ruling on admissibility. If the case is admis-

sible, the requested State shall proceed with the execution of the request. If an admissibility ruling is pending, the requested State may postpone the execution of the request for surrender of the person until the Court makes a determination on admissibility.

(3) (a) A State Party shall authorize, in accordance with its national procedural law, transportation through its territory of a person being surrendered to the Court by another State, except where transit through that State would impede or delay the surrender.
(b) A request by the Court for transit shall be transmitted in accordance with article 87. The request for transit shall contain:
(i) A description of the person being transported;
(ii) A brief statement of the facts of the case and their legal characterization; and
(iii) The warrant for arrest and surrender;
(c) A person being transported shall be detained in custody during the period of transit;
(d) No authorization is required if the person is transported by air and no landing is scheduled on the territory of the transit State;
(e) If an unscheduled landing occurs on the territory of the transit State, that State may require a request for transit from the Court as provided for in subparagraph (b). The transit State shall detain the person being transported until the request for transit is received and the transit is effected, provided that detention for purposes of this subparagraph may not be extended beyond 96 hours from the unscheduled landing unless the request is received within that time.
(4) If the person sought is being proceeded against or is serving a sentence in the requested State for a crime different from that for which surrender to the Court is sought, the requested State, after making its decision to grant the request, shall consult with the Court.

Article 90. Competing requests
(1) A State Party which receives a request from the Court for the surrender of a person under article 89 shall, if it also receives a request from any other State for the extradition of the same person for the same conduct which forms the basis of the crime for which the Court seeks the person's surrender, notify the Court and the requesting State of that fact.
(2) Where the requesting State is a State Party, the requested State shall give priority to the request from the Court if:
(a) The Court has, pursuant to article 18 or 19, made a determination that the case in respect of which surrender is sought is admissible and that determination takes into account the investigation or prosecution conducted by the requesting State in respect of its request for extradition; or
(b) The Court makes the determination described in subparagraph (a) pursuant to the requested State's notification under paragraph (1).
(3) Where a determination under paragraph (2) (a) has not been made, the requested State may, at its discretion, pending the determination of the Court under paragraph (2) (b), proceed to deal with the request for extradition from the requesting State but shall not extradite the person until the Court has determined that the case is inadmissible. The Court's determination shall be made on an expedited basis.
(4) If the requesting State is a State not Party to this Statute the requested State, if it is not under an international obligation to extradite the person to the requesting State, shall give priority to the request for surrender from the Court, if the Court has determined that the case is admissible.
(5) Where a case under paragraph (4) has not been determined to be admissible by the Court, the requested State may, at its discretion, proceed to deal with the request for extradition from the requesting State.
(6) In cases where paragraph (4) applies except that the requested State is under an existing international obligation to extradite the person to the requesting State not Party to this Statute, the requested State shall determine whether to surrender the person to the Court or extradite the person to the requesting State. In making its decision, the requested State shall consider all the relevant factors, including but not limited to:
(a) The respective dates of the requests;
(b) The interests of the requesting State including, where relevant, whether the crime was committed in its territory and the nationality of the victims and of the person sought; and
(c) The possibility of subsequent surrender between the Court and the requesting State.
(7) Where a State Party which receives a request from the Court for the surrender of a person also receives a request from any State for the extradition of the same person for conduct other than that which constitutes the crime for which the Court seeks the person's surrender:
(a) The requested State shall, if it is not under an existing international obligation to extradite the person to the requesting State, give priority to the request from the Court;

(b) The requested State shall, if it is under an existing international obligation to extradite the person to the requesting State, determine whether to surrender the person to the Court or to extradite the person to the requesting State. In making its decision, the requested State shall consider all the relevant factors, including but not limited to those set out in paragraph (6), but shall give special consideration to the relative nature and gravity of the conduct in question. Where pursuant to a notification under this article, the Court has determined a case to be inadmissible, and subsequently extradition to the requesting State is refused, the requested State shall notify the Court of this decision.

Article 91. Contents of request for arrest and surrender

(1) A request for arrest and surrender shall be made in writing. In urgent cases, a request may be made by any medium capable of delivering a written record, provided that the request shall be confirmed through the channel provided for in article 87, paragraph (1) (a).

(2) In the case of a request for the arrest and surrender of a person for whom a warrant of arrest has been issued by the Pre-Trial Chamber under article 58, the request shall contain or be supported by:
(a) Information describing the person sought, sufficient to identify the person, and information as to that person's probable location;
(b) A copy of the warrant of arrest; and
(c) Such documents, statements or information as may be necessary to meet the requirements for the surrender process in the requested State, except that those requirements should not be more burdensome than those applicable to requests for extradition pursuant to treaties or arrangements between the requested State and other States and should, if possible, be less burdensome, taking into account the distinct nature of the Court.

(3) In the case of a request for the arrest and surrender of a person already convicted, the request shall contain or be supported by:
(a) A copy of any warrant of arrest for that person;
(b) A copy of the judgement of conviction;
(c) Information to demonstrate that the person sought is the one referred to in the judgement of conviction; and
(d) If the person sought has been sentenced, a copy of the sentence imposed and, in the case of a sentence for imprisonment, a statement of any time already served and the time remaining to be served.

(4) Upon the request of the Court, a State Party shall consult with the Court, either generally or with respect to a specific matter, regarding any requirements under its national law that may apply under paragraph (2) (c). During the consultations, the State Party shall advise the Court of the specific requirements of its national law.

Article 92. Provisional arrest

(1) In urgent cases, the Court may request the provisional arrest of the person sought, pending presentation of the request for surrender and the documents supporting
the request as specified in article 91.

(2) The request for provisional arrest shall be made by any medium capable of delivering a written record and shall contain:
(a) Information describing the person sought, sufficient to identify the person, and information as to that person's probable location;
(b) A concise statement of the crimes for which the person's arrest is sought and of the facts which are alleged to constitute those crimes, including, where possible, the date and location of the crime;
(c) A statement of the existence of a warrant of arrest or a judgement of conviction against the person sought; and
(d) A statement that a request for surrender of the person sought will follow.

(3) A person who is provisionally arrested may be released from custody if the requested State has not received the request for surrender and the documents supporting the request as specified in article 91 within the time limits specified in the Rules of Procedure and Evidence. However, the person may consent to surrender before the expiration of this period if permitted by the law of the requested State. In such a case, the requested State shall proceed to surrender the person to the Court as soon as possible.

(4) The fact that the person sought has been released from custody pursuant to paragraph (3) shall not prejudice the subsequent arrest and surrender of that person if the request for surrender and the documents supporting the request are delivered at a later date.

Article 93. Other forms of cooperation

(1) States Parties shall, in accordance with the provisions of this Part and under procedures of national law, comply with requests by the Court to provide the following assistance in relation to

investigations or prosecutions:
(a) The identification and whereabouts of persons or the location of items;
(b) The taking of evidence, including testimony under oath, and the production of evidence, including expert opinions and reports necessary to the Court;
(c) The questioning of any person being investigated or prosecuted;
(d) The service of documents, including judicial documents;
(e) Facilitating the voluntary appearance of persons as witnesses or experts before the Court;
(f) The temporary transfer of persons as provided in paragraph (7);
(g) The examination of places or sites, including the exhumation and examination of grave sites;
(h) The execution of searches and seizures;
(i) The provision of records and documents, including official records and documents;
(j) The protection of victims and witnesses and the preservation of evidence;
(k) The identification, tracing and freezing or seizure of proceeds, property and assets and instrumentalities of crimes for the purpose of eventual forfeiture, without prejudice to the rights of bona fide third parties; and
(l) Any other type of assistance which is not prohibited by the law of the requested State, with a view to facilitating the investigation and prosecution of crimes within the jurisdiction of the Court.
(2) The Court shall have the authority to provide an assurance to a witness or an expert appearing before the Court that he or she will not be prosecuted, detained or subjected to any restriction of personal freedom by the Court in respect of any act or omission that preceded the departure of that person from the requested State.
(3) Where execution of a particular measure of assistance detailed in a request presented under paragraph (1), is prohibited in the requested State on the basis of an existing fundamental legal principle of general application, the requested State shall promptly consult with the Court to try to resolve the matter. In the consultations, consideration should be given to whether the assistance can be rendered in another manner or subject to conditions. If after consultations the matter cannot be resolved, the Court shall modify the request as necessary.
(4) In accordance with article 72, a State Party may deny a request for assistance, in whole or in part, only if the request concerns the production of any documents or disclosure of evidence which relates to its national security.
(5) Before denying a request for assistance under paragraph (1) (l), the requested State shall consider whether the assistance can be provided subject to specified conditions, or whether the assistance can be provided at a later date or in an alternative manner, provided that if the Court or the Prosecutor accepts the assistance subject to conditions, the Court or the Prosecutor shall abide by them.
(6) If a request for assistance is denied, the requested State Party shall promptly inform the Court or the Prosecutor of the reasons for such denial.
(7) (a) The Court may request the temporary transfer of a person in custody for purposes of identification or for obtaining testimony or other assistance.
The person may be transferred if the following conditions are fulfilled:
(i) The person freely gives his or her informed consent to the transfer;and
(ii) The requested State agrees to the transfer, subject to such conditions as that State and the Court may agree.
(b) The person being transferred shall remain in custody. When the purposes of the transfer have been fulfilled, the Court shall return the person without delay to the requested State.
(8) (a) The Court shall ensure the confidentiality of documents and information,
except as required for the investigation and proceedings described in the request.
(b) The requested State may, when necessary, transmit documents or information to the Prosecutor on a confidential basis. The Prosecutor may then use them solely for the purpose of generating new evidence.
(c) The requested State may, on its own motion or at the request of the Prosecutor, subsequently consent to the disclosure of such documents or information. They may then be used as evidence pursuant to the provisions of Parts 5 and 6 and in accordance with the Rules of Procedure and Evidence.
(9) (a) (i) In the event that a State Party receives competing requests, other than for surrender or extradition, from the Court and from another State pursuant to an international obligation, the State Party shall endeavour, in consultation with the Court and the other State, to meet both requests, if necessary by postponing or attaching conditions to one or the other request.
(ii) Failing that, competing requests shall be resolved in accordance with the principles established in article 90.
(b) Where, however, the request from the Court concerns information, property or persons which are subject to the control of a third State or an international organization by virtue of an international

PART I   INTERNATIONAL LAW

agreement, the requested States shall so inform the Court and the Court shall direct its request to the third State or international organization.
(10) (a) The Court may, upon request, cooperate with and provide assistance to a State Party conducting an investigation into or trial in respect of conduct which constitutes a crime within the jurisdiction of the Court or which constitutes a serious crime under the national law of the requesting State.
(b)
(i) The assistance provided under subparagraph (a) shall include, inter alia:
(a) The transmission of statements, documents or other types of evidence obtained in the course of an investigation or a trial conducted by the Court; and
(b) The questioning of any person detained by order of the Court;
(ii) In the case of assistance under subparagraph (b) (i) a:
(a) If the documents or other types of evidence have been obtained with the assistance of a State, such transmission shall require the consent of that State;
(b) If the statements, documents or other types of evidence have been provided by a witness or expert, such transmission shall be subject to the provisions of article 68.
(c) The Court may, under the conditions set out in this paragraph, grant a request for assistance under this paragraph from a State which is not a Party to this Statute.

Article 94. Postponement of execution of a request in respect of ongoing investigation or prosecution
(1) If the immediate execution of a request would interfere with an ongoing investigation or prosecution of a case different from that to which the request relates, the requested State may postpone the execution of the request for a period of time agreed upon with the Court. However, the postponement shall be no longer than is necessary to complete the relevant investigation or prosecution in the requested State. Before making a decision to postpone, the requested State should consider whether the assistance may be immediately provided subject to certain conditions.
(2) If a decision to postpone is taken pursuant to paragraph (1), the Prosecutor may, however, seek measures to preserve evidence, pursuant to article 93, paragraph (1) (j).

Article 95. Postponement of execution of a request in respect of an admissibility challenge
Where there is an admissibility challenge under consideration by the Court pursuant to Article 18 or 19, the requested State may postpone the execution of a request under this Part pending a determination by the Court, unless the Court has specifically ordered that the Prosecutor may pursue the collection of such evidence pursuant to article 18 or 19.

Article 96. Contents of request for other forms of assistance under article 93
(1) A request for other forms of assistance referred to in article 93 shall be made in writing. In urgent cases, a request may be made by any medium capable of delivering a written record, provided that the request shall be confirmed through the channel provided for in article 87, paragraph (1) (a).
(2) The request shall, as applicable, contain or be supported by the following:
(a) A concise statement of the purpose of the request and the assistance sought, including the legal basis and the grounds for the request;
(b) As much detailed information as possible about the location or identification of any person or place that must be found or identified in order for the assistance sought to be provided;
(c) A concise statement of the essential facts underlying the request;
(d) The reasons for and details of any procedure or requirement to be followed;
(e) Such information as may be required under the law of the requested State in order to execute the request; and
(f) Any other information relevant in order for the assistance sought to be provided.
(3) Upon the request of the Court, a State Party shall consult with the Court, either generally or with respect to a specific matter, regarding any requirements under its national law that may apply under paragraph (2) (e). During the consultations, the State Party shall advise the Court of the specific requirements of its national law.
(4) The provisions of this article shall, where applicable, also apply in respect of a request for assistance made to the Court.

Article 97. Consultations
Where a State Party receives a request under this Part in relation to which it identifies problems which may impede or prevent the execution of the request, that State shall consult with the Court without delay in order to resolve the matter. Such problems may include, inter alia:
(a) Insufficient information to execute the request;
(b) In the case of a request for surrender, the fact that despite best efforts, the person sought cannot

be located or that the investigation conducted has determined that the person in the requested State is clearly not the person named in the warrant; or
(c) The fact that execution of the request in its current form would require the requested State to breach a pre-existing treaty obligation undertaken with respect to another State.

Article 98. Cooperation with respect to waiver of immunity and consent to surrender
(1) The Court may not proceed with a request for surrender or assistance which would require the requested State to act inconsistently with its obligations under international law with respect to the State or diplomatic immunity of a person or property of a third State, unless the Court can first obtain the cooperation of that third State for the waiver of the immunity.
(2) The Court may not proceed with a request for surrender which would require the requested State to act inconsistently with its obligations under international agreements pursuant to which the consent of a sending State is required to surrender a person of that State to the Court, unless the Court can first obtain the cooperation of the sending State for the giving of consent for the surrender.

Article 99. Execution of requests under articles 93 and 96
(1) Requests for assistance shall be executed in accordance with the relevant procedure under the law of the requested State and, unless prohibited by such law, in the manner specified in the request, including following any procedure outlined therein or permitting persons specified in the request to be present at and assist in the execution process.
(2) In the case of an urgent request, the documents or evidence produced in response shall, at the request of the Court, be sent urgently.
(3) Replies from the requested State shall be transmitted in their original language and form.
(4) Without prejudice to other articles in this Part, where it is necessary for the successful execution of a request which can be executed without any compulsory measures, including specifically the interview of or taking evidence from a person on a voluntary basis, including doing so without the presence of the authorities of the requested State Party if it is essential for the request to be executed, and the examination without modification of a public site or other public place, the Prosecutor may execute such request directly on the territory of a State as follows:
(a) When the State Party requested is a State on the territory of which the crime is alleged to have been committed, and there has been a determination of admissibility pursuant to article 18 or 19, the Prosecutor
may directly execute such request following all possible consultations with the requested State Party;
(b) In other cases, the Prosecutor may execute such request following consultations with the requested State Party and subject to any reasonable conditions or concerns raised by that State Party. Where the requested State Party identifies problems with the execution of a request pursuant to this subparagraph it shall, without delay, consult with the Court to resolve the matter.
(5) Provisions allowing a person heard or examined by the Court under article 72 to invoke restrictions designed to prevent disclosure of confidential information connected with national security shall also apply to the execution of requests for assistance under this article.

Article 100. Costs
(1) The ordinary costs for execution of requests in the territory of the requested State shall be borne by that State, except for the following, which shall be borne by the Court:
(a) Costs associated with the travel and security of witnesses and experts or the transfer under article 93 of persons in custody;
(b) Costs of translation, interpretation and transcription;
(c) Travel and subsistence costs of the judges, the Prosecutor, the Deputy Prosecutors, the Registrar, the Deputy Registrar and staff of any organ of the Court;
(d) Costs of any expert opinion or report requested by the Court;
(e) Costs associated with the transport of a person being surrendered to the Court by a custodial State; and
(f) Following consultations, any extraordinary costs that may result from the execution of a request.
(2) The provisions of paragraph (1) shall, as appropriate, apply to requests from States Parties to the Court. In that case, the Court shall bear the ordinary costs of execution.

Article 101. Rule of speciality
(1) A person surrendered to the Court under this Statute shall not be proceeded against, punished or detained for any conduct committed prior to surrender, other than the conduct or course of conduct which forms the basis of the crimes for which that person has been surrendered.
(2) The Court may request a waiver of the requirements of paragraph (1) from the State which surrendered the person to the Court and, if necessary, the Court shall provide additional information in

accordance with article 91. States Parties shall have the authority to provide a waiver to the Court and should endeavour to do so.

Article 102. Use of terms
For the purposes of this Statute:
(a) "surrender" means the delivering up of a person by a State to the Court, pursuant to this Statute.
(b) "extradition" means the delivering up of a person by one State to another as provided by treaty, convention or national legislation.

Part X. Enforcement

Article 103. Role of States in enforcement of sentences of imprisonment
(1) (a) A sentence of imprisonment shall be served in a State designated by the Court from a list of States which have indicated to the Court their willingness to accept sentenced persons.
(b) At the time of declaring its willingness to accept sentenced persons, a State may attach conditions to its acceptance as agreed by the Court and in accordance with this Part.
(c) A State designated in a particular case shall promptly inform the Court whether it accepts the Court's designation.
(2) (a) The State of enforcement shall notify the Court of any circumstances, including the exercise of any conditions agreed under paragraph (1), which could materially affect the terms or extent of the imprisonment. The Court shall be given at least 45 days' notice of any such known or foreseeable circumstances. During this period, the State of enforcement shall take no action that might prejudice its obligations under article 110.
(b) Where the Court cannot agree to the circumstances referred to in subparagraph (a), it shall notify the State of enforcement and proceed in accordance with article 104, paragraph (1).
(3) In exercising its discretion to make a designation under paragraph (1), the Court shall take into account the following:
(a) The principle that States Parties should share the responsibility for enforcing sentences of imprisonment, in accordance with principles of equitable distribution, as provided in the Rules of Procedure and Evidence;
(b) The application of widely accepted international treaty standards governing the treatment of prisoners;
(c) The views of the sentenced person;
(d) The nationality of the sentenced person;
(e) Such other factors regarding the circumstances of the crime or the person sentenced, or the effective enforcement of the sentence, as may be appropriate in designating the State of enforcement.
(4) If no State is designated under paragraph (1), the sentence of imprisonment shall be served in a prison facility made available by the host State, in accordance with the conditions set out in the headquarters agreement referred to in article 3, paragraph (2). In such a case, the costs arising out of the enforcement of a sentence
of imprisonment shall be borne by the Court.

Article 104. Change in designation of State of enforcement
(1) The Court may, at any time, decide to transfer a sentenced person to a prison of another State.
(2) A sentenced person may, at any time, apply to the Court to be transferred from the State of enforcement.

Article 105. Enforcement of the sentence
(1) Subject to conditions which a State may have specified in accordance with article 103, paragraph (1) (b), the sentence of imprisonment shall be binding on the States Parties, which shall in no case modify it.
(2) The Court alone shall have the right to decide any application for appeal and revision. The State of enforcement shall not impede the making of any such application by a sentenced person.

Article 106. Supervision of enforcement of sentences and conditions of imprisonment
(1) The enforcement of a sentence of imprisonment shall be subject to the supervision of the Court and shall be consistent with widely accepted international treaty standards governing treatment of prisoners.
(2) The conditions of imprisonment shall be governed by the law of the State of enforcement and shall be consistent with widely accepted international treaty standards governing treatment of prisoners; in no case shall such conditions be more or less favourable than those available to prisoners convicted of similar offences in the State of enforcement.

(3) Communications between a sentenced person and the Court shall be unimpeded and confidential.

Article 107. Transfer of the person upon completion of sentence
(1) Following completion of the sentence, a person who is not a national of the State of enforcement may, in accordance with the law of the State of enforcement, be transferred to a State which is obliged to receive him or her, or to another State which agrees to receive him or her, taking into account any wishes of the person to
be transferred to that State, unless the State of enforcement authorizes the person to remain in its territory.
(2) If no State bears the costs arising out of transferring the person to another State pursuant to paragraph (1), such costs shall be borne by the Court.
(3) Subject to the provisions of article 108, the State of enforcement may also, in accordance with its national law, extradite or otherwise surrender the person to a State which has requested the extradition or surrender of the person for purposes of trial or enforcement of a sentence.

Article 108. Limitation on the prosecution or punishment of other offences
(1) A sentenced person in the custody of the State of enforcement shall not be subject to prosecution or punishment or to extradition to a third State for any conduct engaged in prior to that person's delivery to the State of enforcement, unless such prosecution, punishment or extradition has been approved by the Court at the request of the State of enforcement.
(2) The Court shall decide the matter after having heard the views of the sentenced person.
(3) Paragraph (1) shall cease to apply if the sentenced person remains voluntarily for more than 30 days in the territory of the State of enforcement after having served the full sentence imposed by the Court, or returns to the territory of that State after having left it.

Article 109. Enforcement of fines and forfeiture measures
(1) States Parties shall give effect to fines or forfeitures ordered by the Court under Part 7, without prejudice to the rights of bona fide third parties, and in accordance with the procedure of their national law.
(2) If a State Party is unable to give effect to an order for forfeiture, it shall take measures to recover the value of the proceeds, property or assets ordered by the Court to be forfeited, without prejudice to the rights of bona fide third parties.
(3) Property, or the proceeds of the sale of real property or, where appropriate, the sale of other property, which is obtained by a State Party as a result of its enforcement of a judgement of the Court shall be transferred to the Court.

Article 110. Review by the Court concerning reduction of sentence
(1) The State of enforcement shall not release the person before expiry of the sentence pronounced by the Court.
(2) The Court alone shall have the right to decide any reduction of sentence, and shall rule on the matter after having heard the person.
(3) When the person has served two thirds of the sentence, or 25 years in the case of life imprisonment, the Court shall review the sentence to determine whether it should be reduced. Such a review shall not be conducted before that time.
(4) In its review under paragraph 3, the Court may reduce the sentence if it finds that one or more of the following factors are present:
(a) The early and continuing willingness of the person to cooperate with the Court in its investigations and prosecutions;
(b) The voluntary assistance of the person in enabling the enforcement of the judgements and orders of the Court in other cases, and in particular providing assistance in locating assets subject to orders of fine, forfeiture or reparation which may be used for the benefit of victims; or
(c) Other factors establishing a clear and significant change of circumstances sufficient to justify the reduction of sentence, as provided in the Rules of Procedure and Evidence.
(5) If the Court determines in its initial review under paragraph (3) that it is not appropriate to reduce the sentence, it shall thereafter review the question of reduction of sentence at such intervals and applying such criteria as provided for in the Rules of Procedure and Evidence.

Article 111. Escape
If a convicted person escapes from custody and flees the State of enforcement, that State may, after consultation with the Court, request the person's surrender from the State in which the person is located pursuant to existing bilateral or multilateral arrangements, or may request that the Court seek the person's surrender, in accordance with Part 9. It may direct that the person be delivered to the State in which he or she was serving the sentence or to another State designated by the Court.

Part XI. Assembly of States Parties

Article 112. Assembly of States Parties

(1) An Assembly of States Parties to this Statute is hereby established. Each State Party shall have one representative in the Assembly who may be accompanied by alternates and advisers. Other States which have signed this Statute or the Final Act may be observers in the Assembly.

(2) The Assembly shall:

(a) Consider and adopt, as appropriate, recommendations of the Preparatory Commission;

(b) Provide management oversight to the Presidency, the Prosecutor and the Registrar regarding the administration of the Court;

(c) Consider the reports and activities of the Bureau established under paragraph (3) and take appropriate action in regard thereto;

(d) Consider and decide the budget for the Court;

(e) Decide whether to alter, in accordance with article 36, the number of judges;

(f) Consider pursuant to article 87, paragraphs (5) and (7), any question relating to non-cooperation;

(g) Perform any other function consistent with this Statute or the Rules of Procedure and Evidence.

(3) (a) The Assembly shall have a Bureau consisting of a President, two Vice-Presidents and 18 members elected by the Assembly for three-year terms.

(b) The Bureau shall have a representative character, taking into account, in particular, equitable geographical distribution and the adequate representation of the principal legal systems of the world.

(c) The Bureau shall meet as often as necessary, but at least once a year. It shall assist the Assembly in the discharge of its responsibilities.

(4) The Assembly may establish such subsidiary bodies as may be necessary, including an independent oversight mechanism for inspection, evaluation and investigation of the Court, in order to enhance its efficiency and economy.

(5) The President of the Court, the Prosecutor and the Registrar or their representatives may participate, as appropriate, in meetings of the Assembly and of the Bureau.

(6) The Assembly shall meet at the seat of the Court or at the Headquarters of the United Nations once a year and, when circumstances so require, hold special sessions. Except as otherwise specified in this Statute, special sessions shall be convened by the Bureau on its own initiative or at the request of one third of the States Parties.

(7) Each State Party shall have one vote. Every effort shall be made to reach decisions by consensus in the Assembly and in the Bureau. If consensus cannot be reached, except as otherwise provided in the Statute:

(a) Decisions on matters of substance must be approved by a two-thirds majority of those present and voting provided that an absolute majority of States Parties constitutes the quorum for voting;

(b) Decisions on matters of procedure shall be taken by a simple majority of States Parties present and voting.

(8) A State Party which is in arrears in the payment of its financial contributions towards the costs of the Court shall have no vote in the Assembly and in the Bureau if the amount of its arrears equals or exceeds the amount of the contributions due from it for the preceding two full years. The Assembly may, nevertheless, permit such a State Party to vote in the Assembly and in the Bureau if it is satisfied that the failure to pay is due to conditions beyond the control of the State Party.

(9) The Assembly shall adopt its own rules of procedure.

(10) The official and working languages of the Assembly shall be those of the General Assembly of the United Nations.

Part XII. Financing

Article 113. Financial Regulations

Except as otherwise specifically provided, all financial matters related to the Court and the meetings of the Assembly of States Parties, including its Bureau and subsidiary bodies, shall be governed by this Statute and the Financial Regulations and Rules adopted by the Assembly of States Parties.

Article 114. Payment of expenses

Expenses of the Court and the Assembly of States Parties, including its Bureau and subsidiary bodies, shall be paid from the funds of the Court.

Article 115. Funds of the Court and of the Assembly of States Parties

The expenses of the Court and the Assembly of States Parties, including its Bureau and subsidiary bodies, as provided for in the budget decided by the Assembly of States Parties, shall be provided by the following sources:

(a) Assessed contributions made by States Parties;
(b) Funds provided by the United Nations, subject to the approval of the General Assembly, in particular in relation to the expenses incurred due to referrals by the Security Council.

Article 116. Voluntary contributions
Without prejudice to article 115, the Court may receive and utilize, as additional funds, voluntary contributions from Governments, international organizations, individuals, corporations and other entities, in accordance with relevant criteria adopted by the Assembly of States Parties.

Article 117. Assessment of contributions
The contributions of States Parties shall be assessed in accordance with an agreed scale of assessment, based on the scale adopted by the United Nations for its regular budget and adjusted in accordance with the principles on which that scale is based.

Article 118. Annual audit
The records, books and accounts of the Court, including its annual financial statements, shall be audited annually by an independent auditor.

Part XIII. Final clauses

Article 119. Settlement of disputes
(1) Any dispute concerning the judicial functions of the Court shall be settled by the decision of the Court.
(2) Any other dispute between two or more States Parties relating to the interpretation or application of this Statute which is not settled through negotiations within three months of their commencement shall be referred to the Assembly of States Parties. The Assembly may itself seek to settle the dispute or may make recommendations on further means of settlement of the dispute, including referral to the International Court of Justice in conformity with the Statute of that Court.

Article 120. Reservations
No reservations may be made to this Statute.

Article 121. Amendments
(1) After the expiry of seven years from the entry into force of this Statute, any State Party may propose amendments thereto. The text of any proposed amendment shall be submitted to the Secretary-General of the United Nations, who shall promptly circulate it to all States Parties.
(2) No sooner than three months from the date of notification, the Assembly of States Parties, at its next meeting, shall, by a majority of those present and voting, decide whether to take up the proposal. The Assembly may deal with the proposal directly or convene a Review Conference if the issue involved so warrants.
(3) The adoption of an amendment at a meeting of the Assembly of States Parties or at a Review Conference on which consensus cannot be reached shall require a two-thirds majority of States Parties.
(4) Except as provided in paragraph (5), an amendment shall enter into force for all States Parties one year after instruments of ratification or acceptance have been deposited with the Secretary-General of the United Nations by seven-eighths of them.
(5) Any amendment to articles 5, 6, 7 and 8 of this Statute shall enter into force for those States Parties which have accepted the amendment one year after the deposit of their instruments of ratification or acceptance. In respect of a State Party which has not accepted the amendment, the Court shall not exercise its jurisdiction regarding a crime covered by the amendment when committed by that State Party's nationals or on its territory.
(6) If an amendment has been accepted by seven-eighths of States Parties in accordance with paragraph (4),
any State Party which has not accepted the amendment may withdraw from this Statute with immediate effect, notwithstanding article 127, paragraph (1), but subject to article 127, paragraph (2), by giving notice no later than one year after the entry into force of such amendment.
(7) The Secretary-General of the United Nations shall circulate to all States Parties any amendment adopted at a meeting of the Assembly of States Parties or at a Review Conference.

Article 122. Amendments to provisions of an institutional nature
(1) Amendments to provisions of this Statute which are of an exclusively institutional nature, namely, article 35, article 36, paragraphs (8) and (9), article 37, article 38, article 39, paragraphs (1) (first two sentences), (2) and (4), article 42, paragraphs (4) to (9), article 43, paragraphs (2) and (3), and articles 44, 46, 47 and 49, may be proposed at any time, notwithstanding article 121, paragraph (1), by any

State Party. The text of any proposed amendment shall be submitted to the Secretary-General of the United Nations or such other person designated by the Assembly of States Parties who shall promptly circulate it to all States Parties and to others participating in the Assembly.

(2) Amendments under this article on which consensus cannot be reached shall be adopted by the Assembly of States Parties or by a Review Conference, by a two thirds majority of States Parties. Such amendments shall enter into force for all States Parties six months after their adoption by the Assembly or, as the case may be, by the Conference.

Article 123. Review of the Statute

(1) Seven years after the entry into force of this Statute the Secretary-General of the United Nations shall convene a Review Conference to consider any amendments to this Statute. Such review may include, but is not limited to, the list of crimes contained in article 5. The Conference shall be open to those participating in the Assembly of States Parties and on the same conditions.

(2) At any time thereafter, at the request of a State Party and for the purposes set out in paragraph (1), the Secretary-General of the United Nations shall, upon approval by a majority of States Parties, convene a Review Conference.

(3) The provisions of article 121, paragraphs (3) to (7), shall apply to the adoption and entry into force of any amendment to the Statute considered at a Review Conference.

Article 124. Transitional Provision

Notwithstanding article 12, paragraphs (1) and (2), a State, on becoming a party to this Statute, may declare that, for a period of seven years after the entry into force of this Statute for the State concerned, it does not accept the jurisdiction of the Court with respect to the category of crimes referred to in article 8 when a crime is alleged to have been committed by its nationals or on its territory. A declaration under this article may be withdrawn at any time. The provisions of this article shall be reviewed at the Review Conference convened in accordance with article 123, paragraph (1).

Article 125. Signature, ratification, acceptance, approval or accession

(1) This Statute shall be open for signature by all States in Rome, at the headquarters of the Food and Agriculture Organization of the United Nations, on 17 July 1998. Thereafter, it shall remain open for signature in Rome at the Ministry of Foreign Affairs of Italy until 17 October 1998. After that date, the Statute shall remain open for signature in New York, at United Nations Headquarters, until 31 December 2000.

(2) This Statute is subject to ratification, acceptance or approval by signatory States. Instruments of ratification, acceptance or approval shall be deposited with the Secretary-General of the United Nations.

(3) This Statute shall be open to accession by all States. Instruments of accession shall be deposited with the Secretary-General of the United Nations.

AMENDMENTS TO THE ROME STATUTE

Amendments to the Rome Statute of the ICC (Crime of Aggression; Elements of Crimes)

Amendments to the Rome Statute of the Internaional Criminal Court on the Crime of Aggression and the Elements of Crimes, 11 June 2010Adopted at the 13th plenary meeting, on 11 June 2010
RC/Resl 6

The crime of aggression

The Review Conference,
Recalling paragraph (1) of article 12 of the Rome Statute,
Recalling paragraph (2) of article 5 of the Rome Statute,
Recalling also paragraph (7) of resolution F, adopted by the United Nations Diplomatic Conference of Plenipotentiaries on the Establishment of an International Criminal Court on 17 July 1998,
Recalling further resolution ICC-ASP/1/Res.1 on the continuity of work in respect of the crime of aggression, and expressing its appreciation to the Special Working Group on the Crime of Aggression for having elaborated proposals on a provision on the crime of aggression,
Taking note of resolution ICC-ASP/8/Res.6, by which the Assembly of States Parties forwarded proposals on a provision on the crime of aggression to the Review Conference for its consideration,
Resolved to activate the Court's jurisdiction over the crime of aggression as early as possible,
(1) Decides to adopt, in accordance with article 5, paragraph (2), of the Rome Statute of the International Criminal Court (hereinafter: "the Statute") the amendments to the Statute contained in annex I of the present resolution, which are subject to ratification or acceptance and shall enter into force in accordance with
article 121, paragraph (5); and notes that any State Party may lodge a declaration referred to in article 15 bis prior to ratification or acceptance;
(2) Also decides to adopt the amendments to the Elements of Crimes contained in annex II of the present resolution;
(3) Also decides to adopt the understandings regarding the interpretation of the abovementioned amendments contained in annex III of the present resolution;
(4) Further decides to review the amendments on the crime of aggression seven years after the beginning of the Court's exercise of jurisdiction;
(5) Calls upon all States Parties to ratify or accept the amendments contained in annex I.

Annex I.

Amendments to the Rome Statute of the International Criminal Court on the crime of aggression
(1) Article 5, paragraph (2), of the Statute is deleted.
(2) The following text is inserted after article 8 of the Statute:

Article 8 bis Crime of aggression
(1) For the purpose of this Statute, "crime of aggression" means the planning, preparation, initiation or execution, by a person in a position effectively to exercise control over or to direct the political or military action of a State, of an act of aggression which, by its character, gravity and scale, constitutes a manifest violation of the Charter of the United Nations.
(2) For the purpose of paragraph (1), "act of aggression" means the use of armed force by a State against the sovereignty, territorial integrity or political independence of another State, or in any other manner inconsistent with the Charter of the United Nations. Any of the following acts, regardless of a declaration of war, shall, in accordance with United Nations General Assembly resolution 3314 (XXIX) of 14 December 1974, qualify as an act of aggression:
(a) The invasion or attack by the armed forces of a State of the territory of another State, or any military occupation, however temporary, resulting from such invasion or attack, or any annexation by the use of force of the territory of another State or part thereof;
(b) Bombardment by the armed forces of a State against the territory of another State or the use of any weapons by a State against the territory of another State;
(c) The blockade of the ports or coasts of a State by the armed forces of another State;
(d) An attack by the armed forces of a State on the land, sea or air forces, or marine and air fleets of another State;
(e) The use of armed forces of one State which are within the territory of another State with the agreement of the receiving State, in contravention of the conditions provided for in the agreement or

PART I   INTERNATIONAL LAW

any extension of their presence in such territory beyond the termination of the agreement;
(f) The action of a State in allowing its territory, which it has placed at the disposal of another State, to be used by that other State for perpetrating an act of aggression against a third State;
(g) The sending by or on behalf of a State of armed bands, groups, irregulars or mercenaries, which carry out acts of armed force against another State of such gravity as to amount to the acts listed above, or its substantial involvement therein.
(3) The following text is inserted after article 15 of the Statute:

Article 15 bis Exercise of jurisdiction over the crime of aggression (State referral, proprio motu)
(1) The Court may exercise jurisdiction over the crime of aggression in accordance with article 13, paragraphs (a) and (c), subject to the provisions of this article.
(2) The Court may exercise jurisdiction only with respect to crimes of aggression committed one year after the ratification or acceptance of the amendments by thirty States Parties.
(3) The Court shall exercise jurisdiction over the crime of aggression in accordance with this article, subject to a decision to be taken after 1 January 2017 by the same majority of States Parties as is required for the adoption of an amendment to the Statute.
(4) The Court may, in accordance with article 12, exercise jurisdiction over a crime of aggression, arising from an act of aggression committed by a State Party, unless that State Party has previously declared that it does not accept such jurisdiction by lodging a declaration with the Registrar. The withdrawal of such a declaration may be effected at any time and shall be considered by the State Party within three years.
(5) In respect of a State that is not a party to this Statute, the Court shall not exercise its jurisdiction over the crime of aggression when committed by that State's nationals or on its territory.
(6) Where the Prosecutor concludes that there is a reasonable basis to proceed with an investigation in respect of a crime of aggression, he or she shall first ascertain whether the Security Council has made a determination of an act of aggression committed by the State concerned. The Prosecutor shall notify the Secretary-General of the United Nations of the situation before the Court, including any relevant information and documents.
(7) Where the Security Council has made such a determination, the Prosecutor may proceed with the investigation in respect of a crime of aggression.
(8) Where no such determination is made within six months after the date of notification, the Prosecutor may proceed with the investigation in respect of a crime of aggression, provided that the Pre-Trial Division has authorized the commencement of the investigation in respect of a crime of aggression in accordance with the procedure contained in article 15, and the Security Council has not decided otherwise in accordance with
article 16.
(9) A determination of an act of aggression by an organ outside the Court shall be without prejudice to the Court's own findings under this Statute.
(10) This article is without prejudice to the provisions relating to the exercise of jurisdiction with respect to other crimes referred to in article 5.
(4) The following text is inserted after article 15 bis of the Statute:

Article 15 ter Exercise of jurisdiction over the crime of aggression (Security Council referral)
(1) The Court may exercise jurisdiction over the crime of aggression in accordance with article 13, paragraph (b), subject to the provisions of this article.
(2) The Court may exercise jurisdiction only with respect to crimes of aggression committed one year after the ratification or acceptance of the amendments by thirty States Parties.
(3) The Court shall exercise jurisdiction over the crime of aggression in accordance with this article, subject to a decision to be taken after 1 January 2017 by the same majority of States Parties as is required for the adoption of an amendment to the Statute.
(4) A determination of an act of aggression by an organ outside the Court shall be without prejudice to the Court's own findings under this Statute.
(5) This article is without prejudice to the provisions relating to the exercise of jurisdiction with respect to other crimes referred to in article 5.
(5) The following text is inserted after article 25, paragraph (3), of the Statute:
(3) bis. In respect of the crime of aggression, the provisions of this article shall apply only to persons in a position effectively to exercise control over or to direct the political or military action of a State.
6. The first sentence of article 9, paragraph (1), of the Statute is replaced by the following sentence:
1. Elements of Crimes shall assist the Court in the interpretation and application of articles 6, 7, 8 and 8 bis.
7. The chapeau of article 20, paragraph (3), of the Statute is replaced by the following paragraph; the rest of the paragraph remains unchanged:

AMENDMENTS TO THE ROME STATUTE

3. No person who has been tried by another court for conduct also proscribed under article 6, 7, 8 or 8 bis shall be tried by the Court with respect to the same conduct unless the proceedings in the other court:

Annex II.

Amendments to the Elements of Crimes

Article 8 bis Crime of aggression

Introduction
(1) It is understood that any of the acts referred to in article 8 bis, paragraph (2), qualify as an act of aggression.
(2) There is no requirement to prove that the perpetrator has made a legal evaluation as to whether the use of armed force was inconsistent with the Charter of the United Nations.
(3) The term "manifest" is an objective qualification.
(4) There is no requirement to prove that the perpetrator has made a legal evaluation as to the "manifest" nature of the violation of the Charter of the United Nations.

Elements
(1) The perpetrator planned, prepared, initiated or executed an act of aggression.
(2) The perpetrator was a person1 in a position effectively to exercise control over or to direct the political or military action of the State which committed the act of aggression.
(3) The act of aggression – the use of armed force by a State against the sovereignty, territorial integrity or political independence of another State, or in any other manner inconsistent with the Charter of the United Nations – was committed.
(4) The perpetrator was aware of the factual circumstances that established that such a use of armed force was inconsistent with the Charter of the United Nations.
(5) The act of aggression, by its character, gravity and scale, constituted a manifest violation of the Charter of the United Nations.
(6) The perpetrator was aware of the factual circumstances that established such a manifest violation of the Charter of the United Nations.
1 With respect to an act of aggression, more than one person may be in a position that meets these criteria.
RC/11

Annex III.

Understandings regarding the amendments to the Rome Statute of the International Criminal Court on the crime of aggression

Referrals by the Security Council
(1) It is understood that the Court may exercise jurisdiction on the basis of a Security Council referral in accordance with article 13, paragraph (b), of the Statute only with respect to crimes of aggression committed after a decision in accordance with article 15 ter, paragraph (3,) is taken, and one year after the ratification or acceptance of the amendments by thirty States Parties, whichever is later.
(2) It is understood that the Court shall exercise jurisdiction over the crime of aggression on the basis of a Security Council referral in accordance with article 13, paragraph (b), of the Statute irrespective of whether the State concerned has accepted the Court's jurisdiction in this regard.

Jurisdiction ratione temporis
(3) It is understood that in case of article 13, paragraph (a) or (c), the Court may exercise its jurisdiction only with respect to crimes of aggression committed after a decision in accordance with article 15 bis, paragraph (3), is taken, and one year after the ratification or acceptance of the amendments by thirty States Parties, whichever is later.

Domestic jurisdiction over the crime of aggression
(4) It is understood that the amendments that address the definition of the act of aggression and the crime of aggression do so for the purpose of this Statute only. The amendments shall, in accordance with article 10 of the Rome Statute, not be interpreted as limiting or prejudicing in any way existing or developing rules of international law for purposes other than this Statute.
(5) It is understood that the amendments shall not be interpreted as creating the right or obligation to exercise domestic jurisdiction with respect to an act of aggression committed by another State.

PART I   INTERNATIONAL LAW

Other understandings
(6) It is understood that aggression is the most serious and dangerous form of the illegal use of force; and that a determination whether an act of aggression has been committed requires consideration of all the circumstances of each particular case, including the gravity of the acts concerned and their consequences, in accordance with the Charter of the United Nations.

(7) It is understood that in establishing whether an act of aggression constitutes a manifest violation of the Charter of the United Nations, the three components of character, gravity and scale must be sufficient to justify a "manifest" determination. No one component can be significant enough to satisfy the manifest standard by itself.

Elements of Crimes, ICC-ASP1/3
Adoption and Entry into Force. 9 September 2002

B. Elements of Crimes

Explanatory note.
The structure of the elements of the crimes of genocide, crimes against humanity and war crimes follows the structure of the corresponding provisions of articles 6, 7 and 8 of the Rome Statute. Some paragraphs of those articles of the Rome Statute list multiple crimes. In those instances, the elements of crimes appear in separate paragraphs which correspond to each of those crimes to facilitate the identification of the respective elements.

Contents

General introduction

Article 6 Genocide
Introduction
6 (a) Genocide by killing
6 (b) Genocide by causing serious bodily or mental harm
6 (c) Genocide by deliberately inflicting conditions of life calculated to bring about physical destruction
6 (d) Genocide by imposing measures intended to prevent births
6 (e) Genocide by forcibly transferring children

Article 7 Crimes against humanity
Introduction 5
7 (1) (a) Crime against humanity of murder
7 (1) (b) Crime against humanity of extermination
7 (1) (c) Crime against humanity of enslavement
7 (1) (d) Crime against humanity of deportation or forcible transfer of population
7 (1) (e) Crime against humanity of imprisonment or other severe deprivation of physical liberty
7 (1) (f) Crime against humanity of torture
7 (1) (g)-1 Crime against humanity of rape
7 (1) (g)-2 Crime against humanity of sexual slavery
7 (1) (g)-3 Crime against humanity of enforced prostitution
7 (1) (g)-4 Crime against humanity of forced pregnancy
7 (1) (g)-5 Crime against humanity of enforced sterilization
7 (1) (g)-6 Crime against humanity of sexual violence
7 (1) (h) Crime against humanity of persecution
7 (1) (i) Crime against humanity of enforced disappearance of persons,
7 (1) (j) Crime against humanity of apartheid
7 (1) (k) Crime against humanity of other inhumane acts

Article 8 War crimes
Introduction

Article 8 (2) (a)
8 (2) (a) (i) War crime of wilful killing
8 (2) (a) (ii)-1 War crime of torture
8 (2) (a) (ii)-2 War crime of inhuman treatment
8 (2) (a) (ii)-3 War crime of biological experiments
8 (2) (a) (iii) War crime of wilfully causing great suffering
8 (2) (a) (iv) War crime of destruction and appropriation of property
8 (2) (a) (v) War crime of compelling service in hostile forces
8 (2) (a) (vi) War crime of denying a fair trial
8 (2) (a) (vii)-1 War crime of unlawful deportation and transfer
8 (2) (a) (vii)-2 War crime of unlawful confinement
Elements of Crimes
8 (2) (a) (viii) War crime of taking hostages

Article 8 (2) (b)
8 (2) (b) (i) War crime of attacking civilians

PART I   INTERNATIONAL LAW

8 (2) (b) (ii) War crime of attacking civilian objects
8 (2) (b) (iii) War crime of attacking personnel or objects involved in a humanitarian assistance or peacekeeping mission
8 (2) (b) (iv) War crime of excessive incidental death, injury, or damage
8 (2) (b) (v) War crime of attacking undefended places
8 (2) (b) (vi) War crime of killing or wounding a person hors de combat
8 (2) (b) (vii)-1 War crime of improper use of a flag of truce
8 (2) (b) (vii)-2 War crime of improper use of a flag, insignia or uniform of the hostile party
8 (2) (b) (vii)-3 War crime of improper use of a flag, insignia or uniform of the United Nations
8 (2) (b) (vii)-4 War crime of improper use of the distinctive emblems of the Geneva Conventions
8 (2) (b) (viii) The transfer, directly or indirectly, by the Occupying Power of parts of its own civilian population into the territory it occupies, or the deportation or transfer of all or parts of the population of the occupied territory within or outside this territory
8 (2) (b) (ix) War crime of attacking protected objects
8 (2) (b) (x)-1 War crime of mutilation
8 (2) (b) (x)-2 War crime of medical or scientific experiments
8 (2) (b) (xi) War crime of treacherously killing or wounding
8 (2) (b) (xii) War crime of denying quarter
8 (2) (b) (xiii) War crime of destroying or seizing the enemy's property
8 (2) (b) (xiv) War crime of depriving the nationals of the hostile power of rights or actions 25
8 (2) (b) (xv) War crime of compelling participation in military operations
8 (2) (b) (xvi) War crime of pillaging
8 (2) (b) (xvii) War crime of employing poison or poisoned weapons
8 (2) (b) (xviii) War crime of employing prohibited gases, liquids, materials or devices
8 (2) (b) (xix) War crime of employing prohibited bullets
8 (2) (b) (xx) War crime of employing weapons, projectiles or materials or methods of warfare listed in the Annex to the Statute
8 (2) (b) (xxi) War crime of outrages upon personal dignity
8 (2) (b) (xxii)-1 War crime of rape
8 (2) (b) (xxii)-2 War crime of sexual slavery
8 (2) (b) (xxii)-3 War crime of enforced prostitution
8 (2) (b) (xxii)-4 War crime of forced pregnancy
8 (2) (b) (xxii)-5 War crime of enforced sterilization
8 (2) (b) (xxii)-6 War crime of sexual violence
8 (2) (b) (xxiii) War crime of using protected persons as shields
8 (2) (b) (xxiv) War crime of attacking objects or persons using the distinctive emblems of the Geneva Conventions
8 (2) (b) (xxv) War crime of starvation as a method of warfare
8 (2) (b) (xxvi) War crime of using, conscripting or enlisting children

Article 8 (2) (c) 31
8 (2) (c) (i)-1 War crime of murder
8 (2) (c) (i)-2 War crime of mutilation
8 (2) (c) (i)-3 War crime of cruel treatment
8 (2) (c) (i)-4 War crime of torture
8 (2) (c) (ii) War crime of outrages upon personal dignity
8 (2) (c) (iii) War crime of taking hostages
8 (2) (c) (iv) War crime of sentencing or execution without due process

Article 8 (2) (e)
8 (2) (e) (i) War crime of attacking civilians
8 (2) (e) (ii) War crime of attacking objects or persons using the distinctive emblems of the Geneva Conventions
8 (2) (e) (iii) War crime of attacking personnel or objects involved in a humanitarian assistance or peacekeeping mission
8 (2) (e) (iv) War crime of attacking protected objects

8 (2) (e) (v) War crime of pillaging
8 (2) (e) (vi)-1 War crime of rape
8 (2) (e) (vi)-2 War crime of sexual slavery
8 (2) (e) (vi)-3 War crime of enforced prostitution
8 (2) (e) (vi)-4 War crime of forced pregnancy
8 (2) (e) (vi)-5 War crime of enforced sterilization
8 (2) (e) (vi)-6 War crime of sexual violence
8 (2) (e) (vii) War crime of using, conscripting and enlisting children
8 (2) (e) (viii) War crime of displacing civilians
8 (2) (e) (ix) War crime of treacherously killing or wounding
8 (2) (e) (x) War crime of denying quarter
8 (2) (e) (xi)-1 War crime of mutilation
8 (2) (e) (xi)-2 War crime of medical or scientific experiments
8 (2) (e) (xii) War crime of destroying or seizing the enemy's property
8 (2) (e) (xiii) War crime of employing poison or poisoned weapons
8 (2) (e) (xiv) War crime of employing prohibited gases, liquids, materials or devices
8 (2) (e) (xv) War crime of employing prohibited bullets

Article 8 bis Crime of aggression
General introduction
(1) Pursuant to article 9, the following Elements of Crimes shall assist the Court in the interpretation and application of articles 6, 7 and 8, consistent with the Statute. The provisions of the Statute, including article 21 and the general principles set out in Part 3, are applicable to the Elements of Crimes.
(2) As stated in article 30, unless otherwise provided, a person shall be criminally responsible and liable for punishment for a crime within the jurisdiction of the Court only if the material elements are committed with intent and knowledge. Where no reference is made in the Elements of Crimes to a mental element for any particular conduct, consequence or circumstance listed, it is understood that the relevant mental element, i.e., intent, knowledge or both, set out in article 30 applies. Exceptions to the article 30 standard, based on the Statute, including applicable law under its relevant provisions, are indicated below.
(3) Existence of intent and knowledge can be inferred from relevant facts and circumstances.
(4) With respect to mental elements associated with elements involving value judgement, such as those using the terms 'inhumane' or 'severe', it is not necessary that the perpetrator personally completed a particular value judgement, unless otherwise indicated.
(5) Grounds for excluding criminal responsibility or the absence thereof are generally not specified in the elements of crimes listed under each crime.
(6) The requirement of 'unlawfulness' found in the Statute or in other parts of international law, in particular international humanitarian law, is generally not specified in the elements of crimes.
(7) The elements of crimes are generally structured in accordance with the following principles:
As the elements of crimes focus on the conduct, consequences and circumstances associated with each crime, they are generally listed in that order;
When required, a particular mental element is listed after the affected conduct, consequence or circumstance;
Contextual circumstances are listed last.
(8) As used in the Elements of Crimes, the term 'perpetrator' is neutral as to guilt or innocence. The elements, including the appropriate mental elements, apply, *mutatis mutandis*, to all those whose criminal responsibility may fall under articles 25 and 28 of the Statute.
(9) A particular conduct may constitute one or more crimes.
(10) The use of short titles for the crimes has no legal effect.

Article 6. Genocide
Introduction
With respect to the last element listed for each crime:
The term 'in the context of' would include the initial acts in an emerging pattern;
The term 'manifest' is an objective qualification;
Notwithstanding the normal requirement for a mental element provided for in article 30, and recognizing that knowledge of the circumstances will usually be addressed in proving genocidal intent, the appropriate requirement, if any, for a mental element regarding this circumstance will need to be decided by the Court on a case-by-case basis.

Article 6 (a). Genocide by killing
Elements
(1) The perpetrator killed one or more persons.
(2) Such person or persons belonged to a particular national, ethnical, racial or religious group.
(3) The perpetrator intended to destroy, in whole or in part, that national, ethnical, racial or religious group, as such.
(4) The conduct took place in the context of a manifest pattern of similar conduct directed against that group or was conduct that could itself effect such destruction.

Article 6 (b). Genocide by causing serious bodily or mental harm
Elements
(1) The perpetrator caused serious bodily or mental harm to one or more persons.
(2) Such person or persons belonged to a particular national, ethnical, racial or religious group.
(3) The perpetrator intended to destroy, in whole or in part, that national, ethnical, racial or religious group, as such.
(4) The conduct took place in the context of a manifest pattern of similar conduct directed against that group or was conduct that could itself effect such destruction.

Article 6 (c). Genocide by deliberately inflicting conditions of life calculated to bring about physical destruction
Elements
(1) The perpetrator inflicted certain conditions of life upon one or more persons.
(2) Such person or persons belonged to a particular national, ethnical, racial or religious group.
(3) The perpetrator intended to destroy, in whole or in part, that national, ethnical, racial or religious group, as such.
(4) The conditions of life were calculated to bring about the physical destruction of that group, in whole or in part.
(5) The conduct took place in the context of a manifest pattern of similar conduct directed against that group or was conduct that could itself effect such destruction.

Article 6 (d). Genocide by imposing measures intended to prevent births
Elements
(1) The perpetrator imposed certain measures upon one or more persons.
(2) Such person or persons belonged to a particular national, ethnical, racial or religious group.
(3) The perpetrator intended to destroy, in whole or in part, that national, ethnical, racial or religious group, as such.
(4) The measures imposed were intended to prevent births within that group.
(5) The conduct took place in the context of a manifest pattern of similar conduct directed against that group or was conduct that could itself effect such destruction.

Article 6 (e). Genocide by forcibly transferring children
Elements
(1) The perpetrator forcibly transferred one or more persons.
(2) Such person or persons belonged to a particular national, ethnical, racial or religious group.
(3) The perpetrator intended to destroy, in whole or in part, that national, ethnical, racial or religious group, as such.
(4) The transfer was from that group to another group.
(5) The person or persons were under the age of 18 years.
(6) The perpetrator knew, or should have known, that the person or persons were under the age of 18 years.
(7) The conduct took place in the context of a manifest pattern of similar conduct directed against that group or was conduct that could itself effect such destruction.

Article 7. Crimes against humanity
Introduction
(1) Since article 7 pertains to international criminal law, its provisions, consistent with article 22, must be strictly construed, taking into account that crimes against humanity as defined in article 7 are among the most serious crimes of concern to the international community as a whole, warrant and entail individual criminal
responsibility, and require conduct which is impermissible under generally applicable international law, as recognized by the principal legal systems of the world.
(2) The last two elements for each crime against humanity describe the context in which the conduct must take place. These elements clarify the requisite participation in and knowledge of a widespread

or systematic attack against a civilian population. However, the last element should not be interpreted as requiring proof that the
perpetrator had knowledge of all characteristics of the attack or the precise details of the plan or policy of the State or organization. In the case of an emerging widespread or systematic attack against a civilian population, the intent clause of the last element indicates that this mental element is satisfied if the perpetrator intended to further such an attack.

(3) 'Attack directed against a civilian population' in these context elements is understood to mean a course of conduct involving the multiple commission of acts referred to in article 7, paragraph (1), of the Statute against any civilian population, pursuant to or in furtherance of a State or organizational policy to commit such attack. The acts need not constitute a military attack. It is understood that "policy to commit such attack" requires that the State or organization actively promote or encourage such an attack against a civilian population.

Article 7 (1) (a). Crime against humanity of murder
Elements
(1) The perpetrator killed one or more persons.
(2) The conduct was committed as part of a widespread or systematic attack directed against a civilian population.
(3) The perpetrator knew that the conduct was part of or intended the conduct to be part of a widespread or systematic attack against a civilian population.

Article 7 (1) (b). Crime against humanity of extermination
Elements
(1) The perpetrator killed one or more persons, including by inflicting conditions of life calculated to bring about the destruction of part of a population.
(2) The conduct constituted, or took place as part of, a mass killing of members of a civilian population.
(3) The conduct was committed as part of a widespread or systematic attack directed against a civilian population.
(4) The perpetrator knew that the conduct was part of or intended the conduct to be part of a widespread or systematic attack directed against a civilian population.

Article 7 (1) (c). Crime against humanity of enslavement
Elements
(1) The perpetrator exercised any or all of the powers attaching to the right of ownership over one or more persons, such as by purchasing, selling, lending or bartering such a person or persons, or by imposing on them a similar deprivation of liberty.
(2) The conduct was committed as part of a widespread or systematic attack directed against a civilian population.
(3) The perpetrator knew that the conduct was part of or intended the conduct to be part of a widespread or systematic attack directed against a civilian population.

Article 7 (1) (d). Crime against humanity of deportation or forcible transfer of population
Elements
(1) The perpetrator deported or forcibly12 transferred,13 without grounds permitted under international law, one or more persons to another State or location, by expulsion or other coercive acts.
(2) Such person or persons were lawfully present in the area from which they were so deported or transferred.
(3) The perpetrator was aware of the factual circumstances that established the lawfulness of such presence.
(4) The conduct was committed as part of a widespread or systematic attack directed against a civilian population.
(5) The perpetrator knew that the conduct was part of or intended the conduct to be part of a widespread or systematic attack directed against a civilian population.

Article 7 (1) (e). Crime against humanity of imprisonment or other severe deprivation of physical liberty
Elements
(1) The perpetrator imprisoned one or more persons or otherwise severely deprived one or more persons of physical liberty.
(2) The gravity of the conduct was such that it was in violation of fundamental rules of international law.

(3) The perpetrator was aware of the factual circumstances that established the gravity of the conduct.
(4) The conduct was committed as part of a widespread or systematic attack directed against a civilian population.
(5) The perpetrator knew that the conduct was part of or intended the conduct to be part of a widespread or systematic attack directed against a civilian population.

Article 7 (1) (f). Crime against humanity of torture14
Elements

(1) The perpetrator inflicted severe physical or mental pain or suffering upon one or more persons.
(2) Such person or persons were in the custody or under the control of the perpetrator.
(3) Such pain or suffering did not arise only from, and was not inherent in or incidental to, lawful sanctions.
(4) The conduct was committed as part of a widespread or systematic attack directed against a civilian population.
(5) The perpetrator knew that the conduct was part of or intended the conduct to be part of a widespread or systematic attack directed against a civilian population.

Article 7 (1) (g)-1. Crime against humanity of rape
Elements

(1) The perpetrator invaded the body of a person by conduct resulting in penetration, however slight, of any part of the body of the victim or of the perpetrator with a sexual organ, or of the anal or genital opening of the victim with any object or any other part of the body.
(2) The invasion was committed by force, or by threat of force or coercion, such as that caused by fear of violence, duress, detention, psychological oppression or abuse of power, against such person or another person, or by taking advantage of a coercive environment, or the invasion was committed against a person incapable of
giving genuine consent.
(3) The conduct was committed as part of a widespread or systematic attack directed against a civilian population.
(4) The perpetrator knew that the conduct was part of or intended the conduct to
be part of a widespread or systematic attack directed against a civilian population.

Article 7 (1) (g)-2. Crime against humanity of sexual slavery
Elements

(1) The perpetrator exercised any or all of the powers attaching to the right of ownership over one or more persons, such as by purchasing, selling, lending or bartering such a person or persons, or by imposing on them a similar deprivation of liberty.
(2) The perpetrator caused such person or persons to engage in one or more acts of a sexual nature.
(3) The conduct was committed as part of a widespread or systematic attack directed against a civilian population.
(4) The perpetrator knew that the conduct was part of or intended the conduct to be part of a widespread or systematic attack directed against a civilian population.

Article 7 (1) (g)-3. Crime against humanity of enforced prostitution
Elements

(1) The perpetrator caused one or more persons to engage in one or more acts of a sexual nature by force, or by threat of force or coercion, such as that caused by fear of violence, duress, detention, psychological oppression or abuse of power, against such person or persons or another person, or by taking advantage of a coercive
environment or such person's or persons' incapacity to give genuine consent.
(2) The perpetrator or another person obtained or expected to obtain pecuniary or other advantage in exchange for or in connection with the acts of a sexual nature.
(3) The conduct was committed as part of a widespread or systematic attack directed against a civilian population.
(4) The perpetrator knew that the conduct was part of or intended the conduct to be part of a widespread or systematic attack directed against a civilian population.

Article 7 (1) (g)-4. Crime against humanity of forced pregnancy
Elements

(1) The perpetrator confined one or more women forcibly made pregnant, with the intent of affecting the ethnic composition of any population or carrying out other grave violations of international law.
(2) The conduct was committed as part of a widespread or systematic attack directed against a civilian population.

ELEMENTS OF CRIME

(3) The perpetrator knew that the conduct was part of or intended the conduct to be part of a widespread or systematic attack directed against a civilian population.

Article 7 (1) (g)-5. Crime against humanity of enforced sterilization
Elements

(1) The perpetrator deprived one or more persons of biological reproductive capacity.
(2) The conduct was neither justified by the medical or hospital treatment of the person or persons concerned nor carried out with their genuine consent.
(3) The conduct was committed as part of a widespread or systematic attack directed against a civilian population.
(4) The perpetrator knew that the conduct was part of or intended the conduct to be part of a widespread or systematic attack directed against a civilian population.

Article 7 (1) (g)-6. Crime against humanity of sexual violence
Elements

(1) The perpetrator committed an act of a sexual nature against one or more persons or caused such person or persons to engage in an act of a sexual nature by force, or by threat of force or coercion, such as that caused by fear of violence, duress, detention, psychological oppression or abuse of power, against such person
or persons or another person, or by taking advantage of a coercive environment or such person's or persons' incapacity to give genuine consent.
(2) Such conduct was of a gravity comparable to the other offences in article 7, paragraph (1) (g), of the Statute.
(3) The perpetrator was aware of the factual circumstances that established the gravity of the conduct.
(4) The conduct was committed as part of a widespread or systematic attack directed against a civilian population.
(5) The perpetrator knew that the conduct was part of or intended the conduct to be part of a widespread or systematic attack directed against a civilian population.

Article 7 (1) (h). Crime against humanity of persecution
Elements

(1) The perpetrator severely deprived, contrary to international law, one or more persons of fundamental rights.
(2) The perpetrator targeted such person or persons by reason of the identity of a group or collectivity or targeted the group or collectivity as such.
(3) Such targeting was based on political, racial, national, ethnic, cultural, religious, gender as defined in
article 7, paragraph (3), of the Statute, or other grounds that are universally recognized as impermissible under international law.
(4) The conduct was committed in connection with any act referred to in article 7, paragraph (1), of the Statute or any crime within the jurisdiction of the Court.
(5) The conduct was committed as part of a widespread or systematic attack directed against a civilian population.
(6) The perpetrator knew that the conduct was part of or intended the conduct to be part of a widespread or systematic attack directed against a civilian population.

Article 7 (1) (i). Crime against humanity of enforced disappearance of persons
Elements

(1) The perpetrator:
(a) Arrested, detained, or abducted one or more persons; or
(b) Refused to acknowledge the arrest, detention or abduction, or to give information on the fate or whereabouts of such person or persons.
(2) (a) Such arrest, detention or abduction was followed or accompanied by a refusal to acknowledge that deprivation of freedom or to give information on the fate or whereabouts of such person or persons; or
(b) Such refusal was preceded or accompanied by that deprivation of
freedom.
(3) The perpetrator was aware that:
(a) Such arrest, detention or abduction would be followed in the ordinary course of events by a refusal to acknowledge that deprivation of freedom or to give information on the fate or whereabouts of such person or persons; or
(b) Such refusal was preceded or accompanied by that deprivation of freedom.

PART I INTERNATIONAL LAW

(4) Such arrest, detention or abduction was carried out by, or with the authorization, support or acquiescence of, a State or a political organization.
(5) Such refusal to acknowledge that deprivation of freedom or to give information on the fate or whereabouts of such person or persons was carried out by, or with the authorization or support of, such State or political organization.
(6) The perpetrator intended to remove such person or persons from the protection of the law for a prolonged period of time.
(7) The conduct was committed as part of a widespread or systematic attack directed against a civilian population.
(8) The perpetrator knew that the conduct was part of or intended the conduct to be part of a widespread or systematic attack directed against a civilian population.

Article 7 (1) (j). Crime against humanity of apartheid
Elements
(1) The perpetrator committed an inhumane act against one or more persons.
(2) Such act was an act referred to in article 7, paragraph (1), of the Statute, or was an act of a character similar to any of those acts.
(3) The perpetrator was aware of the factual circumstances that established the character of the act.
(4.) The conduct was committed in the context of an institutionalized regime of systematic oppression and domination by one racial group over any other racial group or groups.
(5) The perpetrator intended to maintain such regime by that conduct.
(6) The conduct was committed as part of a widespread or systematic attack directed against a civilian population.
(7) The perpetrator knew that the conduct was part of or intended the conduct to be part of a widespread or systematic attack directed against a civilian population.

Article 7 (1) (k). Crime against humanity of other inhumane acts
Elements
(1) The perpetrator inflicted great suffering, or serious injury to body or to mental or physical health, by means of an inhumane act.
(2) Such act was of a character similar to any other act referred to in article 7, paragraph (1), of the Statute.30
(3) The perpetrator was aware of the factual circumstances that established the character of the act.
(4) The conduct was committed as part of a widespread or systematic attack directed against a civilian population.
(5) The perpetrator knew that the conduct was part of or intended the conduct to be part of a widespread or systematic attack directed against a civilian population.

Article 8. War crimes
Introduction
The elements for war crimes under article 8, paragraph (2) (c) and (e), are subject to the limitations addressed in article 8, paragraph (2) (d) and (f), which are not elements of crimes.
The elements for war crimes under article 8, paragraph (2), of the Statute shall be interpreted within the established framework of the international law of armed conflict including, as appropriate, the international law of armed conflict applicable to armed conflict at sea.
With respect to the last two elements listed for each crime:
- There is no requirement for a legal evaluation by the perpetrator as to the existence of an armed conflict or its character as international or non-international;
- In that context there is no requirement for awareness by the perpetrator of the facts that established the character of the conflict as international or non-international;
- There is only a requirement for the awareness of the factual circumstances that established the existence of an armed conflict that is implicit in the terms "took place in the context of and was associated with".

Article 8 (2) (a)

Article 8 (2) (a) (i). War crime of wilful killing
Elements
(1) The perpetrator killed one or more persons.
(2) Such person or persons were protected under one or more of the Geneva Conventions of 1949.
(3) The perpetrator was aware of the factual circumstances that established that protected status.
(4) The conduct took place in the context of and was associated with an international armed conflict.

ELEMENTS OF CRIME

(5) The perpetrator was aware of factual circumstances that established the existence of an armed conflict.

Article 8 (2) (a) (ii)-1. War crime of torture
Elements
(1) The perpetrator inflicted severe physical or mental pain or suffering upon one or more persons.
(2) The perpetrator inflicted the pain or suffering for such purposes as: obtaining information or a confession, punishment, intimidation or coercion or for any reason based on discrimination of any kind.
(3) Such person or persons were protected under one or more of the Geneva Conventions of 1949.
(4) The perpetrator was aware of the factual circumstances that established that protected status.
(5) The conduct took place in the context of and was associated with an international armed conflict.
(6) The perpetrator was aware of factual circumstances that established the existence of an armed conflict.

Article 8 (2) (a) (ii)-2. War crime of inhuman treatment
Elements
(1) The perpetrator inflicted severe physical or mental pain or suffering upon one or more persons.
(2) Such person or persons were protected under one or more of the Geneva Conventions of 1949.
(3) The perpetrator was aware of the factual circumstances that established that protected status.
(4) The conduct took place in the context of and was associated with an international armed conflict.
(5) The perpetrator was aware of factual circumstances that established the existence of an armed conflict.

Article 8 (2) (a) (ii)-3. War crime of biological experiments
Elements
(1) The perpetrator subjected one or more persons to a particular biological experiment.
(2) The experiment seriously endangered the physical or mental health or integrity of such person or persons.
(3) The intent of the experiment was non-therapeutic and it was neither justified by medical reasons nor carried out in such person's or persons' interest.
(4) Such person or persons were protected under one or more of the Geneva Conventions of 1949.
(5) The perpetrator was aware of the factual circumstances that established that protected status.
(6) The conduct took place in the context of and was associated with an international armed conflict.
(7) The perpetrator was aware of factual circumstances that established the existence of an armed conflict.

Article 8 (2) (a) (iii). War crime of wilfully causing great suffering
Elements
(1) The perpetrator caused great physical or mental pain or suffering to, or serious injury to body or health of, one or more persons.
(2) Such person or persons were protected under one or more of the Geneva Conventions of 1949.
(3) The perpetrator was aware of the factual circumstances that established that protected status.
(4) The conduct took place in the context of and was associated with an international armed conflict.
(5) The perpetrator was aware of factual circumstances that established the existence of an armed conflict.

Article 8 (2) (a) (iv). War crime of destruction and appropriation of property
Elements
(1) The perpetrator destroyed or appropriated certain property.
(2) The destruction or appropriation was not justified by military necessity.
(3) The destruction or appropriation was extensive and carried out wantonly.
(4) Such property was protected under one or more of the Geneva Conventions of 1949.
(5) The perpetrator was aware of the factual circumstances that established that protected status.
(6) The conduct took place in the context of and was associated with an international armed conflict.
(7) The perpetrator was aware of factual circumstances that established the existence of an armed conflict.

Article 8 (2) (a) (v). War crime of compelling service in hostile forces
Elements
(1) The perpetrator coerced one or more persons, by act or threat, to take part in military operations against that person's own country or forces or otherwise serve in the forces of a hostile power.

PART I   INTERNATIONAL LAW

(2) Such person or persons were protected under one or more of the Geneva Conventions of 1949.
(3) The perpetrator was aware of the factual circumstances that established that protected status.
(4) The conduct took place in the context of and was associated with an international armed conflict.
(5) The perpetrator was aware of factual circumstances that established the existence of an armed conflict.

Article 8 (2) (a) (vi). War crime of denying a fair trial
Elements
(1) The perpetrator deprived one or more persons of a fair and regular trial by denying judicial guarantees as defined, in particular, in the third and the fourth Geneva Conventions of 1949.
(2) Such person or persons were protected under one or more of the Geneva Conventions of 1949.
(3) The perpetrator was aware of the factual circumstances that established that protected status.
(4) The conduct took place in the context of and was associated with an international armed conflict.
(5) The perpetrator was aware of factual circumstances that established the existence of an armed conflict.

Article 8 (2) (a) (vii)-1. War crime of unlawful deportation and transfer
Elements
(1) The perpetrator deported or transferred one or more persons to another State or to another location.
(2) Such person or persons were protected under one or more of the Geneva Conventions of 1949.
(3) The perpetrator was aware of the factual circumstances that established that protected status.
(4) The conduct took place in the context of and was associated with an international armed conflict.
(5) The perpetrator was aware of factual circumstances that established the existence of an armed conflict.

Article 8 (2) (a) (vii)-2. War crime of unlawful confinement
Elements
(1) The perpetrator confined or continued to confine one or more persons to a certain location.
(2) Such person or persons were protected under one or more of the Geneva Conventions of 1949.
(3) The perpetrator was aware of the factual circumstances that established that protected status.
(4) The conduct took place in the context of and was associated with an international armed conflict.
5. The perpetrator was aware of factual circumstances that established the existence of an armed conflict.

Article 8 (2) (a) (viii). War crime of taking hostages
Elements
(1) The perpetrator seized, detained or otherwise held hostage one or more persons.
(2) The perpetrator threatened to kill, injure or continue to detain such person or persons.
(3) The perpetrator intended to compel a State, an international organization, a natural or legal person or a group of persons to act or refrain from acting as an explicit or implicit condition for the safety or the release of such person or persons.
(4) Such person or persons were protected under one or more of the Geneva Conventions of 1949.
(5) The perpetrator was aware of the factual circumstances that established that protected status.
(6) The conduct took place in the context of and was associated with an international armed conflict.
(7) The perpetrator was aware of factual circumstances that established the existence of an armed conflict.

Article 8 (2) (b)

Article 8 (2) (b) (i). War crime of attacking civilians
Elements
(1) The perpetrator directed an attack.
(2) The object of the attack was a civilian population as such or individual civilians not taking direct part in hostilities.
(3) The perpetrator intended the civilian population as such or individual civilians not taking direct part in hostilities to be the object of the attack.
(4) The conduct took place in the context of and was associated with an international armed conflict.
(5) The perpetrator was aware of factual circumstances that established the existence of an armed conflict.

Article 8 (2) (b) (ii). War crime of attacking civilian objects
Elements

(1) The perpetrator directed an attack.
(2) The object of the attack was civilian objects, that is, objects which are not military objectives.
(3) The perpetrator intended such civilian objects to be the object of the attack.
(4) The conduct took place in the context of and was associated with an international armed conflict.
(5) The perpetrator was aware of factual circumstances that established the existence of an armed conflict.

Article 8 (2) (b) (iii). War crime of attacking personnel or objects involved in a humanitarian assistance or peacekeeping mission
Elements
(1) The perpetrator directed an attack.
(2) The object of the attack was personnel, installations, material, units or vehicles involved in a humanitarian assistance or peacekeeping mission in accordance with the Charter of the United Nations.
(3) The perpetrator intended such personnel, installations, material, units or vehicles so involved to be the object of the attack.
(4) Such personnel, installations, material, units or vehicles were entitled to that protection given to civilians or civilian objects under the international law of armed conflict.
(5) The perpetrator was aware of the factual circumstances that established that protection.
(6) The conduct took place in the context of and was associated with an international armed conflict.
(7) The perpetrator was aware of factual circumstances that established the existence of an armed conflict.

Article 8 (2) (b) (iv). War crime of excessive incidental death, injury, or damage
Elements
(1) The perpetrator launched an attack.
(2) The attack was such that it would cause incidental death or injury to civilians or damage to civilian objects or widespread, long-term and severe damage to the natural environment and that such death, injury or damage would be of such an extent as to be clearly excessive in relation to the concrete and direct overall military advantage anticipated.
(3) The perpetrator knew that the attack would cause incidental death or injury to civilians or damage to civilian objects or widespread, long-term and severe damage to the natural environment and that such death, injury or damage would be of such an extent as to be clearly excessive in relation to the concrete and direct overall
military advantage anticipated.
(4) The conduct took place in the context of and was associated with an international armed conflict.
(5) The perpetrator was aware of factual circumstances that established the existence of an armed conflict.

Article 8 (2) (b) (v). War crime of attacking undefended places
Elements
(1) The perpetrator attacked one or more towns, villages, dwellings or buildings.
(2) Such towns, villages, dwellings or buildings were open for unresisted occupation.
(3) Such towns, villages, dwellings or buildings did not constitute military objectives.
(4) The conduct took place in the context of and was associated with an international armed conflict.
(5) The perpetrator was aware of factual circumstances that established the existence of an armed conflict.

Article 8 (2) (b) (vi). War crime of killing or wounding a person hors de combat
Elements
(1) The perpetrator killed or injured one or more persons.
(2) Such person or persons were hors de combat.
(3) The perpetrator was aware of the factual circumstances that established this status.
(4) The conduct took place in the context of and was associated with an international armed conflict.
(5) The perpetrator was aware of factual circumstances that established the existence of an armed conflict.

Article 8 (2) (b) (vii)-1. War crime of improper use of a flag of truce
Elements
(1) The perpetrator used a flag of truce.
(2) The perpetrator made such use in order to feign an intention to negotiate when there was no such intention on the part of the perpetrator.

(3) The perpetrator knew or should have known of the prohibited nature of such use.
(4) The conduct resulted in death or serious personal injury.
(5) The perpetrator knew that the conduct could result in death or serious personal injury.
(6) The conduct took place in the context of and was associated with an international armed conflict.
(7) The perpetrator was aware of factual circumstances that established the existence of an armed conflict.

Article 8 (2) (b) (vii)-2. War crime of improper use of a flag, insignia or uniform of the hostile party
Elements
(1) The perpetrator used a flag, insignia or uniform of the hostile party.
(2) The perpetrator made such use in a manner prohibited under the international law of armed conflict while engaged in an attack.
(3) The perpetrator knew or should have known of the prohibited nature of such use.
(4) The conduct resulted in death or serious personal injury.
(5) The perpetrator knew that the conduct could result in death or serious personal injury.
(6) The conduct took place in the context of and was associated with an international armed conflict.
(7) The perpetrator was aware of factual circumstances that established the existence of an armed conflict.

Article 8 (2) (b) (vii)-3. War crime of improper use of a flag, insignia or uniform of the United Nations
Elements
(1) The perpetrator used a flag, insignia or uniform of the United Nations.
(2) The perpetrator made such use in a manner prohibited under the international law of armed conflict.
(3) The perpetrator knew of the prohibited nature of such use.
(4) The conduct resulted in death or serious personal injury.
(5) The perpetrator knew that the conduct could result in death or serious personal injury.
(6) The conduct took place in the context of and was associated with an international armed conflict.
(7) The perpetrator was aware of factual circumstances that established the existence of an armed conflict.

Article 8 (2) (b) (vii)-4. War crime of improper use of the distinctive emblems of the Geneva Conventions
Elements
(1) The perpetrator used the distinctive emblems of the Geneva Conventions.
(2) The perpetrator made such use for combatant purposes in a manner prohibited under the international law of armed conflict.
(3) The perpetrator knew or should have known of the prohibited nature of such use.
(4) The conduct resulted in death or serious personal injury.
(5) The perpetrator knew that the conduct could result in death or serious personal injury.
(6) The conduct took place in the context of and was associated with an international armed conflict.
(7) The perpetrator was aware of factual circumstances that established the existence of an armed conflict.

Article 8 (2) (b) (viii). The transfer, directly or indirectly, by the Occupying Power of parts of its own civilian population into the territory it occupies, or the deportation or transfer of all or parts of the population of the occupied territory within or outside this territory
Elements
(1) The perpetrator:
(a) Transferred, directly or indirectly, parts of its own population into the territory it occupies; or
(b) Deported or transferred all or parts of the population of the occupied territory within or outside this territory.
(2) The conduct took place in the context of and was associated with an international armed conflict.
(3) The perpetrator was aware of factual circumstances that established the existence of an armed conflict.

Article 8 (2) (b) (ix). War crime of attacking protected objects
Elements
(1) The perpetrator directed an attack.

(2) The object of the attack was one or more buildings dedicated to religion, education, art, science or charitable purposes, historic monuments, hospitals or places where the sick and wounded are collected, which were not military objectives.
(3) The perpetrator intended such building or buildings dedicated to religion, education, art, science or charitable purposes, historic monuments, hospitals or places where the sick and wounded are collected, which were not military objectives, to be the object of the attack.
(4) The conduct took place in the context of and was associated with an international armed conflict.
(5) The perpetrator was aware of factual circumstances that established the existence of an armed conflict.

Article 8 (2) (b) (x)-1. War crime of mutilation
Elements
(1) The perpetrator subjected one or more persons to mutilation, in particular by permanently disfiguring the person or persons, or by permanently disabling or removing an organ or appendage.
(2) The conduct caused death or seriously endangered the physical or mental health of such person or persons.
(3) The conduct was neither justified by the medical, dental or hospital treatment of the person or persons concerned nor carried out in such person's or persons' interest.
(4) Such person or persons were in the power of an adverse party.
(5) The conduct took place in the context of and was associated with an international armed conflict.
(6) The perpetrator was aware of factual circumstances that established the existence of an armed conflict.

Article 8 (2) (b) (x)-2. War crime of medical or scientific experiments
Elements
(1) The perpetrator subjected one or more persons to a medical or scientific experiment.
(2) The experiment caused death or seriously endangered the physical or mental health or integrity of such person or persons.
(3) The conduct was neither justified by the medical, dental or hospital treatment of such person or persons concerned nor carried out in such person's or persons' interest.
(4) Such person or persons were in the power of an adverse party.
(5) The conduct took place in the context of and was associated with an international armed conflict.
(6) The perpetrator was aware of factual circumstances that established the
existence of an armed conflict.

Article 8 (2) (b) (xi). War crime of treacherously killing or wounding
Elements
(1) The perpetrator invited the confidence or belief of one or more persons that they were entitled to, or were obliged to accord, protection under rules of international law applicable in armed conflict.
(2) The perpetrator intended to betray that confidence or belief.
(3) The perpetrator killed or injured such person or persons.
(4) The perpetrator made use of that confidence or belief in killing or injuring such person or persons.
(5) Such person or persons belonged to an adverse party.
(6) The conduct took place in the context of and was associated with an international armed conflict.
(7) The perpetrator was aware of factual circumstances that established the existence of an armed conflict.

Article 8 (2) (b) (xii). War crime of denying quarter
Elements
(1) The perpetrator declared or ordered that there shall be no survivors.
(2) Such declaration or order was given in order to threaten an adversary or to conduct hostilities on the basis that there shall be no survivors.
(3) The perpetrator was in a position of effective command or control over the subordinate forces to which the declaration or order was directed.
(4) The conduct took place in the context of and was associated with an international armed conflict.
(5) The perpetrator was aware of factual circumstances that established the existence of an armed conflict.

Article 8 (2) (b) (xiii). War crime of destroying or seizing the enemy's property
Elements
(1) The perpetrator destroyed or seized certain property.
(2) Such property was property of a hostile party.

(3) Such property was protected from that destruction or seizure under the international law of armed conflict.
(4) The perpetrator was aware of the factual circumstances that established the status of the property.
(5) The destruction or seizure was not justified by military necessity.
(6) The conduct took place in the context of and was associated with an international armed conflict.
(7) The perpetrator was aware of factual circumstances that established the existence of an armed conflict.

Article 8 (2) (b) (xiv). War crime of depriving the nationals of the hostile power of rights or actions
Elements
(1) The perpetrator effected the abolition, suspension or termination of admissibility in a court of law of certain rights or actions.
(2) The abolition, suspension or termination was directed at the nationals of a hostile party.
(3) The perpetrator intended the abolition, suspension or termination to be directed at the nationals of a hostile party.
(4) The conduct took place in the context of and was associated with an international armed conflict.
(5) The perpetrator was aware of factual circumstances that established the existence of an armed conflict.

Article 8 (2) (b) (xv). War crime of compelling participation in military operations
Elements
(1) The perpetrator coerced one or more persons by act or threat to take part in military operations against that person's own country or forces.
(2) Such person or persons were nationals of a hostile party.
(3) The conduct took place in the context of and was associated with an international armed conflict.
(4) The perpetrator was aware of factual circumstances that established the existence of an armed conflict.

Article 8 (2) (b) (xvi). War crime of pillaging
Elements
(1) The perpetrator appropriated certain property.
(2) The perpetrator intended to deprive the owner of the property and to appropriate it for private or personal use.
(3) The appropriation was without the consent of the owner.
(4) The conduct took place in the context of and was associated with an international armed conflict.
(5) The perpetrator was aware of factual circumstances that established the existence of an armed conflict.

Article 8 (2) (b) (xvii). War crime of employing poison or poisoned weapons
Elements
(1) The perpetrator employed a substance or a weapon that releases a substance as a result of its employment.
(2) The substance was such that it causes death or serious damage to health in the ordinary course of events, through its toxic properties.
(3) The conduct took place in the context of and was associated with an international armed conflict.
(4) The perpetrator was aware of factual circumstances that established the existence of an armed conflict.

Article 8 (2) (b) (xviii). War crime of employing prohibited gases, liquids, materials or devices
Elements
(1) The perpetrator employed a gas or other analogous substance or device.
(2) The gas, substance or device was such that it causes death or serious damage to health in the ordinary course of events, through its asphyxiating or toxic properties.
(3) The conduct took place in the context of and was associated with an international armed conflict.
(4) The perpetrator was aware of factual circumstances that established the existence of an armed conflict.

Article 8 (2) (b) (xix). War crime of employing prohibited bullets
Elements
(1) The perpetrator employed certain bullets.
(2) The bullets were such that their use violates the international law of armed conflict because they

ELEMENTS OF CRIME

expand or flatten easily in the human body.
(3) The perpetrator was aware that the nature of the bullets was such that their employment would uselessly aggravate suffering or the wounding effect.
(4) The conduct took place in the context of and was associated with an international armed conflict.
(5) The perpetrator was aware of factual circumstances that established the existence of an armed conflict.

Article 8 (2) (b) (xx). War crime of employing weapons, projectiles or materials or methods of warfare listed in the Annex to the Statute
Elements
[Elements will have to be drafted once weapons, projectiles or material or methods of warfare have been included in an annex to the Statute.]

Article 8 (2) (b) (xxi). War crime of outrages upon personal dignity
Elements
(1) The perpetrator humiliated, degraded or otherwise violated the dignity of one or more persons.
(2) The severity of the humiliation, degradation or other violation was of such degree as to be generally recognized as an outrage upon personal dignity.
(3) The conduct took place in the context of and was associated with an international armed conflict.
(4) The perpetrator was aware of factual circumstances that established the existence of an armed conflict.

Article 8 (2) (b) (xxii)-1. War crime of rape
Elements
(1) The perpetrator invaded the body of a person by conduct resulting in penetration, however slight, of any part of the body of the victim or of the perpetrator with a sexual organ, or of the anal or genital opening of the victim with any object or any other part of the body.
(2) The invasion was committed by force, or by threat of force or coercion, such as that caused by fear of violence, duress, detention, psychological oppression or abuse of power, against such person or another person, or by taking advantage of a coercive environment, or the invasion was committed against a person incapable of
giving genuine consent.
(3) The conduct took place in the context of and was associated with an international armed conflict.
(4) The perpetrator was aware of factual circumstances that established the existence of an armed conflict.

Article 8 (2) (b) (xxii)-2. War crime of sexual slavery
Elements
(1) The perpetrator exercised any or all of the powers attaching to the right of ownership over one or more persons, such as by purchasing, selling, lending or bartering such a person or persons, or by imposing on them a similar deprivation of liberty.
(2) The perpetrator caused such person or persons to engage in one or more acts of a sexual nature.
(3) The conduct took place in the context of and was associated with an international armed conflict.
(4) The perpetrator was aware of factual circumstances that established the existence of an armed conflict.

Article 8 (2) (b) (xxii)-3. War crime of enforced prostitution
Elements
(1) The perpetrator caused one or more persons to engage in one or more acts of a sexual nature by force, or by threat of force or coercion, such as that caused by fear of violence, duress, detention, psychological oppression or abuse of power, against such person or persons or another person, or by taking advantage of a coercive environment or such person's or persons' incapacity to give genuine consent.
(2) The perpetrator or another person obtained or expected to obtain pecuniary or other advantage in exchange for or in connection with the acts of a sexual nature.
(3) The conduct took place in the context of and was associated with an international armed conflict.
(4) The perpetrator was aware of factual circumstances that established the existence of an armed conflict.

Article 8 (2) (b) (xxii)-4. War crime of forced pregnancy
Elements
(1) The perpetrator confined one or more women forcibly made pregnant, with the intent of affecting

the ethnic composition of any population or carrying out other grave violations of international law.
(2) The conduct took place in the context of and was associated with an international armed conflict.
(3) The perpetrator was aware of factual circumstances that established the existence of an armed conflict.

Article 8 (2) (b) (xxii)-5. War crime of enforced sterilization
Elements
(1) The perpetrator deprived one or more persons of biological reproductive capacity.
(2) The conduct was neither justified by the medical or hospital treatment of the person or persons concerned nor carried out with their genuine consent.
(3) The conduct took place in the context of and was associated with an international armed conflict.
(4) The perpetrator was aware of factual circumstances that established the existence of an armed conflict.

Article 8 (2) (b) (xxii)-6. War crime of sexual violence
Elements
(1) The perpetrator committed an act of a sexual nature against one or more persons or caused such person or persons to engage in an act of a sexual nature by force, or by threat of force or coercion, such as that caused by fear of violence, duress, detention, psychological oppression or abuse of power, against such person
or persons or another person, or by taking advantage of a coercive environment or such person's or persons' incapacity to give genuine consent.
(2) The conduct was of a gravity comparable to that of a grave breach of the Geneva Conventions.
(3) The perpetrator was aware of the factual circumstances that established the gravity of the conduct.
(4) The conduct took place in the context of and was associated with an international armed conflict.
(5) The perpetrator was aware of factual circumstances that established the existence of an armed conflict.

Article 8 (2) (b) (xxiii). War crime of using protected persons as shields
Elements
(1) The perpetrator moved or otherwise took advantage of the location of one or more civilians or other persons protected under the international law of armed conflict.
(2) The perpetrator intended to shield a military objective from attack or shield, favour or impede military operations.
(3) The conduct took place in the context of and was associated with an international armed conflict.
(4) The perpetrator was aware of factual circumstances that established the existence of an armed conflict.

Article 8 (2) (b) (xxiv). War crime of attacking objects or persons using the distinctive emblems of the Geneva Conventions
Elements
(1) The perpetrator attacked one or more persons, buildings, medical units or transports or other objects using, in conformity with international law, a distinctive emblem or other method of identification indicating protection under the Geneva Conventions.
(2) The perpetrator intended such persons, buildings, units or transports or other objects so using such identification to be the object of the attack.
(3) The conduct took place in the context of and was associated with an international armed conflict.
(4) The perpetrator was aware of factual circumstances that established the existence of an armed conflict.

Article 8 (2) (b) (xxv) War crime of starvation as a method of warfare
Elements
(1) The perpetrator deprived civilians of objects indispensable to their survival.
(2) The perpetrator intended to starve civilians as a method of warfare.
(3) The conduct took place in the context of and was associated with an international armed conflict.
(4) The perpetrator was aware of factual circumstances that established the existence of an armed conflict.

Article 8 (2) (b) (xxvi). War crime of using, conscripting or enlisting children
Elements
(1) The perpetrator conscripted or enlisted one or more persons into the national armed forces or used one or more persons to participate actively in hostilities.

(2) Such person or persons were under the age of 15 years.
(3) The perpetrator knew or should have known that such person or persons were under the age of 15 years.
(4) The conduct took place in the context of and was associated with an international armed conflict.
(5) The perpetrator was aware of factual circumstances that established the existence of an armed conflict.

Article 8 (2) (c)

Article 8 (2) (c) (i)-1. War crime of murder
Elements
(1) The perpetrator killed one or more persons.
(2) Such person or persons were either hors de combat, or were civilians, medical personnel, or religious personnel taking no active part in the hostilities.
(3) The perpetrator was aware of the factual circumstances that established this status.
(4) The conduct took place in the context of and was associated with an armed conflict not of an international character.
(5) The perpetrator was aware of factual circumstances that established the existence of an armed conflict.

Article 8 (2) (c) (i)-2. War crime of mutilation
Elements
(1) The perpetrator subjected one or more persons to mutilation, in particular by permanently disfiguring the person or persons, or by permanently disabling or removing an organ or appendage.
(2) The conduct was neither justified by the medical, dental or hospital treatment of the person or persons concerned nor carried out in such person's or persons' interests.
(3) Such person or persons were either hors de combat, or were civilians, medical personnel or religious personnel taking no active part in the hostilities.
(4) The perpetrator was aware of the factual circumstances that established this status.
(5) The conduct took place in the context of and was associated with an armed conflict not of an international character.
(6) The perpetrator was aware of factual circumstances that established the existence of an armed conflict.

Article 8 (2) (c) (i)-3. War crime of cruel treatment
Elements
(1) The perpetrator inflicted severe physical or mental pain or suffering upon one or more persons.
(2) Such person or persons were either hors de combat, or were civilians, medical personnel, or religious personnel taking no active part in the hostilities.
(3) The perpetrator was aware of the factual circumstances that established this status.
(4) The conduct took place in the context of and was associated with an armed conflict not of an international character.
(5) The perpetrator was aware of factual circumstances that established the existence of an armed conflict.

Article 8 (2) (c) (i)-4. War crime of torture
Elements
(1) The perpetrator inflicted severe physical or mental pain or suffering upon one or more persons.
(2) The perpetrator inflicted the pain or suffering for such purposes as: obtaining information or a confession, punishment, intimidation or coercion or for any reason based on discrimination of any kind.
(3) Such person or persons were either hors de combat, or were civilians, medical personnel or religious personnel taking no active part in the hostilities.
(4) The perpetrator was aware of the factual circumstances that established this status.
(5) The conduct took place in the context of and was associated with an armed conflict not of an international character.
(6) The perpetrator was aware of factual circumstances that established the existence of an armed conflict.

Article 8 (2) (c) (ii). War crime of outrages upon personal dignity
Elements

PART I INTERNATIONAL LAW

(1) The perpetrator humiliated, degraded or otherwise violated the dignity of one or more persons.
(2) The severity of the humiliation, degradation or other violation was of such degree as to be generally recognized as an outrage upon personal dignity.
(3) Such person or persons were either hors de combat, or were civilians, medical personnel or religious personnel taking no active part in the hostilities.
(4) The perpetrator was aware of the factual circumstances that established this status.
(5) The conduct took place in the context of and was associated with an armed conflict not of an international character.
(6) The perpetrator was aware of factual circumstances that established the existence of an armed conflict.

Article 8 (2) (c) (iii). War crime of taking hostages
Elements
(1) The perpetrator seized, detained or otherwise held hostage one or more persons.
(2) The perpetrator threatened to kill, injure or continue to detain such person or persons.
(3) The perpetrator intended to compel a State, an international organization, a natural or legal person or a group of persons to act or refrain from acting as an explicit or implicit condition for the safety or the release of such person or persons.
(4) Such person or persons were either hors de combat, or were civilians, medical personnel or religious personnel taking no active part in the hostilities.
(5) The perpetrator was aware of the factual circumstances that established this status.
(6) The conduct took place in the context of and was associated with an armed conflict not of an international character.
(7) The perpetrator was aware of factual circumstances that established the existence of an armed conflict.

Article 8 (2) (c) (iv). War crime of sentencing or execution without due process
Elements
(1) The perpetrator passed sentence or executed one or more persons.
(2) Such person or persons were either hors de combat, or were civilians, medical personnel or religious personnel taking no active part in the hostilities.
(3) The perpetrator was aware of the factual circumstances that established this status.
(4) There was no previous judgement pronounced by a court, or the court that rendered judgement was not 'regularly constituted', that is, it did not afford the essential guarantees of independence and impartiality, or the court that rendered judgement did not afford all other judicial guarantees generally recognized as indispensable under international law.
(5) The perpetrator was aware of the absence of a previous judgement or of the denial of relevant guarantees and the fact that they are essential or indispensable to a fair trial.
(6) The conduct took place in the context of and was associated with an armed conflict not of an international character.
(7) The perpetrator was aware of factual circumstances that established the existence of an armed conflict.

Article 8 (2) (e)

Article 8 (2) (e) (i). War crime of attacking civilians
Elements
(1) The perpetrator directed an attack.
(2) The object of the attack was a civilian population as such or individual civilians not taking direct part in hostilities.
(3) The perpetrator intended the civilian population as such or individual civilians not taking direct part in hostilities to be the object of the attack.
(4) The conduct took place in the context of and was associated with an armed conflict not of an international character.
(5) The perpetrator was aware of factual circumstances that established the existence of an armed conflict.

Article 8 (2) (e) (ii). War crime of attacking objects or persons using the distinctive emblems of the Geneva Conventions
Elements
(1) The perpetrator attacked one or more persons, buildings, medical units or transports or other objects using, in conformity with international law, a distinctive emblem or other method of identifi-

cation indicating protection under the Geneva Conventions.
(2) The perpetrator intended such persons, buildings, units or transports or other objects so using such identification to be the object of the attack.
(3) The conduct took place in the context of and was associated with an armed conflict not of an international character.
(4) The perpetrator was aware of factual circumstances that established the existence of an armed conflict.

Article 8 (2) (e) (iii). War crime of attacking personnel or objects involved in a humanitarian assistance or peacekeeping mission
Elements
(1) The perpetrator directed an attack.
(2) The object of the attack was personnel, installations, material, units or vehicles involved in a humanitarian assistance or peacekeeping mission in accordance with the Charter of the United Nations.
(3) The perpetrator intended such personnel, installations, material, units or vehicles so involved to be the object of the attack.
(4) Such personnel, installations, material, units or vehicles were entitled to that protection given to civilians or civilian objects under the international law of armed conflict.
(5) The perpetrator was aware of the factual circumstances that established that protection.
(6) The conduct took place in the context of and was associated with an armed conflict not of an international character.
(7) The perpetrator was aware of factual circumstances that established the existence of an armed conflict.

Article 8 (2) (e) (iv). War crime of attacking protected objects
Elements
(1) The perpetrator directed an attack.
(2) The object of the attack was one or more buildings dedicated to religion, education, art, science or charitable purposes, historic monuments, hospitals or places where the sick and wounded are collected, which were not military objectives.
(3) The perpetrator intended such building or buildings dedicated to religion, education, art, science or charitable purposes, historic monuments, hospitals or places where the sick and wounded are collected, which were not military objectives, to be the object of the attack.
(4) The conduct took place in the context of and was associated with an armed conflict not of an international character.
(5) The perpetrator was aware of factual circumstances that established the
existence of an armed conflict.

Article 8 (2) (e) (v). War crime of pillaging
Elements
(1) The perpetrator appropriated certain property.
(2) The perpetrator intended to deprive the owner of the property and to appropriate it for private or personal use.
(3) The appropriation was without the consent of the owner.
(4) The conduct took place in the context of and was associated with an armed conflict not of an international character.
(5) The perpetrator was aware of factual circumstances that established the existence of an armed conflict.

Article 8 (2) (e) (vi)-1. War crime of rape
Elements
(1) The perpetrator invaded the body of a person by conduct resulting in penetration, however slight, of any part of the body of the victim or of the perpetrator with a sexual organ, or of the anal or genital opening of the victim with any object or any other part of the body.
(2) The invasion was committed by force, or by threat of force or coercion, such as that caused by fear of violence, duress, detention, psychological oppression or abuse of power, against such person or another person, or by taking advantage of a coercive environment, or the invasion was committed against a person incapable of
giving genuine consent.
(3) The conduct took place in the context of and was associated with an armed conflict not of an international character.

(4) The perpetrator was aware of factual circumstances that established the existence of an armed conflict.

Article 8 (2) (e) (vi)-2. War crime of sexual slavery
Elements
(1) The perpetrator exercised any or all of the powers attaching to the right of ownership over one or more persons, such as by purchasing, selling, lending or bartering such a person or persons, or by imposing on them a similar deprivation of liberty.
(2) The perpetrator caused such person or persons to engage in one or more acts of a sexual nature.
(3) The conduct took place in the context of and was associated with an armed conflict not of an international character.
(4) The perpetrator was aware of factual circumstances that established the existence of an armed conflict.

Article 8 (2) (e) (vi)-3. War crime of enforced prostitution
Elements
(1) The perpetrator caused one or more persons to engage in one or more acts of a sexual nature by force, or by threat of force or coercion, such as that caused by fear of violence, duress, detention, psychological oppression or abuse of power, against such person or persons or another person, or by taking advantage of a coercive environment or such person's or persons' incapacity to give genuine consent.
(2) The perpetrator or another person obtained or expected to obtain pecuniary or other advantage in exchange for or in connection with the acts of a sexual nature.
(3) The conduct took place in the context of and was associated with an armed conflict not of an international character.
(4) The perpetrator was aware of factual circumstances that established the existence of an armed conflict.

Article 8 (2) (e) (vi)-4. War crime of forced pregnancy
Elements
(1) The perpetrator confined one or more women forcibly made pregnant, with the intent of affecting the ethnic composition of any population or carrying out other grave violations of international law.
(2) The conduct took place in the context of and was associated with an armed conflict not of an international character.
(3) The perpetrator was aware of factual circumstances that established the existence of an armed conflict.

Article 8 (2) (e) (vi)-5. War crime of enforced sterilization
Elements
(1) The perpetrator deprived one or more persons of biological reproductive capacity.
(2) The conduct was neither justified by the medical or hospital treatment of the person or persons concerned nor carried out with their genuine consent.
(3) The conduct took place in the context of and was associated with an armed conflict not of an international character.
(4) The perpetrator was aware of factual circumstances that established the existence of an armed conflict.

Article 8 (2) (e) (vi)-6. War crime of sexual violence
Elements
(1) The perpetrator committed an act of a sexual nature against one or more persons or caused such person or persons to engage in an act of a sexual nature by force, or by threat of force or coercion, such as that caused by fear of violence, duress, detention, psychological oppression or abuse of power, against such person
or persons or another person, or by taking advantage of a coercive environment or such personís or personsí incapacity to give genuine consent.
(2) The conduct was of a gravity comparable to that of a serious violation of article 3 common to the four Geneva Conventions.
(3) The perpetrator was aware of the factual circumstances that established the gravity of the conduct.
(4) The conduct took place in the context of and was associated with an armed conflict not of an international character.
(5) The perpetrator was aware of factual circumstances that established the existence of an armed conflict.

Article 8 (2) (e) (vii). War crime of using, conscripting and enlisting children
Elements
(1) The perpetrator conscripted or enlisted one or more persons into an armed force or group or used one or more persons to participate actively in hostilities.
(2) Such person or persons were under the age of 15 years.
(3) The perpetrator knew or should have known that such person or persons were under the age of 15 years.
(4) The conduct took place in the context of and was associated with an armed conflict not of an international character.
(5) The perpetrator was aware of factual circumstances that established the existence of an armed conflict.

Article 8 (2) (e) (viii). War crime of displacing civilians
Elements
(1) The perpetrator ordered a displacement of a civilian population.
(2) Such order was not justified by the security of the civilians involved or by military necessity.
(3) The perpetrator was in a position to effect such displacement by giving such order.
(4) The conduct took place in the context of and was associated with an armed conflict not of an international character.
(5) The perpetrator was aware of factual circumstances that established the existence of an armed conflict.

Article 8 (2) (e) (ix). War crime of treacherously killing or wounding
Elements
(1) The perpetrator invited the confidence or belief of one or more combatant adversaries that they were entitled to, or were obliged to accord, protection under rules of international law applicable in armed conflict.
(2) The perpetrator intended to betray that confidence or belief.
(3) The perpetrator killed or injured such person or persons.
(4) The perpetrator made use of that confidence or belief in killing or injuring such person or persons.
(5) Such person or persons belonged to an adverse party.
(6) The conduct took place in the context of and was associated with an armed conflict not of an international character.
(7) The perpetrator was aware of factual circumstances that established the existence of an armed conflict.

Article 8 (2) (e) (x). War crime of denying quarter
Elements
1. The perpetrator declared or ordered that there shall be no survivors.
2. Such declaration or order was given in order to threaten an adversary or to conduct hostilities on the basis that there shall be no survivors.
3. The perpetrator was in a position of effective command or control over the subordinate forces to which the declaration or order was directed.
4. The conduct took place in the context of and was associated with an armed conflict not of an international character.
5. The perpetrator was aware of factual circumstances that established the existence of an armed conflict.

Article 8 (2) (e) (xi)-1. War crime of mutilation
Elements
(1) The perpetrator subjected one or more persons to mutilation, in particular by permanently disfiguring the person or persons, or by permanently disabling or removing an organ or appendage.
(2) The conduct caused death or seriously endangered the physical or mental health of such person or persons.
(3) The conduct was neither justified by the medical, dental or hospital treatment of the person or persons concerned nor carried out in such person's or persons' interest.
(4) Such person or persons were in the power of another party to the conflict.
(5) The conduct took place in the context of and was associated with an armed conflict not of an international character.
(6) The perpetrator was aware of factual circumstances that established the existence of an armed conflict.

Article 8 (2) (e) (xi)-2. War crime of medical or scientific experiments
Elements
(1) The perpetrator subjected one or more persons to a medical or scientific experiment.
(2) The experiment caused the death or seriously endangered the physical or mental health or integrity of such person or persons.
(3) The conduct was neither justified by the medical, dental or hospital treatment of such person or persons concerned nor carried out in such person's or persons' interest.
(4) Such person or persons were in the power of another party to the conflict.
(5) The conduct took place in the context of and was associated with an armed conflict not of an international character.
(6) The perpetrator was aware of factual circumstances that established the existence of an armed conflict.

Article 8 (2) (e) (xii). War crime of destroying or seizing the enemy's property
Elements
(1) The perpetrator destroyed or seized certain property.
(2) Such property was property of an adversary.
(3) Such property was protected from that destruction or seizure under the international law of armed conflict.
(4) The perpetrator was aware of the factual circumstances that established the status of the property.
(5) The destruction or seizure was not required by military necessity.
(6) The conduct took place in the context of and was associated with an armed conflict not of an international character.
(7) The perpetrator was aware of factual circumstances that established the existence of an armed conflict

GENERAL AGREEMENT ON TARIFFS AND TRADE 1947

General Agreement on Tariffs and Trade 1947
Geneva 30 October 1947, Trb. 1966 Nr. 1

The Governments of the Commonwealth of Australia, the Kingdom of Belgium, the United States of Brazil, Burma, Canada, Ceylon, the Republic of Chile, the Republic of China, the Republic of Cuba, the Czechoslovak Republic, the French Republic, India, Lebanon, the Grand-Duchy of Luxemburg, the Kingdom of the Netherlands, New Zealand, the Kingdom of Norway, Pakistan, Southern Rhodesia, Syria, the Union of South Africa, the United Kingdom of Great Britain and Northern Ireland, and the United States of America:
Recognizing that their relations in the field of trade and economic endeavour should be conducted with a view to raising standards of living, ensuring full employment and a large and steadily growing volume of real income and effective demand, developing the full use of the resources of the world and expanding the production and exchange of goods,
Being desirous of contributing to these objectives by entering into reciprocal and mutually advantageous arrangements directed to the substantial reduction of tariffs and other barriers to trade and to the elimination of discriminatory treatment in international commerce,
Have through their Representatives agreed as follows:

Part I.

Article I. General Most-Favoured-Nation Treatment

(1) With respect to customs duties and charges of any kind imposed on or in connection with importation or exportation or imposed on the international transfer of payments for imports or exports, and with respect to the method of levying such duties and charges, and with respect to all rules and formalities in connection with importation and exportation, and with respect to all matters referred to in paragraphs (2) and (4) of Article III, any advantage, favour, privilege or immunity granted by any contracting party to any product originating in or destined for any other country shall be accorded immediately and unconditionally to the like product originating in or destined for the territories of all other contracting parties.

(2) The provisions of paragraph (1) of this Article shall not require the elimination of any preferences in respect of import duties or charges which do not exceed the levels provided for in paragraph (4) of this Article and which fall within the following descriptions:

(a) Preferences in force exclusively between two or more of the territories listed in Annex A, subject to the conditions set forth therein;

(b) Preferences in force exclusively between two or more territories which on July 1, 1939, were connected by common sovereignty or relations of protection or suzerainty and which are listed in Annexes B, C and D, subject to the conditions set forth therein;

(c) Preferences in force exclusively between the United States of America and the Republic of Cuba;

(d) Preferences in force exclusively between neighbouring countries listed in Annexes E and F.

(3) The provisions of paragraph (1) shall not apply to preferences between the countries formerly a part of the Ottoman Empire and detached from it on July 24, 1923, provided such preferences are approved under paragraph (5), of Article XXV which shall be applied in this respect in the light of paragraph (1) of Article XXIX.

(4) The margin of preference on any product in respect of which a preference is permitted under paragraph (2) of this Article but is not specifically set forth as a maximum margin of preference in the appropriate Schedule annexed to this Agreement shall not exceed:

(a) in respect of duties or charges on any product described in such Schedule, the difference between the most-favoured-nation and preferential rates provided for therein; if no preferential rate is provided for, the preferential rate shall for the purposes of this paragraph be taken to be that in force on April 10, 1947, and, if no most-favoured-nation rate is provided for, the margin shall not exceed the difference between the most-favoured-nation and preferential rates existing on April 10, 1947;

(b) in respect of duties or charges on any product not described in the appropriate Schedule, the difference between the most-favoured-nation and preferential rates existing on April 10, 1947.

In the case of the contracting parties named in Annex G, the date of April 10, 1947, referred to in subparagraph (a) and (b) of this paragraph shall be replaced by the respective dates set forth in that Annex.

Article II. Schedules of Concessions

(1) (a) Each contracting party shall accord to the commerce of the other contracting parties treatment no less favourable than that provided for in the appropriate Part of the appropriate Schedule annexed to this Agreement.

PART I INTERNATIONAL LAW

(b) The products described in Part I of the Schedule relating to any contracting party, which are the products of territories of other contracting parties, shall, on their importation into the territory to which the Schedule relates, and subject to the terms, conditions or qualifications set forth in that Schedule, be exempt from ordinary customs duties in excess of those set forth and provided therein. Such products shall also be exempt from all other duties or charges of any kind imposed on or in connection with the importation in excess of those imposed on the date of this Agreement or those directly and mandatorily required to be imposed thereafter by legislation in force in the importing territory on that date.

(c) The products described in Part II of the Schedule relating to any contracting party which are the products of territories entitled under Article I to receive preferential treatment upon importation into the territory to which the Schedule relates shall, on their importation into such territory, and subject to the terms, conditions or qualifications set forth in that Schedule, be exempt from ordinary customs duties in excess of those set forth and provided for in Part II of that Schedule. Such products shall also be exempt from all other duties or charges of any kind imposed on or in connection with importation in excess of those imposed on the date of this Agreement or those directly or mandatorily required to be imposed thereafter by legislation in force in the importing territory on that date. Nothing in this Article shall prevent any contracting party from maintaining its requirements existing on the date of this Agreement as to the eligibility of goods for entry at preferential rates of duty.

(2) Nothing in this Article shall prevent any contracting party from imposing at any time on the importation of any product:

(a) a charge equivalent to an internal tax imposed consistently with the provisions of paragraph (2) of Article III in respect of the like domestic product or in respect of an article from which the imported product has been manufactured or produced in whole or in part;

(b) any anti-dumping or countervailing duty applied consistently with the provisions of Article VI;

(c) fees or other charges commensurate with the cost of services rendered.

(3) No contracting party shall alter its method of determining dutiable value or of converting currencies so as to impair the value of any of the concessions provided for in the appropriate Schedule annexed to this Agreement.

(4) If any contracting party establishes, maintains or authorizes, formally or in effect, a monopoly of the importation of any product described in the appropriate Schedule annexed to this Agreement, such monopoly shall not, except as provided for in that Schedule or as otherwise agreed between the parties which initially negotiated the concession, operate so as to afford protection on the average in excess of the amount of protection provided for in that Schedule. The provisions of this paragraph shall not limit the use by contracting parties of any form of assistance to domestic producers permitted by other provisions of this Agreement.

(5) If any contracting party considers that a product is not receiving from another contracting party the treatment which the first contracting party believes to have been contemplated by a concession provided for in the appropriate Schedule annexed to this Agreement, it shall bring the matter directly to the attention of the other contracting party. If the latter agrees that the treatment contemplated was that claimed by the first contracting party, but declares that such treatment cannot be accorded because a court or other proper authority has ruled to the effect that the product involved cannot be classified under the tariff laws of such contracting party so as to permit the treatment contemplated in this Agreement, the two contracting parties, together with any other contracting parties substantially interested, shall enter promptly into further negotiations with a view to a compensatory adjustment of the matter.

(6) (a) The specific duties and charges included in the Schedules relating to contracting parties members of the International Monetary Fund, and margins of preference in specific duties and charges maintained by such contracting parties, are expressed in the appropriate currency at the par value accepted or provisionally recognized by the Fund at the date of this Agreement. Accordingly, in case this par value is reduced consistently with the Articles of Agreement of the International Monetary Fund by more than twenty per centum, such specific duties and charges and margins of preference may be adjusted to take account of such reduction; provided that the contracting parties (i.e., the contracting parties acting jointly as provided for in Article XXV) concur that such adjustments will not impair the value of the concessions provided for in the appropriate Schedule or elsewhere in this Agreement, due account being taken of all factors which may influence the need for, or urgency of, such adjustments.

(b) Similar provisions shall apply to any contracting party not a member of the Fund, as from the date on which such contracting party becomes a member of the Fund or enters into a special exchange agreement in pursuance of Article XV.

GENERAL AGREEMENT ON TARIFFS AND TRADE 1947

(7) The Schedules annexed to this Agreement are hereby made an integral part of Part I of this Agreement.

PART II

Article III. National Treatment on Internal Taxation and Regulation

(1) The contracting parties recognize that internal taxes and other internal charges, and laws, regulations and requirements affecting the internal sale, offering for sale, purchase, transportation, distribution or use of products, and internal quantitative regulations requiring the mixture, processing or use of products in specified amounts or proportions, should not be applied to imported or domestic products so as to afford protection to domestic production.

(2) The products of the territory of any contracting party imported into the territory of any other contracting party shall not be subject, directly or indirectly, to internal taxes or other internal charges of any kind in excess of those applied, directly or indirectly, to like domestic products. Moreover, no contracting party shall otherwise apply internal taxes or other internal charges to imported or domestic products in a manner contrary to the principles set forth in paragraph (1).

(3) With respect to any existing internal tax which is inconsistent with the provisions of paragraph (2), but which is specifically authorized under a trade agreement, in force on April 10, 1947, in which the import duty on the taxed product is bound against increase, the contracting party imposing the tax shall be free to postpone the application of the provisions of paragraph (2) to such tax until such time as it can obtain release from the obligations of such trade agreement in order to permit the increase of such duty to the extent necessary to compensate for the elimination of the protective element of the tax.

(4) The products of the territory of any contracting party imported into the territory of any other contracting party shall be accorded treatment no less favourable than that accorded to like products of national origin in respect of all laws, regulations and requirements affecting their internal sale, offering for sale, purchase, transportation, distribution or use. The provisions of this paragraph shall not prevent the application of differential internal transportation charges which are based exclusively on the economic operation of the means of transport and not on the nationality of the product.

(5) No contracting party shall establish or maintain any internal quantitative regulation relating to the mixture, processing or use of products in specified amounts or proportions which requires, directly or indirectly, that any specified amount or proportion of any product which is the subject of the regulation must be supplied from domestic sources. Moreover, no contracting party shall otherwise apply internal quantitative regulations in a manner contrary to the principles set forth in paragraph (1).

(6) The provisions of paragraph (5) shall not apply to any internal quantitative regulation in force in the territory of any contracting party on July 1, 1939, April 10, 1947, or March 24, 1948, at the option of that contracting party; Provided that any such regulation which is contrary to the provisions of paragraph (5) shall not be modified to the detriment of imports and shall be treated as a customs duty for the purpose of negotiation.

(7) No internal quantitative regulation relating to the mixture, processing or use of products in specified amounts or proportions shall be applied in such a manner as to allocate any such amount or proportion among external sources of supply.

(8) (a) The provisions of this Article shall not apply to laws, regulations or requirements governing the procurement by governmental agencies of products purchased for governmental purposes and not with a view to commercial resale or with a view to use in the production of goods for commercial sale.

(b) The provisions of this Article shall not prevent the payment of subsidies exclusively to domestic producers, including payments to domestic producers derived from the proceeds of internal taxes or charges applied consistently with the provisions of this Article and subsidies effected through governmental purchases of domestic products.

(9) The contracting parties recognize that internal maximum price control measures, even though conforming to the other provisions of this Article, can have effects prejudicial to the interests of contracting parties supplying imported products. Accordingly, contracting parties applying such measures shall take account of the interests of exporting contracting parties with a view to avoiding to the fullest practicable extent such prejudicial effects.

(10) The provisions of this Article shall not prevent any contracting party from establishing or maintaining internal quantitative regulations relating to exposed cinematograph films and meeting the requirements of Article IV.

Article IV. Special Provisions relating to Cinematograph Films

If any contracting party establishes or maintains internal quantitative regulations relating to exposed cinematograph films, such regulations shall take the form of screen quotas which shall conform to the following requirements:

(a) Screen quotas may require the exhibition of cinematograph films of national origin during a specified minimum proportion of the total screen time actually utilized, over a specified period of not less than one year, in the commercial exhibition of all films of whatever origin, and shall be computed on the basis of screen time per theatre per year or the equivalent thereof;

(b) With the exception of screen time reserved for films of national origin under a screen quota, screen time including that released by administrative action from screen time reserved for films of national origin, shall not be allocated formally or in effect among sources of supply;

(c) Notwithstanding the provisions of subparagraph (b) of this Article, any contracting party may maintain screen quotas conforming to the requirements of subparagraph (a) of this Article which reserve a minimum proportion of screen time for films of a specified origin other than that of the contracting party imposing such screen quotas; Provided that no such minimum proportion of screen time shall be increased above the level in effect on April 10, 1947;

(d) Screen quotas shall be subject to negotiation for their limitation, liberalization or elimination.

Article V. Freedom of Transit

(1) Goods (including baggage), and also vessels and other means of transport, shall be deemed to be in transit across the territory of a contracting party when the passage across such territory, with or without trans-shipment, warehousing, breaking bulk, or change in the mode of transport, is only a portion of a complete journey beginning and terminating beyond the frontier of the contracting party across whose territory the traffic passes. Traffic of this nature is termed in this article "traffic in transit".

(2) There shall be freedom of transit through the territory of each contracting party, via the routes most convenient for international transit, for traffic in transit to or from the territory of other contracting parties. No distinction shall be made which is based on the flag of vessels, the place of origin, departure, entry, exit or destination, or on any circumstances relating to the ownership of goods, of vessels or of other means of transport.

(3) Any contracting party may require that traffic in transit through its territory be entered at the proper custom house, but, except in cases of failure to comply with applicable customs laws and regulations, such traffic coming from or going to the territory of other contracting parties shall not be subject to any unnecessary delays or restrictions and shall be exempt from customs duties and from all transit duties or other charges imposed in respect of transit, except charges for transportation or those commensurate with administrative expenses entailed by transit or with the cost of services rendered.

(4) All charges and regulations imposed by contracting parties on traffic in transit to or from the territories of other contracting parties shall be reasonable, having regard to the conditions of the traffic.

(5) With respect to all charges, regulations and formalities in connection with transit, each contracting party shall accord to traffic in transit to or from the territory of any other contracting party treatment no less favourable than the treatment accorded to traffic in transit to or from any third country.

(6) Each contracting party shall accord to products which have been in transit through the territory of any other contracting party treatment no less favourable than that which would have been accorded to such products had they been transported from their place of origin to their destination without going through the territory of such other contracting party. Any contracting party shall, however, be free to maintain its requirements of direct consignment existing on the date of this Agreement, in respect of any goods in regard to which such direct consignment is a requisite condition of eligibility for entry of the goods at preferential rates of duty or has relation to the contracting party's prescribed method of valuation for duty purposes.

(7) The provisions of this Article shall not apply to the operation of aircraft in transit, but shall apply to air transit of goods (including baggage).

Article VI. Anti-dumping and Countervailing Duties

(1) The contracting parties recognize that dumping, by which products of one country are introduced into the commerce of another country at less than the normal value of the products, is to be condemned if it causes or threatens material injury to an established industry in the territory of a contracting party or materially retards the establishment of a domestic industry. For the purposes of this Article, a product is to be considered as being introduced into the commerce of an importing country at less than its normal value, if the price of the product exported from one country to another

(a) is less than the comparable price, in the ordinary course of trade, for the like product when destined for consumption in the exporting country, or,

(b) in the absence of such domestic price, is less than either
(i) the highest comparable price for the like product for export to any third country in the ordinary course of trade, or
(ii) the cost of production of the product in the country of origin plus a reasonable addition for selling cost and profit.
Due allowance shall be made in each case for differences in conditions and terms of sale, for differences in taxation, and for other differences affecting price comparability.
(2) In order to offset or prevent dumping, a contracting party may levy on any dumped product an anti-dumping duty not greater in amount than the margin of dumping in respect of such product. For the purposes of this Article, the margin of dumping is the price difference determined in accordance with the provisions of paragraph (1).
(3) No countervailing duty shall be levied on any product of the territory of any contracting party imported into the territory of another contracting party in excess of an amount equal to the estimated bounty or subsidy determined to have been granted, directly or indirectly, on the manufacture, production or export of such product in the country of origin or exportation, including any special subsidy to the transportation of a particular product. The term "countervailing duty" shall be understood to mean a special duty levied for the purpose of offsetting any bounty or subsidy bestowed, directly, or indirectly, upon the manufacture, production or export of any merchandise.
(4) No product of the territory of any contracting party imported into the territory of any other contracting party shall be subject to anti-dumping or countervailing duty by reason of the exemption of such product from duties or taxes borne by the like product when destined for consumption in the country of origin or exportation, or by reason of the refund of such duties or taxes.
(5) No product of the territory of any contracting party imported into the territory of any other contracting party shall be subject to both anti-dumping and countervailing duties to compensate for the same situation of dumping or export subsidization.
(6) (a) No contracting party shall levy any anti-dumping or countervailing duty on the importation of any product of the territory of another contracting party unless it determines that the effect of the dumping or subsidization, as the case may be, is such as to cause or threaten material injury to an established domestic industry, or is such as to retard materially the establishment of a domestic industry.
(b) The contracting parties may waive the requirement of subparagraph (a) of this paragraph so as to permit a contracting party to levy an anti-dumping or countervailing duty on the importation of any product for the purpose of offsetting dumping or subsidization which causes or threatens material injury to an industry in the territory of another contracting party exporting the product concerned to the territory of the importing contracting party. The contracting parties shall waive the requirements of subparagraph (a) of this paragraph, so as to permit the levying of a countervailing duty, in cases in which they find that a subsidy is causing or threatening material injury to an industry in the territory of another contracting party exporting the product concerned to the territory of the importing contracting party.
(c) In exceptional circumstances, however, where delay might cause damage which would be difficult to repair, a contracting party may levy a countervailing duty for the purpose referred to in subparagraph (b) of this paragraph without the prior approval of the contracting parties; Provided that such action shall be reported immediately to the contracting parties and that the countervailing duty shall be withdrawn promptly if the contracting parties disapprove.
(7) A system for the stabilization of the domestic price or of the return to domestic producers of a primary commodity, independently of the movements of export prices, which results at times in the sale of the commodity for export at a price lower than the comparable price charged for the like commodity to buyers in the domestic market, shall be presumed not to result in material injury within the meaning of paragraph (6) if it is determined by consultation among the contracting parties substantially interested in the commodity concerned that:
(a) the system has also resulted in the sale of the commodity for export at a price higher than the comparable price charged for the like commodity to buyers in the domestic market, and
(b) the system is so operated, either because of the effective regulation of production, or otherwise, as not to stimulate exports unduly or otherwise seriously prejudice the interests of other contracting parties.

Article VII. Valuation for Customs Purposes

(1) The contracting parties recognize the validity of the general principles of valuation set forth in the following paragraphs of this Article, and they undertake to give effect to such principles, in respect of all products subject to duties or other charges or restrictions on importation and exportation based

PART I INTERNATIONAL LAW

upon or regulated in any manner by value. Moreover, they shall, upon a request by another contracting party review the operation of any of their laws or regulations relating to value for customs purposes in the light of these principles. Contracting parties may request from contracting parties reports on steps taken by them in pursuance of the provisions of this Article.
(2) (a) The value for customs purposes of imported merchandise should be based on the actual value of the imported merchandise on which duty is assessed, or of like merchandise, and should not be based on the value of merchandise of national origin or on arbitrary or fictitious values.
(b) "Actual value" should be the price at which, at a time and place determined by the legislation of the country of importation, such or like merchandise is sold or offered for sale in the ordinary course of trade under fully competitive conditions. To the extent to which the price of such or like merchandise is governed by the quantity in a particular transaction, the price to be considered should uniformly be related to either (i) comparable quantities, or (ii) quantities not less favourable to importers than those in which the greater volume of the merchandise is sold in the trade between the countries of exportation and importation.
(c) When the actual value is not ascertainable in accordance with subparagraph (b) of this paragraph, the value for customs purposes should be based on the nearest ascertainable equivalent of such value.
(3) The value for customs purposes of any imported product should not include the amount of any internal tax, applicable within the country of origin or export, from which the imported product has been exempted or has been or will be relieved by means of refund.
(4) (a) Except as otherwise provided for in this paragraph, where it is necessary for the purposes of paragraph (2) of this Article for a contracting party to convert into its own currency a price expressed in the currency of another country, the conversion rate of exchange to be used shall be based, for each currency involved, on the par value as established pursuant to the Articles of Agreement of the International Monetary Fund or on the rate of exchange recognized by the Fund, or on the par value established in accordance with a special exchange agreement entered into pursuant to Article XV of this Agreement.
(b) Where no such established par value and no such recognized rate of exchange exist, the conversion rate shall reflect effectively the current value of such currency in commercial transactions.
(c) The contracting parties, in agreement with the International Monetary Fund, shall formulate rules governing the conversion by contracting parties of any foreign currency in respect of which multiple rates of exchange are maintained consistently with the Articles of Agreement of the International Monetary Fund. Any contracting party may apply such rules in respect of such foreign currencies for the purposes of paragraph (2) of this Article as an alternative to the use of par values. Until such rules are adopted by the Contracting parties, any contracting party may employ, in respect of any such foreign currency, rules of conversion for the purposes of paragraph (2) of this Article which are designed to reflect effectively the value of such foreign currency in commercial transactions.
(d) Nothing in this paragraph shall be construed to require any contracting party to alter the method of converting currencies for customs purposes which is applicable in its territory on the date of this Agreement, if such alteration would have the effect of increasing generally the amounts of duty payable.
(5) The bases and methods for determining the value of products subject to duties or other charges or restrictions based upon or regulated in any manner by value should be stable and should be given sufficient publicity to enable traders to estimate, with a reasonable degree of certainty, the value for customs purposes.

Article VIII. Fees and Formalities connected with Importation and Exportation
(1)(a) All fees and charges of whatever character (other than import and export duties and other than taxes within the purview of Article III) imposed by contracting parties on or in connection with importation or exportation shall be limited in amount to the approximate cost of services rendered and shall not represent an indirect protection to domestic products or a taxation of imports or exports for fiscal purposes.
(b) The contracting parties recognize the need for reducing the number and diversity of fees and charges referred to in subparagraph (a).
(c) The contracting parties also recognize the need for minimizing the incidence and complexity of import and export formalities and for decreasing and simplifying import and export documentation requirements.
(2) A contracting party shall, upon request by another contracting party or by the contracting parties, review the operation of its laws and regulations in the light of the provisions of this Article.
(3) No contracting party shall impose substantial penalties for minor breaches of customs regulations or procedural requirements. In particular, no penalty in respect of any omission or mistake in customs

documentation which is easily rectifiable and obviously made without fraudulent intent or gross negligence shall be greater than necessary to serve merely as a warning.

(4) The provisions of this Article shall extend to fees, charges, formalities and requirements imposed by governmental authorities in connection with importation and exportation, including those relating to:
(a) consular transactions, such as consular invoices and certificates;
(b) quantitative restrictions;
(c) licensing;
(d) exchange control;
(e) statistical services;
(f) documents, documentation and certification;
(g) analysis and inspection; and
(h) quarantine, sanitation and fumigation.

Article IX. Marks of Origin

(1) Each contracting party shall accord to the products of the territories of other contracting parties treatment with regard to marking requirements no less favourable than the treatment accorded to like products of any third country.

(2) The contracting parties recognize that, in adopting and enforcing laws and regulations relating to marks of origin, the difficulties and inconveniences which such measures may cause to the commerce and industry of exporting countries should be reduced to a minimum, due regard being had to the necessity of protecting consumers against fraudulent or misleading indications.

(3) Whenever it is administratively practicable to do so, contracting parties should permit required marks of origin to be affixed at the time of importation.

(4) The laws and regulations of contracting parties relating to the marking of imported products shall be such as to permit compliance without seriously damaging the products, or materially reducing their value, or unreasonably increasing their cost.

(5) As a general rule, no special duty or penalty should be imposed by any contracting party for failure to comply with marking requirements prior to importation unless corrective marking is unreasonably delayed or deceptive marks have been affixed or the required marking has been intentionally omitted.

(6) The contracting parties shall co-operate with each other with a view to preventing the use of trade names in such manner as to misrepresent the true origin of a product, to the detriment of such distinctive regional or geographical names of products of the territory of a contracting party as are protected by its legislation. Each contracting party shall accord full and sympathetic consideration to such requests or representations as may be made by any other contracting party regarding the application of the undertaking set forth in the preceding sentence to names of products which have been communicated to it by the other contracting party.

Article X. Publication and Administration of Trade Regulations

(1) Laws, regulations, judicial decisions and administrative rulings of general application, made effective by any contracting party, pertaining to the classification or the valuation of products for customs purposes, or to rates of duty, taxes or other charges, or to requirements, restrictions or prohibitions on imports or exports or on the transfer of payments therefor, or affecting their sale, distribution, transportation, insurance, warehousing inspection, exhibition, processing, mixing or other use, shall be published promptly in such a manner as to enable governments and traders to become acquainted with them. Agreements affecting international trade policy which are in force between the government or a governmental agency of any contracting party and the government or governmental agency of any other contracting party shall also be published. The provisions of this paragraph shall not require any contracting party to disclose confidential information which would impede law enforcement or otherwise be contrary to the public interest or would prejudice the legitimate commercial interests of particular enterprises, public or private.

(2) No measure of general application taken by any contracting party effecting an advance in a rate of duty or other charge on imports under an established and uniform practice, or imposing a new or more burdensome requirement, restriction or prohibition on imports, or on the transfer of payments therefor, shall be enforced before such measure has been officially published.

(3)(a) Each contracting party shall administer in a uniform, impartial and reasonable manner all its laws, regulations, decisions and rulings of the kind described in paragraph (1) of this Article.
(b) Each contracting party shall maintain, or institute as soon as practicable, judicial, arbitral or administrative tribunals or procedures for the purpose, inter alia, of the prompt review and correction of administrative action relating to customs matters. Such tribunals or procedures shall be indepen-

dent of the agencies entrusted with administrative enforcement and their decisions shall be implemented by, and shall govern the practice of, such agencies unless an appeal is lodged with a court or tribunal of superior jurisdiction within the time prescribed for appeals to be lodged by importers; Provided that the central administration of such agency may take steps to obtain a review of the matter in another proceeding if there is good cause to believe that the decision is inconsistent with established principles of law or the actual facts.

(c) The provisions of subparagraph (b) of this paragraph shall not require the elimination or substitution of procedures in force in the territory of a contracting party on the date of this Agreement which in fact provide for an objective and impartial review of administrative action even though such procedures are not fully or formally independent of the agencies entrusted with administrative enforcement. Any contracting party employing such procedures shall, upon request, furnish the contracting parties with full information thereon in order that they may determine whether such procedures conform to the requirements of this subparagraph.

Article XI. General Elimination of Quantitative Restrictions

(1) No prohibitions or restrictions other than duties, taxes or other charges, whether made effective through quotas, import or export licences or other measures, shall be instituted or maintained by any contracting party on the importation of any product of the territory of any other contracting party or on the exportation or sale for export of any product destined for the territory of any other contracting party.

(2) The provisions of paragraph (1) of this Article shall not extend to the following:

(a) Export prohibitions or restrictions temporarily applied to prevent or relieve critical shortages of foodstuffs or other products essential to the exporting contracting party;

(b) Import and export prohibitions or restrictions necessary to the application of standards or regulations for the classification, grading or marketing of commodities in international trade;

(c) Import restrictions on any agricultural or fisheries product, imported in any form, necessary to the enforcement of governmental measures which operate:

(i) to restrict the quantities of the like domestic product permitted to be marketed or produced, or, if there is no substantial domestic production of the like product, of a domestic product for which the imported product can be directly substituted; or

(ii) to remove a temporary surplus of the like domestic product, or, if there is no substantial domestic production of the like product, of a domestic product for which the imported product can be directly substituted, by making the surplus available to certain groups of domestic consumers free of charge or at prices below the current market level; or

(iii) to restrict the quantities permitted to be produced of any animal product the production of which is directly dependent, wholly or mainly, on the imported commodity, if the domestic production of that commodity is relatively negligible.

Any contracting party applying restrictions on the importation of any product pursuant to subparagraph (c) of this paragraph shall give public notice of the total quantity or value of the product permitted to be imported during a specified future period and of any change in such quantity or value. Moreover, any restrictions applied under (i) above shall not be such as will reduce the total of imports relative to the total of domestic production, as compared with the proportion which might reasonably be expected to rule between the two in the absence of restrictions. In determining this proportion, the contracting party shall pay due regard to the proportion prevailing during a previous representative period and to any special factors which may have affected or may be affecting the trade in the product concerned.

Article XII. Restrictions to Safeguard the Balance of Payments

(1) Notwithstanding the provisions of paragraph (1) of Article XI, any contracting party, in order to safeguard its external financial position and its balance of payments, may restrict the quantity or value of merchandise permitted to be imported, subject to the provisions of the following paragraphs of this Article.

(2)(a) Import restrictions instituted, maintained or intensified by a contracting party under this Article shall not exceed those necessary:

(i) to forestall the imminent threat of, or to stop, a serious decline in its monetary reserves; or

(ii) in the case of a contracting party with very low monetary reserves, to achieve a reasonable rate of increase in its reserves.

Due regard shall be paid in either case to any special factors which may be affecting the reserves of such contracting party or its need for reserves, including, where special external credits or other resources are available to it, the need to provide for the appropriate use of such credits or resources.

(b) Contracting parties applying restrictions under sub-paragraph (a) of this paragraph shall progressively relax them as such conditions improve, maintaining them only to the extent that the conditions specified in that sub-paragraph still justify their application. They shall eliminate the restrictions when conditions would no longer justify their institution or maintenance under that subparagraph.

(3)(a) Contracting parties undertake, in carrying out their domestic policies, to pay due regard to the need for maintaining or restoring equilibrium in their balance of payments on a sound and lasting basis and to the desirability of avoiding an uneconomic employment of productive resources. They recognize that, in order to achieve these ends, it is desirable so far as possible to adopt measures which expand rather than contract international trade.

(b) Contracting parties applying restrictions under this Article may determine the incidence of the restrictions on imports of different products or classes of products in such a way as to give priority to the importation of those products which are more essential.

(c) Contracting parties applying restrictions under this Article undertake:

(i) to avoid unnecessary damage to the commercial or economic interests of any other contracting party;

(ii) not to apply restrictions so as to prevent unreasonably the importation of any description of goods in minimum commercial quantities the exclusion of which would impair regular channels of trade; and

(iii) not to apply restrictions which would prevent the importations of commercial samples or prevent compliance with patent, trade mark, copyright, or similar procedures.

(d) The contracting parties recognize that, as a result of domestic policies directed towards the achievement and maintenance of full and productive employment or towards the development of economic resources, a contracting party may experience a high level of demand for imports involving a threat to its monetary reserves of the sort referred to in paragraph (2)(a) of this Article. Accordingly, a contracting party otherwise complying with the provisions of this Article shall not be required to withdraw or modify restrictions on the ground that a change in those policies would render unnecessary restrictions which it is applying under this Article.

(4)(a) Any contracting party applying new restrictions or raising the general level of its existing restrictions by a substantial intensification of the measures applied under this Article shall immediately after instituting or intensifying such restrictions (or, in circumstances in which prior consultation is practicable, before doing so) consult with the contracting parties as to the nature of its balance of payments difficulties, alternative corrective measures which may be available, and the possible effect of the restrictions on the economies of other contracting parties.

(b) On a date to be determined by them, the contracting parties shall review all restrictions still applied under this Article on that date. Beginning one year after that date, contracting parties applying import restrictions under this Article shall enter into consultations of the type provided for in subparagraph (a) of this paragraph with the contracting parties annually.

(c) (i) If, in the course of consultations with a contracting party under subparagraph (a) or (b) above, the contracting parties find that the restrictions are not consistent with provisions of this Article or with those of Article XIII (subject to the provisions of Article XIV), they shall indicate the nature of the inconsistency and may advise that the restrictions be suitably modified.

(ii) If, however, as a result of the consultations, the contracting parties determine that the restrictions are being applied in a manner involving an inconsistency of a serious nature with the provisions of this Article or with those of Article XIII (subject to the provisions of Article XIV) and that damage to the trade of any contracting party is caused or threatened thereby, they shall so inform the contracting party applying the restrictions and shall make appropriate recommendations for securing conformity with such provisions within the specified period of time. If such contracting party does not comply with these recommendations within the specified period, the contracting parties may release any contracting party the trade of which is adversely affected by the restrictions from such obligations under this Agreement towards the contracting party applying the restrictions as they determine to be appropriate in the circumstances.

(d) The contracting parties shall invite any contracting party which is applying restrictions under this Article to enter into consultations with them at the request of any contracting party which can establish a prima facie case that the restrictions are inconsistent with the provisions of this Article or with those of Article XIII (subject to the provisions of Article XIV) and that its trade is adversely affected thereby. However, no such invitation shall be issued unless the contracting parties have ascertained that direct discussions between the contracting parties concerned have not been successful. If, as a result of the consultations with the contracting parties, no agreement is reached and they determine that the restrictions are being applied inconsistently with such provisions, and that damage to the trade of the contracting party initiating the procedure is caused or threatened thereby, they shall recommend the withdrawal or modification of the restrictions. If the restrictions are not withdrawn or

PART I   INTERNATIONAL LAW

modified within such time as the contracting parties may prescribe, they may release the contracting party initiating the procedure from such obligations under this Agreement towards the contracting party applying the restrictions as they determine to be appropriate in the circumstances.
(e) In proceeding under this paragraph, the contracting parties shall have due regard to any special external factors adversely affecting the export trade of the contracting party applying the restrictions.
(f) Determinations under this paragraph shall be rendered expeditiously and, if possible, within sixty days of the initiation of the consultations.
(5) If there is a persistent and widespread application of import restrictions under this Article, indicating the existence of a general disequilibrium which is restricting international trade, the contracting parties shall initiate discussions to consider whether other measures might be taken, either by those contracting parties the balance of payments of which are under pressure or by those the balance of payments of which are tending to be exceptionally favourable, or by any appropriate intergovernmental organization, to remove the underlying causes of the disequilibrium. On the invitation of the contracting parties, contracting parties shall participate in such discussions.

Article XIII. Non-discriminatory Administration of Quantitative Restrictions
(1) No prohibition or restriction shall be applied by any contracting party on the importation of any product of the territory of any other contracting party or on the exportation of any product destined for the territory of any other contracting party, unless the importation of the like product of all third countries or the exportation of the like product to all third countries is similarly prohibited or restricted.
(2) In applying import restrictions to any product, contracting parties shall aim at a distribution of trade in such product approaching as closely as possible the shares which the various contracting parties might be expected to obtain in the absence of such restrictions and to this end shall observe the following provisions:
(a) Wherever practicable, quotas representing the total amount of permitted imports (whether allocated among supplying countries or not) shall be fixed, and notice given of their amount in accordance with paragraph (3)(b) of this Article;
(b) In cases in which quotas are not practicable, the restrictions may be applied by means of import licences or permits without a quota;
(c) Contracting parties shall not, except for purposes of operating quotas allocated in accordance with subparagraph (d) of this paragraph, require that import licences or permits be utilized for the importation of the product concerned from a particular country or source;
(d) In cases in which a quota is allocated among supplying countries the contracting party applying the restrictions may seek agreement with respect to the allocation of shares in the quota with all other contracting parties having a substantial interest in supplying the product concerned. In cases in which this method is not reasonably practicable, the contracting party concerned shall allot to contracting parties having a substantial interest in supplying the product shares based upon the proportions, supplied by such contracting parties during a previous representative period, of the total quantity or value of imports of the product, due account being taken of any special factors which may have affected or may be affecting the trade in the product. No conditions or formalities shall be imposed which would prevent any contracting party from utilizing fully the share of any such total quantity or value which has been allotted to it, subject to importation being made within any prescribed period to which the quota may relate.
(3)(a) In cases in which import licences are issued in connection with import restrictions, the contracting party applying the restrictions shall provide, upon the request of any contracting party having an interest in the trade in the product concerned, all relevant information concerning the administration of the restrictions, the import licences granted over a recent period and the distribution of such licences among supplying countries; Provided that there shall be no obligation to supply information as to the names of importing or supplying enterprises.
(b) In the case of import restrictions involving the fixing of quotas, the contracting party applying the restrictions shall give public notice of the total quantity or value of the product or products which will be permitted to be imported during a specified future period and of any change in such quantity or value. Any supplies of the product in question which were en route at the time at which public notice was given shall not be excluded from entry; Provided that they may be counted so far as practicable, against the quantity permitted to be imported in the period in question, and also, where necessary, against the quantities permitted to be imported in the next following period or periods; and Provided further that if any contracting party customarily exempts from such restrictions products entered for consumption or withdrawn from warehouse for consumption during a period of thirty days after the day of such public notice, such practice shall be considered full compliance with this subparagraph.

(c) In the case of quotas allocated among supplying countries, the contracting party applying the restrictions shall promptly inform all other contracting parties having an interest in supplying the product concerned of the shares in the quota currently allocated, by quantity or value, to the various supplying countries and shall give public notice thereof.

(4) With regard to restrictions applied in accordance with paragraph (2)(d) of this Article or under paragraph (2)(c) of Article XI, the selection of a representative period for any product and the appraisal of any special factors affecting the trade in the product shall be made initially by the contracting party applying the restriction; Provided that such contracting party shall, upon the request of any other contracting party having a substantial interest in supplying that product or upon the request of the contracting parties, consult promptly with the other contracting party or the contracting parties regarding the need for an adjustment of the proportion determined or of the base period selected, or for the reappraisal of the special factors involved, or for the elimination of conditions, formalities or any other provisions established unilaterally relating to the allocation of an adequate quota or its unrestricted utilization.

(5) The provisions of this Article shall apply to any tariff quota instituted or maintained by any contracting party, and, in so far as applicable, the principles of this Article shall also extend to export restrictions.

Article XIV. Exceptions to the Rule of Non-discrimination

(1) A contracting party which applies restrictions under Article XII or under Section B of Article XVIII may, in the application of such restrictions, deviate from the provisions of Article XIII in a manner having equivalent effect to restrictions on payments and transfers for current international transactions which that contracting party may at that time apply under Article VIII or XIV of the Articles of Agreement of the International Monetary Fund, or under analogous provisions of a special exchange agreement entered into pursuant to paragraph (6) of Article XV.

(2) A contracting party which is applying import restrictions under Article XII or under Section B of Article XVIII may, with the consent of the contracting parties, temporarily deviate from the provisions of Article XIII in respect of a small part of its external trade where the benefits to the contracting party or contracting parties concerned substantially outweigh any injury which may result to the trade of other contracting parties.

(3) The provisions of Article XIII shall not preclude a group of territories having a common quota in the International Monetary Fund from applying against imports from other countries, but not among themselves, restrictions in accordance with the provisions of Article XII or of Section B of Article XVIII on condition that such restrictions are in all other respects consistent with the provisions of Article XIII.

(4) A contracting party applying import restrictions under Article XII or under Section B of Article XVIII shall not be precluded by Articles XI to XV or Section B of Article XVIII of this Agreement from applying measures to direct its exports in such a manner as to increase its earnings of currencies which it can use without deviation from the provisions of Article XIII.

(5) A contracting party shall not be precluded by Articles XI to XV, inclusive, or by Section B of Article XVIII, of this Agreement from applying quantitative restrictions:

(a) having equivalent effect to exchange restrictions authorized under Section 3 (b) of Article VII of the Articles of Agreement of the International Monetary Fund, or

(b) under the preferential arrangements provided for in Annex A of this Agreement, pending the outcome of the negotiations referred to therein.

Article XV. Exchange Arrangements

(1) The contracting parties shall seek co-operation with the International Monetary Fund to the end that the contracting parties and the Fund may pursue a co-ordinated policy with regard to exchange questions within the jurisdiction of the Fund and questions of quantitative restrictions and other trade measures within the jurisdiction of the contracting parties.

(2) In all cases in which the contracting parties are called upon to consider or deal with problems concerning monetary reserves, balances of payments or foreign exchange arrangements, they shall consult fully with the International Monetary Fund. In such consultations, the contracting parties shall accept all findings of statistical and other facts presented by the Fund relating to foreign exchange, monetary reserves and balances of payments, and shall accept the determination of the Fund as to whether action by a contracting party in exchange matters is in accordance with the Articles of Agreement of the International Monetary Fund, or with the terms of a special exchange agreement between that contracting party and the contracting parties. The contracting parties in reaching their final decision in cases involving the criteria set forth in paragraph (2)(a) of Article XII or in paragraph (9) of Article XVIII, shall accept the determination of the Fund as to what constitutes a serious decline

in the contracting party's monetary reserves, a very low level of its monetary reserves or a reasonable rate of increase in its monetary reserves, and as to the financial aspects of other matters covered in consultation in such cases.

(3) The contracting parties shall seek agreement with the Fund regarding procedures for consultation under paragraph (2) of this Article.

(4) Contracting parties shall not, by exchange action, frustrate the intent of the provisions of this Agreement, nor, by trade action, the intent of the provisions of the Articles of Agreement of the International Monetary Fund.

(5) If the contracting parties consider, at any time, that exchange restrictions on payments and transfers in connection with imports are being applied by a contracting party in a manner inconsistent with the exceptions provided for in this Agreement for quantitative restrictions, they shall report thereon to the Fund.

(6) Any contracting party which is not a member of the Fund shall, within a time to be determined by the contracting parties after consultation with the Fund, become a member of the Fund, or, failing that, enter into a special exchange agreement with the contracting parties. A contracting party which ceases to be a member of the Fund shall forthwith enter into a special exchange agreement with the contracting parties. Any special exchange agreement entered into by a contracting party under this paragraph shall thereupon become part of its obligations under this Agreement.

(7)(a) A special exchange agreement between a contracting party and the contracting parties under paragraph (6) of this Article shall provide to the satisfaction of the contracting parties that the objectives of this Agreement will not be frustrated as a result of action in exchange matters by the contracting party in question.

(b) The terms of any such agreement shall not impose obligations on the contracting party in exchange matters generally more restrictive than those imposed by the Articles of Agreement of the International Monetary Fund on members of the Fund.

(8) A contracting party which is not a member of the Fund shall furnish such information within the general scope of section 5 of Article VIII of the Articles of Agreement of the International Monetary Fund as contracting parties may require in order to carry out their functions under this Agreement.

(9) Nothing in this Agreement shall preclude:

(a) the use by a contracting party of exchange controls or exchange restrictions in accordance with the Articles of Agreement of the International Monetary Fund or with that contracting party's special exchange agreement with the contracting parties, or

(b) the use by a contracting party of restrictions or controls in imports or exports, the sole effect of which, additional to the effects permitted under Articles XI, XII, XIII and XIV, is to make effective such exchange controls or exchange restrictions.

Article XVI. Subsidies

Section A - Subsidies in General

(1) If any contracting party grants or maintains any subsidy, including any form of income or price support, which operates directly or indirectly to increase exports of any product from, or to reduce imports of any product into, its territory, it shall notify the contracting parties in writing of the extent and nature of the subsidization, of the estimated effect of the subsidization on the quantity of the affected product or products imported into or exported from its territory and of the circumstances making the subsidization necessary. In any case in which it is determined that serious prejudice to the interests of any other contracting party is caused or threatened by any such subsidization, the contracting party granting the subsidy shall, upon request, discuss with the other contracting party or parties concerned, or with the contracting parties, the possibility of limiting the subsidization.

Section B - Additional Provisions on Export Subsidies

(2) The contracting parties recognize that the granting by a contracting party of a subsidy on the export of any product may have harmful effects for other contracting parties, both importing and exporting, may cause undue disturbance to their normal commercial interests, and may hinder the achievement of the objectives of this Agreement.

(3) Accordingly, contracting parties should seek to avoid the use of subsidies on the export of primary products. If, however, a contracting party grants directly or indirectly any form of subsidy which operates to increase the export of any primary product from its territory, such subsidy shall not be applied in a manner which results in that contracting party having more than an equitable share of world export trade in that product, account being taken of the shares of the contracting parties in such trade in the product during a previous representative period, and any special factors which may have affected or may be affecting such trade in the product.

(4) Further, as from 1 January 1958 or the earliest practicable date thereafter, contracting parties shall

cease to grant either directly or indirectly any form of subsidy on the export of any product other than a primary product which subsidy results in the sale of such product for export at a price lower than the comparable price charged for the like product to buyers in the domestic market. Until 31 December 1957 no contracting party shall extend the scope of any such subsidization beyond that existing on 1 January 1955 by the introduction of new, or the extension of existing, subsidies.

(5) The contracting parties shall review the operation of the provisions of this Article from time to time with a view to examining its effectiveness, in the light of actual experience, in promoting the objectives of this Agreement and avoiding subsidization seriously prejudicial to the trade or interests of contracting parties.

Article XVII. State Trading Enterprises

(1)(a) Each contracting party undertakes that if it establishes or maintains a State enterprise, wherever located, or grants to any enterprise, formally or in effect, exclusive or special privileges, such enterprise shall, in its purchases or sales involving either imports or exports, act in a manner consistent with the general principles of non-discriminatory treatment prescribed in this Agreement for governmental measures affecting imports or exports by private traders.

(b) The provisions of subparagraph (a) of this paragraph shall be understood to require that such enterprises shall, having due regard to the other provisions of this Agreement, make any such purchases or sales solely in accordance with commercial considerations, including price, quality, availability, marketability, transportation and other conditions of purchase or sale, and shall afford the enterprises of the other contracting parties adequate opportunity, in accordance with customary business practice, to compete for participation in such purchases or sales.

(c) No contracting party shall prevent any enterprise (whether or not an enterprise described in subparagraph (a) of this paragraph) under its jurisdiction from acting in accordance with the principles of subparagraphs (a) and (b) of this paragraph.

(2) The provisions of paragraph (1) of this Article shall not apply to imports of products for immediate or ultimate consumption in governmental use and not otherwise for resale or use in the production of goods for sale. With respect to such imports, each contracting party shall accord to the trade of the other contracting parties fair and equitable treatment.

(3) The contracting parties recognize that enterprises of the kind described in paragraph (1) (a) of this Article might be operated so as to create serious obstacles to trade; thus negotiations on a reciprocal and mutually advantageous basis designed to limit or reduce such obstacles are of importance to the expansion of international trade.

(4)(a) Contracting parties shall notify the contracting parties of the products which are imported into or exported from their territories by enterprises of the kind described in paragraph (1)(a) of this Article.

(b) A contracting party establishing, maintaining or authorizing an import monopoly of a product, which is not the subject of a concession under Article II, shall, on the request of another contracting party having a substantial trade in the product concerned, inform the contracting parties of the import mark-up on the product during a recent representative period, or, when it is not possible to do so, of the price charged on the resale of the product.

(c) The contracting parties may, at the request of a contracting party which has reason to believe that its interest under this Agreement are being adversely affected by the operations of an enterprise of the kind described in paragraph (1)(a), request the contracting party establishing, maintaining or authorizing such enterprise to supply information about its operations related to the carrying out of the provisions of this Agreement.

(d) The provisions of this paragraph shall not require any contracting party to disclose confidential information which would impede law enforcement or otherwise be contrary to the public interest or would prejudice the legitimate commercial interests of particular enterprises.

Article XVIII. Governmental Assistance to Economic Development

(1) The contracting parties recognize that the attainment of the objectives of this Agreement will be facilitated by the progressive development of their economies, particularly of those contracting parties the economies of which can only support low standards of living and are in the early stages of development.

(2) The contracting parties recognize further that it may be necessary for those contracting parties, in order to implement programmes and policies of economic development designed to raise the general standard of living of their people, to take protective or other measures affecting imports, and that such measures are justified in so far as they facilitate the attainment of the objectives of this Agreement. They agree, therefore, that those contracting parties should enjoy additional facilities to enable them (a) to maintain sufficient flexibility in their tariff structure to be able to grant the tariff protec-

tion required for the establishment of a particular industry and (b) to apply quantitative restrictions for balance of payments purposes in a manner which takes full account of the continued high level of demand for imports likely to be generated by their programmes of economic development.

(3) The contracting parties recognize finally that, with those additional facilities which are provided for in Sections A and B of this Article, the provisions of this Agreement would normally be sufficient to enable contracting parties to meet the requirements of their economic development. They agree, however, that there may be circumstances where no measure consistent with those provisions is practicable to permit a contracting party in the process of economic development to grant the governmental assistance required to promote the establishment of particular industries with a view to raising the general standard of living of its people. Special procedures are laid down in Sections C and D of this Article to deal with those cases.

(4)(a) Consequently, a contracting party, the economy of which can only support low standards of living and is in the early stages of development, shall be free to deviate temporarily from the provisions of the other Articles of this Agreement, as provided in Sections A, B and C of this Article.

(b) A contracting party, the economy of which is in the process of development, but which does not come within the scope of subparagraph (a) above, may submit applications to the contracting parties under Section D of this Article.

(5) The contracting parties recognize that the export earnings of contracting parties, the economies of which are of the type described in paragraph (4)(a) and (b) above and which depend on exports of a small number of primary commodities, may be seriously reduced by a decline in the sale of such commodities. Accordingly, when the exports of primary commodities by such a contracting party are seriously affected by measures taken by another contracting party, it may have resort to the consultation provisions of Article XXII of this Agreement.

(6) The contracting parties shall review annually all measures applied pursuant to the provisions of Sections C and D of this Article.

Section A

(7)(a) If a contracting party coming within the scope of paragraph (4)(a) of this Article considers it desirable, in order to promote the establishment of a particular industry with a view to raising the general standard of living of its people, to modify or withdraw a concession included in the appropriate Schedule annexed to this Agreement, it shall notify the CONTRACTING PARTIES to this effect and enter into negotiations with any contracting party with which such concession was initially negotiated, and with any other contracting party determined by the contracting parties to have a substantial interest therein. If agreement is reached between such contracting parties concerned, they shall be free to modify or withdraw concessions under the appropriate Schedules to this Agreement in order to give effect to such agreement, including any compensatory adjustments involved.

(b) If agreement is not reached within sixty days after the notification provided for in subparagraph (a) above, the contracting party which proposes to modify or withdraw the concession may refer the matter to the contracting parties which shall promptly examine it. If they find that the contracting party which proposes to modify or withdraw the concession has made every effort to reach an agreement and that the compensatory adjustment offered by it is adequate, that contracting party shall be free to modify or withdraw the concession if, at the same time, it gives effect to the compensatory adjustment. If the contracting parties do not find that the compensation offered by a contracting party proposing to modify or withdraw the concession is adequate, but find that it has made every reasonable effort to offer adequate compensation, that contracting party shall be free to proceed with such modification or withdrawal. If such action is taken, any other contracting party referred to in subparagraph (a) above shall be free to modify or withdraw substantially equivalent concessions initially negotiated with the contracting party which has taken the action.

Section B

(8) The contracting parties recognize that contracting parties coming within the scope of paragraph (4)(a) of this Article tend, when they are in rapid process of development, to experience balance of payments difficulties arising mainly from efforts to expand their internal markets as well as from the instability in their terms of trade.

(9) In order to safeguard its external financial position and to ensure a level of reserves adequate for the implementation of its programme of economic development, a contracting party coming within the scope of paragraph (4)(a) of this Article may, subject to the provisions of paragraphs (10) to (12), control the general level of its imports by restricting the quantity or value of merchandise permitted to be imported; Provided that the import restrictions instituted, maintained or intensified shall not exceed those necessary:

(a) to forestall the threat of, or to stop, a serious decline in its monetary reserves, or

(b) in the case of a contracting party with inadequate monetary reserves, to achieve a reasonable rate of increase in its reserves.

Due regard shall be paid in either case to any special factors which may be affecting the reserves of the contracting party or its need for reserves, including, where special external credits or other resources are available to it, the need to provide for the appropriate use of such credits or resources.

(10) In applying these restrictions, the contracting party may determine their incidence on imports of different products or classes of products in such a way as to give priority to the importation of those products which are more essential in the light of its policy of economic development; Provided that the restrictions are so applied as to avoid unnecessary damage to the commercial or economic interests of any other contracting party and not to prevent unreasonably the importation of any description of goods in minimum commercial quantities the exclusion of which would impair regular channels of trade; and Provided further that the restrictions are not so applied as to prevent the importation of commercial samples or to prevent compliance with patent, trade mark, copyright or similar procedures.

(11) In carrying out its domestic policies, the contracting party concerned shall pay due regard to the need for restoring equilibrium in its balance of payments on a sound and lasting basis and to the desirability of assuring an economic employment of productive resources. It shall progressively relax any restrictions applied under this Section as conditions improve, maintaining them only to the extent necessary under the terms of paragraph (9) of this Article and shall eliminate them when conditions no longer justify such maintenance; Provided that no contracting party shall be required to withdraw or modify restrictions on the ground that a change in its development policy would render unnecessary the restrictions which it is applying under this Section.

(12)(a) Any contracting party applying new restrictions or raising the general level of its existing restrictions by a substantial intensification of the measures applied under this Section, shall immediately after instituting or intensifying such restrictions (or, in circumstances in which prior consultation is practicable, before doing so) consult with the contracting parties as to the nature of its balance of payments difficulties, alternative corrective measures which may be available, and the possible effect of the restrictions on the economies of other contracting parties.

(b) On a date to be determined by them the contracting parties shall review all restrictions still applied under this Section on that date. Beginning two years after that date, contracting parties applying restrictions under this Section shall enter into consultations of the type provided for in subparagraph (a) above with the contracting parties at intervals of approximately, but not less than, two years according to a programme to be drawn up each year by the contracting parties; Provided that no consultation under this subparagraph shall take place within two years after the conclusion of a consultation of a general nature under any other provision of this paragraph.

(c) (i) If, in the course of consultations with a contracting party under subparagraph (a) or (b) of this paragraph, the contracting parties find that the restrictions are not consistent with the provisions of this Section or with those of Article XIII (subject to the provisions of
Article XIV), they shall indicate the nature of the inconsistency and may advise that the restrictions be suitably modified.

(ii) If, however, as a result of the consultations, the contracting parties determine that the restrictions are being applied in a manner involving an inconsistency of a serious nature with the provisions of this Section or with those of Article XIII (subject to the provisions of Article XIV) and that damage to the trade of any contracting party is caused or threatened thereby, they shall so inform the contracting party applying the restrictions and shall make appropriate recommendations for securing conformity with such provisions within a specified period. If such contracting party does not comply with these recommendations within the specified period, the contracting parties may release any contracting party the trade of which is adversely affected by the restrictions from such obligations under this Agreement towards the contracting party applying the restrictions as they determine to be appropriate in the circumstances.

(d) The contracting parties shall invite any contracting party which is applying restrictions under this Section to enter into consultations with them at the request of any contracting party which can establish a prima facie case that the restrictions are inconsistent with the provisions of this Section or with those of Article XIII (subject to the provisions of Article XIV) and that its trade is adversely affected thereby. However, no such invitation shall be issued unless the contracting parties have ascertained that direct discussions between the contracting parties concerned have not been successful. If, as a result of the consultations with the contracting parties no agreement is reached and they determine that the restrictions are being applied inconsistently with such provisions, and that damage to the trade of the contracting party initiating the procedure is caused or threatened thereby, they shall recommend the withdrawal or modification of the restrictions. If the restrictions are not withdrawn or

PART I   INTERNATIONAL LAW

modified within such time as the contracting parties may prescribe, they may release the contracting party initiating the procedure from such obligations under this Agreement towards the contracting party applying the restrictions as they determine to be appropriate in the circumstances.
(e) If a contracting party against which action has been taken in accordance with the last sentence of subparagraph (c) (ii) or (d) of this paragraph, finds that the release of obligations authorized by the contracting parties adversely affects the operation of its programme and policy of economic development, it shall be free, not later than sixty days after such action is taken, to give written notice to the Executive Secretary to the Contracting parties of its intention to withdraw from this Agreement and such withdrawal shall take effect on the sixtieth day following the day on which the notice is received by him.
(f) In proceeding under this paragraph, the contracting parties shall have due regard to the factors referred to in paragraph (2) of this Article. Determinations under this paragraph shall be rendered expeditiously and, if possible, within sixty days of the initiation of the consultations.

Section C
(13) If a contracting party coming within the scope of paragraph (4)(a) of this Article finds that governmental assistance is required to promote the establishment of a particular industry with a view to raising the general standard of living of its people, but that no measure consistent with the other provisions of this Agreement is practicable to achieve that objective, it may have recourse to the provisions and procedures set out in this Section.
(14) The contracting party concerned shall notify the contracting parties of the special difficulties which it meets in the achievement of the objective outlined in paragraph (13) of this Article and shall indicate the specific measure affecting imports which it proposes to introduce in order to remedy these difficulties. It shall not introduce that measure before the expiration of the time-limit laid down in paragraph (15) or (17), as the case may be, or if the measure affects imports of a product which is the subject of a concession included in the appropriate Schedule annexed to this Agreement, unless it has secured the concurrence of the contracting parties in accordance with provisions of paragraph (18); Provided that, if the industry receiving assistance has already started production, the contracting party may, after informing the contracting parties, take such measures as may be necessary to prevent, during that period, imports of the product or products concerned from increasing substantially above a normal level.
(15) If, within thirty days of the notification of the measure, the contracting parties do not request the contracting party concerned to consult with them, that contracting party shall be free to deviate from the relevant provisions of the other Articles of this Agreement to the extent necessary to apply the proposed measure.
(16) If it is requested by the contracting parties to do so, the contracting party concerned shall consult with them as to the purpose of the proposed measure, as to alternative measures which may be available under this Agreement, and as to the possible effect of the measure proposed on the commercial and economic interests of other contracting parties. If, as a result of such consultation, the contracting parties agree that there is no measure consistent with the other provisions of this Agreement which is practicable in order to achieve the objective outlined in paragraph (13) of this Article, and concur in the proposed measure, the contracting party concerned shall be released from its obligations under the relevant provisions of the other Articles of this Agreement to the extent necessary to apply that measure.
(17) If, within ninety days after the date of the notification of the proposed measure under paragraph (14) of this Article, the contracting parties have not concurred in such measure, the contracting party concerned may introduce the measure proposed after informing the contracting parties.
(18) If the proposed measure affects a product which is the subject of a concession included in the appropriate Schedule annexed to this Agreement, the contracting party concerned shall enter into consultations with any other contracting party with which the concession was initially negotiated, and with any other contracting party determined by the contracting parties to have a substantial interest therein. The contracting parties shall concur in the measure if they agree that there is no measure consistent with the other provisions of this Agreement which is practicable in order to achieve the objective set forth in paragraph (13) of this Article, and if they are satisfied:
(a) that agreement has been reached with such other contracting parties as a result of the consultations referred to above, or
(b) if no such agreement has been reached within sixty days after the notification provided for in paragraph (14) has been received by the contracting parties, that the contracting party having recourse to this Section has made all reasonable efforts to reach an agreement and that the interests of other contracting parties are adequately safeguarded.

The contracting party having recourse to this Section shall thereupon be released from its obligations under the relevant provisions of the other Articles of this Agreement to the extent necessary to permit it to apply the measure.

(19) If a proposed measure of the type described in paragraph (13) of this Article concerns an industry the establishment of which has in the initial period been facilitated by incidental protection afforded by restrictions imposed by the contracting party concerned for balance of payments purposes under the relevant provisions of this Agreement, that contracting party may resort to the provisions and procedures of this Section; Provided that it shall not apply the proposed measure without the concurrence of the contracting parties.

(20) Nothing in the preceding paragraphs of this Section shall authorize any deviation from the provisions of Articles I, II and XIII of this Agreement. The provisos to paragraph (10) of this Article shall also be applicable to any restriction under this Section.

(21) At any time while a measure is being applied under paragraph (17) of this Article any contracting party substantially affected by it may suspend the application to the trade of the contracting party having recourse to this Section of such substantially equivalent concessions or other obligations under this Agreement the suspension of which the contracting parties do not disapprove; Provided that sixty days' notice of such suspension is given to contracting parties not later than six months after the measure has been introduced or changed substantially to the detriment of the contracting party affected. Any such contracting party shall afford adequate opportunity for consultation in accordance with the provisions of Article XXII of this Agreement.

Section D

(22) A contracting party coming within the scope of subparagraph (4)(b) of this Article desiring, in the interest of the development of its economy, to introduce a measure of the type described in paragraph (13) of this Article in respect of the establishment of a particular industry may apply to the contracting parties for approval of such measure. The contracting parties shall promptly consult with such contracting party and shall, in making their decision, be guided by the considerations set out in paragraph (16). If the contracting parties concur in the proposed measure the contracting party concerned shall be released from its obligations under the relevant provisions of the other Articles of this Agreement to the extent necessary to permit it to apply the measure. If the proposed measure affects a product which is the subject of a concession included in the appropriate Schedule annexed to this Agreement, the provisions of paragraph (18) shall apply.

(23) Any measure applied under this Section shall comply with the provisions of paragraph (20) of this Article.

Article XIX. Emergency Action on Imports of Particular Products

(1)(a) If, as a result of unforeseen developments and of the effect of the obligations incurred by a contracting party under this Agreement, including tariff concessions, any product is being imported into the territory of that contracting party in such increased quantities and under such conditions as to cause or threaten serious injury to domestic producers in that territory of like or directly competitive products, the contracting party shall be free, in respect of such product, and to the extent and for such time as may be necessary to prevent or remedy such injury, to suspend the obligation in whole or in part or to withdraw or modify the concession.

(b) If any product, which is the subject of a concession with respect to a preference, is being imported into the territory of a contracting party in the circumstances set forth in subparagraph (a) of this paragraph, so as to cause or threaten serious injury to domestic producers of like or directly competitive products in the territory of a contracting party which receives or received such preference, the importing contracting party shall be free, if that other contracting party so requests, to suspend the relevant obligation in whole or in part or to withdraw or modify the concession in respect of the product, to the extent and for such time as may be necessary to prevent or remedy such injury.

(2) Before any contracting party shall take action pursuant to the provisions of paragraph (1) of this Article, it shall give notice in writing to the contracting parties as far in advance as may be practicable and shall afford the contracting parties and those contracting parties having a substantial interest as exporters of the product concerned an opportunity to consult with it in respect of the proposed action. When such notice is given in relation to a concession with respect to a preference, the notice shall name the contracting party which has requested the action. In critical circumstances, where delay would cause damage which it would be difficult to repair, action under paragraph (1) of this Article may be taken provisionally without prior consultation, on the condition that consultation shall be effected immediately after taking such action.

(3)(a) If agreement among the interested contracting parties with respect to the action is not reached, the contracting party which proposes to take or continue the action shall, nevertheless, be free to do

PART I   INTERNATIONAL LAW

so, and if such action is taken or continued, the affected contracting parties shall then be free, not later than ninety days after such action is taken, to suspend, upon the expiration of thirty days from the day on which written notice of such suspension is received by the contracting parties, the application to the trade of the contracting party taking such action, or, in the case envisaged in paragraph (1) (b) of this Article, to the trade of the contracting party requesting such action, of such substantially equivalent concessions or other obligations under this Agreement the suspension of which the contracting parties do not disapprove.

(b) Notwithstanding the provisions of subparagraph (a) of this paragraph, where action is taken under paragraph (2) of this Article without prior consultation and causes or threatens serious injury in the territory of a contracting party to the domestic producers of products affected by the action, that contracting party shall, where delay would cause damage difficult to repair, be free to suspend, upon the taking of the action and throughout the period of consultation, such concessions or other obligations as may be necessary to prevent or remedy the injury.

Article XX. General Exceptions

Subject to the requirement that such measures are not applied in a manner which would constitute a means of arbitrary or unjustifiable discrimination between countries where the same conditions prevail, or a disguised restriction on international trade, nothing in this Agreement shall be construed to prevent the adoption or enforcement by any contracting party of measures:

(a) necessary to protect public morals;

(b) necessary to protect human, animal or plant life or health;

(c) relating to the importations or exportations of gold or silver;

(d) necessary to secure compliance with laws or regulations which are not inconsistent with the provisions of this Agreement, including those relating to customs enforcement, the enforcement of monopolies operated under paragraph (4) of Article II and Article XVII, the protection of patents, trade marks and copyrights, and the prevention of deceptive practices;

(e) relating to the products of prison labour;

(f) imposed for the protection of national treasures of artistic, historic or archaeological value;

(g) relating to the conservation of exhaustible natural resources if such measures are made effective in conjunction with restrictions on domestic production or consumption;

(h) undertaken in pursuance of obligations under any intergovernmental commodity agreement which conforms to criteria submitted to the contracting parties and not disapproved by them or which is itself so submitted and not so disapproved;

(i) involving restrictions on exports of domestic materials necessary to ensure essential quantities of such materials to a domestic processing industry during periods when the domestic price of such materials is held below the world price as part of a governmental stabilization plan; Provided that such restrictions shall not operate to increase the exports of or the protection afforded to such domestic industry, and shall not depart from the provisions of this Agreement relating to non-discrimination;

(j) essential to the acquisition or distribution of products in general or local short supply; Provided that any such measures shall be consistent with the principle that all contracting parties are entitled to an equitable share of the international supply of such products, and that any such measures, which are inconsistent with the other provisions of the Agreement shall be discontinued as soon as the conditions giving rise to them have ceased to exist. The contracting parties shall review the need for this sub-paragraph not later than 30 June 1960.

Article XXI. Security Exceptions

Nothing in this Agreement shall be construed

(a) to require any contracting party to furnish any information the disclosure of which it considers contrary to its essential security interests; or

(b) to prevent any contracting party from taking any action which it considers necessary for the protection of its essential security interests

(i) relating to fissionable materials or the materials from which they are derived;

(ii) relating to the traffic in arms, ammunition and implements of war and to such traffic in other goods and materials as is carried on directly or indirectly for the purpose of supplying a military establishment;

(iii) taken in time of war or other emergency in international relations; or

(c) to prevent any contracting party from taking any action in pursuance of its obligations under the United Nations Charter for the maintenance of international peace and security.

Article XXII. Consultation

(1) Each contracting party shall accord sympathetic consideration to, and shall afford adequate oppor-

tunity for consultation regarding, such representations as may be made by another contracting party with respect to any matter affecting the operation of this Agreement.

(2) The contracting parties may, at the request of a contracting party, consult with any contracting party or parties in respect of any matter for which it has not been possible to find a satisfactory solution through consultation under paragraph (1).

Article XXIII. Nullification or Impairment

(1) If any contracting party should consider that any benefit accruing to it directly or indirectly under this Agreement is being nullified or impaired or that the attainment of any objective of the Agreement is being impeded as the result of

(a) the failure of another contracting party to carry out its obligations under this Agreement, or

(b) the application by another contracting party of any measure, whether or not it conflicts with the provisions of this Agreement, or

(c) the existence of any other situation,

the contracting party may, with a view to the satisfactory adjustment of the matter, make written representations or proposals to the other contracting party or parties which it considers to be concerned. Any contracting party thus approached shall give sympathetic consideration to the representations or proposals made to it.

(2) If no satisfactory adjustment is effected between the contracting parties concerned within a reasonable time, or if the difficulty is of the type described in paragraph (1)(c) of this Article, the matter may be referred to the contracting parties. The contracting parties shall promptly investigate any matter so referred to them and shall make appropriate recommendations to the contracting parties which they consider to be concerned, or give a ruling on the matter, as appropriate. The contracting parties may consult with contracting parties, with the Economic and Social Council of the United Nations and with any appropriate inter-governmental organization in cases where they consider such consultation necessary. If the contracting parties consider that the circumstances are serious enough to justify such action, they may authorize a contracting party or parties to suspend the application to any other contracting party or parties of such concessions or other obligations under this Agreement as they determine to be appropriate in the circumstances. If the application to any contracting party of any concession or other obligation is in fact suspended, that contracting party shall then be free, not later than sixty days after such action is taken, to give written notice to the Executive Secretary to the Contracting parties of its intention to withdraw from this Agreement and such withdrawal shall take effect upon the sixtieth day following the day on which such notice is received by him.

Part III

Article XXIV. Territorial Application - Frontier Traffic - Customs Unions and Free-trade Areas

(1) The provisions of this Agreement shall apply to the metropolitan customs territories of the contracting parties and to any other customs territories in respect of which this Agreement has been accepted under Article XXVI or is being applied under Article XXXIII or pursuant to the Protocol of Provisional Application. Each such customs territory shall, exclusively for the purposes of the territorial application of this Agreement, be treated as though it were a contracting party; Provided that the provisions of this paragraph shall not be construed to create any rights or obligations as between two or more customs territories in respect of which this Agreement has been accepted under Article XXVI or is being applied under Article XXXIII or pursuant to the Protocol of Provisional Application by a single contracting party.

(2) For the purposes of this Agreement a customs territory shall be understood to mean any territory with respect to which separate tariffs or other regulations of commerce are maintained for a substantial part of the trade of such territory with other territories.

(3) The provisions of this Agreement shall not be construed to prevent:

(a) Advantages accorded by any contracting party to adjacent countries in order to facilitate frontier traffic;

(b) Advantages accorded to the trade with the Free Territory of Trieste by countries contiguous to that territory, provided that such advantages are not in conflict with the Treaties of Peace arising out of the Second World War.

(4) The contracting parties recognize the desirability of increasing freedom of trade by the development, through voluntary agreements, of closer integration between the economies of the countries parties to such agreements. They also recognize that the purpose of a customs union or of a free-trade area should be to facilitate trade between the constituent territories and not to raise barriers to the trade of other contracting parties with such territories.

(5) Accordingly, the provisions of this Agreement shall not prevent, as between the territories of con-

tracting parties, the formation of a customs union or of a free-trade area or the adoption of an interim agreement necessary for the formation of a customs union or of a free-trade area; Provided that:
(a) with respect to a customs union, or an interim agreement leading to a formation of a customs union, the duties and other regulations of commerce imposed at the institution of any such union or interim agreement in respect of trade with contracting parties not parties to such union or agreement shall not on the whole be higher or more restrictive than the general incidence of the duties and regulations of commerce applicable in the constituent territories prior to the formation of such union or the adoption of such interim agreement, as the case may be;
(b) with respect to a free-trade area, or an interim agreement leading to the formation of a free-trade area, the duties and other regulations of commerce maintained in each of the constituent territories and applicable at the formation of such free-trade area or the adoption of such interim agreement to the trade of contracting parties not included in such area or not parties to such agreement shall not be higher or more restrictive than the corresponding duties and other regulations of commerce existing in the same constituent territories prior to the formation of the free-trade area, or interim agreement as the case may be; and
(c) any interim agreement referred to in subparagraphs (a) and (b) shall include a plan and schedule for the formation of such a customs union or of such a free-trade area within a reasonable length of time.
(6) If, in fulfilling the requirements of subparagraph (5)(a), a contracting party proposes to increase any rate of duty inconsistently with the provisions of Article II, the procedure set forth in Article XXVIII shall apply. In providing for compensatory adjustment, due account shall be taken of the compensation already afforded by the reduction brought about in the corresponding duty of the other constituents of the union.
(7)(a) Any contracting party deciding to enter into a customs union or free-trade area, or an interim agreement leading to the formation of such a union or area, shall promptly notify the contracting parties and shall make available to them such information regarding the proposed union or area as will enable them to make such reports and recommendations to contracting parties as they may deem appropriate.
(b) If, after having studied the plan and schedule included in an interim agreement referred to in paragraph (5) in consultation with the parties to that agreement and taking due account of the information made available in accordance with the provisions of subparagraph (a), the contracting parties find that such agreement is not likely to result in the formation of a customs union or of a free-trade area within the period contemplated by the parties to the agreement or that such period is not a reasonable one, the contracting parties shall make recommendations to the parties to the agreement. The parties shall not maintain or put into force, as the case may be, such agreement if they are not prepared to modify it in accordance with these recommendations.
(c) Any substantial change in the plan or schedule referred to in paragraph (5)(c) shall be communicated to the contracting parties, which may request the contracting parties concerned to consult with them if the change seems likely to jeopardize or delay unduly the formation of the customs union or of the free-trade area.
(8) For the purposes of this Agreement:
(a) A customs union shall be understood to mean the substitution of a single customs territory for two or more customs territories, so that
(i) duties and other restrictive regulations of commerce (except, where necessary, those permitted under Articles XI, XII, XIII, XIV, XV and XX) are eliminated with respect to substantially all the trade between the constituent territories of the union or at least with respect to substantially all the trade in products originating in such territories, and,
(ii) subject to the provisions of paragraph (9), substantially the same duties and other regulations of commerce are applied by each of the members of the union to the trade of territories not included in the union;
(b) A free-trade area shall be understood to mean a group of two or more customs territories in which the duties and other restrictive regulations of commerce (except, where necessary, those permitted under Articles XI, XII, XIII, XIV, XV and XX) are eliminated on substantially all the trade between the constituent territories in products originating in such territories.
(9) The preferences referred to in paragraph (2) of Article I shall not be affected by the formation of a customs union or of a free-trade area but may be eliminated or adjusted by means of negotiations with contracting parties affected. This procedure of negotiations with affected contracting parties shall, in particular, apply to the elimination of preferences required to conform with the provisions of paragraph (8)(a)(i) and paragraph (8)(b).
(10) The contracting parties may by a two-thirds majority approve proposals which do not fully

comply with the requirements of paragraphs (5) to (9) inclusive, provided that such proposals lead to the formation of a customs union or a free-trade area in the sense of this Article.
(11) Taking into account the exceptional circumstances arising out of the establishment of India and Pakistan as independent States and recognizing the fact that they have long constituted an economic unit, the contracting parties agree that the provisions of this Agreement shall not prevent the two countries from entering into special arrangements with respect to the trade between them, pending the establishment of their mutual trade relations on a definitive basis.
(12) Each contracting party shall take such reasonable measures as may be available to it to ensure observance of the provisions of this Agreement by the regional and local governments and authorities within its territories.

Article XXV. Joint Action by the Contracting parties
(1) Representatives of the contracting parties shall meet from time to time for the purpose of giving effect to those provisions of this Agreement which involve joint action and, generally, with a view to facilitating the operation and furthering the objectives of this Agreement. Wherever reference is made in this Agreement to the contracting parties acting jointly they are designated as the contracting parties.
(2) The Secretary-General of the United Nations is requested to convene the first meeting of the contracting parties, which shall take place not later than March 1, 1948.
(3) Each contracting party shall be entitled to have one vote at all meetings of the contracting parties.
(4) Except as otherwise provided for in this Agreement, decisions of the contracting parties shall be taken by a majority of the votes cast.

(5) In exceptional circumstances not elsewhere provided for in this Agreement, the contracting parties may waive an obligation imposed upon a contracting party by this Agreement; **Provided** that any such decision shall be approved by a two-thirds majority of the votes cast and that such majority shall comprise more than half of the contracting parties. The contracting parties may also by such a vote
(i) define certain categories of exceptional circumstances to which other voting requirements shall apply for the waiver of obligations, and
(ii) prescribe such criteria as may be necessary for the application of this paragraph.

Article XXVI. Acceptance, Entry into Force and Registration
(1) The date of this Agreement shall be 30 October 1947.
(2) This Agreement shall be open for acceptance by any contracting party which,
on 1 March 1955, was a contracting party or was negotiating with a view to accession to this Agreement.
(3) This Agreement, done in a single English original and a single French original, both texts authentic, shall be deposited with the Secretary-General of the United Nations, who shall furnish certified copies thereof to all interested governments.
(4) Each government accepting this Agreement shall deposit an instrument of acceptance with the Executive Secretary to the Contracting parties, who will inform all interested governments of the date of deposit of each instrument of acceptance and of the day on which this Agreement enters into force under paragraph (6) of this Article.
(5)(a) Each government accepting this Agreement does so in respect of its metropolitan territory
and of the other territories for which it has international responsibility, except such separate customs territories as it shall notify to the Executive Secretary to the contracting parties at the time of its own acceptance.
(b) Any government, which has so notified the Executive Secretary under the exceptions in subparagraph (a) of this paragraph, may at any time give notice to the Executive Secretary5 that its acceptance shall be effective in respect of any separate customs territory or territories so excepted and such notice shall take effect on the thirtieth day following the day on which it is received by the Executive Secretary.
(c) If any of the customs territories, in respect of which a contracting party has accepted this Agreement, possesses or acquires full autonomy in the conduct of its external commercial relations and
of the other matters provided for in this Agreement, such territory shall, upon sponsorship through a declaration by the responsible contracting party establishing the above-mentioned fact, be deemed to be a contracting party.
(6) This Agreement shall enter into force, as among the governments which have accepted it, on the thirtieth day following the day on which instruments of acceptance have been deposited with Executive Secretary to the Contracting parties on behalf of governments named in Annex H, the territories of which account for 85 per centum of the total external trade of the territories of such governments,

computed in accordance with the applicable column of percentages set forth therein. The instrument of acceptance of each other government shall take effect on the thirtieth day following the day on which such instrument has been deposited.

(7) The United Nations is authorized to effect registration of this Agreement as soon as it enters into force.

Article XXVII. Withholding or Withdrawal of Concessions

Any contracting party shall at any time be free to withhold or to withdraw in whole or in part any concession, provided for in the appropriate Schedule annexed to this Agreement, in respect of which such contracting party determines that it was initially negotiated with a government which has not become, or has ceased to be, a contracting party. A contracting party taking such action shall notify the contracting parties and, upon request, consult with contracting parties which have a substantial interest in the product concerned.

Article XXVIII. Modification of Schedules

(1) On the first day of each three-year period, the first period beginning on 1 January 1958 (or on the first day of any other period that may be specified by the contracting parties by two-thirds of the votes cast) a contracting party (hereafter in this Article referred to as the "applicant contracting party") may, by negotiation and agreement with any contracting party with which such concession was initially negotiated and with any other contracting party determined by the contracting parties to have a principal supplying interest (which two preceding categories of contracting parties, together with the applicant contracting party, are in this Article hereinafter referred to as the "contracting parties primarily concerned"), and subject to consultation with any other contracting party determined by the contracting parties to have a substantial interest in such concession, modify or withdraw a concession included in the appropriate schedule annexed to this Agreement.

(2) In such negotiations and agreement, which may include provision for compensatory adjustment with respect to other products, the contracting parties concerned shall endeavour to maintain a general level of reciprocal and mutually advantageous concessions not less favourable to trade than that provided for in this Agreement prior to such negotiations.

(3)(a) If agreement between the contracting parties primarily concerned cannot be reached before 1 January 1958 or before the expiration of a period envisaged in paragraph (1) of this Article, the contracting party which proposes to modify or withdraw the concession shall, nevertheless, be free to do so and if such action is taken any contracting party with which such concession was initially negotiated, any contracting party determined under paragraph (1) to have a principal supplying interest and any contracting party determined under paragraph (1) to have a substantial interest shall then be free not later than six months after such action is taken, to withdraw, upon the expiration of thirty days from the day on which written notice of such withdrawal is received by the contracting parties, substantially equivalent concessions initially negotiated with the applicant contracting party.

(b) If agreement between the contracting parties primarily concerned is reached but any other contracting party determined under paragraph (1) of this Article to have a substantial interest is not satisfied, such other contracting party shall be free, not later than six months after action under such agreement is taken, to withdraw, upon the expiration of thirty days from the day on which written notice of such withdrawal is received by the contracting parties, substantially equivalent concessions initially negotiated with the applicant contracting party.

(4) The contracting parties may, at any time, in special circumstances, authorize a contracting party to enter into negotiations for modification or withdrawal of a concession included in the appropriate Schedule annexed to this Agreement subject to the following procedures and conditions:

(a) Such negotiations and any related consultations shall be conducted in accordance with the provisions of paragraph (1) and (2) of this Article.

(b) If agreement between the contracting parties primarily concerned is reached in the negotiations, the provisions of paragraph (3)(b) of this Article shall apply.

(c) If agreement between the contracting parties primarily concerned is not reached within a period of sixty days after negotiations have been authorized, or within such longer period as the contracting parties may have prescribed, the applicant contracting party may refer the matter to the contracting parties.

(d) Upon such reference, the contracting parties shall promptly examine the matter and submit their views to the contracting parties primarily concerned with the aim of achieving a settlement. If a settlement is reached, the provisions of paragraph (3)(b) shall apply as if agreement between the contracting parties primarily concerned had been reached. If no settlement is reached between the contracting parties primarily concerned, the applicant contracting party shall be free to modify or withdraw the concession, unless the contracting parties determine that the applicant contracting party has unreasonably failed to offer adequate compensation. If such action is taken, any contracting party with which the concession was initially negotiated, any contracting party determined under paragraph (4)(a) to have a principal supplying interest and any contracting party determined under paragraph (4)(a) to have a substantial interest, shall be free, not later than six months after such action is taken, to modify or withdraw, upon the expiration of thirty days from the day on which written notice of such withdrawal is received by the contracting parties, substantially equivalent concessions initially negotiated with applicant contracting party.

(5) Before 1 January 1958 and before the end of any period envisaged in paragraph (1) a contracting party may elect by notifying the contracting parties to reserve the right, for the duration of the next period, to modify the appropriate Schedule in accordance with the procedures of paragraph (1) to (3). If a contracting party so elects, other contracting parties shall have the right, during the same period, to modify or withdraw, in accordance with the same procedures, concessions initially negotiated with that contracting party.

Article XXVIII bis. Tariff Negotiations

(1) The contracting parties recognize that customs duties often constitute serious obstacles to trade; thus negotiations on a reciprocal and mutually advantageous basis, directed to the substantial reduction of the general level of tariffs and other charges on imports and exports and in particular to the reduction of such high tariffs as discourage the importation even of minimum quantities, and conducted with due regard to the objectives of this Agreement and the varying needs of individual contracting parties, are of great importance to the expansion of international trade. The CONTRACTING PARTIES may therefore sponsor such negotiations from time to time.

(2) (a) Negotiations under this Article may be carried out on a selective product-by-product basis or by the application of such multilateral procedures as may be accepted by the contracting parties concerned. Such negotiations may be directed towards the reduction of duties, the binding of duties at then existing levels or undertakings that individual duties or the average duties on specified categories of products shall not exceed specified levels. The binding against increase of low duties or of duty-free treatment shall, in principle, be recognized as a concession equivalent in value to the reduction of high duties.

(b) The contracting parties recognize that in general the success of multilateral negotiations would depend on the participation of all contracting parties which conduct a substantial proportion of their external trade with one another.

(3) Negotiations shall be conducted on a basis which affords adequate opportunity to take into account:

(a) the needs of individual contracting parties and individual industries;

(b) the needs of less-developed countries for a more flexible use of tariff protection to assist their economic development and the special needs of these countries to maintain tariffs for revenue purposes; and

(c) all other relevant circumstances, including the fiscal, developmental, strategic and other needs of the contracting parties concerned.

Article XXIX. The Relation of this Agreement to the Havana Charter

(1) The contracting parties undertake to observe to the fullest extent of their executive authority the general principles of Chapters I to VI inclusive and of Chapter IX of the Havana Charter pending their acceptance of it in accordance with their constitutional procedures.

(2) Part II of this Agreement shall be suspended on the day on which the Havana Charter enters into force.

(3) If by September 30, 1949, the Havana Charter has not entered into force, the contracting parties shall meet before December 31, 1949, to agree whether this Agreement shall be amended, supplemented or maintained.

(4) If at any time the Havana Charter should cease to be in force, the CONTRACTING PARTIES shall meet as soon as practicable thereafter to agree whether this Agreement shall be supplemented, amended or maintained. Pending such agreement, Part II of this Agreement shall again enter into force; Provided that the provisions of Part II other than Article XXIII shall be replaced, *mutatis mutandis*, in the form in which they then appeared in the Havana Charter; and Provided further that no contracting party shall be bound by any provisions which did not bind it at the time when the Havana Charter ceased to be in force.

(5) If any contracting party has not accepted the Havana Charter by the date upon which it enters into force, the contracting parties shall confer to agree whether, and if so in what way, this Agreement in so far as it affects relations between such contracting party and other contracting parties, shall be supplemented or amended. Pending such agreement the provisions of Part II of this Agreement shall,

notwithstanding the provisions of paragraph (2) of this Article, continue to apply as between such contracting party and other contracting parties.
(6) Contracting parties which are Members of the International Trade Organization shall not invoke the provisions of this Agreement so as to prevent the operation of any provision of the Havana Charter. The application of the principle underlying this paragraph to any contracting party which is not a Member of the International Trade Organization shall be the subject of an agreement pursuant to paragraph (5) of this Article.

Article XXX. Amendments

(1) Except where provision for modification is made elsewhere in this Agreement, amendments to the provisions of Part I of this Agreement or the provisions of Article XXIX or of this Article shall become effective upon acceptance by all the contracting parties, and other amendments to this Agreement shall become effective, in respect of those contracting parties which accept them, upon acceptance by two-thirds of the contracting parties and thereafter for each other contracting party upon acceptance by it.
(2) Any contracting party accepting an amendment to this Agreement shall deposit an instrument of acceptance with the Secretary-General of the United Nations within such period as the contracting parties may specify. The contracting parties may decide that any amendment made effective under this Article is of such a nature that any contracting party which has not accepted it within a period specified by the contracting parties shall be free to withdraw from this Agreement, or to remain a contracting party with the consent of the contracting parties.

Article XXXI. Withdrawal

Without prejudice to the provisions of paragraph (12) of Article XVIII, of Article XXIII or of paragraph (2) of Article XXX, any contracting party may withdraw from this Agreement, or may separately withdraw on behalf of any of the separate customs territories for which it has international responsibility and which at the time possesses full autonomy in the conduct of its external commercial relations and of the other matters provided for in this Agreement. The withdrawal shall take effect upon the expiration of six months from the day on which written notice of withdrawal is received by the Secretary-General of the United Nations.

Article XXXII. Contracting parties

(1) The contracting parties to this Agreement shall be understood to mean those governments which are applying the provisions of this Agreement under Articles XXVI or XXXIII or pursuant to the Protocol of Provisional Application.
(2) At any time after the entry into force of this Agreement pursuant to paragraph (6) of Article XXVI, those contracting parties which have accepted this Agreement pursuant to paragraph (4) of Article XXVI may decide that any contracting party which has not so accepted it shall cease to be a contracting party.

Article XXXIII. Accession

A government not party to this Agreement, or a government acting on behalf of a separate customs territory possessing full autonomy in the conduct of its external commercial relations and of the other matters provided for in this Agreement, may accede to this Agreement, on its own behalf or on behalf of that territory, on terms to be agreed between such government and the contracting parties. Decisions of the contracting parties under this paragraph shall be taken by a two-thirds majority.

Article XXXIV. Annexes

The annexes to this Agreement are hereby made an integral part of this Agreement.

Article XXXV. Non-application of the Agreement between Particular Contracting parties

(1) This Agreement, or alternatively Article II of this Agreement, shall not apply as between any contracting party and any other contracting party if:
(a) the two contracting parties have not entered into tariff negotiations with each other, and
(b) either of the contracting parties, at the time either becomes a contracting party, does not consent to such application.
(2) The contracting parties may review the operation of this Article in particular cases at the request of any contracting party and make appropriate recommendations.

Part IV. Trade and Development

Article XXXVI. Principles and Objectives

(1) The contracting parties,

GENERAL AGREEMENT ON TARIFFS AND TRADE 1947

(a) recalling that the basic objectives of this Agreement include the raising of standards of living and the progressive development of the economies of all contracting parties, and considering that the attainment of these objectives is particularly urgent for less-developed contracting parties;
(b) considering that export earnings of the less-developed contracting parties can play a vital part in their economic development and that the extent of this contribution depends on the prices paid by the less-developed contracting parties for essential imports, the volume of their exports, and the prices received for these exports;
(c) noting, that there is a wide gap between standards of living in less-developed countries and in other countries;
(d) recognizing that individual and joint action is essential to further the development of the economies of less-developed contracting parties and to bring about a rapid advance in the standards of living in these countries;
(e) recognizing that international trade as a means of achieving economic and social advancement should be governed by such rules and procedures - and measures in conformity with such rules and procedures - as are consistent with the objectives set forth in this Article;
(f) noting that the contracting parties may enable less-developed contracting parties to use special measures to promote their trade and development;
agree as follows.
(2) There is need for a rapid and sustained expansion of the export earnings of the less-developed contracting parties.
(3) There is need for positive efforts designed to ensure that less-developed contracting parties secure a share in the growth in international trade commensurate with the needs of their economic development.
(4) Given the continued dependence of many less-developed contracting parties on the exportation of a limited range of primary products, there is need to provide in the largest possible measure more favourable and acceptable conditions of access to world markets for these products, and wherever appropriate to devise measures designed to stabilize and improve conditions of world markets in these products, including in particular measures designed to attain stable, equitable and remunerative prices, thus permitting an expansion of world trade and demand and a dynamic and steady growth of the real export earnings of these countries so as to provide them with expanding resources for their economic development.
(5) The rapid expansion of the economies of the less-developed contracting parties will be facilitated by a diversification of the structure of their economies and the avoidance of an excessive dependence on the export of primary products. There is, therefore, need for increased access in the largest possible measure to markets under favourable conditions for processed and manufactured products currently or potentially of particular export interest to less-developed contracting parties.
(6) Because of the chronic deficiency in the export proceeds and other foreign exchange earnings of less-developed contracting parties, there are important inter-relationships between trade and financial assistance to development. There is, therefore, need for close and continuing collaboration between the contracting parties and the international lending agencies so that they can contribute most effectively to alleviating the burdens these less-developed contracting parties assume in the interest of their economic development.
(7) There is need for appropriate collaboration between the contracting parties, other intergovernmental bodies and the organs and agencies of the United Nations system, whose activities relate to the trade and economic development of less-developed countries.
(8) The developed contracting parties do not expect reciprocity for commitments made by them in trade negotiations to reduce or remove tariffs and other barriers to the trade of less-developed contracting parties.
(9) The adoption of measures to give effect to these principles and objectives shall be a matter of conscious and purposeful effort on the part of the contracting parties both individually and jointly.

Article XXXVII. Commitments
(1) The developed contracting parties shall to the fullest extent possible - that is, except when compelling reasons, which may include legal reasons, make it impossible - give effect to the following provisions:
(a) accord high priority to the reduction and elimination of barriers to products currently or potentially of particular export interest to less-developed contracting parties, including customs duties and other restrictions which differentiate unreasonably between such products in their primary and in their processed forms;
(b) refrain from introducing, or increasing the incidence of, customs duties or non-tariff import bar-

PART I   INTERNATIONAL LAW

riers on products currently or potentially of particular export interest to less-developed contracting parties; and
(c)(i) refrain from imposing new fiscal measures, and
(ii) in any adjustments of fiscal policy accord high priority to the reduction and elimination of fiscal measures, which would hamper, or which hamper, significantly the growth of consumption of primary products, in raw or processed form, wholly or mainly produced in the territories of less-developed contracting parties, and which are applied specifically to those products.
(2) (a) Whenever it is considered that effect is not being given to any of the provisions of subparagraph (a), (b) or (c) of paragraph (1), the matter shall be reported to the contracting parties either by the contracting party not so giving effect to the relevant provisions or by any other interested contracting party.
(b) (i) The contracting parties shall, if requested so to do by any interested contracting party, and without prejudice to any bilateral consultations that may be undertaken, consult with the contracting party concerned and all interested contracting parties with respect to the matter with a view to reaching solutions satisfactory to all contracting parties concerned in order to further the objectives set forth in Article XXXVI. In the course of these consultations, the reasons given in cases where effect was not being given to the provisions of subparagraph (a), (b) or (c) of paragraph (1) shall be examined.
(ii) As the implementation of the provisions of subparagraph (a), (b) or (c) of paragraph (1) by individual contracting parties may in some cases be more readily achieved where action is taken jointly with other developed contracting parties, such consultation might, where appropriate, be directed towards this end.
(iii) The consultations by the contracting parties might also, in appropriate cases, be directed towards agreement on joint action designed to further the objectives of this Agreement as envisaged in paragraph (1) of Article XXV.
(3) The developed contracting parties shall:
(a) make every effort, in cases where a government directly or indirectly determines the resale price of products wholly or mainly produced in the territories of less-developed contracting parties, to maintain trade margins at equitable levels;
(b) give active consideration to the adoption of other measures designed to provide greater scope for the development of imports from less-developed contracting parties and collaborate in appropriate international action to this end;
(c) have special regard to the trade interests of less-developed contracting parties when considering the application of other measures permitted under this Agreement to meet particular problems and explore all possibilities of constructive remedies before applying such measures where they would affect essential interests of those contracting parties.
(4) Less-developed contracting parties agree to take appropriate action in implementation of the provisions of Part IV for the benefit of the trade of other less-developed contracting parties, in so far as such action is consistent with their individual present and future development, financial and trade needs taking into account past trade developments as well as the trade interests of less-developed contracting parties as a whole.
(5) In the implementation of the commitments set forth in paragraph (1) to (4) each contracting party shall afford to any other interested contracting party or contracting parties full and prompt opportunity for consultations under the normal procedures of this Agreement with respect to any matter or difficulty which may arise.

Article XXXVIII. Joint Action
(1) The contracting parties shall collaborate jointly, with the framework of this Agreement and elsewhere, as appropriate, to further the objectives set forth in Article XXXVI.
(2) In particular, the contracting parties shall:
(a) where appropriate, take action, including action through international arrangements, to provide improved and acceptable conditions of access to world markets for primary products of particular interest to less-developed contracting parties and to devise measures designed to stabilize and improve conditions of world markets in these products including measures designed to attain stable, equitable and remunerative prices for exports of such products;
(b) seek appropriate collaboration in matters of trade and development policy with the United Nations and its organs and agencies, including any institutions that may be created on the basis of recommendations by the United Nations Conference on Trade and Development;
(c) collaborate in analysing the development plans and policies of individual less-developed contracting parties and in examining trade and aid relationships with a view to devising concrete measures

to promote the development of export potential and to facilitate access to export markets for the products of the industries thus developed and, in this connection, seek appropriate collaboration with governments and international organizations, and in particular with organizations having competence in relation to financial assistance for economic development, in systematic studies of trade and aid relationships in individual less-developed contracting parties aimed at obtaining a clear analysis of export potential, market prospects and any further action that may be required;
(d) keep under continuous review the development of world trade with special reference to the rate of growth of the trade of less-developed contracting parties and make such recommendations to contracting parties as may, in the circumstances, be deemed appropriate;
(e) collaborate in seeking feasible methods to expand trade for the purpose of economic development, through international harmonization and adjustment of national policies and regulations, through technical and commercial standards affecting production, transportation and marketing, and through export promotion by the establishment of facilities for the increased flow of trade information and the development of market research; and
(f) establish such institutional arrangements as may be necessary to further the objectives set forth in Article XXXVI and to give effect to the provision of this Part.

Annex A

List of territories referred to in Paragraph (2)(a) of Article I
United Kingdom of Great Britain and Northern Ireland
Dependent territories of the United Kingdom of Great Britain and Northern Ireland
Canada
Commonwealth of Australia
Dependent territories of the Commonwealth of Australia
New Zealand
Dependent territories of New Zealand
Union of South Africa including South West Africa
Ireland
India (as on April 10, 1947)
Newfoundland
Southern Rhodesia
Burma
Ceylon
Certain of the territories listed above have two or more preferential rates in force for certain products. Any such territory may, by agreement with the other contracting parties which are principal suppliers of such products at the most-favoured-nation rate, substitute for such preferential rates a single preferential rate which shall not on the whole be less favourable to suppliers at the most-favoured-nation rate than the preferences in force prior to such substitution.
The imposition of an equivalent margin of tariff preference to replace a margin of preference in an internal tax existing on April 10, 1947 exclusively between two or more of the territories listed in this Annex or to replace the preferential quantitative arrangements described in the following paragraph, shall not be deemed to constitute an increase in a margin of tariff preference.

The preferential arrangements referred to in paragraph (5)(**b**) of Article XIV are those existing in the United Kingdom on 10 April 1947, under contractual agreements with the Governments of Canada, Australia and New Zealand, in respect of chilled and frozen beef and veal, frozen mutton and lamb, chilled and frozen pork and bacon. It is the intention, without prejudice to any action taken under subparagraph (**h**) of Article XX, that these arrangements shall be eliminated or replaced by tariff preferences, and that negotiations to this end shall take place as soon as practicable among the countries substantially concerned or involved.
The film hire tax in force in New Zealand on 10 April 1947, shall, for the purposes of this Agreement, be treated as a customs duty under Article I. The renters' film quota in force in New Zealand on April 10, 1947, shall, for the purposes of this Agreement, be treated as a screen quota under Article IV.
The Dominions of India and Pakistan have not been mentioned separately in the above list since they had not come into existence as such on the base date of April 10, 1947.

Annex B

List of territories of the French Union referred to in Paragraph (2)(b) of Article I
France
French Equatorial Africa (Treaty Basin of the Congo and other territories)

PART I   INTERNATIONAL LAW

French West Africa
Cameroons under French Trusteeship
French Somali Coast and Dependencies
French Establishments in Oceania
French Establishments in the Condominium of the New Hebrides
Indo-China
Madagascar and Dependencies
Morocco (French zone)
New Caledonia and Dependencies
Saint-Pierre and Miquelon
Togo under French Trusteeship
Tunisia

Annex C

List of territories referred to in Paragraph (2)(b) of Article I as respects the Customs Union of Belgium, Luxemburg and the Netherlands
The Economic Union of Belgium and Luxemburg
Belgian Congo
Ruanda Urundi
Netherlands
New Guinea
Surinam
Netherlands Antilles
Republic of Indonesia
For imports into the territories constituting the Customs Union only.

Annex D

List of territories referred to in Paragraph (2)(b) of Article I as respects the United States of America
United States of America (customs territory)
Dependent territories of the United States of America
Republic of the Philippines
The imposition of an equivalent margin of tariff preference to replace a margin of preference in an internal tax existing on 10 April, 1947, exclusively between two or more of the territories listed in this Annex shall not be deemed to constitute an increase in a margin of tariff preference.

Annex E

List of territories covered by preferential arrangements between Chile and neighbouring countries referred to in Paragraph (2)(d) of Article I.
Preferences in force exclusively between Chile on the one hand, and
1. Argentina
2. Bolivia
3. Peru
on the other hand.

Annex F

List of territories covered by preferential arrangements between Lebanon and Syria and neighbouring countries referred to in Paragraph (2)(d) of Article I
Preferences in force exclusively between the Lebano-Syrian Customs Union, on the one hand, and
1. Palestine
2. Transjordan
on the other hand.

Annex G

Dates establishing maximum margins of preference referred to in Paragraph (4) of Article I

Australia	October 15, 1946
Canada	July 1, 1939
France	January 1, 1939
Lebano-Syrian Customs Union	November 30, 1938

Union of South Africa..	July 1, 1938
Southern Rhodesia	May 1, 1941

Annex H

Percentage shares of total external trade to be used for the purpose of making the determination refereed to in Article XXVI
(Based on average of 1949-1953)
If, prior to the accession of the Government of Japan to the General Agreement, the present Agreement has been accepted by contracting parties the external trade of which under Column I accounts for the percentage of such trade specified in paragraph (6) of Article XXVI, column I shall be applicable for the purposes of that paragraph. If the present Agreement has not been so accepted prior to the accession of the Government of Japan, column II shall be applicable for the purposes of that paragraph.

	Column I (Contracting parties on 1 March 1955)	Column II (Contracting parties on 1 March 1955 and Japan)
Australia	3.1	3.0
Austria	0.9	0.8
Belgium-Luxemburg	4.3	4.2
Brazil	2.5	2.4
Burma	0.3	0.3
Canada	6.7	6.5
Ceylon	0.5	0.5
Chile	0.6	0.6
Cuba	1.1	1.1
Czechoslovakia	1.4	1.4
Denmark	1.4	1.4
Dominican Republic	0.1	0.1
Finland	1.0	1.0
France	8.7	8.5
Germany, Federal Republic of	5.3	5.2
Greece	0.4	0.4
Haiti	0.1	0.1
India	2.4	2.4
Indonesia	1.3	1.3
Italy	2.9	2.8
Netherlands, Kingdom of the	4.7	4.6
New Zealand	1.0	1.0
Nicaragua	0.1	0.1
Norway	1.1	1.1
Pakistan	0.9	0.8
Peru	0.4	0.4
Rhodesia and Nyasaland	0.6	0.6
Sweden	2.5	2.4
Turkey	0.6	0.6
Union of South Africa	1.8	1.8
United Kingdom	20.3	19.8
United States of America	20.6	20.1
Uruguay	0.4	0.4
Japan	-	2.3
	100.0	100.0

Note: These percentages have been computed taking into account the trade of all territories in respect of which the General Agreement on Tariffs and Trade is applied

---

Annex I

Notes and supplementary provisions

Article I. Paragraph (1) The obligations incorporated in paragraph (1) of Article I by reference to paragraphs (2) and (4) of Article III and those incorporated in paragraph (2)(b) of Article II by reference to Article VI shall be considered as falling within Part II for the purposes of the Protocol of Provisional Application.

The cross-references, in the paragraph immediately above and in paragraph (1) of Article I, to paragraphs (2) and (4) of Article III shall only apply after Article III has been modified by the entry into force of the amendment provided for in the Protocol Modifying Part II and Article XXVI of the General Agreement on Tariffs and Trade, dated September 14, 1948.

Paragraph (4). The term "margin of preference" means the absolute difference between the most-favoured-nation rate of duty and the preferential rate of duty for the like product, and not the proportionate relation between those rates. As examples:

(1) If the most-favoured-nation rate were 36 per cent ad valorem and the preferential rate were 24 per cent ad valorem, the margin of preference would be 12 per cent ad valorem, and not one-third of the most-favoured-nation rate;

(2) If the most-favoured-nation rate were 36 per cent ad valorem and the preferential rate were expressed as two-thirds of the most-favoured-nation rate, the margin of preference would be 12 per cent ad valorem;

(3) If the most-favoured-nation rate were 2 francs per kilogramme and the preferential rate were 1.50 francs per kilogramme, the margin of preference would be 0.50 franc per kilogramme.

The following kinds of customs action, taken in accordance with established uniform procedures, would not be contrary to a general binding of margins of preference:

(i) The re-application to an imported product of a tariff classification or rate of duty, properly applicable to such product, in cases in which the application of such classification or rate to such product was temporarily suspended or inoperative on April 10, 1947; and

(ii) The classification of a particular product under a tariff item other than that under which importations of that product were classified on April 10, 1947, in cases in which the tariff law clearly contemplates that such product may be classified under more than one tariff item.

Article II. Paragraph (2)(a). The cross-reference, in paragraph (2)(a) of Article II, to paragraph (2) of Article III shall only apply after Article III has been modified by the entry into force of the amendment provided for in the Protocol Modifying Part II and Article XXVI of the General Agreement on Tariffs and Trade, dated September 14, 1948.

Paragraph (2)(b). See the note relating to paragraph (1) of Article I.

Paragraph (4) Except where otherwise specifically agreed between the contracting parties which initially negotiated the concession, the provisions of this paragraph will be applied in the light of the provisions of Article 31 of the Havana Charter.

Article III. Any internal tax or other internal charge, or any law, regulation or requirement of the kind referred to in paragraph (1) which applies to an imported product and to the like domestic product and is collected or enforced in the case of the imported product at the time or point of importation, is nevertheless to be regarded as an internal tax or other internal charge, or a law, regulation or requirement of the kind referred to in paragraph (1), and is accordingly subject to the provisions of Article III.

Paragraph (1) The application of paragraph (1) to internal taxes imposed by local governments and authorities with the territory of a contracting party is subject to the provisions of the final paragraph of Article XXIV. The term "reasonable measures" in the last-mentioned paragraph would not require, for example, the repeal of existing national legislation authorizing
local governments to impose internal taxes which, although technically inconsistent with the letter of Article III, are not in fact inconsistent with its spirit, if such repeal would result in a serious financial hardship for the local governments or authorities concerned. With regard to taxation by local governments or authorities which is inconsistent with both the letter
and spirit of Article III, the term "reasonable measures" would permit a contracting party to eliminate the inconsistent taxation gradually over a transition period, if abrupt action would create serious administrative and financial difficulties.

Paragraph (2) A tax conforming to the requirements of the first sentence of paragraph (2) would be considered to be inconsistent with the provisions of the second sentence only in cases where competition was involved between, on the one hand, the taxed product and, on the other hand, a directly competitive or substitutable product which was not similarly taxed.

Paragraph (5) Regulations consistent with the provisions of the first sentence of paragraph (5) shall not be considered to be contrary to the provisions of the second sentence in any case in which all of the products subject to the regulations are produced domestically in substantial quantities. A regulation cannot be justified as being consistent with the provisions of the second sentence on the ground that the proportion or amount allocated to each of the products which are the subject of the regulation constitutes an equitable relationship between imported and domestic products.

GENERAL AGREEMENT ON TARIFFS AND TRADE 1947

Article V. Paragraph (5) With regard to transportation charges, the principle laid down in paragraph (5) refers to like products being transported on the same route under like conditions.

Article VI. Paragraph (1) (1) Hidden dumping by associated houses (that is, the sale by an importer at a price below that corresponding to the price invoiced by an exporter with whom the importer is associated, and also below the price in the exporting country) constitutes a form of price dumping with respect to which the margin of dumping may be calculated on the basis of the price at which the goods are resold by the importer.
(2) It is recognized that, in the case of imports from a country which has a complete or substantially complete monopoly of its trade and where all domestic prices are fixed by the State, special difficulties may exist in determining price comparability for the purposes of paragraph (1), and in such cases importing contracting parties may find it necessary to take into account the possibility that a strict comparison with domestic prices in such a country may not always be appropriate.
Paragraphs (2) and (3) (1) As in many other cases in customs administration, a contracting party may require reasonable security (bond or cash deposit) for the payment of anti-dumping or countervailing duty pending final determination of the facts in any case of suspected dumping or subsidization.
(2) Multiple currency practices can in certain circumstances constitute a subsidy to exports which may be met by countervailing duties under paragraph (3) or can constitute a form of dumping by means of a partial depreciation of a country's currency which may be met by action under paragraph (2) By "multiple currency practices" is meant practices by governments or sanctioned by governments.
Paragraph (6)(b). Waivers under the provisions of this subparagraph shall be granted only on application by the contracting party proposing to levy an anti-dumping or countervailing duty, as the case may be.

Article VII. Paragraph (1) The expression "or other charges" is not to be regarded as including internal taxes or equivalent charges imposed on or in connection with imported products.
Paragraph (2) (1) It would be in conformity with Article VII to presume that "actual value" may be represented by the invoice price, plus any non-included charges for legitimate costs which are proper elements of "actual value" and plus any abnormal discount or other reduction from the ordinary competitive price.
(2) It would be in conformity with Article VII, paragraph (2)(b), for a contracting party to construe the phrase "in the ordinary course of trade... under fully competitive conditions", as excluding any transaction wherein the buyer and seller are not independent of each other and price is not the sole consideration.
(3) The standard of "fully competitive conditions" permits a contracting party to exclude from consideration prices involving special discounts limited to exclusive agents.
(4) The wording of subparagraphs (a) and (b) permits a contracting party to determine the value for customs purposes uniformly either (1) on the basis of a particular exporter's prices of the imported merchandise, or (2) on the basis of the general price level of like merchandise.

Article VIII. (1) While Article VIII does not cover the use of multiple rates of exchange as such, paragraphs (1) and (4) condemn the use of exchange taxes or fees as a device for implementing multiple currency practices; if, however, a contracting party is using multiple currency exchange fees for balance of payments reasons with the approval of the International Monetary Fund, the provisions of paragraph (9)(a) of Article XV fully safeguard its position.
(2) It would be consistent with paragraph (1) if, on the importation of products from the territory of a contracting party into the territory of another contracting party, the production of certificates of origin should only be required to the extent that is strictly indispensable.

Articles XI, XII, XIII, XIV and XVIII

Throughout Articles XI, XII, XIII, XIV and XVIII, the terms "import restrictions" or "export restrictions" include restrictions made effective through state-trading operations.

Article XI. Paragraph (2)(c) The term "in any form" in this paragraph covers the same products when in an early stage of processing and still perishable, which compete directly with the fresh product and if freely imported would tend to make the restriction on the fresh product ineffective.
Paragraph (2), last subparagraph. The term "special factors" includes changes in relative productive efficiency as between domestic and foreign producers, or as between different foreign producers, but not changes artificially brought about by means not permitted under the Agreement.

Article XII. The contracting parties shall make provision for the utmost secrecy in the conduct of any consultation under the provisions of this Article.

Paragraph (3)(c)(i). Contracting parties applying restrictions shall endeavour to avoid causing serious prejudice to exports of a commodity on which the economy of a contracting party is largely dependent.

Paragraph (4)(b). It is agreed that the date shall be within ninety days after the entry into force of the amendments of this Article effected by the Protocol Amending the Preamble
and Parts II and III of this Agreement. However, should the contracting parties find that conditions were not suitable for the application of the provisions of this subparagraph at the time envisaged, they may determine a later date; Provided that such date is not more than thirty days after such time as the obligations of Article VIII, Sections 2, 3 and 4, of the Articles of Agreement of the International Monetary Fund become applicable to contracting parties, members of the Fund, the combined foreign trade of which constitutes at least fifty per centum of the aggregate foreign trade of all contracting parties.

Paragraph (4)(e) It is agreed that paragraph (4)(e) does not add any new criteria for the imposition or maintenance of quantitative restrictions for balance of payments reasons. It is solely intended to ensure that all external factors such as changes in the terms of trade, quantitative restrictions, excessive tariffs and subsidies, which may be contributing to the balance of payments difficulties of the contracting party applying restrictions, will be fully taken into account.

Article XIII. Paragraph (2)(d). No mention was made of "commercial considerations" as a rule for the allocation of quotas because it was considered that its application by governmental authorities might not always be practicable. Moreover, in cases where it is practicable, a contracting party could apply these considerations in the process of seeking agreement, consistently with the general rule laid down in the opening sentence of paragraph (2).

Paragraph (4) See note relating to "special factors" in connection with the last subparagraph of paragraph (2) of Article XI.

Article XIV. Paragraph (1) The provisions of this paragraph shall not be so construed as to preclude full consideration by the CONTRACTING PARTIES, in the consultations provided
for in paragraph (4) of Article XII and in paragraph (12) of Article XVIII, of the nature, effects and reasons for discrimination in the field of import restrictions.

Paragraph (2) One of the situations contemplated in paragraph (2) is that of a contracting party holding balances acquired as a result of current transactions which it finds itself unable to use without a measure of discrimination.

Article XV. Paragraph (4) The word "frustrate" is intended to indicate, for example, that infringements of the letter of any Article of this Agreement by exchange action shall not be regarded as a violation of that Article if, in practice, there is no appreciable departure from the intent of the Article. Thus, a contracting party which, as part of its exchange control operated in accordance with the Articles of Agreement of the International Monetary Fund, requires payment to be received for its exports in its own currency or in the currency of one or more members of the International Monetary Fund will not thereby be deemed to contravene Article XI or Article XIII. Another example would be that of a contracting party which specifies on an import licence the country from which the goods may be imported, for the purpose not of introducing any additional element of discrimination in its import licensing system but of enforcing permissible exchange controls.

Article XVI. The exemption of an exported product from duties or taxes borne by the like product when destined for domestic consumption, or the remission of such duties or taxes in amounts not in excess of those which have accrued, shall not be deemed to be a subsidy.

Section B. (1) Nothing in Section B shall preclude the use by a contracting party of multiple rates of exchange in accordance with the Articles of Agreement of the International Monetary Fund.

(2) For the purposes of Section B, a "primary product" is understood to be any product of farm, forest or fishery, or any mineral, in its natural form or which has undergone such processing as is customarily required to prepare it for marketing in substantial volume in international trade.

Paragraph (3)(1) The fact that a contracting party has not exported the product in question during the previous representative period would not in itself preclude that contracting party from establishing its right to obtain a share of the trade in the product concerned.

(2) A system for the stabilization of the domestic price or of the return to domestic producers of a primary product independently of the movements of export prices, which results at times in the sale of the product for export at a price lower than the comparable price charged for the like product to buyers in the domestic market, shall be considered not to involve a subsidy on exports within the

meaning of paragraph (3) if the contracting parties determine that:
(a) the system has also resulted, or is so designed as to result, in the sale of the product for export at a price higher than the comparable price charged for the like product to buyers in the domestic market; and
(b) the system is so operated, or is designed so to operate, either because of the effective regulation of production or otherwise, as not to stimulate exports unduly or otherwise seriously to prejudice the interests of other contracting parties.
Notwithstanding such determination by the contracting parties, operations under such a system shall be subject to the provisions of paragraph (3) where they are wholly or partly financed out of government funds in addition to the funds collected from producers in respect of the product concerned.
Paragraph (4) The intention of paragraph (4) is that the contracting parties should seek before the end of 1957 to reach agreement to abolish all remaining subsidies as from 1 January 1958; or, failing this, to reach agreement to extend the application of the standstill until the earliest date thereafter by which they can expect to reach such agreement.

Article XVII. Paragraph (1) The operations of Marketing Boards, which are established by contracting parties and are engaged in purchasing or selling, are subject to the provisions of subparagraphs (a) and (b).
The activities of Marketing Boards which are established by contracting parties and which do not purchase or sell but lay down regulations covering private trade are governed by the relevant Articles of this Agreement.
The charging by a state enterprise of different prices for its sales of a product in different markets is not precluded by the provisions of this Article, provided that such different prices are charged for commercial reasons, to meet conditions of supply and demand in export markets.
Paragraph (1)(a). Governmental measures imposed to insure standards of quality and efficiency in the operation of external trade, or privileges granted for the exploitation of national natural resources but which do not empower the government to exercise control over the trading activities of the enterprise in question, do not constitute "exclusive or special privileges".
Paragraph (1)(b). A country receiving a "tied loan" is free to take this loan into account as a "commercial consideration" when purchasing requirements abroad.
Paragraph (2) The term "goods" is limited to products as understood in commercial practice, and is not intended to include the purchase or sale of services.
Paragraph (3) Negotiations which contracting parties agree to conduct under this paragraph may be directed towards the reduction of duties and other charges on imports and exports or towards the conclusion of any other mutually satisfactory arrangement consistent with the provisions of this Agreement. (See paragraph (4) of Article II and the note to that paragraph.)
Paragraph (4)(b). The term "import mark-up" in this paragraph shall represent the margin by which the price charged by the import monopoly for the imported product (exclusive of internal taxes within the purview of Article III, transportation, distribution, and other expenses incident to the purchase, sale or further processing, and a reasonable margin of profit) exceeds the landed cost.

Article XVIII. The contracting parties and the contracting parties concerned shall preserve the utmost secrecy in respect of matters arising under this Article.
Paragraphs (1) and (4) (1) When they consider whether the economy of a contracting party "can only support low standards of living", the contracting parties shall take into consideration the normal position of that economy and shall not base their determination on exceptional circumstances such as those which may result from the temporary existence of exceptionally favourable conditions for the staple export product or products of such contracting party.
(2) The phrase "in the early stages of development" is not meant to apply only to contracting parties which have just started their economic development, but also to contracting parties the economies of which are undergoing a process of industrialization to correct an excessive dependence on primary production.
Paragraphs (2), (3), (7), (13) and (22). The reference to the establishment of particular industries shall apply not only to the establishment of a new industry, but also to the establishment of a new branch of production in an existing industry and to the substantial transformation of an existing industry, and to the substantial expansion of an existing industry supplying a relatively small proportion of the domestic demand. It shall also cover the reconstruction of an industry destroyed or substantially damaged as a result of hostilities or natural disasters.
Paragraph (7)(b). A modification or withdrawal, pursuant to paragraph (7)(b), by a contracting party, other than the applicant contracting party, referred to in paragraph (7)(a), shall be made within six

months of the day on which the action is taken by the applicant contracting party, and shall become effective on the thirtieth day following the day on which such modification or withdrawal has been notified to the contracting parties.

Paragraph (11) The second sentence in paragraph (11) shall not be interpreted to mean that a contracting party is required to relax or remove restrictions if such relaxation or removal would thereupon produce conditions justifying the intensification or institution, respectively, of restrictions under paragraph 9 of Article XVIII.

Paragraph (12)(b) The date referred to in paragraph (12)(b) shall be the date determined by the contracting parties in accordance with the provisions of paragraph (4)(b) of Article XII of this Agreement.

Paragraphs (13) and (14) It is recognized that, before deciding on the introduction of a measure and notifying the contracting parties in accordance with paragraph (14), a contracting party may need a reasonable period of time to assess the competitive position of the industry concerned.

Paragraphs (15) and (16). It is understood that the contracting parties shall invite a contracting party proposing to apply a measure under Section C to consult with them pursuant to
paragraph (16) if they are requested to do so by a contracting party the trade of which would be appreciably affected by the measure in question.

Paragraphs (16), (18), (19) and (22) (1) It is understood that the contracting parties may concur in a proposed measure subject to specific conditions or limitations. If the measure as applied does not conform to the terms of the concurrence it will to that extent be deemed a measure in which the contracting parties have not concurred. In cases in which the contracting parties have concurred in a measure for a specified period, the contracting party concerned, if it finds that the maintenance of the measure for a further period of time is required to achieve the objective for which the measure was originally taken, may apply to the contracting parties for an extension of that period in accordance with the provisions and procedures of Section C or D, as the case may be.

(2) It is expected that the contracting parties will, as a rule, refrain from concurring in a measure which is likely to cause serious prejudice to exports of a commodity on which the economy of a contracting party is largely dependent.

Paragraph (18) and (22) The phrase "that the interests of other contracting parties are adequately safeguarded" is meant to provide latitude sufficient to permit consideration in each case of the most appropriate method of safeguarding those interests. The appropriate method may, for instance, take the form of an additional concession to be applied by the contracting party having recourse to Section C or D during such time as the deviation from the other Articles of the Agreement would remain in force or of the temporary suspension by any other contracting party referred to in paragraph (18) of a concession substantially equivalent to the impairment due to the introduction of the measure in question. Such contracting party would have the right to safeguard its interests through such a temporary suspension of a concession; Provided that this right will not be exercised when, in the case of a measure imposed by a contracting party coming within the scope of paragraph (4)(a), the CONTRACTING PARTIES have determined that the extent of the compensatory concession proposed was adequate.

Paragraph (19). The provisions of paragraph (19) are intended to cover the cases where an industry has been in existence beyond the "reasonable period of time" referred to in the note to paragraphs (13) and (14), and should not be so construed as to deprive a contracting party coming within the scope of paragraph (4)(a) of Article XVIII, of its right to resort to the other provisions of
Section C, including paragraph (17), with regard to a newly established industry even though it has benefited from incidental protection afforded by balance of payments import restrictions.

Paragraph (21). Any measure taken pursuant to the provisions of paragraph (21) shall be withdrawn forthwith if the action taken in accordance with paragraph (17) is withdrawn or if the contracting parties concur in the measure proposed after the expiration of the ninety-day time limit specified in paragraph (17).

Article XX. Subparagraph (h). The exception provided for in this subparagraph extends to any commodity agreement which conforms to the principles approved by the Economic and Social Council in its resolution 30 (IV) of 28 March 1947.

Article XXIV. Paragraph (9) It is understood that the provisions of Article I would require that, when a product which has been imported into the territory of a member of a customs union or free-trade area at a preferential rate of duty is re-exported to the territory of another member of such union or area, the latter member should collect a duty equal to the difference between the duty already paid and any higher duty that would be payable if the product were being imported directly into its territory.

Paragraph (11) Measures adopted by India and Pakistan in order to carry out definitive trade arrangements between them, once they have been agreed upon, might depart from particular provisions of this Agreement, but these measures would in general be consistent with the objectives of the Agreement.

Article XXVIII. The contracting parties and each contracting party concerned should arrange to conduct the negotiations and consultations with the greatest possible secrecy in order to avoid premature disclosure of details of prospective tariff changes. The contracting parties shall be informed immediately of all changes in national tariffs resulting from recourse to this Article.
Paragraph (1)(1) If the contracting parties specify a period other than a three-year period, a contracting party may act pursuant to paragraph (1) or paragraph (3)(of Article XXVIII on the first day following the expiration of such other period and, unless the contracting parties have again specified another period, subsequent periods will be three-year periods following the expiration of such specified period.
(2) The provision that on 1 January 1958, and on other days determined pursuant to paragraph (1), a contracting party "may... modify or withdraw a concession" means that on such day, and on the first day after the end of each period, the legal obligation of such contracting party under Article II is altered; it does not mean that the changes in its customs tariff should necessarily be made effective on that day. If a tariff change resulting from negotiations undertaken pursuant to this Article is delayed, the entry into force of any compensatory concessions may be similarly delayed.
(3) Not earlier than six months, nor later than three months, prior to 1 January 1958, or to the termination date of any subsequent period, a contracting party wishing to modify or withdraw any concession embodied in the appropriate Schedule, should notify the contracting parties to this effect. The contracting parties shall then determine the contracting party or contracting parties with which the negotiations or consultations referred to in paragraph (1) shall take place. Any contracting party so determined shall participate in such negotiations or consultations with the applicant contracting party with the aim of reaching agreement before the end of the period. Any extension of the assured life of the Schedules shall relate to the Schedules as modified after such negotiations, in accordance with paragraphs (1), (2), and (3) of Article XXVIII. If the contracting parties are arranging for multilateral tariff negotiations to take place within the period of six months before 1 January 1958, or before any other day determined pursuant
to paragraph (1), they shall include in the arrangements for such negotiations suitable procedures for carrying out the negotiations referred to in this paragraph.
(4) The object of providing for the participation in the negotiation of any contracting party with a principle supplying interest, in addition to any contracting party with which the concession was originally negotiated, is to ensure that a contracting party with a larger share in the trade affected by the concession than a contracting party with which the concession was originally negotiated shall have an effective opportunity to protect the contractual right which it enjoys under this Agreement. On the other hand, it is not intended that the scope of the negotiations should be such as to make negotiations and agreement under Article XXVIII unduly difficult nor to create complications in the application of this Article in the future to concessions which result from negotiations thereunder. Accordingly, the contracting parties TIES should only determine that a contracting party has a principal supplying interest if that contracting party has had, over a reasonable period of time prior to the negotiations, a larger share in the market of the applicant contracting party than a contracting party with which the concession was initially negotiated or would, in the judgement of the contracting parties S, have had such a share in the absence of discriminatory quantitative restrictions maintained by the applicant contracting party. It would therefore not be appropriate for the contracting parties to determine that more than one contracting party, or in those exceptional cases where there is near equality more than two contracting parties, had a principal supplying interest.
(5) Notwithstanding the definition of a principal supplying interest in note 4 to paragraph (1), the contracting parties may exceptionally determine that a contracting party has a principal supplying interest if the concession in question affects trade which constitutes a major part of the total exports of such contracting party.
(6) It is not intended that provision for participation in the negotiations of any contracting party with a principal supplying interest, and for consultation with any contracting party having a substantial interest in the concession which the applicant contracting party is seeking to modify or withdraw, should have the effect that it should have to pay compensation or suffer retaliation greater than the withdrawal or modification sought, judged in the light of the conditions of trade at the time of the proposed withdrawal or modification, making allowance for any discriminatory quantitative restrictions maintained by the applicant contracting party.

PART I   INTERNATIONAL LAW

(7) The expression "substantial interest" is not capable of a precise definition and accordingly may present difficulties for the contracting parties. It is, however, intended to be construed to cover only those contracting parties which have, or in the absence of discriminatory quantitative restrictions affecting their exports could reasonably be expected to have, a significant share in the market of the contracting party seeking to modify or withdraw the concession.

Paragraph (4)(1) Any request for authorization to enter into negotiations shall be accompanied by all relevant statistical and other data. A decision on such request shall be made within thirty days of its submission.

(2) It is recognized that to permit certain contracting parties, depending in large measure on a relatively small number of primary commodities and relying on the tariff as an important aid for furthering diversification of their economies or as an important source of revenue, normally to negotiate for the modification or withdrawal of concessions only under paragraph (1) of Article XXVIII, might cause them at such time to make modifications or withdrawals which in the long run would prove unnecessary. To avoid such a situation the contracting parties shall authorize any such contracting party, under paragraph (4), to enter into negotiations unless they consider this would result in, or contribute substantially towards, such an increase in tariff levels as to threaten the stability of the Schedules to this Agreement or lead to undue disturbance of international trade.

(3) It is expected that negotiations authorized under paragraph (4) for modification or withdrawal of a single item, or a very small group of items, could normally be brought to a conclusion in sixty days. It is recognized, however, that such a period will be inadequate for cases involving negotiations for the modification or withdrawal of a larger number of items and in such cases, therefore, it would be appropriate for the contracting parties to prescribe a longer period.

(4) The determination referred to in paragraph (4)(d) shall be made by the contracting parties within thirty days of the submission of the matter to them unless the applicant contracting party agrees to a longer period.

(5) In determining under paragraph (4)(d) whether an applicant contracting party has unreasonably failed to offer adequate compensation, it is understood that the contracting parties will take due account of the special position of a contracting party which has bound a high proportion of its tariffs at very low rates of duty and to this extent has less scope than other contracting parties to make compensatory adjustment.

Article XXVIII bis. Paragraph (3) It is understood that the reference to fiscal needs would include the revenues aspect of duties and particularly duties imposed primarily for revenue purpose, or duties imposed on products which can be substituted for products subject to revenue duties to prevent the avoidance of such duties.

Article XXIX. Paragraph (1) Chapters VII and VIII of the Havana Charter have been excluded from paragraph (1)because they generally deal with the organization, functions and procedures of the International Trade Organization.

Part IV. The words "developed contracting parties" and the words "less-developed contracting parties" as used in Part IV are to be understood to refer to developed and less-developed countries which are parties to the General Agreement on Tariffs and Trade.

Article XXXVI. Paragraph (1) This Article is based upon the objectives set forth in Article I as it will be amended by Section A of paragraph (1) of the Protocol Amending Part I and Articles XXIX and XXX when that Protocol enters into force.

Paragraph (4) The term "primary products" includes agricultural products, vide paragraph (2) of the note ad Article XVI, Section B.

Paragraph (5) A diversification programme would generally include the intensification of activities for the processing of primary products and the development of manufacturing industries, taking into account the situation of the particular contracting party and the world outlook for production and consumption of different commodities.

Paragraph (8) It is understood that the phrase "do not expect reciprocity" means, in accordance with the objectives set forth in this Article, that the less-developed contracting parties should not be expected, in the course of trade negotiations, to make contributions which are inconsistent with their individual development, financial and trade needs, taking into consideration past trade developments. This paragraph would apply in the event of action under Section A of Article XVIII, Article XXVIII, Article XXVIII bis (Article XXIX after the amendment set forth in Section A of paragraph (1) of the Protocol Amending Part I and Articles XXIX and XXX shall have become effective), Article XXXIII, or any other procedure under this Agreement.

Article XXXVII. Paragraph (1)(a). This paragraph would apply in the event of negotiations for reduction or elimination of tariffs or other restrictive regulations of commerce under Articles XXVIII, XXVIII bis (XXIX after the amendment set forth in Section A of paragraph (1) of the Protocol Amending Part I and Articles XXIX and XXX shall have become effective), and Article XXXIII, as well as in connection with other action to effect such reduction or elimination which contracting parties may be able to undertake.

Paragraph (3) (b). The other measures referred to in this paragraph might include steps to promote domestic structural changes, to encourage the consumption of particular products, or to introduce measures of trade promotion.

PART I   INTERNATIONAL LAW

General Agreement on Tariffs and Trade 1994

(1) The General Agreement on Tariffs and Trade 1994 ("GATT 1994") shall consist of:
(a) the provisions in the General Agreement on Tariffs and Trade, dated 30 October 1947, annexed to the Final Act Adopted at the Conclusion of the Second Session of the Preparatory Committee of the United Nations Conference on Trade and Employment (excluding the Protocol of Provisional Application), as rectified, amended or modified by the terms of legal instruments which have entered into force before the date of entry into force of the WTO Agreement;
(b) the provisions of the legal instruments set forth below that have entered into force under the GATT 1947 before the date of entry into force of the WTO Agreement:
(i) protocols and certifications relating to tariff concessions;
(ii) protocols of accession (excluding the provisions (**a**) concerning provisional application and withdrawal of provisional application and (**b**) providing that Part II of GATT 1947 shall be applied provisionally to the fullest extent not inconsistent with legislation existing on the date of the Protocol);
(iii) decisions on waivers granted under Article XXV of GATT 1947 and still in force on the date of entry into force of the WTO Agreement;
(iv) other decisions of the CONTRACTING PARTIES to GATT 1947;
(c) the Understandings set forth below:
(i) Understanding on the Interpretation of Article II:1(b) of the General Agreement on Tariffs and Trade 1994;
(ii) Understanding on the Interpretation of Article XVII of the General Agreement on Tariffs and Trade 1994;
(iii) Understanding on Balance-of-Payments Provisions of the General Agreement on Tariffs and Trade 1994;
(iv) Understanding on the Interpretation of Article XXIV of the General Agreement on Tariffs and Trade 1994;
(v) Understanding in Respect of Waivers of Obligations under the General Agreement on Tariffs and Trade 1994;
(vi) Understanding on the Interpretation of Article XXVIII of the General Agreement on Tariffs and Trade 1994; and
(d) the Marrakesh Protocol to GATT 1994.

(2) Explanatory Notes
(a) The references to "contracting party" in the provisions of GATT 1994 shall be deemed to read "Member". The references to "less-developed contracting party" and "developed contracting party" shall be deemed to read "developing country Member" and "developed country Member". The references to "Executive Secretary" shall be deemed to read "Director-General of the WTO".
(b) The references to the contracting parties acting jointly in Articles XV:1, XV:2, XV:8, XXXVIII and the Notes Ad Article XII and XVIII; and in the provisions on special exchange agreements in Articles XV:2, XV:3, XV:6, XV:7 and XV:9 of GATT 1994 shall be deemed to be references to the WTO. The other functions that the provisions of GATT 1994 assign to the contracting parties acting jointly shall be allocated by the Ministerial Conference.
(c) (i) The text of GATT 1994 shall be authentic in English, French and Spanish.
(ii) The text of GATT 1994 in the French language shall be subject to the rectifications of terms indicated in Annex A to document MTN.TNC/41.
(iii) The authentic text of GATT 1994 in the Spanish language shall be the text in Volume IV of the Basic Instruments and Selected Documents series, subject to the rectifications of terms indicated in Annex B to document MTN.TNC/41.
(3) (a) The provisions of Part II of GATT 1994 shall not apply to measures taken by a Member under specific mandatory legislation, enacted by that Member before it became a contracting party to GATT 1947, that prohibits the use, sale or lease of foreign-built or foreign-reconstructed vessels in commercial applications between points in national waters or the waters of an exclusive economic zone. This exemption applies to: (a) the continuation or prompt renewal of a non-conforming provision of such legislation; and (b) the amendment to a non-conforming provision of such legislation to the extent that the amendment does not decrease the conformity of the provision with Part II of GATT 1947. This exemption is limited to measures taken under legislation described above that is notified and specified prior to the date of entry into force of the WTO Agreement. If such legislation is subsequently modified to decrease its conformity with Part II of GATT 1994, it will no longer qualify for coverage under this paragraph.
(b) The Ministerial Conference shall review this exemption not later than five years after the date of

entry into force of the WTO Agreement and thereafter every two years for as long as the exemption is in force for the purpose of examining whether the conditions which created the need for the exemption still prevail.

(c) A Member whose measures are covered by this exemption shall annually submit a detailed statistical notification consisting of a five-year moving average of actual and expected deliveries of relevant vessels as well as additional information on the use, sale, lease or repair of relevant vessels covered by this exemption.

(d) A Member that considers that this exemption operates in such a manner as to justify a reciprocal and proportionate limitation on the use, sale, lease or repair of vessels constructed in the territory of the Member invoking the exemption shall be free to introduce such a limitation subject to prior notification to the Ministerial Conference.

(e) This exemption is without prejudice to solutions concerning specific aspects of the legislation covered by this exemption negotiated in sectoral agreements or in other fora.

PART I INTERNATIONAL LAW

Agreement Establishing the World Trade Organization
Marrakesh, 15 April 1994

The Parties to this Agreement,
Recognizing that their relations in the field of trade and economic endeavour should be conducted with a view to raising standards of living, ensuring full employment and a large and steadily growing volume of real income and effective demand, and expanding the production of and trade in goods and services, while allowing for the optimal use of the world's resources in accordance with the objective of sustainable development, seeking both to protect and preserve the environment and to enhance the means for doing so in a manner consistent with their respective needs and concerns at different levels of economic development,
Recognizing further that there is need for positive efforts designed to ensure that developing countries, and especially the least developed among them, secure a share in the growth in international trade commensurate with the needs of their economic development,
Being desirous of contributing to these objectives by entering into reciprocal and mutually advantageous arrangements directed to the substantial reduction of tariffs and other barriers to trade and to the elimination of discriminatory treatment in international trade relations,
Resolved, therefore, to develop an integrated, more viable and durable multilateral trading system encompassing the General Agreement on Tariffs and Trade, the results of past trade liberalization efforts, and all of the results of the Uruguay Round of Multilateral Trade Negotiations,
Determined to preserve the basic principles and to further the objectives underlying this multilateral trading system,
Agree as follows:

Article I. Establishment of the Organization
The World Trade Organization (hereinafter referred to as "the WTO") is hereby established.

Article II. Scope of the WTO
(1) The WTO shall provide the common institutional framework for the conduct of trade relations among its Members in matters related to the agreements and associated legal instruments included in the Annexes to this Agreement.
(2) The agreements and associated legal instruments included in Annexes 1, 2 and 3 (hereinafter referred to as "Multilateral Trade Agreements") are integral parts of this Agreement, binding on all Members.
(3) The agreements and associated legal instruments included in Annex 4 (hereinafter referred to as "Plurilateral Trade Agreements") are also part of this Agreement for those Members that have accepted them, and are binding on those Members. The Plurilateral Trade Agreements do not create either obligations or rights for Members that have not accepted them.
(4) The General Agreement on Tariffs and Trade 1994 as specified in Annex 1A (hereinafter referred to as "GATT 1994") is legally distinct from the General Agreement on Tariffs and Trade, dated 30 October 1947, annexed to the Final Act Adopted at the Conclusion of the Second Session of the Preparatory Committee of the United Nations Conference on Trade and Employment, as subsequently rectified, amended or modified (hereinafter referred to as "GATT 1947").

Article III. Functions of the WTO
(1) The WTO shall facilitate the implementation, administration and operation, and further the objectives, of this Agreement and of the Multilateral Trade Agreements, and shall also provide the framework for the implementation, administration and operation of the Plurilateral Trade Agreements.
(2) The WTO shall provide the forum for negotiations among its Members concerning their multilateral trade relations in matters dealt with under the agreements in the Annexes to this Agreement. The WTO may also provide a forum for further negotiations among its Members concerning their multilateral trade relations, and a framework for the implementation of the results of such negotiations, as may be decided by the Ministerial Conference.
(3) The WTO shall administer the Understanding on Rules and Procedures Governing the Settlement of Disputes (hereinafter referred to as the "Dispute Settlement Understanding" or "DSU") in Annex 2 to this Agreement.
(4) The WTO shall administer the Trade Policy Review Mechanism (hereinafter referred to as the "TPRM") provided for in Annex 3 to this Agreement.
(5) With a view to achieving greater coherence in global economic policy-making, the WTO shall cooperate, as appropriate, with the International Monetary Fund and with the International Bank for Reconstruction and Development and its affiliated agencies.

Article IV. Structure of the WTO

(1) There shall be a Ministerial Conference composed of representatives of all the Members, which shall meet at least once every two years. The Ministerial Conference shall carry out the functions of the WTO and take actions necessary to this effect. The Ministerial Conference shall have the authority to take decisions on all matters under any of the Multilateral Trade Agreements, if so requested by a Member, in accordance with the specific requirements for decision-making in this Agreement and in the relevant Multilateral Trade Agreement.

(2) There shall be a General Council composed of representatives of all the Members, which shall meet as appropriate. In the intervals between meetings of the Ministerial Conference, its functions shall be conducted by the General Council. The General Council shall also carry out the functions assigned to it by this Agreement. The General Council shall establish its rules of procedure and approve the rules of procedure for the Committees provided for in paragraph (7).

(3) The General Council shall convene as appropriate to discharge the responsibilities of the Dispute Settlement Body provided for in the Dispute Settlement Understanding. The Dispute Settlement Body may have its own chairman and shall establish such rules of procedure as it deems necessary for the fulfilment of those responsibilities.

(4) The General Council shall convene as appropriate to discharge the responsibilities of the Trade Policy Review Body provided for in the TPRM. The Trade Policy Review Body may have its own chairman and shall establish such rules of procedure as it deems necessary for the fulfilment of those responsibilities.

(5) There shall be a Council for Trade in Goods, a Council for Trade in Services and a Council for Trade-Related Aspects of Intellectual Property Rights (hereinafter referred to as the "Council for TRIPS"), which shall operate under the general guidance of the General Council. The Council for Trade in Goods shall oversee the functioning of the Multilateral Trade Agreements in Annex 1A. The Council for Trade in Services shall oversee the functioning of the General Agreement on Trade in Services
(hereinafter referred to as "GATS"). The Council for TRIPS shall oversee the functioning of the Agreement on Trade-Related Aspects of Intellectual Property Rights (hereinafter referred to as the "Agreement on TRIPS"). These Councils shall carry out the functions assigned to them by their respective agreements and by the General Council. They shall establish their respective rules of procedure subject to the approval of the General Council. Membership in these Councils shall be open to representatives of all Members. These Councils shall meet as necessary to carry out their functions.

(6) The Council for Trade in Goods, the Council for Trade in Services and the Council for TRIPS shall establish subsidiary bodies as required. These subsidiary bodies shall establish their respective rules of procedure subject to the approval of their respective Councils.

(7) The Ministerial Conference shall establish a Committee on Trade and Development, a Committee on Balance-of-Payments Restrictions and a Committee on Budget, Finance and Administration, which shall carry out the functions assigned to them by this Agreement and by the Multilateral Trade Agreements, and any additional functions assigned to them by the General Council, and may establish such additional Committees with such functions as it may deem appropriate. As part of its functions, the Committee on Trade and Development shall periodically review the special provisions in the Multilateral Trade Agreements in favour of the least-developed country Members and report to the General Council for appropriate action. Membership in these Committees shall be open to representatives of all Members.

(8) The bodies provided for under the Plurilateral Trade Agreements shall carry out the functions assigned to them under those Agreements and shall operate within the institutional framework of the WTO. These bodies shall keep the General Council informed of their activities on a regular basis.

Article V. Relations with Other Organizations
(1) The General Council shall make appropriate arrangements for effective cooperation with other intergovernmental organizations that have responsibilities related to those of the WTO. (2) The General Council may make appropriate arrangements for consultation and cooperation with non-governmental organizations concerned with matters related to those of the WTO.

Article VI. The Secretariat
(1) There shall be a Secretariat of the WTO (hereinafter referred to as "the Secretariat") headed by a Director-General.
(2) The Ministerial Conference shall appoint the Director-General and adopt regulations setting out the powers, duties, conditions of service and term of office of the Director-General.
(3) The Director-General shall appoint the members of the staff of the Secretariat and determine their duties and conditions of service in accordance with regulations adopted by the Ministerial Conference.
(4) The responsibilities of the Director-General and of the staff of the Secretariat shall be exclusively

international in character. In the discharge of their duties, the Director-General and the staff of the Secretariat shall not seek or accept instructions from any government or any other authority external to the WTO. They shall refrain from any action which might adversely reflect on their position as international officials. The Members of the WTO shall respect the international character of the responsibilities of the Director-General and of the staff of the Secretariat and shall not seek to influence them in the discharge of their duties.

Article VII. Budget and Contributions

(1) The Director-General shall present to the Committee on Budget, Finance and Administration the annual budget estimate and financial statement of the WTO. The Committee on Budget, Finance and Administration shall review the annual budget estimate and the financial statement presented by the Director-General and make recommendations thereon to the General Council. The annual budget estimate shall be subject to approval by the General Council.

(2) The Committee on Budget, Finance and Administration shall propose to the General Council financial regulations which shall include provisions setting out: (a) the scale of contributions apportioning the expenses of the WTO among its Members; and (b) the measures to be taken in respect of Members in arrears. The financial regulations shall be based, as far as practicable, on the regulations and practices of GATT 1947.

(3) The General Council shall adopt the financial regulations and the annual budget estimate by a two-thirds majority comprising more than half of the Members of the WTO.

(4) Each Member shall promptly contribute to the WTO its share in the expenses of the WTO in accordance with the financial regulations adopted by the General Council.

Article VIII. Status of the WTO

(1) The WTO shall have legal personality, and shall be accorded by each of its Members such legal capacity as may be necessary for the exercise of its functions.

(2) The WTO shall be accorded by each of its Members such privileges and immunities as are necessary for the exercise of its functions.

(3) The officials of the WTO and the representatives of the Members shall similarly be accorded by each of its Members such privileges and immunities as are necessary for the independent exercise of their functions in connection with the WTO.

(4) The privileges and immunities to be accorded by a Member to the WTO, its officials, and the representatives of its Members shall be similar to the privileges and immunities stipulated in the Convention on the Privileges and Immunities of the Specialized Agencies, approved by the General Assembly of the United Nations on 21 November 1947.

(5) The WTO may conclude a headquarters agreement.

Article IX. Decision-Making

(1) The WTO shall continue the practice of decision-making by consensus followed under GATT 1947.1 Except as otherwise provided, where a decision cannot be arrived at by consensus, the matter at issue shall be decided by voting. At meetings of the Ministerial Conference and the General Council, each Member of the WTO shall have one vote. Where the European Communities exercise their right to vote, they shall have a number of votes equal to the number of their member States which are Members of the WTO. Decisions of the Ministerial Conference and the General Council shall be taken by a majority of the votes cast, unless otherwise provided in this Agreement or in the relevant Multilateral Trade Agreement.

(2) The Ministerial Conference and the General Council shall have the exclusive authority to adopt interpretations of this Agreement and of the Multilateral Trade Agreements. In the case of an interpretation of a Multilateral Trade Agreement in Annex 1, they shall exercise their authority on the basis of a recommendation by the Council overseeing the functioning of that Agreement. The decision to adopt an interpretation shall be taken by a three-fourths majority of the Members. This paragraph shall not be used in a manner that would undermine the amendment provisions in Article X.

(3) In exceptional circumstances, the Ministerial Conference may decide to waive an obligation imposed on a Member by this Agreement or any of the Multilateral Trade Agreements, provided that any such decision shall be taken by three fourths of the Members unless otherwise provided for in this paragraph.

(a) A request for a waiver concerning this Agreement shall be submitted to the Ministerial Conference for consideration pursuant to the practice of decision-making by consensus. The Ministerial Conference shall establish a time-period, which shall not exceed 90 days, to consider the request. If consensus is not reached during the time-period, any decision to grant a waiver shall be taken by three fourths of the Members.

(b) A request for a waiver concerning the Multilateral Trade Agreements in

Annexes 1A or 1B or 1C and their annexes shall be submitted initially to the Council for Trade in Goods, the Council for Trade in Services or the Council for TRIPS, respectively, for consideration during a time-period which shall not exceed 90 days. At the end of the time-period, the relevant Council shall submit a report to the Ministerial Conference.
(4) A decision by the Ministerial Conference granting a waiver shall state the exceptional circumstances justifying the decision, the terms and conditions governing the application of the waiver, and the date on which the waiver shall terminate. Any waiver granted for a period of more than one year shall be reviewed by the Ministerial Conference not later than one year after it is granted, and thereafter annually until the waiver terminates. In each review, the Ministerial Conference shall examine whether the exceptional circumstances justifying the waiver still exist and whether the terms and conditions attached to the waiver have been met. The Ministerial Conference, on the basis of the annual review, may extend, modify or terminate the waiver.
(5) Decisions under a Plurilateral Trade Agreement, including any decisions on interpretations and waivers, shall be governed by the provisions of that Agreement.

Article X. Amendments
(1) Any Member of the WTO may initiate a proposal to amend the provisions of this Agreement or the Multilateral Trade Agreements in Annex 1 by submitting such proposal to the Ministerial Conference. The Councils listed in paragraph (5) of Article IV may also submit to the Ministerial Conference proposals to amend the provisions of the corresponding Multilateral Trade Agreements in Annex 1 the functioning of which they oversee. Unless the Ministerial Conference decides on a longer period, for a period of 90 days after the proposal has been tabled formally at the Ministerial Conference any decision by the Ministerial Conference to submit the proposed amendment to the Members for acceptance shall be taken by consensus. Unless the provisions of paragraphs (2), (5) or (6) apply, that decision shall specify whether the provisions of paragraphs (3) or (4) shall apply. If consensus is reached, the Ministerial Conference shall forthwith submit the proposed amendment to the Members for acceptance. If consensus is not reached at a meeting of the Ministerial Conference within the established period, the Ministerial Conference shall decide by a two-thirds majority of the Members whether to submit the proposed amendment to the Members for acceptance. Except as provided in paragraphs (2), (5) and (6), the provisions of paragraph (3) shall apply to the proposed amendment, unless the Ministerial Conference decides by a three-fourths majority of the Members that the provisions of paragraph (4) shall apply.
(2) Amendments to the provisions of this Article and to the provisions of the following Articles shall take effect only upon acceptance by all Members:
Article IX of this Agreement;
Articles I and II of GATT 1994;
Article II:1 of GATS;
Article 4 of the Agreement on TRIPS.
(3) Amendments to provisions of this Agreement, or of the Multilateral Trade Agreements in Annexes 1A and 1C, other than those listed in paragraphs (2) and (6), of a nature that would alter the rights and obligations of the Members, shall take effect for the Members that have accepted them upon acceptance by two thirds of the Members and thereafter for each other Member upon acceptance by it. The Ministerial Conference may decide by a three-fourths majority of the Members that any amendment made effective under this paragraph is of such a nature that any Member which has not accepted it within a period specified by the Ministerial Conference in each case shall be free to withdraw from the WTO or to remain a Member with the consent of the Ministerial Conference.
(4) Amendments to provisions of this Agreement or of the Multilateral Trade Agreements in Annexes 1A and 1C, other than those listed in paragraphs (2) and (6), of a nature that would not alter the rights and obligations of the Members, shall take effect for all Members upon acceptance by two thirds of the Members.
(5) Except as provided in paragraph (2) above, amendments to Parts I, II and III of GATS and the respective annexes shall take effect for the Members that have accepted them upon acceptance by two thirds of the Members and thereafter for each Member upon acceptance by it. The Ministerial Conference may decide by a three-fourths majority of the Members that any amendment made effective under the preceding provision is of such a nature that any Member which has not accepted it within a period specified by the Ministerial Conference in each case shall be free to withdraw from the WTO or to remain a Member with the consent of the Ministerial Conference. Amendments to Parts IV, V and VI of GATS and the respective annexes shall take effect for all Members upon acceptance by two thirds of the Members.
(6) Notwithstanding the other provisions of this Article, amendments to the Agreement on TRIPS meeting the requirements of paragraph (2) of Article 71 thereof may be adopted by the Ministerial

Conference without further formal acceptance process.

(7) Any Member accepting an amendment to this Agreement or to a Multilateral Trade Agreement in Annex 1 shall deposit an instrument of acceptance with the Director-General of the WTO within the period of acceptance specified by the Ministerial Conference.

(8) Any Member of the WTO may initiate a proposal to amend the provisions of the Multilateral Trade Agreements in Annexes 2 and 3 by submitting such proposal to the Ministerial Conference. The decision to approve amendments to the Multilateral Trade Agreement in Annex 2 shall be made by consensus and these amendments shall take effect for all Members upon approval by the Ministerial Conference. Decisions to approve amendments to the Multilateral Trade Agreement in Annex 3 shall take effect for all Members upon approval by the Ministerial Conference.

(9) The Ministerial Conference, upon the request of the Members parties to a trade agreement, may decide exclusively by consensus to add that agreement to Annex 4. The Ministerial Conference, upon the request of the Members parties to a Plurilateral Trade Agreement, may decide to delete that Agreement from Annex 4.

(10) Amendments to a Plurilateral Trade Agreement shall be governed by the provisions of that Agreement.

Article XI. Original Membership

(1) The contracting parties to GATT 1947 as of the date of entry into force of this Agreement, and the European Communities, which accept this Agreement and the Multilateral Trade Agreements and for which Schedules of Concessions and Commitments are annexed to GATT 1994 and for which Schedules of Specific Commitments are annexed to GATS shall become original Members of the WTO.

(2) The least-developed countries recognized as such by the United Nations will only be required to undertake commitments and concessions to the extent consistent with their individual development, financial and trade needs or their administrative and institutional capabilities.

Article XII. Accession

(1) Any State or separate customs territory possessing full autonomy in the conduct of its external commercial relations and of the other matters provided for in this Agreement and the Multilateral Trade Agreements may accede to this Agreement, on terms to be agreed between it and the WTO. Such accession shall apply to this Agreement and the Multilateral Trade Agreements annexed thereto.

(2) Decisions on accession shall be taken by the Ministerial Conference. The Ministerial Conference shall approve the agreement on the terms of accession by a two-thirds majority of the Members of the WTO.

(3) Accession to a Plurilateral Trade Agreement shall be governed by the provisions of that Agreement.

Article XIII. Non-Application of Multilateral Trade Agreements between Particular Members

(1) This Agreement and the Multilateral Trade Agreements in Annexes 1 and 2 shall not apply as between any Member and any other Member if either of the Members, at the time either becomes a Member, does not consent to such application.

(2) Paragraph (1) may be invoked between original Members of the WTO which were contracting parties to GATT 1947 only where Article XXXV of that Agreement had been invoked earlier and was effective as between those contracting parties at the time of entry into force for them of this Agreement.

(3) Paragraph (1) shall apply between a Member and another Member which has acceded under Article XII only if the Member not consenting to the application has so notified the Ministerial Conference before the approval of the agreement on the terms of accession by the Ministerial Conference.

(4) The Ministerial Conference may review the operation of this Article in particular cases at the request of any Member and make appropriate recommendations. 5. Non-application of a Plurilateral Trade Agreement between parties to that Agreement shall be governed by the provisions of that Agreement

Article XIV. Acceptance, Entry into Force and Deposit

(1) This Agreement shall be open for acceptance, by signature or otherwise, by contracting parties to GATT 1947, and the European Communities, which are eligible to become original Members of the WTO in accordance with Article XI of this Agreement. Such acceptance shall apply to this Agreement and the Multilateral Trade Agreements annexed hereto. This Agreement and the Multilateral Trade Agreements annexed hereto shall enter into force on the date determined by Ministers in accordance with paragraph (3) of the Final Act Embodying the Results of the Uruguay Round of Multilateral Trade Negotiations and shall remain open for acceptance for a period of two years following that date unless the Ministers decide otherwise. An acceptance following the entry into force

of this Agreement shall enter into force on the 30th day following the date of such acceptance.
(2) A Member which accepts this Agreement after its entry into force shall implement those concessions and obligations in the Multilateral Trade Agreements that are to be implemented over a period of time starting with the entry into force of this Agreement as if it had accepted this Agreement on the date of its entry into force.
(3) Until the entry into force of this Agreement, the text of this Agreement and the Multilateral Trade Agreements shall be deposited with the Director-General to the contracting parties to GATT 1947. The Director-General shall promptly furnish a certified true copy of this Agreement and the Multilateral Trade Agreements, and a notification of each acceptance thereof, to each government and the European Communities having accepted this Agreement. This Agreement and the Multilateral Trade Agreements, and any amendments thereto, shall, upon the entry into force of this Agreement, be deposited with the Director-General of the WTO.
(4) The acceptance and entry into force of a Plurilateral Trade Agreement shall be governed by the provisions of that Agreement. Such Agreements shall be deposited with the Director-General to the contracting parties to GATT 1947. Upon the entry into force of this Agreement, such Agreements shall be deposited with the Director-General of the WTO.

Article XV. Withdrawal
(1) Any Member may withdraw from this Agreement. Such withdrawal shall apply both to this Agreement and the Multilateral Trade Agreements and shall take effect upon the expiration of six months from the date on which written notice of withdrawal is received by the Director-General of the WTO.
(2) Withdrawal from a Plurilateral Trade Agreement shall be governed by the provisions of that Agreement.

Article XVI. Miscellaneous Provisions
(1) Except as otherwise provided under this Agreement or the Multilateral Trade Agreements, the WTO shall be guided by the decisions, procedures and customary practices followed by the contracting parties to GATT 1947 and the bodies established in the framework of GATT 1947.
(2) To the extent practicable, the Secretariat of GATT 1947 shall become the Secretariat of the WTO, and the Director-General to the contracting parties to GATT 1947, until such time as the Ministerial Conference has appointed a Director-General in accordance with
paragraph (2) of Article VI of this Agreement, shall serve as Director-General of the WTO.
(3) In the event of a conflict between a provision of this Agreement and a provision of any of the Multilateral Trade Agreements, the provision of this Agreement shall prevail to the extent of the conflict.
(4) Each Member shall ensure the conformity of its laws, regulations and administrative procedures with its obligations as provided in the annexed Agreements.
(5) No reservations may be made in respect of any provision of this Agreement. Reservations in respect of any of the provisions of the Multilateral Trade Agreements may only be made to the extent provided for in those Agreements. Reservations in respect of a provision of a Plurilateral Trade Agreement shall be governed by the provisions of that Agreement.
(6) This Agreement shall be registered in accordance with the provisions of Article 102 of the Charter of the United Nations.
DONE at Marrakesh this fifteenth day of April one thousand nine hundred and ninety-four, in a single copy, in the English, French and Spanish languages, each text being authentic.
Explanatory Notes:
The terms "country" or "countries" as used in this Agreement and the Multilateral Trade Agreements are to be understood to include any separate customs territory Member of the WTO.
In the case of a separate customs territory Member of the WTO, where an expression in this Agreement and the Multilateral Trade Agreements is qualified by the term "national", such expression shall be read as pertaining to that customs territory, unless otherwise specified.

PART I   INTERNATIONAL LAW

UN General Assembly Resolution A/RES/377 (V) "Uniting for Peace", 3 November, 1950

The General Assembly,
Recognizing that the first two stated Purposes of the United Nations are:
"To maintain international peace and security, and to that end: to take effective collective measures for the prevention and removal of threats to the peace, and for the suppression of acts of aggression or other breaches of the peace, and to bring about by peaceful means, and in conformity with the principles of justice and international law, adjustment or settlement of international disputes or situations which might lead to a breach of the peace", and
"To develop friendly relations among nations based on respect for the principle of equal rights and self-determination of peoples, and to take other appropriate measures to strengthen universal peace",
Reaffirming that it remains the primary duty of all Members of the United Nations, when involved in an international dispute, to seek settlement of such a dispute by peaceful means through the procedures laid down in Chapter VI of the Charter, and recalling the successful achievements of the United Nations in this regard on a number of previous occasions,
Finding that international tension exists on a dangerous scale,
Recalling its resolution 290 (IV) entitled "Essentials of peace", which states that disregard of the Principles of the Charter of the United Nations is primarily responsible for the continuance of international tension, and desiring to contribute further to the objectives of that resolution,
Reaffirming the importance of the exercise by the Security Council of its primary responsibility for the maintenance of international peace and security, and the duty of the permanent members to seek unanimity and to exercise restraint in the use of the veto,
Reaffirming that the initiative in negotiating the agreements for armed forces provided for in Article 43 of the Charter belongs to the Security Council, and desiring to ensure that, pending the conclusion of such agreements, the United Nations has at its disposal means for maintaining international peace and security,
Conscious that failure of the Security Council to discharge its responsibilities on behalf of all the Member States, particularly those responsibilities referred to in the two preceding paragraphs, does not relieve Member States of their obligations or the United Nations of its responsibility under the Charter to maintain international peace and security,
Recognizing in particular that such failure does not deprive the General Assembly of its rights or relieve it of its responsibilities under the Charter in regard to the maintenance of international peace and security,
Recognizing that discharge by the General Assembly of its responsibilities in these respects calls for possibilities of observation which would ascertain the facts and expose aggressors; for the existence of armed forces which could be used collectively; and for the possibility of timely recommendation by the General Assembly to Members of the United Nations for collective action which, to be effective, should be prompt,

A

(1) Resolves that if the Security Council, because of lack of unanimity of the permanent members, fails to exercise its primary responsibility for the maintenance of international peace and security in any case where there appears to be a threat to the peace, breach of the peace, or act of aggression, the General Assembly shall consider the matter immediately with a view to making appropriate recommendations to Members for collective measures, including in the case of a breach of the peace or act of aggression the use of armed force when necessary, to maintain or restore international peace and security. If not in session at the time, the General Assembly may meet in emergency special session within twenty-four hours of the request therefor. Such emergency special session shall be called if requested by the Security Council on the vote of any seven members, or by a majority of the Members of the United Nations;
(2) Adopts for this purpose the amendments to its rules of procedure set forth in the annex to the present resolution;

B

(3) Establishes a Peace Observation Commission which, for the calendar years 1951 and 1952, shall be composed of fourteen Members, namely: China, Colombia, Czechoslovakia, France, India, Iraq, Israel, New Zealand, Pakistan, Sweden, the Union of Soviet Socialist Republics, the United Kingdom of Great Britain and Northern Ireland, the United States of America and Uruguay, and which could observe and report on the situation in any area where there exists international tension the continuance of which is likely to endanger the maintenance of international peace and security. Upon the invitation or with the consent of the State into whose territory the Commission would go, the General

RESOLUTION 377 A (V) UNITING FOR PEACE

Assembly, or the Interim Committee when the Assembly is not in session, may utilize the Commission if the Security Council is not exercising the functions assigned to it by the Charter with respect to the matter in question. Decisions to utilize the Commission shall be made on the affirmative vote of two-thirds of the members present and voting. The Security Council may also utilize the Commission in accordance with its authority under the Charter;

(4) Decides that the Commission shall have authority in its discretion to appoint sub-commissions and to utilize the services of observers to assist it in the performance of its functions;

(5) Recommends to all governments and authorities that they co-operate with the Commission and assist it in the performance of its functions;

(6) Requests the Secretary-General to provide the necessary staff and facilities, utilizing, where directed by the Commission, the United Nations Panel of Field Observers envisaged in General Assembly resolution 297 B (IV);

C

(7) Invites each Member of the United Nations to survey its resources in order to determine the nature and scope of the assistance it may be in a position to render in support of any recommendations of the Security Council or of the General Assembly for the restoration of international peace and security;

(8) Recommends to the States Members of the United Nations that each Member maintain within its national armed forces elements so trained, organized and equipped that they could promptly be made available, in accordance with its constitutional processes, for service as a United Nations unit or units, upon recommendation by the Security Council or the General Assembly, without prejudice to the use of such elements in exercise of the right of individual or collective self-defence recognized in Article 51 of the Charter;

(9) Invites the Members of the United Nations to inform the Collective Measures Committee provided for in paragraph (11) as soon as possible of the measures taken in implementation of the preceding paragraph;

(10) Requests the Secretary-General to appoint, with the approval of the Committee provided for in paragraph (11), a panel of military experts who could be made available, on request, to Member States wishing to obtain technical advice regarding the organization, training, and equipment for prompt service as United Nations units or the elements referred to in paragraph (8);

D

(11) Establishes a Collective Measures Committee consisting of fourteen Members, namely: Australia, Belgium, Brazil, Burma, Canada, Egypt, France, Mexico, Philippines, Turkey, the United Kingdom of Great Britain and Northern Ireland, the United States of America, Venezuela and Yugoslavia, and directs the Committee, in consultation with the Secretary-General and with such Member States as the Committee finds appropriate, to study and make a report to the Security Council and the General Assembly, not later than 1 September 1951, on methods, including those in section C of the present resolution, which might be used to maintain and strengthen international peace and security in accordance with the Purposes and Principles of the Charter, taking account of collective self-defence and regional arrangements (Articles 51 and 52 of the Charter);

(12) Recommends to all Member States that they co-operate with the Committee and assist it in the performance of its functions;

(13) Requests the Secretary-General to furnish the staff and facilities necessary for the effective accomplishment of the purposes set forth in sections C and D of the present resolution;

E

(14) Is fully conscious that, in adopting the proposals set forth above, enduring peace will not be secured solely by collective security arrangements against breaches of international peace and acts of aggression but that a genuine and lasting peace depends also upon the observance of all the Principles and Purposes established in the Charter of the United Nations, upon the implementation of the resolutions of the Security Council, the General Assembly and other principal organs of the United Nations intended to achieve the maintenance of international peace and security, and especially upon respect for and observance of human rights and fundamental freedoms for all and on the establishment and maintenance of conditions of economic and social well-being in all countries; and accordingly

(15) Urges Member States to respect fully, and to intensify, joint action, in co-operation with the United Nations, to develop and stimulate universal respect for and observance of human rights and fundamental freedoms, and to intensify individual and collective efforts to achieve conditions of economic stability and social progress, particularly through the development of under-developed countries and areas.

PART I   INTERNATIONAL LAW

Annex

The rules of procedure of the General Assembly are amended in the following respects:

(1) The present text of rule 8 shall become paragraph (a) of that rule, and a new paragraph (b) shall be added to read as follows:

"Emergency special sessions pursuant to resolution 377 A (V) shall be convened within twenty-four hours of the receipt by the Secretary-General of a request for such a session from the Security Council, on the vote of any seven members thereof, or of a request from a majority of the Members of the United Nations expressed by vote in the Interim Committee or otherwise, or of the concurrence of a majority of Members as provided in rule 9."

(2) The present text of rule 9 shall become paragraph (a) of that rule and a new paragraph (b) shall be added to read as follows:

"This rule shall apply also to a request by any Member for an emergency special session pursuant to resolution 377 A (V). In such a case the Secretary-General shall communicate with other Members by the most expeditious means of communication available."

(3) Rule 10 is amended by adding at the end thereof the following:

"... In the case of an emergency special session convened pursuant to rule 8 (b), the Secretary-General shall notify the Members of the United Nations at least twelve hours in advance of the opening of the session."

(4) Rule 16 is amended by adding at the end thereof the following:

"... The provisional agenda of an emergency special session shall be communicated to the Members of the United Nations simultaneously with the communication summoning the session."

(5) Rule 19 is amended by adding at the end thereof the following:

"... During an emergency special session additional items concerning the matters dealt with in resolution 377 A (V) may be added to the agenda by a two-thirds majority of the Members present and voting."

(6) There is added a new rule to precede rule 65 to read as follows:

"Notwithstanding the provisions of any other rule and unless the General Assembly decides otherwise, the Assembly, in case of an emergency special session shall convene in plenary session only and proceed directly to consider the item proposed for consideration in the request for the holding of the session, without previous reference to the General Committee or to any other Committee; the President and Vice-Presidents for such emergency special sessions shall be, respectively, the Chairman of those delegations from which were elected the President and Vice-Presidents of the previous session."

302nd plenary meeting,
3 November 1950

RESOLUTION 3314 (XXIX) DEFINITION OF AGGRESSION

UN General Assembly Resolution A/RES/3314 (XXIX) "Definition of Aggression"
14 December 1974

The General Assembly,
Having considered the report of the Special Committee on the Question of Defining Aggression, established pursuant to its resolution 2330(XXII) of 18 December 1967, covering the work of its seventh session held from 11 March to 12 April 1974, including the draft Definition of Aggression adopted by the Special Committee by consensus and recommended for adoption by the General Assembly,
Deeply, convinced that the adoption of the Definition of Aggression would contribute to the strengthening of international peace and security,

(1) Approves the Definition of Aggression, the text of which is annexed to the present resolution;
(2) Expresses its appreciation to the Special Committee on the Question of Defining Aggression for its work which resulted in the elaboration of the Definition of Aggression;
(3) Calls upon all States to refrain from all acts of aggression and other uses of force contrary to the Charter of the United Nations and the Declaration on Principles of International Law concerning Friendly Relations and Cooperation among States in accordance with the Charter of the United Nations;
(4) Calls the attention of the Security Council to the Definition of Aggression, as set out below, and recommends that it should, as appropriate, take account of that Definition as guidance in determination, in accordance with the Charter, the existence of an act of aggression.
2319th plenary meeting
14 December 1974

Annex. Definition of Aggression

The General Assembly,
Basing itself on the fact that one of the fundamental purposes of the United Nations is to maintain international peace and security and to take effective collective measures for the prevention and removal of threats to the peace, and for the suppression of acts of aggression or other breaches of the peace,
Recalling that the Security Council, in accordance with Article 39 of the Charter of the United Nations, shall determine the existence of any threat to the peace, breach of the peace or act of aggression and shall make recommendations, or decide what measures shall be taken in accordance with Articles 41 and 42, to maintain or restore international peace and security
Recalling also the duty of States under the Charter to settle their international disputes by peaceful means in order not to endanger international peace, security and justice,
Bearing in mind that nothing in this Definition shall be interpreted as in any way affecting the scope of the provisions of the Charter with respect to the functions and powers of the organs of the United Nations,
Considering also that, since aggression is the most serious and dangerous form of the illegal use of force, being fraught, in the conditions created by the existence of all types of weapons of mass destruction, with the possible threat of a world conflict and all its catastrophic consequences, aggression should be defined at the present stage,
Reaffirming the duty of States not to use armed force to deprive peoples of their right to self-determination, freedom and independence, or to disrupt territorial Integrity,
Reaffirming also that the territory of a State shall not be violated by being the object, even temporarily, of military occupation or of other measures of force taken by another State in contravention of the Charter, and that it shall not be the object of acquisition by another State resulting from such measures or the threat thereof,
Reaffirming also the provisions of the Declaration on Principles of Internationa lLaw concerning Friendly Relations and Cooperation among States in accordance with the Charter of the United Nations,
Convinced that the adoption of a definition of aggression ought to have the effect of deterring a potential aggressor, would simplify the determination of acts of aggression and the implementation of measures to suppress them and would also facilitate the protection of the rights and lawful interests of, and the rendering of assistance to, the victim,
Believing that, although the question whether an act of aggression has been committed must be considered in the light of all the circumstances of each particular case, it is nevertheless desirable to formulate basic principles as guidance for such determination,

PART I   INTERNATIONAL LAW

Adopts the following Definition of Aggression:

Article I. Aggression is the use of armed force by a State against the sovereignty, territorial integrity or political independence of another State, or in any other manner inconsistent with the Charter of the United Nations, as set out in this Definition.
Explanatory note: In this Definition the term "State":
(a) Is used without prejudice to questions of recognition or to whether a State is a member of the United Nations;
(b) Includes the concept of a "group of States" where appropriate.

Article 2. The First use of armed force by a State in contravention of the Charter shall constitute prima facie evidence of an act of aggression although the Security Council may, in conformity with the Charter, conclude that a determination that an act of aggression has been committed would not be justified in the light of other relevant circumstances, including the fact that the acts concerned or their consequences are not of sufficient gravity.

Article 3. Any of the following acts, regardless of a declaration of war, shall, subject to and in accordance with the provisions of article 2, qualify as an act of aggression:
(a) The invasion or attack by the armed forces of a State of the territory of another State, or any military occupation, however temporary, resulting from such invasion or attack, or any annexation by the use of force of the territory of another State or part thereof,
(b) Bombardment by the armed forces of a State against the territory of another State or the use of any weapons by a State against the territory of another State;
(c) The blockade of the ports or coasts of a State by the armed forces of another State;
(d) An attack by the armed forces of a State on the land, sea or air forces, or marine and air fleets of another State;
(e) The use of armed forces of one State which are within the territory of another State with the agreement of the receiving State, in contravention of the conditions provided for in the agreement or any extension of their presence in such territory beyond the termination of the agreement;
(f) The action of a State in allowing its territory, which it has placed at the disposal of another State, to be used by that other State for perpetrating an act of aggression against a third State;
(g) The sending by or on behalf of a State of armed bands, groups, irregulars or mercenaries, which carry out acts of armed force against another State of such gravity as to amount to the acts listed above, or its substantial involvement therein.

Article 4. The acts enumerated above are not exhaustive and the Security Council may determine that other acts constitute aggression under the provisions of the Charter.

Article 5. (1) No consideration of whatever nature, whether political, economic, military or otherwise, may serve as a justification for aggression.
(2) A war of aggression is a crime against international peace. Aggression gives rise to international responsibility.
(3) No territorial acquisition or special advantage resulting from aggression is or shall be recognized as lawful.

Article 6. Nothing in this Definition shall be construed as in any way enlarging or diminishing the scope of the Charter, including its provisions concerning cases in which the use of force is lawful.

Article 7. Nothing in this Definition, and in particular article 3, could in any way prejudice the right to self-determination, freedom and independence, as derived from the Charter, of peoples forcibly deprived of that right and referred to in the Declaration on Principles of International Law concerning Friendly Relations and Cooperation among States in accordance with the Charter of the United Nations, particularly peoples under colonial and racist regimes or other forms of alien domination: nor the right of these peoples to struggle to that end and to seek and receive support, in accordance with the principles of the Charter and in conformity with the above-mentioned Declaration.

Article 8. In their interpretation and application the above provisions are interrelated and each provision should be construed in the context of the other provisions.

UN Security Council Resolution S/RES/660 (1990) "Iraq/Kuwait
August 1990

The Security Council,
Alarmed by the invasion of Kuwait on 2 August 1990 by the military forces of Iraq,
Determining that there exists a breach of international peace and security as regards the Iraqi invasion of Kuwait,
Acting under Articles 39 and 40 of the Charter of the United Nations,

(1) Condemns the Iraqi invasion of Kuwait;
(2) Demands that Iraq withdraw immediately and unconditionally all its forces to the positions in which they were located on 1 August 1990;
(3) Calls upon Iraq and Kuwait to begin immediately intensive negotiations for the resolution of their differences and supports all efforts in this regard, and especially those of the League of Arab States;
(4) Decides to meet again as necessary to consider further steps to ensure compliance with the present resolution.

Adopted at the 2932nd meeting by 14 votes to none. One member (Yemen) did not participate in the vote.

PART I INTERNATIONAL LAW

UN Security Council Resolution S/RES/661 (1990) "Iraq Sanctions"
6 August 1990

The Security Council,
Reaffirming its resolution 660 (1990) of 2 August 1990,
Deeply concerned that that resolution has not been implemented and that the invasion by Iraq of Kuwait continues with further loss of human life and material destruction,
Determined to bring the invasion and occupation of Kuwait by Iraq to an end and to restore the sovereignty, independence and territorial integrity of Kuwait,
Noting that the legitimate Government of Kuwait has expressed its readiness to comply with resolution 660 (1990),
Mindful of its responsibilities under the Charter of the United Nations for the maintenance of international peace and security,
Affirming the inherent right of individual or collective self-defence, in response to the armed attack by Iraq against Kuwait, in accordance with Article 51 of the Charter,
Acting under Chapter VII of the Charter of the United Nations,

(1) Determines that Iraq so far has failed to comply with paragraph (2) of resolution 660 (1990) and has usurped the authority of the legitimate Government of Kuwait;

(2) Decides, as a consequence, to take the following measures to secure compliance of Iraq with paragraph (2) of resolution 660 (1990) and to restore the authority of the legitimate Government of Kuwait;

(3) Decides that all States shall prevent:

(a) The import into their territories of all commodities and products originating in Iraq or Kuwait exported therefrom after the date of the present resolution;

(b) Any activities by their nationals or in their territories which would promote or are calculated to promote the export or trans-shipment of any commodities or products from Iraq or Kuwait; and any dealings by their nationals or their flag vessels or in their territories in any commodities or products originating in Iraq or Kuwait and exported therefrom after the date of the present resolution, including in particular any transfer of funds to Iraq or Kuwait for the purposes of such activities or dealings;

(c) The sale or supply by their nationals or from their territories or using their flag vessels of any commodities or products, including weapons or any other military equipment, whether or not originating in their territories but not including supplies intended strictly for medical purposes, and, in humanitarian circumstances, foodstuffs, to any person or body in Iraq or Kuwait or to any person or body for the purposes of any business carried on in or operated from Iraq or Kuwait, and any activities by their nationals or in their territories which promote or are calculated to promote such sale or supply of such commodities or products;

(4) Decides that all States shall not make available to the Government of Iraq or to any commercial, industrial or public utility undertaking in Iraq or Kuwait, any funds or any other financial or economic resources and shall prevent their nationals and any persons within their territories from removing from their territories or otherwise making available to that Government or to any such undertaking any such funds or resources and from remitting any other funds to persons or bodies within Iraq or Kuwait, except payments exclusively for strictly medical or humanitarian purposes and, in humanitarian circumstances, foodstuffs;

(5) Calls upon all States, including States non-members of the United Nations, to act strictly in accordance with the provisions of the present resolution notwithstanding any contract entered into or licence granted before the date of the present resolution;

(6) Decides to establish, in accordance with rule 28 of the provisional rules of procedure of the Security Council, a Committee of the Security Council consisting of all the members of the Council, to undertake the following tasks and to report on its work to the Council with its observations and recommendations:

(a) To examine the reports on the progress of the implementation of the present resolution which will be submitted by the Secretary-General;

(b) To seek from all States further information regarding the action taken by them concerning the effective implementation of the provisions laid down in the present resolution;

(7) Calls upon all States to co-operate fully with the Committee in the fulfilment of its task, including supplying such information as may be sought by the Committee in pursuance of the present resolution;

(8) Requests the Secretary-General to provide all necessary assistance to the Committee and to make the necessary arrangements in the Secretariat for the purpose;

(9) Decides that, notwithstanding paragraphs (4) through (8) above, nothing in the present resolution shall prohibit assistance to the legitimate Government of Kuwait, and calls upon all States:
(a) To take appropriate measures to protect assets of the legitimate Government of Kuwait and its agencies;
(b) Not to recognize any regime set up by the occupying Power;
(10) Requests the Secretary-General to report to the Council on the progress of the implementation of the present resolution, the first report to be submitted within thirty days;
(11) Decides to keep this item on its agenda and to continue its efforts to put an early end to the invasion by Iraq.

Adopted at the 2933rd meeting by 13 votes to none, with 2 abstentions (Cuba and Yemen).

PART I   INTERNATIONAL LAW

UN Security Council Resolution S/RES/678 (1990) "Iraq/Kuwait/all necessary means"
29 November 1990

The Security Council,
Recalling and reaffirming its resolutions 660 (1990) of 2 August (1990), 661 (1990) of 6 August 1990, 662 (1990) of 9 August 1990, 664 (1990) of 18 August 1990, 665 (1990) of 25 August 1990, 666 (1990) of 13 September 1990, 667 (1990) of 16 September 1990, 669 (1990) of 24 September 1990, 670 (1990) of 25 September 1990, 674 (1990) of of 29 October 1990 and 677 (1990) of 28 November 1990.
Noting that, despite all efforts by the United Nations, Iraq refuses to comply with its obligation to implement resolution 660 (1990) and the above-mentioned subsequent relevant resolutions, in flagrant contempt of the Security Council,
Mindful of its duties and responsibilities under the Charter of the United Nations for the maintenance and preservation of international peace and security,
Determined to secure full compliance with its decisions,
Acting under Chapter VII of the Charter,

(1) Demands that Iraq comply fully with resolution 660 (1990) and all subsequent relevant resolutions, and decides, while maintaining all its decisions, to allow Iraq one final opportunity, as a pause of goodwill, to do so;
(2) Authorizes Member States co-operating with the Government of Kuwait, unless Iraq on or before 15 January 1991 fully implements, as set forth in paragraph (1) above, the foregoing resolutions, to use all necessary means to uphold and implement resolution 660 (1990) and all subsequent relevant resolutions and to restore international peace and security in the area;
(3) Requests all States to provide appropriate support for the actions undertaken in pursuance of paragraph (2) of the present resolution;
(4) Requests the States concerned to keep the Security Council regularly informed on the progress of actions undertaken pursuant to paragraphs (2) and (3) of the present resolution;
(5) Decides to remain seized of the matter.

RESOLUTION 687 IRAQ/KUWAIT

UN Security Council Resolution S/RES/687 (1991) "Iraq/Kuwait"
2 April 1991

The Security Council,
Recalling its resolutions 660(1990) of 2 August 1990, 661 (1990) of 6 August 1990, 662 (1990) of 9 August 1990, 664 (1990) of 18 August 1990, 665 (1990) of 25 August (1990), 666 (1990) of 13 September 1990, 669 (1990) of 24 September 1990, 670 (1990) of 25 September 1990, 674 (1990) of 29 October 1990, 677 (1990) of 28 November 1990, 678 (1990) of 29 November 1990 and 686 (1991(of 2 March (1991),
Welcoming the restoration to Kuwait of its sovereignty, independence and territorial integrity and the return of its legitimate Government,
Affirming the commitment of all Member States to the sovereignty, territorial integrity and political independence of Kuwait and Iraq, and noting the intention expressed by the Member States cooperating with Kuwait under paragraph (2) of resolution 678 (1990) to bring their military presence in Iraq to an end as soon as possible consistent with paragraph (8) of resolution 686 (1991),
Reaffirming the need to be assured of Iraq's peaceful intention sin the light of its unlawful invasion and occupation of Kuwait,
Taking note of the letter sent by the Minister of foreign Affairs of Iraq on 27 February 1991 and those sent pursuant to resolution 686 (1991),
Noting that Iraq and Kuwait, as independent sovereign States, signed at Baghdad on 4 October 1963 'Agreed minutes Between the State of Kuwait and the Republic of Iraq Regarding the Restoration of Friendly Relations, Recognition and Related Matters', thereby recognizing formally the boundary between Iraq and Kuwait and the allocation of islands, which were registered with the United Nations in accordance with Article 102 of the Charter of the United Nations and in which Iraq recognized the independence and complete sovereignty of the State of Kuwait within its borders as specified and accepted in the letter of the Prime Minister of Iraq dates 21 July 1932, and as accepted by the Ruler of Kuwait in his letter dated 10 August 1932,
Conscious of the need for demarcation of the said boundary,
Conscious also of the statements by Iraq threatening to use weapons in violation of its obligations under the Geneva Protocol for the Prohibition of the Use in War of Asphyxiating, Poisonous or Other Gases, and of Bacteriological Methods of Warfare, signed at Geneva on 17 June 1925, and of its prior use of chemical weapons and affirming the grave consequences would follow any further use by Iraq of such weapons,
Recalling that Iraq has subscribed to the Declaration adopted by all States participating in the Conference of States Parties to the 1925 Geneva Protocol and Other Interested States, held in Paris from 7 to 11 January 1989, establishing the objective of universal elimination of chemical and biological weapons,
Recalling also that Iraq has signed the Convention on the Prohibition of the Development, Production and Stockpiling of Bacteriological (biological) and Toxin Weapons and on Their Destruction, of April 1972,
Noting the importance of Iraq ratifying this Convention,
Noting moreover the importance of all States adhering to this Convention and encouraging its forthcoming Review Conference to reinforce the authority, efficiency and universal scope of the Convention,
Stressing the importance of an early conclusion by the Conference of Disarmament of its work on a Convention on the Universal Prohibition of Chemical Weapons and of universal adherence thereto,
Aware of the use by Iraq of ballistic missiles in unprovoked attacks and therefore of the need to take specific measures in regard to such missiles located in Iraq,
Concerned by the reports in the hands of Member States that Iraq has attempted to acquire materials for a nuclear weapon programme contrary to its obligations under the Treaty on the Non-Proliferation of Nuclear Weapons of 1 July 1968,
Recalling the objective of the establishment of a nuclear-weapon-free-zone in the region of the Middle East,
Conscious of the threat that all weapons of mass destruction pose to peace and security in the area and of the need to work towards the establishment in the Middle East of a zone free of such weapons,
Conscious also of the objective of achieving balance and comprehensive control of armaments in the region,
Conscious further of the importance of achieving the objectives noted above using all available means, including a dialogue among the States of the region,
Noting that resolution 589 (1991) marked the lifting of the measures imposed by resolution 661(1990)

PART I   INTERNATIONAL LAW

in so far as they applied to Kuwait,
Noting that despite the progress being made in fulfilling the obligations of resolution 585 (1991), many Kuwaiti and third country nationals are still not accounted for and property remains unreturned,
Recalling the International Convention against the Taking of Hostages, opened for signature at New York on 18 December 1979, which categorized all acts of taking hostages as manifestations of international terrorism,
Deploring threats made by Iraq during the recent conflict to make use of terrorism against targets outside Iraq and the taking of hostages by Iraq,
Taking note with grave concern of the reports of the Secretary-General of 20 March 1991 and 28 March 1991, and conscious of the necessity to meet urgently the humanitarian needs in Kuwait and Iraq,
Bearing in mind its objective of restoring international peace and security in the area as set out in recent resolution of the Security Council.
Conscious of the need to take the following measures acting under Chapter VII of the Chapter,

(1) Affirms all thirteen resolutions, noted above, except as expressly changed below to achieve the goals of this resolution, including a formal cease-fire;

A
(2) Demands that Iraq and Kuwait respect the inviolability of the international boundary and the allocation of islands set out in the 'Agreed Minutes Between the State of Kuwait and the Republic of Iraq Regarding the Restoration of Friendly Relations, Recognition and Related Matters', signed by them in the exercise of their sovereignty at Baghdad on 4 October 1963 and registered with the United Nations and published by the United Nations in document 7063, United Nations Treaty Series, 1964;
(3) Calls upon the Secretary-General to lend his assistance to make arrangements with Iraq and Kuwait to demarcate the boundary between Iraq and Kuwait, drawing on appropriate material, including the map transmitted by Security Council document S/22-412 and to report back to the Security Council within one month;
(4) Decides to guarantee the inviolability of the abovementioned international boundary and to take as appropriate all necessary measures to that end in accordance with the Charter of the United Nations;

B
(5) Requests the Secretary-General, after consulting with Iraq and Kuwait, to submit within three days to the Security Council for its approval a plan for the immediate deployment of a United Nations observer unit to monitor the Khor Abdullah and a demilitarized zone, which is thereby established, extending ten kilometres into Iraq and five kilometres into Kuwait from the boundary referred to in the 'Agreed Minutes Between the State of Kuwait and the Republic of Iraq Regarding the Restoration of Friendly Relations, Recognition and Related Matters' of 4 October 1963, to deter violations of the boundary through its presence in and surveillance of the demilitarized zone, to observe any hostile or potentially hostile action mounted from the territory of one State to the other; and for the Secretary-General to report regularly to the Security Council of the operations of the unit, and immediately if there are serious violations of the zone or potential threats to peace;
(6) Notes that as soon as the Secretary-General notifies the Security Council of the completion of the deployment of the United Nations observer unit, the conditions will be established for the Member States cooperating with Kuwait in accordance with resolution 678 (1990) to bring their military presence in Iraq to an end consistent with resolution 686 (1991);

C
(7) Invites Iraq to reaffirm unconditionally its obligations under the Geneva Protocol for the Prohibition of the Use in War of Asphyxiating, Poisonous or Other Gases, and of Bacteriological Methods of Warfare, signed at Geneva on 17 June 1925, and to ratify the Convention on the Prohibition of the Development, Production and Stockpiling of Bacteriological (Biological) and Toxin Weapons and on Their Destruction, of 10 April 1972;
(8) Decides that Iraq shall unconditionally accept the destruction, removal or rendering harmless, under international supervision of;
(a) All chemical and biological weapons and all stock of agents and all related subsystems and components and all research, development, support and manufacturing facilities;
(b) All ballistic missiles with a range greater than 150 kilometres and related major parts, and repair and production facilities;

(9) Decides, for the implementation of paragraph (8) above, the following:
(1) Iraq shall submit to the Secretary-General, within fifteen days of the adoption of the present resolution, a declaration of the locations, amounts and types of all items specified in paragraph (a) and agree to urgent, on-site inspection as specified below;
(b) The Secretary-General, in consultation with the appropriate Governments and, where appropriate, with the Director General of the World Health Organization, within forty-five days of the passage of the present resolution shall develop, and submit to the Council for approval, a plan calling for the completion of the following acts within forty-five days of such approval:
(i) The forming of a Special Commission, which shall carry out immediate on-site inspection of Iraq's biological, chemical and missile capabilities, based on Iraq's declarations and the designation of any additional locations by the Special Commission itself;
(ii) The yielding by Iraq of possession to the Special Commission for destruction, removal or rendering harmless, taking into account the requirements of public safety, of all items specified under paragraph (8)(a) above, including items at the additional locations designated by the Special Commission under paragraph (9)(b)(i) above and the destruction by Iraq, under the supervision of the Special Commission, of all its missile capabilities, including launchers, as specified under paragraph (8)(b) above;
(iii) The provision by the Special Commission of the assistance and cooperation to the Director-General of the International Atomic Energy Agency required in paragraphs (12) and (13) below;
(10) Decides that Iraq shall unconditionally undertake not to use, develop, construct or acquire any of the items specified in paragraphs (8) and (9) above and requests the Secretary-General, in consultation with the Special Commission to develop a plan for the future ongoing monitoring and verification of Iraq's compliance with this paragraph, to be submitted to the Security Council for approval within one hundred and twenty days of the passage of this resolution;
(11) Invites Iraq to reaffirm unconditionally its obligations under the Treaty on the Non-Proliferation of Nuclear Weapons of 1 July 1968;
(12) Decides that Iraq shall unconditionally agree not to acquire or develop nuclear weapons or nuclear-weapons-usable material or any subsystems or components or any research, development, support or manufacturing facilities related to the above; to submit to the Secretary-General and the Director-General of the International Atomic Energy Agency within fifteen days of the adoption of the present resolution a declaration of the locations, amounts, and types of all items specified above; to place all of its nuclear weapons-usable materials under the exclusive control, for custody and removal, of the International Atomic Emergency Agency, with the assistance and cooperation of the Special Commission as provided for in the plan of the Secretary-General discussed in paragraph (9)(b) above; to accept, in accordance with the arrangements provided for in paragraph (13) below, urgent on-site inspections and the destruction, removal or rendering harmless as appropriate of all items specified above; and to accept the plan discussed in paragraph (13) below for future ongoing monitoring and verification of its compliance with these undertakings;
(13) Requests the Director-General of the International Atomic Energy Agency, through the Secretary-General, with the assistance and cooperation of the Special Commission as provided for in plan of the Secretary-General in paragraph (9) (b) above, to carry out immediate on-site inspection of Iraq's nuclear capabilities based on Iraq's declarations and the designation of any additional locations by the Special Commission; to develop a plan for submission to the Security Council within forty-five days calling for destruction, removal, or rendering harmless as appropriate of all items listed in paragraph (12) above; to carry out the plan within forty-five days following approval by the Security Council; and to develop a plan, taking into account the rights and obligations of Iraq under the Treaty on the Non-Proliferation of Nuclear Weapons of 1 July 1968, for the future ongoing monitoring and verification of Iraq's compliance with paragraph (12) above, including an inventory of all nuclear material in Iraq subject to the Agency's verification and inspections of the International Atomic Energy Agency to confirm that the Agency's safeguards cover all relevant nuclear activities in Iraq, to be submitted to the Security Council for approval within one hundred and twenty days of the passage of the present resolution;
(14) Takes note that the actions to be taken by Iraq in paragraph (8), (9), (10), (11), (12), and (13) of the present resolution represent steps towards the goal of establishing in the Middle East a zone free of weapons of mass destruction and all missiles for their delivery and the objective of a global ban on chemical weapons

D
(15) Requests the Secretary-General to report to the Security Council on the steps taken to facilitate the return of all Kuwaiti property seized by Iraq, including a list of any property that Kuwait claims had not been returned or which has not been returned intact;

PART I   INTERNATIONAL LAW

E

(16) Reaffirms that Iraq, without prejudice to the debts and obligations of Iraq arising prior to 2 August 1990, which will be addressed through the normal mechanism, is liable under international law for any direct loss, damage, including environmental damage and the depletion of natural resources, or injury to foreign Governments, nationals and corporations, as a result of Iraq's unlawful invasion and occupation of Kuwait

(17) Decides that all Iraqi statements made since 2 August 1990 repudiating its foreign debt are null and void, and demands that Iraq adhere scrupulously to all of its obligations concerning servicing and repayment of its foreign debt;

(18) Decides also to create a fund to pay compensation for claims that fall within paragraph (16) above and to establish a Commission that will administer the fund;

(19) Directs the Secretary-General to develop and present to the Security Council for decision, no later than thirty days following the adoption of the present resolution, recommendations for the fund to meet the requirement for the payment of claims established in accordance with paragraph (18) above and for a programme to implement the decisions in paragraphs (16), (17) and (18) above, including: administration of the fund; mechanisms for determining the appropriate level of Iraq's contribution to the fund based on a percentage of the value of the exports of petroleum and petroleum products from Iraq not to exceed a figure to be suggested to the Council by the Secretary-General, taking into account the requirements of the people of Iraq, Iraq's payment capacity as assessed in conjunction with the international financial institutions taking into consideration external debt service, and the needs of the Iraqi economy, arrangements for ensuring that payments are made to the fund; the process by which funds will be allocated and claims paid; appropriate procedures for evaluating losses, listing claims and verifying their validity and resolving disputed claims in respect of Iraq's liability as specified in paragraph (16) above; and the composition of the commission designated above;

F

(20) Decides, effective immediately, that the prohibitions against the sale or supply to Iraq of commodities or products, other than medicine and health supplies, and prohibitions against financial transactions related thereto contained in resolution 661 (1990) shall not apply to foodstuff notified by the Security Council Committee established in resolution 661 (1990) concerning the situation between Iraq and Kuwait or, with the approval of that Committee, under the simplified and accelerated 'no-objection' procedure, to materials and supplies for essential civilian needs as identified in the report of the Secretary-General dated 20 March 1991, and in any further findings of humanitarian need by the Committee;

(22) Decides that upon the approval by the Security Council on the programme called for in paragraph (19) above and upon Council agreement that Iraq has completed all actions contemplated in paragraphs (8), (9), (10), (11), (12) and (13) above the prohibitions against the import of commodities and products originating in Iraq and the prohibitions against financial transactions related thereto contained in resolution 661 (1990) shall have no further force or effect;

(23) Decides that, pending action by the Security Council under paragraph (22) above, the Security Council Committee established by resolution 661 (1990) shall be empowered to approve, when required to assure adequate financial resources on the part of Iraq to carry out the activities under paragraph (20) above, exceptions to the prohibition against the import of commodities and products originating in Iraq;

(24) Decides that, in accordance with resolution 661 (1990) and subsequent related resolutions and until a further decision is taken by the Security Council, all States shall continue to prevent the sale or supply, to Iraq by their nations, or from their territories or using their flag vessels or aircraft, of:

(a) Arms and related matériel of all types, specifically including the sale or transfer through other means of all forms of conventional military equipment, including for paramilitary forces, and spare parts and components and their means of production, for such equipment;

(b) Items specified and defined in paragraphs (8) ad (12) above not otherwise covered above;

(c) Technology under licensing or other transfer arrangements used in production, utilization or stockpiling of items specified in subparagraphs (a) and (b) above;

(d) Personnel or materials for training or technical support services relating to the design, development, manufacture, use, maintenance or support of items specified in subparagraphs (a) and (b) above;

(25) Calls upon all States and international organizations to act strictly in accordance with paragraph (24) above, notwithstanding the existence of any contracts, agreements, licences or any other arrangements;

(26) Requests the Secretary-General, in consultation with appropriate Governments, to develop within sixty days, fort the approval of the Security Council, guidelines to facilitate full international implementation of paragraphs (24) and (25) above and paragraph (27) below, and to make them available to all States and to establish a procedure for updating these guidelines periodically;
(27) Calls upon all States to maintain such national controls and procedures and to take such other actions consistent with the guidelines to be established by the Security Council under paragraph (26) above as may be necessary to ensure compliance with the terms of paragraph (24) above, and calls upon international organizations to take all appropriate steps to assist in ensuring such full compliance;
(28) Agrees to review its decisions in paragraphs (22), (23), (24) and (25) above, except from the items specified and defined in paragraphs (8) and (12) above, on a regular basis and in any case on hundred and twenty days following passage of the present resolution, taking into account Iraq's compliance with the resolution and general progress towards the control of armaments in the region;
(29) Decides that all States, including Iraq, shall take the necessary measures to ensure that no claim shall lie at the instance of the Government of Iraq, or of any person or body in Iraq, or of any person claiming through or for the benefit of any such person or body, in connection with any contract or other transaction where its performance was affected by reason of the measures taken by the Security Council in resolution 661 (1990) and related resolutions;

G
(30) Decides that, in furtherance of its commitment to facilitate the reparation of all Kuwaiti and third country nationals, Iraq shall extend all necessary cooperation to the International Committee of the Red Cross, providing lists of such persons, facilitating the access of the International Committee of the Red Cross to all such persons wherever located or detained and facilitating the search by the International Committee of the Red Cross for those Kuwaiti and third country nationals still unaccounted for;
(31) Invites the International Committee of the Red Cross to keep the Secretary-General apprised as appropriate of all activities undertaken in connection with facilitating the repatriation or return of all Kuwaiti and third country nationals or their remains present in Iraq on or after 2 August 1990;

H
(32) Requires Iraq to inform the Security Council that it will not commit or support any act of international terrorism or allow any organization directed towards commission of such acts to operate within its territory and to condemn unequivocally and renounce all acts, methods and practices of terrorism;

I
(33) Declares that, upon official notification by Iraq to the Secretary-General and to the Security-Council of its acceptance of the provisions above, a formal cease fire is effective between Iraq and Kuwait and the Member States cooperating with Kuwait in accordance with resolution 678 (1990);
(34) Decides to remain seized on the matter and to take such further steps as may be required for the implementation of the present resolution and to secure peace and security in the area.

PART I   INTERNATIONAL LAW

UN Security Council Resolution S/RES/688 (1991) "Iraq/Kurdish population"
5 April 1991

The Security Council,
Mindful of its duties and its responsibilities under the Charter of the United Nations for the maintenance of international peace and security,
Recalling of Article 2, paragraph 7, of the Charter of the United Nations,
Gravely concerned by the repression of the Iraqi civilian population in many parts of Iraq, including most recently in Kurdish populated areas, which led to a massive flow of refugees towards and across international frontiers and to cross-border incursions, which threaten international peace and security in the region,
Deeply disturbed by the magnitude of the human suffering involved,
Taking note of the letters sent by the representatives of Turkey and France to the United Nations dated 2 April 1991 and 4 April 1991, respectively (S/22435 and S/22442),
Taking note also of the letters sent by the Permanent Representative of the Islamic Republic of Iran to the United Nations dated 3 and 4 April 1991, respectively (S/22436 and S/22447),
Reaffirming the commitment of all Member States to the sovereignty, territorial integrity and political independence of Iraq and of all States in the area,
Bearing in mind the Secretary-General's report of 20 March 1991 (S/22366),

(1) Condemns the repression of the Iraqi civilian population in many parts of Iraq, including most recently in Kurdish populated areas, the consequences of which threaten international peace and security in the region;
(2) Demands that Iraq, as a contribution to remove the threat to international peace and security in the region, immediately end this repression and expresses the hope in the same context that an open dialogue will take place to ensure that the human and political rights of all Iraqi citizens are respected;
(3) Insists that Iraq allow immediate access by international humanitarian organizations to all those in need of assistance in all parts of Iraq and to make available all necessary facilities for their operations;
(4) Requests the Secretary-General to pursue his humanitarian efforts in Iraq and to report forthwith, if appropriate on the basis of a further mission to the region, on the plight of the Iraqi civilian population, and in particular the Kurdish population, suffering from the repression in all its forms inflicted by the Iraqi authorities;
(5) Requests further the Secretary-General to use all the resources at his disposal, including those of the relevant United Nations agencies, to address urgently the critical needs of the refugees and displaced Iraqi population;
(6) Appeals to all Member States and to all humanitarian organizations to contribute to these humanitarian relief efforts;
(7) Demands that Iraq cooperate with the Secretary-General to these ends;
(8) Decides to remain seized of the matter.

Adopted at the 2982nd meeting by 10 votes to 3 (Cuba, Yemen, Zimbabwe), with 2 abstentions (China, India).

UN Security Council Resolution S/RES/794 (1992) "Somalia"
3 December 1992

The Security Council,
Reaffirming its resolutions 733 (1992) of 23 January 1992, 746 (1992) of 17 March 1992, 751 (1992) of 24 April 1992, 767 (1992) of 27 July 1992 and 775 (1992) of 28 August 1992,
Recognizing the unique character of the present situation in Somalia and mindful of its deteriorating, complex and extraordinary nature, requiring an immediate and exceptional response,
Determining that the magnitude of the human tragedy caused by the conflict in Somalia, further exacerbated by the obstacles being created to the distribution of humanitarian assistance, constitutes a threat to international peace and security,
Gravely alarmed by the deterioration of the humanitarian situation in Somalia and underlining the urgent need for the quick delivery of humanitarian assistance in the whole country,
Noting the efforts of the League of Arab States, the Organization of African Unity, and in particular the proposal made by its Chairman at the forty-seventh regular session of the General Assembly for the organization of an international conference on Somalia, and the Organization of the Islamic Conference and other regional agencies and arrangements to promote reconciliation and political settlement in Somalia and to address the humanitarian needs of the people of that country,
Commending the ongoing efforts of the United Nations, its specialized agencies and humanitarian organizations and of non-governmental organizations and of States to ensure delivery of humanitarian assistance in Somalia,
Responding to the urgent calls from Somalia for the international community to take measures to ensure the delivery of humanitarian assistance in Somalia,
Expressing grave alarm at continuing reports of widespread violations of international humanitarian law occurring in Somalia, including reports of violence and threats of violence against personnel participating lawfully in impartial humanitarian relief activities; deliberate attacks on non-combatants, relief consignments and vehicles, and medical and relief facilities; and impeding the delivery of food and medical supplies essential for the survival of the civilian population,
Dismayed by the continuation of conditions that impede the delivery of humanitarian supplies to destinations within Somalia, and in particular reports of looting of relief supplies destined for starving people, attacks on aircraft and ships bringing in humanitarian relief supplies, and attacks on the Pakistani UNOSOM contingent in Mogadishu,
Taking note with appreciation of the letters of the Secretary-General of 24 November 1992 (S/24859) and of 29 November 1992 (S/24868),
Sharing the Secretary-General's assessment that the situation in Somalia is intolerable and that it has become necessary to review the basic premises and principles of the United Nations effort in Somalia, and that UNOSOM's existing course would not in present circumstances be an adequate response to the tragedy in Somalia,
Determined to establish as soon as possible the necessary conditions for the delivery of humanitarian assistance wherever needed in Somalia, in conformity with resolutions 751 (1992) and 767 (1992),
Noting the offer by Member States aimed at establishing a secure environment for humanitarian relief operations in Somalia as soon as possible,
Determined further to restore peace, stability and law and order with a view to facilitating the process of a political settlement under the auspices of the United Nations, aimed at national reconciliation in Somalia, and encouraging the Secretary-General and his Special Representative to continue and intensify their work at the national and regional levels to promote these objectives,
Recognizing that the people of Somalia bear ultimate responsibility for national reconciliation and the reconstruction of their own country,

(1) *Reaffirms* its demand that all parties, movements and factions in Somalia immediately cease hostilities, maintain a cease-fire throughout the country, and cooperate with the Special Representative of the Secretary-General as well as with the military forces to be established pursuant to the authorization given in paragraph (10) below in order to promote the process of relief distribution, reconciliation and political settlement in Somalia;
(2) *Demands* that all parties, movements and factions in Somalia take all measures necessary to facilitate the efforts of the United Nations, its specialized agencies and humanitarian organizations to provide urgent humanitarian assistance to the affected population in Somalia;
(3) *Also demands* that all parties, movements and factions in Somalia take all measures necessary to ensure the safety of United Nations and all other personnel engaged in the delivery of humanitarian assistance, including the military forces to be established pursuant to the authorization given in

PART I   INTERNATIONAL LAW

paragraph (10) below;
(4) Further demands that all parties, movements and factions in Somalia immediately cease and desist from all breaches of international humanitarian law including from actions such as those described above;
(5) Strongly condemns all violations of international humanitarian law occurring in Somalia, including in particular the deliberate impeding of the delivery of food and medical supplies essential for the survival of the civilian population, and affirms that those who commit or order the commission of such acts will be held individually responsible in respect of such acts;
(6) Decides that the operations and the further deployment of the 3,500 personnel of the United Nations Operation in Somalia (UNOSOM) authorized by paragraph (3) of resolution 775 (1992) should proceed at the discretion of the Secretary-General in the light of his assessment of conditions on the ground; and requests him to keep the Council informed and to make such recommendations as may be appropriate for the fulfilment of its mandate where conditions permit;
(7) Endorses the recommendation by the Secretary-General in his letter of 29 November 1992 (S/24868) that action under Chapter VII of the Charter of the United Nations should be taken in order to establish a secure environment for humanitarian relief operations in Somalia as soon as possible;
(8) Welcomes the offer by a Member State described in the Secretary-General's letter to the Council of 29 November 1992 (S/24868) concerning the establishment of an operation to create such a secure environment;
(9) Welcomes also offers by other Member States to participate in that operation;
(10) Acting under Chapter VII of the Charter of the United Nations, authorizes the Secretary-General and Member States cooperating to implement the offer referred to in paragraph (8) above to use all necessary means to establish as soon as possible a secure environment for humanitarian relief operations in Somalia;
(11) Calls on all Member States which are in a position to do so to provide military forces and to make additional contributions, in cash or in kind, in accordance with paragraph (10) above and requests the Secretary-General to establish a fund through which the contributions, where appropriate, could be channelled to the States or operations concerned;
(12) Authorizes the Secretary-General and the Member States concerned to make the necessary arrangements for the unified command and control of the forces involved, which will reflect the offer referred to in paragraph (8) above;
(13) Requests the Secretary-General and the Member States acting under paragraph (10) above to establish appropriate mechanisms for coordination between the United Nations and their military forces;
(14) Decides to appoint an ad hoc commission composed of members of the Security Council to report to the Council on the implementation of this resolution;
(15) Invites the Secretary-General to attach a small UNOSOM liaison staff to the Field Headquarters of the unified command;
(16) Acting under Chapters VII and VIII of the Charter, calls upon States, nationally or through regional agencies or arrangements, to use such measures as may be necessary to ensure strict implementation of paragraph (5) of the resolution 733 (1992);
(17) Requests all States, in particular those in the region, to provide appropriate support for the actions undertaken by States, nationally or through regional agencies or arrangements, pursuant to this and other relevant resolutions;
(18) Requests the Secretary-General and, as appropriate, the States concerned to report to the Council on a regular basis, the first such report to be made no later than fifteen days after the adoption of this resolution, on the implementation of this resolution and the attainment of the objective of establishing a secure environment so as to enable the Council to make the necessary decision for a prompt transition to continued peace-keeping operations;
(19) Requests the Secretary-General to submit a plan to the Council initially within fifteen days after the adoption of this resolution to ensure that UNOSOM will be able to fulfil its mandate upon the withdrawal of the unified command;
(20) Invites the Secretary-General and his Special Representative to continue their efforts to achieve a political settlement in Somalia;
(21) Decides to remain actively seized of the matter.

Adopted by the Security Council at its 3145th meeting, on 3 December 1992

UN Security Council Resolution S/RES/836 (1993) "Bosnia. Safe Areas"
4 June 1993

The Security Council,
Reaffirming its resolutions 713 (1991) of 25 September 1991 and all subsequent relevant resolutions,
Reaffirming in particular its resolutions 819 (1993) of 16 April 1993 and 824 (1993) of 6 May 1993, which demanded that certain towns and their surrounding areas in the Republic of Bosnia and Herzegovina should be treated as safe areas,
Reaffirming the sovereignty, territorial integrity and political independence of the Republic of Bosnia and Herzegovina and the responsibility of the Security Council in this regard,
Condemning military attacks, and actions that do not respect the sovereignty, territorial integrity and political independence of the Republic of Bosnia and Herzegovina, which, as a State Member of the United Nations, enjoys the rights provided for in the Charter of the United Nations,
Reiterating its alarm at the grave and intolerable situation in the Republic of Bosnia and Herzegovina arising from serious violations of international humanitarian law,
Reaffirming once again that any taking of territory by force or any practice of "ethnic cleansing" is unlawful and totally unacceptable,
Commending the Government of the Republic of Bosnia and Herzegovina and the Bosnian Croat party for having signed the Vance-Owen Plan,
Gravely concerned at the persistent refusal of the Bosnian Serb party to accept the Vance-Owen Plan and calling upon that party to accept the Peace Plan for the Republic of Bosnia and Herzegovina in full,
Deeply concerned by the continuing armed hostilities in the territory of the Republic of Bosnia and Herzegovina which run totally counter to the Peace Plan,
Alarmed by the resulting plight of the civilian population in the territory of the Republic of Bosnia and Herzegovina in particular in Sarajevo, Bihac, Srebrenica. Gorazde, Tuzla and Zepa,
Condemning the obstruction, primarily by the Bosnian Serb party, of the delivery of humanitarian assistance,
Determined to ensure the protection of the civilian population in safe areas and to promote a lasting political solution,
Confirming the ban on military flights in the airspace of the Republic of Bosnia and Herzegovina, established by resolutions 781 (1992) of 9 October 1992, 786 (1992) of 10 November 1992, and 816 (1993) of 31 March 1993,
Affirming that the concept of safe areas in the Republic of Bosnia and Herzegovina as contained in resolutions 819 (1993) and 824 (1993) was adopted to respond to an emergency situation, and noting that the concept proposed by France in document S/25800 and by others could make a valuable contribution and should not in any way be taken as an end in itself, but as part of the Vance-Owen process and as a first step towards a just and lasting political solution,
Convinced that treating the towns and surrounding areas referred to above as safe areas will contribute to the early implementation of that objective,
Stressing that the lasting solution to the conflict in the Republic of Bosnia and Herzegovina must be based on the following principles: immediate and complete cessation of hostilities; withdrawal from territories seized by the use of force and "ethnic cleansing"; reversal of the consequences of "ethnic cleansing" and recognition of the right of all refugees to return to their homes; and respect for sovereignty, territorial integrity and political independence of the Republic of Bosnia and Herzegovina,
Noting also the crucial work being done throughout the Republic of Bosnia and Herzegovina by the United Nations Protection Force (UNPROFOR), and the importance of such work continuing,
Determining that the situation in the Republic of Bosnia and Herzegovina continues to be a threat to international peace and security,
Acting under Chapter VII of the Charter of the United Nations,

(1) Calls for the full and immediate implementation of all its relevant resolutions;
(2) Commends the Peace Plan for the Republic of Bosnia and Herzegovina as contained in document S/25479);
(3) Reaffirms the unacceptability of the acquisition of territory by the use of force and the need to restore the full sovereignty, territorial integrity and political independence of the Republic of Bosnia and Herzegovina,
(4) Decides to ensure full respect for the safe areas referred to in resolution 824 (1993);
(5) Decides to extend to that end the mandate of UNPROFOR in order to enable it, in the safe areas referred to in resolution 824 (1993), to deter attacks against the safe areas, to monitor the cease-fire,

PART I   INTERNATIONAL LAW

to promote the withdrawal of military or paramilitary units other than those of the Government of the Republic of Bosnia and Herzegovina and to occupy some key points on the ground, in addition to participating in the delivery of humanitarian relief to the population as provided for in resolution 776 (1992) of 14 September 1992,

(6) Affirms that these safe areas are a temporary measure and that the primary objective remains to reverse the consequences of the use of force and to allow all persons displaced from their homes in the Republic of Bosnia and Herzegovina to return to their homes in peace, beginning, inter-alia, with the prompt implementation of the provisions of the Vance-Owen Plan in areas where those have been agreed by the parties directly concerned;

(7) Requests the Secretary-General, in consultation, inter alia, with the Governments of the Member States contributing forces to UNPROFOR:

(a) To make the adjustments or reinforcement of UNPROFOR which might be required by the implementation of the present resolution, and to consider assigning UNPROFOR elements in support of the elements entrusted with protection of safe areas, with the agreement of the Governments contributing forces;

(b) To direct the UNPROFOR Force Commander to redeploy to the the extent possible the forces under his command in the Republic of Bosnia and Herzegovina;

(8) Calls upon Member States to contribute forces, including logistic support, to facilitate the implementation of the provisions regarding the safe areas, expresses its gratitude to Members States already providing forces for that purpose and invites the Secretary-General to seek additional contingents from other Member States;

(9) Authorizes UNPROFOR, in addition to the mandate defined in resolutions 770 (1992) of 13 August 1992 and 776 (1992), in carrying out the mandate defined in paragraph (5) above, acting in self-defence, to take the necessary measures, including the use of force, in reply to bombardments against the safe areas by any of the parties or to armed incursion into them or in the event of any deliberate obstruction in or around those areas to the freedom of movement of UNPROFOR or of protected humanitarian convoys;

(10) Decides that, notwithstanding paragraph (1) of resolution 816 (1993), Member States, acting nationally or through regional organizations or arrangements, may take, under the authority of the Security Council and subject to close coordination with the Secretary-General and UNPROFOR, all necessary measures, through the use of air power, in and around the safe areas in the Republic of Bosnia and Herzegovina, to support UNPROFOR in the performance of its mandate set out in paragraphs (5) and (9) above;

(11) Requests the Members States concerned, the Secretary-General and UNPROFOR to coordinate closely on the measures they are taking to implement paragraph (10) above and to report to the Council through the Secretary-General;

(12) Invites the Secretary-General to report to the Council, for decision, if possible within seven days of the adoption of the present resolution, on the modalities of its implementation, including its financial implications;

(13) Further invites the Secretary-General to submit to the Council, not later than two months after the adoption of the present resolution, a report on the implementation of and compliance with the present resolution;

(14) Emphasizes that it will keep open other options for new and tougher measures, none of which is prejudged or excluded from consideration;

(15) Decides to remain actively seized of the matter, and undertakes to take prompt action, as required.

RESOLUTION 929 RWANDA

UN Security Council Resolution S/RES/929 (1994) "Rwanda"
22 June 1994

The Security Council,
Reaffirming all its previous resolutions on the situation in Rwanda, in particular its resolutions 912 (1994) of 21 April 1994, 918 (1994) of 17 May 1994 and 925 (1994) of 8 June 1994, which set out the mandate and force level of the United Nations Assistance Mission for Rwanda (UNAMIR),
Determined to contribute to the resumption of the process of political settlement under the Arusha Peace Agreement and encouraging the Secretary-General and his Special Representative for Rwanda to continue and redouble their efforts at the national, regional and international levels to promote these objectives,
Stressing the importance of the cooperation of all parties for the fulfilment of the objectives of the United Nations in Rwanda,
Having considered the letter of the Secretary-General of 19 June 1994 (S/1994/728), Taking into account the time needed to gather the necessary resources for the effective deployment of UNAMIR, as expanded in resolutions 918 (1994) and 925 (1994),
Noting the offer by Member States to cooperate with the Secretary-General towards the fulfilment of the objectives of the United Nations in Rwanda (S/1994/734), and stressing the strictly humanitarian character of this operation which shall be conducted in an impartial and neutral fashion, and shall not constitute an interposition force between the parties,
Welcoming the cooperation between the United Nations, the Organization of African Unity (OAU) and neighbouring States to bring peace to Rwanda,
Deeply concerned by the continuation of systematic and widespread killings of the civilian population in Rwanda,
Recognizing that the current situation in Rwanda constitutes a unique case which demands an urgent response by the international community,
Determining that the magnitude of the humanitarian crisis in Rwanda constitutes a threat to peace and security in the region,

(1) Welcomes the Secretary-General's letter dated 19 June 1994 (S/1994/728) and agrees that a multinational operation may be set up for humanitarian purposes in Rwanda until UNAMIR is brought up to the necessary strength;
(2) Welcomes also the offer by Member States (S/1994/734) to cooperate with the Secretary-General in order to achieve the objectives of the United Nations in Rwanda through the establishment of a temporary operation under national command and control aimed at contributing, in an impartial way, to the security and protection of displaced persons, refugees and civilians at risk in Rwanda, on the understanding that the costs of implementing the offer will be borne by the Member States concerned;
(3) Acting under Chapter VII of the Charter of the United Nations, authorizes the Member States cooperating with the Secretary-General to conduct the operation referred to in paragraph (2) above using all necessary means to achieve the humanitarian objectives set out in subparagraphs (4) (a) and (b) of
resolution 925 (1994);
(4) Decides that the mission of Member States cooperating with the Secretary-General will be limited to a period of two months following the adoption of the present resolution, unless the Secretary-General determines at an earlier date that the expanded UNAMIR is able to carry out its mandate;
(5) Commends the offers already made by Member States of troops for the expanded UNAMIR;
(6) Calls upon all Member States to respond urgently to the Secretary-General's request for resources, including logistical support, in order to enable expanded UNAMIR to fulfil its mandate effectively as soon as possible and requests the Secretary-General to identify and coordinate the supply of the essential equipment required by troops committed to the expanded UNAMIR;
(7) Welcomes, in this respect, the offers already made by Member States of equipment for troop contributors to UNAMIR and calls on other Members to offer such support, including the possibility of comprehensive provision of equipment to specific troop contributors, to speed UNAMIR's expanded force deployment;
(8) Requests Member States cooperating with the Secretary-General to coordinate closely with UNAMIR and also requests the Secretary-General to set up appropriate mechanisms to this end;
(9) Demands that all parties to the conflict and others concerned immediately bring to an end all killings of civilian populations in areas under their control and allow Member States cooperating with the Secretary-General to implement fully the mission set forth in paragraph (3) above;

PART I   INTERNATIONAL LAW

(10) Requests the States concerned and the Secretary-General, as appropriate, to report to the Council on a regular basis, the first such report to be made no later than fifteen days after the adoption of this resolution, on the implementation of this operation and the progress made towards the fulfilment of the objectives referred to in paragraphs (2) and (3) above;

(11) Also requests the Secretary-General to report on the progress made towards completing the deployment of the expanded UNAMIR within the framework of the report due no later than 9 August 1994 under paragraph (17) of resolution 925 (1994), as well as on progress towards the resumption of the process of political settlement under the Arusha Peace Agreement;

(12) Decides to remain actively seized of the matter.

RESOLUTION 940 HAITI

UN Security Council Resolution S/RES/940 (1994) "Haiti"
31 July 1994

The Security Council, Reaffirming its resolutions 841 (1993) of 16 June 1993, 861 (1993) of 27 August 1993, 862 (1993) of 31 August 1993, 867 (1993) of 23 September 1993, 873 (1993) of 13 October 1993, 875 (1993) of 16 October 1993, 905 (1994) of 23 March 1994, 917 (1994) of 6 May 1994 and 933 (1994) of 30 June 1994,
Recalling the terms of the Governors Island Agreement (S/26063) and the related Pact of New York (S/26297),
Condemning the continuing disregard of those agreements by the illegal de facto regime, and the regime's refusal to cooperate with efforts by the United Nations and the Organization of American States (OAS) to bring about their implementation,
Gravely concerned by the significant further deterioration of the humanitarian situation in Haiti, in particular the continuing escalation by the illegal de facto regime of systematic violations of civil liberties, the desperate plight of Haitian refugees and the recent expulsion of the staff of the International Civilian Mission (MICIVIH), which was condemned in its Presidential statement of 12 July 1994 (S/PRST/1994/32),
Having considered the reports of the Secretary-General of 15 July 1994 (S/1994/828 and Add.1) and 26 July 1994 (S/1994/871),
Taking note of the letter dated 29 July 1994 from the legitimately elected President of Haiti (S/1994/905, annex) and the letter dated 30 July 1994 from the Permanent Representative of Haiti to the United Nations (S/1994/910), Reiterating its commitment for the international community to assist and support the economic, social and institutional development of Haiti,
Reaffirming that the goal of the international community remains the restoration of democracy in Haiti and the prompt return of the legitimately elected President, Jean-Bertrand Aristide, within the framework of the Governors Island Agreement,
Recalling that in resolution 873 (1993) the Council confirmed its readiness to consider the imposition of additional measures if the military authorities in Haiti continued to impede the activities of the United Nations Mission in Haiti (UNMIH) or failed to comply in full with its relevant resolutions and the provisions of the Governors Island Agreement,
Determining that the situation in Haiti continues to constitute a threat to peace and security in the region,

(1) Welcomes the report of the Secretary-General of 15 July 1994 (S/1994/828) and takes note of his support for action under Chapter VII of the Charter of the United Nations in order to assist the legitimate Government of Haiti in the maintenance of public order;
(2) Recognizes the unique character of the present situation in Haiti and its deteriorating, complex and extraordinary nature, requiring an exceptional response;
(3) Determines that the illegal de facto regime in Haiti has failed to comply with the Governors Island Agreement and is in breach of its obligations under the relevant resolutions of the Security Council;
(4) Acting under Chapter VII of the Charter of the United Nations, authorizes Member States to form a multinational force under unified command and control and, in this framework, to use all necessary means to facilitate the departure from Haiti of the military leadership, consistent with the Governors Island Agreement, the prompt return of the legitimately elected President and the restoration of the legitimate authorities of the Government of Haiti, and to establish and maintain a secure and stable environment that will permit implementation of the Governors Island Agreement, on the understanding that the cost of implementing this temporary operation will be borne by the participating Member States;
(5) Approves the establishment, upon adoption of this resolution, of an advance team of UNMIH of not more than sixty personnel, including a group of observers, to establish the appropriate means of coordination with the multinational force, to carry out the monitoring of the operations of the multinational force and other functions described in paragraph (23) of the report of the Secretary-General of 15 July 1994 (S/1994/828), and to assess requirements and to prepare for the deployment of UNMIH upon completion of the mission of the multinational force;
(6) Requests the Secretary-General to report on the activities of the team within thirty days of the date of deployment of the multinational force;
(7) Decides that the tasks of the advance team as defined in paragraph (5) above will expire on the date of termination of the mission of the multinational force;
(8) Decides that the multinational force will terminate its mission and UNMIH will assume the full

range of its functions described in paragraph (9) below when a secure and stable environment has been established and UNMIH has adequate force capability and structure to assume the full range of its functions; the determination will be made by the Security Council, taking into account recommendations from the Member States of the multinational force, which are based on the assessment of the commander of the multinational force, and from the Secretary-General;

(9) Decides to revise and extend the mandate of the United Nations Mission in Haiti (UNMIH) for a period of six months to assist the democratic Government of Haiti in fulfilling its responsibilities in connection with:

(a) sustaining the secure and stable environment established during the multinational phase and protecting international personnel and key installations; and

(b) the professionalization of the Haitian armed forces and the creation of a separate police force;

(10) Requests also that UNMIH assist the legitimate constitutional authorities of Haiti in establishing an environment conducive to the organization of free and fair legislative elections to be called by those authorities and, when requested by them, monitored by the United Nations, in cooperation with the Organization of American States (OAS);

(11) Decides to increase the troop level of UNMIH to 6,000 and establishes the objective of completing UNMIH's mission, in cooperation with the constitutional Government of Haiti, not later than February 1996;

(12) Invites all States, in particular those in the region, to provide appropriate support for the actions undertaken by the United Nations and by Member States pursuant to this and other relevant Security Council resolutions;

(13) Requests the Member States acting in accordance with paragraph (4) above to report to the Council at regular intervals, the first such report to be made not later than seven days following the deployment of the multinational force;

(14) Requests the Secretary-General to report on the implementation of this resolution at sixty-day intervals starting from the date of deployment of the multinational force;

(15) Demands strict respect for the persons and premises of the United Nations, the Organization of American States, other international and humanitarian organizations and diplomatic missions in Haiti, and that no acts of intimidation or violence be directed against personnel engaged in humanitarian or peace-keeping work;

(16) Emphasizes the necessity that, inter alia:

(a) All appropriate steps be taken to ensure the security and safety of the operations and personnel engaged in such operations; and

(b) The security and safety arrangements undertaken extend to all persons engaged in the operations;

(17) Affirms that the Council will review the measures imposed pursuant to resolutions 841 (1993), 873 (1993) and 917 (1994), with a view to lifting them in their entirety, immediately following the return to Haiti of President Jean-Bertrand Aristide;

(18) Decides to remain actively seized of the matter.

UN Security Council Resolution S/RES/1199 (1998) "Kosovo"
23 September 1998

The Security Council,
Recalling its resolution 1160 (1998) of 31 March 1998,
Having considered the reports of the Secretary-General pursuant to that
resolution, and in particular his report of 4 September 1998 (S/1998/834 and Add.1),
Noting with appreciation the statement of the Foreign Ministers of France, Germany, Italy, the Russian Federation, the United Kingdom of Great Britain and Northern Ireland and the United States of America (the Contact Group) of 12 June 1998 at the conclusion of the Contact Group's meeting with the Foreign Ministers of Canada and Japan (S/1998/567, annex), and the further statement of the Contact Group made in Bonn on 8 July 1998 (S/1998/657),
Noting also with appreciation the joint statement by the Presidents of the Russian Federation and the Federal Republic of Yugoslavia of 16 June 1998 (S/1998/526),
Noting further the communication by the Prosecutor of the International Tribunal for the Former Yugoslavia to the Contact Group on 7 July 1998,
Expressing the view that the situation in Kosovo represents an armed conflict within the terms of the mandate of the Tribunal,
Gravely concerned at the recent intense fighting in Kosovo and in particular the excessive and indiscriminate use of force by Serbian security forces and the Yugoslav Army which have resulted in numerous civilian casualties and, according to the estimate of the Secretary-General, the displacement of over 230,000 persons from their homes,
Deeply concerned by the flow of refugees into northern Albania, Bosnia and Herzegovina and other European countries as a result of the use of force in Kosovo, as well as by the increasing numbers of displaced persons within Kosovo, and other parts of the Federal Republic of Yugoslavia, up to 50,000 of whom the United Nations High Commissioner for Refugees has estimated are without shelter and other basic necessities,
Reaffirming the right of all refugees and displaced persons to return to their homes in safety, and underlining the responsibility of the Federal Republic of Yugoslavia for creating the conditions which allow them to do so,
Condemning all acts of violence by any party, as well as terrorism in pursuit of political goals by any group or individual, and all external support for such activities in Kosovo, including the supply of arms and training for terrorist activities in Kosovo and expressing concern at the reports of continuing violations of the prohibitions imposed by resolution 1160 (1998),
Deeply concerned by the rapid deterioration in the humanitarian situation throughout Kosovo, alarmed at the impending humanitarian catastrophe as described in the report of the Secretary-General, and emphasizing the need to prevent this from happening,
Deeply concerned also by reports of increasing violations of human rights and of international humanitarian law, and emphasizing the need to ensure that the rights of all inhabitants of Kosovo are respected,
Reaffirming the objectives of resolution 1160 (1998), in which the Council expressed support for a peaceful resolution of the Kosovo problem which would include an enhanced status for Kosovo, a substantially greater degree of autonomy, and meaningful self-administration,
Reaffirming also the commitment of all Member States to the sovereignty and territorial integrity of the Federal Republic of Yugoslavia,
Affirming that the deterioration of the situation in Kosovo, Federal Republic of Yugoslavia, constitutes a threat to peace and security in the region,
Acting under Chapter VII of the Charter of the United Nations,

(1) Demands that all parties, groups and individuals immediately cease hostilities and maintain a ceasefire in Kosovo, Federal Republic of Yugoslavia, which would enhance the prospects for a meaningful dialogue between the authorities of the Federal Republic of Yugoslavia and the Kosovo Albanian leadership and reduce the risks of a humanitarian catastrophe;
(2) Demands also that the authorities of the Federal Republic of Yugoslavia and the Kosovo Albanian leadership take immediate steps to improve the humanitarian situation and to avert the impending humanitarian catastrophe;
(3) Calls upon the authorities in the Federal Republic of Yugoslavia and the Kosovo Albanian leadership to enter immediately into a meaningful dialogue without preconditions and with international involvement, and to a clear timetable, leading to an end of the crisis and to a negotiated political solu-

PART I   INTERNATIONAL LAW

tion to the issue of Kosovo, and welcomes the current efforts aimed at facilitating such a dialogue;
(4) Demands further that the Federal Republic of Yugoslavia, in addition to the measures called for under resolution 1160 (1998), implement immediately the following concrete measures towards achieving a political solution to the situation in Kosovo as contained in the Contact Group statement of 12 June 1998:
(a) cease all action by the security forces affecting the civilian population and order the withdrawal of security units used for civilian repression;
(b) enable effective and continuous international monitoring in Kosovo by the European Community Monitoring Mission and diplomatic missions accredited to the Federal Republic of Yugoslavia, including access and complete freedom of movement of such monitors to, from and within Kosovo unimpeded by government authorities, and expeditious issuance of appropriate travel documents to international personnel contributing to the monitoring;
(c) facilitate, in agreement with the UNHCR and the International Committee of the Red Cross (ICRC), the safe return of refugees and displaced persons to their homes and allow free and unimpeded access for humanitarian organizations and supplies to Kosovo;
(d) make rapid progress to a clear timetable, in the dialogue referred to in paragraph 3 with the Kosovo Albanian community called for in resolution 1160 (1998), with the aim of agreeing confidence-building measures and finding a political solution to the problems of Kosovo;
(5) Notes, in this connection, the commitments of the President of the Federal Republic of Yugoslavia, in his joint statement with the President of the Russian Federation of 16 June 1998:
(a) to resolve existing problems by political means on the basis of equality for all citizens and ethnic communities in Kosovo;
(b) not to carry out any repressive actions against the peaceful population;
(c) to provide full freedom of movement for and ensure that there will be no restrictions on representatives of foreign States and international institutions accredited to the Federal Republic of Yugoslavia monitoring the situation in Kosovo;
(d) to ensure full and unimpeded access for humanitarian organizations, the ICRC and the UNHCR, and delivery of humanitarian supplies;
(e) to facilitate the unimpeded return of refugees and displaced persons under programmes agreed with the UNHCR and the ICRC, providing State aid for the reconstruction of destroyed homes, and calls for the full implementation of these commitments;
(6) Insists that the Kosovo Albanian leadership condemn all terrorist action, and emphasizes that all elements in the Kosovo Albanian community should pursue their goals by peaceful means only;
(7) Recalls the obligations of all States to implement fully the prohibitions imposed by resolution 1160 (1998);
(8) Endorses the steps taken to establish effective international monitoring of the situation in Kosovo, and in this connection welcomes the establishment of the Kosovo Diplomatic Observer Mission;
(9) Urges States and international organizations represented in the Federal Republic of Yugoslavia to make available personnel to fulfil the responsibility of carrying out effective and continuous international monitoring in Kosovo until the objectives of this resolution and those of resolution 1160 (1998) are achieved;
(10) Reminds the Federal Republic of Yugoslavia that it has the primary responsibility for the security of all diplomatic personnel accredited to the Federal Republic of Yugoslavia as well as the safety and security of all international and non-governmental humanitarian personnel in the Federal Republic of Yugoslavia and calls upon the authorities of the Federal Republic of Yugoslavia and all others concerned in the Federal Republic of Yugoslavia to take all appropriate steps to ensure that monitoring personnel performing functions under this resolution are not subject to the threat or use of force or interference of any kind;
(11) Requests States to pursue all means consistent with their domestic legislation and relevant international law to prevent funds collected on their territory being used to contravene resolution 1160 (1998);
(12) Calls upon Member States and others concerned to provide adequate resources
for humanitarian assistance in the region and to respond promptly and generously
to the United Nations Consolidated Inter-Agency Appeal for Humanitarian Assistance Related to the Kosovo Crisis;
(13) Calls upon the authorities of the Federal Republic of Yugoslavia, the leaders of the Kosovo Albanian community and all others concerned to cooperate fully with the Prosecutor of the International Tribunal for the Former Yugoslavia in the investigation of possible violations within the jurisdiction of the Tribunal;
(14) Underlines also the need for the authorities of the Federal Republic of Yugoslavia to bring to

justice those members of the security forces who have been involved in the mistreatment of civilians and the deliberate destruction of property;

(15) Requests the Secretary-General to provide regular reports to the Council as necessary on his assessment of compliance with this resolution by the authorities of the Federal Republic of Yugoslavia and all elements in the Kosovo Albanian community, including through his regular reports on compliance with resolution 1160 (1998);

(16) Decides, should the concrete measures demanded in this resolution and resolution 1160 (1998) not be taken, to consider further action and additional measures to maintain or restore peace and stability in the region;

(17) Decides to remain seized of the matter.

PART I INTERNATIONAL LAW

UN Security Council Resolution S/RES/1203 (1998) "Kosovo"
24 October 1998

The Security Council,
Recalling its resolutions 1160 (1998) of 31 March 1998 and 1199 (1998) of 23 September 1998, and the importance of the peaceful resolution of the problem of Kosovo, Federal Republic of Yugoslavia,
Having considered the reports of the Secretary-General pursuant to those resolutions, in particular his report of 5 October 1998 (S/1998/912),
Welcoming the agreement signed in Belgrade on 16 October 1998 by the Minister of Foreign Affairs of the Federal Republic of Yugoslavia and the Chairman-in-Office of the Organization for Security and Cooperation in Europe (OSCE) providing for the OSCE to establish a verification mission in Kosovo (S/1998/978), including the undertaking of the Federal Republic of Yugoslavia to comply with resolutions 1160 (1998) and 1199 (1998),
Welcoming also the agreement signed in Belgrade on 15 October 1998 by the Chief of General Staff of the Federal Republic of Yugoslavia and the Supreme Allied Commander, Europe, of the North Atlantic Treaty Organization (NATO) providing for the establishment of an air verification mission over Kosovo (S/1998/991, annex), complementing the OSCE Verification Mission,
Welcoming also the decision of the Permanent Council of the OSCE of 15 October 1998 (S/1998/959, annex),
Welcoming the decision of the Secretary-General to send a mission to the Federal Republic of Yugoslavia to establish a first-hand capacity to assess developments on the ground in Kosovo,
Reaffirming that, under the Charter of the United Nations, primary responsibility for the maintenance of international peace and security is conferred on the Security Council,
Recalling the objectives of resolution 1160 (1998), in which the Council expressed support for a peaceful resolution of the Kosovo problem which would include an enhanced status for Kosovo, a substantially greater degree of autonomy, and meaningful self-administration,
Condemning all acts of violence by any party, as well as terrorism in pursuit of political goals by any group or individual, and all external support for such activities in Kosovo, including the supply of arms and training for terrorist activities in Kosovo, and expressing concern at the reports of continuing violations of the prohibitions imposed by resolution 1160 (1998),
Deeply concerned at the recent closure by the authorities of the Federal Republic of Yugoslavia of independent media outlets in the Federal Republic of Yugoslavia, and emphasizing the need for these to be allowed freely to resume their operations,
Deeply alarmed and concerned at the continuing grave humanitarian situation throughout Kosovo and the impending humanitarian catastrophe, and re-emphasizing the need to prevent this from happening,
Stressing the importance of proper coordination of humanitarian initiatives undertaken by States, the United Nations High Commissioner for Refugees and international organizations in Kosovo,
Emphasizing the need to ensure the safety and security of members of the Verification Mission in Kosovo and the Air Verification Mission over Kosovo,
Reaffirming the commitment of all Member States to the sovereignty and territorial integrity of the Federal Republic of Yugoslavia,
Affirming that the unresolved situation in Kosovo, Federal Republic of Yugoslavia, constitutes a continuing threat to peace and security in the region,
Acting under Chapter VII of the Charter of the United Nations,

(1) Endorses and supports the agreements signed in Belgrade on 16 October 1998 between the Federal Republic of Yugoslavia and the OSCE, and on 15 October 1998 between the Federal Republic of Yugoslavia and NATO, concerning the verification of compliance by the Federal Republic of Yugoslavia and all others concerned in Kosovo with the requirements of its resolution 1199 (1998), and demands the full and prompt implementation of these agreements by the Federal Republic of Yugoslavia;
(2) Notes the endorsement by the Government of Serbia of the accord reached by the President of the Federal Republic of Yugoslavia and the United States Special Envoy (S/1998/953, annex), and the public commitment of the Federal Republic of Yugoslavia to complete negotiations on a framework for a political settlement by 2 November 1998, and calls for the full implementation of these commitments;
(3) Demands that the Federal Republic of Yugoslavia comply fully and swiftly with resolutions 1160 (1998) and 1199 (1998) and cooperate fully with the OSCE Verification Mission in Kosovo and the NATO Air Verification Mission over Kosovo according to the terms of the agreements referred to in

paragraph (1) above;
(4) Demands also that the Kosovo Albanian leadership and all other elements of the Kosovo Albanian community comply fully and swiftly with resolutions 1160 (1998) and 1199 (1998) and cooperate fully with the OSCE Verification Mission in Kosovo;
(5) Stresses the urgent need for the authorities in the Federal Republic of Yugoslavia and the Kosovo Albanian leadership to enter immediately into a meaningful dialogue without preconditions and with international involvement, and to a clear timetable, leading to an end of the crisis and to a negotiated political solution to the issue of Kosovo;
(6) Demands that the authorities of the Federal Republic of Yugoslavia, the Kosovo Albanian leadership and all others concerned respect the freedom of movement of the OSCE Verification Mission and other international personnel;
(7) Urges States and international organizations to make available personnel to the OSCE Verification Mission in Kosovo;
(8) Reminds the Federal Republic of Yugoslavia that it has the primary responsibility for the safety and security of all diplomatic personnel accredited to the Federal Republic of Yugoslavia, including members of the OSCE Verification Mission, as well as the safety and security of all international and non governmental humanitarian personnel in the Federal Republic of Yugoslavia, and calls upon the authorities of the Federal Republic of Yugoslavia, and all others concerned throughout the Federal Republic of Yugoslavia including the Kosovo Albanian leadership, to take all appropriate steps to ensure that personnel performing functions under this resolution and the agreements referred to in paragraph (1) above are not subject to the threat or use of force or interference of any kind;
(9) Welcomes in this context the commitment of the Federal Republic of Yugoslavia to guarantee the safety and security of the Verification Missions as contained in the agreements referred to in paragraph (1) above, notes that, to this end, the OSCE is considering arrangements to be implemented in cooperation with other organizations, and affirms that, in the event of an emergency, action may be needed to ensure their safety and freedom of movement as envisaged in the agreements referred to in paragraph (1) above;
(10) Insists that the Kosovo Albanian leadership condemn all terrorist actions, demands that such actions cease immediately and emphasizes that all elements in the Kosovo Albanian community should pursue their goals by peaceful means only;
(11) Demands immediate action from the authorities of the Federal Republic of Yugoslavia and the Kosovo Albanian leadership to cooperate with international efforts to improve the humanitarian situation and to avert the impending humanitarian catastrophe;
(12) Reaffirms the right of all refugees and displaced persons to return to their homes in safety, and underlines the responsibility of the Federal Republic of Yugoslavia for creating the conditions which allow them to do so;
(13) Urges Member States and others concerned to provide adequate resources for humanitarian assistance in the region and to respond promptly and generously to the United Nations Consolidated Inter-Agency Appeal for Humanitarian
Assistance Related to the Kosovo crisis;
(14) Calls for prompt and complete investigation, including international supervision and participation, of all atrocities committed against civilians and full cooperation with the International Tribunal for the former Yugoslavia, including compliance with its orders, requests for information and investigations;
(15) Decides that the prohibitions imposed by paragraph (8) of resolution 1160 (1998) shall not apply to relevant equipment for the sole use of the Verification Missions in accordance with the agreements referred to in paragraph (1) above;
(16) Requests the Secretary-General, acting in consultation with the parties concerned with the agreements referred to in paragraph (1) above, to report regularly to the Council regarding implementation of this resolution;
(17) Decides to remain seized of the matter.

PART I   INTERNATIONAL LAW

UN Security Council Resolution S/RES/1244 (1999) "Kosovo"
10 June 1999

The Security Council,
Bearing in mind the purposes and principles of the Charter of the United Nations, and the primary responsibility of the Security Council for the maintenance of international peace and security,
Recalling its resolutions 1160 (1998) of 31 March 1998, 1199 (1998) of 23 September 1998, 1203 (1998) of 24 October 1998 and 1239 (1999) of 14 May 1999,
Regretting that there has not been full compliance with the requirements of these resolutions,
Determined to resolve the grave humanitarian situation in Kosovo, Federal Republic of Yugoslavia, and to provide for the safe and free return of all refugees and displaced persons to their homes,
Condemning all acts of violence against the Kosovo population as well as all terrorist acts by any party,
Recalling the statement made by the Secretary-General on 9 April 1999, expressing concern at the humanitarian tragedy taking place in Kosovo,
Reaffirming the right of all refugees and displaced persons to return to their homes in safety,
Recalling the jurisdiction and the mandate of the International Tribunal for the Former Yugoslavia,
Welcoming the general principles on a political solution to the Kosovo crisis adopted on 6 May 1999 (S/1999/516, annex 1 to this resolution) and welcoming also the acceptance by the Federal Republic of Yugoslavia of the principles set forth in points 1 to 9 of the paper presented in Belgrade on 2 June 1999 (S/1999/649, annex 2 to this resolution), and the Federal Republic of Yugoslavia's agreement to that paper,
Reaffirming the commitment of all Member States to the sovereignty and territorial integrity of the Federal Republic of Yugoslavia and the other States of the region, as set out in the Helsinki Final Act and annex 2,
Reaffirming the call in previous resolutions for substantial autonomy and meaningful self-administration for Kosovo,
Determining that the situation in the region continues to constitute a threat to international peace and security,
Determined to ensure the safety and security of international personnel and the implementation by all concerned of their responsibilities under the present resolution, and acting for these purposes under Chapter VII of the Charter of the United Nations,

(1) Decides that a political solution to the Kosovo crisis shall be based on the general principles in annex 1 and as further elaborated in the principles and other required elements in annex 2;
(2) Welcomes the acceptance by the Federal Republic of Yugoslavia of the principles and other required elements referred to in paragraph (1) above, and demands the full cooperation of the Federal Republic of Yugoslavia in their rapid implementation;
(3) Demands in particular that the Federal Republic of Yugoslavia put an immediate and verifiable end to violence and repression in Kosovo, and begin and complete verifiable phased withdrawal from Kosovo of all military, police and paramilitary forces according to a rapid timetable, with which the deployment of the international security presence in Kosovo will be synchronized;
(4) Confirms that after the withdrawal an agreed number of Yugoslav and Serb military and police personnel will be permitted to return to Kosovo to perform the functions in accordance with annex 2;
(5) Decides on the deployment in Kosovo, under United Nations auspices, of international civil and security presences, with appropriate equipment and personnel as required, and welcomes the agreement of the Federal Republic of Yugoslavia to such presences;
(6) Requests the Secretary-General to appoint, in consultation with the Security Council, a Special Representative to control the implementation of the international civil presence, and further requests the Secretary-General to instruct his Special Representative to coordinate closely with the international security presence to ensure that both presences operate towards the same goals and in a mutually supportive manner;
(7) Authorizes Member States and relevant international organizations to establish the international security presence in Kosovo as set out in point 4 of annex 2 with all necessary means to fulfil its responsibilities under paragraph (9) below;
(8) Affirms the need for the rapid early deployment of effective international civil and security presences to Kosovo, and demands that the parties cooperate fully in their deployment;
(9) Decides that the responsibilities of the international security presence to be deployed and acting in Kosovo will include:
(a) Deterring renewed hostilities, maintaining and where necessary enforcing a ceasefire, and ensur-

RESOLUTION 1244 KOSOVO

ing the withdrawal and preventing the return into Kosovo of Federal and Republic military, police and paramilitary forces, except as provided in point 6 of annex 2;
(b) Demilitarizing the Kosovo Liberation Army (KLA) and other armed Kosovo Albanian groups as required in paragraph (15) below;
(c) Establishing a secure environment in which refugees and displaced persons can return home in safety, the international civil presence can operate, a transitional administration can be established, and humanitarian aid can be delivered;
(d) Ensuring public safety and order until the international civil presence can take responsibility for this task;
(e) Supervising demining until the international civil presence can, as appropriate, take over responsibility for this task;
(f) Supporting, as appropriate, and coordinating closely with the work of the international civil presence;
(g) Conducting border monitoring duties as required;
(h) Ensuring the protection and freedom of movement of itself, the international civil presence, and other international organizations;
(10) Authorizes the Secretary-General, with the assistance of relevant international organizations, to establish an international civil presence in Kosovo in order to provide an interim administration for Kosovo under which the people of Kosovo can enjoy substantial autonomy within the Federal Republic of Yugoslavia, and which will provide transitional administration while establishing and overseeing the development of provisional democratic selfgoverning institutions to ensure conditions for a peaceful and normal life for all inhabitants of Kosovo;
(11) Decides that the main responsibilities of the international civil presence will include:
(a) Promoting the establishment, pending a final settlement, of substantial autonomy and self-government in Kosovo, taking full account of annex 2 and of the Rambouillet
accords (S/1999/648);
(b) Performing basic civilian administrative functions where and as long as required;
(c) Organizing and overseeing the development of provisional institutions for democratic and autonomous self-government pending a political settlement, including the holding of elections;
(d) Transferring, as these institutions are established, its administrative responsibilities while overseeing and supporting the consolidation of Kosovo's local provisional institutions and other peacebuilding activities;
(e) Facilitating a political process designed to determine Kosovo's future status, taking into account the Rambouillet accords (S/1999/648);
(f) In a final stage, overseeing the transfer of authority from Kosovo's provisional institutions to institutions established under a political settlement;
(g) Supporting the reconstruction of key infrastructure and other economic reconstruction;
(h) Supporting, in coordination with international humanitarian organizations, humanitarian and disaster relief aid;
(i) Maintaining civil law and order, including establishing local police forces and meanwhile through the deployment of international police personnel to serve in Kosovo;
(j) Protecting and promoting human rights;
(k) Assuring the safe and unimpeded return of all refugees and displaced persons to their homes in Kosovo;
(12) Emphasizes the need for coordinated humanitarian relief operations, and for the Federal Republic of Yugoslavia to allow unimpeded access to Kosovo by humanitarian aid organizations and to cooperate with such organizations so as to ensure the fast and effective delivery of international aid;
(13) Encourages all Member States and international organizations to contribute to economic and social reconstruction as well as to the safe return of refugees and displaced persons, and emphasizes in this context the importance of convening an international donors' conference, particularly for the purposes set out in paragraph (11)(g) above, at the earliest possible date;
(14) Demands full cooperation by all concerned, including the international security presence, with the International Tribunal for the Former Yugoslavia;
(15) Demands that the KLA and other armed Kosovo Albanian groups end immediately all offensive actions and comply with the requirements for demilitarization as laid down by the head of the international security presence in consultation with the Special Representative of the Secretary-General;
(16) Decides that the prohibitions imposed by paragraph (8) of resolution 1160 (1998) shall not apply to arms and related matériel for the use of the international civil and security presences;
(17) Welcomes the work in hand in the European Union and other international organizations to develop a comprehensive approach to the economic development and stabilization of the region

affected by the Kosovo crisis, including the implementation of a Stability Pact for South Eastern Europe with broad international participation in order to further the promotion of democracy, economic prosperity, stability and regional cooperation;

(18) Demands that all States in the region cooperate fully in the implementation of all aspects of this resolution;

(19) Decides that the international civil and security presences are established for an initial period of 12 months, to continue thereafter unless the Security Council decides otherwise;

(20) Requests the Secretary-General to report to the Council at regular intervals on the implementation of this resolution, including reports from the leaderships of the international civil and security presences, the first reports to be submitted within 30 days of the adoption of this resolution;

(21) Decides to remain actively seized of the matter.

Annex 1

Statement by the Chairman on the conclusion of the meeting of the G-8 Foreign Ministers held at the Petersberg Centre on 6 May 1999

The G-8 Foreign Ministers adopted the following general principles on the
political solution to the Kosovo crisis:
- Immediate and verifiable end of violence and repression in Kosovo;
- Withdrawal from Kosovo of military, police and paramilitary forces;
- Deployment in Kosovo of effective international civil and security presences, endorsed and adopted by the United Nations, capable of guaranteeing the achievement of the common objectives;
- Establishment of an interim administration for Kosovo to be decided by the Security Council of the United Nations to ensure conditions for a peaceful and normal life for all inhabitants in Kosovo;
- The safe and free return of all refugees and displaced persons and unimpeded access to Kosovo by humanitarian aid organizations;
- A political process towards the establishment of an interim political framework agreement providing for a substantial self-government for Kosovo, taking full account of the Rambouillet accords and the principles of sovereignty and territorial integrity of the Federal Republic of Yugoslavia and the other countries of the region, and the demilitarization of the KLA;
- Comprehensive approach to the economic development and stabilization
of the crisis region.

Annex 2

Agreement should be reached on the following principles to move towards a resolution of the Kosovo crisis:

(1) An immediate and verifiable end of violence and repression in Kosovo.

(2) Verifiable withdrawal from Kosovo of all military, police and paramilitary forces according to a rapid timetable.

(3) Deployment in Kosovo under United Nations auspices of effective international civil and security presences, acting as may be decided under Chapter VII of the Charter, capable of guaranteeing the achievement of common objectives.

(4) The international security presence with substantial North Atlantic Treaty Organization participation must be deployed under unified command and control and authorized to establish a safe environment for all people in Kosovo and to facilitate the safe return to their homes of all displaced persons and refugees.

(5) Establishment of an interim administration for Kosovo as a part of the international civil presence under which the people of Kosovo can enjoy substantial autonomy within the Federal Republic of Yugoslavia, to be decided by the Security Council of the United Nations. The interim administration to provide transitional administration while establishing and overseeing the development of provisional democratic self-governing institutions to ensure conditions for a peaceful and normal life for all inhabitants in Kosovo.

(6) After withdrawal, an agreed number of Yugoslav and Serbian personnel will be permitted to return to perform the following functions:
- Liaison with the international civil mission and the international
security presence;
- Marking/clearing minefields;
- Maintaining a presence at Serb patrimonial sites;
- Maintaining a presence at key border crossings.

(7) Safe and free return of all refugees and displaced persons under the supervision of the Office of the United Nations High Commissioner for Refugees and unimpeded access to Kosovo by humanitar-

ian aid organizations.

(8) A political process towards the establishment of an interim political framework agreement providing for substantial self-government for Kosovo, taking full account of the Rambouillet accords and the principles of sovereignty and territorial integrity of the Federal Republic of Yugoslavia and the other countries of the region, and the demilitarization of UCK. Negotiations between the parties for a settlement should not delay or disrupt the establishment of democratic self-governing institutions.

(9) A comprehensive approach to the economic development and stabilization of the crisis region. This will include the implementation of a stability pact for South-Eastern Europe with broad international participation in order to further promotion of democracy, economic prosperity, stability and regional cooperation.

(10) Suspension of military activity will require acceptance of the principles set forth above in addition to agreement to other, previously identified, required elements, which are specified in the footnote below. A military-technical agreement will then be rapidly concluded that would, among other things, specify additional modalities, including the roles and functions of Yugoslav/Serb personnel in Kosovo:

Withdrawal
- Procedures for withdrawals, including the phased, detailed schedule and delineation of a buffer area in Serbia beyond which forces will be withdrawn;
Returning personnel
- Equipment associated with returning personnel;
- Terms of reference for their functional responsibilities;
- Timetable for their return;
- Delineation of their geographical areas of operation;
- Rules governing their relationship to the international security presence and the international civil mission.

PART I INTERNATIONAL LAW

UN Security Council Resolution S/RES/1325 (2001) "Women and Security"
31 October 2001

The Security Council,
Recalling its resolutions 1261 (1999) of 25 August 1999, 1265 (1999) of 17 September 1999, 1296 (2000) of 19 April 2000 and 1314 (2000) of 11 August 2000, as well as relevant statements of its President, and recalling also the statement of its President to the press on the occasion of the United Nations Day for Women's Rights and International Peace (International Women's Day) of 8 March 2000 (SC/6816),
Recalling also the commitments of the Beijing Declaration and Platform for Action (A/52/231) as well as those contained in the outcome document of the twenty-third Special Session of the United Nations General Assembly entitled "Women 2000: Gender Equality, Development and Peace for the Twenty-First Century" (A/S-23/10/Rev.1), in particular those concerning women and armed conflict,
Bearing in mind the purposes and principles of the Charter of the United Nations and the primary responsibility of the Security Council under the Charter for the maintenance of international peace and security,
Expressing concern that civilians, particularly women and children, account for the vast majority of those adversely affected by armed conflict, including as refugees and internally displaced persons, and increasingly are targeted by combatants and armed elements, and recognizing the consequent impact this has on durable peace and reconciliation,
Reaffirming the important role of women in the prevention and resolution of conflicts and in peace-building, and stressing the importance of their equal participation and full involvement in all efforts for the maintenance and promotion of peace and security, and the need to increase their role in decision-making with regard to conflict prevention and resolution,
Reaffirming also the need to implement fully international humanitarian and human rights law that protects the rights of women and girls during and after conflicts,
Emphasizing the need for all parties to ensure that mine clearance and mine awareness programmes take into account the special needs of women and girls,
Recognizing the urgent need to mainstream a gender perspective into peacekeeping operations, and in this regard noting the Windhoek Declaration and the Namibia Plan of Action on Mainstreaming a Gender Perspective in Multidimensional Peace Support Operations (S/2000/693),
Recognizing also the importance of the recommendation contained in the statement of its President to the press of 8 March 2000 for specialized training for all peacekeeping personnel on the protection, special needs and human rights of women and children in conflict situations,
Recognizing that an understanding of the impact of armed conflict on women and girls, effective institutional arrangements to guarantee their protection and full participation in the peace process can significantly contribute to the maintenance and promotion of international peace and security,
Noting the need to consolidate data on the impact of armed conflict on women and girls,

(1) Urges Member States to ensure increased representation of women at all decision-making levels in national, regional and international institutions and mechanisms for the prevention, management, and resolution of conflict;
(2) Encourages the Secretary-General to implement his strategic plan of action (A/49/587) calling for an increase in the participation of women at decision making levels in conflict resolution and peace processes;
(3) Urges the Secretary-General to appoint more women as special representatives and envoys to pursue good offices on his behalf, and in this regard calls on Member States to provide candidates to the Secretary-General, for inclusion in a regularly updated centralized roster;
(4) Further urges the Secretary-General to seek to expand the role and contribution of women in United Nations field-based operations, and especially among military observers, civilian police, human rights and humanitarian personnel;
(5) Expresses its willingness to incorporate a gender perspective into peacekeeping operations, and urges the Secretary-General to ensure that, where appropriate, field operations include a gender component;
(6) Requests the Secretary-General to provide to Member States training guidelines and materials on the protection, rights and the particular needs of women, as well as on the importance of involving women in all peacekeeping and peacebuilding measures, invites Member States to incorporate these elements as well as HIV/AIDS awareness training into their national training programmes for military and civilian police personnel in preparation for deployment, and further requests the Secretary-General to ensure that civilian personnel of peacekeeping operations receive similar training;

(7) Urges Member States to increase their voluntary financial, technical and logistical support for gender-sensitive training efforts, including those undertaken by relevant funds and programmes, inter alia, the United Nations Fund for Women and United Nations Children's Fund, and by the Office of the United Nations High Commissioner for Refugees and other relevant bodies;
(8) Calls on all actors involved, when negotiating and implementing peace agreements, to adopt a gender perspective, including, inter alia:
(a) The special needs of women and girls during repatriation and resettlement and for rehabilitation, reintegration and post-conflict reconstruction;
(b) Measures that support local women's peace initiatives and indigenous processes for conflict resolution, and that involve women in all of the implementation mechanisms of the peace agreements;
(c) Measures that ensure the protection of and respect for human rights of women and girls, particularly as they relate to the constitution, the electoral system, the police and the judiciary;
(9) Calls upon all parties to armed conflict to respect fully international law applicable to the rights and protection of women and girls, especially as civilians, in particular the obligations applicable to them under the Geneva Conventions of 1949 and the Additional Protocols thereto of 1977, the Refugee Convention of 1951 and the Protocol thereto of 1967, the Convention on the Elimination of All Forms of Discrimination against Women of 1979 and the Optional Protocol thereto of 1999 and the United Nations Convention on the Rights of the Child of 1989 and the two Optional Protocols thereto of 25 May 2000, and to bear in mind the relevant provisions of the Rome Statute of the International Criminal Court;
(10) Calls on all parties to armed conflict to take special measures to protect women and girls from gender-based violence, particularly rape and other forms of sexual abuse, and all other forms of violence in situations of armed conflict;
(11) Emphasizes the responsibility of all States to put an end to impunity and to prosecute those responsible for genocide, crimes against humanity, and war crimes including those relating to sexual and other violence against women and girls, and in this regard stresses the need to exclude these crimes, where feasible from amnesty provisions;
(12) Calls upon all parties to armed conflict to respect the civilian and humanitarian character of refugee camps and settlements, and to take into account the particular needs of women and girls, including in their design, and recalls its resolutions 1208 (1998) of 19 November 1998 and 1296 (2000) of 19 April 2000;
(13) Encourages all those involved in the planning for disarmament, demobilization and reintegration to consider the different needs of female and male ex-combatants and to take into account the needs of their dependants;
(14) Reaffirms its readiness, whenever measures are adopted under Article 41 of the Charter of the United Nations, to give consideration to their potential impact on the civilian population, bearing in mind the special needs of women and girls, in order to consider appropriate humanitarian exemptions;
(15) Expresses its willingness to ensure that Security Council missions take into account gender considerations and the rights of women, including through consultation with local and international women's groups;
(16) Invites the Secretary-General to carry out a study on the impact of armed conflict on women and girls, the role of women in peace-building and the gender dimensions of peace processes and conflict resolution, and further invites him to submit a report to the Security Council on the results of this study and to make this available to all Member States of the United Nations;
(17) Requests the Secretary-General, where appropriate, to include in his reporting to the Security Council progress on gender mainstreaming throughout peacekeeping missions and all other aspects relating to women and girls;
(18) Decides to remain actively seized of the matter.

PART I INTERNATIONAL LAW

UN Security Council Resolution S/RES/1441 (2002) "Iraq"
08 November 2002

The Security Council,
Recalling all its previous relevant resolutions, in particular its resolutions 661 (1990) of 6 August 1990, 678 (1990) of 29 November 1990, 686 (1991) of 2 March 1991, 687 (1991) of 3 April 1991, 688 (1991) of 5 April 1991, 707 (1991) of 15 August 1991, 715 (1991) of 11 October 1991, 986 (1995) of 14 April 1995, and 1284 (1999) of 17 December 1999, and all the relevant statements of its President,
Recalling also its resolution 1382 (2001) of 29 November 2001 and its intention to implement it fully, Recognizing the threat Iraq's non-compliance with Council resolutions and proliferation of weapons of mass destruction and long-range missiles poses to international peace and security,
Recalling that its resolution 678 (1990) authorized Member States to use all necessary means to uphold and implement its resolution 660 (1990) of 2 August 1990 and all relevant resolutions subsequent to resolution 660 (1990) and to restore international peace and security in the area,
Further recalling that its resolution 687 (1991) imposed obligations on Iraq as a necessary step for achievement of its stated objective of restoring international peace and security in the area,
Deploring the fact that Iraq has not provided an accurate, full, final, and complete disclosure, as required by resolution 687 (1991), of all aspects of its programmes to develop weapons of mass destruction and ballistic missiles with a range greater than one hundred and fifty kilometres, and of all holdings of such weapons, their components and production facilities and locations, as well as all other nuclear programmes, including any which it claims are for purposes not related to nuclear-weapons-usable material,
Deploring further that Iraq repeatedly obstructed immediate, unconditional, and unrestricted access to sites designated by the United Nations Special Commission (UNSCOM) and the International Atomic Energy Agency (IAEA), failed to cooperate fully and unconditionally with UNSCOM and IAEA weapons inspectors, as required by resolution 687 (1991), and ultimately ceased all cooperation with UNSCOM and the IAEA in 1998,
Deploring the absence, since December 1998, in Iraq of international monitoring, inspection, and verification, as required by relevant resolutions, of weapons of mass destruction and ballistic missiles, in spite of the Council's repeated demands that Iraq provide immediate, unconditional, and unrestricted access to the United Nations Monitoring, Verification and Inspection Commission (UNMOVIC), established in resolution 1284 (1999) as the successor organization to UNSCOM, and the IAEA, and regretting the consequent prolonging of the crisis in the region and the suffering of the Iraqi people,
Deploring also that the Government of Iraq has failed to comply with its commitments pursuant to resolution 687 (1991) with regard to terrorism, pursuant to resolution 688 (1991) to end repression of its civilian population and to provide access by international humanitarian organizations to all those in need of assistance in Iraq, and pursuant to resolutions 686 (1991), 687 (1991), and 1284 (1999) to return or cooperate in accounting for Kuwaiti and third country nationals wrongfully detained by Iraq, or to return Kuwaiti property wrongfully seized by Iraq,
Recalling that in its resolution 687 (1991) the Council declared that a ceasefire would be based on acceptance by Iraq of the provisions of that resolution, including the obligations on Iraq contained therein,
Determined to ensure full and immediate compliance by Iraq without conditions or restrictions with its obligations under resolution 687 (1991) and other relevant resolutions and recalling that the resolutions of the Council constitute the governing standard of Iraqi compliance,
Recalling that the effective operation of UNMOVIC, as the successor organization to the Special Commission, and the IAEA is essential for the implementation of resolution 687 (1991) and other relevant resolutions,
Noting that the letter dated 16 September 2002 from the Minister for Foreign Affairs of Iraq addressed to the Secretary-General is a necessary first step toward rectifying Iraq's continued failure to comply with relevant Council resolutions,
Noting further the letter dated 8 October 2002 from the Executive Chairman of UNMOVIC and the Director-General of the IAEA to General Al-Saadi of the Government of Iraq laying out the practical arrangements, as a follow-up to their meeting in Vienna, that are prerequisites for the resumption of inspections in Iraq by UNMOVIC and the IAEA, and expressing the gravest concern at the continued failure by the Government of Iraq to provide confirmation of the arrangements as laid out in that letter,
Reaffirming the commitment of all Member States to the sovereignty and territorial integrity of Iraq,

RESOLUTION 1441 IRAQ

Kuwait, and the neighbouring States,
Commending the Secretary-General and members of the League of Arab States and its Secretary-General for their efforts in this regard,
Determined to secure full compliance with its decisions,
Acting under Chapter VII of the Charter of the United Nations,

(1) Decides that Iraq has been and remains in material breach of its obligations under relevant resolutions, including resolution 687 (1991), in particular through Iraq's failure to cooperate with United Nations inspectors and the IAEA, and to complete the actions required under paragraphs (8) to (13) of resolution 687 (1991);

(2) Decides, while acknowledging paragraph (1) above, to afford Iraq, by this resolution, a final opportunity to comply with its disarmament obligations under relevant resolutions of the Council; and accordingly decides to set up an enhanced inspection regime with the aim of bringing to full and verified completion the disarmament process established by resolution 687 (1991) and subsequent resolutions of the Council;

(3) Decides that, in order to begin to comply with its disarmament obligations, in addition to submitting the required biannual declarations, the Government of Iraq shall provide to UNMOVIC, the IAEA, and the Council, not later than 30 days from the date of this resolution, a currently accurate, full, and complete declaration of all aspects of its programmes to develop chemical, biological, and nuclear weapons, ballistic missiles, and other delivery systems such as unmanned aerial vehicles and dispersal systems designed for use on aircraft, including any holdings and precise locations of such weapons, components, subcomponents, stocks of agents, and related material and equipment, the locations and work of its research, development and production facilities, as well as all other chemical, biological, and nuclear programmes, including any which it claims are for purposes not related to weapon production or material;

(4) Decides that false statements or omissions in the declarations submitted by Iraq pursuant to this resolution and failure by Iraq at any time to comply with, and cooperate fully in the implementation of, this resolution shall constitute a further material breach of Iraq's obligations and will be reported to the Council for assessment in accordance with paragraphs (11) and (12) below;

(5) Decides that Iraq shall provide UNMOVIC and the IAEA immediate, unimpeded, unconditional, and unrestricted access to any and all, including underground, areas, facilities, buildings, equipment, records, and means of transport which they wish to inspect, as well as immediate, unimpeded, unrestricted, and private access to all officials and other persons whom UNMOVIC or the IAEA wish to interview in the mode or location of UNMOVIC's or the IAEA's choice pursuant to any aspect of their mandates; further decides that UNMOVIC and the IAEA may at their discretion conduct interviews inside or outside of Iraq, may facilitate the travel of those interviewed and family members outside of Iraq, and that, at the sole discretion of UNMOVIC and the IAEA, such interviews may occur without the presence of observers from the Iraqi Government; and instructs UNMOVIC and requests the IAEA to resume inspections no later than 45 days following adoption of this resolution and to update the Council 60 days thereafter;

(6) Endorses the 8 October 2002 letter from the Executive Chairman of UNMOVIC and the Director-General of the IAEA to General Al-Saadi of the Government of Iraq, which is annexed hereto, and decides that the contents of the letter shall be binding upon Iraq;

(7) Decides further that, in view of the prolonged interruption by Iraq of the presence of UNMOVIC and the IAEA and in order for them to accomplish the tasks set forth in this resolution and all previous relevant resolutions and notwithstanding prior understandings, the Council hereby establishes the following revised or additional authorities, which shall be binding upon Iraq, to facilitate their work in Iraq:

– UNMOVIC and the IAEA shall determine the composition of their inspection teams and ensure that these teams are composed of the most qualified and experienced experts available;

– All UNMOVIC and IAEA personnel shall enjoy the privileges and immunities, corresponding to those of experts on mission, provided in the Convention on Privileges and Immunities of the United Nations and the Agreement on the Privileges and Immunities of the IAEA;

– UNMOVIC and the IAEA shall have unrestricted rights of entry into and out of Iraq, the right to free, unrestricted, and immediate movement to and from inspection sites, and the right to inspect any sites and buildings, including immediate, unimpeded, unconditional, and unrestricted access to Presidential Sites equal to that at other sites, notwithstanding the provisions of resolution 1154 (1998) of 2 March 1998;

– UNMOVIC and the IAEA shall have the right to be provided by Iraq the names of all personnel currently and formerly associated with Iraq's chemical, biological, nuclear, and ballistic missile

PART I INTERNATIONAL LAW

programmes and the associated research, development, and production facilities;
– Security of UNMOVIC and IAEA facilities shall be ensured by sufficient United Nations security guards;
– UNMOVIC and the IAEA shall have the right to declare, for the purposes of freezing a site to be inspected, exclusion zones, including surrounding areas and transit corridors, in which Iraq will suspend ground and aerial movement so that nothing is changed in or taken out of a site being inspected;
– UNMOVIC and the IAEA shall have the free and unrestricted use and landing of fixed- and rotary-winged aircraft, including manned and unmanned reconnaissance vehicles;
– UNMOVIC and the IAEA shall have the right at their sole discretion verifiably to remove, destroy, or render harmless all prohibited weapons, subsystems, components, records, materials, and other related items, and the right to impound or close any facilities or equipment for the production thereof; and
– UNMOVIC and the IAEA shall have the right to free import and use of equipment or materials for inspections and to seize and export any equipment, materials, or documents taken during inspections, without search of UNMOVIC or IAEA personnel or official or personal baggage;
(8) Decides further that Iraq shall not take or threaten hostile acts directed against any representative or personnel of the United Nations or the IAEA or of any Member State taking action to uphold any Council resolution;
(9) Requests the Secretary-General immediately to notify Iraq of this resolution, which is binding on Iraq; demands that Iraq confirm within seven days of that notification its intention to comply fully with this resolution; and demands further that Iraq cooperate immediately, unconditionally, and actively with UNMOVIC and the IAEA;
(10) Requests all Member States to give full support to UNMOVIC and the IAEA in the discharge of their mandates, including by providing any information related to prohibited programmes or other aspects of their mandates, including on Iraqi attempts since 1998 to acquire prohibited items, and by recommending sites to be inspected, persons to be interviewed, conditions of such interviews, and data to be collected, the results of which shall be reported to the Council by UNMOVIC and the IAEA;
(11) Directs the Executive Chairman of UNMOVIC and the Director-General of the IAEA to report immediately to the Council any interference by Iraq with inspection activities, as well as any failure by Iraq to comply with its disarmament obligations, including its obligations regarding inspections under this resolution;
(12) Decides to convene immediately upon receipt of a report in accordance with paragraphs (4) or (11) above, in order to consider the situation and the need for full compliance with all of the relevant Council resolutions in order to secure international peace and security;
(13) Recalls, in that context, that the Council has repeatedly warned Iraq that it will face serious consequences as a result of its continued violations of its obligations;
(14) Decides to remain seized of the matter.

Annex

Text of Blix/El-Baradei letter
United Nations Monitoring, Verification and Inspection Commission
The Executive Chairman
International Atomic Energy Agency
The Director General
8 October 2002

Dear General Al-Saadi,
During our recent meeting in Vienna, we discussed practical arrangements that are prerequisites for the resumption of inspections in Iraq by UNMOVIC and the IAEA. As you recall, at the end of our meeting in Vienna we agreed on a statement which listed some of the principal results achieved, particularly Iraq's acceptance of all the rights of inspection provided for in all of the relevant Security Council resolutions. This acceptance was stated to be without any conditions attached.
During our 3 October 2002 briefing to the Security Council, members of the Council suggested that we prepare a written document on all of the conclusions we reached in Vienna. This letter lists those conclusions and seeks your confirmation thereof. We shall report accordingly to the Security Council.
In the statement at the end of the meeting, it was clarified that UNMOVIC and the IAEA will be granted immediate, unconditional and unrestricted access to sites, including what was termed "sensitive sites" in the past. As we noted, however, eight presidential sites have been the subject of special procedures under a Memorandum of Understanding of 1998. Should these sites be subject, as all

other sites, to immediate, unconditional and unrestricted access, UNMOVIC and the IAEA would conduct inspections there with the same professionalism.

H.E. General Amir H. Al-Saadi
Advisor
Presidential Office
Baghdad
Iraq

We confirm our understanding that UNMOVIC and the IAEA have the right to determine the number of inspectors required for access to any particular site. This determination will be made on the basis of the size and complexity of the site being inspected. We also confirm that Iraq will be informed of the designation of additional sites, i.e. sites not declared by Iraq or previously inspected by either UNSCOM or the IAEA, through a Notification of Inspection (NIS) provided upon arrival of the inspectors at such sites.

Iraq will ensure that no proscribed material, equipment, records or other relevant items will be destroyed except in the presence of UNMOVIC and/or IAEA inspectors, as appropriate, and at their request.

UNMOVIC and the IAEA may conduct interviews with any person in Iraq whom they believe may have information relevant to their mandate. Iraq will facilitate such interviews. It is for UNMOVIC and the IAEA to choose the mode and location for interviews.

The National Monitoring Directorate (NMD) will, as in the past, serve as the Iraqi counterpart for the inspectors. The Baghdad Ongoing Monitoring and Verification Centre (BOMVIC) will be maintained on the same premises and under the same conditions as was the former Baghdad Monitoring and Verification Centre. The NMD will make available services as before, cost free, for the refurbishment of the premises.

The NMD will provide free of cost: (a) escorts to facilitate access to sites to be inspected and communication with personnel to be interviewed; (b) a hotline for BOMVIC which will be staffed by an English speaking person on a 24 hour a day/seven days a week basis; (c) support in terms of personnel and ground transportation within the country, as requested; and (d) assistance in the movement of materials and equipment at inspectors' request (construction, excavation equipment, etc.). NMD will also ensure that escorts are available in the event of inspections outside normal working hours, including at night and on holidays.

Regional UNMOVIC/IAEA offices may be established, for example, in Basra and Mosul, for the use of their inspectors. For this purpose, Iraq will provide, without cost, adequate office buildings, staff accommodation, and appropriate escort personnel.

UNMOVIC and the IAEA may use any type of voice or data transmission, including satellite and/or inland networks, with or without encryption capability. UNMOVIC and the IAEA may also install equipment in the field with the capability for transmission of data directly to the BOMVIC, New York and Vienna (e.g. sensors, surveillance cameras). This will be facilitated by Iraq and there will be no interference by Iraq with UNMOVIC or IAEA communications.

Iraq will provide, without cost, physical protection of all surveillance equipment, and construct antennae for remote transmission of data, at the request of UNMOVIC and the IAEA. Upon request by UNMOVIC through the NMD, Iraq will allocate frequencies for communications equipment.

Iraq will provide security for all UNMOVIC and IAEA personnel. Secure and suitable accommodations will be designated at normal rates by Iraq for these personnel. For their part, UNMOVIC and the IAEA will require that their staff not stay at any accommodation other than those identified in consultation with Iraq.

On the use of fixed-wing aircraft for transport of personnel and equipment and for inspection purposes, it was clarified that aircraft used by UNMOVIC and IAEA staff arriving in Baghdad may land at Saddam International Airport. The points of departure of incoming aircraft will be decided by UNMOVIC. The Rasheed airbase will continue to be used for UNMOVIC and IAEA helicopter operations. UNMOVIC and Iraq will establish air liaison offices at the airbase. At both Saddam International Airport and Rasheed airbase, Iraq will provide the necessary support premises and facilities. Aircraft fuel will be provided by Iraq, as before, free of charge.

On the wider issue of air operations in Iraq, both fixed-wing and rotary, Iraq will guarantee the safety of air operations in its air space outside the no-fly zones. With regard to air operations in the no-fly zones, Iraq will take all steps within its control to ensure the safety of such operations.

Helicopter flights may be used, as needed, during inspections and for technical activities, such as gamma detection, without limitation in all parts of Iraq and without any area excluded. Helicopters may also be used for medical evacuation.

PART I   INTERNATIONAL LAW

On the question of aerial imagery, UNMOVIC may wish to resume the use of U-2 or Mirage overflights. The relevant practical arrangements would be similar to those implemented in the past. As before, visas for all arriving staff will be issued at the point of entry on the basis of the UN Laissez-Passer or UN Certificate; no other entry or exit formalities will be required. The aircraft passenger manifest will be provided one hour in advance of the arrival of the aircraft in Baghdad. There will be no searching of UNMOVIC or IAEA personnel or of official or personal baggage. UNMOVIC and the IAEA will ensure that their personnel respect the laws of Iraq restricting the export of certain items, for example, those related to Iraq's national cultural heritage. UNMOVIC and the IAEA may bring into, and remove from, Iraq all of the items and materials they require, including satellite phones and other equipment. With respect to samples, UNMOVIC and IAEA will, where feasible, split samples so that Iraq may receive a portion while another portion is kept for reference purposes. Where appropriate, the organizations will send the samples to more than one laboratory for analysis. We would appreciate your confirmation of the above as a correct reflection of our talks in Vienna. Naturally, we may need other practical arrangements when proceeding with inspections. We would expect in such matters, as with the above, Iraq's co-operation in all respect.

Yours sincerely,

(Signed) (Signed)

Hans Blix Mohamed ElBaradei
Executive Chairman Director General
United Nations Monitoring, International Atomic Energy Agency

RESOLUTION 1540 WEAPONS OF MASS DESTRUCTION

**UN Security Council Resolution S/RES/1540 (2004) "Weapons of Mass Destruction"
28 April 2004**

*The Security Council,
Affirming that proliferation of nuclear, chemical and biological weapons, as well as their means of delivery, constitutes a threat to international peace and security,
Reaffirming, in this context, the Statement of its President adopted at the Council's meeting at the level of Heads of State and Government on 31 January 1992 (S/23500), including the need for all Member States to fulfil their obligations in relation to arms control and disarmament and to prevent proliferation in all its aspects of all weapons of mass destruction,
Recalling also that the Statement underlined the need for all Member States to resolve peacefully in accordance with the Charter any problems in that context threatening or disrupting the maintenance of regional and global stability,
Affirming its resolve to take appropriate and effective actions against any threat to international peace and security caused by the proliferation of nuclear, chemical and biological weapons and their means of delivery, in conformity with its primary responsibilities, as provided for in the United Nations Charter,
Affirming its support for the multilateral treaties whose aim is to eliminate or prevent the proliferation of nuclear, chemical or biological weapons and the importance for all States parties to these treaties to implement them fully in order to promote international stability,
Welcoming efforts in this context by multilateral arrangements which contribute to non-proliferation,
Affirming that prevention of proliferation of nuclear, chemical and biological weapons should not hamper international cooperation in materials, equipment and technology for peaceful purposes while goals of peaceful utilization should not be used as a cover for proliferation,
Gravely concerned by the threat of terrorism and the risk that non-State actors such as those identified in the United Nations list established and maintained by the Committee established under Security Council resolution 1267 and those to whom resolution 1373 applies, may acquire, develop, traffic in or use nuclear, chemical and biological weapons and their means of delivery,
Gravely concerned by the threat of illicit trafficking in nuclear, chemical, or biological weapons and their means of delivery, and related materials, which adds a new dimension to the issue of proliferation of such weapons and also poses a threat to international peace and security,
Recognizing the need to enhance coordination of efforts on national, subregional, regional and international levels in order to strengthen a global response to this serious challenge and threat to international security,
Recognizing that most States have undertaken binding legal obligations under treaties to which they are parties, or have made other commitments aimed at preventing the proliferation of nuclear, chemical or biological weapons, and have taken effective measures to account for, secure and physically protect sensitive materials, such as those required by the Convention on the Physical Protection of Nuclear Materials and those recommended by the IAEA Code of Conduct on the Safety and Security of Radioactive Sources,
Recognizing further the urgent need for all States to take additional effective measures to prevent the proliferation of nuclear, chemical or biological weapons and their means of delivery,
Encouraging all Member States to implement fully the disarmament treaties and agreements to which they are party,
Reaffirming the need to combat by all means, in accordance with the Charter of the United Nations, threats to international peace and security caused by terrorist acts,
Determined to facilitate henceforth an effective response to global threats in the area of non-proliferation,
Acting under Chapter VII of the Charter of the United Nations,*

(1) Decides that all States shall refrain from providing any form of support to non-State actors that attempt to develop, acquire, manufacture, possess, transport, transfer or use nuclear, chemical or biological weapons and their means of delivery;
(2) Decides also that all States, in accordance with their national procedures, shall adopt and enforce appropriate effective laws which prohibit any non-State actor to manufacture, acquire, possess, develop, transport, transfer or use nuclear, chemical or biological weapons and their means of delivery, in particular for terrorist purposes, as well as attempts to engage in any of the foregoing activities, participate in them as an accomplice, assist or finance them;
(3) Decides also that all States shall take and enforce effective measures to establish domestic controls to prevent the proliferation of nuclear, chemical, or biological weapons and their means of

PART I INTERNATIONAL LAW

delivery, including by establishing appropriate controls over related materials and to this end shall:
(a) Develop and maintain appropriate effective measures to account for and secure such items in production, use, storage or transport;
(b) Develop and maintain appropriate effective physical protection measures;
(c) Develop and maintain appropriate effective border controls and law enforcement efforts to detect, deter, prevent and combat, including through international cooperation when necessary, the illicit trafficking and brokering in such items in accordance with their national legal authorities and legislation and consistent with international law;
(d) Establish, develop, review and maintain appropriate effective national export and trans-shipment controls over such items, including appropriate laws and regulations to control export, transit, trans-shipment and re-export and controls on providing funds and services related to such export and trans-shipment such as financing, and transporting that would contribute to proliferation, as well as establishing end-user controls; and establishing and enforcing appropriate criminal or civil penalties for violations of such export control laws and regulations;
(4) Decides to establish, in accordance with rule 28 of its provisional rules of procedure, for a period of no longer than two years, a Committee of the Security Council, consisting of all members of the Council, which will, calling as appropriate on other expertise, report to the Security Council for its examination, on the implementation of this resolution, and to this end calls upon States to present a first report no later than six months from the adoption of this resolution to the Committee on steps they have taken or intend to take to implement this resolution;
(5) Decides that none of the obligations set forth in this resolution shall be interpreted so as to conflict with or alter the rights and obligations of State Parties to the Nuclear Non-Proliferation Treaty, the Chemical Weapons Convention and the Biological and Toxin Weapons Convention or alter the responsibilities of the International Atomic Energy Agency or the Organization for the Prohibition of Chemical Weapons;
(6) Recognizes the utility in implementing this resolution of effective national control lists and calls upon all Member States, when necessary, to pursue at the earliest opportunity the development of such lists;
(7) Recognizes that some States may require assistance in implementing the provisions of this resolution within their territories and invites States in a position to do so to offer assistance as appropriate in response to specific requests to the States lacking the legal and regulatory infrastructure, implementation experience and/or resources for fulfilling the above provisions;
(8) Calls upon all States:
(a) To promote the universal adoption and full implementation, and, where necessary, strengthening of multilateral treaties to which they are parties, whose aim is to prevent the proliferation of nuclear, biological or chemical weapons;
(b) To adopt national rules and regulations, where it has not yet been done, to ensure compliance with their commitments under the key multilateral non-proliferation
treaties;
(c) To renew and fulfil their commitment to multilateral cooperation, in particular within the framework of the International Atomic Energy Agency, the Organization for the Prohibition of Chemical Weapons and the Biological and Toxin Weapons Convention, as important means of pursuing and achieving their common objectives in the area of non-proliferation and of promoting international cooperation for peaceful purposes;
(d) To develop appropriate ways to work with and inform industry and the public regarding their obligations under such laws;
(9) Calls upon all States to promote dialogue and cooperation on non-proliferation so as to address the threat posed by proliferation of nuclear, chemical, or biological weapons, and their means of delivery;
(10) Further to counter that threat, calls upon all States, in accordance with their national legal authorities and legislation and consistent with international law, to take cooperative action to prevent illicit trafficking in nuclear, chemical or biological weapons, their means of delivery, and related materials;
(11) Expresses its intention to monitor closely the implementation of this resolution and, at the appropriate level, to take further decisions which may be required to this end;
(12) Decides to remain seized of the matter.

UN Security Council Resolution S/RES/1851 (2008) "Somalia"
16 December 2008

The Security Council,
Recalling its previous resolutions concerning the situation in Somalia, especially resolutions 1814 (2008), 1816 (2008), 1838 (2008), 1844 (2008), and 1846 (2008),
Continuing to be gravely concerned by the dramatic increase in the incidents of piracy and armed robbery at sea off the coast of Somalia in the last six months, and by the threat that piracy and armed robbery at sea against vessels pose to the prompt, safe and effective delivery of humanitarian aid to Somalia, and noting that pirate attacks off the coast of Somalia have become more sophisticated and daring and have expanded in their geographic scope, notably evidenced by the hijacking of the M/V Sirius Star 500 nautical miles off the coast of Kenya and subsequent unsuccessful attempts well east of Tanzania,
Reaffirming its respect for the sovereignty, territorial integrity, political independence and unity of Somalia, including Somalia's rights with respect to offshore natural resources, including fisheries, in accordance with international law,
Further reaffirming that international law, as reflected in the United Nations Convention on the Law of the Sea of 10 December 1982 (UNCLOS), sets out the legal framework applicable to combating piracy and armed robbery at sea, as well as other ocean activities,
Again taking into account the crisis situation in Somalia, and the lack of capacity of the Transitional Federal Government (TFG) to interdict, or upon interdiction to prosecute pirates or to patrol and secure the waters off the coast of Somalia, including the international sea lanes and Somalia's territorial waters,
Noting the several requests from the TFG for international assistance to counter piracy off its coast, including the letter of 9 December 2008 from the President of Somalia requesting the international community to assist the TFG in taking all necessary measures to interdict those who use Somali territory and airspace to plan, facilitate or undertake acts of piracy and armed robbery at sea, and the 1 September 2008 letter from the President of Somalia to the Secretary-General of the UN expressing the appreciation of the TFG to the Security Council for its assistance and expressing the TFG's willingness to consider working with other States and regional organizations to combat piracy and armed robbery off the coast
of Somalia,
Welcoming the launching of the EU operation Atalanta to combat piracy off the coast of Somalia and to protect vulnerable ships bound for Somalia, as well as the efforts by the North Atlantic Treaty Organization, and other States acting in a national capacity in cooperation with the TFG to suppress piracy off the coast of Somalia,
Also welcoming the recent initiatives of the Governments of Egypt, Kenya, and the Secretary-General's Special Representative for Somalia, and the United Nations Office on Drugs and Crime (UNODC) to achieve effective measures to remedy the causes, capabilities, and incidents of piracy and armed robbery off the coast of Somalia, and emphasizing the need for current and future counter-piracy operations to effectively coordinate their activities,
Noting with concern that the lack of capacity, domestic legislation, and clarity about how to dispose of pirates after their capture, has hindered more robust international action against the pirates off the coast of Somalia and in some cases led to pirates being released without facing justice, and reiterating that the 1988 Convention for the Suppression of Unlawful Acts Against the Safety of Maritime Navigation ("SUA Convention") provides for parties to create criminal offences, establish jurisdiction, and accept delivery of persons responsible for or suspected of seizing or exercising control over a ship by force or threat thereof or any other form of intimidation,
Welcoming the report of the Monitoring Group on Somalia of 20 November 2008 (S/2008/769), and noting the role piracy may play in financing embargo violations by armed groups,
Determining that the incidents of piracy and armed robbery at sea in the waters off the coast of Somalia exacerbate the situation in Somalia which continues to constitute a threat to international peace and security in the region,
Acting under Chapter VII of the Charter of the United Nations,

(1) Reiterates that it condemns and deplores all acts of piracy and armed robbery against vessels in waters off the coast of Somalia;
(2) Calls upon States, regional and international organizations that have the capacity to do so, to take part actively in the fight against piracy and armed robbery at sea off the coast of Somalia, in particular, consistent with this resolution, resolution 1846 (2008), and international law, by deploying

PART I   INTERNATIONAL LAW

naval vessels and military aircraft and through seizure and disposition of boats, vessels, arms and other related equipment used in the commission of piracy and armed robbery at sea off the coast of Somalia, or for which there are reasonable grounds for suspecting such use;
(3) Invites all States and regional organizations fighting piracy off the coast of Somalia to conclude special agreements or arrangements with countries willing to take custody of pirates in order to embark law enforcement officials ("shipriders") from the latter countries, in particular countries in the region, to facilitate the investigation and prosecution of persons detained as a result of operations conducted under this resolution for acts of piracy and armed robbery at sea off the coast of Somalia, provided that the advance consent of the TFG is obtained for the exercise of third state jurisdiction by shipriders in Somali territorial waters and that such agreements or arrangements do not prejudice the effective implementation of the SUA Convention;
(4) Encourages all States and regional organizations fighting piracy and armed robbery at sea off the coast of Somalia to establish an international cooperation mechanism to act as a common point of contact between and among states, regional and international organizations on all aspects of combating piracy and armed robbery at sea off Somalia's coast; and recalls that future recommendations on ways to ensure the long-term security of international navigation off the coast of Somalia, including the long-term security of WFP maritime deliveries to Somalia and a possible coordination and leadership role for the United Nations in this regard to rally Member States and regional organizations to counter piracy and armed robbery at sea off the coast of Somalia are to be detailed in a report by the Secretary-General no later than three months after the adoption of resolution 1846;
(5) Further encourages all states and regional organizations fighting piracy and armed robbery at sea off the coast of Somalia to consider creating a centre in the region to coordinate information relevant to piracy and armed robbery at sea off the coast of Somalia, to increase regional capacity with assistance of UNODC to arrange effective shiprider agreements or arrangements consistent with UNCLOS and to implement the SUA Convention, the United Nations Convention against Transnational Organized Crime and other relevant instruments to which States in the region are party, in order to effectively investigate and prosecute piracy and armed robbery at sea offences;
(6) In response to the letter from the TFG of 9 December 2008, encourages Member States to continue to cooperate with the TFG in the fight against piracy and armed robbery at sea, notes the primary role of the TFG in rooting out piracy and armed robbery at sea, and decides that for a period of twelve months from the date of adoption of resolution 1846, States and regional organizations cooperating in the fight against piracy and armed robbery at sea off the coast of Somalia for which advance notification has been provided by the TFG to the Secretary-General may undertake all necessary measures that are appropriate in Somalia, for the purpose of suppressing acts of piracy and armed robbery at sea, pursuant to the request of the TFG, provided, however, that any measures undertaken pursuant to the authority of this paragraph shall be undertaken consistent with applicable international humanitarian and human rights law;
(7) Calls on Member States to assist the TFG, at its request and with notification to the Secretary-General, to strengthen its operational capacity to bring to justice those who are using Somali territory to plan, facilitate or undertake criminal acts of piracy and armed robbery at sea, and stresses that any measures undertaken pursuant to this paragraph shall be consistent with applicable international human rights law;
(8) Welcomes the communiqué issued by the International Conference on Piracy around Somalia held in Nairobi, Kenya, on 11 December 2008 and encourages Member States to work to enhance the capacity of relevant states in the region to combat piracy, including judicial capacity;
(9) Notes with concern the findings contained in the 20 November 2008 report of the Monitoring Group on Somalia that escalating ransom payments are fuelling the growth of piracy in waters off the coast of Somalia, and that the lack of enforcement of the arms embargo established by resolution 733 (1992) has permitted ready access to the arms and ammunition used by the pirates and driven in part the phenomenal growth in piracy;
(10) Affirms that the authorization provided in this resolution apply only with respect to the situation in Somalia and shall not affect the rights or obligations or responsibilities of Member States under international law, including any rights or obligations under UNCLOS, with respect to any other situation, and underscores in particular that this resolution shall not be considered as establishing customary international law, and affirms further that such authorizations have been provided only following the receipt of the 9 December 2008 letter conveying the consent of the TFG;
(11) Affirms that the measures imposed by paragraph (5) of resolution 733 (1992) and further elaborated upon by paragraphs (1) and (2) or resolution 1425 (2002) shall not apply to weapons and military equipment destined for the sole use of Member States and regional organizations undertaking measures in accordance with paragraph (6) above;

(12) Urges States in collaboration with the shipping and insurance industries, and the IMO to continue to develop avoidance, evasion, and defensive best practices and advisories to take when under attack or when sailing in waters off the coast of Somalia, and further urges States to make their citizens and vessels available for forensic investigation as appropriate at the first port of call immediately following an act or attempted act of piracy or armed robbery at sea or release from captivity;
(13) Decides to remain seized of the matter.

PART I INTERNATIONAL LAW

UN Security Council Resolution S/RES/1970 (2011) "Peace and Security in Africa"
26 February 2011

The Security Council,
Expressing grave concern at the situation in the Libyan Arab Jamahiriya and condemning the violence and use of force against civilians,
Deploring the gross and systematic violation of human rights, including the repression of peaceful demonstrators, expressing deep concern at the deaths of civilians, and rejecting unequivocally the incitement to hostility and violence against the civilian population made from the highest level of the Libyan government,
Welcoming the condemnation by the Arab League, the African Union, and the Secretary General of the Organization of the Islamic Conference of the serious violations of human rights and international humanitarian law that are being committed in the Libyan Arab Jamahiriya,
Taking note of the letter to the President of the Security Council from the Permanent Representative of the Libyan Arab Jamahiriya dated 26 February 2011,
Welcoming the Human Rights Council resolution A/HRC/S-15/2 of 25 February 2011, including the decision to urgently dispatch an independent international commission of inquiry to investigate all alleged violations of international human rights law in the Libyan Arab Jamahiriya, to establish the facts and circumstances of such violations and of the crimes perpetrated, and where possible identify those responsible,
Considering that the widespread and systematic attacks currently taking place in the Libyan Arab Jamahiriya against the civilian population may amount to crimes against humanity,
Expressing concern at the plight of refugees forced to flee the violence in the Libyan Arab Jamahiriya,
Expressing concern also at the reports of shortages of medical supplies to treat the wounded,
Recalling the Libyan authorities' responsibility to protect its population,
Underlining the need to respect the freedoms of peaceful assembly and of expression, including freedom of the media,
Stressing the need to hold to account those responsible for attacks, including by forces under their control, on civilians,
Recalling article 16 of the Rome Statute under which no investigation or prosecution may be commenced or proceeded with by the International Criminal Court for a period of 12 months after a Security Council request to that effect,
Expressing concern for the safety of foreign nationals and their rights in the Libyan Arab Jamahiriya,
Reaffirming its strong commitment to the sovereignty, independence, territorial integrity and national unity of the Libyan Arab Jamahiriya.
Mindful of its primary responsibility for the maintenance of international peace and security under the Charter of the United Nations,
Acting under Chapter VII of the Charter of the United Nations, and taking measures under its Article 41,

(1) Demands an immediate end to the violence and calls for steps to fulfil the legitimate demands of the population;
(2) Urges the Libyan authorities to:
(a) Act with the utmost restraint, respect human rights and international humanitarian law, and allow immediate access for international human rights monitors;
(b) Ensure the safety of all foreign nationals and their assets and facilitate the departure of those wishing to leave the country;
(c) Ensure the safe passage of humanitarian and medical supplies, and humanitarian agencies and workers, into the country; and
(d) Immediately lift restrictions on all forms of media;
(3) Requests all Member States, to the extent possible, to cooperate in the evacuation of those foreign nationals wishing to leave the country;
ICC referral
(4) Decides to refer the situation in the Libyan Arab Jamahiriya since 15 February 2011 to the Prosecutor of the International Criminal Court;
(5) Decides that the Libyan authorities shall cooperate fully with and provide any necessary assistance to the Court and the Prosecutor pursuant to this resolution and, while recognizing that States not party to the Rome Statute have no obligation under the Statute, urges all States and concerned regional and other international organizations to cooperate fully with the Court and the Prosecutor;

(6) Decides that nationals, current or former officials or personnel from a State outside the Libyan Arab Jamahiriya which is not a party to the Rome Statute of the International Criminal Court shall be subject to the exclusive jurisdiction of that State for all alleged acts or omissions arising out of or related to operations in the Libyan Arab Jamahiriya established or authorized by the Council, unless such exclusive jurisdiction has been expressly waived by the State;
(7) Invites the Prosecutor to address the Security Council within two months of the adoption of this resolution and every six months thereafter on actions taken pursuant to this resolution;
(8) Recognizes that none of the expenses incurred in connection with the referral, including expenses related to investigations or prosecutions in connection with that referral, shall be borne by the United Nations and that such costs shall be borne by the parties to the Rome Statute and those States that wish to contribute voluntarily;

Arms embargo
(9) Decides that all Member States shall immediately take the necessary measures to prevent the direct or indirect supply, sale or transfer to the Libyan Arab Jamahiriya, from or through their territories or by their nationals, or using their flag vessels or aircraft, of arms and related materiel of all types, including weapons and ammunition, military vehicles and equipment, paramilitary equipment, and spare parts for the aforementioned, and technical assistance, training, financial or other assistance, related to military activities or the provision, maintenance or use of any arms and related materiel, including the provision of armed mercenary personnel whether or not originating in their territories, and decides further that this measure shall not apply to:
(a) Supplies of non-lethal military equipment intended solely for humanitarian or protective use, and related technical assistance or training, as approved in advance by the Committee established pursuant to paragraph (24) below;
(b) Protective clothing, including flak jackets and military helmets, temporarily exported to the Libyan Arab Jamahiriya by United Nations personnel, representatives of the media and humanitarian and development works and associated personnel, for their personal use only; or
(c) Other sales or supply of arms and related materiel, or provision of assistance or personnel, as approved in advance by the Committee;
(10) Decides that the Libyan Arab Jamahiriya shall cease the export of all arms and related materiel and that all Member States shall prohibit the procurement of such items from the Libyan Arab Jamahiriya by their nationals, or using their flagged vessels or aircraft, and whether or not originating in the territory of the Libyan Arab Jamahiriya;
(11) Calls upon all States, in particular States neighbouring the Libyan Arab Jamahiriya, to inspect, in accordance with their national authorities and legislation and consistent with international law, in particular the law of the sea and relevant international civil aviation agreements, all cargo to and from the Libyan Arab Jamahiriya, in their territory, including seaports and airports, if the State concerned has information that provides reasonable grounds to believe the cargo contains items the supply, sale, transfer, or export of which is prohibited by paragraphs (9) or (10) of this resolution for the purpose of ensuring strict implementation of those provisions;
(12) Decides to authorize all Member States to, and that all Member States shall, upon discovery of items prohibited by paragraph (9) or (10) of this resolution, seize and dispose (such as through destruction, rendering inoperable, storage or transferring to a State other than the originating or destination States for disposal) items the supply, sale, transfer or export of which is prohibited by paragraph (9) or (10) of this resolution and decides further that all Member States shall cooperate in such efforts;
(13) Requires any Member State when it undertakes an inspection pursuant to paragraph (11) above, to submit promptly an initial written report to the Committee containing, in particular, explanation of the grounds for the inspections, the results of such inspections, and whether or not cooperation was provided, and, if prohibited items for transfer are found, further requires such Member States to submit to the Committee, at a later stage, a subsequent written report containing relevant details on the inspection, seizure, and disposal, and relevant details of the transfer, including a description of the items, their origin and intended destination, if this information is not in the initial report;
(14) Encourages Member States to take steps to strongly discourage their nationals from travelling to the Libyan Arab Jamahiriya to participate in activities on behalf of the Libyan authorities that could reasonably contribute to the violation of human rights;

Travel ban
(15) Decides that all Member States shall take the necessary measures to prevent the entry into or transit through their territories of individuals listed in Annex I of this resolution or designated by the

PART I   INTERNATIONAL LAW

Committee established pursuant to paragraph (24) below, provided that nothing in this paragraph shall oblige a State to refuse its own nationals entry into its territory;
(16) Decides that the measures imposed by paragraph (15) above shall not apply:
(a) Where the Committee determines on a case-by-case basis that such travel is justified on the grounds of humanitarian need, including religious obligation;
(b) Where entry or transit is necessary for the fulfilment of a judicial process;
(c) Where the Committee determines on a case-by-case basis that an exemption would further the objectives of peace and national reconciliation in the Libyan Arab Jamahiriya and stability in the region; or
(d) Where a State determines on a case-by-case basis that such entry or transit is required to advance peace and stability in the Libyan Arab Jamahiriya and the States subsequently notifies the Committee within forty-eight hours after making such a determination;

Asset freeze
(17) Decides that all Member States shall freeze without delay all funds, other financial assets and economic resources which are on their territories, which are owned or controlled, directly or indirectly, by the individuals or entities listed in Annex II of this resolution or designated by the Committee established pursuant to paragraph (24) below, or by individuals or entities acting on their behalf or at their direction, or by entities owned or controlled by them, and decides further that all Member States shall ensure that any funds, financial assets or economic resources are prevented from being made available by their nationals or by any individuals or entities within their territories, to or for the benefit of the individuals or entities listed in Annex II of this resolution or individuals designated by the Committee;
(18) Expresses its intention to ensure that assets frozen pursuant to paragraph (17) shall at a later stage be made available to and for the benefit of the people of the Libyan Arab Jamahiriya;
(19) Decides that the measures imposed by paragraph (17) above do not apply to funds, other financial assets or economic resources that have been determined by relevant Member States:
(a) To be necessary for basic expenses, including payment for foodstuffs, rent or mortgage, medicines and medical treatment, taxes, insurance premiums, and public utility charges or exclusively for payment of reasonable professional fees and reimbursement of incurred expenses associated with the provision of legal services in accordance with national laws, or fees or service charges, in accordance with national laws, for routine holding or maintenance of frozen funds, other financial assets and economic resources, after notification by the relevant State to the Committee of the intention to authorize, where appropriate, access to such funds, other financial assets or economic resources and in the absence of a negative decision by the Committee within five working days of such notification;
(b) To be necessary for extraordinary expenses, provided that such determination has been notified by the relevant State or Member States to the Committee and has been approved by the Committee; or
(c) To be the subject of a judicial, administrative or arbitral lien or judgment, in which case the funds, other financial assets and economic resources may be used to satisfy that lien or judgment provided that the lien or judgment was entered into prior to the date of the present resolution, is not for the benefit of a person or entity designated pursuant to paragraph (17) above, and has been notified by the relevant State or Member States to the Committee;
(20) Decides that Member States may permit the addition to the accounts frozen pursuant to the provisions of paragraph (17) above of interests or other earnings due on those accounts or payments due under contracts, agreements or obligations that arose prior to the date on which those accounts became subject to the provisions of this resolution, provided that any such interest, other earnings and payments continue to be subject to these provisions and are frozen;
(21) Decides that the measures in paragraph (17) above shall not prevent a designated person or entity from making payment due under a contract entered into prior to the listing of such a person or entity, provided that the relevant States have determined that the payment is not directly or indirectly received by a person or entity designated pursuant to paragraph (17) above, and after notification by the relevant States to the Committee of the intention to make or receive such payments or to authorize, where appropriate, the unfreezing of funds, other financial assets or economic resources for this purpose, 10 working days prior to such authorization;

Designation criteria
(22) Decides that the measures contained in paragraphs (15) and (17) shall apply to the individuals and entities designated by the Committee, pursuant to paragraph (24)(b) and (c), respectively;
(a) Involved in or complicit in ordering, controlling, or otherwise directing, the commission of serious human rights abuses against persons in the Libyan Arab Jamahiriya, including by being involved in or complicit in planning, commanding, ordering or conducting attacks, in violation of international

RESOLUTION 1970 PEACE AND SECURITY IN AFRICA

law, including aerial bombardments, on civilian populations and facilities; or
(b) Acting for or on behalf of or at the direction of individuals or entities identified in subparagraph (a).
(23) Strongly encourages Member States to submit to the Committee names of individuals who meet the criteria set out in paragraph (22) above;

New Sanctions Committee
(24) Decides to establish, in accordance with rule 28 of its provisional rules of procedure, a Committee of the Security Council consisting of all the members of the Council (herein "the Committee"), to undertake to following tasks:
(a) To monitor implementation of the measures imposed in paragraphs (9), (10), (15), and (17);
(b) To designate those individuals subject to the measures imposed by paragraphs (15) and to consider requests for exemptions in accordance with paragraph (16) above;
(c) To designate those individuals subject to the measures imposed by paragraph (17) above and to consider requests for exemptions in accordance with paragraphs (19) and (20) above;
(d) To establish such guidelines as may be necessary to facilitate the implementation of the measures imposed above;
(e) To report within thirty days to the Security Council on its work for the first report and thereafter to report as deemed necessary by the Committee;
(f) To encourage a dialogue between the Committee and interested Member States, in particular those in the region, including by inviting representatives of such States to meet with the Committee to discuss implementation of the measures;
(g) To seek from all States whatever information it may consider useful regarding the actions taken by them to implement effectively the measures imposed above;
(h) To examine and take appropriate action on information regarding alleged violations or non-compliance with the measures contained in this resolution;
(25) Calls upon all Member States to report to the Committee within 120 days of the adoption of this resolution on the steps they have taken with a view to implementing effectively paragraphs (9), (10), (15) and (17) above;

Humanitarian assistance
(26) Calls upon all Member States, working together and acting in cooperation with the Secretary General, to facilitate and support the return of humanitarian agencies and make available humanitarian and related assistance in the Libyan Arab Jamahiriya, and requests the States concerned to keep the Security Council regularly informed on the progress of actions undertaken pursuant to this paragraph, and expresses its readiness to consider taking additional appropriate measures, as necessary, to achieve this;

Commitment to review
(27) Affirms that it shall keep the Libyan authorities' actions under continuous review and that it shall be prepared to review the appropriateness of the measures contained in this resolution, including the strengthening, modification, suspension or lifting of the measures, as may be needed at any time in light of the Libyan authorities' compliance with relevant provisions of this resolution;
(28) Decides to remain actively seized of the matter.

Annex I

Travel ban
(1) Al-Baghdadi, Dr Abdulqader Mohammed
Passport number: B010574. Date of birth: 01/07/1950.
Head of the Liaison Office of the Revolutionary Committees. Revolutionary Committees involved in violence against demonstrators.
(2) Dibri, Abdulqader Yusef
Date of birth: 1946. Place of birth: Houn, Libya.
Head of Muammar Qadhafi's personal security. Responsibility for regime security. History of directing violence against dissidents.
(3) Dorda, Abu Zayd Umar
Director, External Security Organisation. Regime loyalist. Head of external intelligence agency.
(4) Jabir, Major General Abu Bakr Yunis
Date of birth: 1952. Place of birth: Jalo, Libya.
Defence Minister. Overall responsibility for actions of armed forces.

PART I   INTERNATIONAL LAW

(5) Matuq, Matuq Mohammed
Date of birth: 1956. Place of birth: Khoms.
Secretary for Utilities. Senior member of regime. Involvement with Revolutionary Committees. Past history of involvement in suppression of dissent and violence.
(6) Qadhaf Al-dam, Sayyid Mohammed
Date of birth: 1948. Place of birth: Sirte, Libya.
Cousin of Muammar Qadhafi. In the 1980s, Sayyid was involved in the dissident assassination campaign and allegedly responsible for several deaths in Europe. He is also thought to have been involved in arms procurement.
(7) Qadhafi, Aisha Muammar
Date of birth: 1978. Place of birth: Tripoli, Libya.
Daughter of Muammar Qadhafi. Closeness of association with regime.
(8) Qadhafi, Hannibal Muammar
Passport number: B/002210. Date of birth: 20/09/1975. Place of birth: Tripoli,
Libya. Son of Muammar Qadhafi. Closeness of association with regime.
(9) Qadhafi, Khamis Muammar
Date of birth: 1978. Place of birth: Tripoli, Libya.
Son of Muammar Qadhafi. Closeness of association with regime. Command of military units involved in repression of demonstrations.
(10) Qadhafi, Mohammed Muammar
Date of birth: 1970. Place of birth: Tripoli, Libya.
Son of Muammar Qadhafi. Closeness of association with regime.
(11) Qadhafi, Muammar Mohammed Abu Minyar
Date of birth: 1942. Place of birth: Sirte, Libya.
Leader of the Revolution, Supreme Commander of Armed Forces.
Responsibility for ordering repression of demonstrations, human rights abuses.
(12) Qadhafi, Mutassim
Date of birth: 1976. Place of birth: Tripoli, Libya.
National Security Adviser. Son of Muammar Qadhafi. Closeness of association with regime.
(13) Qadhafi, Saadi
Passport number: 014797. Date of birth: 25/05/1973. Place of birth: Tripoli,
Libya.
Commander Special Forces. Son of Muammar Qadhafi. Closeness of association with regime. Command of military units involved in repression of demonstrations.
(14) Qadhafi, Saif al-Arab
Date of birth: 1982. Place of birth: Tripoli, Libya.
Son of Muammar Qadhafi. Closeness of association with regime.
(15) Qadhafi, Saif al-Islam
Passport number: B014995. Date of birth: 25/06/1972. Place of birth: Tripoli, Libya.
Director, Qadhafi Foundation. Son of Muammar Qadhafi. Closeness of association with regime. Inflammatory public statements encouraging violence against demonstrators.
(16) Al-Senussi, Colonel Abdullah
Date of birth: 1949. Place of birth: Sudan.
Director Military Intelligence. Military Intelligence involvement in suppression of demonstrations. Past history includes suspicion of involvement in Abu Selim prison massacre. Convicted in absentia for bombing of UTA flight. Brother -in-law of Muammar Qadhafi.

Annex II

Asset freeze
(1) Qadhafi, Aisha Muammar
Date of birth: 1978. Place of birth: Tripoli, Libya.
Daughter of Muammar Qadhafi. Closeness of association with regime.
(2) Qadhafi, Hannibal Muammar
Passport number: B/002210. Date of birth: 20/09/1975. Place of birth: Tripoli,
Libya. Son of Muammar Qadhafi. Closeness of association with regime.
(3) Qadhafi, Khamis Muammar
Date of birth: 1978. Place of birth: Tripoli, Libya.
Son of Muammar Qadhafi. Closeness of association with regime. Command of military units involved in repression of demonstrations.
(4) Qadhafi, Muammar Mohammed Abu Minyar

Date of birth: 1942. Place of birth: Sirte, Libya.
Leader of the Revolution, Supreme Commander of Armed Forces.
Responsibility for ordering repression of demonstrations, human rights abuses.
(5) Qadhafi, Mutassim
Date of birth: 1976. Place of birth: Tripoli, Libya.
National Security Adviser. Son of Muammar Qadhafi. Closeness of association with regime.
(6) Qadhafi, Saif al-Islam
Passport number: B014995. Date of birth: 25/06/1972. Place of birth: Tripoli, Libya.
Director, Qadhafi Foundation. Son of Muammar Qadhafi. Closeness of association with regime. Inflammatory public statements encouraging violence against demonstrators.

PART I   INTERNATIONAL LAW

UN Security Council Resolution S/RES/1973 (2011) "Situation in Libya"
17 March 2011

The Security Council,
Recalling its resolution 1970 (2011) of 26 February 2011,
Deploring the failure of the Libyan authorities to comply with resolution 1970 (2011),
Expressing grave concern at the deteriorating situation, the escalation of violence, and the heavy civilian casualties,
Reiterating the responsibility of the Libyan authorities to protect the Libyan population and reaffirming that parties to armed conflicts bear the primary responsibility to take all feasible steps to ensure the protection of civilians,
Condemning the gross and systematic violation of human rights, including arbitrary detentions, enforced disappearances, torture and summary executions,
Further condemning acts of violence and intimidation committed by the Libyan authorities against journalists, media professionals and associated personnel and urging these authorities to comply with their obligations under international humanitarian law as outlined in resolution 1738 (2006),
Considering that the widespread and systematic attacks currently taking place in the Libyan Arab Jamahiriya against the civilian population may amount to crimes against humanity,
Recalling paragraph (26) of resolution 1970 (2011) in which the Council expressed its readiness to consider taking additional appropriate measures, as necessary, to facilitate and support the return of humanitarian agencies and make available humanitarian and related assistance in the Libyan Arab Jamahiriya,
Expressing its determination to ensure the protection of civilians and civilian populated areas and the rapid and unimpeded passage of humanitarian assistance and the safety of humanitarian personnel,
Recalling the condemnation by the League of Arab States, the African Union, and the Secretary General of the Organization of the Islamic Conference of the serious violations of human rights and international humanitarian law that have been and are being committed in the Libyan Arab Jamahiriya,
Taking note of the final communiqué of the Organisation of the Islamic Conference of 8 March 2011, and the communiqué of the Peace and Security Council of the African Union of 10 March 2011 which established an ad hoc High Level Committee on Libya,
Taking note also of the decision of the Council of the League of Arab States of 12 March 2011 to call for the imposition of a no-fly zone on Libyan military aviation, and to establish safe areas in places exposed to shelling as a precautionary measure that allows the protection of the Libyan people and foreign nationals residing in the Libyan Arab Jamahiriya,
Taking note further of the Secretary-General's call on 16 March 2011 for an immediate cease-fire,
Recalling its decision to refer the situation in the Libyan Arab Jamahiriya since 15 February 2011 to the Prosecutor of the International Criminal Court, and stressing that those responsible for or complicit in attacks targeting the civilian population, including aerial and naval attacks, must be held to account,
Reiterating its concern at the plight of refugees and foreign workers forced to flee the violence in the Libyan Arab Jamahiriya, welcoming the response of neighbouring States, in particular Tunisia and Egypt, to address the needs of those refugees and foreign workers, and calling on the international community to support those efforts,
Deploring the continuing use of mercenaries by the Libyan authorities,
Considering that the establishment of a ban on all flights in the airspace of the Libyan Arab Jamahiriya constitutes an important element for the protection of civilians as well as the safety of the delivery of humanitarian assistance and a decisive step for the cessation of hostilities in Libya,
Expressing concern also for the safety of foreign nationals and their rights in the Libyan Arab Jamahiriya,
Welcoming the appointment by the Secretary General of his Special Envoy to Libya, Mr. Abdel-Elah Mohamed Al-Khatib and supporting his efforts to find a sustainable and peaceful solution to the crisis in the Libyan Arab Jamahiriya,
Reaffirming its strong commitment to the sovereignty, independence, territorial integrity and national unity of the Libyan Arab Jamahiriya,
Determining that the situation in the Libyan Arab Jamahiriya continues to constitute a threat to international peace and security,
Acting under Chapter VII of the Charter of the United Nations,

RESOLUTION 1973 THE SITUATION IN LYBIA

(1) Demands the immediate establishment of a cease-fire and a complete end to violence and all attacks against, and abuses of, civilians;
(2) Stresses the need to intensify efforts to find a solution to the crisis which responds to the legitimate demands of the Libyan people and notes the decisions of the Secretary-General to send his Special Envoy to Libya and of the Peace and Security Council of the African Union to send its ad hoc High Level Committee to Libya with the aim of facilitating dialogue to lead to the political reforms necessary to find a peaceful and sustainable solution;
(3) Demands that the Libyan authorities comply with their obligations under international law, including international humanitarian law, human rights and refugee law and take all measures to protect civilians and meet their basic needs, and to ensure the rapid and unimpeded passage of humanitarian assistance;

Protection of civilians
(4) Authorizes Member States that have notified the Secretary-General, acting nationally or through regional organizations or arrangements, and acting in cooperation with the Secretary-General, to take all necessary measures, notwithstanding paragraph (9) of resolution 1970 (2011), to protect civilians and civilian populated areas under threat of attack in the Libyan Arab Jamahiriya, including Benghazi, while excluding a foreign occupation force of any form on any part of Libyan territory, and requests the Member States concerned to inform the Secretary-General immediately of the measures they take pursuant to the authorization conferred by this paragraph which shall be immediately reported to the Security Council;
(5) Recognizes the important role of the League of Arab States in matters relating to the maintenance of international peace and security in the region, and bearing in mind Chapter VIII of the Charter of the United Nations, requests the Member States of the League of Arab States to cooperate with other Member States in the implementation of paragraph (4);

No Fly Zone
(6) Decides to establish a ban on all flights in the airspace of the Libyan Arab Jamahiriya in order to help protect civilians;
(7) Decides further that the ban imposed by paragraph (6) shall not apply to flights whose sole purpose is humanitarian, such as delivering or facilitating the delivery of assistance, including medical supplies, food, humanitarian workers and related assistance, or evacuating foreign nationals from the Libyan Arab Jamahiriya, nor shall it apply to flights authorised by paragraphs (4) or (8), nor other flights which are deemed necessary by States acting under the authorisation conferred in paragraph (8) to be for the benefit of the Libyan people, and that these flights shall be coordinated with any mechanism established under paragraph (8);
(8) Authorizes Member States that have notified the Secretary-General and the Secretary-General of the League of Arab States, acting nationally or through regional organizations or arrangements, to take all necessary measures to enforce compliance with the ban on flights imposed by paragraph (6) above, as necessary, and requests the States concerned in cooperation with the League of Arab States to coordinate closely with the Secretary General on the measures they are taking to implement this ban, including by establishing an appropriate mechanism for implementing the provisions of paragraphs (6) and (7) above,
(9) Calls upon all Member States, acting nationally or through regional organizations or arrangements, to provide assistance, including any necessary over-flight approvals, for the purposes of implementing paragraphs (4), (6), (7) and (8) above;
(10) Requests the Member States concerned to coordinate closely with each other and the Secretary-General on the measures they are taking to implement paragraphs (4), (6), (7) and (8) above, including practical measures for the monitoring and approval of authorised humanitarian or evacuation flights;
(11) Decides that the Member States concerned shall inform the Secretary General and the Secretary-General of the League of Arab States immediately of measures taken in exercise of the authority conferred by paragraph (8) above, including to supply a concept of operations;
(12) Requests the Secretary-General to inform the Council immediately of any actions taken by the Member States concerned in exercise of the authority conferred by paragraph (8) above and to report to the Council within 7 days and every month thereafter on the implementation of this resolution, including information on any violations of the flight ban imposed by paragraph (6) above;

Enforcement of the arms embargo
(13) Decides that paragraph (11) of resolution 1970 (2011) shall be replaced by
the following paragraph: "Calls upon all Member States, in particular States of the region, acting

PART I   INTERNATIONAL LAW

nationally or through regional organisations or arrangements, in order to ensure strict implementation of the arms embargo established by paragraphs (9) and (10) of resolution 1970 (2011), to inspect in their territory, including seaports and airports, and on the high seas, vessels and aircraft bound to or from the Libyan Arab Jamahiriya, if the State concerned has information that provides reasonable grounds to believe that the cargo contains items the supply, sale, transfer or export of which is prohibited by paragraphs (9) or (10) of resolution 1970 (2011) as modified by this resolution, including the provision of armed mercenary personnel, calls upon all flag States of such vessels and aircraft to cooperate with such inspections and authorises Member States to use all measures commensurate to the specific circumstances to carry out such inspections";

(14) Requests Member States which are taking action under paragraph (13) above on the high seas to coordinate closely with each other and the Secretary General and further requests the States concerned to inform the Secretary-General and the Committee established pursuant to paragraph (24) of resolution 1970 (2011) ("the Committee") immediately of measures taken in the exercise of the authority conferred by paragraph (13) above;

(15) Requires any Member State whether acting nationally or through regional organisations or arrangements, when it undertakes an inspection pursuant to paragraph (13) above, to submit promptly an initial written report to the Committee containing, in particular, explanation of the grounds for the inspection, the results of such inspection, and whether or not cooperation was provided, and, if prohibited items for transfer are found, further requires such Member States to submit to the Committee, at a later stage, a subsequent written report containing relevant details on the inspection, seizure, and disposal, and relevant details of the transfer, including a description of the items, their origin and intended destination, if this information is not in the initial report;

(16) Deplores the continuing flows of mercenaries into the Libyan Arab Jamahiriya and calls upon all Member States to comply strictly with their obligations under paragraph 9 of resolution 1970 (2011) to prevent the provision of armed mercenary personnel to the Libyan Arab Jamahiriya;

Ban on flights

(17) Decides that all States shall deny permission to any aircraft registered in the Libyan Arab Jamahiriya or owned or operated by Libyan nationals or companies to take off from, land in or overfly their territory unless the particular flight has been approved in advance by the Committee, or in the case of an emergency landing;

(18) Decides that all States shall deny permission to any aircraft to take off from, land in or overfly their territory, if they have information that provides reasonable grounds to believe that the aircraft contains items the supply, sale, transfer, or export of which is prohibited by paragraphs (9) and (10) of resolution 1970
(2011) as modified by this resolution, including the provision of armed mercenary personnel, except in the case of an emergency landing;

Asset freeze

(19) Decides that the asset freeze imposed by paragraph (17), (19), (20) and (21) of resolution 1970 (2011) shall apply to all funds, other financial assets and economic resources which are on their territories, which are owned or controlled, directly or indirectly, by the Libyan authorities, as designated by the Committee, or by individuals or entities acting on their behalf or at their direction, or by entities owned or controlled by them, as designated by the Committee, and decides further that all States shall ensure that any funds, financial assets or economic resources are prevented from being made available by their nationals or by any individuals or entities within their territories, to or for the benefit of the Libyan authorities, as designated by the Committee, or individuals or entities acting on their behalf or at their direction, or entities owned or controlled by them, as designated by the Committee, and directs the Committee to designate such Libyan authorities, individuals or entities within 30 days of the date of the adoption of this resolution and as appropriate thereafter;

(20) Affirms its determination to ensure that assets frozen pursuant to paragraph (17) of resolution 1970 (2011) shall, at a later stage, as soon as possible be made available to and for the benefit of the people of the Libyan Arab Jamahiriya;

(21) Decides that all States shall require their nationals, persons subject to their jurisdiction and firms incorporated in their territory or subject to their jurisdiction to exercise vigilance when doing business with entities incorporated in the Libyan Arab Jamahiriya or subject to its jurisdiction, and any individuals or
entities acting on their behalf or at their direction, and entities owned or controlled by them, if the States have information that provides reasonable grounds to believe that such business could contribute to violence and use of force against civilians;

Designations
(22) Decides that the individuals listed in Annex I shall be subject to the travel restrictions imposed in paragraphs (15) and (16) of resolution 1970 (2011), and decides further that the individuals and entities listed in Annex II shall be subject to the asset freeze imposed in paragraphs (17), (19), (20) and (21) of resolution 1970 (2011);
(23) Decides that the measures specified in paragraphs (15), (16), (17), (19), (20) and (21) of resolution 1970 (2011) shall apply also to individuals and entities determined by the Council or the Committee to have violated the provisions of resolution 1970 (2011), particularly paragraphs 9 and 10 thereof, or to have assisted others in doing so;

Panel of Experts
(24) Requests the Secretary-General to create for an initial period of one year, in consultation with the Committee, a group of up to eight experts ("Panel of Experts"), under the direction of the Committee to carry out the following tasks:
(a) Assist the Committee in carrying out its mandate as specified in paragraph (24) of resolution 1970 (2011) and this resolution;
(b) Gather, examine and analyse information from States, relevant United Nations bodies, regional organisations and other interested parties regarding the implementation of the measures decided in resolution 1970 (2011) and this resolution, in particular incidents of non-compliance;
(c) Make recommendations on actions the Council, or the Committee or State, may consider to improve implementation of the relevant measures;
(d) Provide to the Council an interim report on its work no later than 90 days after the Panel's appointment, and a final report to the Council no later than 30 days prior to the termination of its mandate with its findings and recommendations;
(25) Urges all States, relevant United Nations bodies and other interested parties, to cooperate fully with the Committee and the Panel of Experts, in particular by supplying any information at their disposal on the implementation of the measures decided in resolution 1970 (2011) and this resolution, in particular incidents of non-compliance;
(26) Decides that the mandate of the Committee as set out in paragraph 24 of resolution 1970 (2011) shall also apply to the measures decided in this resolution;
(27) Decides that all States, including the Libyan Arab Jamahiriya, shall take the necessary measures to ensure that no claim shall lie at the instance of the Libyan authorities, or of any person or body in the Libyan Arab Jamahiriya, or of any person claiming through or for the benefit of any such person or body, in connection with any contract or other transaction where its performance was affected by reason of the measures taken by the Security Council in resolution 1970 (2011), this resolution and related resolutions;
(28) Reaffirms its intention to keep the actions of the Libyan authorities under continuous review and underlines its readiness to review at any time the measures imposed by this resolution and resolution 1970 (2011), including by strengthening, suspending or lifting those measures, as appropriate, based on compliance by the Libyan authorities with this resolution and resolution 1970 (2011).
(29) Decides to remain actively seized of the matter.
Libya: UNSCR proposed designations
Number Name Justification Identifiers

Annex I. Travel Ban
1 QUREN SALIH QUREN AL QADHAFI
Libyan Ambassador to Chad. Has left Chad for Sabha. Involved directly in recruiting and coordinating mercenaries for the regime.
2 Colonel AMID HUSAIN AL KUNI
Governor of Ghat (South Libya). Directly involved in recruiting mercenaries. Number Name Justification Identifiers

Annex II. Asset Freeze
1 Dorda, Abu Zayd Umar Position: Director, External Security Organisation
2 Jabir, Major General Abu Bakr Yunis
Position: Defence Minister Title: Major General DOB: --/--/1952.
POB: Jalo, Libya
3 Matuq, Matuq Mohammed
Position: Secretary for Utilities DOB: --/--/1956. POB: Khoms
4 Qadhafi, Mohammed Muammar
Son of Muammar Qadhafi.

PART I   INTERNATIONAL LAW

Closeness of association with regime DOB: --/--/1970. POB: Tripoli, Libya
5 Qadhafi, Saadi Commander Special Forces. Son of Muammar Qadhafi. Closeness
of association with regime. Command of military units involved in repression of demonstrations
DOB: 25/05/1973. POB: Tripoli, Libya
6 Qadhafi, Saif al-Arab Son of Muammar Qadhafi.
Closeness of association with regime DOB: --/--/1982. POB: Tripoli, Libya
7 Al-Senussi, Colonel Abdullah
Position: Director Military Intelligence
Title: Colonel DOB: --/--/1949.
POB: Sudan

Entities
1 Central Bank of Libya Under control of Muammar Qadhafi and his family, and potential source of funding for his regime. Number Name Justification Identifiers
2 Libyan Investment Authority
Under control of Muammar Qadhafi and his family, and potential source of funding for his regime.
a.k.a: Libyan Arab Foreign Investment Company (LAFICO)
Address: 1 Fateh Tower Office, No 99 22nd Floor, Borgaida Street, Tripoli, Libya, 1103
3 Libyan Foreign Bank Under control of Muammar Qadhafi and his family and a potential source of funding for his regime.
4 Libyan Africa Investment Portfolio
Under control of Muammar Qadhafi and his family, and potential source of funding for his regime.
Address: Jamahiriya Street, LAP, Building, PO Box 91330, Tripoli, Libya
5 Libyan National Oil Corporation
Under control of Muammar Qadhafi and his family, and potential source of funding for his regime.
Address: Bashir Saadwi Street, Tripoli, Tarabulus, Libya

RESOLUTION 68/262 TERRITORIAL INTEGRITY UKRAINE

UN General Assembly Resolution A/RES/68/262 (2014) "Territorial integrity Ukraine"
27 March 2014

The General Assembly,
Reaffirming the paramount importance of the Charter of the United Nations in the promotion of the rule of law among nations,
Recalling the obligations of all States under Article 2 of the Charter to refrain in their international relations from the threat or use of force against the territorial integrity or political independence of any State, and to settle their international disputes by peaceful means,
Recalling also its resolution 2625 (XXV) of 24 October 1970, in which it approved the Declaration on Principles of International Law concerning Friendly Relations and Cooperation among States in accordance with the Charter of the United Nations, and reaffirming the principles contained therein that the territory of a State shall not be the object of acquisition by another State resulting from the threat or use of force, and that any attempt aimed at the partial or total disruption of the national unity and territorial integrity of a State or country or at its political independence is incompatible with the purposes and principles of the Charter,
Recalling further the Final Act of the Conference on Security and Cooperation in Europe, signed in Helsinki on 1 August 1975, the Memorandum on Security Assurances in Connection with Ukraine's Accession to the Treaty on the Non-Proliferation of Nuclear Weapons (Budapest Memorandum) of 5 December 1994, the Treaty on Friendship, Cooperation and Partnership between Ukraine and the Russian Federation of 31 May 1997 and the Alma-Ata Declaration of 21 December 1991,
Stressing the importance of maintaining the inclusive political dialogue in Ukraine that reflects the diversity of its society and includes representation from all parts of Ukraine,
Welcoming the continued efforts by the Secretary-General and the Organization for Security and Cooperation in Europe and other international and regional organizations to support de-escalation of the situation with respect to Ukraine,
Noting that the referendum held in the Autonomous Republic of Crimea and the city of Sevastopol on 16 March 2014 was not authorized by Ukraine,

(1) Affirms its commitment to the sovereignty, political independence, unity and territorial integrity of Ukraine within its internationally recognized borders;
(2) Calls upon all States to desist and refrain from actions aimed at the partial or total disruption of the national unity and territorial integrity of Ukraine, including any attempts to modify Ukraine's borders through the threat or use of force or other unlawful means;
(3) Urges all parties to pursue immediately the peaceful resolution of the situation with respect to Ukraine through direct political dialogue, to exercise restraint, to refrain from unilateral actions and inflammatory rhetoric that may increase tensions and to engage fully with international mediation efforts;
(4) Welcomes the efforts of the United Nations, the Organization for Security and Cooperation in Europe and other international and regional organizations to assist Ukraine in protecting the rights of all persons in Ukraine, including the rights of persons belonging to minorities;
(5) Underscores that the referendum held in the Autonomous Republic of Crimea and the city of Sevastopol on 16 March 2014, having no validity, cannot form the basis for any alteration of the status of the Autonomous Republic of Crimea or of the city of Sevastopol;
(6) Calls upon all States, international organizations and specialized agencies not to recognize any alteration of the status of the Autonomous Republic of Crimea and the city of Sevastopol on the basis of the above-mentioned referendum and to refrain from any action or dealing that might be interpreted as recognizing any such altered status.

PART I   INTERNATIONAL LAW

UN Security Council Resolution S/RES/1368 (2001), 12 September 2011
Adopted by the Security Council at its 4370th meeting, on 12 September 2001

The Security Council,
Reaffirming the principles and purposes of the Charter of the United Nations,
Determined to combat by all means threats to international peace and security caused by terrorist acts,
Recognizing the inherent right of individual or collective self-defence in accordance with the Charter,

1. Unequivocally condemns in the strongest terms the horrifying terrorist attacks which took place on 11 September 2001 in New York, Washington, D.C. and Pennsylvania and regards such acts, like any act of international terrorism, as a threat to international peace and security;
2. Expresses its deepest sympathy and condolences to the victims and their families and to the people and Government of the United States of America;
3. Calls on all States to work together urgently to bring to justice the perpetrators, organizers and sponsors of these terrorist attacks and stresses that those responsible for aiding, supporting or harbouring the perpetrators, organizers and sponsors of these acts will be held accountable;
4. Calls also on the international community to redouble their efforts to prevent and suppress terrorist acts including by increased cooperation and full implementation of the relevant international anti-terrorist conventions and Security Council resolutions, in particular resolution 1269 (1999) of 19 October 1999;
5. Expresses its readiness to take all necessary steps to respond to the terrorist attacks of 11 September 2001, and to combat all forms of terrorism, in accordance with its responsibilities under the Charter of the United Nations;
6. Decides to remain seized of the matter.

RESOLUTION 1373 TERRORISM

UN Security Council Resolution S/RES/1373 (2001), 28 September 2011
Adopted by the Security Council at its 4385th meeting, on 28 September 2001

The Security Council,
Reaffirming its resolutions 1269 (1999) of 19 October 1999 and 1368 (2001) of 12 September 2001,
Reaffirming also its unequivocal condemnation of the terrorist attacks which took place in New York, Washington, D.C. and Pennsylvania on 11 September 2001,
and expressing its determination to prevent all such acts,
Reaffirming further that such acts, like any act of international terrorism, constitute a threat to international peace and security,
Reaffirming the inherent right of individual or collective self-defence as recognized by the Charter of the United Nations as reiterated in resolution 1368 (2001),
Reaffirming the need to combat by all means, in accordance with the Charter of the United Nations, threats to international peace and security caused by terrorist acts,
Deeply concerned by the increase, in various regions of the world, of acts of terrorism motivated by intolerance or extremism,
Calling on States to work together urgently to prevent and suppress terrorist acts, including through increased cooperation and full implementation of the relevant international conventions relating to terrorism,
Recognizing the need for States to complement international cooperation by taking additional measures to prevent and suppress, in their territories through all lawful means, the financing and preparation of any acts of terrorism,
Reaffirming the principle established by the General Assembly in its declaration of October 1970 (resolution 2625 (XXV)) and reiterated by the Security Council in its resolution 1189 (1998) of 13 August 1998, namely that every State has the duty to refrain from organizing, instigating, assisting or participating in terrorist acts in another State or acquiescing in organized activities within its territory directed towards the commission of such acts,
Acting under Chapter VII of the Charter of the United Nations,

(1) Decides that all States shall:
(a) Prevent and suppress the financing of terrorist acts;
(b) Criminalize the wilful provision or collection, by any means, directly or indirectly, of funds by their nationals or in their territories with the intention that the funds should be used, or in the knowledge that they are to be used, in order to carry out terrorist acts;
(c) Freeze without delay funds and other financial assets or economic resources of persons who commit, or attempt to commit, terrorist acts or participate in or facilitate the commission of terrorist acts; of entities owned or controlled directly or indirectly by such persons; and of persons and entities acting on behalf of, or at the direction of such persons and entities, including funds derived or generated from property owned or controlled directly or indirectly by such persons and associated persons and entities;
(d) Prohibit their nationals or any persons and entities within their territories from making any funds, financial assets or economic resources or financial or other related services available, directly or indirectly, for the benefit of persons who commit or attempt to commit or facilitate or participate in the commission of terrorist acts, of entities owned or controlled, directly or indirectly, by such persons and of persons and entities acting on behalf of or at the direction of such persons;
(2) Decides also that all States shall:
(a) Refrain from providing any form of support, active or passive, to entities or persons involved in terrorist acts, including by suppressing recruitment of members of terrorist groups and eliminating the supply of weapons to terrorists;
(b) Take the necessary steps to prevent the commission of terrorist acts, including by provision of early warning to other States by exchange of information;
(c) Deny safe haven to those who finance, plan, support, or commit terrorist acts, or provide safe havens;
(d) Prevent those who finance, plan, facilitate or commit terrorist acts from using their respective territories for those purposes against other States or their citizens;
(e) Ensure that any person who participates in the financing, planning, preparation or perpetration of terrorist acts or in supporting terrorist acts is brought to justice and ensure that, in addition to any other measures against them, such terrorist acts are established as serious criminal offences in domestic laws and regulations and that the punishment duly reflects the seriousness of such terrorist acts;
(f) Afford one another the greatest measure of assistance in connection with criminal investigations or criminal proceedings relating to the financing or support of terrorist acts, including assistance in

obtaining evidence in their possession necessary for the proceedings;

(g) Prevent the movement of terrorists or terrorist groups by effective border controls and controls on issuance of identity papers and travel documents, and through measures for preventing counterfeiting, forgery or fraudulent use of identity papers and travel documents;

(3) Calls upon all States to:

(a) Find ways of intensifying and accelerating the exchange of operational information, especially regarding actions or movements of terrorist persons or networks; forged or falsified travel documents; traffic in arms, explosives or sensitive materials; use of communications technologies by terrorist groups; and the threat posed by the possession of weapons of mass destruction by terrorist groups;

(b) Exchange information in accordance with international and domestic law and cooperate on administrative and judicial matters to prevent the commission of terrorist acts;

(c) Cooperate, particularly through bilateral and multilateral arrangements and agreements, to prevent and suppress terrorist attacks and take action against perpetrators of such acts;

(d) Become parties as soon as possible to the relevant international conventions and protocols relating to terrorism, including the International Convention for the Suppression of the Financing of Terrorism of 9 December 1999;

(e) Increase cooperation and fully implement the relevant international conventions and protocols relating to terrorism and Security Council resolutions 1269 (1999) and 1368 (2001);

(f) Take appropriate measures in conformity with the relevant provisions of national and international law, including international standards of human rights, before granting refugee status, for the purpose of ensuring that the asylum-seeker has not planned, facilitated or participated in the commission of terrorist acts;

(g) Ensure, in conformity with international law, that refugee status is not abused by the perpetrators, organizers or facilitators of terrorist acts, and that claims of political motivation are not recognized as grounds for refusing requests for the extradition of alleged terrorists;

(4) Notes with concern the close connection between international terrorism and transnational organized crime, illicit drugs, money-laundering, illegal arms-trafficking, and illegal movement of nuclear, chemical, biological and other potentially deadly materials, and in this regard emphasizes the need to enhance coordination of efforts on national, subregional, regional and international levels in order to strengthen a global response to this serious challenge and threat to international security;

(5) Declares that acts, methods, and practices of terrorism are contrary to the purposes and principles of the United Nations and that knowingly financing, planning and inciting terrorist acts are also contrary to the purposes and principles of the United Nations;

(6) Decides to establish, in accordance with rule 28 of its provisional rules of procedure, a Committee of the Security Council, consisting of all the members of the Council, to monitor implementation of this resolution, with the assistance of appropriate expertise, and calls upon all States to report to the Committee, no later than 90 days from the date of adoption of this resolution and thereafter according to a timetable to be proposed by the Committee, on the steps they have taken to implement this resolution;

(7) Directs the Committee to delineate its tasks, submit a work programme within 30 days of the adoption of this resolution, and to consider the support it requires, in consultation with the Secretary-General;

(8) Expresses its determination to take all necessary steps in order to ensure the full implementation of this resolution, in accordance with its responsibilities under the Charter;

(9) Decides to remain seized of this matter.

Fundamental Rights

PART II FUNDAMENTAL RIGHTS

Universal Declaration of Human Rights
UN General Assembly Resolution 217 A (III). 10 December 1948
UN Doc. A/810 (III)

Whereas recognition of the inherent dignity and of the equal and inalienable rights of all members of the human family is the foundation of freedom, justice and peace in the world,
Whereas disregard and contempt for human rights have resulted in barbarous acts which have outraged the conscience of mankind, and the advent of a world in which human beings shall enjoy freedom of speech and belief and freedom from fear and want has been proclaimed as the highest aspiration of the common people,
Whereas it is essential, if man is not to be compelled to have recourse, as a last resort, to rebellion against tyranny and oppression, that human rights should be protected by the rule of law,
Whereas it is essential to promote the development of friendly relations between nations,
Whereas the peoples of the United Nations have in the Charter reaffirmed their faith in fundamental human rights, in the dignity and worth of the human person and in the equal rights of men and women and have determined to promote social progress and better standards of life in larger freedom,
Whereas Member States have pledged themselves to achieve, in cooperation with the United Nations, the promotion of universal respect for and observance of human rights and fundamental freedoms,
Whereas a common understanding of these rights and freedoms is of the greatest importance for the full realization of this pledge,
Now, therefore,
The General Assembly,
Proclaims this Universal Declaration of Human Rights as a common standard of achievement for all peoples and all nations, to the end that every individual and every organ of society, keeping this Declaration constantly in mind, shall strive by teaching and education to promote respect for these rights and freedoms and by progressive measures, national and international, to secure their universal and effective recognition and observance, both among the peoples of Member States themselves and among the peoples of territories under their jurisdiction.

Article 1. All human beings are born free and equal in dignity and rights. They are endowed with reason and conscience and should act towards one another in a spirit of brotherhood.

Article 2. Everyone is entitled to all the rights and freedoms set forth in this Declaration, without distinction of any kind, such as race, colour, sex, language, religion, political or other opinion, national or social origin, property, birth or other status.
Furthermore, no distinction shall be made on the basis of the political, jurisdictional or international status of the country or territory to which a person belongs, whether it be independent, trust, non-self-governing or under any other limitation of sovereignty.

Article 3. Everyone has the right to life, liberty and security of person.

Article 4. No one shall be held in slavery or servitude; slavery and the slave trade shall be prohibited in all their forms.

Article 5. No one shall be subjected to torture or to cruel, inhuman or degrading treatment or punishment.

Article 6. Everyone has the right to recognition everywhere as a person before the law.

Article 7. All are equal before the law and are entitled without any discrimination to equal protection of the law. All are entitled to equal protection against any discrimination in violation of this Declaration and against any incitement to such discrimination.

Article 8. Everyone has the right to an effective remedy by the competent national tribunals for acts violating the fundamental rights granted him by the constitution or by law.

Article 9. No one shall be subjected to arbitrary arrest, detention or exile.

Article 10. Everyone is entitled in full equality to a fair and public hearing by an independent and impartial tribunal, in the determination of his rights and obligations and of any criminal charge against him.

Article 11. (1) Everyone charged with a penal offence has the right to be presumed innocent until

proved guilty according to law in a public trial at which he has had all the guarantees necessary for his defence.
(2) No one shall be held guilty of any penal offence on account of any act or omission which did not constitute a penal offence, under national or international law, at the time when it was committed. Nor shall a heavier penalty be imposed than the one that was applicable at the time the penal offence was committed.

Article 12. No one shall be subjected to arbitrary interference with his privacy, family, home or correspondence, nor to attacks upon his honour and reputation. Everyone has the right to the protection of the law against such interference or attacks.

Article 13. (1) Everyone has the right to freedom of movement and residence within the borders of each State.
(2) Everyone has the right to leave any country, including his own, and to return to his country.

Article 14. (1) Everyone has the right to seek and to enjoy in other countries asylum from persecution.
(2) This right may not be invoked in the case of prosecutions genuinely arising from non-political crimes or from acts contrary to the purposes and principles of the United Nations.

Article 15. (1) Everyone has the right to a nationality.
(2) No one shall be arbitrarily deprived of his nationality nor denied the right to change his nationality.

Article 16. (1) Men and women of full age, without any limitation due to race, nationality or religion, have the right to marry and to found a family. They are entitled to equal rights as to marriage, during marriage and at its dissolution.
(2) Marriage shall be entered into only with the free and full consent of the intending spouses.
(3) The family is the natural and fundamental group unit of society and is entitled to protection by society and the State.

Article 17. (1) Everyone has the right to own property alone as well as in association with others.
(2) No one shall be arbitrarily deprived of his property.

Article 18. Everyone has the right to freedom of thought, conscience and religion; this right includes freedom to change his religion or belief, and freedom, either alone or in community with others and in public or private, to manifest his religion or belief in teaching, practice, worship and observance.

Article 19. Everyone has the right to freedom of opinion and expression; this right includes freedom to hold opinions without interference and to seek, receive and impart information and ideas through any media and regardless of frontiers.

Article 20. (1) Everyone has the right to freedom of peaceful assembly and association.
(2) No one may be compelled to belong to an association.

Article 21. (1) Everyone has the right to take part in the government of his country, directly or through freely chosen representatives.
(2) Everyone has the right to equal access to public service in his country.
(3) The will of the people shall be the basis of the authority of government; this will shall be expressed in periodic and genuine elections which shall be by universal and equal suffrage and shall be held by secret vote or by equivalent free voting procedures.

Article 22. Everyone, as a member of society, has the right to social security and is entitled to realization, through national effort and international co-operation and in accordance with the organization and resources of each State, of the economic, social and cultural rights indispensable for his dignity and the free development of his personality.

Article 23. (1) Everyone has the right to work, to free choice of employment, to just and favourable conditions of work and to protection against unemployment.
(2) Everyone, without any discrimination, has the right to equal pay for equal work.
(3) Everyone who works has the right to just and favourable remuneration ensuring for himself and his family an existence worthy of human dignity, and supplemented, if necessary, by other means of social protection.
(4) Everyone has the right to form and to join trade unions for the protection of his interests.

PART II   FUNDAMENTAL RIGHTS

Article 24. Everyone has the right to rest and leisure, including reasonable limitation of working hours and periodic holidays with pay.

Article 25. (1) Everyone has the right to a standard of living adequate for the health and well-being of himself and of his family, including food, clothing, housing and medical care and necessary social services, and the right to security in the event of unemployment, sickness, disability, widowhood, old age or other lack of livelihood in circumstances beyond his control.
(2) Motherhood and childhood are entitled to special care and assistance. All children, whether born in or out of wedlock, shall enjoy the same social protection.

Article 26. (1) Everyone has the right to education. Education shall be free, at least in the elementary and fundamental stages. Elementary education shall be compulsory. Technical and professional education shall be made generally available and higher education shall be equally accessible to all on the basis of merit.
(2) Education shall be directed to the full development of the human personality and to the strengthening of respect for human rights and fundamental freedoms. It shall promote understanding, tolerance and friendship among all nations, racial or religious groups, and shall further the activities of the United Nations for the maintenance of peace.
(3) Parents have a prior right to choose the kind of education that shall be given to their children.

Article 27. (1) Everyone has the right freely to participate in the cultural life of the community, to enjoy the arts and to share in scientific advancement and its benefits.
(2) Everyone has the right to the protection of the moral and material interests resulting from any scientific, literary or artistic production of which he is the author.

Article 28. Everyone is entitled to a social and international order in which the rights and freedoms set forth in this Declaration can be fully realized.

Article 29. (1) Everyone has duties to the community in which alone the free and full development of his personality is possible.
(2) In the exercise of his rights and freedoms, everyone shall be subject only to such limitations as are determined by law solely for the purpose of securing due recognition and respect for the rights and freedoms of others and of meeting the just requirements of morality, public order and the general welfare in a democratic society.
(3) These rights and freedoms may in no case be exercised contrary to the purposes and principles of the United Nations.

Article 30. Nothing in this Declaration may be interpreted as implying for any State, group or person any right to engage in any activity or to perform any act aimed at the destruction of any of the rights and freedoms set forth herein.

Convention relating to the Status of Refugees
Geneva, 28 July 1951, Entry into force. 22 April 1954

The High Contracting Parties
Considering that the Charter of the United Nations and the Universal Declaration of Human Rights approved on 10 December 1948 by the General Assembly have affirmed the principle that human beings shall enjoy fundamental rights and freedoms without discrimination,
Considering that the United Nations has, on various occasions, manifested its profound concern for refugees and endeavoured to assure refugees the widest possible exercise of these fundamental rights and freedoms,
Considering that it is desirable to revise and consolidate previous international agreements relating to the status of refugees and to extend the scope of and the protection accorded by such instruments by means of a new agreement,
Considering that the grant of asylum may place unduly heavy burdens on certain countries, and that a satisfactory solution of a problem of which the United Nations has recognized the international scope and nature cannot therefore be achieved without international co-operation,
Expressing the wish that all States, recognizing the social and humanitarian nature of the problem of refugees, will do everything within their power to prevent this problem from becoming a cause of tension between States,
Noting that the United Nations High Commissioner for Refugees is charged with the task of supervising international conventions providing for the protection of refugees, and recognizing that the effective co-ordination of measures taken to deal with this problem will depend upon the co-operation of States with the High Commissioner,
Have agreed as follows:

Chapter I. General provisions

Article 1. Definition of the term *"refugee"*

A. For the purposes of the present Convention, the term "refugee" shall apply to any person who: (1) Has been considered a refugee under the Arrangements of 12 May 1926 and 30 June 1928 or under the Conventions of 28 October 1933 and 10 February 1938, the Protocol of 14 September 1939 or the Constitution of the International Refugee Organization; Decisions of non-eligibility taken by the International Refugee Organization during the period of its activities shall not prevent the status of refugee being accorded to persons who fulfil the conditions of paragraph (2) of this section;
(2) As a result of events occurring before 1 January 1951 and owing to well-founded fear of being persecuted for reasons of race, religion, nationality, membership of a particular social group or political opinion, is outside the country of his nationality and is unable or, owing to such fear, is unwilling to avail himself of the protection of that country; or who, not having a nationality and being outside the country of his former habitual residence as a result of such events, is unable or, owing to such fear, is unwilling to return to it. In the case of a person who has more than one nationality, the term "the country of his nationality" shall mean each of the countries of which he is a national, and a person shall not be deemed to be lacking the protection of the country of his nationality if, without any valid reason based on well-founded fear, he has not availed himself of the protection of one of the countries of which he is a national.
B. (1) For the purposes of this Convention, the words "events occurring before 1 January 1951" in article 1, section A, shall be understood to mean either (a) "events occurring in Europe before 1 January 1951"; or (b) "events occurring in Europe or elsewhere before 1 January 1951"; and each Contracting State shall make a declaration at the time of signature, ratification or accession, specifying which of these meanings it applies for the purpose of its obligations under this Convention.
(2) Any Contracting State which has adopted alternative (a) may at any time extend its obligations by adopting alternative (b) by means of a notification addressed to the Secretary-General of the United Nations.
C. This Convention shall cease to apply to any person falling under the terms of section A if: (1) He has voluntarily re-availed himself of the protection of the country of his nationality; or (2) Having lost his nationality, he has voluntarily reacquired it; or
(3) He has acquired a new nationality, and enjoys the protection of the country of his new nationality; or
(4) He has voluntarily re-established himself in the country which he left or outside which he remained owing to fear of persecution; or
(5) He can no longer, because the circumstances in connection with which he has been recognized as a refugee have ceased to exist, continue to refuse to avail himself of the protection of the country of his nationality;

PART II FUNDAMENTAL RIGHTS

Provided that this paragraph shall not apply to a refugee falling under section A (1) of this article who is able to invoke compelling reasons arising out of previous persecution for refusing to avail himself of the protection of the country of nationality;

(6) Being a person who has no nationality he is, because the circumstances in connection with which he has been recognized as a refugee have ceased to exist, able to return to the country of his former habitual residence;

Provided that this paragraph shall not apply to a refugee falling under section A (1) of this article who is able to invoke compelling reasons arising out of previous persecution for refusing to return to the country of his former habitual residence.

D. This Convention shall not apply to persons who are at present receiving from organs or agencies of the United Nations other than the United Nations High Commissioner for Refugees protection or assistance. When such protection or assistance has ceased for any reason, without the position of such persons being definitively settled in accordance with the relevant resolutions adopted by the General Assembly of the United Nations, these persons shall ipso facto be entitled to the benefits of this Convention.

E. This Convention shall not apply to a person who is recognized by the competent authorities of the country in which he has taken residence as having the rights and obligations which are attached to the possession of the nationality of that country.

F. The provisions of this Convention shall not apply to any person with respect to whom there are serious reasons for considering that:

(a) He has committed a crime against peace, a war crime, or a crime against humanity, as defined in the international instruments drawn up to make provision in respect of such crimes;

(b) He has committed a serious non-political crime outside the country of refuge prior to his admission to that country as a refugee;

(c) He has been guilty of acts contrary to the purposes and principles of the United Nations.

Article 2. General obligations

Every refugee has duties to the country in which he finds himself, which require in particular that he conform to its laws and regulations as well as to measures taken for the maintenance of public order.

Article 3. Non-discrimination

The Contracting States shall apply the provisions of this Convention to refugees without discrimination as to race, religion or country of origin.

Article 4. Religion

The Contracting States shall accord to refugees within their territories treatment at least as favourable as that accorded to their nationals with respect to freedom to practise their religion and freedom as regards the religious education of their children.

Article 5. Rights granted apart from this Convention

Nothing in this Convention shall be deemed to impair any rights and benefits granted by a Contracting State to refugees apart from this Convention.

Article 6. The term *"in the same circumstances"*

For the purposes of this Convention, the term "in the same circumstances" implies that any requirements (including requirements as to length and conditions of sojourn or residence) which the particular individual would have to fulfil for the enjoyment of the right in question, if he were not a refugee, must be fulfilled by him, with the exception of requirements which by their nature a refugee is incapable of fulfilling.

Article 7. Exemption from reciprocity

(1) Except where this Convention contains more favourable provisions, a Contracting State shall accord to refugees the same treatment as is accorded to aliens generally.

(2) After a period of three years' residence, all refugees shall enjoy exemption from legislative reciprocity in the territory of the Contracting States.

(3) Each Contracting State shall continue to accord to refugees the rights and benefits to which they were already entitled, in the absence of reciprocity, at the date of entry into force of this Convention for that State.

(4) The Contracting States shall consider favourably the possibility of according to refugees, in the absence of reciprocity, rights and benefits beyond those to which they are entitled according to paragraphs (2) and (3), and to extending exemption from reciprocity to refugees who do not fulfil the conditions provided for in paragraphs (2) and (3).

(5) The provisions of paragraphs (2) and (3) apply both to the rights and benefits referred to in articles 13, 18, 19, 21 and 22 of this Convention and to rights and benefits for which this Convention does not provide.

Article 8. Exemption from exceptional measures
With regard to exceptional measures which may be taken against the person, property or interests of nationals of a foreign State, the Contracting States shall not apply such measures to a refugee who is formally a national of the said State solely on account of such nationality. Contracting States which, under their legislation, are prevented from applying the general principle expressed in this article, shall, in appropriate cases, grant exemptions in favour of such refugees.

Article 9. Provisional measures
Nothing in this Convention shall prevent a Contracting State, in time of war or other grave and exceptional circumstances, from taking provisionally measures which it considers to be essential to the national security in the case of a particular person, pending a determination by the Contracting State that that person is in fact a refugee and that the continuance of such measures is necessary in his case in the interests of national security.

Article 10. Continuity of residence
(1) Where a refugee has been forcibly displaced during the Second World War and removed to the territory of a Contracting State, and is resident there, the period of such enforced sojourn shall be considered to have been lawful residence within that territory.
(2) Where a refugee has been forcibly displaced during the Second World War from the territory of a Contracting State and has, prior to the date of entry into force of this Convention, returned there for the purpose of taking up residence, the period of residence before and after such enforced displacement shall be regarded as one uninterrupted period for any purposes for which uninterrupted residence is required.

Article 11. Refugee seamen
In the case of refugees regularly serving as crew members on board a ship flying the flag of a Contracting State, that State shall give sympathetic consideration to their establishment on its territory and the issue of travel documents to them or their temporary admission to its territory particularly with a view to facilitating their establishment in another country.

Chapter II. Juridical status

Article 12. Personal status
(1) The personal status of a refugee shall be governed by the law of the country of his domicile or, if he has no domicile, by the law of the country of his residence.
(2) Rights previously acquired by a refugee and dependent on personal status, more particularly rights attaching to marriage, shall be respected by a Contracting State, subject to compliance, if this be necessary, with the formalities required by the law of that State, provided that the right in question is one which would have been recognized by the law of that State had he not become a refugee.

Article 13. Movable and immovable property
The Contracting States shall accord to a refugee treatment as favourable as possible and, in any event, not less favourable than that accorded to aliens generally in the same circumstances, as regards the acquisition of movable and immovable property and other rights pertaining thereto, and to leases and other contracts relating to movable and immovable property.

Article 14. Artistic rights and industrial property
In respect of the protection of industrial property, such as inventions, designs or models, trade marks, trade names, and of rights in literary, artistic and scientific works, a refugee shall be accorded in the country in which he has his habitual residence the same protection as is accorded to nationals of that country. In the territory of any other Contracting States, he shall be accorded the same protection as is accorded in that territory to nationals of the country in which he has his habitual residence.

Article 15. Right of association
As regards non-political and non-profit-making associations and trade unions the Contracting States shall accord to refugees lawfully staying in their territory the most favourable treatment accorded to nationals of a foreign country, in the same circumstances.

Article 16. Access to courts
(1) A refugee shall have free access to the courts of law on the territory of all Contracting States.

PART II FUNDAMENTAL RIGHTS

(2) A refugee shall enjoy in the Contracting State in which he has his habitual residence the same treatment as a national in matters pertaining to access to the courts, including legal assistance and exemption from *cautio judicatum solvi*.

(3) A refugee shall be accorded in the matters referred to in paragraph (2) in countries other than that in which he has his habitual residence the treatment granted to a national of the country of his habitual residence.

Chapter III. Gainful employment

Article 17. Wage-earning employment

(1) The Contracting States shall accord to refugees lawfully staying in their territory the most favourable treatment accorded to nationals of a foreign country in the same circumstances, as regards the right to engage in wage-earning employment.

(2) In any case, restrictive measures imposed on aliens or the employment of aliens for the protection of the national labour market shall not be applied to a refugee who was already exempt from them at the date of entry into force of this Convention for the Contracting State concerned, or who fulfils one of the following conditions:

(a) He has completed three years' residence in the country;

(b) He has a spouse possessing the nationality of the country of residence. A refugee may not invoke the benefit of this provision if he has abandoned his spouse;

(c) He has one or more children possessing the nationality of the country of residence.

(3) The Contracting States shall give sympathetic consideration to assimilating the rights of all refugees with regard to wage-earning employment to those of nationals, and in particular of those refugees who have entered their territory pursuant to programmes of labour recruitment or under immigration schemes.

Article 18. Self-employment

The Contracting States shall accord to a refugee lawfully in their territory treatment as favourable as possible and, in any event, not less favourable than that accorded to aliens generally in the same circumstances, as regards the right to engage on his own account in agriculture, industry, handicrafts and commerce and to establish commercial and industrial companies.

Article 19. Liberal professions

1. Each Contracting State shall accord to refugees lawfully staying in their territory who hold diplomas recognized by the competent authorities of that State, and who are desirous of practising a liberal profession, treatment as favourable as possible and, in any event, not less favourable than that accorded to aliens generally in the same circumstances.

2. The Contracting States shall use their best endeavours consistently with their laws and constitutions to secure the settlement of such refugees in the territories, other than the metropolitan territory, for whose international relations they are responsible.

Chapter IV. Welfare

Article 20. Rationing

Where a rationing system exists, which applies to the population at large and regulates the general distribution of products in short supply, refugees shall be accorded the same treatment as nationals.

Article 21. Housing

As regards housing, the Contracting States, in so far as the matter is regulated by laws or regulations or is subject to the control of public authorities, shall accord to refugees lawfully staying in their territory treatment as favourable as possible and, in any event, not less favourable than that accorded to aliens generally in the same circumstances.

Article 22. Public education

(1) The Contracting States shall accord to refugees the same treatment as is accorded to nationals with respect to elementary education.

(2) The Contracting States shall accord to refugees treatment as favourable as possible, and, in any event, not less favourable than that accorded to aliens generally in the same circumstances, with respect to education other than elementary education and, in particular, as regards access to studies, the recognition of foreign school certificates, diplomas and degrees, the remission of fees and charges and the award of scholarships.

Article 23. Public relief

The Contracting States shall accord to refugees lawfully staying in their territory the same treatment with respect to public relief and assistance as is accorded to their nationals.

Article 24. Labour legislation and social security

(1) The Contracting States shall accord to refugees lawfully staying in their territory the same treatment as is accorded to nationals in respect of the following matters;
(a) In so far as such matters are governed by laws or regulations or are subject to the control of administrative authorities: remuneration, including family allowances where these form part of remuneration, hours of work, overtime arrangements, holidays with pay, restrictions on home work, minimum age of employment, apprenticeship and training, women's work and the work of young persons, and the enjoyment of the benefits of collective bargaining;
(b) Social security (legal provisions in respect of employment injury, occupational diseases, maternity, sickness, disability, old age, death, unemployment, family responsibilities and any other contingency which, according to national laws or regulations, is covered by a social security scheme), subject to the following limitations:
(i) There may be appropriate arrangements for the maintenance of acquired rights and rights in course of acquisition;
(ii) National laws or regulations of the country of residence may prescribe special arrangements concerning benefits or portions of benefits which are payable wholly out of public funds, and concerning allowances paid to persons who do not fulfil the contribution conditions prescribed for the award of a normal pension.
(2) The right to compensation for the death of a refugee resulting from employment injury or from occupational disease shall not be affected by the fact that the residence of the beneficiary is outside the territory of the Contracting State.
(3) The Contracting States shall extend to refugees the benefits of agreements concluded between them, or which may be concluded between them in the future, concerning the maintenance of acquired rights and rights in the process of acquisition in regard to social security, subject only to the conditions which apply to nationals of the States signatory to the agreements in question.
(4) The Contracting States will give sympathetic consideration to extending to refugees so far as possible the benefits of similar agreements which may at any time be in force between such Contracting States and non-contracting States.

Chapter V. Administrative measures

Article 25. Administrative assistance

(1) When the exercise of a right by a refugee would normally require the assistance of authorities of a foreign country to whom he cannot have recourse, the Contracting States in whose territory he is residing shall arrange that such assistance be afforded to him by their own authorities or by an international authority.
(2) The authority or authorities mentioned in paragraph (1) shall deliver or cause to be delivered under their supervision to refugees such documents or certifications as would normally be delivered to aliens by or through their national authorities.
(3) Documents or certifications so delivered shall stand in the stead of the official instruments delivered to aliens by or through their national authorities, and shall be given credence in the absence of proof to the contrary.
(4) Subject to such exceptional treatment as may be granted to indigent persons, fees may be charged for the services mentioned herein, but such fees shall be moderate and commensurate with those charged to nationals for similar services.
(5) The provisions of this article shall be without prejudice to articles 27 and 28.

Article 26. Freedom of movement

Each Contracting State shall accord to refugees lawfully in its territory the right to choose their place of residence and to move freely within its territory subject to any regulations applicable to aliens generally in the same circumstances.

Article 27. Identity papers

The Contracting States shall issue identity papers to any refugee in their territory who does not possess a valid travel document.

Article 28. Travel documents

(1) The Contracting States shall issue to refugees lawfully staying in their territory travel documents for the purpose of travel outside their territory, unless compelling reasons of national security or public order otherwise require, and the provisions of the Schedule to this Convention shall apply with respect to such documents. The Contracting States may issue such a travel document to any other refugee in their territory; they shall in particular give sympathetic consideration to the issue of such

PART II FUNDAMENTAL RIGHTS

a travel document to refugees in their territory who are unable to obtain a travel document from the country of their lawful residence.
(2) Travel documents issued to refugees under previous international agreements by Parties thereto shall be recognized and treated by the Contracting States in the same way as if they had been issued pursuant to this article.

Article 29. Fiscal charges
(1) The Contracting States shall not impose upon refugees duties, charges or taxes, of any description whatsoever, other or higher than those which are or may be levied on their nationals in similar situations.
(2) Nothing in the above paragraph shall prevent the application to refugees of the laws and regulations concerning charges in respect of the issue to aliens of administrative documents including identity papers.

Article 30. Transfer of assets
(1) A Contracting State shall, in conformity with its laws and regulations, permit refugees to transfer assets which they have brought into its territory, to another country where they have been admitted for the purposes of resettlement.
(2) A Contracting State shall give sympathetic consideration to the application of refugees for permission to transfer assets wherever they may be and which are necessary for their resettlement in another country to which they have been admitted.

Article 31. Refugees unlawfully in the country of refuge
(1) The Contracting States shall not impose penalties, on account of their illegal entry or presence, on refugees who, coming directly from a territory where their life or freedom was threatened in the sense of article 1, enter or are present in their territory without authorization, provided they present themselves without delay to the authorities and show good cause for their illegal entry or presence.
(2) The Contracting States shall not apply to the movements of such refugees restrictions other than those which are necessary and such restrictions shall only be applied until their status in the country is regularized or they obtain admission into another country. The Contracting States shall allow such refugees a reasonable period and all the necessary facilities to obtain admission into another country.

Article 32. Expulsion
(1) The Contracting States shall not expel a refugee lawfully in their territory save on grounds of national security or public order.
(2) The expulsion of such a refugee shall be only in pursuance of a decision reached in accordance with due process of law. Except where compelling reasons of national security otherwise require, the refugee shall be allowed to submit evidence to clear himself, and to appeal to and be represented for the purpose before competent authority or a person or persons specially designated by the competent authority.
(3) The Contracting States shall allow such a refugee a reasonable period within which to seek legal admission into another country. The Contracting States reserve the right to apply during that period such internal measures as they may deem necessary.

Article 33. Prohibition of expulsion or return *("refoulement")*
(1) No Contracting State shall expel or return (" refouler ") a refugee in any manner whatsoever to the frontiers of territories where his life or freedom would be threatened on account of his race, religion, nationality, membership of a particular social group or political opinion.
(2) The benefit of the present provision may not, however, be claimed by a refugee whom there are reasonable grounds for regarding as a danger to the security of the country in which he is, or who, having been convicted by a final judgement of a particularly serious crime, constitutes a danger to the community of that country.

Article 34. Naturalization
The Contracting States shall as far as possible facilitate the assimilation and naturalization of refugees. They shall in particular make every effort to expedite naturalization proceedings and to reduce as far as possible the charges and costs of such proceedings.

Chapter VI. Executory and transitory provisions

Article 35. Co-operation of the national authorities with the United Nations
(1) The Contracting States undertake to co-operate with the Office of the United Nations High Commissioner for Refugees, or any other agency of the United Nations which may succeed it, in the

exercise of its functions, and shall in particular facilitate its duty of supervising the application of the provisions of this Convention.
(2) In order to enable the Office of the High Commissioner or any other agency of the United Nations which may succeed it, to make reports to the competent organs of the United Nations, the Contracting States undertake to provide them in the appropriate form with information and statistical data requested concerning:
(a) The condition of refugees,
(b) The implementation of this Convention, and
(c) Laws, regulations and decrees which are, or may hereafter be, in force relating to refugees.

Article 36. Information on national legislation
The Contracting States shall communicate to the Secretary-General of the United Nations the laws and regulations which they may adopt to ensure the application of this Convention.

Article 37. Relation to previous conventions
Without prejudice to article 28, paragraph (2), of this Convention, this Convention replaces, as between Parties to it, the Arrangements of 5 July 1922, 31 May 1924, 12 May 1926, 30 June 1928 and 30 July 1935, the Conventions of 28 October 1933 and 10 February 1938, the Protocol of 14 September 1939 and the Agreement of 15 October 1946.

Chapter VII. Final clauses

Article 38. Settlement of disputes
Any dispute between Parties to this Convention relating to its interpretation or application, which cannot be settled by other means, shall be referred to the International Court of Justice at the request of any one of the parties to the dispute.

Article 39. Signature, ratification and accession
(1) This Convention shall be opened for signature at Geneva on 28 July 1951 and shall thereafter be deposited with the Secretary-General of the United Nations. It shall be open for signature at the European Office of the United Nations from 28 July to 31 August 1951 and shall be re-opened for signature at the Headquarters of the United Nations from 17 September 1951 to 31 December 1952.
(2) This Convention shall be open for signature on behalf of all States Members of the United Nations, and also on behalf of any other State invited to attend the Conference of Plenipotentiaries on the Status of Refugees and Stateless Persons or to which an invitation to sign will have been addressed by the General Assembly. It shall be ratified and the instruments of ratification shall be deposited with the Secretary-General of the United Nations.
(3) This Convention shall be open from 28 July 1951 for accession by the States referred to in paragraph (2) of this article. Accession shall be effected by the deposit of an instrument of accession with the Secretary-General of the United Nations.

Article 40. Territorial application clause
(1) Any State may, at the time of signature, ratification or accession, declare that this Convention shall extend to all or any of the territories for the international relations of which it is responsible. Such a declaration shall take effect when the Convention enters into force for the State concerned.
(2) At any time thereafter any such extension shall be made by notification addressed to the Secretary General of the United Nations and shall take effect as from the ninetieth day after the day of receipt by the Secretary-General of the United Nations of this notification, or as from the date of entry into force of the Convention for the State concerned, whichever is the later.
(3) With respect to those territories to which this Convention is not extended at the time of signature, ratification or accession, each State concerned shall consider the possibility of taking the necessary steps in order to extend the application of this Convention to such territories, subject, where necessary for constitutional reasons, to the consent of the Governments of such territories.

Article 41. Federal clause
In the case of a Federal or non-unitary State, the following provisions shall apply:
(a) With respect to those articles of this Convention that come within the legislative jurisdiction of the federal legislative authority, the obligations of the Federal Government shall to this extent be the same as those of parties which are not Federal States;
(b) With respect to those articles of this Convention that come within the legislative jurisdiction of constituent States, provinces or cantons which are not, under the constitutional system of the Federation, bound to take legislative action, the Federal Government shall bring such articles with a favourable recommendation to the notice of the appropriate authorities of States, provinces or cantons at the earliest possible moment;

PART II   FUNDAMENTAL RIGHTS

(c) A Federal State Party to this Convention shall, at the request of any other Contracting State transmitted through the Secretary-General of the United Nations, supply a statement of the law and practice of the Federation and its constituent units in regard to any particular provision of the Convention showing the extent to which effect has been given to that provision by legislative or other action.

Article 42. Reservations
(1) At the time of signature, ratification or accession, any State may make reservations to articles of the Convention other than to articles 1, 3, 4, 16 (1), 33, 36-46 inclusive.
(2) Any State making a reservation in accordance with paragraph (1) of this article may at any time withdraw the reservation by a communication to that effect addressed to the Secretary-General of the United Nations.

Article 43. Entry into force
(1) This Convention shall come into force on the ninetieth day following the day of deposit of the sixth instrument of ratification or accession.
(2) For each State ratifying or acceding to the Convention after the deposit of the sixth instrument of ratification or accession, the Convention shall enter into force on the ninetieth day following the date of deposit by such State of its instrument of ratification or accession.

Article 44. Denunciation
(1) Any Contracting State may denounce this Convention at any time by a notification addressed to the Secretary-General of the United Nations.
(2) Such denunciation shall take effect for the Contracting State concerned one year from the date upon which it is received by the Secretary-General of the United Nations.
(3) Any State which has made a declaration or notification under article 40 may, at any time thereafter, by a notification to the Secretary-General of the United Nations, declare that the Convention shall cease to extend to such territory one year after the date of receipt of the notification by the Secretary General.

Article 45. Revision
(1) Any Contracting State may request revision of this Convention at any time by a notification addressed to the Secretary-General of the United Nations.
(2) The General Assembly of the United Nations shall recommend the steps, if any, to be taken in respect of such request.

Article 46. Notifications by the Secretary-General of the United Nations
The Secretary-General of the United Nations shall inform all Members of the United Nations and non-member States referred to in article 39:
(a) Of declarations and notifications in accordance with section B of article 1;
(b) Of signatures, ratifications and accessions in accordance with article 39;
(c) Of declarations and notifications in accordance with article 40;
(d) Of reservations and withdrawals in accordance with article 42;
(e) Of the date on which this Convention will come into force in accordance with article 43;
(f) Of denunciations and notifications in accordance with article 44;
(g) Of requests for revision in accordance with article 45.
In faith whereof the undersigned, duly authorized, have signed this Convention on behalf of their respective Governments.
Done at Geneva, this twenty-eighth day of July, one thousand nine hundred and fifty-one, in a single copy, of which the English and French texts are equally authentic and which shall remain deposited in the archives of the United Nations, and certified true copies of which shall be delivered to all Members of the United Nations and to the non-member States referred to in article 39.

Protocol relating to the Status of Refugees
New York, 31 January 1967
Trb. 1951 Nr. 131M 1967 Nr. 76

The Protocol was taken note of with approval by the Economic and Social Council in resolution 1186 (XLI) of 18 November 1966 and was taken note of by the General Assembly in resolution 2198 (XXI) of 16 December 1966. In the same resolution the General Assembly requested the Secretary-General to transmit the text of the Protocol to the States mentioned in article V thereof, with a view to enabling them to accede to the Protocol
entry into force 4 October 1967, in accordance with article VIII
The States Parties to the present Protocol,
Considering that the Convention relating to the Status of Refugees done at Geneva on 28 July 1951 (hereinafter referred to as the Convention) covers only those persons who have become refugees as a result of events occurring before I January 1951,
Considering that new refugee situations have arisen since the Convention was adopted and that the refugees concerned may therefore not fall within the scope of the Convention,
Considering that it is desirable that equal status should be enjoyed by all refugees covered by the definition in the Convention irrespective of the dateline I January 1951,
Have agreed as follows:

Article 1. General provision
(1) The States Parties to the present Protocol undertake to apply articles 2 to 34 inclusive of the Convention to refugees as hereinafter defined.
(2) For the purpose of the present Protocol, the term "refugee" shall, except as regards the application of paragraph (3) of this article, mean any person within the definition of article 1 of the Convention as if the words "As a result of events occurring before 1 January 1951 and..." and the words "...as a result of such events", in article 1 A (2) were omitted.
(3) The present Protocol shall be applied by the States Parties hereto without any geographic limitation, save that existing declarations made by States already Parties to the Convention in accordance with article 1 B (I) (a) of the Convention, shall, unless extended under
article 1 B (2) thereof, apply also under the present Protocol.

Article 2. Co-operation of the national authorities with the United Nations
(1) The States Parties to the present Protocol undertake to co-operate with the Office of the United Nations High Commissioner for Refugees, or any other agency of the United Nations which may succeed it, in the exercise of its functions, and shall in particular facilitate its duty of supervising the application of the provisions of the present Protocol.
(2) In order to enable the Office of the High Commissioner or any other agency of the United Nations which may succeed it, to make reports to the competent organs of the United Nations, the States Parties to the present Protocol undertake to provide them with the information and statistical data requested, in the appropriate form, concerning:
(a) The condition of refugees;
(b) The implementation of the present Protocol;
(c) Laws, regulations and decrees which are, or may hereafter be, in force relating to refugees.

Article 3. Information on national legislation
The States Parties to the present Protocol shall communicate to the Secretary-General of the United Nations the laws and regulations which they may adopt to ensure the application of the present Protocol.

Article 4. Settlement of disputes
Any dispute between States Parties to the present Protocol which relates to its interpretation or application and which cannot be settled by other means shall be referred to the International Court of Justice at the request of any one of the parties to the dispute.

Article 5. Accession
The present Protocol shall be open for accession on behalf of all States Parties to the Convention and of any other State Member of the United Nations or member of any of the specialized agencies or to which an invitation to accede may have been addressed by the General Assembly of the United Nations. Accession shall be effected by the deposit of an instrument of accession with the Secretary-General of the United Nations.

PART II FUNDAMENTAL RIGHTS

Article 6. Federal clause
In the case of a Federal or non-unitary State, the following provisions shall apply:
(a) With respect to those articles of the Convention to be applied in accordance with article 1, paragraph (1), of the present Protocol that come within the legislative jurisdiction of the federal legislative authority, the obligations of the Federal Government shall to this extent be the same as those of States Parties which are not Federal States;
(b) With respect to those articles of the Convention to be applied in accordance with article 1, paragraph (1), of the present Protocol that come within the legislative jurisdiction of constituent States, provinces or cantons which are not, under the constitutional system of the Federation, bound to take legislative action, the Federal Government shall bring such articles with a favourable recommendation to the notice of the appropriate authorities of States, provinces or cantons at the earliest possible moment;
(c) A Federal State Party to the present Protocol shall, at the request of any other State Party hereto transmitted through the Secretary-General of the United Nations, supply a statement of the law and practice of the Federation and its constituent units in regard to any particular provision of the Convention to be applied in accordance with article 1, paragraph (1), of the present Protocol, showing the extent to which effect has been given to that provision by legislative or other action.

Article 7. Reservations and declarations
(1) At the time of accession, any State may make reservations in respect of article IV of the present Protocol and in respect of the application in accordance with article I of the present Protocol of any provisions of the Convention other than those contained in
articles 1, 3, 4, 16(1) and 33 thereof, provided that in the case of a State Party to the Convention reservations made under this article shall not extend to refugees in respect of whom the Convention applies.
(2) Reservations made by States Parties to the Convention in accordance with article 42 thereof shall, unless withdrawn, be applicable in relation to their obligations under the present Protocol.
(3) Any State making a reservation in accordance with paragraph (1) of this article may at any time withdraw such reservation by a communication to that effect addressed to the Secretary General of the United Nations.
(4) Declarations made under article 40, paragraphs (1) and (2), of the Convention by a State Party thereto which accedes to the present Protocol shall be deemed to apply in respect of the present Protocol, unless upon accession a notification to the contrary is addressed by the State Party concerned to the Secretary-General of the United Nations. The provisions of article 40, paragraphs (2) and (3), and of article 44, paragraph (3), of the Convention shall be deemed to apply muratis mutandis to the present Protocol.

Article 8. Entry into Protocol
(1) The present Protocol shall come into force on the day of deposit of the sixth instrument of accession.
(2) For each State acceding to the Protocol after the deposit of the sixth instrument of accession, the Protocol shall come into force on the date of deposit by such State of its instrument of accession.

Article 9. Denunciation
(1) Any State Party hereto may denounce this Protocol at any time by a notification addressed to the Secretary-General of the United Nations.
(2) Such denunciation shall take effect for the State Party concerned one year from the date on which it is received by the Secretary-General of the United Nations.

Article 10. Notifications by the Secretary-General of the United Nations
The Secretary-General of the United Nations shall inform the States referred to in article V above of the date of entry into force, accessions, reservations and withdrawals of reservations to and denunciations of the present Protocol, and of declarations and notifications relating hereto.

Article 11. Deposit in the archives of the Secretariat of the United Nations
A copy of the present Protocol, of which the Chinese, English, French, Russian and Spanish texts are equally authentic, signed by the President of the General Assembly and by the Secretary-General of the United Nations, shall be deposited in the archives of the Secretariat of the United Nations. The Secretary-General will transmit certified copies thereof to all States Members of the United Nations and to the other States referred to in article 5 above.

COVENTION ON THE ELIMINATION OF RACIAL DISCRIMINATION

International Convention on the Elimination of All Forms of Racial Discrimination (ICERD)
New York, 7 March 1966, Entry into force 4 January 1969
Trb. 1966 Nr. 237

The States Parties to this Convention,
Considering that the Charter of the United Nations is based on the principles of the dignity and equality inherent in all human beings, and that all Member States have pledged themselves to take joint and separate action, in co-operation with the Organization, for the achievement of one of the purposes of the United Nations which is to promote and encourage universal respect for and observance of human rights and fundamental freedoms for all, without distinction as to race, sex, language or religion,
Considering that the Universal Declaration of Human Rights proclaims that all human beings are born free and equal in dignity and rights and that everyone is entitled to all the rights and freedoms set out therein, without distinction of any kind, in particular as to race, colour or national origin,
Considering that all human beings are equal before the law and are entitled to equal protection of the law against any discrimination and against any incitement to discrimination,
Considering that the United Nations has condemned colonialism and all practices of segregation and discrimination associated therewith, in whatever form and wherever they exist, and that the Declaration on the Granting of Independence to Colonial Countries and Peoples of 14 December 1960 (General Assembly resolution 1514 (XV)) has affirmed and solemnly proclaimed the necessity of bringing them to a speedy and unconditional end,
Considering that the United Nations Declaration on the Elimination of All Forms of Racial Discrimination of 20 November 1963 (General Assembly resolution 1904 (XVIII)) solemnly affirms the necessity of speedily eliminating racial discrimination throughout the world in all its forms and manifestations and of securing understanding of and respect for the dignity of the human person,
Convinced that any doctrine of superiority based on racial differentiation is scientifically false, morally condemnable, socially unjust and dangerous, and that there is no justification for racial discrimination, in theory or in practice, anywhere,
Reaffirming that discrimination between human beings on the grounds of race, colour or ethnic origin is an obstacle to friendly and peaceful relations among nations and is capable of disturbing peace and security among peoples and the harmony of persons living side by side even within one and the same State, Convinced that the existence of racial barriers is repugnant to the ideals of any human society,
Alarmed by manifestations of racial discrimination still in evidence in some areas of the world and by governmental policies based on racial superiority or hatred, such as policies of apartheid, segregation or separation,
Resolved to adopt all necessary measures for speedily eliminating racial discrimination in all its forms and manifestations, and to prevent and combat racist doctrines and practices in order to promote understanding between races and to build an international community free from all forms of racial segregation and racial discrimination,
Bearing in mind the Convention concerning Discrimination in respect of Employment and Occupation adopted by the International Labour Organisation in 1958, and the Convention against Discrimination in Education adopted by the United Nations Educational, Scientific and Cultural Organization in 1960,
Desiring to implement the principles embodied in the United Nations Declaration on the Elimination of All Forms of Racial Discrimination and to secure the earliest adoption of practical measures to that end,
Have agreed as follows:

Part I

Article 1. (1) In this Convention, the term "racial discrimination" shall mean any distinction, exclusion, restriction or preference based on race, colour, descent, or national or ethnic origin which has the purpose or effect of nullifying or impairing the recognition, enjoyment or exercise, on an equal footing, of human rights and fundamental freedoms in the political, economic, social, cultural or any other field of public life.
(2) This Convention shall not apply to distinctions, exclusions, restrictions or preferences made by a State Party to this Convention between citizens and non-citizens.
(3) Nothing in this Convention may be interpreted as affecting in any way the legal provisions of States Parties concerning nationality, citizenship or naturalization, provided that such provisions do not discriminate against any particular nationality.

PART II FUNDAMENTAL RIGHTS

(4) Special measures taken for the sole purpose of securing adequate advancement of certain racial or ethnic groups or individuals requiring such protection as may be necessary in order to ensure such groups or individuals equal enjoyment or exercise of human rights and fundamental freedoms shall not be deemed racial discrimination, provided, however, that such measures do not, as a consequence, lead to the maintenance of separate rights for different racial groups and that they shall not be continued after the objectives for which they were taken have been achieved.

Article 2. (1) States Parties condemn racial discrimination and undertake to pursue by all appropriate means and without delay a policy of eliminating racial discrimination in all its forms and promoting understanding among all races, and, to this end:
(a) Each State Party undertakes to engage in no act or practice of racial discrimination against persons, groups of persons or institutions and to en sure that all public authorities and public institutions, national and local, shall act in conformity with this obligation;
(b) Each State Party undertakes not to sponsor, defend or support racial discrimination by any persons or organizations;
(c) Each State Party shall take effective measures to review governmental, national and local policies, and to amend, rescind or nullify any laws and regulations which have the effect of creating or perpetuating racial discrimination wherever it exists;
(d) Each State Party shall prohibit and bring to an end, by all appropriate means, including legislation as required by circumstances, racial discrimination by any persons, group or organization;
(e) Each State Party undertakes to encourage, where appropriate, integrationist multiracial organizations and movements and other means of eliminating barriers between races, and to discourage anything which tends to strengthen racial division.
(2) States Parties shall, when the circumstances so warrant, take, in the social, economic, cultural and other fields, special and concrete measures to ensure the adequate development and protection of certain racial groups or individuals belonging to them, for the purpose of guaranteeing them the full and equal enjoyment of human rights and fundamental freedoms. These measures shall in no case en tail as a con sequence the maintenance of unequal or separate rights for different racial groups after the objectives for which they were taken have been achieved.

Article 3. States Parties particularly condemn racial segregation and apartheid and undertake to prevent, prohibit and eradicate all practices of this nature in territories under their jurisdiction.

Article 4. States Parties condemn all propaganda and all organizations which are based on ideas or theories of superiority of one race or group of persons of one colour or ethnic origin, or which attempt to justify or promote racial hatred and discrimination in any form, and undertake to adopt immediate and positive measures designed to eradicate all incitement to, or acts of, such discrimination and, to this end, with due regard to the principles embodied in the Universal Declaration of Human Rights and the rights expressly set forth in article 5 of this Convention, inter alia:
(a) Shall declare an offence punishable by law all dissemination of ideas based on racial superiority or hatred, incitement to racial discrimination, as well as all acts of violence or incitement to such acts against any race or group of persons of another colour or ethnic origin, and also the provision of any assistance to racist activities, including the financing thereof;
(b) Shall declare illegal and prohibit organizations, and also organized and all other propaganda activities, which promote and incite racial discrimination, and shall recognize participation in such organizations or activities as an offence punishable by law; (c) Shall not permit public authorities or public institutions, national or local, to promote or incite racial discrimination.

Article 5. In compliance with the fundamental obligations laid down in article 2 of this Convention, States Parties undertake to prohibit and to eliminate racial discrimination in all its forms and to guarantee the right of everyone, without distinction as to race, colour, or national or ethnic origin, to equality before the law, notably in the enjoyment of the following rights:
(a) The right to equal treatment before the tribunals and all other organs administering justice;
(b) The right to security of person and protection by the State against violence or bodily harm, whether inflicted by government officials or by any individual group or institution;
(c) Political rights, in particular the right to participate in elections-to vote and to stand for election-on the basis of universal and equal suffrage, to take part in the Government as well as in the conduct of public affairs at any level and to have equal access to public service;
(d) Other civil rights, in particular:
(i) The right to freedom of movement and residence within the border of the State;
(ii) The right to leave any country, including one's own, and to return to one's country;
(iii) The right to nationality;

(iv) The right to marriage and choice of spouse;
(v) The right to own property alone as well as in association with others;
(vi) The right to inherit;
(vii) The right to freedom of thought, conscience and religion;
(viii) The right to freedom of opinion and expression;
(ix) The right to freedom of peaceful assembly and association;
(e) Economic, social and cultural rights, in particular:
(i) The rights to work, to free choice of employment, to just and favourable conditions of work, to protection against unemployment, to equal pay for equal work, to just and favourable remuneration;
(ii) The right to form and join trade unions;
(iii) The right to housing;
(iv) The right to public health, medical care, social security and social services;
(v) The right to education and training;
(vi) The right to equal participation in cultural activities;
(f) The right of access to any place or service intended for use by the general public, such as transport hotels, restaurants, cafes, theatres and parks.

Article 6. States Parties shall assure to everyone within their jurisdiction effective protection and remedies, through the competent national tribunals and other State institutions, against any acts of racial discrimination which violate his human rights and fundamental freedoms contrary to this Convention, as well as the right to seek from such tribunals just and adequate reparation or satisfaction for any damage suffered as a result of such discrimination.

Article 7. States Parties undertake to adopt immediate and effective measures, particularly in the fields of teaching, education, culture and information, with a view to combating prejudices which lead to racial discrimination and to promoting understanding, tolerance and friendship among nations and racial or ethnical groups, as well as to propagating the purposes and principles of the Charter of the United Nations, the Universal Declaration of Human Rights, the United Nations Declaration on the Elimination of All Forms of Racial Discrimination, and this Convention.

Part II

Article 8. (1) There shall be established a Committee on the Elimination of Racial Discrimination (hereinafter referred to as the Committee) consisting of eighteen experts of high moral standing and acknowledged impartiality elected by States Parties from among their nationals, who shall serve in their personal capacity, consideration being given to equitable geographical distribution and to the representation of the different forms of civilization as well as of the principal legal systems.
(2) The members of the Committee shall be elected by secret ballot from a list of persons nominated by the States Parties. Each State Party may nominate one person from among its own nationals.
(3) The initial election shall be held six months after the date of the entry into force of this Convention. At least three months before the date of each election the Secretary-General of the United Nations shall address a letter to the States Parties inviting them to submit their nominations within two months. The Secretary-General shall prepare a list in alphabetical order of all persons thus nominated, indicating the States Parties which have nominated them, and shall submit it to the States Parties.
(4) Elections of the members of the Committee shall be held at a meeting of States Parties convened by the Secretary-General at United Nations Headquarters. At that meeting, for which two thirds of the States Parties shall constitute a quorum, the persons elected to the Committee shall be nominees who obtain the largest number of votes and an absolute majority of the votes of the representatives of States Parties present and voting.
(5) (a) The members of the Committee shall be elected for a term of four years. However, the terms of nine of the members elected at the first election shall expire at the end of two years; immediately after the first election the names of these nine members shall be chosen by lot by the Chairman of the Committee;
(b) For the filling of casual vacancies, the State Party whose expert has ceased to function as a member of the Committee shall appoint another expert from among its nationals, subject to the approval of the Committee.
(6) States Parties shall be responsible for the expenses of the members of the Committee while they are in performance of Committee duties.

Article 9. (1) States Parties undertake to submit to the Secretary-General of the United Nations, for consideration by the Committee, a report on the legislative, judicial, administrative or other measures

PART II   FUNDAMENTAL RIGHTS

which they have adopted and which give effect to the provisions of this Convention:
(a) within one year after the entry into force of the Convention for the State concerned; and (b) thereafter every two years and whenever the Committee so requests. The Committee may request further information from the States Parties.
(2) The Committee shall report annually, through the Secretary General, to the General Assembly of the United Nations on its activities and may make suggestions and general recommendations based on the examination of the reports and information received from the States Parties. Such suggestions and general recommendations shall be reported to the General Assembly together with comments, if any, from States Parties.

Article 10. (1) The Committee shall adopt its own rules of procedure.
(2) The Committee shall elect its officers for a term of two years.
(3) The secretariat of the Committee shall be provided by the Secretary General of the United Nations.
(4) The meetings of the Committee shall normally be held at United Nations Headquarters.

Article 11. (1) If a State Party considers that another State Party is not giving effect to the provisions of this Convention, it may bring the matter to the attention of the Committee. The Committee shall then transmit the communication to the State Party concerned. Within three months, the receiving State shall submit to the Committee written explanations or statements clarifying the matter and the remedy, if any, that may have been taken by that State.
(2) If the matter is not adjusted to the satisfaction of both parties, either by bilateral negotiations or by any other procedure open to them, within six months after the receipt by the receiving State of the initial communication, either State shall have the right to refer the matter again to the Committee by notifying the Committee and also the other State.
(3) The Committee shall deal with a matter referred to it in accordance with paragraph (2) of this article after it has ascertained that all available domestic remedies have been invoked and exhausted in the case, in conformity with the generally recognized principles of international law. This shall not be the rule where the application of the remedies is unreasonably prolonged.
(4) In any matter referred to it, the Committee may call upon the States Parties concerned to supply any other relevant information.
(5) When any matter arising out of this article is being considered by the Committee, the States Parties concerned shall be entitled to send a representative to take part in the proceedings of the Committee, without voting rights, while the matter is under consideration.

Article 12. (1) (a) After the Committee has obtained and collated all the information it deems necessary, the Chairman shall appoint an ad hoc Conciliation Commission (hereinafter referred to as the Commission) comprising five persons who may or may not be members of the Committee. The members of the Commission shall be appointed with the unanimous consent of the parties to the dispute, and its good offices shall be made available to the States concerned with a view to an amicable solution of the matter on the basis of respect for this Convention;
(b) If the States parties to the dispute fail to reach agreement within three months on all or part of the composition of the Commission, the members of the Commission not agreed upon by the States parties to the dispute shall be elected by secret ballot by a two-thirds majority vote of the Committee from among its own members.
(2) The members of the Commission shall serve in their personal capacity. They shall not be nationals of the States parties to the dispute or of a State not Party to this Convention.
(3) The Commission shall elect its own Chairman and adopt its own rules of procedure.
(4) The meetings of the Commission shall normally be held at United Nations Headquarters or at any other convenient place as determined by the Commission.
(5) The secretariat provided in accordance with article 10, paragraph (3), of this Convention shall also service the Commission whenever a dispute among States Parties brings the Commission into being.
(6) The States parties to the dispute shall share equally all the expenses of the members of the Commission in accordance with estimates to be provided by the Secretary-General of the United Nations.
(7) The Secretary-General shall be empowered to pay the expenses of the members of the Commission, if necessary, before reimbursement by the States parties to the dispute in accordance with paragraph (6) of this article.
(8) The information obtained and collated by the Committee shall be made available to the Commission, and the Commission may call upon the States concerned to supply any other relevant information.

Article 13. (1) When the Commission has fully considered the matter, it shall prepare and submit to the Chairman of the Committee a report embodying its findings on all questions of fact relevant to the issue between the parties and containing such recommendations as it may think proper for the amicable solution of the dispute.

(2) The Chairman of the Committee shall communicate the report of the Commission to each of the States parties to the dispute. These States shall, within three months, inform the Chairman of the Committee whether or not they accept the recommendations contained in the report of the Commission.

(3) After the period provided for in paragraph (2) of this article, the Chairman of the Committee shall communicate the report of the Commission and the declarations of the States Parties concerned to the other States Parties to this Convention.

Article 14. (1) A State Party may at any time declare that it recognizes the competence of the Committee to receive and consider communications from individuals or groups of individuals within its jurisdiction claiming to be victims of a violation by that State Party of any of the rights set forth in this Convention. No communication shall be received by the Committee if it concerns a State Party which has not made such a declaration.

(2) Any State Party which makes a declaration as provided for in paragraph (1) of this article may establish or indicate a body within its national legal order which shall be competent to receive and consider petitions from individuals and groups of individuals within its jurisdiction who claim to be victims of a violation of any of the rights set forth in this Convention and who have exhausted other available local remedies.

(3) A declaration made in accordance with paragraph (1) of this article and the name of any body established or indicated in accordance with paragraph (2) of this article shall be deposited by the State Party concerned with the Secretary-General of the United Nations, who shall transmit copies thereof to the other States Parties. A declaration may be withdrawn at any time by notification to the Secretary General, but such a withdrawal shall not affect communications pending before the Committee.

(4) A register of petitions shall be kept by the body established or indicated in accordance with paragraph (2) of this article, and certified copies of the register shall be filed annually through appropriate channels with the Secretary-General on the understanding that the contents shall not be publicly disclosed.

(5) In the event of failure to obtain satisfaction from the body established or indicated in accordance with paragraph (2) of this article, the petitioner shall have the right to communicate the matter to the Committee within six months.

(6) (a) The Committee shall confidentially bring any communication referred to it to the attention of the State Party alleged to be violating any provision of this Convention, but the identity of the individual or groups of individuals concerned shall not be revealed without his or their express consent. The Committee shall not receive anonymous communications;

(b) Within three months, the receiving State shall submit to the Committee written explanations or statements clarifying the matter and the remedy, if any, that may have been taken by that State.

(7) (a) The Committee shall consider communications in the light of all information made available to it by the State Party concerned and by the petitioner. The Committee shall not consider any communication from a petitioner unless it has ascertained that the petitioner has exhausted all available domestic remedies. However, this shall not be the rule where the application of the remedies is unreasonably prolonged;

(b) The Committee shall forward its suggestions and recommendations, if any, to the State Party concerned and to the petitioner.

(8) The Committee shall include in its annual report a summary of such communications and, where appropriate, a summary of the explanations and statements of the States Parties concerned and of its own suggestions and recommendations.

(9) The Committee shall be competent to exercise the functions provided for in this article only when at least ten States Parties to this Convention are bound by declarations in accordance with paragraph (1) of this article.

Article 15. (1) Pending the achievement of the objectives of the Declaration on the Granting of Independence to Colonial Countries and Peoples, contained in General Assembly resolution 1514 (XV) of 14 December 1960, the provisions of this Convention shall in no way limit the right of petition granted to these peoples by other international instruments or by the United Nations and its specialized agencies.

(2) (a) The Committee established under article 8, paragraph (1), of this Convention shall receive copies of the petitions from, and submit expressions of opinion and recommendations on these peti-

tions to, the bodies of the United Nations which deal with matters directly related to the principles and objectives of this Convention in their consideration of petitions from the inhabitants of Trust and Non-Self-Governing Territories and all other territories to which General Assembly resolution 1514 (XV) applies, relating to matters covered by this Convention which are before these bodies;
(b) The Committee shall receive from the competent bodies of the United Nations copies of the reports concerning the legislative, judicial, administrative or other measures directly related to the principles and objectives of this Convention applied by the administering Powers within the Territories mentioned in subparagraph (a) of this paragraph, and shall express opinions and make recommendations to these bodies.
(3) The Committee shall include in its report to the General Assembly a summary of the petitions and reports it has received from United Nations bodies, and the expressions of opinion and recommendations of the Committee relating to the said petitions and reports.
(4) The Committee shall request from the Secretary-General of the United Nations all information relevant to the objectives of this Convention and available to him regarding the Territories mentioned in paragraph (2)(a) of this article.

Article 16. The provisions of this Convention concerning the settlement of disputes or complaints shall be applied without prejudice to other procedures for settling disputes or complaints in the field of discrimination laid down in the constituent instruments of, or conventions adopted by, the United Nations and its specialized agencies, and shall not prevent the States Parties from having recourse to other procedures for settling a dispute in accordance with general or special international agreements in force between them.

Part III

Article 17. (1) This Convention is open for signature by any State Member of the United Nations or member of any of its specialized agencies, by any State Party to the Statute of the International Court of Justice, and by any other State which has been invited by the General Assembly of the United Nations to become a Party to this Convention.
(2) This Convention is subject to ratification. Instruments of ratification shall be deposited with the Secretary-General of the United Nations.

Article 18. (1) This Convention shall be open to accession by any State referred to in article 17, paragraph (1), of the Convention.
(2) Accession shall be effected by the deposit of an instrument of accession with the Secretary-General of the United Nations.

Article 19. (1) This Convention shall enter into force on the thirtieth day after the date of the deposit with the Secretary-General of the United Nations of the twenty-seventh instrument of ratification or instrument of accession.
(2) For each State ratifying this Convention or acceding to it after the deposit of the twenty-seventh instrument of ratification or instrument of accession, the Convention shall enter into force on the thirtieth day after the date of the deposit of its own instrument of ratification or instrument of accession.

Article 20. (1) The Secretary-General of the United Nations shall receive and circulate to all States which are or may become Parties to this Convention reservations made by States at the time of ratification or accession. Any State which objects to the reservation shall, within a period of ninety days from the date of the said communication, notify the Secretary-General that it does not accept it.
(2) A reservation incompatible with the object and purpose of this Convention shall not be permitted, nor shall a reservation the effect of which would inhibit the operation of any of the bodies established by this Convention be allowed. A reservation shall be considered incompatible or inhibitive if at least two thirds of the States Parties to this Convention object to it.
(3) Reservations may be withdrawn at any time by notification to this effect addressed to the Secretary General. Such notification shall take effect on the date on which it is received.

Article 21. A State Party may denounce this Convention by written notification to the Secretary-General of the United Nations. Denunciation shall take effect one year after the date of receipt of the notification by the Secretary General.

Article 22. Any dispute between two or more States Parties with respect to the interpretation or application of this Convention, which is not settled by negotiation or by the procedures expressly provided for in this Convention, shall, at the request of any of the parties to the dispute, be referred to the International Court of Justice for decision, unless the disputants agree to another mode of settlement.

COVENTION ON THE ELIMINATION OF RACIAL DISCRIMINATION

Article 23. (1) A request for the revision of this Convention may be made at any time by any State Party by means of a notification in writing addressed to the Secretary-General of the United Nations.
2. The General Assembly of the United Nations shall decide upon the steps, if any, to be taken in respect of such a request.

Article 24. The Secretary-General of the United Nations shall inform all States referred to in article 17, paragraph (1), of this Convention of the following particulars:
(a) Signatures, ratifications and accessions under articles 17 and 18;
(b) The date of entry into force of this Convention under article 19;
(c) Communications and declarations received under articles 14, 20 and 23;
(d) Denunciations under article 21.

Article 25. (1) This Convention, of which the Chinese, English, French, Russian and Spanish texts are equally authentic, shall be deposited in the archives of the United Nations.
(2) The Secretary-General of the United Nations shall transmit certified copies of this Convention to all States belonging to any of the categories mentioned in article 17,
paragraph (1), of the Convention.

PART II FUNDAMENTAL RIGHTS

International Covenant on Economic, Social and Cultural Rights (ICESCR)
New York 19 December 1966, Entry into force 3 January 1976
Trb. 1969 Nr. 100

The States Parties to the present Covenant,
Considering that, in accordance with the principles proclaimed in the Charter of the United Nations, recognition of the inherent dignity and of the equal and inalienable rights of all members of the human family is the foundation of freedom, justice and peace in the world,
Recognizing that these rights derive from the inherent dignity of the human person,
Recognizing that, in accordance with the Universal Declaration of Human Rights, the ideal of free human beings enjoying freedom from fear and want can only be achieved if conditions are created whereby everyone may enjoy his economic, social and cultural rights, as well as his civil and political rights,
Considering the obligation of States under the Charter of the United Nations to promote universal respect for, and observance of, human rights and freedoms,
Realizing that the individual, having duties to other individuals and to the community to which he belongs, is under a responsibility to strive for the promotion and observance of the rights recognized in the present Covenant,
Agree upon the following articles:

Part I

Article 1. (1) All peoples have the right of self-determination. By virtue of that right they freely determine their political status and freely pursue their economic, social and cultural development.
(2) All peoples may, for their own ends, freely dispose of their natural wealth and resources without prejudice to any obligations arising out of international economic co-operation, based upon the principle of mutual benefit, and international law. In no case may a people be deprived of its own means of subsistence.
(3) The States Parties to the present Covenant, including those having responsibility for the administration of Non-Self-Governing and Trust Territories, shall promote the realization of the right of self-determination, and shall respect that right, in conformity with the provisions of the Charter of the United Nations.

Part II

Article 2. (1) Each State Party to the present Covenant undertakes to take steps, individually and through international assistance and co-operation, especially economic and technical, to the maximum of its available resources, with a view to achieving progressively the full realization of the rights recognized in the present Covenant by all appropriate means, including particularly the adoption of legislative measures.
(2) The States Parties to the present Covenant undertake to guarantee that the rights enunciated in the present Covenant will be exercised without discrimination of any kind as to race, colour, sex, language, religion, political or other opinion, national or social origin, property, birth or other status.
(3) Developing countries, with due regard to human rights and their national economy, may determine to what extent they would guarantee the economic rights recognized in the present Covenant to non-nationals.

Article 3. The States Parties to the present Covenant undertake to ensure the equal right of men and women to the enjoyment of all economic, social and cultural rights set forth in the present Covenant.

Article 4. The States Parties to the present Covenant recognize that, in the enjoyment of those rights provided by the State in conformity with the present Covenant, the State may subject such rights only to such limitations as are determined by law only in so far as this may be compatible with the nature of these rights and solely for the purpose of promoting the general welfare in a democratic society.

Article 5. (1) Nothing in the present Covenant may be interpreted as implying for any State, group or person any right to engage in any activity or to perform any act aimed at the destruction of any of the rights or freedoms recognized herein, or at their limitation to a greater extent than is provided for in the present Covenant.
(2) No restriction upon or derogation from any of the fundamental human rights recognized or existing in any country in virtue of law, conventions, regulations or custom shall be admitted on the pretext that the present Covenant does not recognize such rights or that it recognizes them to a lesser extent.

Part III

Article 6. (1) The States Parties to the present Covenant recognize the right to work, which includes the right of everyone to the opportunity to gain his living by work which he freely chooses or accepts, and will take appropriate steps to safeguard this right.
(2) The steps to be taken by a State Party to the present Covenant to achieve the full realization of this right shall include technical and vocational guidance and training programmes, policies and techniques to achieve steady economic, social and cultural development and full and productive employment under conditions safeguarding fundamental political and economic freedoms to the individual.

Article 7. The States Parties to the present Covenant recognize the right of everyone to the enjoyment of just and favourable conditions of work which ensure, in particular:
(a) Remuneration which provides all workers, as a minimum, with:
(i) Fair wages and equal remuneration for work of equal value without distinction of any kind, in particular women being guaranteed conditions of work not inferior to those enjoyed by men, with equal pay for equal work;
(ii) A decent living for themselves and their families in accordance with the provisions of the present Covenant;
(b) Safe and healthy working conditions;
(c) Equal opportunity for everyone to be promoted in his employment to an appropriate higher level, subject to no considerations other than those of seniority and competence;
(d) Rest, leisure and reasonable limitation of working hours and periodic holidays with pay, as well as remuneration for public holidays

Article 8. (1) The States Parties to the present Covenant undertake to ensure:
(a) The right of everyone to form trade unions and join the trade union of his choice, subject only to the rules of the organization concerned, for the promotion and protection of his economic and social interests. No restrictions may be placed on the exercise of this right other than those prescribed by law and which are necessary in a democratic society in the interests of national security or public order or for the protection of the rights and freedoms of others;
(b) The right of trade unions to establish national federations or confederations and the right of the latter to form or join international trade-union organizations;
(c) The right of trade unions to function freely subject to no limitations other than those prescribed by law and which are necessary in a democratic society in the interests of national security or public order or for the protection of the rights and freedoms of others;
(d) The right to strike, provided that it is exercised in conformity with the laws of the particular country.
(2) This article shall not prevent the imposition of lawful restrictions on the exercise of these rights by members of the armed forces or of the police or of the administration of the State.
(3) Nothing in this article shall authorize States Parties to the International Labour Organisation Convention of 1948 concerning Freedom of Association and Protection of the Right to Organize to take legislative measures which would prejudice, or apply the law in such a manner as would prejudice, the guarantees provided for in that Convention.

Article 9. The States Parties to the present Covenant recognize the right of everyone to social security, including social insurance.

Article 10. The States Parties to the present Covenant recognize that:
(1) The widest possible protection and assistance should be accorded to the family, which is the natural and fundamental group unit of society, particularly for its establishment and while it is responsible for the care and education of dependent children. Marriage must be entered into with the free consent of the intending spouses.
(2) Special protection should be accorded to mothers during a reasonable period before and after childbirth. During such period working mothers should be accorded paid leave or leave with adequate social security benefits.
(3) Special measures of protection and assistance should be taken on behalf of all children and young persons without any discrimination for reasons of parentage or other conditions. Children and young persons should be protected from economic and social exploitation. Their employment in work harmful to their morals or health or dangerous to life or likely to hamper their normal development should be punishable by law. States should also set age limits below which the paid employment of child labour should be prohibited and punishable by law.

PART II FUNDAMENTAL RIGHTS

Article 11. (1) The States Parties to the present Covenant recognize the right of everyone to an adequate standard of living for himself and his family, including adequate food, clothing and housing, and to the continuous improvement of living conditions. The States Parties will take appropriate steps to ensure the realization of this right, recognizing to this effect the essential importance of international cooperation based on free consent.
(2) The States Parties to the present Covenant, recognizing the fundamental right of everyone to be free from hunger, shall take, individually and through international co-operation, the measures, including specific programmes, which are needed:
(a) To improve methods of production, conservation and distribution of food by making full use of technical and scientific knowledge, by disseminating knowledge of the principles of nutrition and by developing or reforming agrarian systems in such a way as to achieve the most efficient development and utilization of natural resources;
(b) Taking into account the problems of both food-importing and food-exporting countries, to ensure an equitable distribution of world food supplies in relation to need.

Article 12. (1) The States Parties to the present Covenant recognize the right of everyone to the enjoyment of the highest attainable standard of physical and mental health.
(2) The steps to be taken by the States Parties to the present Covenant to achieve the full realization of this right shall include those necessary for:
(a) The provision for the reduction of the stillbirth-rate and of infant mortality and for the healthy development of the child;
(b) The improvement of all aspects of environmental and industrial hygiene;
(c) The prevention, treatment and control of epidemic, endemic, occupational and other diseases;
(d) The creation of conditions which would assure to all medical service and medical attention in the event of sickness.

Article 13. (1) The States Parties to the present Covenant recognize the right of everyone to education. They agree that education shall be directed to the full development of the human personality and the sense of its dignity, and shall strengthen the respect for human rights and fundamental freedoms. They further agree that education shall enable all persons to participate effectively in a free society, promote understanding, tolerance and friendship among all nations and all racial, ethnic or religious groups, and further the activities of the United Nations for the maintenance of peace.
(2) The States Parties to the present Covenant recognize that, with a view to achieving the full realization of this right:
(a) Primary education shall be compulsory and available free to all;
(b) Secondary education in its different forms, including technical and vocational secondary education, shall be made generally available and accessible to all by every appropriate means, and in particular by the progressive introduction of free education;
(c) Higher education shall be made equally accessible to all, on the basis of capacity, by every appropriate means, and in particular by the progressive introduction of free education; (d) Fundamental education shall be encouraged or intensified as far as possible for those persons who have not received or completed the whole period of their primary education;
(e) The development of a system of schools at all levels shall be actively pursued, an adequate fellowship system shall be established, and the material conditions of teaching staff shall be continuously improved.
(3) The States Parties to the present Covenant undertake to have respect for the liberty of parents and, when applicable, legal guardians to choose for their children schools, other than those established by the public authorities, which conform to such minimum educational standards as may be laid down or approved by the State and to ensure the religious and moral education of their children in conformity with their own convictions.
(4) No part of this article shall be construed so as to interfere with the liberty of individuals and bodies to establish and direct educational institutions, subject always to the observance of the principles set forth in paragraph (1) of this article and to the requirement that the education given in such institutions shall conform to such minimum standards as may be laid down by the State.

Article 14. Each State Party to the present Covenant which, at the time of becoming a Party, has not been able to secure in its metropolitan territory or other territories under its jurisdiction compulsory primary education, free of charge, undertakes, within two years, to work out and adopt a detailed plan of action for the progressive implementation, within a reasonable number of years, to be fixed in the plan, of the principle of compulsory education free of charge for all.

Article 15. (1) The States Parties to the present Covenant recognize the right of everyone:

(a) To take part in cultural life;
(b) To enjoy the benefits of scientific progress and its applications;
(c) To benefit from the protection of the moral and material interests resulting from any scientific, literary or artistic production of which he is the author.
(2) The steps to be taken by the States Parties to the present Covenant to achieve the full realization of this right shall include those necessary for the conservation, the development and the diffusion of science and culture.
(3) The States Parties to the present Covenant undertake to respect the freedom indispensable for scientific research and creative activity. 4. The States Parties to the present Covenant recognize the benefits to be derived from the encouragement and development of international contacts and co-operation in the scientific and cultural fields.

Part IV

Article 16. (1) The States Parties to the present Covenant undertake to submit in conformity with this part of the Covenant reports on the measures which they have adopted and the progress made in achieving the observance of the rights recognized herein.
(2) (a) All reports shall be submitted to the Secretary-General of the United Nations, who shall transmit copies to the Economic and Social Council for consideration in accordance with the provisions of the present Covenant;
(b) The Secretary-General of the United Nations shall also transmit to the specialized agencies copies of the reports, or any relevant parts therefrom, from States Parties to the present Covenant which are also members of these specialized agencies in so far as these reports, or parts therefrom, relate to any matters which fall within the responsibilities of the said agencies in accordance with their constitutional instruments.

Article 17. (1) The States Parties to the present Covenant shall furnish their reports in stages, in accordance with a programme to be established by the Economic and Social Council within one year of the entry into force of the present Covenant after consultation with the States Parties and the specialized agencies concerned.
(2) Reports may indicate factors and difficulties affecting the degree of fulfilment of obligations under the present Covenant.
(3) Where relevant information has previously been furnished to the United Nations or to any specialized agency by any State Party to the present Covenant, it will not be necessary to reproduce that information, but a precise reference to the information so furnished will suffice.

Article 18. Pursuant to its responsibilities under the Charter of the United Nations in the field of human rights and fundamental freedoms, the Economic and Social Council may make arrangements with the specialized agencies in respect of their reporting to it on the progress made in achieving the observance of the provisions of the present Covenant falling within the scope of their activities. These reports may include particulars of decisions and recommendations on such implementation adopted by their competent organs.

Article 19. The Economic and Social Council may transmit to the Commission on Human Rights for study and general recommendation or, as appropriate, for information the reports concerning human rights submitted by States in accordance with articles 16 and 17, and those concerning human rights submitted by the specialized agencies in accordance with article 18.

Article 20. The States Parties to the present Covenant and the specialized agencies concerned may submit comments to the Economic and Social Council on any general recommendation under article 19 or reference to such general recommendation in any report of the Commission on Human Rights or any documentation referred to therein.

Article 21. The Economic and Social Council may submit from time to time to the General Assembly reports with recommendations of a general nature and a summary of the information received from the States Parties to the present Covenant and the specialized agencies on the measures taken and the progress made in achieving general observance of the rights recognized in the present Covenant.

Article 22. The Economic and Social Council may bring to the attention of other organs of the United Nations, their subsidiary organs and specialized agencies concerned with furnishing technical assistance any matters arising out of the reports referred to in this part of the present Covenant which may assist such bodies in deciding, each within its field of competence, on the advisability of international measures likely to contribute to the effective progressive implementation of the present Covenant.

PART II   FUNDAMENTAL RIGHTS

Article 23. The States Parties to the present Covenant agree that international action for the achievement of the rights recognized in the present Covenant includes such methods as the conclusion of conventions, the adoption of recommendations, the furnishing of technical assistance and the holding of regional meetings and technical meetings for the purpose of consultation and study organized in conjunction with the Governments concerned.

Article 24. Nothing in the present Covenant shall be interpreted as impairing the provisions of the Charter of the United Nations and of the constitutions of the specialized agencies which define the respective responsibilities of the various organs of the United Nations and of the specialized agencies in regard to the matters dealt with in the present Covenant.

Article 25. Nothing in the present Covenant shall be interpreted as impairing the inherent right of all peoples to enjoy and utilize fully and freely their natural wealth and resources.

Part V

Article 26. (1) The present Covenant is open for signature by any State Member of the United Nations or member of any of its specialized agencies, by any State Party to the Statute of the International Court of Justice, and by any other State which has been invited by the General Assembly of the United Nations to become a party to the present Covenant.
(2) The present Covenant is subject to ratification. Instruments of ratification shall be deposited with the Secretary-General of the United Nations.
(3) The present Covenant shall be open to accession by any State referred to in paragraph (1) of this article.
(4) Accession shall be effected by the deposit of an instrument of accession with the Secretary-General of the United Nations.
(5) The Secretary-General of the United Nations shall inform all States which have signed the present Covenant or acceded to it of the deposit of each instrument of ratification or accession.

Article 27. (1) The present Covenant shall enter into force three months after the date of the deposit with the Secretary-General of the United Nations of the thirty-fifth instrument of ratification or instrument of accession.
(2) For each State ratifying the present Covenant or acceding to it after the deposit of the thirty-fifth instrument of ratification or instrument of accession, the present Covenant shall enter into force three months after the date of the deposit of its own instrument of ratification or instrument of accession.

Article 28. The provisions of the present Covenant shall extend to all parts of federal States without any limitations or exceptions.

Article 29. (1) Any State Party to the present Covenant may propose an amendment and file it with the Secretary General of the United Nations. The Secretary-General shall thereupon communicate any proposed amendments to the States Parties to the present Covenant with a request that they notify him whether they favour a conference of States Parties for the purpose of considering and voting upon the proposals. In the event that at least one third of the States Parties favours such a conference, the Secretary-General shall convene the conference under the auspices of the United Nations. Any amendment adopted by a majority of the States Parties present and voting at the conference shall be submitted to the General Assembly of the United Nations for approval.
(2) Amendments shall come into force when they have been approved by the General Assembly of the United Nations and accepted by a two-thirds majority of the States Parties to the present Covenant in accordance with their respective constitutional processes.
(3) When amendments come into force they shall be binding on those States Parties which have accepted them, other States Parties still being bound by the provisions of the present Covenant and any earlier amendment which they have accepted. Article 30 Irrespective of the notifications made under article 26, paragraph (5), the Secretary-General of the United Nations shall inform all States referred to in paragraph (1) of the same article of the following particulars:
(a) Signatures, ratifications and accessions under article 26;
(b) The date of the entry into force of the present Covenant under article 27 and the date of the entry into force of any amendments under article 29.

Article 31. (1) The present Covenant, of which the Chinese, English, French, Russian and Spanish texts are equally authentic, shall be deposited in the archives of the United Nations. (2) The Secretary-General of the United Nations shall transmit certified copies of the present Covenant to all States referred to in article 26.

OPTIONAL PROTOCOL ON ECONOMIC, SOCIAL AND CULTURAL RIGHTS

Optional Protocol to the (ICESCR)
Adopted by General Assembly Resolution 63/117 of March 2009

The General Assembly,
Taking note of the adoption by the Human Rights Council, by its resolution 8/2 of 18 June 2008, of the Optional Protocol to the International Covenant on Economic, Social and Cultural Rights,
1. Adopts the Optional Protocol to the International Covenant on Economic, Social and Cultural Rights, the text of which is annexed to the present resolution;
2. Recommends that the Optional Protocol be opened for signature at a signing ceremony to be held in 2009, and requests the Secretary-General and the United Nations High Commissioner for Human Rights to provide the necessary assistance.
Annex
Optional Protocol to the International Covenant on Economic, Social and Cultural Rights
Preamble. The States Parties to the present Protocol,
Considering that, in accordance with the principles proclaimed in the Charter of the United Nations, recognition of the inherent dignity and of the equal and inalienable rights of all members of the human family is the foundation of freedom, justice and peace in the world,
Noting that the Universal Declaration of Human Rights proclaims that all human beings are born free and equal in dignity and rights and that everyone is entitled to all the rights and freedoms set forth therein, without distinction of any kind, such as race, colour, sex, language, religion, political or other opinion, national or social origin, property, birth or other status,
Recalling that the Universal Declaration of Human Rights and the International Covenants on Human Rights recognize that the ideal of free human beings enjoying freedom from fear and want can only be achieved if conditions are created whereby everyone may enjoy civil, cultural, economic, political and social rights,
Reaffirming the universality, indivisibility, interdependence and interrelatedness of all human rights and fundamental freedoms,
Recalling that each State Party to the International Covenant on Economic, Social and Cultural Rights (hereinafter referred to as the Covenant) undertakes to take steps, individually and through international assistance and cooperation, especially economic and technical, to the maximum of its available resources, with a view to achieving progressively the full realization of the rights recognized in the Covenant by all appropriate means, including particularly the adoption of legislative measures,
Considering that, in order further to achieve the purposes of the Covenant and the implementation of its provisions, it would be appropriate to enable the Committee on Economic, Social and Cultural Rights (hereinafter referred to as the Committee) to carry out the functions provided for in the present Protocol,
Have agreed as follows:

Article 1. Competence of the Committee to receive and consider communications
(1) A State Party to the Covenant that becomes a Party to the present Protocol recognizes the competence of the Committee to receive and consider communications as provided for by the provisions of the present Protocol.
(2) No communication shall be received by the Committee if it concerns a State Party to the Covenant which is not a Party to the present Protocol.

Article 2. Communications
Communications may be submitted by or on behalf of individuals or groups of individuals, under the jurisdiction of a State Party, claiming to be victims of a violation of any of the economic, social and cultural rights set forth in the Covenant by that State Party. Where a communication is submitted on behalf of individuals or groups of individuals, this shall be with their consent unless the author can justify acting on their behalf without such consent.

Article 3. Admissibility
(1) The Committee shall not consider a communication unless it has ascertained that all available domestic remedies have been exhausted. This shall not be the rule where the application of such remedies is unreasonably prolonged.
(2) The Committee shall declare a communication inadmissible when:
(a) It is not submitted within one year after the exhaustion of domestic remedies, except in cases where the author can demonstrate that it had not been possible to submit the communication within that time limit;

PART II FUNDAMENTAL RIGHTS

(b) The facts that are the subject of the communication occurred prior to the entry into force of the present Protocol for the State Party concerned unless those facts continued after that date;
(c) The same matter has already been examined by the Committee or has been or is being examined under another procedure of international investigation or settlement;
(d) It is incompatible with the provisions of the Covenant;
(e) It is manifestly ill-founded, not sufficiently substantiated or exclusively based on reports disseminated by mass media;
(f) It is an abuse of the right to submit a communication; or when
(g) It is anonymous or not in writing.

Article 4. Communications not revealing a clear disadvantage
The Committee may, if necessary, decline to consider a communication where it does not reveal that the author has suffered a clear disadvantage, unless the Committee considers that the communication raises a serious issue of general importance.

Article 5. Interim measures
(1) At any time after the receipt of a communication and before a determination on the merits has been reached, the Committee may transmit to the State Party concerned for its urgent consideration a request that the State Party take such interim measures as may be necessary in exceptional circumstances to avoid possible irreparable damage to the victim or victims of the alleged violations.
(2) Where the Committee exercises its discretion under paragraph (1) of the present article, this does not imply a determination on admissibility or on the merits of the communication.

Article 6. Transmission of the communication
(1) Unless the Committee considers a communication inadmissible without reference to the State Party concerned, the Committee shall bring any communication submitted to it under the present Protocol confidentially to the attention of the State Party concerned.
(2) Within six months, the receiving State Party shall submit to the Committee written explanations or statements clarifying the matter and the remedy, if any, that may have been provided by that State Party.

Article 7. Friendly settlement
(1) The Committee shall make available its good offices to the parties concerned with a view to reaching a friendly settlement of the matter on the basis of the respect for the obligations set forth in the Covenant.
(2) An agreement on a friendly settlement closes consideration of the communication under the present Protocol.

Article 8. Examination of communications
(1) The Committee shall examine communications received under article 2 of the present Protocol in the light of all documentation submitted to it, provided that this documentation is transmitted to the parties concerned.
(2) The Committee shall hold closed meetings when examining communications under the present Protocol.
(3) When examining a communication under the present Protocol, the Committee may consult, as appropriate, relevant documentation emanating from other United Nations bodies, specialized agencies, funds, programmes and mechanisms, and other international organizations, including from regional human rights systems, and any observations or comments by the State Party concerned.
(4) When examining communications under the present Protocol, the Committee shall consider the reasonableness of the steps taken by the State Party in accordance with part II of the Covenant. In doing so, the Committee shall bear in mind that the State Party may adopt a range of possible policy measures for the implementation of the rights set forth in the Covenant.

Article 9. Follow-up to the views of the Committee
(1) After examining a communication, the Committee shall transmit its views on the communication, together with its recommendations, if any, to the parties concerned.
(2) The State Party shall give due consideration to the views of the Committee, together with its recommendations, if any, and shall submit to the Committee, within six months, a written response, including information on any action taken in the light of the views and recommendations of the Committee.
(3) The Committee may invite the State Party to submit further information about any measures the State Party has taken in response to its views or recommendations, if any, including as deemed

appropriate by the Committee, in the State Party's subsequent reports under articles 16 and 17 of the Covenant.

Article 10. Inter-State communications
(1) A State Party to the present Protocol may at any time declare under the present article that it recognizes the competence of the Committee to receive and consider communications to the effect that a State Party claims that another State Party is not fulfilling its obligations under the Covenant. Communications under the present article may be received and considered only if submitted by a State Party that has made a declaration recognizing in regard to itself the competence of the Committee. No communication shall be received by the Committee if it concerns a State Party which has not made such a declaration. Communications received under the present article shall be dealt with in accordance with the following procedure:
(a) If a State Party to the present Protocol considers that another State Party is not fulfilling its obligations under the Covenant, it may, by written communication, bring the matter to the attention of that State Party. The State Party may also inform the Committee of the matter. Within three months after the receipt of the communication the receiving State shall afford the State that sent the communication an explanation, or any other statement in writing clarifying the matter, which should include, to the extent possible and pertinent, reference to domestic procedures and remedies taken, pending or available in the matter;
(b) If the matter is not settled to the satisfaction of both States Parties concerned within six months after the receipt by the receiving State of the initial communication, either State shall have the right to refer the matter to the Committee, by notice given to the Committee and to the other State;
(c) The Committee shall deal with a matter referred to it only after it has ascertained that all available domestic remedies have been invoked and exhausted in the matter. This shall not be the rule where the application of the remedies is unreasonably prolonged;
(d) Subject to the provisions of subparagraph (c) of the present paragraph the Committee shall make available its good offices to the States Parties concerned with a view to a friendly solution of the matter on the basis of the respect for the obligations set forth in the Covenant; (e) The Committee shall hold closed meetings when examining communications under the present article;
(f) In any matter referred to it in accordance with subparagraph (b) of the present paragraph, the Committee may call upon the States Parties concerned, referred to in subparagraph (b), to supply any relevant information;
(g) The States Parties concerned, referred to in subparagraph (b) of the present paragraph, shall have the right to be represented when the matter is being considered by the Committee and to make submissions orally and/or in writing;
(h) The Committee shall, with all due expediency after the date of receipt of notice under subparagraph (b) of the present paragraph, submit a report, as follows:
(i) If a solution within the terms of subparagraph (d) of the present paragraph is reached, the Committee shall confine its report to a brief statement of the facts and of the solution reached;
(ii) If a solution within the terms of subparagraph (d) is not reached, the Committee shall, in its report, set forth the relevant facts concerning the issue between the States Parties concerned. The written submissions and record of the oral submissions made by the States Parties concerned shall be attached to the report. The Committee may also communicate only to the States Parties concerned any views that it may consider relevant to the issue between them. In every matter, the report shall be communicated to the States Parties concerned.
(2) A declaration under paragraph (1) of the present article shall be deposited by the States Parties with the Secretary-General of the United Nations, who shall transmit copies thereof to the other States Parties. A declaration may be withdrawn at any time by notification to the Secretary-General. Such a withdrawal shall not prejudice the consideration of any matter that is the subject of a communication already transmitted under the present article; no further communication by any State Party shall be received under the present article after the notification of withdrawal of the declaration has been received by the Secretary-General, unless the State Party concerned has made a new declaration.

Article 11. Inquiry procedure
(1) A State Party to the present Protocol may at any time declare that it recognizes the competence of the Committee provided for under the present article.
(2) If the Committee receives reliable information indicating grave or systematic violations by a State Party of any of the economic, social and cultural rights set forth in the Covenant, the Committee shall invite that State Party to cooperate in the examination of the information and to this end to submit observations with regard to the information concerned.
(3) Taking into account any observations that may have been submitted by the State Party concerned

PART II FUNDAMENTAL RIGHTS

as well as any other reliable information available to it, the Committee may designate one or more of its members to conduct an inquiry and to report urgently to the Committee. Where warranted and with the consent of the State Party, the inquiry may include a visit to its territory.

(4) Such an inquiry shall be conducted confidentially and the cooperation of the State Party shall be sought at all stages of the proceedings.

(5) After examining the findings of such an inquiry, the Committee shall transmit these findings to the State Party concerned together with any comments and recommendations.

(6) The State Party concerned shall, within six months of receiving the findings, comments and recommendations transmitted by the Committee, submit its observations to the Committee.

(7) After such proceedings have been completed with regard to an inquiry made in accordance with paragraph (2) of the present article, the Committee may, after consultations with the State Party concerned, decide to include a summary account of the results of the proceedings in its annual report provided for in article 15 of the present Protocol.

(8) Any State Party having made a declaration in accordance with paragraph (1) of the present article may, at any time, withdraw this declaration by notification to the Secretary-General.

Article 12. Follow-up to the inquiry procedure

(1) The Committee may invite the State Party concerned to include in its report under articles 16 and 17 of the Covenant details of any measures taken in response to an inquiry conducted under article 11 of the present Protocol.

(2) The Committee may, if necessary, after the end of the period of six months referred to in article 11, paragraph (6), invite the State Party concerned to inform it of the measures taken in response to such an inquiry.

Article 13. Protection measures

A State Party shall take all appropriate measures to ensure that individuals under its jurisdiction are not subjected to any form of ill-treatment or intimidation as a consequence of communicating with the Committee pursuant to the present Protocol.

Article 14. International assistance and cooperation

(1) The Committee shall transmit, as it may consider appropriate, and with the consent of the State Party concerned, to United Nations specialized agencies, funds and programmes and other competent bodies, its views or recommendations concerning communications and inquiries that indicate a need for technical advice or assistance, along with the State Party's observations and suggestions, if any, on these views or recommendations.

(2) The Committee may also bring to the attention of such bodies, with the consent of the State Party concerned, any matter arising out of communications considered under the present Protocol which may assist them in deciding, each within its field of competence, on the advisability of international measures likely to contribute to assisting States Parties in achieving progress in implementation of the rights recognized in the Covenant.

(3) A trust fund shall be established in accordance with the relevant procedures of the General Assembly, to be administered in accordance with the financial regulations and rules of the United Nations, with a view to providing expert and technical assistance to States Parties, with the consent of the State Party concerned, for the enhanced implementation of the rights contained in the Covenant, thus contributing to building national capacities in the area of economic, social and cultural rights in the context of the present Protocol.

(4) The provisions of the present article are without prejudice to the obligations of each State Party to fulfil its obligations under the Covenant.

Article 15. Annual report

The Committee shall include in its annual report a summary of its activities under the present Protocol.

Article 16. Dissemination and information

Each State Party undertakes to make widely known and to disseminate the Covenant and the present Protocol and to facilitate access to information about the views and recommendations of the Committee, in particular, on matters involving that State Party, and to do so in accessible formats for persons with disabilities.

Article 17. Signature, ratification and accession

(1) The present Protocol is open for signature by any State that has signed, ratified or acceded to the Covenant.

(2) The present Protocol is subject to ratification by any State that has ratified or acceded to the Covenant. Instruments of ratification shall be deposited with the Secretary-General of the United Nations.
(3) The present Protocol shall be open to accession by any State that has ratified or acceded to the Covenant.
(4) Accession shall be effected by the deposit of an instrument of accession with the Secretary-General of the United Nations.

Article 18. Entry into force
(1) The present Protocol shall enter into force three months after the date of the deposit with the Secretary-General of the United Nations of the tenth instrument of ratification or accession.
(2) For each State ratifying or acceding to the present Protocol, after the deposit of the tenth instrument of ratification or accession, the Protocol shall enter into force three months after the date of the deposit of its instrument of ratification or accession.

Article 19. Amendments
(1) Any State Party may propose an amendment to the present Protocol and submit it to the Secretary-General of the United Nations. The Secretary-General shall communicate any proposed amendments to States Parties, with a request to be notified whether they favour a meeting of States Parties for the purpose of considering and deciding upon the proposals. In the event that, within four months from the date of such communication, at least one third of the States Parties favour such a meeting, the Secretary-General shall convene the meeting under the auspices of the United Nations. Any amendment adopted by a majority of two thirds of the States Parties present and voting shall be submitted by the Secretary-General to the General Assembly for approval and thereafter to all States Parties for acceptance.
(2) An amendment adopted and approved in accordance with paragraph (1) of the present article shall enter into force on the thirtieth day after the number of instruments of acceptance deposited reaches two thirds of the number of States Parties at the date of adoption of the amendment. Thereafter, the amendment shall enter into force for any State Party on the thirtieth day following the deposit of its own instrument of acceptance. An amendment shall be binding only on those States Parties which have accepted it.

Article 20. Denunciation
(1) Any State Party may denounce the present Protocol at any time by written notification addressed to the Secretary-General of the United Nations. Denunciation shall take effect six months after the date of receipt of the notification by the Secretary-General.
(2) Denunciation shall be without prejudice to the continued application of the provisions of the present Protocol to any communication submitted under articles 2 and 10 or to any procedure initiated under article 11 before the effective date of denunciation.

Article 21. Notification by the Secretary-General
The Secretary-General of the United Nations shall notify all States referred to in article 26, paragraph (1), of the Covenant of the following particulars:
(a) Signatures, ratifications and accessions under the present Protocol;
(b) The date of entry into force of the present Protocol and of any amendment under article 19;
(c) Any denunciation under article 20.

Article 22. Official languages
(1) The present Protocol, of which the Arabic, Chinese, English, French, Russian and Spanish texts are equally authentic, shall be deposited in the archives of the United Nations.
(2) The Secretary-General of the United Nations shall transmit certified copies of the present Protocol to all States referred to in article 26 of the Covenant.

PART II FUNDAMENTAL RIGHTS

International Covenant on Civil and Political Rights (ICCPR)
New York 19 December 1966, Entry into force 23 March 1976
Trb. 1969 Nr. 99

The States Parties to the present Covenant,
Considering that, in accordance with the principles proclaimed in the Charter of the United Nations, recognition of the inherent dignity and of the equal and inalienable rights of all members of the human family is the foundation of freedom, justice and peace in the world,
Recognizing that these rights derive from the inherent dignity of the human person,
Recognizing that, in accordance with the Universal Declaration of Human Rights, the ideal of free human beings enjoying civil and political freedom and freedom from fear and want can only be achieved if conditions are created whereby everyone may enjoy his civil and political rights, as well as his economic, social and cultural rights,
Considering the obligation of States under the Charter of the United Nations to promote universal respect for, and observance of, human rights and freedoms,
Realizing that the individual, having duties to other individuals and to the community to which he belongs, is under a responsibility to strive for the promotion and observance of the rights recognized in the present Covenant,
Agree upon the following articles:

Part I

Article 1. (1) All peoples have the right of self-determination. By virtue of that right they freely determine their political status and freely pursue their economic, social and cultural development.
(2) All peoples may, for their own ends, freely dispose of their natural wealth and resources without prejudice to any obligations arising out of international economic co-operation, based upon the principle of mutual benefit, and international law. In no case may a people be deprived of its own means of subsistence.
(3) The States Parties to the present Covenant, including those having responsibility for the administration of Non-Self-Governing and Trust Territories, shall promote the realization of the right of self-determination, and shall respect that right, in conformity with the provisions of the Charter of the United Nations.

Part II

Article 2. (1) Each State Party to the present Covenant undertakes to respect and to ensure to all individuals within its territory and subject to its jurisdiction the rights recognized in the present Covenant, without distinction of any kind, such as race, colour, sex, language, religion, political or other opinion, national or social origin, property, birth or other status.
(2) Where not already provided for by existing legislative or other measures, each State Party to the present Covenant undertakes to take the necessary steps, in accordance with its constitutional processes and with the provisions of the present Covenant, to adopt such laws or other measures as may be necessary to give effect to the rights recognized in the present Covenant.
(3) Each State Party to the present Covenant undertakes:
(a) To ensure that any person whose rights or freedoms as herein recognized are violated shall have an effective remedy, notwithstanding that the violation has been committed by persons acting in an official capacity;
(b) To ensure that any person claiming such a remedy shall have his right thereto determined by competent judicial, administrative or legislative authorities, or by any other competent authority provided for by the legal system of the State, and to develop the possibilities of judicial remedy;
(c) To ensure that the competent authorities shall enforce such remedies when granted.

Article 3. The States Parties to the present Covenant undertake to ensure the equal right of men and women to the enjoyment of all civil and political rights set forth in the present Covenant.

Article 4. (1) In time of public emergency which threatens the life of the nation and the existence of which is officially proclaimed, the States Parties to the present Covenant may take measures derogating from their obligations under the present Covenant to the extent strictly required by the exigencies of the situation, provided that such measures are not inconsistent with their other obligations under international law and do not involve discrimination solely on the ground of race, colour, sex, language, religion or social origin.
(2) No derogation from articles 6, 7, 8 (paragraphs (1) and (2)), 11, 15, 16 and 18 may be made under this provision.

INTERNATIONAL COVENANT ON CIVIL AND POLITICAL RIGHTS

(3) Any State Party to the present Covenant availing itself of the right of derogation shall immediately inform the other States Parties to the present Covenant, through the intermediary of the Secretary General of the United Nations, of the provisions from which it has derogated and of the reasons by which it was actuated. A further communication shall be made, through the same intermediary, on the date on which it terminates such derogation.

Article 5. (1) Nothing in the present Covenant may be interpreted as implying for any State, group or person any right to engage in any activity or perform any act aimed at the destruction of any of the rights and freedoms recognized herein or at their limitation to a greater extent than is provided for in the present Covenant.
(2) There shall be no restriction upon or derogation from any of the fundamental human rights recognized or existing in any State Party to the present Covenant pursuant to law, conventions, regulations or custom on the pretext that the present Covenant does not recognize such rights or that it recognizes them to a lesser extent.

Part III

Article 6. (1) Every human being has the inherent right to life. This right shall be protected by law. No one shall be arbitrarily deprived of his life.
(2) In countries which have not abolished the death penalty, sentence of death may be imposed only for the most serious crimes in accordance with the law in force at the time of the commission of the crime and not contrary to the provisions of the present Covenant and to the Convention on the Prevention and Punishment of the Crime of Genocide. This penalty can only be carried out pursuant to a final judgement rendered by a competent court.
(3) When deprivation of life constitutes the crime of genocide, it is understood that nothing in this article shall authorize any State Party to the present Covenant to derogate in any way from any obligation assumed under the provisions of the Convention on the Prevention and Punishment of the Crime of Genocide.
(4) Anyone sentenced to death shall have the right to seek pardon or commutation of the sentence. Amnesty, pardon or commutation of the sentence of death may be granted in all cases.
(5) Sentence of death shall not be imposed for crimes committed by persons below eighteen years of age and shall not be carried out on pregnant women.
(6) Nothing in this article shall be invoked to delay or to prevent the abolition of capital punishment by any State Party to the present Covenant.

Article 7. No one shall be subjected to torture or to cruel, inhuman or degrading treatment or punishment. In particular, no one shall be subjected without his free consent to medical or scientific experimentation.

Article 8. (1) No one shall be held in slavery; slavery and the slave-trade in all their forms shall be prohibited.
(2) No one shall be held in servitude.
(3) (a) No one shall be required to perform forced or compulsory labour;
(b) Paragraph (3)(a) shall not be held to preclude, in countries where imprisonment with hard labour may be imposed as a punishment for a crime, the performance of hard labour in pursuance of a sentence to such punishment by a competent court;
(c) For the purpose of this paragraph the term "forced or compulsory labour" shall not include:
(i) Any work or service, not referred to in subparagraph (b), normally required of a person who is under detention in consequence of a lawful order of a court, or of a person during conditional release from such detention;
(ii) Any service of a military character and, in countries where conscientious objection is recognized, any national service required by law of conscientious objectors;
(iii) Any service exacted in cases of emergency or calamity threatening the life or well-being of the community;
(iv) Any work or service which forms part of normal civil obligations.

Article 9. (1) Everyone has the right to liberty and security of person. No one shall be subjected to arbitrary arrest or detention. No one shall be deprived of his liberty except on such grounds and in accordance with such procedure as are established by law.
(2) Anyone who is arrested shall be informed, at the time of arrest, of the reasons for his arrest and shall be promptly informed of any charges against him.
(3) Anyone arrested or detained on a criminal charge shall be brought promptly before a judge or

PART II FUNDAMENTAL RIGHTS

other officer authorized by law to exercise judicial power and shall be entitled to trial within a reasonable time or to release. It shall not be the general rule that persons awaiting trial shall be detained in custody, but release may be subject to guarantees to appear for trial, at any other stage of the judicial proceedings, and, should occasion arise, for execution of the judgement.
(4) Anyone who is deprived of his liberty by arrest or detention shall be entitled to take proceedings before a court, in order that that court may decide without delay on the lawfulness of his detention and order his release if the detention is not lawful.
(5) Anyone who has been the victim of unlawful arrest or detention shall have an enforceable right to compensation.

Article 10. (1) All persons deprived of their liberty shall be treated with humanity and with respect for the inherent dignity of the human person.
(2) (a) Accused persons shall, save in exceptional circumstances, be segregated from convicted persons and shall be subject to separate treatment appropriate to their status as unconvicted persons;
(b) Accused juvenile persons shall be separated from adults and brought as speedily as possible for adjudication.
(3) The penitentiary system shall comprise treatment of prisoners the essential aim of which shall be their reformation and social rehabilitation. Juvenile offenders shall be segregated from adults and be accorded treatment appropriate to their age and legal status.

Article 11. No one shall be imprisoned merely on the ground of inability to fulfil a contractual obligation.

Article 12. (1) Everyone lawfully within the territory of a State shall, within that territory, have the right to liberty of movement and freedom to choose his residence.
(2) Everyone shall be free to leave any country, including his own.
(3) The above-mentioned rights shall not be subject to any restrictions except those which are provided by law, are necessary to protect national security, public order (ordre public), public health or morals or the rights and freedoms of others, and are consistent with the other rights recognized in the present Covenant.
(4) No one shall be arbitrarily deprived of the right to enter his own country.

Article 13. An alien lawfully in the territory of a State Party to the present Covenant may be expelled therefrom only in pursuance of a decision reached in accordance with law and shall, except where compelling reasons of national security otherwise require, be allowed to submit the reasons against his expulsion and to have his case reviewed by, and be represented for the purpose before, the competent authority or a person or persons especially designated by the competent authority.

Article 14. (1) All persons shall be equal before the courts and tribunals. In the determination of any criminal charge against him, or of his rights and obligations in a suit at law, everyone shall be entitled to a fair and public hearing by a competent, independent and impartial tribunal established by law. The press and the public may be excluded from all or part of a trial for reasons of morals, public order (ordre public) or national security in a democratic society, or when the interest of the private lives of the parties so requires, or to the extent strictly necessary in the opinion of the court in special circumstances where publicity would prejudice the interests of justice; but any judgement rendered in a criminal case or in a suit at law shall be made public except where the interest of juvenile persons otherwise requires or the proceedings concern matrimonial disputes or the guardianship of children.
(2) Everyone charged with a criminal offence shall have the right to be presumed innocent until proved guilty according to law.
(3) In the determination of any criminal charge against him, everyone shall be entitled to the following minimum guarantees, in full equality:
(a) To be informed promptly and in detail in a language which he understands of the nature and cause of the charge against him;
(b) To have adequate time and facilities for the preparation of his defence and to communicate with counsel of his own choosing;
(c) To be tried without undue delay;
(d) To be tried in his presence, and to defend himself in person or through legal assistance of his own choosing; to be informed, if he does not have legal assistance, of this right; and to have legal assistance assigned to him, in any case where the interests of justice so require, and without payment by him in any such case if he does not have sufficient means to pay for it;
(e) To examine, or have examined, the witnesses against him and to obtain the attendance and examination of witnesses on his behalf under the same conditions as witnesses against him; (f) To have the

free assistance of an interpreter if he cannot understand or speak the language used in court;
(g) Not to be compelled to testify against himself or to confess guilt.
(4) In the case of juvenile persons, the procedure shall be such as will take account of their age and the desirability of promoting their rehabilitation.
(5) Everyone convicted of a crime shall have the right to his conviction and sentence being reviewed by a higher tribunal according to law.
(6) When a person has by a final decision been convicted of a criminal offence and when subsequently his conviction has been reversed or he has been pardoned on the ground that a new or newly discovered fact shows conclusively that there has been a miscarriage of justice, the person who has suffered punishment as a result of such conviction shall be compensated according to law, unless it is proved that the non-disclosure of the unknown fact in time is wholly or partly attributable to him.
(7) No one shall be liable to be tried or punished again for an offence for which he has already been finally convicted or acquitted in accordance with the law and penal procedure of each country.

Article 15. (1) No one shall be held guilty of any criminal offence on account of any act or omission which did not constitute a criminal offence, under national or international law, at the time when it was committed. Nor shall a heavier penalty be imposed than the one that was applicable at the time when the criminal offence was committed. If, subsequent to the commission of the offence, provision is made by law for the imposition of the lighter penalty, the offender shall benefit thereby.
2. Nothing in this article shall prejudice the trial and punishment of any person for any act or omission which, at the time when it was committed, was criminal according to the general principles of law recognized by the community of nations.

Article 16. Everyone shall have the right to recognition everywhere as a person before the law.

Article 17. (1) No one shall be subjected to arbitrary or unlawful interference with his privacy, family, home or correspondence, nor to unlawful attacks on his honour and reputation.
(2) Everyone has the right to the protection of the law against such interference or attacks.

Article 18. (1) Everyone shall have the right to freedom of thought, conscience and religion. This right shall include freedom to have or to adopt a religion or belief of his choice, and freedom, either individually or in community with others and in public or private, to manifest his religion or belief in worship, observance, practice and teaching.
(2) No one shall be subject to coercion which would impair his freedom to have or to adopt a religion or belief of his choice.
(3) Freedom to manifest one's religion or beliefs may be subject only to such limitations as are prescribed by law and are necessary to protect public safety, order, health, or morals or the fundamental rights and freedoms of others.
(4) The States Parties to the present Covenant undertake to have respect for the liberty of parents and, when applicable, legal guardians to ensure the religious and moral education of their children in conformity with their own convictions.

Article 19. (1) Everyone shall have the right to hold opinions without interference.
(2) Everyone shall have the right to freedom of expression; this right shall include freedom to seek, receive and impart information and ideas of all kinds, regardless of frontiers, either orally, in writing or in print, in the form of art, or through any other media of his choice.
(3) The exercise of the rights provided for in paragraph (2) of this article carries with it special duties and responsibilities. It may therefore be subject to certain restrictions, but these shall only be such as are provided by law and are necessary:
(a) For respect of the rights or reputations of others;
(b) For the protection of national security or of public order (ordre public), or of public health or morals.

Article 20. (1) Any propaganda for war shall be prohibited by law.
(2) Any advocacy of national, racial or religious hatred that constitutes incitement to discrimination, hostility or violence shall be prohibited by law.

Article 21. The right of peaceful assembly shall be recognized. No restrictions may be placed on the exercise of this right other than those imposed in conformity with the law and which are necessary in a democratic society in the interests of national security or public safety, public order (ordre public), the protection of public health or morals or the protection of the rights and freedoms of others.

Article 22. (1) Everyone shall have the right to freedom of association with others, including the

PART II FUNDAMENTAL RIGHTS

right to form and join trade unions for the protection of his interests.
(2) No restrictions may be placed on the exercise of this right other than those which are prescribed by law and which are necessary in a democratic society in the interests of national security or public safety, public order (ordre public), the protection of public health or morals or the protection of the rights and freedoms of others. This article shall not prevent the imposition of lawful restrictions on members of the armed forces and of the police in their exercise of this right.
(3) Nothing in this article shall authorize States Parties to the International Labour Organisation Convention of 1948 concerning Freedom of Association and Protection of the Right to Organize to take legislative measures which would prejudice, or to apply the law in such a manner as to prejudice, the guarantees provided for in that Convention.

Article 23. (1) The family is the natural and fundamental group unit of society and is entitled to protection by society and the State.
(2) The right of men and women of marriageable age to marry and to found a family shall be recognized.
(3) No marriage shall be entered into without the free and full consent of the intending spouses.
(4) States Parties to the present Covenant shall take appropriate steps to ensure equality of rights and responsibilities of spouses as to marriage, during marriage and at its dissolution. In the case of dissolution, provision shall be made for the necessary protection of any children.

Article 24. (1) Every child shall have, without any discrimination as to race, colour, sex, language, religion, national or social origin, property or birth, the right to such measures of protection as are required by his status as a minor, on the part of his family, society and the State.
(2) Every child shall be registered immediately after birth and shall have a name.
(3) Every child has the right to acquire a nationality.

Article 25. Every citizen shall have the right and the opportunity, without any of the distinctions mentioned in article 2 and without unreasonable restrictions:
(a) To take part in the conduct of public affairs, directly or through freely chosen representatives;
(b) To vote and to be elected at genuine periodic elections which shall be by universal and equal suffrage and shall be held by secret ballot, guaranteeing the free expression of the will of the electors;
(c) To have access, on general terms of equality, to public service in his country.

Article 26. All persons are equal before the law and are entitled without any discrimination to the equal protection of the law. In this respect, the law shall prohibit any discrimination and guarantee to all persons equal and effective protection against discrimination on any ground such as race, colour, sex, language, religion, political or other opinion, national or social origin, property, birth or other status.

Article 27. In those States in which ethnic, religious or linguistic minorities exist, persons belonging to such minorities shall not be denied the right, in community with the other members of their group, to enjoy their own culture, to profess and practise their own religion, or to use their own language.

Part IV

Article 28. (1) There shall be established a Human Rights Committee (hereafter referred to in the present Covenant as the Committee). It shall consist of eighteen members and shall carry out the functions hereinafter provided.
(2) The Committee shall be composed of nationals of the States Parties to the present Covenant who shall be persons of high moral character and recognized competence in the field of human rights, consideration being given to the usefulness of the participation of some persons having legal experience.
(3) The members of the Committee shall be elected and shall serve in their personal capacity.

Article 29. (1) The members of the Committee shall be elected by secret ballot from a list of persons possessing the qualifications prescribed in article 28 and nominated for the purpose by the States Parties to the present Covenant.
(2) Each State Party to the present Covenant may nominate not more than two persons. These persons shall be nationals of the nominating State.
(3) A person shall be eligible for re-nomination.

Article 30. (1) The initial election shall be held no later than six months after the date of the entry into force of the present Covenant.
(2) At least four months before the date of each election to the Committee, other than an election to fill a vacancy declared in accordance with article 34, the Secretary-General of the United Nations

shall address a written invitation to the States Parties to the present Covenant to submit their nominations for membership of the Committee within three months.

(3) The Secretary-General of the United Nations shall prepare a list in alphabetical order of all the persons thus nominated, with an indication of the States Parties which have nominated them, and shall submit it to the States Parties to the present Covenant no later than one month before the date of each election.

(4) Elections of the members of the Committee shall be held at a meeting of the States Parties to the present Covenant convened by the Secretary General of the United Nations at the Headquarters of the United Nations. At that meeting, for which two thirds of the States Parties to the present Covenant shall constitute a quorum, the persons elected to the Committee shall be those nominees who obtain the largest number of votes and an absolute majority of the votes of the representatives of States Parties present and voting.

Article 31. (1) The Committee may not include more than one national of the same State.

(2) In the election of the Committee, consideration shall be given to equitable geographical distribution of membership and to the representation of the different forms of civilization and of the principal legal systems.

Article 32. (1) The members of the Committee shall be elected for a term of four years. They shall be eligible for re-election if renominated. However, the terms of nine of the members elected at the first election shall expire at the end of two years; immediately after the first election, the names of these nine members shall be chosen by lot by the Chairman of the meeting referred to in article 30, paragraph (4).

(2) Elections at the expiry of office shall be held in accordance with the preceding articles of this part of the present Covenant.

Article 33. (1) If, in the unanimous opinion of the other members, a member of the Committee has ceased to carry out his functions for any cause other than absence of a temporary character, the Chairman of the Committee shall notify the Secretary-General of the United Nations, who shall then declare the seat of that member to be vacant.

(2) In the event of the death or the resignation of a member of the Committee, the Chairman shall immediately notify the Secretary-General of the United Nations, who shall declare the seat vacant from the date of death or the date on which the resignation takes effect.

Article 34. (1) When a vacancy is declared in accordance with article 33 and if the term of office of the member to be replaced does not expire within six months of the declaration of the vacancy, the Secretary General of the United Nations shall notify each of the States Parties to the present Covenant, which may within two months submit nominations in accordance with article 29 for the purpose of filling the vacancy.

(2) The Secretary-General of the United Nations shall prepare a list in alphabetical order of the persons thus nominated and shall submit it to the States Parties to the present Covenant. The election to fill the vacancy shall then take place in accordance with the relevant provisions of this part of the present Covenant.

(3) A member of the Committee elected to fill a vacancy declared in accordance with article 33 shall hold office for the remainder of the term of the member who vacated the seat on the Committee under the provisions of that article.

Article 35. The members of the Committee shall, with the approval of the General Assembly of the United Nations, receive emoluments from United Nations resources on such terms and conditions as the General Assembly may decide, having regard to the importance of the Committee's responsibilities.

Article 36. The Secretary-General of the United Nations shall provide the necessary staff and facilities for the effective performance of the functions of the Committee under the present Covenant.

Article 37. (1) The Secretary-General of the United Nations shall convene the initial meeting of the Committee at the Headquarters of the United Nations.

(2) After its initial meeting, the Committee shall meet at such times as shall be provided in its rules of procedure.

(3) The Committee shall normally meet at the Headquarters of the United Nations or at the United Nations Office at Geneva.

Article 38. Every member of the Committee shall, before taking up his duties, make a solemn declaration in open committee that he will perform his functions impartially and conscientiously.

PART II   FUNDAMENTAL RIGHTS

Article 39. (1) The Committee shall elect its officers for a term of two years. They may be re-elected.
(2) The Committee shall establish its own rules of procedure, but these rules shall provide, inter alia, that:
(a) Twelve members shall constitute a quorum;
(b) Decisions of the Committee shall be made by a majority vote of the members present.

Article 40. (1) The States Parties to the present Covenant undertake to submit reports on the measures they have adopted which give effect to the rights recognized herein and on the progress made in the enjoyment of those rights:
(a) Within one year of the entry into force of the present Covenant for the States Parties concerned;
(b) Thereafter whenever the Committee so requests.
(2) All reports shall be submitted to the Secretary-General of the United Nations, who shall transmit them to the Committee for consideration. Reports shall indicate the factors and difficulties, if any, affecting the implementation of the present Covenant.
(3) The Secretary-General of the United Nations may, after consultation with the Committee, transmit to the specialized agencies concerned copies of such parts of the reports as may fall within their field of competence.
(4) The Committee shall study the reports submitted by the States Parties to the present Covenant. It shall transmit its reports, and such general comments as it may consider appropriate, to the States Parties. The Committee may also transmit to the Economic and Social Council these comments along with the copies of the reports it has received from States Parties to the present Covenant.
(5) The States Parties to the present Covenant may submit to the Committee observations on any comments that may be made in accordance with paragraph (4) of this article.

Article 41. (1) A State Party to the present Covenant may at any time declare under this article that it recognizes the competence of the Committee to receive and consider communications to the effect that a State Party claims that another State Party is not fulfilling its obligations under the present Covenant. Communications under this article may be received and considered only if submitted by a State Party which has made a declaration recognizing in regard to itself the competence of the Committee. No communication shall be received by the Committee if it concerns a State Party which has not made such a declaration. Communications received under this article shall be dealt with in accordance with the following procedure:
(a) If a State Party to the present Covenant considers that another State Party is not giving effect to the provisions of the present Covenant, it may, by written communication, bring the matter to the attention of that State Party. Within three months after the receipt of the communication the receiving State shall afford the State which sent the communication an explanation, or any other statement in writing clarifying the matter which should include, to the extent possible and pertinent, reference to domestic procedures and remedies taken, pending, or available in the matter;
(b) If the matter is not adjusted to the satisfaction of both States Parties concerned within six months after the receipt by the receiving State of the initial communication, either State shall have the right to refer the matter to the Committee, by notice given to the Committee and to the other State;
(c) The Committee shall deal with a matter referred to it only after it has ascertained that all available domestic remedies have been invoked and exhausted in the matter, in conformity with the generally recognized principles of international law. This shall not be the rule where the application of the remedies is unreasonably prolonged;
(d) The Committee shall hold closed meetings when examining communications under this article;
(e) Subject to the provisions of subparagraph (c), the Committee shall make available its good offices to the States Parties concerned with a view to a friendly solution of the matter on the basis of respect for human rights and fundamental freedoms as recognized in the present Covenant;
(f) In any matter referred to it, the Committee may call upon the States Parties concerned, referred to in subparagraph (b), to supply any relevant information;
(g) The States Parties concerned, referred to in subparagraph (b), shall have the right to be represented when the matter is being considered in the Committee and to make submissions orally and/or in writing;
(h) The Committee shall, within twelve months after the date of receipt of notice under subparagraph (b), submit a report:
(i) If a solution within the terms of subparagraph (e) is reached, the Committee shall confine its report to a brief statement of the facts and of the solution reached;
(ii) If a solution within the terms of subparagraph (e) is not reached, the Committee shall confine its report to a brief statement of the facts; the written submissions and record of the oral submissions made by the States Parties concerned shall be attached to the report. In every matter, the report shall

be communicated to the States Parties concerned.

(2) The provisions of this article shall come into force when ten States Parties to the present Covenant have made declarations under paragraph (1) of this article. Such declarations shall be deposited by the States Parties with the Secretary-General of the United Nations, who shall transmit copies thereof to the other States Parties. A declaration may be withdrawn at any time by notification to the Secretary General.

Such a withdrawal shall not prejudice the consideration of any matter which is the subject of a communication already transmitted under this article; no further communication by any State Party shall be received after the notification of withdrawal of the declaration has been received by the Secretary-General, unless the State Party concerned has made a new declaration.

Article 42. (1) (a) If a matter referred to the Committee in accordance with article 41 is not resolved to the satisfaction of the States Parties concerned, the Committee may, with the prior consent of the States Parties concerned, appoint an ad hoc Conciliation Commission (hereinafter referred to as the Commission). The good offices of the Commission shall be made available to the States Parties concerned with a view to an amicable solution of the matter on the basis of respect for the present Covenant;
(b) The Commission shall consist of five persons acceptable to the States Parties concerned. If the States Parties concerned fail to reach agreement within three months on all or part of the composition of the Commission, the members of the Commission concerning whom no agreement has been reached shall be elected by secret ballot by a two-thirds majority vote of the Committee from among its members.
(2) The members of the Commission shall serve in their personal capacity. They shall not be nationals of the States Parties concerned, or of a State not Party to the present Covenant, or of a State Party which has not made a declaration under article 41.
(3) The Commission shall elect its own Chairman and adopt its own rules of procedure.
(4) The meetings of the Commission shall normally be held at the Headquarters of the United Nations or at the United Nations Office at Geneva. However, they may be held at such other convenient places as the Commission may determine in consultation with the Secretary-General of the United Nations and the States Parties concerned.
(5) The secretariat provided in accordance with article 36 shall also service the commissions appointed under this article.
(6) The information received and collated by the Committee shall be made available to the Commission and the Commission may call upon the States Parties concerned to supply any other relevant information.
(7) When the Commission has fully considered the matter, but in any event not later than twelve months after having been seized of the matter, it shall submit to the Chairman of the Committee a report for communication to the States Parties concerned:
(a) If the Commission is unable to complete its consideration of the matter within twelve months, it shall confine its report to a brief statement of the status of its consideration of the matter;
(b) If an amicable solution to the matter on tie basis of respect for human rights as recognized in the present Covenant is reached, the Commission shall confine its report to a brief statement of the facts and of the solution reached;
(c) If a solution within the terms of subparagraph (b) is not reached, the Commission's report shall embody its findings on all questions of fact relevant to the issues between the States Parties concerned, and its views on the possibilities of an amicable solution of the matter. This report shall also contain the written submissions and a record of the oral submissions made by the States Parties concerned;
(d) If the Commission's report is submitted under subparagraph (c), the States Parties concerned shall, within three months of the receipt of the report, notify the Chairman of the Committee whether or not they accept the contents of the report of the Commission.
(8) The provisions of this article are without prejudice to the responsibilities of the Committee under article 41.
(9) The States Parties concerned shall share equally all the expenses of the members of the Commission in accordance with estimates to be provided by the Secretary-General of the United Nations.
(10) The Secretary-General of the United Nations shall be empowered to pay the expenses of the members of the Commission, if necessary, before reimbursement by the States Parties concerned, in accordance with paragraph (9) of this article.

Article 43. The members of the Committee, and of the ad hoc conciliation commissions which may be appointed under article 42, shall be entitled to the facilities, privileges and immunities of experts

PART II   FUNDAMENTAL RIGHTS

on mission for the United Nations as laid down in the relevant sections of the Convention on the Privileges and Immunities of the United Nations.

Article 44. The provisions for the implementation of the present Covenant shall apply without prejudice to the procedures prescribed in the field of human rights by or under the constituent instruments and the conventions of the United Nations and of the specialized agencies and shall not prevent the States Parties to the present Covenant from having recourse to other procedures for settling a dispute in accordance with general or special international agreements in force between them.

Article 45. The Committee shall submit to the General Assembly of the United Nations, through the Economic and Social Council, an annual report on its activities.

Part V

Article 46. Nothing in the present Covenant shall be interpreted as impairing the provisions of the Charter of the United Nations and of the constitutions of the specialized agencies which define the respective responsibilities of the various organs of the United Nations and of the specialized agencies in regard to the matters dealt with in the present Covenant.

Article 47. Nothing in the present Covenant shall be interpreted as impairing the inherent right of all peoples to enjoy and utilize fully and freely their natural wealth and resources.

Part VI

Article 48. (1) The present Covenant is open for signature by any State Member of the United Nations or member of any of its specialized agencies, by any State Party to the Statute of the International Court of Justice, and by any other State which has been invited by the General Assembly of the United Nations to become a Party to the present Covenant.
(2) The present Covenant is subject to ratification. Instruments of ratification shall be deposited with the Secretary-General of the United Nations.
(3) The present Covenant shall be open to accession by any State referred to in paragraph (1) of this article.
(4) Accession shall be effected by the deposit of an instrument of accession with the Secretary General of the United Nations.
(5) The Secretary-General of the United Nations shall inform all States which have signed this Covenant or acceded to it of the deposit of each instrument of ratification or accession.

Article 49. (1) The present Covenant shall enter into force three months after the date of the deposit with the Secretary-General of the United Nations of the thirty-fifth instrument of ratification or instrument of accession.
(2) For each State ratifying the present Covenant or acceding to it after the deposit of the thirty-fifth instrument of ratification or instrument of accession, the present Covenant shall enter into force three months after the date of the deposit of its own instrument of ratification or instrument of accession.

Article 50. The provisions of the present Covenant shall extend to all parts of federal States without any limitations or exceptions.

Article 51. (1) Any State Party to the present Covenant may propose an amendment and file it with the Secretary-General of the United Nations. The Secretary-General of the United Nations shall thereupon communicate any proposed amendments to the States Parties to the present Covenant with a request that they notify him whether they favour a conference of States Parties for the purpose of considering and voting upon the proposals. In the event that at least one third of the States Parties favours such a conference, the Secretary-General shall convene the conference under the auspices of the United Nations. Any amendment adopted by a majority of the States Parties present and voting at the conference shall be submitted to the General Assembly of the United Nations for approval.
(2) Amendments shall come into force when they have been approved by the General Assembly of the United Nations and accepted by a two-thirds majority of the States Parties to the present Covenant in accordance with their respective constitutional processes.
(3) When amendments come into force, they shall be binding on those States Parties which have accepted them, other States Parties still being bound by the provisions of the present Covenant and any earlier amendment which they have accepted.

Article 52. (1) Irrespective of the notifications made under article 48, paragraph (5), the Secretary-General of the United Nations shall inform all States referred to in paragraph (1) of the same article of the following particulars:

(a) Signatures, ratifications and accessions under article 48;
(b) The date of the entry into force of the present Covenant under article 49 and the date of the entry into force of any amendments under article 51.

Article 53. (1) The present Covenant, of which the Chinese, English, French, Russian and Spanish texts are equally authentic, shall be deposited in the archives of the United Nations. (2) The Secretary-General of the United Nations shall transmit certified copies of the present Covenant to all States referred to in article 48.

PART II FUNDAMENTAL RIGHTS

Optional Protocol to the ICCPR
New York, 16 December 1966, entry into force 23 March 1976

The States Parties to the present Protocol,
Considering that in order further to achieve the purposes of the International Covenant on Civil and Political Rights (hereinafter referred to as the Covenant) and the implementation of its provisions it would be appropriate to enable the Human Rights Committee set up in part IV of the Covenant (hereinafter referred to as the Committee) to receive and consider, as provided in the present Protocol, communications from individuals claiming to be victims of violations of any of the rights set forth in the Covenant.
Have agreed as follows:

Article 1. A State Party to the Covenant that becomes a Party to the present Protocol recognizes the competence of the Committee to receive and consider communications from individuals subject to its jurisdiction who claim to be victims of a violation by that State Party of any of the rights set forth in the Covenant. No communication shall be received by the Committee if it concerns a State Party to the Covenant which is not a Party to the present Protocol.

Article 2. Subject to the provisions of article 1, individuals who claim that any of their rights enumerated in the Covenant have been violated and who have exhausted all available domestic remedies may submit a written communication to the Committee for consideration.

Article 3. The Committee shall consider inadmissible any communication under the present Protocol which is anonymous, or which it considers to be an abuse of the right of submission of such communications or to be incompatible with the provisions of the Covenant.

Article 4. (1) Subject to the provisions of article 3, the Committee shall bring any communications submitted to it under the present Protocol to the attention of the State Party to the present Protocol alleged to be violating any provision of the Covenant.
(2) Within six months, the receiving State shall submit to the Committee written explanations or statements clarifying the matter and the remedy, if any, that may have been taken by that State.

Article 5. (1) The Committee shall consider communications received under the present Protocol in the light of all written information made available to it by the individual and by the State Party concerned.
(2) The Committee shall not consider any communication from an individual unless it has ascertained that:
(a) The same matter is not being examined under another procedure of international investigation or settlement;
(b) The individual has exhausted all available domestic remedies. This shall not be the rule where the application of the remedies is unreasonably prolonged.
(3) The Committee shall hold closed meetings when examining communications under the present Protocol.
(4) The Committee shall forward its views to the State Party concerned and to the individual.

Article 6. The Committee shall include in its annual report under article 45 of the Covenant a summary of its activities under the present Protocol.

Article 7. Pending the achievement of the objectives of resolution 1514(XV) adopted by the General Assembly of the United Nations on 14 December 1960 concerning the Declaration on the Granting of Independence to Colonial Countries and Peoples, the provisions of the present Protocol shall in no way limit the right of petition granted to these peoples by the Charter of the United Nations and other international conventions and instruments under the United Nations and its specialized agencies.

Article 8. (1) The present Protocol is open for signature by any State which has signed the Covenant.
(2) The present Protocol is subject to ratification by any State which has ratified or acceded to the Covenant. Instruments of ratification shall be deposited with the Secretary-General of the United Nations.
(3) The present Protocol shall be open to accession by any State which has ratified or acceded to the Covenant.
(4) Accession shall be effected by the deposit of an instrument of accession with the Secretary General of the United Nations.
(5) The Secretary-General of the United Nations shall inform all States which have signed the present Protocol or acceded to it of the deposit of each instrument of ratification or accession.

Article 9. (1) Subject to the entry into force of the Covenant, the present Protocol shall enter into force three months after the date of the deposit with the Secretary-General of the United Nations of the tenth instrument of ratification or instrument of accession.
(2) For each State ratifying the present Protocol or acceding to it after the deposit of the tenth instrument of ratification or instrument of accession, the present Protocol shall enter into force three months after the date of the deposit of its own instrument of ratification or instrument of accession.

Article 10. The provisions of the present Protocol shall extend to all parts of federal States without any limitations or exceptions.

Article 11. (1) Any State Party to the present Protocol may propose an amendment and file it with the Secretary-General of the United Nations. The Secretary-General shall thereupon communicate any proposed amendments to the States Parties to the present Protocol with a request that they notify him whether they favour a conference of States Parties for the purpose of considering and voting upon the proposal. In the event that at least one third of the States Parties favours such a conference, the Secretary-General shall convene the conference under the auspices of the United Nations. Any amendment adopted by a majority of the States Parties present and voting at the conference shall be submitted to the General Assembly of the United Nations for approval.
(2) Amendments shall come into force when they have been approved by the General Assembly of the United Nations and accepted by a two-thirds majority of the States Parties to the present Protocol in accordance with their respective constitutional processes. 3. When amendments come into force, they shall be binding on those States Parties which have accepted them, other States Parties still being bound by the provisions of the present Protocol and any earlier amendment which they have accepted.

Article 12. (1) Any State Party may denounce the present Protocol at any time by written notification addressed to the Secretary-General of the United Nations. Denunciation shall take effect three months after the date of receipt of the notification by the Secretary-General. 2. Denunciation shall be without prejudice to the continued application of the provisions of the present Protocol to any communication submitted under article 2 before the effective date of denunciation.

Article 13. Irrespective of the notifications made under article 8, paragraph (5), of the present Protocol, the Secretary-General of the United Nations shall inform all States referred to in article 48, paragraph (1), of the Covenant of the following particulars:
(a) Signatures, ratifications and accessions under article 8;
(b) The date of the entry into force of the present Protocol under article 9 and the date of the entry into force of any amendments under article 11;
(c) Denunciations under article 12.

Article 14. (1) The present Protocol, of which the Chinese, English, French, Russian and Spanish texts are equally authentic, shall be deposited in the archives of the United Nations. (2) The Secretary-General of the United Nations shall transmit certified copies of the present Protocol to all States referred to in article 48 of the Covenant.

PART II   FUNDAMENTAL RIGHTS

Second Optional Protocol to the ICCPR (Abolition of the Death Penalty)
New York 15 December 1989, Entry into Force 11 July 1991
Trb. 1990 No. 125

The States Parties to the present Protocol,
Believing that abolition of the death penalty contributes to enhancement of human dignity and progressive development of human rights,
Recalling article 3 of the Universal Declaration of Human Rights, adopted on 10 December 1948, and article 6 of the International Covenant on Civil and Political Rights, adopted on 16 December 1966,
Noting that article 6 of the International Covenant on Civil and Political Rights refers to abolition of the death penalty in terms that strongly suggest that abolition is desirable,
Convinced that all measures of abolition of the death penalty should be considered as progress in the enjoyment of the right to life,
Desirous to undertake hereby an international commitment to abolish the death penalty,
Have agreed as follows:

Article 1. (1) No one within the jurisdiction of a State Party to the present Protocol shall be executed.
(2) Each State Party shall take all necessary measures to abolish the death penalty within its jurisdiction.

Article 2. (1) No reservation is admissible to the present Protocol, except for a reservation made at the time of ratification or accession that provides for the application of the death penalty in time of war pursuant to a conviction for a most serious crime of a military nature committed during wartime.
(2) The State Party making such a reservation shall at the time of ratification or accession communicate to the Secretary-General of the United Nations the relevant provisions of its national legislation applicable during wartime.
(3) The State Party having made such a reservation shall notify the Secretary-General of the United Nations of any beginning or ending of a state of war applicable to its territory.

Article 3. The States Parties to the present Protocol shall include in the reports they submit to the Human Rights Committee, in accordance with article 40 of the Covenant, information on the measures that they have adopted to give effect to the present Protocol.

Article 4. With respect to the States Parties to the Covenant that have made a declaration under article 41, the competence of the Human Rights Committee to receive and consider communications when a State Party claims that another State Party is not fulfilling its obligations shall extend to the provisions of the present Protocol, unless the State Party concerned has made a statement to the contrary at the moment of ratification or accession.

Article 5. With respect to the States Parties to the first Optional Protocol to the International Covenant on Civil and Political Rights adopted on 16 December 1966, the competence of the Human Rights Committee to receive and consider communications from individuals subject to its jurisdiction shall extend to the provisions of the present Protocol, unless the State Party concerned has made a statement to the contrary at the moment of ratification or accession.

Article 6. (1) The provisions of the present Protocol shall apply as additional provisions to the Covenant.
(2) Without prejudice to the possibility of a reservation under article 2 of the present Protocol, the right guaranteed in article 1, paragraph (1), of the present Protocol shall not be subject to any derogation under article 4 of the Covenant.

Article 7. (1) The present Protocol is open for signature by any State that has signed the Covenant.
(2) The present Protocol is subject to ratification by any State that has ratified the Covenant or acceded to it. Instruments of ratification shall be deposited with the Secretary-General of the United Nations.
(3) The present Protocol shall be open to accession by any State that has ratified the Covenant or acceded to it.
(4) Accession shall be effected by the deposit of an instrument of accession with the Secretary General of the United Nations.
(5) The Secretary-General of the United Nations shall inform all States that have signed the present Protocol or acceded to it of the deposit of each instrument of ratification or accession.

Article 8. (1) The present Protocol shall enter into force three months after the date of the deposit with the Secretary-General of the United Nations of the tenth instrument of ratification or accession.
(2) For each State ratifying the present Protocol or acceding to it after the deposit of the tenth instrument of ratification or accession, the present Protocol shall enter into force three months after the date of the deposit of its own instrument of ratification or accession.

Article 9. The provisions of the present Protocol shall extend to all parts of federal States without any limitations or exceptions.

Article 10. The Secretary-General of the United Nations shall inform all States referred to in article 48, paragraph (1), of the Covenant of the following particulars:
(a) Reservations, communications and notifications under article 2 of the present Protocol; (b) Statements made under articles 4 or 5 of the present Protocol;
(c) Signatures, ratifications and accessions under article 7 of the present Protocol:
(d) The date of the entry into force of the present Protocol under article 8 thereof.

Article 11. (1) The present Protocol, of which the Arabic, Chinese, English, French, Russian and Spanish texts are equally authentic, shall be deposited in the archives of the United Nations.
(2) The Secretary-General of the United Nations shall transmit certified copies of the present Protocol to all States referred to in article 48 of the Covenant.

PART II   FUNDAMENTAL RIGHTS

**Convention on the Elimination of all Forms of Discrimination against Women (CEDAW)
Adopted by General Assembly Resolution 34/180 of 1979, Entry into force 3 September 1981**

The States Parties to the present Convention,
Noting that the Charter of the United Nations reaffirms faith in fundamental human rights, in the dignity and worth of the human person and in the equal rights of men and women,
Noting that the Universal Declaration of Human Rights affirms the principle of the inadmissibility of discrimination and proclaims that all human beings are born free and equal in dignity and rights and that everyone is entitled to all the rights and freedoms set forth therein, without distinction of any kind, including distinction based on sex,
Noting that the States Parties to the International Covenants on Human Rights have the obligation to ensure the equal rights of men and women to enjoy all economic, social, cultural, civil and political rights,
Considering the international conventions concluded under the auspices of the United Nations and the specialized agencies promoting equality of rights of men and women,
Noting also the resolutions, declarations and recommendations adopted by the United Nations and the specialized agencies promoting equality of rights of men and women,
Concerned, however, that despite these various instruments extensive discrimination against women continues to exist,
Recalling that discrimination against women violates the principles of equality of rights and respect for human dignity, is an obstacle to the participation of women, on equal terms with men, in the political, social, economic and cultural life of their countries, hampers the growth of the prosperity of society and the family and makes more difficult the full development of the potentialities of women in the service of their countries and of humanity,
Concerned that in situations of poverty women have the least access to food, health, education, training and opportunities for employment and other needs,
Convinced that the establishment of the new international economic order based on equity and justice will contribute significantly towards the promotion of equality between men and women,
Emphasizing that the eradication of apartheid, all forms of racism, racial discrimination, colonialism, neo-colonialism, aggression, foreign occupation and domination and interference in the internal affairs of States is essential to the full enjoyment of the rights of men and women,
Affirming that the strengthening of international peace and security, the relaxation of international tension, mutual co-operation among all States irrespective of their social and economic systems, general and complete disarmament, in particular nuclear disarmament under strict and effective international control, the affirmation of the principles of justice, equality and mutual benefit in relations among countries and the realization of the right of peoples under alien and colonial domination and foreign occupation to self-determination and independence, as well as respect for national sovereignty and territorial integrity, will promote social progress and development and as a consequence will contribute to the attainment of full equality between men and women,
Convinced that the full and complete development of a country, the welfare of the world and the cause of peace require the maximum participation of women on equal terms with men in all fields,
Bearing in mind the great contribution of women to the welfare of the family and to the development of society, so far not fully recognized, the social significance of maternity and the role of both parents in the family and in the upbringing of children, and aware that the role of women in procreation should not be a basis for discrimination but that the upbringing of children requires a sharing of responsibility between men and women and society as a whole,
Aware that a change in the traditional role of men as well as the role of women in society and in the family is needed to achieve full equality between men and women,
Determined to implement the principles set forth in the Declaration on the Elimination of Discrimination against Women and, for that purpose, to adopt the measures required for the elimination of such discrimination in all its forms and manifestations,
Have agreed on the following:

Part I

Article I. For the purposes of the present Convention, the term "discrimination against women" shall mean any distinction, exclusion or restriction made on the basis of sex which has the effect or purpose of impairing or nullifying the recognition, enjoyment or exercise by women, irrespective of their marital status, on a basis of equality of men and women, of human rights and fundamental freedoms in the political, economic, social, cultural, civil or any other field.

CONVENTION ON THE ELIMINATION OF DISCRIMINATION AGAINST WOMEN

Article 2. States Parties condemn discrimination against women in all its forms, agree to pursue by all appropriate means and without delay a policy of eliminating discrimination against women and, to this end, undertake:
(a) To embody the principle of the equality of men and women in their national constitutions or other appropriate legislation if not yet incorporated therein and to ensure, through law and other appropriate means, the practical realization of this principle;
(b) To adopt appropriate legislative and other measures, including sanctions where appropriate, prohibiting all discrimination against women;

(c) To establish legal protection of the rights of women on an equal basis with men and to ensure through competent national tribunals and other public institutions the effective protection of women against any act of discrimination;
(d) To refrain from engaging in any act or practice of discrimination against women and to ensure that public authorities and institutions shall act in conformity with this obligation;
(e) To take all appropriate measures to eliminate discrimination against women by any person, organization or enterprise;
(f) To take all appropriate measures, including legislation, to modify or abolish existing laws, regulations, customs and practices which constitute discrimination against women;
(g) To repeal all national penal provisions which constitute discrimination against women.

Article 3. States Parties shall take in all fields, in particular in the political, social, economic and cultural fields, all appropriate measures, including legislation, to en sure the full development and advancement of women, for the purpose of guaranteeing them the exercise and enjoyment of human rights and fundamental freedoms on a basis of equality with men.

Article 4. (1) Adoption by States Parties of temporary special measures aimed at accelerating de facto equality between men and women shall not be considered discrimination as defined in the present Convention, but shall in no way entail as a consequence the maintenance of unequal or separate standards; these measures shall be discontinued when the objectives of equality of opportunity and treatment have been achieved.
(2) Adoption by States Parties of special measures, including those measures contained in the present Convention, aimed at protecting maternity shall not be considered discriminatory.

Article 5. States Parties shall take all appropriate measures:
(a) To modify the social and cultural patterns of conduct of men and women, with a view to achieving the elimination of prejudices and customary and all other practices which are based on the idea of the inferiority or the superiority of either of the sexes or on stereotyped roles for men and women;
(b) To ensure that family education includes a proper understanding of maternity as a social function and the recognition of the common responsibility of men and women in the upbringing and development of their children, it being understood that the interest of the children is the primordial consideration in all cases.

Article 6
States Parties shall take all appropriate measures, including legislation, to suppress all forms of traffic in women and exploitation of prostitution of women.

Part II

Article 7. States Parties shall take all appropriate measures to eliminate discrimination against women in the political and public life of the country and, in particular, shall ensure to women, on equal terms with men, the right:
(a) To vote in all elections and public referenda and to be eligible for election to all publicly elected bodies;
(b) To participate in the formulation of government policy and the implementation thereof and to hold public office and perform all public functions at all levels of government;
(c) To participate in non-governmental organizations and associations concerned with the public and political life of the country.

Article 8. States Parties shall take all appropriate measures to ensure to women, on equal terms with men and without any discrimination, the opportunity to represent their Governments at the international level and to participate in the work of international organizations.

Article 9
(1) States Parties shall grant women equal rights with men to acquire, change or retain their national-

PART II   FUNDAMENTAL RIGHTS

ity. They shall ensure in particular that neither marriage to an alien nor change of nationality by the husband during marriage shall automatically change the nationality of the wife, render her stateless or force upon her the nationality of the husband.
(2) States Parties shall grant women equal rights with men with respect to the nationality of their children.

Part III

Article 10. States Parties shall take all appropriate measures to eliminate discrimination against women in order to ensure to them equal rights with men in the field of education and in particular to ensure, on a basis of equality of men and women:
(a) The same conditions for career and vocational guidance, for access to studies and for the achievement of diplomas in educational establishments of all categories in rural as well as in urban areas; this equality shall be ensured in pre-school, general, technical, professional and higher technical education, as well as in all types of vocational training;
(b) Access to the same curricula, the same examinations, teaching staff with qualifications of the same standard and school premises and equipment of the same quality;
(c) The elimination of any stereotyped concept of the roles of men and women at all levels and in all forms of education by encouraging coeducation and other types of education which will help to achieve this aim and, in particular, by the revision of textbooks and school programmes and the adaptation of teaching methods;
(d) The same opportunities to benefit from scholarships and other study grants;
(e) The same opportunities for access to programmes of continuing education, including adult and functional literacy programmes, particulary those aimed at reducing, at the earliest possible time, any gap in education existing between men and women;
(f) The reduction of female student drop-out rates and the organization of programmes for girls and women who have left school prematurely;
(g) The same Opportunities to participate actively in sports and physical education;
(h) Access to specific educational information to help to ensure the health and well-being of families, including information and advice on family planning.

Article 11. (1) States Parties shall take all appropriate measures to eliminate discrimination against women in the field of employment in order to ensure, on a basis of equality of men and women, the same rights, in particular:
(a) The right to work as an inalienable right of all human beings;
(b) The right to the same employment opportunities, including the application of the same criteria for selection in matters of employment;
(c) The right to free choice of profession and employment, the right to promotion, job security and all benefits and conditions of service and the right to receive vocational training and retraining, including apprenticeships, advanced vocational training and recurrent training;
(d) The right to equal remuneration, including benefits, and to equal treatment in respect of work of equal value, as well as equality of treatment in the evaluation of the quality of work;
(e) The right to social security, particularly in cases of retirement, unemployment, sickness, invalidity and old age and other incapacity to work, as well as the right to paid leave;
(f) The right to protection of health and to safety in working conditions, including the safeguarding of the function of reproduction.
(2) In order to prevent discrimination against women on the grounds of marriage or maternity and to ensure their effective right to work, States Parties shall take appropriate measures:
(a) To prohibit, subject to the imposition of sanctions, dismissal on the grounds of pregnancy or of maternity leave and discrimination in dismissals on the basis of marital status;
(b) To introduce maternity leave with pay or with comparable social benefits without loss of former employment, seniority or social allowances;
(c) To encourage the provision of the necessary supporting social services to enable parents to combine family obligations with work responsibilities and participation in public life, in particular through promoting the establishment and development of a network of child-care facilities;
(d) To provide special protection to women during pregnancy in types of work proved to be harmful to them.
(3) Protective legislation relating to matters covered in this article shall be reviewed periodically in the light of scientific and technological knowledge and shall be revised, repealed or extended as necessary.

Article 12. (1) States Parties shall take all appropriate measures to eliminate discrimination against

women in the field of health care in order to ensure, on a basis of equality of men and women, access to health care services, including those related to family planning.
(2) Notwithstanding the provisions of paragraph I of this article, States Parties shall ensure to women appropriate services in connection with pregnancy, confinement and the post-natal period, granting free services where necessary, as well as adequate nutrition during pregnancy and lactation.

Article 13. States Parties shall take all appropriate measures to eliminate discrimination against women in other areas of economic and social life in order to ensure, on a basis of equality of men and women, the same rights, in particular:
(a) The right to family benefits;
(b) The right to bank loans, mortgages and other forms of financial credit;
(c) The right to participate in recreational activities, sports and all aspects of cultural life.

Article 14. (1) States Parties shall take into account the particular problems faced by rural women and the significant roles which rural women play in the economic survival of their families, including their work in the non-monetized sectors of the economy, and shall take all appropriate measures to ensure the application of the provisions of the present Convention to women in rural areas.
(2) States Parties shall take all appropriate measures to eliminate discrimination against women in rural areas in order to ensure, on a basis of equality of men and women, that they participate in and benefit from rural development and, in particular, shall ensure to such women the right:
(a) To participate in the elaboration and implementation of development planning at all levels;
(b) To have access to adequate health care facilities, including information, counselling and services in family planning;
(c) To benefit directly from social security programmes;
(d) To obtain all types of training and education, formal and non-formal, including that relating to functional literacy, as well as, inter alia, the benefit of all community and extension services, in order to increase their technical proficiency;
(e) To organize self-help groups and co-operatives in order to obtain equal access to economic opportunities through employment or self employment;
(f) To participate in all community activities;
(g) To have access to agricultural credit and loans, marketing facilities, appropriate technology and equal treatment in land and agrarian reform as well as in land resettlement schemes;
(h) To enjoy adequate living conditions, particularly in relation to housing, sanitation, electricity and water supply, transport and communications.

Part IV

Article 15. (1) States Parties shall accord to women equality with men before the law.
(2) States Parties shall accord to women, in civil matters, a legal capacity identical to that of men and the same opportunities to exercise that capacity. In particular, they shall give women equal rights to conclude contracts and to administer property and shall treat them equally in all stages of procedure in courts and tribunals.
(3) States Parties agree that all contracts and all other private instruments of any kind with a legal effect which is directed at restricting the legal capacity of women shall be deemed null and void.
(4) States Parties shall accord to men and women the same rights with regard to the law relating to the movement of persons and the freedom to choose their residence and domicile.

Article 16. (1) States Parties shall take all appropriate measures to eliminate discrimination against women in all matters relating to marriage and family relations and in particular shall ensure, on a basis of equality of men and women:
(a) The same right to enter into marriage;
(b) The same right freely to choose a spouse and to enter into marriage only with their free and full consent;
(c) The same rights and responsibilities during marriage and at its dissolution;
(d) The same rights and responsibilities as parents, irrespective of their marital status, in matters relating to their children; in all cases the interests of the children shall be paramount;
(e) The same rights to decide freely and responsibly on the number and spacing of their children and to have access to the information, education and means to enable them to exercise these rights;
(f) The same rights and responsibilities with regard to guardianship, wardship, trusteeship and adoption of children, or similar institutions where these concepts exist in national legislation; in all cases the interests of the children shall be paramount;
(g) The same personal rights as husband and wife, including the right to choose a family name, a

PART II   FUNDAMENTAL RIGHTS

profession and an occupation;
(h) The same rights for both spouses in respect of the ownership, acquisition, management, administration, enjoyment and disposition of property, whether free of charge or for a valuable consideration.
(2) The betrothal and the marriage of a child shall have no legal effect, and all necessary action, including legislation, shall be taken to specify a minimum age for marriage and to make the registration of marriages in an official registry compulsory.

Part V

Article 17. (1) For the purpose of considering the progress made in the implementation of the present Convention, there shall be established a Committee on the Elimination of Discrimination against Women (hereinafter referred to as the Committee) consisting, at the time of entry into force of the Convention, of eighteen and, after ratification of or accession to the Convention by the thirty-fifth State Party, of twenty-three experts of high moral standing and competence in the field covered by the Convention. The experts shall be elected by States Parties from among their nationals and shall serve in their personal capacity, consideration being given to equitable geographical distribution and to the representation of the different forms of civilization as well as the principal legal systems.
(2) The members of the Committee shall be elected by secret ballot from a list of persons nominated by States Parties. Each State Party may nominate one person from among its own nationals.
(3) The initial election shall be held six months after the date of the entry into force of the present Convention. At least three months before the date of each election the Secretary-General of the United Nations shall address a letter to the States Parties inviting them to submit their nominations within two months. The Secretary-General shall prepare a list in alphabetical order of all persons thus nominated, indicating the States Parties which have nominated them, and shall submit it to the States Parties.
(4) Elections of the members of the Committee shall be held at a meeting of States Parties convened by the Secretary-General at United Nations Headquarters. At that meeting, for which two thirds of the States Parties shall constitute a quorum, the persons elected to the Committee shall be those nominees who obtain the largest number of votes and an absolute majority of the votes of the representatives of States Parties present and voting.
(5) The members of the Committee shall be elected for a term of four years. However, the terms of nine of the members elected at the first election shall expire at the end of two years; immediately after the first election the names of these nine members shall be chosen by lot by the Chairman of the Committee.
(6) The election of the five additional members of the Committee shall be held in accordance with the provisions of paragraphs (2), (3) and (4) of this article, following the thirty-fifth ratification or accession. The terms of two of the additional members elected on this occasion shall expire at the end of two years, the names of these two members having been chosen by lot by the Chairman of the Committee.
(7) For the filling of casual vacancies, the State Party whose expert has ceased to function as a member of the Committee shall appoint another expert from among its nationals, subject to the approval of the Committee.
(8) The members of the Committee shall, with the approval of the General Assembly, receive emoluments from United Nations resources on such terms and conditions as the Assembly may decide, having regard to the importance of the Committee's responsibilities.
9. The Secretary-General of the United Nations shall provide the necessary staff and facilities for the effective performance of the functions of the Committee under the present Convention.

Article 18. (1) States Parties undertake to submit to the Secretary-General of the United Nations, for consideration by the Committee, a report on the legislative, judicial, administrative or other measures which they have adopted to give effect to the provisions of the present Convention and on the progress made in this respect:
(a) Within one year after the entry into force for the State concerned;
(b) Thereafter at least every four years and further whenever the Committee so requests.
(2) Reports may indicate factors and difficulties affecting the degree of fulfilment of obligations under the present Convention.

Article 19. (1) The Committee shall adopt its own rules of procedure.
(2) The Committee shall elect its officers for a term of two years.

Article 20. (1) The Committee shall normally meet for a period of not more than two weeks annually in order to consider the reports submitted in accordance with article 18 of the present Convention.

(2) The meetings of the Committee shall normally be held at United Nations Headquarters or at any other convenient place as determined by the Committee. (amendment, status of ratification)

Article 21. (1) The Committee shall, through the Economic and Social Council, report annually to the General Assembly of the United Nations on its activities and may make suggestions and general recommendations based on the examination of reports and information received from the States Parties. Such suggestions and general recommendations shall be included in the report of the Committee together with comments, if any, from States Parties.
(2) The Secretary-General of the United Nations shall transmit the reports of the Committee to the Commission on the Status of Women for its information.

Article 22. The specialized agencies shall be entitled to be represented at the consideration of the implementation of such provisions of the present Convention as fall within the scope of their activities. The Committee may invite the specialized agencies to submit reports on the implementation of the Convention in areas falling within the scope of their activities.

Part VI

Article 23. Nothing in the present Convention shall affect any provisions that are more conducive to the achievement of equality between men and women which may be contained:
(a) In the legislation of a State Party; or
(b) In any other international convention, treaty or agreement in force for that State.
Article 24. States Parties undertake to adopt all necessary measures at the national level aimed at achieving the full realization of the rights recognized in the present Convention.

Article 25. (1) The present Convention shall be open for signature by all States.
(2) The Secretary-General of the United Nations is designated as the depositary of the present Convention.
(3) The present Convention is subject to ratification. Instruments of ratification shall be deposited with the Secretary-General of the United Nations.
(4) The present Convention shall be open to accession by all States. Accession shall be effected by the deposit of an instrument of accession with the Secretary-General of the United Nations.

Article 26. (1) A request for the revision of the present Convention may be made at any time by any State Party by means of a notification in writing addressed to the Secretary-General of the United Nations.
(2) The General Assembly of the United Nations shall decide upon the steps, if any, to be taken in respect of such a request.

Article 27. (1) The present Convention shall enter into force on the thirtieth day after the date of deposit with the Secretary-General of the United Nations of the twentieth instrument of ratification or accession.
(2) For each State ratifying the present Convention or acceding to it after the deposit of the twentieth instrument of ratification or accession, the Convention shall enter into force on the thirtieth day after the date of the deposit of its own instrument of ratification or accession.

Article 28. (1) The Secretary-General of the United Nations shall receive and circulate to all States the text of reservations made by States at the time of ratification or accession.
(2) A reservation incompatible with the object and purpose of the present Convention shall not be permitted.
(3) Reservations may be withdrawn at any time by notification to this effect addressed to the Secretary-General of the United Nations, who shall then inform all States thereof. Such notification shall take effect on the date on which it is received.

Article 29. (1) Any dispute between two or more States Parties concerning the interpretation or application of the present Convention which is not settled by negotiation shall, at the request of one of them, be submitted to arbitration. If within six months from the date of the request for arbitration the parties are unable to agree on the organization of the arbitration, any one of those parties may refer the dispute to the International Court of Justice by request in conformity with the Statute of the Court.
(2) Each State Party may at the time of signature or ratification of the present Convention or accession thereto declare that it does not consider itself bound by paragraph (I) of this article. The other States Parties shall not be bound by that paragraph with respect to any State Party which has made such a reservation.

PART II   FUNDAMENTAL RIGHTS

(3) Any State Party which has made a reservation in accordance with paragraph (2) of this article may at any time withdraw that reservation by notification to the Secretary-General of the United Nations.

Article 30. The present Convention, the Arabic, Chinese, English, French, Russian and Spanish texts of which are equally authentic, shall be deposited with the Secretary-General of the United Nations.

Optional Protocol to the CEDAW
Adopted by General Assembly Resolution A/54/4 on 6 October 1999 and opened for signature on 10 December 1999, Human Rights Day, Entry into force 22 December 2000

The States Parties to the present Protocol,
Noting that the Charter of the United Nations reaffirms faith in fundamental human rights, in the dignity and worth of the human person and in the equal rights of men and women,
Also noting that the Universal Declaration of Human Rights proclaims that all human beings are born free and equal in dignity and rights and that everyone is entitled to all the rights and freedoms set forth therein, without distinction of any kind, including distinction based on sex,
Recalling that the International Covenants on Human Rights Resolution 2200 A (XXI), annex. and other international human rights instruments prohibit discrimination on the basis of sex,
Also recalling the Convention on the Elimination of All Forms of Discrimination against Women4 ("the Convention"), in which the States Parties thereto condemn discrimination against women in all its forms and agree to pursue by all appropriate means and without delay a policy of eliminating discrimination against women,
Reaffirming their determination to ensure the full and equal enjoyment by women of all human rights and fundamental freedoms and to take effective action to prevent violations of these rights and freedoms,
Have agreed as follows:

Article 1. A State Party to the present Protocol ("State Party") recognizes the competence of the Committee on the Elimination of Discrimination against Women ("the Committee") to receive and consider communications submitted in accordance with article 2.

Article 2. Communications may be submitted by or on behalf of individuals or groups of individuals, under the jurisdiction of a State Party, claiming to be victims of a violation of any of the rights set forth in the Convention by that State Party. Where a communication is submitted on behalf of individuals or groups of individuals, this shall be with their consent unless the author can justify acting on their behalf without such consent.

Article 3. Communications shall be in writing and shall not be anonymous. No communication shall be received by the Committee if it concerns a State Party to the Convention that is not a party to the present Protocol.

Article 4. (1) The Committee shall not consider a communication unless it has ascertained that all available domestic remedies have been exhausted unless the application of such remedies is unreasonably prolonged or unlikely to bring effective relief.
(2) The Committee shall declare a communication inadmissible where:
(a) The same matter has already been examined by the Committee or has been or is being examined under another procedure of international investigation or settlement;
(b) It is incompatible with the provisions of the Convention;
(c) It is manifestly ill-founded or not sufficiently substantiated;
(d) It is an abuse of the right to submit a communication;
(e) The facts that are the subject of the communication occurred prior to the entry into force of the present Protocol for the State Party concerned unless those facts continued after that date.

Article 5. (1) At any time after the receipt of a communication and before a determination on the merits has been reached, the Committee may transmit to the State Party concerned for its urgent consideration a request that the State Party take such interim measures as may be necessary to avoid possible irreparable damage to the victim or victims of the alleged violation.
(2) Where the Committee exercises its discretion under paragraph (1) of the present article, this does not imply a determination on admissibility or on the merits of the communication.

Article 6. (1) Unless the Committee considers a communication inadmissible without reference to the State Party concerned, and provided that the individual or individuals consent to the disclosure of their identity to that State Party, the Committee shall bring any communication submitted to it under the present Protocol confidentially to the attention of the State Party concerned.
(2) Within six months, the receiving State Party shall submit to the Committee written explanations or statements clarifying the matter and the remedy, if any, that may have been provided by that State Party.

Article 7. (1) The Committee shall consider communications received under the present Protocol in

PART II   FUNDAMENTAL RIGHTS

the light of all information made available to it by or on behalf of individuals or groups of individuals and by the State Party concerned, provided that this information is transmitted to the parties concerned.
(2) The Committee shall hold closed meetings when examining communications under the present Protocol.
(3) After examining a communication, the Committee shall transmit its views on the communication, together with its recommendations, if any, to the parties concerned.
(4) The State Party shall give due consideration to the views of the Committee, together with its recommendations, if any, and shall submit to the Committee, within six months, a written response, including information on any action taken in the light of the views and recommendations of the Committee.
(5) The Committee may invite the State Party to submit further information about any measures the State Party has taken in response to its views or recommendations, if any, including as deemed appropriate by the Committee, in the State Party's subsequent reports under article 18 of the Convention.

Article 8. (1) If the Committee receives reliable information indicating grave or systematic violations by a State Party of rights set forth in the Convention, the Committee shall invite that State Party to cooperate in the examination of the information and to this end to submit observations with regard to the information concerned.
(2) Taking into account any observations that may have been submitted by the State Party concerned as well as any other reliable information available to it, the Committee may designate one or more of its members to conduct an inquiry and to report urgently to the Committee. Where warranted and with the consent of the State Party, the inquiry may include a visit to its territory.
(3) After examining the findings of such an inquiry, the Committee shall transmit these findings to the State Party concerned together with any comments and recommendations.
(4) The State Party concerned shall, within six months of receiving the findings, comments and recommendations transmitted by the Committee, submit its observations to the Committee. 5. Such an inquiry shall be conducted confidentially and the cooperation of the State Party shall be sought at all stages of the proceedings.

Article 9. (1) The Committee may invite the State Party concerned to include in its report under article 18 of the Convention details of any measures taken in response to an inquiry conducted under article 8 of the present Protocol.
(2) The Committee may, if necessary, after the end of the period of six months referred to in article 8.4, invite the State Party concerned to inform it of the measures taken in response to such an inquiry.

Article 10. (1) Each State Party may, at the time of signature or ratification of the present Protocol or accession thereto, declare that it does not recognize the competence of the Committee provided for in articles 8 and 9.
(2) Any State Party having made a declaration in accordance with paragraph (1) of the present article may, at any time, withdraw this declaration by notification to the Secretary-General.

Article 11. A State Party shall take all appropriate steps to ensure that individuals under its jurisdiction are not subjected to ill treatment or intimidation as a consequence of communicating with the Committee pursuant to the present Protocol.

Article 12. The Committee shall include in its annual report under article 21 of the Convention a summary of its activities under the present Protocol.

Article 13. Each State Party undertakes to make widely known and to give publicity to the Convention and the present Protocol and to facilitate access to information about the views and recommendations of the Committee, in particular, on matters involving that State Party.

Article 14. The Committee shall develop its own rules of procedure to be followed when exercising the functions conferred on it by the present Protocol.

Article 15. (1) The present Protocol shall be open for signature by any State that has signed, ratified or acceded to the Convention.
(2) The present Protocol shall be subject to ratification by any State that has ratified or acceded to the Convention. Instruments of ratification shall be deposited with the Secretary-General of the United Nations.
(3) The present Protocol shall be open to accession by any State that has ratified or acceded to the Convention.

(4) Accession shall be effected by the deposit of an instrument of accession with the Secretary-General of the United Nations.

Article 16. (1) The present Protocol shall enter into force three months after the date of the deposit with the Secretary-General of the United Nations of the tenth instrument of ratification or accession.
(2) For each State ratifying the present Protocol or acceding to it after its entry into force, the present Protocol shall enter into force three months after the date of the deposit of its own instrument of ratification or accession.

Article 17. No reservations to the present Protocol shall be permitted.

Article 18. (1) Any State Party may propose an amendment to the present Protocol and file it with the Secretary General of the United Nations. The Secretary-General shall thereupon communicate any proposed amendments to the States Parties with a request that they notify her or him whether they favour a conference of States Parties for the purpose of considering and voting on the proposal. In the event that at least one third of the States Parties favour such a conference, the Secretary-General shall convene the conference under the auspices of the United Nations. Any amendment adopted by a majority of the States Parties present and voting at the conference shall be submitted to the General Assembly of the United Nations for approval.
(2) Amendments shall come into force when they have been approved by the General Assembly of the United Nations and accepted by a two-thirds majority of the States Parties to the present Protocol in accordance with their respective constitutional processes.
(3) When amendments come into force, they shall be binding on those States Parties that have accepted them, other States Parties still being bound by the provisions of the present Protocol and any earlier amendments that they have accepted.

Article 19. (1) Any State Party may denounce the present Protocol at any time by written notification addressed to the Secretary-General of the United Nations. Denunciation shall take effect six months after the date of receipt of the notification by the Secretary-General.
(2) Denunciation shall be without prejudice to the continued application of the provisions of the present Protocol to any communication submitted under article 2 or any inquiry initiated under article 8 before the effective date of denunciation.

Article 20. The Secretary-General of the United Nations shall inform all States of:
(a) Signatures, ratifications and accessions under the present Protocol;
(b) The date of entry into force of the present Protocol and of any amendment under article 18;
(c) Any denunciation under article 19.

Article 21. (1) The present Protocol, of which the Arabic, Chinese, English, French, Russian and Spanish texts are equally authentic, shall be deposited in the archives of the United Nations.
(2) The Secretary-General of the United Nations shall transmit certified copies of the present Protocol to all States referred to in article 25 of the Convention.

PART II   FUNDAMENTAL RIGHTS

Convention against Torture and Other Cruel, Inhuman or Degrading Treatment or Punishment (CAT)
New York 10 December 1984,
1465 UNTS 85

The States Parties to this Convention,
Considering that, in accordance with the principles proclaimed in the Charter of the United Nations, recognition of the equal and inalienable rights of all members of the human family is the foundation of freedom, justice and peace in the world,
Recognizing that those rights derive from the inherent dignity of the human person,
Considering the obligation of States under the Charter, in particular Article 55, to promote universal respect for, and observance of, human rights and fundamental freedoms,
Having regard to article 5 of the Universal Declaration of Human Rights and article 7 of the International Covenant on Civil and Political Rights, both of which provide that no one shall be subjected to torture or to cruel, inhuman or degrading treatment or punishment,
Having regard also to the Declaration on the Protection of All Persons from Being Subjected to Torture and Other Cruel, Inhuman or Degrading Treatment or Punishment, adopted by the General Assembly on 9 December 1975,
Desiring to make more effective the struggle against torture and other cruel, inhuman or degrading treatment or punishment throughout the world,
Have agreed as follows:

Part I

Article 1. (1) For the purposes of this Convention, the term "torture" means any act by which severe pain or suffering, whether physical or mental, is intentionally inflicted on a person for such purposes as obtaining from him or a third person information or a confession, punishing him for an act he or a third person has committed or is suspected of having committed, or intimidating or coercing him or a third person, or for any reason based on discrimination of any kind, when such pain or suffering is inflicted by or at the instigation of or with the consent or acquiescence of a public official or other person acting in an official capacity. It does not include pain or suffering arising only from, inherent in or incidental to lawful sanctions.
(2) This article is without prejudice to any international instrument or national legislation which does or may contain provisions of wider application.

Article 2. (1) Each State Party shall take effective legislative, administrative, judicial or other measures to prevent acts of torture in any territory under its jurisdiction.
(2) No exceptional circumstances whatsoever, whether a state of war or a threat of war, internal political instability or any other public emergency, may be invoked as a justification of torture.
(3) An order from a superior officer or a public authority may not be invoked as a justification of torture.

Article 3. (1) No State Party shall expel, return ("refouler") or extradite a person to another State where there are substantial grounds for believing that he would be in danger of being subjected to torture.
(2) For the purpose of determining whether there are such grounds, the competent authorities shall take into account all relevant considerations including, where applicable, the existence in the State concerned of a consistent pattern of gross, flagrant or mass violations of human rights.

Article 4. (1) Each State Party shall ensure that all acts of torture are offences under its criminal law. The same shall apply to an attempt to commit torture and to an act by any person which constitutes complicity or participation in torture.
2. Each State Party shall make these offences punishable by appropriate penalties which take into account their grave nature.

Article 5. (1) Each State Party shall take such measures as may be necessary to establish its jurisdiction over the offences referred to in article 4 in the following cases:
(a) When the offences are committed in any territory under its jurisdiction or on board a ship or aircraft registered in that State;
(b) When the alleged offender is a national of that State;
(c) When the victim is a national of that State if that State considers it appropriate.
(2) Each State Party shall likewise take such measures as may be necessary to establish its jurisdic-

tion over such offences in cases where the alleged offender is present in any territory under its jurisdiction and it does not extradite him pursuant to article 8 to any of the States mentioned in paragraph (I) of this article.
(3) This Convention does not exclude any criminal jurisdiction exercised in accordance with internal law.

Article 6. (1) Upon being satisfied, after an examination of information available to it, that the circumstances so warrant, any State Party in whose territory a person alleged to have committed any offence referred to in
article 4 is present shall take him into custody or take other legal measures to ensure his presence. The custody and other legal measures shall be as provided in the law of that State but may be continued only for such time as is necessary to enable any criminal or extradition proceedings to be instituted.
(2) Such State shall immediately make a preliminary inquiry into the facts.
(3) Any person in custody pursuant to paragraph (I) of this article shall be assisted in communicating immediately with the nearest appropriate representative of the State of which he is a national, or, if he is a stateless person, with the representative of the State where he usually resides.
(4) When a State, pursuant to this article, has taken a person into custody, it shall immediately notify the States referred to in article 5, paragraph (1), of the fact that such person is in custody and of the circumstances which warrant his detention. The State which makes the preliminary inquiry contemplated in paragraph (2) of this article shall promptly report its findings to the said States and shall indicate whether it intends to exercise jurisdiction.

Article 7. (1) The State Party in the territory under whose jurisdiction a person alleged to have committed any offence referred to in article 4 is found shall in the cases contemplated in article 5, if it does not extradite him, submit the case to its competent authorities for the purpose of prosecution.
(2) These authorities shall take their decision in the same manner as in the case of any ordinary offence of a serious nature under the law of that State. In the cases referred to in article 5, paragraph (2), the standards of evidence required for prosecution and conviction shall in no way be less stringent than those which apply in the cases referred to in article 5, paragraph (1).
(3) Any person regarding whom proceedings are brought in connection with any of the offences referred to in article 4 shall be guaranteed fair treatment at all stages of the proceedings.

Article 8. (1) The offences referred to in article 4 shall be deemed to be included as extraditable offences in any extradition treaty existing between States Parties. States Parties undertake to include such offences as extraditable offences in every extradition treaty to be concluded between them.
(2) If a State Party which makes extradition conditional on the existence of a treaty receives a request for extradition from another State Party with which it has no extradition treaty, it may consider this Convention as the legal basis for extradition in respect of such offences. Extradition shall be subject to the other conditions provided by the law of the requested State. (3) States Parties which do not make extradition conditional on the existence of a treaty shall recognize such offences as extraditable offences between themselves subject to the conditions provided by the law of the requested State.
(4) Such offences shall be treated, for the purpose of extradition between States Parties, as if they had been committed not only in the place in which they occurred but also in the territories of the States required to establish their jurisdiction in accordance with article 5, paragraph (1).

Article 9. (1) States Parties shall afford one another the greatest measure of assistance in connection with criminal proceedings brought in respect of any of the offences referred to in article 4, including the supply of all evidence at their disposal necessary for the proceedings. (2) States Parties shall carry out their obligations under paragraph (I) of this article in conformity with any treaties on mutual judicial assistance that may exist between them.

Article 10. (1) Each State Party shall ensure that education and information regarding the prohibition against torture are fully included in the training of law enforcement personnel, civil or military, medical personnel, public officials and other persons who may be involved in the custody, interrogation or treatment of any individual subjected to any form of arrest, detention or imprisonment.
(2) Each State Party shall include this prohibition in the rules or instructions issued in regard to the duties and functions of any such person.

Article 11. Each State Party shall keep under systematic review interrogation rules, instructions, methods and practices as well as arrangements for the custody and treatment of persons subjected to any form of arrest, detention or imprisonment in any territory under its jurisdiction, with a view to preventing any cases of torture.

PART II   FUNDAMENTAL RIGHTS

Article 12. Each State Party shall ensure that its competent authorities proceed to a prompt and impartial investigation, wherever there is reasonable ground to believe that an act of torture has been committed in any territory under its jurisdiction.

Article 13. Each State Party shall ensure that any individual who alleges he has been subjected to torture in any territory under its jurisdiction has the right to complain to, and to have his case promptly and impartially examined by, its competent authorities. Steps shall be taken to ensure that the complainant and witnesses are protected against all ill-treatment or intimidation as a consequence of his complaint or any evidence given.

Article 14. (1) Each State Party shall ensure in its legal system that the victim of an act of torture obtains redress and has an enforceable right to fair and adequate compensation, including the means for as full rehabilitation as possible. In the event of the death of the victim as a result of an act of torture, his dependants shall be entitled to compensation.
(2) Nothing in this article shall affect any right of the victim or other persons to compensation which may exist under national law.

Article 15. Each State Party shall ensure that any statement which is established to have been made as a result of torture shall not be invoked as evidence in any proceedings, except against a person accused of torture as evidence that the statement was made.

Article 16. (1) Each State Party shall undertake to prevent in any territory under its jurisdiction other acts of cruel, inhuman or degrading treatment or punishment which do not amount to torture as defined in article I, when such acts are committed by or at the instigation of or with the consent or acquiescence of a public official or other person acting in an official capacity. In particular, the obligations contained in articles 10, 11, 12 and 13 shall apply with the substitution for references to torture of references to other forms of cruel, inhuman or degrading treatment or punishment.
(2) The provisions of this Convention are without prejudice to the provisions of any other international instrument or national law which prohibits cruel, inhuman or degrading treatment or punishment or which relates to extradition or expulsion.

Part II

Article 17. (1) There shall be established a Committee against Torture (hereinafter referred to as the Committee) which shall carry out the functions hereinafter provided. The Committee shall consist of ten experts of high moral standing and recognized competence in the field of human rights, who shall serve in their personal capacity. The experts shall be elected by the States Parties, consideration being given to equitable geographical distribution and to the usefulness of the participation of some persons having legal experience.
(2) The members of the Committee shall be elected by secret ballot from a list of persons nominated by States Parties. Each State Party may nominate one person from among its own nationals. States Parties shall bear in mind the usefulness of nominating persons who are also members of the Human Rights Committee established under the International Covenant on Civil and Political Rights and who are willing to serve on the Committee against Torture.
(3) Elections of the members of the Committee shall be held at biennial meetings of States Parties convened by the Secretary-General of the United Nations. At those meetings, for which two thirds of the States Parties shall constitute a quorum, the persons elected to the Committee shall be those who obtain the largest number of votes and an absolute majority of the votes of the representatives of States Parties present and voting.
(4) The initial election shall be held no later than six months after the date of the entry into force of this Convention. At least four months before the date of each election, the Secretary-General of the United Nations shall address a letter to the States Parties inviting them to submit their nominations within three months. The Secretary-General shall prepare a list in alphabetical order of all persons thus nominated, indicating the States Parties which have nominated them, and shall submit it to the States Parties.
(5) The members of the Committee shall be elected for a term of four years. They shall be eligible for re-election if renominated. However, the term of five of the members elected at the first election shall expire at the end of two years; immediately after the first election the names of these five members shall be chosen by lot by the chairman of the meeting referred to in paragraph (3) of this article.
(6) If a member of the Committee dies or resigns or for any other cause can no longer perform his Committee duties, the State Party which nominated him shall appoint another expert from among its nationals to serve for the remainder of his term, subject to the approval of the majority of the States

Parties. The approval shall be considered given unless half or more of the States Parties respond negatively within six weeks after having been informed by the Secretary-General of the United Nations of the proposed appointment.
(7) States Parties shall be responsible for the expenses of the members of the Committee while they are in performance of Committee duties.

Article 18. (1) The Committee shall elect its officers for a term of two years. They may be re-elected.
(2) The Committee shall establish its own rules of procedure, but these rules shall provide, inter alia, that: (a) Six members shall constitute a quorum; (b) Decisions of the Committee shall be made by a majority vote of the members present.
(3) The Secretary-General of the United Nations shall provide the necessary staff and facilities for the effective performance of the functions of the Committee under this Convention.
(4) The Secretary-General of the United Nations shall convene the initial meeting of the Committee. After its initial meeting, the Committee shall meet at such times as shall be provided in its rules of procedure.
(5) The States Parties shall be responsible for expenses incurred in connection with the holding of meetings of the States Parties and of the Committee, including reimbursement to the United Nations for any expenses, such as the cost of staff and facilities, incurred by the United Nations pursuant to paragraph (3) of this article.

Article 19. (1) The States Parties shall submit to the Committee, through the Secretary-General of the United Nations, reports on the measures they have taken to give effect to their undertakings under this Convention, within one year after the entry into force of the Convention for the State Party concerned. Thereafter the States Parties shall submit supplementary reports every four years on any new measures taken and such other reports as the Committee may request.
(2) The Secretary-General of the United Nations shall transmit the reports to all States Parties.
(3) Each report shall be considered by the Committee which may make such general comments on the report as it may consider appropriate and shall forward these to the State Party concerned. That State Party may respond with any observations it chooses to the Committee.
(4) The Committee may, at its discretion, decide to include any comments made by it in accordance with paragraph (3) of this article, together with the observations thereon received from the State Party concerned, in its annual report made in accordance with article 24. If so requested by the State Party concerned, the Committee may also include a copy of the report submitted under paragraph (I) of this article.

Article 20. (1) If the Committee receives reliable information which appears to it to contain well-founded indications that torture is being systematically practised in the territory of a State Party, the Committee shall invite that State Party to co-operate in the examination of the information and to this end to submit observations with regard to the information concerned. (2) Taking into account any observations which may have been submitted by the State Party concerned, as well as any other relevant information available to it, the Committee may, if it decides that this is warranted, designate one or more of its members to make a confidential inquiry and to report to the Committee urgently.
(3) If an inquiry is made in accordance with paragraph (2) of this article, the Committee shall seek the co-operation of the State Party concerned. In agreement with that State Party, such an inquiry may include a visit to its territory.
(4) After examining the findings of its member or members submitted in accordance with paragraph (2) of this article, the Commission shall transmit these findings to the State Party concerned together with any comments or suggestions which seem appropriate in view of the situation.
(5) All the proceedings of the Committee referred to in paragraphs (1) to (4) of this article s hall be confidential, and at all stages of the proceedings the co-operation of the State Party shall be sought. After such proceedings have been completed with regard to an inquiry made in accordance with paragraph (2), the Committee may, after consultations with the State Party concerned, decide to include a summary account of the results of the proceedings in its annual report made in accordance with article 24.

Article 21. (1) A State Party to this Convention may at any time declare under this article that it recognizes the competence of the Committee to receive and consider communications to the effect that a State Party claims that another State Party is not fulfilling its obligations under this Convention. Such communications may be received and considered according to the procedures laid down in this article only if submitted by a State Party which has made a declaration recognizing in regard to itself the competence of the Committee. No communication shall be dealt with by the Committee under this article if it concerns a State Party which has not made such a declaration. Communications received

PART II FUNDAMENTAL RIGHTS

under this article shall be dealt with in accordance with the following procedure;
(a) If a State Party considers that another State Party is not giving effect to the provisions of this Convention, it may, by written communication, bring the matter to the attention of that State Party. Within three months after the receipt of the communication the receiving State shall afford the State which sent the communication an explanation or any other statement in writing clarifying the matter, which should include, to the extent possible and pertinent, reference to domestic procedures and remedies taken, pending or available in the matter;
(b) If the matter is not adjusted to the satisfaction of both States Parties concerned within six months after the receipt by the receiving State of the initial communication, either State shall have the right to refer the matter to the Committee, by notice given to the Committee and to the other State;
(c) The Committee shall deal with a matter referred to it under this article only after it has ascertained that all domestic remedies have been invoked and exhausted in the matter, in conformity with the generally recognized principles of international law. This shall not be the rule where the application of the remedies is unreasonably prolonged or is unlikely to bring effective relief to the person who is the victim of the violation of this Convention;
(d) The Committee shall hold closed meetings when examining communications under this article;
(e) Subject to the provisions of subparagraph (e), the Committee shall make available its good offices to the States Parties concerned with a view to a friendly solution of the matter on the basis of respect for the obligations provided for in this Convention. For this purpose, the Committee may, when appropriate, set up an ad hoc conciliation commission;
(f) In any matter referred to it under this article, the Committee may call upon the States Parties concerned, referred to in subparagraph (b), to supply any relevant information;
(g) The States Parties concerned, referred to in subparagraph (b), shall have the right to be represented when the matter is being considered by the Committee and to make submissions orally and/or in writing;
(h) The Committee shall, within twelve months after the date of receipt of notice under subparagraph (b), submit a report:
(i) If a solution within the terms of subparagraph (e) is reached, the Committee shall confine its report to a brief statement of the facts and of the solution reached;
(ii) If a solution within the terms of subparagraph (e) is not reached, the Committee shall confine its report to a brief statement of the facts; the written submissions and record of the oral submissions made by the States Parties concerned shall be attached to the report. In every matter, the report shall be communicated to the States Parties concerned.
(2) The provisions of this article shall come into force when five States Parties to this Convention have made declarations under paragraph (1) of this article. Such declarations shall be deposited by the States Parties with the Secretary-General of the United Nations, who shall transmit copies thereof to the other States Parties. A declaration may be withdrawn at any time by notification to the Secretary-General. Such a withdrawal shall not prejudice the consideration of any matter which is the subject of a communication already transmitted under this article; no further communication by any State Party shall be received under this article after the notification of withdrawal of the declaration has been received by the Secretary-General, unless the State Party concerned has made a new declaration.

Article 22. (1) A State Party to this Convention may at any time declare under this article that it recognizes the competence of the Committee to receive and consider communications from or on behalf of individuals subject to its jurisdiction who claim to be victims of a violation by a State Party of the provisions of the Convention. No communication shall be received by the Committee if it concerns a State Party which has not made such a declaration.
(2) The Committee shall consider inadmissible any communication under this article which is anonymous or which it considers to be an abuse of the right of submission of such communications or to be incompatible with the provisions of this Convention.
(3) Subject to the provisions of paragraph (2), the Committee shall bring any communications submitted to it under this article to the attention of the State Party to this Convention which has made a declaration under paragraph (I) and is alleged to be violating any provisions of the Convention. Within six months, the receiving State shall submit to the Committee written explanations or statements clarifying the matter and the remedy, if any, that may have been taken by that State.
(4) The Committee shall consider communications received under this article in the light of all information made available to it by or on behalf of the individual and by the State Party concerned.
(5) The Committee shall not consider any communications from an individual under this article unless it has ascertained that:

(a) The same matter has not been, and is not being, examined under another procedure of international investigation or settlement;
(b) The individual has exhausted all available domestic remedies; this shall not be the rule where the application of the remedies is unreasonably prolonged or is unlikely to bring effective relief to the person who is the victim of the violation of this Convention.
(6) The Committee shall hold closed meetings when examining communications under this article.
(7) The Committee shall forward its views to the State Party concerned and to the individual. (8) The provisions of this article shall come into force when five States Parties to this Convention have made declarations under paragraph (1) of this article. Such declarations shall be deposited by the States Parties with the Secretary-General of the United Nations, who shall transmit copies thereof to the other States Parties. A declaration may be withdrawn at any time by notification to the Secretary-General. Such a withdrawal shall not prejudice the consideration of any matter which is the subject of a communication already transmitted under this article; no further communication by or on behalf of an individual shall be received under this article after the notification of withdrawal of the declaration has been received by the Secretary General, unless the State Party has made a new declaration.

Article 23. The members of the Committee and of the ad hoc conciliation commissions which may be appointed under article 21, paragraph (I) (e), shall be entitled to the facilities, privileges and immunities of experts on mission for the United Nations as laid down in the relevant sections of the Convention on the Privileges and Immunities of the United Nations.

Article 24. The Committee shall submit an annual report on its activities under this Convention to the States Parties and to the General Assembly of the United Nations.

Part III

Article 25. (1) This Convention is open for signature by all States.
(2) This Convention is subject to ratification. Instruments of ratification shall be deposited with the Secretary-General of the United Nations.

Article 26. This Convention is open to accession by all States. Accession shall be effected by the deposit of an instrument of accession with the Secretary General of the United Nations.

Article 27. (1) This Convention shall enter into force on the thirtieth day after the date of the deposit with the Secretary-General of the United Nations of the twentieth instrument of ratification or accession.
(2) For each State ratifying this Convention or acceding to it after the deposit of the twentieth instrument of ratification or accession, the Convention shall enter into force on the thirtieth day after the date of the deposit of its own instrument of ratification or accession.

Article 28. (1) Each State may, at the time of signature or ratification of this Convention or accession thereto, declare that it does not recognize the competence of the Committee provided for in article 20.
(2) Any State Party having made a reservation in accordance with paragraph (I) of this article may, at any time, withdraw this reservation by notification to the Secretary-General of the United Nations.

Article 29. (1) Any State Party to this Convention may propose an amendment and file it with the Secretary General of the United Nations. The Secretary General shall thereupon communicate the proposed amendment to the States Parties with a request that they notify him whether they favour a conference of States Parties for the purpose of considering and voting upon the proposal. In the event that within four months from the date of such communication at least one third of the States Parties favours such a conference, the Secretary General shall convene the conference under the auspices of the United Nations. Any amendment adopted by a majority of the States Parties present and voting at the conference shall be submitted by the Secretary-General to all the States Parties for acceptance.
(2) An amendment adopted in accordance with paragraph (I) of this article shall enter into force when two thirds of the States Parties to this Convention have notified the Secretary-General of the United Nations that they have accepted it in accordance with their respective constitutional processes.
(3) When amendments enter into force, they shall be binding on those States Parties which have accepted them, other States Parties still being bound by the provisions of this Convention and any earlier amendments which they have accepted.

Article 30. (1) Any dispute between two or more States Parties concerning the interpretation or application of this Convention which cannot be settled through negotiation shall, at the request of one of them, be submitted to arbitration. If within six months from the date of the request for arbitration the Parties are unable to agree on the organization of the arbitration, any one of those Parties may refer

PART II   FUNDAMENTAL RIGHTS

the dispute to the International Court of Justice by request in conformity with the Statute of the Court.
(2) Each State may, at the time of signature or ratification of this Convention or accession thereto, declare that it does not consider itself bound by paragraph I of this article. The other States Parties shall not be bound by paragraph (I) of this article with respect to any State Party having made such a reservation.
(3) Any State Party having made a reservation in accordance with paragraph (2) of this article may at any time withdraw this reservation by notification to the Secretary-General of the United Nations.

Article 31. (1) A State Party may denounce this Convention by written notification to the Secretary-General of the United Nations. Denunciation becomes effective one year after the date of receipt of the notification by the Secretary-General.
(2) Such a denunciation shall not have the effect of releasing the State Party from its obligations under this Convention in regard to any act or omission which occurs prior to the date at which the denunciation becomes effective, nor shall denunciation prejudice in any way the continued consideration of any matter which is already under consideration by the Committee prior to the date at which the denunciation becomes effective.
(3) Following the date at which the denunciation of a State Party becomes effective, the Committee shall not commence consideration of any new matter regarding that State.

Article 32. The Secretary-General of the United Nations shall inform all States Members of the United Nations and all States which have signed this Convention or acceded to it of the following:
(a) Signatures, ratifications and accessions under articles 25 and 26;
(b) The date of entry into force of this Convention under article 27 and the date of the entry into force of any amendments under article 29;
(c) Denunciations under article 31.

Article 33. (1) This Convention, of which the Arabic, Chinese, English, French, Russian and Spanish texts are equally authentic, shall be deposited with the Secretary-General of the United Nations.
(2) The Secretary-General of the United Nations shall transmit certified copies of this Convention to all States.

OPTIONAL PROTOCOL TO THE CONVENTION AGAINST TORTURE

Optional Protocol to the CAT
18 December 2002, Entry into force on 22 June 2006
United Nations General Assembly Resolution A/RES757/199

The States Parties to the present Protocol,
Reaffirming that torture and other cruel, inhuman or degrading treatment or punishment are prohibited and constitute serious violations of human rights,
Convinced that further measures are necessary to achieve the purposes of the Convention against Torture and Other Cruel, Inhuman or Degrading Treatment or Punishment (hereinafter referred to as the Convention) and to strengthen the protection of persons deprived of their liberty against torture and other cruel, inhuman or degrading treatment or punishment,
Recalling that articles 2 and 16 of the Convention oblige each State Party to take effective measures to prevent acts of torture and other cruel, inhuman or degrading treatment or punishment in any territory under its jurisdiction,
Recognizing that States have the primary responsibility for implementing those articles, that strengthening the protection of people deprived of their liberty and the full respect for their human rights is a common responsibility shared by all and that international implementing bodies complement and strengthen national measures,
Recalling that the effective prevention of torture and other cruel, inhuman or degrading treatment or punishment requires education and a combination of various legislative, administrative, judicial and other measures,
Recalling also that the World Conference on Human Rights firmly declared that efforts to eradicate torture should first and foremost be concentrated on prevention and called for the adoption of an optional protocol to the Convention, intended to establish a preventive system of regular visits to places of detention,
Convinced that the protection of persons deprived of their liberty against torture and other cruel, inhuman or degrading treatment or punishment can be strengthened by non-judicial means of a preventive nature, based on regular visits to places of detention,
Have agreed as follows:

Part I. General principles

Article 1. The objective of the present Protocol is to establish a system of regular visits undertaken by independent international and national bodies to places where people are deprived of their liberty, in order to prevent torture and other cruel, inhuman or degrading treatment or punishment.

Article 2. (1) A Subcommittee on Prevention of Torture and Other Cruel, Inhuman or Degrading Treatment or Punishment of the Committee against Torture (hereinafter referred to as the Subcommittee on Prevention) shall be established and shall carry out the functions laid down in the present Protocol.
(2) The Subcommittee on Prevention shall carry out its work within the framework of the Charter of the United Nations and shall be guided by the purposes and principles thereof, as well as the norms of the United Nations concerning the treatment of people deprived of their liberty.
(3) Equally, the Subcommittee on Prevention shall be guided by the principles of confidentiality, impartiality, non-selectivity, universality and objectivity.
(4) The Subcommittee on Prevention and the States Parties shall cooperate in the implementation of the present Protocol.

Article 3. Each State Party shall set up, designate or maintain at the domestic level one or several visiting bodies for the prevention of torture and other cruel, inhuman or degrading treatment or punishment (hereinafter referred to as the national preventive mechanism).

Article 4. (1) Each State Party shall allow visits, in accordance with the present Protocol, by the mechanisms referred to in articles 2 and 3 to any place under its jurisdiction and control where persons are or may be deprived of their liberty, either by virtue of an order given by a public authority or at its instigation or with its consent or acquiescence (hereinafter referred to as places of detention). These visits shall be undertaken with a view to strengthening, if necessary, the protection of these persons against torture and other cruel, inhuman or degrading treatment or punishment.
(2) For the purposes of the present Protocol, deprivation of liberty means any form of detention or imprisonment or the placement of a person in a public or private custodial setting which that person is not permitted to leave at will by order of any judicial, administrative or other authority.

PART II   FUNDAMENTAL RIGHTS

Part II. Subcommittee on Prevention

Article 5. (1) The Subcommittee on Prevention shall consist of ten members. After the fiftieth ratification of or accession to the present Protocol, the number of the members of the Subcommittee on Prevention shall increase to twenty-five.
(2) The members of the Subcommittee on Prevention shall be chosen from among persons of high moral character, having proven professional experience in the field of the administration of justice, in particular criminal law, prison or police administration, or in the various fields relevant to the treatment of persons deprived of their liberty.
(3) In the composition of the Subcommittee on Prevention due consideration shall be given to equitable geographic distribution and to the representation of different forms of civilization and legal systems of the States Parties.
(4) In this composition consideration shall also be given to balanced gender representation on the basis of the principles of equality and non-discrimination.
(5) No two members of the Subcommittee on Prevention may be nationals of the same State. (6) The members of the Subcommittee on Prevention shall serve in their individual capacity, shall be independent and impartial and shall be available to serve the Subcommittee on Prevention efficiently.

Article 6. (1) Each State Party may nominate, in accordance with paragraph (2) of the present article, up to two candidates possessing the qualifications and meeting the requirements set out in article 5, and in doing so shall provide detailed information on the qualifications of the nominees.
(2) (a) The nominees shall have the nationality of a State Party to the present Protocol;
(b) At least one of the two candidates shall have the nationality of the nominating State Party; (c) No more than two nationals of a State Party shall be nominated;
(d) Before a State Party nominates a national of another State Party, it shall seek and obtain the consent of that State Party.
(3) At least five months before the date of the meeting of the States Parties during which the elections will be held, the Secretary-General of the United Nations shall address a letter to the States Parties inviting them to submit their nominations within three months. The Secretary General shall submit a list, in alphabetical order, of all persons thus nominated, indicating the States Parties that have nominated them.

Article 7. (1) The members of the Subcommittee on Prevention shall be elected in the following manner:
(a) Primary consideration shall be given to the fulfilment of the requirements and criteria of article 5 of the present Protocol;
(b) The initial election shall be held no later than six months after the entry into force of the present Protocol;
(c) The States Parties shall elect the members of the Subcommittee on Prevention by secret ballot;
(d) Elections of the members of the Subcommittee on Prevention shall be held at biennial meetings of the States Parties convened by the Secretary-General of the United Nations. At those meetings, for which two thirds of the States Parties shall constitute a quorum, the persons elected to the Subcommittee on Prevention shall be those who obtain the largest number of votes and an absolute majority of the votes of the representatives of the States Parties present and voting.
(2) If during the election process two nationals of a State Party have become eligible to serve as members of the Subcommittee on Prevention, the candidate receiving the higher number of votes shall serve as the member of the Subcommittee on Prevention. Where nationals have received the same number of votes, the following procedure applies:
(a) Where only one has been nominated by the State Party of which he or she is a national, that national shall serve as the member of the Subcommittee on Prevention;
(b) Where both candidates have been nominated by the State Party of which they are nationals, a separate vote by secret ballot shall be held to determine which national shall become the member;
(c) Where neither candidate has been nominated by the State Party of which he or she is a national, a separate vote by secret ballot shall be held to determine which candidate shall be the member.

Article 8. If a member of the Subcommittee on Prevention dies or resigns, or for any cause can no longer perform his or her duties, the State Party that nominated the member shall nominate another eligible person possessing the qualifications and meeting the requirements set out in article 5, taking into account the need for a proper balance among the various fields of competence, to serve until the next meeting of the States Parties, subject to the approval of the majority of the States Parties. The approval shall be considered given unless half or more of the States Parties respond negatively within six weeks after having been informed by the Secretary-General of the United Nations of the proposed appointment.

Article 9. The members of the Subcommittee on Prevention shall be elected for a term of four years. They shall be eligible for re-election once if renominated. The term of half the members elected at the first election shall expire at the end of two years; immediately after the first election the names of those members shall be chosen by lot by the Chairman of the meeting referred to in article 7, paragraph (1)(d).

Article 10. (1) The Subcommittee on Prevention shall elect its officers for a term of two years. They may be re-elected.
(2) The Subcommittee on Prevention shall establish its own rules of procedure. These rules shall provide, inter alia, that:
(a) Half the members plus one shall constitute a quorum;
(b) Decisions of the Subcommittee on Prevention shall be made by a majority vote of the members present;
(c) The Subcommittee on Prevention shall meet in camera.
(3) The Secretary-General of the United Nations shall convene the initial meeting of the Subcommittee on Prevention. After its initial meeting, the Subcommittee on Prevention shall meet at such times as shall be provided by its rules of procedure. The Subcommittee on Prevention and the Committee against Torture shall hold their sessions simultaneously at least once a year.

Part III. Mandate of the Subcommittee on Prevention

Article 11. (1) The Subcommittee on Prevention shall:
(a) Visit the places referred to in article 4 and make recommendations to States Parties concerning the protection of persons deprived of their liberty against torture and other cruel, inhuman or degrading treatment or punishment;
(b) In regard to the national preventive mechanisms:
(i) Advise and assist States Parties, when necessary, in their establishment;
(ii) Maintain direct, and if necessary confidential, contact with the national preventive mechanisms and offer them training and technical assistance with a view to strengthening their capacities;
(iii) Advise and assist them in the evaluation of the needs and the means necessary to strengthen the protection of persons deprived of their liberty against torture and other cruel, inhuman or degrading treatment or punishment;
(iv) Make recommendations and observations to the States Parties with a view to strengthening the capacity and the mandate of the national preventive mechanisms for the prevention of torture and other cruel, inhuman or degrading treatment or punishment;
(c) Cooperate, for the prevention of torture in general, with the relevant United Nations organs and mechanisms as well as with the international, regional and national institutions or organizations working towards the strengthening of the protection of all persons against torture and other cruel, inhuman or degrading treatment or punishment.

Article 12. In order to enable the Subcommittee on Prevention to comply with its mandate as laid down in article 11, the States Parties undertake:
(a) To receive the Subcommittee on Prevention in their territory and grant it access to the places of detention as defined in article 4 of the present Protocol;
(b) To provide all relevant information the Subcommittee on Prevention may request to evaluate the needs and measures that should be adopted to strengthen the protection of persons deprived of their liberty against torture and other cruel, inhuman or degrading treatment or punishment;
(c) To encourage and facilitate contacts between the Subcommittee on Prevention and the national preventive mechanisms;
(d) To examine the recommendations of the Subcommittee on Prevention and enter into dialogue with it on possible implementation measures.

Article 13. (1) The Subcommittee on Prevention shall establish, at first by lot, a programme of regular visits to the States Parties in order to fulfil its mandate as established in article 11.
(2) After consultations, the Subcommittee on Prevention shall notify the States Parties of its programme in order that they may, without delay, make the necessary practical arrangements for the visits to be conducted.
(3) The visits shall be conducted by at least two members of the Subcommittee on Prevention. These members may be accompanied, if needed, by experts of demonstrated professional experience and

PART II   FUNDAMENTAL RIGHTS

knowledge in the fields covered by the present Protocol who shall be selected from a roster of experts prepared on the basis of proposals made by the States Parties, the Office of the United Nations High Commissioner for Human Rights and the United Nations Centre for International Crime Prevention. In preparing the roster, the States Parties 6 concerned shall propose no more than five national experts. The State Party concerned may oppose the inclusion of a specific expert in the visit, whereupon the Subcommittee on Prevention shall propose another expert.

(4) If the Subcommittee on Prevention considers it appropriate, it may propose a short follow up visit after a regular visit.

Article 14. (1) In order to enable the Subcommittee on Prevention to fulfil its mandate, the States Parties to the present Protocol undertake to grant it:

(a) Unrestricted access to all information concerning the number of persons deprived of their liberty in places of detention as defined in article 4, as well as the number of places and their location;

(b) Unrestricted access to all information referring to the treatment of those persons as well as their conditions of detention;

(c) Subject to paragraph (2) below, unrestricted access to all places of detention and their installations and facilities;

(d) The opportunity to have private interviews with the persons deprived of their liberty without witnesses, either personally or with a translator if deemed necessary, as well as with any other person who the Subcommittee on Prevention believes may supply relevant information;

(e) The liberty to choose the places it wants to visit and the persons it wants to interview.

(2) Objection to a visit to a particular place of detention may be made only on urgent and compelling grounds of national defence, public safety, natural disaster or serious disorder in the place to be visited that temporarily prevent the carrying out of such a visit. The existence of a declared state of emergency as such shall not be invoked by a State Party as a reason to object to a visit.

Article 15. No authority or official shall order, apply, permit or tolerate any sanction against any person or organization for having communicated to the Subcommittee on Prevention or to its delegates any information, whether true or false, and no such person or organization shall be otherwise prejudiced in any way.

Article 16. (1) The Subcommittee on Prevention shall communicate its recommendations and observations confidentially to the State Party and, if relevant, to the national preventive mechanism.

(2) The Subcommittee on Prevention shall publish its report, together with any comments of the State Party concerned, whenever requested to do so by that State Party. If the State Party makes part of the report public, the Subcommittee on Prevention may publish the report in whole or in part. However, no personal data shall be published without the express consent of the person concerned.

(3) The Subcommittee on Prevention shall present a public annual report on its activities to the Committee against Torture.

(4) If the State Party refuses to cooperate with the Subcommittee on Prevention according to articles 12 and 14, or to take steps to improve the situation in the light of the recommendations of the Subcommittee on Prevention, the Committee against Torture may, at the request of the Subcommittee on Prevention, decide, by a majority of its members, after the State Party has had an opportunity to make its views known, to make a public statement on the matter or to publish the report of the Subcommittee on Prevention.

Part IV. National preventive mechanisms

Article 17. Each State Party shall maintain, designate or establish, at the latest one year after the entry into force of the present Protocol or of its ratification or accession, one or several independent national preventive mechanisms for the prevention of torture at the domestic level. Mechanisms established by decentralized units may be designated as national preventive mechanisms for the purposes of the present Protocol if they are in conformity with its provisions.

Article 18. (1) The States Parties shall guarantee the functional independence of the national preventive mechanisms as well as the independence of their personnel.

(2) The States Parties shall take the necessary measures to ensure that the experts of the national preventive mechanism have the required capabilities and professional knowledge. They shall strive for a gender balance and the adequate representation of ethnic and minority groups in the country.

(3) The States Parties undertake to make available the necessary resources for the functioning of the national preventive mechanisms.

(4) When establishing national preventive mechanisms, States Parties shall give due consideration to

the Principles relating to the status of national institutions for the promotion and protection of human rights.

Article 19. The national preventive mechanisms shall be granted at a minimum the power:
(a) To regularly examine the treatment of the persons deprived of their liberty in places of detention as defined in article 4, with a view to strengthening, if necessary, their protection against torture and other cruel, inhuman or degrading treatment or punishment;
(b) To make recommendations to the relevant authorities with the aim of improving the treatment and the conditions of the persons deprived of their liberty and to prevent torture and other cruel, inhuman or degrading treatment or punishment, taking into consideration the relevant norms of the United Nations;
(c) To submit proposals and observations concerning existing or draft legislation.

Article 20. In order to enable the national preventive mechanisms to fulfil their mandate, the States Parties to the present Protocol undertake to grant them:
(a) Access to all information concerning the number of persons deprived of their liberty in places of detention as defined in article 4, as well as the number of places and their location; (b) Access to all information referring to the treatment of those persons as well as their conditions of detention;
(c) Access to all places of detention and their installations and facilities;
(d) The opportunity to have private interviews with the persons deprived of their liberty without witnesses, either personally or with a translator if deemed necessary, as well as with any other person who the national preventive mechanism believes may supply relevant information;
(e) The liberty to choose the places they want to visit and the persons they want to interview; (f) The right to have contacts with the Subcommittee on Prevention, to send it information and to meet with it.

Article 21. (1) No authority or official shall order, apply, permit or tolerate any sanction against any person or organization for having communicated to the national preventive mechanism any information, whether true or false, and no such person or organization shall be otherwise prejudiced in any way.
(2) Confidential information collected by the national preventive mechanism shall be privileged. No personal data shall be published without the express consent of the person concerned.

Article 22. The competent authorities of the State Party concerned shall examine the recommendations of the national preventive mechanism and enter into a dialogue with it on possible implementation measures.

Article 23. The States Parties to the present Protocol undertake to publish and disseminate the annual reports of the national preventive mechanisms.

Part V. Declaration

Article 24. (1) Upon ratification, States Parties may make a declaration postponing the implementation of their obligations under either part III or part IV of the present Protocol.
2. This postponement shall be valid for a maximum of three years. After due representations made by the State Party and after consultation with the Subcommittee on Prevention, the Committee against Torture may extend that period for an additional two years.

Part VI. Financial provisions

Article 25. (1) The expenditure incurred by the Subcommittee on Prevention in the implementation of the present Protocol shall be borne by the United Nations.
(2) The Secretary-General of the United Nations shall provide the necessary staff and facilities for the effective performance of the functions of the Subcommittee on Prevention under the present Protocol.

Article 26. (1) A Special Fund shall be set up in accordance with the relevant procedures of the General Assembly, to be administered in accordance with the financial regulations and rules of the United Nations, to help finance the implementation of the recommendations made by the Subcommittee on Prevention after a visit to a State Party, as well as education programmes of the national preventive mechanisms.
(2) The Special Fund may be financed through voluntary contributions made by Governments, intergovernmental and non-governmental organizations and other private or public entities.

PART II FUNDAMENTAL RIGHTS

Part VII. Final provisions

Article 27. (1) The present Protocol is open for signature by any State that has signed the Convention.
(2) The present Protocol is subject to ratification by any State that has ratified or acceded to the Convention. Instruments of ratification shall be deposited with the Secretary-General of the United Nations.
(3) The present Protocol shall be open to accession by any State that has ratified or acceded to the Convention.
(4) Accession shall be effected by the deposit of an instrument of accession with the Secretary General of the United Nations.
(5) The Secretary-General of the United Nations shall inform all States that have signed the present Protocol or acceded to it of the deposit of each instrument of ratification or accession.

Article 28. (1) The present Protocol shall enter into force on the thirtieth day after the date of deposit with the Secretary-General of the United Nations of the twentieth instrument of ratification or accession.
(2) For each State ratifying the present Protocol or acceding to it after the deposit with the Secretary-General of the United Nations of the twentieth instrument of ratification or accession, the present Protocol shall enter into force on the thirtieth day after the date of deposit of its own instrument of ratification or accession.

Article 29. The provisions of the present Protocol shall extend to all parts of federal States without any limitations or exceptions.

Article 30. No reservations shall be made to the present Protocol.

Article 31. The provisions of the present Protocol shall not affect the obligations of States Parties under any regional convention instituting a system of visits to places of detention. The Subcommittee on Prevention and the bodies established under such regional conventions are encouraged to consult and cooperate with a view to avoiding duplication and promoting effectively the objectives of the present Protocol.

Article 32. The provisions of the present Protocol shall not affect the obligations of States Parties to the four Geneva Conventions of 12 August 1949 and the Additional Protocols thereto of 8 June 1977, nor the opportunity available to any State Party to authorize the International Committee of the Red Cross to visit places of detention in situations not covered by international humanitarian law.

Article 33. (1) Any State Party may denounce the present Protocol at any time by written notification addressed to the Secretary-General of the United Nations, who shall thereafter inform the other States Parties to the present Protocol and the Convention. Denunciation shall take effect one year after the date of receipt of the notification by the Secretary-General.
(2) Such a denunciation shall not have the effect of releasing the St ate Party from its obligations under the present Protocol in regard to any act or situation that may occur prior to the date on which the denunciation becomes effective, or to the actions that the Subcommittee on Prevention has decided or may decide to take with respect to the State Party concerned, nor shall denunciation prejudice in any way the continued consideration of any matter already under consideration by the Subcommittee on Prevention prior to the date on which the denunciation becomes effective.
(3) Following the date on which the denunciation of the State Party becomes effective, the Subcommittee on Prevention shall not commence consideration of any new matter regarding that State.

Article 34. (1) Any State Party to the present Protocol may propose an amendment and file it with the Secretary-General of the United Nations. The Secretary-General shall thereupon communicate the proposed amendment to the States Parties to the present Protocol with a request that they notify him whether they favour a conference of States Parties for the purpose of considering and voting upon the proposal. In the event that within four months from the date of such communication at least one third of the States Parties favour such a conference, the Secretary-General shall convene the conference under the auspices of the United Nations. Any amendment adopted by a majority of two thirds of the States Parties present and voting at the conference shall be submitted by the Secretary-General of the United Nations to all States Parties for acceptance.
(2) An amendment adopted in accordance with paragraph (1) of the present article shall come into force when it has been accepted by a two -thirds majority of the States Parties to the present Protocol in accordance with their respective constitutional processes.

(3) When amendments come into force, they shall be binding on those States Parties that have accepted them, other States Parties still being bound by the provisions of the present Protocol and any earlier amendment that they have accepted.

Article 35. Members of the Subcommittee on Prevention and of the national preventive mechanisms shall be accorded such privileges and immunities as are necessary for the independent exercise of their functions. Members of the Subcommittee on Prevention shall be accorded the privileges and immunities specified in section 22 of the Convention on the Privileges and Immunities of the United Nations of 13 February 1946, subject to the provisions of section 23 of that Convention.

Article 36. When visiting a State Party, the members of the Subcommittee on Prevention shall, without prejudice to the provisions and purposes of the present Protocol and such privileges and immunities as they may enjoy:
(a) Respect the laws and regulations of the visited State;
(b) Refrain from any action or activity incompatible with the impartial and international nature of their duties.

Article 37. (1) The present Protocol, of which the Arabic, Chinese, English, French, Russian and Spanish texts are equally authentic, shall be deposited with the Secretary-General of the United Nations.
(2) The Secretary-General of the United Nations shall transmit certified copies of the present Protocol to all States.

PART II FUNDAMENTAL RIGHTS

Declaration on the Right to Development
Adopted by General Assembly resolution 41/128 of 4 December 1986

The General Assembly,
Having considered the question of the right to development,
Decides to adopt the Declaration on the Right to Development, the text of which is annexed to the present resolution.

Annex. Declaration on the Right to Development

The General Assembly,
Bearing in mind the purposes and principles of the Charter of the United Nations relating to the achievement of international co-operation in solving international problems of an economic, social, cultural or humanitarian nature, and in promoting and encouraging respect for human rights and fundamental freedoms for all without distinction as to race, sex, language or religion,
Recognizing that development is a comprehensive economic, social, cultural and political process, which aims at the constant improvement of the well-being of the entire population and of all individuals on the basis of their active, free and meaningful participation in development and in the fair distribution of benefits resulting therefrom,
Considering that under the provisions of the Universal Declaration of Human Rights everyone is entitled to a social and international order in which the rights and freedoms set forth in that Declaration can be fully realized,
Recalling the provisions of the International Covenant on Economic, Social and Cultural Rights and of the International Covenant on Civil and
Political Rights,
Recalling further the relevant agreements, conventions, resolutions, recommendations and other instruments of the United Nations and its specialized agencies concerning the integral development of the human being, economic and social progress and development of all peoples, including those instruments concerning decolonization, the prevention of discrimination, respect for and observance of, human rights and fundamental freedoms, the maintenance of international peace and security and the further promotion of friendly relations and co-operation among States in accordance with the Charter,
Recalling the right of peoples to self-determination, by virtue of which they have the right freely to determine their political status and to pursue their economic, social and cultural development,
Recalling also the right of peoples to exercise, subject to the relevant provisions of both International Covenants on Human Rights, full and complete sovereignty over all their natural wealth and resources,
Mindful of the obligation of States under the Charter to promote universal respect for and observance of human rights and fundamental freedoms for all without distinction of any kind such as race, colour, sex, language, religion, political or other opinion, national or social origin, property, birth or other status,
Considering that the elimination of the massive and flagrant violations of the human rights of the peoples and individuals affected by situations such as those resulting from colonialism, neo-colonialism, apartheid, all forms of racism and racial discrimination, foreign domination and occupation, aggression and threats against national sovereignty, national unity and territorial integrity and threats of war would contribute to the establishment of circumstances propitious to the development of a great part of mankind,
Concerned at the existence of serious obstacles to development, as well as to the complete fulfilment of human beings and of peoples, constituted, inter alia, by the denial of civil, political, economic, social and cultural rights, and considering that all human rights and fundamental freedoms are indivisible and interdependent and that, in order to promote development, equal attention and urgent consideration should be given to the implementation, promotion and protection of civil, political, economic, social and cultural rights and that, accordingly, the promotion of, respect for and enjoyment of certain human rights and fundamental freedoms cannot justify the denial of other human rights and fundamental freedoms,
Considering that international peace and security are essential elements for the realization of the right to development,
Reaffirming that there is a close relationship between disarmament and development and that progress in the field of disarmament would considerably promote progress in the field of development and that resources released through disarmament measures should be devoted to the economic and

social development and well-being of all peoples and, in particular, those of the developing countries,
Recognizing that the human person is the central subject of the development process and that development policy should therefore make the human being the main participant and beneficiary of development,
Recognizing that the creation of conditions favourable to the development of peoples and individuals is the primary responsibility of their States,
Aware that efforts at the international level to promote and protect human rights should be accompanied by efforts to establish a new international economic order,
Confirming that the right to development is an inalienable human right and that equality of opportunity for development is a prerogative both of nations and of individuals who make up nations,
Proclaims the following Declaration on the Right to Development:

Article 1. (1) The right to development is an inalienable human right by virtue of which every human person and all peoples are entitled to participate in, contribute to, and enjoy economic, social, cultural and political development, in which all human rights and fundamental freedoms can be fully realized.
(2) The human right to development also implies the full realization of the right of peoples to self-determination, which includes, subject to the relevant provisions of both International Covenants on Human Rights, the exercise of their inalienable right to full sovereignty over all their natural wealth and resources.

Article 2. (1) The human person is the central subject of development and should be the active participant and beneficiary of the right to development.
(2) All human beings have a responsibility for development, individually and collectively, taking into account the need for full respect for their human rights and fundamental freedoms as well as their duties to the community, which alone can ensure the free and complete fulfilment of the human being, and they should therefore promote and protect an appropriate political, social and economic order for development.
(3) States have the right and the duty to formulate appropriate national development policies that aim at the constant improvement of the well-being of the entire population and of all individuals, on the basis of their active, free and meaningful participation in development and in the fair distribution of the benefits resulting therefrom.

Article 3. (1) States have the primary responsibility for the creation of national and international conditions favourable to the realization of the right to development.
(2) The realization of the right to development requires full respect for the principles of international law concerning friendly relations and co-operation among States in accordance with the Charter of the United Nations.
(3) States have the duty to co-operate with each other in ensuring development and eliminating obstacles to development. States should realize their rights and fulfil their duties in such a manner as to promote a new international economic order based on sovereign equality, interdependence, mutual interest and co-operation among all States, as well as to encourage the observance and realization of human rights.

Article 4. (1) States have the duty to take steps, individually and collectively, to formulate international development policies with a view to facilitating the full realization of the right to development.
(2) Sustained action is required to promote more rapid development of developing countries. As a complement to the efforts of developing countries, effective international co-operation is essential in providing these countries with appropriate means and facilities to foster their comprehensive development.

Article 5. States shall take resolute steps to eliminate the massive and flagrant violations of the human rights of peoples and human beings affected by situations such as those resulting from apartheid, all forms of racism and racial discrimination, colonialism, foreign domination and occupation, aggression, foreign interference and threats against national sovereignty, national unity and territorial integrity, threats of war and refusal to recognize the fundamental right of peoples to self-determination.

Article 6. (1) All States should co-operate with a view to promoting, encouraging and strengthening universal respect for and observance of all human rights and fundamental freedoms for all without any distinction as to race, sex, language or religion.
(2) All human rights and fundamental freedoms are indivisible and interdependent; equal attention and urgent consideration should be given to the implementation, promotion and protection of civil,

PART II FUNDAMENTAL RIGHTS

political, economic, social and cultural rights.
(3) States should take steps to eliminate obstacles to development resulting from failure to observe civil and political rights, as well as economic, social and cultural rights.

Article 7. All States should promote the establishment, maintenance and strengthening of international peace and security and, to that end, should do their utmost to achieve general and complete disarmament under effective international control, as well as to ensure that the resources released by effective disarmament measures are used for comprehensive development, in particular that of the developing countries.

Article 8. (1) States should undertake, at the national level, all necessary measures for the realization of the right to development and shall ensure, inter alia, equality of opportunity for all in their access to basic resources, education, health services, food, housing, employment and the fair distribution of income. Effective measures should be undertaken to ensure that women have an active role in the development process. Appropriate economic and social reforms should be carried out with a view to eradicating all social injustices.
(2) States should encourage popular participation in all spheres as an important factor in development and in the full realization of all human rights.

Article 9. (1) All the aspects of the right to development set forth in the present Declaration are indivisible and interdependent and each of them should be considered in the context of the whole.
(2) Nothing in the present Declaration shall be construed as being contrary to the purposes and principles of the United Nations, or as implying that any State, group or person has a right to engage in any activity or to perform any act aimed at the violation of the rights set forth in the Universal Declaration of Human Rights and in the International Covenants on Human Rights.

Article 10. Steps should be taken to ensure the full exercise and progressive enhancement of the right to development, including the formulation, adoption and implementation of policy, legislative and other measures at the national and international levels.

CONVENTION ON THE RIGHTS OF THE CHILD

Convention on the Rights of the Child (CRC)
Adopted and opened for signature, ratification and accession by General Assembly resolution 44/25 of 20 November 1989, Entry into force 2 September 1990, in accordance with Article 49

The States Parties to the present Convention,
Considering that, in accordance with the principles proclaimed in the Charter of the United Nations, recognition of the inherent dignity and of the equal and inalienable rights of all members of the human family is the foundation of freedom, justice and peace in the world,
Bearing in mind that the peoples of the United Nations have, in the Charter, reaffirmed their faith in fundamental human rights and in the dignity and worth of the human person, and have determined to promote social progress and better standards of life in larger freedom,
Recognizing that the United Nations has, in the Universal Declaration of Human Rights and in the International Covenants on Human Rights, proclaimed and agreed that everyone is entitled to all the rights and freedoms set forth therein, without distinction of any kind, such as race, colour, sex, language, religion, political or other opinion, national or social origin, property, birth or other status,
Recalling that, in the Universal Declaration of Human Rights, the United Nations has proclaimed that childhood is entitled to special care and assistance,
Convinced that the family, as the fundamental group of society and the natural environment for the growth and well-being of all its members and particularly children, should be afforded the necessary protection and assistance so that it can fully assume its responsibilities within the community,
Recognizing that the child, for the full and harmonious development of his or her personality, should grow up in a family environment, in an atmosphere of happiness, love and understanding,
Considering that the child should be fully prepared to live an individual life in society, and brought up in the spirit of the ideals proclaimed in the Charter of the United Nations, and in particular in the spirit of peace, dignity, tolerance, freedom, equality and solidarity,
Bearing in mind that the need to extend particular care to the child has been stated in the Geneva Declaration of the Rights of the Child of 1924 and in the Declaration of the Rights of the Child adopted by the General Assembly on 20 November 1959 and recognized in the Universal Declaration of Human Rights, in the International Covenant on Civil and Political Rights (in particular in articles 23 and 24), in the International Covenant on Economic, Social and Cultural Rights (in particular in article 10) and in the statutes and relevant instruments of specialized agencies and international organizations concerned with the welfare of children,
Bearing in mind that, as indicated in the Declaration of the Rights of the Child, "the child, by reason of his physical and mental immaturity, needs special safeguards and care, including appropriate legal protection, before as well as after birth", Recalling the provisions of the
Declaration on Social and Legal Principles relating to the Protection and Welfare of Children, with Special Reference to Foster Placement and Adoption Nationally and Internationally; the United Nations Standard Minimum Rules for the Administration of Juvenile Justice (The Beijing Rules); and the Declaration on the Protection of Women and Children in Emergency and Armed Conflict,
Recognizing that, in all countries in the world, there are children living in exceptionally difficult conditions, and that such children need special consideration,
Taking due account of the importance of the traditions and cultural values of each people for the protection and harmonious development of the child,
Recognizing the importance of international cooperation for improving the living conditions of children in every country, in particular in the developing countries,
Have agreed as follows:

Part I

Article 1. For the purposes of the present Convention, a child means every human being below the age of eighteen years unless under the law applicable to the child, majority is attained earlier.

Article 2. (1) States Parties shall respect and ensure the rights set forth in the present Convention to each child within their jurisdiction without discrimination of any kind, irrespective of the child's or his or her parent's or legal guardian's race, colour, sex, language, religion, political or other opinion, national, ethnic or social origin, property, disability, birth or other status.
(2) States Parties shall take all appropriate measures to ensure that the child is protected against all forms of discrimination or punishment on the basis of the status, activities, expressed opinions, or beliefs of the child's parents, legal guardians, or family members.

Article 3. (1) In all actions concerning children, whether undertaken by public or private social

PART II FUNDAMENTAL RIGHTS

welfare institutions, courts of law, administrative authorities or legislative bodies, the best interests of the child shall be a primary consideration.

(2) States Parties undertake to ensure the child such protection and care as is necessary for his or her well-being, taking into account the rights and duties of his or her parents, legal guardians, or other individuals legally responsible for him or her, and, to this end, shall take all appropriate legislative and administrative measures.

(3) States Parties shall ensure that the institutions, services and facilities responsible for the care or protection of children shall conform with the standards established by competent authorities, particularly in the areas of safety, health, in the number and suitability of their staff, as well as competent supervision.

Article 4. States Parties shall undertake all appropriate legislative, administrative, and other measures for the implementation of the rights recognized in the present Convention.

With regard to economic, social and cultural rights, States Parties shall undertake such measures to the maximum extent of their available resources and, where needed, within the framework of international co-operation.

Article 5. States Parties shall respect the responsibilities, rights and duties of parents or, where applicable, the members of the extended family or community as provided for by local custom, legal guardians or other persons legally responsible for the child, to provide, in a manner consistent with the evolving capacities of the child, appropriate direction and guidance in the exercise by the child of the rights recognized in the present Convention.

Article 6. (1) States Parties recognize that every child has the inherent right to life.

(2) States Parties shall ensure to the maximum extent possible the survival and development of the child.

Article 7. (1) The child shall be registered immediately after birth and shall have the right from birth to a name, the right to acquire a nationality and. as far as possible, the right to know and be cared for by his or her parents.

(2) States Parties shall ensure the implementation of these rights in accordance with their national law and their obligations under the relevant international instruments in this field, in particular where the child would otherwise be stateless.

Article 8. (1) States Parties undertake to respect the right of the child to preserve his or her identity, including nationality, name and family relations as recognized by law without unlawful interference.

(2) Where a child is illegally deprived of some or all of the elements of his or her identity, States Parties shall provide appropriate assistance and protection, with a view to re-establishing speedily his or her identity.

Article 9. (1) States Parties shall ensure that a child shall not be separated from his or her parents against their will, except when competent authorities subject to judicial review determine, in accordance with applicable law and procedures, that such separation is necessary for the best interests of the child. Such determination may be necessary in a particular case such as one involving abuse or neglect of the child by the parents, or one where the parents are living separately and a decision must be made as to the child's place of residence.

(2) In any proceedings pursuant to paragraph (1) of the present article, all interested parties shall be given an opportunity to participate in the proceedings and make their views known.

(3) States Parties shall respect the right of the child who is separated from one or both parents to maintain personal relations and direct contact with both parents on a regular basis, except if it is contrary to the child's best interests.

(4) Where such separation results from any action initiated by a State Party, such as the detention, imprisonment, exile, deportation or death (including death arising from any cause while the person is in the custody of the State) of one or both parents or of the child, that State Party shall, upon request, provide the parents, the child or, if appropriate, another member of the family with the essential information concerning the whereabouts of the absent member(s) of the family unless the provision of the information would be detrimental to the well-being of the child. States Parties shall further ensure that the submission of such a request shall of itself entail no adverse consequences for the person(s) concerned.

Article 10. (1) In accordance with the obligation of States Parties under article 9, paragraph (1), applications by a child or his or her parents to enter or leave a State Party for the purpose of family reunification shall be dealt with by States Parties in a positive, humane and expeditious manner.

States Parties shall further ensure that the submission of such a request shall entail no adverse consequences for the applicants and for the members of their family. (2) A child whose parents reside in different States shall have the right to maintain on a regular basis, save in exceptional circumstances personal relations and direct contacts with both parents. Towards that end and in accordance with the obligation of States Parties under article 9, paragraph (1), States Parties shall respect the right of the child and his or her parents to leave any country, including their 4 own, and to enter their own country. The right to leave any country shall be subject only to such restrictions as are prescribed by law and which are necessary to protect the national security, public order (ordre public), public health or morals or the rights and freedoms of others and are consistent with the other rights recognized in the present Convention.

Article 11. (1) States Parties shall take measures to combat the illicit transfer and non-return of children abroad.
(2) To this end, States Parties shall promote the conclusion of bilateral or multilateral agreements or accession to existing agreements.

Article 12. (1) States Parties shall assure to the child who is capable of forming his or her own views the right to express those views freely in all matters affecting the child, the views of the child being given due weight in accordance with the age and maturity of the child.
(2) For this purpose, the child shall in particular be provided the opportunity to be heard in any judicial and administrative proceedings affecting the child, either directly, or through a representative or an appropriate body, in a manner consistent with the procedural rules of national law.

Article 13. (1) The child shall have the right to freedom of expression; this right shall include freedom to seek, receive and impart information and ideas of all kinds, regardless of frontiers, either orally, in writing or in print, in the form of art, or through any other media of the child's choice.
(2) The exercise of this right may be subject to certain restrictions, but these shall only be such as are provided by law and are necessary:
(a) For respect of the rights or reputations of others; or
(b) For the protection of national security or of public order (*ordre public*), or of public health or morals.

Article 14. (1) States Parties shall respect the right of the child to freedom of thought, conscience and religion.
(2) States Parties shall respect the rights and duties of the parents and, when applicable, legal guardians, to provide direction to the child in the exercise of his or her right in a manner consistent with the evolving capacities of the child.
(3) Freedom to manifest one's religion or beliefs may be subject only to such limitations as are prescribed by law and are necessary to protect public safety, order, health or morals, or the fundamental rights and freedoms of others.

Article 15. (1) States Parties recognize the rights of the child to freedom of association and to freedom of peaceful assembly.
(2) No restrictions may be placed on the exercise of these rights other than those imposed in conformity with the law and which are necessary in a democratic society in the interests of national security or public safety, public order (*ordre public*), the protection of public health or morals or the protection of the rights and freedoms of others.

Article 16. (1) No child shall be subjected to arbitrary or unlawful interference with his or her privacy, family, home or correspondence, nor to unlawful attacks on his or her honour and reputation.
(2) The child has the right to the protection of the law against such interference or attacks.

Article 17. States Parties recognize the important function performed by the mass media and shall ensure that the child has access to information and material from a diversity of national and international sources, especially those aimed at the promotion of his or her social, spiritual and moral well-being and physical and mental health. To this end, States Parties shall:
(a) Encourage the mass media to disseminate information and material of social and cultural benefit to the child and in accordance with the spirit of article 29;
(b) Encourage international co-operation in the production, exchange and dissemination of such information and material from a diversity of cultural, national and international sources; (c) Encourage the production and dissemination of children's books;
(d) Encourage the mass media to have particular regard to the linguistic needs of the child who belongs to a minority group or who is indigenous;

PART II FUNDAMENTAL RIGHTS

(e) Encourage the development of appropriate guidelines for the protection of the child from information and material injurious to his or her well-being, bearing in mind the provisions of articles 13 and 18.

Article 18. (1) States Parties shall use their best efforts to ensure recognition of the principle that both parents have common responsibilities for the upbringing and development of the child. Parents or, as the case may be, legal guardians, have the primary responsibility for the upbringing and development of the child. The best interests of the child will be their basic concern.
(2) For the purpose of guaranteeing and promoting the rights set forth in the present Convention, States Parties shall render appropriate assistance to parents and legal guardians in the performance of their child-rearing responsibilities and shall ensure the development of institutions, facilities and services for the care of children.
(3) States Parties shall take all appropriate measures to ensure that children of working parents have the right to benefit from child-care services and facilities for which they are eligible.

Article 19. (1) States Parties shall take all appropriate legislative, administrative, social and educational measures to protect the child from all forms of physical or mental violence, injury or abuse, neglect or negligent treatment, maltreatment or exploitation, including sexual abuse, while in the care of parent(s), legal guardian(s) or any other person who has the care of the child.
(2) Such protective measures should, as appropriate, include effective procedures for the establishment of social programmes to provide necessary support for the child and for those who have the care of the child, as well as for other forms of prevention and for identification, reporting, referral, investigation, treatment and follow-up of instances of child maltreatment described heretofore, and, as appropriate, for judicial involvement.

Article 20. (1) A child temporarily or permanently deprived of his or her family environment, or in whose own best interests cannot be allowed to remain in that environment, shall be entitled to special protection and assistance provided by the State.
(2) States Parties shall in accordance with their national laws ensure alternative care for such a child.
(3) Such care could include, inter alia, foster placement, kafalah of Islamic law, adoption or if necessary placement in suitable institutions for the care of children. When considering solutions, due regard shall be paid to the desirability of continuity in a child's upbringing and to the child's ethnic, religious, cultural and linguistic background.

Article 21. States Parties that recognize and/or permit the system of adoption shall ensure that the best interests of the child shall be the paramount consideration and they shall:
(a) Ensure that the adoption of a child is authorized only by competent authorities who determine, in accordance with applicable law and procedures and on the basis of all pertinent and reliable information, that the adoption is permissible in view of the child's status concerning parents, relatives and legal guardians and that, if required, the persons concerned have given their informed consent to the adoption on the basis of such counselling as may be necessary;
(b) Recognize that inter-country adoption may be considered as an alternative means of child's care, if the child cannot be placed in a foster or an adoptive family or cannot in any suitable manner be cared for in the child's country of origin;
(c) Ensure that the child concerned by inter-country adoption enjoys safeguards and standards equivalent to those existing in the case of national adoption;
(d) Take all appropriate measures to ensure that, in inter-country adoption, the placement does not result in improper financial gain for those involved in it;
(e) Promote, where appropriate, the objectives of the present article by concluding bilateral or multilateral arrangements or agreements, and endeavour, within this framework, to ensure that the placement of the child in another country is carried out by competent authorities or organs.

Article 22. (1) States Parties shall take appropriate measures to ensure that a child who is seeking refugee status or who is considered a refugee in accordance with applicable international or domestic law and procedures shall, whether unaccompanied or accompanied by his or her parents or by any other person, receive appropriate protection and humanitarian assistance in the enjoyment of applicable rights set forth in the present Convention and in other international human rights or humanitarian instruments to which the said States are Parties.
(2) For this purpose, States Parties shall provide, as they consider appropriate, co-operation in any efforts by the United Nations and other competent intergovernmental organizations or nongovernmental organizations co-operating with the United Nations to protect and assist such a child and to trace the parents or other members of the family of any refugee child in order to obtain information

necessary for reunification with his or her family. In cases where no parents or other members of the family can be found, the child shall be accorded the same protection as any other child permanently or temporarily deprived of his or her family environment for any reason, as set forth in the present Convention.

Article 23. (1) States Parties recognize that a mentally or physically disabled child should enjoy a full and decent life, in conditions which ensure dignity, promote self-reliance and facilitate the child's active participation in the community.
(2) States Parties recognize the right of the disabled child to special care and shall encourage and ensure the extension, subject to available resources, to the eligible child and those responsible for his or her care, of assistance for which application is made and which is appropriate to the child's condition and to the circumstances of the parents or others caring for the child.
(3) Recognizing the special needs of a disabled child, assistance extended in accordance with paragraph (2) of the present article shall be provided free of charge, whenever possible, taking into account the financial resources of the parents or others caring for the child, and shall be designed to ensure that the disabled child has effective access to and receives education, training, health care services, rehabilitation services, preparation for employment and recreation opportunities in a manner conducive to the child's achieving the fullest possible social integration and individual development, including his or her cultural and spiritual development
(4) States Parties shall promote, in the spirit of international cooperation, the exchange of appropriate information in the field of preventive health care and of medical, psychological and functional treatment of disabled children, including dissemination of and access to information concerning methods of rehabilitation, education and vocational services, with the aim of enabling States Parties to improve their capabilities and skills and to widen their experience in these areas. In this regard, particular account shall be taken of the needs of developing countries.

Article 24. (1) States Parties recognize the right of the child to the enjoyment of the highest attainable standard of health and to facilities for the treatment of illness and rehabilitation of health. States Parties shall strive to ensure that no child is deprived of his or her right of access to such health care services.
(2) States Parties shall pursue full implementation of this right and, in particular, shall take appropriate measures:
(a) To diminish infant and child mortality;
(b) To ensure the provision of necessary medical assistance and health care to all children with emphasis on the development of primary health care;
(c) To combat disease and malnutrition, including within the framework of primary health care, through, inter alia, the application of readily available technology and through the provision of adequate nutritious foods and clean drinking-water, taking into consideration the dangers and risks of environmental pollution;
(d) To ensure appropriate pre-natal and post-natal health care for mothers;
(e) To ensure that all segments of society, in particular parents and children, are informed, have access to education and are supported in the use of basic knowledge of child health and nutrition, the advantages of breastfeeding, hygiene and environmental sanitation and the prevention of accidents;
(f) To develop preventive health care, guidance for parents and family planning education and services.
(3) States Parties shall take all effective and appropriate measures with a view to abolishing traditional practices prejudicial to the health of children.
(4) States Parties undertake to promote and encourage international co-operation with a view to achieving progressively the full realization of the right recognized in the present article. In this regard, particular account shall be taken of the needs of developing countries.

Article 25. States Parties recognize the right of a child who has been placed by the competent authorities for the purposes of care, protection or treatment of his or her physical or mental health, to a periodic review of the treatment provided to the child and all other circumstances relevant to his or her placement.

Article 26. (1) States Parties shall recognize for every child the right to benefit from social security, including social insurance, and shall take the necessary measures to achieve the full realization of this right in accordance with their national law.
(2) The benefits should, where appropriate, be granted, taking into account the resources and the circumstances of the child and persons having responsibility for the maintenance of the child, as well as any other consideration relevant to an application for benefits made by or on behalf of the child.

PART II FUNDAMENTAL RIGHTS

Article 27. (1) States Parties recognize the right of every child to a standard of living adequate for the child's physical, mental, spiritual, moral and social development.
(2) The parent(s) or others responsible for the child have the primary responsibility to secure, within their abilities and financial capacities, the conditions of living necessary for the child's development.
(3) States Parties, in accordance with national conditions and within their means, shall take appropriate measures to assist parents and others responsible for the child to implement this right and shall in case of need provide material assistance and support programmes, particularly with regard to nutrition, clothing and housing.
(4) States Parties shall take all appropriate measures to secure the recovery of maintenance for the child from the parents or other persons having financial responsibility for the child, both within the State Party and from abroad. In particular, where the person having financial responsibility for the child lives in a State different from that of the child, States Parties shall promote the accession to international agreements or the conclusion of such agreements, as well as the making of other appropriate arrangements.

Article 28. (1) States Parties recognize the right of the child to education, and with a view to achieving this right progressively and on the basis of equal opportunity, they shall, in particular:
(a) Make primary education compulsory and available free to all;
(b) Encourage the development of different forms of secondary education, including general and vocational education, make them available and accessible to every child, and take appropriate measures such as the introduction of free education and offering financial assistance in case of need;
(c) Make higher education accessible to all on the basis of capacity by every appropriate means;
(d) Make educational and vocational information and guidance available and accessible to all children;
(e) Take measures to encourage regular attendance at schools and the reduction of drop-out rates.
(2) States Parties shall take all appropriate measures to ensure that school discipline is administered in a manner consistent with the child's human dignity and in conformity with the present Convention.
(3) States Parties shall promote and encourage international cooperation in matters relating to education, in particular with a view to contributing to the elimination of ignorance and illiteracy throughout the world and facilitating access to scientific and technical knowledge and modern teaching methods. In this regard, particular account shall be taken of the needs of developing countries.

Article 29. (1) States Parties agree that the education of the child shall be directed to:
(a) The development of the child's personality, talents and mental and physical abilities to their fullest potential;
(b) The development of respect for human rights and fundamental freedoms, and for the principles enshrined in the Charter of the United Nations;
(c) The development of respect for the child's parents, his or her own cultural identity, language and values, for the national values of the country in which the child is living, the country from which he or she may originate, and for civilizations different from his or her own;
(d) The preparation of the child for responsible life in a free society, in the spirit of understanding, peace, tolerance, equality of sexes, and friendship among all peoples, ethnic, national and religious groups and persons of indigenous origin;
(e) The development of respect for the natural environment.
(2) No part of the present article or article 28 shall be construed so as to interfere with the liberty of individuals and bodies to establish and direct educational institutions, subject always to the observance of the principle set forth in paragraph (1) of the present article and to the requirements that the education given in such institutions shall conform to such minimum standards as may be laid down by the State.

Article 30. In those States in which ethnic, religious or linguistic minorities or persons of indigenous origin exist, a child belonging to such a minority or who is indigenous shall not be denied the right, in community with other members of his or her group, to enjoy his or her own culture, to profess and practise his or her own religion, or to use his or her own language.

Article 31. (1) States Parties recognize the right of the child to rest and leisure, to engage in play and recreational activities appropriate to the age of the child and to participate freely in cultural life and the arts.
(2) States Parties shall respect and promote the right of the child to participate fully in cultural and artistic life and shall encourage the provision of appropriate and equal opportunities for cultural, artistic, recreational and leisure activity.

Article 32. (1) States Parties recognize the right of the child to be protected from economic exploitation and from performing any work that is likely to be hazardous or to interfere with the child's education, or to be harmful to the child's health or physical, mental, spiritual, moral or social development.
(2) States Parties shall take legislative, administrative, social and educational measures to ensure the implementation of the present article. To this end, and having regard to the relevant provisions of other international instruments,
States Parties shall in particular:
(a) Provide for a minimum age or minimum ages for admission to employment;
(b) Provide for appropriate regulation of the hours and conditions of employment;
(c) Provide for appropriate penalties or other sanctions to ensure the effective enforcement of the present article.

Article 33. States Parties shall take all appropriate measures, including legislative, administrative, social and educational measures, to protect children from the illicit use of narcotic drugs and psychotropic substances as defined in the relevant international treaties, and to prevent the use of children in the illicit production and trafficking of such substances.

Article 34. States Parties undertake to protect the child from all forms of sexual exploitation and sexual abuse. For these purposes, States Parties shall in particular take all appropriate national, bilateral and multilateral measures to prevent:
(a) The inducement or coercion of a child to engage in any unlawful sexual activity;
(b) The exploitative use of children in prostitution or other unlawful sexual practices;
(c) The exploitative use of children in pornographic performances and materials.

Article 35. States Parties shall take all appropriate national, bilateral and multilateral measures to prevent the abduction of, the sale of or traffic in children for any purpose or in any form. Article 36 States Parties shall protect the child against all other forms of exploitation prejudicial to any aspects of the child's welfare.

Article 37. States Parties shall ensure that:
(a) No child shall be subjected to torture or other cruel, inhuman or degrading treatment or punishment. Neither capital punishment nor life imprisonment without possibility of release shall be imposed for offences committed by persons below eighteen years of age;
(b) No child shall be deprived of his or her liberty unlawfully or arbitrarily. The arrest, detention or imprisonment of a child shall be in conformity with the law and shall be used only as a measure of last resort and for the shortest appropriate period of time;
(c) Every child deprived of liberty shall be treated with humanity and respect for the inherent dignity of the human person, and in a manner which takes into account the needs of persons of his or her age. In particular, every child deprived of liberty shall be separated from adults unless it is considered in the child's best interest not to do so and shall have the right to maintain contact with his or her family through correspondence and visits, save in exceptional circumstances;
(d) Every child deprived of his or her liberty shall have the right to prompt access to legal and other appropriate assistance, as well as the right to challenge the legality of the deprivation of his or her liberty before a court or other competent, independent and impartial authority, and to a prompt decision on any such action.

Article 38. (1) States Parties undertake to respect and to ensure respect for rules of international humanitarian law applicable to them in armed conflicts which are relevant to the child.
(2) States Parties shall take all feasible measures to ensure that persons who have not attained the age of fifteen years do not take a direct part in hostilities.
(3) States Parties shall refrain from recruiting any person who has not attained the age of fifteen years into their armed forces. In recruiting among those persons who have attained the age of fifteen years but who have not attained the age of eighteen years, States Parties shall endeavour to give priority to those who are oldest.
(4) In accordance with their obligations under international humanitarian law to protect the civilian population in armed conflicts, States Parties shall take all feasible measures to ensure protection and care of children who are affected by an armed conflict.

Article 39. States Parties shall take all appropriate measures to promote physical and psychological recovery and social reintegration of a child victim of: any form of neglect, exploitation, or abuse; torture or any other form of cruel, inhuman or degrading treatment or punishment; or armed conflicts.

PART II FUNDAMENTAL RIGHTS

Such recovery and reintegration shall take place in an environment which fosters the health, self-respect and dignity of the child.

Article 40. (1) States Parties recognize the right of every child alleged as, accused of, or recognized as having infringed the penal law to be treated in a manner consistent with the promotion of the child's sense of dignity and worth, which reinforces the child's respect for the human rights and fundamental freedoms of others and which takes into account the child's age and the desirability of promoting the child's reintegration and the child's assuming a constructive role in society.
(2) To this end, and having regard to the relevant provisions of international instruments, States Parties shall, in particular, ensure that:
(a) No child shall be alleged as, be accused of, or recognized as having infringed the penal law by reason of acts or omissions that were not prohibited by national or international law at the time they were committed;
(b) Every child alleged as or accused of having infringed the penal law has at least the following guarantees:
(i) To be presumed innocent until proven guilty according to law;
(ii) To be informed promptly and directly of the charges against him or her, and, if appropriate, through his or her parents or legal guardians, and to have legal or other appropriate assistance in the preparation and presentation of his or her defence;
(iii) To have the matter determined without delay by a competent, independent and impartial authority or judicial body in a fair hearing according to law, in the presence of legal or other appropriate assistance and, unless it is considered not to be in the best interest of the child, in particular, taking into account his or her age or situation, his or her parents or legal guardians; (iv) Not to be compelled to give testimony or to confess guilt; to examine or have examined adverse witnesses and to obtain the participation and examination of witnesses on his or her behalf under conditions of equality;
(v) If considered to have infringed the penal law, to have this decision and any measures imposed in consequence thereof reviewed by a higher competent, independent and impartial authority or judicial body according to law;
(vi) To have the free assistance of an interpreter if the child cannot understand or speak the language used;
(vii) To have his or her privacy fully respected at all stages of the proceedings.
(3) States Parties shall seek to promote the establishment of laws, procedures, authorities and institutions specifically applicable to children alleged as, accused of, or recognized as having infringed the penal law, and, in particular:
(a) The establishment of a minimum age below which children shall be presumed not to have the capacity to infringe the penal law;
(b) Whenever appropriate and desirable, measures for dealing with such children without resorting to judicial proceedings, providing that human rights and legal safeguards are fully respected.
(4) A variety of dispositions, such as care, guidance and supervision orders; counselling; probation; foster care; education and vocational training programmes and other alternatives to institutional care shall be available to ensure that children are dealt with in a manner appropriate to their well-being and proportionate both to their circumstances and the offence.

Article 41. Nothing in the present Convention shall affect any provisions which are more conducive to the realization of the rights of the child and which may be contained in:
(a) The law of a State party; or
(b) International law in force for that State.

Part II

Article 42. States Parties undertake to make the principles and provisions of the Convention widely known, by appropriate and active means, to adults and children alike.

Article 43. (1) For the purpose of examining the progress made by States Parties in achieving the realization of the obligations undertaken in the present Convention, there shall be established a Committee on the Rights of the Child, which shall carry out the functions hereinafter provided.
(2) The Committee shall consist of ten experts of high moral standing and recognized competence in the field covered by this Convention. The members of the Committee shall be elected by States Parties from among their nationals and shall serve in their personal capacity, consideration being given to equitable geographical distribution, as well as to the principal legal systems.
(3) The members of the Committee shall be elected by secret ballot from a list of persons nominated by States Parties. Each State Party may nominate one person from among its own nationals.

(4) The initial election to the Committee shall be held no later than six months after the date of the entry into force of the present Convention and thereafter every second year. At least four months before the date of each election, the Secretary-General of the United Nations shall address a letter to States Parties inviting them to submit their nominations within two months. The Secretary-General shall subsequently prepare a list in alphabetical order of all persons thus nominated, indicating States Parties which have nominated them, and shall submit it to the States Parties to the present Convention.
(5) The elections shall be held at meetings of States Parties convened by the Secretary-General at United Nations Headquarters. At those meetings, for which two thirds of States Parties shall constitute a quorum, the persons elected to the Committee shall be those who obtain the largest number of votes and an absolute majority of the votes of the representatives of States Parties present and voting.
(6) The members of the Committee shall be elected for a term of four years. They shall be eligible for re-election if renominated. The term of five of the members elected at the first election shall expire at the end of two years; immediately after the first election, the names of these five members shall be chosen by lot by the Chairman of the meeting.
(7) If a member of the Committee dies or resigns or declares that for any other cause he or she can no longer perform the duties of the Committee, the State Party which nominated the member shall appoint another expert from among its nationals to serve for the remainder of the term, subject to the approval of the Committee.
(8) The Committee shall establish its own rules of procedure.
(9) The Committee shall elect its officers for a period of two years.
(10) The meetings of the Committee shall normally be held at United Nations Headquarters or at any other convenient place as determined by the Committee. The Committee shall normally meet annually. The duration of the meetings of the Committee shall be determined, and reviewed, if necessary, by a meeting of the States Parties to the present Convention, subject to the approval of the General Assembly.
(11) The Secretary-General of the United Nations shall provide the necessary staff and facilities for the effective performance of the functions of the Committee under the present Convention.
(12) With the approval of the General Assembly, the members of the Committee established under the present Convention shall receive emoluments from United Nations resources on such terms and conditions as the Assembly may decide.

Article 44. (1) States Parties undertake to submit to the Committee, through the Secretary-General of the United Nations, reports on the measures they have adopted which give effect to the rights recognized herein and on the progress made on the enjoyment of those rights (a) Within two years of the entry into force of the Convention for the State Party concerned; (b) Thereafter every five years.
(2) Reports made under the present article shall indicate factors and difficulties, if any, affecting the degree of fulfilment of the obligations under the present Convention. Reports shall also contain sufficient information to provide the Committee with a comprehensive understanding of the implementation of the Convention in the country concerned.
(3) A State Party which has submitted a comprehensive initial report to the Committee need not, in its subsequent reports submitted in accordance with paragraph (1) (b) of the present article, repeat basic information previously provided.
(4) The Committee may request from States Parties further information relevant to the implementation of the Convention.
(5) The Committee shall submit to the General Assembly, through the Economic and Social Council, every two years, reports on its activities. 6. States Parties shall make their reports widely available to the public in their own countries.

Article 45. In order to foster the effective implementation of the Convention and to encourage international cooperation in the field covered by the Convention:
(a) The specialized agencies, the United Nations Children's Fund, and other United Nations organs shall be entitled to be represented at the consideration of the implementation of such provisions of the present Convention as fall within the scope of their mandate. The Committee may invite the specialized agencies, the United Nations Children's Fund and other competent bodies as it may consider appropriate to provide expert advice on the implementation of the Convention in areas falling within the scope of their respective mandates. The Committee may invite the specialized agencies, the United Nations Children's Fund, and other United Nations organs to submit reports on the implementation of the Convention in areas falling within the scope of their activities;
(b) The Committee shall transmit, as it may consider appropriate, to the specialized agencies, the United Nations Children's Fund and other competent bodies, any reports from States Parties that

PART II FUNDAMENTAL RIGHTS

contain a request, or indicate a need, for technical advice or assistance, along with the Committee's observations and suggestions, if any, on these requests or indications;
(c) The Committee may recommend to the General Assembly to request the Secretary-General to undertake on its behalf studies on specific issues relating to the rights of the child; (d) The Committee may make suggestions and general recommendations based on information received pursuant to articles 44 and 45 of the present Convention. Such suggestions and general recommendations shall be transmitted to any State Party concerned and reported to the General Assembly, together with comments, if any, from States Parties.

Part III

Article 46. The present Convention shall be open for signature by all States.

Article 47. The present Convention is subject to ratification. Instruments of ratification shall be deposited with the Secretary-General of the United Nations.

Article 48. The present Convention shall remain open for accession by any State. The instruments of accession shall be deposited with the Secretary-General of the United Nations.

Article 49. (1) The present Convention shall enter into force on the thirtieth day following the date of deposit with the Secretary-General of the United Nations of the twentieth instrument of ratification or accession.
(2) For each State ratifying or acceding to the Convention after the deposit of the twentieth instrument of ratification or accession, the Convention shall enter into force on the thirtieth day after the deposit by such State of its instrument of ratification or accession.

Article 50. (1) Any State Party may propose an amendment and file it with the Secretary-General of the United Nations. The Secretary-General shall thereupon communicate the proposed amendment to States Parties, with a request that they indicate whether they favour a conference of States Parties for the purpose of considering and voting upon the proposals. In the event that, within four months from the date of such communication, at least one third of the States Parties favour such a conference, the Secretary-General shall convene the conference under the auspices of the United Nations. Any amendment adopted by a majority of States Parties present and voting at the conference shall be submitted to the General Assembly for approval.
(2) An amendment adopted in accordance with paragraph (1) of the present article shall enter into force when it has been approved by the General Assembly of the United Nations and accepted by a two thirds majority of States Parties.
(3) When an amendment enters into force, it shall be binding on those States Parties which have accepted it, other States Parties still being bound by the provisions of the present Convention and any earlier amendments which they have accepted.

Article 51. (1) The Secretary-General of the United Nations shall receive and circulate to all States the text of reservations made by States at the time of ratification or accession.
(2) A reservation incompatible with the object and purpose of the present Convention shall not be permitted.
(3) Reservations may be withdrawn at any time by notification to that effect addressed to the Secretary-General of the United Nations, who shall then inform all States. Such notification shall take effect on the date on which it is received by the Secretary-General

Article 52. A State Party may denounce the present Convention by written notification to the Secretary-General of the United Nations. Denunciation becomes effective one year after the date of receipt of the notification by the Secretary-General.

Article 53. The Secretary-General of the United Nations is designated as the depositary of the present Convention.

Article 54. The original of the present Convention, of which the Arabic, Chinese, English, French, Russian and Spanish texts are equally authentic, shall be deposited with the Secretary-General of the United Nations.

IN WITNESS THEREOF the undersigned plenipotentiaries, being duly authorized thereto by their respective governments, have signed the present Convention.

OPTIONAL PROTOCOL TO THE CRC

Optional Protocol to the CRC on the sale of children, child prostitution and child pornography
Adopted by General Assembly Resolution A/RES/54/263 of 25 May 2000; entered into force on 18 January 2002

The States Parties to the present Protocol,
Considering that, in order further to achieve the purposes of the Convention on the Rights of the Child and the implementation of its provisions, especially articles 1, 11, 21, 32, 33, 34, 35 and 36, it would be appropriate to extend the measures that States Parties should undertake in order to guarantee the protection of the child from the sale of children, child prostitution and child pornography,
Considering also that the Convention on the Rights of the Child recognizes the right of the child to be protected from economic exploitation and from performing any work that is likely to be hazardous or to interfere with the child's education, or to be harmful to the child's health or physical, mental, spiritual, moral or social development,
Gravely concerned at the significant and increasing international traffic in children for the purpose of the sale of children, child prostitution and child pornography,
Deeply concerned at the widespread and continuing practice of sex tourism, to which children are especially vulnerable, as it directly promotes the sale of children, child prostitution and child pornography,
Recognizing that a number of particularly vulnerable groups, including girl children, are at greater risk of sexual exploitation and that girl children are disproportionately represented among the sexually exploited,
Concerned about the growing availability of child pornography on the Internet and other evolving technologies, and recalling the International Conference on Combating Child Pornography on the Internet, held in Vienna in 1999, in particular its conclusion calling for the worldwide criminalization of the production, distribution, exportation, transmission, importation, intentional possession and advertising of child pornography, and stressing the importance of closer cooperation and partnership between Governments and the Internet industry,
Believing that the elimination of the sale of children, child prostitution and child pornography will be facilitated by adopting a holistic approach, addressing the contributing factors, including underdevelopment, poverty, economic disparities, inequitable socio-economic structure, dysfunctioning families, lack of education, urban-rural migration, gender discrimination, irresponsible adult sexual behaviour, harmful traditional practices, armed conflicts and trafficking in children,
Believing also that efforts to raise public awareness are needed to reduce consumer demand for the sale of children, child prostitution and child pornography, and believing further in the importance of strengthening global partnership among all actors and of improving law enforcement at the national level,
Noting the provisions of international legal instruments relevant to the protection of children, including the Hague Convention on Protection of Children and Cooperation in Respect of Intercountry Adoption, the Hague Convention on the Civil Aspects of International Child Abduction, the Hague Convention on Jurisdiction, Applicable Law, Recognition, Enforcement and Cooperation in Respect of Parental Responsibility and Measures for the Protection of Children, and International Labour Organization Convention No. 182 on the Prohibition and Immediate Action for the Elimination of the Worst Forms of Child Labour,
Encouraged by the overwhelming support for the Convention on the Rights of the Child, demonstrating the widespread commitment that exists for the promotion and protection of the rights of the child,
Recognizing the importance of the implementation of the provisions of the Programme of Action for the Prevention of the Sale of Children, Child Prostitution and Child Pornography and the Declaration and Agenda for Action adopted at the World Congress against Commercial Sexual Exploitation of Children, held in Stockholm from 27 to 31 August 1996, and the other relevant decisions and recommendations of pertinent international bodies,
Taking due account of the importance of the traditions and cultural values of each people for the protection and harmonious development of the child,
Have agreed as follows:

Article 1. States Parties shall prohibit the sale of children, child prostitution and child pornography as provided for by the present Protocol.

Article 2. For the purposes of the present Protocol:
(a) Sale of children means any act or transaction whereby a child is transferred by any person or group of persons to another for remuneration or any other consideration;

PART II   FUNDAMENTAL RIGHTS

(b) Child prostitution means the use of a child in sexual activities for remuneration or any other form of consideration;
(c) Child pornography means any representation, by whatever means, of a child engaged in real or simulated explicit sexual activities or any representation of the sexual parts of a child for primarily sexual purposes.

Article 3. (1) Each State Party shall ensure that, as a minimum, the following acts and activities are fully covered under its criminal or penal law, whether such offences are committed domestically or transnationally or on an individual or organized basis:
(a) In the context of sale of children as defined in article 2:
(i) Offering, delivering or accepting, by whatever means, a child for the purpose of:
(a) Sexual exploitation of the child;
(b) Transfer of organs of the child for profit;
(c) Engagement of the child in forced labour;
(ii) Improperly inducing consent, as an intermediary, for the adoption of a child in violation of applicable international legal instruments on adoption;
(b) Offering, obtaining, procuring or providing a child for child prostitution, as defined in article 2;
(c) Producing, distributing, disseminating, importing, exporting, offering, selling or possessing for the above purposes child pornography as defined in article 2.
(2) Subject to the provisions of the national law of a State Party, the same shall apply to an attempt to commit any of the said acts and to complicity or participation in any of the said acts.
(3) Each State Party shall make such offences punishable by appropriate penalties that take into account their grave nature.
(4) Subject to the provisions of its national law, each State Party shall take measures, where appropriate, to establish the liability of legal persons for offences established in paragraph (1) of the present article. Subject to the legal principles of the State Party, such liability of legal persons may be criminal, civil or administrative.
(5) States Parties shall take all appropriate legal and administrative measures to ensure that all persons involved in the adoption of a child act in conformity with applicable international legal instruments.

Article 4. (1) Each State Party shall take such measures as may be necessary to establish its jurisdiction over the offences referred to in article 3, paragraph (1), when the offences are committed in its territory or on board a ship or aircraft registered in that State.
(2) Each State Party may take such measures as may be necessary to establish its jurisdiction over the offences referred to in article 3, paragraph (1), in the following cases:
(a) When the alleged offender is a national of that State or a person who has his habitual residence in its territory;
(b) When the victim is a national of that State.
(3) Each State Party shall also take such measures as may be necessary to establish its jurisdiction over the aforementioned offences when the alleged offender is present in its territory and it does not extradite him or her to another State Party on the ground that the offence has been committed by one of its nationals.
(4) The present Protocol does not exclude any criminal jurisdiction exercised in accordance with internal law.

Article 5. (1) The offences referred to in article 3, paragraph (1), shall be deemed to be included as extraditable offences in any extradition treaty existing between States Parties and shall be included as extraditable offences in every extradition treaty subsequently concluded between them, in accordance with the conditions set forth in such treaties.
(2) If a State Party that makes extradition conditional on the existence of a treaty receives a request for extradition from another State Party with which it has no extradition treaty, it may consider the present Protocol to be a legal basis for extradition in respect of such offences. Extradition shall be subject to the conditions provided by the law of the requested State.
(3) States Parties that do not make extradition conditional on the existence of a treaty shall recognize such offences as extraditable offences between themselves subject to the conditions provided by the law of the requested State.
(4) Such offences shall be treated, for the purpose of extradition between States Parties, as if they had been committed not only in the place in which they occurred but also in the territories of the States required to establish their jurisdiction in accordance with article 4.
(5) If an extradition request is made with respect to an offence described in article 3, paragraph

(1), and the requested State Party does not or will not extradite on the basis of the nationality of the offender, that State shall take suitable measures to submit the case to its competent authorities for the purpose of prosecution.

Article 6. (1) States Parties shall afford one another the greatest measure of assistance in connection with investigations or criminal or extradition proceedings brought in respect of the offences set forth in article 3, paragraph (1), including assistance in obtaining evidence at their disposal necessary for the proceedings.
(2) States Parties shall carry out their obligations under paragraph (1) of the present article in conformity with any treaties or other arrangements on mutual legal assistance that may exist between them. In the absence of such treaties or arrangements, States Parties shall afford one another assistance in accordance with their domestic law.

Article 7. States Parties shall, subject to the provisions of their national law:
(a) Take measures to provide for the seizure and confiscation, as appropriate, of:
(i) Goods, such as materials, assets and other instrumentalities used to commit or facilitate offences under the present protocol;
(ii) Proceeds derived from such offences;
(b) Execute requests from another State Party for seizure or confiscation of goods or proceeds referred to in subparagraph (a);
(c) Take measures aimed at closing, on a temporary or definitive basis, premises used to commit such offences.

Article 8. (1) States Parties shall adopt appropriate measures to protect the rights and interests of child victims of the practices prohibited under the present Protocol at all stages of the criminal justice process, in particular by:
(a) Recognizing the vulnerability of child victims and adapting procedures to recognize their special needs, including their special needs as witnesses;
(b) Informing child victims of their rights, their role and the scope, timing and progress of the proceedings and of the disposition of their cases;
(c) Allowing the views, needs and concerns of child victims to be presented and considered in proceedings where their personal interests are affected, in a manner consistent with the procedural rules of national law;
(d) Providing appropriate support services to child victims throughout the legal process;
(e) Protecting, as appropriate, the privacy and identity of child victims and taking measures in accordance with national law to avoid the inappropriate dissemination of information that could lead to the identification of child victims;
(f) Providing, in appropriate cases, for the safety of child victims, as well as that of their families and witnesses on their behalf, from intimidation and retaliation;
(g) Avoiding unnecessary delay in the disposition of cases and the execution of orders or decrees granting compensation to child victims.
(2) States Parties shall ensure that uncertainty as to the actual age of the victim shall not prevent the initiation of criminal investigations, including investigations aimed at establishing the age of the victim.
(3) States Parties shall ensure that, in the treatment by the criminal justice system of children who are victims of the offences described in the present Protocol, the best interest of the child shall be a primary consideration.
(4) States Parties shall take measures to ensure appropriate training, in particular legal and psychological training, for the persons who work with victims of the offences prohibited under the present Protocol.
(5) States Parties shall, in appropriate cases, adopt measures in order to protect the safety and integrity of those persons and/or organizations involved in the prevention and/or protection and rehabilitation of victims of such offences.
(6) Nothing in the present article shall be construed to be prejudicial to or inconsistent with the rights of the accused to a fair and impartial trial.

Article 9. (1) States Parties shall adopt or strengthen, implement and disseminate laws, administrative measures, social policies and programmes to prevent the offences referred to in the present Protocol. Particular attention shall be given to protect children who are especially vulnerable to such practices.
(2) States Parties shall promote awareness in the public at large, including children, through information by all appropriate means, education and training, about the preventive measures and harmful

PART II   FUNDAMENTAL RIGHTS

effects of the offences referred to in the present Protocol. In fulfilling their obligations under this article, States Parties shall encourage the participation of the community and, in particular, children and child victims, in such information and education and training programmes, including at the international level.
(3) States Parties shall take all feasible measures with the aim of ensuring all appropriate assistance to victims of such offences, including their full social reintegration and their full physical and psychological recovery.
(4) States Parties shall ensure that all child victims of the offences described in the present Protocol have access to adequate procedures to seek, without discrimination, compensation for damages from those legally responsible.
(5) States Parties shall take appropriate measures aimed at effectively prohibiting the production and dissemination of material advertising the offences described in the present Protocol.

Article 10. (1) States Parties shall take all necessary steps to strengthen international cooperation by multilateral, regional and bilateral arrangements for the prevention, detection, investigation, prosecution and punishment of those responsible for acts involving the sale of children, child prostitution, child pornography and child sex tourism. States Parties shall also promote international cooperation and coordination between their authorities, national and international non-governmental organizations and international organizations.
(2) States Parties shall promote international cooperation to assist child victims in their physical and psychological recovery, social reintegration and repatriation.
(3) States Parties shall promote the strengthening of international cooperation in order to address the root causes, such as poverty and underdevelopment, contributing to the vulnerability of children to the sale of children, child prostitution, child pornography and child sex tourism.
(4) States Parties in a position to do so shall provide financial, technical or other assistance through existing multilateral, regional, bilateral or other programmes.

Article 11. Nothing in the present Protocol shall affect any provisions that are more conducive to the realization of the rights of the child and that may be contained in:
(a) The law of a State Party;
(b) International law in force for that State.

Article 12. (1) Each State Party shall, within two years following the entry into force of the present Protocol for that State Party, submit a report to the Committee on the Rights of the Child providing comprehensive information on the measures it has taken to implement the provisions of the Protocol.
(2) Following the submission of the comprehensive report, each State Party shall include in the reports they submit to the Committee on the Rights of the Child, in accordance with article 44 of the Convention, any further information with respect to the implementation of the present Protocol. Other States Parties to the Protocol shall submit a report every five years.
(3) The Committee on the Rights of the Child may request from States Parties further information relevant to the implementation of the present Protocol.

Article 13. (1) The present Protocol is open for signature by any State that is a party to the Convention or has signed it.
(2) The present Protocol is subject to ratification and is open to accession by any State that is a party to the Convention or has signed it. Instruments of ratification or accession shall be deposited with the Secretary- General of the United Nations.

Article 14. (1) The present Protocol shall enter into force three months after the deposit of the tenth instrument of ratification or accession.
(2) For each State ratifying the present Protocol or acceding to it after its entry into force, the Protocol shall enter into force one month after the date of the deposit of its own instrument of ratification or accession.

Article 15. (1) Any State Party may denounce the present Protocol at any time by written notification to the Secretary- General of the United Nations, who shall thereafter inform the other States Parties to the Convention and all States that have signed the Convention. The denunciation shall take effect one year after the date of receipt of the notification by the Secretary-General.
(2) Such a denunciation shall not have the effect of releasing the State Party from its obligations under the present Protocol in regard to any offence that occurs prior to the date on which the denunciation becomes effective. Nor shall such a denunciation prejudice in any way the continued consideration of any matter that is already under consideration by the Committee on the Rights of the Child prior to the date on which the denunciation becomes effective.

Article 16. (1) Any State Party may propose an amendment and file it with the Secretary-General of the United Nations. The Secretary-General shall thereupon communicate the proposed amendment to States Parties with a request that they indicate whether they favour a conference of States Parties for the purpose of considering and voting upon the proposals. In the event that, within four months from the date of such communication, at least one third of the States Parties favour such a conference, the Secretary-General shall convene the conference under the auspices of the United Nations. Any amendment adopted by a majority of States Parties present and voting at the conference shall be submitted to the General Assembly of the United Nations for approval.
(2) An amendment adopted in accordance with paragraph (1) of the present article shall enter into force when it has been approved by the General Assembly and accepted by a two-thirds majority of States Parties.
(3) When an amendment enters into force, it shall be binding on those States Parties that have accepted it, other States Parties still being bound by the provisions of the present Protocol and any earlier amendments they have accepted.

Article 17. (1) The present Protocol, of which the Arabic, Chinese, English, French, Russian and Spanish texts are equally authentic, shall be deposited in the archives of the United Nations.
(2) The Secretary-General of the United Nations shall transmit certified copies of the present Protocol to all States Parties to the Convention and all States that have signed the Convention.

PART II   FUNDAMENTAL RIGHTS

UN General Assembly Resolution A/RES/60/251 on the Human Rights Council
General Assembly Distr. General 3 April 2006, sixtieth session,
Agenda items 46 and 120 05-50266

The General Assembly,
Reaffirming the purposes and principles contained in the Charter of the United Nations, including developing friendly relations among nations based on respect for the principle of equal rights and self-determination of peoples, and achieving international cooperation in solving international problems of an economic, social, cultural or humanitarian character and in promoting and encouraging respect for human rights and fundamental freedoms for all,
Reaffirming also the Universal Declaration of Human Rights and the Vienna Declaration and Programme of Action, and recalling the International Covenant on Civil and Political Rights, the International Covenant on Economic, Social and Cultural Rights and other human rights instruments,
Reaffirming further that all human rights are universal, indivisible, interrelated, interdependent and mutually reinforcing, and that all human rights must be treated in a fair and equal manner, on the same footing and with the same emphasis,
Reaffirming that, while the significance of national and regional particularities and various historical, cultural and religious backgrounds must be borne in mind, all States, regardless of their political, economic and cultural systems, have the duty to promote and protect all human rights and fundamental freedoms,
Emphasizing the responsibilities of all States, in conformity with the Charter, to respect human rights and fundamental freedoms for all, without distinction of any kind as to race, colour, sex, language or religion, political or other opinion, national or social origin, property, birth or other status,
Acknowledging that peace and security, development and human rights are the pillars of the United Nations system and the foundations for collective security and well-being, and recognizing that development, peace and security and human rights are interlinked and mutually reinforcing,
Affirming the need for all States to continue international efforts to enhance dialogue and broaden understanding among civilizations, cultures and religions, and emphasizing that States, regional organizations, non-governmental organizations, religious bodies and the media have an important role to play in promoting tolerance, respect for and freedom of religion and belief,
Recognizing the work undertaken by the Commission on Human Rights and the need to preserve and build on its achievements and to redress its shortcomings,
Recognizing also the importance of ensuring universality, objectivity and non-selectivity in the consideration of human rights issues, and the elimination of double standards and politicization,
Recognizing further that the promotion and protection of human rights should be based on the principles of cooperation and genuine dialogue and aimed at strengthening the capacity of Member States to comply with their human rights obligations for the benefit of all human beings,
Acknowledging that non-governmental organizations play an important role at the national, regional and international levels, in the promotion and protection of human rights,
Reaffirming the commitment to strengthen the United Nations human rights machinery, with the aim of ensuring effective enjoyment by all of all human rights, civil, political, economic, social and cultural rights, including the right to development, and to that end, the resolve to create a Human Rights Council,

(1) Decides to establish the Human Rights Council, based in Geneva, in replacement of the Commission on Human Rights, as a subsidiary organ of the General Assembly; the Assembly shall review the status of the Council within five years;
(2) Decides that the Council shall be responsible for promoting universal respect for the protection of all human rights and fundamental freedoms for all, without distinction of any kind and in a fair and equal manner;
(3) Decides also that the Council should address situations of violations of human rights, including gross and systematic violations, and make recommendations thereon. It should also promote the effective coordination and the mainstreaming of human rights within the United Nations system;
(4) Decides further that the work of the Council shall be guided by the principles of universality, impartiality, objectivity and non-selectivity, constructive international dialogue and cooperation, with a view to enhancing the promotion and protection of all human rights, civil, political, economic, social and cultural rights, including the right to development;
(5) Decides that the Council shall, inter alia:
(a) Promote human rights education and learning as well as advisory services, technical assistance and capacity-building, to be provided in consultation with and with the consent of Member States concerned;

(b) Serve as a forum for dialogue on thematic issues on all human rights;
(c) Make recommendations to the General Assembly for the further development of international law in the field of human rights;
(d) Promote the full implementation of human rights obligations undertaken by States and follow-up to the goals and commitments related to the promotion and protection of human rights emanating from United Nations conferences and summits;
(e) Undertake a universal periodic review, based on objective and reliable information, of the fulfilment by each State of its human rights obligations and commitments in a manner which ensures universality of coverage and equal treatment with respect to all States; the review shall be a cooperative mechanism, based on an interactive dialogue, with the full involvement of the country concerned and with consideration given to its capacity-building needs; such a mechanism shall complement and not duplicate the work of treaty bodies; the Council shall develop the modalities and necessary time allocation for the universal periodic review mechanism within one year after the holding of its first session;
(f) Contribute, through dialogue and cooperation, towards the prevention of human rights violations and respond promptly to human rights emergencies;
(g) Assume the role and responsibilities of the Commission on Human Rights relating to the work of the Office of the United Nations High Commissioner for Human Rights, as decided by the General Assembly in its resolution 48/141 of 20 December 1993;
(h) Work in close cooperation in the field of human rights with Governments, regional organizations, national human rights institutions and civil society;
(i) Make recommendations with regard to the promotion and protection of human rights;
(j) Submit an annual report to the General Assembly;
(6) Decides also that the Council shall assume, review and, where necessary, improve and rationalize all mandates, mechanisms, functions and responsibilities of the Commission on Human Rights in order to maintain a system of special procedures, expert advice and a complaint procedure; the Council shall complete this review within one year after the holding of its first session;
(7) Decides further that the Council shall consist of forty-seven Member States, which shall be elected directly and individually by secret ballot by the majority of the members of the General Assembly; the membership shall be based on equitable geographical distribution, and seats shall be distributed as follows among regional groups: Group of African States, thirteen; Group of Asian States, thirteen; Group of Eastern European States, six; Group of Latin American and Caribbean States, eight; and Group of Western European and other States, seven; the members of the Council shall serve for a period of three years and shall not be eligible for immediate re-election after two consecutive terms;
(8) Decides that the membership in the Council shall be open to all States Members of the United Nations; when electing members of the Council, Member States shall take into account the contribution of candidates to the promotion and protection of human rights and their voluntary pledges and commitments made thereto; the General Assembly, by a two-thirds majority of the members present and voting, may suspend the rights of membership in the Council of a member of the Council that commits gross and systematic violations of human rights;
(9) Decides also that members elected to the Council shall uphold the highest standards in the promotion and protection of human rights, shall fully cooperate with the Council and be reviewed under the universal periodic review mechanism during their term of membership;
(10) Decides further that the Council shall meet regularly throughout the year and schedule no fewer than three sessions per year, including a main session, for a total duration of no less than ten weeks, and shall be able to hold special sessions, when needed, at the request of a member of the Council with the support of one third of the membership of the Council;
(11) Decides that the Council shall apply the rules of procedure established for committees of the General Assembly, as applicable, unless subsequently otherwise decided by the Assembly or the Council, and also decides that the participation of and consultation with observers, including States that are not members of the Council, the specialized agencies, other intergovernmental organizations and national human rights institutions, as well as non-governmental organizations, shall be based on arrangements, including Economic and Social Council resolution 1996/31 of 25 July 1996 and practices observed by the Commission on Human Rights, while ensuring the most effective contribution of these entities;
(12) Decides also that the methods of work of the Council shall be transparent, fair and impartial and shall enable genuine dialogue, be results-oriented, allow for subsequent follow-up discussions to recommendations and their implementation and also allow for substantive interaction with special procedures and mechanisms;

PART II   FUNDAMENTAL RIGHTS

(13) Recommends that the Economic and Social Council request the Commission on Human Rights to conclude its work at its sixty-second session, and that it abolish the Commission on 16 June 2006;
(14) Decides to elect the new members of the Council; the terms of membership shall be staggered, and such decision shall be taken for the first election by the drawing of lots, taking into consideration equitable geographical distribution;
(15) Decides also that elections of the first members of the Council shall take place on 9 May 2006, and that the first meeting of the Council shall be convened on 19 June 2006;
(16) Decides further that the Council shall review its work and functioning five years after its establishment and report to the General Assembly. 72nd plenary meeting 15 March 2006

HUMAN RIGHTS COUNCIL: INSTITUTION BUILDING

Human Rights Council Resolution A/HRC/RES/5/1 on Institution-building
18 June 2007

The Human Rights Council,
Acting in compliance with the mandate entrusted to it by the United Nations General Assembly in resolution 60/251 of 15 March 2006,
Having considered the draft text on institution-building submitted by the President of the Council,
1. Adopts the draft text entitled "United Nations Human Rights Council: Institution-Building", as contained in the annex to the present resolution, including its appendix(ces);
2. Decides to submit the following draft resolution to the General Assembly for its adoption as a matter of priority in order to facilitate the timely implementation of the text contained thereafter:
"The General Assembly,
"Taking note of Human Rights Council resolution 5/1 of 18 June 2007, "
1. Welcomes the text entitled 'United Nations Human Rights Council: Institution-Building', as contained in the annex to the present resolution, including its appendix(ces)."

Annex United Nations Human Rights Council. Institution-Building

I. Universal Periodic Review Mechanism

A. Basis of the review

(1) The basis of the review is:
(a) The Charter of the United Nations;
(b) The Universal Declaration of Human Rights;
(c) Human rights instruments to which a State is party;
(2) In addition to the above and given the complementary and mutually interrelated nature of international human rights law and international humanitarian law, the review shall take into account applicable international humanitarian law.

B. Principles and objectives

1. Principles

(3) The universal periodic review should:
(a) Promote the universality, interdependence, indivisibility and interrelatedness of all human rights;
(b) Be a cooperative mechanism based on objective and reliable information and on interactive dialogue;
(c) Ensure universal coverage and equal treatment of all States;
(d) Be an intergovernmental process, United Nations Member-driven and action-oriented;
(e) Fully involve the country under review;
(f) Complement and not duplicate other human rights mechanisms, thus representing an added value;
(g) Be conducted in an objective, transparent, non-selective, constructive, non-confrontational and non-politicized manner;
(h) Not be overly burdensome to the concerned State or to the agenda of the Council;
(i) Not be overly long; it should be realistic and not absorb a disproportionate amount of time, human and financial resources;
(j) Not diminish the Council's capacity to respond to urgent human rights situations;
(k) Fully integrate a gender perspective;
(l) Without prejudice to the obligations contained in the elements provided for in the basis of review, take into account the level of development and specificities of countries;
(m) Ensure the participation of all relevant stakeholders, including non-governmental organizations and national human rights institutions, in accordance with General Assembly resolution 60/251 of 15 March 2006 and Economic and Social Council resolution 1996/31 of 25 July 1996, as well as any decisions that the Council may take in this regard.

2. Objectives

(4) The objectives of the review are:
(a) The improvement of the human rights situation on the ground;
(b) The fulfilment of the State's human rights obligations and commitments and assessment of positive developments and challenges faced by the State;
(c) The enhancement of the State's capacity and of technical assistance, in consultation with, and with the consent of, the State concerned;
(d) The sharing of best practice among States and other stakeholders;

PART II FUNDAMENTAL RIGHTS

(e) Support for cooperation in the promotion and protection of human rights;
(f) The encouragement of full cooperation and engagement with the Council, other human rights bodies and the Office of the United Nations High Commissioner for Human Rights.

C. Periodicity and order of the review

(5) The review begins after the adoption of the universal periodic review mechanism by the Council.
(6) The order of review should reflect the principles of universality and equal treatment.
(7) The order of the review should be established as soon as possible in order to allow States to prepare adequately.
(8) All member States of the Council shall be reviewed during their term of membership.
(9) The initial members of the Council, especially those elected for one or two-year terms, should be reviewed first.
(10) A mix of member and observer States of the Council should be reviewed.
(11) Equitable geographic distribution should be respected in the selection of countries for review.
(12) The first member and observer States to be reviewed will be chosen by the drawing of lots from each Regional Group in such a way as to ensure full respect for equitable geographic distribution. Alphabetical order will then be applied beginning with those countries thus selected, unless other countries volunteer to be reviewed.
(13) The period between review cycles should be reasonable so as to take into account the capacity of States to prepare for, and the capacity of other stakeholders to respond to, the requests arising from the review.
(14) The periodicity of the review for the first cycle will be of four years. This will imply the consideration of 48 States per year during three sessions of the working group of two weeks each.

D. Process and modalities of the review

1. Documentation

(15) The documents on which the review would be based are:
(a) Information prepared by the State concerned, which can take the form of a national report, on the basis of general guidelines to be adopted by the Council at its sixth session (first session of the second cycle), and any other information considered relevant by the State concerned, which could be presented either orally or in writing, provided that the written presentation summarizing the information will not exceed 20 pages, to guarantee equal treatment to all States and not to overburden the mechanism. States are encouraged to prepare the information through a broad consultation process at the national level with all relevant stakeholders;
(b) Additionally a compilation prepared by the Office of the High Commissioner for Human Rights of the information contained in the reports of treaty bodies, special procedures, including observations and comments by the State concerned, and other relevant official United Nations documents, which shall not exceed 10 pages; a The universal periodic review is an evolving process; the Council, after the conclusion of the first review cycle, may review the modalities and the periodicity of this mechanism, based on best practices and lessons learned.
(c) Additional, credible and reliable information provided by other relevant stakeholders to the universal periodic review which should also be taken into consideration by the Council in the review. The Office of the High Commissioner for Human Rights will prepare a summary of such information which shall not exceed 10 pages.
(16) The documents prepared by the Office of the High Commissioner for Human Rights should be elaborated following the structure of the general guidelines adopted by the Council regarding the information prepared by the State concerned.
(17) Both the State's written presentation and the summaries prepared by the Office of the High Commissioner for Human Rights shall be ready six weeks prior to the review by the working group to ensure the distribution of documents simultaneously in the six official languages of the United Nations, in accordance with General Assembly resolution 53/208 of 14 January 1999.

2. Modalities

(18) The modalities of the review shall be as follows:
(a) The review will be conducted in one working group, chaired by the President of the Council and composed of the 47 member States of the Council. Each member State will decide on the composition of its delegation;
(b) Observer States may participate in the review, including in the interactive dialogue;
(c) Other relevant stakeholders may attend the review in the Working Group;
(d) A group of three rapporteurs, selected by the drawing of lots among the members of the Council and from different Regional Groups (troika) will be formed to facilitate each review, including the

preparation of the report of the working group. The Office of the High Commissioner for Human Rights will provide the necessary assistance and expertise to the rapporteurs.
(19) The country concerned may request that one of the rapporteurs be from its own Regional Group and may also request the substitution of a rapporteur on only one occasion.
(20) A rapporteur may request to be excused from participation in a specific review process.
(21) Interactive dialogue between the country under review and the Council will take place in the working group. The rapporteurs may collate issues or questions to be transmitted to the State under review to facilitate its preparation and focus the interactive dialogue, while guaranteeing fairness and transparency.
(22) The duration of the review will be three hours for each country in the working group. Additional time of up to one hour will be allocated for the consideration of the outcome by the plenary of the Council.
(23) Half an hour will be allocated for the adoption of the report of each country under review in the working group.
(24) A reasonable time frame should be allocated between the review and the adoption of the report of each State in the working group.
(25) The final outcome will be adopted by the plenary of the Council.

E. Outcome of the review

1. Format of the outcome
(26) The format of the outcome of the review will be a report consisting of a summary of the proceedings of the review process; conclusions and/or recommendations, and the voluntary commitments of the State concerned.

2. Content of the outcome
(27) The universal periodic review is a cooperative mechanism. Its outcome may include, inter alia:
(a) An assessment undertaken in an objective and transparent manner of the human rights situation in the country under review, including positive developments and the challenges faced by the country;
(b) Sharing of best practices;
(c) An emphasis on enhancing cooperation for the promotion and protection of human rights; (d) The provision of technical assistance and capacity-building in consultation with, and with the consent of, the country concerned;
(e) Voluntary commitments and pledges made by the country under review.

3. Adoption of the outcome
(28) The country under review should be fully involved in the outcome.
(29) Before the adoption of the outcome by the plenary of the Council, the State concerned should be offered the opportunity to present replies to questions or issues that were not sufficiently addressed during the interactive dialogue.
(30) The State concerned and the member States of the Council, as well as observer States, will be given the opportunity to express their views on the outcome of the review before the plenary takes action on it.
(31) Other relevant stakeholders will have the opportunity to make general comments before the adoption of the outcome by the plenary.
(32) Recommendations that enjoy the support of the State concerned will be identified as such. Other recommendations, together with the comments of the State concerned thereon, will be noted. Both will be included in the outcome report to be adopted by the Council.

F. Follow-up to the review
(33.) The outcome of the universal periodic review, as a cooperative mechanism, should be implemented primarily by the State concerned and, as appropriate, by other relevant stakeholders.
(34) The subsequent review should focus, inter alia, on the implementation of the preceding outcome.
(35) The Council should have a standing item on its agenda devoted to the universal periodic review.
(36) The international community will assist in implementing the recommendations and conclusions regarding capacity-building and technical assistance, in consultation with, and with the consent of, the country concerned.
(37) In considering the outcome of the universal periodic review, the Council will decide if and when any specific follow-up is necessary.
(38) After exhausting all efforts to encourage a State to cooperate with the universal periodic review mechanism, the Council will address, as appropriate, cases of persistent non-cooperation with the mechanism.

PART II   FUNDAMENTAL RIGHTS

II. Special Procedures

A. Selection and appointment of mandate-holders

(39) The following general criteria will be of paramount importance while nominating, selecting and appointing mandate-holders:
(a) expertise;
(b) experience in the field of the mandate;
(c) independence;
(d) impartiality;
(e) personal integrity; and
(f) objectivity.
(40) Due consideration should be given to gender balance and equitable geographic representation, as well as to an appropriate representation of different legal systems.
(41) Technical and objective requirements for eligible candidates for mandate-holders will be approved by the Council at its sixth session (first session of the second cycle), in order to ensure that eligible candidates are highly qualified individuals who possess established competence, relevant expertise and extensive professional experience in the field of human rights.
(42) The following entities may nominate candidates as special procedures mandate-holders: (a) Governments;
(b) Regional Groups operating within the United Nations human rights system;
(c) international organizations or their offices (e.g. the Office of the High Commissioner for Human Rights);
(d) nongovernmental organizations;
(e) other human rights bodies;
(f) individual nominations.
(43) The Office of the High Commissioner for Human Rights shall immediately prepare, maintain and periodically update a public list of eligible candidates in a standardized format, which shall include personal data, areas of expertise and professional experience. Upcoming vacancies of mandates shall be publicized.
(44) The principle of non-accumulation of human rights functions at a time shall be respected.
(45) A mandate-holder's tenure in a given function, whether a thematic or country mandate, will be no longer than six years (two terms of three years for thematic mandate-holders).
(46) Individuals holding decision-making positions in Government or in any other organization or entity which may give rise to a conflict of interest with the responsibilities inherent to the mandate shall be excluded. Mandate-holders will act in their personal capacity.
(47) A consultative group would be established to propose to the President, at least one month before the beginning of the session in which the Council would consider the selection of mandate-holders, a list of candidates who possess the highest qualifications for the mandates in question and meet the general criteria and particular requirements.
(48) The consultative group shall also give due consideration to the exclusion of nominated candidates from the public list of eligible candidates brought to its attention.
(49) At the beginning of the annual cycle of the Council, Regional Groups would be invited to appoint a member of the consultative group, who would serve in his/her personal capacity. The Group will be assisted by the Office of the High Commissioner for Human Rights.
(50) The consultative group will consider candidates included in the public list; however, under exceptional circumstances and if a particular post justifies it, the Group may consider additional nominations with equal or more suitable qualifications for the post. Recommendations to the President shall be public and substantiated.
(51) The consultative group should take into account, as appropriate, the views of stakeholders, including the current or outgoing mandate-holders, in determining the necessary expertise, experience, skills, and other relevant requirements for each mandate.
(52) On the basis of the recommendations of the consultative group and following broad consultations, in particular through the regional coordinators, the President of the Council will identify an appropriate candidate for each vacancy. The President will present to member States and observers a list of candidates to be proposed at least two weeks prior to the beginning of the session in which the Council will consider the appointments.
(53) If necessary, the President will conduct further consultations to ensure the endorsement of the proposed candidates. The appointment of the special procedures mandate-holders will be completed upon the subsequent approval of the Council. Mandate-holders shall be appointed before the end of the session. B. Review, rationalization and improvement of mandates

(54) The review, rationalization and improvement of mandates, as well as the creation of new ones, must be guided by the principles of universality, impartiality, objectivity and non-selectivity, constructive international dialogue and cooperation, with a view to enhancing the promotion and protection of all human rights, civil, political, economic, social and cultural rights, including the right to development.
(55) The review, rationalization and improvement of each mandate would take place in the context of the negotiations of the relevant resolutions. An assessment of the mandate may take place in a separate segment of the interactive dialogue between the Council and special procedures mandate-holders.
(56) The review, rationalization and improvement of mandates would focus on the relevance, scope and contents of the mandates, having as a framework the internationally recognized human rights standards, the system of special procedures and General Assembly resolution 60/251.
(57) Any decision to streamline, merge or possibly discontinue mandates should always be guided by the need for improvement of the enjoyment and protection of human rights.
(58) The Council should always strive for improvements:
(a) Mandates should always offer a clear prospect of an increased level of human rights protection and promotion as well as being coherent within the system of human rights;
(b) Equal attention should be paid to all human rights. The balance of thematic mandates should broadly reflect the accepted equal importance of civil, political, economic, social and cultural rights, including the right to development;
(c) Every effort should be made to avoid unnecessary duplication;
(d) Areas which constitute thematic gaps will be identified and addressed, including by means other than the creation of special procedures mandates, such as by expanding an existing mandate, bringing a cross-cutting issue to the attention of mandate-holders or by requesting a joint action to the relevant mandate-holders;
(e) Any consideration of merging mandates should have regard to the content and predominant functions of each mandate, as well as to the workload of individual mandate-holders;
(f) In creating or reviewing mandates, efforts should be made to identify whether the structure of the mechanism (expert, rapporteur or working group) is the most effective in terms of increasing human rights protection;
(g) New mandates should be as clear and specific as possible, so as to avoid ambiguity.
(59) It should be considered desirable to have a uniform nomenclature of mandate-holders, titles of mandates as well as a selection and appointment process, to make the whole system more understandable.
(60) Thematic mandate periods will be of three years. Country mandate periods will be of one year.
(61) Mandates included in Appendix I, where applicable, will be renewed until the date on which they are considered by the Council according to the programme of work.
(62) Current mandate-holders may continue serving, provided they have not exceeded the six-year term limit (Appendix II). On an exceptional basis, the term of those mandate-holders who have served more than six years may be extended until the relevant mandate is considered by the Council and the selection and appointment process has concluded.
(63) Decisions to create, review or discontinue country mandates should also take into account the principles of cooperation and genuine dialogue aimed at strengthening the capacity of Member States to comply with their human rights obligations.
(64) In case of situations of violations of human rights or a lack of cooperation that require the Council's attention, the principles of objectivity, non-selectivity, and the elimination of double standards and politicization should apply.

III. Human Rights Council Advisory Committee
(65) The Human Rights Council Advisory Committee (hereinafter "the Advisory Committee"), composed of 18 experts serving in their personal capacity, will function as a think-tank for the Council and work at its direction. The establishment of this subsidiary body and its functioning will be executed according to the guidelines stipulated below.

A. Nomination
(66) All Member States of the United Nations may propose or endorse candidates from their own region. When selecting their candidates, States should consult their national human rights institutions and civil society organizations and, in this regard, include the names of those supporting their candidates.
(67) The aim is to ensure that the best possible expertise is made available to the Council. For this purpose, technical and objective requirements for the submission of candidatures will be established

PART II FUNDAMENTAL RIGHTS

and approved by the Council at its sixth session (first session of the second cycle). These should include:
(a) Recognized competence and experience in the field of human rights;
(b) High moral standing;
(c) Independence and impartiality.
(68) Individuals holding decision-making positions in Government or in any other organization or entity which might give rise to a conflict of interest with the responsibilities inherent in the mandate shall be excluded. Elected members of the Committee will act in their personal capacity.
(69) The principle of non-accumulation of human rights functions at the same time shall be respected.

B. Election

(70) The Council shall elect the members of the Advisory Committee, in secret ballot, from the list of candidates whose names have been presented in accordance with the agreed requirements. d Country mandates meet the following criteria: − There is a pending mandate of the Council to be accomplished; or − There is a pending mandate of the General Assembly to be accomplished; or − The nature of the mandate is for advisory services and technical assistance.
(71) The list of candidates shall be closed two months prior to the election date. The Secretariat will make available the list of candidates and relevant information to member States and to the public at least one month prior to their election.
(72) Due consideration should be given to gender balance and appropriate representation of different civilizations and legal systems.
(73) The geographic distribution will be as follows:
African States: 5
Asian States: 5
Eastern European States: 2
Latin American and Caribbean States: 3
Western European and other States: 3
(74) The members of the Advisory Committee shall serve for a period of three years. They shall be eligible for re-election once. In the first term, one third of the experts will serve for one year and another third for two years. The staggering of terms of membership will be defined by the drawing of lots. C. Functions
(75) The function of the Advisory Committee is to provide expertise to the Council in the manner and form requested by the Council, focusing mainly on studies and research-based advice. Further, such expertise shall be rendered only upon the latter's request, in compliance with its resolutions and under its guidance.
(76) The Advisory Committee should be implementation-oriented and the scope of its advice should be limited to thematic issues pertaining to the mandate of the Council; namely promotion and protection of all human rights.
(77) The Advisory Committee shall not adopt resolutions or decisions. The Advisory Committee may propose within the scope of the work set out by the Council, for the latter's consideration and approval, suggestions for further enhancing its procedural efficiency, as well as further research proposals within the scope of the work set out by the Council.
(78) The Council shall issue specific guidelines for the Advisory Committee when it requests a substantive contribution from the latter and shall review all or any portion of those guidelines if it deems necessary in the future.

D. Methods of work

(79) The Advisory Committee shall convene up to two sessions for a maximum of 10 working days per year. Additional sessions may be scheduled on an ad hoc basis with prior approval of the Council.
(80) The Council may request the Advisory Committee to undertake certain tasks that could be performed collectively, through a smaller team or individually. The Advisory Committee will report on such efforts to the Council.
(81) Members of the Advisory Committee are encouraged to communicate between sessions, individually or in teams. However, the Advisory Committee shall not establish subsidiary bodies unless the Council authorizes it to do so.
(82) In the performance of its mandate, the Advisory Committee is urged to establish interaction with States, national human rights institutions, non-governmental organizations and other civil society entities in accordance with the modalities of the Council.
(83) Member States and observers, including States that are not members of the Council, the specialized agencies, other intergovernmental organizations and national human rights institutions, as well as nongovernmental organizations shall be entitled to participate in the work of the Advisory

HUMAN RIGHTS COUNCIL: INSTITUTION BUILDING

Committee based on arrangements, including Economic and Social Council resolution 1996/31 and practices observed by the Commission on Human Rights and the Council, while ensuring the most effective contribution of these entities.
(84) The Council will decide at its sixth session (first session of its second cycle) on the most appropriate mechanisms to continue the work of the Working Groups on Indigenous Populations; Contemporary Forms of Slavery; Minorities; and the Social Forum.

IV. Complaint Procedure

A. Objective and scope

(85) A complaint procedure is being established to address consistent patterns of gross and reliably attested violations of all human rights and all fundamental freedoms occurring in any part of the world and under any circumstances.
(86) Economic and Social Council resolution 1503 (XLVIII) of 27 May 1970 as revised by resolution 2000/3
of 19 June 2000 served as a working basis and was improved where necessary, so as to ensure that the complaint procedure is impartial, objective, efficient, victims-oriented and conducted in a timely manner. The procedure will retain its confidential nature, with a view to enhancing cooperation with the State concerned. B. Admissibility criteria for communications
(87) A communication related to a violation of human rights and fundamental freedoms, for the purpose of this procedure, shall be admissible, provided that:
(a) It is not manifestly politically motivated and its object is consistent with the Charter of the United Nations, the Universal Declaration of Human Rights and other applicable instruments in the field of human rights law;
(b) It gives a factual description of the alleged violations, including the rights which are alleged to be violated;
(c) Its language is not abusive. However, such a communication may be considered if it meets the other criteria for admissibility after deletion of the abusive language;
(d) It is submitted by a person or a group of persons claiming to be the victims of violations of human rights and fundamental freedoms, or by any person or group of persons, including non-governmental organizations, acting in good faith in accordance with the principles of human rights, not resorting to politically motivated stands contrary to the provisions of the Charter of the United Nations and claiming to have direct and reliable knowledge of the violations concerned. Nonetheless, reliably attested communications shall not be inadmissible solely because the knowledge of the individual authors is second-hand, provided that they are accompanied by clear evidence;
(e) It is not exclusively based on reports disseminated by mass media;
(f) It does not refer to a case that appears to reveal a consistent pattern of gross and reliably attested violations of human rights already being dealt with by a special procedure, a treaty body or other United Nations or similar regional complaints procedure in the field of human rights;
(g) Domestic remedies have been exhausted, unless it appears that such remedies would be ineffective or unreasonably prolonged.
(88) National human rights institutions, established and operating under the Principles Relating to the Status of National Institutions (the Paris Principles), in particular in regard to quasi-judicial competence, may serve as effective means of addressing individual human rights violations.

C. Working groups

(89) Two distinct working groups shall be established with the mandate to examine the communications and to bring to the attention of the Council consistent patterns of gross and reliably attested violations of human rights and fundamental freedoms.
(90) Both working groups shall, to the greatest possible extent, work on the basis of consensus. In the absence of consensus, decisions shall be taken by simple majority of the votes. They may establish their own rules of procedure.

1. Working Group on Communications. composition, mandate and powers

(91) The Human Rights Council Advisory Committee shall appoint five of its members, one from each Regional Group, with due consideration to gender balance, to constitute the Working Group on Communications.
(92) In case of a vacancy, the Advisory Committee shall appoint an independent and highly qualified expert of the same Regional Group from the Advisory Committee.
(93) Since there is a need for independent expertise and continuity with regard to the examination and assessment of communications received, the independent and highly qualified experts of the Working Group on Communications shall be appointed for three years. Their mandate is renewable only once.

PART II FUNDAMENTAL RIGHTS

(94) The Chairperson of the Working Group on Communications is requested, together with the secretariat, to undertake an initial screening of communications received, based on the admissibility criteria, before transmitting them to the States concerned. Manifestly ill-founded or anonymous communications shall be screened out by the Chairperson and shall therefore not be transmitted to the State concerned. In a perspective of accountability and transparency, the Chairperson of the Working Group on Communications shall provide all its members with a list of all communications rejected after initial screening. This list should indicate the grounds of all decisions resulting in the rejection of a communication. All other communications, which have not been screened out, shall be transmitted to the State concerned, so as to obtain the views of the latter on the allegations of violations.

(95) The members of the Working Group on Communications shall decide on the admissibility of a communication and assess the merits of the allegations of violations, including whether the communication alone or in combination with other communications appear to reveal a consistent pattern of gross and reliably attested violations of human rights and fundamental freedoms. The Working Group on Communications shall provide the Working Group on Situations with a file containing all admissible communications as well as recommendations thereon. When the Working Group on Communications requires further consideration or additional information, it may keep a case under review until its next session and request such information from the State concerned. The Working Group on Communications may decide to dismiss a case. All decisions of the Working Group on Communications shall be based on a rigorous application of the admissibility criteria and duly justified.

2. Working Group on Situations. composition, mandate and powers

(96) Each Regional Group shall appoint a representative of a member State of the Council, with due consideration to gender balance, to serve on the Working Group on Situations. Members shall be appointed for one year. Their mandate may be renewed once, if the State concerned is a member of the Council.

(97) Members of the Working Group on Situations shall serve in their personal capacity. In order to fill a vacancy, the respective Regional Group to which the vacancy belongs, shall appoint a representative from member States of the same Regional Group.

(98) The Working Group on Situations is requested, on the basis of the information and recommendations provided by the Working Group on Communications, to present the Council with a report on consistent patterns of gross and reliably attested violations of human rights and fundamental freedoms and to make recommendations to the Council on the course of action to take, normally in the form of a draft resolution or decision with respect to the situations referred to it. When the Working Group on Situations requires further consideration or additional information, its members may keep a case under review until its next session. The Working Group on Situations may also decide to dismiss a case.

(99) All decisions of the Working Group on Situations shall be duly justified and indicate why the consideration of a situation has been discontinued or action recommended thereon. Decisions to discontinue should be taken by consensus; if that is not possible, by simple majority of the votes.

D. Working modalities and confidentiality

(100) Since the complaint procedure is to be, inter alia, victims-oriented and conducted in a confidential and timely manner, both Working Groups shall meet at least twice a year for five working days each session, in order to promptly examine the communications received, including replies of States thereon, and the situations of which the Council is already seized under the complaint procedure.

(101) The State concerned shall cooperate with the complaint procedure and make every effort to provide substantive replies in one of the United Nations official languages to any of the requests of the Working Groups or the Council. The State concerned shall also make every effort to provide a reply not later than three months after the request has been made. If necessary, this deadline may however be extended at the request of the State concerned.

(102) The Secretariat is requested to make the confidential files available to all members of the Council, at least two weeks in advance, so as to allow sufficient time for the consideration of the files.

(103). The Council shall consider consistent patterns of gross and reliably attested violations of human rights and fundamental freedoms brought to its attention by the Working Group on Situations as frequently as needed, but at least once a year.

(104) The reports of the Working Group on Situations referred to the Council shall be examined in a confidential manner, unless the Council decides otherwise. When the Working Group on Situations recommends to the Council that it consider a situation in a public meeting, in particular in the case of manifest and unequivocal lack of cooperation, the Council shall consider such recommendation on a priority basis at its next session.

(105) So as to ensure that the complaint procedure is victims-oriented, efficient and conducted in a

timely manner, the period of time between the transmission of the complaint to the State concerned and consideration by the Council shall not, in principle, exceed 24 months.

E. Involvement of the complainant and of the State concerned

(106) The complaint procedure shall ensure that both the author of a communication and the State concerned are informed of the proceedings at the following key stages:
(a) When a communication is deemed inadmissible by the Working Group on Communications or when it is taken up for consideration by the Working Group on Situations; or when a communication is kept pending by one of the Working Groups or by the Council;
(b) At the final outcome.
(107) In addition, the complainant shall be informed when his/her communication is registered by the complaint procedure.
(108) Should the complainant request that his/her identity be kept confidential, it will not be transmitted to the State concerned.

F. Measures

(109) In accordance with established practice the action taken in respect of a particular situation should be one of the following options:
(a) To discontinue considering the situation when further consideration or action is not warranted;
(b) To keep the situation under review and request the State concerned to provide further information within a reasonable period of time;
(c) To keep the situation under review and appoint an independent and highly qualified expert to monitor the situation and report back to the Council;
(d) To discontinue reviewing the matter under the confidential complaint procedure in order to take up public consideration of the same;
(e) To recommend to OHCHR to provide technical cooperation, capacity-building assistance or advisory services to the State concerned.

V. Agenda and Framework for the Programme of Work

A. Principles

Universality
Impartiality
Objectivity
Non-selectiveness
Constructive dialogue and cooperation
Predictability
Flexibility
Transparency
Accountability
Balance
Inclusive/comprehensive
Gender perspective
Implementation and follow-up of decisions

B. Agenda Item

(1) Organizational and procedural matters Item
(2) Annual report of the United Nations High Commissioner for Human Rights and reports of the Office of the High Commissioner and the Secretary-General Item
(3) Promotion and protection of all human rights, civil, political, economic, social and cultural rights, including the right to development Item
(4) Human rights situations that require the Council's attention Item
(5) Human rights bodies and mechanisms Item
(6) Universal Periodic Review Item
(7) Human rights situation in Palestine and other occupied Arab territories Item
(8) Follow-up and implementation of the Vienna Declaration and Programme of Action Item
(9) Racism, racial discrimination, xenophobia and related forms of intolerance, follow-up and implementation of the Durban Declaration and Programme of Action Item
(10) Technical assistance and capacity-building

C. Framework for the programme of work Item

(1) Organizational and procedural matters Election of the Bureau Adoption of the annual programme

PART II   FUNDAMENTAL RIGHTS

of work Adoption of the programme of work of the session, including other business Selection and appointment of mandate-holders Election of members of the Human Rights Council Advisory Committee Adoption of the report of the session Adoption of the annual report Item

(2) Annual report of the United Nations High Commissioner for Human Rights and reports of the Office of the High Commissioner and the Secretary-General Presentation of the annual report and updates Item

(3) Promotion and protection of all human rights, civil, political, economic, social and cultural rights, including the right to development Economic, social and cultural rights Civil and political rights Rights of peoples, and specific groups and individuals Right to development Interrelation of human rights and human rights thematic issues Item

(4) Human rights situations that require the Council's attention Item

(5) Human rights bodies and mechanisms Report of the Human Rights Council Advisory Committee Report of the complaint procedure Item

(6) Universal Periodic Review Item

(7) Human rights situation in Palestine and other occupied Arab territories Human rights violations and implications of the Israeli occupation of Palestine and other occupied Arab territories Right to self-determination of the Palestinian people Item

(8) Follow-up and implementation of the Vienna Declaration and Programme of Action Item

(9) Racism, racial discrimination, xenophobia and related forms of intolerance, follow-up and implementation of the Durban Declaration and Programme of Action Item

(10) Technical assistance and capacity-building

VI. Methods of Work

(110) The methods of work, pursuant to General Assembly resolution 60/251 should be transparent, impartial, equitable, fair, pragmatic; lead to clarity, predictability, and inclusiveness. They may also be updated and adjusted over time.

A. Institutional arrangements

1. Briefings on prospective resolutions or decisions

(111) The briefings on prospective resolutions or decisions would be informative only, whereby delegations would be apprised of resolutions and/or decisions tabled or intended to be tabled. These briefings will be organized by interested delegations.

2. President's open-ended information meetings on resolutions, decisions and other related business

(112) The President's open-ended information meetings on resolutions, decisions and other related business shall provide information on the status of negotiations on draft resolutions and/or decisions so that delegations may gain a bird's eye view of the status of such drafts. The consultations shall have a purely informational function, combined with information on the extranet, and be held in a transparent and inclusive manner. They shall not serve as a negotiating forum.

3. Informal consultations on proposals convened by main sponsors

(113) Informal consultations shall be the primary means for the negotiation of draft resolutions and/or decisions, and their convening shall be the responsibility of the sponsor(s). At least one informal open-ended consultation should be held on each draft resolution and/or decision before it is considered for action by the Council. Consultations should, as much as possible, be scheduled in a timely, transparent and inclusive manner that takes into account the constraints faced by delegations, particularly smaller ones.

4. Role of the Bureau

(114) The Bureau shall deal with procedural and organizational matters. The Bureau shall regularly communicate the contents of its meetings through a timely summary report. 5. Other work formats may include panel debates, seminars and round tables

(115) Utilization of these other work formats, including topics and modalities, would be decided by the Council on a case-by-case basis. They may serve as tools of the Council for enhancing dialogue and mutual understanding on certain issues. They should be utilized in the context of the Council's agenda and annual programme of work, and reinforce and/or complement its intergovernmental nature. They shall not be used to substitute or replace existing human rights mechanisms and established methods of work. 6. High-Level Segment

(116) The High-Level Segment shall be held once a year during the main session of the Council. It shall be followed by a general segment wherein delegations that did not participate in the High-Level

Segment may deliver general statements. B. Working culture
(117) There is a need for:
(a) Early notification of proposals;
(b) Early submission of draft resolutions and decisions, preferably by the end of the penultimate week of a session;
(c) Early distribution of all reports, particularly those of special procedures, to be transmitted to delegations in a timely fashion, at least 15 days in advance of their consideration by the Council, and in all official United Nations languages;
(d) Proposers of a country resolution to have the responsibility to secure the broadest possible support for their initiatives (preferably 15 members), before action is taken;
(e) Restraint in resorting to resolutions, in order to avoid proliferation of resolutions without prejudice to the right of States to decide on the periodicity of presenting their draft proposals by:
(i) Minimizing unnecessary duplication of initiatives with the General Assembly/Third Committee;
(ii) Clustering of agenda items;
(iii) Staggering the tabling of decisions and/or resolutions and consideration of action on agenda items/issues.

C. Outcomes other than resolutions and decisions
(118) These may include recommendations, conclusions, summaries of discussions and President's Statement. As such outcomes would have different legal implications, they should supplement and not replace resolutions and decisions.

D. Special sessions of the Council
(119) The following provisions shall complement the general framework provided by General Assembly resolution 60/251 and the rules of procedure of the Human Rights Council.
(120) The rules of procedure of special sessions shall be in accordance with the rules of procedure applicable for regular sessions of the Council.
(121) The request for the holding of a special session, in accordance with the requirement established in paragraph (10) of General Assembly resolution 60/251, shall be submitted to the President and to the secretariat of the Council. The request shall specify the item proposed for consideration and include any other relevant information the sponsors may wish to provide.
(122) The special session shall be convened as soon as possible after the formal request is communicated, but, in principle, not earlier than two working days, and not later than five working days after the formal receipt of the request. The duration of the special session shall not exceed three days (six working sessions), unless the Council decides otherwise.
(123) The secretariat of the Council shall immediately communicate the request for the holding of a special session and any additional information provided by the sponsors in the request, as well as the date for the convening of the special session, to all United Nations Member States and make the information available to the specialized agencies, other intergovernmental organizations and national human rights institutions, as well as to non-governmental organizations in consultative status by the most expedient and expeditious means of communication. Special session documentation, in particular draft resolutions and decisions, should be made available in all official United Nations languages to all States in an equitable, timely and transparent manner.
(124) The President of the Council should hold open-ended informative consultations before the special session on its conduct and organization. In this regard, the secretariat may also be requested to provide additional information, including, on the methods of work of previous special sessions.
(125) Members of the Council, concerned States, observer States, specialized agencies, other intergovernmental organizations and national human rights institutions, as well as non-governmental organizations in consultative status may contribute to the special session in accordance with the rules of procedure of the Council.
(126) If the requesting or other States intend to present draft resolutions or decisions at the special session, texts should be made available in accordance with the Council's relevant rules of procedure. Nevertheless, sponsors are urged to present such texts as early as possible.
(127) The sponsors of a draft resolution or decision should hold open-ended consultations on the text of their draft resolution(s) or decision(s) with a view to achieving the widest participation in their consideration and, if possible, achieving consensus on them.
(128) A special session should allow participatory debate, be results-oriented and geared to achieving practical outcomes, the implementation of which can be monitored and reported on at the following regular session of the Council for possible follow-up decision.

VII. Rules of Procedure Sessions

PART II FUNDAMENTAL RIGHTS

Rules of procedure

Rule 1. The Human Rights Council shall apply the rules of procedure established for the Main Committees of the General Assembly, as applicable, unless subsequently otherwise decided by the Assembly or the Council.

Regular Sessions

Number of sessions

Rule 2. The Human Rights Council shall meet regularly throughout the year and schedule no fewer than three sessions per Council year, including a main session, for a total duration of no less than 10 weeks. Assumption of membership

Rule 3. Newly-elected member States of the Human Rights Council shall assume their membership on the first day of the Council year, replacing member States that have concluded their respective membership terms.

Place of meeting

Rule 4. The Human Rights Council shall be based in Geneva.

Special Sessions

Convening of special sessions

Rule 5. The rules of procedure of special sessions of the Human Rights Council will be the same as the rules of procedure applicable for regular sessions of the Human Rights Council.

Rule 6. The Human Rights Council shall hold special sessions, when needed, at the request of a member of the Council with the support of one third of the membership of the Council. Participation of and Consultation with Observers of the Council

Rule 7. (a) The Council shall apply the rules of procedure established for committees of the General Assembly, as applicable, unless subsequently otherwise decided by the Assembly or the Council, and the participation of and consultation with observers, including States that are not members of the Council, the specialized agencies, other intergovernmental organizations and national human rights institutions, as well as non-governmental organizations, shall be based on arrangements, including Economic and Social Council resolution 1996/31 of 25 July 1996, and practices observed by the Commission on Human Rights, while ensuring the most effective contribution of these entities.
(b) Participation of national human rights institutions shall be based on arrangements and practices agreed upon by the Commission on Human Rights, including resolution 2005/74 of 20 April 2005, while ensuring the most effective contribution of these entities.

Organization of Work and Agenda for Regular Sessions

Organizational meetings

Rule 8. (a) At the beginning of each Council year, the Council shall hold an organizational meeting to elect its Bureau and to consider and adopt the agenda, programme of work, and calendar of regular sessions for the Council year indicating, if possible, a target date for the conclusion of its work, the approximate dates of consideration of items and the number of meetings to be allocated to each item.
(b) The President of the Council shall also convene organizational meetings two weeks before the beginning of each session and, if necessary, during the Council sessions to discuss organizational and procedural issues pertinent to that session.

President and Vice-Presidents

Elections

Rule 9. (a) At the beginning of each Council year, at its organizational meeting, the Council shall elect, from among the representatives of its members, a President and four Vice-Presidents. The President and the Vice-Presidents shall constitute the Bureau. One of the Vice-Presidents shall serve as Rapporteur.
(b) In the election of the President of the Council, regard shall be had for the equitable geographical rotation of this office among the following Regional Groups: African States, Asian States, Eastern European States, Latin American and Caribbean States, and Western European and other States. The

HUMAN RIGHTS COUNCIL: INSTITUTION BUILDING

four Vice-Presidents of the Council shall be elected on the basis of equitable geographical distribution from the Regional Groups other than the one to which the President belongs. The selection of the Rapporteur shall be based on geographic rotation.

Bureau

Rule 10. The Bureau shall deal with procedural and organizational matters. Term of office

Rule 11. The President and the Vice-Presidents shall, subject to rule 13, hold office for a period of one year. They shall not be eligible for immediate re-election to the same post.

Absence of officers

Rule 12 [105]. If the President finds it necessary to be absent during a meeting or any part thereof, he/she shall designate one of the Vice-Presidents to take his/her place. A Vice-President acting as President shall have the same powers and duties as the President. If the President ceases to hold office pursuant to rule 13, the remaining members of the Bureau shall designate one of the Vice-Presidents to take his/her place until the election of a new President.

Replacement of the President or a Vice-President

Rule 13 If the President or any Vice-President ceases to be able to carry out his/her functions or ceases to be a representative of a member of the Council, or if the Member of the United Nations of which he/she is a representative ceases to be a member of the Council, he/she shall cease to hold such office and a new President or Vice-President shall be elected for the unexpired term.

Secretariat

Duties of the secretariat

Rule 14 [47]. The Office of the United Nations High Commissioner for Human Rights shall act as secretariat for the Council. In this regard, it shall receive, translate, print and circulate in all official United Nations languages, documents, reports and resolutions of the Council, its committees and its organs; interpret speeches made at the meetings; prepare, print and circulate the records of the session; have the custody and proper preservation of the documents in the archives of the Council; distribute all documents of the Council to the members of the Council and observers and, generally, perform all other support functions which the Council may require.

Records and Reports

Report to the General Assembly

Rule 15. The Council shall submit an annual report to the General Assembly.

Public and Private Meetings of the Human Rights Council

General principles

Rule 16 [60]. The meetings of the Council shall be held in public unless the Council decides that exceptional circumstances require the meeting be held in private.

Private meetings

Rule 17 [61]. All decisions of the Council taken at a private meeting shall be announced at an early public meeting of the Council.

Conduct of Business

Working groups and other arrangements

Rule 18. The Council may set up working groups and other arrangements. Participation in these bodies shall be decided upon by the members, based on rule 7. The rules of procedure of these bodies shall follow those of the Council, as applicable, unless decided otherwise by the Council.

Quorum

Rule 19 [67]. The President may declare a meeting open and permit the debate to proceed when at least one third of the members of the Council are present. The presence of a majority of the members shall be required for any decision to be taken. Majority required Rule 20 [125] Decisions of the Council shall be made by a simple majority of the members present and voting, subject to rule 19.

PART II   FUNDAMENTAL RIGHTS

Appendix I Renewed Mandates until they could be considered by the Human Rights Council according to its Annual Programme of Work
Independent expert appointed by the Secretary-General on the situation of human rights in Haiti
Independent expert appointed by the Secretary-General on the situation of human rights in Somalia
Independent expert on the situation of human rights in Burundi
Independent expert on technical cooperation and advisory services in Liberia
Independent expert on the situation of human rights in the Democratic Republic of the Congo
Independent expert on human rights and international solidarity Independent expert on minority issues
Independent expert on the effects of economic reform policies and foreign debt on the full enjoyment of all human rights, particularly economic, social and cultural rights Independent expert on the question of human rights and extreme poverty
Special Rapporteur on the situation of human rights in the Sudan
Special Rapporteur on the situation of human rights in Myanmar
Special Rapporteur on the situation of human rights in the Democratic People's Republic of Korea
Special Rapporteur on the situation of human rights in the Palestinian territories occupied since 1967 (The duration of this mandate has been established until the end of the occupation.)
Special Rapporteur on adequate housing as a component of the right to an adequate standard of living
Special Rapporteur on contemporary forms of racism, racial discrimination, xenophobia and related intolerance
Special Rapporteur on extrajudicial, summary or arbitrary executions Special Rapporteur on freedom of religion or belief
Special Rapporteur on the adverse effects of the illicit movement and dumping of toxic and dangerous products and wastes on the enjoyment of human rights
Special Rapporteur on the human rights aspects of the victims of trafficking in persons, especially women and children
Special Rapporteur on the human rights of migrants
Special Rapporteur on the independence of judges and lawyers
Special Rapporteur on the promotion and protection of human rights and fundamental freedoms while countering terrorism
Special Rapporteur on the promotion and protection of the right to freedom of opinion and expression
Special Rapporteur on the right of everyone to the enjoyment of the highest attainable standard of physical and mental health
Special Rapporteur on the right to education
Special Rapporteur on the right to food
Special Rapporteur on the sale of children, child prostitution and child pornography
Special Rapporteur on the situation of human rights and fundamental freedoms of indigenous people
Special Rapporteur on torture and other cruel, inhuman or degrading treatment or punishment
Special Rapporteur on violence against women, its causes and consequences
Special Representative of the Secretary-General on the issue of human rights and transnational corporations and other business enterprises
Special Representative of the Secretary-General for human rights in Cambodia Special Representative of the Secretary-General on the situation of human rights defenders Representative of the Secretary-General on human rights of internally displaced persons Working Group of Experts on People of African Descent
Working Group on Arbitrary Detention
Working Group on Enforced or Involuntary Disappearances
Working Group on the question of the use of mercenaries as a means of violating human rights and impeding the exercise of the right of peoples to self-determination

Appendix II *[omitted]*.

CONVENTION ON RIGHTS OF PERSONS WITH DISABILITIES

UN Convention on the Rights of Persons with Disabilities (CRPD)
New York, 13 December 2006; entered into force on 3 May 2008
GA Doc. A/61/611
The States Parties to the present Convention,

(a) Recalling the principles proclaimed in the Charter of the United Nations which recognize the inherent dignity and worth and the equal and inalienable rights of all members of the human family as the foundation of freedom, justice and peace in the world,
(b) Recognizing that the United Nations, in the Universal Declaration of Human Rights and in the International Covenants on Human Rights, has proclaimed and agreed that everyone is entitled to all the rights and freedoms set forth therein, without distinction of any kind,
(c) Reaffirming the universality, indivisibility, interdependence and interrelatedness of all human rights and fundamental freedoms and the need for persons with disabilities to be guaranteed their full enjoyment without discrimination,
(d) Recalling the International Covenant on Economic, Social and Cultural Rights, the International Covenant on Civil and Political Rights, the International Convention on the Elimination of All Forms of Racial Discrimination, the Convention on the Elimination of All Forms of Discrimination against Women, the Convention against Torture and Other Cruel, Inhuman or Degrading Treatment or Punishment, the Convention on the Rights of the Child, and the International Convention on the Protection of the Rights of All Migrant Workers and Members of Their Families,
(e) Recognizing that disability is an evolving concept and that disability results from the interaction between persons with impairments and attitudinal and environmental barriers that hinders their full and effective participation in society on an equal basis with others,
(f) Recognizing the importance of the principles and policy guidelines contained in the World Programme of Action concerning Disabled Persons and in the Standard Rules on the Equalization of Opportunities for Persons with Disabilities in influencing the promotion, formulation and evaluation of the policies, plans, programmes and actions at the national, regional and international levels to further equalize opportunities for persons with disabilities, (g) Emphasizing the importance of mainstreaming disability issues as an integral part of relevant strategies of sustainable development,
(h) Recognizing also that discrimination against any person on the basis of disability is a violation of the inherent dignity and worth of the human person,
(i) Recognizing further the diversity of persons with disabilities,
(j) Recognizing the need to promote and protect the human rights of all persons with disabilities, including those who require more intensive support,
(k) Concerned that, despite these various instruments and undertakings, persons with disabilities continue to face barriers in their participation as equal members of society and violations of their human rights in all parts of the world,
(l) Recognizing the importance of international cooperation for improving the living conditions of persons with disabilities in every country, particularly in developing countries, (m) Recognizing the valued existing and potential contributions made by persons with disabilities to the overall well-being and diversity of their communities, and that the promotion of the full enjoyment by persons with disabilities of their human rights and fundamental freedoms and of full participation by persons with disabilities will result in their enhanced sense of belonging and in significant advances in the human, social and economic development of society and the eradication of poverty,
(n) Recognizing the importance for persons with disabilities of their individual autonomy and independence, including the freedom to make their own choices,
(o) Considering that persons with disabilities should have the opportunity to be actively involved in decision-making processes about policies and programmes, including those directly concerning them,
(p) Concerned about the difficult conditions faced by persons with disabilities who are subject to multiple or aggravated forms of discrimination on the basis of race, colour, sex, language, religion, political or other opinion, national, ethnic, indigenous or social origin, property, birth, age or other status,
(q) Recognizing that women and girls with disabilities are often at greater risk, both within and outside the home of violence, injury or abuse, neglect or negligent treatment, maltreatment or exploitation,
(r) Recognizing that children with disabilities should have full enjoyment of all human rights and fundamental freedoms on an equal basis with other children, and recalling obligations to that end undertaken by States Parties to the Convention on the Rights of the Child,
(s) Emphasizing the need to incorporate a gender perspective in all efforts to promote the full enjoyment of human rights and fundamental freedoms by persons with disabilities,

PART II   FUNDAMENTAL RIGHTS

(t) Highlighting the fact that the majority of persons with disabilities live in conditions of poverty, and in this regard recognizing the critical need to address the negative impact of poverty on persons with disabilities,

(u) Bearing in mind that conditions of peace and security based on full respect for the purposes and principles contained in the Charter of the United Nations and observance of applicable human rights instruments are indispensable for the full protection of persons with disabilities, in particular during armed conflicts and foreign occupation,

(v) Recognizing the importance of accessibility to the physical, social, economic and cultural environment, to health and education and to information and communication, in enabling persons with disabilities to fully enjoy all human rights and fundamental freedoms,

(w) Realizing that the individual, having duties to other individuals and to the community to which he or she belongs, is under a responsibility to strive for the promotion and observance of the rights recognized in the International Bill of Human Rights,

(x) Convinced that the family is the natural and fundamental group unit of society and is entitled to protection by society and the State, and that persons with disabilities and their family members should receive the necessary protection and assistance to enable families to contribute towards the full and equal enjoyment of the rights of persons with disabilities,

(y) Convinced that a comprehensive and integral international convention to promote and protect the rights and dignity of persons with disabilities will make a significant contribution to redressing the profound social disadvantage of persons with disabilities and promote their participation in the civil, political, economic, social and cultural spheres with equal opportunities, in both developing and developed countries,

Have agreed as follows:

Article 1. Purpose

The purpose of the present Convention is to promote, protect and ensure the full and equal enjoyment of all human rights and fundamental freedoms by all persons with disabilities, and to promote respect for their inherent dignity. Persons with disabilities include those who have long-term physical, mental, intellectual or sensory impairments which in interaction with various barriers may hinder their full and effective participation in society on an equal basis with others.

Article 2. Definitions

For the purposes of the present Convention:

"Communication" includes languages, display of text, Braille, tactile communication, large print, accessible multimedia as well as written, audio, plain-language, human-reader and augmentative and alternative modes, means and formats of communication, including accessible information and communication technology;

"Language" includes spoken and signed languages and other forms of non spoken languages; "Discrimination on the basis of disability" means any distinction, exclusion or restriction on the basis of disability which has the purpose or effect of impairing or nullifying the recognition, enjoyment or exercise, on an equal basis with others, of all human rights and fundamental freedoms in the political, economic, social, cultural, civil or any other field. It includes all forms of discrimination, including denial of reasonable accommodation; "Reasonable accommodation" means necessary and appropriate modification and adjustments not imposing a disproportionate or undue burden, where needed in a particular case, to ensure to persons with disabilities the enjoyment or exercise on an equal basis with others of all human rights and fundamental freedoms;

"Universal design" means the design of products, environments, programmes and services to be usable by all people, to the greatest extent possible, without the need for adaptation or specialized design.

"Universal design" shall not exclude assistive devices for particular groups of persons with disabilities where this is needed.

Article 3. General principles

The principles of the present Convention shall be:
(a) Respect for inherent dignity, individual autonomy including the freedom to make one's own choices, and independence of persons;
(b) Non-discrimination;
(c) Full and effective participation and inclusion in society;
(d) Respect for difference and acceptance of persons with disabilities as part of human diversity and humanity;
(e) Equality of opportunity;

(f) Accessibility;
(g) Equality between men and women;
(h) Respect for the evolving capacities of children with disabilities and respect for the right of children with disabilities to preserve their identities.

Article 4. General obligations
(1) States Parties undertake to ensure and promote the full realization of all human rights and fundamental freedoms for all persons with disabilities without discrimination of any kind on the basis of disability. To this end, States Parties undertake:
(a) To adopt all appropriate legislative, administrative and other measures for the implementation of the rights recognized in the present Convention;
(b) To take all appropriate measures, including legislation, to modify or abolish existing laws, regulations, customs and practices that constitute discrimination against persons with disabilities;
(c) To take into account the protection and promotion of the human rights of persons with disabilities in all policies and programmes;
(d) To refrain from engaging in any act or practice that is inconsistent with the present Convention and to ensure that public authorities and institutions act in conformity with the present Convention;
(e) To take all appropriate measures to eliminate discrimination on the basis of disability by any person, organization or private enterprise;
(f) To undertake or promote research and development of universally designed goods, services, equipment and facilities, as defined in article 2 of the present Convention, which should require the minimum possible adaptation and the least cost to meet the specific needs of a person with disabilities, to promote their availability and use, and to promote universal design in the development of standards and guidelines;
(g) To undertake or promote research and development of, and to promote the availability and use of new technologies, including information and communications technologies, mobility aids, devices and assistive technologies, suitable for persons with disabilities, giving priority to technologies at an affordable cost;
(h) To provide accessible information to persons with disabilities about mobility aids, devices and assistive technologies, including new technologies, as well as other forms of assistance, support services and facilities;
(i) To promote the training of professionals and staff working with persons with disabilities in the rights recognized in this Convention so as to better provide the assistance and services guaranteed by those rights.
(2) With regard to economic, social and cultural rights, each State Party undertakes to take measures to the maximum of its available resources and, where needed, within the framework of international cooperation, with a view to achieving progressively the full realization of these rights, without prejudice to those obligations contained in the present Convention that are immediately applicable according to international law.
(3) In the development and implementation of legislation and policies to implement the present Convention, and in other decision-making processes concerning issues relating to persons with disabilities, States Parties shall closely consult with and actively involve persons with disabilities, including children with disabilities, through their representative organizations.
(4) Nothing in the present Convention shall affect any provisions which are more conducive to the realization of the rights of persons with disabilities and which may be contained in the law of a State Party or international law in force for that State. There shall be no restriction upon or derogation from any of the human rights and fundamental freedoms recognized or existing in any State Party to the present Convention pursuant to law, conventions, regulation or custom on the pretext that the present Convention does not recognize such rights or freedoms or that it recognizes them to a lesser extent.
(5) The provisions of the present Convention shall extend to all parts of federal states without any limitations or exceptions.

Article 5. Equality and non-discrimination
(1) States Parties recognize that all persons are equal before and under the law and are entitled without any discrimination to the equal protection and equal benefit of the law.
(2) States Parties shall prohibit all discrimination on the basis of disability and guarantee to persons with disabilities equal and effective legal protection against discrimination on all grounds.
(3) In order to promote equality and eliminate discrimination, States Parties shall take all appropriate steps to ensure that reasonable accommodation is provided.
(4) Specific measures which are necessary to accelerate or achieve de facto equality of persons with disabilities shall not be considered discrimination under the terms of the present Convention.

PART II   FUNDAMENTAL RIGHTS

Article 6. Women with disabilities
(1) States Parties recognize that women and girls with disabilities are subject to multiple discrimination, and in this regard shall take measures to ensure the full and equal enjoyment by them of all human rights and fundamental freedoms.
(2) States Parties shall take all appropriate measures to ensure the full development, advancement and empowerment of women, for the purpose of guaranteeing them the exercise and enjoyment of the human rights and fundamental freedoms set out in the present
Convention.

Article 7. Children with disabilities
(1) States Parties shall take all necessary measures to ensure the full enjoyment by children with disabilities of all human rights and fundamental freedoms on an equal basis with other children.
(2) In all actions concerning children with disabilities, the best interests of the child shall be a primary consideration.
(3) States Parties shall ensure that children with disabilities have the right to express their views freely on all matters affecting them, their views being given due weight in accordance with their age and maturity, on an equal basis with other children, and to be provided with disability and age-appropriate assistance to realize that right.

Article 8. Awareness-raising
(1) States Parties undertake to adopt immediate, effective and appropriate measures:
(a) To raise awareness throughout society, including at the family level, regarding persons with disabilities, and to foster respect for the rights and dignity of persons with disabilities;
(b) To combat stereotypes, prejudices and harmful practices relating to persons with disabilities, including those based on sex and age, in all areas of life;
(c) To promote awareness of the capabilities and contributions of persons with disabilities.
(2) Measures to this end include:
(a) Initiating and maintaining effective public awareness campaigns designed:
(i) To nurture receptiveness to the rights of persons with disabilities;
(ii) To promote positive perceptions and greater social awareness towards persons with disabilities;
(iii) To promote recognition of the skills, merits and abilities of persons with disabilities, and of their contributions to the workplace and the labour market;
(b) Fostering at all levels of the education system, including in all children from an early age, an attitude of respect for the rights of persons with disabilities;
(c) Encouraging all organs of the media to portray persons with disabilities in a manner consistent with the purpose of the present Convention;
(d) Promoting awareness-training programmes regarding persons with disabilities and the rights of persons with disabilities.

Article 9. Accessibility
(1) To enable persons with disabilities to live independently and participate fully in all aspects of life, States Parties shall take appropriate measures to ensure to persons with disabilities access, on an equal basis with others, to the physical environment, to transportation, to information and communications, including information and communications technologies and systems, and to other facilities and services open or provided to the public, both in urban and in rural areas. These measures, which shall include the identification and elimination of obstacles and barriers to accessibility, shall apply to, inter alia:
(a) Buildings, roads, transportation and other indoor and outdoor facilities, including schools, housing, medical facilities and workplaces;
(b) Information, communications and other services, including electronic services and emergency services.
(2) States Parties shall also take appropriate measures to:
(a) Develop, promulgate and monitor the implementation of minimum standards and guidelines for the accessibility of facilities and services open or provided to the public;
(b) Ensure that private entities that offer facilities and services which are open or provided to the public take into account all aspects of accessibility for persons with disabilities;
(c) Provide training for stakeholders on accessibility issues facing persons with disabilities;
(d) Provide in buildings and other facilities open to the public signage in Braille and in easy to read and understand forms;
(e) Provide forms of live assistance and intermediaries, including guides, readers and professional sign language interpreters, to facilitate accessibility to buildings and other facilities open to the

public;
(f) Promote other appropriate forms of assistance and support to persons with disabilities to ensure their access to information;
(g) Promote access for persons with disabilities to new information and communications technologies and systems, including the Internet;
(h) Promote the design, development, production and distribution of accessible information and communications technologies and systems at an early stage, so that these technologies and systems become accessible at minimum cost.

Article 10. Right to life
States Parties reaffirm that every human being has the inherent right to life and shall take all necessary measures to ensure its effective enjoyment by persons with disabilities on an equal basis with others.

Article 11. Situations of risk and humanitarian emergencies
States Parties shall take, in accordance with their obligations under international law, including international humanitarian law and international human rights law, all necessary measures to ensure the protection and safety of persons with disabilities in situations of risk, including situations of armed conflict, humanitarian emergencies and the occurrence of natural disasters.

Article 12. Equal recognition before the law
(1) States Parties reaffirm that persons with disabilities have the right to recognition everywhere as persons before the law.
(2) States Parties shall recognize that persons with disabilities enjoy legal capacity on an equal basis with others in all aspects of life.
(3) States Parties shall take appropriate measures to provide access by persons with disabilities to the support they may require in exercising their legal capacity.
(4) States Parties shall ensure that all measures that relate to the exercise of legal capacity provide for appropriate and effective safeguards to prevent abuse in accordance with international human rights law. Such safeguards shall ensure that measures relating to the exercise of legal capacity respect the rights, will and preferences of the person, are free of conflict of interest and undue influence, are proportional and tailored to the person's circumstances, apply for the shortest time possible and are subject to regular review by a competent, independent and impartial authority or judicial body. The safeguards shall be proportional to the degree to which such measures affect the person's rights and interests.
(5) Subject to the provisions of this article, States Parties shall take all appropriate and effective measures to ensure the equal right of persons with disabilities to own or inherit property, to control their own financial affairs and to have equal access to bank loans, mortgages and other forms of financial credit, and shall ensure that persons with disabilities are not arbitrarily deprived of their property.

Article 13. Access to justice
(1) States Parties shall ensure effective access to justice for persons with disabilities on an equal basis with others, including through the provision of procedural and age-appropriate accommodations, in order to facilitate their effective role as direct and indirect participants, including as witnesses, in all legal proceedings, including at investigative and other preliminary stages.
(2) In order to help to ensure effective access to justice for persons with disabilities, States Parties shall promote appropriate training for those working in the field of administration of justice, including police and prison staff.

Article 14. Liberty and security of the person
(1) States Parties shall ensure that persons with disabilities, on an equal basis with others:
(a) Enjoy the right to liberty and security of person;
(b) Are not deprived of their liberty unlawfully or arbitrarily, and that any deprivation of liberty is in conformity with the law, and that the existence of a disability shall in no case justify a deprivation of liberty.
(2) States Parties shall ensure that if persons with disabilities are deprived of their liberty through any process, they are, on an equal basis with others, entitled to guarantees in accordance with international human rights law and shall be treated in compliance with the objectives and principles of this Convention, including by provision of reasonable accommodation.

Article 15. Freedom from torture or cruel, inhuman or degrading treatment or punishment
(1) No one shall be subjected to torture or to cruel, inhuman or degrading treatment or punishment. In

particular, no one shall be subjected without his or her free consent to medical or scientific experimentation.
(2) States Parties shall take all effective legislative, administrative, judicial or other measures to prevent persons with disabilities, on an equal basis with others, from being subjected to torture or cruel, inhuman or degrading treatment or punishment.

Article 16. Freedom from exploitation, violence and abuse
(1) States Parties shall take all appropriate legislative, administrative, social, educational and other measures to protect persons with disabilities, both within and outside the home, from all forms of exploitation, violence and abuse, including their gender-based aspects.
(2) States Parties shall also take all appropriate measures to prevent all forms of exploitation, violence and abuse by ensuring, inter alia, appropriate forms of gender- and age-sensitive assistance and support for persons with disabilities and their families and caregivers, including through the provision of information and education on how to avoid, recognize and report instances of exploitation, violence and abuse. States Parties shall ensure that protection services are age-, gender- and disability-sensitive.
(3) In order to prevent the occurrence of all forms of exploitation, violence and abuse, States Parties shall ensure that all facilities and programmes designed to serve persons with disabilities are effectively monitored by independent authorities.
(4) States Parties shall take all appropriate measures to promote the physical, cognitive and psychological recovery, rehabilitation and social reintegration of persons with disabilities who become victims of any form of exploitation, violence or abuse, including through the provision of protection services. Such recovery and reintegration shall take place in an environment that fosters the health, welfare, self-respect, dignity and autonomy of the person and takes into account gender- and age-specific needs.
(5) States Parties shall put in place effective legislation and policies, including women- and child-focused legislation and policies, to ensure that instances of exploitation, violence and abuse against persons with disabilities are identified, investigated and, where appropriate, prosecuted.

Article 17. Protecting the integrity of the person
Every person with disabilities has a right to respect for his or her physical and mental integrity on an equal basis with others.

Article 18. Liberty of movement and nationality
(1) States Parties shall recognize the rights of persons with disabilities to liberty of movement, to freedom to choose their residence and to a nationality, on an equal basis with others, including by ensuring that persons with disabilities:
(a) Have the right to acquire and change a nationality and are not deprived of their nationality arbitrarily or on the basis of disability;
(b) Are not deprived, on the basis of disability, of their ability to obtain, possess and utilize documentation of their nationality or other documentation of identification, or to utilize relevant processes such as immigration proceedings, that may be needed to facilitate exercise of the right to liberty of movement;
(c) Are free to leave any country, including their own;
(d) Are not deprived, arbitrarily or on the basis of disability, of the right to enter their own country.
(2) Children with disabilities shall be registered immediately after birth and shall have the right from birth to a name, the right to acquire a nationality and, as far as possible, the right to know and be cared for by their parents.

Article 19. Living independently and being included in the community
States Parties to this Convention recognize the equal right of all persons with disabilities to live in the community, with choices equal to others, and shall take effective and appropriate measures to facilitate full enjoyment by persons with disabilities of this right and their full inclusion and participation in the community, including by ensuring that:
(a) Persons with disabilities have the opportunity to choose their place of residence and where and with whom they live on an equal basis with others and are not obliged to live in a particular living arrangement;
(b) Persons with disabilities have access to a range of in-home, residential and other community support services, including personal assistance necessary to support living and inclusion in the community, and to prevent isolation or segregation from the community;
(c) Community services and facilities for the general population are available on an equal basis to persons with disabilities and are responsive to their needs.

Article 20. Personal mobility

States Parties shall take effective measures to ensure personal mobility with the greatest possible independence for persons with disabilities, including by:
(a) Facilitating the personal mobility of persons with disabilities in the manner and at the time of their choice, and at affordable cost;
(b) Facilitating access by persons with disabilities to quality mobility aids, devices, assistive technologies and forms of live assistance and intermediaries, including by making them available at affordable cost;
(c) Providing training in mobility skills to persons with disabilities and to specialist staff working with persons with disabilities;
(d) Encouraging entities that produce mobility aids, devices and assistive technologies to take into account all aspects of mobility for persons with disabilities.

Article 21. Freedom of expression and opinion, and access to information

States Parties shall take all appropriate measures to ensure that persons with disabilities can exercise the right to freedom of expression and opinion, including the freedom to seek, receive and impart information and ideas on an equal basis with others and through all forms of communication of their choice, as defined in article 2 of the present Convention, including by:
(a) Providing information intended for the general public to persons with disabilities in accessible formats and technologies appropriate to different kinds of disabilities in a timely manner and without additional cost;
(b) Accepting and facilitating the use of sign languages, Braille, augmentative and alternative communication, and all other accessible means, modes and formats of communication of their choice by persons with disabilities in official interactions;
(c) Urging private entities that provide services to the general public, including through the Internet, to provide information and services in accessible and usable formats for persons with disabilities;
(d) Encouraging the mass media, including providers of information through the Internet, to make their services accessible to persons with disabilities;
(e) Recognizing and promoting the use of sign languages.

Article 22. Respect for privacy

(1) No person with disabilities, regardless of place of residence or living arrangements, shall be subjected to arbitrary or unlawful interference with his or her privacy, family, home or correspondence or other types of communication or to unlawful attacks on his or her honour and reputation. Persons with disabilities have the right to the protection of the law against such interference or attacks.
(2) States Parties shall protect the privacy of personal, health and rehabilitation information of persons with disabilities on an equal basis with others.

Article 23. Respect for home and the family

(1) States Parties shall take effective and appropriate measures to eliminate discrimination against persons with disabilities in all matters relating to marriage, family, parenthood and relationships, on an equal basis with others, so as to ensure that:
(a) The right of all persons with disabilities who are of marriageable age to marry and to found a family on the basis of free and full consent of the intending spouses is recognized;
(b) The rights of persons with disabilities to decide freely and responsibly on the number and spacing of their children and to have access to age-appropriate information, reproductive and family planning education are recognized, and the means necessary to enable them to exercise these rights are provided;
(c) Persons with disabilities, including children, retain their fertility on an equal basis with others.
(2) States Parties shall ensure the rights and responsibilities of persons with disabilities, with regard to guardianship, wardship, trusteeship, adoption of children or similar institutions, where these concepts exist in national legislation; in all cases the best interests of the child shall be paramount. States Parties shall render appropriate assistance to persons with disabilities in the performance of their child-rearing responsibilities.
(3) States Parties shall ensure that children with disabilities have equal rights with respect to family life. With a view to realizing these rights, and to prevent concealment, abandonment, neglect and segregation of children with disabilities, States Parties shall undertake to provide early and comprehensive information, services and support to children with disabilities and their families.
(4) States Parties shall ensure that a child shall not be separated from his or her parents against their will, except when competent authorities subject to judicial review determine, in accordance with applicable law and procedures, that such separation is necessary for the best interests of the child. In

PART II   FUNDAMENTAL RIGHTS

no case shall a child be separated from parents on the basis of a disability of either the child or one or both of the parents.
(5) States Parties shall, where the immediate family is unable to care for a child with disabilities, undertake every effort to provide alternative care within the wider family, and failing that, within the community in a family setting.

Article 24. Education
(1) States Parties recognize the right of persons with disabilities to education. With a view to realizing this right without discrimination and on the basis of equal opportunity, States Parties shall ensure an inclusive education system at all levels and life long learning directed to:
(a) The full development of human potential and sense of dignity and self-worth, and the strengthening of respect for human rights, fundamental freedoms and human diversity;
(b) The development by persons with disabilities of their personality, talents and creativity, as well as their mental and physical abilities, to their fullest potential;
(c) Enabling persons with disabilities to participate effectively in a free society.
(2) In realizing this right, States Parties shall ensure that:
(a) Persons with disabilities are not excluded from the general education system on the basis of disability, and that children with disabilities are not excluded from free and compulsory primary education, or from secondary education, on the basis of disability;
(b) Persons with disabilities can access an inclusive, quality and free primary education and secondary education on an equal basis with others in the communities in which they live;
(c) Reasonable accommodation of the individual's requirements is provided;
(d) Persons with disabilities receive the support required, within the general education system, to facilitate their effective education;
(e) Effective individualized support measures are provided in environments that maximize academic and social development, consistent with the goal of full inclusion.
(3) States Parties shall enable persons with disabilities to learn life and social development skills to facilitate their full and equal participation in education and as members of the community. To this end, States Parties shall take appropriate measures, including:
(a) Facilitating the learning of Braille, alternative script, augmentative and alternative modes, means and formats of communication and orientation and mobility skills, and facilitating peer support and mentoring;
(b) Facilitating the learning of sign language and the promotion of the linguistic identity of the deaf community;
(c) Ensuring that the education of persons, and in particular children, who are blind, deaf or deafblind, is delivered in the most appropriate languages and modes and means of communication for the individual, and in environments which maximize academic and social development.
(4) In order to help ensure the realization of this right, States Parties shall take appropriate measures to employ teachers, including teachers with disabilities, who are qualified in sign language and/or Braille, and to train professionals and staff who work at all levels of education. Such training shall incorporate disability awareness and the use of appropriate augmentative and alternative modes, means and formats of communication, educational techniques and materials to support persons with disabilities.
(5) States Parties shall ensure that persons with disabilities are able to access general tertiary education, vocational training, adult education and lifelong learning without discrimination and on an equal basis with others. To this end, States Parties shall ensure that reasonable accommodation is provided to persons with disabilities.

Article 25. Health States
Parties recognize that persons with disabilities have the right to the enjoyment of the highest attainable standard of health without discrimination on the basis of disability. States Parties shall take all appropriate measures to ensure access for persons with disabilities to health services that are gender-sensitive, including health-related rehabilitation. In particular, States Parties shall:
(a) Provide persons with disabilities with the same range, quality and standard of free or affordable health care and programmes as provided to other persons, including in the area of sexual and reproductive health and population-based public health programmes;
(b) Provide those health services needed by persons with disabilities specifically because of their disabilities, including early identification and intervention as appropriate, and services designed to minimize and prevent further disabilities, including among children and older persons;
(c) Provide these health services as close as possible to people's own communities, including in rural areas;

(d) Require health professionals to provide care of the same quality to persons with disabilities as to others, including on the basis of free and informed consent by, inter alia, raising awareness of the human rights, dignity, autonomy and needs of persons with disabilities through training and the promulgation of ethical standards for public and private health care;
(e) Prohibit discrimination against persons with disabilities in the provision of health insurance, and life insurance where such insurance is permitted by national law, which shall be provided in a fair and reasonable manner;
(f) Prevent discriminatory denial of health care or health services or food and fluids on the basis of disability.

Article 26. Habilitation and rehabilitation

(1) States Parties shall take effective and appropriate measures, including through peer support, to enable persons with disabilities to attain and maintain maximum independence, full physical, mental, social and vocational ability, and full inclusion and participation in all aspects of life. To that end, States Parties shall organize, strengthen and extend comprehensive habilitation and rehabilitation services and programmes, particularly in the areas of health, employment, education and social services, in such a way that these services and programmes:
(a) Begin at the earliest possible stage, and are based on the multidisciplinary assessment of individual needs and strengths;
(b) Support participation and inclusion in the community and all aspects of society, are voluntary, and are available to persons with disabilities as close as possible to their own communities, including in rural areas.
(2) States Parties shall promote the development of initial and continuing training for professionals and staff working in habilitation and rehabilitation services.
(3) States Parties shall promote the availability, knowledge and use of assistive devices and technologies, designed for persons with disabilities, as they relate to habilitation and rehabilitation.

Article 27. Work and employment

(1) States Parties recognize the right of persons with disabilities to work, on an equal basis with others; this includes the right to the opportunity to gain a living by work freely chosen or accepted in a labour market and work environment that is open, inclusive and accessible to persons with disabilities. States Parties shall safeguard and promote the realization of the right to work, including for those who acquire a disability during the course of employment, by taking appropriate steps, including through legislation, to, inter alia:
(a) Prohibit discrimination on the basis of disability with regard to all matters concerning all forms of employment, including conditions of recruitment, hiring and employment, continuance of employment, career advancement and safe and healthy working conditions;
(b) Protect the rights of persons with disabilities, on an equal basis with others, to just and favourable conditions of work, including equal opportunities and equal remuneration for work of equal value, safe and healthy working conditions, including protection from harassment, and the redress of grievances;
(c) Ensure that persons with disabilities are able to exercise their labour and trade union rights on an equal basis with others;
(d) Enable persons with disabilities to have effective access to general technical and vocational guidance programmes, placement services and vocational and continuing training;
(e) Promote employment opportunities and career advancement for persons with disabilities in the labour market, as well as assistance in finding, obtaining, maintaining and returning to employment;
(f) Promote opportunities for self-employment, entrepreneurship, the development of cooperatives and starting one's own business;
(g) Employ persons with disabilities in the public sector;
(h) Promote the employment of persons with disabilities in the private sector through appropriate policies and measures, which may include affirmative action programmes, incentives and other measures;
(i) Ensure that reasonable accommodation is provided to persons with disabilities in the workplace;
(j) Promote the acquisition by persons with disabilities of work experience in the open labour market;
(k) Promote vocational and professional rehabilitation, job retention and return-to-work programmes for persons with disabilities.
(2) States Parties shall ensure that persons with disabilities are not held in slavery or in servitude, and are protected, on an equal basis with others, from forced or compulsory labour.

PART II   FUNDAMENTAL RIGHTS

Article 28. Adequate standard of living and social protection

(1) States Parties recognize the right of persons with disabilities to an adequate standard of living for themselves and their families, including adequate food, clothing and housing, and to the continuous improvement of living conditions, and shall take appropriate steps to safeguard and promote the realization of this right without discrimination on the basis of disability.

(2) States Parties recognize the right of persons with disabilities to social protection and to the enjoyment of that right without discrimination on the basis of disability, and shall take appropriate steps to safeguard and promote the realization of this right, including measures: (a) To ensure equal access by persons with disabilities to clean water services, and to ensure access to appropriate and affordable services, devices and other assistance for disability-related needs;

(b) To ensure access by persons with disabilities, in particular women and girls with disabilities and older persons with disabilities, to social protection programmes and poverty reduction programmes;

(c) To ensure access by persons with disabilities and their families living in situations of poverty to assistance from the State with disability-related expenses, including adequate training, counselling, financial assistance and respite care;

(d) To ensure access by persons with disabilities to public housing programmes;

(e) To ensure equal access by persons with disabilities to retirement benefits and programmes.

Article 29. Participation in political and public life

States Parties shall guarantee to persons with disabilities political rights and the opportunity to enjoy them on an equal basis with others, and shall undertake to:

(a) Ensure that persons with disabilities can effectively and fully participate in political and public life on an equal basis with others, directly or through freely chosen representatives, including the right and opportunity for persons with disabilities to vote and be elected, inter alia, by:

(i) Ensuring that voting procedures, facilities and materials are appropriate, accessible and easy to understand and use;

(ii) Protecting the right of persons with disabilities to vote by secret ballot in elections and public referendums without intimidation, and to stand for elections, to effectively hold office and perform all public functions at all levels of government, facilitating the use of assistive and new technologies where appropriate;

(iii) Guaranteeing the free expression of the will of persons with disabilities as electors and to this end, where necessary, at their request, allowing assistance in voting by a person of their own choice;

(b) Promote actively an environment in which persons with disabilities can effectively and fully participate in the conduct of public affairs, without discrimination and on an equal basis with others, and encourage their participation in public affairs, including:

(i) Participation in non-governmental organizations and associations concerned with the public and political life of the country, and in the activities and administration of political parties;

(ii) Forming and joining organizations of persons with disabilities to represent persons with disabilities at international, national, regional and local levels.

Article 30. Participation in cultural life, recreation, leisure and sport

(1) States Parties recognize the right of persons with disabilities to take part on an equal basis with others in cultural life, and shall take all appropriate measures to ensure that persons with disabilities:

(a) Enjoy access to cultural materials in accessible formats;

(b) Enjoy access to television programmes, films, theatre and other cultural activities, in accessible formats;

(c) Enjoy access to places for cultural performances or services, such as theatres, museums, cinemas, libraries and tourism services, and, as far as possible, enjoy access to monuments and sites of national cultural importance.

(2) States Parties shall take appropriate measures to enable persons with disabilities to have the opportunity to develop and utilize their creative, artistic and intellectual potential, not only for their own benefit, but also for the enrichment of society.

(3) States Parties shall take all appropriate steps, in accordance with international law, to ensure that laws protecting intellectual property rights do not constitute an unreasonable or discriminatory barrier to access by persons with disabilities to cultural materials.

(4) Persons with disabilities shall be entitled, on an equal basis with others, to recognition and support of their specific cultural and linguistic identity, including sign languages and deaf culture.

(5) With a view to enabling persons with disabilities to participate on an equal basis with others in recreational, leisure and sporting activities, States Parties shall take appropriate measures:

(a) To encourage and promote the participation, to the fullest extent possible, of persons with disabilities in mainstream sporting activities at all levels;

(b) To ensure that persons with disabilities have an opportunity to organize, develop and participate in disability-specific sporting and recreational activities and, to this end, encourage the provision, on an equal basis with others, of appropriate instruction, training and resources;
(c) To ensure that persons with disabilities have access to sporting, recreational and tourism venues;
(d) To ensure that children with disabilities have equal access with other children to participation in play, recreation and leisure and sporting activities, including those activities in the school system;
(e) To ensure that persons with disabilities have access to services from those involved in the organization of recreational, tourism, leisure and sporting activities.

Article 31. Statistics and data collection
(1) States Parties undertake to collect appropriate information, including statistical and research data, to enable them to formulate and implement policies to give effect to the present Convention. The process of collecting and maintaining this information shall:
(a) Comply with legally established safeguards, including legislation on data protection, to ensure confidentiality and respect for the privacy of persons with disabilities;
(b) Comply with internationally accepted norms to protect human rights and fundamental freedoms and ethical principles in the collection and use of statistics.
(2) The information collected in accordance with this article shall be disaggregated, as appropriate, and used to help assess the implementation of States Parties' obligations under the present Convention and to identify and address the barriers faced by persons with disabilities in exercising their rights.
(3) States Parties shall assume responsibility for the dissemination of these statistics and ensure their accessibility to persons with disabilities and others.

Article 32. International cooperation
(1) States Parties recognize the importance of international cooperation and its promotion, in support of national efforts for the realization of the purpose and objectives of the present Convention, and will undertake appropriate and effective measures in this regard, between and among States and, as appropriate, in partnership with relevant international and regional organizations and civil society, in particular organizations of persons with disabilities. Such measures could include, inter alia:
(a) Ensuring that international cooperation, including international development programmes, is inclusive of and accessible to persons with disabilities;
(b) Facilitating and supporting capacity-building, including through the exchange and sharing of information, experiences, training programmes and best practices;
(c) Facilitating cooperation in research and access to scientific and technical knowledge;
(d) Providing, as appropriate, technical and economic assistance, including by facilitating access to and sharing of accessible and assistive technologies, and through the transfer of technologies.
(2) The provisions of this article are without prejudice to the obligations of each State Party to fulfil its obligations under the present Convention.

Article 33. National implementation and monitoring
(1) States Parties, in accordance with their system of organization, shall designate one or more focal points within government for matters relating to the implementation of the present Convention, and shall give due consideration to the establishment or designation of a coordination mechanism within government to facilitate related action in different sectors and at different levels.
(2) States Parties shall, in accordance with their legal and administrative systems, maintain, strengthen, designate or establish within the State Party, a framework, including one or more independent mechanisms, as appropriate, to promote, protect and monitor implementation of the present Convention. When designating or establishing such a mechanism, States Parties shall take into account the principles relating to the status and functioning of national institutions for protection and promotion of human rights.
(3) Civil society, in particular persons with disabilities and their representative organizations, shall be involved and participate fully in the monitoring process.

Article 34. Committee on the Rights of Persons with Disabilities
(1) There shall be established a Committee on the Rights of Persons with Disabilities (hereafter referred to as "the Committee"), which shall carry out the functions hereinafter provided.
(2) The Committee shall consist, at the time of entry into force of the present Convention, of twelve experts. After an additional sixty ratifications or accessions to the Convention, the membership of the Committee shall increase by six members, attaining a maximum number of eighteen members.
(3) The members of the Committee shall serve in their personal capacity and shall be of high moral standing and recognized competence and experience in the field covered by the present Convention.

PART II   FUNDAMENTAL RIGHTS

When nominating their candidates, States Parties are invited to give due consideration to the provision set out in article 4.3 of the present Convention.
(4) The members of the Committee shall be elected by States Parties, consideration being given to equitable geographical distribution, representation of the different forms of civilization and of the principal legal systems, balanced gender representation and participation of experts with disabilities.
(5) The members of the Committee shall be elected by secret ballot from a list of persons nominated by the States Parties from among their nationals at meetings of the Conference of States Parties. At those meetings, for which two thirds of States Parties shall constitute a quorum, the persons elected to the Committee shall be those who obtain the largest number of votes and an absolute majority of the votes of the representatives of States Parties present and voting.
(6) The initial election shall be held no later than six months after the date of entry into force of the present Convention. At least four months before the date of each election, the Secretary-General of the United Nations shall address a letter to the States Parties inviting them to submit the nominations within two months. The Secretary-General shall subsequently prepare a list in alphabetical order of all persons thus nominated, indicating the State Parties which have nominated them, and shall submit it to the States Parties to the present Convention.
(7) The members of the Committee shall be elected for a term of four years. They shall be eligible for re-election once. However, the term of six of the members elected at the first election shall expire at the end of two years; immediately after the first election, the names of these six members shall be chosen by lot by the chairperson of the meeting referred to in paragraph (5) of this article.
(8) The election of the six additional members of the Committee shall be held on the occasion of regular elections, in accordance with the relevant provisions of this article.
(9) If a member of the Committee dies or resigns or declares that for any other cause she or he can no longer perform her or his duties, the State Party which nominated the member shall appoint another expert possessing the qualifications and meeting the requirements set out in the relevant provisions of this article, to serve for the remainder of the term.
(10) The Committee shall establish its own rules of procedure.
(11) The Secretary-General of the United Nations shall provide the necessary staff and facilities for the effective performance of the functions of the Committee under the present Convention, and shall convene its initial meeting.
(12) With the approval of the General Assembly, the members of the Committee established under the present Convention shall receive emoluments from United Nations resources on such terms and conditions as the Assembly may decide, having regard to the importance of the Committee's responsibilities.
(13) The members of the Committee shall be entitled to the facilities, privileges and immunities of experts on mission for the United Nations as laid down in the relevant sections of the Convention on the Privileges and Immunities of the United Nations.

Article 35. Reports by States Parties

(1) Each State Party shall submit to the Committee, through the Secretary-General of the United Nations, a comprehensive report on measures taken to give effect to its obligations under the present Convention and on the progress made in that regard, within two years after the entry into force of the present Convention for the State Party concerned.
(2) Thereafter, States Parties shall submit subsequent reports at least every four years and further whenever the Committee so requests.
(3) The Committee shall decide any guidelines applicable to the content of the reports.
(4) A State Party which has submitted a comprehensive initial report to the Committee need not, in its subsequent reports, repeat information previously provided. When preparing reports to the Committee, States Parties are invited to consider doing so in an open and transparent process and to give due consideration to the provision set out in article 4.3 of the present Convention.
(5) Reports may indicate factors and difficulties affecting the degree of fulfilment of obligations under the present Convention.

Article 36. Consideration of reports

(1) Each report shall be considered by the Committee, which shall make such suggestions and general recommendations on the report as it may consider appropriate and shall forward these to the State Party concerned. The State Party may respond with any information it chooses to the Committee. The Committee may request further information from States Parties relevant to the implementation of the present Convention.
(2) If a State Party is significantly overdue in the submission of a report, the Committee may notify the State Party concerned of the need to examine the implementation of the present Convention in

that State Party, on the basis of reliable information available to the Committee, if the relevant report is not submitted within three months following the notification. The Committee shall invite the State Party concerned to participate in such examination. Should the State Party respond by submitting the relevant report, the provisions of paragraph (1) of this article will apply.
(3) The Secretary-General of the United Nations shall make available the reports to all States Parties.
(4) States Parties shall make their reports widely available to the public in their own countries and facilitate access to the suggestions and general recommendations relating to these reports.
(5) The Committee shall transmit, as it may consider appropriate, to the specialized agencies, funds and programmes of the United Nations, and other competent bodies, reports from States Parties in order to address a request or indication of a need for technical advice or assistance contained therein, along with the Committee's observations and recommendations, if any, on these requests or indications.

Article 37. Cooperation between States Parties and the Committee
(1) Each State Party shall cooperate with the Committee and assist its members in the fulfilment of their mandate.
(2) In its relationship with States Parties, the Committee shall give due consideration to ways and means of enhancing national capacities for the implementation of the present Convention, including through international cooperation.

Article 38. Relationship of the Committee with other bodies
In order to foster the effective implementation of the present Convention and to encourage international cooperation in the field covered by the present Convention:
(a) The specialized agencies and other United Nations organs shall be entitled to be represented at the consideration of the implementation of such provisions of the present Convention as fall within the scope of their mandate. The Committee may invite the specialized agencies and other competent bodies as it may consider appropriate to provide expert advice on the implementation of the Convention in areas falling within the scope of their respective mandates. The Committee may invite specialized agencies and other United Nations organs to submit reports on the implementation of the Convention in areas falling within the scope of their activities;
(b) The Committee, as it discharges its mandate, shall consult, as appropriate, other relevant bodies instituted by international human rights treaties, with a view to ensuring the consistency of their respective reporting guidelines, suggestions and general recommendations, and avoiding duplication and overlap in the performance of their functions.

Article 39. Report of the Committee
The Committee shall report every two years to the General Assembly and to the Economic and Social Council on its activities, and may make suggestions and general recommendations based on the examination of reports and information received from the States Parties. Such suggestions and general recommendations shall be included in the report of the Committee together with comments, if any, from States Parties.

Article 40. Conference of States Parties
(1) The States Parties shall meet regularly in a Conference of States Parties in order to consider any matter with regard to the implementation of the present Convention.
(2) No later than six months after the entry into force of the present Convention, the Conference of the States Parties shall be convened by the Secretary-General of the United Nations. The subsequent meetings shall be convened by the Secretary-General of the United Nations biennially or upon the decision of the Conference of States Parties.

Article 41. Depositary
The Secretary-General of the United Nations shall be the depositary of the present Convention.

Article 42. Signature
The present Convention shall be open for signature by all States and by regional integration organizations at United Nations Headquarters in New York as of 30 March 2007.

Article 43. Consent to be bound
The present Convention shall be subject to ratification by signatory States and to formal confirmation by signatory regional integration organizations. It shall be open for accession by any State or regional integration organization which has not signed the Convention.

Article 44. Regional integration organizations

PART II   FUNDAMENTAL RIGHTS

(1) "Regional integration organization" shall mean an organization constituted by sovereign States of a given region, to which its member States have transferred competence in respect of matters governed by this Convention. Such organizations shall declare, in their instruments of formal confirmation or accession, the extent of their competence with respect to matters governed by this Convention. Subsequently, they shall inform the depositary of any substantial modification in the extent of their competence.
(2) References to "States Parties" in the present Convention shall apply to such organizations within the limits of their competence.
(3) For the purposes of article 45, paragraph (1), and article 47, paragraphs (2) and (3), any instrument deposited by a regional integration organization shall not be counted.
(4) Regional integration organizations, in matters within their competence, may exercise their right to vote in the Conference of States Parties, with a number of votes equal to the number of their member States that are Parties to this Convention. Such an organization shall not exercise its right to vote if any of its member States exercises its right, and vice versa.

Article 45. Entry into force
(1) The present Convention shall enter into force on the thirtieth day after the deposit of the twentieth instrument of ratification or accession.
(2) For each State or regional integration organization ratifying, formally confirming or acceding to the Convention after the deposit of the twentieth such instrument, the Convention shall enter into force on the thirtieth day after the deposit of its own such instrument.

Article 46. Reservations
(1) Reservations incompatible with the object and purpose of the present Convention shall not be permitted.
(2) Reservations may be withdrawn at any time.

Article 47. Amendments
(1) Any State Party may propose an amendment to the present Convention and submit it to the Secretary-General of the United Nations. The Secretary-General shall communicate any proposed amendments to States Parties, with a request to be notified whether they favour a conference of States Parties for the purpose of considering and deciding upon the proposals. In the event that, within four months from the date of such communication, at least one third of the States Parties favour such a conference, the Secretary-General shall convene the conference under the auspices of the United Nations. Any amendment adopted by a majority of two thirds of the States Parties present and voting shall be submitted by the Secretary-General to the General Assembly for approval and thereafter to all States Parties for acceptance.
(2) An amendment adopted and approved in accordance with paragraph (1) of this article shall enter into force on the thirtieth day after the number of instruments of acceptance deposited reaches two thirds of the number of States Parties at the date of adoption of the amendment. Thereafter, the amendment shall enter into force for any State Party on the thirtieth day following the deposit of its own instrument of acceptance. An amendment shall be binding only on those States Parties which have accepted it.
(3) If so decided by the Conference of States Parties by consensus, an amendment adopted and approved in accordance with paragraph (1) of this article which relates exclusively to articles 34, 38, 39 and 40 shall enter into force for all States Parties on the thirtieth day after the number of instruments of acceptance deposited reaches two thirds of the number of States Parties at the date of adoption of the amendment.

Article 48. Denunciation
A State Party may denounce the present Convention by written notification to the Secretary-General of the United Nations. The denunciation shall become effective one year after the date of receipt of the notification by the Secretary-General.

Article 49. Accessible format
The text of the present Convention shall be made available in accessible formats.

Article 50. Authentic texts
The Arabic, Chinese, English, French, Russian and Spanish texts of the present Convention shall be equally authentic. In witness thereof the undersigned plenipotentiaries, being duly authorized thereto by their respective Governments, have signed the present Convention.

Optional Protocol to the CRPD

The States Parties to the present Protocol have agreed as follows:

Article 1. (1) A State Party to the present Protocol ("State Party") recognizes the competence of the Committee on the Rights of Persons with Disabilities ("the Committee") to receive and consider communications from or on behalf of individuals or groups of individuals subject to its jurisdiction who claim to be victims of a violation by that State Party of the provisions of the Convention.
(2) No communication shall be received by the Committee if it concerns a State Party to the Convention that is not a party to the present Protocol.

Article 2. The Committee shall consider a communication inadmissible when:
(a) The communication is anonymous;
(b) The communication constitutes an abuse of the right of submission of such communications or is incompatible with the provisions of the Convention;
(c) The same matter has already been examined by the Committee or has been or is being examined under another procedure of international investigation or settlement;
(d) All available domestic remedies have not been exhausted. This shall not be the rule where the application of the remedies is unreasonably prolonged or unlikely to bring effective relief;
(e) It is manifestly ill-founded or not sufficiently substantiated; or when
(f) The facts that are the subject of the communication occurred prior to the entry into force of the present Protocol for the State Party concerned unless those facts continued after that date.

Article 3. Subject to the provisions of article 2 of the present Protocol, the Committee shall bring any communications submitted to it confidentially to the attention of the State Party. Within six months, the receiving State shall submit to the Committee written explanations or statements clarifying the matter and the remedy, if any, that may have been taken by that State.

Article 4. (1) At any time after the receipt of a communication and before a determination on the merits has been reached, the Committee may transmit to the State Party concerned for its urgent consideration a request that the State Party take such interim measures as may be necessary to avoid possible irreparable damage to the victim or victims of the alleged violation.
(2) Where the Committee exercises its discretion under paragraph (1) of this article, this does not imply a determination on admissibility or on the merits of the communication.

Article 5. The Committee shall hold closed meetings when examining communications under the present Protocol. After examining a communication, the Committee shall forward its suggestions and recommendations, if any, to the State Party concerned and to the petitioner.

Article 6. (1) If the Committee receives reliable information indicating grave or systematic violations by a State Party of rights set forth in the Convention, the Committee shall invite that State Party to cooperate in the examination of the information and to this end submit observations with regard to the information concerned.
(2) Taking into account any observations that may have been submitted by the State Party concerned as well as any other reliable information available to it, the Committee may designate one or more of its members to conduct an inquiry and to report urgently to the Committee. Where warranted and with the consent of the State Party, the inquiry may include a visit to its territory.
(3) After examining the findings of such an inquiry, the Committee shall transmit these findings to the State Party concerned together with any comments and recommendations.
(4) The State Party concerned shall, within six months of receiving the findings, comments and recommendations transmitted by the Committee, submit its observations to the Committee.
(5) Such an inquiry shall be conducted confidentially and the cooperation of the State Party shall be sought at all stages of the proceedings.

Article 7. (1) The Committee may invite the State Party concerned to include in its report under article 35 of the Convention details of any measures taken in response to an inquiry conducted under article 6 of the present Protocol.
(2) The Committee may, if necessary, after the end of the period of six months referred to in article 6.4, invite the State Party concerned to inform it of the measures taken in response to such an inquiry.

Article 8. Each State Party may, at the time of signature or ratification of the present Protocol or accession thereto, declare that it does not recognize the competence of the Committee provided for in articles 6 and 7.

PART II   FUNDAMENTAL RIGHTS

Article 9. The Secretary-General of the United Nations shall be the depositary of the present Protocol.

Article 10. The present Protocol shall be open for signature by signatory States and regional integration organizations of the Convention at United Nations Headquarters in New York as of 30 March 2007.

Article 11. The present Protocol shall be subject to ratification by signatory States of this Protocol which have ratified or acceded to the Convention. It shall be subject to formal confirmation by signatory regional integration organizations of this Protocol which have formally confirmed or acceded to the Convention. It shall be open for accession by any State or regional integration organization which has ratified, formally confirmed or acceded to the Convention and which has not signed the Protocol.

Article 12. (1) "Regional integration organization" shall mean an organization constituted by sovereign States of a given region, to which its member States have transferred competence in respect of matters governed by the Convention and this Protocol. Such organizations shall declare, in their instruments of formal confirmation or accession, the extent of their competence with respect to matters governed by the Convention and this Protocol. Subsequently, they shall inform the depositary of any substantial modification in the extent of their competence.
(2) References to "States Parties" in the present Protocol shall apply to such organizations within the limits of their competence.
(3) For the purposes of article 13, paragraph (1), and article 15, paragraph (2), any instrument deposited by a regional integration organization shall not be counted.
(4) Regional integration organizations, in matters within their competence, may exercise their right to vote in the meeting of States Parties, with a number of votes equal to the number of their member States that are Parties to this Protocol. Such an organization shall not exercise its right to vote if any of its member States exercises its right, and vice versa.

Article 13. (1) Subject to the entry into force of the Convention, the present Protocol shall enter into force on the thirtieth day after the deposit of the tenth instrument of ratification or accession.
(2) For each State or regional integration organization ratifying, formally confirming or acceding to the Protocol after the deposit of the tenth such instrument, the Protocol shall enter into force on the thirtieth day after the deposit of its own such instrument.

Article 14. (1) Reservations incompatible with the object and purpose of the present Protocol shall not be permitted.
(2) Reservations may be withdrawn at any time.

Article 15. (1) Any State Party may propose an amendment to the present Protocol and submit it to the Secretary-General of the United Nations. The Secretary-General shall communicate any proposed amendments to States Parties, with a request to be notified whether they favour a meeting of States Parties for the purpose of considering and deciding upon the proposals. In the event that, within four months from the date of such communication, at least one third of the States Parties favour such a meeting, the Secretary-General shall convene the meeting under the auspices of the United Nations. Any amendment adopted by a majority of two thirds of the States Parties present and voting shall be submitted by the Secretary-General to the General Assembly for approval and thereafter to all States Parties for acceptance.
(2) An amendment adopted and approved in accordance with paragraph (1) of this article shall enter into force on the thirtieth day after the number of instruments of acceptance deposited reaches two thirds of the number of States Parties at the date of adoption of the amendment. Thereafter, the amendment shall enter into force for any State Party on the thirtieth day following the deposit of its own instrument of acceptance. An amendment shall be binding only on those States Parties which have accepted it.

Article 16. A State Party may denounce the present Protocol by written notification to the Secretary-General of the United Nations. The denunciation shall become effective one year after the date of receipt of the notification by the Secretary-General.

Article 17. The text of the present Protocol shall be made available in accessible formats.

Article 18. The Arabic, Chinese, English, French, Russian and Spanish texts of the present Protocol shall be equally authentic.
In witness thereof the undersigned plenipotentiaries, being duly authorized thereto by their respective Governments, have signed the present Protocol.

EUROPEAN CONVENTION ON HUMAN RIGHTS

European Convention for the Protection of Human Rights and Fundamental Freedoms (ECHR), Rome, 4 November 1950, as last amended by Protocol 14 (1 June 2010).

The governments signatory hereto, being members of the Council of Europe, Considering the Universal Declaration of Human Rights proclaimed by the General Assembly of the United Nations on 10 December 1948;
Considering that this Declaration aims at securing the universal and effective recognition and observance of the Rights therein declared;
Considering that the aim of the Council of Europe is the achievement of greater unity between its members and that one of the methods by which that aim is to be pursued is the maintenance and further realisation of human rights and fundamental freedoms;
Reaffirming their profound belief in those fundamental freedoms which are the foundation of justice and peace in the world and are best maintained on the one hand by an effective political democracy and on the other by a common understanding and observance of the human rights upon which they depend;
Being resolved, as the governments of European countries which are likeminded and have a common heritage of political traditions, ideals, freedom and the rule of law, to take the first steps for the collective enforcement of certain of the rights stated in the Universal Declaration,
Have agreed as follows:

Article 1. The High Contracting Parties shall secure to everyone within their jurisdiction the rights and freedoms defined in Section I of this Convention.

Section I. Rights and freedoms

Article 2. (1) Everyone's right to life shall be protected by law. No one shall be deprived of his life intentionally save in the execution of a sentence of a court following his conviction of a crime for which this penalty is provided by law.
(2) Deprivation of life shall not be regarded as inflicted in contravention of this Article when it results from the use of force which is no more than abso-lutely necessary:
(a) in defence of any person from unlawful violence;
(b) in order to effect a lawful arrest or to prevent the escape of a person lawfully detained;
(c) in action lawfully taken for the purpose of quelling a riot or insurrection.

Article 3. No one shall be subjected to torture or to inhuman or degrading treatment or punishment.

Article 4. (1) No one shall be held in slavery or servitude.
(2) No one shall be required to perform forced or compulsory labour.
(3) For the purpose of this Article the term "forced or compulsory labour" shall not include:
(a) any work required to be done in the ordinary course of detention imposed according to the provisions of Article 5 of this Convention or during conditional release from such detention;
(b) any service of a military character or, in case of conscientious objectors in countries where they are recognised, service exacted instead of compulsory military service;
(c) any service exacted in case of an emergency or calamity threatening the life or well-being of the community;
(d) any work or service which forms part of normal civic obligations.

Article 5. (1) Everyone has the right to liberty and security of person. No one shall be deprived of his liberty save in the following cases and in accordance with a procedure prescribed by law:
(a) the lawful detention of a person after conviction by a competent court;
(b) the lawful arrest or detention of a person for non-compliance with the lawful order of a court or in order to secure the fulfilment of any obligation prescribed by law;
(c) the lawful arrest or detention of a person effected for the purpose of bringing him before the competent legal authority on reasonable suspicion of having committed an offence or when it is reasonably considered necessary to prevent his committing an offence or fleeing after having done so;
(d) the detention of a minor by lawful order for the purpose of educational supervision or his lawful detention for the purpose of bringing him before the competent legal authority;
(e) the lawful detention of persons for the prevention of the spreading of infectious diseases, of persons of un-sound mind, alcoholics or drug addicts or vagrants;
(f) the lawful arrest or detention of a person to prevent his effecting an unauthorised entry into the country or of a person against whom action is being taken with a view to deportation or extradition.
(2) Everyone who is arrested shall be informed promptly, in a language which he understands, of the

PART II   FUNDAMENTAL RIGHTS

reasons for his arrest and of any charge against him.
(3) Everyone arrested or detained in accordance with the provisions of paragraph (1) (c) of this Article shall be brought promptly before a judge or other officer authorised by law to exercise judicial power and shall be entitled to trial within a reasonable time or to release pending trial. Release may be conditioned by guarantees to appear for trial.
(4) Everyone who is deprived of his liberty by arrest or detention shall be entitled to take proceedings by which the lawfulness of his detention shall be decided speedily by a court and his release ordered if the detention is not lawful.
(5) Everyone who has been the victim of arrest or detention in contravention of the provisions of this Article shall have an enforceable right to compensation.

Article 6. (1) In the determination of his civil rights and obligations or of any criminal charge against him, everyone is entitled to a fair and public hearing within a reasonable time by an independent and impartial tribunal established by law. Judgment shall be pronounced publicly but the press and public may be excluded from all or part of the trial in the interests of morals, public order or national security in a democratic society, where the interests of juveniles or the protection of the private life of the parties so require, or to the extent strictly necessary in the opinion of the court in special circumstances where publicity would prejudice the interests of justice.
(2) Everyone charged with a criminal offence shall be presumed innocent until proved guilty according to law.
(3) Everyone charged with a criminal offence has the following minimum rights:
(a) to be informed promptly, in a language which he understands and in detail, of the nature and cause of the accusation against him;
(b) to have adequate time and facilities for the preparation of his defence;
(c) to defend himself in person or through legal assistance of his own choosing or, if he has not sufficient means to pay for legal assistance, to be given it free when the interests of justice so require;
(d) to examine or have examined witnesses against him and to obtain the attendance and examination of wit-nesses on his behalf under the same conditions as witnesses against him;
(e) to have the free assistance of an interpreter if he cannot understand or speak the language used in court.

Article 7. (1) No one shall be held guilty of any criminal offence on account of any act or omission which did not constitute a criminal offence under national or international law at the time when it was committed. Nor shall a heavier penalty be imposed than the one that was applicable at the time the criminal offence was committed.
(2) This Article shall not prejudice the trial and punishment of any person for any act or omission which, at the time when it was committed, was criminal according to the general principles of law recognised by civilised nations.

Article 8. (1) Everyone has the right to respect for his private and family life, his home and his correspondence.
(2) There shall be no interference by a public authority with the exercise of this right except such as is in accordance with the law and is necessary in a democratic society in the interests of national security, public safety or the economic well-being of the country, for the prevention of disorder or crime, for the protection of health or morals, or for the protection of the rights and freedoms of others.

Article 9. (1) Everyone has the right to freedom of thought, conscience and religion; this right includes freedom to change his religion or belief and freedom, either alone or in community with others and in public or private, to manifest his religion or belief, in worship, teaching, practice and observance.
(2) Freedom to manifest one's religion or beliefs shall be subject only to such limitations as are prescribed by law and are necessary in a democratic society in the interests of public safety, for the protection of public order, health or morals, or for the protection of the rights and freedoms of others.

Article 10. (1) Everyone has the right to freedom of expression. This right shall include freedom to hold opinions and to receive and impart information and ideas without interference by public authority and regardless of frontiers. This Article shall not prevent States from requiring the licensing of broadcasting, television or cinema enterprises.
(2) The exercise of these freedoms, since it carries with it duties and responsibilities, may be subject to such formalities, conditions, restrictions or penalties as are prescribed by law and are necessary in a democratic society, in the interests of national security, territorial integrity or public safety, for the prevention of disorder or crime, for the protection of health or morals, for the protection of the

reputation or rights of others, for preventing the disclosure of information received in confidence, or for maintaining the authority and im-partiality of the judiciary.

Article 11. (1) Everyone has the right to freedom of peaceful assembly and to freedom of association with others, including the right to form and to join trade unions for the protection of his interests. (2) No restrictions shall be placed on the exercise of these rights other than such as are prescribed by law and are necessary in a democratic society in the interests of national security or public safety, for the prevention of disorder or crime, for the protection of health or morals or for the protection of the rights and freedoms of others. This Article shall not prevent the imposition of lawful restrictions on the exercise of these rights by members of the armed forces, of the police or of the administration of the State.

Article 12. Men and women of marriageable age have the right to marry and to found a family, according to the national laws governing the exercise of this right.

Article 13. Everyone whose rights and freedoms as set forth in this Convention are violated shall have an effective remedy before a national authority notwithstanding that the violation has been committed by persons acting in an official capacity.

Article 14. The enjoyment of the rights and freedoms set forth in this Convention shall be secured without discrimination on any ground such as sex, race, colour, language, religion, political or other opinion, national or social origin, association with a national minority, property, birth or other status.

Article 15. (1) In time of war or other public emergency threatening the life of the nation any High Contracting Party may take measures derogating from its obligations under this Convention to the extent strictly required by the exigencies of the situation, provided that such measures are not inconsistent with its other obligations under international law.
(2) No derogation from Article 2, except in respect of deaths resulting from lawful acts of war, or from Articles 3, 4 § 1 and 7 shall be made under this provision.
(3) Any High Contracting Party availing itself of this right of derogation shall keep the Secretary General of the Council of Europe fully informed of the measures which it has taken and the reasons therefor. It shall also inform the Secretary General of the Council of Europe when such measures have ceased to operate and the provisions of the Convention are again being fully executed.

Article 16. Nothing in Articles 10, 11 and 14 shall be regarded as preventing the High Contracting Parties from imposing restrictions on the political activity of aliens.

Article 17. Nothing in this Convention may be interpreted as implying for any State, group or person any right to engage in any activity or perform any act aimed at the destruction of any of the rights and freedoms set forth herein or at their limitation to a greater extent than is provided for in the Convention.

Article 18. The restrictions permitted under this Convention to the said rights and freedoms shall not be applied for any purpose other than those for which they have been prescribed.

Section II. European Court of Human Rights

Article 19. To ensure the observance of the engagements undertaken by the High Contracting Parties in the Convention and the Protocols thereto, there shall be set up a European Court of Human Rights, hereinafter referred to as "the Court". It shall function on a permanent basis.

Article 20. The Court shall consist of a number of judges equal to that of the High Contracting Parties.

Article 21. (1) The judges shall be of high moral character and must either possess the qualifications required for appointment to high judicial office or be jurisconsults of recognised competence.
(2) The judges shall sit on the Court in their individual capacity.
(3) During their term of office the judges shall not engage in any activity which is incompatible with their independence, impartiality or with the demands of a full-time office; all questions arising from the application of this paragraph shall be decided by the Court.

Article 22. The judges shall be elected by the Parliamentary Assembly with respect to each High Contracting Party by a majority of votes cast from a list of three candidates nominated by the High Contracting Party.

Article 23. (1) The judges shall be elected for a period of nine years. They may not be re-elected.

PART II   FUNDAMENTAL RIGHTS

(2) The terms of office of judges shall expire when they reach the age of 70.
(3) The judges shall hold office until replaced. They shall, however, continue to deal with such cases as they already have under consideration.
(4) No judge may be dismissed from office unless the other judges decide by a majority of two-thirds that that judge has ceased to fulfil the required conditions.

Article 24. (1) The Court shall have a Registry, the functions and organisation of which shall be laid down in the rules of the Court.
(2) When sitting in a single-judge formation, the Court shall be assisted by rapporteurs who shall function under the authority of the President of the Court. They shall form part of the Court's Registry.

Article 25. The plenary Court shall
(a) elect its President and one or two Vice-Presidents for a period of three years; they may be re-elected;
(b) set up Chambers, constituted for a fixed period of time;
(c) elect the Presidents of the Chambers of the Court; they may be re-elected;
(d) adopt the rules of the Court;
(e) elect the Registrar and one or more Deputy Registrars;
(f) make any request under Article 26 § 2.

Article 26. (1) To consider cases brought before it, the Court shall sit in a single-judge formation, in Committees of three judges, in Chambers of seven judges and in a Grand Chamber of seventeen judges. The Court's Chambers shall set up Committees for a fixed period of time.
(2) At the request of the plenary Court, the Committee of Ministers may, by a unanimous decision and for a fixed period, reduce to five the number of judges of the Chambers.
(3) When sitting as a single judge, a judge shall not examine any application against the High Contracting Party in respect of which that judge has been elected.
(4) There shall sit as an ex officio member of the Chamber and the Grand Chamber the judge elected in respect of the High Contracting Party concerned. If there is none or if that judge is unable to sit, a person chosen by the President of the Court from a list submitted in advance by that Party shall sit in the capacity of judge.
(5) The Grand Chamber shall also include the President of the Court, the Vice-Presidents, the Presidents of the Chambers and other judges chosen in accordance with the rules of the Court. When a case is referred to the Grand Chamber under Article 43, no judge from the Chamber which rendered the judgment shall sit in the Grand Chamber, with the exception of the President of the Chamber and the judge who sat in respect of the High Contracting Party concerned.

Article 27. (1) A single judge may declare inadmissible or strike out of the Court's list of cases an application submitted under Article 34, where such a decision can be taken without further examination.
(2) The decision shall be final.
(3) If the single judge does not declare an application inadmissible or strike it out, that judge shall forward it to a Committee or to a Chamber for further examination.

Article 28. (1) In respect of an application sub-mitted under Article 34, a Committee may, by a unanimous vote,
(a) declare it inadmissible or strike it out of its list of cases, where such decision can be taken without further examination; or
(b) declare it admissible and render at the same time a judgment on the merits, if the underlying question in the case, concerning the interpretation or the application of the Convention or the Protocols thereto, is already the subject of well-established case-law of the Court.
(2) Decisions and judgments under paragraph (1) shall be final.
(3) If the judge elected in respect of the High Contracting Party concerned is not a member of the Committee, the Committee may at any stage of the proceedings invite that judge to take the place of one of the members of the Committee, having regard to all relevant factors, including whether that Party has contested the application of the procedure under paragraph (1) (b).

Article 29. (1) If no decision is taken under Article 27 or 28, or no judgment rendered under Article 28, a Chamber shall decide on the admissibility and merits of individual applications submitted under Article 34. The decision on admissibility may be taken separately.
(2) A Chamber shall decide on the admissibility and merits of inter-State applications submitted

PART II FUNDAMENTAL RIGHTS

However, the Court shall continue the examination of the application if respect for human rights as defined in the Convention and the Protocols thereto so requires.
(2) The Court may decide to restore an application to its list of cases if it considers that the circumstances justify such a course.

Article 38. The Court shall examine the case together with the representatives of the parties and, if need be, undertake an investigation, for the effective conduct of which the High Contracting Parties concerned shall furnish all necessary facilities.

Article 39. (1) At any stage of the proceedings, the Court may place itself at the disposal of the parties concerned with a view to securing a friendly settlement of the matter on the basis of respect for human rights as defined in the Convention and the Protocols thereto.
(2) Proceedings conducted under paragraph 1 shall be confidential.
(3) If a friendly settlement is effected, the Court shall strike the case out of its list by means of a decision which shall be confined to a brief statement of the facts and of the solution reached.
(4) This decision shall be transmitted to the Committee of Ministers, which shall supervise the execution of the terms of the friendly settlement as set out in the decision.

Article 40. (1) Hearings shall be in public unless the Court in exceptional circumstances decides otherwise.
(2) Documents deposited with the Registrar shall be accessible to the public unless the President of the Court decides otherwise.

Article 41. If the Court finds that there has been a violation of the Convention or the Protocols thereto, and if the internal law of the High Contracting Party concerned allows only partial reparation to be made, the Court shall, if necessary, afford just satisfaction to the injured party.

Article 42. Judgments of Chambers shall become final in accordance with the provisions of Article 44 § 2.

Article 43. (1) Within a period of three months from the date of the judgment of the Chamber, any party to the case may, in exceptional cases, request that the case be referred to the Grand Chamber.
(2) A panel of five judges of the Grand Chamber shall accept the request if the case raises a serious question affecting the interpretation or application of the Convention or the Protocols thereto, or a serious issue of general importance.
(3) If the panel accepts the request, the Grand Chamber shall decide the case by means of a judgment.

Article 44. (1) The judgment of the Grand Chamber shall be final.
(2) The judgment of a Chamber shall become final
(a) when the parties declare that they will not request that the case be referred to the Grand Chamber; or
(b) three months after the date of the judgment, if reference of the case to the Grand Chamber has not been requested; or
(c) when the panel of the Grand Chamber rejects the request to refer under Article 43.
(3) The final judgment shall be published.

Article 45. (1) Reasons shall be given for judgments as well as for decisions declaring applications admissible or inadmissible.
(2) If a judgment does not represent, in whole or in part, the unanimous opinion of the judges, any judge shall be entitled to deliver a separate opinion.

Article 46. (1). The High Contracting Parties under-take to abide by the final judgment of the Court in any case to which they are parties.
(2) The final judgment of the Court shall be transmitted to the Committee of Ministers, which shall supervise its execution.
(3) If the Committee of Ministers considers that the supervision of the execution of a final judgment is hindered by a problem of interpretation of the judgment, it may refer the matter to the Court for a ruling on the question of
interpretation. A referral decision shall require a majority vote of two thirds of the representatives entitled to sit on the Committee.
(4) If the Committee of Ministers considers that a High Contracting Party refuses to abide by a final judgment in a case to which it is a party, it may, after serving formal notice on that Party and by decision adopted by a majority vote of two-thirds of the representatives entitled to sit on the Committee,

under Article 33. The decision on admissibility shall be taken separately unless the Court, in exceptional cases, decides otherwise.

Article 30. Where a case pending before a Chamber raises a serious question affecting the interpretation of the Convention or the Protocols thereto, or where the resolution of a question before the Chamber might have a result inconsistent with a judgment previously delivered by the Court, the Chamber may, at any time before it has rendered its judgment, relinquish jurisdiction in favour of the Grand Chamber, unless one of the parties to the case objects.

Article 31. The Grand Chamber shall
(a) determine applications submitted either under Article 33 or Article 34 when a Chamber has relinquished jurisdiction under Article 30 or when the case has been referred to it under Article 43;
(b) decide on issues referred to the Court by the Committee of Ministers in accordance with Article 46 § 4; and
(c) consider requests for advisory opinions submitted under Article 47.

Article 32. (1) The jurisdiction of the Court shall extend to all matters concerning the interpretation and application of the Convention and the Protocols thereto which are referred to it as provided in Articles 33, 34, 46 and 47.
(2) In the event of dispute as to whether the Court has jurisdiction, the Court shall decide.

Article 33. Any High Contracting Party may refer to the Court any alleged breach of the provisions of the Convention and the Protocols thereto by another High Contracting Party.

Article 34. The Court may receive applications from any person, non-governmental organisation or group of individuals claiming to be the victim of a violation by one of the High Contracting Parties of the rights set forth in the Convention or the Protocols thereto. The High Contracting Parties undertake not to hinder in any way the effective exercise of this right.

Article 35. (1) The Court may only deal with the matter after all domestic remedies have been exhausted, according to the generally recognised rules of inter-national law, and within a period of six months from the date on which the final decision was taken.
(2) The Court shall not deal with any application submitted under Article 34 that
(a) is anonymous; or
(b) is substantially the same as a matter that has already been examined by the Court or has already been submitted to another procedure of international investigation or settlement and contains no relevant new information.
(3) The Court shall declare inadmissible any individual application submitted under Article 34 if it considers that:
(a) the application is incompatible with the provisions of the Convention or the Protocols thereto, manifestly ill-founded, or an abuse of the right of individual application; or
(b) the applicant has not suffered a significant disadvantage, unless respect for human rights as defined in the Convention and the Protocols thereto requires an examination of the application on the merits and provided that no case may be rejected on this ground which has not been duly considered by a domestic tribunal.
(4) The Court shall reject any application which it considers inadmissible under this Article. It may do so at any stage of the proceedings.

Article 36. (1) In all cases before a Chamber or the Grand Chamber, a High Contracting Party one of whose nationals is an applicant shall have the right to submit written comments and to take part in hearings.
(2) The President of the Court may, in the interest of the proper administration of justice, invite any High Contracting Party which is not a party to the proceedings or any person concerned who is not the applicant to submit written comments or take part in hearings.
(3) In all cases before a Chamber or the Grand Chamber, the Council of Europe Commissioner for Human Rights may submit written comments and take part in hearings.

Article 37. (1) The Court may at any stage of the proceedings decide to strike an application out of its list of cases where the circumstances lead to the conclusion that
(a) the applicant does not intend to pursue his application; or
(b) the matter has been resolved; or
(c) for any other reason established by the Court, it is no longer justified to continue the examination of the application.

refer to the Court the question whether that Party has failed to fulfil its obligation under paragraph (1).
(5) If the Court finds a violation of paragraph (1), it shall refer the case to the Committee of Ministers for consideration of the measures to be taken. If the Court finds no violation of paragraph (1), it shall refer the case to the Committee of Ministers, which shall close its examination of the case.

Article 47. (1) The Court may, at the request of the Committee of Ministers, give advisory opinions on legal questions concerning the interpretation of the Convention and the Protocols thereto.
(2) Such opinions shall not deal with any question relating to the content or scope of the rights or freedoms defined in Section I of the Convention and the Protocols thereto, or with any other question which the Court or the Committee of Ministers might have to consider in consequence of any such proceedings as could be instituted in accordance with the Convention.
(3) Decisions of the Committee of Ministers to request an advisory opinion of the Court shall require a majority vote of the representatives entitled to sit on the Committee.

Article 48. The Court shall decide whether a request for an advisory opinion submitted by the Committee of Ministers is within its competence as defined in Article 47.

Article 49. (1) Reasons shall be given for advisory opinions of the Court.
(2) If the advisory opinion does not represent, in whole or in part, the unanimous opinion of the judges, any judge shall be entitled to deliver a separate opinion.
(3) Advisory opinions of the Court shall be communicated to the Committee of Ministers.

Article 50. The expenditure on the Court shall be borne by the Council of Europe.

Article 51. The judges shall be entitled, during the exercise of their functions, to the privileges and immunities provided for in Article 40 of the Statute of the Council of Europe and in the agreements made thereunder.

Article 52. On receipt of a request from the Secretary General of the Council of Europe any High Contracting Party shall furnish an explanation of the manner in which its internal law ensures the effective implementation of any of the provisions of the Convention.

Article 53. Nothing in this Convention shall be construed as limiting or derogating from any of the human rights and fundamental freedoms which may be ensured under the laws of any High Contracting Party or under any other agreement to which it is a party.

Article 54. Nothing in this Convention shall prejudice the powers conferred on the Committee of Ministers by the Statute of the Council of Europe.

Article 55. The High Contracting Parties agree that, except by special agreement, they will not avail themselves of treaties, conventions or declarations in force between them for the purpose of submitting, by way of petition, a dispute arising out of the interpretation or application of this Convention to a means of settlement other than those provided for in this Convention.

Article 56. (1) Any State may at the time of its ratification or at any time thereafter declare by notification addressed to the Secretary General of the Council of Europe that the present Convention shall, subject to paragraph (4) of this Article, extend to all or any of the territories for whose international relations it is responsible.
(2) The Convention shall extend to the territory or territories named in the notification as from the thirtieth day after the receipt of this notification by the Secretary General of the Council of Europe.
(3) The provisions of this Convention shall be applied in such territories with due regard, however, to local requirements.
(4) Any State which has made a declaration in accordance with paragraph 1 of this Article may at any time thereafter declare on behalf of one or more of the territories to which the declaration relates that it accepts the competence of the Court to receive applications from individuals, non-governmental organisations or groups of individuals as provided by Article 34 of the Convention.

Article 57. (1) Any State may, when signing this Convention or when depositing its instrument of ratification, make a reservation in respect of any particular provision of the Convention to the extent that any law then in force in its territory is not in conformity with the provision. Reservations of a general character shall not be permitted under this Article.
(2) Any reservation made under this Article shall contain a brief statement of the law concerned.

Article 58. (1) A High Contracting Party may denounce the present Convention only after the expiry

PART II   FUNDAMENTAL RIGHTS

of five years from the date on which it became a party to it and after six months' notice contained in a notification addressed to the Secretary General of the Council of Europe, who shall inform the other High Contracting Parties.
(2) Such a denunciation shall not have the effect of releasing the High
Contracting Party concerned from its obligations under this Convention in respect of any act which, being capable of constituting a violation of such obligations, may have been performed by it before the date at which the denunciation became effective.
(3) Any High Contracting Party which shall cease to be a member of the Council of Europe shall cease to be a party to this Convention under the same conditions.
(4) The Convention may be denounced in accordance with the provisions of the preceding paragraphs in respect of any territory to which it has been declared to extend under the terms of Article 56.

Article 59. (1) This Convention shall be open to the signature of the members of the Council of Europe. It shall be ratified. Ratifications shall be deposited with the Secretary General of the Council of Europe.
(2) The European Union may accede to this Convention.
(3) The present Convention shall come into force after the deposit of ten instruments of ratification.
(4) As regards any signatory ratifying subsequently, the Convention shall come into force at the date of the deposit of its instrument of ratification.
(5) The Secretary General of the Council of Europe shall notify all the members of the Council of Europe of the entry into force of the Convention, the names of the High Contracting Parties who have ratified it, and the deposit of all instruments of ratification which may be effected subsequently.

Protocols to the ECHR

Protocol (No. 1) to the Convention for the Protection of Human Rights and Fundamental Freedoms. Paris, 20 March 1952.

The governments signatory hereto, being members of the Council of Europe,
Being resolved to take steps to ensure the collective enforcement of certain rights and freedoms other than those already included in Section I of the Convention for the Protection of Human Rights and Fundamental Freedoms signed at Rome on 4 November 1950 (hereinafter referred to as 'the Convention'),
Have agreed as follows:

Article 1. Every natural or legal person is entitled to the peaceful enjoyment of his possessions. No one shall be deprived of his possessions except in the public interest and subject to the conditions provided for by law and by the general principles of international law.
The preceding provisions shall not, however, in any way impair the right of a State to enforce such laws as it deems necessary to control the use of property in accordance with the general interest or to secure the payment of taxes or other contributions or penalties.

Article 2. No person shall be denied the right to education. In the exercise of any functions which it assumes in relation to education and to teaching, the State shall respect the right of parents to ensure such education and teaching in conformity with their own religious and philosophical convictions.

Article 3. The High Contracting Parties undertake to hold free elections at reasonable intervals by secret ballot, under conditions which will ensure the free expression of the opinion of the people in the choice of the legislature.
[Articles 4 – 6 are omitted.]

Protocol No. 4 to the Convention for the Protection of Human Rights and Fundamental Freedoms securing certain rights and freedoms other than those already included in the Convention and in the first Protocol thereto. Strasbourg, 16 September 1963.

[The Preamble is omitted.]

Article 1. No one shall be deprived of his liberty merely on the ground of inability to fulfil a contractual obligation.

Article 2. (1) Everyone lawfully within the territory of a State shall, within that territory, have the right to liberty of movement and freedom to choose his residence.
(2) Everyone shall be free to leave any country, including his own.
(3) No restrictions shall be placed on the exercise of these rights other than such as are in accordance with law and are necessary in a democratic society in the interests of national security or public safety, for the maintenance of ordre public, for the prevention of crime, for the protection of health or morals, or for the protection of the rights and freedoms of others.
(4) The rights set forth in paragraph (1) may also be subject, in particular areas, to restrictions imposed in accordance with law and justified by the public interest in a democratic society.

Article 3. (1) No one shall be expelled, by means either of an individual or of a collective measure, from the territory of the State of which he is a national.
(2) No one shall be deprived of the right to enter the territory of the state of which he is a national.

Article 4. Collective expulsion of aliens is prohibited.
[Articles 5 – 7 are omitted.]

Protocol No. 6 to the Convention for the Protection of Human Rights and Fundamental Freedoms concerning the abolition of the death penalty. Strasbourg, 28 April 1983.

[The Preamble is omitted.]

Article 1. The death penalty shall be abolished. No-one shall be condemned to such penalty or executed.

Article 2. A State may make provision in its law for the death penalty in respect of acts committed

PART II FUNDAMENTAL RIGHTS

in time of war or of imminent threat of war; such penalty shall be applied only in the instances laid down in the law and in accordance with its provisions. The State shall communicate to the Secretary General of the Council of Europe the relevant provisions of that law.
[Articles 3 – 9 are omitted.]

Protocol No. 7 to the Convention for the Protection of Human Rights and Fundamental Freedoms. Strasbourg, 22 November 1984.

[The Preamble is omitted.]

Article 1. (1) An alien lawfully resident in the territory of a State shall not be expelled therefrom except in pursuance of a decision reached in accordance with law and shall be allowed:
a. to submit reasons against his expulsion,
b. to have his case reviewed, and
c. to be represented for these purposes before the competent authority or a person or persons designated by that authority.
(2) An alien may be expelled before the exercise of his rights under paragraph (1)(a), (b) and (c) of this Article, when such expulsion is necessary in the interests of public order or is grounded on reasons of national security.

Article 2. (1) Everyone convicted of a criminal offence by a tribunal shall have the right to have his conviction or sentence reviewed by a higher tribunal. The exercise of this right, including the grounds on which it may be exercised, shall be governed by law.
(2) This right may be subject to exceptions in regard to offences of a minor character, as prescribed by law, or in cases in which the person concerned was tried in the first instance by the highest tribunal or was convicted following an appeal against acquittal.

Article 3. When a person has by a final decision been convicted of a criminal offence and when subsequently his conviction has been reversed, or he has been pardoned, on the ground that a new or newly discovered fact shows conclusively that there has been a miscarriage of justice, the person who has suffered punishment as a result of such conviction shall be compensated according to the law or the practice of the State concerned, unless it is proved that the non-disclosure of the unknown fact in time is wholly or partly attributable to him.

Article 4. (1) No one shall be liable to be tried or punished again in criminal proceedings under the jurisdiction of the same State for an offence for which he has already been finally acquitted or convicted in accordance with the law and penal procedure of that State.
(2) The provisions of the preceding paragraph shall not prevent the reopening of the case in accordance with the law and penal procedure of the State concerned, if there is evidence of new or newly discovered facts, or if there has been a fundamental defect in the previous proceedings, which could affect the outcome of the case.
(3) No derogation from this Article shall be made under Article 15 of the Convention.

Article 5. Spouses shall enjoy equality of rights and responsibilities of a private law character between them, and in their relations with their children, as to marriage, during marriage and in the event of its dissolution. This Article shall not prevent States from taking such measures as are necessary in the interests of the children.
[Articles 6 – 10 are omitted.]

Protocol No. 12 to the Convention for the Protection of Human Rights and Fundamental Freedoms. Rome, 4 November 2000.

[The Preamble is omitted.]

Article 1. (1) The enjoyment of any right set forth by law shall be secured without discrimination on any ground such as sex, race, colour, language, religion, political or other opinion, national or social origin, association with a national minority, property, birth or other status.
(2) No one shall be discriminated against by any public authority on any ground such as those mentioned in paragraph (1).
[Articles 2 – 6 are omitted.]

Protocol No. 13 to the Convention for the Protection of Human Rights and Fundamental Freedoms Concerning the abolition of the death penalty in all circumstances. Vilnius, 3 May 2002.

[The Preamble is omitted.]

Article 1. The death penalty shall be abolished. No one shall be condemned to such penalty or executed.
[Articles 2 – 8 are omitted.]

Protocol No. 15 amending the Convention on the Protection of Human Rights and Fundamental Freedoms. Strasbourg, 24 June 2013.

The member States of the Council of Europe and the other High Contracting Parties to the Convention for the Protection of Human Rights and Fundamental Freedoms, signed at Rome on 4 November 1950 (hereinafter referred to as "the Convention"), signatory hereto,
Having regard to the declaration adopted at the High Level Conference on the Future of the European Court of Human Rights, held in Brighton on 19 and 20 April 2012, as well as the declarations adopted at the conferences held in Interlaken on 18 and 19 February 2010 and ??zmir on 26 and 27 April 2011;
Having regard to Opinion No. 283 (2013) adopted by the Parliamentary Assembly of the Council of Europe on 26 April 2013;
Considering the need to ensure that the European Court of Human Rights (hereinafter referred to as "the Court") can continue to play its pre-eminent role in protecting human rights in Europe,
Have agreed as follows:

Article 1. At the end of the preamble to the Convention, a new recital shall be added, which shall read as follows:
"Affirming that the High Contracting Parties, in accordance with the principle of subsidiarity, have the primary responsibility to secure the rights and freedoms defined in this Convention and the Protocols thereto, and that in doing so they enjoy a margin of appreciation, subject to the supervisory jurisdiction of the European Court of Human Rights established by this Convention,"

Article 2. (1) In Article 21 of the Convention, a new paragraph (2) shall be inserted, which shall read as follows:
"Candidates shall be less than 65 years of age at the date by which the list of three candidates has been requested by the Parliamentary Assembly, further to Article 22."
(2) Paragraphs (2) and (3) of Article 21 of the Convention shall become paragraphs (3) and (4) of Article 21 respectively.
(3) Paragraph (2) of Article 23 of the Convention shall be deleted. Paragraphs (3) and (4) of Article 23 shall become paragraphs (2) and (3) of Article 23 respectively.

Article 3. In Article 30 of the Convention, the words "unless one of the parties to the case objects" shall be deleted.

Article 4. In Article 35, paragraph (1) of the Convention, the words "within a period of six months" shall be replaced by the words "within a period of four months".

Article 5. In Article 35, paragraph (3), sub-paragraph (b) of the Convention, the words "and provided that no case may be rejected on this ground which has not been duly considered by a domestic tribunal" shall be deleted.
Final and transitional provisions

Article 6. (1) This Protocol shall be open for signature by the High Contracting Parties to the Convention, which may express their consent to be bound by:
(a) signature without reservation as to ratification, acceptance or approval; or
(b) signature subject to ratification, acceptance or approval, followed by ratification, acceptance or approval.
(2) The instruments of ratification, acceptance or approval shall be deposited with the Secretary General of the Council of Europe.

Article 7. This Protocol shall enter into force on the first day of the month following the expiration of a period of three months after the date on which all High Contracting Parties to the Convention have expressed their consent to be bound by the Protocol, in accordance with the provisions of Article 6.

PART II   FUNDAMENTAL RIGHTS

Article 8. (1) The amendments introduced by Article 2 of this Protocol shall apply only to candidates on lists submitted to the Parliamentary Assembly by the High Contracting Parties under Article 22 of the Convention after the entry into force of this Protocol.
(2) The amendment introduced by Article 3 of this Protocol shall not apply to any pending case in which one of the parties has objected, prior to the date of entry into force of this Protocol, to a proposal by a Chamber of the Court to relinquish jurisdiction in favour of the Grand Chamber.
(3) Article 4 of this Protocol shall enter into force following the expiration of a period of six months after the date of entry into force of this Protocol. Article 4 of this Protocol shall not apply to applications in respect of which the final decision within the meaning of Article 35, paragraph (1) of the Convention was taken prior to the date of entry into force of Article 4 of this Protocol.
(4) All other provisions of this Protocol shall apply from its date of entry into force, in accordance with the provisions of Article 7.

Article 9. The Secretary General of the Council of Europe shall notify the member States of the Council of Europe and the other High Contracting Parties to the Convention of:
(a) any signature;
(b) the deposit of any instrument of ratification, acceptance or approval;
(c) the date of entry into force of this Protocol in accordance with Article 7; and
(d) any other act, notification or communication relating to this Protocol.

Protocol No. 16 to the Convention on the Protection of Human Rights and Fundamental Freedoms. Strasbourg, 2 October 2013.

The member States of the Council of Europe and other High Contracting Parties to the Convention for the Protection of Human Rights and Fundamental Freedoms, signed at Rome on 4 November 1950 (hereinafter referred to as "the Convention"), signatories hereto,
Having regard to the provisions of the Convention and, in particular, Article 19 establishing the European Court of Human Rights (hereinafter referred to as "the Court");
Considering that the extension of the Court's competence to give advisory opinions will further enhance the interaction between the Court and national authorities and thereby reinforce implementation of the Convention, in accordance with the principle of subsidiarity;
Having regard to Opinion No. 285 (2013) adopted by the Parliamentary Assembly of the Council of Europe on 28 June 2013,
Have agreed as follows:

Article 1. (1) Highest courts and tribunals of a High Contracting Party, as specified in accordance with Article 10, may request the Court to give advisory opinions on questions of principle relating to the interpretation or application of the rights and freedoms defined in the Convention or the protocols thereto.
(2) The requesting court or tribunal may seek an advisory opinion only in the context of a case pending before it.
(3) The requesting court or tribunal shall give reasons for its request and shall provide the relevant legal and factual background of the pending case.

Article 2. (1) A panel of five judges of the Grand Chamber shall decide whether to accept the request for an advisory opinion, having regard to Article 1. The panel shall give reasons for any refusal to accept the request.
(2) If the panel accepts the request, the Grand Chamber shall deliver the advisory opinion.
(3) The panel and the Grand Chamber, as referred to in the preceding paragraphs, shall include ex officio the judge elected in respect of the High Contracting Party to which the requesting court or tribunal pertains. If there is none or if that judge is unable to sit, a person chosen by the President of the Court from a list submitted in advance by that Party shall sit in the capacity of judge.

Article 3. The Council of Europe Commissioner for Human Rights and the High Contracting Party to which the requesting court or tribunal pertains shall have the right to submit written comments and take part in any hearing. The President of the Court may, in the interest of the proper administration of justice, invite any other High Contracting Party or person also to submit written comments or take part in any hearing.

Article 4. (1) Reasons shall be given for advisory opinions.
(2) If the advisory opinion does not represent, in whole or in part, the unanimous opinion of the

judges, any judge shall be entitled to deliver a separate opinion.
(3) Advisory opinions shall be communicated to the requesting court or tribunal and to the High Contracting Party to which that court or tribunal pertains.
(4) Advisory opinions shall be published.

Article 5. Advisory opinions shall not be binding.

Article 6. As between the High Contracting Parties the provisions of Articles 1 to 5 of this Protocol shall be regarded as additional articles to the Convention, and all the provisions of the Convention shall apply accordingly.

Article 7. (1) This Protocol shall be open for signature by the High Contracting Parties to the Convention, which may express their consent to be bound by:
(a) signature without reservation as to ratification, acceptance or approval; or
(b) signature subject to ratification, acceptance or approval, followed by ratification, acceptance or approval.
(2) The instruments of ratification, acceptance or approval shall be deposited with the Secretary General of the Council of Europe.

Article 8. (1) This Protocol shall enter into force on the first day of the month following the expiration of a period of three months after the date on which ten High Contracting Parties to the Convention have expressed their consent to be bound by the Protocol in accordance with the provisions of Article 7.
(2) In respect of any High Contracting Party to the Convention which subsequently expresses its consent to be bound by it, the Protocol shall enter into force on the first day of the month following the expiration of a period of three months after the date of the expression of its consent to be bound by the Protocol in accordance with the provisions of Article 7.

Article 9. No reservation may be made under Article 57 of the Convention in respect of the provisions of this Protocol.

Article 10. Each High Contracting Party to the Convention shall, at the time of signature or when depositing its instrument of ratification, acceptance or approval, by means of a declaration addressed to the Secretary General of the Council of Europe, indicate the courts or tribunals that it designates for the purposes of Article 1, paragraph (1), of this Protocol. This declaration may be modified at any later date and in the same manner.

Article 11. The Secretary General of the Council of Europe shall notify the member States of the Council of Europe and the other High Contracting Parties to the Convention of:
(a) any signature;
(b) the deposit of any instrument of ratification, acceptance or approval;
(c) any date of entry into force of this Protocol in accordance with Article 8;
(d) any declaration made in accordance with Article 10; and
(e) any other act, notification or communication relating to this Protocol.
In witness whereof the undersigned, being duly authorised thereto, have signed this Protocol.
Done at Strasbourg, this 2nd day of October 2013, in English and French, both texts being equally authentic, in a single copy which shall be deposited in the archives of the Council of Europe. The Secretary General of the Council of Europe shall transmit certified copies to each member State of the Council of Europe and to the other High Contracting Parties to the Convention.

PART II FUNDAMENTAL RIGHTS

Rules of Court of the European Court of Human Rights, as last amended on 3 June 2019.

The European Court of Human Rights,
Having regard to the Convention for the Protection of Human Rights and Fundamental Freedoms and the Protocols thereto,
Makes the present Rules:

Rule 1. For the purposes of these Rules unless the context otherwise requires:
(a) the term "Convention" means the Convention for the Protection of Human Rights and Fundamental Freedoms and the Protocols thereto;
(b) the expression "plenary Court" means the European Court of Human Rights sitting in plenary session;
(c) the expression "Grand Chamber" means the Grand Chamber of seventeen judges constituted in pursuance of Article 26 § 1 of the Convention;
(d) the term "Section" means a Chamber set up by the plenary Court for a fixed period in pursuance of Article 25 (b) of the Convention and the expression "President of the Section" means the judge elected by the plenary Court in pursuance of Article 25 (c) of the Convention as President of such a Section;
(e) the term "Chamber" means any Chamber of seven judges constituted in pursuance of Article 26 § 1 of the Convention and the expression "President of the Chamber" means the judge presiding over such a "Chamber";
(f) the term "Committee" means a Committee of three judges set up in pursuance of Article 26 § 1 of the Convention and the expression "President of the Committee" means the judge presiding over such a "Committee";
(g) the expression "single-judge formation" means a single judge sitting in accordance with Article 26 § 1 of the Convention;
(h) the term "Court" means either the plenary Court, the Grand Chamber, a Section, a Chamber, a Committee, a single judge or the panel of five judges referred to in Article 43 § 2 of the Convention;
(i) the expression "ad hoc judge" means any person chosen in pursuance of Article 26 § 4 of the Convention and in accordance with Rule 29 to sit as a member of the Grand Chamber or as a member of a Chamber;
(j) the terms "judge" and "judges" mean the judges elected by the Parliamentary Assembly of the Council of Europe or ad hoc judges;
(k) the expression "Judge Rapporteur" means a judge appointed to carry out the tasks provided for in Rules 48 and 49;
(l) the term "non-judicial rapporteur" means a member of the Registry charged with assisting the single-judge formations provided for in Article 24 § 2 of the Convention;
(m) the term "delegate" means a judge who has been appointed to a delegation by the Chamber and the expression "head of the delegation" means the delegate appointed by the Chamber to lead its delegation;
(n) the term "delegation" means a body composed of delegates, Registry members and any other person appointed by the Chamber to assist the delegation;
(o) the term "Registrar" denotes the Registrar of the Court or the Registrar of a Section according to the context;
(p) the terms "party" and "parties" mean
- the applicant or respondent Contracting Parties;
- the applicant (the person, non-governmental organisation or group of individuals) that lodged a complaint under Article 34 of the Convention;
(q) the expression "third party" means any Contracting Party or any person concerned or the Council of Europe Commissioner for Human Rights who, as provided for in Article 36 §§ 1, 2 and 3 of the Convention, has exercised the right to submit written comments and take part in a hearing, or has been invited to do so;
(r) the terms "hearing" and "hearings" mean oral proceedings held on the admissibility and/or merits of an application or in connection with a request for revision or an advisory opinion, a request for interpretation by a party or by the Committee of Ministers, or a question whether there has been a failure to fulfil an obligation which may be referred to the Court by virtue of Article 46 § 4 of the Convention;
(s) the expression "Committee of Ministers" means the Committee of Ministers of the Council of Europe;
(t) the terms "former Court" and "Commission" mean respectively the European Court and European Commission of Human Rights set up under former Article 19 of the Convention.

[Title I is omitted.]

Title II. Procedure

Chapter I. General Rules

Rule 31. The provisions of this Title shall not prevent the Court from derogating from them for the consideration of a particular case after having consulted the parties where appropriate.

Rule 32. The President of the Court may issue practice directions, notably in relation to such matters as appearance at hearings and the filing of pleadings and other documents.

Rule 33. 1. All documents deposited with the Registry by the parties or by any third party in connection with an application, except those deposited within the framework of friendly-settlement negotiations as provided for in Rule 62, shall be accessible to the public in accordance with arrangements determined by the Registrar, unless the President of the Chamber, for the reasons set out in paragraph (2) of this Rule, decides otherwise, either of his or her own motion or at the request of a party or any other person concerned.
2. Public access to a document or to any part of it may be restricted in the interests of morals, public order or national security in a democratic society, where the interests of juveniles or the protection of the private life of the parties or of any person concerned so require, or to the extent strictly necessary in the opinion of the President of the Chamber in special circumstances where publicity would prejudice the interests of justice.
3. Any request for confidentiality made under paragraph (1) of this Rule must include reasons and specify whether it is requested that all or part of the documents be inaccessible to the public.
4. Decisions and judgments given by a Chamber shall be accessible to the public. Decisions and judgments given by a Committee, including decisions covered by the proviso to Rule 53 § 5, shall be accessible to the public. The Court shall periodically make accessible to the public general information about decisions taken by single-judge formations pursuant to Rule 52A § 1 and by Committees in application of Rule 53 § 5.

Rule 34. 1. The official languages of the Court shall be English and French.
2. In connection with applications lodged under Article 34 of the Convention, and for as long as no Contracting Party has been given notice of such an application in accordance with these Rules, all communications with and oral and written submissions by applicants or their representatives, if not in one of the Court's official languages, shall be in one of the official languages of the Contracting Parties. If a Contracting Party is informed or given notice of an application in accordance with these Rules, the application and any accompanying documents shall be communicated to that State in the language in which they were lodged with the Registry by the applicant.
3. (a) All communications with and oral and written submissions by applicants or their representatives in respect of a hearing, or after notice of an application has been given to a Contracting Party, shall be in one of the Court's official languages, unless the President of the Chamber grants leave for the continued use of the official language of a Contracting Party.
(b) If such leave is granted, the Registrar shall make the necessary arrangements for the interpretation and translation into English or French of the applicant's oral and written submissions respectively, in full or in part, where the President of the Chamber considers it to be in the interests of the proper conduct of the proceedings.
(c) Exceptionally the President of the Chamber may make the grant of leave subject to the condition that the applicant bear all or part of the costs of making such arrangements.
(d) Unless the President of the Chamber decides otherwise, any decision made under the foregoing provisions of this paragraph shall remain valid in all subsequent proceedings in the case, including those in respect of requests for referral of the case to the Grand Chamber and requests for interpretation or revision of a judgment under Rules 73, 79 and 80 respectively.
4. (a) All communications with and oral and written submissions by a Contracting Party which is a party to the case shall be in one of the Court's official languages. The President of the Chamber may grant the Contracting Party concerned leave to use one of its official languages for its oral and written submissions.
(b) If such leave is granted, it shall be the responsibility of the requesting Party
(i) to file a translation of its written submissions into one of the official languages of the Court within a time-limit to be fixed by the President of the Chamber. Should that Party not file the translation within that time-limit, the Registrar may make the necessary arrangements for such translation, the expenses to be charged to the requesting Party;

PART II   FUNDAMENTAL RIGHTS

(ii) to bear the expenses of interpreting its oral submissions into English or French. The Registrar shall be responsible for making the necessary arrangements for such interpretation.
(c) The President of the Chamber may direct that a Contracting Party which is a party to the case shall, within a specified time, provide a translation into, or a summary in, English or French of all or certain annexes to its written submissions or of any other relevant document, or of extracts therefrom.
(d) The preceding sub-paragraphs of this paragraph shall also apply, *mutatis mutandis*, to third- party intervention under Rule 44 and to the use of a non-official language by a third party.
5. The President of the Chamber may invite the respondent Contracting Party to provide a translation of its written submissions in the or an official language of that Party in order to facilitate the applicant's understanding of those submissions.
6. Any witness, expert or other person appearing before the Court may use his or her own language if he or she does not have sufficient knowledge of either of the two official languages. In that event the Registrar shall make the necessary arrangements for interpreting or translation.

Rule 35. The Contracting Parties shall be represented by Agents, who may have the assistance of advocates or advisers.

Rule 36. 1. Persons, non-governmental organisations or groups of individuals may initially present applications under Article 34 of the Convention themselves or through a representative.
2. Following notification of the application to the respondent Contracting Party under Rule 54 § 2 (b), the applicant should be represented in accordance with paragraph (4) of this Rule, unless the President of the Chamber decides otherwise.
3. The applicant must be so represented at any hearing decided on by the Chamber, unless the President of the Chamber exceptionally grants leave to the applicant to present his or her own case, subject, if necessary, to being assisted by an advocate or other approved representative.
4. (a) The representative acting on behalf of the applicant pursuant to paragraphs (2) and (3) of this Rule shall be an advocate authorised to practise in any of the Contracting Parties and resident in the territory of one of them, or any other person approved by the President of the Chamber.
(b) In exceptional circumstances and at any stage of the procedure, the President of the Chamber may, where he or she considers that the circumstances or the conduct of the advocate or other person appointed under the preceding sub-paragraph so warrant, direct that the latter may no longer represent or assist the applicant and that the applicant should seek alternative representation.
5. (a) The advocate or other approved representative, or the applicant in person who seeks leave to present his or her own case, must even if leave is granted under the following sub-paragraph have an adequate understanding of one of the Court's official languages.
(b) If he or she does not have sufficient proficiency to express himself or herself in one of the Court's official languages, leave to use one of the official languages of the Contracting Parties may be given by the President of the Chamber under Rule 34 § 3.

Rule 37. 1. Communications or notifications addressed to the Agents or advocates of the parties shall be deemed to have been addressed to the parties.
2. If, for any communication, notification or summons addressed to persons other than the Agents or advocates of the parties, the Court considers it necessary to have the assistance of the Government of the State on whose territory such communication, notification or summons is to have effect, the President of the Court shall apply directly to that Government in order to obtain the necessary facilities.

Rule 38. 1. No written observations or other documents may be filed after the time-limit set by the President of the Chamber or the Judge Rapporteur, as the case may be, in accordance with these Rules. No written observations or other documents filed outside that time-limit or contrary to any practice direction issued under Rule 32 shall be included in the case file unless the President of the Chamber decides otherwise.
2. For the purposes of observing the time-limit referred to in paragraph (1) of this Rule, the material date is the certified date of dispatch of the document or, if there is none, the actual date of receipt at the Registry.

Rule 38A. Questions of procedure requiring a decision by the Chamber shall be considered simultaneously with the examination of the case, unless the President of the Chamber decides otherwise.

Rule 39. 1. The Chamber or, where appropriate, the President of the Section or a duty judge appointed pursuant to paragraph 4 of this Rule may, at the request of a party or of any other person concerned, or of their own motion, indicate to the parties any interim measure which they consider should be adopted in the interests of the parties or of the proper conduct of the proceedings.

2. Where it is considered appropriate, immediate notice of the measure adopted in a particular case may be given to the Committee of Ministers.
3. The Chamber or, where appropriate, the President of the Section or a duty judge appointed pursuant to paragraph (4) of this Rule may request information from the parties on any matter connected with the implementation of any interim measure indicated.
4. The President of the Court may appoint Vice-Presidents of Sections as duty judges to decide on requests for interim measures.

Rule 40. In any case of urgency the Registrar, with the authorisation of the President of the Chamber, may, without prejudice to the taking of any other procedural steps and by any available means, inform a Contracting Party concerned in an application of the introduction of the application and of a summary of its objects.

Rule 41. In determining the order in which cases are to be dealt with, the Court shall have regard to the importance and urgency of the issues raised on the basis of criteria fixed by it. The Chamber, or its President, may, however, derogate from these criteria so as to give priority to a particular application.

Rule 42 (former Rule 43). 1. The Chamber may, either at the request of the parties or of its own motion, order the joinder of two or more applications.
2. The President of the Chamber may, after consulting the parties, order that the proceedings in applications assigned to the same Chamber be conducted simultaneously, without prejudice to the decision of the Chamber on the joinder of the applications.

Rule 43 (former Rule 44). 1. The Court may at any stage of the proceedings decide to strike an application out of its list of cases in accordance with Article 37 of the Convention.
2. When an applicant Contracting Party notifies the Registrar of its intention not to proceed with the case, the Chamber may strike the application out of the Court's list under Article 37 of the Convention if the other Contracting Party or Parties concerned in the case agree to such discontinuance.
3. If a friendly settlement is effected in accordance with Article 39 of the Convention, the application shall be struck out of the Court's list of cases by means of a decision. In accordance with Article 39 § 4 of the Convention, this decision shall be transmitted to the Committee of Ministers, which shall supervise the execution of the terms of the friendly settlement as set out in the decision. In other cases provided for in Article 37 of the Convention, the application shall be struck out by means of a judgment if it has been declared admissible or, if not declared admissible, by means of a decision. Where the application has been struck out by means of a judgment, the President of the Chamber shall forward that judgment, once it has become final, to the Committee of Ministers in order to allow the latter to supervise, in accordance with Article 46 § 2 of the Convention, the execution of any undertakings which may have been attached to the discontinuance or solution of the matter.
4. When an application has been struck out in accordance with Article 37 of the Convention, the costs shall be at the discretion of the Court. If an award of costs is made in a decision striking out an application which has not been declared admissible, the President of the Chamber shall forward the decision to the Committee of Ministers.
5. Where an application has been struck out in accordance with Article 37 of the Convention, the Court may restore it to its list if it considers that exceptional circumstances so justify.

Rule 44. 1. (a) When notice of an application lodged under Article 33 or 34 of the Convention is given to the respondent Contracting Party under Rules 51 § 1 or 54 § 2 (b), a copy of the application shall at the same time be transmitted by the Registrar to any other Contracting Party one of whose nationals is an applicant in the case. The Registrar shall similarly notify any such Contracting Party of a decision to hold an oral hearing in the case.
(b) If a Contracting Party wishes to exercise its right under Article 36 § 1 of the Convention to submit written comments or to take part in a hearing, it shall so advise the Registrar in writing not later than twelve weeks after the transmission or notification referred to in the preceding sub-paragraph. Another time-limit may be fixed by the President of the Chamber for exceptional reasons.
2. If the Council of Europe Commissioner for Human Rights wishes to exercise the right under Article 36 § 3 of the Convention to submit written observations or take part in a hearing, he or she shall so advise the Registrar in writing not later than twelve weeks after transmission of the application to the respondent Contracting Party or notification to it of the decision to hold an oral hearing. Another time-limit may be fixed by the President of the Chamber for exceptional reasons.
Should the Commissioner for Human Rights be unable to take part in the proceedings before the Court himself, he or she shall indicate the name of the person or persons from his or her Office whom

PART II FUNDAMENTAL RIGHTS

he or she has appointed to represent him. He or she may be assisted by an advocate.
3. (a) Once notice of an application has been given to the respondent Contracting Party under Rules 51 § 1 or 54 § 2 (b), the President of the Chamber may, in the interests of the proper administration of justice, as provided in Article 36 § 2 of the Convention, invite, or grant leave to, any Contracting Party which is not a party to the proceedings, or any person concerned who is not the applicant, to submit written comments or, in exceptional cases, to take part in a hearing.
(b) Requests for leave for this purpose must be duly reasoned and submitted in writing in one of the official languages as provided in Rule 34 § 4 not later than twelve weeks after notice of the application has been given to the respondent Contracting Party. Another time-limit may be fixed by the President of the Chamber for exceptional reasons.
4. (a) In cases to be considered by the Grand Chamber, the periods of time prescribed in the preceding paragraphs shall run from the notification to the parties of the decision of the Chamber under Rule 72 § 1 to relinquish jurisdiction in favour of the Grand Chamber or of the decision of the panel of the Grand Chamber under Rule 73 § 2 to accept a request by a party for referral of the case to the Grand Chamber.
(b) The time-limits laid down in this Rule may exceptionally be extended by the President of the Chamber if sufficient cause is shown.
5. Any invitation or grant of leave referred to in paragraph 3 (a) of this Rule shall be subject to any conditions, including time-limits, set by the President of the Chamber. Where such conditions are not complied with, the President may decide not to include the comments in the case file or to limit participation in the hearing to the extent that he or she considers appropriate.
6. Written comments submitted under this Rule shall be drafted in one of the official languages as provided in Rule 34 § 4. They shall be forwarded by the Registrar to the parties to the case, who shall be entitled, subject to any conditions, including time-limits, set by the President of the Chamber, to file written observations in reply or, where appropriate, to reply at the hearing.

Rule 44A. The parties have a duty to cooperate fully in the conduct of the proceedings and, in particular, to take such action within their power as the Court considers necessary for the proper administration of justice. This duty shall also apply to a Contracting Party not party to the proceedings where such cooperation is necessary.

Rule 44B. Where a party fails to comply with an order of the Court concerning the conduct of the proceedings, the President of the Chamber may take any steps which he or she considers appropriate.

Rule 44C. 1. Where a party fails to adduce evidence or provide information requested by the Court or to divulge relevant information of its own motion or otherwise fails to participate effectively in the proceedings, the Court may draw such inferences as it deems appropriate.
2. Failure or refusal by a respondent Contracting Party to participate effectively in the proceedings shall not, in itself, be a reason for the Chamber to discontinue the examination of the application.

Rule 44D. If the representative of a party makes abusive, frivolous, vexatious, misleading or prolix submissions, the President of the Chamber may exclude that representative from the proceedings, refuse to accept all or part of the submissions or make any other order which he or she considers it appropriate to make, without prejudice to Article 35 § 3 of the Convention.

Rule 44E. In accordance with Article 37 § 1 (a) of the Convention, if an applicant Contracting Party or an individual applicant fails to pursue the application, the Chamber may strike the application out of the Court's list under Rule 43.

Chapter II. Institution of Proceedings

Rule 45. 1. Any application made under Articles 33 or 34 of the Convention shall be submitted in writing and shall be signed by the applicant or by the applicant's representative.
2. Where an application is made by a non-governmental organisation or by a group of individuals, it shall be signed by those persons competent to represent that organisation or group. The Chamber or Committee concerned shall determine any question as to whether the persons who have signed an application are competent to do so.
3. Where applicants are represented in accordance with Rule 36, a power of attorney or written authority to act shall be supplied by their representative or representatives.

Rule 46. Any Contracting Party or Parties intending to bring a case before the Court under Article 33 of the Convention shall file with the Registry an application setting out
(a) the name of the Contracting Party against which the application is made;

(b) a statement of the facts;
(c) a statement of the alleged violation(s) of the Convention and the relevant arguments;
(d) a statement on compliance with the admissibility criteria (exhaustion of domestic remedies and the six-month rule) laid down in Article 35 § 1 of the Convention;
(e) the object of the application and a general indication of any claims for just satisfaction made under Article 41 of the Convention on behalf of the alleged injured party or parties; and
(f) the name and address of the person or persons appointed as Agent; and accompanied by
(g) copies of any relevant documents and in particular the decisions, whether judicial or not, relating to the object of the application.

Rule 47. 1. An application under Article 34 of the Convention shall be made on the application form provided by the Registry, unless the Court decides otherwise. It shall contain all of the information requested in the relevant parts of the application form and set out
(a) the name, date of birth, nationality and address of the applicant and, where the applicant is a legal person, the full name, date of incorporation or registration, the official registration number (if any) and the official address;
(b) the name, occupation, address, telephone and fax numbers and e-mail address of the representative, if any;
(c) the name of the Contracting Party or Parties against which the application is made;
(d) a concise and legible statement of the facts;
(e) a concise and legible statement of the alleged violation(s) of the Convention and the relevant arguments; and
(f) a concise and legible statement confirming the applicant's compliance with the admissibility criteria laid down in Article 35 § 1 of the Convention.
2. (a) All of the information referred to in paragraph 1 (d) to (f) above that is set out in the relevant part of the application form should be sufficient to enable the Court to determine the nature and scope of the application without recourse to any other document.
(b) The applicant may however supplement the information by appending to the application form further details on the facts, alleged violations of the Convention and the relevant arguments. Such information shall not exceed 20 pages.
3.1 The application form shall be signed by the applicant or the applicant's representative and shall be accompanied by
(a) copies of documents relating to the decisions or measures complained of, judicial or otherwise;
(b) copies of documents and decisions showing that the applicant has complied with the exhaustion of domestic remedies requirement and the time-limit contained in Article 35 § 1 of the Convention;
(c) where appropriate, copies of documents relating to any other procedure of international investigation or settlement;
(d) where represented, the original of the power of attorney or form of authority signed by the applicant.
3.2 Documents submitted in support of the application shall be listed in order by date, numbered consecutively and be identified clearly.
4. Applicants who do not wish their identity to be disclosed to the public shall so indicate and shall submit a statement of the reasons justifying such a departure from the normal rule of public access to information in proceedings before the Court. The Court may authorise anonymity or grant it of its own motion.
5.1 Failure to comply with the requirements set out in paragraphs 1 to 3 of this Rule will result in the application not being examined by the Court, unless
(a) the applicant has provided an adequate explanation for the failure to comply;
(b) the application concerns a request for an interim measure;
(c) the Court otherwise directs of its own motion or at the request of an applicant.
5.2. The Court may in any case request an applicant to provide information or documents in any form or manner which may be appropriate within a fixed time-limit.
6. (a) The date of introduction of the application for the purposes of Article 35 § 1 of the Convention shall be the date on which an application form satisfying the requirements of this Rule is sent to the Court. The date of dispatch shall be the date of the postmark.
(b) Where it finds it justified, the Court may nevertheless decide that a different date shall be considered to be the date of introduction.
7. Applicants shall keep the Court informed of any change of address and of all circumstances relevant to the application.

PART II   FUNDAMENTAL RIGHTS

Chapter III – Judge Rapporteurs

Rule 48. 1. Where an application is made under Article 33 of the Convention, the Chamber constituted to consider the case shall designate one or more of its judges as Judge Rapporteur(s), who shall submit a report on admissibility when the written observations of the Contracting Parties concerned have been received.
2. The Judge Rapporteur(s) shall submit such reports, drafts and other documents as may assist the Chamber and its President in carrying out their functions.

Rule 49. 1. Where the material submitted by the applicant is on its own sufficient to disclose that the application is inadmissible or should be struck out of the list, the application shall be considered by a single-judge formation unless there is some special reason to the contrary.
2. Where an application is made under Article 34 of the Convention and its examination by a Chamber or a Committee exercising the functions attributed to it under Rule 53 § 2 seems justified, the President of the Section to which the case has been assigned shall designate a judge as Judge Rapporteur, who shall examine the application.
3. In their examination of applications, Judge Rapporteurs
(a) may request the parties to submit, within a specified time, any factual information, documents or other material which they consider to be relevant;
(b) shall, subject to the President of the Section directing that the case be considered by a Chamber or a Committee, decide whether the application is to be considered by a single-judge formation, by a Committee or by a Chamber;
(c) shall submit such reports, drafts and other documents as may assist the Chamber or the Committee or the respective President in carrying out their functions.

Rule 50. Where a case has been submitted to the Grand Chamber either under Article 30 or under Article 43 of the Convention, the President of the Grand Chamber shall designate as Judge Rapporteur(s) one or, in the case of an inter-State application, one or more of its members.
Chapter IV – Proceedings on Admissibility
Inter-State applications

Rule 51. 1. When an application is made under Article 33 of the Convention, the President of the Court shall immediately give notice of the application to the respondent Contracting Party and shall assign the application to one of the Sections.
2. In accordance with Rule 26 § 1 (a), the judges elected in respect of the applicant and respondent Contracting Parties shall sit as ex officio members of the Chamber constituted to consider the case. Rule 30 shall apply if the application has been brought by several Contracting Parties or if applications with the same object brought by several Contracting Parties are being examined jointly under Rule 42.
3. On assignment of the case to a Section, the President of the Section shall constitute the Chamber in accordance with Rule 26 § 1 and shall invite the respondent Contracting Party to submit its observations in writing on the admissibility of the application. The observations so obtained shall be communicated by the Registrar to the applicant Contracting Party, which may submit written observations in reply.
4. Before the ruling on the admissibility of the application is given, the Chamber or its President may decide to invite the Parties to submit further observations in writing.
5. A hearing on the admissibility shall be held if one or more of the Contracting Parties concerned so requests or if the Chamber so decides of its own motion.
6. Before fixing the written and, where appropriate, oral procedure, the President of the Chamber shall consult the Parties.
Individual applications

Rule 52. 1. Any application made under Article 34 of the Convention shall be assigned to a Section by the President of the Court, who in so doing shall endeavour to ensure a fair distribution of cases between the Sections.
2. The Chamber of seven judges provided for in Article 26 § 1 of the Convention shall be constituted by the President of the Section concerned in accordance with Rule 26 § 1.
3. Pending the constitution of a Chamber in accordance with paragraph (2) of this Rule, the President of the Section shall exercise any powers conferred on the President of the Chamber by these Rules.

Rule 52A. 1. In accordance with Article 27 of the Convention, a single judge may declare inadmissible or strike out of the Court's list of cases an application submitted under Article 34, where such a

decision can be taken without further examination. The decision shall be final. The applicant shall be informed of the decision by letter.
2. In accordance with Article 26 § 3 of the Convention, a single judge may not examine any application against the Contracting Party in respect of which that judge has been elected.
3. If the single judge does not take a decision of the kind provided for in the first paragraph of the present Rule, that judge shall forward the application to a Committee or to a Chamber for further examination.

Rule 53. 1. In accordance with Article 28 § 1 (a) of the Convention, the Committee may, by a unanimous vote and at any stage of the proceedings, declare an application inadmissible or strike it out of the Court's list of cases where such a decision can be taken without further examination.
2. If the Committee is satisfied, in the light of the parties' observations received pursuant to Rule 54 § 2 (b), that the case falls to be examined in accordance with the procedure under Article 28 § 1 (b) of the Convention, it shall, by a unanimous vote, adopt a judgment including its decision on admissibility and, as appropriate, on just satisfaction.
3. If the judge elected in respect of the Contracting Party concerned is not a member of the Committee, the Committee may at any stage of the proceedings before it, by a unanimous vote, invite that judge to take the place of one of its members, having regard to all relevant factors, including whether that Party has contested the application of the procedure under Article 28 § 1 (b) of the Convention.
4. Decisions and judgments under Article 28 § 1 of the Convention shall be final.
5. The applicant, as well as the Contracting Parties concerned where these have previously been involved in the application in accordance with the present Rules, shall be informed of the decision of the Committee pursuant to Article 28 § 1 (a) of the Convention by letter, unless the Committee decides otherwise.
6. If no decision or judgment is adopted by the Committee, the application shall be forwarded to the Chamber constituted under Rule 52 § 2 to examine the case.
7. The provisions of Rule 42 § 1 and Rules 79 to 81 shall apply, *mutatis mutandis*, to proceedings before a Committee.

Rule 54. 1. The Chamber may at once declare the application inadmissible or strike it out of the Court's list of cases. The decision of the Chamber may relate to all or part of the application.
2. Alternatively, the Chamber or the President of the Section may decide to
(a) request the parties to submit any factual information, documents or other material considered by the Chamber or its President to be relevant;
(b) give notice of the application or part of the application to the respondent Contracting Party and invite that Party to submit written observations thereon and, upon receipt thereof, invite the applicant to submit observations in reply;
(c) invite the parties to submit further observations in writing.
3. In the exercise of the competences under paragraph (2) (b) of this Rule, the President of the Section, acting as a single judge, may at once declare part of the application inadmissible or strike part of the application out of the Court's list of cases. The decision shall be final. The applicant shall be informed of the decision by letter.
4. Paragraphs (2) and (3) of this Rule shall also apply to Vice-Presidents of Sections appointed as duty judges in accordance with Rule 39 § 4 to decide on requests for interim measures.
5. Before taking a decision on admissibility, the Chamber may decide, either at the request of a party or of its own motion, to hold a hearing if it considers that the discharge of its functions under the Convention so requires. In that event, unless the Chamber shall exceptionally decide otherwise, the parties shall also be invited to address the issues arising in relation to the merits of the application.

Rule 54A. 1. When giving notice of the application to the respondent Contracting Party pursuant to Rule 54 § 2 (b), the Chamber may also decide to examine the admissibility and merits at the same time in accordance with Article 29 § 1 of the Convention. The parties shall be invited to include in their observations any submissions concerning just satisfaction and any proposals for a friendly settlement. The conditions laid down in Rules 60 and 62 shall apply, *mutatis mutandis*. The Court may, however, decide at any stage, if necessary, to take a separate decision on admissibility.
2. If no friendly settlement or other solution is reached and the Chamber is satisfied, in the light of the parties' arguments, that the case is admissible and ready for a determination on the merits, it shall immediately adopt a judgment including the Chamber's decision on admissibility, save in cases where it decides to take such a decision separately.
Inter-State and individual applications

Rule 55. Any plea of inadmissibility must, in so far as its character and the circumstances permit, be raised by the respondent Contracting Party in its written or oral observations on the admissibility of the application submitted as provided in Rule 51 or 54, as the case may be.

Rule 56. 1. The decision of the Chamber shall state whether it was taken unanimously or by a majority and shall be accompanied or followed by reasons.

2. The decision of the Chamber shall be communicated by the Registrar to the applicant. It shall also be communicated to the Contracting Party or Parties concerned and to any third party, including the Council of Europe Commissioner for Human Rights, where these have previously been informed of the application in accordance with the present Rules. If a friendly settlement is effected, the decision to strike an application out of the list of cases shall be forwarded to the Committee of Ministers in accordance with Rule 43 § 3.

Rule 57. 1. Unless the Court decides that a decision shall be given in both official languages, all decisions of Chambers shall be given either in English or in French.

2. Publication of such decisions in the official reports of the Court, as provided for in Rule 78, shall be in both official languages of the Court.

Chapter V. Proceedings after the admission of an application

Rule 58. 1. Once the Chamber has decided to admit an application made under Article 33 of the Convention, the President of the Chamber shall, after consulting the Contracting Parties concerned, lay down the time-limits for the filing of written observations on the merits and for the production of any further evidence. The President may however, with the agreement of the Contracting Parties concerned, direct that a written procedure is to be dispensed with.

2. A hearing on the merits shall be held if one or more of the Contracting Parties concerned so requests or if the Chamber so decides of its own motion. The President of the Chamber shall fix the oral procedure.

Rule 59. 1. Once an application made under Article 34 of the Convention has been declared admissible, the Chamber or its President may invite the parties to submit further evidence and written observations.

2. Unless decided otherwise, the parties shall be allowed the same time for submission of their observations.

3. The Chamber may decide, either at the request of a party or of its own motion, to hold a hearing on the merits if it considers that the discharge of its functions under the Convention so requires.

4. The President of the Chamber shall, where appropriate, fix the written and oral procedure.

Rule 60. 1. An applicant who wishes to obtain an award of just satisfaction under Article 41 of the Convention in the event of the Court finding a violation of his or her Convention rights must make a specific claim to that effect.

2. The applicant must submit itemised particulars of all claims, together with any relevant supporting documents, within the time-limit fixed for the submission of the applicant's observations on the merits unless the President of the Chamber directs otherwise.

3. If the applicant fails to comply with the requirements set out in the preceding paragraphs the Chamber may reject the claims in whole or in part.

4. The applicant's claims shall be transmitted to the respondent Contracting Party for comment.

Rule 61. 1. The Court may initiate a pilot-judgment procedure and adopt a pilot judgment where the facts of an application reveal in the Contracting Party concerned the existence of a structural or systemic problem or other similar dysfunction which has given rise or may give rise to similar applications.

2. (a) Before initiating a pilot-judgment procedure, the Court shall first seek the views of the parties on whether the application under examination results from the existence of such a problem or dysfunction in the Contracting Party concerned and on the suitability of processing the application in accordance with that procedure.

(b) A pilot-judgment procedure may be initiated by the Court of its own motion or at the request of one or both parties.

(c) Any application selected for pilot-judgment treatment shall be processed as a matter of priority in accordance with Rule 41 of the Rules of Court.

3. The Court shall in its pilot judgment identify both the nature of the structural or systemic problem or other dysfunction as established as well as the type of remedial measures which the Contracting Party concerned is required to take at the domestic level by virtue of the operative provisions of the judgment.

RULES OF COURT OF THE ECTHR

4. The Court may direct in the operative provisions of the pilot judgment that the remedial measures referred to in paragraph (3) above be adopted within a specified time, bearing in mind the nature of the measures required and the speed with which the problem which it has identified can be remedied at the domestic level.

5. When adopting a pilot judgment, the Court may reserve the question of just satisfaction either in whole or in part pending the adoption by the respondent Contracting Party of the individual and general measures specified in the pilot judgment.

6. (a) As appropriate, the Court may adjourn the examination of all similar applications pending the adoption of the remedial measures required by virtue of the operative provisions of the pilot judgment.

(b) The applicants concerned shall be informed in a suitable manner of the decision to adjourn. They shall be notified as appropriate of all relevant developments affecting their cases.

(c) The Court may at any time examine an adjourned application where the interests of the proper administration of justice so require.

7. Where the parties to the pilot case reach a friendly-settlement agreement, such agreement shall comprise a declaration by the respondent Contracting Party on the implementation of the general measures identified in the pilot judgment as well as the redress to be afforded to other actual or potential applicants.

8. Subject to any decision to the contrary, in the event of the failure of the Contracting Party concerned to comply with the operative provisions of a pilot judgment, the Court shall resume its examination of the applications which have been adjourned in accordance with paragraph (6) above.

9. The Committee of Ministers, the Parliamentary Assembly of the Council of Europe, the Secretary General of the Council of Europe, and the Council of Europe Commissioner for Human Rights shall be informed of the adoption of a pilot judgment as well as of any other judgment in which the Court draws attention to the existence of a structural or systemic problem in a Contracting Party.

10. Information about the initiation of pilot-judgment procedures, the adoption of pilot judgments and their execution as well as the closure of such procedures shall be published on the Court's website.

Rule 62. 1. Once an application has been declared admissible, the Registrar, acting on the instructions of the Chamber or its President, shall enter into contact with the parties with a view to securing a friendly settlement of the matter in accordance with Article 39 § 1 of the Convention. The Chamber shall take any steps that appear appropriate to facilitate such a settlement.

2. In accordance with Article 39 § 2 of the Convention, the friendly-settlement negotiations shall be confidential and without prejudice to the parties' arguments in the contentious proceedings. No written or oral communication and no offer or concession made in the framework of the attempt to secure a friendly settlement may be referred to or relied on in the contentious proceedings.

3. If the Chamber is informed by the Registrar that the parties have agreed to a friendly settlement, it shall, after verifying that the settlement has been reached on the basis of respect for human rights as defined in the Convention and the Protocols thereto, strike the case out of the Court's list in accordance with Rule 43 § 3.

4. Paragraphs (2) and (3) apply, *mutatis mutandis*, to the procedure under Rule 54A. Rule 62A1 – Unilateral declaration

1. (a) Where an applicant has refused the terms of a friendly-settlement proposal made pursuant to Rule 62, the Contracting Party concerned may file with the Court a request to strike the application out of the list in accordance with Article 37 § 1 of the Convention.

(b) Such request shall be accompanied by a declaration clearly acknowledging that there has been a violation of the Convention in the applicant's case together with an undertaking to provide adequate redress and, as appropriate, to take necessary remedial measures.

(c) The filing of a declaration under paragraph (1) (b) of this Rule must be made in public and adversarial proceedings conducted separately from and with due respect for the confidentiality of any friendly-settlement proceedings referred to in Article 39 § 2 of the Convention and Rule 62 § 2.

2. Where exceptional circumstances so justify, a request and accompanying declaration may be filed with the Court even in the absence of a prior attempt to reach a friendly settlement.

3. If it is satisfied that the declaration offers a sufficient basis for finding that respect for human rights as defined in the Convention and the Protocols thereto does not require it to continue its examination of the application, the Court may strike it out of the list, either in whole or in part, even if the applicant wishes the examination of the application to be continued.

4. This Rule applies, *mutatis mutandis*, to the procedure under Rule 54A.

PART II   FUNDAMENTAL RIGHTS

Chapter VI. Hearings

Rule 63. 1. Hearings shall be public unless, in accordance with paragraph (2) of this Rule, the Chamber in exceptional circumstances decides otherwise, either of its own motion or at the request of a party or any other person concerned.
2. The press and the public may be excluded from all or part of a hearing in the interests of morals, public order or national security in a democratic society, where the interests of juveniles or the protection of the private life of the parties so require, or to the extent strictly necessary in the opinion of the Chamber in special circumstances where publicity would prejudice the interests of justice.
3. Any request for a hearing to be held in camera made under paragraph (1) of this Rule must include reasons and specify whether it concerns all or only part of the hearing.

Rule 64. 1. The President of the Chamber shall organise and direct hearings and shall prescribe the order in which those appearing before the Chamber shall be called upon to speak.
2. Any judge may put questions to any person appearing before the Chamber.

Rule 65. Where a party or any other person due to appear fails or declines to do so, the Chamber may, provided that it is satisfied that such a course is consistent with the proper administration of justice, nonetheless proceed with the hearing.

[Rules 66 to 69 deleted]

Rule 70. 1. If the President of the Chamber so directs, the Registrar shall be responsible for the making of a verbatim record of the hearing. Any such record shall include:
(a) the composition of the Chamber;
(b) a list of those appearing before the Chamber;
(c) the text of the submissions made, questions put and replies given;
(d) the text of any ruling delivered during the hearing.
2. If all or part of the verbatim record is in a non-official language, the Registrar shall arrange for its translation into one of the official languages.
3. The representatives of the parties shall receive a copy of the verbatim record in order that they may, subject to the control of the Registrar or the President of the Chamber, make corrections, but in no case may such corrections affect the sense and bearing of what was said. The Registrar shall lay down, in accordance with the instructions of the President of the Chamber, the time-limits granted for this purpose.
4. The verbatim record, once so corrected, shall be signed by the President of the Chamber and the Registrar and shall then constitute certified matters of record.

Chapter VII. Proceedings before the Grand Chamber

Rule 71. 1. Any provisions governing proceedings before the Chambers shall apply, *mutatis mutandis*, to proceedings before the Grand Chamber.
2. The powers conferred on a Chamber by Rules 54 § 5 and 59 § 3 in relation to the holding of a hearing may, in proceedings before the Grand Chamber, also be exercised by the President of the Grand Chamber.

Rule 72. 1. Where a case pending before a Chamber raises a serious question affecting the interpretation of the Convention or the Protocols thereto, the Chamber may relinquish jurisdiction in favour of the Grand Chamber, unless one of the parties to the case has objected in accordance with paragraph (4) of this Rule.
2. Where the resolution of a question raised in a case before the Chamber might have a result inconsistent with the Court's case-law, the Chamber shall relinquish jurisdiction in favour of the Grand Chamber, unless one of the parties to the case has objected in accordance with paragraph (4) of this Rule.
3. Reasons need not be given for the decision to relinquish.
4. The Registrar shall notify the parties of the Chamber's intention to relinquish jurisdiction. The parties shall have one month from the date of that notification within which to file at the Registry a duly reasoned objection. An objection which does not fulfil these conditions shall be considered invalid by the Chamber.

Rule 73. 1. In accordance with Article 43 of the Convention, any party to a case may exceptionally, within a period of three months from the date of delivery of the judgment of a Chamber, file in writing at the Registry a request that the case be referred to the Grand Chamber. The party shall specify in its request the serious question affecting the interpretation or application of the Convention or the

Protocols thereto, or the serious issue of general importance, which in its view warrants consideration by the Grand Chamber.
2. A panel of five judges of the Grand Chamber constituted in accordance with Rule 24 § 5 shall examine the request solely on the basis of the existing case file. It shall accept the request only if it considers that the case does raise such a question or issue. Reasons need not be given for a refusal of the request.
3. If the panel accepts the request, the Grand Chamber shall decide the case by means of a judgment.

Chapter VIII. Judgments

Rule 74. 1. A judgment as referred to in Articles 28, 42 and 44 of the Convention shall contain
(a) the names of the President and the other judges constituting the Chamber or the Committee concerned, and the name of the Registrar or the Deputy Registrar;
(b) the dates on which it was adopted and delivered;
(c) a description of the parties;
(d) the names of the Agents, advocates or advisers of the parties; (e) an account of the procedure followed;
(f) the facts of the case;
(g) a summary of the submissions of the parties;
(h) the reasons in point of law;
(i) the operative provisions;
(j) the decision, if any, in respect of costs;
(k) the number of judges constituting the majority;
(l) where appropriate, a statement as to which text is authentic.
2. Any judge who has taken part in the consideration of the case by a Chamber or by the Grand Chamber shall be entitled to annex to the judgment either a separate opinion, concurring with or dissenting from that judgment, or a bare statement of dissent.

Rule 75. 1. Where the Chamber or the Committee finds that there has been a violation of the Convention or the Protocols thereto, it shall give in the same judgment a ruling on the application of Article 41 of the Convention if a specific claim has been submitted in accordance with Rule 60 and the question is ready for decision; if the question is not ready for decision, the Chamber or the Committee shall reserve it in whole or in part and shall fix the further procedure.
2. For the purposes of ruling on the application of Article 41 of the Convention, the Chamber or the Committee shall, as far as possible, be composed of those judges who sat to consider the merits of the case. Where it is not possible to constitute the original Chamber or Committee, the President of the Section shall complete or compose the Chamber or Committee by drawing lots.
3. The Chamber or the Committee may, when affording just satisfaction under Article 41 of the Convention, direct that if settlement is not made within a specified time, interest is to be payable on any sums awarded.
4. If the Court is informed that an agreement has been reached between the injured party and the Contracting Party liable, it shall verify the equitable nature of the agreement and, where it finds the agreement to be equitable, strike the case out of the list in accordance with Rule 43 § 3.

Rule 76. 1. Unless the Court decides that a judgment shall be given in both official languages, all judgments shall be given either in English or in French.
2. Publication of such judgments in the official reports of the Court, as provided for in Rule 78, shall be in both official languages of the Court.

Rule 77. 1. Judgments shall be signed by the President of the Chamber or the Committee and the Registrar.
2. The judgment adopted by a Chamber may be read out at a public hearing by the President of the Chamber or by another judge delegated by him or her. The Agents and representatives of the parties shall be informed in due time of the date of the hearing. Otherwise, and in respect of judgments adopted by Committees, the notification provided for in paragraph (3) of this Rule shall constitute delivery of the judgment.
3. The judgment shall be transmitted to the Committee of Ministers. The Registrar shall send copies to the parties, to the Secretary General of the Council of Europe, to any third party, including the Council of Europe Commissioner for Human Rights, and to any other person directly concerned. The original copy, duly signed, shall be placed in the archives of the Court.

Rule 78. In accordance with Article 44 § 3 of the Convention, final judgments of the Court shall be

PART II   FUNDAMENTAL RIGHTS

published, under the responsibility of the Registrar, in an appropriate form. The Registrar shall in addition be responsible for the publication of official reports of selected judgments and decisions and of any document which the President of the Court considers it useful to publish.

Rule 79. 1. A party may request the interpretation of a judgment within a period of one year following the delivery of that judgment.
2. The request shall be filed with the Registry. It shall state precisely the point or points in the operative provisions of the judgment on which interpretation is required.
3. The original Chamber may decide of its own motion to refuse the request on the ground that there is no reason to warrant considering it. Where it is not possible to constitute the original Chamber, the President of the Court shall complete or compose the Chamber by drawing lots.
4. If the Chamber does not refuse the request, the Registrar shall communicate it to the other party or parties and shall invite them to submit any written comments within a time-limit laid down by the President of the Chamber. The President of the Chamber shall also fix the date of the hearing should the Chamber decide to hold one. The Chamber shall decide by means of a judgment.

Rule 80. 1. A party may, in the event of the discovery of a fact which might by its nature have a decisive influence and which, when a judgment was delivered, was unknown to the Court and could not reasonably have been known to that party, request the Court, within a period of six months after that party acquired knowledge of the fact, to revise that judgment.
2. The request shall mention the judgment of which revision is requested and shall contain the information necessary to show that the conditions laid down in paragraph (1) of this Rule have been complied with. It shall be accompanied by a copy of all supporting documents. The request and supporting documents shall be filed with the Registry.
3. The original Chamber may decide of its own motion to refuse the request on the ground that there is no reason to warrant considering it. Where it is not possible to constitute the original Chamber, the President of the Court shall complete or compose the Chamber by drawing lots.
4. If the Chamber does not refuse the request, the Registrar shall communicate it to the other party or parties and shall invite them to submit any written comments within a time-limit laid down by the President of the Chamber. The President of the Chamber shall also fix the date of the hearing should the Chamber decide to hold one. The Chamber shall decide by means of a judgment.

Rule 81. Without prejudice to the provisions on revision of judgments and on restoration to the list of applications, the Court may, of its own motion or at the request of a party made within one month of the delivery of a decision or a judgment, rectify clerical errors, errors in calculation or obvious mistakes.

Chapter IX. Advisory Opinions

Rule 82. In proceedings relating to advisory opinions the Court shall apply, in addition to the provisions of Articles 47, 48 and 49 of the Convention, the provisions which follow. It shall also apply the other provisions of these Rules to the extent to which it considers this to be appropriate.

Rule 83. The request for an advisory opinion shall be filed with the Registrar. It shall state fully and precisely the question on which the opinion of the Court is sought, and also
(a) the date on which the Committee of Ministers adopted the decision referred to in Article 47 § 3 of the Convention;
(b) the name and address of the person or persons appointed by the Committee of Ministers to give the Court any explanations which it may require.
The request shall be accompanied by all documents likely to elucidate the question.

Rule 84. 1. On receipt of a request, the Registrar shall transmit a copy of it and of the accompanying documents to all members of the Court.
2. The Registrar shall inform the Contracting Parties that they may submit written comments on the request.

Rule 85. 1. The President of the Court shall lay down the time-limits for filing written comments or other documents.
2. Written comments or other documents shall be filed with the Registrar. The Registrar shall transmit copies of them to all the members of the Court, to the Committee of Ministers and to each of the Contracting Parties.

Rule 86. After the close of the written procedure, the President of the Court shall decide whether the Contracting Parties which have submitted written comments are to be given an opportunity to develop them at an oral hearing held for the purpose.

Rule 87. 1. A Grand Chamber shall be constituted to consider the request for an advisory opinion.
2. If the Grand Chamber considers that the request is not within its competence as defined in Article 47 of the Convention, it shall so declare in a reasoned decision.

Rule 88. 1. Reasoned decisions and advisory opinions shall be given by a majority vote of the Grand Chamber. They shall mention the number of judges constituting the majority.
2. Any judge may, if he or she so desires, attach to the reasoned decision or advisory opinion of the Court either a separate opinion, concurring with or dissenting from the reasoned decision or advisory opinion, or a bare statement of dissent.

Rule 89. The reasoned decision or advisory opinion may be read out in one of the two official languages by the President of the Grand Chamber, or by another judge delegated by the President, at a public hearing, prior notice having been given to the Committee of Ministers and to each of the Contracting Parties. Otherwise the notification provided for in Rule 90 shall constitute delivery of the opinion or reasoned decision.

Rule 90. The advisory opinion or reasoned decision shall be signed by the President of the Grand Chamber and by the Registrar. The original copy, duly signed, shall be placed in the archives of the Court. The Registrar shall send certified copies to the Committee of Ministers, to the Contracting Parties and to the Secretary General of the Council of Europe.

Chapter X. Proceedings under Article 46 §§ 3, 4 and 5 of the Convention

Sub-Chapter I. Proceedings under Article 46 § 3 of the Convention

Rule 91. Any request for interpretation under Article 46 § 3 of the Convention shall be filed with the Registrar. The request shall state fully and precisely the nature and source of the question of interpretation that has hindered execution of the judgment mentioned in the request and shall be accompanied by
(a) information about the execution proceedings, if any, before the Committee of Ministers in respect of the judgment;
(b) a copy of the decision referred to in Article 46 § 3 of the Convention;
(c) the name and address of the person or persons appointed by the Committee of Ministers to give the Court any explanations which it may require.

Rule 92. 1. The request shall be examined by the Grand Chamber, Chamber or Committee which rendered the judgment in question.
2. Where it is not possible to constitute the original Grand Chamber, Chamber or Committee, the President of the Court shall complete or compose it by drawing lots.

Rule 93. The decision of the Court on the question of interpretation referred to it by the Committee of Ministers is final. No separate opinion of the judges may be delivered thereto. Copies of the ruling shall be transmitted to the Committee of Ministers and to the parties concerned as well as to any third party, including the Council of Europe Commissioner for Human Rights.

Sub-Chapter II. Proceedings under Article 46 §§ 4 and 5 of the Convention

Rule 94. In proceedings relating to a referral to the Court of a question whether a Contracting Party has failed to fulfil its obligation under Article 46 § 1 of the Convention the Court shall apply, in addition to the provisions of Article 31 (b) and Article 46 §§ 4 and 5 of the Convention, the provisions which follow. It shall also apply the other provisions of these Rules to the extent to which it considers this to be appropriate.

Rule 95. Any request made pursuant to Article 46 § 4 of the Convention shall be reasoned and shall be filed with the Registrar. It shall be accompanied by
(a) the judgment concerned;
(b) information about the execution proceedings before the Committee of Ministers in respect of the judgment concerned, including, if any, the views expressed in writing by the parties concerned and communications submitted in those proceedings;
(c) copies of the formal notice served on the respondent Contracting Party or Parties and the decision referred to in Article 46 § 4 of the Convention;
(d) the name and address of the person or persons appointed by the Committee of Ministers to give the Court any explanations which it may require;
(e) copies of all other documents likely to elucidate the question.

PART II FUNDAMENTAL RIGHTS

Rule 96. A Grand Chamber shall be constituted, in accordance with Rule 24 § 2 (g), to consider the question referred to the Court.

Rule 97. The President of the Grand Chamber shall inform the Committee of Ministers and the parties concerned that they may submit written comments on the question referred.

Rule 98. 1. The President of the Grand Chamber shall lay down the time-limits for filing written comments or other documents.
2. The Grand Chamber may decide to hold a hearing.

Rule 99. The Grand Chamber shall decide by means of a judgment. Copies of the judgment shall be transmitted to the Committee of Ministers and to the parties concerned as well as to any third party, including the Council of Europe Commissioner for Human Rights.

Chapter XI. Legal Aid

Rule 100 (former Rule 91). 1. The President of the Chamber may, either at the request of an applicant having lodged an application under Article 34 of the Convention or of his or her own motion, grant free legal aid to the applicant in connection with the presentation of the case from the moment when observations in writing on the admissibility of that application are received from the respondent Contracting Party in accordance with Rule 54 § 2 b, or where the time-limit for their submission has expired.
2. Subject to Rule 105, where the applicant has been granted legal aid in connection with the presentation of his or her case before the Chamber, that grant shall continue in force for the purposes of his or her representation before the Grand Chamber.

Rule 101 (former Rule 92). Legal aid shall be granted only where the President of the Chamber is satisfied
(a) that it is necessary for the proper conduct of the case before the Chamber;
(b) that the applicant has insufficient means to meet all or part of the costs entailed.

Rule 102 (former Rule 93). 1. In order to determine whether or not applicants have sufficient means to meet all or part of the costs entailed, they shall be required to complete a form of declaration stating their income, capital assets and any financial commitments in respect of dependants, or any other financial obligations. The declaration shall be certified by the appropriate domestic authority or authorities.
2. The President of the Chamber may invite the Contracting Party concerned to submit its comments in writing.
3. After receiving the information mentioned in paragraph (1) of this Rule, the President of the Chamber shall decide whether or not to grant legal aid. The Registrar shall inform the parties accordingly.

Rule 103 (former Rule 94). 1. Fees shall be payable to the advocates or other persons appointed in accordance with Rule 36 § 4. Fees may, where appropriate, be paid to more than one such representative.
2. Legal aid may be granted to cover not only representatives' fees but also travelling and subsistence expenses and other necessary expenses incurred by the applicant or appointed representative.

Rule 104 (former Rule 95). On a decision to grant legal aid, the Registrar shall fix
(a) the rate of fees to be paid in accordance with the legal-aid scales in force; (b) the level of expenses to be paid.

Rule 105 (former Rule 96). The President of the Chamber may, if satisfied that the conditions stated in Rule 101 are no longer fulfilled, revoke or vary a grant of legal aid at any time.

Title III. Transitional Rules

(Former Rules 97 and 98 deleted)

Rule 106 (former Rule 99). 1. In cases brought before the Court under Article 5 §§ 4 and 5 of Protocol No. 11 to the Convention, the Court may invite the Commission to delegate one or more of its members to take part in the consideration of the case before the Court.
2. In cases referred to in paragraph (1) of this Rule, the Court shall take into consideration the report of the Commission adopted pursuant to former Article 31 of the Convention.
3. Unless the President of the Chamber decides otherwise, the said report shall be made available to the public through the Registrar as soon as possible after the case has been brought before the Court.

4. The remainder of the case file of the Commission, including all pleadings, in cases brought before the Court under Article 5 §§ 2 to 5 of Protocol No. 11 shall remain confidential unless the President of the Chamber decides otherwise.

5. In cases where the Commission has taken evidence but has been unable to adopt a report in accordance with former Article 31 of the Convention, the Court shall take into consideration the verbatim records, documentation and opinion of the Commission's delegations arising from such investigations.

Rule 107 (former Rule 100). 1. In cases referred to the Court under Article 5 § 4 of Protocol No. 11 to the Convention, a panel of the Grand Chamber constituted in accordance with Rule 24 § 5 shall determine, solely on the basis of the existing case file, whether a Chamber or the Grand Chamber is to decide the case.

2. If the case is decided by a Chamber, the judgment of the Chamber shall, in accordance with Article 5 § 4 of Protocol No. 11, be final and Rule 73 shall be inapplicable.

3. Cases transmitted to the Court under Article 5 § 5 of Protocol No. 11 shall be forwarded by the President of the Court to the Grand Chamber.

4. For each case transmitted to the Grand Chamber under Article 5 § 5 of Protocol No. 11, the Grand Chamber shall be completed by judges designated by rotation within one of the groups mentioned in Rule 24 § 31, the cases being allocated to the groups on an alternate basis.

Rule 108 (former Rule 101). Subject to Rule 96, in cases brought before the Court under Article 5 §§ 2 to 5 of Protocol No. 11 to the Convention, a grant of legal aid made to an applicant in the proceedings before the Commission or the former Court shall continue in force for the purposes of his or her representation before the Court.

Rule 109 (former Rule 102). 1. Where a party requests revision of a judgment delivered by the former Court, the President of the Court shall assign the request to one of the Sections in accordance with the conditions laid down in Rule 51 or 52, as the case may be.

2. The President of the relevant Section shall, notwithstanding Rule 80 § 3, constitute a new Chamber to consider the request.

3. The Chamber to be constituted shall include as ex officio members
(a) the President of the Section;
and, whether or not they are members of the relevant Section,
(b) the judge elected in respect of any Contracting Party concerned or, if he or she is unable to sit, any judge appointed under Rule 29;
(c) any judge of the Court who was a member of the original Chamber that delivered the judgment in the former Court.

4. (a) The other members of the Chamber shall be designated by the President of the Section by means of a drawing of lots from among the members of the relevant Section.
(b) The members of the Section who are not so designated shall sit in the case as substitute judges.

Rules of Court – 1 June 2015

Title IV. Final Clauses

Rule 110 (former Rule 103). 1. Any Rule may be amended upon a motion made after notice where such a motion is carried at the next session of the plenary Court by a majority of all the members of the Court. Notice of such a motion shall be delivered in writing to the Registrar at least one month before the session at which it is to be discussed. On receipt of such a notice of motion, the Registrar shall inform all members of the Court at the earliest possible moment.

2. A Rule relating to the internal working of the Court may be suspended upon a motion made without notice, provided that this decision is taken unanimously by the Chamber concerned. The suspension of a Rule shall in this case be limited in its operation to the particular purpose for which it was sought.

Rule 111 (former Rule 104). The present Rules shall enter into force on 1 November 1998.

[The Annex and Practice Directions are omitted.]

PART II   FUNDAMENTAL RIGHTS

European Convention for the Prevention of Torture and Inhuman or Degrading Treatment or Punishment (CPT)
Opened for signature in Strasbourg on 26 November 1987, entered into force on 1 February 1989

The member States of the Council of Europe, signatory hereto,
Having regard to the provisions of the Convention for the Protection of Human Rights and Fundamental Freedoms,
Recalling that, under Article 3 of the same Convention, "no one shall be subjected to torture or to inhuman or degrading treatment or punishment";
Noting that the machinery provided for in that Convention operates in relation to persons who allege that they are victims of violations of Article 3;
Convinced that the protection of persons deprived of their liberty against torture and inhuman or degrading treatment or punishment could be strengthened by non-judicial means of a preventive character based on visits,
Have agreed as follows:

Chapter I

Article 1. There shall be established a European Committee for the Prevention of Torture and Inhuman or Degrading Treatment or Punishment (hereinafter referred to as "the Committee"). The Committee shall, by means of visits, examine the treatment of persons deprived of their liberty with a view to strengthening, if necessary, the protection of such persons from torture and from inhuman or degrading treatment or punishment.

Article 2. Each Party shall permit visits, in accordance with this Convention, to any place within its jurisdiction where persons are deprived of their liberty by a public authority.

Article 3. In the application of this Convention, the Committee and the competent national authorities of the Party concerned shall co-operate with each other.

Chapter II

Article 4. (1) The Committee shall consist of a number of members equal to that of the Parties.
(2) The members of the Committee shall be chosen from among persons of high moral character, known for their competence in the field of human rights or having professional experience in the areas covered by this Convention.
(3) No two members of the Committee may be nationals of the same State.
(4) The members shall serve in their individual capacity, shall be independent and impartial, and shall be available to serve the Committee effectively.

Article 5. (1) The members of the Committee shall be elected by the Committee of Ministers of the Council of Europe by an absolute majority of votes, from a list of names drawn up by the Bureau of the Consultative Assembly of the Council of Europe; each national delegation of the Parties in the Consultative Assembly shall put forward three candidates, of whom two at least shall be its nationals. Where a member is to be elected to the Committee in respect of a non-member State of the Council of Europe, the Bureau of the Consultative Assembly shall invite the Parliament of that State to put forward three candidates, of whom two at least shall be its nationals. The election by the Committee of Ministers shall take place after consultation with the Party concerned.
(2) The same procedure shall be followed in filling casual vacancies.
(3) The members of the Committee shall be elected for a period of four years. They may be re-elected twice. However, among the members elected at the first election, the terms of three members shall expire at the end of two years. The members whose terms are to expire at the end of the initial period of two years shall be chosen by lot by the Secretary General of the Council of Europe immediately after the first election has been completed.
(4) In order to ensure that, as far as possible, one half of the membership of the Committee shall be renewed every two years, the Committee of Ministers may decide, before proceeding to any subsequent election, that the term or terms of office of one or more members to be elected shall be for a period other than four years but not more than six and not less than two years.
(5) In cases where more than one term of office is involved and the Committee of Ministers applies the preceding paragraph, the allocation of the terms of office shall be effected by the drawing of lots by the Secretary General, immediately after the election.

Article 6. (1) The Committee shall meet in camera. A quorum shall be equal to the majority of its members. The decisions of the Committee shall be taken by a majority of the members present, subject to the provisions of Article 10, paragraph (2).
(2) The Committee shall draw up its own rules of procedure.
(3) The Secretariat of the Committee shall be provided by the Secretary General of the Council of Europe.

Chapter III

Article 7. (1) The Committee shall organise visits to places referred to in Article 2. Apart from periodic visits, the Committee may organise such other visits as appear to it to be required in the circumstances.
(2) As a general rule, the visits shall be carried out by at least two members of the Committee. The Committee may, if it considers it necessary, be assisted by experts and interpreters.

Article 8. (1) The Committee shall notify the Government of the Party concerned of its intention to carry out a visit. After such notification, it may at any time visit any place referred to in Article 2.
(2) A Party shall provide the Committee with the following facilities to carry out its task:
(a) access to its territory and the right to travel without restriction;
(b) full information on the places where persons deprived of their liberty are being held;
(c) unlimited access to any place where persons are deprived of their liberty, including the right to move inside such places without restriction;
(d) other information available to the Party which is necessary for the Committee to carry out its task. In seeking such information, the Committee shall have regard to applicable rules of national law and professional ethics.
(3) The Committee may interview in private persons deprived of their liberty.
(4) The Committee may communicate freely with any person whom it believes can supply relevant information.
(5) If necessary, the Committee may immediately communicate observations to the competent authorities of the Party concerned.

Article 9. (1) In exceptional circumstances, the competent authorities of the Party concerned may make representations to the Committee against a visit at the time or to the particular place proposed by the Committee. Such representations may only be made on grounds of national defence, public safety, serious disorder in places where persons are deprived of their liberty, the medical condition of a person or that an urgent interrogation relating to a serious crime is in progress.
(2) Following such representations, the Committee and the Party shall immediately enter into consultations in order to clarify the situation and seek agreement on arrangements to enable the Committee to exercise its functions expeditiously. Such arrangements may include the transfer to another place of any person whom the Committee proposed to visit. Until the visit takes place, the Party shall provide information to the Committee about any person concerned.

Article 10. (1) After each visit, the Committee shall draw up a report on the facts found during the visit, taking account of any observations which may have been submitted by the Party concerned. It shall transmit to the latter its report containing any recommendations it considers necessary. The Committee may consult with the Party with a view to suggesting, if necessary, improvements in the protection of persons deprived of their liberty.
(2) If the Party fails to co-operate or refuses to improve the situation in the light of the Committee's recommendations, the Committee may decide, after the Party has had an opportunity to make known its views, by a majority of two-thirds of its members to make a public statement on the matter.

Article 11. (1) The information gathered by the Committee in relation to a visit, its report and its consultations with the Party concerned shall be confidential.
(2) The Committee shall publish its report, together with any comments of the Party concerned, whenever requested to do so by that Party.
(3) However, no personal data shall be published without the express consent of the person concerned.

Article 12. (1) Subject to the rules of confidentiality in Article 11, the Committee shall every year submit to the Committee of Ministers a general report on its activities which shall be transmitted to the Consultative Assembly and to any non-member State of the Council of Europe which is a party to the Convention, and made public.

PART II FUNDAMENTAL RIGHTS

Article 13. The members of the Committee, experts and other persons assisting the Committee are required, during and after their terms of office, to maintain the confidentiality of the facts or information of which they have become aware during the discharge of their functions

Article 14. (1) The names of persons assisting the Committee shall be specified in the notification under
Article 8, paragraph (1).
(2) Experts shall act on the instructions and under the authority of the Committee. They shall have particular knowledge and experience in the areas covered by this Convention and shall be bound by the same duties of independence, impartiality and availability as the members of the Committee.
3A Party may exceptionally declare that an expert or other person assisting the Committee may not be allowed to take part in a visit to a place within its jurisdiction.

Chapter IV

Article 15. Each Party shall inform the Committee of the name and address of the authority competent to receive notifications to its Government, and of any liaison officer it may appoint.

Article 16. The Committee, its members and experts referred to in Article 7, paragraph (2) shall enjoy the privileges and immunities set out in the annex to this Convention.

Article 17. (1) This Convention shall not prejudice the provisions of domestic law or any international agreement which provide greater protection for persons deprived of their liberty.
(2) Nothing in this Convention shall be construed as limiting or derogating from the competence of the organs of the European Convention on Human Rights or from the obligations assumed by the Parties under that Convention.
(3) The Committee shall not visit places which representatives or delegates of Protecting Powers or the International Committee of the Red Cross effectively visit on a regular basis by virtue of the Geneva Conventions of 12 August 1949 and the Additional Protocols of 8 June 1977 thereto.

Chapter V

Article 18. (1) This Convention shall be open for signature by the member States of the Council of Europe. It is subject to ratification, acceptance or approval. Instruments of ratification, acceptance or approval shall be deposited with the Secretary General of the Council of Europe.
(2) The Committee of Ministers of the Council of Europe may invite any non-member State of the Council of Europe to accede to the Convention.

Article 19. (1) This Convention shall enter into force on the first day of the month following the expiration of a period of three months after the date on which seven member States of the Council of Europe have expressed their consent to be bound by the Convention in accordance with the provisions of
Article 18.
(2) In respect of any State which subsequently expresses its consent to be bound by it, the Convention shall enter into force on the first day of the month following the expiration of a period of three months after the date of the deposit of the instrument of ratification, acceptance, approval or accession.

Article 20. (1) Any State may at the time of signature or when depositing its instrument of ratification, acceptance, approval or accession, specify the territory or territories to which this Convention shall apply.
(2) Any State may at any later date, by a declaration addressed to the Secretary General of the Council of Europe, extend the application of this Convention to any other territory specified in the declaration. In respect of such territory the Convention shall enter into force on the first day of the month following the expiration of a period of three months after the date of receipt of such declaration by the Secretary General.
(3) Any declaration made under the two preceding paragraphs may, in respect of any territory specified in such declaration, be withdrawn by a notification addressed to the Secretary General. The withdrawal shall become effective on the first day of the month following the expiration of a period of three months after the date of receipt of such notification by the Secretary General.

Article 21. No reservation may be made in respect of the provisions of this Convention.

Article 22. (1) Any Party may, at any time, denounce this Convention by means of a notification

addressed to the Secretary General of the Council of Europe.
(2) Such denunciation shall become effective on the first day of the month following the expiration of a period of twelve months after the date of receipt of the notification by the Secretary General.

Article 23. (1) The Secretary General of the Council of Europe shall notify the member States and any non-member State of the Council of Europe party to the Convention of:
(a) any signature;
(b) the deposit of any instrument of ratification, acceptance, approval or accession;
(c) any date of entry into force of this Convention in accordance with Articles 19 and 20;
(d) any other act, notification or communication relating to this Convention, except for action taken in pursuance of Articles 8 and 10.

In witness whereof, the undersigned, being duly authorised thereto, have signed this Convention.
Done at Strasbourg, the 26 November 1987, in English and in French, both texts being equally authentic, in a single copy which shall be deposited in the archives of the Council of Europe. The Secretary General of the Council of Europe shall transmit certified copies to each member State of the Council of Europe.

PART II   FUNDAMENTAL RIGHTS

European Social Charter
Opened for signature in Strasbourg on 3 May 1996, entered into force on 1 July 1999

The governments signatory hereto, being members of the Council of Europe,
Considering that the aim of the Council of Europe is the achievement of greater unity between its members for the purpose of safeguarding and realising the ideals and principles which are their common heritage and of facilitating their economic and social progress, in particular by the maintenance and further realisation of human rights and fundamental freedoms;
Considering that in the European Convention for the Protection of Human Rights and Fundamental Freedoms signed at Rome on 4 November 1950, and the Protocols thereto, the member States of the Council of Europe agreed to secure to their populations the civil and political rights and freedoms therein specified;
Considering that in the European Social Charter opened for signature in Turin on 18 October 1961 and the Protocols thereto, the member States of the Council of Europe agreed to secure to their populations the social rights specified therein in order to improve their standard of living and their social well-being;
Recalling that the Ministerial Conference on Human Rights held in Rome on 5 November 1990 stressed the need, on the one hand, to preserve the indivisible nature of all human rights, be they civil, political, economic, social or cultural and, on the other hand, to give the European Social Charter fresh impetus;
Resolved, as was decided during the Ministerial Conference held in Turin on 21 and 22 October 1991, to update and adapt the substantive contents of the Charter in order to take account in particular of the fundamental social changes which have occurred since the text was adopted;
Recognising the advantage of embodying in a Revised Charter, designed progressively to take the place of the European Social Charter, the rights guaranteed by the Charter as amended, the rights guaranteed by the Additional Protocol of 1988 and to add new rights,
Have agreed as follows:

Part I
The Parties accept as the aim of their policy, to be pursued by all appropriate means both national and international in character, the attainment of conditions in which the following rights and principles may be effectively realised:
(1) Everyone shall have the opportunity to earn his living in an occupation freely entered upon.
(2) All workers have the right to just conditions of work.
(3) All workers have the right to safe and healthy working conditions.
(4) All workers have the right to a fair remuneration sufficient for a decent standard of living for themselves and their families.
(5) All workers and employers have the right to freedom of association in national or international organisations for the protection of their economic and social interests.
(6) All workers and employers have the right to bargain collectively.
(7) Children and young persons have the right to a special protection against the physical and moral hazards to which they are exposed.
(8) Employed women, in case of maternity, have the right to a special protection.
(9) Everyone has the right to appropriate facilities for vocational guidance with a view to helping him choose an occupation suited to his personal aptitude and interests.
(10) Everyone has the right to appropriate facilities for vocational training.
(11) Everyone has the right to benefit from any measures enabling him to enjoy the highest possible standard of health attainable.
(12) All workers and their dependents have the right to social security.
(13) Anyone without adequate resources has the right to social and medical assistance.
(14) Everyone has the right to benefit from social welfare services.
(15) Disabled persons have the right to independence, social integration and participation in the life of the community.
(16) The family as a fundamental unit of society has the right to appropriate social, legal and economic protection to ensure its full development.
(17) Children and young persons have the right to appropriate social, legal and economic protection.
(18) The nationals of any one of the Parties have the right to engage in any gainful occupation in the territory of any one of the others on a footing of equality with the nationals of the latter, subject to restrictions based on cogent economic or social reasons.
(19) Migrant workers who are nationals of a Party and their families have the right to protection and

assistance in the territory of any other Party.
(20) All workers have the right to equal opportunities and equal treatment in matters of employment and occupation without discrimination on the grounds of sex.
(21) Workers have the right to be informed and to be consulted within the undertaking.
(22) Workers have the right to take part in the determination and improvement of the working conditions and working environment in the undertaking.
(23) Every elderly person has the right to social protection.
(24) All workers have the right to protection in cases of termination of employment.
(25) All workers have the right to protection of their claims in the event of the insolvency of their employer.
(26) All workers have the right to dignity at work.
27 All persons with family responsibilities and who are engaged or wish to engage in employment have a right to do so without being subject to discrimination and as far as possible without conflict between their employment and family responsibilities.
(28) Workers' representatives in undertakings have the right to protection against acts prejudicial to them and should be afforded appropriate facilities to carry out their functions.
(29) All workers have the right to be informed and consulted in collective redundancy procedures.
(30) Everyone has the right to protection against poverty and social exclusion.
(31) Everyone has the right to housing.

Part II

The Parties undertake, as provided for in Part III, to consider themselves bound by the obligations laid down in the following articles and paragraphs.

Article 1. The right to work

With a view to ensuring the effective exercise of the right to work, the Parties undertake:
(1) to accept as one of their primary aims and responsibilities the achievement and maintenance of as high and stable a level of employment as possible, with a view to the attainment of full employment;
(2) to protect effectively the right of the worker to earn his living in an occupation freely entered upon;
(3) to establish or maintain free employment services for all workers;
(4) to provide or promote appropriate vocational guidance, training and rehabilitation.

Article 2. The right to just conditions of work

With a view to ensuring the effective exercise of the right to just conditions of work, the Parties undertake:
(1) to provide for reasonable daily and weekly working hours, the working week to be progressively reduced to the extent that the increase of productivity and other relevant factors permit;
(2) to provide for public holidays with pay;
(3) to provide for a minimum of four weeks' annual holiday with pay;
(4) to eliminate risks in inherently dangerous or unhealthy occupations, and where it has not yet been possible to eliminate or reduce sufficiently these risks, to provide for either a reduction of working hours or additional paid holidays for workers engaged in such occupations;
(5) to ensure a weekly rest period which shall, as far as possible, coincide with the day recognised by tradition or custom in the country or region concerned as a day of rest;
(6) to ensure that workers are informed in written form, as soon as possible, and in any event not later than two months after the date of commencing their employment, of the essential aspects of the contract or employment relationship;
(7) to ensure that workers performing night work benefit from measures which take account of the special nature of the work.

Article 3. The right to safe and healthy working conditions

With a view to ensuring the effective exercise of the right to safe and healthy working conditions, the Parties undertake, in consultation with employers' and workers' organisations:
(1) to formulate, implement and periodically review a coherent national policy on occupational safety, occupational health and the working environment. The primary aim of this policy shall be to improve occupational safety and health and to prevent accidents and injury to health arising out of, linked with or occurring in the course of work, particularly by minimising the causes of hazards inherent in the working environment;
(2) to issue safety and health regulations;
(3) to provide for the enforcement of such regulations by measures of supervision;
(4) to promote the progressive development of occupational health services for all workers with essentially preventive and advisory functions.

PART II FUNDAMENTAL RIGHTS

Article 4. The right to a fair remuneration
With a view to ensuring the effective exercise of the right to a fair remuneration, the Parties undertake:
(1) to recognise the right of workers to a remuneration such as will give them and their families a decent standard of living;
(2) to recognise the right of workers to an increased rate of remuneration for overtime work, subject to exceptions in particular cases;
(3) to recognise the right of men and women workers to equal pay for work of equal value;
(4) to recognise the right of all workers to a reasonable period of notice for termination of employment;
(5) to permit deductions from wages only under conditions and to the extent prescribed by national laws or regulations or fixed by collective agreements or arbitration awards. The exercise of these rights shall be achieved by freely concluded collective agreements, by statutory wage-fixing machinery, or by other means appropriate to national conditions.

Article 5. The right to organise
With a view to ensuring or promoting the freedom of workers and employers to form local, national or international organisations for the protection of their economic and social interests and to join those organisations, the Parties undertake that national law shall not be such as to impair, nor shall it be so applied as to impair, this freedom. The extent to which the guarantees provided for in this article shall apply to the police shall be determined by national laws or regulations. The principle governing the application to the members of the armed forces of these guarantees and the extent to which they shall apply to persons in this category shall equally be determined by national laws or regulations.

Article 6. The right to bargain collectively
With a view to ensuring the effective exercise of the right to bargain collectively, the Parties undertake:
(1) to promote joint consultation between workers and employers;
(2) to promote, where necessary and appropriate, machinery for voluntary negotiations between employers or employers' organisations and workers' organisations, with a view to the regulation of terms and conditions of employment by means of collective agreements;
(3) to promote the establishment and use of appropriate machinery for conciliation and voluntary arbitration for the settlement of labour disputes; and recognise:
(4) the right of workers and employers to collective action in cases of conflicts of interest, including the right to strike, subject to obligations that might arise out of collective agreements previously entered into.

Article 7. The right of children and young persons to protection
With a view to ensuring the effective exercise of the right of children and young persons to protection, the Parties undertake:
(1) to provide that the minimum age of admission to employment shall be 15 years, subject to exceptions for children employed in prescribed light work without harm to their health, morals or education;
(2) to provide that the minimum age of admission to employment shall be 18 years with respect to prescribed occupations regarded as dangerous or unhealthy;
(3) to provide that persons who are still subject to compulsory education shall not be employed in such work as would deprive them of the full benefit of their education;
(4) to provide that the working hours of persons under 18 years of age shall be limited in accordance with the needs of their development, and particularly with their need for vocational training;
(5) to recognise the right of young workers and apprentices to a fair wage or other appropriate allowances;
(6) to provide that the time spent by young persons in vocational training during the normal working hours with the consent of the employer shall be treated as forming part of the working day;
(7) to provide that employed persons of under 18 years of age shall be entitled to a minimum of four weeks' annual holiday with pay;
(8) to provide that persons under 18 years of age shall not be employed in night work with the exception of certain occupations provided for by national laws or regulations;
(9) to provide that persons under 18 years of age employed in occupations prescribed by national laws or regulations shall be subject to regular medical control;
(10) to ensure special protection against physical and moral dangers to which children and young persons are exposed, and particularly against those resulting directly or indirectly from their work.

Article 8. The right of employed women to protection of maternity

With a view to ensuring the effective exercise of the right of employed women to the protection of maternity, the Parties undertake:

(1) to provide either by paid leave, by adequate social security benefits or by benefits from public funds for employed women to take leave before and after childbirth up to a total of at least fourteen weeks;

(2) to consider it as unlawful for an employer to give a woman notice of dismissal during the period from the time she notifies her employer that she is pregnant until the end of her maternity leave, or to give her notice of dismissal at such a time that the notice would expire during such a period;

(3) to provide that mothers who are nursing their infants shall be entitled to sufficient time off for this purpose;

(4) to regulate the employment in night work of pregnant women, women who have recently given birth and women nursing their infants;

(5) to prohibit the employment of pregnant women, women who have recently given birth or who are nursing their infants in underground mining and all other work which is unsuitable by reason of its dangerous, unhealthy or arduous nature and to take appropriate measures to protect the employment rights of these women.

Article 9. The right to vocational guidance

With a view to ensuring the effective exercise of the right to vocational guidance, the Parties undertake to provide or promote, as necessary, a service which will assist all persons, including the handicapped, to solve problems related to occupational choice and progress, with due regard to the individual's characteristics and their relation to occupational opportunity: this assistance should be available free of charge, both to young persons, including schoolchildren, and to adults.

Article 10. The right to vocational training

With a view to ensuring the effective exercise of the right to vocational training, the Parties undertake:

(1) to provide or promote, as necessary, the technical and vocational training of all persons, including the handicapped, in consultation with employers' and workers' organisations, and to grant facilities for access to higher technical and university education, based solely on individual aptitude;

(2) to provide or promote a system of apprenticeship and other systematic arrangements for training young boys and girls in their various employments;

(3) to provide or promote, as necessary:

(a) adequate and readily available training facilities for adult workers;

(b) special facilities for the retraining of adult workers needed as a result of technological development or new trends in employment;

(4) to provide or promote, as necessary, special measures for the retraining and reintegration of the long-term unemployed;

(5) to encourage the full utilisation of the facilities provided by appropriate measures such as:

(a) reducing or abolishing any fees or charges;

(b) granting financial assistance in appropriate cases;

(c) including in the normal working hours time spent on supplementary training taken by the worker, at the request of his employer, during employment;

(d) ensuring, through adequate supervision, in consultation with the employers' and workers' organisations, the efficiency of apprenticeship and other training arrangements for young workers, and the adequate protection of young workers generally.

Article 11. The right to protection of health

With a view to ensuring the effective exercise of the right to protection of health, the Parties undertake, either directly or in co-operation with public or private organisations, to take appropriate measures designed inter alia:

(1) to remove as far as possible the causes of ill-health;

(2) to provide advisory and educational facilities for the promotion of health and the encouragement of individual responsibility in matters of health;

(3) to prevent as far as possible epidemic, endemic and other diseases, as well as accidents.

Article 12. The right to social security

With a view to ensuring the effective exercise of the right to social security, the Parties undertake:

(1) to establish or maintain a system of social security;

PART II   FUNDAMENTAL RIGHTS

(2) to maintain the social security system at a satisfactory level at least equal to that necessary for the ratification of the European Code of Social Security;
(3) to endeavour to raise progressively the system of social security to a higher level;
(4) to take steps, by the conclusion of appropriate bilateral and multilateral agreements or by other means, and subject to the conditions laid down in such agreements, in order to ensure:
(a) equal treatment with their own nationals of the nationals of other Parties in respect of social security rights, including the retention of benefits arising out of social security legislation, whatever movements the persons protected may undertake between the territories of the Parties;
(b) the granting, maintenance and resumption of social security rights by such means as the accumulation of insurance or employment periods completed under the legislation of each of the Parties.

Article 13. The right to social and medical assistance
With a view to ensuring the effective exercise of the right to social and medical assistance, the Parties undertake:
(1) to ensure that any person who is without adequate resources and who is unable to secure such resources either by his own efforts or from other sources, in particular by benefits under a social security scheme, be granted adequate assistance, and, in case of sickness, the care necessitated by his condition;
(2) to ensure that persons receiving such assistance shall not, for that reason, suffer from a diminution of their political or social rights;
(3) to provide that everyone may receive by appropriate public or private services such advice and personal help as may be required to prevent, to remove, or to alleviate personal or family want;
(4) to apply the provisions referred to in paragraphs (1), (2) and (3) of this article on an equal footing with their nationals to nationals of other Parties lawfully within their territories, in accordance with their obligations under the European Convention on Social and Medical Assistance, signed at Paris on 11 December 1953.

Article 14. The right to benefit from social welfare services
With a view to ensuring the effective exercise of the right to benefit from social welfare services, the Parties undertake:
(1) to promote or provide services which, by using methods of social work, would contribute to the welfare and development of both individuals and groups in the community, and to their adjustment to the social environment;
(2) to encourage the participation of individuals and voluntary or other organisations in the establishment and maintenance of such services.

Article 15. The right of persons with disabilities to independence, social integration and participation in the life of the community
With a view to ensuring to persons with disabilities, irrespective of age and the nature and origin of their disabilities, the effective exercise of the right to independence, social integration and participation in the life of the community, the Parties undertake, in particular:
(1) to take the necessary measures to provide persons with disabilities with guidance, education and vocational training in the framework of general schemes wherever possible or, where this is not possible, through specialised bodies, public or private;
(2) to promote their access to employment through all measures tending to encourage employers to hire and keep in employment persons with disabilities in the ordinary working environment and to adjust the working conditions to the needs of the disabled or, where this is not possible by reason of the disability, by arranging for or creating sheltered employment according to the level of disability. In certain cases, such measures may require recourse to specialised placement and support services;
(3) to promote their full social integration and participation in the life of the community in particular through measures, including technical aids, aiming to overcome barriers to communication and mobility and enabling access to transport, housing, cultural activities and leisure.

Article 16. The right of the family to social, legal and economic protection
With a view to ensuring the necessary conditions for the full development of the family, which is a fundamental unit of society, the Parties undertake to promote the economic, legal and social protection of family life by such means as social and family benefits, fiscal arrangements, provision of family housing, benefits for the newly married and other appropriate means.

Article 17. The right of children and young persons to social, legal and economic protection
With a view to ensuring the effective exercise of the right of children and young persons to
row up in an environment which encourages the full development of their personality and of their

physical and mental capacities, the Parties undertake, either directly or in co-operation with public and private organisations, to take all appropriate and necessary measures designed:
(1) (a) to ensure that children and young persons, taking account of the rights and duties of their parents, have the care, the assistance, the education and the training they need, in particular by providing for the establishment or maintenance of institutions and services sufficient and adequate for this purpose;
(b) to protect children and young persons against negligence, violence or exploitation;
(c) to provide protection and special aid from the state for children and young persons temporarily or definitively deprived of their family's support;
(2) to provide to children and young persons a free primary and secondary education as well as to encourage regular attendance at schools.

Article 18. The right to engage in a gainful occupation in the territory of other Parties

With a view to ensuring the effective exercise of the right to engage in a gainful occupation in the territory of any other Party, the Parties undertake:
(1) to apply existing regulations in a spirit of liberality;
(2) to simplify existing formalities and to reduce or abolish chancery dues and other charges payable by foreign workers or their employers;
(3) to liberalise, individually or collectively, regulations governing the employment of foreign workers; and recognise:
(4) the right of their nationals to leave the country to engage in a gainful occupation in the territories of the other Parties.

Article 19. The right of migrant workers and their families to protection and assistance

With a view to ensuring the effective exercise of the right of migrant workers and their families to protection and assistance in the territory of any other Party, the Parties undertake:
(1) to maintain or to satisfy themselves that there are maintained adequate and free services to assist such workers, particularly in obtaining accurate information, and to take all appropriate steps, so far as national laws and regulations permit, against misleading propaganda relating to emigration and immigration;
(2) to adopt appropriate measures within their own jurisdiction to facilitate the departure, journey and reception of such workers and their families, and to provide, within their own jurisdiction, appropriate services for health, medical attention and good hygienic conditions during the journey;
(3) to promote co-operation, as appropriate, between social services, public and private, in emigration and immigration countries;
(4) to secure for such workers lawfully within their territories, insofar as such matters are regulated by law or regulations or are subject to the control of administrative authorities, treatment not less favourable than that of their own nationals in respect of the following matters:
(a) remuneration and other employment and working conditions;
(b) membership of trade unions and enjoyment of the benefits of collective bargaining;
(c) accommodation;
(5) to secure for such workers lawfully within their territories treatment not less favourable than that of their own nationals with regard to employment taxes, dues or contributions payable in respect of employed persons;
(6) to facilitate as far as possible the reunion of the family of a foreign worker permitted to establish himself in the territory;
(7) to secure for such workers lawfully within their territories treatment not less favourable than that of their own nationals in respect of legal proceedings relating to matters referred to in this article;
(8) to secure that such workers lawfully residing within their territories are not expelled unless they endanger national security or offend against public interest or morality;
(9) to permit, within legal limits, the transfer of such parts of the earnings and savings of such workers as they may desire;
(10) to extend the protection and assistance provided for in this article to self-employed migrants insofar as such measures apply;
(11) to promote and facilitate the teaching of the national language of the receiving state or, if there are several, one of these languages, to migrant workers and members of their families;
(12) to promote and facilitate, as far as practicable, the teaching of the migrant worker's mother tongue to the children of the migrant worker.

Article 20. The right to equal opportunities and equal treatment in matters of employment and occupation without discrimination on the grounds of sex

PART II   FUNDAMENTAL RIGHTS

With a view to ensuring the effective exercise of the right to equal opportunities and equal treatment in matters of employment and occupation without discrimination on the grounds of sex, the Parties undertake to recognise that right and to take appropriate measures to ensure or promote its application in the following fields:
(a) access to employment, protection against dismissal and occupational reintegration;
(b) vocational guidance, training, retraining and rehabilitation;
(c) terms of employment and working conditions, including remuneration;
(d) career development, including promotion.

Article 21. The right to information and consultation

With a view to ensuring the effective exercise of the right of workers to be informed and consulted within the undertaking, the Parties undertake to adopt or encourage measures enabling workers or their representatives, in accordance with national legislation and practice:
(a) to be informed regularly or at the appropriate time and in a comprehensible way about the economic and financial situation of the undertaking employing them, on the understanding that the disclosure of certain information which could be prejudicial to the undertaking may be refused or subject to confidentiality; and
(b) to be consulted in good time on proposed decisions which could substantially affect the interests of workers, particularly on those decisions which could have an important impact on the employment situation in the undertaking.

Article 22. The right to take part in the determination and improvement of the working conditions and working environment

With a view to ensuring the effective exercise of the right of workers to take part in the determination and improvement of the working conditions and working environment in the undertaking, the Parties undertake to adopt or encourage measures enabling workers or their representatives, in accordance with national legislation and practice, to contribute:
(a) to the determination and the improvement of the working conditions, work organisation and working environment;
(b) to the protection of health and safety within the undertaking;
(c) to the organisation of social and socio-cultural services and facilities within the undertaking;
(d) to the supervision of the observance of regulations on these matters.

Article 23. The right of elderly persons to social protection

With a view to ensuring the effective exercise of the right of elderly persons to social protection, the Parties undertake to adopt or encourage, either directly or in co-operation with public or private organisations, appropriate measures designed in particular:
- to enable elderly persons to remain full members of society for as long as possible, by means of:
(a) adequate resources enabling them to lead a decent life and play an active part in public, social and cultural life;
(b) provision of information about services and facilities available for elderly persons and their opportunities to make use of them;
- to enable elderly persons to choose their life-style freely and to lead independent lives in their familiar surroundings for as long as they wish and are able, by means of:
(a) provision of housing suited to their needs and their state of health or of adequate support for adapting their housing;
(b) the health care and the services necessitated by their state;
- to guarantee elderly persons living in institutions appropriate support, while respecting their privacy, and participation in decisions concerning living conditions in the institution.

Article 24. The right to protection in cases of termination of employment

With a view to ensuring the effective exercise of the right of workers to protection in cases of termination of employment, the Parties undertake to recognise:
(a) the right of all workers not to have their employment terminated without valid reasons for such termination connected with their capacity or conduct or based on the operational requirements of the undertaking, establishment or service;
(b) the right of workers whose employment is terminated without a valid reason to adequate compensation or other appropriate relief.
To this end the Parties undertake to ensure that a worker who considers that his employment has been terminated without a valid reason shall have the right to appeal to an impartial body.

Article 25. The right of workers to the protection of their claims in the event of the insolvency of their employer

With a view to ensuring the effective exercise of the right of workers to the protection of their claims in the event of the insolvency of their employer, the Parties undertake to provide that workers' claims arising from contracts of employment or employment relationships be guaranteed by a guarantee institution or by any other effective form of protection.

Article 26. The right to dignity at work

With a view to ensuring the effective exercise of the right of all workers to protection of their dignity at work, the Parties undertake, in consultation with employers' and workers' organisations:
(1) to promote awareness, information and prevention of sexual harassment in the workplace or in relation to work and to take all appropriate measures to protect workers from such conduct;
(2) to promote awareness, information and prevention of recurrent reprehensible or distinctly negative and offensive actions directed against individual workers in the workplace or in relation to work and to take all appropriate measures to protect workers from such conduct.

Article 27. The right of workers with family responsibilities to equal opportunities and equal treatment

With a view to ensuring the exercise of the right to equality of opportunity and treatment for men and women workers with family responsibilities and between such workers and other workers, the Parties undertake:
(1) to take appropriate measures:
(a) to enable workers with family responsibilities to enter and remain in employment, as well as to re-enter employment after an absence due to those responsibilities, including measures in the field of vocational guidance and training;
(b) to take account of their needs in terms of conditions of employment and social security;
(c) to develop or promote services, public or private, in particular child daycare services and other childcare arrangements;
(2) to provide a possibility for either parent to obtain, during a period after maternity leave, parental leave to take care of a child, the duration and conditions of which should be determined by national legislation, collective agreements or practice;
(3) to ensure that family responsibilities shall not, as such, constitute a valid reason for termination of employment.

Article 28. The right of workers' representatives to protection in the undertaking and facilities to be accorded to them

With a view to ensuring the effective exercise of the right of workers' representatives to carry out their functions, the Parties undertake to ensure that in the undertaking:
(a) they enjoy effective protection against acts prejudicial to them, including dismissal, based on their status or activities as workers' representatives within the undertaking;
(b) they are afforded such facilities as may be appropriate in order to enable them to carry out their functions promptly and efficiently, account being taken of the industrial relations system of the country and the needs, size and capabilities of the undertaking concerned.

Article 29. The right to information and consultation in collective redundancy procedures

With a view to ensuring the effective exercise of the right of workers to be informed and consulted in situations of collective redundancies, the Parties undertake to ensure that employers shall inform and consult workers' representatives, in good time prior to such collective redundancies, on ways and means of avoiding collective redundancies or limiting their occurrence and mitigating their consequences, for example by recourse to accompanying social measures aimed, in particular, at aid for the redeployment or retraining of the workers concerned.

Article 30. The right to protection against poverty and social exclusion

With a view to ensuring the effective exercise of the right to protection against poverty and social exclusion, the Parties undertake:
(a) to take measures within the framework of an overall and co-ordinated approach to promote the effective access of persons who live or risk living in a situation of social exclusion or poverty, as well as their families, to, in particular, employment, housing, training, education, culture and social and medical assistance;
(b) to review these measures with a view to their adaptation if necessary.

Article 31. The right to housing

PART II   FUNDAMENTAL RIGHTS

With a view to ensuring the effective exercise of the right to housing, the Parties undertake to take measures designed:
(1) to promote access to housing of an adequate standard;
(2) to prevent and reduce homelessness with a view to its gradual elimination;
(3) to make the price of housing accessible to those without adequate resources.

Part III

Article A. Undertakings

(1) Subject to the provisions of Article B below, each of the Parties undertakes:
(a) to consider Part I of this Charter as a declaration of the aims which it will pursue by all appropriate means, as stated in the introductory paragraph of that part;
(b) to consider itself bound by at least six of the following nine articles of Part II of this Charter: Articles 1, 5, 6, 7, 12, 13, 16, 19 and 20;
(c) to consider itself bound by an additional number of articles or numbered paragraphs of Part II of the Charter which it may select, provided that the total number of articles or numbered paragraphs by which it is bound is not less than sixteen articles or sixty-three numbered paragraphs.
(2) The articles or paragraphs selected in accordance with sub-paragraphs (b) and( )c of paragraph (1) of this article shall be notified to the Secretary General of the Council of Europe at the time when the instrument of ratification, acceptance or approval is deposited.
(3) Any Party may, at a later date, declare by notification addressed to the Secretary General that it considers itself bound by any articles or any numbered paragraphs of Part II of the Charter which it has not already accepted under the terms of paragraph (1) of this article. Such undertakings subsequently given shall be deemed to be an integral part of the ratification, acceptance or approval and shall have the same effect as from the first day of the month following the expiration of a period of one month after the date of the notification.
(4) Each Party shall maintain a system of labour inspection appropriate to national conditions.

Article B. Links with the European Social Charter and the 1988 Additional Protocol

(1) No Contracting Party to the European Social Charter or Party to the Additional Protocol of 5 May 1988 may ratify, accept or approve this Charter without considering itself bound by at least the provisions corresponding to the provisions of the European Social Charter and, where appropriate, of the Additional Protocol, to which it was bound.
(2) Acceptance of the obligations of any provision of this Charter shall, from the date of entry into force of those obligations for the Party concerned, result in the corresponding provision of the European Social Charter and, where appropriate, of its Additional Protocol of 1988 ceasing to apply to the Party concerned in the event of that Party being bound by the first of those instruments or by both instruments.

Part IV

Article C. Supervision of the implementation of the undertakings contained in this Charter

The implementation of the legal obligations contained in this Charter shall be submitted to the same supervision as the European Social Charter.

Article D. Collective complaints

(1) The provisions of the Additional Protocol to the European Social Charter providing for a system of collective complaints shall apply to the undertakings given in this Charter for the States which have ratified the said Protocol.
(2) Any State which is not bound by the Additional Protocol to the European Social Charter providing for a system of collective complaints may when depositing its instrument of ratification, acceptance or approval of this Charter or at any time thereafter, declare by notification addressed to the Secretary General of the Council of Europe, that it accepts the supervision of its obligations under this Charter following the procedure provided for in the said Protocol.

Part V

Article E. Non-discrimination

The enjoyment of the rights set forth in this Charter shall be secured without discrimination on any ground such as race, colour, sex, language, religion, political or other opinion, national extraction or social origin, health, association with a national minority, birth or other status.

Article F. Derogations in time of war or public emergency

(1) In time of war or other public emergency threatening the life of the nation any Party may take

measures derogating from its obligations under this Charter to the extent strictly required by the exigencies of the situation, provided that such measures are not inconsistent with its other obligations under international law.

(2) Any Party which has availed itself of this right of derogation shall, within a reasonable lapse of time, keep the Secretary General of the Council of Europe fully informed of the measures taken and of the reasons therefor. It shall likewise inform the Secretary General when such measures have ceased to operate and the provisions of the Charter which it has accepted are again being fully executed.

Article G. Restrictions

(1) The rights and principles set forth in Part I when effectively realised, and their effective exercise as provided for in Part II, shall not be subject to any restrictions or limitations not specified in those parts, except such as are prescribed by law and are necessary in a democratic society for the protection of the rights and freedoms of others or for the protection of public interest, national security, public health, or morals.

(2) The restrictions permitted under this Charter to the rights and obligations set forth herein shallnot be applied for any purpose other than that for which they have been prescribed.

Article H. Relations between the Charter and domestic law or international agreements

The provisions of this Charter shall not prejudice the provisions of domestic law or of any bilateral or multilateral treaties, conventions or agreements which are already in force, or may come into force, under which more favourable treatment would be accorded to the persons protected.

Article I. Implementation of the undertakings given

(1) Without prejudice to the methods of implementation foreseen in these articles the relevant provisions of Articles 1 to 31 of Part II of this Charter shall be implemented by:
(a) laws or regulations;
(b) agreements between employers or employers' organisations and workers' organisations;
(c) a combination of those two methods;
(d) other appropriate means.

(2) Compliance with the undertakings deriving from the provisions of paragraphs (1), (2), (3), (4), (5) and (7) of Article 2, paragraphs (4), (6) and (7) of Article 7, paragraphs (1), (2), (3) and (5) of Article 10 and Articles 21 and 22 of Part II of this Charter shall be regarded as effective if the provisions are applied, in accordance with paragraph (1) of this article, to the great majority of the workers concerned.

Article J. Amendments

(1) Any amendment to Parts I and II of this Charter with the purpose of extending the rights guaranteed in this Charter as well as any amendment to Parts III to VI, proposed by a Party or by the Governmental Committee, shall be communicated to the Secretary General of the Council of Europe and forwarded by the Secretary General to the Parties to this Charter.

(2) Any amendment proposed in accordance with the provisions of the preceding paragraph shall be examined by the Governmental Committee which shall submit the text adopted to the Committee of Ministers for approval after consultation with the Parliamentary Assembly. After its approval by the Committee of Ministers this text shall be forwarded to the Parties for acceptance.

(3) Any amendment to Part I and to Part II of this Charter shall enter into force, in respect of those Parties which have accepted it, on the first day of the month following the expiration of a period of one month after the date on which three Parties have informed the Secretary General that they have accepted it.
In respect of any Party which subsequently accepts it, the amendment shall enter into force on the first day of the month following the expiration of a period of one month after the date on which that Party has informed the Secretary General of its acceptance.

(4) Any amendment to Parts III to VI of this Charter shall enter into force on the first day of the month following the expiration of a period of one month after the date on which all Parties have informed the Secretary General that they have accepted it.

Part VI

Article K. Signature, ratification and entry into force

(1) This Charter shall be open for signature by the member States of the Council of Europe. It shall be subject to ratification, acceptance or approval. Instruments of ratification, acceptance or approval shall be deposited with the Secretary General of the Council of Europe.

PART II   FUNDAMENTAL RIGHTS

(2) This Charter shall enter into force on the first day of the month following the expiration of a period of one month after the date on which three member States of the Council of Europe have expressed their consent to be bound by this Charter in accordance with the preceding paragraph.
(3) In respect of any member State which subsequently expresses its consent to be bound by this Charter, it shall enter into force on the first day of the month following the expiration of a period of one month after the date of the deposit of the instrument of ratification, acceptance or approval.

Article L. Territorial application
(1) This Charter shall apply to the metropolitan territory of each Party. Each signatory may, at the time of signature or of the deposit of its instrument of ratification, acceptance or approval, specify, by declaration addressed to the Secretary General of the Council of Europe, the territory which shall be considered to be its metropolitan territory for this purpose.
(2) Any signatory may, at the time of signature or of the deposit of its instrument of ratification, acceptance or approval, or at any time thereafter, declare by notification addressed to the Secretary General of the Council of Europe, that the Charter shall extend in whole or in part to a non-metropolitan territory or territories specified in the said declaration for whose international relations it is responsible or for which it assumes international responsibility. It shall specify in the declaration the articles or paragraphs of Part II of the Charter which it accepts as binding in respect of the territories named in the declaration.
(3) The Charter shall extend its application to the territory or territories named in the aforesaid declaration as from the first day of the month following the expiration of a period of one month after the date of receipt of the notification of such declaration by the Secretary General.
(4) Any Party may declare at a later date by notification addressed to the Secretary General of the Council of Europe that, in respect of one or more of the territories to which the Charter has been applied in accordance with paragraph (2) of this article, it accepts as binding any articles or any numbered paragraphs which it has not already accepted in respect of that territory or territories. Such undertakings subsequently given shall be deemed to be an integral part of the original declaration in respect of the territory concerned, and shall have the same effect as from
the first day of the month following the expiration of a period of one month after the date of receipt of such notification by the Secretary General.

Article M. Denunciation
(1) Any Party may denounce this Charter only at the end of a period of five years from the date on which the Charter entered into force for it, or at the end of any subsequent period of two years, and in either case after giving six months' notice to the Secretary General of the Council of Europe who shall inform the other Parties accordingly.
(2) Any Party may, in accordance with the provisions set out in the preceding paragraph, denounce any article or paragraph of Part II of the Charter accepted by it provided that the number of articles or paragraphs by which this Party is bound shall never be less than sixteen in the former case and sixty-three in the latter and that this number of articles or paragraphs shall continue to include the articles selected by the Party among those to which special
reference is made in Article A, paragraph (1), sub-paragraph (b).
(3) Any Party may denounce the present Charter or any of the articles or paragraphs of Part II of the Charter under the conditions specified in paragraph (1) of this article in respect of any territory to which the said Charter is applicable, by virtue of a declaration made in accordance with paragraph (2) of Article L.

Article N. Appendix
The appendix to this Charter shall form an integral part of it.

Article O. Notifications
The Secretary General of the Council of Europe shall notify the member States of the Council and the Director General of the International Labour Office of:
(a) any signature;
(b) the deposit of any instrument of ratification, acceptance or approval;
(c) any date of entry into force of this Charter in accordance with Article K;
(d) any declaration made in application of Articles A, paragraphs (2) and 3, D, paragraphs (1) and (2), F,
paragraph (2), L, paragraphs (1), (2), (3) and (4);
(e) any amendment in accordance with Article J;
(f) any denunciation in accordance with Article M;
(g) any other act, notification or communication relating to this Charter.

In witness whereof, the undersigned, being duly authorised thereto, have signed this revised Charter.
Done at Strasbourg, this 3rd day of May 1996, in English and French, both texts being equally
authentic, in a single copy which shall be deposited in the archives of the Council of Europe.
The Secretary General of the Council of Europe shall transmit certified copies to each member State
of the Council of Europe and to the Director General of the International Labour Office.

Appendix to the Revised European Social Charter

Scope of the Revised European Social Charter in terms of persons protected
(1) Without prejudice to Article 12, paragraph (4), and Article 13, paragraph (4), the persons covered
by Articles 1 to 17 and 20 to 31 include foreigners only in so far as they are nationals of other Parties lawfully resident or working regularly within the territory of the Party concerned, subject to the
understanding that these articles are to be interpreted in the light of the provisions of Articles 18 and
19. This interpretation would not prejudice the extension of similar facilities to other persons by any
of the Parties.
(2) Each Party will grant to refugees as defined in the Convention relating to the Status of Refugees,
signed in Geneva on 28 July 1951 and in the Protocol of 31 January 1967, and lawfully staying in
its territory, treatment as favourable as possible, and in any case not less favourable than under the
obligations accepted by the Party under the said convention and under any other existing international
instruments applicable to those refugees.
(3) Each Party will grant to stateless persons as defined in the Convention on the Status of Stateless
Persons done in New York on 28 September 1954 and lawfully staying in its territory, treatment as
favourable as possible and in any case not less favourable than under the obligations accepted by the
Party under the said instrument and under any other existing international instruments applicable to
those stateless persons.

Part I, paragraph 18, and Part II, Article 18, paragraph 1
It is understood that these provisions are not concerned with the question of entry into the territories
of the Parties and do not prejudice the provisions of the European Convention on Establishment,
signed in Paris on 13 December 1955.

Part II

Article 1, paragraph 2
This provision shall not be interpreted as prohibiting or authorising any union security clause or
practice.

Article 2, paragraph 6
Parties may provide that this provision shall not apply:
(a) to workers having a contract or employment relationship with a total duration not exceeding one
month and/or with a working week not exceeding eight hours;
(b) where the contract or employment relationship is of a casual and/or specific nature, provided, in
these cases, that its non-application is justified by objective considerations.

Article 3, paragraph 4
It is understood that for the purposes of this provision the functions, organisation and conditions of
operation of these services shall be determined by national laws or regulations,
collective agreements or other means appropriate to national conditions.

Article 4, paragraph 4
This provision shall be so understood as not to prohibit immediate dismissal for any serious offence.

Article 4, paragraph 5
It is understood that a Party may give the undertaking required in this paragraph if the great majority
of workers are not permitted to suffer deductions from wages either by law or through collective
agreements or arbitration awards, the exceptions being those persons not so covered.

Article 6, paragraph 4
It is understood that each Party may, insofar as it is concerned, regulate the exercise of the right to
strike by law, provided that any further restriction that this might place on the right can be justified
under the terms of Article G.

Article 7, paragraph 2
This provision does not prevent Parties from providing in their legislation that young persons not

PART II FUNDAMENTAL RIGHTS

having reached the minimum age laid down may perform work in so far as it is absolutely necessary for their vocational training where such work is carried out in accordance with conditions prescribed by the competent authority and measures are taken to protect the health and safety of these young persons.

Article 7, paragraph 8

It is understood that a Party may give the undertaking required in this paragraph if it fulfils the spirit of the undertaking by providing by law that the great majority of persons under eighteen years of age shall not be employed in night work.

Article 8, paragraph 2

This provision shall not be interpreted as laying down an absolute prohibition. Exceptions could be made, for instance, in the following cases:
(a) if an employed woman has been guilty of misconduct which justifies breaking off the employment relationship;
(b) if the undertaking concerned ceases to operate;
(c) if the period prescribed in the employment contract has expired.

Article 12, paragraph 4

The words "and subject to the conditions laid down in such agreements" in the introduction to this paragraph are taken to imply inter alia that with regard to benefits which are available independently of any insurance contribution, a Party may require the completion of a prescribed period of residence before granting such benefits to nationals of other Parties.

Article 13, paragraph 4

Governments not Parties to the European Convention on Social and Medical Assistance may ratify the Charter in respect of this paragraph provided that they grant to nationals of other Parties a treatment which is in conformity with the provisions of the said convention.

Article 16

It is understood that the protection afforded in this provision covers single-parent families.

Article 17

It is understood that this provision covers all persons below the age of 18 years, unless under the law applicable to the child majority is attained earlier, without prejudice to the other specific provisions provided by the Charter, particularly Article 7.
This does not imply an obligation to provide compulsory education up to the above-mentioned age.

Article 19, paragraph 6

For the purpose of applying this provision, the term "family of a foreign worker" is understood to mean at least the worker's spouse and unmarried children, as long as the latter are considered to be minors by the receiving State and are dependent on the migrant worker.

Article 20

(1) It is understood that social security matters, as well as other provisions relating to unemployment benefit, old age benefit and survivor's benefit, may be excluded from the scope of this article.
(2) Provisions concerning the protection of women, particularly as regards pregnancy, confinement and the post-natal period, shall not be deemed to be discrimination as referred to in this article.
(3) This article shall not prevent the adoption of specific measures aimed at removing de facto inequalities.
(4) Occupational activities which, by reason of their nature or the context in which they are carried out, can be entrusted only to persons of a particular sex may be excluded from the scope of this article or some of its provisions. This provision is not to be interpreted as requiring the Parties to embody in laws or regulations a list of occupations which, by reason of their nature or the context in which they are carried out, may be reserved to persons of a particular sex.

Articles 21 and 22

(1) For the purpose of the application of these articles, the term "workers' representatives" means persons who are recognised as such under national legislation or practice.
(2) The terms "national legislation and practice" embrace as the case may be, in addition to laws and regulations, collective agreements, other agreements between employers and workers' representatives, customs as well as relevant case law.
(3) For the purpose of the application of these articles, the term "undertaking" is understood as refer-

ring to a set of tangible and intangible components, with or without legal personality, formed to produce goods or provide services for financial gain and with power to determine its own market policy.
(4) It is understood that religious communities and their institutions may be excluded from the application of these articles, even if these institutions are "undertakings" within the meaning of paragraph (3). Establishments pursuing activities which are inspired by certain ideals or guided by certain moral concepts, ideals and concepts which are protected by national legislation, may be excluded from the application of these articles to such an extent as is necessary to protect the orientation of the undertaking.
(5) It is understood that where in a state the rights set out in these articles are exercised in the various establishments of the undertaking, the Party concerned is to be considered as fulfilling the obligations deriving from these provisions.
(6) The Parties may exclude from the field of application of these articles, those undertakings employing less than a certain number of workers, to be determined by national legislation or practice.

Article 22
(1) This provision affects neither the powers and obligations of states as regards the adoption of health and safety regulations for workplaces, nor the powers and responsibilities of the bodies in charge of monitoring their application.
(2) The terms "social and socio-cultural services and facilities" are understood as referring to the social and/or cultural facilities for workers provided by some undertakings such as welfare assistance, sports fields, rooms for nursing mothers, libraries, children's holiday camps, etc.

Article 23, paragraph 1
For the purpose of the application of this paragraph, the term "for as long as possible" refers to the elderly person's physical, psychological and intellectual capacities.

Article 24
(1) It is understood that for the purposes of this article the terms "termination of employment" and "terminated" mean termination of employment at the initiative of the employer.
(2) It is understood that this article covers all workers but that a Party may exclude from some or all of its protection the following categories of employed persons:
(a) workers engaged under a contract of employment for a specified period of time or a specified task;
(b) workers undergoing a period of probation or a qualifying period of employment, provided that this is determined in advance and is of a reasonable duration;
(c) workers engaged on a casual basis for a short period.
(3) For the purpose of this article the following, in particular, shall not constitute valid reasons for termination of employment:
(a) trade union membership or participation in union activities outside working hours, or, with the consent of the employer, within working hours;
(b) seeking office as, acting or having acted in the capacity of a workers' representative;
(c) the filing of a complaint or the participation in proceedings against an employer involving alleged violation of laws or regulations or recourse to competent administrative authorities;
(d) race, colour, sex, marital status, family responsibilities, pregnancy, religion, political opinion, national extraction or social origin;
(e) maternity or parental leave;
(f) temporary absence from work due to illness or injury.
(4) It is understood that compensation or other appropriate relief in case of termination of employment without valid reasons shall be determined by national laws or regulations, collective agreements or other means appropriate to national conditions.

Article 25.
(1) It is understood that the competent national authority may, by way of exemption and after consulting organisations of employers and workers, exclude certain categories of workers from the protection provided in this provision by reason of the special nature of their employment relationship.
(2) It is understood that the definition of the term "insolvency" must be determined by national law and practice.
(3) The workers' claims covered by this provision shall include at least:
(a) the workers' claims for wages relating to a prescribed period, which shall not be less than three months under a privilege system and eight weeks under a guarantee system, prior to the insolvency or to the termination of employment;
(b) the workers' claims for holiday pay due as a result of work performed during the year in which the insolvency or the termination of employment occurred;

PART II   FUNDAMENTAL RIGHTS

(c) the workers' claims for amounts due in respect of other types of paid absence relating to a prescribed period, which shall not be less than three months under a privilege system and eight weeks under a guarantee system, prior to the insolvency or the termination of the employment.
(4) National laws or regulations may limit the protection of workers' claims to a prescribed amount, which shall be of a socially acceptable level.

Article 26
It is understood that this article does not require that legislation be enacted by the Parties.
It is understood that paragraph 2 does not cover sexual harassment.

Article 27
It is understood that this article applies to men and women workers with family responsibilities in relation to their dependent children as well as in relation to other members of their immediate family who clearly need their care or support where such responsibilities restrict their possibilities of preparing for, entering, participating in or advancing in economic activity. The terms "dependent children" and "other members of their immediate family who clearly need their care and support" mean persons defined as such by the national legislation of the Party concerned.

Articles 28 and 29
For the purpose of the application of this article, the term "workers' representatives" means persons who are recognised as such under national legislation or practice.

Part III
It is understood that the Charter contains legal obligations of an international character, the application of which is submitted solely to the supervision provided for in Part IV thereof.

Article A, paragraph 1
It is understood that the numbered paragraphs may include articles consisting of only one paragraph.

Article B, paragraph 2
For the purpose of paragraph (2) of Article B, the provisions of the revised Charter correspond to the provisions of the Charter with the same article or paragraph number with the exception of:
(a) Article 3, paragraph (2), of the revised Charter which corresponds to Article 3, paragraphs (1) and (3), of the Charter;
(b) Article 3, paragraph (3), of the revised Charter which corresponds to Article 3, paragraphs (2) and (3), of the Charter;
(c) Article 10, paragraph (5), of the revised Charter which corresponds to Article 10, paragraph (4), of the Charter;
(d) Article 17, paragraph (1), of the revised Charter which corresponds to Article 17 of the Charter.

Part V

Article E
A differential treatment based on an objective and reasonable justification shall not be deemed discriminatory.

Article F
The terms "in time of war or other public emergency" shall be so understood as to cover also the threat of war.

Article I
It is understood that workers excluded in accordance with the appendix to Articles 21 and 22 are not taken into account in establishing the number of workers concerned.

Article J
The term "amendment" shall be extended so as to cover also the addition of new articles to the Charter.

OPTIONAL PROTOCOL TO THE EUROPEAN SOCIAL CHARTER

Additional Protocol to the European Social Charter Providing for a System of Collective Complaints
Strasbourg, 9 September 1995

The member States of the Council of Europe, signatories to this Protocol to the European Social Charter, opened for signature in Turin on 18 October 1961 (hereinafter referred to as "the Charter"),
Resolved to take new measures to improve the effective enforcement of the social rights guaranteed by the Charter;
Considering that this aim could be achieved in particular by the establishment of a collective complaints procedure, which, inter alia, would strengthen the participation of management and labour and of non-governmental organisations,
Have agreed as follows:

Article 1. The Contracting Parties to this Protocol recognise the right of the following organisations to submit complaints alleging unsatisfactory application of the Charter:
(a) international organisations of employers and trade unions referred to in paragraph (2) of Article 27 of the Charter;
(b) other international non-governmental organisations which have consultative status with the Council of Europe and have been put on a list established for this purpose by the Governmental Committee;
(c) representative national organisations of employers and trade unions within the jurisdiction of the Contracting Party against which they have lodged a complaint.

Article 2. (1) Any Contracting State may also, when it expresses its consent to be bound by this Protocol, in accordance with the provisions of Article 13, or at any moment thereafter, declare that it recognises the right of any other representative national non-governmental organisation within its jurisdiction which has particular competence in the matters governed by the Charter, to lodge complaints against it.
(2) Such declarations may be made for a specific period.
(3) The declarations shall be deposited with the Secretary General of the Council of Europe who shall transmit copies thereof to the Contracting Parties and publish them.

Article 3. The international non-governmental organisations and the national non-governmental organisations referred to in Article 1.b and Article 2 respectively may submit complaints in accordance with the procedure prescribed by the aforesaid provisions only in respect of those matters regarding which they have been recognised as having particular competence.

Article 4. The complaint shall be lodged in writing, relate to a provision of the Charter accepted by the Contracting Party concerned and indicate in what respect the latter has not ensured the satisfactory application of this provision.

Article 5. Any complaint shall be addressed to the Secretary General who shall acknowledge receipt of it, notify it to the Contracting Party concerned and immediately transmit it to the Committee of Independent Experts.

Article 6. The Committee of Independent Experts may request the Contracting Party concerned and the organisation which lodged the complaint to submit written information and observations on the admissibility of the complaint within such time-limit as it shall prescribe.

Article 7. (1) If it decides that a complaint is admissible, the Committee of Independent Experts shall notify the Contracting Parties to the Charter through the Secretary General. It shall request the Contracting Party concerned and the organisation which lodged the complaint to submit, within such time-limit as it shall prescribe, all relevant written explanations or information, and the other Contracting Parties to this Protocol, the comments they wish to submit, within the same time-limit.
(2) If the complaint has been lodged by a national organisation of employers or a national trade union or by another national or international non-governmental organisation, the Committee of Independent Experts shall notify the international organisations of employers or trade unions referred to in paragraph (2) of Article 27 of the Charter, through the Secretary General, and invite them to submit observations within such time-limit as it shall prescribe.
(3) On the basis of the explanations, information or observations submitted under paragraphs (1) and (2) above, the Contracting Party concerned and the organisation which lodged the complaint may submit any additional written information or observations within such time- limit as the Committee of Independent Experts shall prescribe.

PART II   FUNDAMENTAL RIGHTS

(4) In the course of the examination of the complaint, the Committee of Independent Experts may organise a hearing with the representatives of the parties.

Article 8. (1) The Committee of Independent Experts shall draw up a report in which it shall describe the steps taken by it to examine the complaint and present its conclusions as to whether or not the Contracting Party concerned has ensured the satisfactory application of the provision of the Charter referred to in the complaint.

ETS 158 – European Social Charter (Additional Protocol), 9.XI.1995

(2) The report shall be transmitted to the Committee of Ministers. It shall also be transmitted to the organisation that lodged the complaint and to the Contracting Parties to the Charter, which shall not be at liberty to publish it.

It shall be transmitted to the Parliamentary Assembly and made public at the same time as the resolution referred to in Article 9 or no later than four months after it has been transmitted to the Committee of Ministers.

Article 9. (1) On the basis of the report of the Committee of Independent Experts, the Committee of Ministers shall adopt a resolution by a majority of those voting. If the Committee of Independent Experts finds that the Charter has not been applied in a satisfactory manner, the Committee of Ministers shall adopt, by a majority of two-thirds of those voting, a recommendation addressed to the Contracting Party concerned. In both cases, entitlement to voting shall be limited to the Contracting Parties to the Charter.

(2) At the request of the Contracting Party concerned, the Committee of Ministers may decide, where the report of the Committee of Independent Experts raises new issues, by a two-thirds majority of the Contracting Parties to the Charter, to consult the Governmental Committee.

Article 10. The Contracting Party concerned shall provide information on the measures it has taken to give effect to the Committee of Ministers' recommendation, in the next report which it submits to the Secretary General under Article 21 of the Charter.

Article 11. Articles 1 to 10 of this Protocol shall apply also to the articles of Part II of the first Additional Protocol to the Charter in respect of the States Parties to that Protocol, to the extent that these articles have been accepted.

Article 12. The States Parties to this Protocol consider that the first paragraph of the appendix to the Charter, relating to Part III, reads as follows:

"It is understood that the Charter contains legal obligations of an international character, the application of which is submitted solely to the supervision provided for in Part IV thereof and in the provisions of this Protocol."

Article 13. (1) This Protocol shall be open for signature by member States of the Council of Europe signatories to the Charter, which may express their consent to be bound by:

(a) signature without reservation as to ratification, acceptance or approval; or

(b) signature subject to ratification, acceptance or approval, followed by ratification, acceptance or approval.

(2) A member State of the Council of Europe may not express its consent to be bound by this Protocol without previously or simultaneously ratifying the Charter.

(3) Instruments of ratification, acceptance or approval shall be deposited with the Secretary General of the Council of Europe.

Article 14. (1) This Protocol shall enter into force on the first day of the month following the expiration of a period of one month after the date on which five member States of the Council of Europe have expressed their consent to be bound by the Protocol in accordance with the provisions of Article 13.

(2) In respect of any member State which subsequently expresses its consent to be bound by it, the Protocol shall enter into force on the first day of the month following the expiration of a period of one month after the date of the deposit of the instrument of ratification, acceptance or approval.

Article 15. (1) Any Party may at any time denounce this Protocol by means of a notification addressed to the Secretary General of the Council of Europe.

(2) Such denunciation shall become effective on the first day of the month following the expiration of a period of twelve months after the date of receipt of such notification by the Secretary General.

Article 16. The Secretary General of the Council of Europe shall notify all the member States of the Council of:

OPTIONAL PROTOCOL TO THE EUROPEAN SOCIAL CHARTER

(a) any signature;
(b) the deposit of any instrument of ratification, acceptance or approval;
(c) the date of entry into force of this Protocol in accordance with Article 14;
(d) any other act, notification or declaration relating to this Protocol.

In witness whereof the undersigned, being duly authorised thereto, have signed this Protocol.
Done at Strasbourg, this 9th day of November 1995, in English and French, both texts being equally authentic, in a single copy which shall be deposited in the archives of the Council of Europe. The Secretary General of the Council of Europe shall transmit certified copies to each member State of the Council of Europe.

PART II   FUNDAMENTAL RIGHTS

Charter of Fundamental Rights of the European Union
(2000/C 364/01)

The peoples of Europe, in creating an ever closer union among them, are resolved to share a peaceful future based on common values.
Conscious of its spiritual and moral heritage, the Union is founded on the indivisible, universal values of human dignity, freedom, equality and solidarity; it is based on the principles of democracy and the rule of law. It places the individual at the heart of its activities, by establishing the citizenship of the Union and by creating an area of freedom, security and justice.
The Union contributes to the preservation and to the development of these common values while respecting the diversity of the cultures and traditions of the peoples of Europe as well as the national identities of the Member States and the organisation of their public authorities at national, regional and local levels; it seeks to promote balanced and sustainable development and ensures free movement of persons, services, goods and capital, and the freedom of establishment.
To this end, it is necessary to strengthen the protection of fundamental rights in the light of changes in society, social progress and scientific and technological developments by making those rights more visible in a Charter.
This Charter reaffirms, with due regard for the powers and tasks of the Union and for the principle of subsidiarity, the rights as they result, in particular, from the constitutional traditions and international obligations common to the Member States, the European Convention for the Protection of Human Rights and Fundamental Freedoms, the Social Charters adopted by the Union and by the Council of Europe and the case-law of the Court of Justice of the European Union and of the European Court of Human Rights. In this context the Charter will be interpreted by the courts of the Union and the Member States with due regard to the explanations prepared under the authority of the Praesidium of the Convention which drafted the Charter and updated under the responsibility of the Praesidium of the European Convention.
Enjoyment of these rights entails responsibilities and duties with regard to other persons, to the human community and to future generations.
The Union therefore recognises the rights, freedoms and principles set out hereafter.

Title I. Dignity

Article 1. Human dignity is inviolable. It must be respected and protected.

Article 2. (1) Everyone has the right to life.
(2) No one shall be condemned to the death penalty, or executed.

Article 3. (1) Everyone has the right to respect for his or her physical and mental integrity.
(2) In the fields of medicine and biology, the following must be respected in particular:
(a) the free and informed consent of the person concerned, according to the procedures laid down by law;
(b) the prohibition of eugenic practices, in particular those aiming at the selection of persons;
(c) the prohibition on making the human body and its parts as such a source of financial gain;
(d) the prohibition of the reproductive cloning of human beings.

Article 4. No one shall be subjected to torture or to inhuman or degrading treatment or punishment.

Article 5. (1) No one shall be held in slavery or servitude.
(2) No one shall be required to perform forced or compulsory labour.
(3) Trafficking in human beings is prohibited.

Title II. Freedoms

Article 6. Everyone has the right to liberty and security of person.

Article 7. Everyone has the right to respect for his or her private and family life, home and communications.

Article 8. (1) Everyone has the right to the protection of personal data concerning him or her.
(2) Such data must be processed fairly for specified purposes and on the basis of the consent of the person concerned or some other legitimate basis laid down by law. Everyone has the right of access to data which has been collected concerning him or her, and the right to have it rectified.
(3) Compliance with these rules shall be subject to control by an independent authority.

CHARTER OF FUNDAMENTAL RIGHTS OF THE EU

Article 9. The right to marry and the right to found a family shall be guaranteed in accordance with the national laws governing the exercise of these rights.

Article 10. (1) Everyone has the right to freedom of thought, conscience and religion. This right includes freedom to change religion or belief and freedom, either alone or in community with others and in public or in private, to manifest religion or belief, in worship, teaching, practice and observance.
(2) The right to conscientious objection is recognised, in accordance with the national laws governing the exercise of this right.

Article 11. (1) Everyone has the right to freedom of expression. This right shall include freedom to hold opinions and to receive and impart information and ideas without interference by public authority and regardless of frontiers.
(2) The freedom and pluralism of the media shall be respected.

Article 12. (1) Everyone has the right to freedom of peaceful assembly and to freedom of association at all levels, in particular in political, trade union and civic matters, which implies the right of everyone to form and to join trade unions for the protection of his or her interests.
(2) Political parties at Union level contribute to expressing the political will of the citizens of the Union.

Article 13. The arts and scientific research shall be free of constraint. Academic freedom shall be respected.

Article 14. (1) Everyone has the right to education and to have access to vocational and continuing training.
(2) This right includes the possibility to receive free compulsory education.
(3) The freedom to found educational establishments with due respect for democratic principles and the right of parents to ensure the education and teaching of their children in conformity with their religious, philosophical and pedagogical convictions shall be respected, in accordance with the national laws governing the exercise of such freedom and right.

Article 15. (1) Everyone has the right to engage in work and to pursue a freely chosen or accepted occupation.
(2) Every citizen of the Union has the freedom to seek employment, to work, to exercise the right of establishment and to provide services in any Member State.
(3) Nationals of third countries who are authorised to work in the territories of the Member States are entitled to working conditions equivalent to those of citizens of the Union.

Article 16. The freedom to conduct a business in accordance with Union law and national laws and practices is recognised.

Article 17. (1) Everyone has the right to own, use, dispose of and bequeath his or her lawfully acquired possessions. No one may be deprived of his or her possessions, except in the public interest and in the cases and under the conditions provided for by law, subject to fair compensation being paid in good time for their loss. The use of property may be regulated by law in so far as is necessary for the general interest.
(2) Intellectual property shall be protected.

Article 18. The right to asylum shall be guaranteed with due respect for the rules of the Geneva Convention of 28 July 1951 and the Protocol of 31 January 1967 relating to the status of refugees and in accordance with the Treaty on European Union and the Treaty on the Functioning of the European Union (hereinafter referred to as 'the Treaties').

Article 19. (1) Collective expulsions are prohibited.
(2) No one may be removed, expelled or extradited to a State where there is a serious risk that he or she would be subjected to the death penalty, torture or other inhuman or degrading treatment or punishment.

Title III. Equality

Article 20. Everyone is equal before the law.

Article 21. (1) Any discrimination based on any ground such as sex, race, colour, ethnic or social origin, genetic features, language, religion or belief, political or any other opinion, membership of a

PART II   FUNDAMENTAL RIGHTS

national minority, property, birth, disability, age or sexual orientation shall be prohibited.
(2) Within the scope of application of the Treaties and without prejudice to any of their specific provisions, any discrimination on grounds of nationality shall be prohibited.

Article 22. The Union shall respect cultural, religious and linguistic diversity.

Article 23. Equality between women and men must be ensured in all areas, including employment, work and pay.
The principle of equality shall not prevent the maintenance or adoption of measures providing for specific advantages in favour of the under-represented sex.

Article 24. (1) Children shall have the right to such protection and care as is necessary for their well-being. They may express their views freely. Such views shall be taken into consideration on matters which concern them in accordance with their age and maturity.
(2) In all actions relating to children, whether taken by public authorities or private institutions, the child's best interests must be a primary consideration.
(3) Every child shall have the right to maintain on a regular basis a personal relationship and direct contact with both his or her parents, unless that is contrary to his or her interests.

Article 25. The Union recognises and respects the rights of the elderly to lead a life of dignity and independence and to participate in social and cultural life.

Article 26. The Union recognises and respects the right of persons with disabilities to benefit from measures designed to ensure their independence, social and occupational integration and participation in the life of the community.

Title IV. Solidarity

Article 27. Workers or their representatives must, at the appropriate levels, be guaranteed information and consultation in good time in the cases and under the conditions provided for by Union law and national laws and practices.

Article 28. Workers and employers, or their respective organisations, have, in accordance with Union law and national laws and practices, the right to negotiate and conclude collective agreements at the appropriate levels and, in cases of conflicts of interest, to take collective action to defend their interests, including strike action.

Article 29. Everyone has the right of access to a free placement service.

Article 30. Every worker has the right to protection against unjustified dismissal, in accordance with Union law and national laws and practices.

Article 31. (1) Every worker has the right to working conditions which respect his or her health, safety and dignity.
(2) Every worker has the right to limitation of maximum working hours, to daily and weekly rest periods and to an annual period of paid leave.

Article 32. The employment of children is prohibited. The minimum age of admission to employment may not be lower than the minimum school-leaving age, without prejudice to such rules as may be more favourable to young people and except for limited derogations.
Young people admitted to work must have working conditions appropriate to their age and be protected against economic exploitation and any work likely to harm their safety, health or physical, mental, moral or social development or to interfere with their education.

Article 33. (1) The family shall enjoy legal, economic and social protection.
(2) To reconcile family and professional life, everyone shall have the right to protection from dismissal for a reason connected with maternity and the right to paid maternity leave and to parental leave following the birth or adoption of a child.

Article 34. (1) The Union recognises and respects the entitlement to social security benefits and social services providing protection in cases such as maternity, illness, industrial accidents, dependency or old age, and in the case of loss of employment, in accordance with the rules laid down by Union law and national laws and practices.
(2) Everyone residing and moving legally within the European Union is entitled to social security benefits and social advantages in accordance with Union law and national laws and practices.
(3) In order to combat social exclusion and poverty, the Union recognises and respects the right to

social and housing assistance so as to ensure a decent existence for all those who lack sufficient resources, in accordance with the rules laid down by Union law and national laws and practices.

Article 35. Everyone has the right of access to preventive health care and the right to benefit from medical treatment under the conditions established by national laws and practices. A high level of human health protection shall be ensured in the definition and implementation of all the Union's policies and activities.

Article 36. The Union recognises and respects access to services of general economic interest as provided for in national laws and practices, in accordance with the Treaties, in order to promote the social and territorial cohesion of the Union.

Article 37. A high level of environmental protection and the improvement of the quality of the environment must be integrated into the policies of the Union and ensured in accordance with the principle of sustainable development.

Article 38. Union policies shall ensure a high level of consumer protection.

Title V. Citizens' Rights

Article 39. (1) Every citizen of the Union has the right to vote and to stand as a candidate at elections to the European Parliament in the Member State in which he or she resides, under the same conditions as nationals of that State.
(2) Members of the European Parliament shall be elected by direct universal suffrage in a free and secret ballot.

Article 40. Every citizen of the Union has the right to vote and to stand as a candidate at municipal elections in the Member State in which he or she resides under the same conditions as nationals of that State.

Article 41. (1) Every person has the right to have his or her affairs handled impartially, fairly and within a reasonable time by the institutions, bodies, offices and agencies of the Union.
(2) This right includes:
(a) the right of every person to be heard, before any individual measure which would affect him or her adversely is taken;
(b) the right of every person to have access to his or her file, while respecting the legitimate interests of confidentiality and of professional and business secrecy;
(c) the obligation of the administration to give reasons for its decisions.
(3) Every person has the right to have the Union make good any damage caused by its institutions or by its servants in the performance of their duties, in accordance with the general principles common to the laws of the Member States.
(4) Every person may write to the institutions of the Union in one of the languages of the Treaties and must have an answer in the same language.

Article 42. Any citizen of the Union, and any natural or legal person residing or having its registered office in a Member State, has a right of access to documents of the institutions, bodies, offices and agencies of the Union, whatever their medium.

Article 43. Any citizen of the Union and any natural or legal person residing or having its registered office in a Member State has the right to refer to the European Ombudsman cases of maladministration in the activities of the institutions, bodies, offices or agencies of the Union, with the exception of the Court of Justice of the European Union acting in its judicial role.

Article 44. Any citizen of the Union and any natural or legal person residing or having its registered office in a Member State has the right to petition the European Parliament.

Article 45. (1) Every citizen of the Union has the right to move and reside freely within the territory of the Member States.
(2) Freedom of movement and residence may be granted, in accordance with the Treaties, to nationals of third countries legally resident in the territory of a Member State.

Article 46. Every citizen of the Union shall, in the territory of a third country in which the Member State of which he or she is a national is not represented, be entitled to protection by the diplomatic or consular authorities of any Member State, on the same conditions as the nationals of that Member State.

PART II   FUNDAMENTAL RIGHTS

Title VI. Justice

Article 47. Everyone whose rights and freedoms guaranteed by the law of the Union are violated has the right to an effective remedy before a tribunal in compliance with the conditions laid down in this Article.
Everyone is entitled to a fair and public hearing within a reasonable time by an independent and impartial tribunal previously established by law. Everyone shall have the possibility of being advised, defended and represented.
Legal aid shall be made available to those who lack sufficient resources in so far as such aid is necessary to ensure effective access to justice.

Article 48. (1) Everyone who has been charged shall be presumed innocent until proved guilty according to law.
(2) Respect for the rights of the defence of anyone who has been charged shall be guaranteed.

Article 49. (1) No one shall be held guilty of any criminal offence on account of any act or omission which did not constitute a criminal offence under national law or international law at the time when it was committed. Nor shall a heavier penalty be imposed than the one that was applicable at the time the criminal offence was committed. If, subsequent to the commission of a criminal offence, the law provides for a lighter penalty, that penalty shall be applicable.
(2) This Article shall not prejudice the trial and punishment of any person for any act or omission which, at the time when it was committed, was criminal according to the general principles recognised by the community of nations.
(3) The severity of penalties must not be disproportionate to the criminal offence.

Article 50. No one shall be liable to be tried or punished again in criminal proceedings for an offence for which he or she has already been finally acquitted or convicted within the Union in accordance with the law.

Title VII. General Provisions Governing the Interpretation and Application of the Charter

Article 51. (1) The provisions of this Charter are addressed to the institutions, bodies, offices and agencies of the Union with due regard for the principle of subsidiarity and to the Member States only when they are implementing Union law. They shall therefore respect the rights, observe the principles and promote the application thereof in accordance with their respective powers and respecting the limits of the powers of the Union as conferred on it in the Treaties.
(2) The Charter does not extend the field of application of Union law beyond the powers of the Union or establish any new power or task for the Union, or modify powers and tasks as defined in the Treaties.

Article 52. (1) Any limitation on the exercise of the rights and freedoms recognised by this Charter must be provided for by law and respect the essence of those rights and freedoms. Subject to the principle of proportionality, limitations may be made only if they are necessary and genuinely meet objectives of general interest recognised by the Union or the need to protect the rights and freedoms of others.
(2) Rights recognised by this Charter for which provision is made in the Treaties shall be exercised under the conditions and within the limits defined by those Treaties.
(3) In so far as this Charter contains rights which correspond to rights guaranteed by the Convention for the Protection of Human Rights and Fundamental Freedoms, the meaning and scope of those rights shall be the same as those laid down by the said Convention. This provision shall not prevent Union law providing more extensive protection.
(4) In so far as this Charter recognises fundamental rights as they result from the constitutional traditions common to the Member States, those rights shall be interpreted in harmony with those traditions.
(5) The provisions of this Charter which contain principles may be implemented by legislative and executive acts taken by institutions, bodies, offices and agencies of the Union, and by acts of Member States when they are implementing Union law, in the exercise of their respective powers. They shall be judicially cognisable only in the interpretation of such acts and in the ruling on their legality.
(6) Full account shall be taken of national laws and practices as specified in this Charter.
(7) The explanations drawn up as a way of providing guidance in the interpretation of this Charter shall be given due regard by the courts of the Union and of the Member States.

Article 53. Nothing in this Charter shall be interpreted as restricting or adversely affecting human rights and fundamental freedoms as recognised, in their respective fields of application, by Union law and international law and by international agreements to which the Union or all the Member States are party, including the European Convention for the Protection of Human Rights and Fundamental Freedoms, and by the Member States' constitutions.

Article 54. Nothing in this Charter shall be interpreted as implying any right to engage in any activity or to perform any act aimed at the destruction of any of the rights and freedoms recognised in this Charter or at their limitation to a greater extent than is provided for herein.

VOL I PART III

European Union

PART III EUROPEAN UNION

Treaty on European Union
Consolidated version as published in the Official Journal of the European Union on 26 October 2012, including tables of equivalences.

HIS MAJESTY THE KING OF THE BELGIANS, HER MAJESTY THE QUEEN OF DENMARK, THE PRESIDENT OF THE FEDERAL REPUBLIC OF GERMANY, THE PRESIDENT OF IRELAND, THE PRESIDENT OF THE HELLENIC REPUBLIC, HIS MAJESTY THE KING OF SPAIN, THE PRESIDENT OF THE FRENCH REPUBLIC, THE PRESIDENT OF THE ITALIAN REPUBLIC, HIS ROYAL HIGHNESS THE GRAND DUKE OF LUXEMBOURG, HER MAJESTY THE QUEEN OF THE NETHERLANDS, THE PRESIDENT OF THE PORTUGUESE REPUBLIC, HER MAJESTY THE QUEEN OF THE UNITED KINGDOM OF GREAT BRITAIN AND NORTHERN IRELAND[1],

RESOLVED to mark a new stage in the process of European integration undertaken with the establishment of the European Communities,
DRAWING INSPIRATION from the cultural, religious and humanist inheritance of Europe, from which have developed the universal values of the inviolable and inalienable rights of the human person, freedom, democracy, equality and the rule of law,
RECALLING the historic importance of the ending of the division of the European continent and the need to create firm bases for the construction of the future Europe,
CONFIRMING their attachment to the principles of liberty, democracy and respect for human rights and fundamental freedoms and of the rule of law,
CONFIRMING their attachment to fundamental social rights as defined in the European Social Charter signed at Turin on 18 October 1961 and in the 1989 Community Charter of the Fundamental Social Rights of Workers,
DESIRING to deepen the solidarity between their peoples while respecting their history, their culture and their traditions,
DESIRING to enhance further the democratic and efficient functioning of the institutions so as to enable them better to carry out, within a single institutional framework, the tasks entrusted to them,
RESOLVED to achieve the strengthening and the convergence of their economies and to establish an economic and monetary union including, in accordance with the provisions of this Treaty and of the Treaty on the Functioning of the European Union, a single and stable currency,
DETERMINED to promote economic and social progress for their peoples, taking into account the principle of sustainable development and within the context of the accomplishment of the internal market and of reinforced cohesion and environmental protection, and to implement policies ensuring that advances in economic integration are accompanied by parallel progress in other fields,
RESOLVED to establish a citizenship common to nationals of their countries,
RESOLVED to implement a common foreign and security policy including the progressive framing of a common defence policy, which might lead to a common defence in accordance with the provisions of Article 42, thereby reinforcing the European identity and its independence in order to promote peace, security and progress in Europe and in the world,
RESOLVED to facilitate the free movement of persons, while ensuring the safety and security of their peoples, by establishing an area of freedom, security and justice, in accordance with the provisions of this Treaty and of the Treaty on the Functioning of the European Union,
RESOLVED to continue the process of creating an ever closer union among the peoples of Europe, in which decisions are taken as closely as possible to the citizen in accordance with the principle of subsidiarity,
IN VIEW of further steps to be taken in order to advance European integration,
HAVE DECIDED to establish a European Union and to this end have designated as their Plenipotentiaries:
[List of plenipotentiaries not reproduced]
WHO, having exchanged their full powers, found in good and due form, have agreed as follows:

Title I. Common Provisions

Article 1 (ex Article 1 TEU)[2]**.** By this Treaty, the HIGH CONTRACTING PARTIES establish among themselves a EUROPEAN UNION, hereinafter called «the Union», on which the Member

---

[1] The Republic of Bulgaria, the Czech Republic, the Republic of Estonia, the Republic of Cyprus, The Republic of Latvia, the Republic of Lithuania, the Republic of Hungary, the Republic of Malta, the Republic of Austria, the Republic of Poland, Romania, the Republic of Slovenia, the Slovak Republic, the Republic of Finland and the Kingdom of Sweden have since become members of the European Union.

[2] These references are merely indicative. For ample information, please refer to the tables of equivalences between the old and new numbering of the Treaties.

States confer competences to attain objectives they have in common.
This Treaty marks a new stage in the process of creating an ever closer union among the peoples of Europe, in which decisions are taken as openly as possible and as closely as possible to the citizen. The Union shall be founded on the present Treaty and on the Treaty on the Functioning of the European Union (hereinafter referred to as «the Treaties»). Those two Treaties shall have the same legal value. The Union shall replace and succeed the European Community.

Article 2. The Union is founded on the values of respect for human dignity, freedom, democracy, equality, the rule of law and respect for human rights, including the rights of persons belonging to minorities. These values are common to the Member States in a society in which pluralism, non–discrimination, tolerance, justice, solidarity and equality between women and men prevail.

Article 3 (ex Article 2 TEU). (1) The Union's aim is to promote peace, its values and the well–being of its peoples.
(2) The Union shall offer its citizens an area of freedom, security and justice without internal frontiers, in which the free movement of persons is ensured in conjunction with appropriate measures with respect to external border controls, asylum, immigration and the prevention and combating of crime.
(3) The Union shall establish an internal market. It shall work for the sustainable development of Europe based on balanced economic growth and price stability, a highly competitive social market economy, aiming at full employment and social progress, and a high level of protection and improvement of the quality of the environment. It shall promote scientific and technological advance.
It shall combat social exclusion and discrimination, and shall promote social justice and protection, equality between women and men, solidarity between generations and protection of the rights of the child.
It shall promote economic, social and territorial cohesion, and solidarity among Member States.
It shall respect its rich cultural and linguistic diversity, and shall ensure that Europe's cultural heritage is safeguarded and enhanced.
(4) The Union shall establish an economic and monetary union whose currency is the euro.
(5) In its relations with the wider world, the Union shall uphold and promote its values and interests and contribute to the protection of its citizens. It shall contribute to peace, security, the sustainable development of the Earth, solidarity and mutual respect among peoples, free and fair trade, eradication of poverty and the protection of human rights, in particular the rights of the child, as well as to the strict observance and the development of international law, including respect for the principles of the United Nations Charter.
(6) The Union shall pursue its objectives by appropriate means commensurate with the competences which are conferred upon it in the Treaties.

Article 4. (1) In accordance with Article 5, competences not conferred upon the Union in the Treaties remain with the Member States.
(2) The Union shall respect the equality of Member States before the Treaties as well as their national identities, inherent in their fundamental structures, political and constitutional, inclusive of regional and local self–government. It shall respect their essential State functions, including ensuring the territorial integrity of the State, maintaining law and order and safeguarding national security. In particular, national security remains the sole responsibility of each Member State.
(3) Pursuant to the principle of sincere cooperation, the Union and the Member States shall, in full mutual respect, assist each other in carrying out tasks which flow from the Treaties.
The Member States shall take any appropriate measure, general or particular, to ensure fulfilment of the obligations arising out of the Treaties or resulting from the acts of the institutions of the Union.
The Member States shall facilitate the achievement of the Union's tasks and refrain from any measure which could jeopardise the attainment of the Union's objectives.

Article 5 (ex Article 5 TEC). (1) The limits of Union competences are governed by the principle of conferral. The use of Union competences is governed by the principles of subsidiarity and proportionality.
(2) Under the principle of conferral, the Union shall act only within the limits of the competences conferred upon it by the Member States in the Treaties to attain the objectives set out therein. Competences not conferred upon the Union in the Treaties remain with the Member States.
(3) Under the principle of subsidiarity, in areas which do not fall within its exclusive competence, the Union shall act only if and in so far as the objectives of the proposed action cannot be sufficiently achieved by the Member States, either at central level or at regional and local level, but can rather, by reason of the scale or effects of the proposed action, be better achieved at Union level.

PART III   EUROPEAN UNION

The institutions of the Union shall apply the principle of subsidiarity as laid down in the Protocol on the application of the principles of subsidiarity and proportionality. National Parliaments ensure compliance with the principle of subsidiarity in accordance with the procedure set out in that Protocol.
(4) Under the principle of proportionality, the content and form of Union action shall not exceed what is necessary to achieve the objectives of the Treaties.
The institutions of the Union shall apply the principle of proportionality as laid down in the Protocol on the application of the principles of subsidiarity and proportionality.

Article 6 (ex Article 6 TEU). (1) The Union recognises the rights, freedoms and principles set out in the Charter of Fundamental Rights of the European Union of 7 December 2000, as adapted at Strasbourg, on 12 December 2007, which shall have the same legal value as the Treaties.
The provisions of the Charter shall not extend in any way the competences of the Union as defined in the Treaties.
The rights, freedoms and principles in the Charter shall be interpreted in accordance with the general provisions in Title VII of the Charter governing its interpretation and application and with due regard to the explanations referred to in the Charter, that set out the sources of those provisions.
(2) The Union shall accede to the European Convention for the Protection of Human Rights and Fundamental Freedoms. Such accession shall not affect the Union's competences as defined in the Treaties.
(3) Fundamental rights, as guaranteed by the European Convention for the Protection of Human Rights and Fundamental Freedoms and as they result from the constitutional traditions common to the Member States, shall constitute general principles of the Union's law.

Article 7 (ex Article 7 TEU). (1) On a reasoned proposal by one third of the Member States, by the European Parliament or by the European Commission, the Council, acting by a majority of four fifths of its members after obtaining the consent of the European Parliament, may determine that there is a clear risk of a serious breach by a Member State of the values referred to in Article 2. Before making such a determination, the Council shall hear the Member State in question and may address recommendations to it, acting in accordance with the same procedure.
The Council shall regularly verify that the grounds on which such a determination was made continue to apply.
(2) The European Council, acting by unanimity on a proposal by one third of the Member States or by the Commission and after obtaining the consent of the European Parliament, may determine the existence of a serious and persistent breach by a Member State of the values referred to in Article 2, after inviting the Member State in question to submit its observations.
(3) Where a determination under paragraph 2 has been made, the Council, acting by a qualified majority, may decide to suspend certain of the rights deriving from the application of the Treaties to the Member State in question, including the voting rights of the representative of the government of that Member State in the Council. In doing so, the Council shall take into account the possible consequences of such a suspension on the rights and obligations of natural and legal persons.
The obligations of the Member State in question under the Treaties shall in any case continue to be binding on that State.
(4) The Council, acting by a qualified majority, may decide subsequently to vary or revoke measures taken under paragraph 3 in response to changes in the situation which led to their being imposed.
(5) The voting arrangements applying to the European Parliament, the European Council and the Council for the purposes of this Article are laid down in Article 354 of the Treaty on the Functioning of the European Union.

Article 8. (1) The Union shall develop a special relationship with neighbouring countries, aiming to establish an area of prosperity and good neighbourliness, founded on the values of the Union and characterised by close and peaceful relations based on cooperation.
(2) For the purposes of paragraph 1, the Union may conclude specific agreements with the countries concerned. These agreements may contain reciprocal rights and obligations as well as the possibility of undertaking activities jointly. Their implementation shall be the subject of periodic consultation.

Title II. Provisions on Democratic Principles

Article 9. In all its activities, the Union shall observe the principle of the equality of its citizens, who shall receive equal attention from its institutions, bodies, offices and agencies. Every national of a Member State shall be a citizen of the Union. Citizenship of the Union shall be additional to and not replace national citizenship.

Article 10. (1) The functioning of the Union shall be founded on representative democracy.
(2) Citizens are directly represented at Union level in the European Parliament.
Member States are represented in the European Council by their Heads of State or Government and in the Council by their governments, themselves democratically accountable either to their national Parliaments, or to their citizens.
(3) Every citizen shall have the right to participate in the democratic life of the Union. Decisions shall be taken as openly and as closely as possible to the citizen.
(4) Political parties at European level contribute to forming European political awareness and to expressing the will of citizens of the Union.

Article 11. (1) The institutions shall, by appropriate means, give citizens and representative associations the opportunity to make known and publicly exchange their views in all areas of Union action.
(2) The institutions shall maintain an open, transparent and regular dialogue with representative associations and civil society.
(3) The European Commission shall carry out broad consultations with parties concerned in order to ensure that the Union's actions are coherent and transparent.
(4) Not less than one million citizens who are nationals of a significant number of Member States may take the initiative of inviting the European Commission, within the framework of its powers, to submit any appropriate proposal on matters where citizens consider that a legal act of the Union is required for the purpose of implementing the Treaties.
The procedures and conditions required for such a citizens' initiative shall be determined in accordance with the first paragraph of Article 24 of the Treaty on the Functioning of the European Union.

Article 12. National Parliaments contribute actively to the good functioning of the Union:
(a) through being informed by the institutions of the Union and having draft legislative acts of the Union forwarded to them in accordance with the Protocol on the role of national Parliaments in the European Union;
(b) by seeing to it that the principle of subsidiarity is respected in accordance with the procedures provided for in the Protocol on the application of the principles of subsidiarity and proportionality;
(c) by taking part, within the framework of the area of freedom, security and justice, in the evaluation mechanisms for the implementation of the Union policies in that area, in accordance with Article 70 of the Treaty on the Functioning of the European Union, and through being involved in the political monitoring of Europol and the evaluation of Eurojust's activities in accordance with Articles 88 and 85 of that Treaty;
(d) by taking part in the revision procedures of the Treaties, in accordance with Article 48 of this Treaty;
(e) by being notified of applications for accession to the Union, in accordance with Article 49 of this Treaty;
(f) by taking part in the inter–parliamentary cooperation between national Parliaments and with the European Parliament, in accordance with the Protocol on the role of national Parliaments in the European Union.

Title III. Provisions on the Institutions

Article 13. (1) The Union shall have an institutional framework which shall aim to promote its values, advance its objectives, serve its interests, those of its citizens and those of the Member States, and ensure the consistency, effectiveness and continuity of its policies and actions.
The Union's institutions shall be:
– the European Parliament,
– the European Council,
– the Council,
– the European Commission (hereinafter referred to as "the Commission"),
– the Court of Justice of the European Union,
– the European Central Bank,
– the Court of Auditors.
(2) Each institution shall act within the limits of the powers conferred on it in the Treaties, and in conformity with the procedures, conditions and objectives set out in them. The institutions shall practice mutual sincere cooperation.
(3) The provisions relating to the European Central Bank and the Court of Auditors and detailed provisions on the other institutions are set out in the Treaty on the Functioning of the European Union.
(4) The European Parliament, the Council and the Commission shall be assisted by an Economic and Social Committee and a Committee of the Regions acting in an advisory capacity.

PART III   EUROPEAN UNION

Article 14. (1) The European Parliament shall, jointly with the Council, exercise legislative and budgetary functions. It shall exercise functions of political control and consultation as laid down in the Treaties. It shall elect the President of the Commission.
(2) The European Parliament shall be composed of representatives of the Union's citizens. They shall not exceed seven hundred and fifty in number, plus the President. Representation of citizens shall be degressively proportional, with a minimum threshold of six members per Member State. No Member State shall be allocated more than ninety–six seats.
The European Council shall adopt by unanimity, on the initiative of the European Parliament and with its consent, a decision establishing the composition of the European Parliament, respecting the principles referred to in the first subparagraph.
(3) The members of the European Parliament shall be elected for a term of five years by direct universal suffrage in a free and secret ballot.
(4) The European Parliament shall elect its President and its officers from among its members.

Article 15. (1) The European Council shall provide the Union with the necessary impetus for its development and shall define the general political directions and priorities thereof. It shall not exercise legislative functions.
(2) The European Council shall consist of the Heads of State or Government of the Member States, together with its President and the President of the Commission. The High Representative of the Union for Foreign Affairs and Security Policy shall take part in its work.
(3) The European Council shall meet twice every six months, convened by its President. When the agenda so requires, the members of the European Council may decide each to be assisted by a minister and, in the case of the President of the Commission, by a member of the Commission. When the situation so requires, the President shall convene a special meeting of the European Council.
(4) Except where the Treaties provide otherwise, decisions of the European Council shall be taken by consensus.
(5) The European Council shall elect its President, by a qualified majority, for a term of two and a half years, renewable once. In the event of an impediment or serious misconduct, the European Council can end the President's term of office in accordance with the same procedure.
(6) The President of the European Council:
(a) shall chair it and drive forward its work;
(b) shall ensure the preparation and continuity of the work of the European Council in cooperation with the President of the Commission, and on the basis of the work of the General Affairs Council;
(c) shall endeavour to facilitate cohesion and consensus within the European Council;
(d) shall present a report to the European Parliament after each of the meetings of the European Council.
The President of the European Council shall, at his level and in that capacity, ensure the external representation of the Union on issues concerning its common foreign and security policy, without prejudice to the powers of the High Representative of the Union for Foreign Affairs and Security Policy. The President of the European Council shall not hold a national office.

Article 16. (1) The Council shall, jointly with the European Parliament, exercise legislative and budgetary functions. It shall carry out policy–making and coordinating functions as laid down in the Treaties.
(2) The Council shall consist of a representative of each Member State at ministerial level, who may commit the government of the Member State in question and cast its vote.
(3) The Council shall act by a qualified majority except where the Treaties provide otherwise.
(4) As from 1 November 2014, a qualified majority shall be defined as at least 55 % of the members of the Council, comprising at least fifteen of them and representing Member States comprising at least 65 % of the population of the Union.
A blocking minority must include at least four Council members, failing which the qualified majority shall be deemed attained.
The other arrangements governing the qualified majority are laid down in Article 238(2) of the Treaty on the Functioning of the European Union.
(5) The transitional provisions relating to the definition of the qualified majority which shall be applicable until 31 October 2014 and those which shall be applicable from 1 November 2014 to 31 March 2017 are laid down in the Protocol on transitional provisions.
(6) The Council shall meet in different configurations, the list of which shall be adopted in accordance with Article 236 of the Treaty on the Functioning of the European Union.
The General Affairs Council shall ensure consistency in the work of the different Council configurations. It shall prepare and ensure the follow–up to meetings of the European Council, in liaison with

the President of the European Council and the Commission.

The Foreign Affairs Council shall elaborate the Union's external action on the basis of strategic guidelines laid down by the European Council and ensure that the Union's action is consistent.

(7) A Committee of Permanent Representatives of the Governments of the Member States shall be responsible for preparing the work of the Council.

(8) The Council shall meet in public when it deliberates and votes on a draft legislative act. To this end, each Council meeting shall be divided into two parts, dealing respectively with deliberations on Union legislative acts and non–legislative activities.

(9) The Presidency of Council configurations, other than that of Foreign Affairs, shall be held by Member State representatives in the Council on the basis of equal rotation, in accordance with the conditions established in accordance with Article 236 of the Treaty on the Functioning of the European Union.

Article 17. (1) The Commission shall promote the general interest of the Union and take appropriate initiatives to that end. It shall ensure the application of the Treaties, and of measures adopted by the institutions pursuant to them. It shall oversee the application of Union law under the control of the Court of Justice of the European Union. It shall execute the budget and manage programmes. It shall exercise coordinating, executive and management functions, as laid down in the Treaties. With the exception of the common foreign and security policy, and other cases provided for in the Treaties, it shall ensure the Union's external representation. It shall initiate the Union's annual and multiannual programming with a view to achieving interinstitutional agreements.

(2) Union legislative acts may only be adopted on the basis of a Commission proposal, except where the Treaties provide otherwise. Other acts shall be adopted on the basis of a Commission proposal where the Treaties so provide.

(3) The Commission's term of office shall be five years.

The members of the Commission shall be chosen on the ground of their general competence and European commitment from persons whose independence is beyond doubt.

In carrying out its responsibilities, the Commission shall be completely independent. Without prejudice to Article 18(2), the members of the Commission shall neither seek nor take instructions from any Government or other institution, body, office or entity. They shall refrain from any action incompatible with their duties or the performance of their tasks.

(4) The Commission appointed between the date of entry into force of the Treaty of Lisbon and 31 October 2014, shall consist of one national of each Member State, including its President and the High Representative of the Union for Foreign Affairs and Security Policy who shall be one of its Vice–Presidents.

(5) As from 1 November 2014, the Commission shall consist of a number of members, including its President and the High Representative of the Union for Foreign Affairs and Security Policy, corresponding to two thirds of the number of Member States, unless the European Council, acting unanimously, decides to alter this number.

The members of the Commission shall be chosen from among the nationals of the Member States on the basis of a system of strictly equal rotation between the Member States, reflecting the demographic and geographical range of all the Member States. This system shall be established unanimously by the European Council in accordance with Article 244 of the Treaty on the Functioning of the European Union.

(6) The President of the Commission shall:

(a) lay down guidelines within which the Commission is to work;

(b) decide on the internal organisation of the Commission, ensuring that it acts consistently, efficiently and as a collegiate body;

(c) appoint Vice–Presidents, other than the High Representative of the Union for Foreign Affairs and Security Policy, from among the members of the Commission.

A member of the Commission shall resign if the President so requests. The High Representative of the Union for Foreign Affairs and Security Policy shall resign, in accordance with the procedure set out in Article 18(1), if the President so requests.

(7) Taking into account the elections to the European Parliament and after having held the appropriate consultations, the European Council, acting by a qualified majority, shall propose to the European Parliament a candidate for President of the Commission. This candidate shall be elected by the European Parliament by a majority of its component members. If he does not obtain the required majority, the European Council, acting by a qualified majority, shall within one month propose a new candidate who shall be elected by the European Parliament following the same procedure.

The Council, by common accord with the President–elect, shall adopt the list of the other persons whom it proposes for appointment as members of the Commission. They shall be selected, on the basis of the suggestions made by Member States, in accordance with the criteria set out in paragraph 3, second subparagraph, and paragraph 5, second subparagraph.

The President, the High Representative of the Union for Foreign Affairs and Security Policy and the other members of the Commission shall be subject as a body to a vote of consent by the European Parliament. On the basis of this consent the Commission shall be appointed by the European Council, acting by a qualified majority.

(8) The Commission, as a body, shall be responsible to the European Parliament. In accordance with Article 234 of the Treaty on the Functioning of the European Union, the European Parliament may vote on a motion of censure of the Commission. If such a motion is carried, the members of the Commission shall resign as a body and the High Representative of the Union for Foreign Affairs and Security Policy shall resign from the duties that he carries out in the Commission.

Article 18. (1) The European Council, acting by a qualified majority, with the agreement of the President of the Commission, shall appoint the High Representative of the Union for Foreign Affairs and Security Policy. The European Council may end his term of office by the same procedure.
(2) The High Representative shall conduct the Union's common foreign and security policy. He shall contribute by his proposals to the development of that policy, which he shall carry out as mandated by the Council. The same shall apply to the common security and defence policy.
(3) The High Representative shall preside over the Foreign Affairs Council.
(4) The High Representative shall be one of the Vice–Presidents of the Commission. He shall ensure the consistency of the Union's external action. He shall be responsible within the Commission for responsibilities incumbent on it in external relations and for coordinating other aspects of the Union's external action. In exercising these responsibilities within the Commission, and only for these responsibilities, the High Representative shall be bound by Commission procedures to the extent that this is consistent with paragraphs 2 and 3.

Article 19. (1) The Court of Justice of the European Union shall include the Court of Justice, the General Court and specialised courts. It shall ensure that in the interpretation and application of the Treaties the law is observed.
Member States shall provide remedies sufficient to ensure effective legal protection in the fields covered by Union law.
(2) The Court of Justice shall consist of one judge from each Member State. It shall be assisted by Advocates–General.
The General Court shall include at least one judge per Member State.
The Judges and the Advocates–General of the Court of Justice and the Judges of the General Court shall be chosen from persons whose independence is beyond doubt and who satisfy the conditions set out in Articles 253 and 254 of the Treaty on the Functioning of the European Union. They shall be appointed by common accord of the governments of the Member States for six years. Retiring Judges and Advocates–General may be reappointed.
(3) The Court of Justice of the European Union shall, in accordance with the Treaties:
(a) rule on actions brought by a Member State, an institution or a natural or legal person;
(b) give preliminary rulings, at the request of courts or tribunals of the Member States, on the interpretation of Union law or the validity of acts adopted by the institutions;
(c) rule in other cases provided for in the Treaties.

Title IV. Provisions on Enhanced Cooperation

Article 20 (ex Articles 27a to 27e, 40 to 40b and 43 to 45 TEU and ex Articles 11 and 11a TEC).
(1) Member States which wish to establish enhanced cooperation between themselves within the framework of the Union's non–exclusive competences may make use of its institutions and exercise those competences by applying the relevant provisions of the Treaties, subject to the limits and in accordance with the detailed arrangements laid down in this Article and in Articles 326 to 334 of the Treaty on the Functioning of the European Union.
Enhanced cooperation shall aim to further the objectives of the Union, protect its interests and reinforce its integration process. Such cooperation shall be open at any time to all Member States, in accordance with Article 328 of the Treaty on the Functioning of the European Union.
(2) The decision authorising enhanced cooperation shall be adopted by the Council as a last resort, when it has established that the objectives of such cooperation cannot be attained within a reasonable period by the Union as a whole, and provided that at least nine Member States participate in it. The Council shall act in accordance with the procedure laid down in Article 329 of the Treaty on the Functioning of the European Union.

(3) All members of the Council may participate in its deliberations, but only members of the Council representing the Member States participating in enhanced cooperation shall take part in the vote. The voting rules are set out in Article 330 of the Treaty on the Functioning of the European Union.
(4) Acts adopted in the framework of enhanced cooperation shall bind only participating Member States. They shall not be regarded as part of the acquis which has to be accepted by candidate States for accession to the Union.

Title V. General Provisions on the Union's External Action and Specific Provisions on the Common Foreign and Security Policy

Chapter 1. General Provisions on the Union's External Action

Article 21. (1) The Union's action on the international scene shall be guided by the principles which have inspired its own creation, development and enlargement, and which it seeks to advance in the wider world: democracy, the rule of law, the universality and indivisibility of human rights and fundamental freedoms, respect for human dignity, the principles of equality and solidarity, and respect for the principles of the United Nations Charter and international law.
The Union shall seek to develop relations and build partnerships with third countries, and international, regional or global organisations which share the principles referred to in the first subparagraph. It shall promote multilateral solutions to common problems, in particular in the framework of the United Nations.
(2) The Union shall define and pursue common policies and actions, and shall work for a high degree of cooperation in all fields of international relations, in order to:
(a) safeguard its values, fundamental interests, security, independence and integrity;
(b) consolidate and support democracy, the rule of law, human rights and the principles of international law;
(c) preserve peace, prevent conflicts and strengthen international security, in accordance with the purposes and principles of the United Nations Charter, with the principles of the Helsinki Final Act and with the aims of the Charter of Paris, including those relating to external borders;
(d) foster the sustainable economic, social and environmental development of developing countries, with the primary aim of eradicating poverty;
(e) encourage the integration of all countries into the world economy, including through the progressive abolition of restrictions on international trade;
(f) help develop international measures to preserve and improve the quality of the environment and the sustainable management of global natural resources, in order to ensure sustainable development;
(g) assist populations, countries and regions confronting natural or man–made disasters; and
(h) promote an international system based on stronger multilateral cooperation and good global governance.
(3) The Union shall respect the principles and pursue the objectives set out in paragraphs 1 and 2 in the development and implementation of the different areas of the Union's external action covered by this Title and by Part Five of the Treaty on the Functioning of the European Union, and of the external aspects of its other policies.
The Union shall ensure consistency between the different areas of its external action and between these and its other policies. The Council and the Commission, assisted by the High Representative of the Union for Foreign Affairs and Security Policy, shall ensure that consistency and shall cooperate to that effect.

Article 22. (1) On the basis of the principles and objectives set out in Article 21, the European Council shall identify the strategic interests and objectives of the Union.
Decisions of the European Council on the strategic interests and objectives of the Union shall relate to the common foreign and security policy and to other areas of the external action of the Union. Such decisions may concern the relations of the Union with a specific country or region or may be thematic in approach. They shall define their duration, and the means to be made available by the Union and the Member States.
The European Council shall act unanimously on a recommendation from the Council, adopted by the latter under the arrangements laid down for each area. Decisions of the European Council shall be implemented in accordance with the procedures provided for in the Treaties.
(2) The High Representative of the Union for Foreign Affairs and Security Policy, for the area of common foreign and security policy, and the Commission, for other areas of external action, may submit joint proposals to the Council.

PART III   EUROPEAN UNION

Chapter 2. Specific Provisions on the Common Foreign and Security Policy

Section 1. Common Provisions

Article 23. The Union's action on the international scene, pursuant to this Chapter, shall be guided by the principles, shall pursue the objectives of, and be conducted in accordance with, the general provisions laid down in Chapter 1.

Article 24 (ex Article 11 TEU). (1) The Union's competence in matters of common foreign and security policy shall cover all areas of foreign policy and all questions relating to the Union's security, including the progressive framing of a common defence policy that might lead to a common defence.

The common foreign and security policy is subject to specific rules and procedures. It shall be defined and implemented by the European Council and the Council acting unanimously, except where the Treaties provide otherwise. The adoption of legislative acts shall be excluded. The common foreign and security policy shall be put into effect by the High Representative of the Union for Foreign Affairs and Security Policy and by Member States, in accordance with the Treaties. The specific role of the European Parliament and of the Commission in this area is defined by the Treaties. The Court of Justice of the European Union shall not have jurisdiction with respect to these provisions, with the exception of its jurisdiction to monitor compliance with Article 40 of this Treaty and to review the legality of certain decisions as provided for by the second paragraph of Article 275 of the Treaty on the Functioning of the European Union.

(2) Within the framework of the principles and objectives of its external action, the Union shall conduct, define and implement a common foreign and security policy, based on the development of mutual political solidarity among Member States, the identification of questions of general interest and the achievement of an ever–increasing degree of convergence of Member States' actions.

(3) The Member States shall support the Union's external and security policy actively and unreservedly in a spirit of loyalty and mutual solidarity and shall comply with the Union's action in this area. The Member States shall work together to enhance and develop their mutual political solidarity. They shall refrain from any action which is contrary to the interests of the Union or likely to impair its effectiveness as a cohesive force in international relations.

The Council and the High Representative shall ensure compliance with these principles.

Article 25 (ex Article 12 TEU). The Union shall conduct the common foreign and security policy by:
(a) defining the general guidelines;
(b) adopting decisions defining:
(i) actions to be undertaken by the Union;
(ii) positions to be taken by the Union;
(iii) arrangements for the implementation of the decisions referred to in points (i) and (ii);
and by
(c) strengthening systematic cooperation between Member States in the conduct of policy.

Article 26 (ex Article 13 TEU). (1) The European Council shall identify the Union's strategic interests, determine the objectives of and define general guidelines for the common foreign and security policy, including for matters with defence implications. It shall adopt the necessary decisions.

If international developments so require, the President of the European Council shall convene an extraordinary meeting of the European Council in order to define the strategic lines of the Union's policy in the face of such developments.

(2) The Council shall frame the common foreign and security policy and take the decisions necessary for defining and implementing it on the basis of the general guidelines and strategic lines defined by the European Council.

The Council and the High Representative of the Union for Foreign Affairs and Security Policy shall ensure the unity, consistency and effectiveness of action by the Union.

(3) The common foreign and security policy shall be put into effect by the High Representative and by the Member States, using national and Union resources.

Article 27. (1) The High Representative of the Union for Foreign Affairs and Security Policy, who shall chair the Foreign Affairs Council, shall contribute through his proposals to the development of the common foreign and security policy and shall ensure implementation of the decisions adopted by the European Council and the Council.

(2) The High Representative shall represent the Union for matters relating to the common foreign and

security policy. He shall conduct political dialogue with third parties on the Union's behalf and shall express the Union's position in international organisations and at international conferences.

(3) In fulfilling his mandate, the High Representative shall be assisted by a European External Action Service. This service shall work in cooperation with the diplomatic services of the Member States and shall comprise officials from relevant departments of the General Secretariat of the Council and of the Commission as well as staff seconded from national diplomatic services of the Member States. The organisation and functioning of the European External Action Service shall be established by a decision of the Council. The Council shall act on a proposal from the High Representative after consulting the European Parliament and after obtaining the consent of the Commission.

Article 28 (ex Article 14 TEU). (1) Where the international situation requires operational action by the Union, the Council shall adopt the necessary decisions. They shall lay down their objectives, scope, the means to be made available to the Union, if necessary their duration, and the conditions for their implementation.

If there is a change in circumstances having a substantial effect on a question subject to such a decision, the Council shall review the principles and objectives of that decision and take the necessary decisions.

(2) Decisions referred to in paragraph 1 shall commit the Member States in the positions they adopt and in the conduct of their activity.

(3) Whenever there is any plan to adopt a national position or take national action pursuant to a decision as referred to in paragraph 1, information shall be provided by the Member State concerned in time to allow, if necessary, for prior consultations within the Council. The obligation to provide prior information shall not apply to measures which are merely a national transposition of Council decisions.

(4) In cases of imperative need arising from changes in the situation and failing a review of the Council decision as referred to in paragraph 1, Member States may take the necessary measures as a matter of urgency having regard to the general objectives of that decision. The Member State concerned shall inform the Council immediately of any such measures.

(5) Should there be any major difficulties in implementing a decision as referred to in this Article, a Member State shall refer them to the Council which shall discuss them and seek appropriate solutions. Such solutions shall not run counter to the objectives of the decision referred to in paragraph 1 or impair its effectiveness.

Article 29 (ex Article 15 TEU). The Council shall adopt decisions which shall define the approach of the Union to a particular matter of a geographical or thematic nature. Member States shall ensure that their national policies conform to the Union positions.

Article 30 (ex Article 22 TEU). (1) Any Member State, the High Representative of the Union for Foreign Affairs and Security Policy, or the High Representative with the Commission's support, may refer any question relating to the common foreign and security policy to the Council and may submit to it, respectively, initiatives or proposals.

(2) In cases requiring a rapid decision, the High Representative, of his own motion, or at the request of a Member State, shall convene an extraordinary Council meeting within 48 hours or, in an emergency, within a shorter period.

Article 31 (ex Article 23 TEU). (1) Decisions under this Chapter shall be taken by the European Council and the Council acting unanimously, except where this Chapter provides otherwise. The adoption of legislative acts shall be excluded.

When abstaining in a vote, any member of the Council may qualify its abstention by making a formal declaration under the present subparagraph. In that case, it shall not be obliged to apply the decision, but shall accept that the decision commits the Union. In a spirit of mutual solidarity, the Member State concerned shall refrain from any action likely to conflict with or impede Union action based on that decision and the other Member States shall respect its position. If the members of the Council qualifying their abstention in this way represent at least one third of the Member States comprising at least one third of the population of the Union, the decision shall not be adopted.

(2) By derogation from the provisions of paragraph 1, the Council shall act by qualified majority:
– when adopting a decision defining a Union action or position on the basis of a decision of the European Council relating to the Union's strategic interests and objectives, as referred to in Article 22(1),
– when adopting a decision defining a Union action or position, on a proposal which the High Representative of the Union for Foreign Affairs and Security Policy has presented following a specific request from the European Council, made on its own initiative or that of the High Representative,
– when adopting any decision implementing a decision defining a Union action or position,
– when appointing a special representative in accordance with Article 33.

PART III EUROPEAN UNION

If a member of the Council declares that, for vital and stated reasons of national policy, it intends to oppose the adoption of a decision to be taken by qualified majority, a vote shall not be taken. The High Representative will, in close consultation with the Member State involved, search for a solution acceptable to it. If he does not succeed, the Council may, acting by a qualified majority, request that the matter be referred to the European Council for a decision by unanimity.
(3) The European Council may unanimously adopt a decision stipulating that the Council shall act by a qualified majority in cases other than those referred to in paragraph 2.
(4) Paragraphs 2 and 3 shall not apply to decisions having military or defence implications.
(5) For procedural questions, the Council shall act by a majority of its members.

Article 32 (ex Article 16 TEU). Member States shall consult one another within the European Council and the Council on any matter of foreign and security policy of general interest in order to determine a common approach. Before undertaking any action on the international scene or entering into any commitment which could affect the Union's interests, each Member State shall consult the others within the European Council or the Council. Member States shall ensure, through the convergence of their actions, that the Union is able to assert its interests and values on the international scene. Member States shall show mutual solidarity.
When the European Council or the Council has defined a common approach of the Union within the meaning of the first paragraph, the High Representative of the Union for Foreign Affairs and Security Policy and the Ministers for Foreign Affairs of the Member States shall coordinate their activities within the Council.
The diplomatic missions of the Member States and the Union delegations in third countries and at international organisations shall cooperate and shall contribute to formulating and implementing the common approach.

Article 33 (ex Article 18 TEU). The Council may, on a proposal from the High Representative of the Union for Foreign Affairs and Security Policy, appoint a special representative with a mandate in relation to particular policy issues. The special representative shall carry out his mandate under the authority of the High Representative.

Article 34 (ex Article 19 TEU). (1) Member States shall coordinate their action in international organisations and at international conferences. They shall uphold the Union's positions in such forums. The High Representative of the Union for Foreign Affairs and Security Policy shall organise this coordination.
In international organisations and at international conferences where not all the Member States participate, those which do take part shall uphold the Union's positions.
(2) In accordance with Article 24(3), Member States represented in international organisations or international conferences where not all the Member States participate shall keep the other Member States and the High Representative informed of any matter of common interest.
Member States which are also members of the United Nations Security Council will concert and keep the other Member States and the High Representative fully informed. Member States which are members of the Security Council will, in the execution of their functions, defend the positions and the interests of the Union, without prejudice to their responsibilities under the provisions of the United Nations Charter.
When the Union has defined a position on a subject which is on the United Nations Security Council agenda, those Member States which sit on the Security Council shall request that the High Representative be invited to present the Union's position.

Article 35 (ex Article 20 TEU). The diplomatic and consular missions of the Member States and the Union delegations in third countries and international conferences, and their representations to international organisations, shall cooperate in ensuring that decisions defining Union positions and actions adopted pursuant to this Chapter are complied with and implemented.
They shall step up cooperation by exchanging information and carrying out joint assessments.
They shall contribute to the implementation of the right of citizens of the Union to protection in the territory of third countries as referred to in Article 20(2)(c) of the Treaty on the Functioning of the European Union and of the measures adopted pursuant to Article 23 of that Treaty.

Article 36 (ex Article 21 TEU). The High Representative of the Union for Foreign Affairs and Security Policy shall regularly consult the European Parliament on the main aspects and the basic choices of the common foreign and security policy and the common security and defence policy and inform it of how those policies evolve. He shall ensure that the views of the European Parliament are duly taken into consideration. Special representatives may be involved in briefing the European Parliament.

The European Parliament may address questions or make recommendations to the Council or the High Representative. Twice a year it shall hold a debate on progress in implementing the common foreign and security policy, including the common security and defence policy.

Article 37 (ex Article 24 TEU). The Union may conclude agreements with one or more States or international organisations in areas covered by this Chapter.

Article 38 (ex Article 25 TEU). Without prejudice to Article 240 of the Treaty on the Functioning of the European Union, a Political and Security Committee shall monitor the international situation in the areas covered by the common foreign and security policy and contribute to the definition of policies by delivering opinions to the Council at the request of the Council or of the High Representative of the Union for Foreign Affairs and Security Policy or on its own initiative. It shall also monitor the implementation of agreed policies, without prejudice to the powers of the High Representative.
Within the scope of this Chapter, the Political and Security Committee shall exercise, under the responsibility of the Council and of the High Representative, the political control and strategic direction of the crisis management operations referred to in Article 43.
The Council may authorise the Committee, for the purpose and for the duration of a crisis management operation, as determined by the Council, to take the relevant decisions concerning the political control and strategic direction of the operation.

Article 39. In accordance with Article 16 of the Treaty on the Functioning of the European Union and by way of derogation from paragraph 2 thereof, the Council shall adopt a decision laying down the rules relating to the protection of individuals with regard to the processing of personal data by the Member States when carrying out activities which fall within the scope of this Chapter, and the rules relating to the free movement of such data. Compliance with these rules shall be subject to the control of independent authorities.

Article 40 (ex Article 47 TEU). The implementation of the common foreign and security policy shall not affect the application of the procedures and the extent of the powers of the institutions laid down by the Treaties for the exercise of the Union competences referred to in Articles 3 to 6 of the Treaty on the Functioning of the European Union.
Similarly, the implementation of the policies listed in those Articles shall not affect the application of the procedures and the extent of the powers of the institutions laid down by the Treaties for the exercise of the Union competences under this Chapter.

Article 41 (ex Article 28 TEU). (1) Administrative expenditure to which the implementation of this Chapter gives rise for the institutions shall be charged to the Union budget.
(2) Operating expenditure to which the implementation of this Chapter gives rise shall also be charged to the Union budget, except for such expenditure arising from operations having military or defence implications and cases where the Council acting unanimously decides otherwise.
In cases where expenditure is not charged to the Union budget, it shall be charged to the Member States in accordance with the gross national product scale, unless the Council acting unanimously decides otherwise. As for expenditure arising from operations having military or defence implications, Member States whose representatives in the Council have made a formal declaration under Article 31(1), second subparagraph, shall not be obliged to contribute to the financing thereof.
(3) The Council shall adopt a decision establishing the specific procedures for guaranteeing rapid access to appropriations in the Union budget for urgent financing of initiatives in the framework of the common foreign and security policy, and in particular for preparatory activities for the tasks referred to in Article 42(1) and Article 43. It shall act after consulting the European Parliament.
Preparatory activities for the tasks referred to in Article 42(1) and Article 43 which are not charged to the Union budget shall be financed by a start–up fund made up of Member States' contributions.
The Council shall adopt by a qualified majority, on a proposal from the High Representative of the Union for Foreign Affairs and Security Policy, decisions establishing:
(a) the procedures for setting up and financing the start–up fund, in particular the amounts allocated to the fund;
(b) the procedures for administering the start–up fund;
(c) the financial control procedures.
When the task planned in accordance with Article 42(1) and Article 43 cannot be charged to the Union budget, the Council shall authorise the High Representative to use the fund. The High Representative shall report to the Council on the implementation of this remit.

PART III   EUROPEAN UNION

Section 2. Provisions on the Common Security and Defence Policy

Article 42 (ex Article 17 TEU). (1) The common security and defence policy shall be an integral part of the common foreign and security policy. It shall provide the Union with an operational capacity drawing on civilian and military assets. The Union may use them on missions outside the Union for peace–keeping, conflict prevention and strengthening international security in accordance with the principles of the United Nations Charter. The performance of these tasks shall be undertaken using capabilities provided by the Member States.
(2) The common security and defence policy shall include the progressive framing of a common Union defence policy. This will lead to a common defence, when the European Council, acting unanimously, so decides. It shall in that case recommend to the Member States the adoption of such a decision in accordance with their respective constitutional requirements.
The policy of the Union in accordance with this Section shall not prejudice the specific character of the security and defence policy of certain Member States and shall respect the obligations of certain Member States, which see their common defence realised in the North Atlantic Treaty Organisation (NATO), under the North Atlantic Treaty and be compatible with the common security and defence policy established within that framework.
(3) Member States shall make civilian and military capabilities available to the Union for the implementation of the common security and defence policy, to contribute to the objectives defined by the Council. Those Member States which together establish multinational forces may also make them available to the common security and defence policy.
Member States shall undertake progressively to improve their military capabilities. The Agency in the field of defence capabilities development, research, acquisition and armaments (hereinafter referred to as "the European Defence Agency") shall identify operational requirements, shall promote measures to satisfy those requirements, shall contribute to identifying and, where appropriate, implementing any measure needed to strengthen the industrial and technological base of the defence sector, shall participate in defining a European capabilities and armaments policy, and shall assist the Council in evaluating the improvement of military capabilities.
(4) Decisions relating to the common security and defence policy, including those initiating a mission as referred to in this Article, shall be adopted by the Council acting unanimously on a proposal from the High Representative of the Union for Foreign Affairs and Security Policy or an initiative from a Member State. The High Representative may propose the use of both national resources and Union instruments, together with the Commission where appropriate.
(5) The Council may entrust the execution of a task, within the Union framework, to a group of Member States in order to protect the Union's values and serve its interests. The execution of such a task shall be governed by Article 44.
(6) Those Member States whose military capabilities fulfil higher criteria and which have made more binding commitments to one another in this area with a view to the most demanding missions shall establish permanent structured cooperation within the Union framework. Such cooperation shall be governed by Article 46. It shall not affect the provisions of Article 43.
(7) If a Member State is the victim of armed aggression on its territory, the other Member States shall have towards it an obligation of aid and assistance by all the means in their power, in accordance with Article 51 of the United Nations Charter. This shall not prejudice the specific character of the security and defence policy of certain Member States.
Commitments and cooperation in this area shall be consistent with commitments under the North Atlantic Treaty Organisation, which, for those States which are members of it, remains the foundation of their collective defence and the forum for its implementation.

Article 43. (1) The tasks referred to in Article 42(1), in the course of which the Union may use civilian and military means, shall include joint disarmament operations, humanitarian and rescue tasks, military advice and assistance tasks, conflict prevention and peace–keeping tasks, tasks of combat forces in crisis management, including peace–making and post–conflict stabilisation. All these tasks may contribute to the fight against terrorism, including by supporting third countries in combating terrorism in their territories.
(2) The Council shall adopt decisions relating to the tasks referred to in paragraph 1, defining their objectives and scope and the general conditions for their implementation. The High Representative of the Union for Foreign Affairs and Security Policy, acting under the authority of the Council and in close and constant contact with the Political and Security Committee, shall ensure coordination of the civilian and military aspects of such tasks.

Article 44. (1) Within the framework of the decisions adopted in accordance with Article 43, the

Council may entrust the implementation of a task to a group of Member States which are willing and have the necessary capability for such a task. Those Member States, in association with the High Representative of the Union for Foreign Affairs and Security Policy, shall agree among themselves on the management of the task.

(2) Member States participating in the task shall keep the Council regularly informed of its progress on their own initiative or at the request of another Member State. Those States shall inform the Council immediately should the completion of the task entail major consequences or require amendment of the objective, scope and conditions determined for the task in the decisions referred to in paragraph 1. In such cases, the Council shall adopt the necessary decisions.

Article 45. (1) The European Defence Agency referred to in Article 42(3), subject to the authority of the Council, shall have as its task to:
(a) contribute to identifying the Member States' military capability objectives and evaluating observance of the capability commitments given by the Member States;
(b) promote harmonisation of operational needs and adoption of effective, compatible procurement methods;
(c) propose multilateral projects to fulfil the objectives in terms of military capabilities, ensure coordination of the programmes implemented by the Member States and management of specific cooperation programmes;
(d) support defence technology research, and coordinate and plan joint research activities and the study of technical solutions meeting future operational needs;
(e) contribute to identifying and, if necessary, implementing any useful measure for strengthening the industrial and technological base of the defence sector and for improving the effectiveness of military expenditure.
(2) The European Defence Agency shall be open to all Member States wishing to be part of it. The Council, acting by a qualified majority, shall adopt a decision defining the Agency's statute, seat and operational rules. That decision should take account of the level of effective participation in the Agency's activities. Specific groups shall be set up within the Agency bringing together Member States engaged in joint projects. The Agency shall carry out its tasks in liaison with the Commission where necessary.

Article 46. (1) Those Member States which wish to participate in the permanent structured cooperation referred to in Article 42(6), which fulfil the criteria and have made the commitments on military capabilities set out in the Protocol on permanent structured cooperation, shall notify their intention to the Council and to the High Representative of the Union for Foreign Affairs and Security Policy.
(2) Within three months following the notification referred to in paragraph 1 the Council shall adopt a decision establishing permanent structured cooperation and determining the list of participating Member States. The Council shall act by a qualified majority after consulting the High Representative.
(3) Any Member State which, at a later stage, wishes to participate in the permanent structured cooperation shall notify its intention to the Council and to the High Representative.
The Council shall adopt a decision confirming the participation of the Member State concerned which fulfils the criteria and makes the commitments referred to in Articles 1 and 2 of the Protocol on permanent structured cooperation. The Council shall act by a qualified majority after consulting the High Representative. Only members of the Council representing the participating Member States shall take part in the vote.
A qualified majority shall be defined in accordance with Article 238(3)(a) of the Treaty on the Functioning of the European Union.
(4) If a participating Member State no longer fulfils the criteria or is no longer able to meet the commitments referred to in Articles 1 and 2 of the Protocol on permanent structured cooperation, the Council may adopt a decision suspending the participation of the Member State concerned.
The Council shall act by a qualified majority. Only members of the Council representing the participating Member States, with the exception of the Member State in question, shall take part in the vote.
A qualified majority shall be defined in accordance with Article 238(3)(a) of the Treaty on the Functioning of the European Union.
(5) Any participating Member State which wishes to withdraw from permanent structured cooperation shall notify its intention to the Council, which shall take note that the Member State in question has ceased to participate.
(6) The decisions and recommendations of the Council within the framework of permanent structured cooperation, other than those provided for in paragraphs 2 to 5, shall be adopted by unanimity. For the purposes of this paragraph, unanimity shall be constituted by the votes of the representatives of the participating Member States only.

PART III   EUROPEAN UNION

Title VI. Final Provisions

Article 47. The Union shall have legal personality.

Article 48 (ex Article 48 TEU). (1) The Treaties may be amended in accordance with an ordinary revision procedure. They may also be amended in accordance with simplified revision procedures.
Ordinary revision procedure
(2) The Government of any Member State, the European Parliament or the Commission may submit to the Council proposals for the amendment of the Treaties. These proposals may, inter alia, serve either to increase or to reduce the competences conferred on the Union in the Treaties. These proposals shall be submitted to the European Council by the Council and the national Parliaments shall be notified.
(3) If the European Council, after consulting the European Parliament and the Commission, adopts by a simple majority a decision in favour of examining the proposed amendments, the President of the European Council shall convene a Convention composed of representatives of the national Parliaments, of the Heads of State or Government of the Member States, of the European Parliament and of the Commission. The European Central Bank shall also be consulted in the case of institutional changes in the monetary area. The Convention shall examine the proposals for amendments and shall adopt by consensus a recommendation to a conference of representatives of the governments of the Member States as provided for in paragraph 4.
The European Council may decide by a simple majority, after obtaining the consent of the European Parliament, not to convene a Convention should this not be justified by the extent of the proposed amendments. In the latter case, the European Council shall define the terms of reference for a conference of representatives of the governments of the Member States.
(4) A conference of representatives of the governments of the Member States shall be convened by the President of the Council for the purpose of determining by common accord the amendments to be made to the Treaties.
The amendments shall enter into force after being ratified by all the Member States in accordance with their respective constitutional requirements.
(5) If, two years after the signature of a treaty amending the Treaties, four fifths of the Member States have ratified it and one or more Member States have encountered difficulties in proceeding with ratification, the matter shall be referred to the European Council.
Simplified revision procedures
(6) The Government of any Member State, the European Parliament or the Commission may submit to the European Council proposals for revising all or part of the provisions of Part Three of the Treaty on the Functioning of the European Union relating to the internal policies and action of the Union.
The European Council may adopt a decision amending all or part of the provisions of Part Three of the Treaty on the Functioning of the European Union. The European Council shall act by unanimity after consulting the European Parliament and the Commission, and the European Central Bank in the case of institutional changes in the monetary area. That decision shall not enter into force until it is approved by the Member States in accordance with their respective constitutional requirements.
The decision referred to in the second subparagraph shall not increase the competences conferred on the Union in the Treaties.
(7) Where the Treaty on the Functioning of the European Union or Title V of this Treaty provides for the Council to act by unanimity in a given area or case, the European Council may adopt a decision authorising the Council to act by a qualified majority in that area or in that case. This subparagraph shall not apply to decisions with military implications or those in the area of defence.
Where the Treaty on the Functioning of the European Union provides for legislative acts to be adopted by the Council in accordance with a special legislative procedure, the European Council may adopt a decision allowing for the adoption of such acts in accordance with the ordinary legislative procedure.
Any initiative taken by the European Council on the basis of the first or the second subparagraph shall be notified to the national Parliaments. If a national Parliament makes known its opposition within six months of the date of such notification, the decision referred to in the first or the second subparagraph shall not be adopted. In the absence of opposition, the European Council may adopt the decision.
For the adoption of the decisions referred to in the first and second subparagraphs, the European Council shall act by unanimity after obtaining the consent of the European Parliament, which shall be given by a majority of its component members.

Article 49 (ex Article 49 TEU). Any European State which respects the values referred to in Article

2 and is committed to promoting them may apply to become a member of the Union. The European Parliament and national Parliaments shall be notified of this application. The applicant State shall address its application to the Council, which shall act unanimously after consulting the Commission and after receiving the consent of the European Parliament, which shall act by a majority of its component members. The conditions of eligibility agreed upon by the European Council shall be taken into account.

The conditions of admission and the adjustments to the Treaties on which the Union is founded, which such admission entails, shall be the subject of an agreement between the Member States and the applicant State. This agreement shall be submitted for ratification by all the contracting States in accordance with their respective constitutional requirements.

Article 50. (1) Any Member State may decide to withdraw from the Union in accordance with its own constitutional requirements.

(2) A Member State which decides to withdraw shall notify the European Council of its intention. In the light of the guidelines provided by the European Council, the Union shall negotiate and conclude an agreement with that State, setting out the arrangements for its withdrawal, taking account of the framework for its future relationship with the Union. That agreement shall be negotiated in accordance with Article 218(3) of the Treaty on the Functioning of the European Union. It shall be concluded on behalf of the Union by the Council, acting by a qualified majority, after obtaining the consent of the European Parliament.

(3) The Treaties shall cease to apply to the State in question from the date of entry into force of the withdrawal agreement or, failing that, two years after the notification referred to in paragraph 2, unless the European Council, in agreement with the Member State concerned, unanimously decides to extend this period.

(4) For the purposes of paragraphs 2 and 3, the member of the European Council or of the Council representing the withdrawing Member State shall not participate in the discussions of the European Council or Council or in decisions concerning it.

A qualified majority shall be defined in accordance with Article 238(3)(b) of the Treaty on the Functioning of the European Union.

(5) If a State which has withdrawn from the Union asks to rejoin, its request shall be subject to the procedure referred to in Article 49.

Article 51. The Protocols and Annexes to the Treaties shall form an integral part thereof.

Article 52. (1) The Treaties shall apply to the Kingdom of Belgium, the Republic of Bulgaria, the Czech Republic, the Kingdom of Denmark, the Federal Republic of Germany, the Republic of Estonia, Ireland, the Hellenic Republic, the Kingdom of Spain, the French Republic, the Republic of Croatia, the Italian Republic, the Republic of Cyprus, the Republic of Latvia, the Republic of Lithuania, the Grand Duchy of Luxembourg, the Republic of Hungary, the Republic of Malta, the Kingdom of the Netherlands, the Republic of Austria, the Republic of Poland, the Portuguese Republic, Romania, the Republic of Slovenia, the Slovak Republic, the Republic of Finland, the Kingdom of Sweden and the United Kingdom of Great Britain and Northern Ireland.

(2) The territorial scope of the Treaties is specified in Article 355 of the Treaty on the Functioning of the European Union.

Article 53. (ex Article 51 TEU). This Treaty is concluded for an unlimited period.

Article 54. (ex Article 52 TEU). (1) This Treaty shall be ratified by the High Contracting Parties in accordance with their respective constitutional requirements. The instruments of ratification shall be deposited with the Government of the Italian Republic.

(2) This Treaty shall enter into force on 1 January 1993, provided that all the Instruments of ratification have been deposited, or, failing that, on the first day of the month following the deposit of the Instrument of ratification by the last signatory State to take this step.

Article 55. (ex Article 53 TEU). (1) This Treaty, drawn up in a single original in the Bulgarian, Czech, Danish, Dutch, English, Estonian, Finnish, French, German, Greek, Hungarian, Irish, Italian, Latvian, Lithuanian, Maltese, Polish, Portuguese, Romanian, Slovak, Slovenian, Spanish and Swedish languages, the texts in each of these languages being equally authentic, shall be deposited in the archives of the Government of the Italian Republic, which will transmit a certified copy to each of the governments of the other signatory States.

(2) This Treaty may also be translated into any other languages as determined by Member States among those which, in accordance with their constitutional order, enjoy official status in all or part of

PART III   EUROPEAN UNION

their territory. A certified copy of such translations shall be provided by the Member States concerned to be deposited in the archives of the Council.

IN WITNESS WHEREOF the undersigned Plenipotentiaries have signed this Treaty.
Done at Maastricht on the seventh day of February in the year one thousand nine hundred and ninety–two.
[The List of signatories is not reproduced.]

TREATY ON EUROPEAN UNION

Tables of equivalences (TEU).

Treaty on European Union
Old numbering of the Treaty on European Union | New numbering of the Treaty on European Union |

TITLE I – COMMON PROVISIONS | TITLE I – COMMON PROVISIONS |
Article 1 | Article 1 |
| Article 2 |
Article 2 | Article 3 |
Article 3 (repealed) [2] | |
| Article 4 |
| Article 5 [3] |
Article 4 (repealed) [4] | |
Article 5 (repealed) [5] | |
Article 6 | Article 6 |
Article 7 | Article 7 |
| Article 8 |

TITLE II – PROVISIONS AMENDING THE TREATY ESTABLISHING THE EUROPEAN ECONOMIC COMMUNITY WITH A VIEW TO ESTABLISHING THE EUROPEAN COMMUNITY | TITLE II – PROVISIONS ON DEMOCRATIC PRINCIPLES |
Article 8 (repealed) [6] | Article 9 |
| Article 10 [7] |
| Article 11 |
| Article 12 |

TITLE III – PROVISIONS AMENDING THE TREATY ESTABLISHING THE EUROPEAN COAL AND STEEL COMMUNITY | TITLE III – PROVISIONS ON THE INSTITUTIONS |
Article 9 (repealed) [8] | Article 13 |
| Article 14 [9] |
| Article 15 [10] |
| Article 16 [11] |
| Article 17 [12] |
| Article 18 |
| Article 19 [13] |

TITLE IV – PROVISIONS AMENDING THE TREATY ESTABLISHING THE EUROPEAN ATOMIC ENERGY COMMUNITY | TITLE IV – PROVISIONS ON ENHANCED COOPERATION |
Article 10 (repealed) [14] Articles 27a to 27e (replaced) Articles 40 to 40b (replaced) Articles 43 to 45 (replaced) | Article 20 [15] |

TITLE V – PROVISIONS ON A COMMON FOREIGN AND SECURITY POLICY | TITLE V – GENERAL PROVISIONS ON THE UNION'S EXTERNAL ACTION AND SPECIFIC PROVISIONS ON THE COMMON FOREIGN AND SECURITY POLICY |
| Chapter 1 – General provisions on the Union's external action |
| Article 21 |
| Article 22 |
| Chapter 2 – Specific provisions on the common foreign and security policy |
| Section 1 – Common provisions |
| Article 23 |
Article 11 | Article 24 |
Article 12 | Article 25 |
Article 13 | Article 26 |
| Article 27 |
Article 14 | Article 28 |
Article 15 | Article 29 |
Article 22 (moved) | Article 30 |
Article 23 (moved) | Article 31 |
Article 16 | Article 32 |
Article 17 (moved) | Article 42 |
Article 18 | Article 33 |

PART III   EUROPEAN UNION

Article 19 | Article 34 |
Article 20 | Article 35 |
Article 21 | Article 36 |
Article 22 (moved) | Article 30 |
Article 23 (moved) | Article 31 |
Article 24 | Article 37 |
Article 25 | Article 38 |
| Article 39 |
Article 47 (moved) | Article 40 |
Article 26 (repealed) | |
Article 27 (repealed) | |
Article 27a (replaced) [16] | Article 20 |
Article 27b (replaced) [16] | Article 20 |
Article 27c (replaced) [16] | Article 20 |
Article 27d (replaced) [16] | Article 20 |
Article 27e (replaced) [16] | Article 20 |
Article 28 | Article 41 |
| Section 2 – Provisions on the common security and defence policy |
Article 17 (moved) | Article 42 |
| Article 43 |
| Article 44 |
| Article 45 |
| Article 46 |

TITLE VI – PROVISIONS ON POLICE AND JUDICIAL COOPERATION IN CRIMINAL MATTERS (repealed) [17] | |
Article 29 (replaced) [18] | |
Article 30 (replaced) [19] | |
Article 31 (replaced) [20] | |
|
Article 32 (replaced) [21] | |
Article 33 (replaced) [22] | |
Article 34 (repealed) | |
Article 35 (repealed) | |
Article 36 (replaced) [23] | |
Article 37 (repealed) | |
Article 38 (repealed) | |
Article 39 (repealed) | |
Article 40 (replaced) [24] | Article 20 |
Article 40 A (replaced) [24] | Article 20 |
Article 40 B (replaced) [24] | Article 20 |
Article 41 (repealed) | |
Article 42 (repealed) | |

TITLE VII – PROVISIONS ON ENHANCED COOPERATION (replaced) [25] | TITLE IV – PROVISIONS ON ENHANCED COOPERATION |
Article 43 (replaced) [25] | Article 20 |
Article 43 A (replaced) [25] | Article 20 |
Article 43 B (replaced) [25] | Article 20 |
Article 44 (replaced) [25] | Article 20 |
Article 44 A (replaced) [25] | Article 20 |
Article 45 (replaced) [25] | Article 20 |

TITLE VIII – FINAL PROVISIONS | TITLE VI – FINAL PROVISIONS |
Article 46 (repealed) | |
| Article 47 |
|
Article 47 (replaced) | Article 40 |
Article 48 | Article 48 |
Article 49 | Article 49 |
| Article 50 |

| Article 51 |
| Article 52 |
Article 50 (repealed) | |
Article 51 | Article 53 |
Article 52 | Article 54 |
Article 53 | Article 55 |

[*] Tables of equivalences as referred to in Article 5 of the Treaty of Lisbon. The original centre column, which set out the intermediate numbering as used in that Treaty, has been omitted.
[2] Replaced, in substance, by Article 7 of the Treaty on the Functioning of the European Union («TFEU») and by Articles 13(1) and 21, paragraph 3, second subparagraph of the Treaty on European Union («TEU»).
[3] Replaces Article 5 of the Treaty establishing the European Community («TEC»).
[4] Replaced, in substance, by Article 15.
[5] Replaced, in substance, by Article 13, paragraph 2.
[6] Article 8 TEU, which was in force until the entry into force of the Treaty of Lisbon (hereinafter «current»), amended the TEC. Those amendments are incorporated into the latter Treaty and Article 8 is repealed. Its number is used to insert a new provision.
[7] Paragraph 4 replaces, in substance, the first subparagraph of Article 191 TEC.
[8] The current Article 9 TEU amended the Treaty establishing the European Coal and Steel Community. This latter expired on 23 July 2002. Article 9 is repealed and the number thereof is used to insert another provision.
[9]
– Paragraphs 1 and 2 replace, in substance, Article 189 TEC;
– paragraphs 1 to 3 replace, in substance, paragraphs 1 to 3 of Article 190 TEC;
– paragraph 1 replaces, in substance, the first subparagraph of Article 192 TEC;
– paragraph 4 replaces, in substance, the first subparagraph of Article 197 TEC.
[10] Replaces, in substance, Article 4.
[11]
– Paragraph 1 replaces, in substance, the first and second indents of Article 202 TEC;
– paragraphs 2 and 9 replace, in substance, Article 203 TEC;
– paragraphs 4 and 5 replace, in substance, paragraphs 2 and 4 of Article 205 TEC.
[12]
– Paragraph 1 replaces, in substance, Article 211 TEC;
– paragraphs 3 and 7 replace, in substance, Article 214 TEC.
– paragraph 6 replaces, in substance, paragraphs 1, 3 and 4 of Article 217 TEC.
[13]
– Replaces, in substance, Article 220 TEC.
– the first subparagraph of paragraph 2 replaces, in substance, the first subparagraph of Article 221 TEC.
[14] The current Article 10 TEU amended the Treaty establishing the European Atomic Energy Community. Those amendments are incorporated into the Treaty of Lisbon. Article 10 is repealed and the number thereof is used to insert another provision.
[15] Also replaces Articles 11 and 11a TEC.
[16] The current Articles 27a to 27e, on enhanced cooperation, are also replaced by Articles 326 to 334 TFEU.
[17] The current provisions of Title VI of the TEU, on police and judicial cooperation in criminal matters, are replaced by the provisions of Chapters 1, 4 and 5 of Title IV (renumbered V) of Part Three of the TFEU.
[18] Replaced by Article 67 TFEU.
[19] Replaced by Articles 87 and 88 TFEU.
[20] Replaced by Articles 82, 83 and 85 TFEU.
[21] Replaced by Article 89 TFEU.
[22] Replaced by Article 72 TFEU.
[23] Replaced by Article 71 TFEU.
[24] The current Articles 40 to 40 B TEU, on enhanced cooperation, are also replaced by Articles 326 to 334 TFEU.
[25] The current Articles 43 to 45 and Title VII of the TEU, on enhanced cooperation, are also replaced by Articles 326 to 334 TFEU.
[26] Replaced, in substance, by Article 3 TEU.

PART III   EUROPEAN UNION

[27] Replaced, in substance, by Articles 3 to 6 TFEU.
[28] Replaced by Article 5 TEU.
[29] Insertion of the operative part of the protocol on protection and welfare of animals.
[30] Replaced, in substance, by Article 13 TEU.
[31] Replaced, in substance, by Article 13 TEU and Article 282, paragraph 1, TFEU.
[32] Replaced, in substance, by Article 4, paragraph 3, TEU.
[33] Also replaced by Article 20 TEU.
[34] Also replaces the current Article 29 TEU.
[35] Replaces the current Article 36 TEU.
[36] Also replaces the current Article 33 TEU.
[37] Points 1 and 2 of Article 63 EC are replaced by paragraphs 1 and 2 of Article 78 TFEU, and paragraph 2 of Article 64 is replaced by paragraph 3 of Article 78 TFEU.
[38] Replaces the current Article 31 TEU.
[39] Replaces the current Article 30 TEU.
[40] Replaces the current Article 32 TEU.
[41]
– Article 140, paragraph 1 takes over the wording of paragraph 1 of Article 121.
– Article 140, paragraph 2 takes over the second sentence of paragraph 2 of Article 122.
– Article 140, paragraph 3 takes over paragraph 5 of Article 123.
[42]
– Article 141, paragraph 1 takes over paragraph 3 of Article 123.
– Article 141, paragraph 2 takes over the first five indents of paragraph 2 of Article 117.
[43] Replaced, in substance, by the second sentence of the second subparagraph of paragraph 1 of Article 208 TFEU.
[44] The second sentence of the second subparagraph of paragraph 1 replaces, in substance, Article 178 TEC.
[45] Replaced, in substance, by Article 14, paragraphs 1 and 2, TEU.
[46] Replaced, in substance, by Article 14, paragraphs 1 to 3, TEU.
[47] Replaced, in substance, by Article 11, paragraph 4, TEU.
[48] Replaced, in substance, by Article 14, paragraph 1, TEU.
[49] Replaced, in substance, by Article 14, paragraph 4, TEU.
[50] Replaced, in substance, by Article 16, paragraph 1, TEU and by Articles 290 and 291 TFEU.
[51] Replaced, in substance, by Article 16, paragraphs 2 and 9 TEU.
[52] Replaced, in substance, by Article 16, paragraphs 4 and 5 TEU.
[53] Replaced, in substance, by Article 17, paragraph 1 TEU.
[54] Replaced, in substance, by Article 17, paragraphs 3 and 7 TEU.
[55] Replaced, in substance, by Article 17, paragraph 6, TEU.
[56] Replaced, in substance, by Article 295 TFEU.
[57] Replaced, in substance, by Article 19 TEU.
[58] Replaced, in substance, by Article 19, paragraph 2, first subparagraph, of the TEU.
[59] The first sentence of the first subparagraph is replaced, in substance, by Article 19, paragraph 2, second subparagraph of the TEU.
[60] Replaces, in substance, the third indent of Article 202 TEC.
[61] Replaced, in substance, by Article 300, paragraph 2 of the TFEU.
[62] Replaced, in substance, by Article 300, paragraph 4 of the TFEU.
[63] Replaced, in substance, by Article 300, paragraphs 3 and 4, TFEU.
[64] Replaced, in substance, by Article 310, paragraph 4, TFEU.
[65] Also replaces the current Articles 27a to 27e, 40 to 40b, and 43 to 45 TEU.
[66] Replaced, in substance, by Article 47 TEU.
[67] Replaced, in substance by Article 52 TEU.
[68] Replaced, in substance by Article 51 TEU.
[69] Replaced, in substance by Article 55 TEU.

Treaty on the Functioning of the European Union.
Consolidated Version as published in the Official Journal of the European Union on 26 October 2012.
The text of the consolidated version is reproduced, followed by Protocols, Annexes, Declarations annexed to the Final Act of the Intergovernmental Conference which adopted the Treaty of Lisbon, signed on 13 December 2007, and tables of equivalences.

HIS MAJESTY THE KING OF THE BELGIANS, THE PRESIDENT OF THE FEDERAL REPUBLIC OF GERMANY, THE PRESIDENT OF THE FRENCH REPUBLIC, THE PRESIDENT OF THE ITALIAN REPUBLIC, HER ROYAL HIGHNESS THE GRAND DUCHESS OF LUXEMBOURG, HER MAJESTY THE QUEEN OF THE NETHERLANDS[1],

DETERMINED to lay the foundations of an ever closer union among the peoples of Europe,
RESOLVED to ensure the economic and social progress of their States by common action to eliminate the barriers which divide Europe,
AFFIRMING as the essential objective of their efforts the constant improvements of the living and working conditions of their peoples,
RECOGNISING that the removal of existing obstacles calls for concerted action in order to guarantee steady expansion, balanced trade and fair competition,
ANXIOUS to strengthen the unity of their economies and to ensure their harmonious development by reducing the differences existing between the various regions and the backwardness of the less favoured regions,
DESIRING to contribute, by means of a common commercial policy, to the progressive abolition of restrictions on international trade,
INTENDING to confirm the solidarity which binds Europe and the overseas countries and desiring to ensure the development of their prosperity, in accordance with the principles of the Charter of the United Nations,
RESOLVED by thus pooling their resources to preserve and strengthen peace and liberty, and calling upon the other peoples of Europe who share their ideal to join in their efforts,
DETERMINED to promote the development of the highest possible level of knowledge for their peoples through a wide access to education and through its continuous updating,
and to this end HAVE DESIGNATED as their Plenipotentiaries:
[List of plenipotentiaries not reproduced]
WHO, having exchanged their full powers, found in good and due form, have agreed as follows.

Part One. Principles

Article 1. (1) This Treaty organises the functioning of the Union and determines the areas of, delimitation of, and arrangements for exercising its competences.
(2) This Treaty and the Treaty on European Union constitute the Treaties on which the Union is founded. These two Treaties, which have the same legal value, shall be referred to as "the Treaties".

Title I. Categories and Areas of Union Competence

Article 2. (1) When the Treaties confer on the Union exclusive competence in a specific area, only the Union may legislate and adopt legally binding acts, the Member States being able to do so themselves only if so empowered by the Union or for the implementation of Union acts.
(2) When the Treaties confer on the Union a competence shared with the Member States in a specific area, the Union and the Member States may legislate and adopt legally binding acts in that area. The Member States shall exercise their competence to the extent that the Union has not exercised its competence. The Member States shall again exercise their competence to the extent that the Union has decided to cease exercising its competence.
(3) The Member States shall coordinate their economic and employment policies within arrangements as determined by this Treaty, which the Union shall have competence to provide.
(4) The Union shall have competence, in accordance with the provisions of the Treaty on European

---

[1] The Republic of Bulgaria, the Czech Republic, the Kingdom of Denmark, the Republic of Estonia, Ireland, the Hellenic Republic, the Kingdom of Spain, the Republic of Cyprus, the Republic of Latvia, the Republic of Lithuania, the Republic of Hungary, the Republic of Malta, the Republic of Austria, the Republic of Poland, the Portuguese Republic, Romania, the Republic of Slovenia, the Slovak Republic, the Republic of Finland, the Kingdom of Sweden and the United Kingdom of Great Britain and Norther Ireland have since become members of the European Union.

PART III EUROPEAN UNION

Union, to define and implement a common foreign and security policy, including the progressive framing of a common defence policy.

(5) In certain areas and under the conditions laid down in the Treaties, the Union shall have competence to carry out actions to support, coordinate or supplement the actions of the Member States, without thereby superseding their competence in these areas.

Legally binding acts of the Union adopted on the basis of the provisions of the Treaties relating to these areas shall not entail harmonisation of Member States' laws or regulations.

(6) The scope of and arrangements for exercising the Union's competences shall be determined by the provisions of the Treaties relating to each area.

Article 3. (1) The Union shall have exclusive competence in the following areas:
(a) customs union;
(b) the establishing of the competition rules necessary for the functioning of the internal market;
(c) monetary policy for the Member States whose currency is the euro;
(d) the conservation of marine biological resources under the common fisheries policy;
(e) common commercial policy.
(2) The Union shall also have exclusive competence for the conclusion of an international agreement when its conclusion is provided for in a legislative act of the Union or is necessary to enable the Union to exercise its internal competence, or in so far as its conclusion may affect common rules or alter their scope.

Article 4. (1) The Union shall share competence with the Member States where the Treaties confer on it a competence which does not relate to the areas referred to in Articles 3 and 6.
(2) Shared competence between the Union and the Member States applies in the following principal areas:
(a) internal market;
(b) social policy, for the aspects defined in this Treaty;
(c) economic, social and territorial cohesion;
(d) agriculture and fisheries, excluding the conservation of marine biological resources;
(e) environment;
(f) consumer protection;
(g) transport;
(h) trans–European networks;
(i) energy;
(j) area of freedom, security and justice;
(k) common safety concerns in public health matters, for the aspects defined in this Treaty.
(3) In the areas of research, technological development and space, the Union shall have competence to carry out activities, in particular to define and implement programmes; however, the exercise of that competence shall not result in Member States being prevented from exercising theirs.
(4) In the areas of development cooperation and humanitarian aid, the Union shall have competence to carry out activities and conduct a common policy; however, the exercise of that competence shall not result in Member States being prevented from exercising theirs.

Article 5. (1) The Member States shall coordinate their economic policies within the Union. To this end, the Council shall adopt measures, in particular broad guidelines for these policies.
Specific provisions shall apply to those Member States whose currency is the euro.
(2) The Union shall take measures to ensure coordination of the employment policies of the Member States, in particular by defining guidelines for these policies.
(3) The Union may take initiatives to ensure coordination of Member States' social policies.

Article 6. The Union shall have competence to carry out actions to support, coordinate or supplement the actions of the Member States. The areas of such action shall, at European level, be:
(a) protection and improvement of human health;
(b) industry;
(c) culture;
(d) tourism;
(e) education, vocational training, youth and sport;
(f) civil protection;
(g) administrative cooperation.

Title II. Provisions Having General Application

Article 7. The Union shall ensure consistency between its policies and activities, taking all of its objectives into account and in accordance with the principle of conferral of powers.

Article 8 (ex Article 3(2) TEC)[1]. In all its activities, the Union shall aim to eliminate inequalities, and to promote equality, between men and women.

Article 9. In defining and implementing its policies and activities, the Union shall take into account requirements linked to the promotion of a high level of employment, the guarantee of adequate social protection, the fight against social exclusion, and a high level of education, training and protection of human health.

Article 10. In defining and implementing its policies and activities, the Union shall aim to combat discrimination based on sex, racial or ethnic origin, religion or belief, disability, age or sexual orientation.

Article 11 (ex Article 6 TEC). Environmental protection requirements must be integrated into the definition and implementation of the Union's policies and activities, in particular with a view to promoting sustainable development.

Article 12 (ex Article 153(2) TEC). Consumer protection requirements shall be taken into account in defining and implementing other Union policies and activities.

Article 13. In formulating and implementing the Union's agriculture, fisheries, transport, internal market, research and technological development and space policies, the Union and the Member States shall, since animals are sentient beings, pay full regard to the welfare requirements of animals, while respecting the legislative or administrative provisions and customs of the Member States relating in particular to religious rites, cultural traditions and regional heritage.

Article 14 (ex Article 16 TEC). Without prejudice to Article 4 of the Treaty on European Union or to Articles 93, 106 and 107 of this Treaty, and given the place occupied by services of general economic interest in the shared values of the Union as well as their role in promoting social and territorial cohesion, the Union and the Member States, each within their respective powers and within the scope of application of the Treaties, shall take care that such services operate on the basis of principles and conditions, particularly economic and financial conditions, which enable them to fulfil their missions. The European Parliament and the Council, acting by means of regulations in accordance with the ordinary legislative procedure, shall establish these principles and set these conditions without prejudice to the competence of Member States, in compliance with the Treaties, to provide, to commission and to fund such services.

Article 15 (ex Article 255 TEC). (1) In order to promote good governance and ensure the participation of civil society, the Union's institutions, bodies, offices and agencies shall conduct their work as openly as possible.
(2) The European Parliament shall meet in public, as shall the Council when considering and voting on a draft legislative act.
(3) Any citizen of the Union, and any natural or legal person residing or having its registered office in a Member State, shall have a right of access to documents of the Union's institutions, bodies, offices and agencies, whatever their medium, subject to the principles and the conditions to be defined in accordance with this paragraph.
General principles and limits on grounds of public or private interest governing this right of access to documents shall be determined by the European Parliament and the Council, by means of regulations, acting in accordance with the ordinary legislative procedure.
Each institution, body, office or agency shall ensure that its proceedings are transparent and shall elaborate in its own Rules of Procedure specific provisions regarding access to its documents, in accordance with the regulations referred to in the second subparagraph.
The Court of Justice of the European Union, the European Central Bank and the European Investment Bank shall be subject to this paragraph only when exercising their administrative tasks.
The European Parliament and the Council shall ensure publication of the documents relating to the legislative procedures under the terms laid down by the regulations referred to in the second subparagraph.

Article 16 (ex Article 286 TEC). (1) Everyone has the right to the protection of personal data concerning them.
(2) The European Parliament and the Council, acting in accordance with the ordinary legislative pro-

---

[1] These references are merely indicative. For ample information, please refer to the tables of equivalences between the old and the new numbering of the Treaties.

cedure, shall lay down the rules relating to the protection of individuals with regard to the processing of personal data by Union institutions, bodies, offices and agencies, and by the Member States when carrying out activities which fall within the scope of Union law, and the rules relating to the free movement of such data. Compliance with these rules shall be subject to the control of independent authorities.

The rules adopted on the basis of this Article shall be without prejudice to the specific rules laid down in Article 39 of the Treaty on European Union.

Article 17. (1) The Union respects and does not prejudice the status under national law of churches and religious associations or communities in the Member States.

(2) The Union equally respects the status under national law of philosophical and non–confessional organisations.

(3) Recognising their identity and their specific contribution, the Union shall maintain an open, transparent and regular dialogue with these churches and organisations.

Part Two. Non–Discrimination and Citizenship of the Union

Article 18 (ex Article 12 TEC). Within the scope of application of the Treaties, and without prejudice to any special provisions contained therein, any discrimination on grounds of nationality shall be prohibited.

The European Parliament and the Council, acting in accordance with the ordinary legislative procedure, may adopt rules designed to prohibit such discrimination.

Article 19 (ex Article 13 TEC). (1) Without prejudice to the other provisions of the Treaties and within the limits of the powers conferred by them upon the Union, the Council, acting unanimously in accordance with a special legislative procedure and after obtaining the consent of the European Parliament, may take appropriate action to combat discrimination based on sex, racial or ethnic origin, religion or belief, disability, age or sexual orientation.

(2) By way of derogation from paragraph 1, the European Parliament and the Council, acting in accordance with the ordinary legislative procedure, may adopt the basic principles of Union incentive measures, excluding any harmonisation of the laws and regulations of the Member States, to support action taken by the Member States in order to contribute to the achievement of the objectives referred to in paragraph 1.

Article 20 (ex Article 17 TEC). (1) Citizenship of the Union is hereby established. Every person holding the nationality of a Member State shall be a citizen of the Union. Citizenship of the Union shall be additional to and not replace national citizenship.

(2) Citizens of the Union shall enjoy the rights and be subject to the duties provided for in the Treaties. They shall have, inter alia:

(a) the right to move and reside freely within the territory of the Member States;

(b) the right to vote and to stand as candidates in elections to the European Parliament and in municipal elections in their Member State of residence, under the same conditions as nationals of that State;

(c) the right to enjoy, in the territory of a third country in which the Member State of which they are nationals is not represented, the protection of the diplomatic and consular authorities of any Member State on the same conditions as the nationals of that State;

(d) the right to petition the European Parliament, to apply to the European Ombudsman, and to address the institutions and advisory bodies of the Union in any of the Treaty languages and to obtain a reply in the same language.

These rights shall be exercised in accordance with the conditions and limits defined by the Treaties and by the measures adopted thereunder.

Article 21 (ex Article 18 TEC). (1) Every citizen of the Union shall have the right to move and reside freely within the territory of the Member States, subject to the limitations and conditions laid down in the Treaties and by the measures adopted to give them effect.

(2) If action by the Union should prove necessary to attain this objective and the Treaties have not provided the necessary powers, the European Parliament and the Council, acting in accordance with the ordinary legislative procedure, may adopt provisions with a view to facilitating the exercise of the rights referred to in paragraph 1.

(3) For the same purposes as those referred to in paragraph 1 and if the Treaties have not provided the necessary powers, the Council, acting in accordance with a special legislative procedure, may adopt measures concerning social security or social protection. The Council shall act unanimously after consulting the European Parliament.

Article 22 (ex Article 19 TEC). (1) Every citizen of the Union residing in a Member State of which he is not a national shall have the right to vote and to stand as a candidate at municipal elections in the Member State in which he resides, under the same conditions as nationals of that State. This right shall be exercised subject to detailed arrangements adopted by the Council, acting unanimously in accordance with a special legislative procedure and after consulting the European Parliament; these arrangements may provide for derogations where warranted by problems specific to a Member State.
(2) Without prejudice to Article 223(1) and to the provisions adopted for its implementation, every citizen of the Union residing in a Member State of which he is not a national shall have the right to vote and to stand as a candidate in elections to the European Parliament in the Member State in which he resides, under the same conditions as nationals of that State. This right shall be exercised subject to detailed arrangements adopted by the Council, acting unanimously in accordance with a special legislative procedure and after consulting the European Parliament; these arrangements may provide for derogations where warranted by problems specific to a Member State.

Article 23 (ex Article 20 TEC). Every citizen of the Union shall, in the territory of a third country in which the Member State of which he is a national is not represented, be entitled to protection by the diplomatic or consular authorities of any Member State, on the same conditions as the nationals of that State. Member States shall adopt the necessary provisions and start the international negotiations required to secure this protection.
The Council, acting in accordance with a special legislative procedure and after consulting the European Parliament, may adopt directives establishing the coordination and cooperation measures necessary to facilitate such protection.

Article 24 (ex Article 21 TEC). The European Parliament and the Council, acting by means of regulations in accordance with the ordinary legislative procedure, shall adopt the provisions for the procedures and conditions required for a citizens' initiative within the meaning of Article 11 of the Treaty on European Union, including the minimum number of Member States from which such citizens must come.
Every citizen of the Union shall have the right to petition the European Parliament in accordance with Article 227.
Every citizen of the Union may apply to the Ombudsman established in accordance with Article 228.
Every citizen of the Union may write to any of the institutions or bodies referred to in this Article or in Article 13 of the Treaty on European Union in one of the languages mentioned in Article 55(1) of the Treaty on European Union and have an answer in the same language.

Article 25 (ex Article 22 TEC). The Commission shall report to the European Parliament, to the Council and to the Economic and Social Committee every three years on the application of the provisions of this Part. This report shall take account of the development of the Union.
On this basis, and without prejudice to the other provisions of the Treaties, the Council, acting unanimously in accordance with a special legislative procedure and after obtaining the consent of the European Parliament, may adopt provisions to strengthen or to add to the rights listed in Article 20(2). These provisions shall enter into force after their approval by the Member States in accordance with their respective constitutional requirements.

Part Three. Union Policies and Internal Actions

Title I. The Internal Market

Article 26 (ex Article 14 TEC). (1) The Union shall adopt measures with the aim of establishing or ensuring the functioning of the internal market, in accordance with the relevant provisions of the Treaties.
(2) The internal market shall comprise an area without internal frontiers in which the free movement of goods, persons, services and capital is ensured in accordance with the provisions of the Treaties.
(3) The Council, on a proposal from the Commission, shall determine the guidelines and conditions necessary to ensure balanced progress in all the sectors concerned.

Article 27 (ex Article 15 TEC). When drawing up its proposals with a view to achieving the objectives set out in Article 26, the Commission shall take into account the extent of the effort that certain economies showing differences in development will have to sustain for the establishment of the internal market and it may propose appropriate provisions.
If these provisions take the form of derogations, they must be of a temporary nature and must cause the least possible disturbance to the functioning of the internal market.

PART III   EUROPEAN UNION

Title II. Free Movement of Goods

Article 28 (ex Article 23 TEC). (1) The Union shall comprise a customs union which shall cover all trade in goods and which shall involve the prohibition between Member States of customs duties on imports and exports and of all charges having equivalent effect, and the adoption of a common customs tariff in their relations with third countries.
(2) The provisions of Article 30 and of Chapter 3 of this Title shall apply to products originating in Member States and to products coming from third countries which are in free circulation in Member States.

Article 29 (ex Article 24 TEC). Products coming from a third country shall be considered to be in free circulation in a Member State if the import formalities have been complied with and any customs duties or charges having equivalent effect which are payable have been levied in that Member State, and if they have not benefited from a total or partial drawback of such duties or charges.

Chapter 1. The Customs Union

Article 30 (ex Article 25 TEC). Customs duties on imports and exports and charges having equivalent effect shall be prohibited between Member States. This prohibition shall also apply to customs duties of a fiscal nature.

Article 31 (ex Article 26 TEC). Common Customs Tariff duties shall be fixed by the Council on a proposal from the Commission.

Article 32 (ex Article 27 TEC). In carrying out the tasks entrusted to it under this Chapter the Commission shall be guided by:
(a) the need to promote trade between Member States and third countries;
(b) developments in conditions of competition within the Union in so far as they lead to an improvement in the competitive capacity of undertakings;
(c) the requirements of the Union as regards the supply of raw materials and semi–finished goods; in this connection the Commission shall take care to avoid distorting conditions of competition between Member States in respect of finished goods;
(d) the need to avoid serious disturbances in the economies of Member States and to ensure rational development of production and an expansion of consumption within the Union.

Chapter 2. Customs Cooperation

Article 33 (ex Article 135 TEC). Within the scope of application of the Treaties, the European Parliament and the Council, acting in accordance with the ordinary legislative procedure, shall take measures in order to strengthen customs cooperation between Member States and between the latter and the Commission.

Chapter 3. Prohibition of Quantitative Restrictions between Member States

Article 34 (ex Article 28 TEC). Quantitative restrictions on imports and all measures having equivalent effect shall be prohibited between Member States.

Article 35 (ex Article 29 TEC). Quantitative restrictions on exports, and all measures having equivalent effect, shall be prohibited between Member States.

Article 36 (ex Article 30 TEC). The provisions of Articles 34 and 35 shall not preclude prohibitions or restrictions on imports, exports or goods in transit justified on grounds of public morality, public policy or public security; the protection of health and life of humans, animals or plants; the protection of national treasures possessing artistic, historic or archaeological value; or the protection of industrial and commercial property. Such prohibitions or restrictions shall not, however, constitute a means of arbitrary discrimination or a disguised restriction on trade between Member States.

Article 37 (ex Article 31 TEC). (1) Member States shall adjust any State monopolies of a commercial character so as to ensure that no discrimination regarding the conditions under which goods are procured and marketed exists between nationals of Member States.
The provisions of this Article shall apply to any body through which a Member State, in law or in fact, either directly or indirectly supervises, determines or appreciably influences imports or exports between Member States. These provisions shall likewise apply to monopolies delegated by the State to others.
(2) Member States shall refrain from introducing any new measure which is contrary to the principles

TREATY ON THE FUNCTIONING OF THE EU

laid down in paragraph 1 or which restricts the scope of the articles dealing with the prohibition of customs duties and quantitative restrictions between Member States.
(3) If a State monopoly of a commercial character has rules which are designed to make it easier to dispose of agricultural products or obtain for them the best return, steps should be taken in applying the rules contained in this Article to ensure equivalent safeguards for the employment and standard of living of the producers concerned.

Title III. Agriculture and Fisheries

Article 38 (ex Article 32 TEC). (1) The Union shall define and implement a common agriculture and fisheries policy.
The internal market shall extend to agriculture, fisheries and trade in agricultural products. "Agricultural products" means the products of the soil, of stockfarming and of fisheries and products of first-stage processing directly related to these products. References to the common agricultural policy or to agriculture, and the use of the term "agricultural", shall be understood as also referring to fisheries, having regard to the specific characteristics of this sector.
(2) Save as otherwise provided in Articles 39 to 44, the rules laid down for the establishment and functioning of the internal market shall apply to agricultural products.
(3) The products subject to the provisions of Articles 39 to 44 are listed in Annex I.
(4) The operation and development of the internal market for agricultural products must be accompanied by the establishment of a common agricultural policy.

Article 39 (ex Article 33 TEC). (1) The objectives of the common agricultural policy shall be:
(a) to increase agricultural productivity by promoting technical progress and by ensuring the rational development of agricultural production and the optimum utilisation of the factors of production, in particular labour;
(b) thus to ensure a fair standard of living for the agricultural community, in particular by increasing the individual earnings of persons engaged in agriculture;
(c) to stabilise markets;
(d) to assure the availability of supplies;
(e) to ensure that supplies reach consumers at reasonable prices.
(2) In working out the common agricultural policy and the special methods for its application, account shall be taken of:
(a) the particular nature of agricultural activity, which results from the social structure of agriculture and from structural and natural disparities between the various agricultural regions;
(b) the need to effect the appropriate adjustments by degrees;
(c) the fact that in the Member States agriculture constitutes a sector closely linked with the economy as a whole.

Article 40 (ex Article 34 TEC). (1) In order to attain the objectives set out in Article 39, a common organisation of agricultural markets shall be established.
This organisation shall take one of the following forms, depending on the product concerned:
(a) common rules on competition;
(b) compulsory coordination of the various national market organisations;
(c) a European market organisation.
(2) The common organisation established in accordance with paragraph 1 may include all measures required to attain the objectives set out in Article 39, in particular regulation of prices, aids for the production and marketing of the various products, storage and carryover arrangements and common machinery for stabilising imports or exports.
The common organisation shall be limited to pursuit of the objectives set out in Article 39 and shall exclude any discrimination between producers or consumers within the Union.
Any common price policy shall be based on common criteria and uniform methods of calculation.
(3) In order to enable the common organisation referred to in paragraph 1 to attain its objectives, one or more agricultural guidance and guarantee funds may be set up.

Article 41 (ex Article 35 TEC). To enable the objectives set out in Article 39 to be attained, provision may be made within the framework of the common agricultural policy for measures such as:
(a) an effective coordination of efforts in the spheres of vocational training, of research and of the dissemination of agricultural knowledge; this may include joint financing of projects or institutions;
(b) joint measures to promote consumption of certain products.

Article 42 (ex Article 36 TEC). The provisions of the Chapter relating to rules on competition shall

apply to production of and trade in agricultural products only to the extent determined by the European Parliament and the Council within the framework of Article 43(2) and in accordance with the procedure laid down therein, account being taken of the objectives set out in Article 39.
The Council, on a proposal from the Commission, may authorise the granting of aid:
(a) for the protection of enterprises handicapped by structural or natural conditions;
(b) within the framework of economic development programmes.

Article 43 (ex Article 37 TEC). (1) The Commission shall submit proposals for working out and implementing the common agricultural policy, including the replacement of the national organisations by one of the forms of common organisation provided for in Article 40(1), and for implementing the measures specified in this Title.
These proposals shall take account of the interdependence of the agricultural matters mentioned in this Title.
(2) The European Parliament and the Council, acting in accordance with the ordinary legislative procedure and after consulting the Economic and Social Committee, shall establish the common organisation of agricultural markets provided for in Article 40(1) and the other provisions necessary for the pursuit of the objectives of the common agricultural policy and the common fisheries policy.
(3) The Council, on a proposal from the Commission, shall adopt measures on fixing prices, levies, aid and quantitative limitations and on the fixing and allocation of fishing opportunities.
(4) In accordance with paragraph 2, the national market organisations may be replaced by the common organisation provided for in Article 40(1) if:
(a) the common organisation offers Member States which are opposed to this measure and which have an organisation of their own for the production in question equivalent safeguards for the employment and standard of living of the producers concerned, account being taken of the adjustments that will be possible and the specialisation that will be needed with the passage of time;
(b) such an organisation ensures conditions for trade within the Union similar to those existing in a national market.
(5) If a common organisation for certain raw materials is established before a common organisation exists for the corresponding processed products, such raw materials as are used for processed products intended for export to third countries may be imported from outside the Union.

Article 44 (ex Article 38 TEC). Where in a Member State a product is subject to a national market organisation or to internal rules having equivalent effect which affect the competitive position of similar production in another Member State, a countervailing charge shall be applied by Member States to imports of this product coming from the Member State where such organisation or rules exist, unless that State applies a countervailing charge on export.
The Commission shall fix the amount of these charges at the level required to redress the balance; it may also authorise other measures, the conditions and details of which it shall determine.

Title IV. Free Movement of Persons, Services and Capital

Chapter 1. Workers

Article 45 (ex Article 39 TEC). (1) Freedom of movement for workers shall be secured within the Union.
(2) Such freedom of movement shall entail the abolition of any discrimination based on nationality between workers of the Member States as regards employment, remuneration and other conditions of work and employment.
(3) It shall entail the right, subject to limitations justified on grounds of public policy, public security or public health:
(a) to accept offers of employment actually made;
(b) to move freely within the territory of Member States for this purpose;
(c) to stay in a Member State for the purpose of employment in accordance with the provisions governing the employment of nationals of that State laid down by law, regulation or administrative action;
(d) to remain in the territory of a Member State after having been employed in that State, subject to conditions which shall be embodied in regulations to be drawn up by the Commission.
(4) The provisions of this Article shall not apply to employment in the public service.

Article 46 (ex Article 40 TEC). The European Parliament and the Council shall, acting in accordance with the ordinary legislative procedure and after consulting the Economic and Social Committee, issue directives or make regulations setting out the measures required to bring about freedom of

movement for workers, as defined in Article 45, in particular:
(a) by ensuring close cooperation between national employment services;
(b) by abolishing those administrative procedures and practices and those qualifying periods in respect of eligibility for available employment, whether resulting from national legislation or from agreements previously concluded between Member States, the maintenance of which would form an obstacle to liberalisation of the movement of workers;
(c) by abolishing all such qualifying periods and other restrictions provided for either under national legislation or under agreements previously concluded between Member States as imposed on workers of other Member States conditions regarding the free choice of employment other than those imposed on workers of the State concerned;
(d) by setting up appropriate machinery to bring offers of employment into touch with applications for employment and to facilitate the achievement of a balance between supply and demand in the employment market in such a way as to avoid serious threats to the standard of living and level of employment in the various regions and industries.

Article 47 (ex Article 41 TEC). Member States shall, within the framework of a joint programme, encourage the exchange of young workers.

Article 48 (ex Article 42 TEC). The European Parliament and the Council shall, acting in accordance with the ordinary legislative procedure, adopt such measures in the field of social security as are necessary to provide freedom of movement for workers; to this end, they shall make arrangements to secure for employed and self–employed migrant workers and their dependants:
(a) aggregation, for the purpose of acquiring and retaining the right to benefit and of calculating the amount of benefit, of all periods taken into account under the laws of the several countries;
(b) payment of benefits to persons resident in the territories of Member States.
Where a member of the Council declares that a draft legislative act referred to in the first subparagraph would affect important aspects of its social security system, including its scope, cost or financial structure, or would affect the financial balance of that system, it may request that the matter be referred to the European Council. In that case, the ordinary legislative procedure shall be suspended. After discussion, the European Council shall, within four months of this suspension, either:
(a) refer the draft back to the Council, which shall terminate the suspension of the ordinary legislative procedure; or
(b) take no action or request the Commission to submit a new proposal; in that case, the act originally proposed shall be deemed not to have been adopted.

Chapter 2. Right of Establishment

Article 49 (ex Article 43 TEC). Within the framework of the provisions set out below, restrictions on the freedom of establishment of nationals of a Member State in the territory of another Member State shall be prohibited. Such prohibition shall also apply to restrictions on the setting–up of agencies, branches or subsidiaries by nationals of any Member State established in the territory of any Member State.
Freedom of establishment shall include the right to take up and pursue activities as self–employed persons and to set up and manage undertakings, in particular companies or firms within the meaning of the second paragraph of Article 54, under the conditions laid down for its own nationals by the law of the country where such establishment is effected, subject to the provisions of the Chapter relating to capital.

Article 50 (ex Article 44 TEC). (1) In order to attain freedom of establishment as regards a particular activity, the European Parliament and the Council, acting in accordance with the ordinary legislative procedure and after consulting the Economic and Social Committee, shall act by means of directives.
(2) The European Parliament, the Council and the Commission shall carry out the duties devolving upon them under the preceding provisions, in particular:
(a) by according, as a general rule, priority treatment to activities where freedom of establishment makes a particularly valuable contribution to the development of production and trade;
(b) by ensuring close cooperation between the competent authorities in the Member States in order to ascertain the particular situation within the Union of the various activities concerned;
(c) by abolishing those administrative procedures and practices, whether resulting from national legislation or from agreements previously concluded between Member States, the maintenance of which would form an obstacle to freedom of establishment;
(d) by ensuring that workers of one Member State employed in the territory of another Member State

may remain in that territory for the purpose of taking up activities therein as self–employed persons, where they satisfy the conditions which they would be required to satisfy if they were entering that State at the time when they intended to take up such activities;

(e) by enabling a national of one Member State to acquire and use land and buildings situated in the territory of another Member State, in so far as this does not conflict with the principles laid down in Article 39(2);

(f) by effecting the progressive abolition of restrictions on freedom of establishment in every branch of activity under consideration, both as regards the conditions for setting up agencies, branches or subsidiaries in the territory of a Member State and as regards the subsidiaries in the territory of a Member State and as regards the conditions governing the entry of personnel belonging to the main establishment into managerial or supervisory posts in such agencies, branches or subsidiaries;

(g) by coordinating to the necessary extent the safeguards which, for the protection of the interests of members and others, are required by Member States of companies or firms within the meaning of the second paragraph of Article 54 with a view to making such safeguards equivalent throughout the Union;

(h) by satisfying themselves that the conditions of establishment are not distorted by aids granted by Member States.

Article 51 (ex Article 45 TEC). The provisions of this Chapter shall not apply, so far as any given Member State is concerned, to activities which in that State are connected, even occasionally, with the exercise of official authority.

The European Parliament and the Council, acting in accordance with the ordinary legislative procedure, may rule that the provisions of this Chapter shall not apply to certain activities.

Article 52 (ex Article 46 TEC). (1) The provisions of this Chapter and measures taken in pursuance thereof shall not prejudice the applicability of provisions laid down by law, regulation or administrative action providing for special treatment for foreign nationals on grounds of public policy, public security or public health.

(2) The European Parliament and the Council shall, acting in accordance with the ordinary legislative procedure, issue directives for the coordination of the abovementioned provisions.

Article 53 (ex Article 47 TEC). (1) In order to make it easier for persons to take up and pursue activities as self–employed persons, the European Parliament and the Council shall, acting in accordance with the ordinary legislative procedure, issue directives for the mutual recognition of diplomas, certificates and other evidence of formal qualifications and for the coordination of the provisions laid down by law, regulation or administrative action in Member States concerning the taking–up and pursuit of activities as self–employed persons.

(2) In the case of the medical and allied and pharmaceutical professions, the progressive abolition of restrictions shall be dependent upon coordination of the conditions for their exercise in the various Member States.

Article 54 (ex Article 48 TEC). Companies or firms formed in accordance with the law of a Member State and having their registered office, central administration or principal place of business within the Union shall, for the purposes of this Chapter, be treated in the same way as natural persons who are nationals of Member States.

"Companies or firms" means companies or firms constituted under civil or commercial law, including cooperative societies, and other legal persons governed by public or private law, save for those which are non–profit–making.

Article 55 (ex Article 294 TEC). Member States shall accord nationals of the other Member States the same treatment as their own nationals as regards participation in the capital of companies or firms within the meaning of Article 54, without prejudice to the application of the other provisions of the Treaties.

Chapter 3. Services

Article 56 (ex Article 49 TEC). Within the framework of the provisions set out below, restrictions on freedom to provide services within the Union shall be prohibited in respect of nationals of Member States who are established in a Member State other than that of the person for whom the services are intended.

The European Parliament and the Council, acting in accordance with the ordinary legislative procedure, may extend the provisions of the Chapter to nationals of a third country who provide services and who are established within the Union.

TREATY ON THE FUNCTIONING OF THE EU

Article 57 (ex Article 50 TEC). Services shall be considered to be "services" within the meaning of the Treaties where they are normally provided for remuneration, in so far as they are not governed by the provisions relating to freedom of movement for goods, capital and persons.
"Services" shall in particular include:
(a) activities of an industrial character;
(b) activities of a commercial character;
(c) activities of craftsmen;
(d) activities of the professions.
Without prejudice to the provisions of the Chapter relating to the right of establishment, the person providing a service may, in order to do so, temporarily pursue his activity in the Member State where the service is provided, under the same conditions as are imposed by that State on its own nationals.

Article 58 (ex Article 51 TEC). (1) Freedom to provide services in the field of transport shall be governed by the provisions of the Title relating to transport.
(2) The liberalisation of banking and insurance services connected with movements of capital shall be effected in step with the liberalisation of movement of capital.

Article 59 (ex Article 52 TEC). (1) In order to achieve the liberalisation of a specific service, the European Parliament and the Council, acting in accordance with the ordinary legislative procedure and after consulting the Economic and Social Committee, shall issue directives.
(2) As regards the directives referred to in paragraph 1, priority shall as a general rule be given to those services which directly affect production costs or the liberalisation of which helps to promote trade in goods.

Article 60 (ex Article 53 TEC). The Member States shall endeavour to undertake the liberalisation of services beyond the extent required by the directives issued pursuant to Article 59(1), if their general economic situation and the situation of the economic sector concerned so permit.
To this end, the Commission shall make recommendations to the Member States concerned.

Article 61 (ex Article 54 TEC). As long as restrictions on freedom to provide services have not been abolished, each Member State shall apply such restrictions without distinction on grounds of nationality or residence to all persons providing services within the meaning of the first paragraph of Article 56.

Article 62 (ex Article 55 TEC). The provisions of Articles 51 to 54 shall apply to the matters covered by this Chapter.

Chapter 4. Capital and Payments

Article 63 (ex Article 56 TEC). (1) Within the framework of the provisions set out in this Chapter, all restrictions on the movement of capital between Member States and between Member States and third countries shall be prohibited.
(2) Within the framework of the provisions set out in this Chapter, all restrictions on payments between Member States and between Member States and third countries shall be prohibited.

Article 64 (ex Article 57 TEC). (1) The provisions of Article 63 shall be without prejudice to the application to third countries of any restrictions which exist on 31 December 1993 under national or Union law adopted in respect of the movement of capital to or from third countries involving direct investment – including in real estate – establishment, the provision of financial services or the admission of securities to capital markets. In respect of restrictions existing under national law in Bulgaria, Estonia and Hungary, the relevant date shall be 31 December 1999. In respect of restrictions existing under national law in Croatia, the relevant date shall be 31 December 2002.
(2) Whilst endeavouring to achieve the objective of free movement of capital between Member States and third countries to the greatest extent possible and without prejudice to the other Chapters of the Treaties, the European Parliament and the Council, acting in accordance with the ordinary legislative procedure, shall adopt the measures on the movement of capital to or from third countries involving direct investment – including investment in real estate – establishment, the provision of financial services or the admission of securities to capital markets.
(3) Notwithstanding paragraph 2, only the Council, acting in accordance with a special legislative procedure, may unanimously, and after consulting the European Parliament, adopt measures which constitute a step backwards in Union law as regards the liberalisation of the movement of capital to or from third countries.

Article 65 (ex Article 58 TEC). (1) The provisions of Article 63 shall be without prejudice to the right of Member States:

(a) to apply the relevant provisions of their tax law which distinguish between taxpayers who are not in the same situation with regard to their place of residence or with regard to the place where their capital is invested;
(b) to take all requisite measures to prevent infringements of national law and regulations, in particular in the field of taxation and the prudential supervision of financial institutions, or to lay down procedures for the declaration of capital movements for purposes of administrative or statistical information, or to take measures which are justified on grounds of public policy or public security.
(2) The provisions of this Chapter shall be without prejudice to the applicability of restrictions on the right of establishment which are compatible with the Treaties.
(3) The measures and procedures referred to in paragraphs 1 and 2 shall not constitute a means of arbitrary discrimination or a disguised restriction on the free movement of capital and payments as defined in Article 63.
(4) In the absence of measures pursuant to Article 64(3), the Commission or, in the absence of a Commission decision within three months from the request of the Member State concerned, the Council, may adopt a decision stating that restrictive tax measures adopted by a Member State concerning one or more third countries are to be considered compatible with the Treaties in so far as they are justified by one of the objectives of the Union and compatible with the proper functioning of the internal market. The Council shall act unanimously on application by a Member State.

Article 66 (ex Article 59 TEC). Where, in exceptional circumstances, movements of capital to or from third countries cause, or threaten to cause, serious difficulties for the operation of economic and monetary union, the Council, on a proposal from the Commission and after consulting the European Central Bank, may take safeguard measures with regard to third countries for a period not exceeding six months if such measures are strictly necessary.

Title V. Area of Freedom, Security and Justice

Chapter 1. General provisions

Article 67 (ex Article 61 TEC and ex Article 29 TEU). (1) The Union shall constitute an area of freedom, security and justice with respect for fundamental rights and the different legal systems and traditions of the Member States.
(2) It shall ensure the absence of internal border controls for persons and shall frame a common policy on asylum, immigration and external border control, based on solidarity between Member States, which is fair towards third–country nationals. For the purpose of this Title, stateless persons shall be treated as third–country nationals.
(3) The Union shall endeavour to ensure a high level of security through measures to prevent and combat crime, racism and xenophobia, and through measures for coordination and cooperation between police and judicial authorities and other competent authorities, as well as through the mutual recognition of judgments in criminal matters and, if necessary, through the approximation of criminal laws.
(4) The Union shall facilitate access to justice, in particular through the principle of mutual recognition of judicial and extrajudicial decisions in civil matters.

Article 68. The European Council shall define the strategic guidelines for legislative and operational planning within the area of freedom, security and justice.

Article 69. National Parliaments ensure that the proposals and legislative initiatives submitted under Chapters 4 and 5 comply with the principle of subsidiarity, in accordance with the arrangements laid down by the Protocol on the application of the principles of subsidiarity and proportionality.

Article 70. Without prejudice to Articles 258, 259 and 260, the Council may, on a proposal from the Commission, adopt measures laying down the arrangements whereby Member States, in collaboration with the Commission, conduct objective and impartial evaluation of the implementation of the Union policies referred to in this Title by Member States' authorities, in particular in order to facilitate full application of the principle of mutual recognition. The European Parliament and national Parliaments shall be informed of the content and results of the evaluation.

Article 71 (ex Article 36 TEU). A standing committee shall be set up within the Council in order to ensure that operational cooperation on internal security is promoted and strengthened within the Union. Without prejudice to Article 240, it shall facilitate coordination of the action of Member States' competent authorities. Representatives of the Union bodies, offices and agencies concerned may be involved in the proceedings of this committee. The European Parliament and national Parliaments shall be kept informed of the proceedings.

Article 72 (ex Article 64(1) TEC and ex Article 33 TEU). This Title shall not affect the exercise of the responsibilities incumbent upon Member States with regard to the maintenance of law and order and the safeguarding of internal security.

Article 73. It shall be open to Member States to organise between themselves and under their responsibility such forms of cooperation and coordination as they deem appropriate between the competent departments of their administrations responsible for safeguarding national security.

Article 74 (ex Article 66 TEC). The Council shall adopt measures to ensure administrative cooperation between the relevant departments of the Member States in the areas covered by this Title, as well as between those departments and the Commission. It shall act on a Commission proposal, subject to Article 76, and after consulting the European Parliament.

Article 75 (ex Article 60 TEC). Where necessary to achieve the objectives set out in Article 67, as regards preventing and combating terrorism and related activities, the European Parliament and the Council, acting by means of regulations in accordance with the ordinary legislative procedure, shall define a framework for administrative measures with regard to capital movements and payments, such as the freezing of funds, financial assets or economic gains belonging to, or owned or held by, natural or legal persons, groups or non–State entities.

The Council, on a proposal from the Commission, shall adopt measures to implement the framework referred to in the first paragraph.

The acts referred to in this Article shall include necessary provisions on legal safeguards.

Article 76. The acts referred to in Chapters 4 and 5, together with the measures referred to in Article 74 which ensure administrative cooperation in the areas covered by these Chapters, shall be adopted:
(a) on a proposal from the Commission, or
(b) on the initiative of a quarter of the Member States.

Chapter 2. Policies on Border Checks, Asylum and Immigration

Article 77 (ex Article 62 TEC). (1) The Union shall develop a policy with a view to:
(a) ensuring the absence of any controls on persons, whatever their nationality, when crossing internal borders;
(b) carrying out checks on persons and efficient monitoring of the crossing of external borders;
(c) the gradual introduction of an integrated management system for external borders.
(2) For the purposes of paragraph 1, the European Parliament and the Council, acting in accordance with the ordinary legislative procedure, shall adopt measures concerning:
(a) the common policy on visas and other short–stay residence permits;
(b) the checks to which persons crossing external borders are subject;
(c) the conditions under which nationals of third countries shall have the freedom to travel within the Union for a short period;
(d) any measure necessary for the gradual establishment of an integrated management system for external borders;
(e) the absence of any controls on persons, whatever their nationality, when crossing internal borders.
(3) If action by the Union should prove necessary to facilitate the exercise of the right referred to in Article 20(2)(a), and if the Treaties have not provided the necessary powers, the Council, acting in accordance with a special legislative procedure, may adopt provisions concerning passports, identity cards, residence permits or any other such document. The Council shall act unanimously after consulting the European Parliament.
(4) This Article shall not affect the competence of the Member States concerning the geographical demarcation of their borders, in accordance with international law.

Article 78 (ex Articles 63, points 1 and 2, and 64(2) TEC). (1) The Union shall develop a common policy on asylum, subsidiary protection and temporary protection with a view to offering appropriate status to any third–country national requiring international protection and ensuring compliance with the principle of non–refoulement. This policy must be in accordance with the Geneva Convention of 28 July 1951 and the Protocol of 31 January 1967 relating to the status of refugees, and other relevant treaties.
(2) For the purposes of paragraph 1, the European Parliament and the Council, acting in accordance with the ordinary legislative procedure, shall adopt measures for a common European asylum system comprising:
(a) a uniform status of asylum for nationals of third countries, valid throughout the Union;
(b) a uniform status of subsidiary protection for nationals of third countries who, without obtaining

European asylum, are in need of international protection;
(c) a common system of temporary protection for displaced persons in the event of a massive inflow;
(d) common procedures for the granting and withdrawing of uniform asylum or subsidiary protection status;
(e) criteria and mechanisms for determining which Member State is responsible for considering an application for asylum or subsidiary protection;
(f) standards concerning the conditions for the reception of applicants for asylum or subsidiary protection;
(g) partnership and cooperation with third countries for the purpose of managing inflows of people applying for asylum or subsidiary or temporary protection.
(3) In the event of one or more Member States being confronted by an emergency situation characterised by a sudden inflow of nationals of third countries, the Council, on a proposal from the Commission, may adopt provisional measures for the benefit of the Member State(s) concerned. It shall act after consulting the European Parliament.

Article 79 (ex Article 63, points 3 and 4, TEC). (1) The Union shall develop a common immigration policy aimed at ensuring, at all stages, the efficient management of migration flows, fair treatment of third–country nationals residing legally in Member States, and the prevention of, and enhanced measures to combat, illegal immigration and trafficking in human beings.
(2) For the purposes of paragraph 1, the European Parliament and the Council, acting in accordance with the ordinary legislative procedure, shall adopt measures in the following areas:
(a) the conditions of entry and residence, and standards on the issue by Member States of long–term visas and residence permits, including those for the purpose of family reunification;
(b) the definition of the rights of third–country nationals residing legally in a Member State, including the conditions governing freedom of movement and of residence in other Member States;
(c) illegal immigration and unauthorised residence, including removal and repatriation of persons residing without authorisation;
(d) combating trafficking in persons, in particular women and children.
(3) The Union may conclude agreements with third countries for the readmission to their countries of origin or provenance of third–country nationals who do not or who no longer fulfil the conditions for entry, presence or residence in the territory of one of the Member States.
(4) The European Parliament and the Council, acting in accordance with the ordinary legislative procedure, may establish measures to provide incentives and support for the action of Member States with a view to promoting the integration of third–country nationals residing legally in their territories, excluding any harmonisation of the laws and regulations of the Member States.
(5) This Article shall not affect the right of Member States to determine volumes of admission of third–country nationals coming from third countries to their territory in order to seek work, whether employed or self–employed.

Article 80. The policies of the Union set out in this Chapter and their implementation shall be governed by the principle of solidarity and fair sharing of responsibility, including its financial implications, between the Member States. Whenever necessary, the Union acts adopted pursuant to this Chapter shall contain appropriate measures to give effect to this principle.

Chapter 3. Judicial Cooperation in Civil Matters

Article 81 (ex Article 65 TEC). (1) The Union shall develop judicial cooperation in civil matters having cross–border implications, based on the principle of mutual recognition of judgments and of decisions in extrajudicial cases. Such cooperation may include the adoption of measures for the approximation of the laws and regulations of the Member States.
(2) For the purposes of paragraph 1, the European Parliament and the Council, acting in accordance with the ordinary legislative procedure, shall adopt measures, particularly when necessary for the proper functioning of the internal market, aimed at ensuring:
(a) the mutual recognition and enforcement between Member States of judgments and of decisions in extrajudicial cases;
(b) the cross–border service of judicial and extrajudicial documents;
(c) the compatibility of the rules applicable in the Member States concerning conflict of laws and of jurisdiction;
(d) cooperation in the taking of evidence;
(e) effective access to justice;
(f) the elimination of obstacles to the proper functioning of civil proceedings, if necessary by promoting the compatibility of the rules on civil procedure applicable in the Member States;

(g) the development of alternative methods of dispute settlement;
(h) support for the training of the judiciary and judicial staff.
(3) Notwithstanding paragraph 2, measures concerning family law with cross–border implications shall be established by the Council, acting in accordance with a special legislative procedure. The Council shall act unanimously after consulting the European Parliament.
The Council, on a proposal from the Commission, may adopt a decision determining those aspects of family law with cross–border implications which may be the subject of acts adopted by the ordinary legislative procedure. The Council shall act unanimously after consulting the European Parliament.
The proposal referred to in the second subparagraph shall be notified to the national Parliaments. If a national Parliament makes known its opposition within six months of the date of such notification, the decision shall not be adopted. In the absence of opposition, the Council may adopt the decision.

Chapter 4. Judicial Cooperation in Criminal Matters

Article 82 (ex Article 31 TEU). (1) Judicial cooperation in criminal matters in the Union shall be based on the principle of mutual recognition of judgments and judicial decisions and shall include the approximation of the laws and regulations of the Member States in the areas referred to in paragraph 2 and in Article 83.
The European Parliament and the Council, acting in accordance with the ordinary legislative procedure, shall adopt measures to:
(a) lay down rules and procedures for ensuring recognition throughout the Union of all forms of judgments and judicial decisions;
(b) prevent and settle conflicts of jurisdiction between Member States;
(c) support the training of the judiciary and judicial staff;
(d) facilitate cooperation between judicial or equivalent authorities of the Member States in relation to proceedings in criminal matters and the enforcement of decisions.
(2) To the extent necessary to facilitate mutual recognition of judgments and judicial decisions and police and judicial cooperation in criminal matters having a cross–border dimension, the European Parliament and the Council may, by means of directives adopted in accordance with the ordinary legislative procedure, establish minimum rules. Such rules shall take into account the differences between the legal traditions and systems of the Member States.
They shall concern:
(a) mutual admissibility of evidence between Member States;
(b) the rights of individuals in criminal procedure;
(c) the rights of victims of crime;
(d) any other specific aspects of criminal procedure which the Council has identified in advance by a decision; for the adoption of such a decision, the Council shall act unanimously after obtaining the consent of the European Parliament.
Adoption of the minimum rules referred to in this paragraph shall not prevent Member States from maintaining or introducing a higher level of protection for individuals.
(3) Where a member of the Council considers that a draft directive as referred to in paragraph 2 would affect fundamental aspects of its criminal justice system, it may request that the draft directive be referred to the European Council. In that case, the ordinary legislative procedure shall be suspended. After discussion, and in case of a consensus, the European Council shall, within four months of this suspension, refer the draft back to the Council, which shall terminate the suspension of the ordinary legislative procedure.
Within the same timeframe, in case of disagreement, and if at least nine Member States wish to establish enhanced cooperation on the basis of the draft directive concerned, they shall notify the European Parliament, the Council and the Commission accordingly. In such a case, the authorisation to proceed with enhanced cooperation referred to in Article 20(2) of the Treaty on European Union and Article 329(1) of this Treaty shall be deemed to be granted and the provisions on enhanced cooperation shall apply.

Article 83 (ex Article 31 TEU). (1) The European Parliament and the Council may, by means of directives adopted in accordance with the ordinary legislative procedure, establish minimum rules concerning the definition of criminal offences and sanctions in the areas of particularly serious crime with a cross–border dimension resulting from the nature or impact of such offences or from a special need to combat them on a common basis.
These areas of crime are the following: terrorism, trafficking in human beings and sexual exploitation of women and children, illicit drug trafficking, illicit arms trafficking, money laundering, corruption, counterfeiting of means of payment, computer crime and organised crime.

PART III EUROPEAN UNION

On the basis of developments in crime, the Council may adopt a decision identifying other areas of crime that meet the criteria specified in this paragraph. It shall act unanimously after obtaining the consent of the European Parliament.

(2) If the approximation of criminal laws and regulations of the Member States proves essential to ensure the effective implementation of a Union policy in an area which has been subject to harmonisation measures, directives may establish minimum rules with regard to the definition of criminal offences and sanctions in the area concerned. Such directives shall be adopted by the same ordinary or special legislative procedure as was followed for the adoption of the harmonisation measures in question, without prejudice to Article 76.

(3) Where a member of the Council considers that a draft directive as referred to in paragraph 1 or 2 would affect fundamental aspects of its criminal justice system, it may request that the draft directive be referred to the European Council. In that case, the ordinary legislative procedure shall be suspended. After discussion, and in case of a consensus, the European Council shall, within four months of this suspension, refer the draft back to the Council, which shall terminate the suspension of the ordinary legislative procedure.

Within the same timeframe, in case of disagreement, and if at least nine Member States wish to establish enhanced cooperation on the basis of the draft directive concerned, they shall notify the European Parliament, the Council and the Commission accordingly. In such a case, the authorisation to proceed with enhanced cooperation referred to in Article 20(2) of the Treaty on European Union and Article 329(1) of this Treaty shall be deemed to be granted and the provisions on enhanced cooperation shall apply.

Article 84. The European Parliament and the Council, acting in accordance with the ordinary legislative procedure, may establish measures to promote and support the action of Member States in the field of crime prevention, excluding any harmonisation of the laws and regulations of the Member States.

Article 85 (ex Article 31 TEU). (1) Eurojust's mission shall be to support and strengthen coordination and cooperation between national investigating and prosecuting authorities in relation to serious crime affecting two or more Member States or requiring a prosecution on common bases, on the basis of operations conducted and information supplied by the Member States' authorities and by Europol. In this context, the European Parliament and the Council, by means of regulations adopted in accordance with the ordinary legislative procedure, shall determine Eurojust's structure, operation, field of action and tasks. These tasks may include:

(a) the initiation of criminal investigations, as well as proposing the initiation of prosecutions conducted by competent national authorities, particularly those relating to offences against the financial interests of the Union;

(b) the coordination of investigations and prosecutions referred to in point (a);

(c) the strengthening of judicial cooperation, including by resolution of conflicts of jurisdiction and by close cooperation with the European Judicial Network.

These regulations shall also determine arrangements for involving the European Parliament and national Parliaments in the evaluation of Eurojust's activities.

(2) In the prosecutions referred to in paragraph 1, and without prejudice to Article 86, formal acts of judicial procedure shall be carried out by the competent national officials.

Article 86. (1) In order to combat crimes affecting the financial interests of the Union, the Council, by means of regulations adopted in accordance with a special legislative procedure, may establish a European Public Prosecutor's Office from Eurojust. The Council shall act unanimously after obtaining the consent of the European Parliament.

In the absence of unanimity in the Council, a group of at least nine Member States may request that the draft regulation be referred to the European Council. In that case, the procedure in the Council shall be suspended. After discussion, and in case of a consensus, the European Council shall, within four months of this suspension, refer the draft back to the Council for adoption.

Within the same timeframe, in case of disagreement, and if at least nine Member States wish to establish enhanced cooperation on the basis of the draft regulation concerned, they shall notify the European Parliament, the Council and the Commission accordingly. In such a case, the authorisation to proceed with enhanced cooperation referred to in Article 20(2) of the Treaty on European Union and Article 329(1) of this Treaty shall be deemed to be granted and the provisions on enhanced cooperation shall apply.

(2) The European Public Prosecutor's Office shall be responsible for investigating, prosecuting and bringing to judgment, where appropriate in liaison with Europol, the perpetrators of, and accomplices

in, offences against the Union's financial interests, as determined by the regulation provided for in paragraph 1. It shall exercise the functions of prosecutor in the competent courts of the Member States in relation to such offences.

(3) The regulations referred to in paragraph 1 shall determine the general rules applicable to the European Public Prosecutor's Office, the conditions governing the performance of its functions, the rules of procedure applicable to its activities, as well as those governing the admissibility of evidence, and the rules applicable to the judicial review of procedural measures taken by it in the performance of its functions.

(4) The European Council may, at the same time or subsequently, adopt a decision amending paragraph 1 in order to extend the powers of the European Public Prosecutor's Office to include serious crime having a cross–border dimension and amending accordingly paragraph 2 as regards the perpetrators of, and accomplices in, serious crimes affecting more than one Member State. The European Council shall act unanimously after obtaining the consent of the European Parliament and after consulting the Commission.

Chapter 5. Police Cooperation

Article 87 (ex Article 30 TEU). (1) The Union shall establish police cooperation involving all the Member States' competent authorities, including police, customs and other specialised law enforcement services in relation to the prevention, detection and investigation of criminal offences.

(2) For the purposes of paragraph 1, the European Parliament and the Council, acting in accordance with the ordinary legislative procedure, may establish measures concerning:
(a) the collection, storage, processing, analysis and exchange of relevant information;
(b) support for the training of staff, and cooperation on the exchange of staff, on equipment and on research into crime–detection;
(c) common investigative techniques in relation to the detection of serious forms of organised crime.

(3) The Council, acting in accordance with a special legislative procedure, may establish measures concerning operational cooperation between the authorities referred to in this Article. The Council shall act unanimously after consulting the European Parliament.

In case of the absence of unanimity in the Council, a group of at least nine Member States may request that the draft measures be referred to the European Council. In that case, the procedure in the Council shall be suspended. After discussion, and in case of a consensus, the European Council shall, within four months of this suspension, refer the draft back to the Council for adoption.

Within the same timeframe, in case of disagreement, and if at least nine Member States wish to establish enhanced cooperation on the basis of the draft measures concerned, they shall notify the European Parliament, the Council and the Commission accordingly. In such a case, the authorisation to proceed with enhanced cooperation referred to in Article 20(2) of the Treaty on European Union and Article 329(1) of this Treaty shall be deemed to be granted and the provisions on enhanced cooperation shall apply.

The specific procedure provided for in the second and third subparagraphs shall not apply to acts which constitute a development of the Schengen acquis.

Article 88 (ex Article 30 TEU). (1) Europol's mission shall be to support and strengthen action by the Member States' police authorities and other law enforcement services and their mutual cooperation in preventing and combating serious crime affecting two or more Member States, terrorism and forms of crime which affect a common interest covered by a Union policy.

(2) The European Parliament and the Council, by means of regulations adopted in accordance with the ordinary legislative procedure, shall determine Europol's structure, operation, field of action and tasks. These tasks may include:
(a) the collection, storage, processing, analysis and exchange of information, in particular that forwarded by the authorities of the Member States or third countries or bodies;
(b) the coordination, organisation and implementation of investigative and operational action carried out jointly with the Member States' competent authorities or in the context of joint investigative teams, where appropriate in liaison with Eurojust.

These regulations shall also lay down the procedures for scrutiny of Europol's activities by the European Parliament, together with national Parliaments.

(3) Any operational action by Europol must be carried out in liaison and in agreement with the authorities of the Member State or States whose territory is concerned. The application of coercive measures shall be the exclusive responsibility of the competent national authorities.

Article 89 (ex Article 32 TEU). The Council, acting in accordance with a special legislative procedure, shall lay down the conditions and limitations under which the competent authorities of the

PART III EUROPEAN UNION

Member States referred to in Articles 82 and 87 may operate in the territory of another Member State in liaison and in agreement with the authorities of that State. The Council shall act unanimously after consulting the European Parliament.

Title VI. Transport

Article 90 (ex Article 70 TEC). The objectives of the Treaties shall, in matters governed by this Title, be pursued within the framework of a common transport policy.

Article 91 (ex Article 71 TEC). (1) For the purpose of implementing Article 90, and taking into account the distinctive features of transport, the European Parliament and the Council shall, acting in accordance with the ordinary legislative procedure and after consulting the Economic and Social Committee and the Committee of the Regions, lay down:
(a) common rules applicable to international transport to or from the territory of a Member State or passing across the territory of one or more Member States;
(b) the conditions under which non–resident carriers may operate transport services within a Member State;
(c) measures to improve transport safety;
(d) any other appropriate provisions.
(2) When the measures referred to in paragraph 1 are adopted, account shall be taken of cases where their application might seriously affect the standard of living and level of employment in certain regions, and the operation of transport facilities.

Article 92 (ex Article 72 TEC). Until the provisions referred to in Article 91(1) have been laid down, no Member State may, unless the Council has unanimously adopted a measure granting a derogation, make the various provisions governing the subject on 1 January 1958 or, for acceding States, the date of their accession less favourable in their direct or indirect effect on carriers of other Member States as compared with carriers who are nationals of that State.

Article 93 (ex Article 73 TEC). Aids shall be compatible with the Treaties if they meet the needs of coordination of transport or if they represent reimbursement for the discharge of certain obligations inherent in the concept of a public service.

Article 94 (ex Article 74 TEC). Any measures taken within the framework of the Treaties in respect of transport rates and conditions shall take account of the economic circumstances of carriers.

Article 95 (ex Article 75 TEC). (1) In the case of transport within the Union, discrimination which takes the form of carriers charging different rates and imposing different conditions for the carriage of the same goods over the same transport links on grounds of the country of origin or of destination of the goods in question shall be prohibited.
(2) Paragraph 1 shall not prevent the European Parliament and the Council from adopting other measures pursuant to Article 91(1).
(3) The Council shall, on a proposal from the Commission and after consulting the European Parliament and the Economic and Social Committee, lay down rules for implementing the provisions of paragraph 1.
The Council may in particular lay down the provisions needed to enable the institutions of the Union to secure compliance with the rule laid down in paragraph 1 and to ensure that users benefit from it to the full.
(4) The Commission shall, acting on its own initiative or on application by a Member State, investigate any cases of discrimination falling within paragraph 1 and, after consulting any Member State concerned, shall take the necessary decisions within the framework of the rules laid down in accordance with the provisions of paragraph 3.

Article 96 (ex Article 76 TEC). (1) The imposition by a Member State, in respect of transport operations carried out within the Union, of rates and conditions involving any element of support or protection in the interest of one or more particular undertakings or industries shall be prohibited, unless authorised by the Commission.
(2) The Commission shall, acting on its own initiative or on application by a Member State, examine the rates and conditions referred to in paragraph 1, taking account in particular of the requirements of an appropriate regional economic policy, the needs of underdeveloped areas and the problems of areas seriously affected by political circumstances on the one hand, and of the effects of such rates and conditions on competition between the different modes of transport on the other.
After consulting each Member State concerned, the Commission shall take the necessary decisions.

(3) The prohibition provided for in paragraph 1 shall not apply to tariffs fixed to meet competition.

Article 97 (ex Article 77 TEC). Charges or dues in respect of the crossing of frontiers which are charged by a carrier in addition to the transport rates shall not exceed a reasonable level after taking the costs actually incurred thereby into account.
Member States shall endeavour to reduce these costs progressively.
The Commission may make recommendations to Member States for the application of this Article.

Article 98 (ex Article 78 TEC). The provisions of this Title shall not form an obstacle to the application of measures taken in the Federal Republic of Germany to the extent that such measures are required in order to compensate for the economic disadvantages caused by the division of Germany to the economy of certain areas of the Federal Republic affected by that division. Five years after the entry into force of the Treaty of Lisbon, the Council, acting on a proposal from the Commission, may adopt a decision repealing this Article.

Article 99 (ex Article 79 TEC). An Advisory Committee consisting of experts designated by the governments of Member States shall be attached to the Commission. The Commission, whenever it considers it desirable, shall consult the Committee on transport matters.

Article 100 (ex Article 80 TEC). (1) The provisions of this Title shall apply to transport by rail, road and inland waterway.
(2) The European Parliament and the Council, acting in accordance with the ordinary legislative procedure, may lay down appropriate provisions for sea and air transport. They shall act after consulting the Economic and Social Committee and the Committee of the Regions.

Title VII. Common Rules on Competition, Taxation and Approximation of Laws

Chapter 1. Rules on Competition

Section 1. Rules Applying to Undertakings

Article 101 (ex Article 81 TEC). (1) The following shall be prohibited as incompatible with the internal market: all agreements between undertakings, decisions by associations of undertakings and concerted practices which may affect trade between Member States and which have as their object or effect the prevention, restriction or distortion of competition within the internal market, and in particular those which:
(a) directly or indirectly fix purchase or selling prices or any other trading conditions;
(b) limit or control production, markets, technical development, or investment;
(c) share markets or sources of supply;
(d) apply dissimilar conditions to equivalent transactions with other trading parties, thereby placing them at a competitive disadvantage;
(e) make the conclusion of contracts subject to acceptance by the other parties of supplementary obligations which, by their nature or according to commercial usage, have no connection with the subject of such contracts.
(2) Any agreements or decisions prohibited pursuant to this Article shall be automatically void.
(3) The provisions of paragraph 1 may, however, be declared inapplicable in the case of:
– any agreement or category of agreements between undertakings,
– any decision or category of decisions by associations of undertakings,
– any concerted practice or category of concerted practices,
which contributes to improving the production or distribution of goods or to promoting technical or economic progress, while allowing consumers a fair share of the resulting benefit, and which does not:
(a) impose on the undertakings concerned restrictions which are not indispensable to the attainment of these objectives;
(b) afford such undertakings the possibility of eliminating competition in respect of a substantial part of the products in question.

Article 102 (ex Article 82 TEC). Any abuse by one or more undertakings of a dominant position within the internal market or in a substantial part of it shall be prohibited as incompatible with the internal market in so far as it may affect trade between Member States.
Such abuse may, in particular, consist in:
(a) directly or indirectly imposing unfair purchase or selling prices or other unfair trading conditions;
(b) limiting production, markets or technical development to the prejudice of consumers;
(c) applying dissimilar conditions to equivalent transactions with other trading parties, thereby plac-

ing them at a competitive disadvantage;
(d) making the conclusion of contracts subject to acceptance by the other parties of supplementary obligations which, by their nature or according to commercial usage, have no connection with the subject of such contracts.

Article 103 (ex Article 83 TEC). (1) The appropriate regulations or directives to give effect to the principles set out in Articles 101 and 102 shall be laid down by the Council, on a proposal from the Commission and after consulting the European Parliament.
(2) The regulations or directives referred to in paragraph 1 shall be designed in particular:
(a) to ensure compliance with the prohibitions laid down in Article 101(1) and in Article 102 by making provision for fines and periodic penalty payments;
(b) to lay down detailed rules for the application of Article 101(3), taking into account the need to ensure effective supervision on the one hand, and to simplify administration to the greatest possible extent on the other;
(c) to define, if need be, in the various branches of the economy, the scope of the provisions of Articles 101 and 102;
(d) to define the respective functions of the Commission and of the Court of Justice of the European Union in applying the provisions laid down in this paragraph;
(e) to determine the relationship between national laws and the provisions contained in this Section or adopted pursuant to this Article.

Article 104 (ex Article 84 TEC). Until the entry into force of the provisions adopted in pursuance of Article 103, the authorities in Member States shall rule on the admissibility of agreements, decisions and concerted practices and on abuse of a dominant position in the internal market in accordance with the law of their country and with the provisions of Article 101, in particular paragraph 3, and of Article 102.

Article 105 (ex Article 85 TEC). (1) Without prejudice to Article 104, the Commission shall ensure the application of the principles laid down in Articles 101 and 102. On application by a Member State or on its own initiative, and in cooperation with the competent authorities in the Member States, which shall give it their assistance, the Commission shall investigate cases of suspected infringement of these principles. If it finds that there has been an infringement, it shall propose appropriate measures to bring it to an end.
(2) If the infringement is not brought to an end, the Commission shall record such infringement of the principles in a reasoned decision. The Commission may publish its decision and authorise Member States to take the measures, the conditions and details of which it shall determine, needed to remedy the situation.
(3) The Commission may adopt regulations relating to the categories of agreement in respect of which the Council has adopted a regulation or a directive pursuant to Article 103(2)(b).

Article 106 (ex Article 86 TEC). (1) In the case of public undertakings and undertakings to which Member States grant special or exclusive rights, Member States shall neither enact nor maintain in force any measure contrary to the rules contained in the Treaties, in particular to those rules provided for in Article 18 and Articles 101 to 109.
(2) Undertakings entrusted with the operation of services of general economic interest or having the character of a revenue–producing monopoly shall be subject to the rules contained in the Treaties, in particular to the rules on competition, in so far as the application of such rules does not obstruct the performance, in law or in fact, of the particular tasks assigned to them. The development of trade must not be affected to such an extent as would be contrary to the interests of the Union.
(3) The Commission shall ensure the application of the provisions of this Article and shall, where necessary, address appropriate directives or decisions to Member States.

Section 2. Aids Granted by States

Article 107 (ex Article 87 TEC). (1) Save as otherwise provided in the Treaties, any aid granted by a Member State or through State resources in any form whatsoever which distorts or threatens to distort competition by favouring certain undertakings or the production of certain goods shall, in so far as it affects trade between Member States, be incompatible with the internal market.
(2) The following shall be compatible with the internal market:
(a) aid having a social character, granted to individual consumers, provided that such aid is granted without discrimination related to the origin of the products concerned;
(b) aid to make good the damage caused by natural disasters or exceptional occurrences;

(c) aid granted to the economy of certain areas of the Federal Republic of Germany affected by the division of Germany, in so far as such aid is required in order to compensate for the economic disadvantages caused by that division. Five years after the entry into force of the Treaty of Lisbon, the Council, acting on a proposal from the Commission, may adopt a decision repealing this point.
(3) The following may be considered to be compatible with the internal market:
(a) aid to promote the economic development of areas where the standard of living is abnormally low or where there is serious underemployment, and of the regions referred to in Article 349, in view of their structural, economic and social situation;
(b) aid to promote the execution of an important project of common European interest or to remedy a serious disturbance in the economy of a Member State;
(c) aid to facilitate the development of certain economic activities or of certain economic areas, where such aid does not adversely affect trading conditions to an extent contrary to the common interest;
(d) aid to promote culture and heritage conservation where such aid does not affect trading conditions and competition in the Union to an extent that is contrary to the common interest;
(e) such other categories of aid as may be specified by decision of the Council on a proposal from the Commission.

Article 108 (ex Article 88 TEC). (1) The Commission shall, in cooperation with Member States, keep under constant review all systems of aid existing in those States. It shall propose to the latter any appropriate measures required by the progressive development or by the functioning of the internal market.
(2) If, after giving notice to the parties concerned to submit their comments, the Commission finds that aid granted by a State or through State resources is not compatible with the internal market having regard to Article 107, or that such aid is being misused, it shall decide that the State concerned shall abolish or alter such aid within a period of time to be determined by the Commission.
If the State concerned does not comply with this decision within the prescribed time, the Commission or any other interested State may, in derogation from the provisions of Articles 258 and 259, refer the matter to the Court of Justice of the European Union direct.
On application by a Member State, the Council may, acting unanimously, decide that aid which that State is granting or intends to grant shall be considered to be compatible with the internal market, in derogation from the provisions of Article 107 or from the regulations provided for in Article 109, if such a decision is justified by exceptional circumstances. If, as regards the aid in question, the Commission has already initiated the procedure provided for in the first subparagraph of this paragraph, the fact that the State concerned has made its application to the Council shall have the effect of suspending that procedure until the Council has made its attitude known.
If, however, the Council has not made its attitude known within three months of the said application being made, the Commission shall give its decision on the case.
(3) The Commission shall be informed, in sufficient time to enable it to submit its comments, of any plans to grant or alter aid. If it considers that any such plan is not compatible with the internal market having regard to Article 107, it shall without delay initiate the procedure provided for in paragraph 2. The Member State concerned shall not put its proposed measures into effect until this procedure has resulted in a final decision.
(4) The Commission may adopt regulations relating to the categories of State aid that the Council has, pursuant to Article 109, determined may be exempted from the procedure provided for by paragraph 3 of this Article.

Article 109 (ex Article 89 TEC). The Council, on a proposal from the Commission and after consulting the European Parliament, may make any appropriate regulations for the application of Articles 107 and 108 and may in particular determine the conditions in which Article 108(3) shall apply and the categories of aid exempted from this procedure.

Chapter 2. Tax Provisions

Article 110 (ex Article 90 TEC). No Member State shall impose, directly or indirectly, on the products of other Member States any internal taxation of any kind in excess of that imposed directly or indirectly on similar domestic products.
Furthermore, no Member State shall impose on the products of other Member States any internal taxation of such a nature as to afford indirect protection to other products.

Article 111 (ex Article 91 TEC). Where products are exported to the territory of any Member State, any repayment of internal taxation shall not exceed the internal taxation imposed on them whether directly or indirectly.

PART III   EUROPEAN UNION

Article 112 (ex Article 92 TEC). In the case of charges other than turnover taxes, excise duties and other forms of indirect taxation, remissions and repayments in respect of exports to other Member States may not be granted and countervailing charges in respect of imports from Member States may not be imposed unless the measures contemplated have been previously approved for a limited period by the Council on a proposal from the Commission.

Article 113 (ex Article 93 TEC). The Council shall, acting unanimously in accordance with a special legislative procedure and after consulting the European Parliament and the Economic and Social Committee, adopt provisions for the harmonisation of legislation concerning turnover taxes, excise duties and other forms of indirect taxation to the extent that such harmonisation is necessary to ensure the establishment and the functioning of the internal market and to avoid distortion of competition.

Chapter 3. Approximation of Laws

Article 114 (ex Article 95 TEC). (1) Save where otherwise provided in the Treaties, the following provisions shall apply for the achievement of the objectives set out in Article 26. The European Parliament and the Council shall, acting in accordance with the ordinary legislative procedure and after consulting the Economic and Social Committee, adopt the measures for the approximation of the provisions laid down by law, regulation or administrative action in Member States which have as their object the establishment and functioning of the internal market.
(2) Paragraph 1 shall not apply to fiscal provisions, to those relating to the free movement of persons nor to those relating to the rights and interests of employed persons.
(3) The Commission, in its proposals envisaged in paragraph 1 concerning health, safety, environmental protection and consumer protection, will take as a base a high level of protection, taking account in particular of any new development based on scientific facts. Within their respective powers, the European Parliament and the Council will also seek to achieve this objective.
(4) If, after the adoption of a harmonisation measure by the European Parliament and the Council, by the Council or by the Commission, a Member State deems it necessary to maintain national provisions on grounds of major needs referred to in Article 36, or relating to the protection of the environment or the working environment, it shall notify the Commission of these provisions as well as the grounds for maintaining them.
(5) Moreover, without prejudice to paragraph 4, if, after the adoption of a harmonisation measure by the European Parliament and the Council, by the Council or by the Commission, a Member State deems it necessary to introduce national provisions based on new scientific evidence relating to the protection of the environment or the working environment on grounds of a problem specific to that Member State arising after the adoption of the harmonisation measure, it shall notify the Commission of the envisaged provisions as well as the grounds for introducing them.
(6) The Commission shall, within six months of the notifications as referred to in paragraphs 4 and 5, approve or reject the national provisions involved after having verified whether or not they are a means of arbitrary discrimination or a disguised restriction on trade between Member States and whether or not they shall constitute an obstacle to the functioning of the internal market.
In the absence of a decision by the Commission within this period the national provisions referred to in paragraphs 4 and 5 shall be deemed to have been approved.
When justified by the complexity of the matter and in the absence of danger for human health, the Commission may notify the Member State concerned that the period referred to in this paragraph may be extended for a further period of up to six months.
(7) When, pursuant to paragraph 6, a Member State is authorised to maintain or introduce national provisions derogating from a harmonisation measure, the Commission shall immediately examine whether to propose an adaptation to that measure.
(8) When a Member State raises a specific problem on public health in a field which has been the subject of prior harmonisation measures, it shall bring it to the attention of the Commission which shall immediately examine whether to propose appropriate measures to the Council.
(9) By way of derogation from the procedure laid down in Articles 258 and 259, the Commission and any Member State may bring the matter directly before the Court of Justice of the European Union if it considers that another Member State is making improper use of the powers provided for in this Article.
(10) The harmonisation measures referred to above shall, in appropriate cases, include a safeguard clause authorising the Member States to take, for one or more of the non–economic reasons referred to in Article 36, provisional measures subject to a Union control procedure.

Article 115 (ex Article 94 TEC). Without prejudice to Article 114, the Council shall, acting unanimously in accordance with a special legislative procedure and after consulting the European Parliament and the Economic and Social Committee, issue directives for the approximation of such laws, regulations or administrative provisions of the Member States as directly affect the establishment or functioning of the internal market.

Article 116 (ex Article 96 TEC). Where the Commission finds that a difference between the provisions laid down by law, regulation or administrative action in Member States is distorting the conditions of competition in the internal market and that the resultant distortion needs to be eliminated, it shall consult the Member States concerned.

If such consultation does not result in an agreement eliminating the distortion in question, the European, Parliament and the Council, acting in accordance with the ordinary legislative procedure, shall issue the necessary directives. Any other appropriate measures provided for in the Treaties may be adopted.

Article 117 (ex Article 97 TEC). (1) Where there is a reason to fear that the adoption or amendment of a provision laid down by law, regulation or administrative action may cause distortion within the meaning of Article 116, a Member State desiring to proceed therewith shall consult the Commission. After consulting the Member States, the Commission shall recommend to the States concerned such measures as may be appropriate to avoid the distortion in question.

(2) If a State desiring to introduce or amend its own provisions does not comply with the recommendation addressed to it by the Commission, other Member States shall not be required, pursuant to Article 116, to amend their own provisions in order to eliminate such distortion. If the Member State which has ignored the recommendation of the Commission causes distortion detrimental only to itself, the provisions of Article 116 shall not apply.

Article 118. In the context of the establishment and functioning of the internal market, the European Parliament and the Council, acting in accordance with the ordinary legislative procedure, shall establish measures for the creation of European intellectual property rights to provide uniform protection of intellectual property rights throughout the Union and for the setting up of centralised Union–wide authorisation, coordination and supervision arrangements.

The Council, acting in accordance with a special legislative procedure, shall by means of regulations establish language arrangements for the European intellectual property rights. The Council shall act unanimously after consulting the European Parliament.

Title VIII. Economic and Monetary Policy

Article 119 (ex Article 4 TEC). (1) For the purposes set out in Article 3 of the Treaty on European Union, the activities of the Member States and the Union shall include, as provided in the Treaties, the adoption of an economic policy which is based on the close coordination of Member States' economic policies, on the internal market and on the definition of common objectives, and conducted in accordance with the principle of an open market economy with free competition.

(2) Concurrently with the foregoing, and as provided in the Treaties and in accordance with the procedures set out therein, these activities shall include a single currency, the euro, and the definition and conduct of a single monetary policy and exchange–rate policy the primary objective of both of which shall be to maintain price stability and, without prejudice to this objective, to support the general economic policies in the Union, in accordance with the principle of an open market economy with free competition.

(3) These activities of the Member States and the Union shall entail compliance with the following guiding principles: stable prices, sound public finances and monetary conditions and a sustainable balance of payments.

Chapter 1. Economic Policy

Article 120 (ex Article 98 TEC). Member States shall conduct their economic policies with a view to contributing to the achievement of the objectives of the Union, as defined in Article 3 of the Treaty on European Union, and in the context of the broad guidelines referred to in Article 121(2). The Member States and the Union shall act in accordance with the principle of an open market economy with free competition, favouring an efficient allocation of resources, and in compliance with the principles set out in Article 119.

Article 121 (ex Article 99 TEC). (1) Member States shall regard their economic policies as a matter of common concern and shall coordinate them within the Council, in accordance with the provisions of Article 120.

(2) The Council shall, on a recommendation from the Commission, formulate a draft for the broad

PART III EUROPEAN UNION

guidelines of the economic policies of the Member States and of the Union, and shall report its findings to the European Council.

The European Council shall, acting on the basis of the report from the Council, discuss a conclusion on the broad guidelines of the economic policies of the Member States and of the Union.

On the basis of this conclusion, the Council shall adopt a recommendation setting out these broad guidelines. The Council shall inform the European Parliament of its recommendation.

(3) In order to ensure closer coordination of economic policies and sustained convergence of the economic performances of the Member States, the Council shall, on the basis of reports submitted by the Commission, monitor economic developments in each of the Member States and in the Union as well as the consistency of economic policies with the broad guidelines referred to in paragraph 2, and regularly carry out an overall assessment.

For the purpose of this multilateral surveillance, Member States shall forward information to the Commission about important measures taken by them in the field of their economic policy and such other information as they deem necessary.

(4) Where it is established, under the procedure referred to in paragraph 3, that the economic policies of a Member State are not consistent with the broad guidelines referred to in paragraph 2 or that they risk jeopardising the proper functioning of economic and monetary union, the Commission may address a warning to the Member State concerned. The Council, on a recommendation from the Commission, may address the necessary recommendations to the Member State concerned. The Council may, on a proposal from the Commission, decide to make its recommendations public.

Within the scope of this paragraph, the Council shall act without taking into account the vote of the member of the Council representing the Member State concerned.

A qualified majority of the other members of the Council shall be defined in accordance with Article 238(3)(a).

(5) The President of the Council and the Commission shall report to the European Parliament on the results of multilateral surveillance. The President of the Council may be invited to appear before the competent committee of the European Parliament if the Council has made its recommendations public.

(6) The European Parliament and the Council, acting by means of regulations in accordance with the ordinary legislative procedure, may adopt detailed rules for the multilateral surveillance procedure referred to in paragraphs 3 and 4.

Article 122 (ex Article 100 TEC). (1) Without prejudice to any other procedures provided for in the Treaties, the Council, on a proposal from the Commission, may decide, in a spirit of solidarity between Member States, upon the measures appropriate to the economic situation, in particular if severe difficulties arise in the supply of certain products, notably in the area of energy.

(2) Where a Member State is in difficulties or is seriously threatened with severe difficulties caused by natural disasters or exceptional occurrences beyond its control, the Council, on a proposal from the Commission, may grant, under certain conditions, Union financial assistance to the Member State concerned. The President of the Council shall inform the European Parliament of the decision taken.

Article 123 (ex Article 101 TEC). (1) Overdraft facilities or any other type of credit facility with the European Central Bank or with the central banks of the Member States (hereinafter referred to as "national central banks") in favour of Union institutions, bodies, offices or agencies, central governments, regional, local or other public authorities, other bodies governed by public law, or public undertakings of Member States shall be prohibited, as shall the purchase directly from them by the European Central Bank or national central banks of debt instruments.

(2) Paragraph 1 shall not apply to publicly owned credit institutions which, in the context of the supply of reserves by central banks, shall be given the same treatment by national central banks and the European Central Bank as private credit institutions.

Article 124 (ex Article 102 TEC). Any measure, not based on prudential considerations, establishing privileged access by Union institutions, bodies, offices or agencies, central governments, regional, local or other public authorities, other bodies governed by public law, or public undertakings of Member States to financial institutions, shall be prohibited.

Article 125 (ex Article 103 TEC). (1) The Union shall not be liable for or assume the commitments of central governments, regional, local or other public authorities, other bodies governed by public law, or public undertakings of any Member State, without prejudice to mutual financial guarantees for the joint execution of a specific project. A Member State shall not be liable for or assume the commitments of central governments, regional, local or other public authorities, other bodies governed by public law, or public undertakings of another Member State, without prejudice to mutual financial

guarantees for the joint execution of a specific project.
(2) The Council, on a proposal from the Commission and after consulting the European Parliament, may, as required, specify definitions for the application of the prohibitions referred to in Articles 123 and 124 and in this Article.

Article 126 (ex Article 104 TEC). (1) Member States shall avoid excessive government deficits.
(2) The Commission shall monitor the development of the budgetary situation and of the stock of government debt in the Member States with a view to identifying gross errors. In particular it shall examine compliance with budgetary discipline on the basis of the following two criteria:
(a) whether the ratio of the planned or actual government deficit to gross domestic product exceeds a reference value, unless:
– either the ratio has declined substantially and continuously and reached a level that comes close to the reference value,
– or, alternatively, the excess over the reference value is only exceptional and temporary and the ratio remains close to the reference value;
(b) whether the ratio of government debt to gross domestic product exceeds a reference value, unless the ratio is sufficiently diminishing and approaching the reference value at a satisfactory pace.
The reference values are specified in the Protocol on the excessive deficit procedure annexed to the Treaties.
(3) If a Member State does not fulfil the requirements under one or both of these criteria, the Commission shall prepare a report. The report of the Commission shall also take into account whether the government deficit exceeds government investment expenditure and take into account all other relevant factors, including the medium–term economic and budgetary position of the Member State. The Commission may also prepare a report if, notwithstanding the fulfilment of the requirements under the criteria, it is of the opinion that there is a risk of an excessive deficit in a Member State.
(4) The Economic and Financial Committee shall formulate an opinion on the report of the Commission.
(5) If the Commission considers that an excessive deficit in a Member State exists or may occur, it shall address an opinion to the Member State concerned and shall inform the Council accordingly.
(6) The Council shall, on a proposal from the Commission, and having considered any observations which the Member State concerned may wish to make, decide after an overall assessment whether an excessive deficit exists.
(7) Where the Council decides, in accordance with paragraph 6, that an excessive deficit exists, it shall adopt, without undue delay, on a recommendation from the Commission, recommendations addressed to the Member State concerned with a view to bringing that situation to an end within a given period. Subject to the provisions of paragraph 8, these recommendations shall not be made public.
(8) Where it establishes that there has been no effective action in response to its recommendations within the period laid down, the Council may make its recommendations public.
(9) If a Member State persists in failing to put into practice the recommendations of the Council, the Council may decide to give notice to the Member State to take, within a specified time limit, measures for the deficit reduction which is judged necessary by the Council in order to remedy the situation.
In such a case, the Council may request the Member State concerned to submit reports in accordance with a specific timetable in order to examine the adjustment efforts of that Member State.
(10) The rights to bring actions provided for in Articles 258 and 259 may not be exercised within the framework of paragraphs 1 to 9 of this Article.
(11) As long as a Member State fails to comply with a decision taken in accordance with paragraph 9, the Council may decide to apply or, as the case may be, intensify one or more of the following measures:
– to require the Member State concerned to publish additional information, to be specified by the Council, before issuing bonds and securities,
– to invite the European Investment Bank to reconsider its lending policy towards the Member State concerned,
– to require the Member State concerned to make a non–interest–bearing deposit of an appropriate size with the Union until the excessive deficit has, in the view of the Council, been corrected,
– to impose fines of an appropriate size.
The President of the Council shall inform the European Parliament of the decisions taken.
(12) The Council shall abrogate some or all of its decisions or recommendations referred to in paragraphs 6 to 9 and 11 to the extent that the excessive deficit in the Member State concerned has, in the

view of the Council, been corrected. If the Council has previously made public recommendations, it shall, as soon as the decision under paragraph 8 has been abrogated, make a public statement that an excessive deficit in the Member State concerned no longer exists.

(13) When taking the decisions or recommendations referred to in paragraphs 8, 9, 11 and 12, the Council shall act on a recommendation from the Commission.

When the Council adopts the measures referred to in paragraphs 6 to 9, 11 and 12, it shall act without taking into account the vote of the member of the Council representing the Member State concerned. A qualified majority of the other members of the Council shall be defined in accordance with Article 238(3)(a).

(14) Further provisions relating to the implementation of the procedure described in this Article are set out in the Protocol on the excessive deficit procedure annexed to the Treaties.

The Council shall, acting unanimously in accordance with a special legislative procedure and after consulting the European Parliament and the European Central Bank, adopt the appropriate provisions which shall then replace the said Protocol.

Subject to the other provisions of this paragraph, the Council shall, on a proposal from the Commission and after consulting the European Parliament, lay down detailed rules and definitions for the application of the provisions of the said Protocol.

Chapter 2. Monetary Policy

Article 127 (ex Article 105 TEC). (1) The primary objective of the European System of Central Banks (hereinafter referred to as "the ESCB") shall be to maintain price stability. Without prejudice to the objective of price stability, the ESCB shall support the general economic policies in the Union with a view to contributing to the achievement of the objectives of the Union as laid down in Article 3 of the Treaty on European Union. The ESCB shall act in accordance with the principle of an open market economy with free competition, favouring an efficient allocation of resources, and in compliance with the principles set out in Article 119.

(2) The basic tasks to be carried out through the ESCB shall be:
– to define and implement the monetary policy of the Union,
– to conduct foreign–exchange operations consistent with the provisions of Article 219,
– to hold and manage the official foreign reserves of the Member States,
– to promote the smooth operation of payment systems.

(3) The third indent of paragraph 2 shall be without prejudice to the holding and management by the governments of Member States of foreign–exchange working balances.

(4) The European Central Bank shall be consulted:
– on any proposed Union act in its fields of competence,
– by national authorities regarding any draft legislative provision in its fields of competence, but within the limits and under the conditions set out by the Council in accordance with the procedure laid down in Article 129(4).

The European Central Bank may submit opinions to the appropriate Union institutions, bodies, offices or agencies or to national authorities on matters in its fields of competence.

(5) The ESCB shall contribute to the smooth conduct of policies pursued by the competent authorities relating to the prudential supervision of credit institutions and the stability of the financial system.

(6) The Council, acting by means of regulations in accordance with a special legislative procedure, may unanimously, and after consulting the European Parliament and the European Central Bank, confer specific tasks upon the European Central Bank concerning policies relating to the prudential supervision of credit institutions and other financial institutions with the exception of insurance undertakings.

Article 128 (ex Article 106 TEC). (1) The European Central Bank shall have the exclusive right to authorise the issue of euro banknotes within the Union. The European Central Bank and the national central banks may issue such notes. The banknotes issued by the European Central Bank and the national central banks shall be the only such notes to have the status of legal tender within the Union.

(2) Member States may issue euro coins subject to approval by the European Central Bank of the volume of the issue. The Council, on a proposal from the Commission and after consulting the European Parliament and the European Central Bank, may adopt measures to harmonise the denominations and technical specifications of all coins intended for circulation to the extent necessary to permit their smooth circulation within the Union.

Article 129 (ex Article 107 TEC). (1) The ESCB shall be governed by the decision–making bodies of the European Central Bank which shall be the Governing Council and the Executive Board.

(2) The Statute of the European System of Central Banks and of the European Central Bank (herein-

after referred to as "the Statute of the ESCB and of the ECB") is laid down in a Protocol annexed to the Treaties.

(3) Articles 5.1, 5.2, 5.3, 17, 18, 19.1, 22, 23, 24, 26, 32.2, 32.3, 32.4, 32.6, 33.1(a) and 36 of the Statute of the ESCB and of the ECB may be amended by the European Parliament and the Council, acting in accordance with the ordinary legislative procedure. They shall act either on a recommendation from the European Central Bank and after consulting the Commission or on a proposal from the Commission and after consulting the European Central Bank.

(4) The Council, either on a proposal from the Commission and after consulting the European Parliament and the European Central Bank or on a recommendation from the European Central Bank and after consulting the European Parliament and the Commission, shall adopt the provisions referred to in Articles 4, 5.4, 19.2, 20, 28.1, 29.2, 30.4 and 34.3 of the Statute of the ESCB and of the ECB.

Article 130 (ex Article 108 TEC). When exercising the powers and carrying out the tasks and duties conferred upon them by the Treaties and the Statute of the ESCB and of the ECB, neither the European Central Bank, nor a national central bank, nor any member of their decision–making bodies shall seek or take instructions from Union institutions, bodies, offices or agencies, from any government of a Member State or from any other body. The Union institutions, bodies, offices or agencies and the governments of the Member States undertake to respect this principle and not to seek to influence the members of the decision–making bodies of the European Central Bank or of the national central banks in the performance of their tasks.

Article 131 (ex Article 109 TEC). Each Member State shall ensure that its national legislation including the statutes of its national central bank is compatible with the Treaties and the Statute of the ESCB and of the ECB.

Article 132 (ex Article 110 TEC). (1) In order to carry out the tasks entrusted to the ESCB, the European Central Bank shall, in accordance with the provisions of the Treaties and under the conditions laid down in the Statute of the ESCB and of the ECB:
– make regulations to the extent necessary to implement the tasks defined in Article 3.1, first indent, Articles 19.1, 22 and 25.2 of the Statute of the ESCB and of the ECB in cases which shall be laid down in the acts of the Council referred to in Article 129(4),
– take decisions necessary for carrying out the tasks entrusted to the ESCB under the Treaties and the Statute of the ESCB and of the ECB,
– make recommendations and deliver opinions.

(2) The European Central Bank may decide to publish its decisions, recommendations and opinions.

(3) Within the limits and under the conditions adopted by the Council under the procedure laid down in Article 129(4), the European Central Bank shall be entitled to impose fines or periodic penalty payments on undertakings for failure to comply with obligations under its regulations and decisions.

Article 133. Without prejudice to the powers of the European Central Bank, the European Parliament and the Council, acting in accordance with the ordinary legislative procedure, shall lay down the measures necessary for the use of the euro as the single currency. Such measures shall be adopted after consultation of the European Central Bank.

Chapter 3. Institutional Provisions

Article 134 (ex Article 114 TEC). (1) In order to promote coordination of the policies of Member States to the full extent needed for the functioning of the internal market, an Economic and Financial Committee is hereby set up.

(2) The Economic and Financial Committee shall have the following tasks:
– to deliver opinions at the request of the Council or of the Commission, or on its own initiative for submission to those institutions,
– to keep under review the economic and financial situation of the Member States and of the Union and to report regularly thereon to the Council and to the Commission, in particular on financial relations with third countries and international institutions,
– without prejudice to Article 240, to contribute to the preparation of the work of the Council referred to in Articles 66, 75, 121(2), (3), (4) and (6), 122, 124, 125, 126, 127(6), 128(2), 129(3) and (4), 138, 140(2) and (3), 143, 144(2) and (3), and in Article 219, and to carry out other advisory and preparatory tasks assigned to it by the Council,
– to examine, at least once a year, the situation regarding the movement of capital and the freedom of payments, as they result from the application of the Treaties and of measures adopted by the Council; the examination shall cover all measures relating to capital movements and payments; the Committee

PART III   EUROPEAN UNION

shall report to the Commission and to the Council on the outcome of this examination.
The Member States, the Commission and the European Central Bank shall each appoint no more than two members of the Committee.
(3) The Council shall, on a proposal from the Commission and after consulting the European Central Bank and the Committee referred to in this Article, lay down detailed provisions concerning the composition of the Economic and Financial Committee. The President of the Council shall inform the European Parliament of such a decision.
(4) In addition to the tasks set out in paragraph 2, if and as long as there are Member States with a derogation as referred to in Article 139, the Committee shall keep under review the monetary and financial situation and the general payments system of those Member States and report regularly thereon to the Council and to the Commission.

Article 135 (ex Article 115 TEC). For matters within the scope of Articles 121(4), 126 with the exception of paragraph 14, 138, 140(1), 140(2), first subparagraph, 140(3) and 219, the Council or a Member State may request the Commission to make a recommendation or a proposal, as appropriate. The Commission shall examine this request and submit its conclusions to the Council without delay.

Chapter 4. Provisions Specific to Member States whose Currency is the Euro

Article 136. (1) In order to ensure the proper functioning of economic and monetary union, and in accordance with the relevant provisions of the Treaties, the Council shall, in accordance with the relevant procedure from among those referred to in Articles 121 and 126, with the exception of the procedure set out in Article 126(14), adopt measures specific to those Member States whose currency is the euro:
(a) to strengthen the coordination and surveillance of their budgetary discipline;
(b) to set out economic policy guidelines for them, while ensuring that they are compatible with those adopted for the whole of the Union and are kept under surveillance.
(2) For those measures set out in paragraph 1, only members of the Council representing Member States whose currency is the euro shall take part in the vote.
A qualified majority of the said members shall be defined in accordance with Article 238(3)(a).
(3) The Member States whose currency is the euro may establish a stability mechanism to be activated if indispensable to safeguard the stability of the euro area as a whole. The granting of any required financial assistance under the mechanism will be made subject to strict conditionality.

Article 137. Arrangements for meetings between ministers of those Member States whose currency is the euro are laid down by the Protocol on the Euro Group.

Article 138 (ex Article 111(4) TEC). (1) In order to secure the euro's place in the international monetary system, the Council, on a proposal from the Commission, shall adopt a decision establishing common positions on matters of particular interest for economic and monetary union within the competent international financial institutions and conferences. The Council shall act after consulting the European Central Bank.
(2) The Council, on a proposal from the Commission, may adopt appropriate measures to ensure unified representation within the international financial institutions and conferences. The Council shall act after consulting the European Central Bank.
(3) For the measures referred to in paragraphs 1 and 2, only members of the Council representing Member States whose currency is the euro shall take part in the vote.
A qualified majority of the said members shall be defined in accordance with Article 238(3)(a).

Chapter 5. Transitional Provisions

Article 139. (1) Member States in respect of which the Council has not decided that they fulfil the necessary conditions for the adoption of the euro shall hereinafter be referred to as "Member States with a derogation".
(2) The following provisions of the Treaties shall not apply to Member States with a derogation:
(a) adoption of the parts of the broad economic policy guidelines which concern the euro area generally (Article 121(2));
(b) coercive means of remedying excessive deficits (Article 126(9) and (11));
(c) the objectives and tasks of the ESCB (Article 127(1) to (3) and (5));
(d) issue of the euro (Article 128);
(e) acts of the European Central Bank (Article 132);
(f) measures governing the use of the euro (Article 133);
(g) monetary agreements and other measures relating to exchange–rate policy (Article 219);

(h) appointment of members of the Executive Board of the European Central Bank (Article 283(2));
(i) decisions establishing common positions on issues of particular relevance for economic and monetary union within the competent international financial institutions and conferences (Article 138(1));
(j) measures to ensure unified representation within the international financial institutions and conferences (Article 138(2)).
In the Articles referred to in points (a) to (j), "Member States" shall therefore mean Member States whose currency is the euro.
(3) Under Chapter IX of the Statute of the ESCB and of the ECB, Member States with a derogation and their national central banks are excluded from rights and obligations within the ESCB.
(4) The voting rights of members of the Council representing Member States with a derogation shall be suspended for the adoption by the Council of the measures referred to in the Articles listed in paragraph 2, and in the following instances:
(a) recommendations made to those Member States whose currency is the euro in the framework of multilateral surveillance, including on stability programmes and warnings (Article 121(4));
(b) measures relating to excessive deficits concerning those Member States whose currency is the euro (Article 126(6), (7), (8), (12) and (13)).
A qualified majority of the other members of the Council shall be defined in accordance with Article 238(3)(a).

Article 140 (ex Articles 121(1), 122(2), second sentence, and 123(5) TEC). (1) At least once every two years, or at the request of a Member State with a derogation, the Commission and the European Central Bank shall report to the Council on the progress made by the Member States with a derogation in fulfilling their obligations regarding the achievement of economic and monetary union. These reports shall include an examination of the compatibility between the national legislation of each of these Member States, including the statutes of its national central bank, and Articles 130 and 131 and the Statute of the ESCB and of the ECB. The reports shall also examine the achievement of a high degree of sustainable convergence by reference to the fulfilment by each Member State of the following criteria:
– the achievement of a high degree of price stability; this will be apparent from a rate of inflation which is close to that of, at most, the three best performing Member States in terms of price stability,
– the sustainability of the government financial position; this will be apparent from having achieved a government budgetary position without a deficit that is excessive as determined in accordance with Article 126(6),
– the observance of the normal fluctuation margins provided for by the exchange–rate mechanism of the European Monetary System, for at least two years, without devaluing against the euro,
– the durability of convergence achieved by the Member State with a derogation and of its participation in the exchange–rate mechanism being reflected in the long–term interest–rate levels.
The four criteria mentioned in this paragraph and the relevant periods over which they are to be respected are developed further in a Protocol annexed to the Treaties. The reports of the Commission and the European Central Bank shall also take account of the results of the integration of markets, the situation and development of the balances of payments on current account and an examination of the development of unit labour costs and other price indices.
(2) After consulting the European Parliament and after discussion in the European Council, the Council shall, on a proposal from the Commission, decide which Member States with a derogation fulfil the necessary conditions on the basis of the criteria set out in paragraph 1, and abrogate the derogations of the Member States concerned.
The Council shall act having received a recommendation of a qualified majority of those among its members representing Member States whose currency is the euro. These members shall act within six months of the Council receiving the Commission's proposal.
The qualified majority of the said members, as referred to in the second subparagraph, shall be defined in accordance with Article 238(3)(a).
(3) If it is decided, in accordance with the procedure set out in paragraph 2, to abrogate a derogation, the Council shall, acting with the unanimity of the Member States whose currency is the euro and the Member State concerned, on a proposal from the Commission and after consulting the European Central Bank, irrevocably fix the rate at which the euro shall be substituted for the currency of the Member State concerned, and take the other measures necessary for the introduction of the euro as the single currency in the Member State concerned.

Article 141 (ex Articles 123(3) and 117(2) first five indents, TEC). (1) If and as long as there are Member States with a derogation, and without prejudice to Article 129(1), the General Council of the European Central Bank referred to in Article 44 of the Statute of the ESCB and of the ECB shall be constituted as a third decision–making body of the European Central Bank.

(2) If and as long as there are Member States with a derogation, the European Central Bank shall, as regards those Member States:
– strengthen cooperation between the national central banks,
– strengthen the coordination of the monetary policies of the Member States, with the aim of ensuring price stability,
– monitor the functioning of the exchange–rate mechanism,
– hold consultations concerning issues falling within the competence of the national central banks and affecting the stability of financial institutions and markets,
– carry out the former tasks of the European Monetary Cooperation Fund which had subsequently been taken over by the European Monetary Institute.

Article 142 (ex Article 124(1) TEC). Each Member State with a derogation shall treat its exchange–rate policy as a matter of common interest. In so doing, Member States shall take account of the experience acquired in cooperation within the framework of the exchange–rate mechanism.

Article 143 (ex Article 119 TEC). (1) Where a Member State with a derogation is in difficulties or is seriously threatened with difficulties as regards its balance of payments either as a result of an overall disequilibrium in its balance of payments, or as a result of the type of currency at its disposal, and where such difficulties are liable in particular to jeopardise the functioning of the internal market or the implementation of the common commercial policy, the Commission shall immediately investigate the position of the State in question and the action which, making use of all the means at its disposal, that State has taken or may take in accordance with the provisions of the Treaties. The Commission shall state what measures it recommends the State concerned to take.
If the action taken by a Member State with a derogation and the measures suggested by the Commission do not prove sufficient to overcome the difficulties which have arisen or which threaten, the Commission shall, after consulting the Economic and Financial Committee, recommend to the Council the granting of mutual assistance and appropriate methods therefor.
The Commission shall keep the Council regularly informed of the situation and of how it is developing.
(2) The Council shall grant such mutual assistance; it shall adopt directives or decisions laying down the conditions and details of such assistance, which may take such forms as:
(a) a concerted approach to or within any other international organisations to which Member States with a derogation may have recourse;
(b) measures needed to avoid deflection of trade where the Member State with a derogation which is in difficulties maintains or reintroduces quantitative restrictions against third countries;
(c) the granting of limited credits by other Member States, subject to their agreement.
(3) If the mutual assistance recommended by the Commission is not granted by the Council or if the mutual assistance granted and the measures taken are insufficient, the Commission shall authorise the Member State with a derogation which is in difficulties to take protective measures, the conditions and details of which the Commission shall determine.
Such authorisation may be revoked and such conditions and details may be changed by the Council.

Article 144 (ex Article 120 TEC). (1) Where a sudden crisis in the balance of payments occurs and a decision within the meaning of Article 143(2) is not immediately taken, a Member State with a derogation may, as a precaution, take the necessary protective measures. Such measures must cause the least possible disturbance in the functioning of the internal market and must not be wider in scope than is strictly necessary to remedy the sudden difficulties which have arisen.
(2) The Commission and the other Member States shall be informed of such protective measures not later than when they enter into force. The Commission may recommend to the Council the granting of mutual assistance under Article 143.
(3) After the Commission has delivered a recommendation and the Economic and Financial Committee has been consulted, the Council may decide that the Member State concerned shall amend, suspend or abolish the protective measures referred to above.

Title IX. Employment

Article 145 (ex Article 125 TEC). Member States and the Union shall, in accordance with this Title, work towards developing a coordinated strategy for employment and particularly for promoting a skilled, trained and adaptable workforce and labour markets responsive to economic change with a view to achieving the objectives defined in Article 3 of the Treaty on European Union.

Article 146 (ex Article 126 TEC). (1) Member States, through their employment policies, shall contribute to the achievement of the objectives referred to in Article 145 in a way consistent with the broad guidelines of the economic policies of the Member States and of the Union adopted pursuant to Article 121(2).
(2) Member States, having regard to national practices related to the responsibilities of management and labour, shall regard promoting employment as a matter of common concern and shall coordinate their action in this respect within the Council, in accordance with the provisions of Article 148.

Article 147 (ex Article 127 TEC). (1) The Union shall contribute to a high level of employment by encouraging cooperation between Member States and by supporting and, if necessary, complementing their action. In doing so, the competences of the Member States shall be respected.
(2) The objective of a high level of employment shall be taken into consideration in the formulation and implementation of Union policies and activities.

Article 148 (ex Article 128 TEC). (1) The European Council shall each year consider the employment situation in the Union and adopt conclusions thereon, on the basis of a joint annual report by the Council and the Commission.
(2) On the basis of the conclusions of the European Council, the Council, on a proposal from the Commission and after consulting the European Parliament, the Economic and Social Committee, the Committee of the Regions and the Employment Committee referred to in Article 150, shall each year draw up guidelines which the Member States shall take into account in their employment policies. These guidelines shall be consistent with the broad guidelines adopted pursuant to Article 121(2).
(3) Each Member State shall provide the Council and the Commission with an annual report on the principal measures taken to implement its employment policy in the light of the guidelines for employment as referred to in paragraph 2.
(4) The Council, on the basis of the reports referred to in paragraph 3 and having received the views of the Employment Committee, shall each year carry out an examination of the implementation of the employment policies of the Member States in the light of the guidelines for employment. The Council, on a recommendation from the Commission, may, if it considers it appropriate in the light of that examination, make recommendations to Member States.
(5) On the basis of the results of that examination, the Council and the Commission shall make a joint annual report to the European Council on the employment situation in the Union and on the implementation of the guidelines for employment.

Article 149 (ex Article 129 TEC). The European Parliament and the Council, acting in accordance with the ordinary legislative procedure and after consulting the Economic and Social Committee and the Committee of the Regions, may adopt incentive measures designed to encourage cooperation between Member States and to support their action in the field of employment through initiatives aimed at developing exchanges of information and best practices, providing comparative analysis and advice as well as promoting innovative approaches and evaluating experiences, in particular by recourse to pilot projects.
Those measures shall not include harmonisation of the laws and regulations of the Member States.

Article 150 (ex Article 130 TEC). The Council, acting by a simple majority after consulting the European Parliament, shall establish an Employment Committee with advisory status to promote coordination between Member States on employment and labour market policies. The tasks of the Committee shall be:
– to monitor the employment situation and employment policies in the Member States and the Union,
– without prejudice to Article 240, to formulate opinions at the request of either the Council or the Commission or on its own initiative, and to contribute to the preparation of the Council proceedings referred to in Article 148.
In fulfilling its mandate, the Committee shall consult management and labour.
Each Member State and the Commission shall appoint two members of the Committee.

Title X. Social Policy

Article 151 (ex Article 136 TEC). The Union and the Member States, having in mind fundamental social rights such as those set out in the European Social Charter signed at Turin on 18 October 1961 and in the 1989 Community Charter of the Fundamental Social Rights of Workers, shall have as their objectives the promotion of employment, improved living and working conditions, so as to make possible their harmonisation while the improvement is being maintained, proper social protection, dialogue between management and labour, the development of human resources with a view to lasting high employment and the combating of exclusion.

To this end the Union and the Member States shall implement measures which take account of the diverse forms of national practices, in particular in the field of contractual relations, and the need to maintain the competitiveness of the Union economy.

They believe that such a development will ensue not only from the functioning of the internal market, which will favour the harmonisation of social systems, but also from the procedures provided for in the Treaties and from the approximation of provisions laid down by law, regulation or administrative action.

Article 152. The Union recognises and promotes the role of the social partners at its level, taking into account the diversity of national systems. It shall facilitate dialogue between the social partners, respecting their autonomy.

The Tripartite Social Summit for Growth and Employment shall contribute to social dialogue.

Article 153 (ex Article 137 TEC). (1) With a view to achieving the objectives of Article 151, the Union shall support and complement the activities of the Member States in the following fields:
(a) improvement in particular of the working environment to protect workers' health and safety;
(b) working conditions;
(c) social security and social protection of workers;
(d) protection of workers where their employment contract is terminated;
(e) the information and consultation of workers;
(f) representation and collective defence of the interests of workers and employers, including co–determination, subject to paragraph 5;
(g) conditions of employment for third–country nationals legally residing in Union territory;
(h) the integration of persons excluded from the labour market, without prejudice to Article 166;
(i) equality between men and women with regard to labour market opportunities and treatment at work;
(j) the combating of social exclusion;
(k) the modernisation of social protection systems without prejudice to point (c).
(2) To this end, the European Parliament and the Council:
(a) may adopt measures designed to encourage cooperation between Member States through initiatives aimed at improving knowledge, developing exchanges of information and best practices, promoting innovative approaches and evaluating experiences, excluding any harmonisation of the laws and regulations of the Member States;
(b) may adopt, in the fields referred to in paragraph 1(a) to (i), by means of directives, minimum requirements for gradual implementation, having regard to the conditions and technical rules obtaining in each of the Member States. Such directives shall avoid imposing administrative, financial and legal constraints in a way which would hold back the creation and development of small and medium–sized undertakings.

The European Parliament and the Council shall act in accordance with the ordinary legislative procedure after consulting the Economic and Social Committee and the Committee of the Regions.

In the fields referred to in paragraph 1(c), (d), (f) and (g), the Council shall act unanimously, in accordance with a special legislative procedure, after consulting the European Parliament and the said Committees.

The Council, acting unanimously on a proposal from the Commission, after consulting the European Parliament, may decide to render the ordinary legislative procedure applicable to paragraph 1(d), (f) and (g).

(3) A Member State may entrust management and labour, at their joint request, with the implementation of directives adopted pursuant to paragraph 2, or, where appropriate, with the implementation of a Council decision adopted in accordance with Article 155.

In this case, it shall ensure that, no later than the date on which a directive or a decision must be transposed or implemented, management and labour have introduced the necessary measures by agreement, the Member State concerned being required to take any necessary measure enabling it at any time to be in a position to guarantee the results imposed by that directive or that decision.

(4) The provisions adopted pursuant to this Article:
– shall not affect the right of Member States to define the fundamental principles of their social security systems and must not significantly affect the financial equilibrium thereof,
– shall not prevent any Member State from maintaining or introducing more stringent protective measures compatible with the Treaties.

(5) The provisions of this Article shall not apply to pay, the right of association, the right to strike or the right to impose lock–outs.

Article 154 (ex Article 138 TEC). (1) The Commission shall have the task of promoting the consultation of management and labour at Union level and shall take any relevant measure to facilitate their dialogue by ensuring balanced support for the parties.
(2) To this end, before submitting proposals in the social policy field, the Commission shall consult management and labour on the possible direction of Union action.
(3) If, after such consultation, the Commission considers Union action advisable, it shall consult management and labour on the content of the envisaged proposal. Management and labour shall forward to the Commission an opinion or, where appropriate, a recommendation.
(4) On the occasion of the consultation referred to in paragraphs 2 and 3, management and labour may inform the Commission of their wish to initiate the process provided for in Article 155. The duration of this process shall not exceed nine months, unless the management and labour concerned and the Commission decide jointly to extend it.

Article 155 (ex Article 139 TEC). (1) Should management and labour so desire, the dialogue between them at Union level may lead to contractual relations, including agreements.
(2) Agreements concluded at Union level shall be implemented either in accordance with the procedures and practices specific to management and labour and the Member States or, in matters covered by Article 153, at the joint request of the signatory parties, by a Council decision on a proposal from the Commission. The European Parliament shall be informed.
The Council shall act unanimously where the agreement in question contains one or more provisions relating to one of the areas for which unanimity is required pursuant to Article 153(2).

Article 156 (ex Article 140 TEC). With a view to achieving the objectives of Article 151 and without prejudice to the other provisions of the Treaties, the Commission shall encourage cooperation between the Member States and facilitate the coordination of their action in all social policy fields under this Chapter, particularly in matters relating to:
– employment,
– labour law and working conditions,
– basic and advanced vocational training,
– social security,
– prevention of occupational accidents and diseases,
– occupational hygiene,
– the right of association and collective bargaining between employers and workers.
To this end, the Commission shall act in close contact with Member States by making studies, delivering opinions and arranging consultations both on problems arising at national level and on those of concern to international organisations, in particular initiatives aiming at the establishment of guidelines and indicators, the organisation of exchange of best practice, and the preparation of the necessary elements for periodic monitoring and evaluation. The European Parliament shall be kept fully informed.
Before delivering the opinions provided for in this Article, the Commission shall consult the Economic and Social Committee.

Article 157 (ex Article 141 TEC). (1) Each Member State shall ensure that the principle of equal pay for male and female workers for equal work or work of equal value is applied.
(2) For the purpose of this Article, "pay" means the ordinary basic or minimum wage or salary and any other consideration, whether in cash or in kind, which the worker receives directly or indirectly, in respect of his employment, from his employer.
Equal pay without discrimination based on sex means:
(a) that pay for the same work at piece rates shall be calculated on the basis of the same unit of measurement;
(b) that pay for work at time rates shall be the same for the same job.
(3) The European Parliament and the Council, acting in accordance with the ordinary legislative procedure, and after consulting the Economic and Social Committee, shall adopt measures to ensure the application of the principle of equal opportunities and equal treatment of men and women in matters of employment and occupation, including the principle of equal pay for equal work or work of equal value.
(4) With a view to ensuring full equality in practice between men and women in working life, the principle of equal treatment shall not prevent any Member State from maintaining or adopting measures providing for specific advantages in order to make it easier for the underrepresented sex to pursue a vocational activity or to prevent or compensate for disadvantages in professional careers.

Article 158 (ex Article 142 TEC). Member States shall endeavour to maintain the existing equivalence between paid holiday schemes.

PART III   EUROPEAN UNION

Article 159 (ex Article 143 TEC). The Commission shall draw up a report each year on progress in achieving the objectives of Article 151, including the demographic situation in the Union. It shall forward the report to the European Parliament, the Council and the Economic and Social Committee.

Article 160 (ex Article 144 TEC). The Council, acting by a simple majority after consulting the European Parliament, shall establish a Social Protection Committee with advisory status to promote cooperation on social protection policies between Member States and with the Commission. The tasks of the Committee shall be:
– to monitor the social situation and the development of social protection policies in the Member States and the Union,
– to promote exchanges of information, experience and good practice between Member States and with the Commission,
– without prejudice to Article 240, to prepare reports, formulate opinions or undertake other work within its fields of competence, at the request of either the Council or the Commission or on its own initiative.
In fulfilling its mandate, the Committee shall establish appropriate contacts with management and labour.
Each Member State and the Commission shall appoint two members of the Committee.

Article 161 (ex Article 145 TEC). The Commission shall include a separate chapter on social developments within the Union in its annual report to the European Parliament.
The European Parliament may invite the Commission to draw up reports on any particular problems concerning social conditions.

Title XI. The European Social Fund

Article 162 (ex Article 146 TEC). In order to improve employment opportunities for workers in the internal market and to contribute thereby to raising the standard of living, a European Social Fund is hereby established in accordance with the provisions set out below; it shall aim to render the employment of workers easier and to increase their geographical and occupational mobility within the Union, and to facilitate their adaptation to industrial changes and to changes in production systems, in particular through vocational training and retraining.

Article 163 (ex Article 147 TEC). The Fund shall be administered by the Commission.
The Commission shall be assisted in this task by a Committee presided over by a Member of the Commission and composed of representatives of governments, trade unions and employers' organisations.

Article 164 (ex Article 148 TEC). The European Parliament and the Council, acting in accordance with the ordinary legislative procedure and after consulting the Economic and Social Committee and the Committee of the Regions, shall adopt implementing regulations relating to the European Social Fund.

Title XII. Education, Vocational Training, Youth and Sport

Article 165 (ex Article 149 TEC). (1) The Union shall contribute to the development of quality education by encouraging cooperation between Member States and, if necessary, by supporting and supplementing their action, while fully respecting the responsibility of the Member States for the content of teaching and the organisation of education systems and their cultural and linguistic diversity.
The Union shall contribute to the promotion of European sporting issues, while taking account of the specific nature of sport, its structures based on voluntary activity and its social and educational function.
(2) Union action shall be aimed at:
– developing the European dimension in education, particularly through the teaching and dissemination of the languages of the Member States,
– encouraging mobility of students and teachers, by encouraging inter alia, the academic recognition of diplomas and periods of study,
– promoting cooperation between educational establishments,
– developing exchanges of information and experience on issues common to the education systems of the Member States,
– encouraging the development of youth exchanges and of exchanges of socio–educational instructors, and encouraging the participation of young people in democratic life in Europe,
– encouraging the development of distance education,

– developing the European dimension in sport, by promoting fairness and openness in sporting competitions and cooperation between bodies responsible for sports, and by protecting the physical and moral integrity of sportsmen and sportswomen, especially the youngest sportsmen and sportswomen.
(3) The Union and the Member States shall foster cooperation with third countries and the competent international organisations in the field of education and sport, in particular the Council of Europe.
(4) In order to contribute to the achievement of the objectives referred to in this Article:
– the European Parliament and the Council, acting in accordance with the ordinary legislative procedure, after consulting the Economic and Social Committee and the Committee of the Regions, shall adopt incentive measures, excluding any harmonisation of the laws and regulations of the Member States,
– the Council, on a proposal from the Commission, shall adopt recommendations.

Article 166 (ex Article 150 TEC). (1) The Union shall implement a vocational training policy which shall support and supplement the action of the Member States, while fully respecting the responsibility of the Member States for the content and organisation of vocational training.
(2) Union action shall aim to:
– facilitate adaptation to industrial changes, in particular through vocational training and retraining,
– improve initial and continuing vocational training in order to facilitate vocational integration and reintegration into the labour market,
– facilitate access to vocational training and encourage mobility of instructors and trainees and particularly young people,
– stimulate cooperation on training between educational or training establishments and firms,
– develop exchanges of information and experience on issues common to the training systems of the Member States.
(3) The Union and the Member States shall foster cooperation with third countries and the competent international organisations in the sphere of vocational training.
(4) The European Parliament and the Council, acting in accordance with the ordinary legislative procedure and after consulting the Economic and Social Committee and the Committee of the Regions, shall adopt measures to contribute to the achievement of the objectives referred to in this Article, excluding any harmonisation of the laws and regulations of the Member States, and the Council, on a proposal from the Commission, shall adopt recommendations.

Title XIII. Culture

Article 167 (ex Article 151 TEC). (1) The Union shall contribute to the flowering of the cultures of the Member States, while respecting their national and regional diversity and at the same time bringing the common cultural heritage to the fore.
(2) Action by the Union shall be aimed at encouraging cooperation between Member States and, if necessary, supporting and supplementing their action in the following areas:
– improvement of the knowledge and dissemination of the culture and history of the European peoples,
– conservation and safeguarding of cultural heritage of European significance,
– non–commercial cultural exchanges,
– artistic and literary creation, including in the audiovisual sector.
(3) The Union and the Member States shall foster cooperation with third countries and the competent international organisations in the sphere of culture, in particular the Council of Europe.
(4) The Union shall take cultural aspects into account in its action under other provisions of the Treaties, in particular in order to respect and to promote the diversity of its cultures.
(5) In order to contribute to the achievement of the objectives referred to in this Article:
– the European Parliament and the Council acting in accordance with the ordinary legislative procedure and after consulting the Committee of the Regions, shall adopt incentive measures, excluding any harmonisation of the laws and regulations of the Member States,
– the Council, on a proposal from the Commission, shall adopt recommendations.

Title XIV. Health

Article 168 (ex Article 152 TEC). (1) A high level of human health protection shall be ensured in the definition and implementation of all Union policies and activities.
Union action, which shall complement national policies, shall be directed towards improving public health, preventing physical and mental illness and diseases, and obviating sources of danger to physical and mental health. Such action shall cover the fight against the major health scourges, by promoting research into their causes, their transmission and their prevention, as well as health infor-

mation and education, and monitoring, early warning of and combating serious cross–border threats to health.

The Union shall complement the Member States' action in reducing drugs–related health damage, including information and prevention.

(2) The Union shall encourage cooperation between the Member States in the areas referred to in this Article and, if necessary, lend support to their action. It shall in particular encourage cooperation between the Member States to improve the complementarity of their health services in cross–border areas.

Member States shall, in liaison with the Commission, coordinate among themselves their policies and programmes in the areas referred to in paragraph 1. The Commission may, in close contact with the Member States, take any useful initiative to promote such coordination, in particular initiatives aiming at the establishment of guidelines and indicators, the organisation of exchange of best practice, and the preparation of the necessary elements for periodic monitoring and evaluation. The European Parliament shall be kept fully informed.

(3) The Union and the Member States shall foster cooperation with third countries and the competent international organisations in the sphere of public health.

(4) By way of derogation from Article 2(5) and Article 6(a) and in accordance with Article 4(2)(k) the European Parliament and the Council, acting in accordance with the ordinary legislative procedure and after consulting the Economic and Social Committee and the Committee of the Regions, shall contribute to the achievement of the objectives referred to in this Article through adopting in order to meet common safety concerns:

(a) measures setting high standards of quality and safety of organs and substances of human origin, blood and blood derivatives; these measures shall not prevent any Member State from maintaining or introducing more stringent protective measures;

(b) measures in the veterinary and phytosanitary fields which have as their direct objective the protection of public health;

(c) measures setting high standards of quality and safety for medicinal products and devices for medical use.

(5) The European Parliament and the Council, acting in accordance with the ordinary legislative procedure and after consulting the Economic and Social Committee and the Committee of the Regions, may also adopt incentive measures designed to protect and improve human health and in particular to combat the major cross–border health scourges, measures concerning monitoring, early warning of and combating serious cross–border threats to health, and measures which have as their direct objective the protection of public health regarding tobacco and the abuse of alcohol, excluding any harmonisation of the laws and regulations of the Member States.

(6) The Council, on a proposal from the Commission, may also adopt recommendations for the purposes set out in this Article.

(7) Union action shall respect the responsibilities of the Member States for the definition of their health policy and for the organisation and delivery of health services and medical care. The responsibilities of the Member States shall include the management of health services and medical care and the allocation of the resources assigned to them. The measures referred to in paragraph 4(a) shall not affect national provisions on the donation or medical use of organs and blood.

Title XV. Consumer Protection

Article 169 (ex Article 153 TEC). (1) In order to promote the interests of consumers and to ensure a high level of consumer protection, the Union shall contribute to protecting the health, safety and economic interests of consumers, as well as to promoting their right to information, education and to organise themselves in order to safeguard their interests.

(2) The Union shall contribute to the attainment of the objectives referred to in paragraph 1 through:
(a) measures adopted pursuant to Article 114 in the context of the completion of the internal market;
(b) measures which support, supplement and monitor the policy pursued by the Member States.

(3) The European Parliament and the Council, acting in accordance with the ordinary legislative procedure and after consulting the Economic and Social Committee, shall adopt the measures referred to in paragraph 2(b).

(4) Measures adopted pursuant to paragraph 3 shall not prevent any Member State from maintaining or introducing more stringent protective measures. Such measures must be compatible with the Treaties. The Commission shall be notified of them.

Title XVI. Trans–European Networks

Article 170 (ex Article 154 TEC). (1) To help achieve the objectives referred to in Articles 26 and

174 and to enable citizens of the Union, economic operators and regional and local communities to derive full benefit from the setting–up of an area without internal frontiers, the Union shall contribute to the establishment and development of trans–European networks in the areas of transport, telecommunications and energy infrastructures.

(2) Within the framework of a system of open and competitive markets, action by the Union shall aim at promoting the interconnection and interoperability of national networks as well as access to such networks. It shall take account in particular of the need to link island, landlocked and peripheral regions with the central regions of the Union.

Article 171 (ex Article 155 TEC). (1) In order to achieve the objectives referred to in Article 170, the Union:
– shall establish a series of guidelines covering the objectives, priorities and broad lines of measures envisaged in the sphere of trans–European networks; these guidelines shall identify projects of common interest,
– shall implement any measures that may prove necessary to ensure the interoperability of the networks, in particular in the field of technical standardisation,
– may support projects of common interest supported by Member States, which are identified in the framework of the guidelines referred to in the first indent, particularly through feasibility studies, loan guarantees or interest–rate subsidies; the Union may also contribute, through the Cohesion Fund set up pursuant to Article 177, to the financing of specific projects in Member States in the area of transport infrastructure.
The Union's activities shall take into account the potential economic viability of the projects.
(2) Member States shall, in liaison with the Commission, coordinate among themselves the policies pursued at national level which may have a significant impact on the achievement of the objectives referred to in Article 170. The Commission may, in close cooperation with the Member State, take any useful initiative to promote such coordination.
3. The Union may decide to cooperate with third countries to promote projects of mutual interest and to ensure the interoperability of networks.

Article 172 (ex Article 156 TEC). The guidelines and other measures referred to in Article 171(1) shall be adopted by the European Parliament and the Council, acting in accordance with the ordinary legislative procedure and after consulting the Economic and Social Committee and the Committee of the Regions.
Guidelines and projects of common interest which relate to the territory of a Member State shall require the approval of the Member State concerned.

Title XVII. Industry

Article 173 (ex Article 157 TEC). (1) The Union and the Member States shall ensure that the conditions necessary for the competitiveness of the Union's industry exist.
For that purpose, in accordance with a system of open and competitive markets, their action shall be aimed at:
– speeding up the adjustment of industry to structural changes,
– encouraging an environment favourable to initiative and to the development of undertakings throughout the Union, particularly small and medium–sized undertakings,
– encouraging an environment favourable to cooperation between undertakings,
– fostering better exploitation of the industrial potential of policies of innovation, research and technological development.
(2) The Member States shall consult each other in liaison with the Commission and, where necessary, shall coordinate their action. The Commission may take any useful initiative to promote such coordination, in particular initiatives aiming at the establishment of guidelines and indicators, the organisation of exchange of best practice, and the preparation of the necessary elements for periodic monitoring and evaluation. The European Parliament shall be kept fully informed.
(3) The Union shall contribute to the achievement of the objectives set out in paragraph 1 through the policies and activities it pursues under other provisions of the Treaties. The European Parliament and the Council, acting in accordance with the ordinary legislative procedure and after consulting the Economic and Social Committee, may decide on specific measures in support of action taken in the Member States to achieve the objectives set out in paragraph 1, excluding any harmonisation of the laws and regulations of the Member States.
This Title shall not provide a basis for the introduction by the Union of any measure which could lead to a distortion of competition or contains tax provisions or provisions relating to the rights and interests of employed persons.

PART III   EUROPEAN UNION

Title XVIII. Economic, Social and Territorial Cohesion

Article 174 (ex Article 158 TEC). In order to promote its overall harmonious development, the Union shall develop and pursue its actions leading to the strengthening of its economic, social and territorial cohesion.

In particular, the Union shall aim at reducing disparities between the levels of development of the various regions and the backwardness of the least favoured regions.

Among the regions concerned, particular attention shall be paid to rural areas, areas affected by industrial transition, and regions which suffer from severe and permanent natural or demographic handicaps such as the northernmost regions with very low population density and island, cross–border and mountain regions.

Article 175 (ex Article 159 TEC). Member States shall conduct their economic policies and shall coordinate them in such a way as, in addition, to attain the objectives set out in Article 174. The formulation and implementation of the Union's policies and actions and the implementation of the internal market shall take into account the objectives set out in Article 174 and shall contribute to their achievement. The Union shall also support the achievement of these objectives by the action it takes through the Structural Funds (European Agricultural Guidance and Guarantee Fund, Guidance Section; European Social Fund; European Regional Development Fund), the European Investment Bank and the other existing Financial Instruments.

The Commission shall submit a report to the European Parliament, the Council, the Economic and Social Committee and the Committee of the Regions every three years on the progress made towards achieving economic, social and territorial cohesion and on the manner in which the various means provided for in this Article have contributed to it. This report shall, if necessary, be accompanied by appropriate proposals.

If specific actions prove necessary outside the Funds and without prejudice to the measures decided upon within the framework of the other Union policies, such actions may be adopted by the European Parliament and the Council acting in accordance with the ordinary legislative procedure and after consulting the Economic and Social Committee and the Committee of the Regions.

Article 176 (ex Article 160 TEC). The European Regional Development Fund is intended to help to redress the main regional imbalances in the Union through participation in the development and structural adjustment of regions whose development is lagging behind and in the conversion of declining industrial regions.

Article 177 (ex Article 161 TEC). Without prejudice to Article 178, the European Parliament and the Council, acting by means of regulations in accordance with the ordinary legislative procedure and consulting the Economic and Social Committee and the Committee of the Regions, shall define the tasks, priority objectives and the organisation of the Structural Funds, which may involve grouping the Funds. The general rules applicable to them and the provisions necessary to ensure their effectiveness and the coordination of the Funds with one another and with the other existing Financial Instruments shall also be defined by the same procedure.

A Cohesion Fund set up in accordance with the same procedure shall provide a financial contribution to projects in the fields of environment and trans–European networks in the area of transport infrastructure.

Article 178 (ex Article 162 TEC). Implementing regulations relating to the European Regional Development Fund shall be taken by the European Parliament and the Council, acting in accordance with the ordinary legislative procedure and after consulting the Economic and Social Committee and the Committee of the Regions.

With regard to the European Agricultural Guidance and Guarantee Fund, Guidance Section, and the European Social Fund, Articles 43 and 164 respectively shall continue to apply.

Title XIX. Research and Technological Development and Space

Article 179 (ex Article 163 TEC). (1) The Union shall have the objective of strengthening its scientific and technological bases by achieving a European research area in which researchers, scientific knowledge and technology circulate freely, and encouraging it to become more competitive, including in its industry, while promoting all the research activities deemed necessary by virtue of other Chapters of the Treaties.

(2) For this purpose the Union shall, throughout the Union, encourage undertakings, including small and medium–sized undertakings, research centres and universities in their research and technological development activities of high quality; it shall support their efforts to cooperate with one

another, aiming, notably, at permitting researchers to cooperate freely across borders and at enabling undertakings to exploit the internal market potential to the full, in particular through the opening–up of national public contracts, the definition of common standards and the removal of legal and fiscal obstacles to that cooperation.

(3) All Union activities under the Treaties in the area of research and technological development, including demonstration projects, shall be decided on and implemented in accordance with the provisions of this Title.

Article 180 (ex Article 164 TEC). In pursuing these objectives, the Union shall carry out the following activities, complementing the activities carried out in the Member States:
(a) implementation of research, technological development and demonstration programmes, by promoting cooperation with and between undertakings, research centres and universities;
(b) promotion of cooperation in the field of Union research, technological development and demonstration with third countries and international organisations;
(c) dissemination and optimisation of the results of activities in Union research, technological development and demonstration;
(d) stimulation of the training and mobility of researchers in the Union.

Article 181 (ex Article 165 TEC). (1) The Union and the Member States shall coordinate their research and technological development activities so as to ensure that national policies and Union policy are mutually consistent.
(2) In close cooperation with the Member State, the Commission may take any useful initiative to promote the coordination referred to in paragraph 1, in particular initiatives aiming at the establishment of guidelines and indicators, the organisation of exchange of best practice, and the preparation of the necessary elements for periodic monitoring and evaluation. The European Parliament shall be kept fully informed.

Article 182 (ex Article 166 TEC). (1) A multiannual framework programme, setting out all the activities of the Union, shall be adopted by the European Parliament and the Council, acting in accordance with the ordinary legislative procedure after consulting the Economic and Social Committee.
The framework programme shall:
– establish the scientific and technological objectives to be achieved by the activities provided for in Article 180 and fix the relevant priorities,
– indicate the broad lines of such activities,
– fix the maximum overall amount and the detailed rules for Union financial participation in the framework programme and the respective shares in each of the activities provided for.
(2) The framework programme shall be adapted or supplemented as the situation changes.
(3) The framework programme shall be implemented through specific programmes developed within each activity. Each specific programme shall define the detailed rules for implementing it, fix its duration and provide for the means deemed necessary. The sum of the amounts deemed necessary, fixed in the specific programmes, may not exceed the overall maximum amount fixed for the framework programme and each activity.
(4) The Council, acting in accordance with a special legislative procedure and after consulting the European Parliament and the Economic and Social Committee, shall adopt the specific programmes.
(5) As a complement to the activities planned in the multiannual framework programme, the European Parliament and the Council, acting in accordance with the ordinary legislative procedure and after consulting the Economic and Social Committee, shall establish the measures necessary for the implementation of the European research area.

Article 183 (ex Article 167 TEC). For the implementation of the multiannual framework programme the Union shall:
– determine the rules for the participation of undertakings, research centres and universities,
– lay down the rules governing the dissemination of research results.

Article 184 (ex Article 168 TEC). In implementing the multiannual framework programme, supplementary programmes may be decided on involving the participation of certain Member States only, which shall finance them subject to possible Union participation.
The Union shall adopt the rules applicable to supplementary programmes, particularly as regards the dissemination of knowledge and access by other Member States.

Article 185 (ex Article 169 TEC). In implementing the multiannual framework programme, the Union may make provision, in agreement with the Member States concerned, for participation in research and development programmes undertaken by several Member States, including participation in the structures created for the execution of those programmes.

Article 186 (ex Article 170 TEC). In implementing the multiannual framework programme the Union may make provision for cooperation in Union research, technological development and demonstration with third countries or international organisations.
The detailed arrangements for such cooperation may be the subject of agreements between the Union and the third parties concerned.

Article 187 (ex Article 171 TEC). The Union may set up joint undertakings or any other structure necessary for the efficient execution of Union research, technological development and demonstration programmes.

Article 188 (ex Article 172 TEC). The Council, on a proposal from the Commission and after consulting the European Parliament and the Economic and Social Committee, shall adopt the provisions referred to in Article 187.
The European Parliament and the Council, acting in accordance with the ordinary legislative procedure and after consulting the Economic and Social Committee, shall adopt the provisions referred to in Articles 183, 184 and 185. Adoption of the supplementary programmes shall require the agreement of the Member States concerned.

Article 189. (1) To promote scientific and technical progress, industrial competitiveness and the implementation of its policies, the Union shall draw up a European space policy. To this end, it may promote joint initiatives, support research and technological development and coordinate the efforts needed for the exploration and exploitation of space.
(2) To contribute to attaining the objectives referred to in paragraph 1, the European Parliament and the Council, acting in accordance with the ordinary legislative procedure, shall establish the necessary measures, which may take the form of a European space programme, excluding any harmonisation of the laws and regulations of the Member States.
(3) The Union shall establish any appropriate relations with the European Space Agency.
(4) This Article shall be without prejudice to the other provisions of this Title.

Article 190 (ex Article 173 TEC). At the beginning of each year the Commission shall send a report to the European Parliament and to the Council. The report shall include information on research and technological development activities and the dissemination of results during the previous year, and the work programme for the current year.

Title XX. Environment

Article 191 (ex Article 174 TEC). (1) Union policy on the environment shall contribute to pursuit of the following objectives:
– preserving, protecting and improving the quality of the environment,
– protecting human health,
– prudent and rational utilisation of natural resources,
– promoting measures at international level to deal with regional or worldwide environmental problems, and in particular combating climate change.
(2) Union policy on the environment shall aim at a high level of protection taking into account the diversity of situations in the various regions of the Union. It shall be based on the precautionary principle and on the principles that preventive action should be taken, that environmental damage should as a priority be rectified at source and that the polluter should pay.
In this context, harmonisation measures answering environmental protection requirements shall include, where appropriate, a safeguard clause allowing Member States to take provisional measures, for non–economic environmental reasons, subject to a procedure of inspection by the Union.
(3) In preparing its policy on the environment, the Union shall take account of:
– available scientific and technical data,
– environmental conditions in the various regions of the Union,
– the potential benefits and costs of action or lack of action,
– the economic and social development of the Union as a whole and the balanced development of its regions.
(4) Within their respective spheres of competence, the Union and the Member States shall cooperate with third countries and with the competent international organisations. The arrangements for Union cooperation may be the subject of agreements between the Union and the third parties concerned.
The previous subparagraph shall be without prejudice to Member States' competence to negotiate in international bodies and to conclude international agreements.

Article 192 (ex Article 175 TEC). (1) The European Parliament and the Council, acting in accordance with the ordinary legislative procedure and after consulting the Economic and Social Committee and the Committee of the Regions, shall decide what action is to be taken by the Union in order to achieve the objectives referred to in Article 191.

(2) By way of derogation from the decision–making procedure provided for in paragraph 1 and without prejudice to Article 114, the Council acting unanimously in accordance with a special legislative procedure and after consulting the European Parliament, the Economic and Social Committee and the Committee of the Regions, shall adopt:

(a) provisions primarily of a fiscal nature;

(b) measures affecting:

– town and country planning,

– quantitative management of water resources or affecting, directly or indirectly, the availability of those resources,

– land use, with the exception of waste management;

(c) measures significantly affecting a Member State's choice between different energy sources and the general structure of its energy supply.

The Council, acting unanimously on a proposal from the Commission and after consulting the European Parliament, the Economic and Social Committee and the Committee of the Regions, may make the ordinary legislative procedure applicable to the matters referred to in the first subparagraph.

(3) General action programmes setting out priority objectives to be attained shall be adopted by the European Parliament and the Council, acting in accordance with the ordinary legislative procedure and after consulting the Economic and Social Committee and the Committee of the Regions.

The measures necessary for the implementation of these programmes shall be adopted under the terms of paragraph 1 or 2, as the case may be.

(4) Without prejudice to certain measures adopted by the Union, the Member States shall finance and implement the environment policy.

(5) Without prejudice to the principle that the polluter should pay, if a measure based on the provisions of paragraph 1 involves costs deemed disproportionate for the public authorities of a Member State, such measure shall lay down appropriate provisions in the form of:

– temporary derogations, and/or

– financial support from the Cohesion Fund set up pursuant to Article 177.

Article 193 (ex Article 176 TEC). The protective measures adopted pursuant to Article 192 shall not prevent any Member State from maintaining or introducing more stringent protective measures. Such measures must be compatible with the Treaties. They shall be notified to the Commission.

Title XXI. Energy

Article 194. (1) In the context of the establishment and functioning of the internal market and with regard for the need to preserve and improve the environment, Union policy on energy shall aim, in a spirit of solidarity between Member States, to:

(a) ensure the functioning of the energy market;

(b) ensure security of energy supply in the Union;

(c) promote energy efficiency and energy saving and the development of new and renewable forms of energy; and

(d) promote the interconnection of energy networks.

(2) Without prejudice to the application of other provisions of the Treaties, the European Parliament and the Council, acting in accordance with the ordinary legislative procedure, shall establish the measures necessary to achieve the objectives in paragraph 1. Such measures shall be adopted after consultation of the Economic and Social Committee and the Committee of the Regions.

Such measures shall not affect a Member State's right to determine the conditions for exploiting its energy resources, its choice between different energy sources and the general structure of its energy supply, without prejudice to Article 192(2)(c).

(3) By way of derogation from paragraph 2, the Council, acting in accordance with a special legislative procedure, shall unanimously and after consulting the European Parliament, establish the measures referred to therein when they are primarily of a fiscal nature.

Title XXII. Tourism

Article 195. (1) The Union shall complement the action of the Member States in the tourism sector, in particular by promoting the competitiveness of Union undertakings in that sector.

To that end, Union action shall be aimed at:

(a) encouraging the creation of a favourable environment for the development of undertakings in this sector;
(b) promoting cooperation between the Member States, particularly by the exchange of good practice.
(2) The European Parliament and the Council, acting in accordance with the ordinary legislative procedure, shall establish specific measures to complement actions within the Member States to achieve the objectives referred to in this Article, excluding any harmonisation of the laws and regulations of the Member States.

Title XXIII. Civil Protection

Article 196. (1) The Union shall encourage cooperation between Member States in order to improve the effectiveness of systems for preventing and protecting against natural or man–made disasters. Union action shall aim to:
(a) support and complement Member States' action at national, regional and local level in risk prevention, in preparing their civil–protection personnel and in responding to natural or man–made disasters within the Union;
(b) promote swift, effective operational cooperation within the Union between national civil–protection services;
(c) promote consistency in international civil–protection work.
(2) The European Parliament and the Council, acting in accordance with the ordinary legislative procedure shall establish the measures necessary to help achieve the objectives referred to in paragraph 1, excluding any harmonisation of the laws and regulations of the Member States.

Title XXIV. Administrative Cooperation

Article 197. (1) Effective implementation of Union law by the Member States, which is essential for the proper functioning of the Union, shall be regarded as a matter of common interest.
(2) The Union may support the efforts of Member States to improve their administrative capacity to implement Union law. Such action may include facilitating the exchange of information and of civil servants as well as supporting training schemes. No Member State shall be obliged to avail itself of such support. The European Parliament and the Council, acting by means of regulations in accordance with the ordinary legislative procedure, shall establish the necessary measures to this end, excluding any harmonisation of the laws and regulations of the Member States.
(3) This Article shall be without prejudice to the obligations of the Member States to implement Union law or to the prerogatives and duties of the Commission. It shall also be without prejudice to other provisions of the Treaties providing for administrative cooperation among the Member States and between them and the Union.

Part Four. Association of the Overseas Countries and Territories

Article 198 (ex Article 182 TEC). The Member States agree to associate with the Union the non–European countries and territories which have special relations with Denmark, France, the Netherlands and the United Kingdom. These countries and territories (hereinafter called the "countries and territories") are listed in Annex II.
The purpose of association shall be to promote the economic and social development of the countries and territories and to establish close economic relations between them and the Union as a whole.
In accordance with the principles set out in the preamble to this Treaty, association shall serve primarily to further the interests and prosperity of the inhabitants of these countries and territories in order to lead them to the economic, social and cultural development to which they aspire.

Article 199 (ex Article 183 TEC). Association shall have the following objectives.
(1) Member States shall apply to their trade with the countries and territories the same treatment as they accord each other pursuant to the Treaties.
(2) Each country or territory shall apply to its trade with Member States and with the other countries and territories the same treatment as that which it applies to the European State with which is has special relations.
(3) The Member States shall contribute to the investments required for the progressive development of these countries and territories.
(4) For investments financed by the Union, participation in tenders and supplies shall be open on equal terms to all natural and legal persons who are nationals of a Member State or of one of the countries and territories.
(5) In relations between Member States and the countries and territories the right of establishment of nationals and companies or firms shall be regulated in accordance with the provisions and procedures

laid down in the Chapter relating to the right of establishment and on a non–discriminatory basis, subject to any special provisions laid down pursuant to Article 203.

Article 200 (ex Article 184 TEC). (1) Customs duties on imports into the Member States of goods originating in the countries and territories shall be prohibited in conformity with the prohibition of customs duties between Member States in accordance with the provisions of the Treaties.
(2) Customs duties on imports into each country or territory from Member States or from the other countries or territories shall be prohibited in accordance with the provisions of Article 30.
(3) The countries and territories may, however, levy customs duties which meet the needs of their development and industrialisation or produce revenue for their budgets.
The duties referred to in the preceding subparagraph may not exceed the level of those imposed on imports of products from the Member State with which each country or territory has special relations.
(4) Paragraph 2 shall not apply to countries and territories which, by reason of the particular international obligations by which they are bound, already apply a non–discriminatory customs tariff.
(5) The introduction of or any change in customs duties imposed on goods imported into the countries and territories shall not, either in law or in fact, give rise to any direct or indirect discrimination between imports from the various Member States.

Article 201 (ex Article 185 TEC). If the level of the duties applicable to goods from a third country on entry into a country or territory is liable, when the provisions of Article 200(1) have been applied, to cause deflections of trade to the detriment of any Member State, the latter may request the Commission to propose to the other Member States the measures needed to remedy the situation.

Article 202 (ex Article 186 TEC). Subject to the provisions relating to public health, public security or public policy, freedom of movement within Member States for workers from the countries and territories, and within the countries and territories for workers from Member States, shall be regulated by acts adopted in accordance with Article 203.

Article 203 (ex Article 187 TEC). The Council, acting unanimously on a proposal from the Commission, shall, on the basis of the experience acquired under the association of the countries and territories with the Union and of the principles set out in the Treaties, lay down provisions as regards the detailed rules and the procedure for the association of the countries and territories with the Union. Where the provisions in question are adopted by the Council in accordance with a special legislative procedure, it shall act unanimously on a proposal from the Commission and after consulting the European Parliament.

Article 204 (ex Article 188 TEC). The provisions of Articles 198 to 203 shall apply to Greenland, subject to the specific provisions for Greenland set out in the Protocol on special arrangements for Greenland, annexed to the Treaties.

Part Five. The Union's External Action

Title I. General Provisions on the Union's External Action

Article 205. The Union's action on the international scene, pursuant to this Part, shall be guided by the principles, pursue the objectives and be conducted in accordance with the general provisions laid down in Chapter 1 of Title V of the Treaty on European Union.

Title II. Common Commercial Policy

Article 206 (ex Article 131 TEC). By establishing a customs union in accordance with Articles 28 to 32, the Union shall contribute, in the common interest, to the harmonious development of world trade, the progressive abolition of restrictions on international trade and on foreign direct investment, and the lowering of customs and other barriers.

Article 207 (ex Article 133 TEC). (1) The common commercial policy shall be based on uniform principles, particularly with regard to changes in tariff rates, the conclusion of tariff and trade agreements relating to trade in goods and services, and the commercial aspects of intellectual property, foreign direct investment, the achievement of uniformity in measures of liberalisation, export policy and measures to protect trade such as those to be taken in the event of dumping or subsidies. The common commercial policy shall be conducted in the context of the principles and objectives of the Union's external action.
(2) The European Parliament and the Council, acting by means of regulations in accordance with the ordinary legislative procedure, shall adopt the measures defining the framework for implementing the

common commercial policy.

(3) Where agreements with one or more third countries or international organisations need to be negotiated and concluded, Article 218 shall apply, subject to the special provisions of this Article. The Commission shall make recommendations to the Council, which shall authorise it to open the necessary negotiations. The Council and the Commission shall be responsible for ensuring that the agreements negotiated are compatible with internal Union policies and rules.

The Commission shall conduct these negotiations in consultation with a special committee appointed by the Council to assist the Commission in this task and within the framework of such directives as the Council may issue to it. The Commission shall report regularly to the special committee and to the European Parliament on the progress of negotiations.

(4) For the negotiation and conclusion of the agreements referred to in paragraph 3, the Council shall act by a qualified majority.

For the negotiation and conclusion of agreements in the fields of trade in services and the commercial aspects of intellectual property, as well as foreign direct investment, the Council shall act unanimously where such agreements include provisions for which unanimity is required for the adoption of internal rules.

The Council shall also act unanimously for the negotiation and conclusion of agreements:

(a) in the field of trade in cultural and audiovisual services, where these agreements risk prejudicing the Union's cultural and linguistic diversity;

(b) in the field of trade in social, education and health services, where these agreements risk seriously disturbing the national organisation of such services and prejudicing the responsibility of Member States to deliver them.

(5) The negotiation and conclusion of international agreements in the field of transport shall be subject to Title VI of Part Three and to Article 218.

(6) The exercise of the competences conferred by this Article in the field of the common commercial policy shall not affect the delimitation of competences between the Union and the Member States, and shall not lead to harmonisation of legislative or regulatory provisions of the Member States in so far as the Treaties exclude such harmonisation.

Title III. Cooperation with Third Countries and Humanitarian Aid

Chapter 1. Development Cooperation

Article 208 (ex Article 177 TEC). (1) Union policy in the field of development cooperation shall be conducted within the framework of the principles and objectives of the Union's external action. The Union's development cooperation policy and that of the Member States complement and reinforce each other.

Union development cooperation policy shall have as its primary objective the reduction and, in the long term, the eradication of poverty. The Union shall take account of the objectives of development cooperation in the policies that it implements which are likely to affect developing countries.

(2) The Union and the Member States shall comply with the commitments and take account of the objectives they have approved in the context of the United Nations and other competent international organisations.

Article 209 (ex Article 179 TEC). (1) The European Parliament and the Council, acting in accordance with the ordinary legislative procedure, shall adopt the measures necessary for the implementation of development cooperation policy, which may relate to multiannual cooperation programmes with developing countries or programmes with a thematic approach.

(2) The Union may conclude with third countries and competent international organisations any agreement helping to achieve the objectives referred to in Article 21 of the Treaty on European Union and in Article 208 of this Treaty.

The first subparagraph shall be without prejudice to Member States' competence to negotiate in international bodies and to conclude agreements.

(3) The European Investment Bank shall contribute, under the terms laid down in its Statute, to the implementation of the measures referred to in paragraph 1.

Article 210 (ex Article 180 TEC). (1) In order to promote the complementarity and efficiency of their action, the Union and the Member States shall coordinate their policies on development cooperation and shall consult each other on their aid programmes, including in international organisations and during international conferences. They may undertake joint action. Member States shall contribute if necessary to the implementation of Union aid programmes.

(2) The Commission may take any useful initiative to promote the coordination referred to in paragraph 1.

TREATY ON THE FUNCTIONING OF THE EU

Article 211 (ex Article 181 TEC). Within their respective spheres of competence, the Union and the Member States shall cooperate with third countries and with the competent international organisations.

Chapter 2. Economic, Financial and Technical Cooperation with Third Countries

Article 212 (ex Article 181a TEC). (1) Without prejudice to the other provisions of the Treaties, and in particular Articles 208 to 211, the Union shall carry out economic, financial and technical cooperation measures, including assistance, in particular financial assistance, with third countries other than developing countries. Such measures shall be consistent with the development policy of the Union and shall be carried out within the framework of the principles and objectives of its external action. The Union's operations and those of the Member States shall complement and reinforce each other.
(2) The European Parliament and the Council, acting in accordance with the ordinary legislative procedure, shall adopt the measures necessary for the implementation of paragraph 1.
(3) Within their respective spheres of competence, the Union and the Member States shall cooperate with third countries and the competent international organisations. The arrangements for Union cooperation may be the subject of agreements between the Union and the third parties concerned.
The first subparagraph shall be without prejudice to the Member States' competence to negotiate in international bodies and to conclude international agreements.

Article 213. When the situation in a third country requires urgent financial assistance from the Union, the Council shall adopt the necessary decisions on a proposal from the Commission.
Chapter 3. Humanitarian aid

Article 214. (1) The Union's operations in the field of humanitarian aid shall be conducted within the framework of the principles and objectives of the external action of the Union. Such operations shall be intended to provide ad hoc assistance and relief and protection for people in third countries who are victims of natural or man–made disasters, in order to meet the humanitarian needs resulting from these different situations. The Union's measures and those of the Member States shall complement and reinforce each other.
(2) Humanitarian aid operations shall be conducted in compliance with the principles of international law and with the principles of impartiality, neutrality and non–discrimination.
(3) The European Parliament and the Council, acting in accordance with the ordinary legislative procedure, shall establish the measures defining the framework within which the Union's humanitarian aid operations shall be implemented.
(4) The Union may conclude with third countries and competent international organisations any agreement helping to achieve the objectives referred to in paragraph 1 and in Article 21 of the Treaty on European Union.
The first subparagraph shall be without prejudice to Member States' competence to negotiate in international bodies and to conclude agreements.
(5) In order to establish a framework for joint contributions from young Europeans to the humanitarian aid operations of the Union, a European Voluntary Humanitarian Aid Corps shall be set up. The European Parliament and the Council, acting by means of regulations in accordance with the ordinary legislative procedure, shall determine the rules and procedures for the operation of the Corps.
(6) The Commission may take any useful initiative to promote coordination between actions of the Union and those of the Member States, in order to enhance the efficiency and complementarity of Union and national humanitarian aid measures.
(7) The Union shall ensure that its humanitarian aid operations are coordinated and consistent with those of international organisations and bodies, in particular those forming part of the United Nations system.

Title IV. Restrictive Measures

Article 215 (ex Article 301 TEC). (1) Where a decision, adopted in accordance with Chapter 2 of Title V of the Treaty on European Union, provides for the interruption or reduction, in part or completely, of economic and financial relations with one or more third countries, the Council, acting by a qualified majority on a joint proposal from the High Representative of the Union for Foreign Affairs and Security Policy and the Commission, shall adopt the necessary measures. It shall inform the European Parliament thereof.
(2) Where a decision adopted in accordance with Chapter 2 of Title V of the Treaty on European Union so provides, the Council may adopt restrictive measures under the procedure referred to in paragraph 1 against natural or legal persons and groups or non–State entities.
(3) The acts referred to in this Article shall include necessary provisions on legal safeguards.

PART III   EUROPEAN UNION

Title V. International Agreements

Article 216. (1) The Union may conclude an agreement with one or more third countries or international organisations where the Treaties so provide or where the conclusion of an agreement is necessary in order to achieve, within the framework of the Union's policies, one of the objectives referred to in the Treaties, or is provided for in a legally binding Union act or is likely to affect common rules or alter their scope.
(2) Agreements concluded by the Union are binding upon the institutions of the Union and on its Member States.

Article 217 (ex Article 310 TEC). The Union may conclude with one or more third countries or international organisations agreements establishing an association involving reciprocal rights and obligations, common action and special procedure.

Article 218 (ex Article 300 TEC). (1) Without prejudice to the specific provisions laid down in Article 207, agreements between the Union and third countries or international organisations shall be negotiated and concluded in accordance with the following procedure.
(2) The Council shall authorise the opening of negotiations, adopt negotiating directives, authorise the signing of agreements and conclude them.
(3) The Commission, or the High Representative of the Union for Foreign Affairs and Security Policy where the agreement envisaged relates exclusively or principally to the common foreign and security policy, shall submit recommendations to the Council, which shall adopt a decision authorising the opening of negotiations and, depending on the subject of the agreement envisaged, nominating the Union negotiator or the head of the Union's negotiating team.
(4) The Council may address directives to the negotiator and designate a special committee in consultation with which the negotiations must be conducted.
(5) The Council, on a proposal by the negotiator, shall adopt a decision authorising the signing of the agreement and, if necessary, its provisional application before entry into force.
(6) The Council, on a proposal by the negotiator, shall adopt a decision concluding the agreement. Except where agreements relate exclusively to the common foreign and security policy, the Council shall adopt the decision concluding the agreement:
(a) after obtaining the consent of the European Parliament in the following cases:
(i) association agreements;
(ii) agreement on Union accession to the European Convention for the Protection of Human Rights and Fundamental Freedoms;
(iii) agreements establishing a specific institutional framework by organising cooperation procedures;
(iv) agreements with important budgetary implications for the Union;
(v) agreements covering fields to which either the ordinary legislative procedure applies, or the special legislative procedure where consent by the European Parliament is required.
The European Parliament and the Council may, in an urgent situation, agree upon a time–limit for consent.
(b) after consulting the European Parliament in other cases. The European Parliament shall deliver its opinion within a time–limit which the Council may set depending on the urgency of the matter. In the absence of an opinion within that time–limit, the Council may act.
(7) When concluding an agreement, the Council may, by way of derogation from paragraphs 5, 6 and 9, authorise the negotiator to approve on the Union's behalf modifications to the agreement where it provides for them to be adopted by a simplified procedure or by a body set up by the agreement. The Council may attach specific conditions to such authorisation.
(8) The Council shall act by a qualified majority throughout the procedure.
However, it shall act unanimously when the agreement covers a field for which unanimity is required for the adoption of a Union act as well as for association agreements and the agreements referred to in Article 212 with the States which are candidates for accession. The Council shall also act unanimously for the agreement on accession of the Union to the European Convention for the Protection of Human Rights and Fundamental Freedoms; the decision concluding this agreement shall enter into force after it has been approved by the Member States in accordance with their respective constitutional requirements.
(9) The Council, on a proposal from the Commission or the High Representative of the Union for Foreign Affairs and Security Policy, shall adopt a decision suspending application of an agreement and establishing the positions to be adopted on the Union's behalf in a body set up by an agreement, when that body is called upon to adopt acts having legal effects, with the exception of acts supplementing or amending the institutional framework of the agreement.

(10) The European Parliament shall be immediately and fully informed at all stages of the procedure.
(11) A Member State, the European Parliament, the Council or the Commission may obtain the opinion of the Court of Justice as to whether an agreement envisaged is compatible with the Treaties. Where the opinion of the Court is adverse, the agreement envisaged may not enter into force unless it is amended or the Treaties are revised.

Article 219 (ex Article 111(1) to (3) and (5) TEC). (1) By way of derogation from Article 218, the Council, either on a recommendation from the European Central Bank or on a recommendation from the Commission and after consulting the European Central Bank, in an endeavour to reach a consensus consistent with the objective of price stability, may conclude formal agreements on an exchange–rate system for the euro in relation to the currencies of third States. The Council shall act unanimously after consulting the European Parliament and in accordance with the procedure provided for in paragraph 3.
The Council may, either on a recommendation from the European Central Bank or on a recommendation from the Commission, and after consulting the European Central Bank, in an endeavour to reach a consensus consistent with the objective of price stability, adopt, adjust or abandon the central rates of the euro within the exchange–rate system. The President of the Council shall inform the European Parliament of the adoption, adjustment or abandonment of the euro central rates.
(2) In the absence of an exchange–rate system in relation to one or more currencies of third States as referred to in paragraph 1, the Council, either on a recommendation from the Commission and after consulting the European Central Bank or on a recommendation from the European Central Bank, may formulate general orientations for exchange–rate policy in relation to these currencies. These general orientations shall be without prejudice to the primary objective of the ESCB to maintain price stability.
(3) By way of derogation from Article 218, where agreements concerning monetary or foreign exchange regime matters need to be negotiated by the Union with one or more third States or international organisations, the Council, on a recommendation from the Commission and after consulting the European Central Bank, shall decide the arrangements for the negotiation and for the conclusion of such agreements. These arrangements shall ensure that the Union expresses a single position. The Commission shall be fully associated with the negotiations.
(4) Without prejudice to Union competence and Union agreements as regards economic and monetary union, Member States may negotiate in international bodies and conclude international agreements.

Title VI. The Union's Relations with International Organisations and Third Countries and Union Delegations

Article 220 (ex Articles 302 to 304 TEC). (1) The Union shall establish all appropriate forms of cooperation with the organs of the United Nations and its specialised agencies, the Council of Europe, the Organisation for Security and Cooperation in Europe and the Organisation for Economic Cooperation and Development.
The Union shall also maintain such relations as are appropriate with other international organisations.
(2) The High Representative of the Union for Foreign Affairs and Security Policy and the Commission shall implement this Article.

Article 221. (1) Union delegations in third countries and at international organisations shall represent the Union.
(2) Union delegations shall be placed under the authority of the High Representative of the Union for Foreign Affairs and Security Policy. They shall act in close cooperation with Member States' diplomatic and consular missions.

Title VII. Solidarity Clause

Article 222. (1) The Union and its Member States shall act jointly in a spirit of solidarity if a Member State is the object of a terrorist attack or the victim of a natural or man–made disaster. The Union shall mobilise all the instruments at its disposal, including the military resources made available by the Member States, to:
(a) – prevent the terrorist threat in the territory of the Member States;
– protect democratic institutions and the civilian population from any terrorist attack;
– assist a Member State in its territory, at the request of its political authorities, in the event of a terrorist attack;
(b) assist a Member State in its territory, at the request of its political authorities, in the event of a natural or man–made disaster.

PART III EUROPEAN UNION

(2) Should a Member State be the object of a terrorist attack or the victim of a natural or man–made disaster, the other Member States shall assist it at the request of its political authorities. To that end, the Member States shall coordinate between themselves in the Council.

(3) The arrangements for the implementation by the Union of the solidarity clause shall be defined by a decision adopted by the Council acting on a joint proposal by the Commission and the High Representative of the Union for Foreign Affairs and Security Policy. The Council shall act in accordance with Article 31(1) of the Treaty on European Union where this decision has defence implications. The European Parliament shall be informed.

For the purposes of this paragraph and without prejudice to Article 240, the Council shall be assisted by the Political and Security Committee with the support of the structures developed in the context of the common security and defence policy and by the Committee referred to in Article 71; the two committees shall, if necessary, submit joint opinions.

(4) The European Council shall regularly assess the threats facing the Union in order to enable the Union and its Member States to take effective action.

Part Six. Institutional and Financial Provisions

Title I. Institutional Provisions

Chapter 1. The Institutions

Section 1. The European Parliament

Article 223 (ex Article 190(4) and (5) TEC). (1) The European Parliament shall draw up a proposal to lay down the provisions necessary for the election of its Members by direct universal suffrage in accordance with a uniform procedure in all Member States or in accordance with principles common to all Member States.

The Council, acting unanimously in accordance with a special legislative procedure and after obtaining the consent of the European Parliament, which shall act by a majority of its component Members, shall lay down the necessary provisions. These provisions shall enter into force following their approval by the Member States in accordance with their respective constitutional requirements.

(2) The European Parliament, acting by means of regulations on its own initiative in accordance with a special legislative procedure after seeking an opinion from the Commission and with the consent of the Council, shall lay down the regulations and general conditions governing the performance of the duties of its Members. All rules or conditions relating to the taxation of Members or former Members shall require unanimity within the Council.

Article 224 (ex Article 191, second subparagraph, TEC). The European Parliament and the Council, acting in accordance with the ordinary legislative procedure, by means of regulations, shall lay down the regulations governing political parties at European level referred to in Article 10(4) of the Treaty on European Union and in particular the rules regarding their funding.

Article 225 (ex Article 192, second subparagraph, TEC). The European Parliament may, acting by a majority of its component Members, request the Commission to submit any appropriate proposal on matters on which it considers that a Union act is required for the purpose of implementing the Treaties. If the Commission does not submit a proposal, it shall inform the European Parliament of the reasons.

Article 226 (ex Article 193 TEC). In the course of its duties, the European Parliament may, at the request of a quarter of its component Members, set up a temporary Committee of Inquiry to investigate, without prejudice to the powers conferred by the Treaties on other institutions or bodies, alleged contraventions or maladministration in the implementation of Union law, except where the alleged facts are being examined before a court and while the case is still subject to legal proceedings.

The temporary Committee of Inquiry shall cease to exist on the submission of its report.

The detailed provisions governing the exercise of the right of inquiry shall be determined by the European Parliament, acting by means of regulations on its own initiative in accordance with a special legislative procedure, after obtaining the consent of the Council and the Commission.

Article 227 (ex Article 194 TEC). Any citizen of the Union, and any natural or legal person residing or having its registered office in a Member State, shall have the right to address, individually or in association with other citizens or persons, a petition to the European Parliament on a matter which comes within the Union's fields of activity and which affects him, her or it directly.

Article 228 (ex Article 195 TEC). (1) A European Ombudsman, elected by the European Parliament, shall be empowered to receive complaints from any citizen of the Union or any natural or legal person residing or having its registered office in a Member State concerning instances of maladministration in the activities of the Union institutions, bodies, offices or agencies, with the exception of the Court of Justice of the European Union acting in its judicial role. He or she shall examine such complaints and report on them.

In accordance with his duties, the Ombudsman shall conduct inquiries for which he finds grounds, either on his own initiative or on the basis of complaints submitted to him direct or through a Member of the European Parliament, except where the alleged facts are or have been the subject of legal proceedings. Where the Ombudsman establishes an instance of maladministration, he shall refer the matter to the institution, body, office or agency concerned, which shall have a period of three months in which to inform him of its views. The Ombudsman shall then forward a report to the European Parliament and the institution, body, office or agency concerned. The person lodging the complaint shall be informed of the outcome of such inquiries.

The Ombudsman shall submit an annual report to the European Parliament on the outcome of his inquiries.

(2) The Ombudsman shall be elected after each election of the European Parliament for the duration of its term of office. The Ombudsman shall be eligible for reappointment.

The Ombudsman may be dismissed by the Court of Justice at the request of the European Parliament if he no longer fulfils the conditions required for the performance of his duties or if he is guilty of serious misconduct.

(3) The Ombudsman shall be completely independent in the performance of his duties. In the performance of those duties he shall neither seek nor take instructions from any Government, institution, body, office or entity. The Ombudsman may not, during his term of office, engage in any other occupation, whether gainful or not.

(4) The European Parliament acting by means of regulations on its own initiative in accordance with a special legislative procedure shall, after seeking an opinion from the Commission and with the consent of the Council, lay down the regulations and general conditions governing the performance of the Ombudsman's duties.

Article 229 (ex Article 196 TEC). The European Parliament shall hold an annual session. It shall meet, without requiring to be convened, on the second Tuesday in March.

The European Parliament may meet in extraordinary part–session at the request of a majority of its component Members or at the request of the Council or of the Commission.

Article 230 (ex Article 197, second, third and fourth paragraph, TEC). The Commission may attend all the meetings and shall, at its request, be heard.

The Commission shall reply orally or in writing to questions put to it by the European Parliament or by its Members.

The European Council and the Council shall be heard by the European Parliament in accordance with the conditions laid down in the Rules of Procedure of the European Council and those of the Council.

Article 231 (ex Article 198 TEC). Save as otherwise provided in the Treaties, the European Parliament shall act by a majority of the votes cast.

The Rules of Procedure shall determine the quorum.

Article 232 (ex Article 199 TEC). The European Parliament shall adopt its Rules of Procedure, acting by a majority of its Members.

The proceedings of the European Parliament shall be published in the manner laid down in the Treaties and in its Rules of Procedure.

Article 233 (ex Article 200 TEC). The European Parliament shall discuss in open session the annual general report submitted to it by the Commission.

Article 234 (ex Article 201 TEC). If a motion of censure on the activities of the Commission is tabled before it, the European Parliament shall not vote thereon until at least three days after the motion has been tabled and only by open vote.

If the motion of censure is carried by a two–thirds majority of the votes cast, representing a majority of the component Members of the European Parliament, the members of the Commission shall resign as a body and the High Representative of the Union for Foreign Affairs and Security Policy shall resign from duties that he or she carries out in the Commission. They shall remain in office and continue to deal with current business until they are replaced in accordance with Article 17 of the Treaty on European Union. In this case, the term of office of the members of the Commission appointed to replace them shall expire on the date on which the term of office of the members of the Commission obliged to resign as a body would have expired.

Section 2. The European Council

Article 235. (1) Where a vote is taken, any member of the European Council may also act on behalf of not more than one other member.

Article 16(4) of the Treaty on European Union and Article 238(2) of this Treaty shall apply to the European Council when it is acting by a qualified majority. Where the European Council decides by vote, its President and the President of the Commission shall not take part in the vote.

Abstentions by members present in person or represented shall not prevent the adoption by the European Council of acts which require unanimity.

(2) The President of the European Parliament may be invited to be heard by the European Council.

(3) The European Council shall act by a simple majority for procedural questions and for the adoption of its Rules of Procedure.

(4) The European Council shall be assisted by the General Secretariat of the Council.

Article 236. The European Council shall adopt by a qualified majority:

(a) a decision establishing the list of Council configurations, other than those of the General Affairs Council and of the Foreign Affairs Council, in accordance with Article 16(6) of the Treaty on European Union;

(b) a decision on the Presidency of Council configurations, other than that of Foreign Affairs, in accordance with Article 16(9) of the Treaty on European Union.

Section 3. The Council

Article 237 (ex Article 204 TEC). The Council shall meet when convened by its President on his own initiative or at the request of one of its Members or of the Commission.

Article 238 (ex Article 205(1) and (2) TEC). (1) Where it is required to act by a simple majority, the Council shall act by a majority of its component members.

(2) By way of derogation from Article 16(4) of the Treaty on European Union, as from 1 November 2014 and subject to the provisions laid down in the Protocol on transitional provisions, where the Council does not act on a proposal from the Commission or from the High Representative of the Union for Foreign Affairs and Security Policy, the qualified majority shall be defined as at least 72 % of the members of the Council, representing Member States comprising at least 65 % of the population of the Union.

(3) As from 1 November 2014 and subject to the provisions laid down in the Protocol on transitional provisions, in cases where, under the Treaties, not all the members of the Council participate in voting, a qualified majority shall be defined as follows:

(a) A qualified majority shall be defined as at least 55 % of the members of the Council representing the participating Member States, comprising at least 65 % of the population of these States. A blocking minority must include at least the minimum number of Council members representing more than 35 % of the population of the participating Member States, plus one member, failing which the qualified majority shall be deemed attained;

(b) By way of derogation from point (a), where the Council does not act on a proposal from the Commission or from the High Representative of the Union for Foreign Affairs and Security Policy, the qualified majority shall be defined as at least 72 % of the members of the Council representing the participating Member States, comprising at least 65 % of the population of these States.

(4) Abstentions by Members present in person or represented shall not prevent the adoption by the Council of acts which require unanimity.

Article 239 (ex Article 206 TEC). Where a vote is taken, any Member of the Council may also act on behalf of not more than one other member.

Article 240 (ex Article 207 TEC). (1) A committee consisting of the Permanent Representatives of the Governments of the Member States shall be responsible for preparing the work of the Council and for carrying out the tasks assigned to it by the latter. The Committee may adopt procedural decisions in cases provided for in the Council's Rules of Procedure.

(2) The Council shall be assisted by a General Secretariat, under the responsibility of a Secretary–General appointed by the Council.

The Council shall decide on the organisation of the General Secretariat by a simple majority.

(3) The Council shall act by a simple majority regarding procedural matters and for the adoption of its Rules of Procedure.

Article 241 (ex Article 208 TEC). The Council, acting by a simple majority, may request the Commission to undertake any studies the Council considers desirable for the attainment of the common objectives, and to submit to it any appropriate proposals. If the Commission does not submit a proposal, it shall inform the Council of the reasons.

Article 242 (ex Article 209 TEC). The Council, acting by a simple majority shall, after consulting the Commission, determine the rules governing the committees provided for in the Treaties.

Article 243 (ex Article 210 TEC). The Council shall determine the salaries, allowances and pensions of the President of the European Council, the President of the Commission, the High Representative of the Union for Foreign Affairs and Security Policy, the Members of the Commission, the Presidents, Members and Registrars of the Court of Justice of the European Union, and the Secretary-General of the Council. It shall also determine any payment to be made instead of remuneration.

Section 4. The Commission

Article 244. In accordance with Article 17(5) of the Treaty on European Union, the Members of the Commission shall be chosen on the basis of a system of rotation established unanimously by the European Council and on the basis of the following principles:
(a) Member States shall be treated on a strictly equal footing as regards determination of the sequence of, and the time spent by, their nationals as members of the Commission; consequently, the difference between the total number of terms of office held by nationals of any given pair of Member States may never be more than one;
(b) subject to point (a), each successive Commission shall be so composed as to reflect satisfactorily the demographic and geographical range of all the Member States.

Article 245 (ex Article 213 TEC). The Members of the Commission shall refrain from any action incompatible with their duties. Member States shall respect their independence and shall not seek to influence them in the performance of their tasks.
The Members of the Commission may not, during their term of office, engage in any other occupation, whether gainful or not. When entering upon their duties they shall give a solemn undertaking that, both during and after their term of office, they will respect the obligations arising therefrom and in particular their duty to behave with integrity and discretion as regards the acceptance, after they have ceased to hold office, of certain appointments or benefits. In the event of any breach of these obligations, the Court of Justice may, on application by the Council acting by a simple majority or the Commission, rule that the Member concerned be, according to the circumstances, either compulsorily retired in accordance with Article 247 or deprived of his right to a pension or other benefits in its stead.

Article 246 (ex Article 215 TEC). Apart from normal replacement, or death, the duties of a Member of the Commission shall end when he resigns or is compulsorily retired.
A vacancy caused by resignation, compulsory retirement or death shall be filled for the remainder of the Member's term of office by a new Member of the same nationality appointed by the Council, by common accord with the President of the Commission, after consulting the European Parliament and in accordance with the criteria set out in the second subparagraph of Article 17(3) of the Treaty on European Union.
The Council may, acting unanimously on a proposal from the President of the Commission, decide that such a vacancy need not be filled, in particular when the remainder of the Member's term of office is short.
In the event of resignation, compulsory retirement or death, the President shall be replaced for the remainder of his term of office. The procedure laid down in the first subparagraph of Article 17(7) of the Treaty on European Union shall be applicable for the replacement of the President.
In the event of resignation, compulsory retirement or death, the High Representative of the Union for Foreign Affairs and Security Policy shall be replaced, for the remainder of his or her term of office, in accordance with Article 18(1) of the Treaty on European Union.
In the case of the resignation of all the Members of the Commission, they shall remain in office and continue to deal with current business until they have been replaced, for the remainder of their term of office, in accordance with Article 17 of the Treaty on European Union.

Article 247 (ex Article 216 TEC). If any Member of the Commission no longer fulfils the conditions required for the performance of his duties or if he has been guilty of serious misconduct, the Court of Justice may, on application by the Council acting by a simple majority or the Commission, compulsorily retire him.

PART III   EUROPEAN UNION

Article 248 (ex Article 217(2) TEC). Without prejudice to Article 18(4) of the Treaty on European Union, the responsibilities incumbent upon the Commission shall be structured and allocated among its members by its President, in accordance with Article 17(6) of that Treaty. The President may reshuffle the allocation of those responsibilities during the Commission's term of office. The Members of the Commission shall carry out the duties devolved upon them by the President under his authority.

Article 249 (ex Articles 218(2) and 212 TEC). (1) The Commission shall adopt its Rules of Procedure so as to ensure that both it and its departments operate. It shall ensure that these Rules are published.
(2) The Commission shall publish annually, not later than one month before the opening of the session of the European Parliament, a general report on the activities of the Union.

Article 250 (ex Article 219 TEC). The Commission shall act by a majority of its Members.
Its Rules of Procedure shall determine the quorum.

Section 5. The Court of Justice of the European Union

Article 251 (ex Article 221 TEC). The Court of Justice shall sit in chambers or in a Grand Chamber, in accordance with the rules laid down for that purpose in the Statute of the Court of Justice of the European Union.
When provided for in the Statute, the Court of Justice may also sit as a full Court.

Article 252 (ex Article 222 TEC). The Court of Justice shall be assisted by eight Advocates–General. Should the Court of Justice so request, the Council, acting unanimously, may increase the number of Advocates–General.
It shall be the duty of the Advocate–General, acting with complete impartiality and independence, to make, in open court, reasoned submissions on cases which, in accordance with the Statute of the Court of Justice of the European Union, require his involvement.

Article 253 (ex Article 223 TEC). The Judges and Advocates–General of the Court of Justice shall be chosen from persons whose independence is beyond doubt and who possess the qualifications required for appointment to the highest judicial offices in their respective countries or who are jurisconsults of recognised competence; they shall be appointed by common accord of the governments of the Member States for a term of six years, after consultation of the panel provided for in Article 255. Every three years there shall be a partial replacement of the Judges and Advocates–General, in accordance with the conditions laid down in the Statute of the Court of Justice of the European Union.
The Judges shall elect the President of the Court of Justice from among their number for a term of three years. He may be re–elected.
Retiring Judges and Advocates–General may be reappointed.
The Court of Justice shall appoint its Registrar and lay down the rules governing his service.
The Court of Justice shall establish its Rules of Procedure. Those Rules shall require the approval of the Council.

Article 254 (ex Article 224 TEC). The number of Judges of the General Court shall be determined by the Statute of the Court of Justice of the European Union. The Statute may provide for the General Court to be assisted by Advocates–General.
The members of the General Court shall be chosen from persons whose independence is beyond doubt and who possess the ability required for appointment to high judicial office. They shall be appointed by common accord of the governments of the Member States for a term of six years, after consultation of the panel provided for in Article 255. The membership shall be partially renewed every three years. Retiring members shall be eligible for reappointment.
The Judges shall elect the President of the General Court from among their number for a term of three years. He may be re–elected.
The General Court shall appoint its Registrar and lay down the rules governing his service.
The General Court shall establish its Rules of Procedure in agreement with the Court of Justice. Those Rules shall require the approval of the Council.
Unless the Statute of the Court of Justice of the European Union provides otherwise, the provisions of the Treaties relating to the Court of Justice shall apply to the General Court.

Article 255. A panel shall be set up in order to give an opinion on candidates' suitability to perform the duties of Judge and Advocate–General of the Court of Justice and the General Court before the governments of the Member States make the appointments referred to in Articles 253 and 254. The panel shall comprise seven persons chosen from among former members of the Court of Justice and the General Court, members of national supreme courts and lawyers of recognised competence, one of whom shall be proposed by the European Parliament. The Council shall adopt a decision establishing the panel's operating rules and a decision appointing its members. It shall act on the initiative of the President of the Court of Justice.

Article 256 (ex Article 225 TEC). (1) The General Court shall have jurisdiction to hear and determine at first instance actions or proceedings referred to in Articles 263, 265, 268, 270 and 272, with the exception of those assigned to a specialised court set up under Article 257 and those reserved in the Statute for the Court of Justice. The Statute may provide for the General Court to have jurisdiction for other classes of action or proceeding.
Decisions given by the General Court under this paragraph may be subject to a right of appeal to the Court of Justice on points of law only, under the conditions and within the limits laid down by the Statute.
(2) The General Court shall have jurisdiction to hear and determine actions or proceedings brought against decisions of the specialised courts.
Decisions given by the General Court under this paragraph may exceptionally be subject to review by the Court of Justice, under the conditions and within the limits laid down by the Statute, where there is a serious risk of the unity or consistency of Union law being affected.
(3) The General Court shall have jurisdiction to hear and determine questions referred for a preliminary ruling under Article 267, in specific areas laid down by the Statute.
Where the General Court considers that the case requires a decision of principle likely to affect the unity or consistency of Union law, it may refer the case to the Court of Justice for a ruling.
Decisions given by the General Court on questions referred for a preliminary ruling may exceptionally be subject to review by the Court of Justice, under the conditions and within the limits laid down by the Statute, where there is a serious risk of the unity or consistency of Union law being affected.

Article 257 (ex Article 225a TEC). The European Parliament and the Council, acting in accordance with the ordinary legislative procedure, may establish specialised courts attached to the General Court to hear and determine at first instance certain classes of action or proceeding brought in specific areas. The European Parliament and the Council shall act by means of regulations either on a proposal from the Commission after consultation of the Court of Justice or at the request of the Court of Justice after consultation of the Commission.
The regulation establishing a specialised court shall lay down the rules on the organisation of the court and the extent of the jurisdiction conferred upon it.
Decisions given by specialised courts may be subject to a right of appeal on points of law only or, when provided for in the regulation establishing the specialised court, a right of appeal also on matters of fact, before the General Court.
The members of the specialised courts shall be chosen from persons whose independence is beyond doubt and who possess the ability required for appointment to judicial office. They shall be appointed by the Council, acting unanimously.
The specialised courts shall establish their Rules of Procedure in agreement with the Court of Justice. Those Rules shall require the approval of the Council.
Unless the regulation establishing the specialised court provides otherwise, the provisions of the Treaties relating to the Court of Justice of the European Union and the provisions of the Statute of the Court of Justice of the European Union shall apply to the specialised courts. Title I of the Statute and Article 64 thereof shall in any case apply to the specialised courts.

Article 258 (ex Article 226 TEC). If the Commission considers that a Member State has failed to fulfil an obligation under the Treaties, it shall deliver a reasoned opinion on the matter after giving the State concerned the opportunity to submit its observations.
If the State concerned does not comply with the opinion within the period laid down by the Commission, the latter may bring the matter before the Court of Justice of the European Union.

Article 259 (ex Article 227 TEC). A Member State which considers that another Member State has failed to fulfil an obligation under the Treaties may bring the matter before the Court of Justice of the European Union.
Before a Member State brings an action against another Member State for an alleged infringement of an obligation under the Treaties, it shall bring the matter before the Commission.
The Commission shall deliver a reasoned opinion after each of the States concerned has been given the opportunity to submit its own case and its observations on the other party's case both orally and

in writing.

If the Commission has not delivered an opinion within three months of the date on which the matter was brought before it, the absence of such opinion shall not prevent the matter from being brought before the Court.

Article 260 (ex Article 228 TEC). (1) If the Court of Justice of the European Union finds that a Member State has failed to fulfil an obligation under the Treaties, the State shall be required to take the necessary measures to comply with the judgment of the Court.

(2) If the Commission considers that the Member State concerned has not taken the necessary measures to comply with the judgment of the Court, it may bring the case before the Court after giving that State the opportunity to submit its observations. It shall specify the amount of the lump sum or penalty payment to be paid by the Member State concerned which it considers appropriate in the circumstances.

If the Court finds that the Member State concerned has not complied with its judgment it may impose a lump sum or penalty payment on it.

This procedure shall be without prejudice to Article 259.

(3) When the Commission brings a case before the Court pursuant to Article 258 on the grounds that the Member State concerned has failed to fulfil its obligation to notify measures transposing a directive adopted under a legislative procedure, it may, when it deems appropriate, specify the amount of the lump sum or penalty payment to be paid by the Member State concerned which it considers appropriate in the circumstances.

If the Court finds that there is an infringement it may impose a lump sum or penalty payment on the Member State concerned not exceeding the amount specified by the Commission. The payment obligation shall take effect on the date set by the Court in its judgment.

Article 261 (ex Article 229 TEC). Regulations adopted jointly by the European Parliament and the Council, and by the Council, pursuant to the provisions of the Treaties, may give the Court of Justice of the European Union unlimited jurisdiction with regard to the penalties provided for in such regulations.

Article 262 (ex Article 229a TEC). Without prejudice to the other provisions of the Treaties, the Council, acting unanimously in accordance with a special legislative procedure and after consulting the European Parliament, may adopt provisions to confer jurisdiction, to the extent that it shall determine, on the Court of Justice of the European Union in disputes relating to the application of acts adopted on the basis of the Treaties which create European intellectual property rights. These provisions shall enter into force after their approval by the Member States in accordance with their respective constitutional requirements.

Article 263 (ex Article 230 TEC). The Court of Justice of the European Union shall review the legality of legislative acts, of acts of the Council, of the Commission and of the European Central Bank, other than recommendations and opinions, and of acts of the European Parliament and of the European Council intended to produce legal effects vis-à-vis third parties. It shall also review the legality of acts of bodies, offices or agencies of the Union intended to produce legal effects vis-à-vis third parties.

It shall for this purpose have jurisdiction in actions brought by a Member State, the European Parliament, the Council or the Commission on grounds of lack of competence, infringement of an essential procedural requirement, infringement of the Treaties or of any rule of law relating to their application, or misuse of powers.

The Court shall have jurisdiction under the same conditions in actions brought by the Court of Auditors, by the European Central Bank and by the Committee of the Regions for the purpose of protecting their prerogatives.

Any natural or legal person may, under the conditions laid down in the first and second paragraphs, institute proceedings against an act addressed to that person or which is of direct and individual concern to them, and against a regulatory act which is of direct concern to them and does not entail implementing measures.

Acts setting up bodies, offices and agencies of the Union may lay down specific conditions and arrangements concerning actions brought by natural or legal persons against acts of these bodies, offices or agencies intended to produce legal effects in relation to them.

The proceedings provided for in this Article shall be instituted within two months of the publication of the measure, or of its notification to the plaintiff, or, in the absence thereof, of the day on which it came to the knowledge of the latter, as the case may be.

Article 264 (ex Article 231 TEC). If the action is well founded, the Court of Justice of the European Union shall declare the act concerned to be void.
However, the Court shall, if it considers this necessary, state which of the effects of the act which it has declared void shall be considered as definitive.

Article 265 (ex Article 232 TEC). Should the European Parliament, the European Council, the Council, the Commission or the European Central Bank, in infringement of the Treaties, fail to act, the Member States and the other institutions of the Union may bring an action before the Court of Justice of the European Union to have the infringement established. This Article shall apply, under the same conditions, to bodies, offices and agencies of the Union which fail to act.
The action shall be admissible only if the institution, body, office or agency concerned has first been called upon to act. If, within two months of being so called upon, the institution, body, office or agency concerned has not defined its position, the action may be brought within a further period of two months.
Any natural or legal person may, under the conditions laid down in the preceding paragraphs, complain to the Court that an institution, body, office or agency of the Union has failed to address to that person any act other than a recommendation or an opinion.

Article 266 (ex Article 233 TEC). The institution whose act has been declared void or whose failure to act has been declared contrary to the Treaties shall be required to take the necessary measures to comply with the judgment of the Court of Justice of the European Union.
This obligation shall not affect any obligation which may result from the application of the second paragraph of Article 340.

Article 267 (ex Article 234 TEC). The Court of Justice of the European Union shall have jurisdiction to give preliminary rulings concerning:
(a) the interpretation of the Treaties;
(b) the validity and interpretation of acts of the institutions, bodies, offices or agencies of the Union;
Where such a question is raised before any court or tribunal of a Member State, that court or tribunal may, if it considers that a decision on the question is necessary to enable it to give judgment, request the Court to give a ruling thereon.
Where any such question is raised in a case pending before a court or tribunal of a Member State against whose decisions there is no judicial remedy under national law, that court or tribunal shall bring the matter before the Court.
If such a question is raised in a case pending before a court or tribunal of a Member State with regard to a person in custody, the Court of Justice of the European Union shall act with the minimum of delay.

Article 268 (ex Article 235 TEC). The Court of Justice of the European Union shall have jurisdiction in disputes relating to compensation for damage provided for in the second and third paragraphs of Article 340.

Article 269. The Court of Justice shall have jurisdiction to decide on the legality of an act adopted by the European Council or by the Council pursuant to Article 7 of the Treaty on European Union solely at the request of the Member State concerned by a determination of the European Council or of the Council and in respect solely of the procedural stipulations contained in that Article.
Such a request must be made within one month from the date of such determination. The Court shall rule within one month from the date of the request.

Article 270 (ex Article 236 TEC). The Court of Justice of the European Union shall have jurisdiction in any dispute between the Union and its servants within the limits and under the conditions laid down in the Staff Regulations of Officials and the Conditions of Employment of other servants of the Union.

Article 271 (ex Article 237 TEC). The Court of Justice of the European Union shall, within the limits hereinafter laid down, have jurisdiction in disputes concerning:
(a) the fulfilment by Member States of obligations under the Statute of the European Investment Bank. In this connection, the Board of Directors of the Bank shall enjoy the powers conferred upon the Commission by Article 258;
(b) measures adopted by the Board of Governors of the European Investment Bank. In this connection, any Member State, the Commission or the Board of Directors of the Bank may institute proceedings under the conditions laid down in Article 263;
(c) measures adopted by the Board of Directors of the European Investment Bank. Proceedings

PART III   EUROPEAN UNION

against such measures may be instituted only by Member States or by the Commission, under the conditions laid down in Article 263, and solely on the grounds of non–compliance with the procedure provided for in Article 19(2), (5), (6) and (7) of the Statute of the Bank;
(d) the fulfilment by national central banks of obligations under the Treaties and the Statute of the ESCB and of the ECB. In this connection the powers of the Governing Council of the European Central Bank in respect of national central banks shall be the same as those conferred upon the Commission in respect of Member States by Article 258. If the Court finds that a national central bank has failed to fulfil an obligation under the Treaties, that bank shall be required to take the necessary measures to comply with the judgment of the Court.

Article 272 (ex Article 238 TEC). The Court of Justice of the European Union shall have jurisdiction to give judgment pursuant to any arbitration clause contained in a contract concluded by or on behalf of the Union, whether that contract be governed by public or private law.

Article 273 (ex Article 239 TEC). The Court of Justice shall have jurisdiction in any dispute between Member States which relates to the subject matter of the Treaties if the dispute is submitted to it under a special agreement between the parties.

Article 274 (ex Article 240 TEC). Save where jurisdiction is conferred on the Court of Justice of the European Union by the Treaties, disputes to which the Union is a party shall not on that ground be excluded from the jurisdiction of the courts or tribunals of the Member States.

Article 275. The Court of Justice of the European Union shall not have jurisdiction with respect to the provisions relating to the common foreign and security policy nor with respect to acts adopted on the basis of those provisions.
However, the Court shall have jurisdiction to monitor compliance with Article 40 of the Treaty on European Union and to rule on proceedings, brought in accordance with the conditions laid down in the fourth paragraph of Article 263 of this Treaty, reviewing the legality of decisions providing for restrictive measures against natural or legal persons adopted by the Council on the basis of Chapter 2 of Title V of the Treaty on European Union.

Article 276. In exercising its powers regarding the provisions of Chapters 4 and 5 of Title V of Part Three relating to the area of freedom, security and justice, the Court of Justice of the European Union shall have no jurisdiction to review the validity or proportionality of operations carried out by the police or other law–enforcement services of a Member State or the exercise of the responsibilities incumbent upon Member States with regard to the maintenance of law and order and the safeguarding of internal security.

Article 277 (ex Article 241 TEC). Notwithstanding the expiry of the period laid down in Article 263, sixth paragraph, any party may, in proceedings in which an act of general application adopted by an institution, body, office or agency of the Union is at issue, plead the grounds specified in Article 263, second paragraph, in order to invoke before the Court of Justice of the European Union the inapplicability of that act.

Article 278 (ex Article 242 TEC). Actions brought before the Court of Justice of the European Union shall not have suspensory effect. The Court may, however, if it considers that circumstances so require, order that application of the contested act be suspended.

Article 279 (ex Article 243 TEC). The Court of Justice of the European Union may in any cases before it prescribe any necessary interim measures.

Article 280 (ex Article 244 TEC). The judgments of the Court of Justice of the European Union shall be enforceable under the conditions laid down in Article 299.

Article 281 (ex Article 245 TEC). The Statute of the Court of Justice of the European Union shall be laid down in a separate Protocol.
The European Parliament and the Council, acting in accordance with the ordinary legislative procedure, may amend the provisions of the Statute, with the exception of Title I and Article 64. The European Parliament and the Council shall act either at the request of the Court of Justice and after consultation of the Commission, or on a proposal from the Commission and after consultation of the Court of Justice.

Section 6. The European Central Bank

Article 282. (1) The European Central Bank, together with the national central banks, shall constitute

the European System of Central Banks (ESCB). The European Central Bank, together with the national central banks of the Member States whose currency is the euro, which constitute the Eurosystem, shall conduct the monetary policy of the Union.
(2) The ESCB shall be governed by the decision–making bodies of the European Central Bank. The primary objective of the ESCB shall be to maintain price stability. Without prejudice to that objective, it shall support the general economic policies in the Union in order to contribute to the achievement of the latter's objectives.
(3) The European Central Bank shall have legal personality. It alone may authorise the issue of the euro. It shall be independent in the exercise of its powers and in the management of its finances. Union institutions, bodies, offices and agencies and the governments of the Member States shall respect that independence.
(4) The European Central Bank shall adopt such measures as are necessary to carry out its tasks in accordance with Articles 127 to 133, with Article 138, and with the conditions laid down in the Statute of the ESCB and of the ECB. In accordance with these same Articles, those Member States whose currency is not the euro, and their central banks, shall retain their powers in monetary matters.
(5) Within the areas falling within its responsibilities, the European Central Bank shall be consulted on all proposed Union acts, and all proposals for regulation at national level, and may give an opinion.

Article 283 (ex Article 112 TEC). (1) The Governing Council of the European Central Bank shall comprise the members of the Executive Board of the European Central Bank and the Governors of the national central banks of the Member States whose currency is the euro.
(2) The Executive Board shall comprise the President, the Vice–President and four other members. The President, the Vice–President and the other members of the Executive Board shall be appointed by the European Council, acting by a qualified majority, from among persons of recognised standing and professional experience in monetary or banking matters, on a recommendation from the Council, after it has consulted the European Parliament and the Governing Council of the European Central Bank.
Their term of office shall be eight years and shall not be renewable.
Only nationals of Member States may be members of the Executive Board.

Article 284 (ex Article 113 TEC). (1) The President of the Council and a Member of the Commission may participate, without having the right to vote, in meetings of the Governing Council of the European Central Bank.
The President of the Council may submit a motion for deliberation to the Governing Council of the European Central Bank.
(2) The President of the European Central Bank shall be invited to participate in Council meetings when the Council is discussing matters relating to the objectives and tasks of the ESCB.
(3) The European Central Bank shall address an annual report on the activities of the ESCB and on the monetary policy of both the previous and current year to the European Parliament, the Council and the Commission, and also to the European Council. The President of the European Central Bank shall present this report to the Council and to the European Parliament, which may hold a general debate on that basis.
The President of the European Central Bank and the other members of the Executive Board may, at the request of the European Parliament or on their own initiative, be heard by the competent committees of the European Parliament.

Section 7. The Court of Auditors

Article 285 (ex Article 246 TEC). The Court of Auditors shall carry out the Union's audit.
It shall consist of one national of each Member State. Its Members shall be completely independent in the performance of their duties, in the Union's general interest.

Article 286 (ex Article 247 TEC). (1) The Members of the Court of Auditors shall be chosen from among persons who belong or have belonged in their respective States to external audit bodies or who are especially qualified for this office. Their independence must be beyond doubt.
(2) The Members of the Court of Auditors shall be appointed for a term of six years. The Council, after consulting the European Parliament, shall adopt the list of Members drawn up in accordance with the proposals made by each Member State. The term of office of the Members of the Court of Auditors shall be renewable.
They shall elect the President of the Court of Auditors from among their number for a term of three years. The President may be re–elected.

(3) In the performance of these duties, the Members of the Court of Auditors shall neither seek nor take instructions from any government or from any other body. The Members of the Court of Auditors shall refrain from any action incompatible with their duties.
(4) The Members of the Court of Auditors may not, during their term of office, engage in any other occupation, whether gainful or not. When entering upon their duties they shall give a solemn undertaking that, both during and after their term of office, they will respect the obligations arising therefrom and in particular their duty to behave with integrity and discretion as regards the acceptance, after they have ceased to hold office, of certain appointments or benefits.
(5) Apart from normal replacement, or death, the duties of a Member of the Court of Auditors shall end when he resigns, or is compulsorily retired by a ruling of the Court of Justice pursuant to paragraph 6.
The vacancy thus caused shall be filled for the remainder of the Member's term of office.
Save in the case of compulsory retirement, Members of the Court of Auditors shall remain in office until they have been replaced.
(6) A Member of the Court of Auditors may be deprived of his office or of his right to a pension or other benefits in its stead only if the Court of Justice, at the request of the Court of Auditors, finds that he no longer fulfils the requisite conditions or meets the obligations arising from his office.
(7) The Council shall determine the conditions of employment of the President and the Members of the Court of Auditors and in particular their salaries, allowances and pensions. It shall also determine any payment to be made instead of remuneration.
(8) The provisions of the Protocol on the privileges and immunities of the European Union applicable to the Judges of the Court of Justice of the European Union shall also apply to the Members of the Court of Auditors.

Article 287 (ex Article 248 TEC). (1) The Court of Auditors shall examine the accounts of all revenue and expenditure of the Union. It shall also examine the accounts of all revenue and expenditure of all bodies, offices or agencies set up by the Union in so far as the relevant constituent instrument does not preclude such examination.
The Court of Auditors shall provide the European Parliament and the Council with a statement of assurance as to the reliability of the accounts and the legality and regularity of the underlying transactions which shall be published in the *Official Journal of the European Union*. This statement may be supplemented by specific assessments for each major area of Union activity.
(2) The Court of Auditors shall examine whether all revenue has been received and all expenditure incurred in a lawful and regular manner and whether the financial management has been sound. In doing so, it shall report in particular on any cases of irregularity.
The audit of revenue shall be carried out on the basis both of the amounts established as due and the amounts actually paid to the Union.
The audit of expenditure shall be carried out on the basis both of commitments undertaken and payments made.
These audits may be carried out before the closure of accounts for the financial year in question.
(3) The audit shall be based on records and, if necessary, performed on the spot in the other institutions of the Union, on the premises of any body, office or agency which manages revenue or expenditure on behalf of the Union and in the Member States, including on the premises of any natural or legal person in receipt of payments from the budget. In the Member States the audit shall be carried out in liaison with national audit bodies or, if these do not have the necessary powers, with the competent national departments. The Court of Auditors and the national audit bodies of the Member States shall cooperate in a spirit of trust while maintaining their independence. These bodies or departments shall inform the Court of Auditors whether they intend to take part in the audit.
The other institutions of the Union, any bodies, offices or agencies managing revenue or expenditure on behalf of the Union, any natural or legal person in receipt of payments from the budget, and the national audit bodies or, if these do not have the necessary powers, the competent national departments, shall forward to the Court of Auditors, at its request, any document or information necessary to carry out its task.
In respect of the European Investment Bank's activity in managing Union expenditure and revenue, the Court's rights of access to information held by the Bank shall be governed by an agreement between the Court, the Bank and the Commission. In the absence of an agreement, the Court shall nevertheless have access to information necessary for the audit of Union expenditure and revenue managed by the Bank.
(4) The Court of Auditors shall draw up an annual report after the close of each financial year. It shall be forwarded to the other institutions of the Union and shall be published, together with the replies of

these institutions to the observations of the Court of Auditors, in the *Official Journal of the European Union*.

The Court of Auditors may also, at any time, submit observations, particularly in the form of special reports, on specific questions and deliver opinions at the request of one of the other institutions of the Union.

It shall adopt its annual reports, special reports or opinions by a majority of its Members. However, it may establish internal chambers in order to adopt certain categories of reports or opinions under the conditions laid down by its Rules of Procedure.

It shall assist the European Parliament and the Council in exercising their powers of control over the implementation of the budget.

The Court of Auditors shall draw up its Rules of Procedure. Those rules shall require the approval of the Council.

Chapter 2. Legal Acts of the Union, Adoption Procedures and other Provisions

Section 1. The Legal Acts of the Union

Article 288 (ex Article 249 TEC). To exercise the Union's competences, the institutions shall adopt regulations, directives, decisions, recommendations and opinions.

A regulation shall have general application. It shall be binding in its entirety and directly applicable in all Member States.

A directive shall be binding, as to the result to be achieved, upon each Member State to which it is addressed, but shall leave to the national authorities the choice of form and methods.

A decision shall be binding in its entirety. A decision which specifies those to whom it is addressed shall be binding only on them.

Recommendations and opinions shall have no binding force.

Article 289. (1) The ordinary legislative procedure shall consist in the joint adoption by the European Parliament and the Council of a regulation, directive or decision on a proposal from the Commission. This procedure is defined in Article 294.

(2) In the specific cases provided for by the Treaties, the adoption of a regulation, directive or decision by the European Parliament with the participation of the Council, or by the latter with the participation of the European Parliament, shall constitute a special legislative procedure.

(3) Legal acts adopted by legislative procedure shall constitute legislative acts.

(4) In the specific cases provided for by the Treaties, legislative acts may be adopted on the initiative of a group of Member States or of the European Parliament, on a recommendation from the European Central Bank or at the request of the Court of Justice or the European Investment Bank.

Article 290. (1) A legislative act may delegate to the Commission the power to adopt non–legislative acts of general application to supplement or amend certain non–essential elements of the legislative act.

The objectives, content, scope and duration of the delegation of power shall be explicitly defined in the legislative acts. The essential elements of an area shall be reserved for the legislative act and accordingly shall not be the subject of a delegation of power.

(2) Legislative acts shall explicitly lay down the conditions to which the delegation is subject; these conditions may be as follows:

(a) the European Parliament or the Council may decide to revoke the delegation;

(b) the delegated act may enter into force only if no objection has been expressed by the European Parliament or the Council within a period set by the legislative act.

For the purposes of (a) and (b), the European Parliament shall act by a majority of its component members, and the Council by a qualified majority.

(3) The adjective "delegated" shall be inserted in the title of delegated acts.

Article 291. (1) Member States shall adopt all measures of national law necessary to implement legally binding Union acts.

(2) Where uniform conditions for implementing legally binding Union acts are needed, those acts shall confer implementing powers on the Commission, or, in duly justified specific cases and in the cases provided for in Articles 24 and 26 of the Treaty on European Union, on the Council.

(3) For the purposes of paragraph 2, the European Parliament and the Council, acting by means of regulations in accordance with the ordinary legislative procedure, shall lay down in advance the rules and general principles concerning mechanisms for control by Member States of the Commission's exercise of implementing powers.

(4) The word "implementing" shall be inserted in the title of implementing acts.

PART III   EUROPEAN UNION

Article 292. The Council shall adopt recommendations. It shall act on a proposal from the Commission in all cases where the Treaties provide that it shall adopt acts on a proposal from the Commission. It shall act unanimously in those areas in which unanimity is required for the adoption of a Union act. The Commission, and the European Central Bank in the specific cases provided for in the Treaties, shall adopt recommendations.

Section 2. Procedures for the Adoption of Acts and other Provisions

Article 293 (ex Article 250 TEC). (1) Where, pursuant to the Treaties, the Council acts on a proposal from the Commission, it may amend that proposal only by acting unanimously, except in the cases referred to in paragraphs 10 and 13 of Article 294, in Articles 310, 312 and 314 and in the second paragraph of Article 315.

(2) As long as the Council has not acted, the Commission may alter its proposal at any time during the procedures leading to the adoption of a Union act.

Article 294 (ex Article 251 TEC). (1) Where reference is made in the Treaties to the ordinary legislative procedure for the adoption of an act, the following procedure shall apply.

(2) The Commission shall submit a proposal to the European Parliament and the Council.

First reading

(3) The European Parliament shall adopt its position at first reading and communicate it to the Council.

(4) If the Council approves the European Parliament's position, the act concerned shall be adopted in the wording which corresponds to the position of the European Parliament.

(5) If the Council does not approve the European Parliament's position, it shall adopt its position at first reading and communicate it to the European Parliament.

(6) The Council shall inform the European Parliament fully of the reasons which led it to adopt its position at first reading. The Commission shall inform the European Parliament fully of its position.

Second reading

(7) If, within three months of such communication, the European Parliament:

(a) approves the Council's position at first reading or has not taken a decision, the act concerned shall be deemed to have been adopted in the wording which corresponds to the position of the Council;

(b) rejects, by a majority of its component members, the Council's position at first reading, the proposed act shall be deemed not to have been adopted;

(c) proposes, by a majority of its component members, amendments to the Council's position at first reading, the text thus amended shall be forwarded to the Council and to the Commission, which shall deliver an opinion on those amendments.

(8) If, within three months of receiving the European Parliament's amendments, the Council, acting by a qualified majority:

(a) approves all those amendments, the act in question shall be deemed to have been adopted;

(b) does not approve all the amendments, the President of the Council, in agreement with the President of the European Parliament, shall within six weeks convene a meeting of the Conciliation Committee.

(9) The Council shall act unanimously on the amendments on which the Commission has delivered a negative opinion.

Conciliation

(10) The Conciliation Committee, which shall be composed of the members of the Council or their representatives and an equal number of members representing the European Parliament, shall have the task of reaching agreement on a joint text, by a qualified majority of the members of the Council or their representatives and by a majority of the members representing the European Parliament within six weeks of its being convened, on the basis of the positions of the European Parliament and the Council at second reading.

(11) The Commission shall take part in the Conciliation Committee's proceedings and shall take all necessary initiatives with a view to reconciling the positions of the European Parliament and the Council.

(12) If, within six weeks of its being convened, the Conciliation Committee does not approve the joint text, the proposed act shall be deemed not to have been adopted.

Third reading

(13) If, within that period, the Conciliation Committee approves a joint text, the European Parliament, acting by a majority of the votes cast, and the Council, acting by a qualified majority, shall each have a period of six weeks from that approval in which to adopt the act in question in accordance with the joint text. If they fail to do so, the proposed act shall be deemed not to have been adopted.

(14) The periods of three months and six weeks referred to in this Article shall be extended by a maximum of one month and two weeks respectively at the initiative of the European Parliament or the Council.

Special provisions

(15) Where, in the cases provided for in the Treaties, a legislative act is submitted to the ordinary legislative procedure on the initiative of a group of Member States, on a recommendation by the European Central Bank, or at the request of the Court of Justice, paragraph 2, the second sentence of paragraph 6, and paragraph 9 shall not apply.

In such cases, the European Parliament and the Council shall communicate the proposed act to the Commission with their positions at first and second readings. The European Parliament or the Council may request the opinion of the Commission throughout the procedure, which the Commission may also deliver on its own initiative. It may also, if it deems it necessary, take part in the Conciliation Committee in accordance with paragraph 11.

Article 295. The European Parliament, the Council and the Commission shall consult each other and by common agreement make arrangements for their cooperation. To that end, they may, in compliance with the Treaties, conclude interinstitutional agreements which may be of a binding nature.

Article 296 (ex Article 253 TEC). Where the Treaties do not specify the type of act to be adopted, the institutions shall select it on a case–by–case basis, in compliance with the applicable procedures and with the principle of proportionality.

Legal acts shall state the reasons on which they are based and shall refer to any proposals, initiatives, recommendations, requests or opinions required by the Treaties.

When considering draft legislative acts, the European Parliament and the Council shall refrain from adopting acts not provided for by the relevant legislative procedure in the area in question.

Article 297 (ex Article 254 TEC). (1) Legislative acts adopted under the ordinary legislative procedure shall be signed by the President of the European Parliament and by the President of the Council. Legislative acts adopted under a special legislative procedure shall be signed by the President of the institution which adopted them.

Legislative acts shall be published in the *Official Journal of the European Union*. They shall enter into force on the date specified in them or, in the absence thereof, on the twentieth day following that of their publication.

(2) Non–legislative acts adopted in the form of regulations, directives or decisions, when the latter do not specify to whom they are addressed, shall be signed by the President of the institution which adopted them.

Regulations and directives which are addressed to all Member States, as well as decisions which do not specify to whom they are addressed, shall be published in the *Official Journal of the European Union*. They shall enter into force on the date specified in them or, in the absence thereof, on the twentieth day following that of their publication.

Other directives, and decisions which specify to whom they are addressed, shall be notified to those to whom they are addressed and shall take effect upon such notification.

Article 298. (1) In carrying out their missions, the institutions, bodies, offices and agencies of the Union shall have the support of an open, efficient and independent European administration.

(2) In compliance with the Staff Regulations and the Conditions of Employment adopted on the basis of Article 336, the European Parliament and the Council, acting by means of regulations in accordance with the ordinary legislative procedure, shall establish provisions to that end.

Article 299 (ex Article 256 TEC). Acts of the Council, the Commission or the European Central Bank which impose a pecuniary obligation on persons other than States, shall be enforceable.

Enforcement shall be governed by the rules of civil procedure in force in the State in the territory of which it is carried out. The order for its enforcement shall be appended to the decision, without other formality than verification of the authenticity of the decision, by the national authority which the government of each Member State shall designate for this purpose and shall make known to the Commission and to the Court of Justice of the European Union.

When these formalities have been completed on application by the party concerned, the latter may proceed to enforcement in accordance with the national law, by bringing the matter directly before the competent authority.

Enforcement may be suspended only by a decision of the Court. However, the courts of the country concerned shall have jurisdiction over complaints that enforcement is being carried out in an irregular manner.

PART III   EUROPEAN UNION

Chapter 3. The Union's Advisory Bodies

Article 300. (1) The European Parliament, the Council and the Commission shall be assisted by an Economic and Social Committee and a Committee of the Regions, exercising advisory functions.
(2) The Economic and Social Committee shall consist of representatives of organisations of employers, of the employed, and of other parties representative of civil society, notably in socio–economic, civic, professional and cultural areas.
(3) The Committee of the Regions shall consist of representatives of regional and local bodies who either hold a regional or local authority electoral mandate or are politically accountable to an elected assembly.
(4) The members of the Economic and Social Committee and of the Committee of the Regions shall not be bound by any mandatory instructions. They shall be completely independent in the performance of their duties, in the Union's general interest.
(5) The rules referred to in paragraphs 2 and 3 governing the nature of the composition of the Committees shall be reviewed at regular intervals by the Council to take account of economic, social and demographic developments within the Union. The Council, on a proposal from the Commission, shall adopt decisions to that end.

Section 1. The Economic and Social Committee

Article 301 (ex Article 258 TEC). The number of members of the Economic and Social Committee shall not exceed 350.
The Council, acting unanimously on a proposal from the Commission, shall adopt a decision determining the Committee's composition.
The Council shall determine the allowances of members of the Committee.

Article 302 (ex Article 259 TEC). (1) The members of the Committee shall be appointed for five years The Council shall adopt the list of members drawn up in accordance with the proposals made by each Member State. The term of office of the members of the Committee shall be renewable.
(2) The Council shall act after consulting the Commission. It may obtain the opinion of European bodies which are representative of the various economic and social sectors and of civil society to which the Union's activities are of concern.

Article 303 (ex Article 260 TEC). The Committee shall elect its chairman and officers from among its members for a term of two and a half years.
It shall adopt its Rules of Procedure.
The Committee shall be convened by its chairman at the request of the European Parliament, the Council or of the Commission. It may also meet on its own initiative.

Article 304 (ex Article 262 TEC). The Committee shall be consulted by the European Parliament, by the Council or by the Commission where the Treaties so provide. The Committee may be consulted by these institutions in all cases in which they consider it appropriate. It may issue an opinion on its own initiative in cases in which it considers such action appropriate.
The European Parliament, the Council or the Commission shall, if it considers it necessary, set the Committee, for the submission of its opinion, a time limit which may not be less than one month from the date on which the chairman receives notification to this effect. Upon expiry of the time limit, the absence of an opinion shall not prevent further action.
The opinion of the Committee, together with a record of the proceedings, shall be forwarded to the European Parliament, to the Council and to the Commission.

Section 2. The Committee of the Regions

Article 305 (ex Article 263, second, third and fourth paragraphs, TEC). The number of members of the Committee of the Regions shall not exceed 350.
The Council, acting unanimously on a proposal from the Commission, shall adopt a decision determining the Committee's composition.
The members of the Committee and an equal number of alternate members shall be appointed for five years. Their term of office shall be renewable. The Council shall adopt the list of members and alternate members drawn up in accordance with the proposals made by each Member State. When the mandate referred to in Article 300(3) on the basis of which they were proposed comes to an end, the term of office of members of the Committee shall terminate automatically and they shall then be replaced for the remainder of the said term of office in accordance with the same procedure. No member of the Committee shall at the same time be a Member of the European Parliament.

Article 306 (ex Article 264 TEC). The Committee of the Regions shall elect its chairman and officers from among its members for a term of two and a half years.
It shall adopt its Rules of Procedure.
The Committee shall be convened by its chairman at the request of the European Parliament, the Council or of the Commission. It may also meet on its own initiative.

Article 307 (ex Article 265 TEC). The Committee of the Regions shall be consulted by the European Parliament, by the Council or by the Commission where the Treaties so provide and in all other cases, in particular those which concern cross–border cooperation, in which one of these institutions considers it appropriate.
The European Parliament, the Council or the Commission shall, if it considers it necessary, set the Committee, for the submission of its opinion, a time limit which may not be less than one month from the date on which the chairman receives notification to this effect. Upon expiry of the time limit, the absence of an opinion shall not prevent further action.
Where the Economic and Social Committee is consulted pursuant to Article 304, the Committee of the Regions shall be informed by the European Parliament, the Council or the Commission of the request for an opinion. Where it considers that specific regional interests are involved, the Committee of the Regions may issue an opinion on the matter.
It may issue an opinion on its own initiative in cases in which it considers such action appropriate.
The opinion of the Committee, together with a record of the proceedings, shall be forwarded to the European Parliament, to the Council and to the Commission.

Chapter 4. The European Investment Bank

Article 308 (ex Article 266 TEC). The European Investment Bank shall have legal personality.
The members of the European Investment Bank shall be the Member States.
The Statute of the European Investment Bank is laid down in a Protocol annexed to the Treaties. The Council acting unanimously in accordance with a special legislative procedure, at the request of the European Investment Bank and after consulting the European Parliament and the Commission, or on a proposal from the Commission and after consulting the European Parliament and the European Investment Bank, may amend the Statute of the Bank.

Article 309 (ex Article 267 TEC). The task of the European Investment Bank shall be to contribute, by having recourse to the capital market and utilising its own resources, to the balanced and steady development of the internal market in the interest of the Union. For this purpose the Bank shall, operating on a non–profit–making basis, grant loans and give guarantees which facilitate the financing of the following projects in all sectors of the economy:
(a) projects for developing less–developed regions;
(b) projects for modernising or converting undertakings or for developing fresh activities called for by the establishment or functioning of the internal market, where these projects are of such a size or nature that they cannot be entirely financed by the various means available in the individual Member States;
(c) projects of common interest to several Member States which are of such a size or nature that they cannot be entirely financed by the various means available in the individual Member States.
In carrying out its task, the Bank shall facilitate the financing of investment programmes in conjunction with assistance from the Structural Funds and other Union Financial Instruments.

Title II. Financial Provisions

Article 310 (ex Article 268 TEC). (1) All items of revenue and expenditure of the Union shall be included in estimates to be drawn up for each financial year and shall be shown in the budget.
The Union's annual budget shall be established by the European Parliament and the Council in accordance with Article 314.
The revenue and expenditure shown in the budget shall be in balance.
(2) The expenditure shown in the budget shall be authorised for the annual budgetary period in accordance with the regulation referred to in Article 322.
(3) The implementation of expenditure shown in the budget shall require the prior adoption of a legally binding Union act providing a legal basis for its action and for the implementation of the corresponding expenditure in accordance with the regulation referred to in Article 322, except in cases for which that law provides.
(4) With a view to maintaining budgetary discipline, the Union shall not adopt any act which is likely to have appreciable implications for the budget without providing an assurance that the expenditure

PART III EUROPEAN UNION

arising from such an act is capable of being financed within the limit of the Union's own resources and in compliance with the multiannual financial framework referred to in Article 312.

(5) The budget shall be implemented in accordance with the principle of sound financial management. Member States shall cooperate with the Union to ensure that the appropriations entered in the budget are used in accordance with this principle.

(6) The Union and the Member States, in accordance with Article 325, shall counter fraud and any other illegal activities affecting the financial interests of the Union.

Chapter 1. The Union's Own Resources

Article 311 (ex Article 269 TEC). The Union shall provide itself with the means necessary to attain its objectives and carry through its policies.

Without prejudice to other revenue, the budget shall be financed wholly from own resources.

The Council, acting in accordance with a special legislative procedure, shall unanimously and after consulting the European Parliament adopt a decision laying down the provisions relating to the system of own resources of the Union. In this context it may establish new categories of own resources or abolish an existing category. That decision shall not enter into force until it is approved by the Member States in accordance with their respective constitutional requirements.

The Council, acting by means of regulations in accordance with a special legislative procedure, shall lay down implementing measures for the Union's own resources system in so far as this is provided for in the decision adopted on the basis of the third paragraph. The Council shall act after obtaining the consent of the European Parliament.

Chapter 2. The Multiannual Financial Framework

Article 312. (1) The multiannual financial framework shall ensure that Union expenditure develops in an orderly manner and within the limits of its own resources.

It shall be established for a period of at least five years.

The annual budget of the Union shall comply with the multiannual financial framework.

(2) The Council, acting in accordance with a special legislative procedure, shall adopt a regulation laying down the multiannual financial framework. The Council shall act unanimously after obtaining the consent of the European Parliament, which shall be given by a majority of its component members.

The European Council may, unanimously, adopt a decision authorising the Council to act by a qualified majority when adopting the regulation referred to in the first subparagraph.

(3) The financial framework shall determine the amounts of the annual ceilings on commitment appropriations by category of expenditure and of the annual ceiling on payment appropriations. The categories of expenditure, limited in number, shall correspond to the Union's major sectors of activity.

The financial framework shall lay down any other provisions required for the annual budgetary procedure to run smoothly.

(4) Where no Council regulation determining a new financial framework has been adopted by the end of the previous financial framework, the ceilings and other provisions corresponding to the last year of that framework shall be extended until such time as that act is adopted.

(5) Throughout the procedure leading to the adoption of the financial framework, the European Parliament, the Council and the Commission shall take any measure necessary to facilitate its adoption.

Chapter 3. The Union's Annual Budget

Article 313 (ex Article 272(1) TEC). The financial year shall run from 1 January to 31 December.

Article 314 (ex Article 272(2) to (10) TEC). The European Parliament and the Council, acting in accordance with a special legislative procedure, shall establish the Union's annual budget in accordance with the following provisions.

(1) With the exception of the European Central Bank, each institution shall, before 1 July, draw up estimates of its expenditure for the following financial year. The Commission shall consolidate these estimates in a draft budget. which may contain different estimates.

The draft budget shall contain an estimate of revenue and an estimate of expenditure.

(2) The Commission shall submit a proposal containing the draft budget to the European Parliament and to the Council not later than 1 September of the year preceding that in which the budget is to be implemented.

The Commission may amend the draft budget during the procedure until such time as the Conciliation Committee, referred to in paragraph 5, is convened.

(3) The Council shall adopt its position on the draft budget and forward it to the European Parliament not later than 1 October of the year preceding that in which the budget is to be implemented. The Council shall inform the European Parliament in full of the reasons which led it to adopt its position.
(4) If, within forty–two days of such communication, the European Parliament:
(a) approves the position of the Council, the budget shall be adopted;
(b) has not taken a decision, the budget shall be deemed to have been adopted;
(c) adopts amendments by a majority of its component members, the amended draft shall be forwarded to the Council and to the Commission. The President of the European Parliament, in agreement with the President of the Council, shall immediately convene a meeting of the Conciliation Committee. However, if within ten days of the draft being forwarded the Council informs the European Parliament that it has approved all its amendments, the Conciliation Committee shall not meet.
(5) The Conciliation Committee, which shall be composed of the members of the Council or their representatives and an equal number of members representing the European Parliament, shall have the task of reaching agreement on a joint text, by a qualified majority of the members of the Council or their representatives and by a majority of the representatives of the European Parliament within twenty–one days of its being convened, on the basis of the positions of the European Parliament and the Council.
The Commission shall take part in the Conciliation Committee's proceedings and shall take all the necessary initiatives with a view to reconciling the positions of the European Parliament and the Council.
(6) If, within the twenty–one days referred to in paragraph 5, the Conciliation Committee agrees on a joint text, the European Parliament and the Council shall each have a period of fourteen days from the date of that agreement in which to approve the joint text.
(7) If, within the period of fourteen days referred to in paragraph 6:
(a) the European Parliament and the Council both approve the joint text or fail to take a decision, or if one of these institutions approves the joint text while the other one fails to take a decision, the budget shall be deemed to be definitively adopted in accordance with the joint text; or
(b) the European Parliament, acting by a majority of its component members, and the Council both reject the joint text, or if one of these institutions rejects the joint text while the other one fails to take a decision, a new draft budget shall be submitted by the Commission; or
(c) the European Parliament, acting by a majority of its component members, rejects the joint text while the Council approves it, a new draft budget shall be submitted by the Commission; or
(d) the European Parliament approves the joint text whilst the Council rejects it, the European Parliament may, within fourteen days from the date of the rejection by the Council and acting by a majority of its component members and three–fifths of the votes cast, decide to confirm all or some of the amendments referred to in paragraph 4(c). Where a European Parliament amendment is not confirmed, the position agreed in the Conciliation Committee on the budget heading which is the subject of the amendment shall be retained. The budget shall be deemed to be definitively adopted on this basis.
(8) If, within the twenty–one days referred to in paragraph 5, the Conciliation Committee does not agree on a joint text, a new draft budget shall be submitted by the Commission.
(9) When the procedure provided for in this Article has been completed, the President of the European Parliament shall declare that the budget has been definitively adopted.
(10) Each institution shall exercise the powers conferred upon it under this Article in compliance with the Treaties and the acts adopted thereunder, with particular regard to the Union's own resources and the balance between revenue and expenditure.

Article 315 (ex Article 273 TEC). If, at the beginning of a financial year, the budget has not yet been definitively adopted, a sum equivalent to not more than one twelfth of the budget appropriations for the preceding financial year may be spent each month in respect of any chapter of the budget in accordance with the provisions of the Regulations made pursuant to Article 322; that sum shall not, however, exceed one twelfth of the appropriations provided for in the same chapter of the draft budget.
The Council on a proposal by the Commission, may, provided that the other conditions laid down in the first paragraph are observed, authorise expenditure in excess of one twelfth in accordance with the regulations made pursuant to Article 322. The Council shall forward the decision immediately to the European Parliament.
The decision referred to in the second paragraph shall lay down the necessary measures relating to resources to ensure application of this Article, in accordance with the acts referred to in Article 311.
It shall enter into force thirty days following its adoption if the European Parliament, acting by a

majority of its component Members, has not decided to reduce this expenditure within that time-limit.

Article 316 (ex Article 271 TEC). In accordance with conditions to be laid down pursuant to Article 322, any appropriations, other than those relating to staff expenditure, that are unexpended at the end of the financial year may be carried forward to the next financial year only.

Appropriations shall be classified under different chapters grouping items of expenditure according to their nature or purpose and subdivided in accordance with the regulations made pursuant to Article 322.

The expenditure of the European Parliament, the European Council and the Council, the Commission and the Court of Justice of the European Union shall be set out in separate parts of the budget, without prejudice to special arrangements for certain common items of expenditure.

Chapter 4. Implementation of the Budget and Discharge

Article 317 (ex Article 274 TEC). The Commission shall implement the budget in cooperation with the Member States, in accordance with the provisions of the regulations made pursuant to Article 322, on its own responsibility and within the limits of the appropriations, having regard to the principles of sound financial management. Member States shall cooperate with the Commission to ensure that the appropriations are used in accordance with the principles of sound financial management.

The regulations shall lay down the control and audit obligations of the Member States in the implementation of the budget and the resulting responsibilities. They shall also lay down the responsibilities and detailed rules for each institution concerning its part in effecting its own expenditure.

Within the budget, the Commission may, subject to the limits and conditions laid down in the regulations made pursuant to Article 322, transfer appropriations from one chapter to another or from one subdivision to another.

Article 318 (ex Article 275 TEC). The Commission shall submit annually to the European Parliament and to the Council the accounts of the preceding financial year relating to the implementation of the budget. The Commission shall also forward to them a financial statement of the assets and liabilities of the Union.

The Commission shall also submit to the European Parliament and to the Council an evaluation report on the Union's finances based on the results achieved, in particular in relation to the indications given by the European Parliament and the Council pursuant to Article 319.

Article 319 (ex Article 276 TEC). (1) The European Parliament, acting on a recommendation from the Council, shall give a discharge to the Commission in respect of the implementation of the budget. To this end, the Council and the European Parliament in turn shall examine the accounts, the financial statement and the evaluation report referred to in Article 318, the annual report by the Court of Auditors together with the replies of the institutions under audit to the observations of the Court of Auditors, the statement of assurance referred to in Article 287(1), second subparagraph and any relevant special reports by the Court of Auditors.

(2) Before giving a discharge to the Commission, or for any other purpose in connection with the exercise of its powers over the implementation of the budget, the European Parliament may ask to hear the Commission give evidence with regard to the execution of expenditure or the operation of financial control systems. The Commission shall submit any necessary information to the European Parliament at the latter's request.

(3) The Commission shall take all appropriate steps to act on the observations in the decisions giving discharge and on other observations by the European Parliament relating to the execution of expenditure, as well as on comments accompanying the recommendations on discharge adopted by the Council.

At the request of the European Parliament or the Council, the Commission shall report on the measures taken in the light of these observations and comments and in particular on the instructions given to the departments which are responsible for the implementation of the budget. These reports shall also be forwarded to the Court of Auditors.

Chapter 5. Common provisions

Article 320 (ex Article 277 TEC). The multiannual financial framework and the annual budget shall be drawn up in euro.

Article 321 (ex Article 278 TEC). The Commission may, provided it notifies the competent authorities of the Member States concerned, transfer into the currency of one of the Member States its holdings in the currency of another Member State, to the extent necessary to enable them to be used for

purposes which come within the scope of the Treaties. The Commission shall as far as possible avoid making such transfers if it possesses cash or liquid assets in the currencies which it needs.
The Commission shall deal with each Member State through the authority designated by the State concerned. In carrying out financial operations the Commission shall employ the services of the bank of issue of the Member State concerned or of any other financial institution approved by that State.

Article 322 (ex Article 279 TEC). (1) The European Parliament and the Council, acting in accordance with the ordinary legislative procedure, and after consulting the Court of Auditors, shall adopt by means of regulations:
(a) the financial rules which determine in particular the procedure to be adopted for establishing and implementing the budget and for presenting and auditing accounts;
(b) rules providing for checks on the responsibility of financial actors, in particular authorising officers and accounting officers.
(2) The Council, acting on a proposal from the Commission and after consulting the European Parliament and the Court of Auditors, shall determine the methods and procedure whereby the budget revenue provided under the arrangements relating to the Union's own resources shall be made available to the Commission, and determine the measures to be applied, if need be, to meet cash requirements.

Article 323. The European Parliament, the Council and the Commission shall ensure that the financial means are made available to allow the Union to fulfil its legal obligations in respect of third parties.

Article 324. Regular meetings between the Presidents of the European Parliament, the Council and the Commission shall be convened, on the initiative of the Commission, under the budgetary procedures referred to in this Title. The Presidents shall take all the necessary steps to promote consultation and the reconciliation of the positions of the institutions over which they preside in order to facilitate the implementation of this Title.

Chapter 6. Combatting Fraud

Article 325 (ex Article 280 TEC). (1) The Union and the Member States shall counter fraud and any other illegal activities affecting the financial interests of the Union through measures to be taken in accordance with this Article, which shall act as a deterrent and be such as to afford effective protection in the Member States, and in all the Union's institutions, bodies, offices and agencies.
(2) Member States shall take the same measures to counter fraud affecting the financial interests of the Union as they take to counter fraud affecting their own financial interests.
(3) Without prejudice to other provisions of the Treaties, the Member States shall coordinate their action aimed at protecting the financial interests of the Union against fraud. To this end they shall organise, together with the Commission, close and regular cooperation between the competent authorities.
(4) The European Parliament and the Council, acting in accordance with the ordinary legislative procedure, after consulting the Court of Auditors, shall adopt the necessary measures in the fields of the prevention of and fight against fraud affecting the financial interests of the Union with a view to affording effective and equivalent protection in the Member States and in all the Union's institutions, bodies, offices and agencies.
(5) The Commission, in cooperation with Member States, shall each year submit to the European Parliament and to the Council a report on the measures taken for the implementation of this Article.

Title III. Enhanced Cooperation

Article 326 (ex Articles 27a to 27e, 40 to 40b and 43 to 45 TEU and ex Articles 11 and 11a TEC). Any enhanced cooperation shall comply with the Treaties and Union law.
Such cooperation shall not undermine the internal market or economic, social and territorial cohesion. It shall not constitute a barrier to or discrimination in trade between Member States, nor shall it distort competition between them.

Article 327 (ex Articles 27a to 27e, 40 to 40b and 43 to 45 TEU and ex Articles 11 and 11a TEC). Any enhanced cooperation shall respect the competences, rights and obligations of those Member States which do not participate in it. Those Member States shall not impede its implementation by the participating Member States.

Article 328 (ex Articles 27a to 27e, 40 to 40b and 43 to 45 TEU and ex Articles 11 and 11a TEC).
(1) When enhanced cooperation is being established, it shall be open to all Member States, subject to compliance with any conditions of participation laid down by the authorising decision. It shall also

be open to them at any other time, subject to compliance with the acts already adopted within that framework, in addition to those conditions.

The Commission and the Member States participating in enhanced cooperation shall ensure that they promote participation by as many Member States as possible.

(2) The Commission and, where appropriate, the High Representative of the Union for Foreign Affairs and Security Policy shall keep the European Parliament and the Council regularly informed regarding developments in enhanced cooperation.

Article 329 (ex Articles 27a to 27e, 40 to 40b and 43 to 45 TEU and ex Articles 11 and 11a TEC).
(1) Member States which wish to establish enhanced cooperation between themselves in one of the areas covered by the Treaties, with the exception of fields of exclusive competence and the common foreign and security policy, shall address a request to the Commission, specifying the scope and objectives of the enhanced cooperation proposed. The Commission may submit a proposal to the Council to that effect. In the event of the Commission not submitting a proposal, it shall inform the Member States concerned of the reasons for not doing so.

Authorisation to proceed with the enhanced cooperation referred to in the first subparagraph shall be granted by the Council, on a proposal from the Commission and after obtaining the consent of the European Parliament.

(2) The request of the Member States which wish to establish enhanced cooperation between themselves within the framework of the common foreign and security policy shall be addressed to the Council. It shall be forwarded to the High Representative of the Union for Foreign Affairs and Security Policy, who shall give an opinion on whether the enhanced cooperation proposed is consistent with the Union's common foreign and security policy, and to the Commission, which shall give its opinion in particular on whether the enhanced cooperation proposed is consistent with other Union policies. It shall also be forwarded to the European Parliament for information.

Authorisation to proceed with enhanced cooperation shall be granted by a decision of the Council acting unanimously.

Article 330 (ex Articles 27a to 27e, 40 to 40b and 43 to 45 TEU and ex Articles 11 and 11a TEC).
All members of the Council may participate in its deliberations, but only members of the Council representing the Member States participating in enhanced cooperation shall take part in the vote.

Unanimity shall be constituted by the votes of the representatives of the participating Member States only.

A qualified majority shall be defined in accordance with Article 238(3).

Article 331 (ex Articles 27a to 27e, 40 to 40b and 43 to 45 TEU and ex Articles 11 and 11a TEC).
(1) Any Member State which wishes to participate in enhanced cooperation in progress in one of the areas referred to in Article 329(1) shall notify its intention to the Council and the Commission.

The Commission shall, within four months of the date of receipt of the notification, confirm the participation of the Member State concerned. It shall note where necessary that the conditions of participation have been fulfilled and shall adopt any transitional measures necessary with regard to the application of the acts already adopted within the framework of enhanced cooperation.

However, if the Commission considers that the conditions of participation have not been fulfilled, it shall indicate the arrangements to be adopted to fulfil those conditions and shall set a deadline for re–examining the request. On the expiry of that deadline, it shall re–examine the request, in accordance with the procedure set out in the second subparagraph. If the Commission considers that the conditions of participation have still not been met, the Member State concerned may refer the matter to the Council, which shall decide on the request. The Council shall act in accordance with Article 330. It may also adopt the transitional measures referred to in the second subparagraph on a proposal from the Commission.

(2) Any Member State which wishes to participate in enhanced cooperation in progress in the framework of the common foreign and security policy shall notify its intention to the Council, the High Representative of the Union for Foreign Affairs and Security Policy and the Commission.

The Council shall confirm the participation of the Member State concerned, after consulting the High Representative of the Union for Foreign Affairs and Security Policy and after noting, where necessary, that the conditions of participation have been fulfilled. The Council, on a proposal from the High Representative, may also adopt any transitional measures necessary with regard to the application of the acts already adopted within the framework of enhanced cooperation. However, if the Council considers that the conditions of participation have not been fulfilled, it shall indicate the arrangements to be adopted to fulfil those conditions and shall set a deadline for re–examining the request for participation.

For the purposes of this paragraph, the Council shall act unanimously and in accordance with Article 330.

Article 332 (ex Articles 27a to 27e, 40 to 40b and 43 to 45 TEU and ex Articles 11 and 11a TEC). Expenditure resulting from implementation of enhanced cooperation, other than administrative costs entailed for the institutions, shall be borne by the participating Member States, unless all members of the Council, acting unanimously after consulting the European Parliament, decide otherwise.

Article 333 (ex Articles 27a to 27e, 40 to 40b and 43 to 45 TEU and ex Articles 11 and 11a TEC).
(1) Where a provision of the Treaties which may be applied in the context of enhanced cooperation stipulates that the Council shall act unanimously, the Council, acting unanimously in accordance with the arrangements laid down in Article 330, may adopt a decision stipulating that it will act by a qualified majority.
(2) Where a provision of the Treaties which may be applied in the context of enhanced cooperation stipulates that the Council shall adopt acts under a special legislative procedure, the Council, acting unanimously in accordance with the arrangements laid down in Article 330, may adopt a decision stipulating that it will act under the ordinary legislative procedure. The Council shall act after consulting the European Parliament.
(3) Paragraphs 1 and 2 shall not apply to decisions having military or defence implications.

Article 334 (ex Articles 27a to 27e, 40 to 40b and 43 to 45 TEU and ex Articles 11 and 11a TEC). The Council and the Commission shall ensure the consistency of activities undertaken in the context of enhanced cooperation and the consistency of such activities with the policies of the Union, and shall cooperate to that end.

Part Seven. General and Final Provisions

Article 335 (ex Article 282 TEC). In each of the Member States, the Union shall enjoy the most extensive legal capacity accorded to legal persons under their laws; it may, in particular, acquire or dispose of movable and immovable property and may be a party to legal proceedings. To this end, the Union shall be represented by the Commission. However, the Union shall be represented by each of the institutions, by virtue of their administrative autonomy, in matters relating to their respective operation.

Article 336 (ex Article 283 TEC). The European Parliament and the Council shall, acting by means of regulations in accordance with the ordinary legislative procedure and after consulting the other institutions concerned, lay down the Staff Regulations of Officials of the European Union and the Conditions of Employment of other servants of the Union.

Article 337 (ex Article 284 TEC). The Commission may, within the limits and under conditions laid down by the Council acting by a simple majority in accordance with the provisions of the Treaties, collect any information and carry out any checks required for the performance of the tasks entrusted to it.

Article 338 (ex Article 285 TEC). (1) Without prejudice to Article 5 of the Protocol on the Statute of the European System of Central Banks and of the European Central Bank, the European Parliament and the Council, acting in accordance with the ordinary legislative procedure, shall adopt measures for the production of statistics where necessary for the performance of the activities of the Union.
(2) The production of Union statistics shall conform to impartiality, reliability, objectivity, scientific independence, cost–effectiveness and statistical confidentiality; it shall not entail excessive burdens on economic operators.

Article 339 (ex Article 287 TEC). The members of the institutions of the Union, the members of committees, and the officials and other servants of the Union shall be required, even after their duties have ceased, not to disclose information of the kind covered by the obligation of professional secrecy, in particular information about undertakings, their business relations or their cost components.

Article 340 (ex Article 288 TEC). The contractual liability of the Union shall be governed by the law applicable to the contract in question.
In the case of non–contractual liability, the Union shall, in accordance with the general principles common to the laws of the Member States, make good any damage caused by its institutions or by its servants in the performance of their duties.
Notwithstanding the second paragraph, the European Central Bank shall, in accordance with the general principles common to the laws of the Member States, make good any damage caused by it or

by its servants in the performance of their duties.
The personal liability of its servants towards the Union shall be governed by the provisions laid down in their Staff Regulations or in the Conditions of Employment applicable to them.

Article 341 (ex Article 289 TEC). The seat of the institutions of the Union shall be determined by common accord of the governments of the Member States.

Article 342 (ex Article 290 TEC). The rules governing the languages of the institutions of the Union shall, without prejudice to the provisions contained in the Statute of the Court of Justice of the European Union, be determined by the Council, acting unanimously by means of regulations.

Article 343 (ex Article 291 TEC). The Union shall enjoy in the territories of the Member States such privileges and immunities as are necessary for the performance of its tasks, under the conditions laid down in the Protocol of 8 April 1965 on the privileges and immunities of the European Union. The same shall apply to the European Central Bank and the European Investment Bank.

Article 344 (ex Article 292 TEC). Member States undertake not to submit a dispute concerning the interpretation or application of the Treaties to any method of settlement other than those provided for therein.

Article 345 (ex Article 295 TEC). The Treaties shall in no way prejudice the rules in Member States governing the system of property ownership.

Article 346 (ex Article 296 TEC). (1) The provisions of the Treaties shall not preclude the application of the following rules:
(a) no Member State shall be obliged to supply information the disclosure of which it considers contrary to the essential interests of its security;
(b) any Member State may take such measures as it considers necessary for the protection of the essential interests of its security which are connected with the production of or trade in arms, munitions and war material; such measures shall not adversely affect the conditions of competition in the internal market regarding products which are not intended for specifically military purposes.
(2) The Council may, acting unanimously on a proposal from the Commission, make changes to the list, which it drew up on 15 April 1958, of the products to which the provisions of paragraph 1(b) apply.

Article 347 (ex Article 297 TEC). Member States shall consult each other with a view to taking together the steps needed to prevent the functioning of the internal market being affected by measures which a Member State may be called upon to take in the event of serious internal disturbances affecting the maintenance of law and order, in the event of war, serious international tension constituting a threat of war, or in order to carry out obligations it has accepted for the purpose of maintaining peace and international security.

Article 348 (ex Article 298 TEC). If measures taken in the circumstances referred to in Articles 346 and 347 have the effect of distorting the conditions of competition in the internal market, the Commission shall, together with the State concerned, examine how these measures can be adjusted to the rules laid down in the Treaties.
By way of derogation from the procedure laid down in Articles 258 and 259, the Commission or any Member State may bring the matter directly before the Court of Justice if it considers that another Member State is making improper use of the powers provided for in Articles 346 and 347. The Court of Justice shall give its ruling in camera.

Article 349 (ex Article 299(2), second, third and fourth subparagraphs, TEC). Taking account of the structural social and economic situation of Guadeloupe, French Guiana, Martinique, Réunion, Saint–Barthélemy, Saint–Martin, the Azores, Madeira and the Canary Islands, which is compounded by their remoteness, insularity, small size, difficult topography and climate, economic dependence on a few products, the permanence and combination of which severely restrain their development, the Council, on a proposal from the Commission and after consulting the European Parliament, shall adopt specific measures aimed, in particular, at laying down the conditions of application of the Treaties to those regions, including common policies. Where the specific measures in question are adopted by the Council in accordance with a special legislative procedure, it shall also act on a proposal from the Commission and after consulting the European Parliament.
The measures referred to in the first paragraph concern in particular areas such as customs and trade policies, fiscal policy, free zones, agriculture and fisheries policies, conditions for supply of raw materials and essential consumer goods, State aids and conditions of access to structural funds and to

horizontal Union programmes.
The Council shall adopt the measures referred to in the first paragraph taking into account the special characteristics and constraints of the outermost regions without undermining the integrity and the coherence of the Union legal order, including the internal market and common policies.

Article 350 (ex Article 306 TEC). The provisions of the Treaties shall not preclude the existence or completion of regional unions between Belgium and Luxembourg, or between Belgium, Luxembourg and the Netherlands, to the extent that the objectives of these regional unions are not attained by application of the Treaties.

Article 351 (ex Article 307 TEC). The rights and obligations arising from agreements concluded before 1 January 1958 or, for acceding States, before the date of their accession, between one or more Member States on the one hand, and one or more third countries on the other, shall not be affected by the provisions of the Treaties.
To the extent that such agreements are not compatible with the Treaties, the Member State or States concerned shall take all appropriate steps to eliminate the incompatibilities established. Member States shall, where necessary, assist each other to this end and shall, where appropriate, adopt a common attitude.
In applying the agreements referred to in the first paragraph, Member States shall take into account the fact that the advantages accorded under the Treaties by each Member State form an integral part of the establishment of the Union and are thereby inseparably linked with the creation of common institutions, the conferring of powers upon them and the granting of the same advantages by all the other Member States.

Article 352 (ex Article 308 TEC). (1) If action by the Union should prove necessary, within the framework of the policies defined in the Treaties, to attain one of the objectives set out in the Treaties, and the Treaties have not provided the necessary powers, the Council, acting unanimously on a proposal from the Commission and after obtaining the consent of the European Parliament, shall adopt the appropriate measures. Where the measures in question are adopted by the Council in accordance with a special legislative procedure, it shall also act unanimously on a proposal from the Commission and after obtaining the consent of the European Parliament.
(2) Using the procedure for monitoring the subsidiarity principle referred to in Article 5(3) of the Treaty on European Union, the Commission shall draw national Parliaments' attention to proposals based on this Article.
(3) Measures based on this Article shall not entail harmonisation of Member States' laws or regulations in cases where the Treaties exclude such harmonisation.
(4) This Article cannot serve as a basis for attaining objectives pertaining to the common foreign and security policy and any acts adopted pursuant to this Article shall respect the limits set out in Article 40, second paragraph, of the Treaty on European Union.

Article 353. Article 48(7) of the Treaty on European Union shall not apply to the following Articles:
– Article 311, third and fourth paragraphs,
– Article 312(2), first subparagraph,
– Article 352, and
– Article 354.

Article 354 (ex Article 309 TEC). For the purposes of Article 7 of the Treaty on European Union on the suspension of certain rights resulting from Union membership, the member of the European Council or of the Council representing the Member State in question shall not take part in the vote and the Member State in question shall not be counted in the calculation of the one third or four fifths of Member States referred to in paragraphs 1 and 2 of that Article. Abstentions by members present in person or represented shall not prevent the adoption of decisions referred to in paragraph 2 of that Article.
For the adoption of the decisions referred to in paragraphs 3 and 4 of Article 7 of the Treaty on European Union, a qualified majority shall be defined in accordance with Article 238(3)(b) of this Treaty. Where, following a decision to suspend voting rights adopted pursuant to paragraph 3 of Article 7 of the Treaty on European Union, the Council acts by a qualified majority on the basis of a provision of the Treaties, that qualified majority shall be defined in accordance with Article 238(3)(b) of this Treaty, or, where the Council acts on a proposal from the Commission or from the High Representative of the Union for Foreign Affairs and Security Policy, in accordance with Article 238(3)(a).
For the purposes of Article 7 of the Treaty on European Union, the European Parliament shall act by a two–thirds majority of the votes cast, representing the majority of its component Members.

PART III EUROPEAN UNION

Article 355. (ex Article 299(2), first subparagraph, and Article 299(3) to (6) TEC).
In addition to the provisions of Article 52 of the Treaty on European Union relating to the territorial scope of the Treaties, the following provisions shall apply:
(1) The provisions of the Treaties shall apply to Guadeloupe, French Guiana, Martinique, Réunion, Saint–Barthélemy, Saint–Martin, the Azores, Madeira and the Canary Islands in accordance with Article 349.
(2) The special arrangements for association set out in Part Four shall apply to the overseas countries and territories listed in Annex II.
The Treaties shall not apply to those overseas countries and territories having special relations with the United Kingdom of Great Britain and Northern Ireland which are not included in the aforementioned list.
(3) The provisions of the Treaties shall apply to the European territories for whose external relations a Member State is responsible.
(4) The provisions of the Treaties shall apply to the Åland Islands in accordance with the provisions set out in Protocol 2 to the Act concerning the conditions of accession of the Republic of Austria, the Republic of Finland and the Kingdom of Sweden.
(5) Notwithstanding Article 52 of the Treaty on European Union and paragraphs 1 to 4 of this Article:
(a) the Treaties shall not apply to the Faeroe Islands;
(b) the Treaties shall not apply to the United Kingdom Sovereign Base Areas of Akrotiri and Dhekelia in Cyprus except to the extent necessary to ensure the implementation of the arrangements set out in the Protocol on the Sovereign Base Areas of the United Kingdom of Great Britain and Northern Ireland in Cyprus annexed to the Act concerning the conditions of accession of the Czech Republic, the Republic of Estonia, the Republic of Cyprus, the Republic of Latvia, the Republic of Lithuania, the Republic of Hungary, the Republic of Malta, the Republic of Poland, the Republic of Slovenia and the Slovak Republic to the European Union and in accordance with the terms of that Protocol;
(c) the Treaties shall apply to the Channel Islands and the Isle of Man only to the extent necessary to ensure the implementation of the arrangements for those islands set out in the Treaty concerning the accession of new Member States to the European Economic Community and to the European Atomic Energy Community signed on 22 January 1972.
(6) The European Council may, on the initiative of the Member State concerned, adopt a decision amending the status, with regard to the Union, of a Danish, French or Netherlands country or territory referred to in paragraphs 1 and 2. The European Council shall act unanimously after consulting the Commission.

Article 356 (ex Article 312 TEC). This Treaty is concluded for an unlimited period.

Article 357 (ex Article 313 TEC). This Treaty shall be ratified by the High Contracting Parties in accordance with their respective constitutional requirements. The Instruments of ratification shall be deposited with the Government of the Italian Republic.
This Treaty shall enter into force on the first day of the month following the deposit of the Instrument of ratification by the last signatory State to take this step. If, however, such deposit is made less than 15 days before the beginning of the following month, this Treaty shall not enter into force until the first day of the second month after the date of such deposit.

Article 358. The provisions of Article 55 of the Treaty on European Union shall apply to this Treaty.

IN WITNESS WHEREOF, the undersigned Plenipotentiaries have signed this Treaty.
Done at Rome this twenty–fifth day of March in the year one thousand nine hundred and fifty–seven.
[List of signatories not reproduced]

Protocols to the Treaties
Protocol (No 1) on the Role of National Parliaments in the European Union

THE HIGH CONTRACTING PARTIES,

RECALLING that the way in which national Parliaments scrutinise their governments in relation to the activities of the Union is a matter for the particular constitutional organisation and practice of each Member State,

DESIRING to encourage greater involvement of national Parliaments in the activities of the European Union and to enhance their ability to express their views on draft legislative acts of the Union as well as on other matters which may be of particular interest to them,

HAVE AGREED UPON the following provisions, which shall be annexed to the Treaty on European Union, to the Treaty on the Functioning of the European Union and to the Treaty establishing the European Atomic Energy Community:

Title I. Information for National Parliaments

Article 1. Commission consultation documents (green and white papers and communications) shall be forwarded directly by the Commission to national Parliaments upon publication. The Commission shall also forward the annual legislative programme as well as any other instrument of legislative planning or policy to national Parliaments, at the same time as to the European Parliament and the Council.

Article 2. Draft legislative acts sent to the European Parliament and to the Council shall be forwarded to national Parliaments.

For the purposes of this Protocol, "draft legislative acts" shall mean proposals from the Commission, initiatives from a group of Member States, initiatives from the European Parliament, requests from the Court of Justice, recommendations from the European Central Bank and requests from the European Investment Bank, for the adoption of a legislative act.

Draft legislative acts originating from the Commission shall be forwarded to national Parliaments directly by the Commission, at the same time as to the European Parliament and the Council.

Draft legislative acts originating from the European Parliament shall be forwarded to national Parliaments directly by the European Parliament.

Draft legislative acts originating from a group of Member States, the Court of Justice, the European Central Bank or the European Investment Bank shall be forwarded to national Parliaments by the Council.

Article 3. National Parliaments may send to the Presidents of the European Parliament, the Council and the Commission a reasoned opinion on whether a draft legislative act complies with the principle of subsidiarity, in accordance with the procedure laid down in the Protocol on the application of the principles of subsidiarity and proportionality.

If the draft legislative act originates from a group of Member States, the President of the Council shall forward the reasoned opinion or opinions to the governments of those Member States.

If the draft legislative act originates from the Court of Justice, the European Central Bank or the European Investment Bank, the President of the Council shall forward the reasoned opinion or opinions to the institution or body concerned.

Article 4. An eight–week period shall elapse between a draft legislative act being made available to national Parliaments in the official languages of the Union and the date when it is placed on a provisional agenda for the Council for its adoption or for adoption of a position under a legislative procedure. Exceptions shall be possible in cases of urgency, the reasons for which shall be stated in the act or position of the Council. Save in urgent cases for which due reasons have been given, no agreement may be reached on a draft legislative act during those eight weeks. Save in urgent cases for which due reasons have been given, a ten–day period shall elapse between the placing of a draft legislative act on the provisional agenda for the Council and the adoption of a position.

Article 5. The agendas for and the outcome of meetings of the Council, including the minutes of meetings where the Council is deliberating on draft legislative acts, shall be forwarded directly to national Parliaments, at the same time as to Member States' governments.

Article 6. When the European Council intends to make use of the first or second subparagraphs of Article 48(7) of the Treaty on European Union, national Parliaments shall be informed of the initiative of the European Council at least six months before any decision is adopted.

PART III   EUROPEAN UNION

Article 7. The Court of Auditors shall forward its annual report to national Parliaments, for information, at the same time as to the European Parliament and to the Council.

Article 8. Where the national Parliamentary system is not unicameral, Articles 1 to 7 shall apply to the component chambers.

Title II. Interparliamentary Cooperation

Article 9. The European Parliament and national Parliaments shall together determine the organisation and promotion of effective and regular interparliamentary cooperation within the Union.

Article 10. A conference of Parliamentary Committees for Union Affairs may submit any contribution it deems appropriate for the attention of the European Parliament, the Council and the Commission. That conference shall in addition promote the exchange of information and best practice between national Parliaments and the European Parliament, including their special committees. It may also organise interparliamentary conferences on specific topics, in particular to debate matters of common foreign and security policy, including common security and defence policy. Contributions from the conference shall not bind national Parliaments and shall not prejudge their positions.

Protocol (No 2) on the Application of the Principles of Subsidiarity and Proportionality

THE HIGH CONTRACTING PARTIES,
WISHING to ensure that decisions are taken as closely as possible to the citizens of the Union,
RESOLVED to establish the conditions for the application of the principles of subsidiarity and proportionality, as laid down in Article 5 of the Treaty on European Union, and to establish a system for monitoring the application of those principles,
HAVE AGREED UPON the following provisions, which shall be annexed to the Treaty on European Union and to the Treaty on the Functioning of the European Union:

Article 1. Each institution shall ensure constant respect for the principles of subsidiarity and proportionality, as laid down in Article 5 of the Treaty on European Union.

Article 2. Before proposing legislative acts, the Commission shall consult widely. Such consultations shall, where appropriate, take into account the regional and local dimension of the action envisaged. In cases of exceptional urgency, the Commission shall not conduct such consultations. It shall give reasons for its decision in its proposal.

Article 3. For the purposes of this Protocol, "draft legislative acts" shall mean proposals from the Commission, initiatives from a group of Member States, initiatives from the European Parliament, requests from the Court of Justice, recommendations from the European Central Bank and requests from the European Investment Bank, for the adoption of a legislative act.

Article 4. The Commission shall forward its draft legislative acts and its amended drafts to national Parliaments at the same time as to the Union legislator.
The European Parliament shall forward its draft legislative acts and its amended drafts to national Parliaments.
The Council shall forward draft legislative acts originating from a group of Member States, the Court of Justice, the European Central Bank or the European Investment Bank and amended drafts to national Parliaments.
Upon adoption, legislative resolutions of the European Parliament and positions of the Council shall be forwarded by them to national Parliaments.

Article 5. Draft legislative acts shall be justified with regard to the principles of subsidiarity and proportionality. Any draft legislative act should contain a detailed statement making it possible to appraise compliance with the principles of subsidiarity and proportionality. This statement should contain some assessment of the proposal's financial impact and, in the case of a directive, of its implications for the rules to be put in place by Member States, including, where necessary, the regional legislation. The reasons for concluding that a Union objective can be better achieved at Union level shall be substantiated by qualitative and, wherever possible, quantitative indicators. Draft legislative acts shall take account of the need for any burden, whether financial or administrative, falling upon the Union, national governments, regional or local authorities, economic operators and citizens, to be minimised and commensurate with the objective to be achieved.

PROTOCOLS TO THE TREATIES

Article 6. Any national Parliament or any chamber of a national Parliament may, within eight weeks from the date of transmission of a draft legislative act, in the official languages of the Union, send to the Presidents of the European Parliament, the Council and the Commission a reasoned opinion stating why it considers that the draft in question does not comply with the principle of subsidiarity. It will be for each national Parliament or each chamber of a national Parliament to consult, where appropriate, regional parliaments with legislative powers.
If the draft legislative act originates from a group of Member States, the President of the Council shall forward the opinion to the governments of those Member States.
If the draft legislative act originates from the Court of Justice, the European Central Bank or the European Investment Bank, the President of the Council shall forward the opinion to the institution or body concerned.

Article 7. (1) The European Parliament, the Council and the Commission, and, where appropriate, the group of Member States, the Court of Justice, the European Central Bank or the European Investment Bank, if the draft legislative act originates from them, shall take account of the reasoned opinions issued by national Parliaments or by a chamber of a national Parliament.
Each national Parliament shall have two votes, shared out on the basis of the national Parliamentary system. In the case of a bicameral Parliamentary system, each of the two chambers shall have one vote.
(2) Where reasoned opinions on a draft legislative act's non–compliance with the principle of subsidiarity represent at least one third of all the votes allocated to the national Parliaments in accordance with the second subparagraph of paragraph 1, the draft must be reviewed. This threshold shall be a quarter in the case of a draft legislative act submitted on the basis of Article 76 of the Treaty on the Functioning of the European Union on the area of freedom, security and justice.
After such review, the Commission or, where appropriate, the group of Member States, the European Parliament, the Court of Justice, the European Central Bank or the European Investment Bank, if the draft legislative act originates from them, may decide to maintain, amend or withdraw the draft. Reasons must be given for this decision.
(3) Furthermore, under the ordinary legislative procedure, where reasoned opinions on the non–compliance of a proposal for a legislative act with the principle of subsidiarity represent at least a simple majority of the votes allocated to the national Parliaments in accordance with the second subparagraph of paragraph 1, the proposal must be reviewed. After such review, the Commission may decide to maintain, amend or withdraw the proposal.
If it chooses to maintain the proposal, the Commission will have, in a reasoned opinion, to justify why it considers that the proposal complies with the principle of subsidiarity. This reasoned opinion, as well as the reasoned opinions of the national Parliaments, will have to be submitted to the Union legislator, for consideration in the procedure:
(a) before concluding the first reading, the legislator (the European Parliament and the Council) shall consider whether the legislative proposal is compatible with the principle of subsidiarity, taking particular account of the reasons expressed and shared by the majority of national Parliaments as well as the reasoned opinion of the Commission;
(b) if, by a majority of 55 % of the members of the Council or a majority of the votes cast in the European Parliament, the legislator is of the opinion that the proposal is not compatible with the principle of subsidiarity, the legislative proposal shall not be given further consideration.

Article 8. The Court of Justice of the European Union shall have jurisdiction in actions on grounds of infringement of the principle of subsidiarity by a legislative act, brought in accordance with the rules laid down in Article 263 of the Treaty on the Functioning of the European Union by Member States, or notified by them in accordance with their legal order on behalf of their national Parliament or a chamber thereof.
In accordance with the rules laid down in the said Article, the Committee of the Regions may also bring such actions against legislative acts for the adoption of which the Treaty on the Functioning of the European Union provides that it be consulted.

Article 9. The Commission shall submit each year to the European Council, the European Parliament, the Council and national Parliaments a report on the application of Article 5 of the Treaty on European Union. This annual report shall also be forwarded to the Economic and Social Committee and the Committee of the Regions.

Protocol (No 3) on the Statute of the Court of Justice of the European Union

PART III   EUROPEAN UNION

THE HIGH CONTRACTING PARTIES,
DESIRING to lay down the Statute of the Court of Justice of the European Union provided for in Article 281 of the Treaty on the Functioning of the European Union,
HAVE AGREED UPON the following provisions, which shall be annexed to the Treaty on European Union, the Treaty on the Functioning of the European Union and the Treaty establishing the European Atomic Energy Community:

Article 1. The Court of Justice of the European Union shall be constituted and shall function in accordance with the provisions of the Treaties, of the Treaty establishing the European Atomic Energy Community (the EAEC Treaty) and of this Statute.

Title I. Judges and Advocates–General

Article 2. Before taking up his duties each Judge shall, before the Court of Justice sitting in open court, take an oath to perform his duties impartially and conscientiously and to preserve the secrecy of the deliberations of the Court.

Article 3. The Judges shall be immune from legal proceedings. After they have ceased to hold office, they shall continue to enjoy immunity in respect of acts performed by them in their official capacity, including words spoken or written.
The Court of Justice, sitting as a full Court, may waive the immunity. If the decision concerns a member of the General Court or of a specialised court, the Court shall decide after consulting the court concerned.
Where immunity has been waived and criminal proceedings are instituted against a Judge, he shall be tried, in any of the Member States, only by the court competent to judge the members of the highest national judiciary.
Articles 11 to 14 and Article 17 of the Protocol on the privileges and immunities of the European Union shall apply to the Judges, Advocates–General, Registrar and Assistant Rapporteurs of the Court of Justice of the European Union, without prejudice to the provisions relating to immunity from legal proceedings of Judges which are set out in the preceding paragraphs.

Article 4. The Judges may not hold any political or administrative office.
They may not engage in any occupation, whether gainful or not, unless exemption is exceptionally granted by the Council, acting by a simple majority.
When taking up their duties, they shall give a solemn undertaking that, both during and after their term of office, they will respect the obligations arising therefrom, in particular the duty to behave with integrity and discretion as regards the acceptance, after they have ceased to hold office, of certain appointments or benefits.
Any doubt on this point shall be settled by decision of the Court of Justice. If the decision concerns a member of the General Court or of a specialised court, the Court shall decide after consulting the court concerned.

Article 5. Apart from normal replacement, or death, the duties of a Judge shall end when he resigns.
Where a Judge resigns, his letter of resignation shall be addressed to the President of the Court of Justice for transmission to the President of the Council. Upon this notification a vacancy shall arise on the bench.
Save where Article 6 applies, a Judge shall continue to hold office until his successor takes up his duties.

Article 6. A Judge may be deprived of his office or of his right to a pension or other benefits in its stead only if, in the unanimous opinion of the Judges and Advocates–General of the Court of Justice, he no longer fulfils the requisite conditions or meets the obligations arising from his office. The Judge concerned shall not take part in any such deliberations. If the person concerned is a member of the General Court or of a specialised court, the Court shall decide after consulting the court concerned.
The Registrar of the Court shall communicate the decision of the Court to the President of the European Parliament and to the President of the Commission and shall notify it to the President of the Council.
In the case of a decision depriving a Judge of his office, a vacancy shall arise on the bench upon this latter notification.

Article 7. A Judge who is to replace a member of the Court whose term of office has not expired shall be appointed for the remainder of his predecessor's term.

Article 8. The provisions of Articles 2 to 7 shall apply to the Advocates–General.

Title II. Organisation of the Court of Justice

Article 9. When, every three years, the Judges are partially replaced, 14 Judges shall be replaced. When, every three years, the Advocates–General are partially replaced, four Advocates–General shall be replaced on each occasion.

Article 10. The Registrar shall take an oath before the Court of Justice to perform his duties impartially and conscientiously and to preserve the secrecy of the deliberations of the Court of Justice.

Article 11. The Court of Justice shall arrange for replacement of the Registrar on occasions when he is prevented from attending the Court of Justice.

Article 12. Officials and other servants shall be attached to the Court of Justice to enable it to function. They shall be responsible to the Registrar under the authority of the President.

Article 13. At the request of the Court of Justice, the European Parliament and the Council may, acting in accordance with the ordinary legislative procedure, provide for the appointment of Assistant Rapporteurs and lay down the rules governing their service. The Assistant Rapporteurs may be required, under conditions laid down in the Rules of Procedure, to participate in preparatory inquiries in cases pending before the Court and to cooperate with the Judge who acts as Rapporteur.
The Assistant Rapporteurs shall be chosen from persons whose independence is beyond doubt and who possess the necessary legal qualifications; they shall be appointed by the Council, acting by a simple majority. They shall take an oath before the Court to perform their duties impartially and conscientiously and to preserve the secrecy of the deliberations of the Court.

Article 14. The Judges, the Advocates–General and the Registrar shall be required to reside at the place where the Court of Justice has its seat.

Article 15. The Court of Justice shall remain permanently in session. The duration of the judicial vacations shall be determined by the Court with due regard to the needs of its business.

Article 16. The Court of Justice shall form chambers consisting of three and five Judges. The Judges shall elect the Presidents of the chambers from among their number. The Presidents of the chambers of five Judges shall be elected for three years. They may be re–elected once.
The Grand Chamber shall consist of 13 Judges. It shall be presided over by the President of the Court. The Presidents of the chambers of five Judges and other Judges appointed in accordance with the conditions laid down in the Rules of Procedure shall also form part of the Grand Chamber.
The Court shall sit in a Grand Chamber when a Member State or an institution of the Union that is party to the proceedings so requests.
The Court shall sit as a full Court where cases are brought before it pursuant to Article 228(2), Article 245(2), Article 247 or Article 286(6) of the Treaty on the Functioning of the European Union. Moreover, where it considers that a case before it is of exceptional importance, the Court may decide, after hearing the Advocate–General, to refer the case to the full Court.

Article 17. Decisions of the Court of Justice shall be valid only when an uneven number of its members is sitting in the deliberations.
Decisions of the chambers consisting of either three or five Judges shall be valid only if they are taken by three Judges.
Decisions of the Grand Chamber shall be valid only if nine Judges are sitting.
Decisions of the full Court shall be valid only if 15 Judges are sitting.
In the event of one of the Judges of a chamber being prevented from attending, a Judge of another chamber may be called upon to sit in accordance with conditions laid down in the Rules of Procedure.

Article 18. No Judge or Advocate–General may take part in the disposal of any case in which he has previously taken part as agent or adviser or has acted for one of the parties, or in which he has been called upon to pronounce as a member of a court or tribunal, of a commission of inquiry or in any other capacity.
If, for some special reason, any Judge or Advocate–General considers that he should not take part in the judgment or examination of a particular case, he shall so inform the President. If, for some special reason, the President considers that any Judge or Advocate–General should not sit or make submissions in a particular case, he shall notify him accordingly.
Any difficulty arising as to the application of this Article shall be settled by decision of the Court of Justice.

PART III   EUROPEAN UNION

A party may not apply for a change in the composition of the Court or of one of its chambers on the grounds of either the nationality of a Judge or the absence from the Court or from the chamber of a Judge of the nationality of that party.

Title III. Procedure before the Court of Justice

Article 19. The Member States and the institutions of the Union shall be represented before the Court of Justice by an agent appointed for each case; the agent may be assisted by an adviser or by a lawyer.

The States, other than the Member States, which are parties to the Agreement on the European Economic Area and also the EFTA Surveillance Authority referred to in that Agreement shall be represented in same manner.

Other parties must be represented by a lawyer.

Only a lawyer authorised to practise before a court of a Member State or of another State which is a party to the Agreement on the European Economic Area may represent or assist a party before the Court.

Such agents, advisers and lawyers shall, when they appear before the Court, enjoy the rights and immunities necessary to the independent exercise of their duties, under conditions laid down in the Rules of Procedure.

As regards such advisers and lawyers who appear before it, the Court shall have the powers normally accorded to courts of law, under conditions laid down in the Rules of Procedure.

University teachers being nationals of a Member State whose law accords them a right of audience shall have the same rights before the Court as are accorded by this Article to lawyers.

Article 20. The procedure before the Court of Justice shall consist of two parts: written and oral.

The written procedure shall consist of the communication to the parties and to the institutions of the Union whose decisions are in dispute, of applications, statements of case, defences and observations, and of replies, if any, as well as of all papers and documents in support or of certified copies of them. Communications shall be made by the Registrar in the order and within the time laid down in the Rules of Procedure.

The oral procedure shall consist of the reading of the report presented by a Judge acting as Rapporteur, the hearing by the Court of agents, advisers and lawyers and of the submissions of the Advocate–General, as well as the hearing, if any, of witnesses and experts.

Where it considers that the case raises no new point of law, the Court may decide, after hearing the Advocate–General, that the case shall be determined without a submission from the Advocate–General.

Article 21. A case shall be brought before the Court of Justice by a written application addressed to the Registrar. The application shall contain the applicant's name and permanent address and the description of the signatory, the name of the party or names of the parties against whom the application is made, the subject–matter of the dispute, the form of order sought and a brief statement of the pleas in law on which the application is based.

The application shall be accompanied, where appropriate, by the measure the annulment of which is sought or, in the circumstances referred to in Article 265 of the Treaty on the Functioning of the European Union, by documentary evidence of the date on which an institution was, in accordance with those Articles, requested to act. If the documents are not submitted with the application, the Registrar shall ask the party concerned to produce them within a reasonable period, but in that event the rights of the party shall not lapse even if such documents are produced after the time limit for bringing proceedings.

Article 22. A case governed by Article 18 of the EAEC Treaty shall be brought before the Court of Justice by an appeal addressed to the Registrar. The appeal shall contain the name and permanent address of the applicant and the description of the signatory, a reference to the decision against which the appeal is brought, the names of the respondents, the subject–matter of the dispute, the submissions and a brief statement of the grounds on which the appeal is based.

The appeal shall be accompanied by a certified copy of the decision of the Arbitration Committee which is contested.

If the Court rejects the appeal, the decision of the Arbitration Committee shall become final.

If the Court annuls the decision of the Arbitration Committee, the matter may be re–opened, where appropriate, on the initiative of one of the parties in the case, before the Arbitration Committee. The latter shall conform to any decisions on points of law given by the Court.

Article 23. In the cases governed by Article 267 of the Treaty on the Functioning of the European Union, the decision of the court or tribunal of a Member State which suspends its proceedings and refers a case to the Court of Justice shall be notified to the Court by the court or tribunal concerned. The decision shall then be notified by the Registrar of the Court to the parties, to the Member States and to the Commission, and to the institution, body, office or agency of the Union which adopted the act the validity or interpretation of which is in dispute.

Within two months of this notification, the parties, the Member States, the Commission and, where appropriate, the institution, body, office or agency which adopted the act the validity or interpretation of which is in dispute, shall be entitled to submit statements of case or written observations to the Court.

In the cases governed by Article 267 of the Treaty on the Functioning of the European Union, the decision of the national court or tribunal shall, moreover, be notified by the Registrar of the Court to the States, other than the Member States, which are parties to the Agreement on the European Economic Area and also to the EFTA Surveillance Authority referred to in that Agreement which may, within two months of notification, where one of the fields of application of that Agreement is concerned, submit statements of case or written observations to the Court.

Where an agreement relating to a specific subject matter, concluded by the Council and one or more non–member States, provides that those States are to be entitled to submit statements of case or written observations where a court or tribunal of a Member State refers to the Court of Justice for a preliminary ruling a question falling within the scope of the agreement, the decision of the national court or tribunal containing that question shall also be notified to the non–member States concerned. Within two months from such notification, those States may lodge at the Court statements of case or written observations.

Article 23a. The Rules of Procedure may provide for an expedited or accelerated procedure and, for references for a preliminary ruling relating to the area of freedom, security and justice, an urgent procedure.

Those procedures may provide, in respect of the submission of statements of case or written observations, for a shorter period than that provided for by Article 23, and, in derogation from the fourth paragraph of Article 20, for the case to be determined without a submission from the Advocate General.

In addition, the urgent procedure may provide for restriction of the parties and other interested persons mentioned in Article 23, authorised to submit statements of case or written observations and, in cases of extreme urgency, for the written stage of the procedure to be omitted.

Article 24. The Court of Justice may require the parties to produce all documents and to supply all information which the Court considers desirable. Formal note shall be taken of any refusal.

The Court may also require the Member States and institutions, bodies, offices and agencies not being parties to the case to supply all information which the Court considers necessary for the proceedings.

Article 25. The Court of Justice may at any time entrust any individual, body, authority, committee or other organisation it chooses with the task of giving an expert opinion.

Article 26. Witnesses may be heard under conditions laid down in the Rules of Procedure.

Article 27. With respect to defaulting witnesses the Court of Justice shall have the powers generally granted to courts and tribunals and may impose pecuniary penalties under conditions laid down in the Rules of Procedure.

Article 28. Witnesses and experts may be heard on oath taken in the form laid down in the Rules of Procedure or in the manner laid down by the law of the country of the witness or expert.

Article 29. The Court of Justice may order that a witness or expert be heard by the judicial authority of his place of permanent residence.

The order shall be sent for implementation to the competent judicial authority under conditions laid down in the Rules of Procedure. The documents drawn up in compliance with the letters rogatory shall be returned to the Court under the same conditions.

The Court shall defray the expenses, without prejudice to the right to charge them, where appropriate, to the parties.

Article 30. A Member State shall treat any violation of an oath by a witness or expert in the same manner as if the offence had been committed before one of its courts with jurisdiction in civil

PART III EUROPEAN UNION

proceedings. At the instance of the Court of Justice, the Member State concerned shall prosecute the offender before its competent court.

Article 31. The hearing in court shall be public, unless the Court of Justice, of its own motion or on application by the parties, decides otherwise for serious reasons.

Article 32. During the hearings the Court of Justice may examine the experts, the witnesses and the parties themselves. The latter, however, may address the Court of Justice only through their representatives.

Article 33. Minutes shall be made of each hearing and signed by the President and the Registrar.

Article 34. The case list shall be established by the President.

Article 35. The deliberations of the Court of Justice shall be and shall remain secret.

Article 36. Judgments shall state the reasons on which they are based. They shall contain the names of the Judges who took part in the deliberations.

Article 37. Judgments shall be signed by the President and the Registrar. They shall be read in open court.

Article 38. The Court of Justice shall adjudicate upon costs.

Article 39. The President of the Court of Justice may, by way of summary procedure, which may, in so far as necessary, differ from some of the rules contained in this Statute and which shall be laid down in the Rules of Procedure, adjudicate upon applications to suspend execution, as provided for in Article 278 of the Treaty on the Functioning of the European Union and Article 157 of the EAEC Treaty, or to prescribe interim measures pursuant to Article 279 of the Treaty on the Functioning of the European Union, or to suspend enforcement in accordance with the fourth paragraph of Article 299 of the Treaty on the Functioning of the European Union or the third paragraph of Article 164 of the EAEC Treaty.

Should the President be prevented from attending, his place shall be taken by another Judge under conditions laid down in the Rules of Procedure.

The ruling of the President or of the Judge replacing him shall be provisional and shall in no way prejudice the decision of the Court on the substance of the case.

Article 40. Member States and institutions of the Union may intervene in cases before the Court of Justice.

The same right shall be open to the bodies, offices and agencies of the Union and to any other person which can establish an interest in the result of a case submitted to the Court. Natural or legal persons shall not intervene in cases between Member States, between institutions of the Union or between Member States and institutions of the Union.

Without prejudice to the second paragraph, the States, other than the Member States, which are parties to the Agreement on the European Economic Area, and also the EFTA Surveillance Authority referred to in that Agreement, may intervene in cases before the Court where one of the fields of application of that Agreement is concerned.

An application to intervene shall be limited to supporting the form of order sought by one of the parties.

Article 41. Where the defending party, after having been duly summoned, fails to file written submissions in defence, judgment shall be given against that party by default. An objection may be lodged against the judgment within one month of it being notified. The objection shall not have the effect of staying enforcement of the judgment by default unless the Court of Justice decides otherwise.

Article 42. Member States, institutions, bodies, offices and agencies of the Union and any other natural or legal persons may, in cases and under conditions to be determined by the Rules of Procedure, institute third–party proceedings to contest a judgment rendered without their being heard, where the judgment is prejudicial to their rights.

Article 43. If the meaning or scope of a judgment is in doubt, the Court of Justice shall construe it on application by any party or any institution of the Union establishing an interest therein.

Article 44. An application for revision of a judgment may be made to the Court of Justice only on discovery of a fact which is of such a nature as to be a decisive factor, and which, when the judgment was given, was unknown to the Court and to the party claiming the revision.

The revision shall be opened by a judgment of the Court expressly recording the existence of a new fact, recognising that it is of such a character as to lay the case open to revision and declaring the application admissible on this ground.

No application for revision may be made after the lapse of 10 years from the date of the judgment.

Article 45. Periods of grace based on considerations of distance shall be determined by the Rules of Procedure.

No right shall be prejudiced in consequence of the expiry of a time limit if the party concerned proves the existence of unforeseeable circumstances or of force majeure.

Article 46. Proceedings against the Union in matters arising from non–contractual liability shall be barred after a period of five years from the occurrence of the event giving rise thereto. The period of limitation shall be interrupted if proceedings are instituted before the Court of Justice or if prior to such proceedings an application is made by the aggrieved party to the relevant institution of the Union. In the latter event the proceedings must be instituted within the period of two months provided for in Article 263 of the Treaty on the Functioning of the European Union; the provisions of the second paragraph of Article 265 of the Treaty on the Functioning of the European Union shall apply where appropriate.

This Article shall also apply to proceedings against the European Central Bank regarding non–contractual liability.

Title IV. General Court

Article 47. The first paragraph of Article 9, Articles 14 and 15, the first, second, fourth and fifth paragraphs of Article 17 and Article 18 shall apply to the General Court and its members.

The fourth paragraph of Article 3 and Articles 10, 11 and 14 shall apply to the Registrar of the General Court *mutatis mutandis*.

Article 48. The General Court shall consist of 27 Judges.

Article 49. The Members of the General Court may be called upon to perform the task of an Advocate–General.

It shall be the duty of the Advocate–General, acting with complete impartiality and independence, to make, in open court, reasoned submissions on certain cases brought before the General Court in order to assist the General Court in the performance of its task.

The criteria for selecting such cases, as well as the procedures for designating the Advocates–General, shall be laid down in the Rules of Procedure of the General Court.

A Member called upon to perform the task of Advocate–General in a case may not take part in the judgment of the case.

Article 50. The General Court shall sit in chambers of three or five Judges. The Judges shall elect the Presidents of the chambers from among their number. The Presidents of the chambers of five Judges shall be elected for three years. They may be re–elected once.

The composition of the chambers and the assignment of cases to them shall be governed by the Rules of Procedure. In certain cases governed by the Rules of Procedure, the General Court may sit as a full court or be constituted by a single Judge.

The Rules of Procedure may also provide that the General Court may sit in a Grand Chamber in cases and under the conditions specified therein.

Article 51. By way of derogation from the rule laid down in Article 256(1) of the Treaty on the Functioning of the European Union, jurisdiction shall be reserved to the Court of Justice in the actions referred to in Articles 263 and 265 of the Treaty on the Functioning of the European Union when they are brought by a Member State against:

(a) an act of or failure to act by the European Parliament or the Council, or by those institutions acting jointly, except for:

– decisions taken by the Council under the third subparagraph of Article 108(2) of the Treaty on the Functioning of the European Union;

– acts of the Council adopted pursuant to a Council regulation concerning measures to protect trade within the meaning of Article 207 of the Treaty on the Functioning of the European Union;

– acts of the Council by which the Council exercises implementing powers in accordance with the second paragraph of Article 291 of the Treaty on the Functioning of the European Union;

(b) against an act of or failure to act by the Commission under the first paragraph of Article 331 of the Treaty on the Functioning of the European Union.

Jurisdiction shall also be reserved to the Court of Justice in the actions referred to in the same Articles when they are brought by an institution of the Union against an act of or failure to act by the European Parliament, the Council, both those institutions acting jointly, or the Commission, or brought by an institution of the Union against an act of or failure to act by the European Central Bank.

Article 52. The President of the Court of Justice and the President of the General Court shall determine, by common accord, the conditions under which officials and other servants attached to the Court of Justice shall render their services to the General Court to enable it to function. Certain officials or other servants shall be responsible to the Registrar of the General Court under the authority of the President of the General Court.

Article 53. The procedure before the General Court shall be governed by Title III.
Such further and more detailed provisions as may be necessary shall be laid down in its Rules of Procedure. The Rules of Procedure may derogate from the fourth paragraph of Article 40 and from Article 41 in order to take account of the specific features of litigation in the field of intellectual property.
Notwithstanding the fourth paragraph of Article 20, the Advocate–General may make his reasoned submissions in writing.

Article 54. Where an application or other procedural document addressed to the General Court is lodged by mistake with the Registrar of the Court of Justice, it shall be transmitted immediately by that Registrar to the Registrar of the General Court; likewise, where an application or other procedural document addressed to the Court of Justice is lodged by mistake with the Registrar of the General Court, it shall be transmitted immediately by that Registrar to the Registrar of the Court of Justice.
Where the General Court finds that it does not have jurisdiction to hear and determine an action in respect of which the Court of Justice has jurisdiction, it shall refer that action to the Court of Justice; likewise, where the Court of Justice finds that an action falls within the jurisdiction of the General Court, it shall refer that action to the General Court, whereupon that Court may not decline jurisdiction.
Where the Court of Justice and the General Court are seised of cases in which the same relief is sought, the same issue of interpretation is raised or the validity of the same act is called in question, the General Court may, after hearing the parties, stay the proceedings before it until such time as the Court of Justice has delivered judgment or, where the action is one brought pursuant to Article 263 of the Treaty on the Functioning of the European Union, may decline jurisdiction so as to allow the Court of Justice to rule on such actions. In the same circumstances, the Court of Justice may also decide to stay the proceedings before it; in that event, the proceedings before the General Court shall continue.
Where a Member State and an institution of the Union are challenging the same act, the General Court shall decline jurisdiction so that the Court of Justice may rule on those applications.

Article 55. Final decisions of the General Court, decisions disposing of the substantive issues in part only or disposing of a procedural issue concerning a plea of lack of competence or inadmissibility, shall be notified by the Registrar of the General Court to all parties as well as all Member States and the institutions of the Union even if they did not intervene in the case before the General Court.

Article 56. An appeal may be brought before the Court of Justice, within two months of the notification of the decision appealed against, against final decisions of the General Court and decisions of that Court disposing of the substantive issues in part only or disposing of a procedural issue concerning a plea of lack of competence or inadmissibility.
Such an appeal may be brought by any party which has been unsuccessful, in whole or in part, in its submissions. However, interveners other than the Member States and the institutions of the Union may bring such an appeal only where the decision of the General Court directly affects them.
With the exception of cases relating to disputes between the Union and its servants, an appeal may also be brought by Member States and institutions of the Union which did not intervene in the proceedings before the General Court. Such Member States and institutions shall be in the same position as Member States or institutions which intervened at first instance.

Article 57. Any person whose application to intervene has been dismissed by the General Court may appeal to the Court of Justice within two weeks from the notification of the decision dismissing the application.
The parties to the proceedings may appeal to the Court of Justice against any decision of the General

Court made pursuant to Article 278 or Article 279 or the fourth paragraph of Article 299 of the Treaty on the Functioning of the European Union or Article 157 or the third paragraph of Article 164 of the EAEC Treaty within two months from their notification.

The appeal referred to in the first two paragraphs of this Article shall be heard and determined under the procedure referred to in Article 39.

Article 58. An appeal to the Court of Justice shall be limited to points of law. It shall lie on the grounds of lack of competence of the General Court, a breach of procedure before it which adversely affects the interests of the appellant as well as the infringement of Union law by the General Court. No appeal shall lie regarding only the amount of the costs or the party ordered to pay them.

Article 59. Where an appeal is brought against a decision of the General Court, the procedure before the Court of Justice shall consist of a written part and an oral part. In accordance with conditions laid down in the Rules of Procedure, the Court of Justice, having heard the Advocate–General and the parties, may dispense with the oral procedure.

Article 60. Without prejudice to Articles 278 and 279 of the Treaty on the Functioning of the European Union or Article 157 of the EAEC Treaty, an appeal shall not have suspensory effect.

By way of derogation from Article 280 of the Treaty on the Functioning of the European Union, decisions of the General Court declaring a regulation to be void shall take effect only as from the date of expiry of the period referred to in the first paragraph of Article 56 of this Statute or, if an appeal shall have been brought within that period, as from the date of dismissal of the appeal, without prejudice, however, to the right of a party to apply to the Court of Justice, pursuant to Articles 278 and 279 of the Treaty on the Functioning of the European Union or Article 157 of the EAEC Treaty, for the suspension of the effects of the regulation which has been declared void or for the prescription of any other interim measure.

Article 61. If the appeal is well founded, the Court of Justice shall quash the decision of the General Court. It may itself give final judgment in the matter, where the state of the proceedings so permits, or refer the case back to the General Court for judgment.

Where a case is referred back to the General Court, that Court shall be bound by the decision of the Court of Justice on points of law.

When an appeal brought by a Member State or an institution of the Union, which did not intervene in the proceedings before the General Court, is well founded, the Court of Justice may, if it considers this necessary, state which of the effects of the decision of the General Court which has been quashed shall be considered as definitive in respect of the parties to the litigation.

Article 62. In the cases provided for in Article 256(2) and (3) of the Treaty on the Functioning of the European Union, where the First Advocate–General considers that there is a serious risk of the unity or consistency of Union law being affected, he may propose that the Court of Justice review the decision of the General Court.

The proposal must be made within one month of delivery of the decision by the General Court. Within one month of receiving the proposal made by the First Advocate–General, the Court of Justice shall decide whether or not the decision should be reviewed.

Article 62a. The Court of Justice shall give a ruling on the questions which are subject to review by means of an urgent procedure on the basis of the file forwarded to it by the General Court.

Those referred to in Article 23 of this Statute and, in the cases provided for in Article 256(2) of the EC Treaty, the parties to the proceedings before the General Court shall be entitled to lodge statements or written observations with the Court of Justice relating to questions which are subject to review within a period prescribed for that purpose.

The Court of Justice may decide to open the oral procedure before giving a ruling.

Article 62b. In the cases provided for in Article 256(2) of the Treaty on the Functioning of the European Union, without prejudice to Articles 278 and 279 of the Treaty on the Functioning of the European Union, proposals for review and decisions to open the review procedure shall not have suspensory effect. If the Court of Justice finds that the decision of the General Court affects the unity or consistency of Union law, it shall refer the case back to the General Court which shall be bound by the points of law decided by the Court of Justice; the Court of Justice may state which of the effects of the decision of the General Court are to be considered as definitive in respect of the parties to the litigation. If, however, having regard to the result of the review, the outcome of the proceedings flows from the findings of fact on which the decision of the General Court was based, the Court of Justice shall give final judgment.

PART III   EUROPEAN UNION

In the cases provided for in Article 256(3) of the Treaty on the Functioning of the European Union, in the absence of proposals for review or decisions to open the review procedure, the answer(s) given by the General Court to the questions submitted to it shall take effect upon expiry of the periods prescribed for that purpose in the second paragraph of Article 62. Should a review procedure be opened, the answer(s) subject to review shall take effect following that procedure, unless the Court of Justice decides otherwise. If the Court of Justice finds that the decision of the General Court affects the unity or consistency of Union law, the answer given by the Court of Justice to the questions subject to review shall be substituted for that given by the General Court.

Title IVa. Specialised Courts

Article 62c. The provisions relating to the jurisdiction, composition, organisation and procedure of the specialised courts established under Article 257 of the Treaty on the Functioning of the European Union are set out in an Annex to this Statute.

Title V. Final provisions

Article 63. The Rules of Procedure of the Court of Justice and of the General Court shall contain any provisions necessary for applying and, where required, supplementing this Statute.

Article 64. The rules governing the language arrangements applicable at the Court of Justice of the European Union shall be laid down by a regulation of the Council acting unanimously. This regulation shall be adopted either at the request of the Court of Justice and after consultation of the Commission and the European Parliament, or on a proposal from the Commission and after consultation of the Court of Justice and of the European Parliament.
Until those rules have been adopted, the provisions of the Rules of Procedure of the Court of Justice and of the Rules of Procedure of the General Court governing language arrangements shall continue to apply. By way of derogation from Articles 253 and 254 of the Treaty on the Functioning of the European Union, those provisions may only be amended or repealed with the unanimous consent of the Council.

Annex. The European Union Civil Service Tribunal

Article 1. The European Union Civil Service Tribunal (hereafter "the Civil Service Tribunal") shall exercise at first instance jurisdiction in disputes between the Union and its servants referred to in Article 270 of the Treaty on the Functioning of the European Union, including disputes between all bodies or agencies and their servants in respect of which jurisdiction is conferred on the Court of Justice of the European Union.

Article 2. The Civil Service Tribunal shall consist of seven judges. Should the Court of Justice so request, the Council, acting by a qualified majority, may increase the number of judges.
The judges shall be appointed for a period of six years. Retiring judges may be reappointed.
Any vacancy shall be filled by the appointment of a new judge for a period of six years.

Article 3. (1) The judges shall be appointed by the Council, acting in accordance with the fourth paragraph of Article 257 of the Treaty on the Functioning of the European Union, after consulting the committee provided for by this Article. When appointing judges, the Council shall ensure a balanced composition of the Civil Service Tribunal on as broad a geographical basis as possible from among nationals of the Member States and with respect to the national legal systems represented.
(2) Any person who is a Union citizen and fulfils the conditions laid down in the fourth paragraph of Article 257 of the Treaty on the Functioning of the European Union may submit an application. The Council, acting on a recommendation from the Court of Justice, shall determine the conditions and the arrangements governing the submission and processing of such applications.
(3) A committee shall be set up comprising seven persons chosen from among former members of the Court of Justice and the General Court and lawyers of recognised competence. The committee's membership and operating rules shall be determined by the Council, acting on a recommendation by the President of the Court of Justice.
(4) The committee shall give an opinion on candidates' suitability to perform the duties of judge at the Civil Service Tribunal. The committee shall append to its opinion a list of candidates having the most suitable high–level experience. Such list shall contain the names of at least twice as many candidates as there are judges to be appointed by the Council.

Article 4. (1) The judges shall elect the President of the Civil Service Tribunal from among their number for a term of three years. He may be re–elected.

(2) The Civil Service Tribunal shall sit in chambers of three judges. It may, in certain cases determined by its rules of procedure, sit in full court or in a chamber of five judges or of a single judge.
(3) The President of the Civil Service Tribunal shall preside over the full court and the chamber of five judges. The Presidents of the chambers of three judges shall be designated as provided in paragraph 1. If the President of the Civil Service Tribunal is assigned to a chamber of three judges, he shall preside over that chamber.
(4) The jurisdiction of and quorum for the full court as well as the composition of the chambers and the assignment of cases to them shall be governed by the Rules of Procedure.

Article 5. Articles 2 to 6, 14, 15, the first, second and fifth paragraphs of Article 17, and Article 18 of the Statute of the Court of Justice of the European Union shall apply to the Civil Service Tribunal and its members.

The oath referred to in Article 2 of the Statute shall be taken before the Court of Justice, and the decisions referred to in Articles 3, 4 and 6 thereof shall be adopted by the Court of Justice after consulting the Civil Service Tribunal.

Article 6. (1) The Civil Service Tribunal shall be supported by the departments of the Court of Justice and of the General Court. The President of the Court of Justice or, in appropriate cases, the President of the General Court, shall determine by common accord with the President of the Civil Service Tribunal the conditions under which officials and other servants attached to the Court of Justice or the General Court shall render their services to the Civil Service Tribunal to enable it to function. Certain officials or other servants shall be responsible to the Registrar of the Civil Service Tribunal under the authority of the President of that Tribunal.
(2) The Civil Service Tribunal shall appoint its Registrar and lay down the rules governing his service. The fourth paragraph of Article 3 and Articles 10, 11 and 14 of the Statute of the Court of Justice of the European Union shall apply to the Registrar of the Tribunal.

Article 7. (1) The procedure before the Civil Service Tribunal shall be governed by Title III of the Statute of the Court of Justice of the European Union, with the exception of Articles 22 and 23. Such further and more detailed provisions as may be necessary shall be laid down in the Rules of Procedure.
(2) The provisions concerning the General Court's language arrangements shall apply to the Civil Service Tribunal.
(3) The written stage of the procedure shall comprise the presentation of the application and of the statement of defence, unless the Civil Service Tribunal decides that a second exchange of written pleadings is necessary. Where there is such second exchange, the Civil Service Tribunal may, with the agreement of the parties, decide to proceed to judgment without an oral procedure.
(4) At all stages of the procedure, including the time when the application is filed, the Civil Service Tribunal may examine the possibilities of an amicable settlement of the dispute and may try to facilitate such settlement.
(5) The Civil Service Tribunal shall rule on the costs of a case. Subject to the specific provisions of the Rules of Procedure, the unsuccessful party shall be ordered to pay the costs should the court so decide.

Article 8. (1) Where an application or other procedural document addressed to the Civil Service Tribunal is lodged by mistake with the Registrar of the Court of Justice or General Court, it shall be transmitted immediately by that Registrar to the Registrar of the Civil Service Tribunal. Likewise, where an application or other procedural document addressed to the Court of Justice or to the General Court is lodged by mistake with the Registrar of the Civil Service Tribunal, it shall be transmitted immediately by that Registrar to the Registrar of the Court of Justice or General Court.
(2) Where the Civil Service Tribunal finds that it does not have jurisdiction to hear and determine an action in respect of which the Court of Justice or the General Court has jurisdiction, it shall refer that action to the Court of Justice or to the General Court. Likewise, where the Court of Justice or the General Court finds that an action falls within the jurisdiction of the Civil Service Tribunal, the Court seised shall refer that action to the Civil Service Tribunal, whereupon that Tribunal may not decline jurisdiction.
(3) Where the Civil Service Tribunal and the General Court are seised of cases in which the same issue of interpretation is raised or the validity of the same act is called in question, the Civil Service Tribunal, after hearing the parties, may stay the proceedings until the judgment of the General Court has been delivered.
Where the Civil Service Tribunal and the General Court are seised of cases in which the same relief is sought, the Civil Service Tribunal shall decline jurisdiction so that the General Court may act on those cases.

PART III EUROPEAN UNION

Article 9. An appeal may be brought before the General Court, within two months of notification of the decision appealed against, against final decisions of the Civil Service Tribunal and decisions of that Tribunal disposing of the substantive issues in part only or disposing of a procedural issue concerning a plea of lack of jurisdiction or inadmissibility.

Such an appeal may be brought by any party which has been unsuccessful, in whole or in part, in its submissions. However, interveners other than the Member States and the institutions of the Union may bring such an appeal only where the decision of the Civil Service Tribunal directly affects them.

Article 10. (1) Any person whose application to intervene has been dismissed by the Civil Service Tribunal may appeal to the General Court within two weeks of notification of the decision dismissing the application.

(2) The parties to the proceedings may appeal to the General Court against any decision of the Civil Service Tribunal made pursuant to Article 278 or Article 279 or the fourth paragraph of Article 299 of the Treaty on the Functioning of the European Union or Article 157 or the third paragraph of Article 164 of the EAEC Treaty within two months of its notification.

(3) The President of the General Court may, by way of summary procedure, which may, in so far as necessary, differ from some of the rules contained in this Annex and which shall be laid down in the rules of procedure of the General Court, adjudicate upon appeals brought in accordance with paragraphs 1 and 2.

Article 11. (1) An appeal to the General Court shall be limited to points of law. It shall lie on the grounds of lack of jurisdiction of the Civil Service Tribunal, a breach of procedure before it which adversely affects the interests of the appellant, as well as the infringement of Union law by the Tribunal.

(2) No appeal shall lie regarding only the amount of the costs or the party ordered to pay them.

Article 12. (1) Without prejudice to Articles 278 and 279 of the Treaty on the Functioning of the European Union or Article 157 of the EAEC Treaty, an appeal before the General Court shall not have suspensory effect.

(2) Where an appeal is brought against a decision of the Civil Service Tribunal, the procedure before the General Court shall consist of a written part and an oral part. In accordance with conditions laid down in the rules of procedure, the General Court, having heard the parties, may dispense with the oral procedure.

Article 13. (1) If the appeal is well founded, the General Court shall quash the decision of the Civil Service Tribunal and itself give judgment in the matter. It shall refer the case back to the Civil Service Tribunal for judgment where the state of the proceedings does not permit a decision by the Court.

(2) Where a case is referred back to the Civil Service Tribunal, the Tribunal shall be bound by the decision of the General Court on points of law.

Protocol (No 4) on the Statute of the European System of Central Banks and of the European Central Bank

THE HIGH CONTRACTING PARTIES,
DESIRING to lay down the Statute of the European System of Central Banks and of the European Central Bank provided for in the second paragraph of Article 129 of the Treaty on the Functioning of the European Union,
HAVE AGREED upon the following provisions, which shall be annexed to the Treaty on European Union and to the Treaty on the Functioning of the European Union:

Chapter I. The European System of Central Banks

Article 1. The European System of Central Banks
In accordance with Article 282(1) of the Treaty on the Functioning of the European Union, the European Central Bank (ECB) and the national central banks shall constitute the European System of Central Banks (ESCB). The ECB and the national central banks of those Member States whose currency is the euro shall constitute the Eurosystem.
The ESCB and the ECB shall perform their tasks and carry on their activities in accordance with the provisions of the Treaties and of this Statute.

Chapter II. Objectives and Tasks of the ESCB

Article 2. In accordance with Article 127(1) and Article 282(2) of the Treaty on the Functioning of the European Union, the primary objective of the ESCB shall be to maintain price stability. Without prejudice to the objective of price stability, it shall support the general economic policies in the Union with a view to contributing to the achievement of the objectives of the Union as laid down in Article 3 of the Treaty on European Union. The ESCB shall act in accordance with the principle of an open market economy with free competition, favouring an efficient allocation of resources, and in compliance with the principles set out in Article 119 of the Treaty on the Functioning of the European Union.

Article 3. (1) In accordance with Article 127(2) of the Treaty on the Functioning of the European Union, the basic tasks to be carried out through the ESCB shall be:
– to define and implement the monetary policy of the Union;
– to conduct foreign–exchange operations consistent with the provisions of Article 219 of that Treaty;
– to hold and manage the official foreign reserves of the Member States;
– to promote the smooth operation of payment systems.
(2) In accordance with Article 127(3) of the Treaty on the Functioning of the European Union, the third indent of Article 3(1) shall be without prejudice to the holding and management by the governments of Member States of foreign–exchange working balances.
(3) In accordance with Article 127(5) of the Treaty on the Functioning of the European Union, the ESCB shall contribute to the smooth conduct of policies pursued by the competent authorities relating to the prudential supervision of credit institutions and the stability of the financial system.

Article 4. In accordance with Article 127(4) of the Treaty on the Functioning of the European Union:
(a) the ECB shall be consulted:
– on any proposed Union act in its fields of competence;
– by national authorities regarding any draft legislative provision in its fields of competence, but within the limits and under the conditions set out by the Council in accordance with the procedure laid down in Article 41;
(b) the ECB may submit opinions to the Union institutions, bodies, offices or agencies or to national authorities on matters in its fields of competence.

Article 5. (1) In order to undertake the tasks of the ESCB, the ECB, assisted by the national central banks, shall collect the necessary statistical information either from the competent national authorities or directly from economic agents. For these purposes it shall cooperate with the Union institutions, bodies, offices or agencies and with the competent authorities of the Member States or third countries and with international organisations.
(2) The national central banks shall carry out, to the extent possible, the tasks described in Article 5(1).
(3) The ECB shall contribute to the harmonisation, where necessary, of the rules and practices governing the collection, compilation and distribution of statistics in the areas within its fields of competence.
(4) The Council, in accordance with the procedure laid down in Article 41, shall define the natural and legal persons subject to reporting requirements, the confidentiality regime and the appropriate provisions for enforcement.

Article 6. (1) In the field of international cooperation involving the tasks entrusted to the ESCB, the ECB shall decide how the ESCB shall be represented.
(2) The ECB and, subject to its approval, the national central banks may participate in international monetary institutions.
(3) Articles 6(1) and 6(2) shall be without prejudice to Article 138 of the Treaty on the Functioning of the European Union.

Chapter III. Organisation of the ESCB

Article 7. In accordance with Article 130 of the Treaty on the Functioning of the European Union, when exercising the powers and carrying out the tasks and duties conferred upon them by the Treaties and this Statute, neither the ECB, nor a national central bank, nor any member of their decision–making bodies shall seek or take instructions from Union institutions, bodies, offices or agencies, from any government of a Member State or from any other body. The Union institutions, bodies, offices or agencies and the governments of the Member States undertake to respect this principle and not to seek to influence the members of the decision–making bodies of the ECB or of the national central banks in the performance of their tasks.

PART III   EUROPEAN UNION

Article 8. The ESCB shall be governed by the decision–making bodies of the ECB.

Article 9. (1) The ECB which, in accordance with Article 282(3) of the Treaty on the Functioning of the European Union, shall have legal personality, shall enjoy in each of the Member States the most extensive legal capacity accorded to legal persons under its law; it may, in particular, acquire or dispose of movable and immovable property and may be a party to legal proceedings.
(2) The ECB shall ensure that the tasks conferred upon the ESCB under Article 127(2), (3) and (5) of the Treaty on the Functioning of the European Union are implemented either by its own activities pursuant to this Statute or through the national central banks pursuant to Articles 12(1) and 14.
(3) In accordance with Article 129(1) of the Treaty on the Functioning of the European Union, the decision making bodies of the ECB shall be the Governing Council and the Executive Board.

Article 10. (1) In accordance with Article 283(1) of the Treaty on the Functioning of the European Union, the Governing Council shall comprise the members of the Executive Board of the ECB and the governors of the national central banks of the Member States whose currency is the euro.
(2) Each member of the Governing Council shall have one vote. As from the date on which the number of members of the Governing Council exceeds 21, each member of the Executive Board shall have one vote and the number of governors with a voting right shall be 15. The latter voting rights shall be assigned and shall rotate as follows:
– as from the date on which the number of governors exceeds 15, until it reaches 22, the governors shall be allocated to two groups, according to a ranking of the size of the share of their national central bank's Member State in the aggregate gross domestic product at market prices and in the total aggregated balance sheet of the monetary financial institutions of the Member States whose currency is the euro. The shares in the aggregate gross domestic product at market prices and in the total aggregated balance sheet of the monetary financial institutions shall be assigned weights of 5/6 and 1/6, respectively. The first group shall be composed of five governors and the second group of the remaining governors. The frequency of voting rights of the governors allocated to the first group shall not be lower than the frequency of voting rights of those of the second group. Subject to the previous sentence, the first group shall be assigned four voting rights and the second group eleven voting rights,
– as from the date on which the number of governors reaches 22, the governors shall be allocated to three groups according to a ranking based on the above criteria. The first group shall be composed of five governors and shall be assigned four voting rights. The second group shall be composed of half of the total number of governors, with any fraction rounded up to the nearest integer, and shall be assigned eight voting rights. The third group shall be composed of the remaining governors and shall be assigned three voting rights,
– within each group, the governors shall have their voting rights for equal amounts of time,
– for the calculation of the shares in the aggregate gross domestic product at market prices Article 29(2) shall apply. The total aggregated balance sheet of the monetary financial institutions shall be calculated in accordance with the statistical framework applying in the Union at the time of the calculation,
– whenever the aggregate gross domestic product at market prices is adjusted in accordance with Article 29(3), or whenever the number of governors increases, the size and/or composition of the groups shall be adjusted in accordance with the above principles,
– the Governing Council, acting by a two–thirds majority of all its members, with and without a voting right, shall take all measures necessary for the implementation of the above principles and may decide to postpone the start of the rotation system until the date on which the number of governors exceeds 18.
The right to vote shall be exercised in person. By way of derogation from this rule, the Rules of Procedure referred to in Article 12(3) may lay down that members of the Governing Council may cast their vote by means of teleconferencing. These rules shall also provide that a member of the Governing Council who is prevented from attending meetings of the Governing Council for a prolonged period may appoint an alternate as a member of the Governing Council.
The provisions of the previous paragraphs are without prejudice to the voting rights of all members of the Governing Council, with and without a voting right, under Articles 10(3), 40(2) and 40(3).
Save as otherwise provided for in this Statute, the Governing Council shall act by a simple majority of the members having a voting right. In the event of a tie, the President shall have the casting vote.
In order for the Governing Council to vote, there shall be a quorum of two–thirds of the members having a voting right. If the quorum is not met, the President may convene an extraordinary meeting at which decisions may be taken without regard to the quorum.
(3) For any decisions to be taken under Articles 28, 29, 30, 32 and 33, the votes in the Governing

Council shall be weighted according to the national central banks' shares in the subscribed capital of the ECB. The weights of the votes of the members of the Executive Board shall be zero. A decision requiring a qualified majority shall be adopted if the votes cast in favour represent at least two thirds of the subscribed capital of the ECB and represent at least half of the shareholders. If a Governor is unable to be present, he may nominate an alternate to cast his weighted vote.
(4) The proceedings of the meetings shall be confidential. The Governing Council may decide to make the outcome of its deliberations public.
(5) The Governing Council shall meet at least 10 times a year.

Article 11. (1) In accordance with the first subparagraph of Article 283(2) of the Treaty on the Functioning of the European Union, the Executive Board shall comprise the President, the Vice–President and four other members.
The members shall perform their duties on a full-time basis. No member shall engage in any occupation, whether gainful or not, unless exemption is exceptionally granted by the Governing Council.
(2) In accordance with the second subparagraph of Article 283(2) of the Treaty on the Functioning of the European Union, the President, the Vice–President and the other members of the Executive Board shall be appointed by the European Council, acting by a qualified majority, from among persons of recognised standing and professional experience in monetary or banking matters, on a recommendation from the Council after it has consulted the European Parliament and the Governing Council.
Their term of office shall be eight years and shall not be renewable.
Only nationals of Member States may be members of the Executive Board.
(3) The terms and conditions of employment of the members of the Executive Board, in particular their salaries, pensions and other social security benefits shall be the subject of contracts with the ECB and shall be fixed by the Governing Council on a proposal from a Committee comprising three members appointed by the Governing Council and three members appointed by the Council. The members of the Executive Board shall not have the right to vote on matters referred to in this paragraph.
(4) If a member of the Executive Board no longer fulfils the conditions required for the performance of his duties or if he has been guilty of serious misconduct, the Court of Justice may, on application by the Governing Council or the Executive Board, compulsorily retire him.
(5) Each member of the Executive Board present in person shall have the right to vote and shall have, for that purpose, one vote. Save as otherwise provided, the Executive Board shall act by a simple majority of the votes cast. In the event of a tie, the President shall have the casting vote. The voting arrangements shall be specified in the Rules of Procedure referred to in Article 12(3).
(6) The Executive Board shall be responsible for the current business of the ECB.
(7) Any vacancy on the Executive Board shall be filled by the appointment of a new member in accordance with Article 11(2).

Article 12. (1) The Governing Council shall adopt the guidelines and take the decisions necessary to ensure the performance of the tasks entrusted to the ESCB under these Treaties and this Statute. The Governing Council shall formulate the monetary policy of the Union including, as appropriate, decisions relating to intermediate monetary objectives, key interest rates and the supply of reserves in the ESCB, and shall establish the necessary guidelines for their implementation.
The Executive Board shall implement monetary policy in accordance with the guidelines and decisions laid down by the Governing Council. In doing so the Executive Board shall give the necessary instructions to national central banks. In addition the Executive Board may have certain powers delegated to it where the Governing Council so decides.
To the extent deemed possible and appropriate and without prejudice to the provisions of this Article, the ECB shall have recourse to the national central banks to carry out operations which form part of the tasks of the ESCB.
(2) The Executive Board shall have responsibility for the preparation of meetings of the Governing Council.
(3) The Governing Council shall adopt Rules of Procedure which determine the internal organisation of the ECB and its decision–making bodies.
(4) The Governing Council shall exercise the advisory functions referred to in Article 4.
(5) The Governing Council shall take the decisions referred to in Article 6.

Article 13. (1) The President or, in his absence, the Vice–President shall chair the Governing Council and the Executive Board of the ECB.
(2) Without prejudice to Article 38, the President or his nominee shall represent the ECB externally.

Article 14. (1) In accordance with Article 131 of the Treaty on the Functioning of the European

PART III   EUROPEAN UNION

Union, each Member State shall ensure that its national legislation, including the statutes of its national central bank, is compatible with these Treaties and this Statute.
(2) The statutes of the national central banks shall, in particular, provide that the term of office of a Governor of a national central bank shall be no less than five years.
A Governor may be relieved from office only if he no longer fulfils the conditions required for the performance of his duties or if he has been guilty of serious misconduct. A decision to this effect may be referred to the Court of Justice by the Governor concerned or the Governing Council on grounds of infringement of these Treaties or of any rule of law relating to their application. Such proceedings shall be instituted within two months of the publication of the decision or of its notification to the plaintiff or, in the absence thereof, of the day on which it came to the knowledge of the latter, as the case may be.
(3) The national central banks are an integral part of the ESCB and shall act in accordance with the guidelines and instructions of the ECB. The Governing Council shall take the necessary steps to ensure compliance with the guidelines and instructions of the ECB, and shall require that any necessary information be given to it.
(4) National central banks may perform functions other than those specified in this Statute unless the Governing Council finds, by a majority of two thirds of the votes cast, that these interfere with the objectives and tasks of the ESCB. Such functions shall be performed on the responsibility and liability of national central banks and shall not be regarded as being part of the functions of the ESCB.

Article 15. (1) The ECB shall draw up and publish reports on the activities of the ESCB at least quarterly.
(2) A consolidated financial statement of the ESCB shall be published each week.
(3) In accordance with Article 284(3) of the Treaty on the Functioning of the European Union, the ECB shall address an annual report on the activities of the ESCB and on the monetary policy of both the previous and the current year to the European Parliament, the Council and the Commission, and also to the European Council.
(4) The reports and statements referred to in this Article shall be made available to interested parties free of charge.

Article 16. In accordance with Article 128(1) of the Treaty on the Functioning of the European Union, the Governing Council shall have the exclusive right to authorise the issue of euro banknotes within the Union. The ECB and the national central banks may issue such notes. The banknotes issued by the ECB and the national central banks shall be the only such notes to have the status of legal tender within the Union.
The ECB shall respect as far as possible existing practices regarding the issue and design of banknotes.

Chapter IV. Monetary Functions and Operations of the ESCB

Article 17. In order to conduct their operations, the ECB and the national central banks may open accounts for credit institutions, public entities and other market participants and accept assets, including book entry securities, as collateral.

Article 18. (1) In order to achieve the objectives of the ESCB and to carry out its tasks, the ECB and the national central banks may:
– operate in the financial markets by buying and selling outright (spot and forward) or under repurchase agreement and by lending or borrowing claims and marketable instruments, whether in euro or other currencies, as well as precious metals;
– conduct credit operations with credit institutions and other market participants, with lending being based on adequate collateral.
(2) The ECB shall establish general principles for open market and credit operations carried out by itself or the national central banks, including for the announcement of conditions under which they stand ready to enter into such transactions.

Article 19. (1) Subject to Article 2, the ECB may require credit institutions established in Member States to hold minimum reserve on accounts with the ECB and national central banks in pursuance of monetary policy objectives. Regulations concerning the calculation and determination of the required minimum reserves may be established by the Governing Council. In cases of non–compliance the ECB shall be entitled to levy penalty interest and to impose other sanctions with comparable effect.
(2) For the application of this Article, the Council shall, in accordance with the procedure laid down in Article 41, define the basis for minimum reserves and the maximum permissible ratios between those reserves and their basis, as well as the appropriate sanctions in cases of non–compliance.

Article 20. The Governing Council may, by a majority of two thirds of the votes cast, decide upon the use of such other operational methods of monetary control as it sees fit, respecting Article 2. The Council shall, in accordance with the procedure laid down in Article 41, define the scope of such methods if they impose obligations on third parties.

Article 21. (1) In accordance with Article 123 of the Treaty on the Functioning of the European Union, overdrafts or any other type of credit facility with the ECB or with the national central banks in favour of Union institutions, bodies, offices or agencies, central governments, regional, local or other public authorities, other bodies governed by public law, or public undertakings of Member States shall be prohibited, as shall the purchase directly from them by the ECB or national central banks of debt instruments.
(2) The ECB and national central banks may act as fiscal agents for the entities referred to in Article 21(1).
(3) The provisions of this Article shall not apply to publicly owned credit institutions which, in the context of the supply of reserves by central banks, shall be given the same treatment by national central banks and the ECB as private credit institutions.

Article 22. The ECB and national central banks may provide facilities, and the ECB may make regulations, to ensure efficient and sound clearing and payment systems, and clearing systems for financial instruments, within the Union and with other countries.

Article 23. The ECB and national central banks may:
– establish relations with central banks and financial institutions in other countries and, where appropriate, with international organisations;
– acquire and sell spot and forward all types of foreign exchange assets and precious metals; the term "foreign exchange asset" shall include securities and all other assets in the currency of any country or units of account and in whatever form held;
– hold and manage the assets referred to in this Article;
– conduct all types of banking transactions in relations with third countries and international organisations, including borrowing and lending operations.

Article 24. In addition to operations arising from their tasks, the ECB and national central banks may enter into operations for their administrative purposes or for their staff.

Chapter V. Prudential Supervision

Article 25. (1) The ECB may offer advice to and be consulted by the Council, the Commission and the competent authorities of the Member States on the scope and implementation of Union legislation relating to the prudential supervision of credit institutions and to the stability of the financial system.
(2) In accordance with any regulation of the Council under Article 127(6) of the Treaty on the Functioning of the European Union, the ECB may perform specific tasks concerning policies relating to the prudential supervision of credit institutions and other financial institutions with the exception of insurance undertakings.

Chapter VI. Financial Provisions of the ESCB

Article 26. (1) The financial year of the ECB and national central banks shall begin on the first day of January and end on the last day of December.
(2) The annual accounts of the ECB shall be drawn up by the Executive Board, in accordance with the principles established by the Governing Council. The accounts shall be approved by the Governing Council and shall thereafter be published.
(3) For analytical and operational purposes, the Executive Board shall draw up a consolidated balance sheet of the ESCB, comprising those assets and liabilities of the national central banks that fall within the ESCB.
(4) For the application of this Article, the Governing Council shall establish the necessary rules for standardising the accounting and reporting of operations undertaken by the national central banks.

Article 27. (1) The accounts of the ECB and national central banks shall be audited by independent external auditors recommended by the Governing Council and approved by the Council. The auditors shall have full power to examine all books and accounts of the ECB and national central banks and obtain full information about their transactions.
(2) The provisions of Article 287 of the Treaty on the Functioning of the European Union shall only apply to an examination of the operational efficiency of the management of the ECB.

PART III   EUROPEAN UNION

Article 28. (1) The capital of the ECB shall be euro 5000 million. The capital may be increased by such amounts as may be decided by the Governing Council acting by the qualified majority provided for in Article 10(3), within the limits and under the conditions set by the Council under the procedure laid down in Article 41.
(2) The national central banks shall be the sole subscribers to and holders of the capital of the ECB. The subscription of capital shall be according to the key established in accordance with Article 29.
(3) The Governing Council, acting by the qualified majority provided for in Article 10(3), shall determine the extent to which and the form in which the capital shall be paid up.
(4) Subject to Article 28(5), the shares of the national central banks in the subscribed capital of the ECB may not be transferred, pledged or attached.
(5) If the key referred to in Article 29 is adjusted, the national central banks shall transfer among themselves capital shares to the extent necessary to ensure that the distribution of capital shares corresponds to the adjusted key. The Governing Council shall determine the terms and conditions of such transfers.

Article 29. (1) The key for subscription of the ECB's capital, fixed for the first time in 1998 when the ESCB was established, shall be determined by assigning to each national central bank a weighting in this key equal to the sum of:
– 50 % of the share of its respective Member State in the population of the Union in the penultimate year preceding the establishment of the ESCB;
– 50 % of the share of its respective Member State in the gross domestic product at market prices of the Union as recorded in the last five years preceding the penultimate year before the establishment of the ESCB.
The percentages shall be rounded up or down to the nearest multiple of 0,0001 percentage points.
(2) The statistical data to be used for the application of this Article shall be provided by the Commission in accordance with the rules adopted by the Council under the procedure provided for in Article 41.
(3) The weightings assigned to the national central banks shall be adjusted every five years after the establishment of the ESCB by analogy with the provisions laid down in Article 29 (1). The adjusted key shall apply with effect from the first day of the following year.
(4) The Governing Council shall take all other measures necessary for the application of this Article.

Article 30. (1) Without prejudice to Article 28, the ECB shall be provided by the national central banks with foreign reserve assets, other than Member States' currencies, euro, IMF reserve positions and SDRs, up to an amount equivalent to euro 50000 million. The Governing Council shall decide upon the proportion to be called up by the ECB following its establishment and the amounts called up at later dates. The ECB shall have the full right to hold and manage the foreign reserves that are transferred to it and to use them for the purposes set out in this Statute.
(2) The contributions of each national central bank shall be fixed in proportion to its share in the subscribed capital of the ECB.
(3) Each national central bank shall be credited by the ECB with a claim equivalent to its contribution. The Governing Council shall determine the denomination and remuneration of such claims.
(4) Further calls of foreign reserve assets beyond the limit set in Article 30(1) may be effected by the ECB, in accordance with Article 30(2), within the limits and under the conditions set by the Council in accordance with the procedure laid down in Article 41.
(5) The ECB may hold and manage IMF reserve positions and SDRs and provide for the pooling of such assets.
(6) The Governing Council shall take all other measures necessary for the application of this Article.

Article 31. (1) The national central banks shall be allowed to perform transactions in fulfilment of their obligations towards international organisations in accordance with Article 23.
(2) All other operations in foreign reserve assets remaining with the national central banks after the transfers referred to in Article 30, and Member States' transactions with their foreign exchange working balances shall, above a certain limit to be established within the framework of Article 31(3), be subject to approval by the ECB in order to ensure consistency with the exchange rate and monetary policies of the Union.
(3) The Governing Council shall issue guidelines with a view to facilitating such operations.

Article 32. (1) The income accruing to the national central banks in the performance of the ESCB's monetary policy function (hereinafter referred to as "monetary income") shall be allocated at the end of each financial year in accordance with the provisions of this Article.
(2) The amount of each national central bank's monetary income shall be equal to its annual income

derived from its assets held against notes in circulation and deposit liabilities to credit institutions. These assets shall be earmarked by national central banks in accordance with guidelines to be established by the Governing Council.

(3) If, after the introduction of the euro, the balance sheet structures of the national central banks do not, in the judgment of the Governing Council, permit the application of Article 32(2), the Governing Council, acting by a qualified majority, may decide that, by way of derogation from Article 32(2), monetary income shall be measured according to an alternative method for a period of not more than five years.

(4) The amount of each national central bank's monetary income shall be reduced by an amount equivalent to any interest paid by that central bank on its deposit liabilities to credit institutions in accordance with Article 19.

The Governing Council may decide that national central banks shall be indemnified against costs incurred in connection with the issue of banknotes or in exceptional circumstances for specific losses arising from monetary policy operations undertaken for the ESCB. Indemnification shall be in a form deemed appropriate in the judgment of the Governing Council; these amounts may be offset against the national central banks' monetary income.

(5) The sum of the national central banks' monetary income shall be allocated to the national central banks in proportion to their paid up shares in the capital of the ECB, subject to any decision taken by the Governing Council pursuant to Article 33(2).

(6) The clearing and settlement of the balances arising from the allocation of monetary income shall be carried out by the ECB in accordance with guidelines established by the Governing Council.

(7) The Governing Council shall take all other measures necessary for the application of this Article.

Article 33. (1) The net profit of the ECB shall be transferred in the following order:
(a) an amount to be determined by the Governing Council, which may not exceed 20 % of the net profit, shall be transferred to the general reserve fund subject to a limit equal to 100 % of the capital;
(b) the remaining net profit shall be distributed to the shareholders of the ECB in proportion to their paid–up shares.

(2) In the event of a loss incurred by the ECB, the shortfall may be offset against the general reserve fund of the ECB and, if necessary, following a decision by the Governing Council, against the monetary income of the relevant financial year in proportion and up to the amounts allocated to the national central banks in accordance with Article 32 (5).

Chapter VII. General Provisions

Article 34. (1) In accordance with Article 132 of the Treaty on the Functioning of the European Union, the ECB shall:
– make regulations to the extent necessary to implement the tasks defined in Article 3(1), first indent, Articles 19(1), 22 or 25(2) and in cases which shall be laid down in the acts of the Council referred to in Article 41;
– take decisions necessary for carrying out the tasks entrusted to the ESCB under these Treaties and this Statute;
– make recommendations and deliver opinions.

(2) The ECB may decide to publish its decisions, recommendations and opinions.

(3) Within the limits and under the conditions adopted by the Council under the procedure laid down in Article 41, the ECB shall be entitled to impose fines or periodic penalty payments on undertakings for failure to comply with obligations under its regulations and decisions.

Article 35. (1) The acts or omissions of the ECB shall be open to review or interpretation by the Court of Justice of the European Union in the cases and under the conditions laid down in the Treaty on the Functioning of the European Union. The ECB may institute proceedings in the cases and under the conditions laid down in the Treaties.

(2) Disputes between the ECB, on the one hand, and its creditors, debtors or any other person, on the other, shall be decided by the competent national courts, save where jurisdiction has been conferred upon the Court of Justice of the European Union.

(3) The ECB shall be subject to the liability regime provided for in Article 340 of the Treaty on the Functioning of the European Union. The national central banks shall be liable according to their respective national laws.

(4) The Court of Justice of the European Union shall have jurisdiction to give judgment pursuant to any arbitration clause contained in a contract concluded by or on behalf of the ECB, whether that contract be governed by public or private law.

(5) A decision of the ECB to bring an action before the Court of Justice of the European Union shall

PART III EUROPEAN UNION

be taken by the Governing Council.

(6) The Court of Justice of the European Union shall have jurisdiction in disputes concerning the fulfilment by a national central bank of obligations under the Treaties and this Statute. If the ECB considers that a national central bank has failed to fulfil an obligation under the Treaties and this Statute, it shall deliver a reasoned opinion on the matter after giving the national central bank concerned the opportunity to submit its observations. If the national central bank concerned does not comply with the opinion within the period laid down by the ECB, the latter may bring the matter before the Court of Justice of the European Union.

Article 36. (1) The Governing Council, on a proposal from the Executive Board, shall lay down the conditions of employment of the staff of the ECB.
(2) The Court of Justice of the European Union shall have jurisdiction in any dispute between the ECB and its servants within the limits and under the conditions laid down in the conditions of employment.

Article 37 (ex Article 38). (1) Members of the governing bodies and the staff of the ECB and the national central banks shall be required, even after their duties have ceased, not to disclose information of the kind covered by the obligation of professional secrecy.
(2) Persons having access to data covered by Union legislation imposing an obligation of secrecy shall be subject to such legislation.

Article 38 (ex Article 39). The ECB shall be legally committed to third parties by the President or by two members of the Executive Board or by the signatures of two members of the staff of the ECB who have been duly authorised by the President to sign on behalf of the ECB.

Article 39 (ex Article 40). The ECB shall enjoy in the territories of the Member States such privileges and immunities as are necessary for the performance of its tasks, under the conditions laid down in the Protocol on the privileges and immunities of the European Union.

Chapter VIII. Amendment of the Statute and Complementary Legislation

Article 40 (ex Article 41). (1) In accordance with Article 129(3) of the Treaty on the Functioning of the European Union, Articles 5(1), 5(2), 5(3), 17, 18, 19(1), 22, 23, 24, 26, 32(2), 32(3), 32(4), 32(6), 33(1)(a) and 36 of this Statute may be amended by the European Parliament and the Council, acting in accordance with the ordinary legislative procedure either on a recommendation from the ECB and after consulting the Commission, or on a proposal from the Commission and after consulting the ECB.
(2) Article 10(2) may be amended by a decision of the European Council, acting unanimously, either on a recommendation from the European Central Bank and after consulting the European Parliament and the Commission, or on a recommendation from the Commission and after consulting the European Parliament and the European Central Bank. These amendments shall not enter into force until they are approved by the Member States in accordance with their respective constitutional requirements.
(3) A recommendation made by the ECB under this Article shall require a unanimous decision by the Governing Council.

Article 41 (ex Article 42). In accordance with Article 129(4) of the Treaty on the Functioning of the European Union, the Council, either on a proposal from the Commission and after consulting the European Parliament and the ECB or on a recommendation from the ECB and after consulting the European Parliament and the Commission, shall adopt the provisions referred to in Articles 4, 5(4), 19(2), 20, 28(1), 29(2), 30(4) and 34(3) of this Statute.

Chapter IX. Transitional and other Provisions for the ESCB

Article 42 (ex Article 43). (1) A derogation as referred to in Article 139 of the Treaty on the Functioning of the European Union shall entail that the following Articles of this Statute shall not confer any rights or impose any obligations on the Member State concerned: 3, 6, 9(2), 12(1), 14(3), 16, 18, 19, 20, 22, 23, 26(2), 27, 30, 31, 32, 33, 34, and 49.
(2) The central banks of Member States with a derogation as specified in Article 139(1) of the Treaty on the Functioning of the European Union shall retain their powers in the field of monetary policy according to national law.
(3) In accordance with Article 139 of the Treaty on the Functioning of the European Union, "Member States" shall be read as "Member States whose currency is the euro" in the following Articles of this Statute: 3, 11(2) and 19.

(4) "National central banks" shall be read as "central banks of Member States whose currency is the euro" in the following Articles of this Statute: 9(2), 10(2), 10(3), 12(1), 16, 17, 18, 22, 23, 27, 30, 31, 32, 33(2) and 49.
(5) "Shareholders" shall be read as "central banks of Member States whose currency is the euro" in Articles 10(3) and 33(1).
(6) "Subscribed capital of the ECB" shall be read as "capital of the ECB subscribed by the central banks of Member States whose currency is the euro" in Articles 10(3) and 30(2).

Article 43 (ex Article 44). The ECB shall take over the former tasks of the EMI referred to in Article 141(2) of the Treaty on the Functioning of the European Union which, because of the derogations of one or more Member States, still have to be performed after the introduction of the euro.
The ECB shall give advice in the preparations for the abrogation of the derogations specified in Article 140 of the Treaty on the Functioning of the European Union.

Article 44 (ex Article 45). (1) Without prejudice to Article 129(1) of the Treaty on the Functioning of the European Union, the General Council shall be constituted as a third decision–making body of the ECB.
(2) The General Council shall comprise the President and Vice–President of the ECB and the Governors of the national central banks. The other members of the Executive Board may participate, without having the right to vote, in meetings of the General Council.
(3) The responsibilities of the General Council are listed in full in Article 46 of this Statute.

Article 45 (ex Article 46). (1) The President or, in his absence, the Vice–President of the ECB shall chair the General Council of the ECB.
(2) The President of the Council and a Member of the Commission may participate, without having the right to vote, in meetings of the General Council.
(3) The President shall prepare the meetings of the General Council.
(4) By way of derogation from Article 12(3), the General Council shall adopt its Rules of Procedure.
(5) The Secretariat of the General Council shall be provided by the ECB.

Article 46 (ex Article 47). (1) The General Council shall:
– perform the tasks referred to in Article 43;
– contribute to the advisory functions referred to in Articles 4 and 25(1).
(2) The General Council shall contribute to:
– the collection of statistical information as referred to in Article 5;
– the reporting activities of the ECB as referred to in Article 15;
– the establishment of the necessary rules for the application of Article 26 as referred to in Article 26(4);
– the taking of all other measures necessary for the application of Article 29 as referred to in Article 29(4);
– the laying down of the conditions of employment of the staff of the ECB as referred to in Article 36.
(3) The General Council shall contribute to the necessary preparations for irrevocably fixing the exchange rates of the currencies of Member States with a derogation against the euro as referred to in Article 140(3) of the Treaty on the Functioning of the European Union.
(4) The General Council shall be informed by the President of the ECB of decisions of the Governing Council.

Article 47 (ex Article 48). In accordance with Article 29(1), each national central bank shall be assigned a weighting in the key for subscription of the ECB's capital. By way of derogation from Article 28(3), central banks of Member States with a derogation shall not pay up their subscribed capital unless the General Council, acting by a majority representing at least two thirds of the subscribed capital of the ECB and at least half of the shareholders, decides that a minimal percentage has to be paid up as a contribution to the operational costs of the ECB.

Article 48 (ex Article 49). (1) The central bank of a Member State whose derogation has been abrogated shall pay up its subscribed share of the capital of the ECB to the same extent as the central banks of other Member States whose currency is the euro, and shall transfer to the ECB foreign reserve assets in accordance with Article 30(1). The sum to be transferred shall be determined by multiplying the euro value at current exchange rates of the foreign reserve assets which have already been transferred to the ECB in accordance with Article 30(1), by the ratio between the number of shares subscribed by the national central bank concerned and the number of shares already paid up by the other national central banks.

(2) In addition to the payment to be made in accordance with Article 48(1), the central bank concerned shall contribute to the reserves of the ECB, to those provisions equivalent to reserves, and to the amount still to be appropriated to the reserves and provisions corresponding to the balance of the profit and loss account as at 31 December of the year prior to the abrogation of the derogation. The sum to be contributed shall be determined by multiplying the amount of the reserves, as defined above and as stated in the approved balance sheet of the ECB, by the ratio between the number of shares subscribed by the central bank concerned and the number of shares already paid up by the other central banks.

(3) Upon one or more countries becoming Member States and their respective national central banks becoming part of the ESCB, the subscribed capital of the ECB and the limit on the amount of foreign reserve assets that may be transferred to the ECB shall be automatically increased. The increase shall be determined by multiplying the respective amounts then prevailing by the ratio, within the expanded capital key, between the weighting of the entering national central banks concerned and the weighting of the national central banks already members of the ESCB. Each national central bank's weighting in the capital key shall be calculated by analogy with Article 29(1) and in compliance with Article 29.(2) The reference periods to be used for the statistical data shall be identical to those applied for the latest quinquennial adjustment of the weightings under Article 29(3).

Article 49 (ex Article 52). Following the irrevocable fixing of exchange rates in accordance with Article 140 of the Treaty on the Functioning of the European Union, the Governing Council shall take the necessary measures to ensure that banknotes denominated in currencies with irrevocably fixed exchange rates are exchanged by the national central banks at their respective par values.

Article 50 (ex Article 53). If and as long as there are Member States with a derogation, Articles 42 to 47 shall be applicable.

Protocol (No 5) on the Statute of the European Investment Bank[1]

THE HIGH CONTRACTING PARTIES,
DESIRING to lay down the Statute of the European Investment Bank provided for in Article 308 of the Treaty on the Functioning of the European Union,
HAVE AGREED upon the following provisions, which shall be annexed to the Treaty on European Union and to the Treaty on the Functioning of the European Union:

Article 1. The European Investment Bank established by Article 308 of the Treaty on the Functioning of the European Union (hereinafter called the "Bank") is hereby constituted; it shall perform its functions and carry on its activities in accordance with the provisions of the Treaties and of this Statute.

Article 2. The task of the Bank shall be that defined in Article 309 of the Treaty on the Functioning of the European Union.

Article 3. In accordance with Article 308 of the Treaty on the Functioning of the European Union, the Bank's members shall be the Member States.

Article 4. (1) The capital of the Bank shall be EUR 23324739000, subscribed by the Member States as follows:
Germany | 37578019000 |
France | 37578019000 |
Italy | 37578019000 |
United Kingdom | 37578019000 |
Spain | 22546811500 |
Belgium | 10416365500 |
Netherlands | 10416365500 |
Sweden | 6910226000 |
Denmark | 5274105000 |
Austria | 5170732500 |
Poland | 4810160500 |
Finland | 2970783000 |

---

[1] This protocol is subject to amendments which will enter into force upon the exit of the United Kingdom from the European Union. These amendments can be found in Council Decision (EU) 2019/654 of 15 April 2019, reproduced below.

Greece | 2825416500 |
Portugal | 1820820000 |
Czech Republic | 1774990500 |
Hungary | 1679222000 |
Ireland | 1318525000 |
Romania | 1217626000 |
Croatia | 854400000 |
Slovakia | 604206500 |
Slovenia | 560951500 |
Bulgaria | 410217500 |
Lithuania | 351981000 |
Luxembourg | 263707000 |
Cyprus | 258583500 |
Latvia | 214805000 |
Estonia | 165882000 |
Malta | 98429500 |

The Member States shall be liable only up to the amount of their share of the capital subscribed and not paid up.

(2) The admission of a new member shall entail an increase in the subscribed capital corresponding to the capital brought in by the new member.

(3) The Board of Governors may, acting unanimously, decide to increase the subscribed capital.

(4) The share of a member in the subscribed capital may not be transferred, pledged or attached.

Article 5. (1) The subscribed capital shall be paid in by Member States to the extent of 5 % on average of the amounts laid down in Article 4(1).

(2) In the event of an increase in the subscribed capital, the Board of Governors, acting unanimously, shall fix the percentage to be paid up and the arrangements for payment. Cash payments shall be made exclusively in euro.

(3) The Board of Directors may require payment of the balance of the subscribed capital, to such extent as may be required for the Bank to meet its obligations.

Each Member State shall make this payment in proportion to its share of the subscribed capital.

Article 6 (ex Article 8). The Bank shall be directed and managed by a Board of Governors, a Board of Directors and a Management Committee.

Article 7 (ex Article 9). (1) The Board of Governors shall consist of the ministers designated by the Member States.

(2) The Board of Governors shall lay down general directives for the credit policy of the Bank, in accordance with the Union's objectives. The Board of Governors shall ensure that these directives are implemented.

(3) The Board of Governors shall in addition:
(a) decide whether to increase the subscribed capital in accordance with Article 4(3) and Article 5(2);
(b) for the purposes of Article 9(1), determine the principles applicable to financing operations undertaken within the framework of the Bank's task;
(c) exercise the powers provided in Articles 9 and 11 in respect of the appointment and the compulsory retirement of the members of the Board of Directors and of the Management Committee, and those powers provided in the second subparagraph of Article 11(1);
(d) take decisions in respect of the granting of finance for investment operations to be carried out, in whole or in part, outside the territories of the Member States in accordance with Article 16(1);
(e) approve the annual report of the Board of Directors;
(f) approve the annual balance sheet and profit and loss account;
(g) exercise the other powers and functions conferred by this Statute;
(h) approve the rules of procedure of the Bank.

(4) Within the framework of the Treaty and this Statute, the Board of Governors shall be competent to take, acting unanimously, any decisions concerning the suspension of the operations of the Bank and, should the event arise, its liquidation.

Article 8 (ex Article 10). Save as otherwise provided in this Statute, decisions of the Board of Governors shall be taken by a majority of its members. This majority must represent at least 50 % of the subscribed capital.

A qualified majority shall require eighteen votes in favour and 68 % of the subscribed capital.

Abstentions by members present in person or represented shall not prevent the adoption of decisions requiring unanimity.

PART III EUROPEAN UNION

Article 9 (ex Article 11). (1) The Board of Directors shall take decisions in respect of granting finance, in particular in the form of loans and guarantees, and raising loans; it shall fix the interest rates on loans granted and the commission and other charges. It may, on the basis of a decision taken by a qualified majority, delegate some of its functions to the Management Committee. It shall determine the terms and conditions for such delegation and shall supervise its execution.
The Board of Directors shall see that the Bank is properly run; it shall ensure that the Bank is managed in accordance with the provisions of the Treaties and of this Statute and with the general directives laid down by the Board of Governors.
At the end of the financial year the Board of Directors shall submit a report to the Board of Governors and shall publish it when approved.
(2) The Board of Directors shall consist of twenty–nine directors and nineteen alternate directors.
The directors shall be appointed by the Board of Governors for five years, one nominated by each Member State, and one nominated by the Commission.
The alternate directors shall be appointed by the Board of Governors for five years as shown below:
– two alternates nominated by the Federal Republic of Germany,
– two alternates nominated by the French Republic,
– two alternates nominated by the Italian Republic,
– two alternates nominated by the United Kingdom of Great Britain and Northern Ireland,
– one alternate nominated by common accord of the Kingdom of Spain and the Portuguese Republic,
– one alternate nominated by common accord of the Kingdom of Belgium, the Grand Duchy of Luxembourg and the Kingdom of the Netherlands,
– two alternates nominated by common accord of the Kingdom of Denmark, the Hellenic Republic, Ireland and Romania,
– two alternates nominated by common accord of the Republic of Estonia, the Republic of Latvia, the Republic of Lithuania, the Republic of Austria, the Republic of Finland and the Kingdom of Sweden,
– four alternates nominated by common accord of the Republic of Bulgaria, the Czech Republic, the Republic of Croatia, the Republic of Cyprus, the Republic of Hungary, the Republic of Malta, the Republic of Poland, the Republic of Slovenia and the Slovak Republic,
– one alternate nominated by the Commission.
The Board of Directors shall co-opt six non–voting experts: three as members and three as alternates.
The appointments of the directors and the alternates shall be renewable.
The Rules of Procedure shall lay down arrangements for participating in the meetings of the Board of Directors and the provisions applicable to alternates and co–opted experts.
The President of the Management Committee or, in his absence, one of the Vice–Presidents, shall preside over meetings of the Board of Directors but shall not vote.
Members of the Board of Directors shall be chosen from persons whose independence and competence are beyond doubt; they shall be responsible only to the Bank.
(3) A director may be compulsorily retired by the Board of Governors only if he no longer fulfils the conditions required for the performance of his duties; the Board must act by a qualified majority.
If the annual report is not approved, the Board of Directors shall resign.
(4) Any vacancy arising as a result of death, voluntary resignation, compulsory retirement or collective resignation shall be filled in accordance with paragraph 2. A member shall be replaced for the remainder of his term of office, save where the entire Board of Directors is being replaced.
(5) The Board of Governors shall determine the remuneration of members of the Board of Directors. The Board of Governors shall lay down what activities are incompatible with the duties of a director or an alternate.

Article 10 (ex Article 12). (1) Each director shall have one vote on the Board of Directors. He may delegate his vote in all cases, according to procedures to be laid down in the Rules of Procedure of the Bank.
(2) Save as otherwise provided in this Statute, decisions of the Board of Directors shall be taken by at least one third of the members entitled to vote representing at least fifty per cent of the subscribed capital. A qualified majority shall require eighteen votes in favour and sixty–eight per cent of the subscribed capital. The rules of procedure of the Bank shall lay down the quorum required for the decisions of the Board of Directors to be valid.

Article 11 (ex Article 13). (1) The Management Committee shall consist of a President and eight Vice–Presidents appointed for a period of six years by the Board of Governors on a proposal from the Board of Directors. Their appointments shall be renewable. The Board of Governors, acting unanimously, may vary the number of members on the Management Committee.
(2) On a proposal from the Board of Directors adopted by a qualified majority, the Board of Gover-

nors may, acting in its turn by a qualified majority, compulsorily retire a member of the Management Committee.

(3) The Management Committee shall be responsible for the current business of the Bank, under the authority of the President and the supervision of the Board of Directors.

It shall prepare the decisions of the Board of Directors, in particular decisions on the raising of loans and the granting of finance, in particular in the form of loans and guarantees; it shall ensure that these decisions are implemented.

(4) The Management Committee shall act by a majority when delivering opinions on proposals for raising loans or granting of finance, in particular in the form of loans and guarantees.

(5) The Board of Governors shall determine the remuneration of members of the Management Committee and shall lay down what activities are incompatible with their duties.

(6) The President or, if he is prevented, a Vice–President shall represent the Bank in judicial and other matters.

(7) The staff of the Bank shall be under the authority of the President. They shall be engaged and discharged by him. In the selection of staff, account shall be taken not only of personal ability and qualifications but also of an equitable representation of nationals of Member States. The Rules of Procedure shall determine which organ is competent to adopt the provisions applicable to staff.

(8) The Management Committee and the staff of the Bank shall be responsible only to the Bank and shall be completely independent in the performance of their duties.

Article 12 (ex Article 14). (1) A Committee consisting of six members, appointed on the grounds of their competence by the Board of Governors, shall verify that the activities of the Bank conform to best banking practice and shall be responsible for the auditing of its accounts.

(2) The Committee referred to in paragraph 1 shall annually ascertain that the operations of the Bank have been conducted and its books kept in a proper manner. To this end, it shall verify that the Bank's operations have been carried out in compliance with the formalities and procedures laid down by this Statute and the Rules of Procedure.

(3) The Committee referred to in paragraph 1 shall confirm that the financial statements, as well as any other financial information contained in the annual accounts drawn up by the Board of Directors, give a true and fair view of the financial position of the Bank in respect of its assets and liabilities, and of the results of its operations and its cash flows for the financial year under review.

(4) The Rules of Procedure shall specify the qualifications required of the members of the Committee and lay down the terms and conditions for the Committee's activity.

Article 13 (ex Article 15). The Bank shall deal with each Member State through the authority designated by that State. In the conduct of financial operations the Bank shall have recourse to the national central bank of the Member State concerned or to other financial institutions approved by that State.

Article 14 (ex Article 16). (1) The Bank shall cooperate with all international organisations active in fields similar to its own.

(2) The Bank shall seek to establish all appropriate contacts in the interests of cooperation with banking and financial institutions in the countries to which its operations extend.

Article 15 (ex Article 17). At the request of a Member State or of the Commission, or on its own initiative, the Board of Governors shall, in accordance with the same provisions as governed their adoption, interpret or supplement the directives laid down by it under Article 7 of this Statute.

Article 16 (ex Article 18). (1) Within the framework of the task set out in Article 309 of the Treaty on the Functioning of the European Union, the Bank shall grant finance, in particular in the form of loans and guarantees to its members or to private or public undertakings for investments to be carried out in the territories of Member States, to the extent that funds are not available from other sources on reasonable terms.

However, by decision of the Board of Governors, acting by a qualified majority on a proposal from the Board of Directors, the Bank may grant financing for investment to be carried out, in whole or in part, outside the territories of Member States.

(2) As far as possible, loans shall be granted only on condition that other sources of finance are also used.

(3) When granting a loan to an undertaking or to a body other than a Member State, the Bank shall make the loan conditional either on a guarantee from the Member State in whose territory the investment will be carried out or on other adequate guarantees, or on the financial strength of the debtor. Furthermore, in accordance with the principles established by the Board of Governors pursuant to Article 7(3)(b), and where the implementation of projects provided for in Article 309 of the Treaty on

PART III   EUROPEAN UNION

the Functioning of the European Union so requires, the Board of Directors shall, acting by a qualified majority, lay down the terms and conditions of any financing operation presenting a specific risk profile and thus considered to be a special activity.

(4) The Bank may guarantee loans contracted by public or private undertakings or other bodies for the purpose of carrying out projects provided for in Article 309 of the Treaty on the Functioning of the European Union.

(5) The aggregate amount outstanding at any time of loans and guarantees granted by the Bank shall not exceed 250 % of its subscribed capital, reserves, non–allocated provisions and profit and loss account surplus. The latter aggregate amount shall be reduced by an amount equal to the amount subscribed (whether or not paid in) for any equity participation of the Bank.

The amount of the Bank's disbursed equity participations shall not exceed at any time an amount corresponding to the total of its paid–in subscribed capital, reserves, non–allocated provisions and profit and loss account surplus.

By way of exception, the special activities of the Bank, as decided by the Board of Governors and the Board of Directors in accordance with paragraph 3, will have a specific allocation of reserve.

This paragraph shall also apply to the consolidated accounts of the Bank.

(6) The Bank shall protect itself against exchange risks by including in contracts for loans and guarantees such clauses as it considers appropriate.

Article 17 (ex Article 19). (1) Interest rates on loans to be granted by the Bank and commission and other charges shall be adjusted to conditions prevailing on the capital market and shall be calculated in such a way that the income therefrom shall enable the Bank to meet its obligations, to cover its expenses and risks and to build up a reserve fund as provided for in Article 22.

(2) The Bank shall not grant any reduction in interest rates. Where a reduction in the interest rate appears desirable in view of the nature of the investment to be financed, the Member State concerned or some other agency may grant aid towards the payment of interest to the extent that this is compatible with Article 107 of the Treaty on the Functioning of the European Union.

Article 18 (ex Article 20). In its financing operations, the Bank shall observe the following principles:

(1) It shall ensure that its funds are employed as rationally as possible in the interests of the Union. It may grant loans or guarantees only:

(a) where, in the case of investments by undertakings in the production sector, interest and amortisation payments are covered out of operating profits or, in the case of other investments, either by a commitment entered into by the State in which the investment is made or by some other means; and

(b) where the execution of the investment contributes to an increase in economic productivity in general and promotes the attainment of the internal market.

(2) It shall neither acquire any interest in an undertaking nor assume any responsibility in its management unless this is required to safeguard the rights of the Bank in ensuring recovery of funds lent. However, in accordance with the principles determined by the Board of Governors pursuant to Article 7(3)(b), and where the implementation of operations provided for in Article 309 of the Treaty on the Functioning of the European Union so requires, the Board of Directors shall, acting by a qualified majority, lay down the terms and conditions for taking an equity participation in a commercial undertaking, normally as a complement to a loan or a guarantee, in so far as this is required to finance an investment or programme.

(3) It may dispose of its claims on the capital market and may, to this end, require its debtors to issue bonds or other securities.

(4) Neither the Bank nor the Member States shall impose conditions requiring funds lent by the Bank to be spent within a specified Member State.

(5) The Bank may make its loans conditional on international invitations to tender being arranged.

(6) The Bank shall not finance, in whole or in part, any investment opposed by the Member State in whose territory it is to be carried out.

(7) As a complement to its lending activity, the Bank may provide technical assistance services in accordance with the terms and conditions laid down by the Board of Governors, acting by a qualified majority, and in compliance with this Statute.

Article 19 (ex Article 21). (1) Any undertaking or public or private entity may apply directly to the Bank for financing. Applications to the Bank may also be made either through the Commission or through the Member State on whose territory the investment will be carried out.

(2) Applications made through the Commission shall be submitted for an opinion to the Member State in whose territory the investment will be carried out. Applications made through a Member

State shall be submitted to the Commission for an opinion. Applications made direct by an undertaking shall be submitted to the Member State concerned and to the Commission.
The Member State concerned and the Commission shall deliver their opinions within two months. If no reply is received within this period, the Bank may assume that there is no objection to the investment in question.
(3) The Board of Directors shall rule on financing operations submitted to it by the Management Committee.
(4) The Management Committee shall examine whether financing operations submitted to it comply with the provisions of this Statute, in particular with Articles 16 and 18. Where the Management Committee is in favour of the financing operation, it shall submit the corresponding proposal to the Board of Directors; the Committee may make its favourable opinion subject to such conditions, as it considers essential. Where the Management Committee is against granting the finance, it shall submit the relevant documents together with its opinion to the Board of Directors.
(5) Where the Management Committee delivers an unfavourable opinion, the Board of Directors may not grant the finance concerned unless its decision is unanimous.
(6) Where the Commission delivers an unfavourable opinion, the Board of Directors may not grant the finance concerned unless its decision is unanimous, the director nominated by the Commission abstaining.
(7) Where both the Management Committee and the Commission deliver an unfavourable opinion, the Board of Directors may not grant the finance.
(8) In the event that a financing operation relating to an approved investment has to be restructured in order to safeguard the Bank's rights and interests, the Management Committee shall take without delay the emergency measures which it deems necessary, subject to immediate reporting thereon to the Board of Directors.

Article 20 (ex Article 22). (1) The Bank shall borrow on the capital markets the funds necessary for the performance of its tasks.
(2) The Bank may borrow on the capital markets of the Member States in accordance with the legal provisions applying to those markets.
The competent authorities of a Member State with a derogation within the meaning of Article 139(1) of the Treaty on the Functioning of the European Union may oppose this only if there is reason to fear serious disturbances on the capital market of that State.

Article 21 (ex Article 23). (1) The Bank may employ any available funds which it does not immediately require to meet its obligations in the following ways:
(a) it may invest on the money markets;
(b) it may, subject to the provisions of Article 18(2), buy and sell securities;
(c) it may carry out any other financial operation linked with its objectives.
(2) Without prejudice to the provisions of Article 23, the Bank shall not, in managing its investments, engage in any currency arbitrage not directly required to carry out its lending operations or fulfil commitments arising out of loans raised or guarantees granted by it.
(3) The Bank shall, in the fields covered by this Article, act in agreement with the competent authorities or with the national central bank of the Member State concerned.

Article 22 (ex Article 24). (1) A reserve fund of up to 10 % of the subscribed capital shall be built up progressively. If the state of the liabilities of the Bank should so justify, the Board of Directors may decide to set aside additional reserves. Until such time as the reserve fund has been fully built up, it shall be fed by:
(a) interest received on loans granted by the Bank out of sums to be paid up by the Member States pursuant to Article 5;
(b) interest received on loans granted by the Bank out of funds derived from repayment of the loans referred to in (a);
to the extent that this income is not required to meet the obligations of the Bank or to cover its expenses.
(2) The resources of the reserve fund shall be so invested as to be available at any time to meet the purpose of the fund.

Article 23 (ex Article 25). (1) The Bank shall at all times be entitled to transfer its assets in the currency of a Member State whose currency is not the euro in order to carry out financial operations corresponding to the task set out in Article 309 of the Treaty on the Functioning of the European Union, taking into account the provisions of Article 21 of this Statute. The Bank shall, as far as possible, avoid making such transfers if it has cash or liquid assets in the currency required.

(2) The Bank may not convert its assets in the currency of a Member State whose currency is not the euro into the currency of a third country without the agreement of the Member State concerned.
(3) The Bank may freely dispose of that part of its capital which is paid up and of any currency borrowed on markets outside the Union.
(4) The Member States undertake to make available to the debtors of the Bank the currency needed to repay the capital and pay the interest on loans or commission on guarantees granted by the Bank for investments to be carried out in their territory.

Article 24 (ex Article 26). If a Member State fails to meet the obligations of membership arising from this Statute, in particular the obligation to pay its share of the subscribed capital or to service its borrowings, the granting of loans or guarantees to that Member State or its nationals may be suspended by a decision of the Board of Governors, acting by a qualified majority.
Such decision shall not release either the State or its nationals from their obligations towards the Bank.

Article 25 (ex Article 27). (1) If the Board of Governors decides to suspend the operations of the Bank, all its activities shall cease forthwith, except those required to ensure the due realisation, protection and preservation of its assets and the settlement of its liabilities.
(2) In the event of liquidation, the Board of Governors shall appoint the liquidators and give them instructions for carrying out the liquidation. It shall ensure that the rights of the members of staff are safeguarded.

Article 26 (ex Article 28). (1) In each of the Member States, the Bank shall enjoy the most extensive legal capacity accorded to legal persons under their laws; it may, in particular, acquire or dispose of movable or immovable property and may be a party to legal proceedings.
(2) The property of the Bank shall be exempt from all forms of requisition or expropriation.

Article 27 (ex Article 29). Disputes between the Bank on the one hand, and its creditors, debtors or any other person on the other, shall be decided by the competent national courts, save where jurisdiction has been conferred on the Court of Justice of the European Union. The Bank may provide for arbitration in any contract.
The Bank shall have an address for service in each Member State. It may, however, in any contract, specify a particular address for service.
The property and assets of the Bank shall not be liable to attachment or to seizure by way of execution except by decision of a court.

Article 28 (ex Article 30). (1) The Board of Governors may, acting unanimously, decide to establish subsidiaries or other entities, which shall have legal personality and financial autonomy.
(2) The Board of Governors shall establish the Statutes of the bodies referred to in paragraph 1. The Statutes shall define, in particular, their objectives, structure, capital, membership, the location of their seat, their financial resources, means of intervention and auditing arrangements, as well as their relationship with the organs of the Bank.
(3) The Bank shall be entitled to participate in the management of these bodies and contribute to their subscribed capital up to the amount determined by the Board of Governors, acting unanimously.
(4) The Protocol on the privileges and immunities of the European Union shall apply to the bodies referred to in paragraph 1 in so far as they are incorporated under the law of the Union, to the members of their organs in the performance of their duties as such and to their staff, under the same terms and conditions as those applicable to the Bank.
Those dividends, capital gains or other forms of revenue stemming from such bodies to which the members, other than the European Union and the Bank, are entitled, shall however remain subject to the fiscal provisions of the applicable legislation.
(5) The Court of Justice of the European Union shall, within the limits hereinafter laid down, have jurisdiction in disputes concerning measures adopted by organs of a body incorporated under Union law. Proceedings against such measures may be instituted by any member of such a body in its capacity as such or by Member States under the conditions laid down in Article 263 of the Treaty on the Functioning of the European Union.
(6) The Board of Governors may, acting unanimously, decide to admit the staff of bodies incorporated under Union law to joint schemes with the Bank, in compliance with the respective internal procedures.

PROTOCOLS TO THE TREATIES

**Council Decision (EU) 2019/654
of 15 April 2019
amending Protocol No 5 on the Statute of the European Investment Bank**

THE COUNCIL OF THE EUROPEAN UNION,
Having regard to the Treaty on the Functioning of the European Union, and in particular Article 308 thereof,
Having regard to the request of the European Investment Bank,
After transmission of the draft legislative act to the national parliaments,
Having regard to the opinion of the European Parliament,
Having regard to the opinion of the European Commission,
Acting in accordance with a special legislative procedure,
Whereas:
(1) On 29 March 2017, the United Kingdom notified the European Council of its intention to withdraw from the Union pursuant to Article 50 of the Treaty on European Union. The Treaties will cease to apply to the United Kingdom from the date of entry into force of the Withdrawal Agreement, or failing that, two years after that notification, i.e. on 30 March 2019, unless the European Council, in agreement with the United Kingdom unanimously decides to extend that period.
(2) In accordance with Article 308 of the Treaty on the Functioning of the European Union, the members of the European Investment Bank (the 'Bank') are the Member States.
(3) The withdrawal of the United Kingdom from the Union will bring an end to the United Kingdom's membership of the Bank, to its subscribed capital in the Bank, to its right to nominate members and alternate members of the Board of Directors, and to the term of office of the members and alternate members of the Board of Directors nominated by the United Kingdom.
(4) The maintenance of the capital of the Bank requires an increase in the capital subscribed by the remaining Member States.
(5) The increase in the capital subscribed by the remaining Member States should occur in parallel with a further strengthening of the governance of the Bank.
(6) The functions of the Board of Directors should be strengthened by allowing for the nomination of additional alternates, and better use should be made of alternate Board members and non-voting experts to enhance their role in supporting the decision-making process of the Board of Directors, in particular with regard to the analysis of financing proposals.
(7) The use of qualified majority voting by the Board of Directors and the Board of Governors should be extended to crucial areas, namely the decision on the Bank's operational plan, the appointment of members of the Management Committee and the approval of the Rules of Procedure.
(8) In order to enhance the effectiveness of the reforms set out in this Decision, the Bank should take further initiatives to reflect, in line with best banking practice, the principles of the 'three lines of defence' at all relevant levels of the Bank, including in the Management Committee.
(9) Furthermore, and in line with Member States' expectations, lending volumes should be kept sustainable and a framework for determining sustainable lending levels should be further developed, while the functions of the Audit Committee should be strengthened by making sure that the Committee includes members with knowledge of supervisory issues. In particular, it should be ensured that the Audit Committee always includes members drawn from a banking supervisory authority from both inside and outside the euro area.
(10) The Statute of the European Investment Bank should therefore be amended accordingly,
HAS ADOPTED THIS DECISION:

Article 1. Protocol No 5 on the Statute of the European Investment Bank, annexed to the Treaty on the Functioning of the European Union, is amended as follows:
(1) the first subparagraph of Article 4(1) is amended as follows:
(a) the introductory part is replaced by the following:
'1. The capital of the Bank shall be EUR 204 089 132 500, subscribed by the Member States as follows:';
(b) the following line in the list is deleted: 'United Kingdom | 39 195 022 000 ';
(2) in Article 7(3), point (h) is replaced by the following: '(h) approve, acting by a qualified majority, the Rules of Procedure of the Bank.';
(3) in the first subparagraph of Article 9(1), the following sentence is added: 'It shall, acting by a qualified majority, decide on the Bank's operational plan.';
(4) Article 9(2) is amended as follows:
(a) the first subparagraph is replaced by the following: '2. The Board of Directors shall consist of 28

PART III EUROPEAN UNION

directors and of 31 alternate directors, nominated in accordance with this paragraph.';
(b) the third subparagraph is replaced by the following: 'The alternate directors shall be appointed by the Board of Governors for five years as shown below:
— two alternates nominated by the Federal Republic of Germany,
— two alternates nominated by the French Republic,
— two alternates nominated by the Italian Republic,
— two alternates nominated by common accord of the Kingdom of Spain and the Portuguese Republic,
— three alternates nominated by common accord of the Kingdom of Belgium, the Grand Duchy of Luxembourg and the Kingdom of the Netherlands,
— four alternates nominated by common accord of the Kingdom of Denmark, the Hellenic Republic, Ireland and Romania,
— six alternates nominated by common accord of the Republic of Estonia, the Republic of Latvia, the Republic of Lithuania, the Republic of Austria, the Republic of Finland and the Kingdom of Sweden,
— nine alternates nominated by common accord of the Republic of Bulgaria, the Czech Republic, the Republic of Croatia, the Republic of Cyprus, Hungary, the Republic of Malta, the Republic of Poland, the Republic of Slovenia and the Slovak Republic,
— one alternate nominated by the Commission.';
(5) the first subparagraph of Article 11(1) is replaced by the following: '1. The Management Committee shall consist of a President and eight Vice-Presidents appointed for a period of six years by the Board of Governors, acting by a qualified majority, on a proposal from the Board of Directors, acting by a qualified majority.'.

Article 2.
1. This Decision shall apply from the day following that on which the Treaties cease to apply to the United Kingdom.
2. Point (1) (a) of Article 1 shall apply from the date referred to in paragraph 1 of this Article unless a decision to increase the capital of the Bank has been adopted with effect from that date or before that date.

Protocol (No 6) on the Location of the Seats of the Institutions and of Certain Bodies, Offices, Agencies and Departments of the European Union

THE REPRESENTATIVES OF THE GOVERNMENTS OF THE MEMBER STATES,
HAVING REGARD to Article 341 of the Treaty on the Functioning of the European Union and Article 189 of the Treaty establishing the European Atomic Energy Community,
RECALLING AND CONFIRMING the Decision of 8 April 1965, and without prejudice to the decisions concerning the seat of future institutions, bodies, offices, agencies and departments,
HAVE AGREED UPON the following provisions, which shall be annexed to the Treaty on European Union and to the Treaty on the Functioning of the European Union, and to the Treaty establishing the European Atomic Energy Community:

Sole Article. (a) The European Parliament shall have its seat in Strasbourg where the 12 periods of monthly plenary sessions, including the budget session, shall be held. The periods of additional plenary sessions shall be held in Brussels. The committees of the European Parliament shall meet in Brussels. The General Secretariat of the European Parliament and its departments shall remain in Luxembourg.
(b) The Council shall have its seat in Brussels. During the months of April, June and October, the Council shall hold its meetings in Luxembourg.
(c) The Commission shall have its seat in Brussels. The departments listed in Articles 7, 8 and 9 of the Decision of 8 April 1965 shall be established in Luxembourg.
(d) The Court of Justice of the European Union shall have its seat in Luxembourg.
(e) The Court of Auditors shall have its seat in Luxembourg.
(f) The Economic and Social Committee shall have its seat in Brussels.
(g) The Committee of the Regions shall have its seat in Brussels.
(h) The European Investment Bank shall have its seat in Luxembourg.
(i) The European Central Bank shall have its seat in Frankfurt.
(j) The European Police Office (Europol) shall have its seat in The Hague.

PROTOCOLS TO THE TREATIES

Protocol (No 7) on the Privileges and Immunities of the European Union

THE HIGH CONTRACTING PARTIES,
CONSIDERING that, in accordance with Article 343 of the Treaty on the Functioning of the European Union and Article 191 of the Treaty establishing the European Atomic Energy Community ("EAEC"), the European Union and the EAEC shall enjoy in the territories of the Member States such privileges and immunities as are necessary for the performance of their tasks,
HAVE AGREED upon the following provisions, which shall be annexed to the Treaty on European Union, the Treaty on the Functioning of the European Union and the Treaty establishing the European Atomic Energy Community:

Chapter I. Property, Funds, Assets and Operations of the European Union

Article 1. The premises and buildings of the Union shall be inviolable. They shall be exempt from search, requisition, confiscation or expropriation. The property and assets of the Union shall not be the subject of any administrative or legal measure of constraint without the authorisation of the Court of Justice.

Article 2. The archives of the Union shall be inviolable.

Article 3. The Union, its assets, revenues and other property shall be exempt from all direct taxes. The governments of the Member States shall, wherever possible, take the appropriate measures to remit or refund the amount of indirect taxes or sales taxes included in the price of movable or immovable property, where the Union makes, for its official use, substantial purchases the price of which includes taxes of this kind. These provisions shall not be applied, however, so as to have the effect of distorting competition within the Union.
No exemption shall be granted in respect of taxes and dues which amount merely to charges for public utility services.

Article 4. The Union shall be exempt from all customs duties, prohibitions and restrictions on imports and exports in respect of articles intended for its official use: articles so imported shall not be disposed of, whether or not in return for payment, in the territory of the country into which they have been imported, except under conditions approved by the government of that country.
The Union shall also be exempt from any customs duties and any prohibitions and restrictions on import and exports in respect of its publications.

Chapter II. Communications and Laissez–Passer

Article 5 (ex Article 6). For their official communications and the transmission of all their documents, the institutions of the Union shall enjoy in the territory of each Member State the treatment accorded by that State to diplomatic missions.
Official correspondence and other official communications of the institutions of the Union shall not be subject to censorship.

Article 6 (ex Article 7). Laissez–passer in a form to be prescribed by the Council, acting by a simple majority, which shall be recognised as valid travel documents by the authorities of the Member States, may be issued to members and servants of the institutions of the Union by the Presidents of these institutions. These laissez–passer shall be issued to officials and other servants under conditions laid down in the Staff Regulations of Officials and the Conditions of Employment of other servants of the Union.
The Commission may conclude agreements for these laissez–passer to be recognised as valid travel documents within the territory of third countries.

Chapter III. Members of the European Parliament

Article 7 (ex Article 8). No administrative or other restriction shall be imposed on the free movement of Members of the European Parliament travelling to or from the place of meeting of the European Parliament.
Members of the European Parliament shall, in respect of customs and exchange control, be accorded:
(a) by their own government, the same facilities as those accorded to senior officials travelling abroad on temporary official missions;
(b) by the government of other Member States, the same facilities as those accorded to representatives of foreign governments on temporary official missions.

PART III EUROPEAN UNION

Article 8 (ex Article 9). Members of the European Parliament shall not be subject to any form of inquiry, detention or legal proceedings in respect of opinions expressed or votes cast by them in the performance of their duties.

Article 9 (ex Article 10). During the sessions of the European Parliament, its Members shall enjoy:
(a) in the territory of their own State, the immunities accorded to members of their parliament;
(b) in the territory of any other Member State, immunity from any measure of detention and from legal proceedings.
Immunity shall likewise apply to Members while they are travelling to and from the place of meeting of the European Parliament.
Immunity cannot be claimed when a Member is found in the act of committing an offence and shall not prevent the European Parliament from exercising its right to waive the immunity of one of its Members.

Chapter IV. Representatives of Member States Taking Part in the Work of the Institutions of the European Union

Article 10 (ex Article 11). Representatives of Member States taking part in the work of the institutions of the Union, their advisers and technical experts shall, in the performance of their duties and during their travel to and from the place of meeting, enjoy the customary privileges, immunities and facilities.
This Article shall also apply to members of the advisory bodies of the Union.

Chapter V. Officials and other Servants of the European Union

Article 11 (ex Article 12). In the territory of each Member State and whatever their nationality, officials and other servants of the Union shall:
(a) subject to the provisions of the Treaties relating, on the one hand, to the rules on the liability of officials and other servants towards the Union and, on the other hand, to the jurisdiction of the Court of Justice of the European Union in disputes between the Union and its officials and other servants, be immune from legal proceedings in respect of acts performed by them in their official capacity, including their words spoken or written. They shall continue to enjoy this immunity after they have ceased to hold office;
(b) together with their spouses and dependent members of their families, not be subject to immigration restrictions or to formalities for the registration of aliens;
(c) in respect of currency or exchange regulations, be accorded the same facilities as are customarily accorded to officials of international organisations;
(d) enjoy the right to import free of duty their furniture and effects at the time of first taking up their post in the country concerned, and the right to re–export free of duty their furniture and effects, on termination of their duties in that country, subject in either case to the conditions considered to be necessary by the government of the country in which this right is exercised;
(e) have the right to import free of duty a motor car for their personal use, acquired either in the country of their last residence or in the country of which they are nationals on the terms ruling in the home market in that country, and to re–export it free of duty, subject in either case to the conditions considered to be necessary by the government of the country concerned.

Article 12 (ex Article 13). Officials and other servants of the Union shall be liable to a tax for the benefit of the Union on salaries, wages and emoluments paid to them by the Union, in accordance with the conditions and procedure laid down by the European Parliament and the Council, acting by means of regulations in accordance with the ordinary legislative procedure and after consultation of the institutions concerned.
They shall be exempt from national taxes on salaries, wages and emoluments paid by the Union.

Article 13 (ex Article 14). In the application of income tax, wealth tax and death duties and in the application of conventions on the avoidance of double taxation concluded between Member States of the Union, officials and other servants of the Union who, solely by reason of the performance of their duties in the service of the Union, establish their residence in the territory of a Member State other than their country of domicile for tax purposes at the time of entering the service of the Union, shall be considered, both in the country of their actual residence and in the country of domicile for tax purposes, as having maintained their domicile in the latter country provided that it is a member of the Union. This provision shall also apply to a spouse, to the extent that the latter is not separately engaged in a gainful occupation, and to children dependent on and in the care of the persons referred to in this Article.

Movable property belonging to persons referred to in the preceding paragraph and situated in the territory of the country where they are staying shall be exempt from death duties in that country; such property shall, for the assessment of such duty, be considered as being in the country of domicile for tax purposes, subject to the rights of third countries and to the possible application of provisions of international conventions on double taxation.

Any domicile acquired solely by reason of the performance of duties in the service of other international organisations shall not be taken into consideration in applying the provisions of this Article.

Article 14 (ex Article 15). The European Parliament and the Council, acting by means of regulations in accordance with the ordinary legislative procedure and after consultation of the institutions concerned, shall lay down the scheme of social security benefits for officials and other servants of the Union.

Article 15 (ex Article 16). The European Parliament and the Council, acting by means of regulations in accordance with the ordinary legislative procedure, and after consulting the other institutions concerned, shall determine the categories of officials and other servants of the Union to whom the provisions of Article 11, the second paragraph of Article 12, and Article 13 shall apply, in whole or in part.

The names, grades and addresses of officials and other servants included in such categories shall be communicated periodically to the governments of the Member States.

Chapter VI. Privileges and Immunities of Missions of Third Countries Accredited to the European Union

Article 16 (ex Article 17). The Member State in whose territory the Union has its seat shall accord the customary diplomatic immunities and privileges to missions of third countries accredited to the Union.

Chapter VII. General Provisions

Article 17 (ex Article 18). Privileges, immunities and facilities shall be accorded to officials and other servants of the Union solely in the interests of the Union.

Each institution of the Union shall be required to waive the immunity accorded to an official or other servant wherever that institution considers that the waiver of such immunity is not contrary to the interests of the Union.

Article 18 (ex Article 19). The institutions of the Union shall, for the purpose of applying this Protocol, cooperate with the responsible authorities of the Member States concerned.

Article 19 (ex Article 20). Articles 11 to 14 and Article 17 shall apply to the President of the European Council.

They shall also apply to Members of the Commission.

Article 20 (ex Article 21). Articles 11 to 14 and Article 17 shall apply to the Judges, the Advocates–General, the Registrars and the Assistant Rapporteurs of the Court of Justice of the European Union, without prejudice to the provisions of Article 3 of the Protocol on the Statute of the Court of Justice of the European Union relating to immunity from legal proceedings of Judges and Advocates–General.

Article 21 (ex Article 22). This Protocol shall also apply to the European Investment Bank, to the members of its organs, to its staff and to the representatives of the Member States taking part in its activities, without prejudice to the provisions of the Protocol on the Statute of the Bank.

The European Investment Bank shall in addition be exempt from any form of taxation or imposition of a like nature on the occasion of any increase in its capital and from the various formalities which may be connected therewith in the State where the Bank has its seat. Similarly, its dissolution or liquidation shall not give rise to any imposition. Finally, the activities of the Bank and of its organs carried on in accordance with its Statute shall not be subject to any turnover tax.

Article 22 (ex Article 23). This Protocol shall also apply to the European Central Bank, to the members of its organs and to its staff, without prejudice to the provisions of the Protocol on the Statute of the European System of Central Banks and the European Central Bank.

The European Central Bank shall, in addition, be exempt from any form of taxation or imposition of a like nature on the occasion of any increase in its capital and from the various formalities which may be connected therewith in the State where the bank has its seat. The activities of the Bank and of its organs carried on in accordance with the Statute of the European System of Central Banks and of the European Central Bank shall not be subject to any turnover tax.

Protocol (No 8) Relating to Article 6(2) of the Treaty on European Union on the Accession of the Union to the European Convention on the Protection of Human Rights and Fundamental Freedoms

THE HIGH CONTRACTING PARTIES,
HAVE AGREED UPON the following provisions, which shall be annexed to the Treaty on European Union and to the Treaty on the Functioning of the European Union:

Article 1. The agreement relating to the accession of the Union to the European Convention on the Protection of Human Rights and Fundamental Freedoms (hereinafter referred to as the "European Convention") provided for in Article 6(2) of the Treaty on European Union shall make provision for preserving the specific characteristics of the Union and Union law, in particular with regard to:
(a) the specific arrangements for the Union's possible participation in the control bodies of the European Convention;
(b) the mechanisms necessary to ensure that proceedings by non–Member States and individual applications are correctly addressed to Member States and/or the Union as appropriate.

Article 2. The agreement referred to in Article 1 shall ensure that accession of the Union shall not affect the competences of the Union or the powers of its institutions. It shall ensure that nothing therein affects the situation of Member States in relation to the European Convention, in particular in relation to the Protocols thereto, measures taken by Member States derogating from the European Convention in accordance with Article 15 thereof and reservations to the European Convention made by Member States in accordance with Article 57 thereof.

Article 3. Nothing in the agreement referred to in Article 1 shall affect Article 344 of the Treaty on the Functioning of the European Union.

Protocol (No 9) on the Decision of the Council Relating to the Implementation of Article 16(4) of the Treaty on European Union and Article 238(2) of the Treaty on the Functioning of the European Union Between 1 November 2014 and 31 March 2017 on the One Hand, And As From 1 April 2017 on the other

THE HIGH CONTRACTING PARTIES,
TAKING INTO ACCOUNT the fundamental importance that agreeing on the Decision of the Council relating to the implementation of Article 16(4) of the Treaty on European Union and Article 238(2) of the Treaty on the Functioning of the European Union between 1 November 2014 and 31 March 2017 on the one hand, and as from 1 April 2017 on the other (hereinafter "the Decision"), had when approving the Treaty of Lisbon,
HAVE AGREED UPON the following provisions, which shall be annexed to the Treaty on European Union and to the Treaty on the Functioning of the European Union:

Sole Article. Before the examination by the Council of any draft which would aim either at amending or abrogating the Decision or any of its provisions, or at modifying indirectly its scope or its meaning through the modification of another legal act of the Union, the European Council shall hold a preliminary deliberation on the said draft, acting by consensus in accordance with Article 15(4) of the Treaty on European Union.

Protocol (No 10) on Permanent Structured Cooperation Established by Article 42 of the Treaty on European Union

THE HIGH CONTRACTING PARTIES,
HAVING REGARD TO Article 42(6) and Article 46 of the Treaty on European Union,
RECALLING that the Union is pursuing a common foreign and security policy based on the achievement of growing convergence of action by Member States,
RECALLING that the common security and defence policy is an integral part of the common foreign and security policy; that it provides the Union with operational capacity drawing on civil and mili-

tary assets; that the Union may use such assets in the tasks referred to in Article 43 of the Treaty on European Union outside the Union for peace–keeping, conflict prevention and strengthening international security in accordance with the principles of the United Nations Charter; that the performance of these tasks is to be undertaken using capabilities provided by the Member States in accordance with the principle of a single set of forces,
RECALLING that the common security and defence policy of the Union does not prejudice the specific character of the security and defence policy of certain Member States,
RECALLING that the common security and defence policy of the Union respects the obligations under the North Atlantic Treaty of those Member States which see their common defence realised in the North Atlantic Treaty Organisation, which remains the foundation of the collective defence of its members, and is compatible with the common security and defence policy established within that framework,
CONVINCED that a more assertive Union role in security and defence matters will contribute to the vitality of a renewed Atlantic Alliance, in accordance with the Berlin Plus arrangements,
DETERMINED to ensure that the Union is capable of fully assuming its responsibilities within the international community,
RECOGNISING that the United Nations Organisation may request the Union's assistance for the urgent implementation of missions undertaken under Chapters VI and VII of the United Nations Charter,
RECOGNISING that the strengthening of the security and defence policy will require efforts by Member States in the area of capabilities,
CONSCIOUS that embarking on a new stage in the development of the European security and defence policy involves a determined effort by the Member States concerned,
RECALLING the importance of the High Representative of the Union for Foreign Affairs and Security Policy being fully involved in proceedings relating to permanent structured cooperation,
HAVE AGREED UPON the following provisions, which shall be annexed to the Treaty on European Union and to the Treaty on the Functioning of the European Union:

Article 1. The permanent structured cooperation referred to in Article 42(6) of the Treaty on European Union shall be open to any Member State which undertakes, from the date of entry into force of the Treaty of Lisbon, to:
(a) proceed more intensively to develop its defence capacities through the development of its national contributions and participation, where appropriate, in multinational forces, in the main European equipment programmes, and in the activity of the Agency in the field of defence capabilities development, research, acquisition and armaments (European Defence Agency), and
(b) have the capacity to supply by 2010 at the latest, either at national level or as a component of multinational force groups, targeted combat units for the missions planned, structured at a tactical level as a battle group, with support elements including transport and logistics, capable of carrying out the tasks referred to in Article 43 of the Treaty on European Union, within a period of five to 30 days, in particular in response to requests from the United Nations Organisation, and which can be sustained for an initial period of 30 days and be extended up to at least 120 days.

Article 2. To achieve the objectives laid down in Article 1, Member States participating in permanent structured cooperation shall undertake to:
(a) cooperate, as from the entry into force of the Treaty of Lisbon, with a view to achieving approved objectives concerning the level of investment expenditure on defence equipment, and regularly review these objectives, in the light of the security environment and of the Union's international responsibilities;
(b) bring their defence apparatus into line with each other as far as possible, particularly by harmonising the identification of their military needs, by pooling and, where appropriate, specialising their defence means and capabilities, and by encouraging cooperation in the fields of training and logistics;
(c) take concrete measures to enhance the availability, interoperability, flexibility and deployability of their forces, in particular by identifying common objectives regarding the commitment of forces, including possibly reviewing their national decision–making procedures;
(d) work together to ensure that they take the necessary measures to make good, including through multinational approaches, and without prejudice to undertakings in this regard within the North Atlantic Treaty Organisation, the shortfalls perceived in the framework of the "Capability Development Mechanism";
(e) take part, where appropriate, in the development of major joint or European equipment programmes in the framework of the European Defence Agency.

PART III   EUROPEAN UNION

Article 3. The European Defence Agency shall contribute to the regular assessment of participating Member States' contributions with regard to capabilities, in particular contributions made in accordance with the criteria to be established, inter alia, on the basis of Article 2, and shall report thereon at least once a year. The assessment may serve as a basis for Council recommendations and decisions adopted in accordance with Article 46 of the Treaty on European Union.

Protocol (No 11) on Article 42 of the Treaty on European Union

THE HIGH CONTRACTING PARTIES,
BEARING IN MIND the need to implement fully the provisions of Article 42(2) of the Treaty on European Union,
BEARING IN MIND that the policy of the Union in accordance with Article 42 shall not prejudice the specific character of the security and defence policy of certain Member States and shall respect the obligations of certain Member States, which see their common defence realised in NATO, under the North Atlantic Treaty and be compatible with the common security and defence policy established within that framework,
HAVE AGREED UPON the following provision, which shall be annexed to the Treaty on European Union and to the Treaty on the Functioning of the European Union:
The European Union shall draw up, together with the Western European Union, arrangements for enhanced cooperation between them.

Protocol (No 12) on the Excessive Deficit Procedure

THE HIGH CONTRACTING PARTIES,
DESIRING TO lay down the details of the excessive deficit procedure referred to in Article 126 of the Treaty on the Functioning of the European Union,
HAVE AGREED upon the following provisions, which shall be annexed to the Treaty on European Union and to the Treaty on the Functioning of the European Union:

Article 1. The reference values referred to in Article 126(2) of the Treaty on the Functioning of the European Union are:
– 3 % for the ratio of the planned or actual government deficit to gross domestic product at market prices;
– 60 % for the ratio of government debt to gross domestic product at market prices.

Article 2. In Article 126 of the said Treaty and in this Protocol:
– "government" means general government, that is central government, regional or local government and social security funds, to the exclusion of commercial operations, as defined in the European System of Integrated Economic Accounts;
– "deficit" means net borrowing as defined in the European System of Integrated Economic Accounts;
– "investment" means gross fixed capital formation as defined in the European System of Integrated Economic Accounts;
– "debt" means total gross debt at nominal value outstanding at the end of the year and consolidated between and within the sectors of general government as defined in the first indent.

Article 3. In order to ensure the effectiveness of the excessive deficit procedure, the governments of the Member States shall be responsible under this procedure for the deficits of general government as defined in the first indent of Article 2. The Member States shall ensure that national procedures in the budgetary area enable them to meet their obligations in this area deriving from these Treaties. The Member States shall report their planned and actual deficits and the levels of their debt promptly and regularly to the Commission.

Article 4. The statistical data to be used for the application of this Protocol shall be provided by the Commission.

Protocol (No 13) on the Convergence Criteria

THE HIGH CONTRACTING PARTIES,
DESIRING to lay down the details of the convergence criteria which shall guide the Union in taking

decisions to end the derogations of those Member States with a derogation, referred to in Article 140 of the Treaty on the Functioning of the European Union,
HAVE AGREED upon the following provisions, which shall be annexed to the Treaty on European Union and to the Treaty on the Functioning of the European Union:

Article 1. The criterion on price stability referred to in the first indent of Article 140(1) of the Treaty on the Functioning of the European Union shall mean that a Member State has a price performance that is sustainable and an average rate of inflation, observed over a period of one year before the examination, that does not exceed by more than 1 ½ percentage points that of, at most, the three best performing Member States in terms of price stability. Inflation shall be measured by means of the consumer price index on a comparable basis taking into account differences in national definitions.

Article 2. The criterion on the government budgetary position referred to in the second indent of Article 140(1) of the said Treaty shall mean that at the time of the examination the Member State is not the subject of a Council decision under Article 126(6) of the said Treaty that an excessive deficit exists.

Article 3. The criterion on participation in the Exchange Rate mechanism of the European Monetary System referred to in the third indent of Article 140(1) of the said Treaty shall mean that a Member State has respected the normal fluctuation margins provided for by the exchange–rate mechanism on the European Monetary System without severe tensions for at least the last two years before the examination. In particular, the Member State shall not have devalued its currency's bilateral central rate against the euro on its own initiative for the same period.

Article 4. The criterion on the convergence of interest rates referred to in the fourth indent of Article 140(1) of the said Treaty shall mean that, observed over a period of one year before the examination, a Member State has had an average nominal long–term interest rate that does not exceed by more than two percentage points that of, at most, the three best performing Member States in terms of price stability. Interest rates shall be measured on the basis of long–term government bonds or comparable securities, taking into account differences in national definitions.

Article 5. The statistical data to be used for the application of this Protocol shall be provided by the Commission.

Article 6. The Council shall, acting unanimously on a proposal from the Commission and after consulting the European Parliament, the ECB and the Economic and Financial Committee, adopt appropriate provisions to lay down the details of the convergence criteria referred to in Article 140(1) of the said Treaty, which shall then replace this Protocol.

Protocol (No 14) on the Euro Group

THE HIGH CONTRACTING PARTIES,
DESIRING to promote conditions for stronger economic growth in the European Union and, to that end, to develop ever–closer coordination of economic policies within the euro area,
CONSCIOUS of the need to lay down special provisions for enhanced dialogue between the Member States whose currency is the euro, pending the euro becoming the currency of all Member States of the Union,
HAVE AGREED UPON the following provisions, which shall be annexed to the Treaty on European Union and to the Treaty on the Functioning of the European Union:

Article 1. The Ministers of the Member States whose currency is the euro shall meet informally. Such meetings shall take place, when necessary, to discuss questions related to the specific responsibilities they share with regard to the single currency. The Commission shall take part in the meetings. The European Central Bank shall be invited to take part in such meetings, which shall be prepared by the representatives of the Ministers with responsibility for finance of the Member States whose currency is the euro and of the Commission.

Article 2. The Ministers of the Member States whose currency is the euro shall elect a president for two and a half years, by a majority of those Member States.

Protocol (No 15) on Certain Provisions Relating to the United Kingdom of Great Britain and Northern Ireland

PART III EUROPEAN UNION

THE HIGH CONTRACTING PARTIES,
RECOGNISING that the United Kingdom shall not be obliged or committed to adopt the euro without a separate decision to do so by its government and parliament,
GIVEN that on 16 October 1996 and 30 October 1997 the United Kingdom government notified the Council of its intention not to participate in the third stage of economic and monetary union,
NOTING the practice of the government of the United Kingdom to fund its borrowing requirement by the sale of debt to the private sector,
HAVE AGREED upon the following provisions, which shall be annexed to the Treaty on European Union and to the Treaty on the Functioning of the European Union:

(1) Unless the United Kingdom notifies the Council that it intends to adopt the euro, it shall be under no obligation to do so.

(2) In view of the notice given to the Council by the United Kingdom government on 16 October 1996 and 30 October 1997, paragraphs 3 to 8 and 10 shall apply to the United Kingdom.

(3) The United Kingdom shall retain its powers in the field of monetary policy according to national law.

(4) Articles 119, second paragraph, 126(1), (9) and (11), 127(1) to (5), 128, 130, 131, 132, 133, 138, 140(3), 219, 282(2), with the exception of the first and last sentences thereof, 282(5), and 283 of the Treaty on the Functioning of the European Union shall not apply to the United Kingdom. The same applies to Article 121(2) of this Treaty as regards the adoption of the parts of the broad economic policy guidelines which concern the euro area generally. In these provisions references to the Union or the Member States shall not include the United Kingdom and references to national central banks shall not include the Bank of England.

(5) The United Kingdom shall endeavour to avoid an excessive government deficit.
Articles 143 and 144 of the Treaty on the Functioning of the European Union shall continue to apply to the United Kingdom. Articles 134(4) and 142 shall apply to the United Kingdom as if it had a derogation.

(6) The voting rights of the United Kingdom shall be suspended in respect of acts of the Council referred to in the Articles listed in paragraph 4 and in the instances referred to in the first subparagraph of Article 139(4) of the Treaty on the Functioning of the European Union. For this purpose the second subparagraph of Article 139(4) of the Treaty shall apply.
The United Kingdom shall also have no right to participate in the appointment of the President, the Vice–President and the other members of the Executive Board of the ECB under the second subparagraph of Article 283(2) of the said Treaty.

(7) Articles 3, 4, 6, 7, 9(2), 10(1), 10(3), 11(2), 12(1), 14, 16, 18 to 20, 22, 23, 26, 27, 30 to 34 and 49 of the Protocol on the Statute of the European System of Central Banks and of the European Central Bank ("the Statute") shall not apply to the United Kingdom.
In those Articles, references to the Union or the Member States shall not include the United Kingdom and references to national central banks or shareholders shall not include the Bank of England. References in Articles 10(3) and 30(2) of the Statute to "subscribed capital of the ECB" shall not include capital subscribed by the Bank of England.

(8) Article 141(1) of the Treaty on the Functioning of the European Union and Articles 43 to 47 of the Statute shall have effect, whether or not there is any Member State with a derogation, subject to the following amendments:

(a) References in Article 43 to the tasks of the ECB and the EMI shall include those tasks that still need to be performed in the third stage owing to any decision of the United Kingdom not to adopt the euro.

(b) In addition to the tasks referred to in Article 46, the ECB shall also give advice in relation to and contribute to the preparation of any decision of the Council with regard to the United Kingdom taken in accordance with paragraphs 9(a) and 9(c).

(c) The Bank of England shall pay up its subscription to the capital of the ECB as a contribution to its operational costs on the same basis as national central banks of Member States with a derogation.

(9) The United Kingdom may notify the Council at any time of its intention to adopt the euro. In that event:

(a) The United Kingdom shall have the right to adopt the euro provided only that it satisfies the necessary conditions. The Council, acting at the request of the United Kingdom and under the conditions and in accordance with the procedure laid down in Article 140(1) and (2) of the Treaty on the Functioning of the European Union, shall decide whether it fulfils the necessary conditions.

(b) The Bank of England shall pay up its subscribed capital, transfer to the ECB foreign reserve assets and contribute to its reserves on the same basis as the national central bank of a Member State whose derogation has been abrogated.

PROTOCOLS TO THE TREATIES

(c) The Council, acting under the conditions and in accordance with the procedure laid down in Article 140(3) of the said Treaty, shall take all other necessary decisions to enable the United Kingdom to adopt the euro.
If the United Kingdom adopts the euro pursuant to the provisions of this Protocol, paragraphs 3 to 8 shall cease to have effect.
(10) Notwithstanding Article 123 of the Treaty on the Functioning of the European Union and Article 21(1) of the Statute, the Government of the United Kingdom may maintain its "ways and means" facility with the Bank of England if and so long as the United Kingdom does not adopt the euro.

Protocol (No 16) on Certain Provisions Relating to Denmark

THE HIGH CONTRACTING PARTIES,
TAKING INTO ACCOUNT that the Danish Constitution contains provisions which may imply a referendum in Denmark prior to Denmark renouncing its exemption,
GIVEN THAT, on 3 November 1993, the Danish Government notified the Council of its intention not to participate in the third stage of economic and monetary union,
HAVE AGREED UPON the following provisions, which shall be annexed to the Treaty on European Union and to the Treaty on the Functioning of the European Union:
(1) In view of the notice given to the Council by the Danish Government on 3 November 1993, Denmark shall have an exemption. The effect of the exemption shall be that all Articles and provisions of the Treaties and the Statute of the ESCB referring to a derogation shall be applicable to Denmark.
(2) As for the abrogation of the exemption, the procedure referred to in Article 140 shall only be initiated at the request of Denmark.
(3) In the event of abrogation of the exemption status, the provisions of this Protocol shall cease to apply.

Protocol (No 17) on Denmark

THE HIGH CONTRACTING PARTIES,
DESIRING to settle certain particular problems relating to Denmark,
HAVE AGREED upon the following provisions, which shall be annexed to the Treaty on European Union and the Treaty on the Functioning of the European Union:
The provisions of Article 14 of the Protocol on the Statute of the European System of Central Banks and of the European Central Bank shall not affect the right of the National Bank of Denmark to carry out its existing tasks concerning those parts of the Kingdom of Denmark which are not part of the Union.

Protocol (No 18) on France

THE HIGH CONTRACTING PARTIES,
DESIRING to take into account a particular point relating to France,
HAVE AGREED UPON the following provisions, which shall be annexed to the Treaty on European Union and to the Treaty on the Functioning of the European Union:
France will keep the privilege of monetary emission in New Caledonia, French Polynesia and Wallis and Futuna under the terms established by its national laws, and will be solely entitled to determine the parity of the CFP franc.

Protocol (No 19) on the Schengen Acquis Integrated into the Framework of the European Union

THE HIGH CONTRACTING PARTIES,
NOTING that the Agreements on the gradual abolition of checks at common borders signed by some Member States of the European Union in Schengen on 14 June 1985 and on 19 June 1990, as well as related agreements and the rules adopted on the basis of these agreements, have been integrated into the framework of the European Union by the Treaty of Amsterdam of 2 October 1997,
DESIRING to preserve the Schengen acquis, as developed since the entry into force of the Treaty of Amsterdam, and to develop this acquis in order to contribute towards achieving the objective of offer-

PART III   EUROPEAN UNION

ing citizens of the Union an area of freedom, security and justice without internal borders,
TAKING INTO ACCOUNT the special position of Denmark,
TAKING INTO ACCOUNT the fact that Ireland and the United Kingdom of Great Britain and Northern Ireland do not participate in all the provisions of the Schengen acquis; that provision should, however, be made to allow those Member States to accept other provisions of this acquis in full or in part,
RECOGNISING that, as a consequence, it is necessary to make use of the provisions of the Treaties concerning closer cooperation between some Member States,
TAKING INTO ACCOUNT the need to maintain a special relationship with the Republic of Iceland and the Kingdom of Norway, both States being bound by the provisions of the Nordic passport union, together with the Nordic States which are members of the European Union,
HAVE AGREED UPON the following provisions, which shall be annexed to the Treaty on European Union and to the Treaty on the Functioning of the European Union:

Article 1. The Kingdom of Belgium, the Republic of Bulgaria, the Czech Republic, the Kingdom of Denmark, the Federal Republic of Germany, the Republic of Estonia, the Hellenic Republic, the Kingdom of Spain, the French Republic, the Italian Republic, the Republic of Cyprus, the Republic of Latvia, the Republic of Lithuania, the Grand Duchy of Luxembourg, the Republic of Hungary, Malta, the Kingdom of the Netherlands, the Republic of Austria, the Republic of Poland, the Portuguese Republic, Romania, the Republic of Slovenia, the Slovak Republic, the Republic of Finland and the Kingdom of Sweden shall be authorised to establish closer cooperation among themselves in areas covered by provisions defined by the Council which constitute the Schengen acquis. This cooperation shall be conducted within the institutional and legal framework of the European Union and with respect for the relevant provisions of the Treaties.

Article 2. The Schengen acquis shall apply to the Member States referred to in Article 1, without prejudice to Article 3 of the Act of Accession of 16 April 2003 or to Article 4 of the Act of Accession of 25 April 2005. The Council will substitute itself for the Executive Committee established by the Schengen agreements.

Article 3. The participation of Denmark in the adoption of measures constituting a development of the Schengen acquis, as well as the implementation of these measures and their application to Denmark, shall be governed by the relevant provisions of the Protocol on the position of Denmark.

Article 4. Ireland and the United Kingdom of Great Britain and Northern Ireland may at any time request to take part in some or all of the provisions of the Schengen acquis.
The Council shall decide on the request with the unanimity of its members referred to in Article 1 and of the representative of the Government of the State concerned.

Article 5. (1) Proposals and initiatives to build upon the Schengen acquis shall be subject to the relevant provisions of the Treaties.
In this context, where either Ireland or the United Kingdom has not notified the Council in writing within a reasonable period that it wishes to take part, the authorisation referred to in Article 329 of the Treaty on the Functioning of the European Union shall be deemed to have been granted to the Member States referred to in Article 1 and to Ireland or the United Kingdom where either of them wishes to take part in the areas of cooperation in question.
(2) Where either Ireland or the United Kingdom is deemed to have given notification pursuant to a decision under Article 4, it may nevertheless notify the Council in writing, within three months, that it does not wish to take part in such a proposal or initiative. In that case, Ireland or the United Kingdom shall not take part in its adoption. As from the latter notification, the procedure for adopting the measure building upon the Schengen acquis shall be suspended until the end of the procedure set out in paragraphs 3 or 4 or until the notification is withdrawn at any moment during that procedure.
(3) For the Member State having made the notification referred to in paragraph 2, any decision taken by the Council pursuant to Article 4 shall, as from the date of entry into force of the proposed measure, cease to apply to the extent considered necessary by the Council and under the conditions to be determined in a decision of the Council acting by a qualified majority on a proposal from the Commission. That decision shall be taken in accordance with the following criteria: the Council shall seek to retain the widest possible measure of participation of the Member State concerned without seriously affecting the practical operability of the various parts of the Schengen acquis, while respecting their coherence. The Commission shall submit its proposal as soon as possible after the notification referred to in paragraph 2. The Council shall, if needed after convening two successive meetings, act within four months of the Commission proposal.

(4) If, by the end of the period of four months, the Council has not adopted a decision, a Member State may, without delay, request that the matter be referred to the European Council. In that case, the European Council shall, at its next meeting, acting by a qualified majority on a proposal from the Commission, take a decision in accordance with the criteria referred to in paragraph 3.

(5) If, by the end of the procedure set out in paragraphs 3 or 4, the Council or, as the case may be, the European Council has not adopted its decision, the suspension of the procedure for adopting the measure building upon the Schengen acquis shall be terminated. If the said measure is subsequently adopted any decision taken by the Council pursuant to Article 4 shall, as from the date of entry into force of that measure, cease to apply for the Member State concerned to the extent and under the conditions decided by the Commission, unless the said Member State has withdrawn its notification referred to in paragraph 2 before the adoption of the measure. The Commission shall act by the date of this adoption. When taking its decision, the Commission shall respect the criteria referred to in paragraph 3.

Article 6. The Republic of Iceland and the Kingdom of Norway shall be associated with the implementation of the Schengen acquis and its further development. Appropriate procedures shall be agreed to that effect in an Agreement to be concluded with those States by the Council, acting by the unanimity of its Members mentioned in Article 1. Such Agreement shall include provisions on the contribution of Iceland and Norway to any financial consequences resulting from the implementation of this Protocol.

A separate Agreement shall be concluded with Iceland and Norway by the Council, acting unanimously, for the establishment of rights and obligations between Ireland and the United Kingdom of Great Britain and Northern Ireland on the one hand, and Iceland and Norway on the other, in domains of the Schengen acquis which apply to these States.

Article 7. For the purposes of the negotiations for the admission of new Member States into the European Union, the Schengen acquis and further measures taken by the institutions within its scope shall be regarded as an acquis which must be accepted in full by all States candidates for admission.

Protocol (No 20) on the Application of Certain Aspects of Article 26 of the Treaty on the Functioning of the European Union to the United Kingdom and to Ireland

THE HIGH CONTRACTING PARTIES,
DESIRING to settle certain questions relating to the United Kingdom and Ireland,
HAVING REGARD to the existence for many years of special travel arrangements between the United Kingdom and Ireland,
HAVE AGREED UPON the following provisions, which shall be annexed to the Treaty on European Union and the Treaty on the Functioning of the European Union:

Article 1. The United Kingdom shall be entitled, notwithstanding Articles 26 and 77 of the Treaty on the Functioning of the European Union, any other provision of that Treaty or of the Treaty on European Union, any measure adopted under those Treaties, or any international agreement concluded by the Union or by the Union and its Member States with one or more third States, to exercise at its frontiers with other Member States such controls on persons seeking to enter the United Kingdom as it may consider necessary for the purpose:
(a) of verifying the right to enter the United Kingdom of citizens of Member States and of their dependants exercising rights conferred by Union law, as well as citizens of other States on whom such rights have been conferred by an agreement by which the United Kingdom is bound; and
(b) of determining whether or not to grant other persons permission to enter the United Kingdom.
Nothing in Articles 26 and 77 of the Treaty on the Functioning of the European Union or in any other provision of that Treaty or of the Treaty on European Union or in any measure adopted under them shall prejudice the right of the United Kingdom to adopt or exercise any such controls. References to the United Kingdom in this Article shall include territories for whose external relations the United Kingdom is responsible.

Article 2. The United Kingdom and Ireland may continue to make arrangements between themselves relating to the movement of persons between their territories ("the Common Travel Area"), while fully respecting the rights of persons referred to in Article 1, first paragraph, point (a) of this Protocol. Accordingly, as long as they maintain such arrangements, the provisions of Article 1 of this Protocol shall apply to Ireland under the same terms and conditions as for the United Kingdom. Nothing in Articles 26 and 77 of the Treaty on the Functioning of the European Union, in any other provision of

PART III   EUROPEAN UNION

that Treaty or of the Treaty on European Union or in any measure adopted under them, shall affect any such arrangements.

Article 3. The other Member States shall be entitled to exercise at their frontiers or at any point of entry into their territory such controls on persons seeking to enter their territory from the United Kingdom or any territories whose external relations are under its responsibility for the same purposes stated in Article 1 of this Protocol, or from Ireland as long as the provisions of Article 1 of this Protocol apply to Ireland.

Nothing in Articles 26 and 77 of the Treaty on the Functioning of the European Union or in any other provision of that Treaty or of the Treaty on European Union or in any measure adopted under them shall prejudice the right of the other Member States to adopt or exercise any such controls.

Protocol (No 21) on the Position of the United Kingdom and Ireland in respect of the Area of Freedom, Security and Justice

THE HIGH CONTRACTING PARTIES,
DESIRING to settle certain questions relating to the United Kingdom and Ireland,
HAVING REGARD to the Protocol on the application of certain aspects of Article 26 of the Treaty on the Functioning of the European Union to the United Kingdom and to Ireland,
HAVE AGREED UPON the following provisions, which shall be annexed to the Treaty on European Union and the Treaty on the Functioning of the European Union:

Article 1. Subject to Article 3, the United Kingdom and Ireland shall not take part in the adoption by the Council of proposed measures pursuant to Title V of Part Three of the Treaty on the Functioning of the European Union. The unanimity of the members of the Council, with the exception of the representatives of the governments of the United Kingdom and Ireland, shall be necessary for decisions of the Council which must be adopted unanimously.

For the purposes of this Article, a qualified majority shall be defined in accordance with Article 238(3) of the Treaty on the Functioning of the European Union.

Article 2. In consequence of Article 1 and subject to Articles 3, 4 and 6, none of the provisions of Title V of Part Three of the Treaty on the Functioning of the European Union, no measure adopted pursuant to that Title, no provision of any international agreement concluded by the Union pursuant to that Title, and no decision of the Court of Justice interpreting any such provision or measure shall be binding upon or applicable in the United Kingdom or Ireland; and no such provision, measure or decision shall in any way affect the competences, rights and obligations of those States; and no such provision, measure or decision shall in any way affect the Community or Union acquis nor form part of Union law as they apply to the United Kingdom or Ireland.

Article 3. (1) The United Kingdom or Ireland may notify the President of the Council in writing, within three months after a proposal or initiative has been presented to the Council pursuant to Title V of Part Three of the Treaty on the Functioning of the European Union, that it wishes to take part in the adoption and application of any such proposed measure, whereupon that State shall be entitled to do so.

The unanimity of the members of the Council, with the exception of a member which has not made such a notification, shall be necessary for decisions of the Council which must be adopted unanimously. A measure adopted under this paragraph shall be binding upon all Member States which took part in its adoption.

Measures adopted pursuant to Article 70 of the Treaty on the Functioning of the European Union shall lay down the conditions for the participation of the United Kingdom and Ireland in the evaluations concerning the areas covered by Title V of Part Three of that Treaty.

For the purposes of this Article, a qualified majority shall be defined in accordance with Article 238(3) of the Treaty on the Functioning of the European Union.

(2) If after a reasonable period of time a measure referred to in paragraph 1 cannot be adopted with the United Kingdom or Ireland taking part, the Council may adopt such measure in accordance with Article 1 without the participation of the United Kingdom or Ireland. In that case Article 2 applies.

Article 4. The United Kingdom or Ireland may at any time after the adoption of a measure by the Council pursuant to Title V of Part Three of the Treaty on the Functioning of the European Union notify its intention to the Council and to the Commission that it wishes to accept that measure. In that case, the procedure provided for in Article 331(1) of the Treaty on the Functioning of the European Union shall apply *mutatis mutandis*.

Article 4a. (1) The provisions of this Protocol apply for the United Kingdom and Ireland also to measures proposed or adopted pursuant to Title V of Part Three of the Treaty on the Functioning of the European Union amending an existing measure by which they are bound.
(2) However, in cases where the Council, acting on a proposal from the Commission, determines that the non–participation of the United Kingdom or Ireland in the amended version of an existing measure makes the application of that measure inoperable for other Member States or the Union, it may urge them to make a notification under Article 3 or 4. For the purposes of Article 3, a further period of two months starts to run as from the date of such determination by the Council.
If at the expiry of that period of two months from the Council's determination the United Kingdom or Ireland has not made a notification under Article 3 or Article 4, the existing measure shall no longer be binding upon or applicable to it, unless the Member State concerned has made a notification under Article 4 before the entry into force of the amending measure. This shall take effect from the date of entry into force of the amending measure or of expiry of the period of two months, whichever is the later.
For the purpose of this paragraph, the Council shall, after a full discussion of the matter, act by a qualified majority of its members representing the Member States participating or having participated in the adoption of the amending measure. A qualified majority of the Council shall be defined in accordance with Article 238(3)(a) of the Treaty on the Functioning of the European Union.
(3) The Council, acting by a qualified majority on a proposal from the Commission, may determine that the United Kingdom or Ireland shall bear the direct financial consequences, if any, necessarily and unavoidably incurred as a result of the cessation of its participation in the existing measure.
(4) This Article shall be without prejudice to Article 4.

Article 5. A Member State which is not bound by a measure adopted pursuant to Title V of Part Three of the Treaty on the Functioning of the European Union shall bear no financial consequences of that measure other than administrative costs entailed for the institutions, unless all members of the Council, acting unanimously after consulting the European Parliament, decide otherwise.

Article 6. Where, in cases referred to in this Protocol, the United Kingdom or Ireland is bound by a measure adopted by the Council pursuant to Title V of Part Three of the Treaty on the Functioning of the European Union, the relevant provisions of the Treaties shall apply to that State in relation to that measure.

Article 6a. The United Kingdom and Ireland shall not be bound by the rules laid down on the basis of Article 16 of the Treaty on the Functioning of the European Union which relate to the processing of personal data by the Member States when carrying out activities which fall within the scope of Chapter 4 or Chapter 5 of Title V of Part Three of that Treaty where the United Kingdom and Ireland are not bound by the rules governing the forms of judicial cooperation in criminal matters or police cooperation which require compliance with the provisions laid down on the basis of Article 16.

Article 7. Articles 3, 4 and 4a shall be without prejudice to the Protocol on the Schengen acquis integrated into the framework of the European Union.

Article 8. Ireland may notify the Council in writing that it no longer wishes to be covered by the terms of this Protocol. In that case, the normal treaty provisions will apply to Ireland.

Article 9. With regard to Ireland, this Protocol shall not apply to Article 75 of the Treaty on the Functioning of the European Union.

Protocol (No 22) on the Position of Denmark

THE HIGH CONTRACTING PARTIES,
RECALLING the Decision of the Heads of State or Government, meeting within the European Council at Edinburgh on 12 December 1992, concerning certain problems raised by Denmark on the Treaty on European Union,
HAVING NOTED the position of Denmark with regard to Citizenship, Economic and Monetary Union, Defence Policy and Justice and Home Affairs as laid down in the Edinburgh Decision,
CONSCIOUS of the fact that a continuation under the Treaties of the legal regime originating in the Edinburgh decision will significantly limit Denmark's participation in important areas of cooperation of the Union, and that it would be in the best interest of the Union to ensure the integrity of the acquis in the area of freedom, security and justice,
WISHING therefore to establish a legal framework that will provide an option for Denmark to

PART III EUROPEAN UNION

participate in the adoption of measures proposed on the basis of Title V of Part Three of the Treaty on the Functioning of the European Union and welcoming the intention of Denmark to avail itself of this option when possible in accordance with its constitutional requirements,
NOTING that Denmark will not prevent the other Member States from further developing their cooperation with respect to measures not binding on Denmark,
BEARING IN MIND Article 3 of the Protocol on the Schengen acquis integrated into the framework of the European Union,
HAVE AGREED UPON the following provisions, which shall be annexed to the Treaty on European Union and the Treaty on the Functioning of the European Union:

Part I.

Article 1. Denmark shall not take part in the adoption by the Council of proposed measures pursuant to Title V of Part Three of the Treaty on the Functioning of the European Union. The unanimity of the members of the Council, with the exception of the representative of the government of Denmark, shall be necessary for the decisions of the Council which must be adopted unanimously.
For the purposes of this Article, a qualified majority shall be defined in accordance with Article 238(3) of the Treaty on the Functioning of the European Union.

Article 2. None of the provisions of Title V of Part Three of the Treaty on the Functioning of the European Union, no measure adopted pursuant to that Title, no provision of any international agreement concluded by the Union pursuant to that Title, and no decision of the Court of Justice of the European Union interpreting any such provision or measure or any measure amended or amendable pursuant to that Title shall be binding upon or applicable in Denmark; and no such provision, measure or decision shall in any way affect the competences, rights and obligations of Denmark; and no such provision, measure or decision shall in any way affect the Community or Union acquis nor form part of Union law as they apply to Denmark. In particular, acts of the Union in the field of police cooperation and judicial cooperation in criminal matters adopted before the entry into force of the Treaty of Lisbon which are amended shall continue to be binding upon and applicable to Denmark unchanged.

Article 2a. Article 2 of this Protocol shall also apply in respect of those rules laid down on the basis of Article 16 of the Treaty on the Functioning of the European Union which relate to the processing of personal data by the Member States when carrying out activities which fall within the scope of Chapter 4 or Chapter 5 of Title V of Part Three of that Treaty.

Article 3. Denmark shall bear no financial consequences of measures referred to in Article 1, other than administrative costs entailed for the institutions.

Article 4. (1) Denmark shall decide within a period of six months after the Council has decided on a proposal or initiative to build upon the Schengen acquis covered by this Part, whether it will implement this measure in its national law. If it decides to do so, this measure will create an obligation under international law between Denmark and the other Member States bound by the measure.
(2) If Denmark decides not to implement a measure of the Council as referred to in paragraph 1, the Member States bound by that measure and Denmark will consider appropriate measures to be taken.

Part II.

Article 5. With regard to measures adopted by the Council pursuant to Article 26(1), Article 42 and Articles 43 to 46 of the Treaty on European Union, Denmark does not participate in the elaboration and the implementation of decisions and actions of the Union which have defence implications. Therefore Denmark shall not participate in their adoption. Denmark will not prevent the other Member States from further developing their cooperation in this area. Denmark shall not be obliged to contribute to the financing of operational expenditure arising from such measures, nor to make military capabilities available to the Union.
The unanimity of the members of the Council, with the exception of the representative of the government of Denmark, shall be necessary for the acts of the Council which must be adopted unanimously.
For the purposes of this Article, a qualified majority shall be defined in accordance with Article 238(3) of the Treaty on the Functioning of the European Union.

Part III.

Article 6. Articles 1, 2 and 3 shall not apply to measures determining the third countries whose nationals must be in possession of a visa when crossing the external borders of the Member States, or measures relating to a uniform format for visas.

PROTOCOLS TO THE TREATIES

Part IV.

Article 7. At any time Denmark may, in accordance with its constitutional requirements, inform the other Member States that it no longer wishes to avail itself of all or part of this Protocol. In that event, Denmark will apply in full all relevant measures then in force taken within the framework of the European Union.

Article 8. (1) At any time and without prejudice to Article 7, Denmark may, in accordance with its constitutional requirements, notify the other Member States that, with effect from the first day of the month following the notification, Part I shall consist of the provisions in the Annex. In that case Articles 5 to 8 shall be renumbered in consequence.
(2) Six months after the date on which the notification referred to in paragraph 1 takes effect all Schengen acquis and measures adopted to build upon this acquis, which until then have been binding on Denmark as obligations under international law, shall be binding upon Denmark as Union law.

Annex.

Article 1. Subject to Article 3, Denmark shall not take part in the adoption by the Council of measures proposed pursuant to Title V of Part Three of the Treaty on the Functioning of the European Union. The unanimity of the members of the Council, with the exception of the representative of the government of Denmark, shall be necessary for the acts of the Council which must be adopted unanimously.
For the purposes of this Article, a qualified majority shall be defined in accordance with Article 238(3) of the Treaty on the Functioning of the European Union.

Article 2. Pursuant to Article 1 and subject to Articles 3, 4 and 8, none of the provisions in Title V of Part Three of the Treaty on the Functioning of the European Union, no measure adopted pursuant to that Title, no provision of any international agreements concluded by the Union pursuant to that Title, no decision of the Court of Justice of the European Union interpreting any such provision or measure shall be binding upon or applicable in Denmark; and no such provision, measure or decision shall in any way affect the competences, rights and obligations of Denmark; and no such provision, measure or decision shall in any way affect the Community or Union acquis nor form part of Union law as they apply to Denmark.

Article 3. (1) Denmark may notify the President of the Council in writing, within three months after a proposal or initiative has been presented to the Council pursuant to Title V of Part Three of the Treaty on the Functioning of the European Union, that it wishes to take part in the adoption and application of any such proposed measure, whereupon Denmark shall be entitled to do so.
(2) If after a reasonable period of time a measure referred to in paragraph 1 cannot be adopted with Denmark taking part, the Council may adopt that measure referred to in paragraph 1 in accordance with Article 1 without the participation of Denmark. In that case Article 2 applies.

Article 4. Denmark may at any time after the adoption of a measure pursuant to Title V of Part Three of the Treaty on the Functioning of the European Union notify its intention to the Council and the Commission that it wishes to accept that measure. In that case, the procedure provided for in Article 331(1) of that Treaty shall apply *mutatis mutandis*.

Article 5. (1) The provisions of this Protocol apply for Denmark also to measures proposed or adopted pursuant to Title V of Part Three of the Treaty on the Functioning of the European Union amending an existing measure by which it is bound.
(2) However, in cases where the Council, acting on a proposal from the Commission, determines that the non–participation of Denmark in the amended version of an existing measure makes the application of that measure inoperable for other Member States or the Union, it may urge it to make a notification under Article 3 or 4. For the purposes of Article 3 a further period of two months starts to run as from the date of such determination by the Council.
If, at the expiry of that period of two months from the Council's determination, Denmark has not made a notification under Article 3 or Article 4, the existing measure shall no longer be binding upon or applicable to it, unless it has made a notification under Article 4 before the entry into force of the amending measure. This shall take effect from the date of entry into force of the amending measure or of expiry of the period of two months, whichever is the later.
For the purpose of this paragraph, the Council shall, after a full discussion of the matter, act by a qualified majority of its members representing the Member States participating or having participated in the adoption of the amending measure. A qualified majority of the Council shall be defined in

PART III EUROPEAN UNION

accordance with Article 238(3)(a) of the Treaty on the Functioning of the European Union.
(3) The Council, acting by a qualified majority on a proposal from the Commission, may determine that Denmark shall bear the direct financial consequences, if any, necessarily and unavoidably incurred as a result of the cessation of its participation in the existing measure.
(4) This Article shall be without prejudice to Article 4.

Article 6. (1) Notification pursuant to Article 4 shall be submitted no later than six months after the final adoption of a measure if this measure builds upon the Schengen acquis.
If Denmark does not submit a notification in accordance with Articles 3 or 4 regarding a measure building upon the Schengen acquis, the Member States bound by that measure and Denmark will consider appropriate measures to be taken.
(2) A notification pursuant to Article 3 with respect to a measure building upon the Schengen acquis shall be deemed irrevocably to be a notification pursuant to Article 3 with respect to any further proposal or initiative aiming to build upon that measure to the extent that such proposal or initiative builds upon the Schengen acquis.

Article 7. Denmark shall not be bound by the rules laid down on the basis of Article 16 of the Treaty on the Functioning of the European Union which relate to the processing of personal data by the Member States when carrying out activities which fall within the scope of Chapter 4 or Chapter 5 of Title V of Part Three of that Treaty where Denmark is not bound by the rules governing the forms of judicial cooperation in criminal matters or police cooperation which require compliance with the provisions laid down on the basis of Article 16.

Article 8. Where, in cases referred to in this Part, Denmark is bound by a measure adopted by the Council pursuant to Title V of Part Three of the Treaty on the Functioning of the European Union, the relevant provisions of the Treaties shall apply to Denmark in relation to that measure.

Article 9. Where Denmark is not bound by a measure adopted pursuant to Title V of Part Three of the Treaty on the Functioning of the European Union, it shall bear no financial consequences of that measure other than administrative costs entailed for the institutions unless the Council, with all its Members acting unanimously after consulting the European Parliament, decides otherwise.

Protocol (No 23) n External Relations of the Member States with regard to the Crossing of External Borders

THE HIGH CONTRACTING PARTIES,
TAKING INTO ACCOUNT the need of the Member States to ensure effective controls at their external borders, in cooperation with third countries where appropriate,
HAVE AGREED UPON the following provisions, which shall be annexed to the Treaty on European Union and to the Treaty on the Functioning of the European Union:
The provisions on the measures on the crossing of external borders included in Article 77(2)(b) of the Treaty on the Functioning of the European Union shall be without prejudice to the competence of Member States to negotiate or conclude agreements with third countries as long as they respect Union law and other relevant international agreements.

Protocol (No 24) on Asylum for Nationals of Member States of the European Union

THE HIGH CONTRACTING PARTIES,
WHEREAS, in accordance with Article 6(1) of the Treaty on European Union, the Union recognises the rights, freedoms and principles set out in the Charter of Fundamental Rights,
WHEREAS pursuant to Article 6(3) of the Treaty on European Union, fundamental rights, as guaranteed by the European Convention for the Protection of Human Rights and Fundamental Freedoms, constitute part of the Union's law as general principles,
WHEREAS the Court of Justice of the European Union has jurisdiction to ensure that in the interpretation and application of Article 6, paragraphs (1) and (3) of the Treaty on European Union the law is observed by the European Union,
WHEREAS pursuant to Article 49 of the Treaty on European Union any European State, when applying to become a Member of the Union, must respect the values set out in Article 2 of the Treaty on European Union,
BEARING IN MIND that Article 7 of the Treaty on European Union establishes a mechanism for

the suspension of certain rights in the event of a serious and persistent breach by a Member State of those values,
RECALLING that each national of a Member State, as a citizen of the Union, enjoys a special status and protection which shall be guaranteed by the Member States in accordance with the provisions of Part Two of the Treaty on the Functioning of the European Union,
BEARING IN MIND that the Treaties establish an area without internal frontiers and grant every citizen of the Union the right to move and reside freely within the territory of the Member States,
WISHING to prevent the institution of asylum being resorted to for purposes alien to those for which it is intended,
WHEREAS this Protocol respects the finality and the objectives of the Geneva Convention of 28 July 1951 relating to the status of refugees,
HAVE AGREED UPON the following provisions, which shall be annexed to the Treaty on European Union and to the Treaty on the Functioning of the European Union:

Sole Article. Given the level of protection of fundamental rights and freedoms by the Member States of the European Union, Member States shall be regarded as constituting safe countries of origin in respect of each other for all legal and practical purposes in relation to asylum matters. Accordingly, any application for asylum made by a national of a Member State may be taken into consideration or declared admissible for processing by another Member State only in the following cases:
(a) if the Member State of which the applicant is a national proceeds after the entry into force of the Treaty of Amsterdam, availing itself of the provisions of Article 15 of the European Convention for the Protection of Human Rights and Fundamental Freedoms, to take measures derogating in its territory from its obligations under that Convention;
(b) if the procedure referred to Article 7(1) of the Treaty on European Union has been initiated and until the Council, or, where appropriate, the European Council, takes a decision in respect thereof with regard to the Member State of which the applicant is a national;
(c) if the Council has adopted a decision in accordance with Article 7(1) of the Treaty on European Union in respect of the Member State of which the applicant is a national or if the European Council has adopted a decision in accordance with Article 7(2) of that Treaty in respect of the Member State of which the applicant is a national;
(d) if a Member State should so decide unilaterally in respect of the application of a national of another Member State; in that case the Council shall be immediately informed; the application shall be dealt with on the basis of the presumption that it is manifestly unfounded without affecting in any way, whatever the cases may be, the decision–making power of the Member State.

Protocol (No 25) on the Exercise of Shared Competence

THE HIGH CONTRACTING PARTIES,
HAVE AGREED UPON the following provisions, which shall be annexed to the Treaty on European Union and to the Treaty on the Functioning of the European Union:

Sole Article. With reference to Article 2(2) of the Treaty on the Functioning of the European Union on shared competence, when the Union has taken action in a certain area, the scope of this exercise of competence only covers those elements governed by the Union act in question and therefore does not cover the whole area.

Protocol (No 26) on Services of General Interest

THE HIGH CONTRACTING PARTIES,
WISHING to emphasise the importance of services of general interest,
HAVE AGREED UPON the following interpretative provisions, which shall be annexed to the Treaty on European Union and to the Treaty on the Functioning of the European Union:

Article 1. The shared values of the Union in respect of services of general economic interest within the meaning of Article 14 of the Treaty on the Functioning of the European Union include in particular:
– the essential role and the wide discretion of national, regional and local authorities in providing, commissioning and organising services of general economic interest as closely as possible to the needs of the users;
– the diversity between various services of general economic interest and the differences in the needs

PART III   EUROPEAN UNION

and preferences of users that may result from different geographical, social or cultural situations;
– a high level of quality, safety and affordability, equal treatment and the promotion of universal access and of user rights.

Article 2. The provisions of the Treaties do not affect in any way the competence of Member States to provide, commission and organise non–economic services of general interest.

Protocol (No 27) on the Internal Market and Competition

THE HIGH CONTRACTING PARTIES,
CONSIDERING that the internal market as set out in Article 3 of the Treaty on European Union includes a system ensuring that competition is not distorted,
HAVE AGREED that:
To this end, the Union shall, if necessary, take action under the provisions of the Treaties, including under Article 352 of the Treaty on the Functioning of the European Union.
This protocol shall be annexed to the Treaty on European Union and to the Treaty on the Functioning of the European Union.

Protocol (No 28) on Economic, Social and Territorial Cohesion

THE HIGH CONTRACTING PARTIES,
RECALLING that Article 3 of the Treaty on European Union includes the objective of promoting economic, social and territorial cohesion and solidarity between Member States and that the said cohesion figures among the areas of shared competence of the Union listed in Article 4(2)(c) of the Treaty on the Functioning of the European Union,
RECALLING that the provisions of Part Three, Title XVIII, on economic, social and territorial cohesion as a whole provide the legal basis for consolidating and further developing the Union's action in the field of economic, social and territorial cohesion, including the creation of a new fund,
RECALLING that the provisions of Article 177 of the Treaty on the Functioning of the European Union envisage setting up a Cohesion Fund,
NOTING that the European Investment Bank is lending large and increasing amounts for the benefit of the poorer regions,
NOTING the desire for greater flexibility in the arrangements for allocations from the Structural Funds,
NOTING the desire for modulation of the levels of Union participation in programmes and projects in certain countries,
NOTING the proposal to take greater account of the relative prosperity of Member States in the system of own resources,
REAFFIRM that the promotion of economic, social and territorial cohesion is vital to the full development and enduring success of the Union,
REAFFIRM their conviction that the Structural Funds should continue to play a considerable part in the achievement of Union objectives in the field of cohesion,
REAFFIRM their conviction that the European Investment Bank should continue to devote the majority of its resources to the promotion of economic, social and territorial cohesion, and declare their willingness to review the capital needs of the European Investment Bank as soon as this is necessary for that purpose,
AGREE that the Cohesion Fund will provide Union financial contributions to projects in the fields of environment and trans–European networks in Member States with a per capita GNP of less than 90 % of the Union average which have a programme leading to the fulfilment of the conditions of economic convergence as set out in Article 126,
DECLARE their intention of allowing a greater margin of flexibility in allocating financing from the Structural Funds to specific needs not covered under the present Structural Funds regulations,
DECLARE their willingness to modulate the levels of Union participation in the context of programmes and projects of the Structural Funds, with a view to avoiding excessive increases in budgetary expenditure in the less prosperous Member States,
RECOGNISE the need to monitor regularly the progress made towards achieving economic, social and territorial cohesion and state their willingness to study all necessary measures in this respect,
DECLARE their intention of taking greater account of the contributive capacity of individual Member States in the system of own resources, and of examining means of correcting, for the less

PROTOCOLS TO THE TREATIES

prosperous Member States, regressive elements existing in the present own resources system,
AGREE to annex this Protocol to the Treaty on European Union and the Treaty on the Functioning of the European Union.

Protocol (No 29) on the System of Public Broadcasting in the Member States

THE HIGH CONTRACTING PARTIES,
CONSIDERING that the system of public broadcasting in the Member States is directly related to the democratic, social and cultural needs of each society and to the need to preserve media pluralism,
HAVE AGREED UPON the following interpretive provisions, which shall be annexed to the Treaty on European Union and to the Treaty on the Functioning of the European Union:
The provisions of the Treaties shall be without prejudice to the competence of Member States to provide for the funding of public service broadcasting and in so far as such funding is granted to broadcasting organisations for the fulfilment of the public service remit as conferred, defined and organised by each Member State, and in so far as such funding does not affect trading conditions and competition in the Union to an extent which would be contrary to the common interest, while the realisation of the remit of that public service shall be taken into account.

Protocol (No 30) on the Application of the Charter of Fundamental Rights of the European Union to Poland and the United Kingdom

THE HIGH CONTRACTING PARTIES,
WHEREAS in Article 6 of the Treaty on European Union, the Union recognises the rights, freedoms and principles set out in the Charter of Fundamental Rights of the European Union,
WHEREAS the Charter is to be applied in strict accordance with the provisions of the aforementioned Article 6 and Title VII of the Charter itself,
WHEREAS the aforementioned Article 6 requires the Charter to be applied and interpreted by the courts of Poland and of the United Kingdom strictly in accordance with the explanations referred to in that Article,
WHEREAS the Charter contains both rights and principles,
WHEREAS the Charter contains both provisions which are civil and political in character and those which are economic and social in character,
WHEREAS the Charter reaffirms the rights, freedoms and principles recognised in the Union and makes those rights more visible, but does not create new rights or principles,
RECALLING the obligations devolving upon Poland and the United Kingdom under the Treaty on European Union, the Treaty on the Functioning of the European Union, and Union law generally,
NOTING the wish of Poland and the United Kingdom to clarify certain aspects of the application of the Charter,
DESIROUS therefore of clarifying the application of the Charter in relation to the laws and administrative action of Poland and of the United Kingdom and of its justiciability within Poland and within the United Kingdom,
REAFFIRMING that references in this Protocol to the operation of specific provisions of the Charter are strictly without prejudice to the operation of other provisions of the Charter,
REAFFIRMING that this Protocol is without prejudice to the application of the Charter to other Member States,
REAFFIRMING that this Protocol is without prejudice to other obligations devolving upon Poland and the United Kingdom under the Treaty on European Union, the Treaty on the Functioning of the European Union, and Union law generally,
HAVE AGREED UPON the following provisions, which shall be annexed to the Treaty on European Union and to the Treaty on the Functioning of the European Union:

Article 1. (1) The Charter does not extend the ability of the Court of Justice of the European Union, or any court or tribunal of Poland or of the United Kingdom, to find that the laws, regulations or administrative provisions, practices or action of Poland or of the United Kingdom are inconsistent with the fundamental rights, freedoms and principles that it reaffirms.
(2) In particular, and for the avoidance of doubt, nothing in Title IV of the Charter creates justiciable rights applicable to Poland or the United Kingdom except in so far as Poland or the United Kingdom has provided for such rights in its national law.

PART III EUROPEAN UNION

Article 2. To the extent that a provision of the Charter refers to national laws and practices, it shall only apply to Poland or the United Kingdom to the extent that the rights or principles that it contains are recognised in the law or practices of Poland or of the United Kingdom.

Protocol (No 31) Concerning Imports into the European Union of Petroleum Products Refined in the Netherlands Antilles

THE HIGH CONTRACTING PARTIES,
BEING DESIROUS of giving fuller details about the system of trade applicable to imports into the European Union of petroleum products refined in the Netherlands Antilles,
HAVE AGREED UPON the following provisions, which shall be annexed to the Treaty on European Union and to the Treaty on the Functioning of the European Union:

Article 1. This Protocol is applicable to petroleum products coming under the Brussels Nomenclature numbers 27(1)0, 27(1)1, 27(1)2, ex 27(1)3 (paraffin wax, petroleum or shale wax and paraffin residues) and 27(1)4, imported for use in Member States.

Article 2. Member States shall undertake to grant to petroleum products refined in the Netherlands Antilles the tariff preferences resulting from the association of the latter with the Union, under the conditions provided for in this Protocol. These provisions shall hold good whatever may be the rules of origin applied by the Member States.

Article 3. (1) When the Commission, at the request of a Member State or on its own initiative, establishes that imports into the Union of petroleum products refined in the Netherlands Antilles under the system provided for in Article 2 above are giving rise to real difficulties on the market of one or more Member States, it shall decide that customs duties on the said imports shall be introduced, increased or re–introduced by the Member States in question, to such an extent and for such a period as may be necessary to meet that situation. The rates of the customs duties thus introduced, increased or re–introduced may not exceed the customs duties applicable to third countries for these same products.
(2) The provisions of paragraph 1 can in any case be applied when imports into the Union of petroleum products refined in the Netherlands Antilles reach two million metric tons a year.
(3) The Council shall be informed of decisions taken by the Commission in pursuance of paragraphs 1 and 2, including those directed at rejecting the request of a Member State. The Council shall, at the request of any Member State, assume responsibility for the matter and may at any time amend or revoke them.

Article 4. (1) If a Member State considers that imports of petroleum products refined in the Netherlands Antilles, made either directly or through another Member State under the system provided for in Article 2 above, are giving rise to real difficulties on its market and that immediate action is necessary to meet them, it may on its own initiative decide to apply customs duties to such imports, the rate of which may not exceed those of the customs duties applicable to third countries in respect of the same products. It shall notify its decision to the Commission which shall decide within one month whether the measures taken by the State should be maintained or must be amended or cancelled. The provisions of Article 3(3) shall be applicable to such decision of the Commission.
(2) When the quantities of petroleum products refined in the Netherlands Antilles imported either directly or through another Member State, under the system provided for in Article 2 above, into a Member State or States of the European Union exceed during a calendar year the tonnage shown in the Annex to this Protocol, the measures taken in pursuance of paragraph 1 by that or those Member States for the current year shall be considered to be justified; the Commission shall, after assuring itself that the tonnage fixed has been reached, formally record the measures taken. In such a case the other Member States shall abstain from formally placing the matter before the Council.

Article 5. If the Union decides to apply quantitative restrictions to petroleum products, no matter whence they are imported, these restrictions may also be applied to imports of such products from the Netherlands Antilles. In such a case preferential treatment shall be granted to the Netherlands Antilles as compared with third countries.

Article 6. (1) The provisions of Articles 2 to 5 shall be reviewed by the Council, by unanimous decision, after consulting the European Parliament and the Commission, when a common definition of origin for petroleum products from third countries and associated countries is adopted, or when decisions are taken within the framework of a common commercial policy for the products in question or when a common energy policy is established.

(2) When such revision is made, however, equivalent preferences must in any case be maintained in favour of the Netherlands Antilles in a suitable form and for a minimum quantity of 21½ million metric tons of petroleum products.

(3) The Union's commitments in regard to equivalent preferences as mentioned in paragraph 2 of this Article may, if necessary, be broken down country by country taking into account the tonnage indicated in the Annex to this Protocol.

Article 7. For the implementation of this Protocol, the Commission is responsible for following the pattern of imports into the Member States of petroleum products refined in the Netherlands Antilles. Member States shall communicate to the Commission, which shall see that it is circulated, all useful information to that end in accordance with the administrative conditions recommended by it.

Annex to the protocol
For the implementation of Article 4(2) of the Protocol concerning imports into the European Union of petroleum products refined in the Netherlands Antilles, the High Contracting Parties have decided that the quantity of 2 million metric tons of petroleum products from the Antilles shall be allocated among the Member States as follows:
Germany … | 625000 metric tons |
Belgo–Luxembourg Economic Union … | 200000 metric tons |
France … | 75000 metric tons |
Italy … | 100000 metric tons |
Netherlands … | 1000000 metric tons |

Protocol (No 32) on the Acquisition of Property in Denmark

THE HIGH CONTRACTING PARTIES,
DESIRING to settle certain particular problems relating to Denmark,
HAVE AGREED UPON the following provisions, which shall be annexed to the Treaty on European Union and to the Treaty on the Functioning of the European Union:
Notwithstanding the provisions of the Treaties, Denmark may maintain the existing legislation on the acquisition of second homes.

Protocol (No 33) Concerning Article 157 of the Treaty on the Functioning of the European Union

THE HIGH CONTRACTING PARTIES,
HAVE AGREED upon the following provision, which shall be annexed to the Treaty on European Union and to the Treaty on the Functioning of the European Union:
For the purposes of Article 157 of the Treaty on the Functioning of the European Union, benefits under occupational social security schemes shall not be considered as remuneration if and in so far as they are attributable to periods of employment prior to 17 May 1990, except in the case of workers or those claiming under them who have before that date initiated legal proceedings or introduced an equivalent claim under the applicable national law.

Protocol (No 34) on Special Arrangements for Greenland

Sole Article. (1) The treatment on import into the Union of products subject to the common organisation of the market in fishery products, originating in Greenland, shall, while complying with the mechanisms of the internal market organisation, involve exemption from customs duties and charges having equivalent effect and the absence of quantitative restrictions or measures having equivalent effect if the possibilities for access to Greenland fishing zones granted to the Union pursuant to an agreement between the Union and the authority responsible for Greenland are satisfactory to the Union.

(2) All measures relating to the import arrangements for such products, including those relating to the adoption of such measures, shall be adopted in accordance with the procedure laid down in Article 43 of the Treaty establishing the European Union.

PART III   EUROPEAN UNION

Protocol (No 35) on Article 40.3.3 of the Constitution of Ireland

THE HIGH CONTRACTING PARTIES,
HAVE AGREED upon the following provision, which shall be annexed to the Treaty on European Union and to the Treaty on the Functioning of the European Union and to the Treaty establishing the European Atomic Energy Community:
Nothing in the Treaties, or in the Treaty establishing the European Atomic Energy Community, or in the Treaties or Acts modifying or supplementing those Treaties, shall affect the application in Ireland of Article 40.3.3 of the Constitution of Ireland.

Protocol (No 36) on Transitional Provisions

THE HIGH CONTRACTING PARTIES,
WHEREAS, in order to organise the transition from the institutional provisions of the Treaties applicable prior to the entry into force of the Treaty of Lisbon to the provisions contained in that Treaty, it is necessary to lay down transitional provisions,
HAVE AGREED UPON the following provisions, which shall be annexed to the Treaty on European Union, to the Treaty on the Functioning of the European Union and to the Treaty establishing the European Atomic Energy Community:

Article 1. In this Protocol, the words "the Treaties" shall mean the Treaty on European Union, the Treaty on the Functioning of the European Union and the Treaty establishing the European Atomic Energy Community.

Title I. Provisions Concerning the European Parliament

Article 2. (1) For the period of the 2009–2014 parliamentary term remaining at the date of entry into force of this Article, and by way of derogation from Articles 189, second paragraph, and 190(2) of the Treaty establishing the European Community and Articles 107, second paragraph, and 108(2) of the Treaty establishing the European Atomic Energy Community, which were in force at the time of the European Parliament elections in June 2009, and by way of derogation from the number of seats provided for in the first subparagraph of Article 14(2) of the Treaty on European Union, the following 18 seats shall be added to the existing 736 seats, thus provisionally bringing the total number of members of the European Parliament to 754 until the end of the 2009–2014 parliamentary term:
Bulgaria | 1 |
Spain | 4 |
France | 2 |
Italy | 1 |
Latvia | 1 |
Malta | 1 |
Netherlands | 1 |
Austria | 2 |
Poland | 1 |
Slovenia | 1 |
Sweden | 2 |
United Kingdom | 1 |
(2) By way of derogation from Article 14(3) of the Treaty on European Union, the Member States concerned shall designate the persons who will fill the additional seats referred to in paragraph 1, in accordance with the legislation of the Member States concerned and provided that the persons in question have been elected by direct universal suffrage:
(a) in ad hoc elections by direct universal suffrage in the Member State concerned, in accordance with the provisions applicable for elections to the European Parliament;
(b) by reference to the results of the European Parliament elections from 4 to 7 June 2009; or
(c) by designation, by the national parliament of the Member State concerned from among its members, of the requisite number of members, according to the procedure determined by each of those Member States.
(3) In accordance with the second subparagraph of Article 14(2) of the Treaty on European Union, the European Council shall adopt a decision determining the composition of the European Parliament in good time before the 2014 European Parliament elections.

Title II. Provisions Concerning the Qualified Majority

PROTOCOLS TO THE TREATIES

Article 3. (1) In accordance with Article 16(4) of the Treaty on European Union, the provisions of that paragraph and of Article 238(2) of the Treaty on the Functioning of the European Union relating to the definition of the qualified majority in the European Council and the Council shall take effect on 1 November 2014.
(2) Between 1 November 2014 and 31 March 2017, when an act is to be adopted by qualified majority, a member of the Council may request that it be adopted in accordance with the qualified majority as defined in paragraph 3. In that case, paragraphs 3 and 4 shall apply.
(3) Until 31 October 2014, the following provisions shall remain in force, without prejudice to the second subparagraph of Article 235(1) of the Treaty on the Functioning of the European Union.
For acts of the European Council and of the Council requiring a qualified majority, members' votes shall be weighted as follows:
Belgium | 12 |
Bulgaria | 10 |
Czech Republic | 12 |
Denmark | 7 |
Germany | 29 |
Estonia | 4 |
Ireland | 7 |
Greece | 12 |
Spain | 27 |
France | 29 |
Croatia | 7 |
Italy | 29 |
Cyprus | 4 |
Latvia | 4 |
Lithuania | 7 |
Luxembourg | 4 |
Hungary | 12 |
Malta | 3 |
Netherlands | 13 |
Austria | 10 |
Poland | 27 |
Portugal | 12 |
Romania | 14 |
Slovenia | 4 |
Slovakia | 7 |
Finland | 7 |
Sweden | 10 |
United Kingdom | 29 |
Acts shall be adopted if there are at least 260 votes in favour representing a majority of the members where, under the Treaties, they must be adopted on a proposal from the Commission. In other cases decisions shall be adopted if there are at least 260 votes in favour representing at least two thirds of the members.
A member of the European Council or the Council may request that, where an act is adopted by the European Council or the Council by a qualified majority, a check is made to ensure that the Member States comprising the qualified majority represent at least 62 % of the total population of the Union. If that proves not to be the case, the act shall not be adopted.
(4) Until 31 October 2014, the qualified majority shall, in cases where, under the Treaties, not all the members of the Council participate in voting, namely in the cases where reference is made to the qualified majority as defined in Article 238(3) of the Treaty on the Functioning of the European Union, be defined as the same proportion of the weighted votes and the same proportion of the number of the Council members and, if appropriate, the same percentage of the population of the Member States concerned as laid down in paragraph 3 of this Article.

Title III. Provisions Concerning the Configurations of the Council

Article 4. Until the entry into force of the decision referred to in the first subparagraph of Article 16(6) of the Treaty on European Union, the Council may meet in the configurations laid down in the second and third subparagraphs of that paragraph and in the other configurations on the list established by a decision of the General Affairs Council, acting by a simple majority.

PART III   EUROPEAN UNION

Title IV. Provisions Concerning the Commission, including the High Representative of the Union for Foreign Affairs and Security Policy

Article 5. The members of the Commission in office on the date of entry into force of the Treaty of Lisbon shall remain in office until the end of their term of office. However, on the day of the appointment of the High Representative of the Union for Foreign Affairs and Security Policy, the term of office of the member having the same nationality as the High Representative shall end.

Title V. Provisions Concerning the Secretary–General of the Council, High Representative for the Common Foreign and Security Policy, and the Deputy Secretary–General of the Council

Article 6. The terms of office of the Secretary–General of the Council, High Representative for the common foreign and security policy, and the Deputy Secretary–General of the Council shall end on the date of entry into force of the Treaty of Lisbon. The Council shall appoint a Secretary–General in conformity with Article 240(2) of the Treaty on the Functioning of the European Union.

Title VI. Provisions Concerning Advisory Bodies

Article 7. Until the entry into force of the decision referred to in Article 301 of the Treaty on the Functioning of the European Union, the allocation of members of the Economic and Social Committee shall be as follows:
Belgium | 12 |
Bulgaria | 12 |
Czech Republic | 12 |
Denmark | 9 |
Germany | 24 |
Estonia | 7 |
Ireland | 9 |
Greece | 12 |
Spain | 21 |
France | 24 |
Croatia | 9 |
Italy | 24 |
Cyprus | 6 |
Latvia | 7 |
Lithuania | 9 |
Luxembourg | 6 |
Hungary | 12 |
Malta | 5 |
Netherlands | 12 |
Austria | 12 |
Poland | 21 |
Portugal | 12 |
Romania | 15 |
Slovenia | 7 |
Slovakia | 9 |
Finland | 9 |
Sweden | 12 |
United Kingdom | 24 |

Article 8. Until the entry into force of the decision referred to in Article 305 of the Treaty on the Functioning of the European Union, the allocation of members of the Committee of the Regions shall be as follows:
Belgium | 12 |
Bulgaria | 12 |
Czech Republic | 12 |
Denmark | 9 |
Germany | 24 |
Estonia | 7 |
Ireland | 9 |
Greece | 12 |
Spain | 21 |

France | 24 |
Croatia | 9 |
Italy | 24 |
Cyprus | 6 |
Latvia | 7 |
Lithuania | 9 |
Luxembourg | 6 |
Hungary | 12 |
Malta | 5 |
Netherlands | 12 |
Austria | 12 |
Poland | 21 |
Portugal | 12 |
Romania | 15 |
Slovenia | 7 |
Slovakia | 9 |
Finland | 9 |
Sweden | 12 |
United Kingdom | 24 |

Title VII. Transitional Provisions Concerning Acts Adopted on the Basis of Titles V and VI of the Treaty on European Union Prior to the Entry into Force of the Treaty of Lisbon

Article 9. The legal effects of the acts of the institutions, bodies, offices and agencies of the Union adopted on the basis of the Treaty on European Union prior to the entry into force of the Treaty of Lisbon shall be preserved until those acts are repealed, annulled or amended in implementation of the Treaties. The same shall apply to agreements concluded between Member States on the basis of the Treaty on European Union.

Article 10. (1) As a transitional measure, and with respect to acts of the Union in the field of police cooperation and judicial cooperation in criminal matters which have been adopted before the entry into force of the Treaty of Lisbon, the powers of the institutions shall be the following at the date of entry into force of that Treaty: the powers of the Commission under Article 258 of the Treaty on the Functioning of the European Union shall not be applicable and the powers of the Court of Justice of the European Union under Title VI of the Treaty on European Union, in the version in force before the entry into force of the Treaty of Lisbon, shall remain the same, including where they have been accepted under Article 35(2) of the said Treaty on European Union.
(2) The amendment of an act referred to in paragraph 1 shall entail the applicability of the powers of the institutions referred to in that paragraph as set out in the Treaties with respect to the amended act for those Member States to which that amended act shall apply.
(3) In any case, the transitional measure mentioned in paragraph 1 shall cease to have effect five years after the date of entry into force of the Treaty of Lisbon.
(4) At the latest six months before the expiry of the transitional period referred to in paragraph 3, the United Kingdom may notify to the Council that it does not accept, with respect to the acts referred to in paragraph 1, the powers of the institutions referred to in paragraph 1 as set out in the Treaties. In case the United Kingdom has made that notification, all acts referred to in paragraph 1 shall cease to apply to it as from the date of expiry of the transitional period referred to in paragraph 3. This subparagraph shall not apply with respect to the amended acts which are applicable to the United Kingdom as referred to in paragraph 2.
The Council, acting by a qualified majority on a proposal from the Commission, shall determine the necessary consequential and transitional arrangements. The United Kingdom shall not participate in the adoption of this decision. A qualified majority of the Council shall be defined in accordance with Article 238(3)(a) of the Treaty on the Functioning of the European Union.
The Council, acting by a qualified majority on a proposal from the Commission, may also adopt a decision determining that the United Kingdom shall bear the direct financial consequences, if any, necessarily and unavoidably incurred as a result of the cessation of its participation in those acts.
(5) The United Kingdom may, at any time afterwards, notify the Council of its wish to participate in acts which have ceased to apply to it pursuant to paragraph 4, first subparagraph. In that case, the relevant provisions of the Protocol on the Schengen acquis integrated into the framework of the European Union or of the Protocol on the position of the United Kingdom and Ireland in respect of the area of freedom, security and justice, as the case may be, shall apply. The powers of the institutions

with regard to those acts shall be those set out in the Treaties. When acting under the relevant Protocols, the Union institutions and the United Kingdom shall seek to re–establish the widest possible measure of participation of the United Kingdom in the acquis of the Union in the area of freedom, security and justice without seriously affecting the practical operability of the various parts thereof, while respecting their coherence.

Protocol (No 37) on the Financial Consequences of the Expiry of the ECSC Treaty and on the Research Fund for Coal and Steel

THE HIGH CONTRACTING PARTIES,
RECALLING that all assets and liabilities of the European Coal and Steel Community, as they existed on 23 July 2002, were transferred to the European Community on 24 July 2002,
TAKING ACCOUNT of the desire to use these funds for research in sectors related to the coal and steel industry and therefore the necessity to provide for certain special rules in this regard,
HAVE AGREED UPON the following provisions, which shall be annexed to the Treaty on European Union and to the Treaty on the Functioning of the European Union:

Article 1. (1) The net worth of these assets and liabilities, as they appear in the balance sheet of the ECSC of 23 July 2002, subject to any increase or decrease which may occur as a result of the liquidation operations, shall be considered as assets intended for research in the sectors related to the coal and steel industry, referred to as the "ECSC in liquidation". On completion of the liquidation they shall be referred to as the "assets of the Research Fund for Coal and Steel".
(2) The revenue from these assets, referred to as the "Research Fund for Coal and Steel", shall be used exclusively for research, outside the research framework programme, in the sectors related to the coal and steel industry in accordance with the provisions of this Protocol and of acts adopted on the basis hereof.

Article 2. The Council, acting in accordance with a special legislative procedure and after obtaining the consent of the European Parliament, shall adopt all the necessary provisions for the implementation of this Protocol, including essential principles.
The Council shall adopt, on a proposal from the Commission and after consulting the European Parliament, measures establishing multiannual financial guidelines for managing the assets of the Research Fund for Coal and Steel and technical guidelines for the research programme of the Research Fund for Coal and Steel.

Article 3. Except as otherwise provided in this Protocol and in the acts adopted on the basis hereof, the provisions of the Treaties shall apply.

ANNEXES TO THE TREATIES

Annexes to the Treaties

Annex I

List referred to in Article 38 of the Treaty on the Functioning of the European Union (1) | (2) |
No in the Brussels nomenclature | Description of products |
Chapter 1 | Live animals |
Chapter 2 | Meat and edible meat offal |
Chapter 3 | Fish, crustaceans and molluscs |
Chapter 4 | Dairy produce; birds' eggs; natural honey |
Chapter 5
05.04 | Guts, bladders and stomachs of animals (other than fish), whole and pieces thereof |
05.15 | Animal products not elsewhere specified or included; dead animals of Chapter 1 or Chapter 3, unfit for human consumption |
Chapter 6 | Live trees and other plants; bulbs, roots and the like; cut flowers and ornamental foliage |
Chapter 7 | Edible vegetables and certain roots and tubers |
Chapter 8 | Edible fruit and nuts; peel of melons or citrus fruit |
Chapter 9 | Coffee, tea and spices, excluding maté (heading No 09.03) |
Chapter 10 | Cereals |
Chapter 11 | Products of the milling industry; malt and starches; gluten; inulin |
Chapter 12 | Oil seeds and oleaginous fruit; miscellaneous grains, seeds and fruit; industrial and medical plants; straw and fodder |
Chapter 13
ex 13.03 | Pectin |
Chapter 15
15.01 | Lard and other rendered pig fat; rendered poultry fat |
15.02 | Unrendered fats of bovine cattle, sheep or goats; tallow (including "premier jus") produced from those fats |
15.03 | Lard stearin, oleostearin and tallow stearin; lard oil, oleo–oil and tallow oil, not emulsified or mixed or prepared in any way |
15.04 | Fats and oil, of fish and marine mammals, whether or not refined |
15.07 | Fixed vegetable oils, fluid or solid, crude, refined or purified |
15.12 | Animal or vegetable fats and oils, hydrogenated, whether or not refined, but not further prepared |
15.13 | Margarine, imitation lard and other prepared edible fats |
15.17 | Residues resulting from the treatment of fatty substances or animal or vegetable waxes |
Chapter 16 | Preparations of meat, of fish, of crustaceans or molluscs |
Chapter 17
17.01 | Beet sugar and cane sugar, solid |
17.02 | Other sugars; sugar syrups; artificial honey (whether or not mixed with natural honey); caramel |
17.03 | Molasses, whether or not decolourised |
17.05 [1] | Flavoured or coloured sugars, syrups and molasses (including vanilla sugar or vanillin), with the exception of fruit juice containing added sugar in any proportion |
Chapter 18
18.01 | Cocoa beans, whole or broken, raw or roasted |
18.02 | Cocoa shells, husks, skins and waste |
Chapter 20 | Preparations of vegetables, fruit or other parts of plants |
Chapter 22
22.04 | Grape must, in fermentation or with fermentation arrested otherwise than by the addition of alcohol |
22.05 | Wine of fresh grapes; grape must with fermentation arrested by the addition of alcohol |
22.07 | Other fermented beverages (for example, cider, perry and mead) |
ex 22.08 [1] ex 22.09 [1] | Ethyl alcohol or neutral spirits, whether or not denatured, of any strength, obtained from agricultural products listed in Annex I, excluding liqueurs and other spirituous beverages and compound alcoholic preparations (known as "concentrated extracts") for the manufacture of beverages |
22.10 [1] | Vinegar and substitutes for vinegar |
Chapter 23 | Residues and waste from the food industries; prepared animal fodder |
Chapter 24

PART III   EUROPEAN UNION

24.01 | Unmanufactured tobacco, tobacco refuse |
Chapter 45
45.01 | Natural cork, unworked, crushed, granulated or ground; waste cork |
Chapter 54
54.01 | Flax, raw or processed but not spun; flax tow and waste (including pulled or garnetted rags) |
Chapter 57
57.01 | True hemp (Cannabis sativa), raw or processed but not spun; tow and waste of true hemp (including pulled or garnetted rags or ropes) |

Annex II

Overseas Countries and Territories to which the Provisions of Part Four of the Treaty on the Functioning of the European Union Apply
– Greenland,
– New Caledonia and Dependencies,
– French Polynesia,
– French Southern and Antarctic Territories,
– Wallis and Futuna Islands,
– Mayotte,
– Saint Pierre and Miquelon,
– Aruba,
– Netherlands Antilles:
– Bonaire,
– Curaçao,
– Saba,
– Sint Eustatius,
– Sint Maarten,
– Anguilla,
– Cayman Islands,
– Falkland Islands,
– South Georgia and the South Sandwich Islands,
– Montserrat,
– Pitcairn,
– Saint Helena and Dependencies,
– British Antarctic Territory,
– British Indian Ocean Territory,
– Turks and Caicos Islands,
– British Virgin Islands,
– Bermuda.

DECLARATIONS ATTACHED TO THE TREATIES

Declarations attached to the Treaties
annexed to the Final Act of the Intergovernmental Conference which adopted the Treaty of Lisbon, signed on 13 December 2007

A. Declarations Concerning Provisions of the Treaties

1. Declaration concerning the Charter of Fundamental Rights of the European Union

The Charter of Fundamental Rights of the European Union, which has legally binding force, confirms the fundamental rights guaranteed by the European Convention for the Protection of Human Rights and Fundamental Freedoms and as they result from the constitutional traditions common to the Member States.

The Charter does not extend the field of application of Union law beyond the powers of the Union or establish any new power or task for the Union,
or modify powers and tasks as defined by the Treaties.

---

2. Declaration on Article 6(2) of the Treaty on European Union

The Conference agrees that the Union's accession to the European Convention for the Protection of Human Rights and Fundamental Freedoms should be arranged in such a way as to preserve the specific features of Union law. In this connection, the Conference notes the existence of a regular dialogue between the Court of Justice of the European Union and the European Court of Human Rights; such dialogue could be reinforced when the Union accedes to that Convention.

---

3. Declaration on Article 8 of the Treaty on European Union

The Union will take into account the particular situation of small–sized countries which maintain specific relations of proximity with it.

---

4. Declaration on the composition of the European Parliament

The additional seat in the European Parliament will be attributed to Italy.

---

5. Declaration on the political agreement by the European Council concerning the draft Decision on the composition of the European Parliament

The European Council will give its political agreement on the revised draft Decision on the composition of the European Parliament for the legislative period 2009–2014, based on the proposal from the European Parliament.

---

6. Declaration on Article 15(5) and (6), Article 17(6) and (7) and Article 18 of the Treaty on European Union

In choosing the persons called upon to hold the offices of President of the European Council, President of the Commission and High Representative of the Union for Foreign Affairs and Security Policy, due account is to be taken of the need to respect the geographical and demographic diversity of the Union and its Member States.

---

7. Declaration on Article 16(4) of the Treaty on European Union and Article 238(2) of the Treaty on the Functioning of the European Union

The Conference declares that the decision relating to the implementation of Article 16(4) of the Treaty on European Union and Article 238(2) of the Treaty on the Functioning of the European Union will be adopted by the Council on the date of the signature of the Treaty of Lisbon and will enter into force on the day that Treaty enters into force. The draft decision is set out below:

PART III   EUROPEAN UNION

*Draft Decision of the Council
relating to the implementation of Article 16(4) of the Treaty on European Union and Article 238(2) of the Treaty on the Functioning of the European Union between 1 November 2014 and 31 March 2017 on the one hand, and as from 1 April 2017 on the other*
THE COUNCIL OF THE EUROPEAN UNION,
Whereas:
(1) Provisions should be adopted allowing for a smooth transition from the system for decision-making in the Council by a qualified majority as defined in Article 3(3) of the Protocol on the transitional provisions, which will continue to apply until 31 October 2014, to the voting system provided for in Article 16(4) of the Treaty on European Union and Article 238(2) of the Treaty on the Functioning of the European Union, which will apply with effect from 1 November 2014, including, during a transitional period until 31 March 2017, specific provisions laid down in Article 3(2) of that Protocol.
(2) It is recalled that it is the practice of the Council to devote every effort to strengthening the democratic legitimacy of decisions taken by a qualified majority,
HAS DECIDED AS FOLLOWS:
Section 1. Provisions to be applied from 1 November 2014 to 31 March 2017
Article 1. *From 1 November 2014 to 31 March 2017, if members of the Council, representing:*
(a) at least three quarters of the population, or
*(b) at least three quarters of the number of Member States
necessary to constitute a blocking minority resulting from the application of Article 16(4), first subparagraph, of the Treaty on European Union or Article 238(2) of the Treaty on the Functioning of the European Union, indicate their opposition to the Council adopting an act by a qualified majority, the Council shall discuss the issue.*
Article 2. *The Council shall, in the course of these discussions, do all in its power to reach, within a reasonable time and without prejudicing obligatory time limits laid down by Union law, a satisfactory solution to address concerns raised by the members of the Council referred to in Article 1.*
Article 3. *To this end, the President of the Council, with the assistance of the Commission and in compliance with the Rules of Procedure of the Council, shall undertake any initiative necessary to facilitate a wider basis of agreement in the Council. The members of the Council shall lend him or her their assistance.*
Section 2. Provisions to be applied as from 1 April 2017
Article 4. *As from 1 April 2017, if members of the Council, representing:*
(a) at least 55 % of the population, or
*(b) at least 55 % of the number of Member States
necessary to constitute a blocking minority resulting from the application of Article 16(4), first subparagraph, of the Treaty on European Union or Article 238(2) of the Treaty on the Functioning of the European Union, indicate their opposition to the Council adopting an act by a qualified majority, the Council shall discuss the issue.*
Article 5. *The Council shall, in the course of these discussions, do all in its power to reach, within a reasonable time and without prejudicing obligatory time limits laid down by Union law, a satisfactory solution to address concerns raised by the members of the Council referred to in Article 4.*
Article 6. *To this end, the President of the Council, with the assistance of the Commission and in compliance with the Rules of Procedure of the Council, shall undertake any initiative necessary to facilitate a wider basis of agreement in the Council. The members of the Council shall lend him or her their assistance.*
Section 3. Entry into force
Article 7. *This Decision shall enter into force on the date of the entry into force of the Treaty of Lisbon.*

---

8. Declaration on practical measures to be taken upon the entry into force of the Treaty of Lisbon as regards the Presidency of the European Council and of the Foreign Affairs Council

In the event that the Treaty of Lisbon enters into force later than 1 January 2009, the Conference requests the competent authorities of the Member State holding the six–monthly Presidency of the Council at that time, on the one hand, and the person elected President of the European Council and the person appointed High Representative of the Union for Foreign Affairs and Security Policy, on the other hand, to take the necessary specific measures, in consultation with the following six–monthly Presidency, to allow an efficient handover of the material and organisational aspects of the Presidency of the European Council and of the Foreign Affairs Council.

DECLARATIONS ATTACHED TO THE TREATIES

9. Declaration on Article 16(9) of the Treaty on European Union concerning the European Council decision on the exercise of the Presidency of the Council

The Conference declares that the Council should begin preparing the decision establishing the procedures for implementing the decision on the exercise of the Presidency of the Council as soon as the Treaty of Lisbon is signed, and should give its political approval within six months. A draft decision of the European Council, which will be adopted on the date of entry into force of the said Treaty, is set out below:

Draft decision of the European Council
on the exercise of the Presidency of the Council

Article 1. *(1) The Presidency of the Council, with the exception of the Foreign Affairs configuration, shall be held by pre–established groups of three Member States for a period of 18 months. The groups shall be made up on a basis of equal rotation among the Member States, taking into account their diversity and geographical balance within the Union.*
(2) Each member of the group shall in turn chair for a six–month period all configurations of the Council, with the exception of the Foreign Affairs configuration. The other members of the group shall assist the Chair in all its responsibilities on the basis of a common programme. Members of the team may decide alternative arrangements among themselves.

Article 2. *The Committee of Permanent Representatives of the Governments of the Member States shall be chaired by a representative of the Member State chairing the General Affairs Council.*
The Chair of the Political and Security Committee shall be held by a representative of the High Representative of the Union for Foreign Affairs and Security Policy.
The chair of the preparatory bodies of the various Council configurations, with the exception of the Foreign Affairs configuration, shall fall to the member of the group chairing the relevant configuration, unless decided otherwise in accordance with Article 4.

Article 3. *The General Affairs Council shall ensure consistency and continuity in the work of the different Council configurations in the framework of multiannual programmes in cooperation with the Commission. The Member States holding the Presidency shall take all necessary measures for the organisation and smooth operation of the Council's work, with the assistance of the General Secretariat of the Council.*

Article 4. *The Council shall adopt a decision establishing the measures for the implementation of this decision.*

10. Declaration on Article 17 of the Treaty on European Union

The Conference considers that when the Commission no longer includes nationals of all Member States, the Commission should pay particular attention to the need to ensure full transparency in relations with all Member States. Accordingly, the Commission should liaise closely with all Member States, whether or not they have a national serving as member of the Commission, and in this context pay special attention to the need to share information and consult with all Member States.

The Conference also considers that the Commission should take all the necessary measures to ensure that political, social and economic realities in all Member States, including those which have no national serving as member of the Commission, are fully taken into account. These measures should include ensuring that the position of those Member States is addressed by appropriate organisational arrangements.

11. Declaration on Article 17(6) and (7) of the Treaty on European Union

The Conference considers that, in accordance with the provisions of the Treaties, the European Parliament and the European Council are jointly responsible for the smooth running of the process leading to the election of the President of the European Commission. Prior to the decision of the European Council, representatives of the European Parliament and of the European Council will thus conduct the necessary consultations in the framework deemed the most appropriate. These consultations will focus on the backgrounds of the candidates for President of the Commission, taking account of the elections to the European Parliament, in accordance with the first subparagraph of Article 17(7). The arrangements for such consultations may be determined, in due course, by common accord between the European Parliament and the European Council.

PART III EUROPEAN UNION

12. Declaration on Article 18 of the Treaty on European Union

(1) The Conference declares that, in the course of the preparatory work preceding the appointment of the High Representative of the Union for Foreign Affairs and Security Policy which is due to take place on the date of entry into force of the Treaty of Lisbon in accordance with Article 18 of the Treaty on European Union and Article 5 of the Protocol on transitional provisions and whose term of office will be from that date until the end of the term of office of the Commission in office on that date, appropriate contacts will be made with the European Parliament.
2. Furthermore, the Conference recalls that, as regards the High Representative of the Union for Foreign Affairs and Security Policy whose term of office will start in November 2009 at the same time and for the same duration as the next Commission, he or she will be appointed in accordance with the provisions of Articles 17 and 18 of the Treaty on European Union.

13. Declaration concerning the common foreign and security policy

The Conference underlines that the provisions in the Treaty on European Union covering the Common Foreign and Security Policy, including the creation of the office of High Representative of the Union for Foreign Affairs and Security Policy and the establishment of an External Action Service, do not affect the responsibilities of the Member States, as they currently exist, for the formulation and conduct of their foreign policy nor of their national representation in third countries and international organisations.
The Conference also recalls that the provisions governing the Common Security and Defence Policy do not prejudice the specific character of the security and defence policy of the Member States.
It stresses that the European Union and its Member States will remain bound by the provisions of the Charter of the United Nations and, in particular, by the primary responsibility of the Security Council and of its Members for the maintenance of international peace and security.

14. Declaration concerning the common foreign and security policy

In addition to the specific rules and procedures referred to in paragraph 1 of Article 24 of the Treaty on European Union, the Conference underlines that the provisions covering the Common Foreign and Security Policy including in relation to the High Representative of the Union for Foreign Affairs and Security Policy and the External Action Service will not affect the existing legal basis, responsibilities, and powers of each Member State in relation to the formulation and conduct of its foreign policy, its national diplomatic service, relations with third countries and participation in international organisations, including a Member State's membership of the Security Council of the United Nations.
The Conference also notes that the provisions covering the Common Foreign and Security Policy do not give new powers to the Commission to initiate decisions nor do they increase the role of the European Parliament.
The Conference also recalls that the provisions governing the Common Security and Defence Policy do not prejudice the specific character of the security and defence policy of the Member States.

15. Declaration on Article 27 of the Treaty on European Union

The Conference declares that, as soon as the Treaty of Lisbon is signed, the Secretary–General of the Council, High Representative for the common foreign and security policy, the Commission and the Member States should begin preparatory work on the European External Action Service.

16. Declaration on Article 55(2) of the Treaty on European Union

The Conference considers that the possibility of producing translations of the Treaties in the languages mentioned in Article 55(2) contributes to fulfilling the objective of respecting the Union's rich cultural and linguistic diversity as set forth in the fourth subparagraph of Article 3(3). In this context, the Conference confirms the attachment of the Union to the cultural diversity of Europe and the special attention it will continue to pay to these and other languages.
The Conference recommends that those Member States wishing to avail themselves of the possibility recognised in Article 55(2) communicate to the Council, within six months from the date of the

signature of the Treaty of Lisbon, the language or languages into which translations of the Treaties will be made.

17. Declaration concerning primacy

The Conference recalls that, in accordance with well settled case law of the Court of Justice of the European Union, the Treaties and the law adopted by the Union on the basis of the Treaties have primacy over the law of Member States, under the conditions laid down by the said case law.
The Conference has also decided to attach as an Annex to this Final Act the Opinion of the Council Legal Service on the primacy of EC law as set out in 11197/07 (JUR 260):
"Opinion of the Council Legal Service
of 22 June 2007
It results from the case–law of the Court of Justice that primacy of EC law is a cornerstone principle of Community law. According to the Court, this principle is inherent to the specific nature of the European Community. At the time of the first judgment of this established case law (Costa/ENEL, 15 July 1964, Case 6/641 [1]) there was no mention of primacy in the treaty. It is still the case today. The fact that the principle of primacy will not be included in the future treaty shall not in any way change the existence of the principle and the existing case–law of the Court of Justice.

18. Declaration in relation to the delimitation of competences

The Conference underlines that, in accordance with the system of division of competences between the Union and the Member States as provided for in the Treaty on European Union and the Treaty on the Functioning of the European Union, competences not conferred upon the Union in the Treaties remain with the Member States.
When the Treaties confer on the Union a competence shared with the Member States in a specific area, the Member States shall exercise their competence to the extent that the Union has not exercised, or has decided to cease exercising, its competence. The latter situation arises when the relevant EU institutions decide to repeal a legislative act, in particular better to ensure constant respect for the principles of subsidiarity and proportionality. The Council may, at the initiative of one or several of its members (representatives of Member States) and in accordance with Article 241 of the Treaty on the Functioning of the European Union, request the Commission to submit proposals for repealing a legislative act. The Conference welcomes the Commission's declaration that it will devote particular attention to these requests.
Equally, the representatives of the governments of the Member States, meeting in an Intergovernmental Conference, in accordance with the ordinary revision procedure provided for in Article 48(2) to (5) of the Treaty on European Union, may decide to amend the Treaties upon which the Union is founded, including either to increase or to reduce the competences conferred on the Union in the said Treaties.

19. Declaration on Article 8 of the Treaty on the Functioning of the European Union

The Conference agrees that, in its general efforts to eliminate inequalities between women and men, the Union will aim in its different policies to combat all kinds of domestic violence. The Member States should take all necessary measures to prevent and punish these criminal acts and to support and protect the victims.

20. Declaration on Article 16 of the Treaty on the Functioning of the European Union

The Conference declares that, whenever rules on protection of personal data to be adopted on the basis of Article 16 could have direct implications for national security, due account will have to be taken of the specific characteristics of the matter. It recalls that the legislation presently applicable (see in particular Directive 95/46/EC) includes specific derogations in this regard.

21. Declaration on the protection of personal data in the fields of judicial cooperation in criminal matters and police cooperation

PART III   EUROPEAN UNION

The Conference acknowledges that specific rules on the protection of personal data and the free movement of such data in the fields of judicial cooperation in criminal matters and police cooperation based on Article 16 of the Treaty on the Functioning of the European Union may prove necessary because of the specific nature of these fields.

22. Declaration on Articles 48 and 79 of the Treaty on the Functioning of the European Union

The Conference considers that in the event that a draft legislative act based on Article 79(2) would affect important aspects of the social security system of a Member State, including its scope, cost or financial structure, or would affect the financial balance of that system as set out in the second paragraph of Article 48, the interests of that Member State will be duly taken into account.

23. Declaration on the second paragraph of Article 48 of the Treaty on the Functioning of the European Union

The Conference recalls that in that case, in accordance with Article 15(4) of the Treaty on European Union, the European Council acts by consensus.

24. Declaration concerning the legal personality of the European Union

The Conference confirms that the fact that the European Union has a legal personality will not in any way authorise the Union to legislate or to act beyond the competences conferred upon it by the Member States in the Treaties.

25. Declaration on Articles 75 and 215 of the Treaty on the Functioning of the European Union

The Conference recalls that the respect for fundamental rights and freedoms implies, in particular, that proper attention is given to the protection and observance of the due process rights of the individuals or entities concerned. For this purpose and in order to guarantee a thorough judicial review of decisions subjecting an individual or entity to restrictive measures, such decisions must be based on clear and distinct criteria. These criteria should be tailored to the specifics of each restrictive measure.

26. Declaration on non–participation by a Member State in a measure based on Title V of Part Three of the Treaty on the Functioning of the European Union

The Conference declares that, where a Member State opts not to participate in a measure based on Title V of Part Three of the Treaty on the Functioning of the European Union, the Council will hold a full discussion on the possible implications and effects of that Member State's non–participation in the measure.
In addition, any Member State may ask the Commission to examine the situation on the basis of Article 116 of the Treaty on the Functioning of the European Union.
The above paragraphs are without prejudice to the entitlement of a Member State to refer the matter to the European Council.

27. Declaration on Article 85(1), second subparagraph, of the Treaty on the Functioning of the European Union

The Conference considers that the regulations referred to in the second subparagraph of Article 85(1) of the Treaty on the Functioning of the European Union should take into account national rules and practices relating to the initiation of criminal investigations.

28. Declaration on Article 98 of the Treaty on the Functioning of the European Union

The Conference notes that the provisions of Article 98 shall be applied in accordance with the current practice. The terms "such measures are required in order to compensate for the economic disadvan-

DECLARATIONS ATTACHED TO THE TREATIES

tages caused by the division of Germany to the economy of certain areas of the Federal Republic affected by that division" shall be interpreted in accordance with the existing case law of the Court of Justice of the European Union.

29. Declaration on Article 107(2)(c) of the Treaty on the Functioning of the European Union

The Conference notes that Article 107(2)(c) shall be interpreted in accordance with the existing case law of the Court of Justice of the European Union regarding the applicability of the provisions to aid granted to certain areas of the Federal Republic of Germany affected by the former division of Germany.

30. Declaration on Article 126 of the Treaty on the Functioning of the European Union

With regard to Article 126, the Conference confirms that raising growth potential and securing sound budgetary positions are the two pillars of the economic and fiscal policy of the Union and the Member States. The Stability and Growth Pact is an important tool to achieve these goals.
The Conference reaffirms its commitment to the provisions concerning the Stability and Growth Pact as the framework for the coordination of budgetary policies in the Member States.
The Conference confirms that a rule–based system is the best guarantee for commitments to be enforced and for all Member States to be treated equally.
Within this framework, the Conference also reaffirms its commitment to the goals of the Lisbon Strategy: job creation, structural reforms, and social cohesion.
The Union aims at achieving balanced economic growth and price stability. Economic and budgetary policies thus need to set the right priorities towards economic reforms, innovation, competitiveness and strengthening of private investment and consumption in phases of weak economic growth. This should be reflected in the orientations of budgetary decisions at the national and Union level in particular through restructuring of public revenue and expenditure while respecting budgetary discipline in accordance with the Treaties and the Stability and Growth Pact.
Budgetary and economic challenges facing the Member States underline the importance of sound budgetary policy throughout the economic cycle.
The Conference agrees that Member States should use periods of economic recovery actively to consolidate public finances and improve their budgetary positions. The objective is to gradually achieve a budgetary surplus in good times which creates the necessary room to accommodate economic downturns and thus contribute to the long–term sustainability of public finances.
The Member States look forward to possible proposals of the Commission as well as further contributions of Member States with regard to strengthening and clarifying the implementation of the Stability and Growth Pact. The Member States will take all necessary measures to raise the growth potential of their economies. Improved economic policy coordination could support this objective. This Declaration does not prejudge the future debate on the Stability and Growth Pact.

31. Declaration on Article 156 of the Treaty on the Functioning of the European Union

The Conference confirms that the policies described in Article 156 fall essentially within the competence of the Member States. Measures to provide encouragement and promote coordination to be taken at Union level in accordance with this Article shall be of a complementary nature. They shall serve to strengthen cooperation between Member States and not to harmonise national systems. The guarantees and practices existing in each Member State as regards the responsibility of the social partners will not be affected.
This Declaration is without prejudice to the provisions of the Treaties conferring competence on the Union, including in social matters.

32. Declaration on Article 168(4)(c) of the Treaty on the Functioning of the European Union

The Conference declares that the measures to be adopted pursuant to Article 168(4)(c) must meet common safety concerns and aim to set high standards of quality and safety where national standards affecting the internal market would otherwise prevent a high level of human health protection being achieved.

PART III   EUROPEAN UNION

33. Declaration on Article 174 of the Treaty on the Functioning of the European Union

The Conference considers that the reference in Article 174 to island regions can include island States in their entirety, subject to the necessary criteria being met.

34. Declaration on Article 179 of the Treaty on the Functioning of the European Union

The Conference agrees that the Union's action in the area of research and technological development will pay due respect to the fundamental orientations and choices of the research policies of the Member States.

35. Declaration on Article 194 of the Treaty on the Functioning of the European Union

The Conference believes that Article 194 does not affect the right of the Member States to take the necessary measures to ensure their energy supply under the conditions provided for in Article 347.

36. Declaration on Article 218 of the Treaty on the Functioning of the European Union concerning the negotiation and conclusion of international agreements by Member States relating to the area of freedom, security and justice

The Conference confirms that Member States may negotiate and conclude agreements with third countries or international organisations in the areas covered by Chapters 3, 4 and 5 of Title V of Part Three in so far as such agreements comply with Union law.

37. Declaration on Article 222 of the Treaty on the Functioning of the European Union

Without prejudice to the measures adopted by the Union to comply with its solidarity obligation towards a Member State which is the object of a terrorist attack or the victim of natural or man–made disaster, none of the provisions of Article 222 is intended to affect the right of another Member State to choose the most appropriate means to comply with its own solidarity obligation towards that Member State.

38. Declaration on Article 252 of the Treaty on the Functioning of the European Union regarding the number of Advocates–General in the Court of Justice

The Conference declares that if, in accordance with Article 252, first paragraph, of the Treaty on the Functioning of the European Union, the Court of Justice requests that the number of Advocates–General be increased by three (eleven instead of eight), the Council will, acting unanimously, agree on such an increase.
In that case, the Conference agrees that Poland will, as is already the case for Germany, France, Italy, Spain and the United Kingdom, have a permanent Advocate–General and no longer take part in the rotation system, while the existing rotation system will involve the rotation of five Advocates–General instead of three.

39. Declaration on Article 290 of the Treaty on the Functioning of the European Union

The Conference takes note of the Commission's intention to continue to consult experts appointed by the Member States in the preparation of draft delegated acts in the financial services area, in accordance with its established practice.

40. Declaration on Article 329 of the Treaty on the Functioning of the European Union

The Conference declares that Member States may indicate, when they make a request to establish enhanced cooperation, if they intend already at that stage to make use of Article 333 providing for the extension of qualified majority voting or to have recourse to the ordinary legislative procedure.

DECLARATIONS ATTACHED TO THE TREATIES

41. Declaration on Article 352 of the Treaty on the Functioning of the European Union

The Conference declares that the reference in Article 352(1) of the Treaty on the Functioning of the European Union to objectives of the Union refers to the objectives as set out in Article 3(2) and (3) of the Treaty on European Union and to the objectives of Article 3(5) of the said Treaty with respect to external action under Part Five of the Treaty on the Functioning of the European Union. It is therefore excluded that an action based on Article 352 of the Treaty on the Functioning of the European Union would only pursue objectives set out in Article 3(1) of the Treaty on European Union. In this connection, the Conference notes that in accordance with Article 31(1) of the Treaty on European Union, legislative acts may not be adopted in the area of the Common Foreign and Security Policy.

42. Declaration on Article 352 of the Treaty on the Functioning of the European Union

The Conference underlines that, in accordance with the settled case law of the Court of Justice of the European Union, Article 352 of the Treaty on the Functioning of the European Union, being an integral part of an institutional system based on the principle of conferred powers, cannot serve as a basis for widening the scope of Union powers beyond the general framework created by the provisions of the Treaties as a whole and, in particular, by those that define the tasks and the activities of the Union. In any event, this Article cannot be used as a basis for the adoption of provisions whose effect would, in substance, be to amend the Treaties without following the procedure which they provide for that purpose.

43. Declaration on Article 355(6) of the Treaty on the Functioning of the European Union

The High Contracting Parties agree that the European Council, pursuant to Article 355(6), will take a decision leading to the modification of the status of Mayotte with regard to the Union in order to make this territory an outermost region within the meaning of Article 355(1) and Article 349, when the French authorities notify the European Council and the Commission that the evolution currently under way in the internal status of the island so allows.

B. Declarations concerning Protocols annexed to the Treaties

44. Declaration on Article 5 of the Protocol on the Schengen acquis integrated into the framework of the European Union

The Conference notes that where a Member State has made a notification under Article 5(2) of the Protocol on the Schengen acquis integrated into the framework of the European Union that it does not wish to take part in a proposal or initiative, that notification may be withdrawn at any moment before the adoption of the measure building upon the Schengen acquis.

45. Declaration on Article 5(2) of the Protocol on the Schengen acquis integrated into the framework of the European Union

The Conference declares that whenever the United Kingdom or Ireland indicates to the Council its intention not to participate in a measure building upon a part of the Schengen acquis in which it participates, the Council will have a full discussion on the possible implications of the non–participation of that Member State in that measure. The discussion within the Council should be conducted in the light of the indications given by the Commission concerning the relationship between the proposal and the Schengen acquis.

46. Declaration on Article 5(3) of the Protocol on the Schengen acquis integrated into the framework of the European Union

The Conference recalls that if the Council does not take a decision after a first substantive discussion of the matter, the Commission may present an amended proposal for a further substantive re–examination by the Council within the deadline of 4 months.

PART III   EUROPEAN UNION

47. Declaration on Article 5(3), (4) and (5) of the Protocol on the Schengen acquis integrated into the framework of the European Union

The Conference notes that the conditions to be determined in the decision referred to in paragraphs 3, 4 or 5 of Article 5 of the Protocol on the Schengen acquis integrated into the framework of the European Union may determine that the Member State concerned shall bear the direct financial consequences, if any, necessarily and unavoidably incurred as a result of the cessation of its participation in some or all of the acquis referred to in any decision taken by the Council pursuant to Article 4 of the said Protocol.

48. Declaration concerning the Protocol on the position of Denmark

The Conference notes that with respect to legal acts to be adopted by the Council acting alone or jointly with the European Parliament and containing provisions applicable to Denmark as well as provisions not applicable to Denmark because they have a legal basis to which Part I of the Protocol on the position of Denmark applies, Denmark declares that it will not use its voting right to prevent the adoption of the provisions which are not applicable to Denmark.

Furthermore, the Conference notes that on the basis of the Declaration by the Conference on Article 222, Denmark declares that Danish participation in actions or legal acts pursuant to Article 222 will take place in accordance with Part I and Part II of the Protocol on the position of Denmark.

49. Declaration concerning Italy

The Conference notes that the Protocol on Italy annexed in 1957 to the Treaty establishing the European Economic Community, as amended upon adoption of the Treaty on European Union, stated that:
"THE HIGH CONTRACTING PARTIES,
DESIRING to settle certain particular problems relating to Italy,
HAVE AGREED UPON the following provisions, which shall be annexed to this Treaty:
THE MEMBER STATES OF THE COMMUNITY
TAKE NOTE of the fact that the Italian Government is carrying out a ten–year programme of economic expansion designed to rectify the disequilibria in the structure of the Italian economy, in particular by providing an infrastructure for the less developed areas in Southern Italy and in the Italian islands and by creating new jobs in order to eliminate unemployment;
RECALL that the principles and objectives of this programme of the Italian Government have been considered and approved by organisations for international cooperation of which the Member States are members;
RECOGNISE that it is in their common interest that the objectives of the Italian programme should be attained;
AGREE, in order to facilitate the accomplishment of this task by the Italian Government, to recommend to the institutions of the Community that they should employ all the methods and procedures provided in this Treaty and, in particular, make appropriate use of the resources of the European Investment Bank and the European Social Fund;
ARE OF THE OPINION that the institutions of the Community should, in applying this Treaty, take account of the sustained effort to be made by the Italian economy in the coming years and of the desirability of avoiding dangerous stresses in particular within the balance of payments or the level of employment, which might jeopardise the application of this Treaty in Italy;
RECOGNISE that in the event of Articles 109 H and 109 I being applied it will be necessary to take care that any measures required of the Italian Government do not prejudice the completion of its programme for economic expansion and for raising the standard of living of the population.".

50. Declaration concerning Article 10 of the Protocol on transitional provisions

The Conference invites the European Parliament, the Council and the Commission, within their respective powers, to seek to adopt, in appropriate cases and as far as possible within the five–year period referred to in Article 10(3) of the Protocol on transitional provisions, legal acts amending or replacing the acts referred to in Article 10(1) of that Protocol.

DECLARATIONS ATTACHED TO THE TREATIES

C. Declarations by Member States

51. Declaration by the Kingdom of Belgium on national Parliaments

Belgium wishes to make clear that, in accordance with its constitutional law, not only the Chamber of Representatives and Senate of the Federal Parliament but also the parliamentary assemblies of the Communities and the Regions act, in terms of the competences exercised by the Union, as components of the national parliamentary system or chambers of the national Parliament.

52. Declaration by the Kingdom of Belgium, the Republic of Bulgaria, the Federal Republic of Germany, the Hellenic Republic, the Kingdom of Spain, the Italian Republic, the Republic of Cyprus, the Republic of Lithuania, the Grand–Duchy of Luxembourg, the Republic of Hungary, the Republic of Malta, the Republic of Austria, the Portuguese Republic, Romania, the Republic of Slovenia and the Slovak Republic on the symbols of the European Union

Belgium, Bulgaria, Germany, Greece, Spain, Italy, Cyprus, Lithuania, Luxemburg, Hungary, Malta, Austria, Portugal, Romania, Slovenia and the Slovak Republic declare that the flag with a circle of twelve golden stars on a blue background, the anthem based on the "Ode to Joy" from the Ninth Symphony by Ludwig van Beethoven, the motto "United in diversity", the euro as the currency of the European Union and Europe Day on 9 May will for them continue as symbols to express the sense of community of the people in the European Union and their allegiance to it.

53. Declaration by the Czech Republic on the Charter of Fundamental Rights of the European Union

(1) The Czech Republic recalls that the provisions of the Charter of Fundamental Rights of the European Union are addressed to the institutions and bodies of the European Union with due regard for the principle of subsidiarity and division of competences between the European Union and its Member States, as reaffirmed in Declaration (No 18) in relation to the delimitation of competences. The Czech Republic stresses that its provisions are addressed to the Member States only when they are implementing Union law, and not when they are adopting and implementing national law independently from Union law.
(2) The Czech Republic also emphasises that the Charter does not extend the field of application of Union law and does not establish any new power for the Union. It does not diminish the field of application of national law and does not restrain any current powers of the national authorities in this field.
(3) The Czech Republic stresses that, in so far as the Charter recognises fundamental rights and principles as they result from constitutional traditions common to the Member States, those rights and principles are to be interpreted in harmony with those traditions.
(4) The Czech Republic further stresses that nothing in the Charter may be interpreted as restricting or adversely affecting human rights and fundamental freedoms as recognised, in their respective field of application, by Union law and by international agreements to which the Union or all the Member States are party, including the European Convention for the Protection of Human Rights and Fundamental Freedoms, and by the Member States' Constitutions.

54. Declaration by the Federal Republic of Germany, Ireland, the Republic of Hungary, the Republic of Austria and the Kingdom of Sweden

Germany, Ireland, Hungary, Austria and Sweden note that the core provisions of the Treaty establishing the European Atomic Energy Community have not been substantially amended since its entry into force and need to be brought up to date. They therefore support the idea of a Conference of the Representatives of the Governments of the Member States, which should be convened as soon as possible.

55. Declaration by the Kingdom of Spain and the United Kingdom of Great Britain and Northern Ireland

The Treaties apply to Gibraltar as a European territory for whose external relations a Member State is responsible. This shall not imply changes in the respective positions of the Member States concerned.

PART III EUROPEAN UNION

56. Declaration by Ireland on Article 3 of the Protocol on the position of the United Kingdom and Ireland in respect of the area of freedom, security and justice

Ireland affirms its commitment to the Union as an area of freedom, security and justice respecting fundamental rights and the different legal systems and traditions of the Member States within which citizens are provided with a high level of safety.

Accordingly, Ireland declares its firm intention to exercise its right under Article 3 of the Protocol on the position of the United Kingdom and Ireland in respect of the area of freedom, security and justice to take part in the adoption of measures pursuant to Title V of Part Three of the Treaty on the Functioning of the European Union to the maximum extent it deems possible.

Ireland will, in particular, participate to the maximum possible extent in measures in the field of police cooperation.

Furthermore, Ireland recalls that in accordance with Article 8 of the Protocol it may notify the Council in writing that it no longer wishes to be covered by the terms of the Protocol. Ireland intends to review the operation of these arrangements within three years of the entry into force of the Treaty of Lisbon.

57. Declaration by the Italian Republic on the composition of the European Parliament

Italy notes that, pursuant to Articles 10 and 14 of the Treaty on European Union, the European Parliament is to be composed of representatives of the Union's citizens; this representation is to be degressively proportional.

Italy likewise notes that on the basis of Article 9 of the Treaty on European Union and Article 20 of the Treaty on the Functioning of the European Union, every national of a Member State is a citizen of the Union.

Italy therefore considers that, without prejudice to the decision on the 2009–2014 legislative period, any decision adopted by the European Council, at the initiative of the European Parliament and with its consent, establishing the composition of the European Parliament, must abide by the principles laid down out in the first subparagraph of Article 14.

58. Declaration by the Republic of Latvia, the Republic of Hungary and the Republic of Malta on the spelling of the name of the single currency in the Treaties

Without prejudice to the unified spelling of the name of the single currency of the European Union referred to in the Treaties as displayed on the banknotes and on the coins, Latvia, Hungary and Malta declare that the spelling of the name of the single currency, including its derivatives as applied throughout the Latvian, Hungarian and Maltese text of the Treaties, has no effect on the existing rules of the Latvian, Hungarian or Maltese languages.

59. Declaration by the Kingdom of the Netherlands on Article 312 of the Treaty on the Functioning of the European Union

The Kingdom of the Netherlands will agree to a decision as referred to in the second subparagraph of Article 312(2) of the Treaty on the Functioning of the European Union once a revision of the decision referred to in the third paragraph of Article 311 of that Treaty has provided the Netherlands with a satisfactory solution for its excessive negative net payment position vis-à-vis the Union budget.

60. Declaration by the Kingdom of the Netherlands on Article 355 of the Treaty on the Functioning of the European Union

The Kingdom of the Netherlands declares that an initiative for a decision, as referred to in Article 355(6) aimed at amending the status of the Netherlands Antilles and/or Aruba with regard to the Union, will be submitted only on the basis of a decision taken in conformity with the Charter for the Kingdom of the Netherlands.

61. Declaration by the Republic of Poland on the Charter of Fundamental Rights of the European Union

DECLARATIONS ATTACHED TO THE TREATIES

The Charter does not affect in any way the right of Member States to legislate in the sphere of public morality, family law, as well as the protection of human dignity and respect for human physical and moral integrity.

62. Declaration by the Republic of Poland concerning the Protocol on the application of the Charter of Fundamental Rights of the European Union in relation to Poland and the United Kingdom

Poland declares that, having regard to the tradition of social movement of "Solidarity" and its significant contribution to the struggle for social and labour rights, it fully respects social and labour rights, as established by European Union law, and in particular those reaffirmed in Title IV of the Charter of Fundamental Rights of the European Union.

63. Declaration by the United Kingdom of Great Britain and Northern Ireland on the definition of the term "nationals"

In respect of the Treaties and the Treaty establishing the European Atomic Energy Community, and in any of the acts deriving from those Treaties or continued in force by those Treaties, the United Kingdom reiterates the Declaration it made on 31 December 1982 on the definition of the term "nationals" with the exception that the reference to "British Dependent Territories Citizens" shall be read as meaning "British overseas territories citizens".

64. Declaration by the United Kingdom of Great Britain and Northern Ireland on the franchise for elections to the European Parliament

The United Kingdom notes that Article 14 of the Treaty on European Union and other provisions of the Treaties are not intended to change the basis for the franchise for elections to the European Parliament.

65. Declaration by the United Kingdom of Great Britain and Northern Ireland on Article 75 of the Treaty on the Functioning of the European Union

The United Kingdom fully supports robust action with regard to adopting financial sanctions designed to prevent and combat terrorism and related activities. Therefore, the United Kingdom declares that it intends to exercise its right under Article 3 of the Protocol on the position of the United Kingdom and Ireland in respect of the area of freedom, security and justice to take part in the adoption of all proposals made under Article 75 of the Treaty on the Functioning of the European Union.
[1] "It follows (…) that the law stemming from the treaty, an independent source of law, could not, because of its special and original nature, be overridden by domestic legal provisions, however framed, without being deprived of its character as Community law and without the legal basis of the Community itself being called into question."

PART III EUROPEAN UNION

Tables of Equivalences (TEU)[1]

Treaty on the Functioning of the European Union

Old numbering of the Treaty establishing the European Community
| New numbering of the Treaty on the Functioning of the European Union |

PART ONE – PRINCIPLES | PART ONE – PRINCIPLES |
Article 1 (repealed) | |
| Article 1 |
Article 2 (repealed) [26] | |
| Title I – Categories and areas of union competence |
| Article 2 |
| Article 3 |
| Article 4 |
| Article 5 |
| Article 6 |
| Title II – Provisions having general application |
|
| Article 7 |
Article 3, paragraph 1 (repealed) [27] | |
Article 3, paragraph 2 | Article 8 |
Article 4 (moved) | Article 119 |
Article 5 (replaced) [28] | |
| Article 9 |
| Article 10 |
Article 6 | Article 11 |
Article 153, paragraph 2 (moved) | Article 12 |
| Article 13 [29] |
Article 7 (repealed) [30] | |
Article 8 (repealed) [31] | |
Article 9 (repealed) | |
Article 10 (repealed) [32] | |
Article 11 (replaced) [33] | Articles 326 to 334 |
Article 11a (replaced) [33] | Articles 326 to 334 |
Article 12 (moved) | Article 18 |
Article 13 (moved) | Article 19 |
Article 14 (moved) | Article 26 |
Article 15 (moved) | Article 27 |
Article 16 | Article 14 |
Article 255 (moved) | Article 15 |
Article 286 (moved) | Article 16 |
|
| Article 17 |

PART TWO – CITIZENSHIP OF THE UNION | PART TWO – NONDISCRIMINATION AND CITIZENSHIP OF THE UNION |
Article 12 (moved) | Article 18 |
Article 13 (moved) | Article 19 |
Article 17 | Article 20 |
Article 18 | Article 21 |
Article 19 | Article 22 |
Article 20 | Article 23 |
Article 21 | Article 24 |
Article 22 | Article 25 |

PART THREE – COMMUNITY POLICIES | PART THREE – POLICIES AND INTERNAL ACTIONS OF THE UNION |
| Title I – The internal market |

---

[1] Tables of equivalences as referred to in Article 5 of the Treaty of Lisbon. The original center column, which set out the intermediate numbering as used in that Treaty, has been omitted.

TABLES OF EQUIVALENCES (TFEU)

Article 14 (moved) | Article 26 |
Article 15 (moved) | Article 27 |
Title I – Free movement of goods | Title II – Free movement of goods |
Article 23 | Article 28 |
Article 24 | Article 29 |
Chapter 1 – The customs union | Chapter 1 – The customs union |
Article 25 | Article 30 |
Article 26 | Article 31 |
Article 27 | Article 32 |
Part Three, Title X, Customs cooperation (moved) | Chapter 2 – Customs cooperation |
Article 135 (moved) | Article 33 |
Chapter 2 – Prohibition of quantitative restrictions between Member States | Chapter 3 – Prohibition of quantitative restrictions between Member States |
Article 28 | Article 34 |
Article 29 | Article 35 |
Article 30 | Article 36 |
Article 31 | Article 37 |
Title II – Agriculture | Title III – Agriculture and fisheries |
Article 32 | Article 38 |
Article 33 | Article 39 |
Article 34 | Article 40 |
Article 35 | Article 41 |
Article 36 | Article 42 |
Article 37 | Article 43 |
Article 38 | Article 44 |
Title III – Free movement of persons, services and capital | Title IV – Free movement of persons, services and capital |
Chapter 1 – Workers | Chapter 1 – Workers |
Article 39 | Article 45 |
Article 40 | Article 46 |
Article 41 | Article 47 |
Article 42 | Article 48 |
Chapter 2 – Right of establishment | Chapter 2 – Right of establishment |
Article 43 | Article 49 |
Article 44 | Article 50 |
Article 45 | Article 51 |
Article 46 | Article 52 |
Article 47 | Article 53 |
Article 48 | Article 54 |
Article 294 (moved) | Article 55 |
Chapter 3 – Services | Chapter 3 – Services |
Article 49 | Article 56 |
Article 50 | Article 57 |
Article 51 | Article 58 |
Article 52 | Article 59 |
Article 53 | Article 60 |
Article 54 | Article 61 |
Article 55 | Article 62 |
Chapter 4 – Capital and payments | Chapter 4 – Capital and payments |
Article 56 | Article 63 |
Article 57 | Article 64 |
Article 58 | Article 65 |
Article 59 | Article 66 |
Article 60 (moved) | Article 75 |
Title IV – Visas, asylum, immigration and other policies related to free movement of persons | Title V – Area of freedom, security and justice |
| Chapter 1 – General provisions |
Article 61 | Article 67 [34] |
| Article 68 |
| Article 69 |

PART III   EUROPEAN UNION

| Article 70 |
| Article 71 [35] |
Article 64, paragraph 1 (replaced) | Article 72 [36] |
| Article 73 |
Article 66 (replaced) | Article 74 |
Article 60 (moved) | Article 75 |
| Article 76 |
|
| Chapter 2 – Policies on border checks, asylum and immigration |
Article 62 | Article 77 |
Article 63, points 1 et 2, and Article 64, paragraph 2 [37] | Article 78 |
Article 63, points 3 and 4 | Article 79 |
| Article 80 |
Article 64, paragraph 1 (replaced) | Article 72 |
| Chapter 3 – Judicial cooperation in civil matters |
Article 65 | Article 81 |
Article 66 (replaced) | Article 74 |
Article 67 (repealed) | |
Article 68 (repealed) | |
Article 69 (repealed) | |
| Chapter 4 – Judicial cooperation in criminal matters |
| Article 82 [38] |
| Article 83 [38] |
| Article 84 |
| Article 85 [38] |
| Article 86 |
| Chapter 5 – Police cooperation |
| Article 87 [39] |
| Article 88 [39] |
| Article 89 [40] |
|
Title V – Transport | Title VI – Transport |
Article 70 | Article 90 |
Article 71 | Article 91 |
Article 72 | Article 92 |
Article 73 | Article 93 |
Article 74 | Article 94 |
Article 75 | Article 95 |
Article 76 | Article 96 |
Article 77 | Article 97 |
Article 78 | Article 98 |
Article 79 | Article 99 |
Article 80 | Article 100 |
Title VI – Common rules on competition, taxation and approximation of laws | Title VII – Common rules on competition, taxation and approximation of laws |
Chapter 1 – Rules on competition | Chapter 1 – Rules on competition |
Section 1 – Rules applying to undertakings | Section 1 – Rules applying to undertakings |
Article 81 | Article 101 |
Article 82 | Article 102 |
Article 83 | Article 103 |
Article 84 | Article 104 |
Article 85 | Article 105 |
Article 86 | Article 106 |
Section 2 – Aids granted by States | Section 2 – Aids granted by States |
Article 87 | Article 107 |
Article 88 | Article 108 |
Article 89 | Article 109 |
Chapter 2 – Tax provisions | Chapter 2 – Tax provisions |
Article 90 | Article 110 |
Article 91 | Article 111 |

TABLES OF EQUIVALENCES (TFEU)

Article 92 | Article 112 |
Article 93 | Article 113 |
Chapter 3 – Approximation of laws | Chapter 3 – Approximation of laws |
Article 95 (moved) | Article 114 |
Article 94 (moved) | Article 115 |
Article 96 | Article 116 |
Article 97 | Article 117 |
| Article 118 |
Title VII – Economic and monetary policy | Title VIII – Economic and monetary policy |
Article 4 (moved) | Article 2 |
Chapter 1 – Economic policy | Chapter 1 – Economic policy |
Article 98 | Article 120 |
Article 99 | Article 121 |
Article 100 | Article 122 |
Article 101 | Article 123 |
Article 102 | Article 124 |
Article 103 | Article 125 |
Article 104 | Article 126 |
Chapter 2 – monetary policy | Chapter 2 – monetary policy |
Article 105 | Article 127 |
Article 106 | Article 128 |
Article 107 | Article 129 |
Article 108 | Article 130 |
Article 109 | Article 131 |
Article 110 | Article 132 |
Article 111, paragraphs 1 to 3 and 5 (moved) | Article 219 |
Article 111, paragraph 4 (moved) | Article 138 |
| Article 133 |
Chapter 3 – Institutional provisions | Chapter 3 – Institutional provisions |
Article 112 (moved) | Article 283 |
Article 113 (moved) | Article 284 |
Article 114 | Article 134 |
Article 115 | Article 135 |
| Chapter 4 – Provisions specific to Member States whose currency is the euro |
| Article 136 |
| Article 137 |
Article 111, paragraph 4 (moved) | Article 138 |
Chapter 4 – Transitional provisions | Chapter 5 – Transitional provisions |
Article 116 (repealed) | |
| Article 139 |
Article 117, paragraphs 1, 2, sixth indent, and 3 to 9 (repealed) | |
Article 117, paragraph 2, first five indents (moved) | Article 141, paragraph 2 |
Article 121, paragraph 1 (moved) Article 122, paragraph 2, second sentence (moved) Article 123, paragraph 5 (moved) | Article 140 [41] |
Article 118 (repealed) | |
Article 123, paragraph 3 (moved) Article 117, paragraph 2, first five indents (moved) | Article 141 [42] |
|
Article 124, paragraph 1 (moved) | Article 142 |
Article 119 | Article 143 |
Article 120 | Article 144 |
Article 121, paragraph 1 (moved) | Article 140, paragraph 1 |
Article 121, paragraphs 2 to 4 (repealed) | |
Article 122, paragraphs 1, 2, first sentence, 3, 4, 5 and 6 (repealed) | |
Article 122, paragraph 2, second sentence (moved) | Article 140, paragraph 2, first subparagraph |
Article 123, paragraphs 1, 2 and 4 (repealed) | |
Article 123, paragraph 3 (moved) | Article 141, paragraph 1 |
Article 123, paragraph 5 (moved) | Article 140, paragraph 3 |
Article 124, paragraph 1 (moved) | Article 142 |
Article 124, paragraph 2 (repealed) | |

PART III   EUROPEAN UNION

Title VIII – Employment | Title IX – Employment |
Article 125 | Article 145 |
Article 126 | Article 146 |
Article 127 | Article 147 |
Article 128 | Article 148 |
Article 129 | Article 149 |
Article 130 | Article 150 |
Title IX – Common commercial policy (moved) | Part Five, Title II, common commercial policy |
Article 131 (moved) | Article 206 |
Article 132 (repealed) | |
Article 133 (moved) | Article 207 |
Article 134 (repealed) | |
Title X – Customs cooperation (moved) | Part Three, Title II, Chapter 2, Customs cooperation |
Article 135 (moved) | Article 33 |
Title XI – Social policy, education, vocational training and youth | Title X – Social policy |
Chapter 1 – social provisions (repealed) | |
Article 136 | Article 151 |
| Article 152 |
Article 137 | Article 153 |
Article 138 | Article 154 |
Article 139 | Article 155 |
Article 140 | Article 156 |
Article 141 | Article 157 |
Article 142 | Article 158 |
Article 143 | Article 159 |
Article 144 | Article 160 |
Article 145 | Article 161 |
Chapter 2 – The European Social Fund | Title XI – The European Social Fund |
Article 146 | Article 162 |
Article 147 | Article 163 |
Article 148 | Article 164 |
Chapter 3 – Education, vocational training and youth | Title XII – Education, vocational training, youth and sport |
Article 149 | Article 165 |
Article 150 | Article 166 |
Title XII – Culture | Title XIII – Culture |
Article 151 | Article 167 |
Title XIII – Public health | Title XIV – Public health |
Article 152 | Article 168 |
Title XIV – Consumer protection | Title XV – Consumer protection |
Article 153, paragraphs 1, 3, 4 and 5 | Article 169 |
Article 153, paragraph 2 (moved) | Article 12 |
Title XV – Trans–European networks | Title XVI – Trans–European networks |
Article 154 | Article 170 |
Article 155 | Article 171 |
Article 156 | Article 172 |
Title XVI – Industry | Title XVII – Industry |
Article 157 | Article 173 |
Title XVII – Economic and social cohesion | Title XVIII – Economic, social and territorial cohesion |
Article 158 | Article 174 |
Article 159 | Article 175 |
Article 160 | Article 176 |
Article 161 | Article 177 |
Article 162 | Article 178 |
Title XVIII – Research and technological development | Title XIX – Research and technological development and space |
Article 163 | Article 179 |
Article 164 | Article 180 |
Article 165 | Article 181 |
Article 166 | Article 182 |

TABLES OF EQUIVALENCES (TFEU)

Article 167 | Article 183 |
Article 168 | Article 184 |
Article 169 | Article 185 |
Article 170 | Article 186 |
Article 171 | Article 187 |
Article 172 | Article 188 |
| Article 189 |
Article 173 | Article 190 |
Title XIX – Environment | Title XX – Environment |
Article 174 | Article 191 |
Article 175 | Article 192 |
Article 176 | Article 193 |
| Titre XXI – Energy |
| Article 194 |
| Title XXII – Tourism |
| Article 195 |
| Title XXIII – Civil protection |
| Article 196 |
| Title XXIV – Administrative cooperation |
| Article 197 |
Title XX – Development cooperation (moved) | Part Five, Title III, Chapter 1, Development cooperation |
Article 177 (moved) | Article 208 |
Article 178 (repealed) [43] | |
Article 179 (moved) | Article 209 |
Article 180 (moved) | Article 210 |
Article 181 (moved) | Article 211 |
Title XXI – Economic, financial and technical cooperation with third countries (moved) | Part Five, Title III, Chapter 2, Economic, financial and technical cooperation with third countries |
Article 181a (moved) | Article 212 |

PART FOUR – ASSOCIATION OF THE OVERSEAS COUNTRIES AND TERRITORIES | PART FOUR – ASSOCIATION OF THE OVERSEAS COUNTRIES AND TERRITORIES |
Article 182 | Article 198 |
Article 183 | Article 199 |
|
Article 184 | Article 200 |
Article 185 | Article 201 |
Article 186 | Article 202 |
Article 187 | Article 203 |
Article 188 | Article 204 |

| PART FIVE – THE UNION'S EXTERNAL ACTION |
| Title I – General provisions on the Union's external action |
| Article 205 |
Part Three, Title IX, Common commercial policy (moved) | Title II – Common commercial policy |
Article 131 (moved) | Article 206 |
Article 133 (moved) | Article 207 |
| Title III – Cooperation with third countries and humanitarian aid |
Part Three, Title XX, Development cooperation (moved) | Chapter 1 – development cooperation |
Article 177 (moved) | Article 208 [44] |
Article 179 (moved) | Article 209 |
Article 180 (moved) | Article 210 |
Article 181 (moved) | Article 211 |
Part Three, Title XXI, Economic, financial and technical cooperation with third countries (moved) | Chapter 2 – Economic, financial and technical cooperation with third countries |
Article 181a (moved) | Article 212 |
| Article 213 |
| Chapter 3 – Humanitarian aid |
| Article 214 |
| Title IV – Restrictive measures |

PART III EUROPEAN UNION

|
Article 301 (replaced) | Article 215 |
| Title V – International agreements |
| Article 216 |
Article 310 (moved) | Article 217 |
Article 300 (replaced) | Article 218 |
Article 111, paragraphs 1 to 3 and 5 (moved) | Article 219 |
| Title VI – The Union's relations with international organisations and third countries and the Union delegations |
Articles 302 to 304 (replaced) | Article 220 |
| Article 221 |
| Title VII – Solidarity clause |
| Article 222 |

PART FIVE – INSTITUTIONS OF THE COMMUNITY | PART SIX – INSTITUTIONAL AND FINANCIAL PROVISIONS |
Title I – Institutional provisions | Title I – Institutional provisions |
Chapter 1 – The institutions | Chapter 1 – The institutions |
Section 1 – The European Parliament | Section 1 – The European Parliament |
Article 189 (repealed) [45] | |
Article 190, paragraphs 1 to 3 (repealed) [46] | |
Article 190, paragraphs 4 and 5 | Article 223 |
Article 191, first paragraph (repealed) [47] | |
Article 191, second paragraph | Article 224 |
Article 192, first paragraph (repealed) [48] | |
Article 192, second paragraph | Article 225 |
Article 193 | Article 226 |
|
Article 194 | Article 227 |
Article 195 | Article 228 |
Article 196 | Article 229 |
Article 197, first paragraph (repealed) [49] | |
Article 197, second, third and fourth paragraphs | Article 230 |
Article 198 | Article 231 |
Article 199 | Article 232 |
Article 200 | Article 233 |
Article 201 | Article 234 |
| Section 2 – The European Council |
| Article 235 |
| Article 236 |
Section 2 – The Council | Section 3 – The Council |
Article 202 (repealed) [50] | |
Article 203 (repealed) [51] | |
Article 204 | Article 237 |
Article 205, paragraphs 2 and 4 (repealed) [52] | |
Article 205, paragraphs 1 and 3 | Article 238 |
Article 206 | Article 239 |
Article 207 | Article 240 |
Article 208 | Article 241 |
Article 209 | Article 242 |
Article 210 | Article 243 |
Section 3 – The Commission | Section 4 – The Commission |
|
Article 211 (repealed) [53] | |
| Article 244 |
Article 212 (moved) | Article 249, paragraph 2 |
Article 213 | Article 245 |
Article 214 (repealed) [54] | |
Article 215 | Article 246 |
Article 216 | Article 247 |

TABLES OF EQUIVALENCES (TFEU)

Article 217, paragraphs 1, 3 and 4 (repealed) [55] | |
Article 217, paragraph 2 | Article 248 |
Article 218, paragraph 1 (repealed) [56] | |
Article 218, paragraph 2 | Article 249 |
Article 219 | Article 250 |
Section 4 – The Court of Justice | Section 5 – The Court of Justice of the European Union |
Article 220 (repealed) [57] | |
Article 221, first paragraph (repealed) [58] | |
Article 221, second and third paragraphs | Article 251 |
Article 222 | Article 252 |
Article 223 | Article 253 |
Article 224 [59] | Article 254 |
| Article 255 |
Article 225 | Article 256 |
Article 225a | Article 257 |
|
Article 226 | Article 258 |
Article 227 | Article 259 |
Article 228 | Article 260 |
Article 229 | Article 261 |
Article 229a | Article 262 |
Article 230 | Article 263 |
Article 231 | Article 264 |
Article 232 | Article 265 |
Article 233 | Article 266 |
Article 234 | Article 267 |
Article 235 | Article 268 |
| Article 269 |
Article 236 | Article 270 |
Article 237 | Article 271 |
Article 238 | Article 272 |
Article 239 | Article 273 |
Article 240 | Article 274 |
| Article 275 |
| Article 276 |
Article 241 | Article 277 |
Article 242 | Article 278 |
Article 243 | Article 279 |
Article 244 | Article 280 |
Article 245 | Article 281 |
| Section 6 – The European Central Bank |
| Article 282 |
Article 112 (moved) | Article 283 |
Article 113 (moved) | Article 284 |
Section 5 – The Court of Auditors | Section 7 – The Court of Auditors |
Article 246 | Article 285 |
Article 247 | Article 286 |
Article 248 | Article 287 |
Chapter 2 – Provisions common to several institutions | Chapter 2 – Legal acts of the Union, adoption procedures and other provisions |
| Section 1 – The legal acts of the Union |
Article 249 | Article 288 |
| Article 289 |
| Article 290 [60] |
| Article 291 [60] |
| Article 292 |
| Section 2 – Procedures for the adoption of acts and other provisions |
Article 250 | Article 293 |
Article 251 | Article 294 |
Article 252 (repealed) | |

PART III   EUROPEAN UNION

| Article 295 |
Article 253 | Article 296 |
Article 254 | Article 297 |
| Article 298 |
Article 255 (moved) | Article 15 |
Article 256 | Article 299 |
| Chapter 3 – The Union's advisory bodies |
| Article 300 |
Chapter 3 – The Economic and Social Committee | Section 1 – The Economic and Social Committee |
|
Article 257 (repealed) [61] | |
Article 258, first, second and fourth paragraphs | Article 301 |
Article 258, third paragraph (repealed) [62] | |
Article 259 | Article 302 |
Article 260 | Article 303 |
Article 261 (repealed) | |
Article 262 | Article 304 |
Chapter 4 – The Committee of the Regions | Section 2 – The Committee of the Regions |
Article 263, first and fifth paragraphs (repealed) [63] | |
Article 263, second to fourth paragraphs | Article 305 |
Article 264 | Article 306 |
Article 265 | Article 307 |
Chapter 5 – The European Investment Bank | Chapter 4 – The European Investment Bank |
Article 266 | Article 308 |
Article 267 | Article 309 |
Title II – Financial provisions | Title II – Financial provisions |
Article 268 | Article 310 |
| Chapter 1 – The Union's own resources |
Article 269 | Article 311 |
Article 270 (repealed) [64] | |
| Chapter 2 – The multiannual financial framework |
| Article 312 |
| Chapter 3 – The Union's annual budget |
|
Article 272, paragraph 1 (moved) | Article 313 |
Article 271 (moved) | Article 316 |
Article 272, paragraph 1 (moved) | Article 313 |
Article 272, paragraphs 2 to 10 | Article 314 |
Article 273 | Article 315 |
Article 271 (moved) | Article 316 |
| Chapter 4 – Implementation of the budget and discharge |
Article 274 | Article 317 |
Article 275 | Article 318 |
Article 276 | Article 319 |
| Chapter 5 – Common provisions |
Article 277 | Article 320 |
Article 278 | Article 321 |
Article 279 | Article 322 |
| Article 323 |
| Article 324 |
| Chapter 6 – Combating fraud |
Article 280 | Article 325 |
| Title III – Enhanced cooperation |
Articles 11 and 11a (replaced) | Article 326 [65] |
Articles 11 and 11a (replaced) | Article 327 [65] |
Articles 11 and 11a (replaced) | Article 328 [65] |
Articles 11 and 11a (replaced) | Article 329 [65] |
Articles 11 and 11a (replaced) | Article 330 [65] |
Articles 11 and 11a (replaced) | Article 331 [65] |
Articles 11 and 11a (replaced) | Article 332 [65] |

Articles 11 and 11a (replaced) | Article 333 [65] |
Articles 11 and 11a (replaced) | Article 334 [65] |

PART SIX – GENERAL AND FINAL PROVISIONS | PART SEVEN – GENERAL AND FINAL PROVISIONS |
Article 281 (repealed) [66] | |
Article 282 | Article 335 |
Article 283 | Article 336 |
Article 284 | Article 337 |
Article 285 | Article 338 |
Article 286 (replaced) | Article 16 |
Article 287 | Article 339 |
Article 288 | Article 340 |
Article 289 | Article 341 |
Article 290 | Article 342 |
Article 291 | Article 343 |
Article 292 | Article 344 |
Article 293 (repealed) | |
Article 294 (moved) | Article 55 |
Article 295 | Article 345 |
Article 296 | Article 346 |
Article 297 | Article 347 |
Article 298 | Article 348 |
Article 299, paragraph 1 (repealed) [67] | |
Article 299, paragraph 2, second, third and fourth subparagraphs | Article 349 |
Article 299, paragraph 2, first subparagraph, and paragraphs 3 to 6 (moved) | Article 355 |
|
Article 300 (replaced) | Article 218 |
Article 301 (replaced) | Article 215 |
Article 302 (replaced) | Article 220 |
Article 303 (replaced) | Article 220 |
Article 304 (replaced) | Article 220 |
Article 305 (repealed) | |
Article 306 | Article 350 |
Article 307 | Article 351 |
Article 308 | Article 352 |
| Article 353 |
Article 309 | Article 354 |
Article 310 (moved) | Article 217 |
Article 311 (repealed) [68] | |
Article 299, paragraph 2, first subparagraph, and paragraphs 3 to 6 (moved) | Article 355 |
Article 312 | Article 356 |
Final Provisions | |
Article 313 | Article 357 |
| Article 358 |
Article 314 (repealed) [69] | |
[2] Replaced, in substance, by Article 7 of the Treaty on the Functioning of the European Union («TFEU») and by Articles 13(1) and 21, paragraph 3, second subparagraph of the Treaty on European Union («TEU»).
[3] Replaces Article 5 of the Treaty establishing the European Community («TEC»).
[4] Replaced, in substance, by Article 15.
[5] Replaced, in substance, by Article 13, paragraph 2.
[6] Article 8 TEU, which was in force until the entry into force of the Treaty of Lisbon (hereinafter «current»), amended the TEC. Those amendments are incorporated into the latter Treaty and Article 8 is repealed. Its number is used to insert a new provision.
[7] Paragraph 4 replaces, in substance, the first subparagraph of Article 191 TEC.
[8] The current Article 9 TEU amended the Treaty establishing the European Coal and Steel Community. This latter expired on 23 July 2002. Article 9 is repealed and the number thereof is used to insert another provision.

PART III   EUROPEAN UNION

[9]
– Paragraphs 1 and 2 replace, in substance, Article 189 TEC;
– paragraphs 1 to 3 replace, in substance, paragraphs 1 to 3 of Article 190 TEC;
– paragraph 1 replaces, in substance, the first subparagraph of Article 192 TEC;
– paragraph 4 replaces, in substance, the first subparagraph of Article 197 TEC.
[10] Replaces, in substance, Article 4.
[11]
– Paragraph 1 replaces, in substance, the first and second indents of Article 202 TEC;
– paragraphs 2 and 9 replace, in substance, Article 203 TEC;
– paragraphs 4 and 5 replace, in substance, paragraphs 2 and 4 of Article 205 TEC.
[12]
– Paragraph 1 replaces, in substance, Article 211 TEC;
– paragraphs 3 and 7 replace, in substance, Article 214 TEC.
– paragraph 6 replaces, in substance, paragraphs 1, 3 and 4 of Article 217 TEC.
[13]
– Replaces, in substance, Article 220 TEC.
– the first subparagraph of paragraph 2 replaces, in substance, the first subparagraph of Article 221 TEC.
[14] The current Article 10 TEU amended the Treaty establishing the European Atomic Energy Community. Those amendments are incorporated into the Treaty of Lisbon. Article 10 is repealed and the number thereof is used to insert another provision.
[15] Also replaces Articles 11 and 11a TEC.
[16] The current Articles 27a to 27e, on enhanced cooperation, are also replaced by Articles 326 to 334 TFEU.
[17] The current provisions of Title VI of the TEU, on police and judicial cooperation in criminal matters, are replaced by the provisions of Chapters 1, 4 and 5 of Title IV (renumbered V) of Part Three of the TFEU.
[18] Replaced by Article 67 TFEU.
[19] Replaced by Articles 87 and 88 TFEU.
[20] Replaced by Articles 82, 83 and 85 TFEU.
[21] Replaced by Article 89 TFEU.
[22] Replaced by Article 72 TFEU.
[23] Replaced by Article 71 TFEU.
[24] The current Articles 40 to 40 B TEU, on enhanced cooperation, are also replaced by Articles 326 to 334 TFEU.
[25] The current Articles 43 to 45 and Title VII of the TEU, on enhanced cooperation, are also replaced by Articles 326 to 334 TFEU.
[26] Replaced, in substance, by Article 3 TEU.
[27] Replaced, in substance, by Articles 3 to 6 TFEU.
[28] Replaced by Article 5 TEU.
[29] Insertion of the operative part of the protocol on protection and welfare of animals.
[30] Replaced, in substance, by Article 13 TEU.
[31] Replaced, in substance, by Article 13 TEU and Article 282, paragraph 1, TFEU.
[32] Replaced, in substance, by Article 4, paragraph 3, TEU.
[33] Also replaced by Article 20 TEU.
[34] Also replaces the current Article 29 TEU.
[35] Replaces the current Article 36 TEU.
[36] Also replaces the current Article 33 TEU.
[37] Points 1 and 2 of Article 63 EC are replaced by paragraphs 1 and 2 of Article 78 TFEU, and paragraph 2 of Article 64 is replaced by paragraph 3 of Article 78 TFEU.
[38] Replaces the current Article 31 TEU.
[39] Replaces the current Article 30 TEU.
[40] Replaces the current Article 32 TEU.
[41]
– Article 140, paragraph 1 takes over the wording of paragraph 1 of Article 121.
– Article 140, paragraph 2 takes over the second sentence of paragraph 2 of Article 122.
– Article 140, paragraph 3 takes over paragraph 5 of Article 123.
[42]
– Article 141, paragraph 1 takes over paragraph 3 of Article 123.
– Article 141, paragraph 2 takes over the first five indents of paragraph 2 of Article 117.

TABLES OF EQUIVALENCES (TFEU)

[43] Replaced, in substance, by the second sentence of the second subparagraph of paragraph 1 of Article 208 TFEU.
[44] The second sentence of the second subparagraph of paragraph 1 replaces, in substance, Article 178 TEC.
[45] Replaced, in substance, by Article 14, paragraphs 1 and 2, TEU.
[46] Replaced, in substance, by Article 14, paragraphs 1 to 3, TEU.
[47] Replaced, in substance, by Article 11, paragraph 4, TEU.
[48] Replaced, in substance, by Article 14, paragraph 1, TEU.
[49] Replaced, in substance, by Article 14, paragraph 4, TEU.
[50] Replaced, in substance, by Article 16, paragraph 1, TEU and by Articles 290 and 291 TFEU.
[51] Replaced, in substance, by Article 16, paragraphs 2 and 9 TEU.
[52] Replaced, in substance, by Article 16, paragraphs 4 and 5 TEU.
[53] Replaced, in substance, by Article 17, paragraph 1 TEU.
[54] Replaced, in substance, by Article 17, paragraphs 3 and 7 TEU.
[55] Replaced, in substance, by Article 17, paragraph 6, TEU.
[56] Replaced, in substance, by Article 295 TFEU.
[57] Replaced, in substance, by Article 19 TEU.
[58] Replaced, in substance, by Article 19, paragraph 2, first subparagraph, of the TEU.
[59] The first sentence of the first subparagraph is replaced, in substance, by Article 19, paragraph 2, second subparagraph of the TEU.
[60] Replaces, in substance, the third indent of Article 202 TEC.
[61] Replaced, in substance, by Article 300, paragraph 2 of the TFEU.
[62] Replaced, in substance, by Article 300, paragraph 4 of the TFEU.
[63] Replaced, in substance, by Article 300, paragraphs 3 and 4, TFEU.
[64] Replaced, in substance, by Article 310, paragraph 4, TFEU.
[65] Also replaces the current Articles 27a to 27e, 40 to 40b, and 43 to 45 TEU.
[66] Replaced, in substance, by Article 47 TEU.
[67] Replaced, in substance by Article 52 TEU.
[68] Replaced, in substance by Article 51 TEU.
[69] Replaced, in substance by Article 55 TEU.

PART III EUROPEAN UNION

Rules of Procedure of the Court of Justice

THE COURT OF JUSTICE
Having regard to the Treaty on European Union, and in particular Article 19 thereof,
Having regard to the Treaty on the Functioning of the European Union, and in particular the sixth paragraph of Article 253 thereof,
Having regard to the Treaty establishing the European Atomic Energy Community, and in particular Article 106a(1) thereof,
Having regard to the Protocol on the Statute of the Court of Justice of the European Union, and in particular Article 63 and the second paragraph of Article 64 thereof,
Whereas:
(1) Despite having been amended on several occasions over the years, the Rules of Procedure of the Court of Justice have remained fundamentally unchanged in structure since their original adoption on 4 March 1953. The Rules of Procedure of 19 June 1991, which are currently in force, still reflect the initial preponderance of direct actions, whereas in fact the majority of such actions now fall within the jurisdiction of the General Court, and references for a preliminary ruling from the courts and tribunals of the Member States represent, quantitatively, the primary category of cases brought before the Court. That fact should be taken into account and the structure and content of the Rules of Procedure of the Court adapted, in consequence, to changes in its caseload.
(2) While references for a preliminary ruling should be given their proper place in the Rules of Procedure, it is also appropriate to draw a clearer distinction between the rules that apply to all types of action and those that are specific to each type, to be contained in separate titles. In the interests of clarification, procedural provisions common to all cases brought before the Court should, therefore, all be contained in an initial title.
(3) In the light of experience gained in the course of implementing the various procedures, it is also necessary to supplement or to clarify, for the benefit of litigants as well as of national courts and tribunals, the rules that apply to each procedure. The rules in question concern, in particular, the concepts of party to the main proceedings, intervener and party to the proceedings before the General Court, or, in preliminary rulings, the rules governing the bringing of matters before the Court and the content of the order for reference. With regard to appeals against decisions of the General Court, a clearer distinction must also be drawn between appeals and cross–appeals in consequence of the service of an appeal on the cross–appellant.
(4) Conversely, the excessive complexity of certain procedures, such as the review procedure, has come to light on their implementation. Accordingly, they should be simplified by providing, inter alia, for a Chamber of five Judges to be designated for a period of one year to be responsible for ruling both on the First Advocate General's proposal to review and on the questions to be reviewed.
(5) Similarly, the procedural arrangements for dealing with requests for Opinions should be eased by aligning them with those that apply to other cases and by providing, in consequence, for a single Advocate General to be involved in dealing with the request for an Opinion. In the interests of making the Rules easier to understand, all the particular procedures currently to be found in a number of separate titles and chapters of the Rules of Procedure should also be brought together in a single title.
(6) In order to maintain the Court's capacity, in the face of an ever–increasing caseload, to dispose within a reasonable period of time of the cases brought before it, it is also necessary to continue the efforts made to reduce the duration of proceedings before the Court, in particular by extending the opportunities for the Court to rule by reasoned order, simplifying the rules relating to the intervention of the States and institutions referred to in the first and third paragraphs of Article 40 of the Statute and providing for the Court to be able to rule without a hearing if it considers that it has sufficient information on the basis of all the written observations lodged in a case.
(7) In the interests of making the Rules applied by the Court easier to understand, lastly, certain rules which are outdated or not applied should be deleted, every paragraph of the present Rules numbered, each article given a specific heading summarising its content and the terminology harmonised.
With the Council's approval given on 24 September 2012.
HAS ADOPTED THESE RULES OF PROCEDURE:

Introductory Provisions

Article 1. Definitions
(1) In these Rules:
(a) provisions of the Treaty on European Union are referred to by the number of the article concerned followed by 'TEU',

(b) provisions of the Treaty on the Functioning of the European Union are referred to by the number of the article concerned followed by 'TFEU',
(c) provisions of the Treaty establishing the European Atomic Energy Community are referred to by the number of the article concerned followed by 'TEAEC',
(d) 'Statute' means the Protocol on the Statute of the Court of Justice of the European Union,
(e) 'EEA Agreement' means the Agreement on the European Economic Area,
(f) 'Council Regulation No 1' means Council Regulation No 1 of 15 April 1958 determining the languages to be used by the European Economic Community.
(2) For the purposes of these Rules:
(a) 'institutions' means the institutions of the European Union referred to in Article 13(1) TEU and bodies, offices and agencies established by the Treaties, or by an act adopted in implementation thereof, which may be parties before the Court,
(b) 'EFTA Surveillance Authority' means the surveillance authority referred to in the EEA Agreement,
(c) 'interested persons referred to in Article 23 of the Statute' means all the parties, States, institutions, bodies, offices and agencies authorised, pursuant to that Article, to submit statements of case or observations in the context of a reference for a preliminary ruling.

Article 2. Purport of these Rules
These Rules implement and supplement, so far as necessary, the relevant provisions of the EU, FEU and EAEC Treaties, and the Statute.

Title I. Organisation of the Court

Chapter 1. Judges and Advocates General

Article 3. Commencement of the term of office of Judges and Advocates General
The term of office of a Judge or Advocate General shall begin on the date fixed for that purpose in the instrument of appointment. In the absence of any provisions in that instrument regarding the date of commencement of the term of office, that term shall begin on the date of publication of the instrument in the *Official Journal of the European Union*.

Article 4. Taking of the oath
Before taking up his duties, a Judge or Advocate General shall, at the first public sitting of the Court which he attends after his appointment, take the following oath provided for in Article 2 of the Statute:
'I swear that I will perform my duties impartially and conscientiously; I swear that I will preserve the secrecy of the deliberations of the Court.'

Article 5. Solemn undertaking
Immediately after taking the oath, a Judge or Advocate General shall sign a declaration by which he gives the solemn undertaking provided for in the third paragraph of Article 4 of the Statute.

Article 6. Depriving a Judge or Advocate General of his office
(1) Where the Court is called upon, pursuant to Article 6 of the Statute, to decide whether a Judge or Advocate General no longer fulfils the requisite conditions or no longer meets the obligations arising from his office, the President shall invite the Judge or Advocate General concerned to make representations.
(2) The Court shall give a decision in the absence of the Registrar.

Article 7. Order of seniority
(1) The seniority of Judges and Advocates General shall be calculated without distinction according to the date on which they took up their duties.
(2) Where there is equal seniority on that basis, the order of seniority shall be determined by age.
(3) Judges and Advocates General whose terms of office are renewed shall retain their former seniority.

Chapter 2. Presidency of the Court, Constitution of the Chambers and Designation of the First Advocate General

Article 8. Election of the President and of the Vice–President of the Court
(1) The Judges shall, immediately after the partial replacement provided for in the second paragraph of Article 253 TFEU, elect one of their number as President of the Court for a term of three years.
(2) If the office of the President falls vacant before the normal date of expiry of the term thereof, the

Court shall elect a successor for the remainder of the term.

(3) The elections provided for in this Article shall be by secret ballot. The Judge obtaining the votes of more than half the Judges of the Court shall be elected. If no Judge obtains that majority, further ballots shall be held until that majority is attained.

(4) The Judges shall then elect one of their number as Vice–President of the Court for a term of three years, in accordance with the procedures laid down in the preceding paragraph. Paragraph 2 shall apply if the office of the Vice–President of the Court falls vacant before the normal date of expiry of the term thereof.

(5) The names of the President and Vice–President elected in accordance with this Article shall be published in the *Official Journal of the European Union*.

Article 9. Responsibilities of the President of the Court

(1) The President shall represent the Court.

(2) The President shall direct the judicial business of the Court. He shall preside at general meetings of the Members of the Court and at hearings before and deliberations of the full Court and the Grand Chamber.

(3) The President shall ensure the proper functioning of the services of the Court.

Article 10. Responsibilities of the Vice–President of the Court

(1) The Vice–President shall assist the President of the Court in the performance of his duties and shall take the President's place when the latter is prevented from acting.

(2) He shall take the President's place, at his request, in performing the duties referred to in Article 9(1) and (3) of these Rules.

(3) The Court shall, by decision, specify the conditions under which the Vice–President shall take the place of the President of the Court in the performance of his judicial duties. That decision shall be published in the *Official Journal of the European Union*.

Article 11. Constitution of Chambers

(1) The Court shall set up Chambers of five and three Judges in accordance with Article 16 of the Statute and shall decide which Judges shall be attached to them.

(2) The Court shall designate the Chambers of five Judges which, for a period of one year, shall be responsible for cases of the kind referred to in Article 107 and Articles 193 and 194.

(3) In respect of cases assigned to a formation of the Court in accordance with Article 60, the word 'Court' in these Rules shall mean that formation.

(4) In respect of cases assigned to a Chamber of five or three Judges, the powers of the President of the Court shall be exercised by the President of the Chamber.

(5) The composition of the Chambers and the designation of the Chambers responsible for cases of the kind referred to in Article 107 and Articles 193 and 194 shall be published in the *Official Journal of the European Union*.

Article 12. Election of Presidents of Chambers

(1) The Judges shall, immediately after the election of the President and Vice–President of the Court, elect the Presidents of the Chambers of five Judges for a term of three years.

(2) The Judges shall then elect the Presidents of the Chambers of three Judges for a term of one year.

(3) The provisions of Article 8(2) and (3) shall apply.

(4) The names of the Presidents of Chambers elected in accordance with this Article shall be published in the *Official Journal of the European Union*.

Article 13. Where the President and Vice–President of the Court are prevented from acting

When the President and the Vice–President of the Court are prevented from acting, the functions of President shall be exercised by one of the Presidents of the Chambers of five Judges or, failing that, by one of the Presidents of the Chambers of three Judges or, failing that, by one of the other Judges, according to the order of seniority laid down in Article 7.

Article 14. Designation of the First Advocate General

(1) The Court shall, after hearing the Advocates General, designate a First Advocate General for a period of one year.

(2) If the office of the First Advocate General falls vacant before the normal date of expiry of the term thereof, the Court shall designate a successor for the remainder of the term.

(3) The name of the First Advocate General designated in accordance with this Article shall be published in the *Official Journal of the European Union*.

Chapter 3. Assignment of Cases to Judge–Rapporteurs and Advocates General

Article 15. Designation of the Judge–Rapporteur

(1) As soon as possible after the document initiating proceedings has been lodged, the President of the Court shall designate a Judge to act as Rapporteur in the case.
(2) For cases of the kind referred to in Article 107 and Articles 193 and 194, the Judge–Rapporteur shall be selected from among the Judges of the Chamber designated in accordance with Article 11(2), on a proposal from the President of that Chamber. If, pursuant to Article 109, the Chamber decides that the reference is not to be dealt with under the urgent procedure, the President of the Court may reassign the case to a Judge–Rapporteur attached to another Chamber.
(3) The President of the Court shall take the necessary steps if a Judge–Rapporteur is prevented from acting.

Article 16. Designation of the Advocate General

(1) The First Advocate General shall assign each case to an Advocate General.
(2) The First Advocate General shall take the necessary steps if an Advocate General is prevented from acting.

Chapter 4. Assistant Rapporteurs

Article 17. Assistant Rapporteurs

(1) Where the Court is of the opinion that the consideration of and preparatory inquiries in cases before it so require, it shall, pursuant to Article 13 of the Statute, propose the appointment of Assistant Rapporteurs.
(2) Assistant Rapporteurs shall in particular:
(a) assist the President of the Court in interim proceedings and
(b) assist the Judge–Rapporteurs in their work.
(3) In the performance of their duties the Assistant Rapporteurs shall be responsible to the President of the Court, the President of a Chamber or a Judge–Rapporteur, as the case may be.
(4) Before taking up his duties, an Assistant Rapporteur shall take before the Court the oath set out in Article 4 of these Rules.

Chapter 5. Registry

Article 18. Appointment of the Registrar

(1) The Court shall appoint the Registrar.
(2) When the post of Registrar is vacant, an advertisement shall be published in the *Official Journal of the European Union*. Interested persons shall be invited to submit their applications within a time–limit of not less than three weeks, accompanied by full details of their nationality, university degrees, knowledge of languages, present and past occupations, and experience, if any, in judicial and international fields.
(3) The vote, in which the Judges and the Advocates General shall take part, shall take place in accordance with the procedure laid down in Article 8(3) of these Rules.
(4) The Registrar shall be appointed for a term of six years. He may be reappointed. The Court may decide to renew the term of office of the incumbent Registrar without availing itself of the procedure laid down in paragraph 2 of this Article.
(5) The Registrar shall take the oath set out in Article 4 and sign the declaration provided for in Article 5.
(6) The Registrar may be deprived of his office only if he no longer fulfils the requisite conditions or no longer meets the obligations arising from his office. The Court shall take its decision after giving the Registrar an opportunity to make representations.
(7) If the office of Registrar falls vacant before the normal date of expiry of the term thereof, the Court shall appoint a new Registrar for a term of six years.
(8) The name of the Registrar elected in accordance with this Article shall be published in the *Official Journal of the European Union*.

Article 19. Deputy Registrar

The Court may, in accordance with the procedure laid down in respect of the Registrar, appoint a Deputy Registrar to assist the Registrar and to take his place if he is prevented from acting.

Article 20. Responsibilities of the Registrar

(1) The Registrar shall be responsible, under the authority of the President of the Court, for the acceptance, transmission and custody of all documents and for effecting service as provided for by these Rules.
(2) The Registrar shall assist the Members of the Court in all their official functions.

(3) The Registrar shall have custody of the seals and shall be responsible for the records. He shall be in charge of the publications of the Court and, in particular, the European Court Reports.
(4) The Registrar shall direct the services of the Court under the authority of the President of the Court. He shall be responsible for the management of the staff and the administration, and for the preparation and implementation of the budget.

Article 21. Keeping of the register

(1) There shall be kept in the Registry, under the responsibility of the Registrar, a register in which all procedural documents and supporting items and documents lodged shall be entered in the order in which they are submitted.
(2) When a document has been registered, the Registrar shall make a note to that effect on the original and, if a party so requests, on any copy submitted for the purpose.
(3) Entries in the register and the notes provided for in the preceding paragraph shall be authentic.
(4) A notice shall be published in the *Official Journal of the European Union* indicating the date of registration of an application initiating proceedings, the names of the parties, the form of order sought by the applicant and a summary of the pleas in law and of the main supporting arguments or, as the case may be, the date of lodging of a request for a preliminary ruling, the identity of the referring court or tribunal and the parties to the main proceedings, and the questions referred to the Court.

Article 22. Consultation of the register and of judgments and orders

(1) Anyone may consult the register at the Registry and may obtain copies or extracts on payment of a charge on a scale fixed by the Court on a proposal from the Registrar.
(2) The parties to a case may, on payment of the appropriate charge, obtain certified copies of procedural documents.
(3) Anyone may, on payment of the appropriate charge, also obtain certified copies of judgments and orders.

Chapter 6. The Working of the Court

Article 23. Location of the sittings of the Court

The Court may choose to hold one or more specific sittings in a place other than that in which it has its seat.

Article 24. Calendar of the Court's judicial business

(1) The judicial year shall begin on 7 October of each calendar year and end on 6 October of the following year.
(2) The judicial vacations shall be determined by the Court.
(3) In a case of urgency, the President may convene the Judges and the Advocates General during the judicial vacations.
(4) The Court shall observe the official holidays of the place in which it has its seat.
(5) The Court may, in proper circumstances, grant leave of absence to any Judge or Advocate General.
(6) The dates of the judicial vacations and the list of official holidays shall be published annually in the *Official Journal of the European Union*.

Article 25. General meeting

Decisions concerning administrative issues or the action to be taken upon the proposals contained in the preliminary report referred to in Article 59 of these Rules shall be taken by the Court at the general meeting in which all the Judges and Advocates General shall take part and have a vote. The Registrar shall be present, unless the Court decides to the contrary.

Article 26. Drawing–up of minutes

Where the Court sits without the Registrar being present it shall, if necessary, instruct the most junior Judge for the purposes of Article 7 of these Rules to draw up minutes, which shall be signed by that Judge and by the President.

Chapter 7. Formations of the Court

Section 1. Composition of the Formations of the Court

Article 27. Composition of the Grand Chamber

(1) The Grand Chamber shall, for each case, be composed of the President and the Vice–President of the Court, three Presidents of Chambers of five Judges, the Judge–Rapporteur and the number of Judges necessary to reach 15. The last–mentioned Judges and the three Presidents of Chambers of

five Judges shall be designated from the lists referred to in paragraphs 3 and 4 of this Article, following the order laid down therein. The starting–point on each of those lists, in every case assigned to the Grand Chamber, shall be the name of the Judge immediately following the last Judge designated from the list concerned for the preceding case assigned to that formation of the Court.
(2) After the election of the President and the Vice–President of the Court, and then of the Presidents of the Chambers of five Judges, a list of the Presidents of Chambers of five Judges and a list of the other Judges shall be drawn up for the purposes of determining the composition of the Grand Chamber.
(3) The list of the Presidents of Chambers of five Judges shall be drawn up according to the order laid down in Article 7 of these Rules.
(4) The list of the other Judges shall be drawn up according to the order laid down in Article 7 of these Rules, alternating with the reverse order: the first Judge on that list shall be the first according to the order laid down in that Article, the second Judge shall be the last according to that order, the third Judge shall be the second according to that order, the fourth Judge the penultimate according to that order, and so on.
(5) The lists referred to in paragraphs 3 and 4 shall be published in the *Official Journal of the European Union*.
(6) In cases which are assigned to the Grand Chamber between the beginning of a calendar year in which there is a partial replacement of Judges and the moment when that replacement has taken place, two substitute Judges may be designated to complete the formation of the Court for so long as the attainment of the quorum referred to in the third paragraph of Article 17 of the Statute is in doubt. Those substitute Judges shall be the two Judges appearing on the list referred to in paragraph 4 immediately after the last Judge designated for the composition of the Grand Chamber in the case.
(7) The substitute Judges shall replace, in the order of the list referred to in paragraph 4, such Judges as are unable to take part in the determination of the case.

Article 28. Composition of the Chambers of five and of three Judges
(1) The Chambers of five Judges and of three Judges shall, for each case, be composed of the President of the Chamber, the Judge–Rapporteur and the number of Judges required to attain the number of five and three Judges respectively. Those last–mentioned Judges shall be designated from the lists referred to in paragraphs 2 and 3, following the order laid down therein. The starting–point on those lists, in every case assigned to a Chamber, shall be the name of the Judge immediately following the last Judge designated from the list for the preceding case assigned to the Chamber concerned.
(2) For the composition of the Chambers of five Judges, after the election of the Presidents of those Chambers lists shall be drawn up including all the Judges attached to the Chamber concerned, with the exception of its President. The lists shall be drawn up in the same way as the list referred to in Article 27(4).
(3) For the composition of the Chambers of three Judges, after the election of the Presidents of those Chambers lists shall be drawn up including all the Judges attached to the Chamber concerned, with the exception of its President. The lists shall be drawn up according to the order laid down in Article 7.
(4) The lists referred to in paragraphs 2 and 3 shall be published in the *Official Journal of the European Union* .

Article 29. Composition of Chambers where cases are related or referred back
(1) Where the Court considers that a number of cases must be heard and determined together by one and the same formation of the Court, the composition of that formation shall be that fixed for the case in respect of which the preliminary report was examined first.
(2) Where a Chamber to which a case has been assigned requests the Court, pursuant to Article 60(3) of these Rules, to assign the case to a formation composed of a greater number of Judges, that formation shall include the members of the Chamber which has referred the case back.

Article 30. Where a President of a Chamber is prevented from acting
(1) When the President of a Chamber of five Judges is prevented from acting, the functions of President of the Chamber shall be exercised by a President of a Chamber of three Judges, where necessary according to the order laid down in Article 7 of these Rules, or, if that formation of the Court does not include a President of a Chamber of three Judges, by one of the other Judges according to the order laid down in Article 7.
(2) When the President of a Chamber of three Judges is prevented from acting, the functions of President of the Chamber shall be exercised by a Judge of that formation of the Court according to the order laid down in Article 7.

PART III   EUROPEAN UNION

Article 31. Where a member of the formation of the Court is prevented from acting

(1) When a member of the Grand Chamber is prevented from acting, he shall be replaced by another Judge according to the order of the list referred to in Article 27(4).

(2) When a member of a Chamber of five Judges is prevented from acting, he shall be replaced by another Judge of that Chamber, according to the order of the list referred to in Article 28(2). If it is not possible to replace the Judge prevented from acting by a Judge of the same Chamber, the President of that Chamber shall so inform the President of the Court who may designate another Judge to complete the Chamber.

(3) When a member of a Chamber of three Judges is prevented from acting, he shall be replaced by another Judge of that Chamber, according to the order of the list referred to in Article 28(3). If it is not possible to replace the Judge prevented from acting by a Judge of the same Chamber, the President of that Chamber shall so inform the President of the Court who may designate another Judge to complete the Chamber.

Section 2. Deliberations

Article 32. Procedures concerning deliberations

(1) The deliberations of the Court shall be and shall remain secret.

(2) When a hearing has taken place, only those Judges who participated in that hearing and, where relevant, the Assistant Rapporteur responsible for the consideration of the case shall take part in the deliberations.

(3) Every Judge taking part in the deliberations shall state his opinion and the reasons for it.

(4) The conclusions reached by the majority of the Judges after final discussion shall determine the decision of the Court.

Article 33. Number of Judges taking part in the deliberations

Where, by reason of a Judge being prevented from acting, there is an even number of Judges, the most junior Judge for the purposes of Article 7 of these Rules shall abstain from taking part in the deliberations unless he is the Judge–Rapporteur. In that case the Judge immediately senior to him shall abstain from taking part in the deliberations.

Article 34. Quorum of the Grand Chamber

(1) If, for a case assigned to the Grand Chamber, it is not possible to attain the quorum referred to in the third paragraph of Article 17 of the Statute, the President of the Court shall designate one or more other Judges according to the order of the list referred to in Article 27(4) of these Rules.

(2) If a hearing has taken place before that designation, the Court shall re–hear oral argument from the parties and the Opinion of the Advocate General.

Article 35. Quorum of the Chambers of five and of three Judges

(1) If, for a case assigned to a Chamber of five or of three Judges, it is not possible to attain the quorum referred to in the second paragraph of Article 17 of the Statute, the President of the Court shall designate one or more other Judges according to the order of the list referred to in Article 28(2) or (3), respectively, of these Rules. If it is not possible to replace the Judge prevented from acting by a Judge of the same Chamber, the President of that Chamber shall so inform the President of the Court forthwith who shall designate another Judge to complete the Chamber.

(2) Article 34(2) shall apply, *mutatis mutandis*, to the Chambers of five and of three Judges.

Chapter 8. Languages

Article 36. Language of a case

The language of a case shall be Bulgarian, Croatian, Czech, Danish, Dutch, English, Estonian, Finnish, French, German, Greek, Hungarian, Irish, Italian, Latvian, Lithuanian, Maltese, Polish, Portuguese, Romanian, Slovak, Slovenian, Spanish or Swedish.

Article 37. Determination of the language of a case

(1) In direct actions, the language of a case shall be chosen by the applicant, except that:

(a) where the defendant is a Member State, the language of the case shall be the official language of that State; where that State has more than one official language, the applicant may choose between them;

(b) at the joint request of the parties, the use of another of the languages mentioned in Article 36 for all or part of the proceedings may be authorised;

(c) at the request of one of the parties, and after the opposite party and the Advocate General have been heard, the use of another of the languages mentioned in Article 36 may be authorised as the

language of the case for all or part of the proceedings by way of derogation from subparagraphs (a) and (b); such a request may not be submitted by one of the institutions of the European Union.
(2) Without prejudice to the provisions of paragraph 1(b) and (c), and of Article 38(4) and (5) of these Rules,
(a) in appeals against decisions of the General Court as referred to in Articles 56 and 57 of the Statute, the language of the case shall be the language of the decision of the General Court against which the appeal is brought;
(b) where, in accordance with the second paragraph of Article 62 of the Statute, the Court decides to review a decision of the General Court, the language of the case shall be the language of the decision of the General Court which is the subject of review;
(c) in the case of challenges concerning the costs to be recovered, applications to set aside judgments by default, third–party proceedings and applications for interpretation or revision of a judgment or for the Court to remedy a failure to adjudicate, the language of the case shall be the language of the decision to which those applications or challenges relate.
(3) In preliminary ruling proceedings, the language of the case shall be the language of the referring court or tribunal. At the duly substantiated request of one of the parties to the main proceedings, and after the other party to the main proceedings and the Advocate General have been heard, the use of another of the languages mentioned in Article 36 may be authorised for the oral part of the procedure. Where granted, such authorisation shall apply in respect of all the interested persons referred to in Article 23 of the Statute.
(4) Requests as above may be decided on by the President; the latter may, and where he wishes to accede to a request without the agreement of all the parties must, refer the request to the Court.

Article 38. Use of the language of the case

(1) The language of the case shall in particular be used in the written and oral pleadings of the parties, including the items and documents produced or annexed to them, and also in the minutes and decisions of the Court.
(2) Any item or document produced or annexed that is expressed in another language must be accompanied by a translation into the language of the case.
(3) However, in the case of substantial items or lengthy documents, translations may be confined to extracts. At any time the Court may, of its own motion or at the request of one of the parties, call for a complete or fuller translation.
(4) Notwithstanding the foregoing provisions, a Member State shall be entitled to use its official language when taking part in preliminary ruling proceedings, when intervening in a case before the Court or when bringing a matter before the Court pursuant to Article 259 TFEU. This provision shall apply both to written documents and to oral statements. The Registrar shall arrange in each instance for translation into the language of the case.
(5) The States, other than the Member States, which are parties to the EEA Agreement, and also the EFTA Surveillance Authority, may be authorised to use one of the languages mentioned in Article 36, other than the language of the case, when they take part in preliminary ruling proceedings or intervene in a case before the Court. This provision shall apply both to written documents and to oral statements. The Registrar shall arrange in each instance for translation into the language of the case.
(6) Non–Member States taking part in preliminary ruling proceedings pursuant to the fourth paragraph of Article 23 of the Statute may be authorised to use one of the languages mentioned in Article 36 other than the language of the case. This provision shall apply both to written documents and to oral statements. The Registrar shall arrange in each instance for translation into the language of the case.
(7) Where a witness or expert states that he is unable adequately to express himself in one of the languages referred to in Article 36, the Court may authorise him to give his evidence in another language. The Registrar shall arrange for translation into the language of the case.
(8) The President and the Vice–President of the Court and also the Presidents of Chambers in conducting oral proceedings, Judges and Advocates General in putting questions and Advocates General in delivering their Opinions may use one of the languages referred to in Article 36 other than the language of the case. The Registrar shall arrange for translation into the language of the case.

Article 39. Responsibility of the Registrar concerning language arrangements

The Registrar shall, at the request of any Judge, of the Advocate General or of a party, arrange for anything said or written in the course of the proceedings before the Court to be translated into the languages chosen from those referred to in Article 36.

Article 40. Languages of the publications of the Court

PART III   EUROPEAN UNION

Publications of the Court shall be issued in the languages referred to in Article 1 of Council Regulation No 1.

Article 41. Authentic texts

The texts of documents drawn up in the language of the case or, where applicable, in another language authorised pursuant to Articles 37 or 38 of these Rules shall be authentic.

Article 42. Language service of the Court

The Court shall set up a language service staffed by experts with adequate legal training and a thorough knowledge of several official languages of the European Union.

Title II. Common Procedural Provisions

Chapter 1. Rights and Obligations of Agents, Advisers and Lawyers

Article 43. Privileges, immunities and facilities

(1) Agents, advisers and lawyers who appear before the Court or before any judicial authority to which the Court has addressed letters rogatory shall enjoy immunity in respect of words spoken or written by them concerning the case or the parties.

(2) Agents, advisers and lawyers shall also enjoy the following privileges and facilities:

(a) any papers and documents relating to the proceedings shall be exempt from both search and seizure. In the event of a dispute, the customs officials or police may seal those papers and documents; they shall then be immediately forwarded to the Court for inspection in the presence of the Registrar and of the person concerned;

(b) agents, advisers and lawyers shall be entitled to travel in the course of duty without hindrance.

Article 44. Status of the parties' representatives

(1) In order to qualify for the privileges, immunities and facilities specified in Article 43, persons entitled to them shall furnish proof of their status as follows:

(a) agents shall produce an official document issued by the party for whom they act, who shall immediately serve a copy thereof on the Registrar;

(b) lawyers shall produce a certificate that they are authorised to practise before a court of a Member State or of another State which is a party to the EEA Agreement, and, where the party which they represent is a legal person governed by private law, an authority to act issued by that person;

(c) advisers shall produce an authority to act issued by the party whom they are assisting.

(2) The Registrar of the Court shall issue them with a certificate, as required. The validity of this certificate shall be limited to a specified period, which may be extended or curtailed according to the duration of the proceedings.

Article 45. Waiver of immunity

(1) The privileges, immunities and facilities specified in Article 43 of these Rules are granted exclusively in the interests of the proper conduct of proceedings.

(2) The Court may waive immunity where it considers that the proper conduct of proceedings will not be hindered thereby.

Article 46. Exclusion from the proceedings

(1) If the Court considers that the conduct of an agent, adviser or lawyer before the Court is incompatible with the dignity of the Court or with the requirements of the proper administration of justice, or that such agent, adviser or lawyer is using his rights for purposes other than those for which they were granted, it shall inform the person concerned. If the Court informs the competent authorities to whom the person concerned is answerable, a copy of the letter sent to those authorities shall be forwarded to the person concerned.

(2) On the same grounds, the Court may at any time, having heard the person concerned and the Advocate General, decide to exclude an agent, adviser or lawyer from the proceedings by reasoned order. That order shall have immediate effect.

(3) Where an agent, adviser or lawyer is excluded from the proceedings, the proceedings shall be suspended for a period fixed by the President in order to allow the party concerned to appoint another agent, adviser or lawyer.

(4) Decisions taken under this Article may be rescinded.

Article 47. University teachers and parties to the main proceedings

(1) The provisions of this Chapter shall apply to university teachers who have a right of audience before the Court in accordance with Article 19 of the Statute.

(2) They shall also apply, in the context of references for a preliminary ruling, to the parties to the

main proceedings where, in accordance with the national rules of procedure applicable, those parties are permitted to bring or defend court proceedings without being represented by a lawyer, and to persons authorised under those rules to represent them.

Chapter 2. Service

Article 48. Methods of service

(1) Where these Rules require that a document be served on a person, the Registrar shall ensure that service is effected at that person's address for service either by the dispatch of a copy of the document by registered post with a form for acknowledgement of receipt or by personal delivery of the copy against a receipt. The Registrar shall prepare and certify the copies of documents to be served, save where the parties themselves supply the copies in accordance with Article 57(2) of these Rules.
(2) Where the addressee has agreed that service is to be effected on him by telefax or any other technical means of communication, any procedural document, including a judgment or order of the Court, may be served by the transmission of a copy of the document by such means.
(3) Where, for technical reasons or on account of the nature or length of the document, such transmission is impossible or impracticable, the document shall be served, if the addressee has not specified an address for service, at his address in accordance with the procedures laid down in paragraph 1 of this Article. The addressee shall be so informed by telefax or any other technical means of communication. Service shall then be deemed to have been effected on the addressee by registered post on the 10th day following the lodging of the registered letter at the post office of the place in which the Court has its seat, unless it is shown by the acknowledgement of receipt that the letter was received on a different date or the addressee informs the Registrar, within three weeks of being informed by telefax or any other technical means of communication, that the document to be served has not reached him.
(4) The Court may, by decision, determine the criteria for a procedural document to be served by electronic means. That decision shall be published in the *Official Journal of the European Union* .

Chapter 3. Time–Limits

Article 49. Calculation of time–limits

(1) Any procedural time–limit prescribed by the Treaties, the Statute or these Rules shall be calculated as follows:
(a) where a time–limit expressed in days, weeks, months or years is to be calculated from the moment at which an event occurs or an action takes place, the day during which that event occurs or that action takes place shall not be counted as falling within the time–limit in question;
(b) a time–limit expressed in weeks, months or years shall end with the expiry of whichever day in the last week, month or year is the same day of the week, or falls on the same date, as the day during which the event or action from which the time–limit is to be calculated occurred or took place. If, in a time–limit expressed in months or years, the day on which it should expire does not occur in the last month, the time–limit shall end with the expiry of the last day of that month;
(c) where a time–limit is expressed in months and days, it shall first be calculated in whole months, then in days;
(d) time–limits shall include Saturdays, Sundays and the official holidays referred to in Article 24(6) of these Rules;
(e) time–limits shall not be suspended during the judicial vacations.
(2) If the time–limit would otherwise end on a Saturday, Sunday or an official holiday, it shall be extended until the end of the first subsequent working day.

Article 50. Proceedings against a measure adopted by an institution

Where the time–limit allowed for initiating proceedings against a measure adopted by an institution runs from the publication of that measure, that time–limit shall be calculated, for the purposes of Article 49(1)(a), from the end of the 14th day after publication of the measure in the *Official Journal of the European Union* .

Article 51. Extension on account of distance

The procedural time–limits shall be extended on account of distance by a single period of 10 days.

Article 52. Setting and extension of time–limits

(1) Any time–limit prescribed by the Court pursuant to these Rules may be extended.
(2) The President and the Presidents of Chambers may delegate to the Registrar power of signature for the purposes of setting certain time–limits which, pursuant to these Rules, it falls to them to prescribe, or of extending such time–limits.

Chapter 4. Different Procedures for Dealing with Cases

Article 53. Procedures for dealing with cases
(1) Without prejudice to the special provisions laid down in the Statute or in these Rules, the procedure before the Court shall consist of a written part and an oral part.
(2) Where it is clear that the Court has no jurisdiction to hear and determine a case or where a request or an application is manifestly inadmissible, the Court may, after hearing the Advocate General, at any time decide to give a decision by reasoned order without taking further steps in the proceedings.
(3) The President may in special circumstances decide that a case be given priority over others.
(4) A case may be dealt with under an expedited procedure in accordance with the conditions provided by these Rules.
(5) A reference for a preliminary ruling may be dealt with under an urgent procedure in accordance with the conditions provided by these Rules.

Article 54. Joinder
(1) Two or more cases of the same type concerning the same subject–matter may at any time be joined, on account of the connection between them, for the purposes of the written or oral part of the procedure or of the judgment which closes the proceedings.
(2) A decision on whether cases should be joined shall be taken by the President after hearing the Judge–Rapporteur and the Advocate General, if the cases concerned have already been assigned, and, save in the case of references for a preliminary ruling, after also hearing the parties. The President may refer the decision on this matter to the Court.
(3) Joined cases may be disjoined, in accordance with the provisions of paragraph 2.

Article 55. Stay of proceedings
(1) The proceedings may be stayed:
(a) in the circumstances specified in the third paragraph of Article 54 of the Statute, by order of the Court, made after hearing the Advocate General;
(b) in all other cases, by decision of the President adopted after hearing the Judge–Rapporteur and the Advocate General and, save in the case of references for a preliminary ruling, the parties.
(2) The proceedings may be resumed by order or decision, following the same procedure.
(3) The orders or decisions referred to in paragraphs 1 and 2 shall be served on the parties or interested persons referred to in Article 23 of the Statute.
(4) The stay of proceedings shall take effect on the date indicated in the order or decision of stay or, in the absence of such indication, on the date of that order or decision.
(5) While proceedings are stayed time shall cease to run for the parties or interested persons referred to in Article 23 of the Statute for the purposes of procedural time–limits.
(6) Where the order or decision of stay does not fix the length of stay, it shall end on the date indicated in the order or decision of resumption or, in the absence of such indication, on the date of the order or decision of resumption.
(7) From the date of resumption of proceedings following a stay, the suspended procedural time–limits shall be replaced by new time–limits and time shall begin to run from the date of that resumption.

Article 56. Deferment of the determination of a case
After hearing the Judge–Rapporteur, the Advocate General and the parties, the President may in special circumstances, either of his own motion or at the request of one of the parties, defer a case to be dealt with at a later date.

Chapter 5. Written Part of the Procedure

Article 57. Lodging of procedural documents
(1) The original of every procedural document must bear the handwritten signature of the party's agent or lawyer or, in the case of observations submitted in the context of preliminary ruling proceedings, that of the party to the main proceedings or his representative, if the national rules of procedure applicable to those main proceedings so permit.
(2) The original, accompanied by all annexes referred to therein, shall be submitted together with five copies for the Court and, in the case of proceedings other than preliminary ruling proceedings, a copy for every other party to the proceedings. Copies shall be certified by the party lodging them.
(3) The institutions shall in addition produce, within time–limits laid down by the Court, translations of any procedural document into the other languages provided for by Article 1 of Council Regulation No 1. The preceding paragraph of this Article shall apply.

(4) To every procedural document there shall be annexed a file containing the items and documents relied on in support of it, together with a schedule listing them.
(5) Where in view of the length of an item or document only extracts from it are annexed to the procedural document, the whole item or document or a full copy of it shall be lodged at the Registry.
(6) All procedural documents shall bear a date. In the calculation of procedural time–limits, only the date and time of lodgment of the original at the Registry shall be taken into account.
(7) Without prejudice to the provisions of paragraphs 1 to 6, the date on and time at which a copy of the signed original of a procedural document, including the schedule of items and documents referred to in paragraph 4, is received at the Registry by telefax or any other technical means of communication available to the Court shall be deemed to be the date and time of lodgment for the purposes of compliance with the procedural time–limits, provided that the signed original of the procedural document, accompanied by the annexes and copies referred to in paragraph 2, is lodged at the Registry no later than 10 days thereafter.
(8) Without prejudice to paragraphs 3 to 6, the Court may, by decision, determine the criteria for a procedural document sent to the Registry by electronic means to be deemed to be the original of that document. That decision shall be published in the *Official Journal of the European Union* .

Article 58. Length of procedural documents

Without prejudice to any special provisions laid down in these Rules, the Court may, by decision, set the maximum length of written pleadings or observations lodged before it. That decision shall be published in the *Official Journal of the European Union* .

Chapter 6. The Preliminary Report and Assignment of Cases to Formations of the Court

Article 59. Preliminary report

(1) When the written part of the procedure is closed, the President shall fix a date on which the Judge–Rapporteur is to present a preliminary report to the general meeting of the Court.
(2) The preliminary report shall contain proposals as to whether particular measures of organisation of procedure, measures of inquiry or, if appropriate, requests to the referring court or tribunal for clarification should be undertaken, and as to the formation to which the case should be assigned. It shall also contain the Judge–Rapporteur's proposals, if any, as to whether to dispense with a hearing and as to whether to dispense with an Opinion of the Advocate General pursuant to the fifth paragraph of Article 20 of the Statute.
(3) The Court shall decide, after hearing the Advocate General, what action to take on the proposals of the Judge–Rapporteur.

Article 60. Assignment of cases to formations of the Court

(1) The Court shall assign to the Chambers of five and of three Judges any case brought before it in so far as the difficulty or importance of the case or particular circumstances are not such as to require that it should be assigned to the Grand Chamber, unless a Member State or an institution of the European Union participating in the proceedings has requested that the case be assigned to the Grand Chamber, pursuant to the third paragraph of Article 16 of the Statute.
(2) The Court shall sit as a full Court where cases are brought before it pursuant to the provisions referred to in the fourth paragraph of Article 16 of the Statute. It may assign a case to the full Court where, in accordance with the fifth paragraph of Article 16 of the Statute, it considers that the case is of exceptional importance.
(3) The formation to which a case has been assigned may, at any stage of the proceedings, request the Court to assign the case to a formation composed of a greater number of Judges.
(4) Where the oral part of the procedure is opened without an inquiry, the President of the formation determining the case shall fix the opening date.

Chapter 7. Measures of Organisation of Procedure and Measures of Inquiry

Section 1. Measures of Organisation of Procedure

Article 61. Measures of organisation prescribed by the Court

(1) In addition to the measures which may be prescribed in accordance with Article 24 of the Statute, the Court may invite the parties or the interested persons referred to in Article 23 of the Statute to answer certain questions in writing, within the time–limit laid down by the Court, or at the hearing. The written replies shall be communicated to the other parties or the interested persons referred to in Article 23 of the Statute.
(2) Where a hearing is organised, the Court shall, in so far as possible, invite the participants in that hearing to concentrate in their oral pleadings on one or more specified issues.

Article 62. Measures of organisation prescribed by the Judge–Rapporteur or the Advocate General

(1) The Judge–Rapporteur or the Advocate General may request the parties or the interested persons referred to in Article 23 of the Statute to submit within a specified time–limit all such information relating to the facts, and all such documents or other particulars, as they may consider relevant. The replies and documents provided shall be communicated to the other parties or the interested persons referred to in Article 23 of the Statute.
(2) The Judge–Rapporteur or the Advocate General may also send to the parties or the interested persons referred to in Article 23 of the Statute questions to be answered at the hearing.

Section 2. Measures of Inquiry

Article 63. Decision on measures of inquiry
(1) The Court shall decide in its general meeting whether a measure of inquiry is necessary.
(2) Where the case has already been assigned to a formation of the Court, the decision shall be taken by that formation.

Article 64. Determination of measures of inquiry
(1) The Court, after hearing the Advocate General, shall prescribe the measures of inquiry that it considers appropriate by means of an order setting out the facts to be proved.
(2) Without prejudice to Articles 24 and 25 of the Statute, the following measures of inquiry may be adopted:
(a) the personal appearance of the parties;
(b) a request for information and production of documents;
(c) oral testimony;
(d) the commissioning of an expert's report;
(e) an inspection of the place or thing in question.
(3) Evidence may be submitted in rebuttal and previous evidence may be amplified.

Article 65. Participation in measures of inquiry
(1) Where the formation of the Court does not undertake the inquiry itself, it shall entrust the task of so doing to the Judge–Rapporteur.
(2) The Advocate General shall take part in the measures of inquiry.
(3) The parties shall be entitled to attend the measures of inquiry.

Article 66. Oral testimony
(1) The Court may, either of its own motion or at the request of one of the parties, and after hearing the Advocate General, order that certain facts be proved by witnesses.
(2) A request by a party for the examination of a witness shall state precisely about what facts and for what reasons the witness should be examined.
(3) The Court shall rule by reasoned order on the request referred to in the preceding paragraph. If the request is granted, the order shall set out the facts to be established and state which witnesses are to be heard in respect of each of those facts.
(4) Witnesses shall be summoned by the Court, where appropriate after lodgment of the security provided for in Article 73(1) of these Rules.

Article 67. Examination of witnesses
(1) After the identity of the witness has been established, the President shall inform him that he will be required to vouch the truth of his evidence in the manner laid down in these Rules.
(2) The witness shall give his evidence to the Court, the parties having been given notice to attend. After the witness has given his evidence the President may, at the request of one of the parties or of his own motion, put questions to him.
(3) The other Judges and the Advocate General may do likewise.
(4) Subject to the control of the President, questions may be put to witnesses by the representatives of the parties.

Article 68. Witnesses' oath
(1) After giving his evidence, the witness shall take the following oath:
'I swear that I have spoken the truth, the whole truth and nothing but the truth.'
(2) The Court may, after hearing the parties, exempt a witness from taking the oath.

Article 69. Pecuniary penalties
(1) Witnesses who have been duly summoned shall obey the summons and attend for examination.

(2) If, without good reason, a witness who has been duly summoned fails to appear before the Court, the Court may impose upon him a pecuniary penalty not exceeding EUR 5 000 and may order that a further summons be served on the witness at his own expense.
(3) The same penalty may be imposed upon a witness who, without good reason, refuses to give evidence or to take the oath.

Article 70. Expert's report
(1) The Court may order that an expert's report be obtained. The order appointing the expert shall define his task and set a time–limit within which he is to submit his report.
(2) After the expert has submitted his report and that report has been served on the parties, the Court may order that the expert be examined, the parties having been given notice to attend. At the request of one of the parties or of his own motion, the President may put questions to the expert.
(3) The other Judges and the Advocate General may do likewise.
(4) Subject to the control of the President, questions may be put to the expert by the representatives of the parties.

Article 71. Expert's oath
(1) After making his report, the expert shall take the following oath:
'I swear that I have conscientiously and impartially carried out my task.'
(2) The Court may, after hearing the parties, exempt the expert from taking the oath.

Article 72. Objection to a witness or expert
(1) If one of the parties objects to a witness or an expert on the ground that he is not a competent or proper person to act as a witness or expert or for any other reason, or if a witness or expert refuses to give evidence or to take the oath, the matter shall be resolved by the Court.
(2) An objection to a witness or an expert shall be raised within two weeks after service of the order summoning the witness or appointing the expert; the statement of objection must set out the grounds of objection and indicate the nature of any evidence offered.

Article 73. Witnesses' and experts' costs
(1) Where the Court orders the examination of witnesses or an expert's report, it may request the parties or one of them to lodge security for the witnesses' costs or the costs of the expert's report.
(2) Witnesses and experts shall be entitled to reimbursement of their travel and subsistence expenses. The cashier of the Court may make an advance payment towards these expenses.
(3) Witnesses shall be entitled to compensation for loss of earnings, and experts to fees for their services. The cashier of the Court shall pay witnesses and experts these sums after they have carried out their respective duties or tasks.

Article 74. Minutes of inquiry hearings
(1) The Registrar shall draw up minutes of every inquiry hearing. The minutes shall be signed by the President and by the Registrar. They shall constitute an official record.
(2) In the case of the examination of witnesses or experts, the minutes shall be signed by the President or by the Judge–Rapporteur responsible for conducting the examination of the witness or expert, and by the Registrar. Before the minutes are thus signed, the witness or expert must be given an opportunity to check the content of the minutes and to sign them.
(3) The minutes shall be served on the parties.

Article 75. Opening of the oral part of the procedure after the inquiry
(1) Unless the Court decides to prescribe a time–limit within which the parties may submit written observations, the President shall fix the date for the opening of the oral part of the procedure after the measures of inquiry have been completed.
(2) Where a time–limit has been prescribed for the submission of written observations, the President shall fix the date for the opening of the oral part of the procedure after that time–limit has expired.

Chapter 8. Oral Part of the Procedure

Article 76. Hearing
(1) Any reasoned requests for a hearing shall be submitted within three weeks after service on the parties or the interested persons referred to in Article 23 of the Statute of notification of the close of the written part of the procedure. That time–limit may be extended by the President.
(2) On a proposal from the Judge–Rapporteur and after hearing the Advocate General, the Court may decide not to hold a hearing if it considers, on reading the written pleadings or observations lodged during the written part of the procedure, that it has sufficient information to give a ruling.

(3) The preceding paragraph shall not apply where a request for a hearing, stating reasons, has been submitted by an interested person referred to in Article 23 of the Statute who did not participate in the written part of the procedure.

Article 77. Joint hearing
If the similarities between two or more cases of the same type so permit, the Court may decide to organise a joint hearing of those cases.

Article 78. Conduct of oral proceedings
Oral proceedings shall be opened and directed by the President, who shall be responsible for the proper conduct of the hearing.

Article 79. Cases heard in camera
(1) For serious reasons related, in particular, to the security of the Member States or to the protection of minors, the Court may decide to hear a case *in camera*.
(2) The oral proceedings in cases heard *in camera* shall not be published.

Article 80. Questions
The members of the formation of the Court and the Advocate General may in the course of the hearing put questions to the agents, advisers or lawyers of the parties and, in the circumstances referred to in Article 47(2) of these Rules, to the parties to the main proceedings or to their representatives.

Article 81. Close of the hearing
After the parties or the interested persons referred to in Article 23 of the Statute have presented oral argument, the President shall declare the hearing closed.

Article 82. Delivery of the Opinion of the Advocate General
(1) Where a hearing takes place, the Opinion of the Advocate General shall be delivered after the close of that hearing.
(2) The President shall declare the oral part of the procedure closed after the Advocate General has delivered his Opinion.

Article 83. Opening or reopening of the oral part of the procedure
The Court may at any time, after hearing the Advocate General, order the opening or reopening of the oral part of the procedure, in particular if it considers that it lacks sufficient information or where a party has, after the close of that part of the procedure, submitted a new fact which is of such a nature as to be a decisive factor for the decision of the Court, or where the case must be decided on the basis of an argument which has not been debated between the parties or the interested persons referred to in Article 23 of the Statute.

Article 84. Minutes of hearings
(1) The Registrar shall draw up minutes of every hearing. The minutes shall be signed by the President and by the Registrar. They shall constitute an official record.
(2) The parties and interested persons referred to in Article 23 of the Statute may inspect the minutes at the Registry and obtain copies.

Article 85. Recording of the hearing
The President may, on a duly substantiated request, authorise a party or an interested person referred to in Article 23 of the Statute who has participated in the written or oral part of the proceedings to listen, on the Court's premises, to the soundtrack of the hearing in the language used by the speaker during that hearing.

Chapter 9. Judgments and Orders

Article 86. Date of delivery of a judgment
The parties or interested persons referred to in Article 23 of the Statute shall be informed of the date of delivery of a judgment.

Article 87. Content of a judgment
A judgment shall contain:
(a) a statement that it is the judgment of the Court,
(b) an indication as to the formation of the Court,
(c) the date of delivery,
(d) the names of the President and of the Judges who took part in the deliberations, with an indication as to the name of the Judge–Rapporteur,

(e) the name of the Advocate General,
(f) the name of the Registrar,
(g) a description of the parties or of the interested persons referred to in Article 23 of the Statute who participated in the proceedings,
(h) the names of their representatives,
(i) in the case of direct actions and appeals, a statement of the forms of order sought by the parties,
(j) where applicable, the date of the hearing,
(k) a statement that the Advocate General has been heard and, where applicable, the date of his Opinion,
(l) a summary of the facts,
(m) the grounds for the decision,
(n) the operative part of the judgment, including, where appropriate, the decision as to costs.

Article 88. Delivery and service of the judgment
(1) The judgment shall be delivered in open court.
(2) The original of the judgment, signed by the President, by the Judges who took part in the deliberations and by the Registrar, shall be sealed and deposited at the Registry; certified copies of the judgment shall be served on the parties and, where applicable, the referring court or tribunal, the interested persons referred to in Article 23 of the Statute and the General Court.

Article 89. Content of an order
(1) An order shall contain:
(a) a statement that it is the order of the Court,
(b) an indication as to the formation of the Court,
(c) the date of its adoption,
(d) an indication as to the legal basis of the order,
(e) the names of the President and, where applicable, the Judges who took part in the deliberations, with an indication as to the name of the Judge–Rapporteur,
(f) the name of the Advocate General,
(g) the name of the Registrar,
(h) a description of the parties or of the parties to the main proceedings,
(i) the names of their representatives,
(j) a statement that the Advocate General has been heard,
(k) the operative part of the order, including, where appropriate, the decision as to costs.
(2) Where, in accordance with these Rules, an order must be reasoned, it shall in addition contain:
(a) in the case of direct actions and appeals, a statement of the forms of order sought by the parties,
(b) a summary of the facts,
(c) the grounds for the decision.

Article 90. Signature and service of the order
The original of the order, signed by the President and by the Registrar, shall be sealed and deposited at the Registry; certified copies of the order shall be served on the parties and, where applicable, the referring court or tribunal, the interested persons referred to in Article 23 of the Statute and the General Court.

Article 91. Binding nature of judgments and orders
(1) A judgment shall be binding from the date of its delivery.
(2) An order shall be binding from the date of its service.

Article 92. Publication in the Official Journal of the European Union
A notice containing the date and the operative part of the judgment or order of the Court which closes the proceedings shall be published in the *Official Journal of the European Union* .

Title III. References for a Preliminary Ruling

Chapter 1. General Provisions

Article 93. Scope
The procedure shall be governed by the provisions of this Title:
(a) in the cases covered by Article 23 of the Statute,
(b) as regards references for interpretation which may be provided for by agreements to which the European Union or the Member States are parties.

Article 94. Content of the request for a preliminary ruling

PART III EUROPEAN UNION

In addition to the text of the questions referred to the Court for a preliminary ruling, the request for a preliminary ruling shall contain:
(a) a summary of the subject–matter of the dispute and the relevant findings of fact as determined by the referring court or tribunal, or, at least, an account of the facts on which the questions are based;
(b) the tenor of any national provisions applicable in the case and, where appropriate, the relevant national case–law;
(c) a statement of the reasons which prompted the referring court or tribunal to inquire about the interpretation or validity of certain provisions of European Union law, and the relationship between those provisions and the national legislation applicable to the main proceedings.

Article 95. Anonymity
(1) Where anonymity has been granted by the referring court or tribunal, the Court shall respect that anonymity in the proceedings pending before it.
(2) At the request of the referring court or tribunal, at the duly reasoned request of a party to the main proceedings or of its own motion, the Court may also, if it considers it necessary, render anonymous one or more persons or entities concerned by the case.

Article 96. Participation in preliminary ruling proceedings
(1) Pursuant to Article 23 of the Statute, the following shall be authorised to submit observations to the Court:
(a) the parties to the main proceedings,
(b) the Member States,
(c) the European Commission,
(d) the institution which adopted the act the validity or interpretation of which is in dispute,
(e) the States, other than the Member States, which are parties to the EEA Agreement, and also the EFTA Surveillance Authority, where a question concerning one of the fields of application of that Agreement is referred to the Court for a preliminary ruling,
(f) non–Member States which are parties to an agreement relating to a specific subject–matter, concluded with the Council, where the agreement so provides and where a court or tribunal of a Member State refers to the Court of Justice for a preliminary ruling a question falling within the scope of that agreement.
(2) Non–participation in the written part of the procedure does not preclude participation in the oral part of the procedure.

Article 97. Parties to the main proceedings
(1) The parties to the main proceedings are those who are determined as such by the referring court or tribunal in accordance with national rules of procedure.
(2) Where the referring court or tribunal informs the Court that a new party has been admitted to the main proceedings, when the proceedings before the Court are already pending, that party must accept the case as he finds it at the time when the Court was so informed. That party shall receive a copy of every procedural document already served on the interested persons referred to in Article 23 of the Statute.
(3) As regards the representation and attendance of the parties to the main proceedings, the Court shall take account of the rules of procedure in force before the court or tribunal which made the reference. In the event of any doubt as to whether a person may under national law represent a party to the main proceedings, the Court may obtain information from the referring court or tribunal on the rules of procedure applicable.

Article 98. Translation and service of the request for a preliminary ruling
(1) The requests for a preliminary ruling referred to in this Title shall be served on the Member States in the original version, accompanied by a translation into the official language of the State to which they are being addressed. Where appropriate, on account of the length of the request, such translation shall be replaced by the translation into the official language of the State to which it is addressed of a summary of that request, which will serve as a basis for the position to be adopted by that State. The summary shall include the full text of the question or questions referred for a preliminary ruling. That summary shall contain, in particular, in so far as that information appears in the request for a preliminary ruling, the subject–matter of the main proceedings, the essential arguments of the parties to those proceedings, a succinct presentation of the reasons for the reference for a preliminary ruling and the case–law and the provisions of national law and European Union law relied on.
(2) In the cases covered by the third paragraph of Article 23 of the Statute, the requests for a preliminary ruling shall be served on the States, other than the Member States, which are parties to the EEA Agreement and also on the EFTA Surveillance Authority in the original version, accompanied by a

translation of the request, or where appropriate of a summary, into one of the languages referred to in Article 36, to be chosen by the addressee.
(3) Where a non–Member State has the right to take part in preliminary ruling proceedings pursuant to the fourth paragraph of Article 23 of the Statute, the original version of the request for a preliminary ruling shall be served on it accompanied by a translation of the request, or where appropriate of a summary, into one of the languages referred to in Article 36, to be chosen by the non–Member State concerned.

Article 99. Reply by reasoned order
Where a question referred to the Court for a preliminary ruling is identical to a question on which the Court has already ruled, where the reply to such a question may be clearly deduced from existing case–law or where the answer to the question referred for a preliminary ruling admits of no reasonable doubt, the Court may at any time, on a proposal from the Judge–Rapporteur and after hearing the Advocate General, decide to rule by reasoned order.

Article 100. Circumstances in which the Court remains seised
(1) The Court shall remain seised of a request for a preliminary ruling for as long as it is not withdrawn by the court or tribunal which made that request to the Court. The withdrawal of a request may be taken into account until notice of the date of delivery of the judgment has been served on the interested persons referred to in Article 23 of the Statute.
(2) However, the Court may at any time declare that the conditions of its jurisdiction are no longer fulfilled.

Article 101. Request for clarification
(1) Without prejudice to the measures of organisation of procedure and measures of inquiry provided for in these Rules, the Court may, after hearing the Advocate General, request clarification from the referring court or tribunal within a time–limit prescribed by the Court.
(2) The reply of the referring court or tribunal to that request shall be served on the interested persons referred to in Article 23 of the Statute.

Article 102. Costs of the preliminary ruling proceedings
It shall be for the referring court or tribunal to decide as to the costs of the preliminary ruling proceedings.

Article 103. Rectification of judgments and orders
(1) Clerical mistakes, errors in calculation and obvious inaccuracies affecting judgments or orders may be rectified by the Court, of its own motion or at the request of an interested person referred to in Article 23 of the Statute made within two weeks after delivery of the judgment or service of the order.
(2) The Court shall take its decision after hearing the Advocate General.
(3) The original of the rectification order shall be annexed to the original of the rectified decision. A note of this order shall be made in the margin of the original of the rectified decision.

Article 104. Interpretation of preliminary rulings
(1) Article 158 of these Rules relating to the interpretation of judgments and orders shall not apply to decisions given in reply to a request for a preliminary ruling.
(2) It shall be for the national courts or tribunals to assess whether they consider that sufficient guidance is given by a preliminary ruling, or whether it appears to them that a further reference to the Court is required.

Chapter 2. Expedited Preliminary Ruling Procedure

Article 105. Expedited procedure
(1) At the request of the referring court or tribunal or, exceptionally, of his own motion, the President of the Court may, where the nature of the case requires that it be dealt with within a short time, after hearing the Judge–Rapporteur and the Advocate General, decide that a reference for a preliminary ruling is to be determined pursuant to an expedited procedure derogating from the provisions of these Rules.
(2) In that event, the President shall immediately fix the date for the hearing, which shall be communicated to the interested persons referred to in Article 23 of the Statute when the request for a preliminary ruling is served.
(3) The interested persons referred to in the preceding paragraph may lodge statements of case or written observations within a time–limit prescribed by the President, which shall not be less than 15

days. The President may request those interested persons to restrict the matters addressed in their statement of case or written observations to the essential points of law raised by the request for a preliminary ruling.
(4) The statements of case or written observations, if any, shall be communicated to all the interested persons referred to in Article 23 of the Statute prior to the hearing.
(5) The Court shall rule after hearing the Advocate General.

Article 106. Transmission of procedural documents
(1) The procedural documents referred to in the preceding Article shall be deemed to have been lodged on the transmission to the Registry, by telefax or any other technical means of communication available to the Court, of a copy of the signed original and the items and documents relied on in support of it, together with the schedule referred to in Article 57(4). The original of the document and the annexes referred to above shall be sent to the Registry immediately.
(2) Where the preceding Article requires that a document be served on or communicated to a person, such service or communication may be effected by transmission of a copy of the document by telefax or any other technical means of communication available to the Court and the addressee.

Chapter 3. Urgent Preliminary Ruling Procedure

Article 107. Scope of the urgent preliminary ruling procedure
(1) A reference for a preliminary ruling which raises one or more questions in the areas covered by Title V of Part Three of the Treaty on the Functioning of the European Union may, at the request of the referring court or tribunal or, exceptionally, of the Court's own motion, be dealt with under an urgent procedure derogating from the provisions of these Rules.
(2) The referring court or tribunal shall set out the matters of fact and law which establish the urgency and justify the application of that exceptional procedure and shall, in so far as possible, indicate the answer that it proposes to the questions referred.
(3) If the referring court or tribunal has not submitted a request for the urgent procedure to be applied, the President of the Court may, if the application of that procedure appears, prima facie, to be required, ask the Chamber referred to in Article 108 to consider whether it is necessary to deal with the reference under that procedure.

Article 108. Decision as to urgency
(1) The decision to deal with a reference for a preliminary ruling under the urgent procedure shall be taken by the designated Chamber, acting on a proposal from the Judge–Rapporteur and after hearing the Advocate General. The composition of that Chamber shall be determined in accordance with Article 28(2) on the day on which the case is assigned to the Judge–Rapporteur if the application of the urgent procedure is requested by the referring court or tribunal, or, if the application of that procedure is considered at the request of the President of the Court, on the day on which that request is made.
(2) If the case is connected with a pending case assigned to a Judge–Rapporteur who is not a member of the designated Chamber, that Chamber may propose to the President of the Court that the case be assigned to that Judge–Rapporteur. Where the case is reassigned to that Judge–Rapporteur, the Chamber of five Judges which includes him shall carry out the duties of the designated Chamber in respect of that case. Article 29(1) shall apply.

Article 109. Written part of the urgent procedure
(1) A request for a preliminary ruling shall, where the referring court or tribunal has requested the application of the urgent procedure or where the President has requested the designated Chamber to consider whether it is necessary to deal with the reference under that procedure, be served forthwith by the Registrar on the parties to the main proceedings, on the Member State from which the reference is made, on the European Commission and on the institution which adopted the act the validity or interpretation of which is in dispute.
(2) The decision as to whether or not to deal with the reference for a preliminary ruling under the urgent procedure shall be served immediately on the referring court or tribunal and on the parties, Member State and institutions referred to in the preceding paragraph. The decision to deal with the reference under the urgent procedure shall prescribe the time–limit within which those parties or entities may lodge statements of case or written observations. The decision may specify the matters of law to which such statements of case or written observations must relate and may specify the maximum length of those documents.
(3) Where a request for a preliminary ruling refers to an administrative procedure or judicial proceedings conducted in a Member State other than that from which the reference is made, the Court may invite that first Member State to provide all relevant information in writing or at the hearing.

(4) As soon as the service referred to in paragraph 1 above has been effected, the request for a preliminary ruling shall also be communicated to the interested persons referred to in Article 23 of the Statute, other than the persons served, and the decision whether or not to deal with the reference for a preliminary ruling under the urgent procedure shall be communicated to those interested persons as soon as the service referred to in paragraph 2 has been effected.
(5) The interested persons referred to in Article 23 of the Statute shall be informed as soon as possible of the likely date of the hearing.
(6) Where the reference is not to be dealt with under the urgent procedure, the proceedings shall continue in accordance with the provisions of Article 23 of the Statute and the applicable provisions of these Rules.

Article 110. Service and information following the close of the written part of the procedure
(1) Where a reference for a preliminary ruling is to be dealt with under the urgent procedure, the request for a preliminary ruling and the statements of case or written observations which have been lodged shall be served on the interested persons referred to in Article 23 of the Statute other than the parties and entities referred to in Article 109(1). The request for a preliminary ruling shall be accompanied by a translation, where appropriate of a summary, in accordance with Article 98.
(2) The statements of case or written observations which have been lodged shall also be served on the parties and other interested persons referred to in Article 109(1).
(3) The date of the hearing shall be communicated to the interested persons referred to in Article 23 of the Statute at the same time as the documents referred to in the preceding paragraphs are served.

Article 111. Omission of the written part of the procedure
The designated Chamber may, in cases of extreme urgency, decide to omit the written part of the procedure referred to in Article 109(2).

Article 112. Decision on the substance
The designated Chamber shall rule after hearing the Advocate General.

Article 113. Formation of the Court
(1) The designated Chamber may decide to sit in a formation of three Judges. In that event, it shall be composed of the President of the designated Chamber, the Judge–Rapporteur and the first Judge or, as the case may be, the first two Judges designated from the list referred to in Article 28(2) on the date on which the composition of the designated Chamber is determined in accordance with Article 108(1).
(2) The designated Chamber may also request the Court to assign the case to a formation composed of a greater number of Judges. The urgent procedure shall continue before the new formation of the Court, where necessary after the reopening of the oral part of the procedure.

Article 114. Transmission of procedural documents
Procedural documents shall be transmitted in accordance with Article 106.

Chapter 4. Legal Aid

Article 115. Application for legal aid
(1) A party to the main proceedings who is wholly or in part unable to meet the costs of the proceedings before the Court may at any time apply for legal aid.
(2) The application shall be accompanied by all information and supporting documents making it possible to assess the applicant's financial situation, such as a certificate issued by a competent national authority attesting to his financial situation.
(3) If the applicant has already obtained legal aid before the referring court or tribunal, he shall produce the decision of that court or tribunal and specify what is covered by the sums already granted.

Article 116. Decision on the application for legal aid
(1) As soon as the application for legal aid has been lodged it shall be assigned by the President to the Judge–Rapporteur responsible for the case in the context of which the application has been made.
(2) The decision to grant legal aid, in full or in part, or to refuse it shall be taken, on a proposal from the Judge–Rapporteur and after hearing the Advocate General, by the Chamber of three Judges to which the Judge–Rapporteur is assigned. The formation of the Court shall, in that event, be composed of the President of that Chamber, the Judge–Rapporteur and the first Judge or, as the case may be, the first two Judges designated from the list referred to in Article 28(3) on the date on which the application for legal aid is brought before that Chamber by the Judge–Rapporteur.
(3) If the Judge–Rapporteur is not a member of a Chamber of three Judges, the decision shall be

taken, under the same conditions, by the Chamber of five Judges to which he is assigned. In addition to the Judge–Rapporteur, the formation of the Court shall be composed of four Judges designated from the list referred to in Article 28(2) on the date on which the application for legal aid is brought before that Chamber by the Judge–Rapporteur.
(4) The formation of the Court shall give its decision by way of order. Where the application for legal aid is refused in whole or in part, the order shall state the reasons for that refusal.

Article 117. Sums to be advanced as legal aid
Where legal aid is granted, the cashier of the Court shall be responsible, where applicable within the limits set by the formation of the Court, for costs involved in the assistance and representation of the applicant before the Court. At the request of the applicant or his representative, an advance on those costs may be paid.

Article 118. Withdrawal of legal aid
The formation of the Court which gave a decision on the application for legal aid may at any time, either of its own motion or on request, withdraw that legal aid if the circumstances which led to its being granted alter during the proceedings.

Title IV. Direct Actions

Chapter 1. Representation of the Parties

Article 119. Obligation to be represented
(1) A party may be represented only by his agent or lawyer.
(2) Agents and lawyers must lodge at the Registry an official document or an authority to act issued by the party whom they represent.
(3) The lawyer acting for a party must also lodge at the Registry a certificate that he is authorised to practise before a court of a Member State or of another State which is a party to the EEA Agreement.
(4) If those documents are not lodged, the Registrar shall prescribe a reasonable time–limit within which the party concerned is to produce them. If the applicant fails to produce the required documents within the time–limit prescribed, the Court shall, after hearing the Judge–Rapporteur and the Advocate General, decide whether the non–compliance with that procedural requirement renders the application or written pleading formally inadmissible.

Chapter 2. Written Part of the Procedure

Article 120. Content of the application
An application of the kind referred to in Article 21 of the Statute shall state:
(a) the name and address of the applicant;
(b) the name of the party against whom the application is made;
(c) the subject–matter of the proceedings, the pleas in law and arguments relied on and a summary of those pleas in law;
(d) the form of order sought by the applicant;
(e) where appropriate, any evidence produced or offered.

Article 121. Information relating to service
(1) For the purpose of the proceedings, the application shall state an address for service. It shall indicate the name of the person who is authorised and has expressed willingness to accept service.
(2) In addition to, or instead of, specifying an address for service as referred to in paragraph 1, the application may state that the lawyer or agent agrees that service is to be effected on him by telefax or any other technical means of communication.
(3) If the application does not comply with the requirements referred to in paragraphs 1 or 2, all service on the party concerned for the purpose of the proceedings shall be effected, for so long as the defect has not been cured, by registered letter addressed to the agent or lawyer of that party. By way of derogation from Article 48, service shall then be deemed to be duly effected by the lodging of the registered letter at the post office of the place in which the Court has its seat.

Article 122. Annexes to the application
(1) The application shall be accompanied, where appropriate, by the documents specified in the second paragraph of Article 21 of the Statute.
(2) An application submitted under Article 273 TFEU shall be accompanied by a copy of the special agreement concluded between the Member States concerned.
(3) If an application does not comply with the requirements set out in paragraphs 1 or 2 of this Article, the Registrar shall prescribe a reasonable time–limit within which the applicant is to produce the

abovementioned documents. If the applicant fails to put the application in order, the Court shall, after hearing the Judge–Rapporteur and the Advocate General, decide whether the non–compliance with these conditions renders the application formally inadmissible.

Article 123. Service of the application
The application shall be served on the defendant. In cases where Article 119(4) or Article 122(3) applies, service shall be effected as soon as the application has been put in order or the Court has declared it admissible notwithstanding the failure to observe the requirements set out in those two Articles.

Article 124. Content of the defence
(1) Within two months after service on him of the application, the defendant shall lodge a defence, stating:
(a) the name and address of the defendant;
(b) the pleas in law and arguments relied on;
(c) the form of order sought by the defendant;
(d) where appropriate, any evidence produced or offered.
(2) Article 121 shall apply to the defence.
(3) The time–limit laid down in paragraph 1 may exceptionally be extended by the President at the duly reasoned request of the defendant.

Article 125. Transmission of documents
Where the European Parliament, the Council or the European Commission is not a party to a case, the Court shall send to them copies of the application and of the defence, without the annexes thereto, to enable them to assess whether the inapplicability of one of their acts is being invoked under Article 277 TFEU.

Article 126. Reply and rejoinder
(1) The application initiating proceedings and the defence may be supplemented by a reply from the applicant and by a rejoinder from the defendant.
(2) The President shall prescribe the time–limits within which those procedural documents are to be produced. He may specify the matters to which the reply or the rejoinder should relate.

Chapter 3. Pleas in Law and Evidence

Article 127. New pleas in law
(1) No new plea in law may be introduced in the course of proceedings unless it is based on matters of law or of fact which come to light in the course of the procedure.
(2) Without prejudice to the decision to be taken on the admissibility of the plea in law, the President may, on a proposal from the Judge–Rapporteur and after hearing the Advocate General, prescribe a time–limit within which the other party may respond to that plea.

Article 128. Evidence produced or offered
(1) In reply or rejoinder a party may produce or offer further evidence in support of his arguments. The party must give reasons for the delay in submitting such evidence.
(2) The parties may, exceptionally, produce or offer further evidence after the close of the written part of the procedure. They must give reasons for the delay in submitting such evidence. The President may, on a proposal from the Judge–Rapporteur and after hearing the Advocate General, prescribe a time–limit within which the other party may comment on such evidence.

Chapter 4. Intervention

Article 129. Object and effects of the intervention
(1) The intervention shall be limited to supporting, in whole or in part, the form of order sought by one of the parties. It shall not confer the same procedural rights as those conferred on the parties and, in particular, shall not give rise to any right to request that a hearing be held.
(2) The intervention shall be ancillary to the main proceedings. It shall become devoid of purpose if the case is removed from the register of the Court as a result of a party's discontinuance or with–drawal from the proceedings or of an agreement between the parties, or where the application is declared inadmissible.
(3) The intervener must accept the case as he finds it at the time of his intervention.
(4) Consideration may be given to an application to intervene which is made after the expiry of the time–limit prescribed in Article 130 but before the decision to open the oral part of the procedure provided for in Article 60(4). In that event, if the President allows the intervention, the intervener may submit his observations during the hearing, if it takes place.

Article 130. Application to intervene

(1) An application to intervene must be submitted within six weeks of the publication of the notice referred to in Article 21(4).

(2) The application to intervene shall contain:

(a) a description of the case;

(b) a description of the main parties;

(c) the name and address of the intervener;

(d) the form of order sought, in support of which the intervener is applying for leave to intervene;

(e) a statement of the circumstances establishing the right to intervene, where the application is submitted pursuant to the second or third paragraph of Article 40 of the Statute.

(3) The intervener shall be represented in accordance with Article 19 of the Statute.

(4) Articles 119, 121 and 122 of these Rules shall apply.

Article 131. Decision on applications to intervene

(1) The application to intervene shall be served on the parties in order to obtain any written or oral observations they may wish to make on that application.

(2) Where the application is submitted pursuant to the first or third paragraph of Article 40 of the Statute, the intervention shall be allowed by decision of the President and the intervener shall receive a copy of every procedural document served on the parties, provided that those parties have not, within 10 days after the service referred to in paragraph 1 has been effected, put forward observations on the application to intervene or identified secret or confidential items or documents which, if communicated to the intervener, the parties claim would be prejudicial to them.

(3) In any other case, the President shall decide on the application to intervene by order or shall refer the application to the Court.

(4) If the application to intervene is granted, the intervener shall receive a copy of every procedural document served on the parties, save, where applicable, for the secret or confidential items or documents excluded from such communication pursuant to paragraph 3.

Article 132. Submission of statements

(1) The intervener may submit a statement in intervention within one month after communication of the procedural documents referred to in the preceding Article. That time–limit may be extended by the President at the duly reasoned request of the intervener.

(2) The statement in intervention shall contain:

(a) the form of order sought by the intervener in support, in whole or in part, of the form of order sought by one of the parties;

(b) the pleas in law and arguments relied on by the intervener;

(c) where appropriate, any evidence produced or offered.

(3) After the statement in intervention has been lodged, the President shall, where necessary, prescribe a time–limit within which the parties may reply to that statement.

Chapter 5. Expedited Procedure

Article 133. Decision relating to the expedited procedure

(1) At the request of the applicant or the defendant, the President of the Court may, where the nature of the case requires that it be dealt with within a short time, after hearing the other party, the Judge–Rapporteur and the Advocate General, decide that a case is to be determined pursuant to an expedited procedure derogating from the provisions of these Rules.

(2) The request for a case to be determined pursuant to an expedited procedure must be made by a separate document submitted at the same time as the application initiating proceedings or the defence, as the case may be, is lodged.

(3) Exceptionally the President may also take such a decision of his own motion, after hearing the parties, the Judge–Rapporteur and the Advocate General.

Article 134. Written part of the procedure

(1) Under the expedited procedure, the application initiating proceedings and the defence may be supplemented by a reply and a rejoinder only if the President, after hearing the Judge–Rapporteur and the Advocate General, considers this to be necessary.

(2) An intervener may submit a statement in intervention only if the President, after hearing the Judge–Rapporteur and the Advocate General, considers this to be necessary.

Article 135. Oral part of the procedure

(1) Once the defence has been submitted or, if the decision to determine the case pursuant to an

expedited procedure is not made until after that pleading has been lodged, once that decision has been taken, the President shall fix a date for the hearing, which shall be communicated forthwith to the parties. He may postpone the date of the hearing where it is necessary to undertake measures of inquiry or where measures of organisation of procedure so require.
(2) Without prejudice to Articles 127 and 128, a party may supplement his arguments and produce or offer evidence during the oral part of the procedure. The party must, however, give reasons for the delay in producing such further arguments or evidence.

Article 136. Decision on the substance
The Court shall give its ruling after hearing the Advocate General.

Chapter 6. Costs

Article 137. Decision as to costs
A decision as to costs shall be given in the judgment or order which closes the proceedings.

Article 138. General rules as to allocation of costs
(1) The unsuccessful party shall be ordered to pay the costs if they have been applied for in the successful party's pleadings.
(2) Where there is more than one unsuccessful party the Court shall decide how the costs are to be shared.
(3) Where each party succeeds on some and fails on other heads, the parties shall bear their own costs. However, if it appears justified in the circumstances of the case, the Court may order that one party, in addition to bearing its own costs, pay a proportion of the costs of the other party.

Article 139. Unreasonable or vexatious costs
The Court may order a party, even if successful, to pay costs which the Court considers that party to have unreasonably or vexatiously caused the opposite party to incur.

Article 140. Costs of interveners
(1) The Member States and institutions which have intervened in the proceedings shall bear their own costs.
(2) The States, other than the Member States, which are parties to the EEA Agreement, and also the EFTA Surveillance Authority, shall similarly bear their own costs if they have intervened in the proceedings.
(3) The Court may order an intervener other than those referred to in the preceding paragraphs to bear his own costs.

Article 141. Costs in the event of discontinuance or withdrawal
(1) A party who discontinues or withdraws from proceedings shall be ordered to pay the costs if they have been applied for in the other party's observations on the discontinuance.
(2) However, at the request of the party who discontinues or withdraws from proceedings, the costs shall be borne by the other party if this appears justified by the conduct of that party.
(3) Where the parties have come to an agreement on costs, the decision as to costs shall be in accordance with that agreement.
(4) If costs are not claimed, the parties shall bear their own costs.

Article 142. Costs where a case does not proceed to judgment
Where a case does not proceed to judgment the costs shall be in the discretion of the Court.

Article 143. Costs of proceedings
Proceedings before the Court shall be free of charge, except that:
(a) where a party has caused the Court to incur avoidable costs the Court may, after hearing the Advocate General, order that party to refund them;
(b) where copying or translation work is carried out at the request of a party, the cost shall, in so far as the Registrar considers it excessive, be paid for by that party on the Registry's scale of charges referred to in Article 22.

Article 144. Recoverable costs
Without prejudice to the preceding Article, the following shall be regarded as recoverable costs:
(a) sums payable to witnesses and experts under Article 73 of these Rules;
(b) expenses necessarily incurred by the parties for the purpose of the proceedings, in particular the travel and subsistence expenses and the remuneration of agents, advisers or lawyers.

Article 145. Dispute concerning the costs to be recovered

(1) If there is a dispute concerning the costs to be recovered, the Chamber of three Judges to which the Judge–Rapporteur who dealt with the case is assigned shall, on application by the party concerned and after hearing the opposite party and the Advocate General, make an order. In that event, the formation of the Court shall be composed of the President of that Chamber, the Judge–Rapporteur and the first Judge or, as the case may be, the first two Judges designated from the list referred to in Article 28(3) on the date on which the dispute is brought before that Chamber by the Judge–Rapporteur.
(2) If the Judge–Rapporteur is not a member of a Chamber of three Judges, the decision shall be taken, under the same conditions, by the Chamber of five Judges to which he is assigned. In addition to the Judge–Rapporteur, the formation of the Court shall be composed of four Judges designated from the list referred to in Article 28(2) on the date on which the dispute is brought before that Chamber by the Judge–Rapporteur.
(3) The parties may, for the purposes of enforcement, apply for an authenticated copy of the order.

Article 146. Procedure for payment

(1) Sums due from the cashier of the Court and from its debtors shall be paid in euro.
(2) Where costs to be recovered have been incurred in a currency other than the euro or where the steps in respect of which payment is due were taken in a country of which the euro is not the currency, the conversion shall be effected at the European Central Bank's official rates of exchange on the day of payment.

Chapter 7. Amicable Settlement, Discontinuance, Cases that do not Proceed to Judgment and Preliminary Issues

Article 147. Amicable settlement

(1) If, before the Court has given its decision, the parties reach a settlement of their dispute and inform the Court of the abandonment of their claims, the President shall order the case to be removed from the register and shall give a decision as to costs in accordance with Article 141, having regard to any proposals made by the parties on the matter.
(2) This provision shall not apply to proceedings under Articles 263 TFEU and 265 TFEU.

Article 148. Discontinuance

If the applicant informs the Court in writing or at the hearing that he wishes to discontinue the proceedings, the President shall order the case to be removed from the register and shall give a decision as to costs in accordance with Article 141.

Article 149. Cases that do not proceed to judgment

If the Court declares that the action has become devoid of purpose and that there is no longer any need to adjudicate on it, the Court may at any time of its own motion, on a proposal from the Judge–Rapporteur and after hearing the parties and the Advocate General, decide to rule by reasoned order. It shall give a decision as to costs.

Article 150. Absolute bar to proceeding with a case

On a proposal from the Judge–Rapporteur, the Court may at any time of its own motion, after hearing the parties and the Advocate General, decide to rule by reasoned order on whether there exists any absolute bar to proceeding with a case.

Article 151. Preliminary objections and issues

(1) A party applying to the Court for a decision on a preliminary objection or issue not going to the substance of the case shall submit the application by a separate document.
(2) The application must state the pleas of law and arguments relied on and the form of order sought by the applicant; any supporting items and documents must be annexed to it.
(3) As soon as the application has been submitted, the President shall prescribe a time–limit within which the opposite party may submit in writing his pleas in law and the form of order which he seeks.
(4) Unless the Court decides otherwise, the remainder of the proceedings on the application shall be oral.
(5) The Court shall, after hearing the Advocate General, decide on the application as soon as possible or, where special circumstances so justify, reserve its decision until it rules on the substance of the case.
(6) If the Court refuses the application or reserves its decision, the President shall prescribe new time–limits for the further steps in the proceedings.

Chapter 8. Judgments by Default

Article 152. Judgments by default

(1) If a defendant on whom an application initiating proceedings has been duly served fails to respond to the application in the proper form and within the time–limit prescribed, the applicant may apply to the Court for judgment by default.

(2) The application for judgment by default shall be served on the defendant. The Court may decide to open the oral part of the procedure on the application.

(3) Before giving judgment by default the Court shall, after hearing the Advocate General, consider whether the application initiating proceedings is admissible, whether the appropriate formalities have been complied with, and whether the applicant's claims appear well founded. The Court may adopt measures of organisation of procedure or order measures of inquiry.

(4) A judgment by default shall be enforceable. The Court may, however, grant a stay of execution until the Court has given its decision on any application under Article 156 to set aside the judgment, or it may make execution subject to the provision of security of an amount and nature to be fixed in the light of the circumstances; this security shall be released if no such application is made or if the application fails.

Chapter 9. Requests and Applications Relating to Judgments and Orders

Article 153. Competent formation of the Court

(1) With the exception of applications referred to in Article 159, the requests and applications referred to in this Chapter shall be assigned to the Judge–Rapporteur who was responsible for the case to which the request or application relates, and shall be assigned to the formation of the Court which gave a decision in that case.

(2) If the Judge–Rapporteur is prevented from acting, the President of the Court shall assign the request or application referred to in this Chapter to a Judge who was a member of the formation of the Court which gave a decision in the case to which that request or application relates.

(3) If the quorum referred to in Article 17 of the Statute can no longer be attained, the Court shall, on a proposal from the Judge–Rapporteur and after hearing the Advocate General, assign the request or application to a new formation of the Court.

Article 154. Rectification

(1) Without prejudice to the provisions relating to the interpretation of judgments and orders, clerical mistakes, errors in calculation and obvious inaccuracies may be rectified by the Court, of its own motion or at the request of a party made within two weeks after delivery of the judgment or service of the order.

(2) Where the request for rectification concerns the operative part or one of the grounds constituting the necessary support for the operative part, the parties, whom the Registrar shall duly inform, may submit written observations within a time–limit prescribed by the President.

(3) The Court shall take its decision after hearing the Advocate General.

(4) The original of the rectification order shall be annexed to the original of the rectified decision. A note of this order shall be made in the margin of the original of the rectified decision.

Article 155. Failure to adjudicate

(1) If the Court has failed to adjudicate on a specific head of claim or on costs, any party wishing to rely on that may, within a month after service of the decision, apply to the Court to supplement its decision.

(2) The application shall be served on the opposite party and the President shall prescribe a time–limit within which that party may submit written observations.

(3) After these observations have been submitted, the Court shall, after hearing the Advocate General, decide both on the admissibility and on the substance of the application.

Article 156. Application to set aside

(1) Application may be made pursuant to Article 41 of the Statute to set aside a judgment delivered by default.

(2) The application to set aside the judgment must be made within one month from the date of service of the judgment and must be submitted in the form prescribed by Articles 120 to 122 of these Rules.

(3) After the application has been served, the President shall prescribe a time–limit within which the other party may submit his written observations.

(4) The proceedings shall be conducted in accordance with Articles 59 to 92 of these Rules.

(5) The Court shall decide by way of a judgment which may not be set aside.

(6) The original of this judgment shall be annexed to the original of the judgment by default. A note of the judgment on the application to set aside shall be made in the margin of the original of the judgment by default.

PART III   EUROPEAN UNION

Article 157. Third–party proceedings

(1) Articles 120 to 122 of these Rules shall apply to an application initiating third–party proceedings made pursuant to Article 42 of the Statute. In addition such an application shall:
(a) specify the judgment or order contested;
(b) state how the contested decision is prejudicial to the rights of the third party;
(c) indicate the reasons for which the third party was unable to take part in the original case.
(2) The application must be made against all the parties to the original case.
(3) The application must be submitted within two months of publication of the decision in the *Official Journal of the European Union* .
(4) The Court may, on application by the third party, order a stay of execution of the contested decision. The provisions of Chapter 10 of this Title shall apply.
(5) The contested decision shall be varied on the points on which the submissions of the third party are upheld.
(6) The original of the judgment in the third–party proceedings shall be annexed to the original of the contested decision. A note of the judgment in the third–party proceedings shall be made in the margin of the original of the contested decision.

Article 158. Interpretation

(1) In accordance with Article 43 of the Statute, if the meaning or scope of a judgment or order is in doubt, the Court shall construe it on application by any party or any institution of the European Union establishing an interest therein.
(2) An application for interpretation must be made within two years after the date of delivery of the judgment or service of the order.
(3) An application for interpretation shall be made in accordance with Articles 120 to 122 of these Rules. In addition it shall specify:
(a) the decision in question;
(b) the passages of which interpretation is sought.
(4) The application must be made against all the parties to the case in which the decision of which interpretation is sought was given.
(5) The Court shall give its decision after having given the parties an opportunity to submit their observations and after hearing the Advocate General.
(6) The original of the interpreting decision shall be annexed to the original of the decision interpreted. A note of the interpreting decision shall be made in the margin of the original of the decision interpreted.

Article 159. Revision

(1) In accordance with Article 44 of the Statute, an application for revision of a decision of the Court may be made only on discovery of a fact which is of such a nature as to be a decisive factor and which, when the judgment was delivered or the order served, was unknown to the Court and to the party claiming the revision.
(2) Without prejudice to the time–limit of 10 years prescribed in the third paragraph of Article 44 of the Statute, an application for revision shall be made within three months of the date on which the facts on which the application is founded came to the applicant's knowledge.
(3) Articles 120 to 122 of these Rules shall apply to an application for revision. In addition such an application shall:
(a) specify the judgment or order contested;
(b) indicate the points on which the decision is contested;
(c) set out the facts on which the application is founded;
(d) indicate the nature of the evidence to show that there are facts justifying revision, and that the time–limits laid down in paragraph 2 have been observed.
(4) The application for revision must be made against all parties to the case in which the contested decision was given.
(5) Without prejudice to its decision on the substance, the Court shall, after hearing the Advocate General, give in the form of an order its decision on the admissibility of the application, having regard to the written observations of the parties.
(6) If the Court declares the application admissible, it shall proceed to consider the substance of the application and shall give its decision in the form of a judgment in accordance with these Rules.
(7) The original of the revising judgment shall be annexed to the original of the decision revised. A note of the revising judgment shall be made in the margin of the original of the decision revised.

Chapter 10. Suspension of Operation or Enforcement and Other Interim Measures

Article 160. Application for suspension or for interim measures

(1) An application to suspend the operation of any measure adopted by an institution, made pursuant to Article 278 TFEU or Article 157 TEAEC, shall be admissible only if the applicant has challenged that measure in an action before the Court.

(2) An application for the adoption of one of the other interim measures referred to in Article 279 TFEU shall be admissible only if it is made by a party to a case before the Court and relates to that case.

(3) An application of a kind referred to in the preceding paragraphs shall state the subject–matter of the proceedings, the circumstances giving rise to urgency and the pleas of fact and law establishing a prima facie case for the interim measure applied for.

(4) The application shall be made by a separate document and in accordance with the provisions of Articles 120 to 122 of these Rules.

(5) The application shall be served on the opposite party, and the President shall prescribe a short time–limit within which that party may submit written or oral observations.

(6) The President may order a preparatory inquiry.

(7) The President may grant the application even before the observations of the opposite party have been submitted. This decision may be varied or cancelled even without any application being made by any party.

Article 161. Decision on the application

(1) The President shall either decide on the application himself or refer it immediately to the Court.

(2) If the President is prevented from acting, Articles 10 and 13 of these Rules shall apply.

(3) Where the application is referred to it, the Court shall give a decision immediately, after hearing the Advocate General.

Article 162. Order for suspension of operation or for interim measures

(1) The decision on the application shall take the form of a reasoned order, from which no appeal shall lie. The order shall be served on the parties forthwith.

(2) The execution of the order may be made conditional on the lodging by the applicant of security, of an amount and nature to be fixed in the light of the circumstances.

(3) Unless the order fixes the date on which the interim measure is to lapse, the measure shall lapse when the judgment which closes the proceedings is delivered.

(4) The order shall have only an interim effect, and shall be without prejudice to the decision of the Court on the substance of the case.

Article 163. Change in circumstances

On application by a party, the order may at any time be varied or cancelled on account of a change in circumstances.

Article 164. New application

Rejection of an application for an interim measure shall not bar the party who made it from making a further application on the basis of new facts.

Article 165. Applications pursuant to Articles 280 TFEU and 299 TFEU and Article 164 TEAEC

(1) The provisions of this Chapter shall apply to applications to suspend the enforcement of a decision of the Court or of any measure adopted by the Council, the European Commission or the European Central Bank, submitted pursuant to Articles 280 TFEU and 299 TFEU or Article 164 TEAEC.

(2) The order granting the application shall fix, where appropriate, a date on which the interim measure is to lapse.

Article 166. Application pursuant to Article 81 TEAEC

(1) An application of a kind referred to in the third and fourth paragraphs of Article 81 TEAEC shall contain:

(a) the names and addresses of the persons or undertakings to be inspected;

(b) an indication of what is to be inspected and of the purpose of the inspection.

(2) The President shall give his decision in the form of an order. Article 162 of these Rules shall apply.

(3) If the President is prevented from acting, Articles 10 and 13 of these Rules shall apply.

Title V. Appeals against Decisions of the General Court

Chapter 1. Form and Content of the Appeal, and Form of Order Sought

PART III   EUROPEAN UNION

Article 167. Lodging of the appeal
(1) An appeal shall be brought by lodging an application at the Registry of the Court of Justice or of the General Court.
(2) The Registry of the General Court shall forthwith transmit to the Registry of the Court of Justice the file in the case at first instance and, where necessary, the appeal.

Article 168. Content of the appeal
(1) An appeal shall contain:
(a) the name and address of the appellant;
(b) a reference to the decision of the General Court appealed against;
(c) the names of the other parties to the relevant case before the General Court;
(d) the pleas in law and legal arguments relied on, and a summary of those pleas in law;
(e) the form of order sought by the appellant.
(2) Articles 119, 121 and 122(1) of these Rules shall apply to appeals.
(3) The appeal shall state the date on which the decision appealed against was served on the appellant.
(4) If an appeal does not comply with paragraphs 1 to 3 of this Article, the Registrar shall prescribe a reasonable time–limit within which the appellant is to put the appeal in order. If the appellant fails to put the appeal in order within the time–limit prescribed, the Court of Justice shall, after hearing the Judge–Rapporteur and the Advocate General, decide whether the non–compliance with that formal requirement renders the appeal formally inadmissible.

Article 169. Form of order sought, pleas in law and arguments of the appeal
(1) An appeal shall seek to have set aside, in whole or in part, the decision of the General Court as set out in the operative part of that decision.
(2) The pleas in law and legal arguments relied on shall identify precisely those points in the grounds of the decision of the General Court which are contested.

Article 170. Form of order sought in the event that the appeal is allowed
(1) An appeal shall seek, in the event that it is declared well founded, the same form of order, in whole or in part, as that sought at first instance and shall not seek a different form of order. The subject–matter of the proceedings before the General Court may not be changed in the appeal.
(2) Where the appellant requests that the case be referred back to the General Court if the decision appealed against is set aside, he shall set out the reasons why the state of the proceedings does not permit a decision by the Court of Justice.

Chapter 1a. Prior determination as to whether Appeals under Article 58a of the Statute should be allowed to proceed

Article 170a. Request that the appeal be allowed to proceed
(1) In the situations referred to in the first and second paragraphs of Article 58a of the Statute, the appellant shall annex to the appeal a request that the appeal be allowed to proceed, setting out the issue raised by the appeal that is significant with respect to the unity, consistency or development of European Union law and containing all the information necessary to enable the Court of Justice to rule on that request. If there is no such request, the Vice-President of the Court shall declare the appeal inadmissible.
(2) The request that the appeal be allowed to proceed shall not exceed seven pages and shall be drawn up taking into account all the formal requirements contained in the Practice Directions to parties concerning cases brought before the Court, adopted on the basis of these Rules.
(3) If the request that the appeal be allowed to proceed does not comply with the requirements set out in the preceding paragraph, the Registrar shall prescribe a reasonable time-limit within which the appellant is to put the request in order. If the appellant fails to put the request in order within the time-limit prescribed, the Vice-President of the Court shall decide, on a proposal from the Judge-Rapporteur and after hearing the Advocate General, whether the non-compliance with that formal requirement renders the appeal formally inadmissible.

Article 170b. Decision on the request that the appeal be allowed to proceed
(1) The Court of Justice shall rule as soon as possible on the request that the appeal be allowed to proceed.
(2) The decision on that request shall be taken, on a proposal from the Judge-Rapporteur and after hearing the Advocate General, by a Chamber specially established for that purpose, presided over by the Vice-President of the Court and including also the Judge-Rapporteur and the President of the

Chamber of three Judges to which the Judge-Rapporteur is attached on the date on which the request is made.
(3) The decision on the request that the appeal be allowed to proceed shall take the form of a reasoned order.
(4) Where the Court of Justice decides that the appeal should be allowed to proceed, wholly or in part, having regard to the criteria set out in the third paragraph of Article 58a of the Statute, the proceedings shall continue in accordance with Articles 171 to 190a of these Rules. The order referred to in the preceding paragraph shall be served, together with the appeal, on the parties to the relevant case before the General Court and shall specify, where the appeal is to be allowed to proceed in part, the pleas in law or parts of the appeal to which the response must relate.
(5) The General Court and, if they were not parties to the proceedings before it, the Member States, the European Parliament, the Council and the European Commission shall forthwith be informed by the Registrar of the decision that the appeal should be allowed to proceed.'

Chapter 2. Responses, Replies and Rejoinders

Article 171. Service of the appeal
(1) The appeal shall be served on the other parties to the relevant case before the General Court.
(2) In a case where Article 168(4) of these Rules applies, service shall be effected as soon as the appeal has been put in order or the Court of Justice has declared it admissible notwithstanding the failure to observe the formal requirements laid down by that Article.

Article 172. Parties authorised to lodge a response
Any party to the relevant case before the General Court having an interest in the appeal being allowed or dismissed may submit a response within two months after service on him of the appeal. The time–limit for submitting a response shall not be extended.

Article 173. Content of the response
(1) A response shall contain:
(a) the name and address of the party submitting it;
(b) the date on which the appeal was served on him;
(c) the pleas in law and legal arguments relied on;
(d) the form of order sought.
(2) Articles 119 and 121 of these Rules shall apply to responses.

Article 174. Form of order sought in the response
A response shall seek to have the appeal allowed or dismissed, in whole or in part.

Article 175. Reply and rejoinder
(1) The appeal and the response may be supplemented by a reply and a rejoinder only where the President, on a duly reasoned application submitted by the appellant within seven days of service of the response, considers it necessary, after hearing the Judge–Rapporteur and the Advocate General, in particular to enable the appellant to present his views on a plea of inadmissibility or on new matters relied on in the response.
(2) The President shall fix the date by which the reply is to be produced and, upon service of that pleading, the date by which the rejoinder is to be produced. He may limit the number of pages and the subject–matter of those pleadings.

Chapter 3. Form and Content of the Cross–Appeal, and Form of Order Sought

Article 176. Cross–appeal
(1) The parties referred to in Article 172 of these Rules may submit a cross–appeal within the same time–limit as that prescribed for the submission of a response.
(2) A cross–appeal must be introduced by a document separate from the response.

Article 177. Content of the cross–appeal
(1) A cross–appeal shall contain:
(a) the name and address of the party bringing the cross–appeal;
(b) the date on which the appeal was served on him;
(c) the pleas in law and legal arguments relied on;
(d) the form of order sought.
(2) Articles 119, 121 and 122(1) and (3) of these Rules shall apply to cross–appeals.

Article 178. Form of order sought, pleas in law and arguments of the cross–appeal

(1) A cross–appeal shall seek to have set aside, in whole or in part, the decision of the General Court.
(2) It may also seek to have set aside an express or implied decision relating to the admissibility of the action before the General Court.
(3) The pleas in law and legal arguments relied on shall identify precisely those points in the grounds of the decision of the General Court which are contested. The pleas in law and arguments must be separate from those relied on in the response.

Chapter 4. Pleadings Consequent on the Cross–Appeal

Article 179. Response to the cross–appeal
Where a cross–appeal is brought, the applicant at first instance or any other party to the relevant case before the General Court having an interest in the cross–appeal being allowed or dismissed may submit a response, which must be limited to the pleas in law relied on in that cross–appeal, within two months after its being served on him. That time–limit shall not be extended.

Article 180. Reply and rejoinder on a cross–appeal
(1) The cross–appeal and the response thereto may be supplemented by a reply and a rejoinder only where the President, on a duly reasoned application submitted by the party who brought the cross–appeal within seven days of service of the response to the cross–appeal, considers it necessary, after hearing the Judge–Rapporteur and the Advocate General, in particular to enable that party to present his views on a plea of inadmissibility or on new matters relied on in the response to the cross–appeal.
(2) The President shall fix the date by which that reply is to be produced and, upon service of that pleading, the date by which the rejoinder is to be produced. He may limit the number of pages and the subject–matter of those pleadings.

Chapter 5. Appeals Determined by Order

Article 181. Manifestly inadmissible or manifestly unfounded appeal or cross–appeal
Where the appeal or cross–appeal is, in whole or in part, manifestly inadmissible or manifestly unfounded, the Court may at any time, acting on a proposal from the Judge–Rapporteur and after hearing the Advocate General, decide by reasoned order to dismiss that appeal or cross–appeal in whole or in part.

Article 182. Manifestly well–founded appeal or cross–appeal
Where the Court has already ruled on one or more questions of law identical to those raised by the pleas in law of the appeal or cross–appeal and considers the appeal or cross–appeal to be manifestly well founded, it may, acting on a proposal from the Judge–Rapporteur and after hearing the parties and the Advocate General, decide by reasoned order in which reference is made to the relevant case–law to declare the appeal or cross–appeal manifestly well founded.

Chapter 6. Effect on a Cross–Appeal of the Removal of the Appeal from the Register

Article 183. Effect on a cross–appeal of the discontinuance or manifest inadmissibility of the appeal
A cross–appeal shall be deemed to be devoid of purpose:
(a) if the appellant discontinues his appeal;
(b) if the appeal is declared manifestly inadmissible for non–compliance with the time–limit for lodging an appeal;
(c) if the appeal is declared manifestly inadmissible on the sole ground that it is not directed against a final decision of the General Court or against a decision disposing of the substantive issues in part only or disposing of a procedural issue concerning a plea of lack of competence or inadmissibility within the meaning of the first paragraph of Article 56 of the Statute.

Chapter 7. Costs and Legal Aid in Appeals

Article 184. Costs in appeals
(1) Subject to the following provisions, Articles 137 to 146 of these Rules shall apply, *mutatis mutandis*, to the procedure before the Court of Justice on an appeal against a decision of the General Court.
(2) Where the appeal is unfounded or where the appeal is well founded and the Court itself gives final judgment in the case, the Court shall make a decision as to the costs.
(3) When an appeal brought by a Member State or an institution of the European Union which did not intervene in the proceedings before the General Court is well founded, the Court of Justice may order that the parties share the costs or that the successful appellant pay the costs which the appeal has caused an unsuccessful party to incur.

(4) Where the appeal has not been brought by an intervener at first instance, he may not be ordered to pay costs in the appeal proceedings unless he participated in the written or oral part of the proceedings before the Court of Justice. Where an intervener at first instance takes part in the proceedings, the Court may decide that he shall bear his own costs.

Article 185. Legal aid
(1) A party who is wholly or in part unable to meet the costs of the proceedings may at any time apply for legal aid.
(2) The application shall be accompanied by all information and supporting documents making it possible to assess the applicant's financial situation, such as a certificate issued by a competent national authority attesting to his financial situation.

Article 186. Prior application for legal aid
(1) If the application is made prior to the appeal which the applicant for legal aid intends to commence, it shall briefly state the subject of the appeal.
(2) The application for legal aid need not be made through a lawyer.
(3) The introduction of an application for legal aid shall, with regard to the person who made that application, suspend the time–limit prescribed for the bringing of the appeal until the date of service of the order making a decision on that application.
(4) The President shall assign the application for legal aid, as soon as it is lodged, to a Judge–Rapporteur who shall put forward, promptly, a proposal as to the action to be taken on it.

Article 187. Decision on the application for legal aid
(1) The decision to grant legal aid, in whole or in part, or to refuse it shall be taken, on a proposal from the Judge–Rapporteur and after hearing the Advocate General, by the Chamber of three Judges to which the Judge–Rapporteur is assigned. In that event, the formation of the Court shall be composed of the President of that Chamber, the Judge–Rapporteur and the first Judge or, as the case may be, the first two Judges designated from the list referred to in Article 28(3) on the date on which the application for legal aid is brought before that Chamber by the Judge–Rapporteur. It shall consider, if appropriate, whether the appeal is manifestly unfounded.
(2) If the Judge–Rapporteur is not a member of a Chamber of three Judges, the decision shall be taken, under the same conditions, by the Chamber of five Judges to which he is assigned. In addition to the Judge–Rapporteur, the formation of the Court shall be composed of four Judges designated from the list referred to in Article 28(2) on the date on which the application for legal aid is brought before that Chamber by the Judge–Rapporteur.
(3) The formation of the Court shall give its decision by way of order. Where the application for legal aid is refused in whole or in part, the order shall state the reasons for that refusal.

Article 188. Sums to be advanced as legal aid
(1) Where legal aid is granted, the cashier of the Court shall be responsible, where applicable within the limits set by the formation of the Court, for costs involved in the assistance and representation of the applicant before the Court. At the request of the applicant or his representative, an advance on those costs may be paid.
(2) In its decision as to costs the Court may order the payment to the cashier of the Court of sums advanced as legal aid.
(3) The Registrar shall take steps to obtain the recovery of these sums from the party ordered to pay them.

Article 189. Withdrawal of legal aid
The formation of the Court which gave a decision on the application for legal aid may at any time, either of its own motion or on request, withdraw that legal aid if the circumstances which led to its being granted alter during the proceedings.

Chapter 8. Other Provisions Applicable to Appeals

Article 190. Other provisions applicable to appeals
(1) Articles 127, 129 to 136, 147 to 150, 153 to 155 and 157 to 166 of these Rules shall apply to the procedure before the Court of Justice on an appeal against decisions of the General Court.
(2) By way of derogation from Article 130(1), an application to intervene shall, however, be made within one month of the publication of the notice referred to in Article 21(4).
(3) Article 95 shall apply, *mutatis mutandis*, to the procedure before the Court of Justice on an appeal against decisions of the General Court.

PART III   EUROPEAN UNION

Article 190a. Treatment of information or material produced before the General Court in accordance with Article 105 of its Rules of Procedure
(1) Where an appeal is brought against a decision of the General Court adopted in proceedings in which information or material has been produced by a main party in accordance with Article 105 of the Rules of Procedure of the General Court and has not been communicated to the other main party, the Registry of the General Court shall make that information or material available to the Court of Justice, on the conditions laid down in the decision referred to in paragraph 11 of that Article.
(2) The information or material referred to in paragraph 1 shall not be communicated to the parties to the proceedings before the Court of Justice.
(3) The Court of Justice shall ensure that the confidential matters contained in the information or material referred to in paragraph 1 are not disclosed in the decision which closes the proceedings or in any Opinion of the Advocate General.
(4) The information or material referred to in paragraph 1 shall be returned to the party that produced it before the General Court as soon as the decision closing the proceedings before the Court of Justice has been served, save where the case is referred back to the General Court. In the latter case, the information or material concerned shall again be made available to the General Court, on the conditions laid down in the decision referred to in paragraph 5.
(5) The Court of Justice shall adopt, by decision, the security rules for protecting the information or material referred to in paragraph 1. That decision shall be published in the *Official Journal of the European Union*.

Title VI. Review of Decisions of the General Court

Article 191. Reviewing Chamber
A Chamber of five Judges shall be designated for a period of one year for the purpose of deciding, in accordance with Articles 193 and 194 of these Rules, whether a decision of the General Court is to be reviewed in accordance with Article 62 of the Statute.

Article 192. Information and communication of decisions which may be reviewed
(1) As soon as the date for the delivery or signature of a decision to be given under Article 256(2) or (3) TFEU is fixed, the Registry of the General Court shall inform the Registry of the Court of Justice.
(2) The decision shall be communicated to the Registry of the Court of Justice immediately upon its delivery or signature, as shall the file in the case, which shall be made available forthwith to the First Advocate General.

Article 193. Review of decisions given on appeal
(1) The proposal of the First Advocate General to review a decision of the General Court given under Article 256(2) TFEU shall be forwarded to the President of the Court of Justice and to the President of the reviewing Chamber. Notice of that transmission shall be given to the Registrar at the same time.
(2) As soon as he is informed of the existence of a proposal, the Registrar shall communicate the file in the case before the General Court to the members of the reviewing Chamber.
(3) As soon as the proposal to review has been received, the President of the Court shall designate the Judge–Rapporteur from among the Judges of the reviewing Chamber on a proposal from the President of that Chamber. The composition of the formation of the Court shall be determined in accordance with Article 28(2) of these Rules on the day on which the case is assigned to the Judge–Rapporteur.
(4) That Chamber, acting on a proposal from the Judge–Rapporteur, shall decide whether the decision of the General Court is to be reviewed. The decision to review the decision of the General Court shall indicate only the questions which are to be reviewed.
(5) The General Court, the parties to the proceedings before it and the other interested persons referred to in the second paragraph of Article 62a of the Statute shall forthwith be informed by the Registrar of the decision of the Court of Justice to review the decision of the General Court.
(6) Notice of the date of the decision to review the decision of the General Court and of the questions which are to be reviewed shall be published in the *Official Journal of the European Union* .

Article 194. Review of preliminary rulings
(1) The proposal of the First Advocate General to review a decision of the General Court given under Article 256(3) TFEU shall be forwarded to the President of the Court of Justice and to the President of the reviewing Chamber. Notice of that transmission shall be given to the Registrar at the same time.
(2) As soon as he is informed of the existence of a proposal, the Registrar shall communicate the file

in the case before the General Court to the members of the reviewing Chamber.
(3) The Registrar shall also inform the General Court, the referring court or tribunal, the parties to the main proceedings and the other interested persons referred to in the second paragraph of Article 62a of the Statute of the existence of a proposal to review.
(4) As soon as the proposal to review has been received, the President of the Court shall designate the Judge–Rapporteur from among the Judges of the reviewing Chamber on a proposal from the President of that Chamber. The composition of the formation of the Court shall be determined in accordance with Article 28(2) of these Rules on the day on which the case is assigned to the Judge–Rapporteur.
(5) That Chamber, acting on a proposal from the Judge–Rapporteur, shall decide whether the decision of the General Court is to be reviewed. The decision to review the decision of the General Court shall indicate only the questions which are to be reviewed.
(6) The General Court, the referring court or tribunal, the parties to the main proceedings and the other interested persons referred to in the second paragraph of Article 62a of the Statute shall forthwith be informed by the Registrar of the decision of the Court of Justice as to whether or not the decision of the General Court is to be reviewed.
(7) Notice of the date of the decision to review the decision of the General Court and of the questions which are to be reviewed shall be published in the *Official Journal of the European Union* .

Article 195. Judgment on the substance of the case after a decision to review
(1) The decision to review a decision of the General Court shall be served on the parties and other interested persons referred to in the second paragraph of Article 62a of the Statute. The decision served on the Member States, and the States, other than the Member States, which are parties to the EEA Agreement, as well as the EFTA Surveillance Authority, shall be accompanied by a translation of the decision of the Court of Justice in accordance with the provisions of Article 98 of these Rules. The decision of the Court of Justice shall also be communicated to the General Court and, if applicable, to the referring court or tribunal.
(2) Within one month of the date of service referred to in paragraph 1, the parties and other interested persons on whom the decision of the Court of Justice has been served may lodge statements or written observations on the questions which are subject to review.
(3) As soon as a decision to review a decision of the General Court has been taken, the First Advocate General shall assign the review to an Advocate General.
(4) The reviewing Chamber shall rule on the substance of the case, after hearing the Advocate General.
(5) It may, however, request the Court of Justice to assign the case to a formation of the Court composed of a greater number of Judges.
(6) Where the decision of the General Court which is subject to review was given under Article 256(2) TFEU, the Court of Justice shall make a decision as to costs.

Title VII. Opinions

Article 196. Written part of the procedure
(1) In accordance with Article 218(11) TFEU, a request for an Opinion may be made by a Member State, by the European Parliament, by the Council or by the European Commission.
(2) A request for an Opinion may relate both to whether the envisaged agreement is compatible with the provisions of the Treaties and to whether the European Union or any institution of the European Union has the power to enter into that agreement.
(3) It shall be served on the Member States and on the institutions referred to in paragraph 1, and the President shall prescribe a time–limit within which they may submit written observations.

Article 197. Designation of the Judge–Rapporteur and of the Advocate General
As soon as the request for an Opinion has been submitted, the President shall designate a Judge–Rapporteur and the First Advocate General shall assign the case to an Advocate General.

Article 198. Hearing
The Court may decide that the procedure before it shall also include a hearing.

Article 199. Time–limit for delivering the Opinion
The Court shall deliver its Opinion as soon as possible, after hearing the Advocate General.

Article 200. Delivery of the Opinion
The Opinion, signed by the President, the Judges who took part in the deliberations and the Registrar, shall be delivered in open court. It shall be served on all the Member States and on the institutions referred to in Article 196(1).

PART III   EUROPEAN UNION

Title VIII. Particular Forms of Procedure

Article 201. Appeals against decisions of the arbitration committee
(1) An application initiating an appeal under the second paragraph of Article 18 TEAEC shall state:
(a) the name and permanent address of the applicant;
(b) the description of the signatory;
(c) a reference to the arbitration committee's decision against which the appeal is made;
(d) the names of the respondents;
(e) a summary of the facts;
(f) the grounds on which the appeal is based and arguments relied on, and a brief statement of those grounds;
(g) the form of order sought by the applicant.
(2) Articles 119 and 121 of these Rules shall apply to the application.
(3) A certified copy of the contested decision shall be annexed to the application.
(4) As soon as the application has been lodged, the Registrar of the Court shall request the arbitration committee registry to transmit to the Court the file in the case.
(5) Articles 123 and 124 of these Rules shall apply to this procedure. The Court may decide that the procedure before it shall also include a hearing.
(6) The Court shall give its decision in the form of a judgment. Where the Court sets aside the decision of the arbitration committee it may refer the case back to the committee.

Article 202. Procedure under Article 103 TEAEC
(1) Four certified copies shall be lodged of an application under the third paragraph of Article 103 TEAEC. The application shall be accompanied by the draft of the agreement or contract concerned, by the observations of the European Commission addressed to the State concerned and by all other supporting documents.
(2) The application and annexes thereto shall be served on the European Commission, which shall have a time–limit of 10 days from such service to submit its written observations. This time–limit may be extended by the President after the State concerned has been heard.
(3) Following the lodging of such observations, which shall be served on the State concerned, the Court shall give its decision promptly, after hearing the Advocate General and, if they so request, the State concerned and the European Commission.

Article 203. Procedures under Articles 104 TEAEC and 105 TEAEC
Applications under the third paragraph of Article 104 TEAEC and the second paragraph of Article 105 TEAEC shall be governed by the provisions of Titles II and IV of these Rules. Such applications shall also be served on the State to which the respondent person or undertaking belongs.

Article 204. Procedure provided for by Article 111(3) of the EEA Agreement
(1) In the case governed by Article 111(3) of the EEA Agreement, the matter shall be brought before the Court by a request submitted by the Contracting Parties which are parties to the dispute. The request shall be served on the other Contracting Parties, on the European Commission, on the EFTA Surveillance Authority and, where appropriate, on the other interested persons on whom a request for a preliminary ruling raising the same question of interpretation of European Union legislation would be served.
(2) The President shall prescribe a time–limit within which the Contracting Parties and the other interested persons on whom the request has been served may submit written observations.
(3) The request shall be made in one of the languages referred to in Article 36 of these Rules. Article 38 shall apply. The provisions of Article 98 shall apply *mutatis mutandis*.
(4) As soon as the request referred to in paragraph 1 of this Article has been submitted, the President shall designate a Judge–Rapporteur. The First Advocate General shall, immediately afterwards, assign the request to an Advocate General.
(5) The Court shall, after hearing the Advocate General, give a reasoned decision on the request.
(6) The decision of the Court, signed by the President, the Judges who took part in the deliberations and the Registrar, shall be served on the Contracting Parties and on the other interested persons referred to in paragraphs 1 and 2.

Article 205. Settlement of the disputes referred to in Article 35 TEU in the version in force before the entry into force of the Treaty of Lisbon
(1) In the case of disputes between Member States as referred to in Article 35(7) TEU in the version in force before the entry into force of the Treaty of Lisbon, as maintained in force by Protocol No 36 annexed to the Treaties, the matter shall be brought before the Court by an application by a party to

the dispute. The application shall be served on the other Member States and on the European Commission.
(2) In the case of disputes between Member States and the European Commission as referred to in Article 35(7) TEU in the version in force before the entry into force of the Treaty of Lisbon, as maintained in force by Protocol No 36 annexed to the Treaties, the matter shall be brought before the Court by an application by a party to the dispute. The application shall be served on the other Member States, the Council and the European Commission if it was submitted by a Member State. The application shall be served on the Member States and on the Council if it was submitted by the European Commission.
(3) The President shall prescribe a time–limit within which the institutions and the Member States on which the application has been served may submit written observations.
(4) As soon as the application referred to in paragraphs 1 and 2 has been submitted, the President shall designate a Judge–Rapporteur. The First Advocate General shall, immediately afterwards, assign the application to an Advocate General.
(5) The Court may decide that the procedure before it shall also include a hearing.
(6) The Court shall, after the Advocate General has delivered his Opinion, give its ruling on the dispute by way of judgment.
(7) The same procedure as that laid down in the preceding paragraphs shall apply where an agreement concluded between the Member States confers jurisdiction on the Court to rule on a dispute between Member States or between Member States and an institution.

Article 206. Requests under Article 269 TFEU

(1) Four certified copies shall be submitted of a request under Article 269 TFEU. The request shall be accompanied by any relevant document and, in particular, any observations and recommendations made pursuant to Article 7 TEU.
(2) The request and annexes thereto shall be served on the European Council or on the Council, as appropriate, each of which shall have a time–limit of 10 days from such service to submit its written observations. This time–limit shall not be extended.
(3) The request and annexes thereto shall also be communicated to the Member States other than the State in question, to the European Parliament and to the European Commission.
(4) Following the lodging of the observations referred to in paragraph 2, which shall be served on the Member State concerned and on the States and institutions referred to in paragraph 3, the Court shall give its decision within a time–limit of one month from the lodging of the request and after hearing the Advocate General. At the request of the Member State concerned, the European Council or the Council, or of its own motion, the Court may decide that the procedure before it shall also include a hearing, which all the States and institutions referred to in this Article shall be given notice to attend.

Final Provisions

Article 207. Supplementary rules

Subject to the provisions of Article 253 TFEU and after consultation with the Governments concerned, the Court shall adopt supplementary rules concerning its practice in relation to:
(a) letters rogatory;
(b) applications for legal aid;
(c) reports by the Court of perjury by witnesses or experts, delivered pursuant to Article 30 of the Statute.

Article 208. Implementing rules

The Court may, by a separate act, adopt practice rules for the implementation of these Rules.

Article 209. Repeal

These Rules replace the Rules of Procedure of the Court of Justice of the European Communities adopted on 19 June 1991, as last amended on 24 May 2011.

Article 210. Publication and entry into force of these Rules

These Rules, which are authentic in the languages referred to in Article 36 of these Rules, shall be published in the *Official Journal of the European Union* and shall enter into force on the first day of the second month following their publication.

PART III   EUROPEAN UNION

Recommendations to National Courts and Tribunals, in Relation to the Initiation of Preliminary Ruling Proceedings

Introduction

1. The reference for a preliminary ruling, provided for in Article 19(3)(b) of the Treaty on European Union ('TEU') and Article 267 of the Treaty on the Functioning of the European Union ('TFEU'), is a fundamental mechanism of EU law. It is designed to ensure the uniform interpretation and application of that law within the European Union, by offering the courts and tribunals of the Member States a means of bringing before the Court of Justice of the European Union ('the Court') for a preliminary ruling questions concerning the interpretation of EU law or the validity of acts adopted by the institutions, bodies, offices or agencies of the Union.

2. The preliminary ruling procedure is based on close cooperation between the Court and the courts and tribunals of the Member States. In order to ensure that that procedure is fully effective, it is necessary to recall its essential characteristics and to provide further information to clarify the provisions of the rules of procedure relating, in particular,
to the originator and scope of a request for a preliminary ruling, as well as to the form and content of such a request. That information – which applies to all requests for a preliminary ruling (I) – is supplemented by the provisions that apply to requests for a preliminary ruling requiring particularly expeditious handling (II) and by an annex which summarises the essential elements of any request for a preliminary ruling.

I. Provisions which Apply to all Requests for a Preliminary Ruling

The originator of the request for a preliminary ruling

3. The jurisdiction of the Court to give a preliminary ruling on the interpretation or validity of EU law is exercised exclusively on the initiative of the national courts and tribunals, whether or not the parties to the main proceedings have expressed the wish that a question be referred to the Court. In so far as it is called upon to assume responsibility for the subsequent judicial decision, it is for the national court or tribunal before which a dispute has been brought
– and for that court or tribunal alone – to determine, in the light of the particular circumstances of each case, both the need for a request for a preliminary ruling in order to enable it to deliver judgment and the relevance of the questions which it submits to the Court.

4. Status as a court or tribunal is interpreted by the Court as a self–standing concept of EU law, the Court taking account of a number of factors such as whether the body making the reference is established by law, whether it is permanent, whether its jurisdiction is compulsory, whether its procedure is *inter partes*, whether it applies rules of law and whether it is independent.

5. The courts and tribunals of the Member States may refer a question to the Court on the interpretation or validity of EU law where they consider that a decision of the Court on the question is necessary to enable them to give judgment (see second paragraph of Article 267 TFEU). A reference for a preliminary ruling may, inter alia, prove particularly useful when a question of interpretation is raised before the national court or tribunal that is new and of general interest for the uniform application of EU law, or where the existing case–law does not appear to provide the necessary guidance in a new legal context or set of facts.

6. Where a question is raised in the context of a case that is pending before a court or tribunal against whose decisions there is no judicial remedy under national law, that court or tribunal is nonetheless required to bring a request for a preliminary ruling before the Court (see third paragraph of Article 267 TFEU), unless there is already well–established case–law on the point or unless the correct interpretation of the rule of law in question admits of no reasonable doubt.

7. It follows, moreover, from settled case–law that although national courts and tribunals may reject pleas raised before them challenging the validity of acts of an institution, body, office or agency of the Union, the Court has exclusive jurisdiction to declare such acts invalid. When it has doubts about the validity of such an act, a court or tribunal of a Member State must therefore refer the matter to the Court, stating the reasons for which it considers that the act is invalid.

The subject matter and scope of the request for a preliminary ruling

8. A request for a preliminary ruling must concern the interpretation or validity of EU law, not the interpretation of rules of national law or issues of fact raised in the main proceedings.

9. The Court can give a preliminary ruling only if EU law applies to the case in the main proceedings. It is essential, in that respect, that the referring court or tribunal set out all the relevant matters of fact and of law that have prompted it to consider that any provisions of EU law may be applicable in the case.

10. With regard to references for a preliminary ruling concerning the interpretation of the Charter of Fundamental Rights of the European Union, it must be noted that, under Article 51(1) of the Charter, the provisions of the Charter are addressed to the Member States only when they are implementing EU law. While the circumstances of such implementation can vary, it must nevertheless be clearly and unequivocally apparent from the request for a preliminary ruling that a rule of EU law other than the Charter is applicable to the case in the main proceedings. Since the Court has no jurisdiction to give a preliminary ruling where a legal situation does not come within the scope of EU law, any provisions of the Charter that may be relied upon by the referring court or tribunal cannot, of themselves, form the basis for such jurisdiction.

11. Lastly, although, in order to deliver its decision, the Court necessarily takes into account the legal and factual context of the dispute in the main proceedings, as defined by the referring court or tribunal in its request for a preliminary ruling, it does not itself apply EU law to that dispute. When ruling on the interpretation or validity of EU law, the Court makes every effort to give a reply which will be of assistance in resolving the dispute in the main proceedings, but it is for the referring court or tribunal to draw case–specific conclusions, if necessary by disapplying the rule of national law held incompatible with EU law.

The appropriate stage at which to make a reference for a preliminary ruling

12. A national court or tribunal may submit a request for a preliminary ruling to the Court as soon as it finds that a ruling on the interpretation or validity of EU law is necessary to enable it to give judgment. It is that court or tribunal which is in fact in the best position to decide at what stage of the proceedings such a request should be made.

13. Since, however, that request will serve as the basis of the proceedings before the Court and the Court must therefore have available to it all the information that will enable it both to assess whether it has jurisdiction to give a reply to the questions raised and, if so, to give a useful reply to those questions, it is necessary that a decision to make a reference for a preliminary ruling be taken when the national proceedings have reached a stage at which the referring court or tribunal is able to define, in sufficient detail, the legal and factual context of the case in the main proceedings, and the legal issues which it raises. In the interests of the proper administration of justice, it may also be desirable for the reference to be made only after both sides have been heard.

The form and content of the request for a preliminary ruling

14. The request for a preliminary ruling may be in any form allowed by national law in respect of procedural issues, but it should be borne in mind that that request serves as the basis of the proceedings before the Court and is served on all the interested persons referred to in Article 23 of the Statute of the Court ('the Statute') and, in particular, on all the Member States, with a view to obtaining any observations they may wish to make. Owing to the consequential need to translate it into all the official languages of the European Union, the request for a preliminary ruling should therefore be drafted simply, clearly and precisely by the referring court or tribunal, avoiding superfluous detail. As experience has shown, about 10 pages are often sufficient to set out adequately the legal and factual context of a request for a preliminary ruling.

15. The content of any request for a preliminary ruling is prescribed by Article 94 of the Rules of Procedure of the Court and is summarised in the annex hereto. In addition to the text of the questions referred to the Court for a preliminary ruling, the request for a preliminary ruling must contain:
– a summary of the subject matter of the dispute and the relevant findings of fact as determined by the referring court or tribunal, or, at the very least, an account of the facts on which the questions referred are based,
– the tenor of any national provisions applicable in the case and, where appropriate, the relevant national case–law, and
– a statement of the reasons which prompted the referring court or tribunal to inquire about the interpretation or validity of certain provisions of EU law, and the relationship between those provisions and the national legislation applicable to the main proceedings.
In the absence of one or more of the above, the Court may have to decline jurisdiction to give a pre-

liminary ruling on the questions referred or dismiss the request for a preliminary ruling as inadmissible.

16. In its request for a preliminary ruling, the referring court or tribunal must provide precise references for the national provisions applicable to the facts of the dispute in the main proceedings, and accurately identify the provisions of EU law whose interpretation is sought or whose validity is challenged. The request should include, if need be, a brief summary of the relevant arguments of the parties to the main proceedings. It is helpful to bear in mind in that context that it is only the request for a preliminary ruling that will be translated, not any annexes to that request.

17. The referring court or tribunal may also briefly state its view on the answer to be given to the questions referred for a preliminary ruling. That information may be useful to the Court, particularly where it is called upon to give a preliminary ruling in an expedited or urgent procedure.

18. Lastly, the questions referred to the Court for a preliminary ruling must appear in a separate and clearly identified section of the order for reference, preferably at the beginning or the end. It must be possible to understand them on their own terms, without it being necessary to refer to the statement of the grounds for the request.

19. In order to make the request for a preliminary ruling easier to read, it is essential that the Court receive it in typewritten form and that the pages and paragraphs of the order for reference be numbered.

20. The request for a preliminary ruling must be dated and signed, then sent, by registered post, to the Court Registry at the following address: Rue du Fort Niedergrünewald, 2925 Luxembourg, LUXEMBOURG. The request must be accompanied by any relevant documents and, in particular, precise contact details for the parties to the main proceedings and their representatives, if any, as well as the file of the case in the main proceedings or a copy of it. The file (or copy file) will be retained at the Registry throughout the proceedings where, unless otherwise indicated by the referring court or tribunal, it may be consulted by the interested persons referred to in Article 23 of the Statute.

21. Under the preliminary ruling procedure, the Court will, as a rule, use the information contained in the order for reference, including nominative or personal data. It is therefore for the referring court or tribunal itself, if it considers it necessary, to redact certain details in its request for a preliminary ruling or to render anonymous one or more persons or entities concerned by the dispute in the main proceedings.

22. After the request for a preliminary ruling has been lodged, the Court may also render such persons or entities anonymous of its own motion, or at the request of the referring court or tribunal or of a party to the main proceedings. In order to maintain its effectiveness, such a request for anonymity must, however, be made at the earliest possible stage of the proceedings, and in any event prior to publication in the *Official Journal of the European Union* of the notice relating to the case concerned, and to service of the request for a preliminary ruling on the interested persons referred to in Article 23 of the Statute, which generally takes place about one month after the request for a preliminary ruling has been lodged. Given the increasing use of new information and communication technologies, any anonymisation after such publication and service would be devoid of practical purpose.

Interaction between the reference for a preliminary ruling and the national proceedings

23. Although the referring court or tribunal may still order protective measures, particularly in connection with a reference on determination of validity, the lodging of a request for a preliminary ruling nevertheless calls for the national proceedings to be stayed until the Court has given its ruling.

24. While the Court, in principle, remains seised of a request for a preliminary ruling for so long as that request is not withdrawn, it must nevertheless be borne in mind that the Court's role in the preliminary ruling procedure is to contribute to the effective administration of justice in the Member States and not to give opinions on general or hypothetical questions. Since the preliminary ruling procedure is predicated on there being proceedings actually pending before the referring court or tribunal, it is incumbent on that court or tribunal to inform the Court of any procedural step that may affect the referral and, in particular, of any discontinuance or withdrawal, amicable settlement or other event leading to the termination of the proceedings. The referring court or tribunal must also inform the Court of any decision delivered in the context of an appeal against the order for reference and of the consequences of that decision for the request for a preliminary ruling.

25. In the interests of the proper conduct of the preliminary ruling proceedings before the Court and in order to maintain their effectiveness, it is important, however, that such information is communicated to the Court with the minimum of delay. The national courts and tribunals should also note that the withdrawal of a request for a preliminary ruling may have an impact on the management of similar cases (or of a series of cases) by the referring court or tribunal. Where the outcome of a number of cases pending before the referring court or tribunal depends on the reply to be given by the Court to the questions submitted by that court or tribunal, it may be appropriate for that court or tribunal to join those cases in the request for a preliminary ruling in order to enable the Court to reply to the questions referred notwithstanding any withdrawal of one or more cases.

Costs and legal aid

26. Preliminary ruling proceedings before the Court are free of charge and the Court does not rule on the costs of the parties to the proceedings pending before the referring court or tribunal; it is for the referring court or tribunal to rule on those costs.

27. If a party to the main proceedings has insufficient means and where it is possible under national rules, the referring court or tribunal may grant that party legal aid to cover the costs, including those of lawyers' fees, which it incurs before the Court. The Court itself may also grant legal aid where the party in question is not already in receipt of aid under national rules or to the extent to which that aid does not cover, or covers only partly, costs incurred before the Court.

Communication between the Court and the national court or tribunal

28. The Court Registry will remain in contact with the referring court or tribunal throughout the proceedings, and will send it copies of all procedural documents and any requests for information or clarification deemed necessary in order for a useful reply to be given to the questions referred by that court or tribunal.

29. At the end of the proceedings, the Registry will send the Court's decision to the referring court or tribunal, which is invited to inform the Court of the action taken upon that decision in the case in the main proceedings and to communicate to the Court its final decision in that case.

II. Provisions Applicable to Requests for a Preliminary Ruling Requiring Particularly Expeditious Handling

30. As provided in Article 23a of the Statute and Articles 105 to 114 of the Rules of Procedure, a reference for a preliminary ruling may, in certain circumstances, be determined pursuant to an expedited procedure or an urgent procedure. The Court will decide whether these procedures are to be applied, either on submission by the referring court or tribunal of a duly reasoned request setting out the matters of fact or of law which justify the application of such procedure(s), or, exceptionally, of its own motion, where that appears to be required by the nature or the particular circumstances of the case.

Conditions for the application of the expedited and urgent procedures

31. Article 105 of the Rules of Procedure provides that a reference for a preliminary ruling may thus be determined pursuant to an expedited procedure derogating from the provisions of those rules where the nature of the case requires that it be dealt with within a short time. Since that procedure imposes significant constraints on all those involved in it, and, in particular, on all the Member States called upon to lodge observations, whether written or oral, within much shorter time limits than would ordinarily apply, its application must be sought only in particular circumstances that warrant the Court giving its ruling quickly on the questions referred. According to settled case–law, the large number of persons or legal situations potentially affected by the decision that the referring court or tribunal has to deliver after bringing the matter before the Court for a preliminary ruling does not, in itself, constitute an exceptional circumstance that would justify the use of the expedited procedure.

32. The same applies a fortiori to the urgent preliminary ruling procedure, provided for in Article 107 of the Rules of Procedure. That procedure, which applies only in the areas covered by Title V of Part Three of the TFEU, relating to the area of freedom, security and justice, imposes even greater constraints on those concerned, since it limits the number of parties authorised to lodge written observations and, in cases of extreme urgency, allows the written part of the procedure before the Court to be omitted altogether. The application of the urgent procedure must therefore be requested only where it is absolutely necessary for the Court to give its ruling very quickly on the questions submitted by the referring court or tribunal.

PART III   EUROPEAN UNION

33. Although it is not possible to provide an exhaustive list of such circumstances, particularly because of the varied and evolving nature of the rules of EU law governing the area of freedom, security and justice, a national court or tribunal may, for example, consider submitting a request for the urgent preliminary ruling procedure to be applied in the case, referred to in the fourth paragraph of Article 267 TFEU, of a person in custody or deprived of his liberty, where the answer to the question raised is decisive as to the assessment of that person's legal situation, or in proceedings concerning parental authority or custody of young children, where the identity of the court having jurisdiction under EU law depends on the answer to the question referred for a preliminary ruling.

The request for application of the expedited procedure or the urgent procedure

34. To enable the Court to decide quickly whether the expedited procedure or the urgent preliminary ruling procedure should be applied, the request must set out precisely the matters of fact and law which establish the urgency and, in particular, the risks involved in following the ordinary procedure. In so far as it is possible to do so, the referring
court or tribunal must also briefly state its view on the answer to be given to the questions referred. Such a statement makes it easier for the parties to the main proceedings and the other interested persons participating in the procedure to define their positions, and therefore contributes to the rapidity of the procedure.

35. The request for the application of the expedited procedure or the urgent procedure must in any event be submitted in an unambiguous form that enables the Registry to establish immediately that the file has to be dealt with in a particular way. Accordingly, the referring court or tribunal is requested to specify which of the two procedures is required in the particular case, and to mention in its request the relevant article of the Rules of Procedure (Article 105 for the expedited procedure or Article 107 for the urgent procedure). That mention must be included in a clearly identifiable place in its order for reference (for example, at the head of the page or in a separate judicial document). Where appropriate, it may be helpful for a covering letter from the referring court or tribunal to refer to that request.

36. As regards the order for reference itself, it is particularly important that it should be concise where the matter is urgent, as this will help to ensure the rapidity of the procedure.

Communication between the Court, the referring court or tribunal and the parties to the main proceedings

37. In order to expedite and facilitate communication with the referring court or tribunal and the parties to the main proceedings, a court or tribunal submitting a request for the expedited procedure or the urgent procedure to be applied is requested to state the email address and any fax number which may be used by the Court, together with the email addresses and any fax numbers of the representatives of the parties to the proceedings.

38. A copy of the signed order for reference together with a request for the expedited procedure or the urgent procedure to be applied can initially be sent to the Court by email (ECJ–Registry@curia.europa.eu) or by fax (+352 433766). Processing of the reference and of the request can then begin upon receipt of the emailed or faxed copy. The originals of those documents must, however, be sent to the Court Registry as soon as possible.

COMMISSION DIRECTIVE 70/50/EEC

Commission Directive 70/50/EEC of 22 December 1969 based on the provisions of Article 33 (7), on the abolition of measures which have an effect equivalent to quantitative restrictions on imports and are not covered by other provisions adopted in pursuance of the EEC Treaty

THE COMMISSION OF THE EUROPEAN COMMUNITIES,
Having regard to the provisions of the Treaty establishing the European Economic Community, and in particular Article 33 (7) thereof;
Whereas for the purpose of Article 30 et seq. "measures" means laws, regulations, administrative provisions, administrative practices, and all instruments issuing from a public authority, including recommendations;
Whereas for the purposes of this Directive "administrative practices" means any standard and regularly followed procedure of a public authority; whereas "recommendations" means any instruments issuing from a public authority which, while not legally binding on the addressees thereof, cause them to pursue a certain conduct;
Whereas the formalities to which imports are subject do not as a general rule have an effect equivalent to that of quantitative restrictions and, consequently, are not covered by this Directive;
Whereas certain measures adopted by Member States, other than those applicable equally to domestic and imported products, which were operative at the date of entry into force of the Treaty and are not covered by other provisions adopted in pursuance of the Treaty, either preclude importation or make it more difficult or costly than the disposal of domestic production;
Whereas such measures must be considered to include those which make access of imported products to the domestic market, at any marketing stage, subject to a condition which is not laid down for domestic products or to a condition differing from that laid down for domestic products, and more difficult to satisfy, so that a burden is thus placed on imported products only;
Whereas such measures must also be considered to include those which, at any marketing stage, grant to domestic products a preference, other than an aid, to which conditions may or may not be attached, and where such measures totally or partially preclude the disposal of imported products;
Whereas such measures hinder imports which could otherwise take place, and thus have an effect equivalent to quantitative restrictions on imports;
Whereas effects on the free movement of goods of measures which relate to the marketing of products and which apply equally to domestic and imported products are not as a general rule equivalent to those of quantitative restrictions, since such effects are normally inherent in the disparities between rules applied by Member States in this respect;
Whereas, however, such measures may have a restrictive effect on the free movement of goods over and above that which is intrinsic to such rules;
Whereas such is the case where imports are either precluded or made more difficult or costly than the disposal of domestic production and where such effect is not necessary for the attainment of an objective within the scope of the powers for the regulation of trade left to Member States by the Treaty ; whereas such is in particular the case where the said objective can be attained just as effectively by other means which are less of a hindrance to trade ; whereas such is also the case where the restrictive effect of these provisions on the free movement of goods is out of proportion to their purpose;
Whereas these measures accordingly have an effect equivalent to that of quantitative restrictions on imports;
Whereas the customs union cannot be achieved without the abolition of such measures having an equivalent effect to quantitative restrictions on imports;
Whereas Member States must abolish all measures having equivalent effect by the end of the transitional period at the latest, even if no Commission Directive expressly requires them to do so;
Whereas the provisions concerning the abolition of quantitative restrictions and measures having equivalent effect between Member States apply both to products originating in and exported by Member States and to products originating in third countries and put into free circulation in the other Member States;
Whereas Article 33 (7) does not apply to measures of the kind referred to which fall under other provisions of the Treaty, and in particular those which fall under Articles 37 (1) and 44 of the Treaty or form an integral part of a national organisation of an agricultural market;
Whereas Article 33 (7) does not apply to the charges and taxation referred to in Article 12 et seq. and Article 95 et seq. or to the aids mentioned in Article 92;
Whereas the provisions of Article 33 (7) do not prevent the application, in particular, of Articles 36 and 223;
HAS ADOPTED THIS DIRECTIVE:

PART III EUROPEAN UNION

Article 1. The purpose of this Directive is to abolish the measures referred to in Articles 2 and 3, which were operative at the date of entry into force of the EEC Treaty.

Article 2. (1) This Directive covers measures, other than those applicable equally to domestic or imported products, which hinder imports which could otherwise take place, including measures which make importation more difficult or costly than the disposal of domestic production.
(2) In particular, it covers measures which make imports or the disposal, at any marketing stage, of imported products subject to a condition–other than a formality–which is required in respect of imported products only, or a condition differing from that required for domestic products and more difficult to satisfy. Equally, it covers, in particular, measures which favour domestic products or grant them a preference, other than an aid, to which conditions may or may not be attached.
(3) The measures referred to must be taken to include those measures which: (a) lay down, for imported products only, minimum or maximum prices below or above which imports are prohibited, reduced or made subject to conditions liable to hinder importation;
(b) lay down less favourable prices for imported products than for domestic products;
(c) fix profit margins or any other price components for imported products only or fix these differently for domestic products and for imported products, to the detriment of the latter;
(d) preclude any increase in the price of the imported product corresponding to the supplementary costs and charges inherent in importation;
(e) fix the prices of products solely on the basis of the cost price or the quality of domestic products at such a level as to create a hindrance to importation;
(f) lower the value of an imported product, in particular by causing a reduction in its intrinsic value, or increase its costs;
(g) make access of imported products to the domestic market conditional upon having an agent or representative in the territory of the importing Member State;
(h) lay down conditions of payment in respect of imported products only, or subject imported products to conditions which are different from those laid down for domestic products and more difficult to satisfy;
(i) require, for imports only, the giving of guarantees or making of payments on account;
(j) subject imported products only to conditions, in respect, in particular of shape, size, weight, composition, presentation, identification or putting up, or subject imported products to conditions which are different from those for domestic products and more difficult to satisfy;
(k) hinder the purchase by private individuals of imported products only, or encourage, require or give preference to the purchase of domestic products only;
(l) totally or partially preclude the use of national facilities or equipment in respect of imported products only, or totally or partially confine the use of such facilities or equipment to domestic products only;
(m) prohibit or limit publicity in respect of imported products only, or totally or partially confine publicity to domestic products only;
(n) prohibit, limit or require stocking in respect of imported products only; totally or partially confine the use of stocking facilities to domestic products only, or make the stocking of imported products subject to conditions which are different from those required for domestic products and more difficult to satisfy;
(o) make importation subject to the granting of reciprocity by one or more Member States;
(p) prescribe that imported products are to conform, totally or partially, to rules other than those of the importing country;
(q) specify time limits for imported products which are insufficient or excessive in relation to the normal course of the various transactions to which these time limits apply;
(r) subject imported products to controls or, other than those inherent in the customs clearance procedure, to which domestic products are not subject or which are stricter in respect of imported products than they are in respect of domestic products, without this being necessary in order to ensure equivalent protection;
(s) confine names which are not indicative of origin or source to domestic products only.

Article 3. This Directive also covers measures governing the marketing of products which deal, in particular, with shape, size, weight, composition, presentation, identification or putting up and which are equally applicable to domestic and imported products, where the restrictive effect of such measures on the free movement of goods exceeds the effects intrinsic to trade rules.
This is the case, in particular, where: – the restrictive effects on the free movement of goods are out of proportion to their purpose;
– the same objective can be attained by other means which are less of a hindrance to trade.

COMMISSION DIRECTIVE 70/50/EEC

Article 4. (1) Member States shall take all necessary steps in respect of products which must be allowed to enjoy free movement pursuant to Articles 9 and 10 of the Treaty to abolish measures having an effect equivalent to quantitative restrictions on imports and covered by this Directive.
(2) Member States shall inform the Commission of measures taken pursuant to this Directive.

Article 5. (1) This Directive does not apply to measures: (a) which fall under Article 37 (1) of the EEC Treaty;
(b) which are referred to in Article 44 of the EEC Treaty or form an integral part of a national organisation of an agricultural market not yet replaced by a common organisation.
(2) This Directive shall apply without prejudice to the application, in particular, of Articles 36 and 223 of the EEC Treaty.

Article 6.
This Directive is addressed to the Member States.

PART III   EUROPEAN UNION

Commission practice note on import prohibitions
Communication from the Commission concerning the consequences of the judgment given by the Court of Justice on 20 February 1979 in Case 120/78 ("Cassis de Dijon"), OJ 1980 C256/2

The following is the text of a letter which has been sent to the Member States; the European Parliament and the Council have also been notified of it.

In the Commission's Communication of 6 November 1978 on "Safeguarding free trade within the Community", it was emphasized that the free movement of goods is being affected by a growing number of restrictive measures.

The judgment delivered by the Court of Justice on 20 February 1979 in Case 120/78 (the "Cassis de Dijon" case), and recently reaffirmed in the judgment of 26 June 1980 in Case 788/79, has given the Commission some interpretative guidance enabling it to monitor more strictly the application of the Treaty rules on the free movement of goods, particularly Articles 30 to 36 of the EEC Treaty.

The Court gives a very general definition of the barriers to free trade which are prohibited by the provisions of Article 30 et seq. of the EEC Treaty. These are taken to include "any national measure capable of hindering, directly or indirectly, actually or potentially, intra–Community trade".

In its judgment of 20 February 1979 the Court indicates the scope of this definition as it applies to technical and commercial rules.

Any product lawfully produced and marketed in one Member State must, in principle, be admitted to the market of any other Member State.

Technical and commercial rules, even those equally applicable to national and imported products, may create barriers to trade only where those rules are necessary to satisfy mandatory requirements and to serve a purpose which is in the general interest and for which they are an essential guarantee. This purpose must be such as to take precedence over the requirements of the free movement of goods, which constitutes one of the fundamental rules of the Community.

The conclusions in terms of policy which the Commission draws from this new guidance are set out below. – Whereas Member States may, with respect to domestic products and in the absence of relevant Community provisions, regulate the terms on which such products are marketed, the case is different for products imported from other Member States.

Any product imported from another Member State must in principle be admitted to the territory of the importing Member State if it has been lawfully produced, that is, conforms to rules and processes of manufacture that are customarily and traditionally accepted in the exporting country, and is marketed in the territory of the latter.

This principle implies that Member States, when drawing up commercial or technical rules liable to affect the free movement of goods, may not take an exclusively national viewpoint and take account only of requirements confined to domestic products. The proper functioning of the common market demands that each Member State also give consideration to the legitimate requirements of the other Member States.

– Only under very strict conditions does the Court accept exceptions to this principle ; barriers to trade resulting from differences between commercial and technical rules are only admissible: – if the rules are necessary, that is appropriate and not excessive, in order to satisfy mandatory requirements (public health, protection of consumers or the environment, the fairness of commercial transactions, etc.);
– if the rules serve a purpose in the general interest which is compelling enough to justify an exception to a fundamental rule of the Treaty such as the free movement of goods;
– if the rules are essential for such a purpose to be attained, i.e. are the means which are the most appropriate and at the same time least hinder trade.

The Court's interpretation has induced the Commission to set out a number of guidelines.

– The principles deduced by the Court imply that a Member State may not in principle prohibit the sale in its territory of a product lawfully produced and marketed in another Member State even if the product is produced according to technical or quality requirements which differ from those imposed on its domestic products. Where a product "suitably and satisfactorily" fulfils the legitimate objective of a Member State's own rules (public safety, protection of the consumer or the environment, etc.), the importing country cannot justify prohibiting its sale in its territory by claiming that the way it fulfils the objective is different from that imposed on domestic products.

In such a case, an absolute prohibition of sale could not be considered "necessary" to satisfy a "mandatory requirement" because it would not be an "essential guarantee" in the sense defined in the Court's judgment.

The Commission will therefore have to tackle a whole body of commercial rules which lay down that products manufactured and marketed in one Member State must fulfil technical or qualitative conditions in order to be admitted to the market of another and specifically in all cases where the trade barriers occasioned by such rules are inadmissible according to the very strict criteria set out by the Court.

The Commission is referring in particular to rules covering the composition, designation, presentation and packaging of products as well as rules requiring compliance with certain technical standards.

– The Commission's work of harmonization will henceforth have to be directed mainly at national laws having an impact on the functioning of the common market where barriers to trade to be removed arise from national provisions which are admissible under the criteria set by the Court.

The Commission will be concentrating on sectors deserving priority because of their economic relevance to the creation of a single internal market.

To forestall later difficulties, the Commission will be informing Member States of potential objections, under the terms of Community law, to provisions they may be considering introducing which come to the attention of the Commission.

It will be producing suggestions soon on the procedures to be followed in such cases.

The Commission is confident that this approach will secure greater freedom of trade for the Community's manufacturers, so strengthening the industrial base of the Community, while meeting the expectations of consumers.

PART III   EUROPEAN UNION

Council Regulation (EC) No 2679/98 of 7 December 1998 on the functioning of the internal market in relation to the free movement of goods among the Member States

THE COUNCIL OF THE EUROPEAN UNION,
Having regard to the Treaty establishing the European Community, and in particular Article 235 thereof,
Having regard to the proposal from the Commission,
Having regard to the opinion of the European Parliament,
Having regard to the opinion of the Economic and Social Committee,
(1) Whereas, as provided for in Article 7a of the Treaty, the internal market comprises an area without internal frontiers in which, in particular, the free movement of goods is ensured in accordance with Articles 30 to 36 of the Treaty;
(2) Whereas breaches of this principle, such as occur when in a given Member State the free movement of goods is obstructed by actions of private individuals, may cause grave disruption to the proper functioning of the internal market and inflict serious losses on the individuals affected;
(3) Whereas, in order to ensure fulfilment of the obligations arising from the Treaty, and, in particular, to ensure the proper functioning of the internal market, Member States should, on the one hand, abstain from adopting measures or engaging in conduct liable to constitute an obstacle to trade and, on the other hand, take all necessary and proportionate measures with a view to facilitating the free movement of goods in their territory;
(4) Whereas such measures must not affect the exercise of fundamental rights, including the right or freedom to strike;
(5) Whereas this Regulation does not prevent any actions which may be necessary in certain cases at Community level to respond to problems in the functioning of the internal market, taking into account, where appropriate, the application of this Regulation;
(6) Whereas Member States have exclusive competence as regards the maintenance of public order and the safeguarding of internal security as well as in determining whether, when and which measures are necessary and proportionate in order to facilitate the free movement of goods in their territory in a given situation;
(7) Whereas there should be adequate and rapid exchange of information between the Member States and the Commission on obstacles to the free movement of goods;
(8) Whereas a Member State on the territory of which obstacles to the free movement of goods occur should take all necessary and proportionate measures to restore as soon as possible the free movement of goods in their territory in order to avoid the risk that the disruption or loss in question will continue, increase or intensify and that there may be a breakdown in trade and in the contractual relations which underlie it; whereas such Member State should inform the Commission and, if requested, other Member States of the measures it has taken or intends to take in order to fulfil this objective;
(9) Whereas the Commission, in fulfilment of its duty under the Treaty, should notify the Member State concerned of its view that a breach has occurred and the Member State should respond to that notification;
(10) Whereas the Treaty provides for no powers, other than those in Article 235 thereof, for the adoption of this Regulation,
HAS ADOPTED THIS REGULATION:

Article 1. For the purpose of this Regulation:
(1) the term 'obstacle' shall mean an obstacle to the free movement of goods among Member States which is attributable to a Member State, whether it involves action or inaction on its part, which may constitute a breach of Articles 30 to 36 of the Treaty and which:
(a) leads to serious disruption of the free movement of goods by physically or otherwise preventing, delaying or diverting their import into, export from or transport across a Member State,
(b) causes serious loss to the individuals affected, and
(c) requires immediate action in order to prevent any continuation, increase or intensification of the disruption or loss in question;
(2) the term 'inaction' shall cover the case when the competent authorities of a Member State, in the presence of an obstacle caused by actions taken by private individuals, fail to take all necessary and proportionate measures within their powers with a view to removing the obstacle and ensuring the free movement of goods in their territory.

Article 2. This Regulation may not be interpreted as affecting in any way the exercise of fundamental rights as recognised in Member States, including the right or freedom to strike. These rights may also

COUNCIL REGULATION 2679/98/EC

include the right or freedom to take other actions covered by the specific industrial relations systems in Member States.

Article 3. (1) When an obstacle occurs or when there is a threat thereof
(a) any Member State (whether or not it is the Member State concerned) which has relevant information shall immediately transmit it to the Commission, and
(b) the Commission shall immediately transmit to the Member States that information and any information from any other source which it may consider relevant.
(2) The Member State concerned shall respond as soon as possible to requests for information from the Commission and from other Member States concerning the nature of the obstacle or threat and the action which it has taken or proposes to take. Information exchange between Member States shall also be transmitted to the Commission.

Article 4. (1) When an obstacle occurs, and subject to Article 2, the Member State concerned shall
(a) take all necessary and proportionate measures so that the free movement of goods is assured in the territory of the Member State in accordance with the Treaty, and
(b) inform the Commission of the actions which its authorities have taken or intend to take.
(2) The Commission shall immediately transmit the information received under paragraph l(b) to the other Member States.

Article 5. (1) Where the Commission considers that an obstacle is occurring in a Member State, it shall notify the Member State concerned of the reasons that have led the Commission to such a conclusion and shall request the Member State to take all necessary and proportionate measures to remove the said obstacle within a period which it shall determine with reference to the urgency of the case.
(2) In reaching its conclusion, the Commission shall have regard to Article 2.
(3) The Commission may publish in the *Official Journal of the European Communities* the text of the notification which it has sent to the Member State concerned and shall immediately transmit the text to any party which requests it.
(4) The Member State shall, within five working days of receipt of the text, either:
– inform the Commission of the steps which it has taken or intends to take to implement paragraph 1, or
– communicate a reasoned submission as to why there is no obstacle constituting a breach of Articles 30 to 36 of the Treaty.
(5) In exceptional cases, the Commission may allow an extension of the deadline mentioned in paragraph 4 if the Member State submits a duly substantiated request and the grounds cited are deemed acceptable.

This Regulation shall be binding in its entirety and directly applicable in all Member States.

PART III EUROPEAN UNION

Council Directive 77/249/EEC of 22 March 1977 to facilitate the effective exercise by lawyers of freedom to provide services

THE COUNCIL OF THE EUROPEAN COMMUNITIES,
Having regard to the Treaty establishing the European Economic Community, and in particular Articles 57 and 66 thereof,
Having regard to the proposal from the Commission,
Having regard to the opinion of the European Parliament,
Having regard to the opinion of the Economic and Social Committee,
Whereas, pursuant to the Treaty, any restriction on the provision of services which is based on nationality or on conditions of residence has been prohibited since the end of the transitional period;
Whereas this Directive deals only with measures to facilitate the effective pursuit of the activities of lawyers by way of provision of services; whereas more detailed measures will be necessary to facilitate the effective exercise of the right of establishment;
Whereas if lawyers are to exercise effectively the freedom to provide services host Member States must recognize as lawyers those persons practising the profession in the various Member States;
Whereas, since this Directive solely concerns provision of services and does not contain provisions on the mutual recognition of diplomas, a person to whom the Directive applies must adopt the professional title used in the Member State in which he is established, hereinafter referred to as "the Member State from which he comes",
HAS ADOPTED THIS DIRECTIVE:

Article 1. (1) This Directive shall apply, within the limits and under the conditions laid down herein, to the activities of lawyers pursued by way of provision of services.
Notwithstanding anything contained in this Directive, Member States may reserve to prescribed categories of lawyers the preparation of formal documents for obtaining title to administer estates of deceased persons, and the drafting of formal documents creating or transferring interests in land.
(2) "Lawyer" means any person entitled to pursue his professional activities under one of the following designations: >PIC FILE= "T0010774">

Article 2. Each Member State shall recognize as a lawyer for the purpose of pursuing the activities specified in Article 1(1) any person listed in paragraph 2 of that Article.

Article 3. A person referred to in Article 1 shall adopt the professional title used in the Member State from which he comes, expressed in the language or one of the languages, of that State, with an indication of the professional organization by which he is authorized to practise or the court of law before which he is entitled to practise pursuant to the laws of that State.

Article 4. (1) Activities relating to the representation of a client in legal proceedings or before public authorities shall be pursued in each host Member State under the conditions laid down for lawyers established in that State, with the exception of any conditions requiring residence, or registration with a professional organization, in that State. OJ No C 103, 5.10.1972, p. 19 and OJ No C 53, 8.3.1976, p. 33. OJ No C 36, 28.3.1970, p. 37 and OJ No C 50, 4.3.1976, p. 17.
(2) A lawyer pursuing these activities shall observe the rules of professional conduct of the host Member State, without prejudice to his obligations in the Member State from which he comes.
(3) When these activities are pursued in the United Kingdom, "rules of professional conduct of the host Member State" means the rules of professional conduct applicable to solicitors, where such activities are not reserved for barristers and advocates. Otherwise the rules of professional conduct applicable to the latter shall apply. However, barristers from Ireland shall always be subject to the rules of professional conduct applicable in the United Kingdom to barristers and advocates.
When these activities are pursued in Ireland "rules of professional conduct of the host Member State" means, in so far as they govern the oral presentation of a case in court, the rules of professional conduct applicable to barristers. In all other cases the rules of professional conduct applicable to solicitors shall apply. However, barristers and advocates from the United Kingdom shall always be subject to the rules of professional conduct applicable in Ireland to barristers.
(4) A lawyer pursuing activities other than those referred to in paragraph 1 shall remain subject to the conditions and rules of professional conduct of the Member State from which he comes without prejudice to respect for the rules, whatever their source, which govern the profession in the host Member State, especially those concerning the incompatibility of the exercise of the activities of a lawyer with the exercise of other activities in that State, professional secrecy, relations with other lawyers, the prohibition on the same lawyer acting for parties with mutually conflicting interests, and publicity. The latter rules are applicable only if they are capable of being observed by a lawyer who

is not established in the host Member State and to the extent to which their observance is objectively justified to ensure, in that State, the proper exercise of a lawyer's activities, the standing of the profession and respect for the rules concerning incompatibility.

Article 5. For the pursuit of activities relating to the representation of a client in legal proceedings, a Member State may require lawyers to whom Article 1 applies: – to be introduced, in accordance with local rules or customs, to the presiding judge and, where appropriate, to the President of the relevant Bar in the host Member State;
– to work in conjunction with a lawyer who practises before the judicial authority in question and who would, where necessary, be answerable to that authority, or with an "avoué" or "procuratore" practising before it.

Article 6. Any Member State may exclude lawyers who are in the salaried employment of a public or private undertaking from pursuing activities relating to the representation of that undertaking in legal proceedings in so far as lawyers established in that State are not permitted to pursue those activities.

Article 7. (1) The competent authority of the host Member State may request the person providing the services to establish his qualifications as a lawyer.
(2) In the event of non–compliance with the obligations referred to in Article 4 and in force in the host Member State, the competent authority of the latter shall determine in accordance with its own rules and procedures the consequences of such non–compliance, and to this end may obtain any appropriate professional information concerning the person providing services. It shall notify the competent authority of the Member State from which the person comes of any decision taken. Such exchanges shall not affect the confidential nature of the information supplied.

Article 8. (1) Member States shall bring into force the measures necessary to comply with this Directive within two years of its notification and shall forthwith inform the Commission thereof.
(2) Member States shall communicate to the Commission the texts of the main provisions of national law which they adopt in the field covered by this Directive.

Article 9. This Directive is addressed to the Member States.

PART III   EUROPEAN UNION

**Directive 96/71/EC of the European Parliament and of the Council
of 16 December 1996 concerning the posting of workers in the framework of the provision of services**

*THE EUROPEAN PARLIAMENT AND THE COUNCIL OF THE EUROPEAN UNION,
Having regard to the Treaty establishing the European Community, and in particular Articles 57 (2) and 66 thereof,
Having regard to the proposal from the Commission,
Having regard to the opinion of the Economic and Social Committee,
Acting in accordance with the procedure laid down in Article 189b of the Treaty,
(1) Whereas, pursuant to Article 3 (c) of the Treaty, the abolition, as between Member States, of obstacles to the free movement of persons and services constitutes one of the objectives of the Community;
(2) Whereas, for the provision of services, any restrictions based on nationality or residence requirements are prohibited under the Treaty with effect from the end of the transitional period;
(3) Whereas the completion of the internal market offers a dynamic environment for the transnational provision of services, prompting a growing number of undertakings to post employees abroad temporarily to perform work in the territory of a Member State other than the State in which they are habitually employed;
(4) Whereas the provision of services may take the form either of performance of work by an undertaking on its account and under its direction, under a contract concluded between that undertaking and the party for whom the services are intended, or of the hiring–out of workers for use by an undertaking in the framework of a public or a private contract;
(5) Whereas any such promotion of the transnational provision of services requires a climate of fair competition and measures guaranteeing respect for the rights of workers;
(6) Whereas the transnationalization of the employment relationship raises problems with regard to the legislation applicable to the employment relationship; whereas it is in the interests of the parties to lay down the terms and conditions governing the employment relationship envisaged;
(7) Whereas the Rome Convention of 19 June 1980 on the law applicable to contractual obligations (4), signed by 12 Member States, entered into force on 1 April 1991 in the majority of Member States;
(8) Whereas Article 3 of that Convention provides, as a general rule, for the free choice of law made by the parties; whereas, in the absence of choice, the contract is to be governed, according to Article 6 (2), by the law of the country, in which the employee habitually carries out his work in performance of the contract, even if he is temporarily employed in another country, or, if the employee does not habitually carry out his work in any one country, by the law of the country in which the place of business through which he was engaged is situated, unless it appears from the circumstances as a whole that the contract is more closely connected with another country, in which case the contract is to be governed by the law of that country;
(9) Whereas, according to Article 6 (1) of the said Convention, the choice of law made by the parties is not to have the result of depriving the employee of the protection afforded to him by the mandatory rules of the law which would be applicable under paragraph 2 of that Article in the absence of choice;
(10) Whereas Article 7 of the said Convention lays down, subject to certain conditions, that effect may be given, concurrently with the law declared applicable, to the mandatory rules of the law of another country, in particular the law of the Member State within whose territory the worker is temporarily posted;
(11) Whereas, according to the principle of precedence of Community law laid down in its Article 20, the said Convention does not affect the application of provisions which, in relation to a particular matter, lay down choice–of–law rules relating to contractual obligations and which are or will be contained in acts of the institutions of the European Communities or in national laws harmonized in implementation of such acts;
(12) Whereas Community law does not preclude Member States from applying their legislation, or collective agreements entered into by employers and labour, to any person who is employed, even temporarily, within their territory, although his employer is established in another Member State; whereas Community law does not forbid Member States to guarantee the observance of those rules by the appropriate means;
(13) Whereas the laws of the Member States must be coordinated in order to lay down a nucleus of mandatory rules for minimum protection to be observed in the host country by employers who post workers to perform temporary work in the territory of a Member State where the services are provided; whereas such coordination can be achieved only by means of Community law;*

(14) Whereas a 'hard core' of clearly defined protective rules should be observed by the provider of the services notwithstanding the duration of the worker's posting;
(15) Whereas it should be laid down that, in certain clearly defined cases of assembly and/or installation of goods, the provisions on minimum rates of pay and minimum paid annual holidays do not apply;
(16) Whereas there should also be some flexibility in application of the provisions concerning minimum rates of pay and the minimum length of paid annual holidays; whereas, when the length of the posting is not more than one month, Member States may, under certain conditions, derogate from the provisions concerning minimum rates of pay or provide for the possibility of derogation by means of collective agreements; whereas, where the amount of work to be done is not significant, Member States may derogate from the provisions concerning minimum rates of pay and the minimum length of paid annual holidays;
(17) Whereas the mandatory rules for minimum protection in force in the host country must not prevent the application of terms and conditions of employment which are more favourable to workers;
(18) Whereas the principle that undertakings established outside the Community must not receive more favourable treatment than undertakings established in the territory of a Member State should be upheld;
(19) Whereas, without prejudice to other provisions of Community law, this Directive does not entail the obligation to give legal recognition to the existence of temporary employment undertakings, nor does it prejudice the application by Member States of their laws concerning the hiring–out of workers and temporary employment undertakings to undertakings not established in their territory but operating therein in the framework of the provision of services;
(20) Whereas this Directive does not affect either the agreements concluded by the Community with third countries or the laws of Member States concerning the access to their territory of third–country providers of services; whereas this Directive is also without prejudice to national laws relating to the entry, residence and access to employment of third–country workers;
(21) Whereas Council Regulation (EEC) No 1408/71 of 14 June 1971 on the application of social security schemes to employed persons and their families moving within the Community (5) lays down the provisions applicable with regard to social security benefits and contributions;
(22) Whereas this Directive is without prejudice to the law of the Member States concerning collective action to defend the interests of trades and professions;
(23) Whereas competent bodies in different Member States must cooperate with each other in the application of this Directive; whereas Member States must provide for appropriate remedies in the event of failure to comply with this Directive;
(24) Whereas it is necessary to guarantee proper application of this Directive and to that end to make provision for close collaboration between the Commission and the Member States;
(25) Whereas five years after adoption of this Directive at the latest the Commission must review the detailed rules for implementing this Directive with a view to proposing, where appropriate, the necessary amendments,
HAVE ADOPTED THIS DIRECTIVE:

Article 1. Subject-matter and scope
(1) This Directive shall ensure the protection of posted workers during their posting in relation to the freedom to provide services, by laying down mandatory provisions regarding working conditions and the protection of workers' health and safety that must be respected.
(1a) This Directive shall not in any way affect the exercise of fundamental rights as recognised in the Member States and at Union level, including the right or freedom to strike or to take other action covered by the specific industrial relations systems in Member States, in accordance with national law and/or practice. Nor does it affect the right to negotiate, to conclude and enforce collective agreements, or to take collective action in accordance with national law and/or practice.
(2) This Directive shall not apply to merchant navy undertakings as regards seagoing personnel.
(3) This Directive shall apply to the extent that the undertakings referred to in paragraph 1 take one of the following transnational measures:
(a) post workers to the territory of a Member State on their account and under their direction, under a contract concluded between the undertaking making the posting and the party for whom the services are intended, operating in that Member State, provided there is an employment relationship between the undertaking making the posting and the worker during the period of posting; or
(b) post workers to an establishment or to an undertaking owned by the group in the territory of a Member State, provided there is an employment relationship between the undertaking making the posting and the worker during the period of posting; or

(c) being a temporary employment undertaking or placement agency, hire out a worker to a user undertaking established or operating in the territory of a Member State, provided there is an employment relationship between the temporary employment undertaking or placement agency and the worker during the period of posting.

Where a worker who has been hired out by a temporary employment undertaking or placement agency to a user undertaking as referred to in point (c) is to carry out work in the framework of the transnational provision of services within the meaning of point (a), (b) or (c) by the user undertaking in the territory of a Member State other than where the worker normally works for the temporary employment undertaking or placement agency, or for the user undertaking, the worker shall be considered to be posted to the territory of that Member State by the temporary employment undertaking or placement agency with which the worker is in an employment relationship. The temporary employment undertaking or placement agency shall be considered to be an undertaking as referred to in paragraph 1 and shall fully comply with the relevant provisions of this Directive and Directive 2014/67/EU of the European Parliament and of the Council.

The user undertaking shall inform the temporary employment undertaking or placement agency which hired out the worker in due time before commencement of the work referred to in the second subparagraph.

(4) Undertakings established in a non–member State must not be given more favourable treatment than undertakings established in a Member State.

Article 2. Definition

(1) For the purposes of this Directive, 'posted worker' means a worker who, for a limited period, carries out his work in the territory of a Member State other than the State in which he normally works.
(2) For the purposes of this Directive, the definition of a worker is that which applies in the law of the Member State to whose territory the worker is posted.

Article 3. Terms and conditions of employment

(1) Member States shall ensure, irrespective of which law applies to the employment relationship, that undertakings as referred to in Article 1(1) guarantee, on the basis of equality of treatment, workers who are posted to their territory the terms and conditions of employment covering the following matters which are laid down in the Member State where the work is carried out:
– by law, regulation or administrative provision, and/or
– by collective agreements or arbitration awards which have been declared universally applicable or otherwise apply in accordance with paragraph 8:
(a) maximum work periods and minimum rest periods;
(b) minimum paid annual leave;
(c) remuneration, including overtime rates; this point does not apply to supplementary occupational retirement pension schemes;
(d) the conditions of hiring–out of workers, in particular the supply of workers by temporary employment undertakings;
(e) health, safety and hygiene at work;
(f) protective measures with regard to the terms and conditions of employment of pregnant women or women who have recently given birth, of children and of young people;
(g) equality of treatment between men and women and other provisions on non–discrimination.
(h) the conditions of workers' accommodation where provided by the employer to workers away from their regular place of work;
(i) allowances or reimbursement of expenditure to cover travel, board and lodging expenses for workers away from home for professional reasons.
Point (i) shall apply exclusively to travel, board and lodging expenditure incurred by posted workers where they are required to travel to and from their regular place of work in the Member State to whose territory they are posted, or where they are temporarily sent by their employer from that regular place of work to another place of work.
For the purposes of this Directive, the concept of remuneration shall be determined by the national law and/or practice of the Member State to whose territory the worker is posted and means all the constituent elements of remuneration rendered mandatory by national law, regulation or administrative provision, or by collective agreements or arbitration awards which, in that Member State, have been declared universally applicable or otherwise apply in accordance with paragraph 8.
Without prejudice to Article 5 of Directive 2014/67/EU, Member States shall publish the information on the terms and conditions of employment, in accordance with national law and/or practice, without undue delay and in a transparent manner, on the single official national website referred to in that Article, including the constituent elements of remuneration as referred to in the third subparagraph

of this paragraph and all the terms and conditions of employment in accordance with paragraph 1a of this Article.

Member States shall ensure that the information provided on the single official national website is accurate and up to date. The Commission shall publish on its website the addresses of the single official national websites.

Where, contrary to Article 5 of Directive 2014/67/EU, the information on the single official national website does not indicate which terms and conditions of employment are to be applied, that circumstance shall be taken into account, in accordance with national law and/or practice, in determining penalties in the event of infringements of the national provisions adopted pursuant to this Directive, to the extent necessary to ensure the proportionality thereof.

(1a) Where the effective duration of a posting exceeds 12 months, Member States shall ensure, irrespective of which law applies to the employment relationship, that undertakings as referred to in Article 1(1) guarantee, on the basis of equality of treatment, workers who are posted to their territory, in addition to the terms and conditions of employment referred to in paragraph 1 of this Article, all the applicable terms and conditions of employment which are laid down in the Member State where the work is carried out:

— by law, regulation or administrative provision, and/or

— by collective agreements or arbitration awards which have been declared universally applicable or otherwise apply in accordance with paragraph 8.

The first subparagraph of this paragraph shall not apply to the following matters:

(a) procedures, formalities and conditions of the conclusion and termination of the employment contract, including non-competition clauses;

(b) supplementary occupational retirement pension schemes.

Where the service provider submits a motivated notification, the Member State where the service is provided shall extend the period referred to in the first subparagraph to 18 months.

Where an undertaking as referred to in Article 1(1) replaces a posted worker by another posted worker performing the same task at the same place, the duration of the posting shall, for the purposes of this paragraph, be the cumulative duration of the posting periods of the individual posted workers concerned.

The concept of "the same task at the same place" referred to in the fourth subparagraph of this paragraph shall be determined taking into consideration, inter alia, the nature of the service to be provided, the work to be performed and the address(es) of the workplace.

(1b) Member States shall provide that the undertakings referred to in point (c) of Article 1(3) guarantee posted workers the terms and conditions of employment which apply pursuant to Article 5 of Directive 2008/104/EC of the European Parliament and of the Council to temporary agency workers hired-out by temporary-work agencies established in the Member State where the work is carried out.

The user undertaking shall inform the undertakings referred to in point (c) of Article 1(3) of the terms and conditions of employment that it applies regarding the working conditions and remuneration to the extent covered by the first subparagraph of this paragraph.

(2) In the case of initial assembly and/or first installation of goods where this is an integral part of a contract for the supply of goods and necessary for taking the goods supplied into use and carried out by the skilled and/or specialist workers of the supplying undertaking, the first subparagraph of paragraph 1 (b) and (c) shall not apply, if the period of posting does not exceed eight days.

This provision shall not apply to activities in the field of building work listed in the Annex.

(3) Member States may, after consulting employers and labour, in accordance with the traditions and practices of each Member State, decide not to apply the first subparagraph of paragraph 1 (c) in the cases referred to in Article 1 (3) (a) and (b) when the length of the posting does not exceed one month.

(4) Member States may, in accordance with national laws and/or practices, provide that exemptions may be made from the first subparagraph of paragraph 1 (c) in the cases referred to in Article 1 (3) (a) and (b) and from a decision by a Member State within the meaning of paragraph 3 of this Article, by means of collective agreements within the meaning of paragraph 8 of this Article, concerning one or more sectors of activity, where the length of the posting does not exceed one month.

(5) Member States may provide for exemptions to be granted from the first subparagraph of paragraph 1 (b) and (c) in the cases referred to in Article 1 (3) (a) and (b) on the grounds that the amount of work to be done is not significant.

Member States availing themselves of the option referred to in the first subparagraph shall lay down the criteria which the work to be performed must meet in order to be considered as 'non–significant'.

(6) The length of the posting shall be calculated on the basis of a reference period of one year from the beginning of the posting.

For the purpose of such calculations, account shall be taken of any previous periods for which the post has been filled by a posted worker.

(7) Paragraphs 1 to 6 shall not prevent application of terms and conditions of employment which are more favourable to workers.

Allowances specific to the posting shall be considered to be part of remuneration, unless they are paid in reimbursement of expenditure actually incurred on account of the posting, such as expenditure on travel, board and lodging. The employer shall, without prejudice to point (h) of the first subparagraph of paragraph 1, reimburse the posted worker for such expenditure in accordance with the national law and/or practice applicable to the employment relationship.

Where the terms and conditions of employment applicable to the employment relationship do not determine whether and, if so, which elements of the allowance specific to the posting are paid in reimbursement of expenditure actually incurred on account of the posting or which are part of remuneration, then the entire allowance shall be considered to be paid in reimbursement of expenditure.

(8) 'Collective agreements or arbitration awards which have been declared universally applicable' means collective agreements or arbitration awards which must be observed by all undertakings in the geographical area and in the profession or industry concerned.

In the absence of, or in addition to, a system for declaring collective agreements or arbitration awards to be of universal application within the meaning of the first subparagraph, Member States may, if they so decide, base themselves on:

— collective agreements or arbitration awards which are generally applicable to all similar undertakings in the geographical area and in the profession or industry concerned, and/or

— collective agreements which have been concluded by the most representative employers' and labour organisations at national level and which are applied throughout national territory,

provided that their application to undertakings as referred to in Article 1(1) ensures equality of treatment on matters listed in the first subparagraph of paragraph 1 of this Article and, where applicable, with regard to the terms and conditions of employment to be guaranteed posted workers in accordance with paragraph 1a of this Article, between those undertakings and the other undertakings referred to in this subparagraph which are in a similar position.

Equality of treatment, within the meaning of this Article, shall be deemed to exist where national undertakings in a similar position:

— are subject, in the place in question or in the sector concerned, to the same obligations as undertakings as referred to in Article 1(1) as regards the matters listed in the first subparagraph of paragraph 1 of this Article and, where applicable, as regards the terms and conditions of employment to be guaranteed posted workers in accordance with paragraph 1a of this Article, and

— are required to fulfil such obligations with the same effects.

(9) Member States may require undertakings as referred to in Article 1(1) to guarantee workers referred to in point (c) of Article 1(3), in addition to the terms and conditions of employment referred to in paragraph 1b of this Article, other terms and conditions that apply to temporary agency workers in the Member State where the work is carried out.

(10)

This Directive shall not preclude the application by Member States, in compliance with the Treaties, to national undertakings and to the undertakings of other Member States, on the basis of equality of treatment, of terms and conditions of employment on matters other than those referred to in the first subparagraph of paragraph 1 in the case of public policy provisions.

Article 4. Cooperation on information

(1) For the purposes of implementing this Directive, Member States shall, in accordance with national legislation and/or practice, designate one or more liaison offices or one or more competent national bodies.

(2) Member States shall make provision for cooperation between the competent authorities or bodies, including public authorities, which, in accordance with national law, are responsible for monitoring the terms and conditions of employment referred to in Article 3, including at Union level. Such cooperation shall in particular consist in replying to reasoned requests from those authorities or bodies for information on the transnational hiring-out of workers, and in tackling manifest abuses or possible cases of unlawful activities, such as transnational cases of undeclared work and bogus self-employment linked to the posting of workers. Where the competent authority or body in the Member State from which the worker is posted does not possess the information requested by the competent authority or body of the Member State to whose territory the worker is posted, it shall seek to obtain that information from other authorities or bodies in that Member State. In the event of persistent delays in the provision of such information to the Member State to whose territory the worker is posted, the

Commission shall be informed and shall take appropriate measures.

(3) Each Member State shall take the appropriate measures to make the information on the terms and conditions of employment referred to in Article 3 generally available.

(4) Each Member State shall notify the other Member States and the Commission of the liaison offices and/or competent bodies referred to in paragraph 1.

Article 5. Monitoring, control and enforcement

The Member State to whose territory the worker is posted and the Member State from which the worker is posted shall be responsible for the monitoring, control and enforcement of the obligations laid down in this Directive and in Directive 2014/67/EU and shall take appropriate measures in the event of failure to comply with this Directive.

Member States shall lay down the rules on penalties applicable to infringements of national provisions adopted pursuant to this Directive and shall take all measures necessary to ensure that they are implemented. The penalties provided for shall be effective, proportionate and dissuasive.

Member States shall in particular ensure that adequate procedures are available to workers and/or workers' representatives for the enforcement of obligations under this Directive.

Where, following an overall assessment made pursuant to Article 4 of Directive 2014/67/EU by a Member State, it is established that an undertaking is improperly or fraudulently creating the impression that the situation of a worker falls within the scope of this Directive, that Member State shall ensure that the worker benefits from relevant law and practice.

Member States shall ensure that this Article does not lead to the worker concerned being subject to less favourable conditions than those applicable to posted workers.

Article 6. Jurisdiction

In order to enforce the right to the terms and conditions of employment guaranteed in Article 3, judicial proceedings may be instituted in the Member State in whose territory the worker is or was posted, without prejudice, where applicable, to the right, under existing international conventions on jurisdiction, to institute proceedings in another State.

Article 7. Implementation

Member States shall adopt the laws, regulations and administrative provisions necessary to comply with this Directive by 16 December 1999 at the latest. They shall forthwith inform the Commission thereof.

When Member States adopt these provisions, they shall contain a reference to this Directive or shall be accompanied by such reference on the occasion of their official publication. The methods of making such reference shall be laid down by Member States.

Article 8. Commission review

By 16 December 2001 at the latest, the Commission shall review the operation of this Directive with a view to proposing the necessary amendments to the Council where appropriate.

Article 9. This Directive is addressed to the Member States.

PART III EUROPEAN UNION

Directive 98/5/EC of the European Parliament and of the Council of 16 February 1998 to facilitate practice of the profession of lawyer on a permanent basis in a Member State other than that in which the qualification was obtained

THE EUROPEAN PARLIAMENT AND THE COUNCIL OF THE EUROPEAN UNION,
Having regard to the Treaty establishing the European Community, and in particular Article 49, Article 57(1) and the first and third sentences of Article 57(2) thereof,
Having regard to the proposal from the Commission,
Having regard to the Opinion of the Economic and Social Committee,
Acting in accordance with the procedure laid down in Article 189b of the Treaty,
(1) Whereas, pursuant to Article 7a of the Treaty, the internal market is to comprise an area without internal frontiers; whereas, pursuant to Article 3(c) of the Treaty, the abolition, as between Member States, of obstacles to freedom of movement for persons and services constitutes one of the objectives of the Community; whereas, for nationals of the Member States, this means among other things the possibility of practising a profession, whether in a self–employed or a salaried capacity, in a Member State other than that in which they obtained their professional qualifications;
(2) Whereas, pursuant to Council Directive 89/48/EEC of 21 December 1988 on a general system for the recognition of higher–education diplomas awarded on completion of professional education and training of at least three years' duration, a lawyer who is fully qualified in one Member State may already ask to have his diploma recognised with a view to establishing himself in another Member State in order to practise the profession of lawyer there under the professional title used in that State; whereas the objective of Directive 89/48/EEC is to ensure that a lawyer is integrated into the profession in the host Member State, and the Directive seeks neither to modify the rules regulating the profession in that State nor to remove such a lawyer from the ambit of those rules;
(3) Whereas while some lawyers may become quickly integrated into the profession in the host Member State, inter alia by passing an aptitude test as provided for in Directive 89/48/EEC, other fully qualified lawyers should be able to achieve such integration after a certain period of professional practice in the host Member State under their home–country professional titles or else continue to practise under their home–country professional titles;
(4) Whereas at the end of that period the lawyer should be able to integrate into the profession in the host Member States after verification that the possesses professional experience in that Member State;
(5) Whereas action along these lines is justified at Community level not only because, compared with the general system for the recognition of diplomas, it provides lawyers with an easier means whereby they can integrate into the profession in a host Member State, but also because, by enabling lawyers to practise under their home–country professional titles on a permanent basis in a host Member State, it meets the needs of consumers of legal services who, owing to the increasing trade flows resulting, in particular, from the internal market, seek advice when carrying out cross–border transactions in which international law, Community law and domestic laws often overlap;
(6) Whereas action is also justified at Community level because only a few Member States already permit in their territory the pursuit of activities of lawyers, otherwise than by way of provision of services, by lawyers from other Member States practising under their home–country professional titles; whereas, however, in the Member States where this possibility exists, the practical details concerning, for example, the area of activity and the obligation to register with the competent authorities differ considerably; whereas such a diversity of situations leads to inequalities and distortions in competition between lawyers from the Member States and constitutes an obstacle to freedom of movement; whereas only a directive laying down the conditions governing practice of the profession, otherwise than by way of provision of services, by lawyers practising under their home–country professional titles is capable of resolving these difficulties and of affording the same opportunities to lawyers and consumers of legal services in all Member States;
(7) Whereas, in keeping with its objective, this Directive does not lay down any rules concerning purely domestic situations, and where it does affect national rules regulating the legal profession it does so no more than is necessary to achieve its purpose effectively; whereas it is without prejudice in particular to national legislation governing access to and practice of the profession of lawyer under the professional title used in the host Member State;
(8) Whereas lawyers covered by the Directive should be required to register with the competent authority in the host Member State in order that that authority may ensure that they comply with the rules of professional conduct in force in that State; whereas the effect of such registration as regards the jurisdictions in which, and the levels and types of court before which, lawyers may practise is determined by the law applicable to lawyers in the host Member State;

(9) Whereas lawyers who are not integrated into the profession in the host Member State should practise in that State under their home–country professional titles so as to ensure that consumers are properly informed and to distinguish between such lawyers and lawyers from the host Member State practising under the professional title used there;

(10) Whereas lawyers covered by this Directive should be permitted to give legal advice in particular on the law of their home Member States, on Community law, on international law and on the law of the host Member State; whereas this is already allowed as regards the provision of services under Council Directive 77/249/EEC of 22 March 1977 to facilitate the effective excercise by lawyers of freedom to provide services; whereas, however, provision should be made, as in Directive 77/249/EEC, for the option of excluding from the activities of lawyers practising under their home–country professional titles in the United Kingdom and Ireland the preparation of certain formal documents in the conveyancing and probate spheres; whereas this Directive in no way affects the provisions under which, in every Member State, certain activities are reserved for professions other than the legal profession; whereas the provision in Directive 77/249/EEC concerning the possibility of the host Member State to require a lawyer practising under his home–country professional title to work in conjunction with a local lawyer when representing or defending a client in legal proceedings should also be incorporated in this Directive; whereas that requirement must be interpreted in the light of the case law of the Court of Justice of the European Communities, in particular its judgment of 25 February 1988 in Case 427/85, Commission v. Germany;

(11) Whereas to ensure the smooth operation of the justice system Member States should be allowed, by means of specific rules, to reserve access to their highest courts to specialist lawyers, without hindering the integration of Member States' lawyers fulfilling the necessary requirements;

(12) Whereas a lawyer registered under his home–country professional title in the host Member State must remain registered with the competent authority in his home Member State if he is to retain his status of lawyer and be covered by this Directive; whereas for that reason close collaboration between the competent authorities is indispensable, in particular in connection with any disciplinary proceedings;

(13) Whereas lawyers covered by this Directive, whether salaried or self–employed in their home Member States, may practise as salaried lawyers in the host Member State, where that Member State offers that possibility to its own lawyers;

(14) Whereas the purpose pursued by this Directive in enabling lawyers to practise in another Member State under their home–country professional titles is also to make it easier for them to obtain the professional title of that host Member State; whereas under Articles 48 and 52 of the Treaty as interpreted by the Court of Justice the host Member State must take into consideration any professional experience gained in its territory; whereas after effectively and regularly pursuing in the host Member State an activity in the law of that State including Community law for a period of three years, a lawyer may reasonably be assumed to have gained the aptitude necessary to become fully integrated into the legal profession there; whereas at the end of that period the lawyer who can, subject to verification, furnish evidence of his professional competence in the host Member State should be able to obtain the professional title of that Member State; whereas if the period of effective and regular professional activity of at least three years includes a shorter period of practice in the law of the host Member State, the authority shall also take into consideration any other knowledge of that State's law, which it may verify during an interview; whereas if evidence of fulfilment of these conditions is not provided, the decision taken by the competent authority of the host State not to grant the State's professional title under the facilitation arrangements linked to those conditions must be substantiated and subject to appeal under national law;

(15) Whereas, for economic and professional reasons, the growing tendency for lawyers in the Community to practise jointly, including in the form of associations, has become a reality; whereas the fact that lawyers belong to a grouping in their home Member State should not be used as a pretext to prevent or deter them from establishing themselves in the host Member State; whereas Member States should be allowed, however, to take appropriate measures with the legitimate aim of safeguarding the profession's independence; whereas certain guarantees should be provided in those Member States which permit joint practice,

HAVE ADOPTED THIS DIRECTIVE:

Article 1. Object, scope and definitions

(1) The purpose of this Directive is to facilitate practice of the profession of lawyer on a permanent basis in a self–employed or salaried capacity in a Member State other than that in which the professional qualification was obtained.

(2) For the purposes of this Directive:

PART III EUROPEAN UNION

(a) 'lawyer' means any person who is a national of a Member State and who is authorised to pursue his professional activities under one of the following professional titles:
<TABLE>
(b) 'home Member State' means the Member State in which a lawyer acquired the right to use one of the professional titles referred to in (a) before practising the profession of lawyer in another Member State;
(c) 'host Member State' means the Member State in which a lawyer practises pursuant to this Directive;
(d) 'home–country professional title' means the professional title used in the Member State in which a lawyer acquired the right to use that title before practising the profession of lawyer in the host Member State;
(e) 'grouping' means any entity, with or without legal personality, formed under the law of a Member State, within which lawyers pursue their professional activities jointly under a joint name;
(f) 'relevant professional title' or 'relevant profession' means the professional title or profession governed by the competent authority with whom a lawyer has registered under Article 3, and 'competent authority' means that authority.
(3) This Directive shall apply both to lawyers practising in a self–employed capacity and to lawyers practising in a salarial capacity in the home Member State and, subject to Article 8, in the host Member State.
(4) Practice of the profession of lawyer within the meaning of this Directive shall not include the provision of services, which is covered by Directive 77/249/EEC.

Article 2. Right to practise under the home–country professional title
Any lawyer shall be entitled to pursue on a permanent basis, in any other Member State under his home–country professional title, the activities specified in Article 5.
Integration into the profession of lawyer in the host Member State shall be subject to Article 10.

Article 3. Registration with the competent authority
(1) A lawyer who wishes to practise in a Member State other than that in which he obtained his professional qualification shall register with the competent authority in that State.
(2) The competent authority in the host Member State shall register the lawyer upon presentation of a certificate attesting to his registration with the competent authority in the home Member State. It may require that, when presented by the competent authority of the home Member State, the certificate be not more than three months old. It shall inform the competent authority in the home Member State of the registration.
(3) For the purpose of applying paragraph 1:
– in the United Kingdom and Ireland, lawyers practising under a professional title other than those used in the United Kingdom or Ireland shall register either with the authority responsible for the profession of barrister or advocate or with the authority responsible for the profession of solicitor,
– in the United Kingdom, the authority responsible for a barrister from Ireland shall be that responsible for the profession of barrister or advocate, and the authority responsible for a solicitor from Ireland shall be that responsible for the profession of solicitor,
– in Ireland, the authority responsible for a barrister or an advocate from the United Kingdom shall be that responsible for the profession of barrister, and the authority responsible for a solicitor from the United Kingdom shall be that responsible for the profession of solicitor.
(4) Where the relevant competent authority in a host Member State publishes the names of lawyers registered with it, it shall also publish the names of lawyers registered pursuant to this Directive.

Article 4. Practice under the home–country professional title
(1) A lawyer practising in a host Member State under his home–country professional title shall do so under that title, which must be expressed in the official language or one of the official languages of his home Member State, in an intelligible manner and in such a way as to avoid confusion with the professional title of the host Member State.
(2) For the purpose of applying paragraph 1, a host Member State may require a lawyer practising under his home–country professional title to indicate the professional body of which he is a member in his home Member State or the judicial authority before which he is entitled to practise pursuant to the laws of his home Member State. A host Member State may also require a lawyer practising under his home–country professional title to include a reference to his registration with the competent authority in that State.

Article 5. Area of activity

(1) Subject to paragraphs 2 and 3, a lawyer practising under his home–country professional title carries on the same professional activities as a lawyer practising under the relevant professional title used in the host Member State and may, inter alia, give advice on the law of his home Member State, on Community law, on international law and on the law of the host Member State. He shall in any event comply with the rules of procedure applicable in the national courts.
(2) Member States which authorise in their territory a prescribed category of lawyers to prepare deeds for obtaining title to administer estates of deceased persons and for creating or transferring interests in land which, in other Member States, are reserved for professions other than that of lawyer may exclude from such activities lawyers practising under a home–country professional title conferred in one of the latter Member States.
(3) For the pursuit of activities relating to the representation or defence of a client in legal proceedings and insofar as the law of the host Member State reserves such activities to lawyers practising under the professional title of that State, the latter may require lawyers practising under their home–country professional titles to work in conjunction with a lawyer who practises before the judicial authority in question and who would, where necessary, be answerable to that authority or with an 'avoué' practising before it.
Nevertheless, in order to ensure the smooth operation of the justice system, Member States may lay down specific rules for access to supreme courts, such as the use of specialist lawyers.

Article 6. Rules of professional conduct applicable
(1) Irrespective of the rules of professional conduct to which he is subject in his home Member State, a lawyer practising under his home–country professional title shall be subject to the same rules of professional conduct as lawyers practising under the relevant professional title of the host Member State in respect of all the activities he pursues in its territory.
(2) Lawyers practising under their home–country professional titles shall be granted appropriate representation in the professional associations of the host Member State. Such representation shall involve at least the right to vote in elections to those associations' governing bodies.
(3) The host Member State may require a lawyer practising under his home–country professional title either to take out professional indemnity insurance or to become a member of a professional guarantee fund in accordance with the rules which that State lays down for professional activities pursued in its territory. Nevertheless, a lawyer practising under his home–country professional title shall be exempted from that requirement if he can prove that he is covered by insurance taken out or a guarantee provided in accordance with the rules of his home Member State, insofar as such insurance or guarantee is equivalent in terms of the conditions and extent of cover. Where the equivalence is only partial, the competent authority in the host Member State may require that additional insurance or an additional guarantee be contracted to cover the elements which are not already covered by the insurance or guarantee contracted in accordance with the rules of the home Member State.

Article 7. Disciplinary proceedings
(1) In the event of failure by a lawyer practising under his home–country professional title to fulfil the obligations in force in the host Member State, the rules of procedure, penalties and remedies provided for in the host Member State shall apply.
(2) Before initiating disciplinary proceedings against a lawyer practising under his home–country professional title, the competent authority in the host Member State shall inform the competent authority in the home Member State as soon as possible, furnishing it with all the relevant details. The first subparagraph shall apply *mutatis mutandis* where disciplinary proceedings are initiated by the competent authority of the home Member State, which shall inform the competent authority of the host Member State(s) accordingly.
(3) Without prejudice to the decision-making power of the competent authority in the host Member State, that authority shall cooperate throughout the disciplinary proceedings with the competent authority in the home Member State. In particular, the host Member State shall take the measures necessary to ensure that the competent authority in the home Member State can make submissions to the bodies responsible for hearing any appeal.
(4) The competent authority in the home Member State shall decide what action to take, under its own procedural and substantive rules, in the light of a decision of the competent authority in the host Member State concerning a lawyer practising under his home–country professional title.
(5) Although it is not a prerequisite for the decision of the competent authority in the host Member State, the temporary or permanent withdrawal by the competent authority in the home Member State of the authorisation to practise the profession shall automatically lead to the lawyer concerned being temporarily or permanently prohibited from practising under his home–country professional title in the host Member State.

PART III   EUROPEAN UNION

Article 8. Salaried practice

A lawyer registered in a host Member State under his home–country professional title may practise as a salaried lawyer in the employ of another lawyer, an association or firm of lawyers, or a public or private enterprise to the extent that the host Member State so permits for lawyers registered under the professional title used in that State.

Article 9. Statement of reasons and remedies

Decisions not to effect the registration referred to in Article 3 or to cancel such registration and decisions imposing disciplinary measures shall state the reasons on which they are based.

A remedy shall be available against such decisions before a court or tribunal in accordance with the provisions of domestic law.

Article 10. Like treatment as a lawyer of the host Member State

(1) A lawyer practising under his home–country professional title who has effectively and regularly pursued for a period of at least three years an activity in the host Member State in the law of that State including Community law shall, with a view to gaining admission to the profession of lawyer in the host Member State, be exempted from the conditions set out in Article 4(1)(b) of Directive 89/48/EEC, 'Effective and regular pursuit' means actual exercise of the activity without any interruption other than that resulting from the events of everyday life.

It shall be for the lawyer concerned to furnish the competent authority in the host Member State with proof of such effective regular pursuit for a period of at least three years of an activity in the law of the host Member State. To that end:

(a) the lawyer shall provide the competent authority in the host Member State with any relevant information and documentation, notably on the number of matters he has dealt with and their nature;

(b) the competent authority of the host Member State may verify the effective and regular nature of the activity pursued and may, if need be, request the lawyer to provide, orally or in writing, clarification of or further details on the information and documentation mentioned in point (a).

Reasons shall be given for a decision by the competent authority in the host Member State not to grant an exemption where proof is not provided that the requirements laid down in the first subparagraph have been fulfilled, and the decision shall be subject to appeal under domestic law.

(2) A lawyer practising under his home–country professional title in a host Member State may, at any time, apply to have his diploma recognised in accordance with Directive 89/48/EEC with a view to gaining admission to the profession of lawyer in the host Member State and practising it under the professional title corresponding to the profession in that Member State.

(3) A lawyer practising under his home–country professional title who has effectively and regularly pursued a professional activity in the host Member State for a period of at least three years but for a lesser period in the law of that Member State may obtain from the competent authority of that State admission to the profession of lawyer in the host Member State and the right to practise it under the professional title corresponding to the profession in that Member State, without having to meet the conditions referred to in Article 4(1)(b) of Directive 89/48/EEC, under the conditions and in accordance with the procedures set out below:

(a) The competent authority of the host Member State shall take into account the effective and regular professional activity pursued during the abovementioned period and any knowledge and professional experience of the law of the host Member State, and any attendance at lectures or seminars on the law of the host Member State, including the rules regulating professional practice and conduct.

(b) The lawyer shall provide the competent authority of the host Member State with any relevant information and documentation, in particular on the matters he has dealt with. Assessment of the lawyer's effective and regular activity in the host Member State and assessment of his capacity to continue the activity he has pursued there shall be carried out by means of an interview with the competent authority of the host Member State in order to verify the regular and effective nature of the activity pursued.

Reasons shall be given for a decision by the competent authority in the host Member State not to grant authorisation where proof is not provided that the requirements laid down in the first subparagraph have been fulfilled, and the decision shall be subject to appeal under domestic law.

(4) The competent authority of the host Member State may, by reasoned decision subject to appeal under domestic law, refuse to allow the lawyer the benefit of the provisions of this Article if it considers that this would be against public policy, in a particular because of disciplinary proceedings, complaints or incidents of any kind.

(5) The representatives of the competent authority entrusted with consideration of the application shall preserve the confidentiality of any information received.

(6) A lawyer who gains admission to the profession of lawyer in the host Member State in accordance

with paragraphs 1, 2 and 3 shall be entitled to use his home–country professional title, expressed in the official language or one of the official languages of his home Member State, alongside the professional title corresponding to the profession of lawyer in the host Member State.

Article 11. Joint practice

Where joint practise is authorised in respect of lawyers carrying on their activities under the relevant professional title in the host Member State, the following provisions shall apply in respect of lawyers wishing to carry on activities under that title or registering with the competent authority:

(1) One or more lawyers who belong to the same grouping in their home Member State and who practise under their home–country professional title in a host Member State may pursue their professional activities in a branch or agency of their grouping in the host Member State. However, where the fundamental rules governing that grouping in the home Member State are incompatible with the fundamental rules laid down by law, regulation or administrative action in the host Member State, the latter rules shall prevail insofar as compliance therewith is justified by the public interest in protecting clients and third parties.

(2) Each Member State shall afford two or more lawyers from the same grouping or the same home Member State who practise in its territory under their home–country professional titles access to a form of joint practice. If the host Member State gives its lawyers a choice between several forms of joint practice, those same forms shall also be made available to the aforementioned lawyers. The manner in which such lawyers practise jointly in the host Member State shall be governed by the laws, regulations and administrative provisions of that State.

(3) The host Member State shall take the measures necessary to permit joint practice also between:
(a) several lawyers from different Member States practising under their home–country professional titles;
(b) one or more lawyers covered by point (a) and one or more lawyers from the host Member State.
The manner in which such lawyers practice jointly in the host Member State shall be governed by the laws, regulations and administrative provisions of that State.

(4) A lawyer who wishes to practise under his home–country professional title shall inform the competent authority in the host Member State of the fact that he is a member of a grouping in his home Member State and furnish any relevant information on that grouping.

(5) Notwithstanding points 1 to 4, a host Member State, insofar as it prohibits lawyers practising under its own relevant professional title from practising the profession of lawyer within a grouping in which some persons are not members of the profession, may refuse to allow a lawyer registered under his home–country professional title to practice in its territory in his capacity as a member of his grouping. The grouping is deemed to include persons who are not members of the profession if
– the capital of the grouping is held entirely or partly, or
– the name under which it practises is used, or
– the decision–making power in that grouping is exercised, de facto or de jure,
by persons who do not have the status of lawyer within the meaning of Article 1(2).
Where the fundamental rules governing a grouping of lawyers in the home Member State are incompatible with the rules in force in the host Member State or with the provisions of the first subparagraph, the host Member State may oppose the opening of a branch or agency within its territory without the restrictions laid down in point (1).

Article 12. Name of the grouping

Whatever the manner in which lawyers practise under their home–country professional titles in the host Member State, they may employ the name of any grouping to which they belong in their home Member State.

The host Member State may require that, in addition to the name referred to in the first subparagraph, mention be made of the legal form of the grouping in the home Member State and/or of the names of any members of the grouping practising in the host Member State.

Article 13. Cooperation between the competent authorities in the home and host Member States and confidentiality

In order to facilitate the application of this Directive and to prevent its provisions from being misapplied for the sole purpose of circumventing the rules applicable in the host Member State, the competent authority in the host Member State and the competent authority in the home Member State shall collaborate closely and afford each other mutual assistance.

They shall preserve the confidentiality of the information they exchange.

Article 14. Designation of the competent authorities

Member States shall designate the competent authorities empowered to receive the applications and to take the decisions referred to in this Directive by 14 March 2000. They shall communicate this information to the other Member States and to the Commission.

Article 15. Report by the Commission

Ten years at the latest from the entry into force of this Directive, the Commission shall report to the European Parliament and to the Council on progress in the implementation of the Directive.

After having held all the necessary consultations, it shall on that occasion present its conclusions and any amendments which could be made to the existing system.

Article 16. Implementation

(1) Member States shall bring into force the laws, regulations and administrative provisions necessary to comply with this Directive by 14 March 2000. They shall forthwith inform the Commission thereof.

When Member States adopt these measures, they shall contain a reference to this Directive or shall be accompanied by such reference on the occasion of their official publication. The methods of making such reference shall be adopted by Member States.

(2) Member States shall communicate to the Commission the texts of the main provisions of domestic law which they adopt in the field covered by this Directive.

Article 17. This Directive shall enter into force on the date of its publication in the Official Journal of the European Communities.

Article 18. Addressees

This Directive is addressed to the Member States.

COUNCIL DIRECTIVE 2003/86/EC

Council Directive 2003/86/EC of 22 September 2003 on the right to family reunification

THE COUNCIL OF THE EUROPEAN UNION,
Having regard to the Treaty establishing the European Community, and in particular Article 63(3)(a) thereof,
Having regard to the proposal from the Commission,
Having regard to the opinion of the European Parliament,
Having regard to the opinion of the European Economic and Social Committee,
Having regard to the opinion of the Committee of the Regions,
Whereas:

(1) With a view to the progressive establishment of an area of freedom, security and justice, the Treaty establishing the European Community provides both for the adoption of measures aimed at ensuring the free movement of persons, in conjunction with flanking measures relating to external border controls, asylum and immigration, and for the adoption of measures relating to asylum, immigration and safeguarding the rights of third country nationals.

(2) Measures concerning family reunification should be adopted in conformity with the obligation to protect the family and respect family life enshrined in many instruments of international law. This Directive respects the fundamental rights and observes the principles recognised in particular in Article 8 of the European Convention for the Protection of Human Rights and Fundamental Freedoms and in the Charter of Fundamental Rights of the European Union.

(3) The European Council, at its special meeting in Tampere on 15 and 16 October 1999, acknowledged the need for harmonisation of national legislation on the conditions for admission and residence of third country nationals. In this context, it has in particular stated that the European Union should ensure fair treatment of third country nationals residing lawfully on the territory of the Member States and that a more vigorous integration policy should aim at granting them rights and obligations comparable to those of citizens of the European Union. The European Council accordingly asked the Council rapidly to adopt the legal instruments on the basis of Commission proposals. The need for achieving the objectives defined at Tampere have been reaffirmed by the Laeken European Council on 14 and 15 December 2001.

(4) Family reunification is a necessary way of making family life possible. It helps to create sociocultural stability facilitating the integration of third country nationals in the Member State, which also serves to promote economic and social cohesion, a fundamental Community objective stated in the Treaty.

(5) Member States should give effect to the provisions of this Directive without discrimination on the basis of sex, race, colour, ethnic or social origin, genetic characteristics, language, religion or beliefs, political or other opinions, membership of a national minority, fortune, birth, disabilities, age or sexual orientation.

(6) To protect the family and establish or preserve family life, the material conditions for exercising the right to family reunification should be determined on the basis of common criteria.

(7) Member States should be able to apply this Directive also when the family enters together.

(8) Special attention should be paid to the situation of refugees on account of the reasons which obliged them to flee their country and prevent them from leading a normal family life there. More favourable conditions should therefore be laid down for the exercise of their right to family reunification.

(9) Family reunification should apply in any case to members of the nuclear family, that is to say the spouse and the minor children.

(10) It is for the Member States to decide whether they wish to authorise family reunification for relatives in the direct ascending line, adult unmarried children, unmarried or registered partners as well as, in the event of a polygamous marriage, minor children of a further spouse and the sponsor. Where a Member State authorises family reunification of these persons, this is without prejudice of the possibility, for Member States which do not recognise the existence of family ties in the cases covered by this provision, of not granting to the said persons the treatment of family members with regard to the right to reside in another Member State, as defined by the relevant EC legislation.

(11) The right to family reunification should be exercised in proper compliance with the values and principles recognised by the Member States, in particular with respect to the rights of women and of children; such compliance justifies the possible taking of restrictive measures against applications for family reunification of polygamous households.

(12) The possibility of limiting the right to family reunification of children over the age of 12, whose primary residence is not with the sponsor, is intended to reflect the children's capacity for integration at early ages and shall ensure that they acquire the necessary education and language skills in school.

PART III EUROPEAN UNION

(13) A set of rules governing the procedure for examination of applications for family reunification and for entry and residence of family members should be laid down. Those procedures should be effective and manageable, taking account of the normal workload of the Member States' administrations, as well as transparent and fair, in order to offer appropriate legal certainty to those concerned.
(14) Family reunification may be refused on duly justified grounds. In particular, the person who wishes to be granted family reunification should not constitute a threat to public policy or public security. The notion of public policy may cover a conviction for committing a serious crime. In this context it has to be noted that the notion of public policy and public security covers also cases in which a third country national belongs to an association which supports terrorism, supports such an association or has extremist aspirations.
(15) The integration of family members should be promoted. For that purpose, they should be granted a status independent of that of the sponsor, in particular in cases of breakup of marriages and partnerships, and access to education, employment and vocational training on the same terms as the person with whom they are reunited, under the relevant conditions.
(16) Since the objectives of the proposed action, namely the establishment of a right to family reunification for third country nationals to be exercised in accordance with common rules, cannot be sufficiently achieved by the Member States and can therefore, by reason of the scale and effects of the action, be better achieved by the Community, the Community may adopt measures, in accordance with the principle of subsidiarity as set out in Article 5 of the Treaty. In accordance with the principle of proportionality as set out in that Article, this Directive does not go beyond what is necessary in order to achieve those objectives.
(17) In accordance with Articles 1 and 2 of the Protocol on the position of the United Kingdom and Ireland, annexed to the Treaty on European Union and to the Treaty establishing the European Community and without prejudice to Article 4 of the said Protocol these Member States are not participating in the adoption of this Directive and are not bound by or subject to its application.
(18) In accordance with Article 1 and 2 of the Protocol on the position of Denmark, annexed to the Treaty on European Union and the Treaty establishing the European Community, Denmark does not take part in the adoption of this Directive, and is not bound by it or subject to its application,
HAS ADOPTED THIS DIRECTIVE:

Chapter I. General Provisions

Article 1. The purpose of this Directive is to determine the conditions for the exercise of the right to family reunification by third country nationals residing lawfully in the territory of the Member States.

Article 2. For the purposes of this Directive:
(a) "third country national" means any person who is not a citizen of the Union within the meaning of Article 17(1) of the Treaty;
(b) "refugee" means any third country national or stateless person enjoying refugee status within the meaning of the Geneva Convention relating to the status of refugees of 28 July 1951, as amended by the Protocol signed in New York on 31 January 1967;
(c) "sponsor" means a third country national residing lawfully in a Member State and applying or whose family members apply for family reunification to be joined with him/her;
(d) "family reunification" means the entry into and residence in a Member State by family members of a third country national residing lawfully in that Member State in order to preserve the family unit, whether the family relationship arose before or after the resident's entry;
(e) "residence permit" means any authorisation issued by the authorities of a Member State allowing a third country national to stay legally in its territory, in accordance with the provisions of Article 1(2)(a) of Council Regulation (EC) No 1030/2002 of 13 June 2002 laying down a uniform format for residence permits for third country nationals;
(f) "unaccompanied minor" means third country nationals or stateless persons below the age of eighteen, who arrive on the territory of the Member States unaccompanied by an adult responsible by law or custom, and for as long as they are not effectively taken into the care of such a person, or minors who are left unaccompanied after they entered the territory of the Member States.

Article 3. (1) This Directive shall apply where the sponsor is holding a residence permit issued by a Member State for a period of validity of one year or more who has reasonable prospects of obtaining the right of permanent residence, if the members of his or her family are third country nationals of whatever status.
(2) This Directive shall not apply where the sponsor is:
(a) applying for recognition of refugee status whose application has not yet given rise to a final decision;

(b) authorised to reside in a Member State on the basis of temporary protection or applying for authorisation to reside on that basis and awaiting a decision on his status;
(c) authorised to reside in a Member State on the basis of a subsidiary form of protection in accordance with international obligations, national legislation or the practice of the Member States or applying for authorisation to reside on that basis and awaiting a decision on his status.
(3) This Directive shall not apply to members of the family of a Union citizen.
(4) This Directive is without prejudice to more favourable provisions of:
(a) bilateral and multilateral agreements between the Community or the Community and its Member States, on the one hand, and third countries, on the other;
(b) the European Social Charter of 18 October 1961, the amended European Social Charter of 3 May 1987 and the European Convention on the legal status of migrant workers of 24 November 1977.
(5) This Directive shall not affect the possibility for the Member States to adopt or maintain more favourable provisions.

Chapter II. Family Members

Article 4. (1) The Member States shall authorise the entry and residence, pursuant to this Directive and subject to compliance with the conditions laid down in Chapter IV, as well as in Article 16, of the following family members:
(a) the sponsor's spouse;
(b) the minor children of the sponsor and of his/her spouse, including children adopted in accordance with a decision taken by the competent authority in the Member State concerned or a decision which is automatically enforceable due to international obligations of that Member State or must be recognised in accordance with international obligations;
(c) the minor children including adopted children of the sponsor where the sponsor has custody and the children are dependent on him or her. Member States may authorise the reunification of children of whom custody is shared, provided the other party sharing custody has given his or her agreement;
(d) the minor children including adopted children of the spouse where the spouse has custody and the children are dependent on him or her. Member States may authorise the reunification of children of whom custody is shared, provided the other party sharing custody has given his or her agreement.
The minor children referred to in this Article must be below the age of majority set by the law of the Member State concerned and must not be married.
By way of derogation, where a child is aged over 12 years and arrives independently from the rest of his/her family, the Member State may, before authorising entry and residence under this Directive, verify whether he or she meets a condition for integration provided for by its existing legislation on the date of implementation of this Directive.
(2) The Member States may, by law or regulation, authorise the entry and residence, pursuant to this Directive and subject to compliance with the conditions laid down in Chapter IV, of the following family members:
(a) first–degree relatives in the direct ascending line of the sponsor or his or her spouse, where they are dependent on them and do not enjoy proper family support in the country of origin;
(b) the adult unmarried children of the sponsor or his or her spouse, where they are objectively unable to provide for their own needs on account of their state of health.
(3) The Member States may, by law or regulation, authorise the entry and residence, pursuant to this Directive and subject to compliance with the conditions laid down in Chapter IV, of the unmarried partner, being a third country national, with whom the sponsor is in a duly attested stable long–term relationship, or of a third country national who is bound to the sponsor by a registered partnership in accordance with Article 5(2), and of the unmarried minor children, including adopted children, as well as the adult unmarried children who are objectively unable to provide for their own needs on account of their state of health, of such persons.
Member States may decide that registered partners are to be treated equally as spouses with respect to family reunification.
(4) In the event of a polygamous marriage, where the sponsor already has a spouse living with him in the territory of a Member State, the Member State concerned shall not authorise the family reunification of a further spouse.
By way of derogation from paragraph 1(c), Member States may limit the family reunification of minor children of a further spouse and the sponsor.
(5) In order to ensure better integration and to prevent forced marriages Member States may require the sponsor and his/her spouse to be of a minimum age, and at maximum 21 years, before the spouse is able to join him/her.
(6) By way of derogation, Member States may request that the applications concerning family reuni-

fication of minor children have to be submitted before the age of 15, as provided for by its existing legislation on the date of the implementation of this Directive. If the application is submitted after the age of 15, the Member States which decide to apply this derogation shall authorise the entry and residence of such children on grounds other than family reunification.

Chapter III. Submission and Examination of the Application

Article 5. (1) Member States shall determine whether, in order to exercise the right to family reunification, an application for entry and residence shall be submitted to the competent authorities of the Member State concerned either by the sponsor or by the family member or members.

(2) The application shall be accompanied by documentary evidence of the family relationship and of compliance with the conditions laid down in Articles 4 and 6 and, where applicable, Articles 7 and 8, as well as certified copies of family member(s)' travel documents.

If appropriate, in order to obtain evidence that a family relationship exists, Member States may carry out interviews with the sponsor and his/her family members and conduct other investigations that are found to be necessary.

When examining an application concerning the unmarried partner of the sponsor, Member States shall consider, as evidence of the family relationship, factors such as a common child, previous cohabitation, registration of the partnership and any other reliable means of proof.

(3) The application shall be submitted and examined when the family members are residing outside the territory of the Member State in which the sponsor resides.

By way of derogation, a Member State may, in appropriate circumstances, accept an application submitted when the family members are already in its territory.

(4) The competent authorities of the Member State shall give the person, who has submitted the application, written notification of the decision as soon as possible and in any event no later than nine months from the date on which the application was lodged.

In exceptional circumstances linked to the complexity of the examination of the application, the time limit referred to in the first subparagraph may be extended.

Reasons shall be given for the decision rejecting the application. Any consequences of no decision being taken by the end of the period provided for in the first subparagraph shall be determined by the national legislation of the relevant Member State.

(5) When examining an application, the Member States shall have due regard to the best interests of minor children.

Chapter IV. Requirements for the Exercise of the Right to Family Reunification

Article 6. (1) The Member States may reject an application for entry and residence of family members on grounds of public policy, public security or public health.

(2) Member States may withdraw or refuse to renew a family member's residence permit on grounds of public policy or public security or public health.

When taking the relevant decision, the Member State shall consider, besides Article 17, the severity or type of offence against public policy or public security committed by the family member, or the dangers that are emanating from such person.

(3) Renewal of the residence permit may not be withheld and removal from the territory may not be ordered by the competent authority of the Member State concerned on the sole ground of illness or disability suffered after the issue of the residence permit.

Article 7. (1) When the application for family reunification is submitted, the Member State concerned may require the person who has submitted the application to provide evidence that the sponsor has:

(a) accommodation regarded as normal for a comparable family in the same region and which meets the general health and safety standards in force in the Member State concerned;

(b) sickness insurance in respect of all risks normally covered for its own nationals in the Member State concerned for himself/herself and the members of his/her family;

(c) stable and regular resources which are sufficient to maintain himself/herself and the members of his/her family, without recourse to the social assistance system of the Member State concerned. Member States shall evaluate these resources by reference to their nature and regularity and may take into account the level of minimum national wages and pensions as well as the number of family members.

(2) Member States may require third country nationals to comply with integration measures, in accordance with national law.

With regard to the refugees and/or family members of refugees referred to in Article 12 the integration measures referred to in the first subparagraph may only be applied once the persons concerned have been granted family reunification.

Article 8. Member States may require the sponsor to have stayed lawfully in their territory for a period not exceeding two years, before having his/her family members join him/her.

By way of derogation, where the legislation of a Member State relating to family reunification in force on the date of adoption of this Directive takes into account its reception capacity, the Member State may provide for a waiting period of no more than three years between submission of the application for family reunification and the issue of a residence permit to the family members.

Chapter V. Family Reunification of Refugees

Article 9. (1) This Chapter shall apply to family reunification of refugees recognised by the Member States.
(2) Member States may confine the application of this Chapter to refugees whose family relationships predate their entry.
(3) This Chapter is without prejudice to any rules granting refugee status to family members.

Article 10. (1) Article 4 shall apply to the definition of family members except that the third subparagraph of paragraph 1 thereof shall not apply to the children of refugees.
(2) The Member States may authorise family reunification of other family members not referred to in Article 4, if they are dependent on the refugee.
(3) If the refugee is an unaccompanied minor, the Member States:
(a) shall authorise the entry and residence for the purposes of family reunification of his/her first–degree relatives in the direct ascending line without applying the conditions laid down in Article 4(2)(a);
(b) may authorise the entry and residence for the purposes of family reunification of his/her legal guardian or any other member of the family, where the refugee has no relatives in the direct ascending line or such relatives cannot be traced.

Article 11. (1) Article 5 shall apply to the submission and examination of the application, subject to paragraph 2 of this Article.
(2) Where a refugee cannot provide official documentary evidence of the family relationship, the Member States shall take into account other evidence, to be assessed in accordance with national law, of the existence of such relationship. A decision rejecting an application may not be based solely on the fact that documentary evidence is lacking.

Article 12. (1) By way of derogation from Article 7, the Member States shall not require the refugee and/or family member(s) to provide, in respect of applications concerning those family members referred to in Article 4(1), the evidence that the refugee fulfils the requirements set out in Article 7. Without prejudice to international obligations, where family reunification is possible in a third country with which the sponsor and/or family member has special links, Member States may require provision of the evidence referred to in the first subparagraph.
Member States may require the refugee to meet the conditions referred to in Article 7(1) if the application for family reunification is not submitted within a period of three months after the granting of the refugee status.
(2) By way of derogation from Article 8, the Member States shall not require the refugee to have resided in their territory for a certain period of time, before having his/her family members join him/her.

Chapter VI. Entry and Residence of Family Members

Article 13. (1) As soon as the application for family reunification has been accepted, the Member State concerned shall authorise the entry of the family member or members. In that regard, the Member State concerned shall grant such persons every facility for obtaining the requisite visas.
(2) The Member State concerned shall grant the family members a first residence permit of at least one year's duration. This residence permit shall be renewable.
(3) The duration of the residence permits granted to the family member(s) shall in principle not go beyond the date of expiry of the residence permit held by the sponsor.

Article 14. (1) The sponsor's family members shall be entitled, in the same way as the sponsor, to:
(a) access to education;
(b) access to employment and self–employed activity;
(c) access to vocational guidance, initial and further training and retraining.

(2) Member States may decide according to national law the conditions under which family members shall exercise an employed or self–employed activity. These conditions shall set a time limit which shall in no case exceed 12 months, during which Member States may examine the situation of their labour market before authorising family members to exercise an employed or self–employed activity.
(3) Member States may restrict access to employment or self–employed activity by first–degree relatives in the direct ascending line or adult unmarried children to whom Article 4(2) applies.

Article 15. (1) Not later than after five years of residence, and provided that the family member has not been granted a residence permit for reasons other than family reunification, the spouse or unmarried partner and a child who has reached majority shall be entitled, upon application, if required, to an autonomous residence permit, independent of that of the sponsor.
Member States may limit the granting of the residence permit referred to in the first subparagraph to the spouse or unmarried partner in cases of breakdown of the family relationship.
(2) The Member States may issue an autonomous residence permit to adult children and to relatives in the direct ascending line to whom Article 4(2) applies.
(3) In the event of widowhood, divorce, separation, or death of first–degree relatives in the direct ascending or descending line, an autonomous residence permit may be issued, upon application, if required, to persons who have entered by virtue of family reunification. Member States shall lay down provisions ensuring the granting of an autonomous residence permit in the event of particularly difficult circumstances.
(4) The conditions relating to the granting and duration of the autonomous residence permit are established by national law.

Chapter VII. Penalties and Redress

Article 16. (1) Member States may reject an application for entry and residence for the purpose of family reunification, or, if appropriate, withdraw or refuse to renew a family member's residence permit, in the following circumstances:
(a) where the conditions laid down by this Directive are not or are no longer satisfied.
When renewing the residence permit, where the sponsor has not sufficient resources without recourse to the social assistance system of the Member State, as referred to in Article 7(1)(c), the Member State shall take into account the contributions of the family members to the household income;
(b) where the sponsor and his/her family member(s) do not or no longer live in a real marital or family relationship;
(c) where it is found that the sponsor or the unmarried partner is married or is in a stable long–term relationship with another person.
(2) Member States may also reject an application for entry and residence for the purpose of family reunification, or withdraw or refuse to renew the family member's residence permits, where it is shown that:
(a) false or misleading information, false or falsified documents were used, fraud was otherwise committed or other unlawful means were used;
(b) the marriage, partnership or adoption was contracted for the sole purpose of enabling the person concerned to enter or reside in a Member State.
When making an assessment with respect to this point, Member States may have regard in particular to the fact that the marriage, partnership or adoption was contracted after the sponsor had been issued his/her residence permit.
(3) The Member States may withdraw or refuse to renew the residence permit of a family member where the sponsor's residence comes to an end and the family member does not yet enjoy an autonomous right of residence under Article 15.
(4) Member States may conduct specific checks and inspections where there is reason to suspect that there is fraud or a marriage, partnership or adoption of convenience as defined by paragraph 2. Specific checks may also be undertaken on the occasion of the renewal of family members' residence permit.

Article 17. Member States shall take due account of the nature and solidity of the person's family relationships and the duration of his residence in the Member State and of the existence of family, cultural and social ties with his/her country of origin where they reject an application, withdraw or refuse to renew a residence permit or decide to order the removal of the sponsor or members of his family.

Article 18. The Member States shall ensure that the sponsor and/or the members of his/her family have the right to mount a legal challenge where an application for family reunification is rejected or a

residence permit is either not renewed or is withdrawn or removal is ordered.
The procedure and the competence according to which the right referred to in the first subparagraph is exercised shall be established by the Member States concerned.

Chapter VIII. Final Provisions

Article 19. Periodically, and for the first time not later than 3 October 2007, the Commission shall report to the European Parliament and the Council on the application of this Directive in the Member States and shall propose such amendments as may appear necessary. These proposals for amendments shall be made by way of priority in relation to Articles 3, 4, 7, 8 and 13.

Article 20. Member States shall bring into force the laws, regulations and administrative provisions necessary to comply with this Directive by not later than 3 October 2005. They shall forthwith inform the Commission thereof.
When Member States adopt these measures, they shall contain a reference to this Directive or be accompanied by such a reference on the occasion of their official publication. The methods of making such reference shall be laid down by the Member States.

Article 21. This Directive shall enter into force on the day of its publication in the *Official Journal of the European Union*.

Article 22. This Directive is addressed to the Member States in accordance with the Treaty establishing the European Community.

PART III   EUROPEAN UNION

Council Directive 2003/109/EC of 25 November 2003 concerning the status of third–country nationals who are long–term residents

THE COUNCIL OF THE EUROPEAN UNION,
Having regard to the Treaty establishing the European Community, and in particular Article 63(3) and (4) thereof,
Having regard to the proposal from the Commission,
Having regard to the opinion of the European Parliament,
Having regard to the opinion of the European Economic and Social Committee,
Having regard to the opinion of the Committee of the Regions,
Whereas:
(1) With a view to the progressive establishment of an area of freedom, security and justice, the Treaty establishing the European Community provides both for the adoption of measures aimed at ensuring the free movement of persons, in conjunction with flanking measures relating to external border controls, asylum and immigration, and for the adoption of measures relating to asylum, immigration and safeguarding the rights of third–country nationals.
(2) The European Council, at its special meeting in Tampere on 15 and 16 October 1999, stated that the legal status of third–country nationals should be approximated to that of Member States' nationals and that a person who has resided legally in a Member State for a period of time to be determined and who holds a long–term residence permit should be granted in that Member State a set of uniform rights which are as near as possible to those enjoyed by citizens of the European Union.
(3) This Directive respects the fundamental rights and observes the principles recognised in particular by the European Convention for the Protection of Human Rights and Fundamental Freedoms and by the Charter of Fundamental Rights of the European Union.
(4) The integration of third–country nationals who are long–term residents in the Member States is a key element in promoting economic and social cohesion, a fundamental objective of the Community stated in the Treaty.
(5) Member States should give effect to the provisions of this Directive without discrimination on the basis of sex, race, colour, ethnic or social origin, genetic characteristics, language, religion or beliefs, political or other opinions, membership of a national minority, fortune, birth, disabilities, age or sexual orientation.
(6) The main criterion for acquiring the status of long–term resident should be the duration of residence in the territory of a Member State. Residence should be both legal and continuous in order to show that the person has put down roots in the country. Provision should be made for a degree of flexibility so that account can be taken of circumstances in which a person might have to leave the territory on a temporary basis.
(7) To acquire long–term resident status, third–country nationals should prove that they have adequate resources and sickness insurance, to avoid becoming a burden for the Member State. Member States, when making an assessment of the possession of stable and regular resources may take into account factors such as contributions to the pension system and fulfilment of tax obligations.
(8) Moreover, third–country nationals who wish to acquire and maintain long–term resident status should not constitute a threat to public policy or public security. The notion of public policy may cover a conviction for committing a serious crime.
(9) Economic considerations should not be a ground for refusing to grant long–term resident status and shall not be considered as interfering with the relevant conditions.
(10) A set of rules governing the procedures for the examination of application for long–term resident status should be laid down. Those procedures should be effective and manageable, taking account of the normal workload of the Member States' administrations, as well as being transparent and fair, in order to offer appropriate legal certainty to those concerned. They should not constitute a means of hindering the exercise of the right of residence.
(11) The acquisition of long–term resident status should be certified by residence permits enabling those concerned to prove their legal status easily and immediately. Such residence permits should also satisfy high–level technical standards, notably as regards protection against falsification and counterfeiting, in order to avoid abuses in the Member State in which the status is acquired and in Member States in which the right of residence is exercised.
(12) In order to constitute a genuine instrument for the integration of long–term residents into society in which they live, long–term residents should enjoy equality of treatment with citizens of the Member State in a wide range of economic and social matters, under the relevant conditions defined by this Directive.
(13) With regard to social assistance, the possibility of limiting the benefits for long–term residents

COUNCIL DIRECTIVE 2003/109/EC

to core benefits is to be understood in the sense that this notion covers at least minimum income support, assistance in case of illness, pregnancy, parental assistance and long–term care. The modalities for granting such benefits should be determined by national law.

(14) The Member States should remain subject to the obligation to afford access for minors to the educational system under conditions similar to those laid down for their nationals.

(15) The notion of study grants in the field of vocational training does not cover measures which are financed under social assistance schemes. Moreover, access to study grants may be dependent on the fact that the person who applies for such grants fulfils on his/her own the conditions for acquiring long–term resident status. As regards the issuing of study grants, Member States may take into account the fact that Union citizens may benefit from this same advantage in the country of origin.

(16) Long–term residents should enjoy reinforced protection against expulsion. This protection is based on the criteria determined by the decisions of the European Court of Human Rights. In order to ensure protection against expulsion Member States should provide for effective legal redress.

(17) Harmonisation of the terms for acquisition of long–term resident status promotes mutual confidence between Member States. Certain Member States issue permits with a permanent or unlimited validity on conditions that are more favourable than those provided for by this Directive. The possibility of applying more favourable national provisions is not excluded by the Treaty. However, for the purposes of this Directive, it should be provided that permits issued on more favourable terms do not confer the right to reside in other Member States.

(18) Establishing the conditions subject to which the right to reside in another Member State may be acquired by third–country nationals who are long–term residents should contribute to the effective attainment of an internal market as an area in which the free movement of persons is ensured. It could also constitute a major factor of mobility, notably on the Union's employment market.

(19) Provision should be made that the right of residence in another Member State may be exercised in order to work in an employed or self–employed capacity, to study or even to settle without exercising any form of economic activity.

(20) Family members should also be able to settle in another Member State with a long–term resident in order to preserve family unity and to avoid hindering the exercise of the long–term resident's right of residence. With regard to the family members who may be authorised to accompany or to join the long–term residents, Member States should pay special attention to the situation of disabled adult children and of first–degree relatives in the direct ascending line who are dependent on them.

(21) The Member State in which a long–term resident intends to exercise his/her right of residence should be able to check that the person concerned meets the conditions for residing in its territory. It should also be able to check that the person concerned does not constitute a threat to public policy, public security or public health.

(22) To avoid rendering the right of residence nugatory, long–term residents should enjoy in the second Member State the same treatment, under the conditions defined by this Directive, they enjoy in the Member State in which they acquired the status. The granting of benefits under social assistance is without prejudice to the possibility for the Member States to withdraw the residence permit if the person concerned no longer fulfils the requirements set by this Directive.

(23) Third–country nationals should be granted the possibility of acquiring long–term resident status in the Member State where they have moved and have decided to settle under comparable conditions to those required for its acquisition in the first Member State.

(24) Since the objectives of the proposed action, namely the determination of terms for granting and withdrawing long–term resident status and the rights pertaining thereto and terms for the exercise of rights of residence by long–term residents in other Member States, cannot be sufficiently achieved by the Member States and can therefore, by reason of the scale and effects of the action, be better achieved by the Community, the Community may adopt measures, in accordance with the principle of subsidiarity as set out in Article 5 of the Treaty. In accordance with the principle of proportionality, as set out in that Article, this Directive does not go beyond what is necessary to achieve those objectives.

(25) In accordance with Articles 1 and 2 of the Protocol on the position of the United Kingdom and Ireland, annexed to the Treaty on European Union and to the Treaty establishing the European Community, and without prejudice to Article 4 of the said Protocol, these Member States are not participating in the adoption of this Directive and are not bound by or subject to its application.

(26) In accordance with Articles 1 and 2 of the Protocol on the position of Denmark, annexed to the Treaty on European Union and the Treaty establishing the European Community, Denmark does not take part in the adoption of this Directive, and is not bound by it or subject to its application,

HAS ADOPTED THIS DIRECTIVE:

PART III EUROPEAN UNION

Chapter I. General Provisions

Article 1. Subject matter

This Directive determines:
(a) the terms for conferring and withdrawing long–term resident status granted by a Member State in relation to third–country nationals legally residing in its territory, and the rights pertaining thereto; and
(b) the terms of residence in Member States other than the one which conferred long–term status on them for third–country nationals enjoying that status.

Article 2. Definitions

For the purposes of this Directive:
(a) "third–country national" means any person who is not a citizen of the Union within the meaning of Article 17(1) of the Treaty;
(b) "long–term resident" means any third–country national who has long–term resident status as provided for under Articles 4 to 7;
(c) "first Member State" means the Member State which for the first time granted long–term resident status to a third–country national;
(d) "second Member State" means any Member State other than the one which for the first time granted long–term resident status to a third–country national and in which that long–term resident exercises the right of residence;
(e) "family members" means the third–country nationals who reside in the Member State concerned in accordance with Council Directive 2003/86/EC of 22 September 2003 on the right to family reunification;
(f) "refugee" means any third–country national enjoying refugee status within the meaning of the Geneva Convention relating to the Status of Refugees of 28 July 1951, as amended by the Protocol signed in New York on 31 January 1967;
(g) "long–term resident's EC residence permit" means a residence permit issued by the Member State concerned upon the acquisition of long–term resident status.

Article 3. Scope

(1) This Directive applies to third–country nationals residing legally in the territory of a Member State.
(2) This Directive does not apply to third–country nationals who:
(a) reside in order to pursue studies or vocational training;
(b) are authorised to reside in a Member State on the basis of temporary protection or have applied for authorisation to reside on that basis and are awaiting a decision on their status;
(c) are authorised to reside in a Member State on the basis of a subsidiary form of protection in accordance with international obligations, national legislation or the practice of the Member States or have applied for authorisation to reside on that basis and are awaiting a decision on their status;
(d) are refugees or have applied for recognition as refugees and whose application has not yet given rise to a final decision;
(e) reside solely on temporary grounds such as au pair or seasonal worker, or as workers posted by a service provider for the purposes of cross–border provision of services, or as cross–border providers of services or in cases where their residence permit has been formally limited;
(f) enjoy a legal status governed by the Vienna Convention on Diplomatic Relations of 1961, the Vienna Convention on Consular Relations of 1963, the Convention of 1969 on Special Missions or the Vienna Convention on the Representation of States in their Relations with International Organisations of a Universal Character of 1975.
(3) This Directive shall apply without prejudice to more favourable provisions of:
(a) bilateral and multilateral agreements between the Community or the Community and its Member States, on the one hand, and third countries, on the other;
(b) bilateral agreements already concluded between a Member State and a third country before the date of entry into force of this Directive;
(c) the European Convention on Establishment of 13 December 1955, the European Social Charter of 18 October 1961, the amended European Social Charter of 3 May 1987 and the European Convention on the Legal Status of Migrant Workers of 24 November 1977.

Chapter II. Long–Term Resident Status in a Member State

Article 4. Duration of residence

(1) Member States shall grant long–term resident status to third–country nationals who have resided

legally and continuously within its territory for five years immediately prior to the submission of the relevant application.

(2) Periods of residence for the reasons referred to in Article 3(2)(e) and (f) shall not be taken into account for the purposes of calculating the period referred to in paragraph 1.

Regarding the cases covered in Article 3(2)(a), where the third–country national concerned has acquired a title of residence which will enable him/her to be granted long–term resident status, only half of the periods of residence for study purposes or vocational training may be taken into account in the calculation of the period referred to in paragraph 1.

(3) Periods of absence from the territory of the Member State concerned shall not interrupt the period referred to in paragraph 1 and shall be taken into account for its calculation where they are shorter than six consecutive months and do not exceed in total 10 months within the period referred to in paragraph 1.

In cases of specific or exceptional reasons of a temporary nature and in accordance with their national law, Member States may accept that a longer period of absence than that which is referred to in the first subparagraph shall not interrupt the period referred to in paragraph 1. In such cases Member States shall not take into account the relevant period of absence in the calculation of the period referred to in paragraph 1.

By way of derogation from the second subparagraph, Member States may take into account in the calculation of the total period referred to in paragraph 1 periods of absence relating to secondment for employment purposes, including the provision of cross–border services.

Article 5. Conditions for acquiring long–term resident status

(1) Member States shall require third–country nationals to provide evidence that they have, for themselves and for dependent family members:

(a) stable and regular resources which are sufficient to maintain himself/herself and the members of his/her family, without recourse to the social assistance system of the Member State concerned. Member States shall evaluate these resources by reference to their nature and regularity and may take into account the level of minimum wages and pensions prior to the application for long–term resident status;

(b) sickness insurance in respect of all risks normally covered for his/her own nationals in the Member State concerned.

(2) Member States may require third–country nationals to comply with integration conditions, in accordance with national law.

Article 6. Public policy and public security

(1) Member States may refuse to grant long–term resident status on grounds of public policy or public security.

When taking the relevant decision, the Member State shall consider the severity or type of offence against public policy or public security, or the danger that emanates from the person concerned, while also having proper regard to the duration of residence and to the existence of links with the country of residence.

(2) The refusal referred to in paragraph 1 shall not be founded on economic considerations.

Article 7. Acquisition of long–term resident status

(1) To acquire long–term resident status, the third–country national concerned shall lodge an application with the competent authorities of the Member State in which he/she resides. The application shall be accompanied by documentary evidence to be determined by national law that he/she meets the conditions set out in Articles 4 and 5 as well as, if required, by a valid travel document or its certified copy.

The evidence referred to in the first subparagraph may also include documentation with regard to appropriate accommodation.

(2) The competent national authorities shall give the applicant written notification of the decision as soon as possible and in any event no later than six months from the date on which the application was lodged. Any such decision shall be notified to the third–country national concerned in accordance with the notification procedures under the relevant national legislation.

In exceptional circumstances linked to the complexity of the examination of the application, the time limit referred to in the first subparagraph may be extended.

In addition, the person concerned shall be informed about his/her rights and obligations under this Directive.

Any consequences of no decision being taken by the end of the period provided for in this provision shall be determined by national legislation of the relevant Member State.

(3) If the conditions provided for by Articles 4 and 5 are met, and the person does not represent a threat within the meaning of Article 6, the Member State concerned shall grant the third–country national concerned long–term resident status.

Article 8. Long–term resident's EC residence permit

(1) The status as long–term resident shall be permanent, subject to Article 9.
(2) Member States shall issue a long–term resident's EC residence permit to long–term residents. The permit shall be valid at least for five years; it shall, upon application if required, be automatically renewable on expiry.
(3) A long–term resident's EC residence permit may be issued in the form of a sticker or of a separate document. It shall be issued in accordance with the rules and standard model as set out in Council Regulation (EC) No 1030/2002 of 13 June 2002 laying down a uniform format for residence permits for third–country nationals(6). Under the heading "type of permit", the Member States shall enter "long–term resident – EC".

Article 9. Withdrawal or loss of status

(1) Long–term residents shall no longer be entitled to maintain long–term resident status in the following cases:
(a) detection of fraudulent acquisition of long–term resident status;
(b) adoption of an expulsion measure under the conditions provided for in Article 12;
(c) in the event of absence from the territory of the Community for a period of 12 consecutive months.
(2) By way of derogation from paragraph 1(c), Member States may provide that absences exceeding 12 consecutive months or for specific or exceptional reasons shall not entail withdrawal or loss of status.
(3) Member States may provide that the long–term resident shall no longer be entitled to maintain his/her long–term resident status in cases where he/she constitutes a threat to public policy, in consideration of the seriousness of the offences he/she committed, but such threat is not a reason for expulsion within the meaning of Article 12.
(4) The long–term resident who has resided in another Member State in accordance with Chapter III shall no longer be entitled to maintain his/her long–term resident status acquired in the first Member State when such a status is granted in another Member State pursuant to Article 23.
In any case after six years of absence from the territory of the Member State that granted long–term resident status the person concerned shall no longer be entitled to maintain his/her long term resident status in the said Member State.
By way of derogation from the second subparagraph the Member State concerned may provide that for specific reasons the long–term resident shall maintain his/her status in the said Member State in case of absences for a period exceeding six years.
(5) With regard to the cases referred to in paragraph 1(c) and in paragraph 4, Member States who have granted the status shall provide for a facilitated procedure for the re–acquisition of long–term resident status.
The said procedure shall apply in particular to the cases of persons that have resided in a second Member State on grounds of pursuit of studies.
The conditions and the procedure for the re–acquisition of long–term resident status shall be determined by national law.
(6) The expiry of a long–term resident's EC residence permit shall in no case entail withdrawal or loss of long–term resident status.
(7) Where the withdrawal or loss of long–term resident status does not lead to removal, the Member State shall authorise the person concerned to remain in its territory if he/she fulfils the conditions provided for in its national legislation and/or if he/she does not constitute a threat to public policy or public security.

Article 10. Procedural guarantees

(1) Reasons shall be given for any decision rejecting an application for long–term resident status or withdrawing that status. Any such decision shall be notified to the third–country national concerned in accordance with the notification procedures under the relevant national legislation. The notification shall specify the redress procedures available and the time within which he/she may act.
(2) Where an application for long–term resident status is rejected or that status is withdrawn or lost or the residence permit is not renewed, the person concerned shall have the right to mount a legal challenge in the Member State concerned.

Article 11. Equal treatment

(1) Long–term residents shall enjoy equal treatment with nationals as regards:
(a) access to employment and self–employed activity, provided such activities do not entail even occasional involvement in the exercise of public authority, and conditions of employment and working conditions, including conditions regarding dismissal and remuneration;
(b) education and vocational training, including study grants in accordance with national law;
(c) recognition of professional diplomas, certificates and other qualifications, in accordance with the relevant national procedures;
(d) social security, social assistance and social protection as defined by national law;
(e) tax benefits;
(f) access to goods and services and the supply of goods and services made available to the public and to procedures for obtaining housing;
(g) freedom of association and affiliation and membership of an organisation representing workers or employers or of any organisation whose members are engaged in a specific occupation, including the benefits conferred by such organisations, without prejudice to the national provisions on public policy and public security;
(h) free access to the entire territory of the Member State concerned, within the limits provided for by the national legislation for reasons of security.
(2) With respect to the provisions of paragraph 1, points (b), (d), (e), (f) and (g), the Member State concerned may restrict equal treatment to cases where the registered or usual place of residence of the long–term resident, or that of family members for whom he/she claims benefits, lies within the territory of the Member State concerned.
(3) Member States may restrict equal treatment with nationals in the following cases:
(a) Member States may retain restrictions to access to employment or self–employed activities in cases where, in accordance with existing national or Community legislation, these activities are reserved to nationals, EU or EEA citizens;
(b) Member States may require proof of appropriate language proficiency for access to education and training. Access to university may be subject to the fulfilment of specific educational prerequisites.
(4) Member States may limit equal treatment in respect of social assistance and social protection to core benefits.
(5) Member States may decide to grant access to additional benefits in the areas referred to in paragraph 1.
Member States may also decide to grant equal treatment with regard to areas not covered in paragraph 1.

Article 12. Protection against expulsion
(1) Member States may take a decision to expel a long–term resident solely where he/she constitutes an actual and sufficiently serious threat to public policy or public security.
(2) The decision referred to in paragraph 1 shall not be founded on economic considerations.
(3) Before taking a decision to expel a long–term resident, Member States shall have regard to the following factors:
(a) the duration of residence in their territory;
(b) the age of the person concerned;
(c) the consequences for the person concerned and family members;
(d) links with the country of residence or the absence of links with the country of origin.
(4) Where an expulsion decision has been adopted, a judicial redress procedure shall be available to the long–term resident in the Member State concerned.
(5) Legal aid shall be given to long–term residents lacking adequate resources, on the same terms as apply to nationals of the State where they reside.

Article 13. More favourable national provisions
Member States may issue residence permits of permanent or unlimited validity on terms that are more favourable than those laid down by this Directive. Such residence permits shall not confer the right of residence in the other Member States as provided by Chapter III of this Directive.

Chapter III. Residence in the Other Member States

Article 14. Principle
(1) A long–term resident shall acquire the right to reside in the territory of Member States other than the one which granted him/her the long–term residence status, for a period exceeding three months, provided that the conditions set out in this chapter are met.
(2) A long–term resident may reside in a second Member State on the following grounds:
(a) exercise of an economic activity in an employed or self–employed capacity;

(b) pursuit of studies or vocational training;
(c) other purposes.
(3) In cases of an economic activity in an employed or self–employed capacity referred to in paragraph 2(a), Member States may examine the situation of their labour market and apply their national procedures regarding the requirements for, respectively, filling a vacancy, or for exercising such activities.
For reasons of labour market policy, Member States may give preference to Union citizens, to third–country nationals, when provided for by Community legislation, as well as to third–country nationals who reside legally and receive unemployment benefits in the Member State concerned.
(4) By way of derogation from the provisions of paragraph 1, Member States may limit the total number of persons entitled to be granted right of residence, provided that such limitations are already set out for the admission of third–country nationals in the existing legislation at the time of the adoption of this Directive.
(5) This chapter does not concern the residence of long–term residents in the territory of the Member States:
(a) as employed workers posted by a service provider for the purposes of cross–border provision of services;
(b) as providers of cross–border services.
Member States may decide, in accordance with national law, the conditions under which long–term residents who wish to move to a second Member State with a view to exercising an economic activity as seasonal workers may reside in that Member State. Cross–border workers may also be subject to specific provisions of national law.
(6) This Chapter is without prejudice to the relevant Community legislation on social security with regard to third–country nationals.

Article 15. Conditions for residence in a second Member State
(1) As soon as possible and no later than three months after entering the territory of the second Member State, the long–term resident shall apply to the competent authorities of that Member State for a residence permit.
Member States may accept that the long–term resident submits the application for a residence permit to the competent authorities of the second Member State while still residing in the territory of the first Member State.
(2) Member States may require the persons concerned to provide evidence that they have:
(a) stable and regular resources which are sufficient to maintain themselves and the members of their families, without recourse to the social assistance of the Member State concerned. For each of the categories referred to in Article 14(2), Member States shall evaluate these resources by reference to their nature and regularity and may take into account the level of minimum wages and pensions;
(b) sickness insurance covering all risks in the second Member State normally covered for its own nationals in the Member State concerned.
(3) Member States may require third–country nationals to comply with integration measures, in accordance with national law.
This condition shall not apply where the third–country nationals concerned have been required to comply with integration conditions in order to be granted long–term resident status, in accordance with the provisions of Article 5(2).
Without prejudice to the second subparagraph, the persons concerned may be required to attend language courses.
(4) The application shall be accompanied by documentary evidence, to be determined by national law, that the persons concerned meets the relevant conditions, as well as by their long–term resident permit and a valid travel document or their certified copies.
The evidence referred to in the first subparagraph may also include documentation with regard to appropriate accommodation.
In particular:
(a) in case of exercise of an economic activity the second Member State may require the persons concerned to provide evidence:
(i) if they are in an employed capacity, that they have an employment contract, a statement by the employer that they are hired or a proposal for an employment contract, under the conditions provided for by national legislation. Member States shall determine which of the said forms of evidence is required;
(ii) if they are in a self–employed capacity, that they have the appropriate funds which are needed, in accordance with national law, to exercise an economic activity in such capacity, presenting the neces-

sary documents and permits;
(b) in case of study or vocational training the second Member State may require the persons concerned to provide evidence of enrolment in an accredited establishment in order to pursue studies or vocational training.

Article 16. Family members
(1) When the long–term resident exercises his/her right of residence in a second Member State and when the family was already constituted in the first Member State, the members of his/her family, who fulfil the conditions referred to in Article 4(1) of Directive 2003/86/EC shall be authorised to accompany or to join the long–term resident.
(2) When the long–term resident exercises his/her right of residence in a second Member State and when the family was already constituted in the first Member State, the members of his/her family, other than those referred to in Article 4(1) of Directive 2003/86/EC may be authorised to accompany or to join the long–term resident.
(3) With respect to the submission of the application for a residence permit, the provisions of Article 15(1) apply.
(4) The second Member State may require the family members concerned to present with their application for a residence permit:
(a) their long–term resident's EC residence permit or residence permit and a valid travel document or their certified copies;
(b) evidence that they have resided as members of the family of the long–term resident in the first Member State;
(c) evidence that they have stable and regular resources which are sufficient to maintain themselves without recourse to the social assistance of the Member State concerned or that the long–term resident has such resources and insurance for them, as well as sickness insurance covering all risks in the second Member State. Member States shall evaluate these resources by reference to their nature and regularity and may take into account the level of minimum wages and pensions.
(5) Where the family was not already constituted in the first Member State, Directive 2003/86/EC shall apply.

Article 17. Public policy and public security
(1) Member States may refuse applications for residence from long–term residents or their family members where the person concerned constitutes a threat to public policy or public security.
When taking the relevant decision, the Member State shall consider the severity or type of offence against public policy or public security committed by the long–term resident or his/her family member(s), or the danger that emanates from the person concerned.
(2) The decision referred to in paragraph 1 shall not be based on economic considerations.

Article 18. Public health
(1) Member States may refuse applications for residence from long–term residents or their family members where the person concerned constitutes a threat to public health.
(2) The only diseases that may justify a refusal to allow entry or the right of residence in the territory of the second Member State shall be the diseases as defined by the relevant applicable instruments of the World Health Organisation's and such other infectious or contagious parasite–based diseases as are the subject of protective provisions in relation to nationals in the host country. Member States shall not introduce new more restrictive provisions or practices.
(3) Diseases contracted after the first residence permit was issued in the second Member State shall not justify a refusal to renew the permit or expulsion from the territory.
(4) A Member State may require a medical examination, for persons to whom this Directive applies, in order to certify that they do not suffer from any of the diseases referred to in paragraph 2. Such medical examinations, which may be free of charge, shall not be performed on a systematic basis.

Article 19. Examination of applications and issue of a residence permit
(1) The competent national authorities shall process applications within four months from the date that these have been lodged.
If an application is not accompanied by the documentary evidence listed in Articles 15 and 16, or in exceptional circumstances linked with the complexity of the examination of the application, the time limit referred to in the first subparagraph may be extended for a period not exceeding three months. In such cases the competent national authorities shall inform the applicant thereof.
(2) If the conditions provided for in Articles 14, 15 and 16 are met, then, subject to the provisions relating to public policy, public security and public health in Articles 17 and 18, the second Member State shall issue the long–term resident with a renewable residence permit. This residence permit

shall, upon application, if required, be renewable on expiry. The second Member State shall inform the first Member State of its decision.

(3) The second Member State shall issue members of the long–term resident's family with renewable residence permits valid for the same period as the permit issued to the long–term resident.

Article 20. Procedural guarantees

(1) Reasons shall be given for any decision rejecting an application for a residence permit. It shall be notified to the third–country national concerned in accordance with the notification procedures under the relevant national legislation. The notification shall specify the possible redress procedures available and the time limit for taking action.

Any consequences of no decision being taken by the end of the period referred to in Article 19(1) shall be determined by the national legislation of the relevant Member State.

(2) Where an application for a residence permit is rejected, or the permit is not renewed or is withdrawn, the person concerned shall have the right to mount a legal challenge in the Member State concerned.

Article 21. Treatment granted in the second Member State

(1) As soon as they have received the residence permit provided for by Article 19 in the second Member State, long–term residents shall in that Member State enjoy equal treatment in the areas and under the conditions referred to in Article 11.

(2) Long–term residents shall have access to the labour market in accordance with the provisions of paragraph 1.

Member States may provide that the persons referred to in Article 14(2)(a) shall have restricted access to employed activities different than those for which they have been granted their residence permit under the conditions set by national legislation for a period not exceeding 12 months.

Member States may decide in accordance with national law the conditions under which the persons referred to in Article 14(2)(b) or (c) may have access to an employed or self–employed activity.

(3) As soon as they have received the residence permit provided for by Article 19 in the second Member State, members of the family of the long–term resident shall in that Member State enjoy the rights listed in Article 14 of Directive 2003/86/EC.

Article 22. Withdrawal of residence permit and obligation to readmit

(1) Until the third–country national has obtained long–term resident status, the second Member State may decide to refuse to renew or to withdraw the resident permit and to oblige the person concerned and his/her family members, in accordance with the procedures provided for by national law, including removal procedures, to leave its territory in the following cases:

(a) on grounds of public policy or public security as defined in Article 17;

(b) where the conditions provided for in Articles 14, 15 and 16 are no longer met;

(c) where the third–country national is not lawfully residing in the Member State concerned.

(2) If the second Member State adopts one of the measures referred to in paragraph 1, the first Member State shall immediately readmit without formalities the long–term resident and his/her family members. The second Member State shall notify the first Member State of its decision.

(3) Until the third–country national has obtained long–term resident status and without prejudice to the obligation to readmit referred to in paragraph 2, the second Member State may adopt a decision to remove the third–country national from the territory of the Union, in accordance with and under the guarantees of Article 12, on serious grounds of public policy or public security.

In such cases, when adopting the said decision the second Member State shall consult the first Member State.

When the second Member State adopts a decision to remove the third–country national concerned, it shall take all the appropriate measures to effectively implement it. In such cases the second Member State shall provide to the first Member State appropriate information with respect to the implementation of the removal decision.

(4) Removal decisions may not be accompanied by a permanent ban on residence in the cases referred to in paragraph 1(b) and (c).

(5) The obligation to readmit referred to in paragraph 2 shall be without prejudice to the possibility of the long–term resident and his/her family members moving to a third Member State.

Article 23. Acquisition of long–term resident status in the second Member State

(1) Upon application, the second Member State shall grant long–term residents the status provided for by Article 7, subject to the provisions of Articles 3, 4, 5 and 6. The second Member State shall notify its decision to the first Member State.

(2) The procedure laid down in Article 7 shall apply to the presentation and examination of applica-

tions for long-term resident status in the second Member State. Article 8 shall apply for the issuance of the residence permit. Where the application is rejected, the procedural guarantees provided for by Article 10 shall apply.

Chapter IV. Final Provisions

Article 24. Report and rendez–vous clause

Periodically, and for the first time no later than 23 January 2011, the Commission shall report to the European Parliament and to the Council on the application of this Directive in the Member States and shall propose such amendments as may be necessary. These proposals for amendments shall be made by way of priority in relation to Articles 4, 5, 9, 11 and to Chapter III.

Article 25. Contact points

Member States shall appoint contact points who will be responsible for receiving and transmitting the information referred to in Article 19(2), Article 22(2) and Article 23(1).

Member States shall provide appropriate cooperation in the exchange of the information and documentation referred to in the first paragraph.

Article 26. Transposition

Member States shall bring into force the laws, regulations and administrative provisions necessary to comply with this Directive by 23 January 2006 at the latest. They shall forthwith inform the Commission thereof.

When Member States adopt these measures, they shall contain a reference to this Directive or shall be accompanied by such reference on the occasion of their official publication. The methods of making such reference shall be laid down by Member States.

Article 27. Entry into force

This Directive shall enter into force on the day of its publication in the *Official Journal of the European Union*.

Article 28. Addressees

This Directive is addressed to the Member States in accordance with the Treaty establishing the European Community.

PART III   EUROPEAN UNION

Directive 2004/38/EC of the European Parliament and of the Council of 29 April 2004 on the right of citizens of the Union and their family members to move and reside freely within the territory of the Member States amending Regulation (EEC) No 1612/68 and repealing Directives 64/221/EEC, 68/360/EEC, 72/194/EEC, 73/148/EEC, 75/34/EEC, 75/35/EEC, 90/364/EEC, 90/365/EEC and 93/96/EEC

THE EUROPEAN PARLIAMENT AND THE COUNCIL OF THE EUROPEAN UNION,
Having regard to the Treaty establishing the European Community, and in particular Articles 12, 18, 40, 44 and 52 thereof,
Having regard to the proposal from the Commission,
Having regard to the Opinion of the European Economic and Social Committee,
Having regard to the Opinion of the Committee of the Regions,
Acting in accordance with the procedure laid down in Article 251 of the Treaty,
Whereas:
(1) Citizenship of the Union confers on every citizen of the Union a primary and individual right to move and reside freely within the territory of the Member States, subject to the limitations and conditions laid down in the Treaty and to the measures adopted to give it effect.
(2) The free movement of persons constitutes one of the fundamental freedoms of the internal market, which comprises an area without internal frontiers, in which freedom is ensured in accordance with the provisions of the Treaty.
(3) Union citizenship should be the fundamental status of nationals of the Member States when they exercise their right of free movement and residence. It is therefore necessary to codify and review the existing Community instruments dealing separately with workers, self–employed persons, as well as students and other inactive persons in order to simplify and strengthen the right of free movement and residence of all Union citizens.
(4) With a view to remedying this sector–by–sector, piecemeal approach to the right of free movement and residence and facilitating the exercise of this right, there needs to be a single legislative act to amend Council Regulation (EEC) No 1612/68 of 15 October 1968 on freedom of movement for workers within the Community and to repeal the following acts: Council Directive 68/360/EEC of 15 October 1968 on the abolition of restrictions on movement and residence within the Community for workers of Member States and their families, Council Directive 73/148/EEC of 21 May 1973 on the abolition of restrictions on movement and residence within the Community for nationals of Member States with regard to establishment and the provision of services, Council Directive 90/364/EEC of 28 June 1990 on the right of residence, Council Directive 90/365/EEC of 28 June 1990 on the right of residence for employees and self–employed persons who have ceased their occupational activity and Council Directive 93/96/EEC of 29 October 1993 on the right of residence for students.
(5) The right of all Union citizens to move and reside freely within the territory of the Member States should, if it is to be exercised under objective conditions of freedom and dignity, be also granted to their family members, irrespective of nationality. For the purposes of this Directive, the definition of "family member" should also include the registered partner if the legislation of the host Member State treats registered partnership as equivalent to marriage.
(6) In order to maintain the unity of the family in a broader sense and without prejudice to the prohibition of discrimination on grounds of nationality, the situation of those persons who are not included in the definition of family members under this Directive, and who therefore do not enjoy an automatic right of entry and residence in the host Member State, should be examined by the host Member State on the basis of its own national legislation, in order to decide whether entry and residence could be granted to such persons, taking into consideration their relationship with the Union citizen or any other circumstances, such as their financial or physical dependence on the Union citizen.
(7) The formalities connected with the free movement of Union citizens within the territory of Member States should be clearly defined, without prejudice to the provisions applicable to national border controls.
(8) With a view to facilitating the free movement of family members who are not nationals of a Member State, those who have already obtained a residence card should be exempted from the requirement to obtain an entry visa within the meaning of Council Regulation (EC) No 539/2001 of 15 March 2001 listing the third countries whose nationals must be in possession of visas when crossing the external borders and those whose nationals are exempt from that requirement or, where appropriate, of the applicable national legislation.
(9) Union citizens should have the right of residence in the host Member State for a period not exceeding three months without being subject to any conditions or any formalities other than the requirement to hold a valid identity card or passport, without prejudice to a more favourable treat-

ment applicable to job–seekers as recognised by the case–law of the Court of Justice.

(10) Persons exercising their right of residence should not, however, become an unreasonable burden on the social assistance system of the host Member State during an initial period of residence. Therefore, the right of residence for Union citizens and their family members for periods in excess of three months should be subject to conditions.

(11) The fundamental and personal right of residence in another Member State is conferred directly on Union citizens by the Treaty and is not dependent upon their having fulfilled administrative procedures.

(12) For periods of residence of longer than three months, Member States should have the possibility to require Union citizens to register with the competent authorities in the place of residence, attested by a registration certificate issued to that effect.

(13) The residence card requirement should be restricted to family members of Union citizens who are not nationals of a Member State for periods of residence of longer than three months.

(14) The supporting documents required by the competent authorities for the issuing of a registration certificate or of a residence card should be comprehensively specified in order to avoid divergent administrative practices or interpretations constituting an undue obstacle to the exercise of the right of residence by Union citizens and their family members.

(15) Family members should be legally safeguarded in the event of the death of the Union citizen, divorce, annulment of marriage or termination of a registered partnership. With due regard for family life and human dignity, and in certain conditions to guard against abuse, measures should therefore be taken to ensure that in such circumstances family members already residing within the territory of the host Member State retain their right of residence exclusively on a personal basis.

(16) As long as the beneficiaries of the right of residence do not become an unreasonable burden on the social assistance system of the host Member State they should not be expelled. Therefore, an expulsion measure should not be the automatic consequence of recourse to the social assistance system. The host Member State should examine whether it is a case of temporary difficulties and take into account the duration of residence, the personal circumstances and the amount of aid granted in order to consider whether the beneficiary has become an unreasonable burden on its social assistance system and to proceed to his expulsion. In no case should an expulsion measure be adopted against workers, self–employed persons or job–seekers as defined by the Court of Justice save on grounds of public policy or public security.

(17) Enjoyment of permanent residence by Union citizens who have chosen to settle long term in the host Member State would strengthen the feeling of Union citizenship and is a key element in promoting social cohesion, which is one of the fundamental objectives of the Union. A right of permanent residence should therefore be laid down for all Union citizens and their family members who have resided in the host Member State in compliance with the conditions laid down in this Directive during a continuous period of five years without becoming subject to an expulsion measure.

(18) In order to be a genuine vehicle for integration into the society of the host Member State in which the Union citizen resides, the right of permanent residence, once obtained, should not be subject to any conditions.

(19) Certain advantages specific to Union citizens who are workers or self–employed persons and to their family members, which may allow these persons to acquire a right of permanent residence before they have resided five years in the host Member State, should be maintained, as these constitute acquired rights, conferred by Commission Regulation (EEC) No 1251/70 of 29 June 1970 on the right of workers to remain in the territory of a Member State after having been employed in that State and Council Directive 75/34/EEC of 17 December 1974 concerning the right of nationals of a Member State to remain in the territory of another Member State after having pursued therein an activity in a self–employed capacity.

(20) In accordance with the prohibition of discrimination on grounds of nationality, all Union citizens and their family members residing in a Member State on the basis of this Directive should enjoy, in that Member State, equal treatment with nationals in areas covered by the Treaty, subject to such specific provisions as are expressly provided for in the Treaty and secondary law.

(21) However, it should be left to the host Member State to decide whether it will grant social assistance during the first three months of residence, or for a longer period in the case of job–seekers, to Union citizens other than those who are workers or self–employed persons or who retain that status or their family members, or maintenance assistance for studies, including vocational training, prior to acquisition of the right of permanent residence, to these same persons.

(22) The Treaty allows restrictions to be placed on the right of free movement and residence on grounds of public policy, public security or public health. In order to ensure a tighter definition of the circumstances and procedural safeguards subject to which Union citizens and their family members

may be denied leave to enter or may be expelled, this Directive should replace Council Directive 64/221/EEC of 25 February 1964 on the coordination of special measures concerning the movement and residence of foreign nationals, which are justified on grounds of public policy, public security or public health.

(23) Expulsion of Union citizens and their family members on grounds of public policy or public security is a measure that can seriously harm persons who, having availed themselves of the rights and freedoms conferred on them by the Treaty, have become genuinely integrated into the host Member State. The scope for such measures should therefore be limited in accordance with the principle of proportionality to take account of the degree of integration of the persons concerned, the length of their residence in the host Member State, their age, state of health, family and economic situation and the links with their country of origin.

(24) Accordingly, the greater the degree of integration of Union citizens and their family members in the host Member State, the greater the degree of protection against expulsion should be. Only in exceptional circumstances, where there are imperative grounds of public security, should an expulsion measure be taken against Union citizens who have resided for many years in the territory of the host Member State, in particular when they were born and have resided there throughout their life. In addition, such exceptional circumstances should also apply to an expulsion measure taken against minors, in order to protect their links with their family, in accordance with the United Nations Convention on the Rights of the Child, of 20 November 1989.

(25) Procedural safeguards should also be specified in detail in order to ensure a high level of protection of the rights of Union citizens and their family members in the event of their being denied leave to enter or reside in another Member State, as well as to uphold the principle that any action taken by the authorities must be properly justified.

(26) In all events, judicial redress procedures should be available to Union citizens and their family members who have been refused leave to enter or reside in another Member State.

(27) In line with the case–law of the Court of Justice prohibiting Member States from issuing orders excluding for life persons covered by this Directive from their territory, the right of Union citizens and their family members who have been excluded from the territory of a Member State to submit a fresh application after a reasonable period, and in any event after a three year period from enforcement of the final exclusion order, should be confirmed.

(28) To guard against abuse of rights or fraud, notably marriages of convenience or any other form of relationships contracted for the sole purpose of enjoying the right of free movement and residence, Member States should have the possibility to adopt the necessary measures.

(29) This Directive should not affect more favourable national provisions.

(30) With a view to examining how further to facilitate the exercise of the right of free movement and residence, a report should be prepared by the Commission in order to evaluate the opportunity to present any necessary proposals to this effect, notably on the extension of the period of residence with no conditions.

(31) This Directive respects the fundamental rights and freedoms and observes the principles recognised in particular by the Charter of Fundamental Rights of the European Union. In accordance with the prohibition of discrimination contained in the Charter, Member States should implement this Directive without discrimination between the beneficiaries of this Directive on grounds such as sex, race, colour, ethnic or social origin, genetic characteristics, language, religion or beliefs, political or other opinion, membership of an ethnic minority, property, birth, disability, age or sexual orientation,

HAVE ADOPTED THIS DIRECTIVE:

Chapter I. General Provisions

Article 1. Subject

This Directive lays down:

(a) the conditions governing the exercise of the right of free movement and residence within the territory of the Member States by Union citizens and their family members;

(b) the right of permanent residence in the territory of the Member States for Union citizens and their family members;

(c) the limits placed on the rights set out in (a) and (b) on grounds of public policy, public security or public health.

Article 2. Definitions

For the purposes of this Directive:

1) "Union citizen" means any person having the nationality of a Member State;

2) "Family member" means:

(a) the spouse;
(b) the partner with whom the Union citizen has contracted a registered partnership, on the basis of the legislation of a Member State, if the legislation of the host Member State treats registered partnerships as equivalent to marriage and in accordance with the conditions laid down in the relevant legislation of the host Member State;
(c) the direct descendants who are under the age of 21 or are dependants and those of the spouse or partner as defined in point (b);
(d) the dependent direct relatives in the ascending line and those of the spouse or partner as defined in point (b);
3) "Host Member State" means the Member State to which a Union citizen moves in order to exercise his/her right of free movement and residence.

Article 3. Beneficiaries
(1) This Directive shall apply to all Union citizens who move to or reside in a Member State other than that of which they are a national, and to their family members as defined in point 2 of Article 2 who accompany or join them.
(2) Without prejudice to any right to free movement and residence the persons concerned may have in their own right, the host Member State shall, in accordance with its national legislation, facilitate entry and residence for the following persons:
(a) any other family members, irrespective of their nationality, not falling under the definition in point 2 of Article 2 who, in the country from which they have come, are dependants or members of the household of the Union citizen having the primary right of residence, or where serious health grounds strictly require the personal care of the family member by the Union citizen;
(b) the partner with whom the Union citizen has a durable relationship, duly attested.
The host Member State shall undertake an extensive examination of the personal circumstances and shall justify any denial of entry or residence to these people.

Chapter II. Right of Exit and Entry

Article 4. Right of exit
(1) Without prejudice to the provisions on travel documents applicable to national border controls, all Union citizens with a valid identity card or passport and their family members who are not nationals of a Member State and who hold a valid passport shall have the right to leave the territory of a Member State to travel to another Member State.
(2) No exit visa or equivalent formality may be imposed on the persons to whom paragraph 1 applies.
(3) Member States shall, acting in accordance with their laws, issue to their own nationals, and renew, an identity card or passport stating their nationality.
(4) The passport shall be valid at least for all Member States and for countries through which the holder must pass when travelling between Member States. Where the law of a Member State does not provide for identity cards to be issued, the period of validity of any passport on being issued or renewed shall be not less than five years.

Article 5. Right of entry
(1) Without prejudice to the provisions on travel documents applicable to national border controls, Member States shall grant Union citizens leave to enter their territory with a valid identity card or passport and shall grant family members who are not nationals of a Member State leave to enter their territory with a valid passport.
No entry visa or equivalent formality may be imposed on Union citizens.
(2) Family members who are not nationals of a Member State shall only be required to have an entry visa in accordance with Regulation (EC) No 539/2001 or, where appropriate, with national law. For the purposes of this Directive, possession of the valid residence card referred to in Article 10 shall exempt such family members from the visa requirement.
Member States shall grant such persons every facility to obtain the necessary visas. Such visas shall be issued free of charge as soon as possible and on the basis of an accelerated procedure.
(3) The host Member State shall not place an entry or exit stamp in the passport of family members who are not nationals of a Member State provided that they present the residence card provided for in Article 10.
(4) Where a Union citizen, or a family member who is not a national of a Member State, does not have the necessary travel documents or, if required, the necessary visas, the Member State concerned shall, before turning them back, give such persons every reasonable opportunity to obtain the necessary documents or have them brought to them within a reasonable period of time or to corroborate or prove by other means that they are covered by the right of free movement and residence.

(5) The Member State may require the person concerned to report his/her presence within its territory within a reasonable and non–discriminatory period of time. Failure to comply with this requirement may make the person concerned liable to proportionate and non–discriminatory sanctions.

Chapter III. Right of Residence

Article 6. Right of residence for up to three months

(1) Union citizens shall have the right of residence on the territory of another Member State for a period of up to three months without any conditions or any formalities other than the requirement to hold a valid identity card or passport.
(2) The provisions of paragraph 1 shall also apply to family members in possession of a valid passport who are not nationals of a Member State, accompanying or joining the Union citizen.

Article 7. Right of residence for more than three months

(1) All Union citizens shall have the right of residence on the territory of another Member State for a period of longer than three months if they:
(a) are workers or self–employed persons in the host Member State; or
(b) have sufficient resources for themselves and their family members not to become a burden on the social assistance system of the host Member State during their period of residence and have comprehensive sickness insurance cover in the host Member State; or
(c) – are enrolled at a private or public establishment, accredited or financed by the host Member State on the basis of its legislation or administrative practice, for the principal purpose of following a course of study, including vocational training; and
– have comprehensive sickness insurance cover in the host Member State and assure the relevant national authority, by means of a declaration or by such equivalent means as they may choose, that they have sufficient resources for themselves and their family members not to become a burden on the social assistance system of the host Member State during their period of residence; or
(d) are family members accompanying or joining a Union citizen who satisfies the conditions referred to in points (a), (b) or (c).
(2) The right of residence provided for in paragraph 1 shall extend to family members who are not nationals of a Member State, accompanying or joining the Union citizen in the host Member State, provided that such Union citizen satisfies the conditions referred to in paragraph l(a), (b) or (c).
(3) For the purposes of paragraph 1(a), a Union citizen who is no longer a worker or self–employed person shall retain the status of worker or self–employed person in the following circumstances:
(a) he/she is temporarily unable to work as the result of an illness or accident;
(b) he/she is in duly recorded involuntary unemployment after having been employed for more than one year and has registered as a job–seeker with the relevant employment office;
(c) he/she is in duly recorded involuntary unemployment after completing a fixed–term employment contract of less than a year or after having become involuntarily unemployed during the first twelve months and has registered as a job–seeker with the relevant employment office. In this case, the status of worker shall be retained for no less than six months;
(d) he/she embarks on vocational training. Unless he/she is involuntarily unemployed, the retention of the status of worker shall require the training to be related to the previous employment.
(4) By way of derogation from paragraphs 1(d) and 2 above, only the spouse, the registered partner provided for in Article 2(2)(b) and dependent children shall have the right of residence as family members of a Union citizen meeting the conditions under 1(c) above. Article 3(2) shall apply to his/her dependent direct relatives in the ascending lines and those of his/her spouse or registered partner.

Article 8. Administrative formalities for Union citizens

(1) Without prejudice to Article 5(5), for periods of residence longer than three months, the host Member State may require Union citizens to register with the relevant authorities.
(2) The deadline for registration may not be less than three months from the date of arrival. A registration certificate shall be issued immediately, stating the name and address of the person registering and the date of the registration. Failure to comply with the registration requirement may render the person concerned liable to proportionate and non–discriminatory sanctions.
(3) For the registration certificate to be issued, Member States may only require that
– Union citizens to whom point (a) of Article 7(1) applies present a valid identity card or passport, a confirmation of engagement from the employer or a certificate of employment, or proof that they are self–employed persons;
– Union citizens to whom point (b) of Article 7(1) applies present a valid identity card or passport and provide proof that they satisfy the conditions laid down therein;
– Union citizens to whom point (c) of Article 7(1) applies present a valid identity card or passport,

provide proof of enrolment at an accredited establishment and of comprehensive sickness insurance cover and the declaration or equivalent means referred to in point (c) of Article 7(1). Member States may not require this declaration to refer to any specific amount of resources.

(4) Member States may not lay down a fixed amount which they regard as "sufficient resources" but they must take into account the personal situation of the person concerned. In all cases this amount shall not be higher than the threshold below which nationals of the host Member State become eligible for social assistance, or, where this criterion is not applicable, higher than the minimum social security pension paid by the host Member State.

(5) For the registration certificate to be issued to family members of Union citizens, who are themselves Union citizens, Member States may require the following documents to be presented:

(a) a valid identity card or passport;
(b) a document attesting to the existence of a family relationship or of a registered partnership;
(c) where appropriate, the registration certificate of the Union citizen whom they are accompanying or joining;
(d) in cases falling under points (c) and (d) of Article 2(2), documentary evidence that the conditions laid down therein are met;
(e) in cases falling under Article 3(2)(a), a document issued by the relevant authority in the country of origin or country from which they are arriving certifying that they are dependants or members of the household of the Union citizen, or proof of the existence of serious health grounds which strictly require the personal care of the family member by the Union citizen;
(f) in cases falling under Article 3(2)(b), proof of the existence of a durable relationship with the Union citizen.

Article 9. Administrative formalities for family members who are not nationals of a Member State

(1) Member States shall issue a residence card to family members of a Union citizen who are not nationals of a Member State, where the planned period of residence is for more than three months.

(2) The deadline for submitting the residence card application may not be less than three months from the date of arrival.

(3) Failure to comply with the requirement to apply for a residence card may make the person concerned liable to proportionate and non–discriminatory sanctions.

Article 10. Issue of residence cards

(1) The right of residence of family members of a Union citizen who are not nationals of a Member State shall be evidenced by the issuing of a document called "Residence card of a family member of a Union citizen" no later than six months from the date on which they submit the application. A certificate of application for the residence card shall be issued immediately.

(2) For the residence card to be issued, Member States shall require presentation of the following documents:

(a) a valid passport;
(b) a document attesting to the existence of a family relationship or of a registered partnership;
(c) the registration certificate or, in the absence of a registration system, any other proof of residence in the host Member State of the Union citizen whom they are accompanying or joining;
(d) in cases falling under points (c) and (d) of Article 2(2), documentary evidence that the conditions laid down therein are met;
(e) in cases falling under Article 3(2)(a), a document issued by the relevant authority in the country of origin or country from which they are arriving certifying that they are dependants or members of the household of the Union citizen, or proof of the existence of serious health grounds which strictly require the personal care of the family member by the Union citizen;
(f) in cases falling under Article 3(2)(b), proof of the existence of a durable relationship with the Union citizen.

Article 11. Validity of the residence card

(1) The residence card provided for by Article 10(1) shall be valid for five years from the date of issue or for the envisaged period of residence of the Union citizen, if this period is less than five years.

(2) The validity of the residence card shall not be affected by temporary absences not exceeding six months a year, or by absences of a longer duration for compulsory military service or by one absence of a maximum of twelve consecutive months for important reasons such as pregnancy and childbirth, serious illness, study or vocational training, or a posting in another Member State or a third country.

Article 12. Retention of the right of residence by family members in the event of death or

departure of the Union citizen

(1) Without prejudice to the second subparagraph, the Union citizen's death or departure from the host Member State shall not affect the right of residence of his/her family members who are nationals of a Member State.

Before acquiring the right of permanent residence, the persons concerned must meet the conditions laid down in points (a), (b), (c) or (d) of Article 7(1).

(2) Without prejudice to the second subparagraph, the Union citizen's death shall not entail loss of the right of residence of his/her family members who are not nationals of a Member State and who have been residing in the host Member State as family members for at least one year before the Union citizen's death.

Before acquiring the right of permanent residence, the right of residence of the persons concerned shall remain subject to the requirement that they are able to show that they are workers or self–employed persons or that they have sufficient resources for themselves and their family members not to become a burden on the social assistance system of the host Member State during their period of residence and have comprehensive sickness insurance cover in the host Member State, or that they are members of the family, already constituted in the host Member State, of a person satisfying these requirements. "Sufficient resources" shall be as defined in Article 8(4).

Such family members shall retain their right of residence exclusively on a personal basis.

(3) The Union citizen's departure from the host Member State or his/her death shall not entail loss of the right of residence of his/her children or of the parent who has actual custody of the children, irrespective of nationality, if the children reside in the host Member State and are enrolled at an educational establishment, for the purpose of studying there, until the completion of their studies.

Article 13. Retention of the right of residence by family members in the event of divorce, annulment of marriage or termination of registered partnership

(1) Without prejudice to the second subparagraph, divorce, annulment of the Union citizen's marriage or termination of his/her registered partnership, as referred to in point 2(b) of Article 2 shall not affect the right of residence of his/her family members who are nationals of a Member State.

Before acquiring the right of permanent residence, the persons concerned must meet the conditions laid down in points (a), (b), (c) or (d) of Article 7(1).

(2) Without prejudice to the second subparagraph, divorce, annulment of marriage or termination of the registered partnership referred to in point 2(b) of Article 2 shall not entail loss of the right of residence of a Union citizen's family members who are not nationals of a Member State where:

(a) prior to initiation of the divorce or annulment proceedings or termination of the registered partnership referred to in point 2(b) of Article 2, the marriage or registered partnership has lasted at least three years, including one year in the host Member State; or

(b) by agreement between the spouses or the partners referred to in point 2(b) of Article 2 or by court order, the spouse or partner who is not a national of a Member State has custody of the Union citizen's children; or

(c) this is warranted by particularly difficult circumstances, such as having been a victim of domestic violence while the marriage or registered partnership was subsisting; or

(d) by agreement between the spouses or partners referred to in point 2(b) of Article 2 or by court order, the spouse or partner who is not a national of a Member State has the right of access to a minor child, provided that the court has ruled that such access must be in the host Member State, and for as long as is required.

Before acquiring the right of permanent residence, the right of residence of the persons concerned shall remain subject to the requirement that they are able to show that they are workers or self–employed persons or that they have sufficient resources for themselves and their family members not to become a burden on the social assistance system of the host Member State during their period of residence and have comprehensive sickness insurance cover in the host Member State, or that they are members of the family, already constituted in the host Member State, of a person satisfying these requirements. "Sufficient resources" shall be as defined in Article 8(4).

Such family members shall retain their right of residence exclusively on personal basis.

Article 14. Retention of the right of residence

(1) Union citizens and their family members shall have the right of residence provided for in Article 6, as long as they do not become an unreasonable burden on the social assistance system of the host Member State.

(2) Union citizens and their family members shall have the right of residence provided for in Articles 7, 12 and 13 as long as they meet the conditions set out therein.

In specific cases where there is a reasonable doubt as to whether a Union citizen or his/her family members satisfies the conditions set out in Articles 7,12 and 13, Member States may verify if these conditions are fulfilled. This verification shall not be carried out systematically.

(3) An expulsion measure shall not be the automatic consequence of a Union citizen's or his or her family member's recourse to the social assistance system of the host Member State.

(4) By way of derogation from paragraphs 1 and 2 and without prejudice to the provisions of Chapter VI, an expulsion measure may in no case be adopted against Union citizens or their family members if:

(a) the Union citizens are workers or self–employed persons, or

(b) the Union citizens entered the territory of the host Member State in order to seek employment. In this case, the Union citizens and their family members may not be expelled for as long as the Union citizens can provide evidence that they are continuing to seek employment and that they have a genuine chance of being engaged.

Article 15. Procedural safeguards

(1) The procedures provided for by Articles 30 and 31 shall apply by analogy to all decisions restricting free movement of Union citizens and their family members on grounds other than public policy, public security or public health.

(2) Expiry of the identity card or passport on the basis of which the person concerned entered the host Member State and was issued with a registration certificate or residence card shall not constitute a ground for expulsion from the host Member State.

(3) The host Member State may not impose a ban on entry in the context of an expulsion decision to which paragraph 1 applies.

Chapter IV. Right of Permanent Residence

Section I. Eligibility

Article 16. General rule for Union citizens and their family members

(1) Union citizens who have resided legally for a continuous period of five years in the host Member State shall have the right of permanent residence there. This right shall not be subject to the conditions provided for in Chapter III.

(2) Paragraph 1 shall apply also to family members who are not nationals of a Member State and have legally resided with the Union citizen in the host Member State for a continuous period of five years.

(3) Continuity of residence shall not be affected by temporary absences not exceeding a total of six months a year, or by absences of a longer duration for compulsory military service, or by one absence of a maximum of twelve consecutive months for important reasons such as pregnancy and childbirth, serious illness, study or vocational training, or a posting in another Member State or a third country.

(4) Once acquired, the right of permanent residence shall be lost only through absence from the host Member State for a period exceeding two consecutive years.

Article 17. Exemptions for persons no longer working in the host Member State and their family members

(1) By way of derogation from Article 16, the right of permanent residence in the host Member State shall be enjoyed before completion of a continuous period of five years of residence by:

(a) workers or self–employed persons who, at the time they stop working, have reached the age laid down by the law of that Member State for entitlement to an old age pension or workers who cease paid employment to take early retirement, provided that they have been working in that Member State for at least the preceding twelve months and have resided there continuously for more than three years.

If the law of the host Member State does not grant the right to an old age pension to certain categories of self–employed persons, the age condition shall be deemed to have been met once the person concerned has reached the age of 60;

(b) workers or self–employed persons who have resided continuously in the host Member State for more than two years and stop working there as a result of permanent incapacity to work.

If such incapacity is the result of an accident at work or an occupational disease entitling the person concerned to a benefit payable in full or in part by an institution in the host Member State, no condition shall be imposed as to length of residence;

(c) workers or self–employed persons who, after three years of continuous employment and residence in the host Member State, work in an employed or self–employed capacity in another Member State, while retaining their place of residence in the host Member State, to which they return, as a rule, each day or at least once a week.

For the purposes of entitlement to the rights referred to in points (a) and (b), periods of employment spent in the Member State in which the person concerned is working shall be regarded as having been spent in the host Member State.

Periods of involuntary unemployment duly recorded by the relevant employment office, periods not worked for reasons not of the person's own making and absences from work or cessation of work due to illness or accident shall be regarded as periods of employment.

(2) The conditions as to length of residence and employment laid down in point (a) of paragraph 1 and the condition as to length of residence laid down in point (b) of paragraph 1 shall not apply if the worker's or the self–employed person's spouse or partner as referred to in point 2(b) of Article 2 is a national of the host Member State or has lost the nationality of that Member State by marriage to that worker or self–employed person.

(3) Irrespective of nationality, the family members of a worker or a self–employed person who are residing with him in the territory of the host Member State shall have the right of permanent residence in that Member State, if the worker or self–employed person has acquired himself the right of permanent residence in that Member State on the basis of paragraph 1.

(4) If, however, the worker or self–employed person dies while still working but before acquiring permanent residence status in the host Member State on the basis of paragraph 1, his family members who are residing with him in the host Member State shall acquire the right of permanent residence there, on condition that:

(a) the worker or self–employed person had, at the time of death, resided continuously on the territory of that Member State for two years; or

(b) the death resulted from an accident at work or an occupational disease; or

(c) the surviving spouse lost the nationality of that Member State following marriage to the worker or self–employed person.

Article 18. Acquisition of the right of permanent residence by certain family members who are not nationals of a Member State

Without prejudice to Article 17, the family members of a Union citizen to whom Articles 12(2) and 13(2) apply, who satisfy the conditions laid down therein, shall acquire the right of permanent residence after residing legally for a period of five consecutive years in the host Member State.

Section II. Administrative Formalities

Article 19. Document certifying permanent residence for Union citizens

(1) Upon application Member States shall issue Union citizens entitled to permanent residence, after having verified duration of residence, with a document certifying permanent residence.

(2) The document certifying permanent residence shall be issued as soon as possible.

Article 20. Permanent residence card for family members who are not nationals of a Member State

(1) Member States shall issue family members who are not nationals of a Member State entitled to permanent residence with a permanent residence card within six months of the submission of the application. The permanent residence card shall be renewable automatically every ten years.

(2) The application for a permanent residence card shall be submitted before the residence card expires. Failure to comply with the requirement to apply for a permanent residence card may render the person concerned liable to proportionate and non–discriminatory sanctions.

(3) Interruption in residence not exceeding two consecutive years shall not affect the validity of the permanent residence card.

Article 21. Continuity of residence

For the purposes of this Directive, continuity of residence may be attested by any means of proof in use in the host Member State. Continuity of residence is broken by any expulsion decision duly enforced against the person concerned.

Chapter V. Provisions Common to the Right of Residence and the Right of Permanent Residence

Article 22. Territorial scope

The right of residence and the right of permanent residence shall cover the whole territory of the host Member State. Member States may impose territorial restrictions on the right of residence and the right of permanent residence only where the same restrictions apply to their–own nationals.

Article 23. Related rights

DIRECTIVE 2004/38/EC

Irrespective of nationality, the family members of a Union citizen who have the right of residence or the right of permanent residence in a Member State shall be entitled to take up employment or self-employment there.

Article 24. Equal treatment

(1) Subject to such specific provisions as are expressly provided for in the Treaty and secondary law, all Union citizens residing on the basis of this Directive in the territory of the host Member State shall enjoy equal treatment with the nationals of that Member State within the scope of the Treaty. The benefit of this right shall be extended to family members who are not nationals of a Member State and who have the right of residence or permanent residence.

(2) By way of derogation from paragraph 1, the host Member State shall not be obliged to confer entitlement to social assistance during the first three months of residence or, where appropriate, the longer period provided for in Article 14(4)(b), nor shall it be obliged, prior to acquisition of the right of permanent residence, to grant maintenance aid for studies, including vocational training, consisting in student grants or student loans to persons other than workers, self-employed persons, persons who retain such status and members of their families.

Article 25. General provisions concerning residence documents

(1) Possession of a registration certificate as referred to in Article 8, of a document certifying permanent residence, of a certificate attesting submission of an application for a family member residence card, of a residence card or of a permanent residence card, may under no circumstances be made a precondition for the exercise of a right or the completion of an administrative formality, as entitlement to rights may be attested by any other means of proof.

(2) All documents mentioned in paragraph 1 shall be issued free of charge or for a charge not exceeding that imposed on nationals for the issuing of similar documents.

Article 26. Checks

Member States may carry out checks on compliance with any requirement deriving from their national legislation for non-nationals always to carry their registration certificate or residence card, provided that the same requirement applies to their own nationals as regards their identity card. In the event of failure to comply with this requirement, Member States may impose the same sanctions as those imposed on their own nationals for failure to carry their identity card.

Chapter VI. Restrictions on the Right of Entry and the Right of Residence on Grounds of Public Policy, Public Security or Public Health

Article 27. General principles

(1) Subject to the provisions of this Chapter, Member States may restrict the freedom of movement and residence of Union citizens and their family members, irrespective of nationality, on grounds of public policy, public security or public health. These grounds shall not be invoked to serve economic ends.

(2) Measures taken on grounds of public policy or public security shall comply with the principle of proportionality and shall be based exclusively on the personal conduct of the individual concerned. Previous criminal convictions shall not in themselves constitute grounds for taking such measures. The personal conduct of the individual concerned must represent a genuine, present and sufficiently serious threat affecting one of the fundamental interests of society. Justifications that are isolated from the particulars of the case or that rely on considerations of general prevention shall not be accepted.

(3) In order to ascertain whether the person concerned represents a danger for public policy or public security, when issuing the registration certificate or, in the absence of a registration system, not later than three months from the date of arrival of the person concerned on its territory or from the date of reporting his/her presence within the territory, as provided for in Article 5(5), or when issuing the residence card, the host Member State may, should it consider this essential, request the Member State of origin and, if need be, other Member States to provide information concerning any previous police record the person concerned may have. Such enquiries shall not be made as a matter of routine. The Member State consulted shall give its reply within two months.

(4) The Member State which issued the passport or identity card shall allow the holder of the document who has been expelled on grounds of public policy, public security, or public health from another Member State to re-enter its territory without any formality even if the document is no longer valid or the nationality of the holder is in dispute.

Article 28. Protection against expulsion

(1) Before taking an expulsion decision on grounds of public policy or public security, the host Member State shall take account of considerations such as how long the individual concerned has resided on its territory, his/her age, state of health, family and economic situation, social and cultural integration into the host Member State and the extent of his/her links with the country of origin.
(2) The host Member State may not take an expulsion decision against Union citizens or their family members, irrespective of nationality, who have the right of permanent residence on its territory, except on serious grounds of public policy or public security.
(3) An expulsion decision may not be taken against Union citizens, except if the decision is based on imperative grounds of public security, as defined by Member States, if they:
(a) have resided in the host Member State for the previous ten years; or
(b) are a minor, except if the expulsion is necessary for the best interests of the child, as provided for in the United Nations Convention on the Rights of the Child of 20 November 1989.

Article 29. Public health

(1) The only diseases justifying measures restricting freedom of movement shall be the diseases with epidemic potential as defined by the relevant instruments of the World Health Organisation and other infectious diseases or contagious parasitic diseases if they are the subject of protection provisions applying to nationals of the host Member State.
(2) Diseases occurring after a three–month period from the date of arrival shall not constitute grounds for expulsion from the territory.
(3) Where there are serious indications that it is necessary, Member States may, within three months of the date of arrival, require persons entitled to the right of residence to undergo, free of charge, a medical examination to certify that they are not suffering from any of the conditions referred to in paragraph 1. Such medical examinations may not be required as a matter of routine.

Article 30. Notification of decisions

(1) The persons concerned shall be notified in writing of any decision taken under Article 27(1), in such a way that they are able to comprehend its content and the implications for them.
(2) The persons concerned shall be informed, precisely and in full, of the public policy, public security or public health grounds on which the decision taken in their case is based, unless this is contrary to the interests of State security.
(3) The notification shall specify the court or administrative authority with which the person concerned may lodge an appeal, the time limit for the appeal and, where applicable, the time allowed for the person to leave the territory of the Member State. Save in duly substantiated cases of urgency, the time allowed to leave the territory shall be not less than one month from the date of notification.

Article 31. Procedural safeguards

(1) The persons concerned shall have access to judicial and, where appropriate, administrative redress procedures in the host Member State to appeal against or seek review of any decision taken against them on the grounds of public policy, public security or public health.
(2) Where the application for appeal against or judicial review of the expulsion decision is accompanied by an application for an interim order to suspend enforcement of that decision, actual removal from the territory may not take place until such time as the decision on the interim order has been taken, except:
– where the expulsion decision is based on a previous judicial decision; or
– where the persons concerned have had previous access to judicial review; or
– where the expulsion decision is based on imperative grounds of public security under Article 28(3).
(3) The redress procedures shall allow for an examination of the legality of the decision, as well as of the facts and circumstances on which the proposed measure is based. They shall ensure that the decision is not disproportionate, particularly in view of the requirements laid down in Article 28.
(4) Member States may exclude the individual concerned from their territory pending the redress procedure, but they may not prevent the individual from submitting his/her defence in person, except when his/her appearance may cause serious troubles to public policy or public security or when the appeal or judicial review concerns a denial of entry to the territory.

Article 32. Duration of exclusion orders

(1) Persons excluded on grounds of public policy or public security may submit an application for lifting of the exclusion order after a reasonable period, depending on the circumstances, and in any event after three years from enforcement of the final exclusion order which has been validly adopted in accordance with Community law, by putting forward arguments to establish that there has been a material change in the circumstances which justified the decision ordering their exclusion.
The Member State concerned shall reach a decision on this application within six months of its submission.

(2) The persons referred to in paragraph 1 shall have no right of entry to the territory of the Member State concerned while their application is being considered.

Article 33. Expulsion as a penalty or legal consequence
(1) Expulsion orders may not be issued by the host Member State as a penalty or legal consequence of a custodial penalty, unless they conform to the requirements of Articles 27, 28 and 29.
(2) If an expulsion order, as provided for in paragraph 1, is enforced more than two years after it was issued, the Member State shall check that the individual concerned is currently and genuinely a threat to public policy or public security and shall assess whether there has been any material change in the circumstances since the expulsion order was issued.

Chapter VII. Final Provisions

Article 34. Publicity
Member States shall disseminate information concerning the rights and obligations of Union citizens and their family members on the subjects covered by this Directive, particularly by means of awareness–raising campaigns conducted through national and local media and other means of communication.

Article 35. Abuse of rights
Member States may adopt the necessary measures to refuse, terminate or withdraw any right conferred by this Directive in the case of abuse of rights or fraud, such as marriages of convenience. Any such measure shall be proportionate and subject to the procedural safeguards provided for in Articles 30 and 31.

Article 36. Sanctions
Member States shall lay down provisions on the sanctions applicable to breaches of national rules adopted for the implementation of this Directive and shall take the measures required for their application. The sanctions laid down shall be effective and proportionate. Member States shall notify the Commission of these provisions not later than two years from the date of entry into force of this Directive and as promptly as possible in the case of any subsequent changes.

Article 37. More favourable national provisions
The provisions of this Directive shall not affect any laws, regulations or administrative provisions laid down by a Member State which would be more favourable to the persons covered by this Directive.

Article 38. Repeals
(1) Articles 10 and 11 of Regulation (EEC) No 1612/68 shall be repealed with effect from two years from the date of entry into force of this Directive.
(2) Directives 64/221/EEC, 68/360/EEC, 72/194/EEC, 73/148/EEC, 75/34/EEC, 75/35/EEC, 90/364/EEC, 90/365/EEC and 93/96/EEC shall be repealed with effect from two years from the date of entry into force of this Directive.
(3) References made to the repealed provisions and Directives shall be construed as being made to this Directive.

Article 39. Report
No later than four years from the date of entry into force of this Directive, the Commission shall submit a report on the application of this Directive to the European Parliament and the Council, together with any necessary proposals, notably on the opportunity to extend the period of time during which Union citizens and their family members may reside in the territory of the host Member State without any conditions. The Member States shall provide the Commission with the information needed to produce the report.

Article 40. Transposition
(1) Member States shall bring into force the laws, regulations and administrative provisions necessary to comply with this Directive by two years from the date of entry into force of this Directive.
When Member States adopt those measures, they shall contain a reference to this Directive or shall be accompanied by such a reference on the occasion of their official publication. The methods of making such reference shall be laid down by the Member States.
(2) Member States shall communicate to the Commission the text of the provisions of national law which they adopt in the field covered by this Directive together with a table showing how the provisions of this Directive correspond to the national provisions adopted.

PART III EUROPEAN UNION

Article 41. Entry into force
This Directive shall enter into force on the day of its publication in the *Official Journal of the European Union*.

Article 42. Addressees
This Directive is addressed to the Member States.

DIRECTIVE 2005/36/EC

Directive 2005/36/EC of the European Parliament and of the Council of 7 September 2005 on the recognition of professional qualifications

THE EUROPEAN PARLIAMENT AND THE COUNCIL OF THE EUROPEAN UNION,
Having regard to the Treaty establishing the European Community, and in particular Article 40, Article 47(1), the first and third sentences of Article 47(2), and Article 55 thereof,
Having regard to the proposal from the Commission,
Having regard to the opinion of the European Economic and Social Committee,
Acting in accordance with the procedure laid down in Article 251 of the Treaty,
Whereas:
(1) Pursuant to Article 3(1)(c) of the Treaty, the abolition, as between Member States, of obstacles to the free movement of persons and services is one of the objectives of the Community. For nationals of the Member States, this includes, in particular, the right to pursue a profession, in a self–employed or employed capacity, in a Member State other than the one in which they have obtained their professional qualifications. In addition, Article 47(1) of the Treaty lays down that directives shall be issued for the mutual recognition of diplomas, certificates and other evidence of formal qualifications.
(2) Following the European Council of Lisbon on 23 and 24 March 2000, the Commission adopted a Communication on 'An Internal Market Strategy for Services', aimed in particular at making the free provision of services within the Community as simple as within an individual Member State. Further to the Communication from the Commission entitled 'New European Labour Markets, Open to All, with Access to All', the European Council of Stockholm on 23 and 24 March 2001 entrusted the Commission with presenting for the 2002 Spring European Council specific proposals for a more uniform, transparent and flexible regime of recognition of qualifications.
(3) The guarantee conferred by this Directive on persons having acquired their professional qualifications in a Member State to have access to the same profession and pursue it in another Member State with the same rights as nationals is without prejudice to compliance by the migrant professional with any non–discriminatory conditions of pursuit which might be laid down by the latter Member State, provided that these are objectively justified and proportionate.
(4) In order to facilitate the free provision of services, there should be specific rules aimed at extending the possibility of pursuing professional activities under the original professional title. In the case of information society services provided at a distance, the provisions of Directive 2000/31/EC of the European Parliament and of the Council of 8 June 2000 on certain legal aspects of information society services, in particular electronic commerce, in the Internal Market, should also apply.
(5) In view of the different systems established for the cross–border provision of services on a temporary and occasional basis on the one hand, and for establishment on the other, the criteria for distinguishing between these two concepts in the event of the movement of the service provider to the territory of the host Member State should be clarified.
(6) The facilitation of service provision has to be ensured in the context of strict respect for public health and safety and consumer protection. Therefore, specific provisions should be envisaged for regulated professions having public health or safety implications, which provide cross–frontier services on a temporary or occasional basis.
(7) Host Member States may, where necessary and in accordance with Community law, provide for declaration requirements. These requirements should not lead to a disproportionate burden on service providers nor hinder or render less attractive the exercise of the freedom to provide services. The need for such requirements should be reviewed periodically in the light of the progress made in establishing a Community framework for administrative cooperation between Member States.
(8) The service provider should be subject to the application of disciplinary rules of the host Member State having a direct and specific link with the professional qualifications, such as the definition of the profession, the scope of activities covered by a profession or reserved to it, the use of titles and serious professional malpractice which is directly and specifically linked to consumer protection and safety.
(9) While maintaining, for the freedom of establishment, the principles and safeguards underlying the different systems for recognition in force, the rules of such systems should be improved in the light of experience. Moreover, the relevant directives have been amended on several occasions, and their provisions should be reorganised and rationalised by standardising the principles applicable. It is therefore necessary to replace Council Directives 89/48/EEC and 92/51/EEC, as well as Directive 1999/42/EC of the European Parliament and of the Council on the general system for the recognition of professional qualifications, and Council Directives 77/452/EEC, 77/453/EEC, 78/686/EEC, 78/687/EEC, 78/1026/EEC, 78/1027/EEC, 80/154/EEC, 80/155/EEC, 85/384/EEC, 85/432/EEC, 85/433/EEC and 93/16/EEC concerning the professions of nurse responsible for general care, dental

practitioner, veterinary surgeon, midwife, architect, pharmacist and doctor, by combining them in a single text.

(10) This Directive does not create an obstacle to the possibility of Member States recognising, in accordance with their rules, the professional qualifications acquired outside the territory of the European Union by third country nationals. All recognition should respect in any case minimum training conditions for certain professions.

(11) In the case of the professions covered by the general system for the recognition of qualifications, hereinafter referred to as 'the general system', Member States should retain the right to lay down the minimum level of qualification required to ensure the quality of the services provided on their territory. However, pursuant to Articles 10, 39 and 43 of the Treaty, they should not require a national of a Member State to obtain qualifications, which they generally lay down only in terms of the diplomas awarded under their national educational system, where the person concerned has already obtained all or part of those qualifications in another Member State. As a result, it should be laid down that any host Member State in which a profession is regulated must take account of the qualifications obtained in another Member State and assess whether they correspond to those which it requires. The general system for recognition, however, does not prevent a Member State from making any person pursuing a profession on its territory subject to specific requirements due to the application of professional rules justified by the general public interest. Rules of this kind relate, for example, to organisation of the profession, professional standards, including those concerning ethics, and supervision and liability. Lastly, this Directive is not intended to interfere with Member States' legitimate interest in preventing any of their citizens from evading enforcement of the national law relating to professions.

(12) This Directive concerns the recognition by Member States of professional qualifications acquired in other Member States. It does not, however, concern the recognition by Member States of recognition decisions adopted by other Member States pursuant to this Directive. Consequently, individuals holding professional qualifications which have been recognised pursuant to this Directive may not use such recognition to obtain in their Member State of origin rights different from those conferred by the professional qualification obtained in that Member State, unless they provide evidence that they have obtained additional professional qualifications in the host Member State.

(13) In order to define the mechanism of recognition under the general system, it is necessary to group the various national education and training schemes into different levels. These levels, which are established only for the purpose of the operation of the general system, have no effect upon the national education and training structures nor upon the competence of Member States in this field.

(14) The mechanism of recognition established by Directives 89/48/EEC and 92/51/EEC remains unchanged. As a consequence, the holder of a diploma certifying successful completion of training at post–secondary level of a duration of at least one year should be permitted access to a regulated profession in a Member State where access is contingent upon possession of a diploma certifying successful completion of higher or university education of four years' duration, regardless of the level to which the diploma required in the host Member State belongs. Conversely, where access to a regulated profession is contingent upon successful completion of higher or university education of more than four years, such access should be permitted only to holders of a diploma certifying successful completion of higher or university education of at least three years' duration.

(15) In the absence of harmonisation of the minimum training conditions for access to the professions governed by the general system, it should be possible for the host Member State to impose a compensation measure. This measure should be proportionate and, in particular, take account of the applicant's professional experience. Experience shows that requiring the migrant to choose between an aptitude test or an adaptation period offers adequate safeguards as regards the latter's level of qualification, so that any derogation from that choice should in each case be justified by an imperative requirement in the general interest.

(16) In order to promote the free movement of professionals, while ensuring an adequate level of qualification, various professional associations and organisations or Member States should be able to propose common platforms at European level. This Directive should take account, under certain conditions, in compliance with the competence of Member States to decide the qualifications required for the pursuit of professions in their territory as well as the contents and the organisation of their systems of education and professional training and in compliance with Community law, and in particular Community law on competition, of those initiatives, while promoting, in this context, a more automatic character of recognition under the general system. Professional associations which are in a position to submit common platforms should be representative at national and European level. A common platform is a set of criteria which make it possible to compensate for the widest range of substantial differences which have been identified between the training requirements in at least two thirds of the Member States including all the Member States which regulate that profession. These

criteria could, for example, include requirements such as additional training, an adaptation period under supervised practice, an aptitude test, or a prescribed minimum level of professional practice, or combinations thereof.

(17) In order to take into account all situations for which there is still no provision relating to the recognition of professional qualifications, the general system should be extended to those cases which are not covered by a specific system, either where the profession is not covered by one of those systems or where, although the profession is covered by such a specific system, the applicant does not for some particular and exceptional reason meet the conditions to benefit from it.

(18) There is a need to simplify the rules allowing access to a number of industrial, commercial and craft activities, in Member States where those professions are regulated, in so far as those activities have been pursued for a reasonable and sufficiently recent period of time in another Member State, while maintaining for those activities a system of automatic recognition based on professional experience.

(19) Freedom of movement and the mutual recognition of the evidence of formal qualifications of doctors, nurses responsible for general care, dental practitioners, veterinary surgeons, midwives, pharmacists and architects should be based on the fundamental principle of automatic recognition of the evidence of formal qualifications on the basis of coordinated minimum conditions for training. In addition, access in the Member States to the professions of doctor, nurse responsible for general care, dental practitioner, veterinary surgeon, midwife and pharmacist should be made conditional upon the possession of a given qualification ensuring that the person concerned has undergone training which meets the minimum conditions laid down. This system should be supplemented by a number of acquired rights from which qualified professionals benefit under certain conditions.

(20) To allow for the characteristics of the qualification system for doctors and dentists and the related acquis communautaire in the area of mutual recognition, the principle of automatic recognition of medical and dental specialities common to at least two Member States should continue to apply to all specialities recognised on the date of adoption of this Directive. To simplify the system, however, automatic recognition should apply after the date of entry into force of this Directive only to those new medical specialities common to at least two fifths of Member States. Moreover, this Directive does not prevent Member States from agreeing amongst themselves on automatic recognition for certain medical and dental specialities common to them but not automatically recognised within the meaning of this Directive, according to their own rules.

(21) Automatic recognition of formal qualifications of doctor with basic training should be without prejudice to the competence of Member States to associate this qualification with professional activities or not.

(22) All Member States should recognise the profession of dental practitioner as a specific profession distinct from that of medical practitioner, whether or not specialised in odontostomatology. Member States should ensure that the training given to dental practitioners equips them with the skills needed for prevention, diagnosis and treatment relating to anomalies and illnesses of the teeth, mouth, jaws and associated tissues. The professional activity of the dental practitioner should be carried out by holders of a qualification as dental practitioner set out in this Directive.

(23) It did not appear desirable to lay down standardised training for midwives for all the Member States. Rather, the latter should have the greatest possible freedom to organise their training.

(24) With a view to simplifying this Directive, reference should be made to the concept of 'pharmacist' in order to delimit the scope of the provisions relating to the automatic recognition of the qualifications, without prejudice to the special features of the national regulations governing those activities.

(25) Holders of qualifications as a pharmacist are specialists in the field of medicines and should, in principle, have access in all Member States to a minimum range of activities in this field. In defining this minimum range, this Directive should neither have the effect of limiting the activities accessible to pharmacists in the Member States, in particular as regards medical biology analyses, nor create a monopoly for those professionals, as this remains a matter solely for the Member States. The provisions of this Directive are without prejudice to the possibility for the Member States to impose supplementary training conditions for access to activities not included in the coordinated minimum range of activities. This means that the host Member State should be able to impose these conditions on the nationals who hold qualifications which are covered by automatic recognition within the meaning of this Directive.

(26) This Directive does not coordinate all the conditions for access to activities in the field of pharmacy and the pursuit of these activities. In particular, the geographical distribution of pharmacies and the monopoly for dispensing medicines should remain a matter for the Member States. This Directive leaves unchanged the legislative, regulatory and administrative provisions of the Member

PART III   EUROPEAN UNION

States forbidding companies from pursuing certain pharmacists' activities or subjecting the pursuit of such activities to certain conditions.

(27) Architectural design, the quality of buildings, their harmonious incorporation into their surroundings, respect for natural and urban landscapes and for the public and private heritage are a matter of public interest. Mutual recognition of qualifications should therefore be based on qualitative and quantitative criteria which ensure that the holders of recognised qualifications are in a position to understand and translate the needs of individuals, social groups and authorities as regards spatial planning, the design, organisation and realisation of structures, conservation and the exploitation of the architectural heritage, and protection of natural balances.

(28) National regulations in the field of architecture and on access to and the pursuit of the professional activities of an architect vary widely in scope. In most Member States, activities in the field of architecture are pursued, de jure or de facto, by persons bearing the title of architect alone or accompanied by another title, without those persons having a monopoly on the pursuit of such activities, unless there are legislative provisions to the contrary. These activities, or some of them, may also be pursued by other professionals, in particular by engineers who have undergone special training in the field of construction or the art of building. With a view to simplifying this Directive, reference should be made to the concept of 'architect' in order to delimit the scope of the provisions relating to the automatic recognition of the qualifications in the field of architecture, without prejudice to the special features of the national regulations governing those activities.

(29) Where a national and European–level professional organisation or association for a regulated profession makes a reasoned request for specific provisions for the recognition of qualifications on the basis of coordination of minimum training conditions, the Commission shall assess the appropriateness of adopting a proposal for the amendment of this Directive.

(30) In order to ensure the effectiveness of the system for the recognition of professional qualifications, uniform formalities and rules of procedure should be defined for its implementation, as well as certain details of the pursuit of the profession.

(31) Since collaboration among the Member States and between them and the Commission is likely to facilitate the implementation of this Directive and compliance with the obligations deriving from it, the means of collaboration should be organised.

(32) The introduction, at European level, of professional cards by professional associations or organisations could facilitate the mobility of professionals, in particular by speeding up the exchange of information between the host Member State and the Member State of origin. This professional card should make it possible to monitor the career of professionals who establish themselves in various Member States. Such cards could contain information, in full respect of data protection provisions, on the professional's professional qualifications (university or institution attended, qualifications obtained, professional experience), his legal establishment, penalties received relating to his profession and the details of the relevant competent authority.

(33) The establishment of a network of contact points with the task of providing the citizens of the Member States with information and assistance will make it possible to ensure that the system of recognition is transparent. These contact points will provide any citizen who so requests and the Commission with all the information and addresses relevant to the recognition procedure. The designation of a single contact point by each Member State within this network does not affect the organisation of competencies at national level. In particular, it does not prevent the designation at national level of several offices, the contact point designated within the aforementioned network being in charge of coordinating with the other offices and informing the citizen, where necessary, of the details of the relevant competent office.

(34) Administering the various systems of recognition set up by the sectoral directives and the general system has proved cumbersome and complex. There is therefore a need to simplify the administration and updating of this Directive to take account of scientific and technical progress, in particular where the minimum conditions of training are coordinated with a view to automatic recognition of qualifications. A single committee for the recognition of professional qualifications should be set up for this purpose, and suitable involvement of representatives of the professional organisations, also at European level, should be ensured.

(35) The measures necessary for the implementation of this Directive should be adopted in accordance with Council Decision 1999/468/EC of 28 June 1999 laying down the procedures for the exercise of implementing powers conferred on the Commission.

(36) The preparation by the Member States of a periodic report on the implementation of this Directive, containing statistical data, will make it possible to determine the impact of the system for the recognition of professional qualifications.

(37) There should be a suitable procedure for adopting temporary measures if the application of any

provision of this Directive were to encounter major difficulties in a Member State.

(38) The provisions of this Directive do not affect the powers of the Member States as regards the organisation of their national social security system and determining the activities which must be pursued under that system.

(39) In view of the speed of technological change and scientific progress, life–long learning is of particular importance for a large number of professions. In this context, it is for the Member States to adopt the detailed arrangements under which, through suitable ongoing training, professionals will keep abreast of technical and scientific progress.

(40) Since the objectives of this Directive, namely the rationalisation, simplification and improvement of the rules for the recognition of professional qualifications, cannot be sufficiently achieved by the Member States and can therefore be better achieved at Community level, the Community may adopt measures, in accordance with the principle of subsidiarity as set out in Article 5 of the Treaty. In accordance with the principle of proportionality, as set out in that Article, this Directive does not go beyond what is necessary in order to achieve those objectives.

(41) This Directive is without prejudice to the application of Articles 39(4) and 45 of the Treaty concerning notably notaries.

(42) This Directive applies, concerning the right of establishment and the provision of services, without prejudice to other specific legal provisions regarding the recognition of professional qualifications, such as those existing in the field of transport, insurance intermediaries and statutory auditors. This Directive does not affect the operation of Council Directive 77/249/EEC of 22 March 1977 to facilitate the effective exercise by lawyers of freedom to provide services, or of Directive 98/5/EC of the European Parliament and of the Council of 16 February 1998 to facilitate practice of the profession of lawyer on a permanent basis in a Member State other than that in which the qualification was obtained. The recognition of professional qualifications for lawyers for the purpose of immediate establishment under the professional title of the host Member State should be covered by this Directive.

(43) To the extent that they are regulated, this Directive includes also liberal professions, which are, according to this Directive, those practised on the basis of relevant professional qualifications in a personal, responsible and professionally independent capacity by those providing intellectual and conceptual services in the interest of the client and the public. The exercise of the profession might be subject in the Member States, in conformity with the Treaty, to specific legal constraints based on national legislation and on the statutory provisions laid down autonomously, within that framework, by the respective professional representative bodies, safeguarding and developing their professionalism and quality of service and the confidentiality of relations with the client.

(44) This Directive is without prejudice to measures necessary to ensure a high level of health and consumer protection,

HAVE ADOPTED THIS DIRECTIVE:

Title I. General Provisions

Article 1. Purpose

This Directive establishes rules according to which a Member State which makes access to or pursuit of a regulated profession in its territory contingent upon possession of specific professional qualifications (referred to hereinafter as the host Member State) shall recognise professional qualifications obtained in one or more other Member States (referred to hereinafter as the home Member State) and which allow the holder of the said qualifications to pursue the same profession there, for access to and pursuit of that profession.

Article 2. Scope

(1) This Directive shall apply to all nationals of a Member State wishing to pursue a regulated profession in a Member State, including those belonging to the liberal professions, other than that in which they obtained their professional qualifications, on either a self–employed or employed basis.

(2) Each Member State may permit Member State nationals in possession of evidence of professional qualifications not obtained in a Member State to pursue a regulated profession within the meaning of Article 3(1)(a) on its territory in accordance with its rules. In the case of professions covered by Title III, Chapter III, this initial recognition shall respect the minimum training conditions laid down in that Chapter.

(3) Where, for a given regulated profession, other specific arrangements directly related to the recognition of professional qualifications are established in a separate instrument of Community law, the corresponding provisions of this Directive shall not apply.

Article 3. Definitions

PART III EUROPEAN UNION

(1) For the purposes of this Directive, the following definitions apply:
(a) 'regulated profession': a professional activity or group of professional activities, access to which, the pursuit of which, or one of the modes of pursuit of which is subject, directly or indirectly, by virtue of legislative, regulatory or administrative provisions to the possession of specific professional qualifications; in particular, the use of a professional title limited by legislative, regulatory or administrative provisions to holders of a given professional qualification shall constitute a mode of pursuit. Where the first sentence of this definition does not apply, a profession referred to in paragraph 2 shall be treated as a regulated profession;
(b) 'professional qualifications': qualifications attested by evidence of formal qualifications, an attestation of competence referred to in Article 11, point (a) (i) and/or professional experience;
(c) 'evidence of formal qualifications': diplomas, certificates and other evidence issued by an authority in a Member State designated pursuant to legislative, regulatory or administrative provisions of that Member State and certifying successful completion of professional training obtained mainly in the Community. Where the first sentence of this definition does not apply, evidence of formal qualifications referred to in paragraph 3 shall be treated as evidence of formal qualifications;
(d) 'competent authority': any authority or body empowered by a Member State specifically to issue or receive training diplomas and other documents or information and to receive the applications, and take the decisions, referred to in this Directive;
(e) 'regulated education and training': any training which is specifically geared to the pursuit of a given profession and which comprises a course or courses complemented, where appropriate, by professional training, or probationary or professional practice.
The structure and level of the professional training, probationary or professional practice shall be determined by the laws, regulations or administrative provisions of the Member State concerned or monitored or approved by the authority designated for that purpose;
(f) 'professional experience': the actual and lawful pursuit of the profession concerned in a Member State;
(g) 'adaptation period': the pursuit of a regulated profession in the host Member State under the responsibility of a qualified member of that profession, such period of supervised practice possibly being accompanied by further training. This period of supervised practice shall be the subject of an assessment. The detailed rules governing the adaptation period and its assessment as well as the status of a migrant under supervision shall be laid down by the competent authority in the host Member State.
The status enjoyed in the host Member State by the person undergoing the period of supervised practice, in particular in the matter of right of residence as well as obligations, social rights and benefits, allowances and remuneration, shall be established by the competent authorities in that Member State in accordance with applicable Community law;
(h) 'aptitude test': a test limited to the professional knowledge of the applicant, made by the competent authorities of the host Member State with the aim of assessing the ability of the applicant to pursue a regulated profession in that Member State. In order to permit this test to be carried out, the competent authorities shall draw up a list of subjects which, on the basis of a comparison of the education and training required in the Member State and that received by the applicant, are not covered by the diploma or other evidence of formal qualifications possessed by the applicant.
The aptitude test must take account of the fact that the applicant is a qualified professional in the home Member State or the Member State from which he comes. It shall cover subjects to be selected from those on the list, knowledge of which is essential in order to be able to pursue the profession in the host Member State. The test may also include knowledge of the professional rules applicable to the activities in question in the host Member State.
The detailed application of the aptitude test and the status, in the host Member State, of the applicant who wishes to prepare himself for the aptitude test in that State shall be determined by the competent authorities in that Member State;
(i) 'manager of an undertaking': any person who in an undertaking in the occupational field in question has pursued an activity:
(i) as a manager of an undertaking or a manager of a branch of an undertaking; or
(ii) as a deputy to the proprietor or the manager of an undertaking where that post involves responsibility equivalent to that of the proprietor or manager represented; or
(iii) in a managerial post with duties of a commercial and/or technical nature and with responsibility for one or more departments of the undertaking.
(2) A profession practised by the members of an association or organisation listed in Annex I shall be treated as a regulated profession.
The purpose of the associations or organisations referred to in the first subparagraph is, in particular,

to promote and maintain a high standard in the professional field concerned. To that end they are recognised in a special form by a Member State and award evidence of formal qualifications to their members, ensure that their members respect the rules of professional conduct which they prescribe, and confer on them the right to use a title or designatory letters or to benefit from a status corresponding to those formal qualifications.

On each occasion that a Member State grants recognition to an association or organisation referred to in the first subparagraph, it shall inform the Commission, which shall publish an appropriate notification in the *Official Journal of the European Union*.

(3) Evidence of formal qualifications issued by a third country shall be regarded as evidence of formal qualifications if the holder has three years' professional experience in the profession concerned on the territory of the Member State which recognised that evidence of formal qualifications in accordance with Article 2(2), certified by that Member State.

Article 4. Effects of recognition

(1) The recognition of professional qualifications by the host Member State allows the beneficiary to gain access in that Member State to the same profession as that for which he is qualified in the home Member State and to pursue it in the host Member State under the same conditions as its nationals.

(2) For the purposes of this Directive, the profession which the applicant wishes to pursue in the host Member State is the same as that for which he is qualified in his home Member State if the activities covered are comparable.

Title II. Free Provision of Services

Article 5. Principle of the free provision of services

(1) Without prejudice to specific provisions of Community law, as well as to Articles 6 and 7 of this Directive, Member States shall not restrict, for any reason relating to professional qualifications, the free provision of services in another Member State:

(a) if the service provider is legally established in a Member State for the purpose of pursuing the same profession there (hereinafter referred to as the Member State of establishment), and

(b) where the service provider moves, if he has pursued that profession in the Member State of establishment for at least two years during the 10 years preceding the provision of services when the profession is not regulated in that Member State. The condition requiring two years' pursuit shall not apply when either the profession or the education and training leading to the profession is regulated.

(2) The provisions of this title shall only apply where the service provider moves to the territory of the host Member State to pursue, on a temporary and occasional basis, the profession referred to in paragraph 1.

The temporary and occasional nature of the provision of services shall be assessed case by case, in particular in relation to its duration, its frequency, its regularity and its continuity.

(3) Where a service provider moves, he shall be subject to professional rules of a professional, statutory or administrative nature which are directly linked to professional qualifications, such as the definition of the profession, the use of titles and serious professional malpractice which is directly and specifically linked to consumer protection and safety, as well as disciplinary provisions which are applicable in the host Member State to professionals who pursue the same profession in that Member State.

Article 6. Exemptions

Pursuant to Article 5(1), the host Member State shall exempt service providers established in another Member State from the requirements which it places on professionals established in its territory relating to:

(a) authorisation by, registration with or membership of a professional organisation or body. In order to facilitate the application of disciplinary provisions in force on their territory according to Article 5(3), Member States may provide either for automatic temporary registration with or for pro forma membership of such a professional organisation or body, provided that such registration or membership does not delay or complicate in any way the provision of services and does not entail any additional costs for the service provider. A copy of the declaration and, where applicable, of the renewal referred to in Article 7(1), accompanied, for professions which have implications for public health and safety referred to in Article 7(4) or which benefit from automatic recognition under Title III Chapter III, by a copy of the documents referred to in Article 7(2) shall be sent by the competent authority to the relevant professional organisation or body, and this shall constitute automatic temporary registration or pro forma membership for this purpose;

(b) registration with a public social security body for the purpose of settling accounts with an insurer relating to activities pursued for the benefit of insured persons.

The service provider shall, however, inform in advance or, in an urgent case, afterwards, the body referred to in point (b) of the services which he has provided.

Article 7. Declaration to be made in advance, if the service provider moves

(1) Member States may require that, where the service provider first moves from one Member State to another in order to provide services, he shall inform the competent authority in the host Member State in a written declaration to be made in advance including the details of any insurance cover or other means of personal or collective protection with regard to professional liability. Such declaration shall be renewed once a year if the service provider intends to provide temporary or occasional services in that Member State during that year. The service provider may supply the declaration by any means.

(2) Moreover, for the first provision of services or if there is a material change in the situation substantiated by the documents, Member States may require that the declaration be accompanied by the following documents:
(a) proof of the nationality of the service provider;
(b) an attestation certifying that the holder is legally established in a Member State for the purpose of pursuing the activities concerned and that he is not prohibited from practising, even temporarily, at the moment of delivering the attestation;
(c) evidence of professional qualifications;
(d) for cases referred to in Article 5(1)(b), any means of proof that the service provider has pursued the activity concerned for at least two years during the previous ten years;
(e) for professions in the security sector, where the Member State so requires for its own nationals, evidence of no criminal convictions.

(3) The service shall be provided under the professional title of the Member State of establishment, in so far as such a title exists in that Member State for the professional activity in question. That title shall be indicated in the official language or one of the official languages of the Member State of establishment in such a way as to avoid any confusion with the professional title of the host Member State. Where no such professional title exists in the Member State of establishment, the service provider shall indicate his formal qualification in the official language or one of the official languages of that Member State. By way of exception, the service shall be provided under the professional title of the host Member State for cases referred to in Title III Chapter III.

(4) For the first provision of services, in the case of regulated professions having public health or safety implications, which do not benefit from automatic recognition under Title III Chapter III, the competent authority of the host Member State may check the professional qualifications of the service provider prior to the first provision of services. Such a prior check shall be possible only where the purpose of the check is to avoid serious damage to the health or safety of the service recipient due to a lack of professional qualification of the service provider and where this does not go beyond what is necessary for that purpose.

Within a maximum of one month of receipt of the declaration and accompanying documents, the competent authority shall endeavour to inform the service provider either of its decision not to check his qualifications or of the outcome of such check. Where there is a difficulty which would result in delay, the competent authority shall notify the service provider within the first month of the reason for the delay and the timescale for a decision, which must be finalised within the second month of receipt of completed documentation.

Where there is a substantial difference between the professional qualifications of the service provider and the training required in the host Member State, to the extent that that difference is such as to be harmful to public health or safety, the host Member State shall give the service provider the opportunity to show, in particular by means of an aptitude test, that he has acquired the knowledge or competence lacking. In any case, it must be possible to provide the service within one month of a decision being taken in accordance with the previous subparagraph.

In the absence of a reaction of the competent authority within the deadlines set in the previous subparagraphs, the service may be provided.

In cases where qualifications have been verified under this paragraph, the service shall be provided under the professional title of the host Member State.

Article 8. Administrative cooperation

(1) The competent authorities of the host Member State may ask the competent authorities of the Member State of establishment, for each provision of services, to provide any information relevant to the legality of the service provider's establishment and his good conduct, as well as the absence of any disciplinary or criminal sanctions of a professional nature. The competent authorities of the Member State of establishment shall provide this information in accordance with the provisions of

Article 56.
(2) The competent authorities shall ensure the exchange of all information necessary for complaints by a recipient of a service against a service provider to be correctly pursued. Recipients shall be informed of the outcome of the complaint.

Article 9. Information to be given to the recipients of the service

In cases where the service is provided under the professional title of the Member State of establishment or under the formal qualification of the service provider, in addition to the other requirements relating to information contained in Community law, the competent authorities of the host Member State may require the service provider to furnish the recipient of the service with any or all of the following information:
(a) if the service provider is registered in a commercial register or similar public register, the register in which he is registered, his registration number, or equivalent means of identification contained in that register;
(b) if the activity is subject to authorisation in the Member State of establishment, the name and address of the competent supervisory authority;
(c) any professional association or similar body with which the service provider is registered;
(d) the professional title or, where no such title exists, the formal qualification of the service provider and the Member State in which it was awarded;
(e) if the service provider performs an activity which is subject to VAT, the VAT identification number referred to in Article 22(1) of the sixth Council Directive 77/388/EEC of 17 May 1977 on the harmonisation of the laws of the Member States relating to turnover taxes – Common system of value added tax: uniform basis of assessment;
(f) details of any insurance cover or other means of personal or collective protection with regard to professional liability.

Title III. Freedom of Establishment

Chapter I. General System for the Recognition of Evidence of Training

Article 10. Scope

This Chapter applies to all professions which are not covered by Chapters II and III of this Title and in the following cases in which the applicant, for specific and exceptional reasons, does not satisfy the conditions laid down in those Chapters:
(a) for activities listed in Annex IV, when the migrant does not meet the requirements set out in Articles 17, 18 and 19;
(b) for doctors with basic training, specialised doctors, nurses responsible for general care, dental practitioners, specialised dental practitioners, veterinary surgeons, midwives, pharmacists and architects, when the migrant does not meet the requirements of effective and lawful professional practice referred to in Articles 23, 27, 33, 37, 39, 43 and 49;
(c) for architects, when the migrant holds evidence of formal qualification not listed in Annex V, point 5.7;
(d) without prejudice to Articles 21(1), 23 and 27, for doctors, nurses, dental practitioners, veterinary surgeons, midwives, pharmacists and architects holding evidence of formal qualifications as a specialist, which must follow the training leading to the possession of a title listed in Annex V, points 5.1.1, 5.2.2, 5.3.2, 5.4.2, 5.5.2, 5.6.2 and 5.7.1, and solely for the purpose of the recognition of the relevant specialty;
(e) for nurses responsible for general care and specialised nurses holding evidence of formal qualifications as a specialist which follows the training leading to the possession of a title listed in Annex V, point 5.2.2, when the migrant seeks recognition in another Member State where the relevant professional activities are pursued by specialised nurses without training as general care nurse;
(f) for specialised nurses without training as general care nurse, when the migrant seeks recognition in another Member State where the relevant professional activities are pursued by nurses responsible for general care, specialised nurses without training as general care nurse or specialised nurses holding evidence of formal qualifications as a specialist which follows the training leading to the possession of the titles listed in Annex V, point 5.2.2;
(g) for migrants meeting the requirements set out in Article 3(3).

Article 11. Levels of qualification

For the purpose of applying Article 13, the professional qualifications are grouped under the following levels as described below:
(a) an attestation of competence issued by a competent authority in the home Member State desig-

nated pursuant to legislative, regulatory or administrative provisions of that Member State, on the basis of:
(i) either a training course not forming part of a certificate or diploma within the meaning of points (b), (c), (d) or (e), or a specific examination without prior training, or full–time pursuit of the profession in a Member State for three consecutive years or for an equivalent duration on a part–time basis during the previous 10 years,
(ii) or general primary or secondary education, attesting that the holder has acquired general knowledge;
(b) a certificate attesting to a successful completion of a secondary course,
(i) either general in character, supplemented by a course of study or professional training other than those referred to in point (c) and/or by the probationary or professional practice required in addition to that course,
(ii) or technical or professional in character, supplemented where appropriate by a course of study or professional training as referred to in point (i), and/or by the probationary or professional practice required in addition to that course;
(c) a diploma certifying successful completion of
(i) either training at post–secondary level other than that referred to in points (d) and (e) of a duration of at least one year or of an equivalent duration on a part–time basis, one of the conditions of entry of which is, as a general rule, the successful completion of the secondary course required to obtain entry to university or higher education or the completion of equivalent school education of the second secondary level, as well as the professional training which may be required in addition to that post–secondary course; or
(ii) in the case of a regulated profession, training with a special structure, included in Annex II, equivalent to the level of training provided for under (i), which provides a comparable professional standard and which prepares the trainee for a comparable level of responsibilities and functions. The list in Annex II may be amended in accordance with the procedure referred to in Article 58(2) in order to take account of training which meets the requirements provided for in the previous sentence;
(d) a diploma certifying successful completion of training at post–secondary level of at least three and not more than four years' duration, or of an equivalent duration on a part–time basis, at a university or establishment of higher education or another establishment providing the same level of training, as well as the professional training which may be required in addition to that post–secondary course;
(e) a diploma certifying that the holder has successfully completed a post–secondary course of at least four years' duration, or of an equivalent duration on a part–time basis, at a university or establishment of higher education or another establishment of equivalent level and, where appropriate, that he has successfully completed the professional training required in addition to the post–secondary course.

Article 12. Equal treatment of qualifications
Any evidence of formal qualifications or set of evidence of formal qualifications issued by a competent authority in a Member State, certifying successful completion of training in the Community which is recognised by that Member State as being of an equivalent level and which confers on the holder the same rights of access to or pursuit of a profession or prepares for the pursuit of that profession, shall be treated as evidence of formal qualifications of the type covered by Article 11, including the level in question.
Any professional qualification which, although not satisfying the requirements contained in the legislative, regulatory or administrative provisions in force in the home Member State for access to or the pursuit of a profession, confers on the holder acquired rights by virtue of these provisions, shall also be treated as such evidence of formal qualifications under the same conditions as set out in the first subparagraph. This applies in particular if the home Member State raises the level of training required for admission to a profession and for its exercise, and if an individual who has undergone former training, which does not meet the requirements of the new qualification, benefits from acquired rights by virtue of national legislative, regulatory or administrative provisions; in such case this former training is considered by the host Member State, for the purposes of the application of Article 13, as corresponding to the level of the new training.

Article 13. Conditions for recognition
(1) If access to or pursuit of a regulated profession in a host Member State is contingent upon possession of specific professional qualifications, the competent authority of that Member State shall permit access to and pursuit of that profession, under the same conditions as apply to its nationals, to applicants possessing the attestation of competence or evidence of formal qualifications required by another Member State in order to gain access to and pursue that profession on its territory.

Attestations of competence or evidence of formal qualifications shall satisfy the following conditions:
(a) they shall have been issued by a competent authority in a Member State, designated in accordance with the legislative, regulatory or administrative provisions of that Member State;
(b) they shall attest a level of professional qualification at least equivalent to the level immediately prior to that which is required in the host Member State, as described in Article 11.
(2) Access to and pursuit of the profession, as described in paragraph 1, shall also be granted to applicants who have pursued the profession referred to in that paragraph on a full–time basis for two years during the previous 10 years in another Member State which does not regulate that profession, providing they possess one or more attestations of competence or documents providing evidence of formal qualifications.
Attestations of competence and evidence of formal qualifications shall satisfy the following conditions:
(a) they shall have been issued by a competent authority in a Member State, designated in accordance with the legislative, regulatory or administrative provisions of that Member State;
(b) they shall attest a level of professional qualification at least equivalent to the level immediately prior to that required in the host Member State, as described in Article 11;
(c) they shall attest that the holder has been prepared for the pursuit of the profession in question.
The two years' professional experience referred to in the first subparagraph may not, however, be required if the evidence of formal qualifications which the applicant possesses certifies regulated education and training within the meaning of Article 3(1)(e) at the levels of qualifications described in Article 11, points (b), (c), (d) or (e). The regulated education and training listed in Annex III shall be considered as such regulated education and training at the level described in Article 11, point (c). The list in Annex III may be amended in accordance with the procedure referred to in Article 58(2) in order to take account of regulated education and training which provides a comparable professional standard and which prepares the trainee for a comparable level of responsibilities and functions.
(3) By way of derogation from paragraph 1, point (b) and to paragraph 2, point (b), the host Member State shall permit access and pursuit of a regulated profession where access to this profession is contingent in its territory upon possession of a qualification certifying successful completion of higher or university education of four years' duration, and where the applicant possesses a qualification referred to in Article 11, point (c).

Article 14. Compensation measures

(1) Article 13 does not preclude the host Member State from requiring the applicant to complete an adaptation period of up to three years or to take an aptitude test if:
(a) the duration of the training of which he provides evidence under the terms of Article 13, paragraph 1 or 2, is at least one year shorter than that required by the host Member State;
(b) the training he has received covers substantially different matters than those covered by the evidence of formal qualifications required in the host Member State;
(c) the regulated profession in the host Member State comprises one or more regulated professional activities which do not exist in the corresponding profession in the applicant's home Member State within the meaning of Article 4(2), and that difference consists in specific training which is required in the host Member State and which covers substantially different matters from those covered by the applicant's attestation of competence or evidence of formal qualifications.
(2) If the host Member State makes use of the option provided for in paragraph 1, it must offer the applicant the choice between an adaptation period and an aptitude test.
Where a Member State considers, with respect to a given profession, that it is necessary to derogate from the requirement, set out in the previous subparagraph, that it give the applicant a choice between an adaptation period and an aptitude test, it shall inform the other Member States and the Commission in advance and provide sufficient justification for the derogation.
If, after receiving all necessary information, the Commission considers that the derogation referred to in the second subparagraph is inappropriate or that it is not in accordance with Community law, it shall, within three months, ask the Member State in question to refrain from taking the envisaged measure. In the absence of a response from the Commission within the abovementioned deadline, the derogation may be applied.
(3) By way of derogation from the principle of the right of the applicant to choose, as laid down in paragraph 2, for professions whose pursuit requires precise knowledge of national law and in respect of which the provision of advice and/or assistance concerning national law is an essential and constant aspect of the professional activity, the host Member State may stipulate either an adaptation period or an aptitude test.
This applies also to the cases provided for in Article 10 points (b) and (c), in Article 10 point (d) con-

cerning doctors and dental practitioners, in Article 10 point (f) when the migrant seeks recognition in another Member State where the relevant professional activities are pursued by nurses responsible for general care or specialised nurses holding evidence of formal qualifications as a specialist which follows the training leading to the possession of the titles listed in Annex V, point 5.2.2 and in Article 10 point (g).

In the cases covered by Article 10 point (a), the host Member State may require an adaptation period or an aptitude test if the migrant envisages pursuing professional activities in a self–employed capacity or as a manager of an undertaking which require the knowledge and the application of the specific national rules in force, provided that knowledge and application of those rules are required by the competent authorities of the host Member State for access to such activities by its own nationals.

(4) For the purpose of applying paragraph 1 points (b) and (c), 'substantially different matters' means matters of which knowledge is essential for pursuing the profession and with regard to which the training received by the migrant shows important differences in terms of duration or content from the training required by the host Member State.

(5) Paragraph 1 shall be applied with due regard to the principle of proportionality. In particular, if the host Member State intends to require the applicant to complete an adaptation period or take an aptitude test, it must first ascertain whether the knowledge acquired by the applicant in the course of his professional experience in a Member State or in a third country, is of a nature to cover, in full or in part, the substantial difference referred to in paragraph 4.

Article 15. Waiving of compensation measures on the basis of common platforms

(1) For the purpose of this Article, 'common platforms' is defined as a set of criteria of professional qualifications which are suitable for compensating for substantial differences which have been identified between the training requirements existing in the various Member States for a given profession. These substantial differences shall be identified by comparison between the duration and contents of the training in at least two thirds of the Member States, including all Member States which regulate this profession. The differences in the contents of the training may result from substantial differences in the scope of the professional activities.

(2) Common platforms as defined in paragraph 1 may be submitted to the Commission by Member States or by professional associations or organisations which are representative at national and European level. If the Commission, after consulting the Member States, is of the opinion that a draft common platform facilitates the mutual recognition of professional qualifications, it may present draft measures with a view to their adoption in accordance with the procedure referred to in Article 58(2).

(3) Where the applicant's professional qualifications satisfy the criteria established in the measure adopted in accordance with paragraph 2, the host Member State shall waive the application of compensation measures under Article 14.

(4) Paragraphs 1 to 3 shall not affect the competence of Member States to decide the professional qualifications required for the pursuit of professions in their territory as well as the contents and the organisation of their systems of education and professional training.

(5) If a Member State considers that the criteria established in a measure adopted in accordance with paragraph 2 no longer offer adequate guarantees with regard to professional qualifications, it shall inform the Commission accordingly, which shall, if appropriate, present a draft measure in accordance with the procedure referred to in Article 58(2).

(6) The Commission shall, by 20 October 2010, submit to the European Parliament and the Council a report on the operation of this Article and, if necessary, appropriate proposals for amending this Article.

Chapter II. Recognition of Professional Experience

Article 16. Requirements regarding professional experience

If, in a Member State, access to or pursuit of one of the activities listed in Annex IV is contingent upon possession of general, commercial or professional knowledge and aptitudes, that Member State shall recognise previous pursuit of the activity in another Member State as sufficient proof of such knowledge and aptitudes. The activity must have been pursued in accordance with Articles 17, 18 and 19.

Article 17. Activities referred to in list I of Annex IV

(1) For the activities in list I of Annex IV, the activity in question must have been previously pursued:
(a) for six consecutive years on a self–employed basis or as a manager of an undertaking; or
(b) for three consecutive years on a self–employed basis or as a manager of an undertaking, where the beneficiary proves that he has received previous training of at least three years for the activity in

question, evidenced by a certificate recognised by the Member State or judged by a competent professional body to be fully valid; or

(c) for four consecutive years on a self–employed basis or as a manager of an undertaking, where the beneficiary can prove that he has received, for the activity in question, previous training of at least two years' duration, attested by a certificate recognised by the Member State or judged by a competent professional body to be fully valid; or

(d) for three consecutive years on a self–employed basis, if the beneficiary can prove that he has pursued the activity in question on an employed basis for at least five years; or

(e) for five consecutive years in an executive position, of which at least three years involved technical duties and responsibility for at least one department of the company, if the beneficiary can prove that he has received, for the activity in question, previous training of at least three years' duration, as attested by a certificate recognised by the Member State or judged by a competent professional body to be fully valid.

(2) In cases (a) and (d), the activity must not have finished more than 10 years before the date on which the complete application was submitted by the person concerned to the competent authority referred to in Article 56.

(3) Paragraph 1(e) shall not apply to activities in Group ex 855, hairdressing establishments, of the ISIC Nomenclature.

Article 18. Activities referred to in list II of Annex IV

(1) For the activities in list II of Annex IV, the activity in question must have been previously pursued:

(2) (a) for five consecutive years on a self–employed basis or as a manager of an undertaking, or

(b) for three consecutive years on a self–employed basis or as a manager of an undertaking, where the beneficiary proves that he has received previous training of at least three years for the activity in question, evidenced by a certificate recognised by the Member State or judged by a competent professional body to be fully valid, or

(c) for four consecutive years on a self–employed basis or as a manager of an undertaking, where the beneficiary can prove that he has received, for the activity in question, previous training of at least two years' duration, attested by a certificate recognised by the Member State or judged by a competent professional body to be fully valid, or

(d) for three consecutive years on a self–employed basis or as a manager of an undertaking, if the beneficiary can prove that he has pursued the activity in question on an employed basis for at least five years, or

(e) for five consecutive years on an employed basis, if the beneficiary can prove that he has received, for the activity in question, previous training of at least three years' duration, as attested by a certificate recognised by the Member State or judged by a competent professional body to be fully valid, or

(f) for six consecutive years on an employed basis, if the beneficiary can prove that he has received previous training in the activity in question of at least two years' duration, as attested by a certificate recognised by the Member State or judged by a competent professional body to be fully valid. In cases (a) and (d), the activity must not have finished more than 10 years before the date on which the complete application was submitted by the person concerned to the competent authority referred to in Article 56.

Article 19. Activities referred to in list III of Annex IV

(1) For the activities in list III of Annex IV, the activity in question must have been previously pursued:

(a) for three consecutive years, either on a self–employed basis or as a manager of an undertaking, or

(b) for two consecutive years, either on a self–employed basis or as a manager of an undertaking, if the beneficiary can prove that he has received previous training for the activity in question, as attested by a certificate recognised by the Member State or judged by a competent professional body to be fully valid, or

(c) for two consecutive years, either on a self–employed basis or as a manager of an undertaking, if the beneficiary can prove that he has pursued the activity in question on an employed basis for at least three years, or

(d) for three consecutive years, on an employed basis, if the beneficiary can prove that he has received previous training for the activity in question, as attested by a certificate recognised by the Member State or judged by a competent professional body to be fully valid.

(2) In cases (a) and (c), the activity must not have finished more than 10 years before the date on which the complete application was submitted by the person concerned to the competent authority referred to in Article 56.

PART III   EUROPEAN UNION

Article 20. Amendment of the lists of activities in Annex IV

The lists of activities in Annex IV which are the subject of recognition of professional experience pursuant to Article 16 may be amended in accordance with the procedure referred to in Article 58(2) with a view to updating or clarifying the nomenclature, provided that this does not involve any change in the activities related to the individual categories.

Chapter III. Recognition on the Basis of Coordination of Minimum Training Conditions

Section 1. General Provisions

Article 21. Principle of automatic recognition

(1) Each Member State shall recognise evidence of formal qualifications as doctor giving access to the professional activities of doctor with basic training and specialised doctor, as nurse responsible for general care, as dental practitioner, as specialised dental practitioner, as veterinary surgeon, as pharmacist and as architect, listed in Annex V, points 5.1.1, 5.1.2, 5.2.2, 5.3.2, 5.3.3, 5.4.2, 5.6.2 and 5.7.1 respectively, which satisfy the minimum training conditions referred to in Articles 24, 25, 31, 34, 35, 38, 44 and 46 respectively, and shall, for the purposes of access to and pursuit of the professional activities, give such evidence the same effect on its territory as the evidence of formal qualifications which it itself issues.

Such evidence of formal qualifications must be issued by the competent bodies in the Member States and accompanied, where appropriate, by the certificates listed in Annex V, points 5.1.1, 5.1.2, 5.2.2, 5.3.2, 5.3.3, 5.4.2, 5.6.2 and 5.7.1 respectively.

The provisions of the first and second subparagraphs do not affect the acquired rights referred to in Articles 23, 27, 33, 37, 39 and 49.

(2) Each Member State shall recognise, for the purpose of pursuing general medical practice in the framework of its national social security system, evidence of formal qualifications listed in Annex V, point 5.1.4 and issued to nationals of the Member States by the other Member States in accordance with the minimum training conditions laid down in Article 28.

The provisions of the previous subparagraph do not affect the acquired rights referred to in Article 30.

(3) Each Member State shall recognise evidence of formal qualifications as a midwife, awarded to nationals of Member States by the other Member States, listed in Annex V, point 5.5.2, which complies with the minimum training conditions referred to in Article 40 and satisfies the criteria set out in Article 41, and shall, for the purposes of access to and pursuit of the professional activities, give such evidence the same effect on its territory as the evidence of formal qualifications which it itself issues. This provision does not affect the acquired rights referred to in Articles 23 and 43.

(4) Member States shall not be obliged to give effect to evidence of formal qualifications referred to in Annex V, point 5.6.2, for the setting up of new pharmacies open to the public. For the purposes of this paragraph, pharmacies which have been open for less than three years shall also be considered as new pharmacies.

(5) Evidence of formal qualifications as an architect referred to in Annex V, point 5.7.1, which is subject to automatic recognition pursuant to paragraph 1, proves completion of a course of training which began not earlier than during the academic reference year referred to in that Annex.

(6) Each Member State shall make access to and pursuit of the professional activities of doctors, nurses responsible for general care, dental practitioners, veterinary surgeons, midwives and pharmacists subject to possession of evidence of formal qualifications referred to in Annex V, points 5.1.1, 5.1.2, 5.1.4, 5.2.2, 5.3.2, 5.3.3, 5.4.2, 5.5.2 and 5.6.2 respectively, attesting that the person concerned has acquired, over the duration of his training, and where appropriate, the knowledge and skills referred to in Articles 24(3), 31(6), 34(3), 38(3), 40(3) and 44(3).

The knowledge and skills referred to in Articles 24(3), 31(6), 34(3), 38(3), 40(3) and 44(3) may be amended in accordance with the procedure referred to in Article 58(2) with a view to adapting them to scientific and technical progress.

Such updates shall not entail, for any Member State, an amendment of its existing legislative principles regarding the structure of professions as regards training and conditions of access by natural persons.

(7) Each Member State shall notify the Commission of the legislative, regulatory and administrative provisions which it adopts with regard to the issuing of evidence of formal qualifications in the area covered by this Chapter. In addition, for evidence of formal qualifications in the area referred to in Section 8, this notification shall be addressed to the other Member States.

The Commission shall publish an appropriate communication in the *Official Journal of the European Union*, indicating the titles adopted by the Member States for evidence of formal qualifications and, where appropriate, the body which issues the evidence of formal qualifications, the certificate which accompanies it and the corresponding professional title referred to in Annex V, points 5.1.1, 5.1.2, 5.1.4, 5.2.2, 5.3.2, 5.3.3, 5.4.2, 5.5.2, 5.6.2 and 5.7.1 respectively.

Article 22. Common provisions on training
With regard to the training referred to in Articles 24, 25, 28, 31, 34, 35, 38, 40, 44 and 46:
(a) Member States may authorise part–time training under conditions laid down by the competent authorities; those authorities shall ensure that the overall duration, level and quality of such training is not lower than that of continuous full–time training;
(b) in accordance with the procedures specific to each Member State, continuing education and training shall ensure that persons who have completed their studies are able to keep abreast of professional developments to the extent necessary to maintain safe and effective practice.

Article 23. Acquired rights
(1) Without prejudice to the acquired rights specific to the professions concerned, in cases where the evidence of formal qualifications as doctor giving access to the professional activities of doctor with basic training and specialised doctor, as nurse responsible for general care, as dental practitioner, as specialised dental practitioner, as veterinary surgeon, as midwife and as pharmacist held by Member States nationals does not satisfy all the training requirements referred to in Articles 24, 25, 31, 34, 35, 38, 40 and 44, each Member State shall recognise as sufficient proof evidence of formal qualifications issued by those Member States insofar as such evidence attests successful completion of training which began before the reference dates laid down in Annex V, points 5.1.1, 5.1.2, 5.2.2, 5.3.2, 5.3.3, 5.4.2, 5.5.2 and 5.6.2 and is accompanied by a certificate stating that the holders have been effectively and lawfully engaged in the activities in question for at least three consecutive years during the five years preceding the award of the certificate.
(2) The same provisions shall apply to evidence of formal qualifications as doctor giving access to the professional activities of doctor with basic training and specialised doctor, as nurse responsible for general care, as dental practitioner, as specialised dental practitioner, as veterinary surgeon, as midwife and as pharmacist, obtained in the territory of the former German Democratic Republic, which does not satisfy all the minimum training requirements laid down in Articles 24, 25, 31, 34, 35, 38, 40 and 44 if such evidence certifies successful completion of training which began before:
(a) 3 October 1990 for doctors with basic training, nurses responsible for general care, dental practitioners with basic training, specialised dental practitioners, veterinary surgeons, midwives and pharmacists, and
(b) 3 April 1992 for specialised doctors.
The evidence of formal qualifications referred to in the first subparagraph confers on the holder the right to pursue professional activities throughout German territory under the same conditions as evidence of formal qualifications issued by the competent German authorities referred to in Annex V, points 5.1.1, 5.1.2, 5.2.2, 5.3.2, 5.3.3, 5.4.2, 5.5.2 and 5.6.2.
(3) Without prejudice to the provisions of Article 37(1), each Member State shall recognise evidence of formal qualifications as doctor giving access to the professional activities of doctor with basic training and specialised doctor, as nurse responsible for general care, as veterinary surgeon, as midwife, as pharmacist and as architect held by Member States nationals and issued by the former Czechoslovakia, or whose training commenced, for the Czech Republic and Slovakia, before 1 January 1993, where the authorities of either of the two aforementioned Member States attest that such evidence of formal qualifications has the same legal validity within their territory as the evidence of formal qualifications which they issue and, with respect to architects, as the evidence of formal qualifications specified for those Member States in Annex VI, point 6, as regards access to the professional activities of doctor with basic training, specialised doctor, nurse responsible for general care, veterinary surgeon, midwife, pharmacist with respect to the activities referred to in Article 45(2), and architect with respect to the activities referred to in Article 48, and the pursuit of such activities.
Such an attestation must be accompanied by a certificate issued by those same authorities stating that such persons have effectively and lawfully been engaged in the activities in question within their territory for at least three consecutive years during the five years prior to the date of issue of the certificate.
(4) Each Member State shall recognise evidence of formal qualifications as doctor giving access to the professional activities of doctor with basic training and specialised doctor, as nurse responsible for general care, as dental practitioner, as specialised dental practitioner, as veterinary surgeon, as midwife, as pharmacist and as architect held by nationals of the Member States and issued by the former Soviet Union, or whose training commenced
(a) for Estonia, before 20 August 1991,
(b) for Latvia, before 21 August 1991,

(c) for Lithuania, before 11 March 1990,
where the authorities of any of the three aforementioned Member States attest that such evidence has the same legal validity within their territory as the evidence which they issue and, with respect to architects, as the evidence of formal qualifications specified for those Member States in Annex VI, point 6, as regards access to the professional activities of doctor with basic training, specialised doctor, nurse responsible for general care, dental practitioner, specialised dental practitioner, veterinary surgeon, midwife, pharmacist with respect to the activities referred to in Article 45(2), and architect with respect to the activities referred to in Article 48, and the pursuit of such activities.

Such an attestation must be accompanied by a certificate issued by those same authorities stating that such persons have effectively and lawfully been engaged in the activities in question within their territory for at least three consecutive years during the five years prior to the date of issue of the certificate.

With regard to evidence of formal qualifications as veterinary surgeons issued by the former Soviet Union or in respect of which training commenced, for Estonia, before 20 August 1991, the attestation referred to in the preceding subparagraph must be accompanied by a certificate issued by the Estonian authorities stating that such persons have effectively and lawfully been engaged in the activities in question within their territory for at least five consecutive years during the seven years prior to the date of issue of the certificate.

(5) Each Member State shall recognise evidence of formal qualifications as doctor giving access to the professional activities of doctor with basic training and specialised doctor, as nurse responsible for general care, as dental practitioner, as specialised dental practitioner, as veterinary surgeon, as midwife, as pharmacist and as architect held by nationals of the Member States and issued by the former Yugoslavia, or whose training commenced, for Slovenia, before 25 June 1991, where the authorities of the aforementioned Member State attest that such evidence has the same legal validity within their territory as the evidence which they issue and, with respect to architects, as the evidence of formal qualifications specified for those Member States in Annex VI, point 6, as regards access to the professional activities of doctor with basic training, specialised doctor, nurse responsible for general care, dental practitioner, specialised dental practitioner, veterinary surgeon, midwife, pharmacist with respect to the activities referred to in Article 45(2), and architect with respect to the activities referred to in Article 48, and the pursuit of such activities.

Such an attestation must be accompanied by a certificate issued by those same authorities stating that such persons have effectively and lawfully been engaged in the activities in question within their territory for at least three consecutive years during the five years prior to the date of issue of the certificate.

(6) Each Member State shall recognise as sufficient proof for Member State nationals whose evidence of formal qualifications as a doctor, nurse responsible for general care, dental practitioner, veterinary surgeon, midwife and pharmacist does not correspond to the titles given for that Member State in Annex V, points 5.1.1, 5.1.2, 5.1.3, 5.1.4, 5.2.2, 5.3.2, 5.3.3, 5.4.2, 5.5.2 and 5.6.2, evidence of formal qualifications issued by those Member States accompanied by a certificate issued by the competent authorities or bodies.

The certificate referred to in the first subparagraph shall state that the evidence of formal qualifications certifies successful completion of training in accordance with Articles 24, 25, 28, 31, 34, 35, 38, 40 and 44 respectively and is treated by the Member State which issued it in the same way as the qualifications whose titles are listed in Annex V, points 5.1.1, 5.1.2, 5.1.3, 5.1.4, 5.2.2, 5.3.2, 5.3.3, 5.4.2, 5.5.2 and 5.6.2.

Section 2. Doctors of Medicine

Article 24. Basic medical training

(1) Admission to basic medical training shall be contingent upon possession of a diploma or certificate providing access, for the studies in question, to universities.

(2) Basic medical training shall comprise a total of at least six years of study or 5 500 hours of theoretical and practical training provided by, or under the supervision of, a university.

For persons who began their studies before 1 January 1972, the course of training referred to in the first subparagraph may comprise six months of full–time practical training at university level under the supervision of the competent authorities.

(3) Basic medical training shall provide an assurance that the person in question has acquired the following knowledge and skills:

(a) adequate knowledge of the sciences on which medicine is based and a good understanding of the scientific methods including the principles of measuring biological functions, the evaluation of scientifically established facts and the analysis of data;

(b) sufficient understanding of the structure, functions and behaviour of healthy and sick persons, as well as relations between the state of health and physical and social surroundings of the human being;
(c) adequate knowledge of clinical disciplines and practices, providing him with a coherent picture of mental and physical diseases, of medicine from the points of view of prophylaxis, diagnosis and therapy and of human reproduction;
(d) suitable clinical experience in hospitals under appropriate supervision.

Article 25. Specialist medical training

(1) Admission to specialist medical training shall be contingent upon completion and validation of six years of study as part of a training programme referred to in Article 24 in the course of which the trainee has acquired the relevant knowledge of basic medicine.
(2) Specialist medical training shall comprise theoretical and practical training at a university or medical teaching hospital or, where appropriate, a medical care establishment approved for that purpose by the competent authorities or bodies.
The Member States shall ensure that the minimum duration of specialist medical training courses referred to in Annex V, point 5.1.3 is not less than the duration provided for in that point. Training shall be given under the supervision of the competent authorities or bodies. It shall include personal participation of the trainee specialised doctor in the activity and responsibilities entailed by the services in question.
(3) Training shall be given on a full–time basis at specific establishments which are recognised by the competent authorities. It shall entail participation in the full range of medical activities of the department where the training is given, including duty on call, in such a way that the trainee specialist devotes all his professional activity to his practical and theoretical training throughout the entire working week and throughout the year, in accordance with the procedures laid down by the competent authorities. Accordingly, these posts shall be the subject of appropriate remuneration.
(4) The Member States shall make the issuance of evidence of specialist medical training contingent upon possession of evidence of basic medical training referred to in Annex V, point 5.1.1.
(5) The minimum periods of training referred to in Annex V, point 5.1.3 may be amended in accordance with the procedure referred to in Article 58(2) with a view to adapting them to scientific and technical progress.

Article 26. Types of specialist medical training

Evidence of formal qualifications as a specialised doctor referred to in Article 21 is such evidence awarded by the competent authorities or bodies referred to in Annex V, point 5.1.2 as corresponds, for the specialised training in question, to the titles in use in the various Member States and referred to in Annex V, point 5.1.3.
The inclusion in Annex V, point 5.1.3 of new medical specialties common to at least two fifths of the Member States may be decided on in accordance with the procedure referred to in Article 58(2) with a view to updating this Directive in the light of changes in national legislation.

Article 27. Acquired rights specific to specialised doctors

(1) A host Member State may require of specialised doctors whose part–time specialist medical training was governed by legislative, regulatory and administrative provisions in force as of 20 June 1975 and who began their specialist training no later than 31 December 1983 that their evidence of formal qualifications be accompanied by a certificate stating that they have been effectively and lawfully engaged in the relevant activities for at least three consecutive years during the five years preceding the award of that certificate.
(2) Every Member State shall recognise the qualification of specialised doctors awarded in Spain to doctors who completed their specialist training before 1 January 1995, even if that training does not satisfy the minimum training requirements provided for in Article 25, in so far as that qualification is accompanied by a certificate issued by the competent Spanish authorities and attesting that the person concerned has passed the examination in specific professional competence held in the context of exceptional measures concerning recognition laid down in Royal Decree 1497/99, with a view to ascertaining that the person concerned possesses a level of knowledge and skill comparable to that of doctors who possess a qualification as a specialised doctor defined for Spain in Annex V, points 5.1.2 and 5.1.3.
(3) Every Member State which has repealed its legislative, regulatory or administrative provisions relating to the award of evidence of formal qualifications as a specialised doctor referred to in Annex V, points 5.1.2 and 5.1.3 and which has adopted measures relating to acquired rights benefiting its nationals, shall grant nationals of other Member States the right to benefit from those measures, in so far as such evidence of formal qualifications was issued before the date on which the host

Member State ceased to issue such evidence for the specialty in question.
The dates on which these provisions were repealed are set out in Annex V, point 5.1.3.

Article 28. Specific training in general medical practice

(1) Admission to specific training in general medical practice shall be contingent on the completion and validation of six years of study as part of a training programme referred to in Article 24.

(2) The specific training in general medical practice leading to the award of evidence of formal qualifications issued before 1 January 2006 shall be of a duration of at least two years on a full–time basis. In the case of evidence of formal qualifications issued after that date, the training shall be of a duration of at least three years on a full–time basis.

Where the training programme referred to in Article 24 comprises practical training given by an approved hospital possessing appropriate general medical equipment and services or as part of an approved general medical practice or an approved centre in which doctors provide primary medical care, the duration of that practical training may, up to a maximum of one year, be included in the duration provided for in the first subparagraph for certificates of training issued on or after 1 January 2006.

The option provided for in the second subparagraph shall be available only for Member States in which the specific training in general medical practice lasted two years as of 1 January 2001.

(3) The specific training in general medical practice shall be carried out on a full–time basis, under the supervision of the competent authorities or bodies. It shall be more practical than theoretical.

The practical training shall be given, on the one hand, for at least six months in an approved hospital possessing appropriate equipment and services and, on the other hand, for at least six months as part of an approved general medical practice or an approved centre at which doctors provide primary health care.

The practical training shall take place in conjunction with other health establishments or structures concerned with general medicine. Without prejudice to the minimum periods laid down in the second subparagraph, however, the practical training may be given during a period of not more than six months in other approved establishments or health structures concerned with general medicine.

The training shall require the personal participation of the trainee in the professional activity and responsibilities of the persons with whom he is working.

(4) Member States shall make the issuance of evidence of formal qualifications in general medical practice subject to possession of evidence of formal qualifications in basic medical training referred to in Annex V, point 5.1.1.

(5) Member States may issue evidence of formal qualifications referred to in Annex V, point 5.1.4 to a doctor who has not completed the training provided for in this Article but who has completed a different, supplementary training, as attested by evidence of formal qualifications issued by the competent authorities in a Member State. They may not, however, award evidence of formal qualifications unless it attests knowledge of a level qualitatively equivalent to the knowledge acquired from the training provided for in this Article.

Member States shall determine, *inter alia*, the extent to which the complementary training and professional experience already acquired by the applicant may replace the training provided for in this Article.

The Member States may only issue the evidence of formal qualifications referred to in Annex V, point 5.1.4 if the applicant has acquired at least six months' experience of general medicine in a general medical practice or a centre in which doctors provide primary health care of the types referred to in paragraph 3.

Article 29. Pursuit of the professional activities of general practitioners

Each Member State shall, subject to the provisions relating to acquired rights, make the pursuit of the activities of a general practitioner in the framework of its national social security system contingent upon possession of evidence of formal qualifications referred to in Annex V, point 5.1.4.

Member States may exempt persons who are currently undergoing specific training in general medicine from this condition.

Article 30. Acquired rights specific to general practitioners

(1) Each Member State shall determine the acquired rights. It shall, however, confer as an acquired right the right to pursue the activities of a general practitioner in the framework of its national social security system, without the evidence of formal qualifications referred to in Annex V, point 5.1.4, on all doctors who enjoy this right as of the reference date stated in that point by virtue of provisions applicable to the medical profession giving access to the professional activities of doctor with basic training and who are established as of that date on its territory, having benefited from the provisions

of Articles 21 or 23.
The competent authorities of each Member State shall, on demand, issue a certificate stating the holder's right to pursue the activities of general practitioner in the framework of their national social security systems, without the evidence of formal qualifications referred to in Annex V, point 5.1.4, to doctors who enjoy acquired rights pursuant to the first subparagraph.
(2) Every Member State shall recognise the certificates referred to in paragraph 1, second subparagraph, awarded to nationals of Member States by the other Member States, and shall give such certificates the same effect on its territory as evidence of formal qualifications which it awards and which permit the pursuit of the activities of a general practitioner in the framework of its national social security system.

Section 3. Nurses Responsible for General Care

Article 31. Training of nurses responsible for general care

(1) Admission to training for nurses responsible for general care shall be contingent upon completion of general education of 10 years, as attested by a diploma, certificate or other evidence issued by the competent authorities or bodies in a Member State or by a certificate attesting success in an examination, of an equivalent level, for admission to a school of nursing.
(2) Training of nurses responsible for general care shall be given on a full–time basis and shall include at least the programme described in Annex V, point 5.2.1.
The content listed in Annex V, point 5.2.1 may be amended in accordance with the procedure referred to in Article 58(2) with a view to adapting it to scientific and technical progress.
Such updates may not entail, for any Member State, any amendment of its existing legislative principles relating to the structure of professions as regards training and the conditions of access by natural persons.
(3) The training of nurses responsible for general care shall comprise at least three years of study or 4 600 hours of theoretical and clinical training, the duration of the theoretical training representing at least one–third and the duration of the clinical training at least one half of the minimum duration of the training. Member States may grant partial exemptions to persons who have received part of their training on courses which are of at least an equivalent level.
The Member States shall ensure that institutions providing nursing training are responsible for the coordination of theoretical and clinical training throughout the entire study programme.
(4) Theoretical training is that part of nurse training from which trainee nurses acquire the professional knowledge, insights and skills necessary for organising, dispensing and evaluating overall health care. The training shall be given by teachers of nursing care and by other competent persons, in nursing schools and other training establishments selected by the training institution.
(5) Clinical training is that part of nurse training in which trainee nurses learn, as part of a team and in direct contact with a healthy or sick individual and/or community, to organise, dispense and evaluate the required comprehensive nursing care, on the basis of the knowledge and skills which they have acquired. The trainee nurse shall learn not only how to work in a team, but also how to lead a team and organise overall nursing care, including health education for individuals and small groups, within the health institute or in the community.
This training shall take place in hospitals and other health institutions and in the community, under the responsibility of nursing teachers, in cooperation with and assisted by other qualified nurses. Other qualified personnel may also take part in the teaching process.
Trainee nurses shall participate in the activities of the department in question insofar as those activities are appropriate to their training, enabling them to learn to assume the responsibilities involved in nursing care.
(6) Training for nurses responsible for general care shall provide an assurance that the person in question has acquired the following knowledge and skills:
(a) adequate knowledge of the sciences on which general nursing is based, including sufficient understanding of the structure, physiological functions and behaviour of healthy and sick persons, and of the relationship between the state of health and the physical and social environment of the human being;
(b) sufficient knowledge of the nature and ethics of the profession and of the general principles of health and nursing;
(c) adequate clinical experience; such experience, which should be selected for its training value, should be gained under the supervision of qualified nursing staff and in places where the number of qualified staff and equipment are appropriate for the nursing care of the patient;
(d) the ability to participate in the practical training of health personnel and experience of working with such personnel;
(e) experience of working with members of other professions in the health sector.

PART III EUROPEAN UNION

Article 32. Pursuit of the professional activities of nurses responsible for general care
For the purposes of this Directive, the professional activities of nurses responsible for general care are the activities pursued on a professional basis and referred to in Annex V, point 5.2.2.

Article 33. Acquired rights specific to nurses responsible for general care
(1) Where the general rules of acquired rights apply to nurses responsible for general care, the activities referred to in Article 23 must have included full responsibility for the planning, organisation and administration of nursing care delivered to the patient.
(2) As regards the Polish qualification of nurse responsible for general care, only the following acquired rights provisions shall apply. In the case of nationals of the Member States whose evidence of formal qualifications as nurse responsible for general care was awarded by, or whose training started in, Poland before 1 May 2004 and who do not satisfy the minimum training requirements laid down in Article 31, Member States shall recognise the following evidence of formal qualifications as nurse responsible for general care as being sufficient proof if accompanied by a certificate stating that those Member State nationals have effectively and lawfully been engaged in the activities of a nurse responsible for general care in Poland for the period specified below:
(a) evidence of formal qualifications as a nurse at degree level (dyplom licencjata pielęgniarstwa) — at least three consecutive years during the five years prior to the date of issue of the certificate,
(b) evidence of formal qualifications as a nurse certifying completion of post–secondary education obtained from a medical vocational school (dyplom pielęgniarki albo pielęgniarki dyplomowanej) — at least five consecutive years during the seven years prior to the date of issue of the certificate.
The said activities must have included taking full responsibility for the planning, organisation and administration of nursing care delivered to the patient.
(3) Member States shall recognise evidence of formal qualifications in nursing awarded in Poland, to nurses who completed training before 1 May 2004, which did not comply with the minimum training requirements laid down in Article 31, attested by the diploma 'bachelor' which has been obtained on the basis of a special upgrading programme contained in Article 11 of the Act of 20 April 2004 on the amendment of the Act on professions of nurse and midwife and on some other legal acts (Official Journal of the Republic of Poland of 30 April 2004 No 92, pos. 885), and the Regulation of the Minister of Health of 11 May 2004 on the detailed conditions of delivering studies for nurses and midwives, who hold a certificate of secondary school (final examination — matura) and are graduates of medical lyceum and medical vocational schools teaching in a profession of a nurse and a midwife (Official Journal of the Republic of Poland of 13 May 2004 No 110, pos. 1170), with the aim of verifying that the person concerned has a level of knowledge and competence comparable to that of nurses holding the qualifications which, in the case of Poland, are defined in Annex V, point 5.2.2.

Section 4. Dental Practitioners

Article 34. Basic dental training
(1) Admission to basic dental training presupposes possession of a diploma or certificate giving access, for the studies in question, to universities or higher institutes of a level recognised as equivalent, in a Member State.
(2) Basic dental training shall comprise a total of at least five years of full–time theoretical and practical study, comprising at least the programme described in Annex V, point 5.3.1 and given in a university, in a higher institute providing training recognised as being of an equivalent level or under the supervision of a university.
The content listed in Annex V, point 5.3.1 may be amended in accordance with the procedure referred to in Article 58(2) with a view to adapting it to scientific and technical progress.
Such updates may not entail, for any Member State, any amendment of its existing legislative principles relating to the system of professions as regards training and the conditions of access by natural persons.
(3) Basic dental training shall provide an assurance that the person in question has acquired the following knowledge and skills:
(a) adequate knowledge of the sciences on which dentistry is based and a good understanding of scientific methods, including the principles of measuring biological functions, the evaluation of scientifically established facts and the analysis of data;
(b) adequate knowledge of the constitution, physiology and behaviour of healthy and sick persons as well as the influence of the natural and social environment on the state of health of the human being, in so far as these factors affect dentistry;
(c) adequate knowledge of the structure and function of the teeth, mouth, jaws and associated tissues, both healthy and diseased, and their relationship to the general state of health and to the physical and

social well-being of the patient;
(d) adequate knowledge of clinical disciplines and methods, providing the dentist with a coherent picture of anomalies, lesions and diseases of the teeth, mouth, jaws and associated tissues and of preventive, diagnostic and therapeutic dentistry;
(e) suitable clinical experience under appropriate supervision.
This training shall provide him with the skills necessary for carrying out all activities involving the prevention, diagnosis and treatment of anomalies and diseases of the teeth, mouth, jaws and associated tissues.

Article 35. Specialist dental training

(1) Admission to specialist dental training shall entail the completion and validation of five years of theoretical and practical instruction within the framework of the training referred to in Article 34, or possession of the documents referred to in Articles 23 and 37.
(2) Specialist dental training shall comprise theoretical and practical instruction in a university centre, in a treatment teaching and research centre or, where appropriate, in a health establishment approved for that purpose by the competent authorities or bodies.
Full-time specialist dental courses shall be of a minimum of three years' duration supervised by the competent authorities or bodies. It shall involve the personal participation of the dental practitioner training to be a specialist in the activity and in the responsibilities of the establishment concerned.
The minimum period of training referred to in the second subparagraph may be amended in accordance with the procedure referred to in Article 58(2) with a view to adapting it to scientific and technical progress.
(3) The Member States shall make the issuance of evidence of specialist dental training contingent upon possession of evidence of basic dental training referred to in Annex V, point 5.3.2.

Article 36. Pursuit of the professional activities of dental practitioners

(1) For the purposes of this Directive, the professional activities of dental practitioners are the activities defined in paragraph 3 and pursued under the professional qualifications listed in Annex V, point 5.3.2.
(2) The profession of dental practitioner shall be based on dental training referred to in Article 34 and shall constitute a specific profession which is distinct from other general or specialised medical professions. Pursuit of the activities of a dental practitioner requires the possession of evidence of formal qualifications referred to in Annex V, point 5.3.2. Holders of such evidence of formal qualifications shall be treated in the same way as those to whom Articles 23 or 37 apply.
(3) The Member States shall ensure that dental practitioners are generally able to gain access to and pursue the activities of prevention, diagnosis and treatment of anomalies and diseases affecting the teeth, mouth, jaws and adjoining tissue, having due regard to the regulatory provisions and rules of professional ethics on the reference dates referred to in Annex V, point 5.3.2.

Article 37. Acquired rights specific to dental practitioners

(1) Every Member State shall, for the purposes of the pursuit of the professional activities of dental practitioners under the qualifications listed in Annex V, point 5.3.2, recognise evidence of formal qualifications as a doctor issued in Italy, Spain, Austria, the Czech Republic and Slovakia to persons who began their medical training on or before the reference date stated in that Annex for the Member State concerned, accompanied by a certificate issued by the competent authorities of that Member State.
The certificate must show that the two following conditions are met:
(a) that the persons in question have been effectively, lawfully and principally engaged in that Member State in the activities referred to in Article 36 for at least three consecutive years during the five years preceding the award of the certificate;
(b) that those persons are authorised to pursue the said activities under the same conditions as holders of evidence of formal qualifications listed for that Member State in Annex V, point 5.3.2.
Persons who have successfully completed at least three years of study, certified by the competent authorities in the Member State concerned as being equivalent to the training referred to in Article 34, shall be exempt from the three–year practical work experience referred to in the second subparagraph, point (a).
With regard to the Czech Republic and Slovakia, evidence of formal qualifications obtained in the former Czechoslovakia shall be accorded the same level of recognition as Czech and Slovak evidence of formal qualifications and under the same conditions as set out in the preceding subparagraphs.
(2) Each Member State shall recognise evidence of formal qualifications as a doctor issued in Italy to persons who began their university medical training after 28 January 1980 and no later than

PART III EUROPEAN UNION

31 December 1984, accompanied by a certificate issued by the competent Italian authorities.
The certificate must show that the three following conditions are met:
(a) that the persons in question passed the relevant aptitude test held by the competent Italian authorities with a view to establishing that those persons possess a level of knowledge and skills comparable to that of persons possessing evidence of formal qualifications listed for Italy in Annex V, point 5.3.2;
(b) that they have been effectively, lawfully and principally engaged in the activities referred to in Article 36 in Italy for at least three consecutive years during the five years preceding the award of the certificate;
(c) that they are authorised to engage in or are effectively, lawfully and principally engaged in the activities referred to in Article 36, under the same conditions as the holders of evidence of formal qualifications listed for Italy in Annex V, point 5.3.2.
Persons who have successfully completed at least three years of study certified by the competent authorities as being equivalent to the training referred to in Article 34 shall be exempt from the aptitude test referred to in the second subparagraph, point (a).
Persons who began their university medical training after 31 December 1984 shall be treated in the same way as those referred to above, provided that the abovementioned three years of study began before 31 December 1994.

Section 5. Veterinary Surgeons

Article 38. The training of veterinary surgeons

(1) The training of veterinary surgeons shall comprise a total of at least five years of full–time theoretical and practical study at a university or at a higher institute providing training recognised as being of an equivalent level, or under the supervision of a university, covering at least the study programme referred to in Annex V, point 5.4.1.
The content listed in Annex V, point 5.4.1 may be amended in accordance with the procedure referred to in Article 58(2) with a view to adapting it to scientific and technical progress.
Such updates may not entail, for any Member State, any amendment of its existing legislative principles relating to the structure of professions as regards training and conditions of access by natural persons.
(2) Admission to veterinary training shall be contingent upon possession of a diploma or certificate entitling the holder to enter, for the studies in question, university establishments or institutes of higher education recognised by a Member State to be of an equivalent level for the purpose of the relevant study.
(3) Training as a veterinary surgeon shall provide an assurance that the person in question has acquired the following knowledge and skills:
(a) adequate knowledge of the sciences on which the activities of the veterinary surgeon are based;
(b) adequate knowledge of the structure and functions of healthy animals, of their husbandry, reproduction and hygiene in general, as well as their feeding, including the technology involved in the manufacture and preservation of foods corresponding to their needs;
(c) adequate knowledge of the behaviour and protection of animals;
(d) adequate knowledge of the causes, nature, course, effects, diagnosis and treatment of the diseases of animals, whether considered individually or in groups, including a special knowledge of the diseases which may be transmitted to humans;
(e) adequate knowledge of preventive medicine;
(f) adequate knowledge of the hygiene and technology involved in the production, manufacture and putting into circulation of animal foodstuffs or foodstuffs of animal origin intended for human consumption;
(g) adequate knowledge of the laws, regulations and administrative provisions relating to the subjects listed above;
(h) adequate clinical and other practical experience under appropriate supervision.

Article 39. Acquired rights specific to veterinary surgeons

Without prejudice to Article 23(4), with regard to nationals of Member States whose evidence of formal qualifications as a veterinary surgeon was issued by, or whose training commenced in, Estonia before 1 May 2004, Member States shall recognise such evidence of formal qualifications as a veterinary surgeon if it is accompanied by a certificate stating that such persons have effectively and lawfully been engaged in the activities in question in Estonia for at least five consecutive years during the seven years prior to the date of issue of the certificate.

Section 6. Midwives

Article 40. The training of midwives

(1) The training of midwives shall comprise a total of at least:
(a) specific full–time training as a midwife comprising at least three years of theoretical and practical study (route I) comprising at least the programme described in Annex V, point 5.5.1, or
(b) specific full–time training as a midwife of 18 months' duration (route II), comprising at least the study programme described in Annex V, point 5.5.1, which was not the subject of equivalent training of nurses responsible for general care.
The Member States shall ensure that institutions providing midwife training are responsible for coordinating theory and practice throughout the programme of study.
The content listed in Annex V, point 5.5.1 may be amended in accordance with the procedure referred to in Article 58(2) with a view to adapting it to scientific and technical progress.
Such updates must not entail, for any Member State, any amendment of existing legislative principles relating to the structure of professions as regards training and the conditions of access by natural persons.
(2) Access to training as a midwife shall be contingent upon one of the following conditions:
(a) completion of at least the first 10 years of general school education for route I, or
(b) possession of evidence of formal qualifications as a nurse responsible for general care referred to in Annex V, point 5.2.2 for route II.
(3) Training as a midwife shall provide an assurance that the person in question has acquired the following knowledge and skills:
(a) adequate knowledge of the sciences on which the activities of midwives are based, particularly obstetrics and gynaecology;
(b) adequate knowledge of the ethics of the profession and the professional legislation;
(c) detailed knowledge of biological functions, anatomy and physiology in the field of obstetrics and of the newly born, and also a knowledge of the relationship between the state of health and the physical and social environment of the human being, and of his behaviour;
(d) adequate clinical experience gained in approved institutions under the supervision of staff qualified in midwifery and obstetrics;
(e) adequate understanding of the training of health personnel and experience of working with such.

Article 41. Procedures for the recognition of evidence of formal qualifications as a midwife

(1) The evidence of formal qualifications as a midwife referred to in Annex V, point 5.5.2 shall be subject to automatic recognition pursuant to Article 21 in so far as they satisfy one of the following criteria:
(a) full–time training of at least three years as a midwife:
(i) either made contingent upon possession of a diploma, certificate or other evidence of qualification giving access to universities or higher education institutes, or otherwise guaranteeing an equivalent level of knowledge; or
(ii) followed by two years of professional practice for which a certificate has been issued in accordance with paragraph 2;
(b) full–time training as a midwife of at least two years or 3 600 hours, contingent upon possession of evidence of formal qualifications as a nurse responsible for general care referred to in Annex V, point 5.2.2;
(c) full–time training as a midwife of at least 18 months or 3 000 hours, contingent upon possession of evidence of formal qualifications as a nurse responsible for general care referred to in Annex V, point 5.2.2 and followed by one year's professional practice for which a certificate has been issued in accordance with paragraph 2.
(2) The certificate referred to in paragraph 1 shall be issued by the competent authorities in the home Member State. It shall certify that the holder, after obtaining evidence of formal qualifications as a midwife, has satisfactorily pursued all the activities of a midwife for a corresponding period in a hospital or a health care establishment approved for that purpose.

Article 42. Pursuit of the professional activities of a midwife

(1) The provisions of this section shall apply to the activities of midwives as defined by each Member State, without prejudice to paragraph 2, and pursued under the professional titles set out in Annex V, point 5.5.2.
(2) The Member States shall ensure that midwives are able to gain access to and pursue at least the following activities:
(a) provision of sound family planning information and advice;
(b) diagnosis of pregnancies and monitoring normal pregnancies; carrying out the examinations necessary for the monitoring of the development of normal pregnancies;

(c) prescribing or advising on the examinations necessary for the earliest possible diagnosis of pregnancies at risk;
(d) provision of programmes of parenthood preparation and complete preparation for childbirth including advice on hygiene and nutrition;
(e) caring for and assisting the mother during labour and monitoring the condition of the foetus in utero by the appropriate clinical and technical means;
(f) conducting spontaneous deliveries including where required episiotomies and in urgent cases breech deliveries;
(g) recognising the warning signs of abnormality in the mother or infant which necessitate referral to a doctor and assisting the latter where appropriate; taking the necessary emergency measures in the doctor's absence, in particular the manual removal of the placenta, possibly followed by manual examination of the uterus;
(h) examining and caring for the new–born infant; taking all initiatives which are necessary in case of need and carrying out where necessary immediate resuscitation;
(i) caring for and monitoring the progress of the mother in the post–natal period and giving all necessary advice to the mother on infant care to enable her to ensure the optimum progress of the new–born infant;
(j) carrying out treatment prescribed by doctors;
(k) drawing up the necessary written reports.

Article 43. Acquired rights specific to midwives

(1) Every Member State shall, in the case of Member State nationals whose evidence of formal qualifications as a midwife satisfies all the minimum training requirements laid down in Article 40 but, by virtue of Article 41, is not recognised unless it is accompanied by a certificate of professional practice referred to in Article 41(2), recognise as sufficient proof evidence of formal qualifications issued by those Member States before the reference date referred to in Annex V, point 5.5.2, accompanied by a certificate stating that those nationals have been effectively and lawfully engaged in the activities in question for at least two consecutive years during the five years preceding the award of the certificate.
(2) The conditions laid down in paragraph 1 shall apply to the nationals of Member States whose evidence of formal qualifications as a midwife certifies completion of training received in the territory of the former German Democratic Republic and satisfying all the minimum training requirements laid down in Article 40 but where the evidence of formal qualifications, by virtue of Article 41, is not recognised unless it is accompanied by the certificate of professional experience referred to in Article 41(2), where it attests a course of training which began before 3 October 1990.
(3) As regards the Polish evidence of formal qualifications as a midwife, only the following acquired rights provisions shall apply.
In the case of Member States nationals whose evidence of formal qualifications as a midwife was awarded by, or whose training commenced in, Poland before 1 May 2004, and who do not satisfy the minimum training requirements as set out in Article 40, Member States shall recognise the following evidence of formal qualifications as a midwife if accompanied by a certificate stating that such persons have effectively and lawfully been engaged in the activities of a midwife for the period specified below:
(a) evidence of formal qualifications as a midwife at degree level (dyplom licencjata położnictwa): at least three consecutive years during the five years prior to the date of issue of the certificate,
(b) evidence of formal qualifications as a midwife certifying completion of post–secondary education obtained from a medical vocational school (dyplom położnej): at least five consecutive years during the seven years prior to the date of issue of the certificate.
(4) Member States shall recognise evidence of formal qualifications in midwifery awarded in Poland, to midwives who completed training before 1 May 2004, which did not comply with the minimum training requirements laid down in Article 40, attested by the diploma 'bachelor' which has been obtained on the basis of a special upgrading programme contained in Article 11 of the Act of 20 April 2004 on the amendment of the Act on professions of nurse and midwife and on some other legal acts (Official Journal of the Republic of Poland of 30 April 2004 No 92, pos. 885), and the Regulation of the Minister of Health of 11 May 2004 on the detailed conditions of delivering studies for nurses and midwives, who hold a certificate of secondary school (final examination — matura) and are graduates of medical lyceum and medical vocational schools teaching in a profession of a nurse and a midwife (Official Journal of the Republic of Poland of 13 May 2004 No 110, pos 1170), with the aim of verifying that the person concerned has a level of knowledge and competence comparable to that of midwives holding the qualifications which, in the case of Poland, are defined in Annex V, point 5.5.2.

Section 7. Pharmacist

Article 44. Training as a pharmacist

(1) Admission to a course of training as a pharmacist shall be contingent upon possession of a diploma or certificate giving access, in a Member State, to the studies in question, at universities or higher institutes of a level recognised as equivalent.

(2) Evidence of formal qualifications as a pharmacist shall attest to training of at least five years' duration, including at least:

(a) four years of full–time theoretical and practical training at a university or at a higher institute of a level recognised as equivalent, or under the supervision of a university;

(b) six–month traineeship in a pharmacy which is open to the public or in a hospital, under the supervision of that hospital's pharmaceutical department.

That training cycle shall include at least the programme described in Annex V, point 5.6.1. The contents listed in Annex V, point 5.6.1 may be amended in accordance with the procedure referred to in Article 58(2) with a view to adapting them to scientific and technical progress.

Such updates must not entail, for any Member State, any amendment of existing legislative principles relating to the structure of professions as regards training and the conditions of access by natural persons.

(3) Training for pharmacists shall provide an assurance that the person concerned has acquired the following knowledge and skills:

(a) adequate knowledge of medicines and the substances used in the manufacture of medicines;

(b) adequate knowledge of pharmaceutical technology and the physical, chemical, biological and microbiological testing of medicinal products;

(c) adequate knowledge of the metabolism and the effects of medicinal products and of the action of toxic substances, and of the use of medicinal products;

(d) adequate knowledge to evaluate scientific data concerning medicines in order to be able to supply appropriate information on the basis of this knowledge;

(e) adequate knowledge of the legal and other requirements associated with the pursuit of pharmacy.

Article 45. Pursuit of the professional activities of a pharmacist

(1) For the purposes of this Directive, the activities of a pharmacist are those, access to which and pursuit of which are contingent, in one or more Member States, upon professional qualifications and which are open to holders of evidence of formal qualifications of the types listed in Annex V, point 5.6.2.

(2) The Member States shall ensure that the holders of evidence of formal qualifications in pharmacy at university level or a level deemed to be equivalent, which satisfies the provisions of Article 44, are able to gain access to and pursue at least the following activities, subject to the requirement, where appropriate, of supplementary professional experience:

(a) preparation of the pharmaceutical form of medicinal products;

(b) manufacture and testing of medicinal products;

(c) testing of medicinal products in a laboratory for the testing of medicinal products;

(d) storage, preservation and distribution of medicinal products at the wholesale stage;

(e) preparation, testing, storage and supply of medicinal products in pharmacies open to the public;

(f) preparation, testing, storage and dispensing of medicinal products in hospitals;

(g) provision of information and advice on medicinal products.

(3) If a Member State makes access to or pursuit of one of the activities of a pharmacist contingent upon supplementary professional experience, in addition to possession of evidence of formal qualifications referred to in Annex V, point 5.6.2, that Member State shall recognise as sufficient proof in this regard a certificate issued by the competent authorities in the home Member State stating that the person concerned has been engaged in those activities in the home Member State for a similar period.

(4) The recognition referred to in paragraph 3 shall not apply with regard to the two–year period of professional experience required by the Grand Duchy of Luxembourg for the grant of a State public pharmacy concession.

(5) If, on 16 September 1985, a Member State had a competitive examination in place designed to select from among the holders referred to in paragraph 2, those who are to be authorised to become owners of new pharmacies whose creation has been decided on as part of a national system of geographical division, that Member State may, by way of derogation from paragraph 1, proceed with that examination and require nationals of Member States who possess evidence of formal qualifications as a pharmacist referred to in Annex V, point 5.6.2 or who benefit from the provisions of Article 23 to take part in it.

Section 8. Architect

PART III   EUROPEAN UNION

Article 46. Training of architects

(1) Training as an architect shall comprise a total of at least four years of full–time study or six years of study, at least three years of which on a full–time basis, at a university or comparable teaching institution. The training must lead to successful completion of a university–level examination.

That training, which must be of university level, and of which architecture is the principal component, must maintain a balance between theoretical and practical aspects of architectural training and guarantee the acquisition of the following knowledge and skills:

(a) ability to create architectural designs that satisfy both aesthetic and technical requirements;

(b) adequate knowledge of the history and theories of architecture and the related arts, technologies and human sciences;

(c) knowledge of the fine arts as an influence on the quality of architectural design;

(d) adequate knowledge of urban design, planning and the skills involved in the planning process;

(e) understanding of the relationship between people and buildings, and between buildings and their environment, and of the need to relate buildings and the spaces between them to human needs and scale;

(f) understanding of the profession of architecture and the role of the architect in society, in particular in preparing briefs that take account of social factors;

(g) understanding of the methods of investigation and preparation of the brief for a design project;

(h) understanding of the structural design, constructional and engineering problems associated with building design;

(i) adequate knowledge of physical problems and technologies and of the function of buildings so as to provide them with internal conditions of comfort and protection against the climate;

(j) the necessary design skills to meet building users' requirements within the constraints imposed by cost factors and building regulations;

(k) adequate knowledge of the industries, organisations, regulations and procedures involved in translating design concepts into buildings and integrating plans into overall planning.

(2) The knowledge and skills listed in paragraph 1 may be amended in accordance with the procedure referred to in Article 58(2) with a view to adapting them to scientific and technical progress.

Such updates must not entail, for any Member State, any amendment of existing legislative principles relating to the structure of professions as regards training and the conditions of access by natural persons.

Article 47. Derogations from the conditions for the training of architects

(1) By way of derogation from Article 46, the following shall also be recognised as satisfying Article 21: training existing as of 5 August 1985, provided by 'Fachhochschulen' in the Federal Republic of Germany over a period of three years, satisfying the requirements referred to in Article 46 and giving access to the activities referred to in Article 48 in that Member State under the professional title of 'architect', in so far as the training was followed by a four–year period of professional experience in the Federal Republic of Germany, as attested by a certificate issued by the professional association in whose roll the name of the architect wishing to benefit from the provisions of this Directive appears.

The professional association must first ascertain that the work performed by the architect concerned in the field of architecture represents convincing application of the full range of knowledge and skills listed in Article 46(1). That certificate shall be awarded in line with the same procedure as that applying to registration in the professional association's roll.

(2) By way of derogation from Article 46, the following shall also be recognised as satisfying Article 21: training as part of social betterment schemes or part–time university studies which satisfies the requirements referred to in Article 46, as attested by an examination in architecture passed by a person who has been working for seven years or more in the field of architecture under the supervision of an architect or architectural bureau. The examination must be of university level and be equivalent to the final examination referred to in Article 46(1), first subparagraph.

Article 48. Pursuit of the professional activities of architects

(1) For the purposes of this Directive, the professional activities of an architect are the activities regularly carried out under the professional title of 'architect'.

(2) Nationals of a Member State who are authorised to use that title pursuant to a law which gives the competent authority of a Member State the power to award that title to Member States nationals who are especially distinguished by the quality of their work in the field of architecture shall be deemed to satisfy the conditions required for the pursuit of the activities of an architect, under the professional title of 'architect'. The architectural nature of the activities of the persons concerned shall be attested by a certificate awarded by their home Member State.

Article 49. Acquired rights specific to architects

(1) Each Member State shall accept evidence of formal qualifications as an architect listed in Annex VI, point 6, awarded by the other Member States, and attesting a course of training which began no later than the reference academic year referred to in that Annex, even if they do not satisfy the minimum requirements laid down in Article 46, and shall, for the purposes of access to and pursuit of the professional activities of an architect, give such evidence the same effect on its territory as evidence of formal qualifications as an architect which it itself issues.

Under these circumstances, certificates issued by the competent authorities of the Federal Republic of Germany attesting that evidence of formal qualifications issued on or after 8 May 1945 by the competent authorities of the German Democratic Republic is equivalent to such evidence listed in that Annex, shall be recognised.

(2) Without prejudice to paragraph 1, every Member State shall recognise the following evidence of formal qualifications and shall, for the purposes of access to and pursuit of the professional activities of an architect performed, give them the same effect on its territory as evidence of formal qualifications which it itself issues: certificates issued to nationals of Member States by the Member States which have enacted rules governing the access to and pursuit of the activities of an architect as of the following dates:

(a) 1 January 1995 for Austria, Finland and Sweden;

(b) 1 May 2004 for the Czech Republic, Estonia, Cyprus, Latvia, Lithuania, Hungary, Malta, Poland, Slovenia and Slovakia;

(c) 5 August 1987 for the other Member States.

The certificates referred to in paragraph 1 shall certify that the holder was authorised, no later than the respective date, to use the professional title of architect, and that he has been effectively engaged, in the context of those rules, in the activities in question for at least three consecutive years during the five years preceding the award of the certificate.

Chapter IV. Common Provisions on Establishment

Article 50. Documentation and formalities

(1) Where the competent authorities of the host Member State decide on an application for authorisation to pursue the regulated profession in question by virtue of this Title, those authorities may demand the documents and certificates listed in Annex VII.

The documents referred to in Annex VII, point 1(d), (e) and (f), shall not be more than three months old by the date on which they are submitted.

The Member States, bodies and other legal persons shall guarantee the confidentiality of the information which they receive.

(2) In the event of justified doubts, the host Member State may require from the competent authorities of a Member State confirmation of the authenticity of the attestations and evidence of formal qualifications awarded in that other Member State, as well as, where applicable, confirmation of the fact that the beneficiary fulfils, for the professions referred to in Chapter III of this Title, the minimum training conditions set out respectively in Articles 24, 25, 28, 31, 34, 35, 38, 40, 44 and 46.

(3) In cases of justified doubt, where evidence of formal qualifications, as defined in Article 3(1)(c), has been issued by a competent authority in a Member State and includes training received in whole or in part in an establishment legally established in the territory of another Member State, the host Member State shall be entitled to verify with the competent body in the Member State of origin of the award:

(a) whether the training course at the establishment which gave the training has been formally certified by the educational establishment based in the Member State of origin of the award;

(b) whether the evidence of formal qualifications issued is the same as that which would have been awarded if the course had been followed entirely in the Member State of origin of the award; and

(c) whether the evidence of formal qualifications confers the same professional rights in the territory of the Member State of origin of the award.

(4) Where a host Member State requires its nationals to swear a solemn oath or make a sworn statement in order to gain access to a regulated profession, and where the wording of that oath or statement cannot be used by nationals of the other Member States, the host Member State shall ensure that the persons concerned can use an appropriate equivalent wording.

Article 51. Procedure for the mutual recognition of professional qualifications

(1) The competent authority of the host Member State shall acknowledge receipt of the application within one month of receipt and inform the applicant of any missing document.

(2) The procedure for examining an application for authorisation to practise a regulated profession

must be completed as quickly as possible and lead to a duly substantiated decision by the competent authority in the host Member State in any case within three months after the date on which the applicant's complete file was submitted. However, this deadline may be extended by one month in cases falling under Chapters I and II of this Title.

(3) The decision, or failure to reach a decision within the deadline, shall be subject to appeal under national law.

Article 52. Use of professional titles

(1) If, in a host Member State, the use of a professional title relating to one of the activities of the profession in question is regulated, nationals of the other Member States who are authorised to practise a regulated profession on the basis of Title III shall use the professional title of the host Member State, which corresponds to that profession in that Member State, and make use of any associated initials.

(2) Where a profession is regulated in the host Member State by an association or organisation within the meaning of Article 3(2), nationals of Member States shall not be authorised to use the professional title issued by that organisation or association, or its abbreviated form, unless they furnish proof that they are members of that association or organisation.

If the association or organisation makes membership contingent upon certain qualifications, it may do so, only under the conditions laid down in this Directive, in respect of nationals of other Member States who possess professional qualifications.

Title IV. Detailed Rules for Pursuing the Profession

Article 53. Knowledge of languages

Persons benefiting from the recognition of professional qualifications shall have a knowledge of languages necessary for practising the profession in the host Member State.

Article 54. Use of academic titles

Without prejudice to Articles 7 and 52, the host Member State shall ensure that the right shall be conferred on the persons concerned to use academic titles conferred on them in the home Member State, and possibly an abbreviated form thereof, in the language of the home Member State. The host Member State may require that title to be followed by the name and address of the establishment or examining board which awarded it. Where an academic title of the home Member State is liable to be confused in the host Member State with a title which, in the latter Member State, requires supplementary training not acquired by the beneficiary, the host Member State may require the beneficiary to use the academic title of the home Member State in an appropriate form, to be laid down by the host Member State.

Article 55. Approval by health insurance funds

Without prejudice to Article 5(1) and Article 6, first subparagraph, point (b), Member States which require persons who acquired their professional qualifications in their territory to complete a preparatory period of in–service training and/or a period of professional experience in order to be approved by a health insurance fund, shall waive this obligation for the holders of evidence of professional qualifications of doctor and dental practitioner acquired in other Member States.

Title V. Administrative Cooperation and Responsibility for Implementation

Article 56. Competent authorities

(1) The competent authorities of the host Member State and of the home Member State shall work in close collaboration and shall provide mutual assistance in order to facilitate application of this Directive. They shall ensure the confidentiality of the information which they exchange.

(2) The competent authorities of the host and home Member States shall exchange information regarding disciplinary action or criminal sanctions taken or any other serious, specific circumstances which are likely to have consequences for the pursuit of activities under this Directive, respecting personal data protection legislation provided for in Directives 95/46/EC of the European Parliament and of the Council of 24 October 1995 on the protection of individuals with regard to the processing of personal data and on the free movement of such data and 2002/58/EC of the European Parliament and of the Council of 12 July 2002 concerning the processing of personal data and the protection of privacy in the electronic communications sector (Directive on privacy and electronic communications).

The home Member State shall examine the veracity of the circumstances and its authorities shall decide on the nature and scope of the investigations which need to be carried out and shall inform the host Member State of the conclusions which it draws from the information available to it.

(3) Each Member State shall, no later than 20 October 2007, designate the authorities and bodies competent to award or receive evidence of formal qualifications and other documents or information, and those competent to receive applications and take the decisions referred to in this Directive, and shall forthwith inform the other Member States and the Commission thereof.
(4) Each Member State shall designate a coordinator for the activities of the authorities referred to in paragraph 1 and shall inform the other Member States and the Commission thereof.
The coordinators' remit shall be:
(a) to promote uniform application of this Directive;
(b) to collect all the information which is relevant for application of this Directive, such as on the conditions for access to regulated professions in the Member States.
For the purpose of fulfilling the remit described in point (b), the coordinators may solicit the help of the contact points referred to in Article 57.

Article 57. Contact points
Each Member State shall designate, no later than 20 October 2007, a contact point whose remit shall be:
(a) to provide the citizens and contact points of the other Member States with such information as is necessary concerning the recognition of professional qualifications provided for in this Directive, such as information on the national legislation governing the professions and the pursuit of those professions, including social legislation, and, where appropriate, the rules of ethics;
(b) to assist citizens in realising the rights conferred on them by this Directive, in cooperation, where appropriate, with the other contact points and the competent authorities in the host Member State.
At the Commission's request, the contact points shall inform the Commission of the result of enquiries with which they are dealing pursuant to the provisions of point (b) within two months of receiving them.

Article 58. Committee on the recognition of professional qualifications
(1) The Commission shall be assisted by a Committee on the recognition of professional qualifications, hereinafter referred to as 'the Committee', made up of representatives of the Member States and chaired by a representative of the Commission.
(2) Where reference is made to this paragraph, Articles 5 and 7 of Decision 1999/468/EC shall apply, having due regard to the provisions of Article 8 thereof.
The period laid down in Article 5(6) of Decision 1999/468/EC shall be set at two months.
(3) The Committee shall adopt its rules of procedure.

Article 59. Consultation
The Commission shall ensure the consultation of experts from the professional groups concerned in an appropriate manner in particular in the context of the work of the committee referred to in Article 58 and shall provide a reasoned report on these consultations to that committee.

Title VI. Other Provisions

Article 60. Reports
(1) As from 20 October 2007, Member States shall, every two years, send a report to the Commission on the application of the system. In addition to general observations, the report shall contain a statistical summary of decisions taken and a description of the main problems arising from the application of this Directive.
(2) As from 20 October 2007, the Commission shall draw up every five years a report on the implementation of this Directive.

Article 61. Derogation clause
If, for the application of one of the provisions of this Directive, a Member State encounters major difficulties in a particular area, the Commission shall examine those difficulties in collaboration with the Member State concerned.
Where appropriate, the Commission shall decide, in accordance with the procedure referred to in Article 58(2), to permit the Member State in question to derogate from the provision in question for a limited period.

Article 62. Repeal
Directives 77/452/EEC, 77/453/EEC, 78/686/EEC, 78/687/EEC, 78/1026/EEC, 78/1027/EEC, 80/154/EEC, 80/155/EEC, 85/384/EEC, 85/432/EEC, 85/433/EEC, 89/48/EEC, 92/51/EEC, 93/16/EEC and 1999/42/EC are repealed with effect from 20 October 2007. References to the repealed Directives shall be understood as references to this Directive and the acts adopted on the basis of

PART III   EUROPEAN UNION

those Directives shall not be affected by the repeal.

Article 63. Transposition

Member States shall bring into force the laws, regulations and administrative provisions necessary to comply with this Directive by 20 October 2007 at the latest. They shall forthwith inform the Commission thereof.

When Member States adopt these measures, they shall contain a reference to this Directive or be accompanied by such a reference on the occasion of their official publication. Member States shall determine how such reference is to be made.

Article 64. Entry into force

This Directive shall enter into force on the 20th day following its publication in the *Official Journal of the European Union*.

Article 65. Addressees

This Directive is addressed to the Member States.

Directive 2006/123/EC of the European Parliament and of the Council of 12 December 2006 on services in the internal market

THE EUROPEAN PARLIAMENT AND THE COUNCIL OF THE EUROPEAN UNION,
Having regard to the Treaty establishing the European Community, and in particular the first and third sentence of Article 47(2) and Article 55 thereof,
Having regard to the proposal from the Commission,
Having regard to the Opinion of the European Economic and Social Committee,
Having regard to the opinion of the Committee of the Regions,
Acting in accordance with the procedure laid down in Article 251 of the Treaty,
Whereas:
(1) The European Community is seeking to forge ever closer links between the States and peoples of Europe and to ensure economic and social progress. In accordance with Article 14(2) of the Treaty, the internal market comprises an area without internal frontiers in which the free movement of services is ensured. In accordance with Article 43 of the Treaty the freedom of establishment is ensured. Article 49 of the Treaty establishes the right to provide services within the Community. The elimination of barriers to the development of service activities between Member States is essential in order to strengthen the integration of the peoples of Europe and to promote balanced and sustainable economic and social progress. In eliminating such barriers it is essential to ensure that the development of service activities contributes to the fulfilment of the task laid down in Article 2 of the Treaty of promoting throughout the Community a harmonious, balanced and sustainable development of economic activities, a high level of employment and of social protection, equality between men and women, sustainable and non–inflationary growth, a high degree of competitiveness and convergence of economic performance, a high level of protection and improvement of the quality of the environment, the raising of the standard of living and quality of life and economic and social cohesion and solidarity among Member States.
(2) A competitive market in services is essential in order to promote economic growth and create jobs in the European Union. At present numerous barriers within the internal market prevent providers, particularly small and medium–sized enterprises (SMEs), from extending their operations beyond their national borders and from taking full advantage of the internal market. This weakens the worldwide competitiveness of European Union providers. A free market which compels the Member States to eliminate restrictions on cross–border provision of services while at the same time increasing transparency and information for consumers would give consumers wider choice and better services at lower prices.
(3) The report from the Commission on 'The State of the Internal Market for Services' drew up an inventory of a large number of barriers which are preventing or slowing down the development of services between Member States, in particular those provided by SMEs, which are predominant in the field of services. The report concludes that a decade after the envisaged completion of the internal market, there is still a huge gap between the vision of an integrated European Union economy and the reality as experienced by European citizens and providers. The barriers affect a wide variety of service activities across all stages of the provider's activity and have a number of common features, including the fact that they often arise from administrative burdens, the legal uncertainty associated with cross–border activity and the lack of mutual trust between Member States.
(4) Since services constitute the engine of economic growth and account for 70 % of GDP and employment in most Member States, this fragmentation of the internal market has a negative impact on the entire European economy, in particular on the competitiveness of SMEs and the movement of workers, and prevents consumers from gaining access to a greater variety of competitively priced services. It is important to point out that the services sector is a key employment sector for women in particular, and that they therefore stand to benefit greatly from new opportunities offered by the completion of the internal market for services. The European Parliament and the Council have emphasised that the removal of legal barriers to the establishment of a genuine internal market is a matter of priority for achieving the goal set by the European Council in Lisbon of 23 and 24 March 2000 of improving employment and social cohesion and achieving sustainable economic growth so as to make the European Union the most competitive and dynamic knowledge–based economy in the world by 2010, with more and better jobs. Removing those barriers, while ensuring an advanced European social model, is thus a basic condition for overcoming the difficulties encountered in implementing the Lisbon Strategy and for reviving the European economy, particularly in terms of employment and investment. It is therefore important to achieve an internal market for services, with the right balance between market opening and preserving public services and social and consumer rights.
(5) It is therefore necessary to remove barriers to the freedom of establishment for providers in

PART III   EUROPEAN UNION

Member States and barriers to the free movement of services as between Member States and to guarantee recipients and providers the legal certainty necessary for the exercise in practice of those two fundamental freedoms of the Treaty. Since the barriers in the internal market for services affect operators who wish to become established in other Member States as well as those who provide a service in another Member State without being established there, it is necessary to enable providers to develop their service activities within the internal market either by becoming established in a Member State or by making use of the free movement of services. Providers should be able to choose between those two freedoms, depending on their strategy for growth in each Member State.

(6) Those barriers cannot be removed solely by relying on direct application of Articles 43 and 49 of the Treaty, since, on the one hand, addressing them on a case–by–case basis through infringement procedures against the Member States concerned would, especially following enlargement, be extremely complicated for national and Community institutions, and, on the other hand, the lifting of many barriers requires prior coordination of national legal schemes, including the setting up of administrative cooperation. As the European Parliament and the Council have recognised, a Community legislative instrument makes it possible to achieve a genuine internal market for services.

(7) This Directive establishes a general legal framework which benefits a wide variety of services while taking into account the distinctive features of each type of activity or profession and its system of regulation. That framework is based on a dynamic and selective approach consisting in the removal, as a matter of priority, of barriers which may be dismantled quickly and, for the others, the launching of a process of evaluation, consultation and complementary harmonisation of specific issues, which will make possible the progressive and coordinated modernisation of national regulatory systems for service activities which is vital in order to achieve a genuine internal market for services by 2010. Provision should be made for a balanced mix of measures involving targeted harmonisation, administrative cooperation, the provision on the freedom to provide services and encouragement of the development of codes of conduct on certain issues. That coordination of national legislative regimes should ensure a high degree of Community legal integration and a high level of protection of general interest objectives, especially protection of consumers, which is vital in order to establish trust between Member States. This Directive also takes into account other general interest objectives, including the protection of the environment, public security and public health as well as the need to comply with labour law.

(8) It is appropriate that the provisions of this Directive concerning the freedom of establishment and the free movement of services should apply only to the extent that the activities in question are open to competition, so that they do not oblige Member States either to liberalise services of general economic interest or to privatise public entities which provide such services or to abolish existing monopolies for other activities or certain distribution services.

(9) This Directive applies only to requirements which affect the access to, or the exercise of, a service activity. Therefore, it does not apply to requirements, such as road traffic rules, rules concerning the development or use of land, town and country planning, building standards as well as administrative penalties imposed for non–compliance with such rules which do not specifically regulate or specifically affect the service activity but have to be respected by providers in the course of carrying out their economic activity in the same way as by individuals acting in their private capacity.

(10) This Directive does not concern requirements governing access to public funds for certain providers. Such requirements include notably those laying down conditions under which providers are entitled to receive public funding, including specific contractual conditions, and in particular quality standards which need to be observed as a condition for receiving public funds, for example for social services.

(11) This Directive does not interfere with measures taken by Member States, in accordance with Community law, in relation to the protection or promotion of cultural and linguistic diversity and media pluralism, including the funding thereof. This Directive does not prevent Member States from applying their fundamental rules and principles relating to the freedom of press and freedom of expression. This Directive does not affect Member State laws prohibiting discrimination on grounds of nationality or on grounds such as those set out in Article 13 of the Treaty.

(12) This Directive aims at creating a legal framework to ensure the freedom of establishment and the free movement of services between the Member States and does not harmonise or prejudice criminal law. However, Member States should not be able to restrict the freedom to provide services by applying criminal law provisions which specifically affect the access to or the exercise of a service activity in circumvention of the rules laid down in this Directive.

(13) It is equally important that this Directive fully respect Community initiatives based on Article 137 of the Treaty with a view to achieving the objectives of Article 136 thereof concerning the promotion of employment and improved living and working conditions.

(14) This Directive does not affect terms and conditions of employment, including maximum work periods and minimum rest periods, minimum paid annual holidays, minimum rates of pay as well as health, safety and hygiene at work, which Member States apply in compliance with Community law, nor does it affect relations between social partners, including the right to negotiate and conclude collective agreements, the right to strike and to take industrial action in accordance with national law and practices which respect Community law, nor does it apply to services provided by temporary work agencies. This Directive does not affect Member States' social security legislation.

(15) This Directive respects the exercise of fundamental rights applicable in the Member States and as recognised in the Charter of fundamental Rights of the European Union and the accompanying explanations, reconciling them with the fundamental freedoms laid down in Articles 43 and 49 of the Treaty. Those fundamental rights include the right to take industrial action in accordance with national law and practices which respect Community law.

(16) This Directive concerns only providers established in a Member State and does not cover external aspects. It does not concern negotiations within international organisations on trade in services, in particular in the framework of the General Agreement on Trade in Services (GATS).

(17) This Directive covers only services which are performed for an economic consideration. Services of general interest are not covered by the definition in Article 50 of the Treaty and therefore do not fall within the scope of this Directive. Services of general economic interest are services that are performed for an economic consideration and therefore do fall within the scope of this Directive. However, certain services of general economic interest, such as those that may exist in the field of transport, are excluded from the scope of this Directive and certain other services of general economic interest, for example, those that may exist in the area of postal services, are the subject of a derogation from the provision on the freedom to provide services set out in this Directive. This Directive does not deal with the funding of services of general economic interest and does not apply to systems of aids granted by Member States, in particular in the social field, in accordance with Community rules on competition. This Directive does not deal with the follow–up to the Commission White Paper on Services of General Interest.

(18) Financial services should be excluded from the scope of this Directive since these activities are the subject of specific Community legislation aimed, as is this Directive, at achieving a genuine internal market for services. Consequently, this exclusion should cover all financial services such as banking, credit, insurance, including reinsurance, occupational or personal pensions, securities, investment funds, payments and investment advice, including the services listed in Annex I to Directive 2006/48/EC of the European Parliament and of the Council of 14 June 2006 relating to the taking up and pursuit of the business of credit institutions.

(19) In view of the adoption in 2002 of a package of legislative instruments relating to electronic communications networks and services, as well as to associated resources and services, which has established a regulatory framework facilitating access to those activities within the internal market, notably through the elimination of most individual authorisation schemes, it is necessary to exclude issues dealt with by those instruments from the scope of this Directive.

(20) The exclusion from the scope of this Directive as regards matters of electronic communications services as covered by Directives 2002/19/EC of the European Parliament and of the Council of 7 March 2002 on access to, and interconnection of, electronic communications networks and associated facilities (Access Directive), 2002/20/EC of the European Parliament and of the Council of 7 March 2002 on the authorisation of electronic communications networks and services (Authorisation Directive), 2002/21/EC of the European Parliament and of the Council of 7 March 2002 on a common regulatory framework for electronic communications networks and services (Framework Directive), 2002/22/EC of the European Parliament and of the Council of 7 March 2002 on universal service and users' rights relating to electronic communications networks and services (Universal Service Directive) and 2002/58/EC of the European Parliament and of the Council of 12 July 2002 concerning the processing of personal data and the protection of privacy in the electronic communications sector (Directive on privacy and electronic communications) should apply not only to questions specifically dealt with in these Directives but also to matters for which the Directives explicitly leave to Member States the possibility of adopting certain measures at national level.

(21) Transport services, including urban transport, taxis and ambulances as well as port services, should be excluded from the scope of this Directive.

(22) The exclusion of healthcare from the scope of this Directive should cover healthcare and pharmaceutical services provided by health professionals to patients to assess, maintain or restore their state of health where those activities are reserved to a regulated health profession in the Member State in which the services are provided.

(23) This Directive does not affect the reimbursement of healthcare provided in a Member State other

PART III EUROPEAN UNION

than that in which the recipient of the care is resident. This issue has been addressed by the Court of Justice on numerous occasions, and the Court has recognised patients' rights. It is important to address this issue in another Community legal instrument in order to achieve greater legal certainty and clarity to the extent that this issue is not already addressed in Council Regulation (EEC) No 1408/71 of 14 June 1971 on the application of social security schemes to employed persons, to self-employed persons and to members of their families moving within the Community.

(24) Audiovisual services, whatever their mode of transmission, including within cinemas, should also be excluded from the scope of this Directive. Furthermore, this Directive should not apply to aids granted by Member States in the audiovisual sector which are covered by Community rules on competition.

(25) Gambling activities, including lottery and betting transactions, should be excluded from the scope of this Directive in view of the specific nature of these activities, which entail implementation by Member States of policies relating to public policy and consumer protection.

(26) This Directive is without prejudice to the application of Article 45 of the Treaty.

(27) This Directive should not cover those social services in the areas of housing, childcare and support to families and persons in need which are provided by the State at national, regional or local level by providers m andated by the State or by charities recognised as such by the State with the objective of ensuring support for those who are permanently or temporarily in a particular state of need because of their insufficient family income or total or partial lack of independence and for those who risk being marginalised. These services are essential in order to guarantee the fundamental right to human dignity and integrity and are a manifestation of the principles of social cohesion and solidarity and should not be affected by this Directive.

(28) This Directive does not deal with the funding of, or the system of aids linked to, social services. Nor does it affect the criteria or conditions set by Member States to ensure that social services effectively carry out a function to the benefit of the public interest and social cohesion. In addition, this Directive should not affect the principle of universal service in Member States' social services.

(29) Given that the Treaty provides specific legal bases for taxation matters and given the Community instruments already adopted in that field, it is necessary to exclude the field of taxation from the scope of this Directive.

(30) There is already a considerable body of Community law on service activities. This Directive builds on, and thus complements, the Community acquis. Conflicts between this Directive and other Community instruments have been identified and are addressed by this Directive, including by means of derogations. However, it is necessary to provide a rule for any residual and exceptional cases where there is a conflict between a provision of this Directive and a provision of another Community instrument. The existence of such a conflict should be determined in compliance with the rules of the Treaty on the right of establishment and the free movement of services.

(31) This Directive is consistent with and does not affect Directive 2005/36/EC of the European Parliament and of the Council of 7 September 2005 on the recognition of professional qualifications. It deals with questions other than those relating to professional qualifications, for example professional liability insurance, commercial communications, multidisciplinary activities and administrative simplification. With regard to temporary cross–border service provision, a derogation from the provision on the freedom to provide services in this Directive ensures that Title II on the free provision of services of Directive 2005/36/EC is not affected. Therefore, none of the measures applicable under that Directive in the Member State where the service is provided is affected by the provision on the freedom to provide services.

(32) This Directive is consistent with Community legislation on consumer protection, such as Directive 2005/29/EC of the European Parliament and of the Council of 11 May 2005 concerning unfair business–to–consumer commercial practices in the internal market (the Unfair Commercial Practices Directive) and Regulation (EC) No 2006/2004 of the European Parliament and of the Council of 27 October 2004 on cooperation between national authorities responsible for the enforcement of consumer protection laws (the Regulation on consumer protection cooperation).

(33) The services covered by this Directive concern a wide variety of ever–changing activities, including business services such as management consultancy, certification and testing; facilities management, including office maintenance; advertising; recruitment services; and the services of commercial agents. The services covered are also services provided both to businesses and to consumers, such as legal or fiscal advice; real estate services such as estate agencies; construction, including the services of architects; distributive trades; the organisation of trade fairs; car rental; and travel agencies. Consumer services are also covered, such as those in the field of tourism, including tour guides; leisure services, sports centres and amusement parks; and, to the extent that they are not excluded from the scope of application of the Directive, household support services, such as help

for the elderly. Those activities may involve services requiring the proximity of provider and recipient, services requiring travel by the recipient or the provider and services which may be provided at a distance, including via the Internet.

(34) According to the case–law of the Court of Justice, the assessment of whether certain activities, in particular activities which are publicly funded or provided by public entities, constitute a 'service' has to be carried out on a case by case basis in the light of all their characteristics, in particular the way they are provided, organised and financed in the Member State concerned. The Court of Justice has held that the essential characteristic of remuneration lies in the fact that it constitutes consideration for the services in question and has recognised that the characteristic of remuneration is absent in the case of activities performed, for no consideration, by the State or on behalf of the State in the context of its duties in the social, cultural, educational and judicial fields, such as courses provided under the national education system, or the management of social security schemes which do not engage in economic activity. The payment of a fee by recipients, for example, a tuition or enrolment fee paid by students in order to make a certain contribution to the operating expenses of a system, does not in itself constitute remuneration because the service is still essentially financed by public funds. These activities are, therefore, not covered by the definition of service in Article 50 of the Treaty and do not therefore fall within the scope of this Directive.

(35) Non–profit making amateur sporting activities are of considerable social importance. They often pursue wholly social or recreational objectives. Thus, they might not constitute economic activities within the meaning of Community law and should fall outside the scope of this Directive.

(36) The concept of 'provider' should cover any natural person who is a national of a Member State or any legal person engaged in a service activity in a Member State, in exercise either of the freedom of establishment or of the free movement of services. The concept of provider should thus not be limited solely to cross–border service provision within the framework of the free movement of services but should also cover cases in which an operator establishes itself in a Member State in order to develop its service activities there. On the other hand, the concept of a provider should not cover the case of branches in a Member State of companies from third countries because, under Article 48 of the Treaty, the freedom of establishment and free movement of services may benefit only companies constituted in accordance with the laws of a Member State and having their registered office, central administration or principal place of business within the Community. The concept of 'recipient' should also cover third country nationals who already benefit from rights conferred upon them by Community acts such as Regulation (EEC) No 1408/71, Council Directive 2003/109/EC of 25 November 2003 concerning the status of third–country nationals who are long–term residents, Council Regulation (EC) No 859/2003 of 14 May 2003 extending the provisions of Regulation (EEC) No 1408/71 and Regulation (EEC) No 574/72 to nationals of third countries who are not already covered by those provisions solely on the ground of their nationality and Directive 2004/38/EC of the European Parliament and of the Council of 29 April 2004 on the right of citizens of the Union and their family members to move and reside freely within the territory of the Member States. Furthermore, Member States may extend the concept of recipient to other third country nationals that are present within their territory.

(37) The place at which a provider is established should be determined in accordance with the case law of the Court of Justice according to which the concept of establishment involves the actual pursuit of an economic activity through a fixed establishment for an indefinite period. This requirement may also be fulfilled where a company is constituted for a given period or where it rents the building or installation through which it pursues its activity. It may also be fulfilled where a Member State grants authorisations for a limited duration only in relation to particular services. An establishment does not need to take the form of a subsidiary, branch or agency, but may consist of an office managed by a provider's own staff or by a person who is independent but authorised to act on a permanent basis for the undertaking, as would be the case with an agency. According to this definition, which requires the actual pursuit of an economic activity at the place of establishment of the provider, a mere letter box does not constitute an establishment. Where a provider has several places of establishment, it is important to determine the place of establishment from which the actual service concerned is provided. Where it is difficult to determine from which of several places of establishment a given service is provided, the location of the provider's centre of activities relating to this particular service should be that place of establishment.

(38) The concept of 'legal persons', according to the Treaty provisions on establishment, leaves operators free to choose the legal form which they deem suitable for carrying out their activity. Accordingly, 'legal persons', within the meaning of the Treaty, means all entities constituted under, or governed by, the law of a Member State, irrespective of their legal form.

(39) The concept of 'authorisation scheme' should cover, inter alia, the administrative procedures for

granting authorisations, licences, approvals or concessions, and also the obligation, in order to be eligible to exercise the activity, to be registered as a member of a profession or entered in a register, roll or database, to be officially appointed to a body or to obtain a card attesting to membership of a particular profession. Authorisation may be granted not only by a formal decision but also by an implicit decision arising, for example, from the silence of the competent authority or from the fact that the interested party must await acknowledgement of receipt of a declaration in order to commence the activity in question or for the latter to become lawful.

(40) The concept of 'overriding reasons relating to the public interest' to which reference is made in certain provisions of this Directive has been developed by the Court of Justice in its case law in relation to Articles 43 and 49 of the Treaty and may continue to evolve. The notion as recognised in the case law of the Court of Justice covers at least the following grounds: public policy, public security and public health, within the meaning of Articles 46 and 55 of the Treaty; the maintenance of order in society; social policy objectives; the protection of the recipients of services; consumer protection; the protection of workers, including the social protection of workers; animal welfare; the preservation of the financial balance of the social security system; the prevention of fraud; the prevention of unfair competition; the protection of the environment and the urban environment, including town and country planning; the protection of creditors; safeguarding the sound administration of justice; road safety; the protection of intellectual property; cultural policy objectives, including safeguarding the freedom of expression of various elements, in particular social, cultural, religious and philosophical values of society; the need to ensure a high level of education, the maintenance of press diversity and the promotion of the national language; the preservation of national historical and artistic heritage; and veterinary policy.

(41) The concept of 'public policy', as interpreted by the Court of Justice, covers the protection against a genuine and sufficiently serious threat affecting one of the fundamental interests of society and may include, in particular, issues relating to human dignity, the protection of minors and vulnerable adults and animal welfare. Similarly, the concept of public security includes issues of public safety.

(42) The rules relating to administrative procedures should not aim at harmonising administrative procedures but at removing overly burdensome authorisation schemes, procedures and formalities that hinder the freedom of establishment and the creation of new service undertakings therefrom.

(43) One of the fundamental difficulties faced, in particular by SMEs, in accessing service activities and exercising them is the complexity, length and legal uncertainty of administrative procedures. For this reason, following the example of certain modernising and good administrative practice initiatives undertaken at Community and national level, it is necessary to establish principles of administrative simplification, inter alia through the limitation of the obligation of prior authorisation to cases in which it is essential and the introduction of the principle of tacit authorisation by the competent authorities after a certain period of time elapsed. Such modernising action, while maintaining the requirements on transparency and the updating of information relating to operators, is intended to eliminate the delays, costs and dissuasive effects which arise, for example, from unnecessary or excessively complex and burdensome procedures, the duplication of procedures, the 'red tape' involved in submitting documents, the arbitrary use of powers by the competent authorities, indeterminate or excessively long periods before a response is given, the limited duration of validity of authorisations granted and disproportionate fees and penalties. Such practices have particularly significant dissuasive effects on providers wishing to develop their activities in other Member States and require coordinated modernisation within an enlarged internal market of twenty-five Member States.

(44) Member States should introduce, where appropriate, forms harmonised at Community level, as established by the Commission, which will serve as an equivalent to certificates, attestations or any other document in relation to establishment.

(45) In order to examine the need for simplifying procedures and formalities, Member States should be able, in particular, to take into account their necessity, number, possible duplication, cost, clarity and accessibility, as well as the delay and practical difficulties to which they could give rise for the provider concerned.

(46) In order to facilitate access to service activities and the exercise thereof in the internal market, it is necessary to establish an objective, common to all Member States, of administrative simplification and to lay down provisions concerning, inter alia, the right to information, procedures by electronic means and the establishment of a framework for authorisation schemes. Other measures adopted at national level to meet that objective could involve reduction of the number of procedures and formalities applicable to service activities and the restriction of such procedures and formalities to those which are essential in order to achieve a general interest objective and which do not duplicate each

other in terms of content or purpose.

(47) With the aim of administrative simplification, general formal requirements, such as presentation of original documents, certified copies or a certified translation, should not be imposed, except where objectively justified by an overriding reason relating to the public interest, such as the protection of workers, public health, the protection of the environment or the protection of consumers. It is also necessary to ensure that an authorisation as a general rule permits access to, or exercise of, a service activity throughout the national territory, unless a new authorisation for each establishment, for example for each new hypermarket, or an authorisation that is restricted to a specific part of the national territory is objectively justified by an overriding reason relating to the public interest.

(48) In order to further simplify administrative procedures, it is appropriate to ensure that each provider has a single point through which he can complete all procedures and formalities (hereinafter referred to as 'points of single contact'). The number of points of single contact per Member State may vary according to regional or local competencies or according to the activities concerned. The creation of points of single contact should not interfere with the allocation of functions among competent authorities within each national system. Where several authorities at regional or local level are competent, one of them may assume the role of point of single contact and coordinator. Points of single contact may be set up not only by administrative authorities but also by chambers of commerce or crafts, or by the professional organisations or private bodies to which a Member State decides to entrust that function. Points of single contact have an important role to play in providing assistance to providers either as the authority directly competent to issue the documents necessary to access a service activity or as an intermediary between the provider and the authorities which are directly competent.

(49) The fee which may be charged by points of single contact should be proportionate to the cost of the procedures and formalities with which they deal. This should not prevent Member States from entrusting the points of single contact with the collection of other administrative fees, such as the fee of supervisory bodies.

(50) It is necessary for providers and recipients of services to have easy access to certain types of information It should be for each Member State to determine, within the framework of this Directive, the way in which providers and recipients are provided with information. In particular, the obligation on Member States to ensure that relevant information is easily accessible to providers and recipients and that it can be accessed by the public without obstacle could be fulfilled by making this information accessible through a website. Any information given should be provided in a clear and unambiguous manner.

(51) The information provided to providers and recipients of services should include, in particular, information on procedures and formalities, contact details of the competent authorities, conditions for access to public registers and data bases and information concerning available remedies and the contact details of associations and organisations from which providers or recipients can obtain practical assistance. The obligation on competent authorities to assist providers and recipients should not include the provision of legal advice in individual cases. Nevertheless, general information on the way in which requirements are usually interpreted or applied should be given. Issues such as liability for providing incorrect or misleading information should be determined by Member States.

(52) The setting up, in the reasonably near future, of electronic means of completing procedures and formalities will be vital for administrative simplification in the field of service activities, for the benefit of providers, recipients and competent authorities. In order to meet that obligation as to results, national laws and other rules applicable to services may need to be adapted. This obligation should not prevent Member States from providing other means of completing such procedures and formalities, in addition to electronic means. The fact that it must be possible to complete those procedures and formalities at a distance means, in particular, that Member States must ensure that they may be completed across borders. The obligation as to results does not cover procedures or formalities which by their very nature are impossible to complete at a distance. Furthermore, this does not interfere with Member States' legislation on the use of languages.

(53) The granting of licences for certain service activities may require an interview with the applicant by the competent authority in order to assess the applicant's personal integrity and suitability for carrying out the service in question. In such cases, the completion of formalities by electronic means may not be appropriate.

(54) The possibility of gaining access to a service activity should be made subject to authorisation by the competent authorities only if that decision satisfies the criteria of non-discrimination, necessity and proportionality. That means, in particular, that authorisation schemes should be permissible only where an a posteriori inspection would not be effective because of the impossibility of ascertaining the defects of the services concerned a posteriori, due account being taken of the risks and dangers

which could arise in the absence of a prior inspection. However, the provision to that effect made by this Directive cannot be relied upon in order to justify authorisation schemes which are prohibited by other Community instruments such as Directive 1999/93/EC of the European Parliament and the Council of 13 December 1999 on a Community framework for electronic signatures, or Directive 2000/31/EC of the European Parliament and of the Council of 8 June 2000 on certain legal aspects of information society services, in particular electronic commerce, in the internal market (Directive on electronic commerce). The results of the process of mutual evaluation will make it possible to determine, at Community level, the types of activity for which authorisation schemes should be eliminated.

(55) This Directive should be without prejudice to the possibility for Member States to withdraw authorisations after they have been issued, if the conditions for the granting of the authorisation are no longer fulfilled.

(56) According to the case law of the Court of Justice, public health, consumer protection, animal health and the protection of the urban environment constitute overriding reasons relating to the public interest. Such overriding reasons may justify the application of authorisation schemes and other restrictions. However, no such authorisation scheme or restriction should discriminate on grounds of nationality. Further, the principles of necessity and proportionality should always be respected.

(57) The provisions of this Directive relating to authorisation schemes should concern cases where the access to or exercise of a service activity by operators requires a decision by a competent authority. This concerns neither decisions by competent authorities to set up a public or private entity for the provision of a particular service nor the conclusion of contracts by competent authorities for the provision of a particular service which is governed by rules on public procurement, since this Directive does not deal with rules on public procurement.

(58) In order to facilitate access to and exercise of service activities, it is important to evaluate and report on authorisation schemes and their justification. This reporting obligation concerns only the existence of authorisation schemes and not the criteria and conditions for the granting of an authorisation.

(59) The authorisation should as a general rule enable the provider to have access to the service activity, or to exercise that activity, throughout the national territory, unless a territorial limit is justified by an overriding reason relating to the public interest. For example, environmental protection may justify the requirement to obtain an individual authorisation for each installation on the national territory. This provision should not affect regional or local competences for the granting of authorisations within the Member States.

(60) This Directive, and in particular the provisions concerning authorisation schemes and the territorial scope of an authorisation, should not interfere with the division of regional or local competences within the Member States, including regional and local self–government and the use of official languages.

(61) The provision relating to the non–duplication of conditions for the granting of an authorisation should not prevent Member States from applying their own conditions as specified in the authorisation scheme. It should only require that competent authorities, when considering whether these conditions are met by the applicant, take into account the equivalent conditions which have already been satisfied by the applicant in another Member State. This provision should not require the application of the conditions for the granting of an authorisation provided for in the authorisation scheme of another Member State.

(62) Where the number of authorisations available for an activity is limited because of scarcity of natural resources or technical capacity, a procedure for selection from among several potential candidates should be adopted with the aim of developing through open competition the quality and conditions for supply of services available to users. Such a procedure should provide guarantees of transparency and impartiality and the authorisation thus granted should not have an excessive duration, be subject to automatic renewal or confer any advantage on the provider whose authorisation has just expired. In particular, the duration of the authorisation granted should be fixed in such a way that it does not restrict or limit free competition beyond what is necessary in order to enable the provider to recoup the cost of investment and to make a fair return on the capital invested. This provision should not prevent Member States from limiting the number of authorisations for reasons other than scarcity of natural resources or technical capacity. These authorisations should remain in any case subject to the other provisions of this Directive relating to authorisation schemes.

(63) In the absence of different arrangements, failing a response within a time period, an authorisation should be deemed to have been granted. However, different arrangements may be put in place in respect of certain activities, where objectively justified by overriding reasons relating to the public

interest, including a legitimate interest of third parties. Such different arrangements could include national rules according to which, in the absence of a response of the competent authority, the application is deemed to have been rejected, this rejection being open to challenge before the courts.

(64) In order to establish a genuine internal market for services, it is necessary to abolish any restrictions on the freedom of establishment and the free movement of services which are still enshrined in the laws of certain Member States and which are incompatible with Articles 43 and 49 of the Treaty respectively. The restrictions to be prohibited particularly affect the internal market for services and should be systematically dismantled as soon as possible.

(65) Freedom of establishment is predicated, in particular, upon the principle of equal treatment, which entails the prohibition not only of any discrimination on grounds of nationality but also of any indirect discrimination based on other grounds but capable of producing the same result. Thus, access to a service activity or the exercise thereof in a Member State, either as a principal or secondary activity, should not be made subject to criteria such as place of establishment, residence, domicile or principal provision of the service activity. However, these criteria should not include requirements according to which a provider or one of his employees or a representative must be present during the exercise of the activity when this is justified by an overriding reason relating to the public interest. Furthermore, a Member State should not restrict the legal capacity or the right of companies, incorporated in accordance with the law of another Member State on whose territory they have their primary establishment, to bring legal proceedings. Moreover, a Member State should not be able to confer any advantages on providers having a particular national or local socio–economic link; nor should it be able to restrict, on grounds of place of establishment, the provider's freedom to acquire, exploit or dispose of rights and goods or to access different forms of credit or accommodation in so far as those choices are useful for access to his activity or for the effective exercise thereof.

(66) Access to or the exercise of a service activity in the territory of a Member State should not be subject to an economic test. The prohibition of economic tests as a prerequisite for the grant of authorisation should cover economic tests as such, but not requirements which are objectively justified by overriding reasons relating to the public interest, such as the protection of the urban environment, social policy or public health. The prohibition should not affect the exercise of the powers of the authorities responsible for applying competition law.

(67) With respect to financial guarantees or insurance, the prohibition of requirements should concern only the obligation that the requested financial guarantees or insurance must be obtained from a financial institution established in the Member State concerned.

(68) With respect to pre–registration, the prohibition of requirements should concern only the obligation that the provider, prior to the establishment, be pre–registered for a given period in a register held in the Member State concerned.

(69) In order to coordinate the modernisation of national rules and regulations in a manner consistent with the requirements of the internal market, it is necessary to evaluate certain non–discriminatory national requirements which, by their very nature, could severely restrict or even prevent access to an activity or the exercise thereof under the freedom of establishment. This evaluation process should be limited to the compatibility of these requirements with the criteria already established by the Court of Justice on the freedom of establishment. It should not concern the application of Community competition law. Where such requirements are discriminatory or not objectively justified by an overriding reason relating to the public interest, or where they are disproportionate, they must be abolished or amended. The outcome of this assessment will be different according to the nature of the activity and the public interest concerned. In particular, such requirements could be fully justified when they pursue social policy objectives.

(70) For the purposes of this Directive, and without prejudice to Article 16 of the Treaty, services may be considered to be services of general economic interest only if they are provided in application of a special task in the public interest entrusted to the provider by the Member State concerned. This assignment should be made by way of one or more acts, the form of which is determined by the Member State concerned, and should specify the precise nature of the special task.

(71) The mutual evaluation process provided for in this Directive should not affect the freedom of Member States to set in their legislation a high level of protection of the public interest, in particular in relation to social policy objectives. Furthermore, it is necessary that the mutual evaluation process take fully into account the specificity of services of general economic interest and of the particular tasks assigned to them. This may justify certain restrictions on the freedom of establishment, in particular where such restrictions pursue the protection of public health and social policy objectives and where they satisfy the conditions set out in Article 15(3)(a), (b) and (c). For example, with regard to the obligation to take a specific legal form in order to exercise certain services in the social field, the Court of Justice has already recognised that it may be justified to subject the provider to a require-

ment to be non–profit making.

(72) Services of a general economic interest are entrusted with important tasks relating to social and territorial cohesion. The performance of these tasks should not be obstructed as a result of the evaluation process provided for in this Directive. Requirements which are necessary for the fulfilment of such tasks should not be affected by this process while, at the same time, unjustified restrictions on the freedom of establishment should be addressed.

(73) The requirements to be examined include national rules which, on grounds other than those relating to professional qualifications, reserve access to certain activities to particular providers. These requirements also include obligations on a provider to take a specific legal form, in particular to be a legal person, to be a company with individual ownership, to be a non–profit making organisation or a company owned exclusively by natural persons, and requirements which relate to the shareholding of a company, in particular obligations to hold a minimum amount of capital for certain service activities or to have a specific qualification in order to hold share capital in or to manage certain companies. The evaluation of the compatibility of fixed minimum and/or maximum tariffs with the freedom of establishment concerns only tariffs imposed by competent authorities specifically for the provision of certain services and not, for example, general rules on price determination, such as for the renting of houses.

(74) The mutual evaluation process means that during the transposition period Member States will first have to conduct a screening of their legislation in order to ascertain whether any of the above mentioned requirements exists in their legal systems. At the latest by the end of the transposition period, Member States should draw up a report on the results of this screening. Each report will be submitted to all other Member States and interested parties. Member States will then have six months in which to submit their observations on these reports. At the latest by one year after the date of transposition of this Directive, the Commission should draw up a summary report, accompanied where appropriate by proposals for further initiatives. If necessary the Commission, in cooperation with the Member States, could assist them to design a common method.

(75) The fact that this Directive specifies a number of requirements to be abolished or evaluated by the Member States during the transposition period is without prejudice to any infringement proceedings against a Member State for failure to fulfil its obligations under Articles 43 or 49 of the Treaty.

(76) This Directive does not concern the application of Articles 28 to 30 of the Treaty relating to the free movement of goods. The restrictions prohibited pursuant to the provision on the freedom to provide services cover the requirements applicable to access to service activities or to the exercise thereof and not those applicable to goods as such.

(77) Where an operator travels to another Member State to exercise a service activity there, a distinction should be made between situations covered by the freedom of establishment and those covered, due to the temporary nature of the activities concerned, by the free movement of services. As regards the distinction between the freedom of establishment and the free movement of services, according to the case law of the Court of Justice the key element is whether or not the operator is established in the Member State where it provides the service concerned. If the operator is established in the Member State where it provides its services, it should come under the scope of application of the freedom of establishment. If, by contrast, the operator is not established in the Member State where the service is provided, its activities should be covered by the free movement of services. The Court of Justice has consistently held that the temporary nature of the activities in question should be determined in the light not only of the duration of the provision of the service, but also of its regularity, periodical nature or continuity. The fact that the activity is temporary should not mean that the provider may not equip itself with some forms of infrastructure in the Member State where the service is provided, such as an office, chambers or consulting rooms, in so far as such infrastructure is necessary for the purposes of providing the service in question.

(78) In order to secure effective implementation of the free movement of services and to ensure that recipients and providers can benefit from and supply services throughout the Community regardless of borders, it is necessary to clarify the extent to which requirements of the Member State where the service is provided can be imposed. It is indispensable to provide that the provision on the freedom to provide services does not prevent the Member State where the service is provided from imposing, in compliance with the principles set out in Article 16(1)(a) to (c), its specific requirements for reasons of public policy or public security or for the protection of public health or the environment.

(79) The Court of Justice has consistently held that Member States retain the right to take measures in order to prevent providers from abusively taking advantage of the internal market principles. Abuse by a provider should be established on a case by case basis.

(80) It is necessary to ensure that providers are able to take equipment which is integral to the provision of their service with them when they travel to provide services in another Member State. In

particular, it is important to avoid cases in which the service could not be provided without the equipment or situations in which providers incur additional costs, for example, by hiring or purchasing different equipment to that which they habitually use or by needing to deviate significantly from the way they habitually carry out their activity.

(81) The concept of equipment does not refer to physical objects which are either supplied by the provider to the client or become part of a physical object as a result of the service activity, such as building materials or spare parts, or which are consumed or left in situ in the course of the service provision, such as combustible fuels, explosives, fireworks, pesticides, poisons or medicines.

(82) The provisions of this Directive should not preclude the application by a Member State of rules on employment conditions. Rules laid down by law, regulation or administrative provisions should, in accordance with the Treaty, be justified for reasons relating to the protection of workers and be non–discriminatory, necessary, and proportionate, as interpreted by the Court of Justice, and comply with other relevant Community law.

(83) It is necessary to ensure that the provision on the freedom to provide services may be departed from only in the areas covered by derogations. Those derogations are necessary in order to take into account the level of integration of the internal market or certain Community instruments relating to services pursuant to which a provider is subject to the application of a law other than that of the Member State of establishment. Moreover, by way of exception, measures against a given provider should also be adopted in certain individual cases and under certain strict procedural and substantive conditions. In addition, any restriction of the free movement of services should be permitted, by way of exception, only if it is consistent with fundamental rights which form an integral part of the general principles of law enshrined in the Community legal order.

(84) The derogation from the provision on the freedom to provide services concerning postal services should cover both activities reserved to the universal service provider and other postal services.

(85) The derogation from the provision on the freedom to provide services relating to the judicial recovery of debts and the reference to a possible future harmonisation instrument should concern only the access to and the exercise of activities which consist, notably, in bringing actions before a court relating to the recovery of debts.

(86) This Directive should not affect terms and conditions of employment which, pursuant to Directive 96/71/EC of the European Parliament and of the Council of 16 December 1996 concerning the posting of workers in the framework of the provision of services, apply to workers posted to provide a service in the territory of another Member State. In such cases, Directive 96/71/EC stipulates that providers have to comply with terms and conditions of employment in a listed number of areas applicable in the Member State where the service is provided. These are: maximum work periods and minimum rest periods, minimum paid annual holidays, minimum rates of pay, including overtime rates, the conditions of hiring out of workers, in particular the protection of workers hired out by temporary employment undertakings, health, safety and hygiene at work, protective measures with regard to the terms and conditions of employment of pregnant women or women who have recently given birth and of children and young people and equality of treatment between men and women and other provisions on non–discrimination. This not only concerns terms and conditions of employment which are laid down by law but also those laid down in collective agreements or arbitration awards that are officially declared or de facto universally applicable within the meaning of Directive 96/71/EC. Moreover, this Directive should not prevent Member States from applying terms and conditions of employment on matters other than those listed in Article 3(1) of Directive 96/71/EC on the grounds of public policy.

(87) Neither should this Directive affect terms and conditions of employment in cases where the worker employed for the provision of a cross–border service is recruited in the Member State where the service is provided. Furthermore, this Directive should not affect the right for the Member State where the service is provided to determine the existence of an employment relationship and the distinction between self–employed persons and employed persons, including 'false self–employed persons'. In that respect the essential characteristic of an employment relationship within the meaning of Article 39 of the Treaty should be the fact that for a certain period of time a person provides services for and under the direction of another person in return for which he receives remuneration. Any activity which a person performs outside a relationship of subordination must be classified as an activity pursued in a self–employed capacity for the purposes of Articles 43 and 49 of the Treaty.

(88) The provision on the freedom to provide services should not apply in cases where, in conformity with Community law, an activity is reserved in a Member State to a particular profession, for example requirements which reserve the provision of legal advice to lawyers.

(89) The derogation from the provision on the freedom to provide services concerning matters relating to the registration of vehicles leased in a Member State other than that in which they are used

follows from the case law of the Court of Justice, which has recognised that a Member State may impose such an obligation, in accordance with proportionate conditions, in the case of vehicles used on its territory. That exclusion does not cover occasional or temporary rental.

(90) Contractual relations between the provider and the client as well as between an employer and employee should not be subject to this Directive. The applicable law regarding the contractual or non contractual obligations of the provider should be determined by the rules of private international law.

(91) It is necessary to afford Member States the possibility, exceptionally and on a case–by–case basis, of taking measures which derogate from the provision on the freedom to provide services in respect of a provider established in another Member State on grounds of the safety of services. However, it should be possible to take such measures only in the absence of harmonisation at Community level.

(92) Restrictions on the free movement of services, contrary to this Directive, may arise not only from measures applied to providers, but also from the many barriers to the use of services by recipients, especially consumers. This Directive mentions, by way of illustration, certain types of restriction applied to a recipient wishing to use a service performed by a provider established in another Member State. This also includes cases where recipients of a service are under an obligation to obtain authorisation from or to make a declaration to their competent authorities in order to receive a service from a provider established in another Member State. This does not concern general authorisation schemes which also apply to the use of a service supplied by a provider established in the same Member State.

(93) The concept of financial assistance provided for the use of a particular service should not apply to systems of aids granted by Member States, in particular in the social field or in the cultural sector, which are covered by Community rules on competition, nor to general financial assistance not linked to the use of a particular service, for example grants or loans to students.

(94) In accordance with the Treaty rules on the free movement of services, discrimination on grounds of the nationality of the recipient or national or local residence is prohibited. Such discrimination could take the form of an obligation, imposed only on nationals of another Member State, to supply original documents, certified copies, a certificate of nationality or official translations of documents in order to benefit from a service or from more advantageous terms or prices. However, the prohibition of discriminatory requirements should not preclude the reservation of advantages, especially as regards tariffs, to certain recipients, if such reservation is based on legitimate and objective criteria.

(95) The principle of non–discrimination within the internal market means that access by a recipient, and especially by a consumer, to a service on offer to the public may not be denied or restricted by application of a criterion, included in general conditions made available to the public, relating to the recipient's nationality or place of residence. It does not follow that it will be unlawful discrimination if provision were made in such general conditions for different tariffs and conditions to apply to the provision of a service, where those tariffs, prices and conditions are justified for objective reasons that can vary from country to country, such as additional costs incurred because of the distance involved or the technical characteristics of the provision of the service, or different market conditions, such as higher or lower demand influenced by seasonality, different vacation periods in the Member States and pricing by different competitors, or extra risks linked to rules differing from those of the Member State of establishment. Neither does it follow that the non–provision of a service to a consumer for lack of the required intellectual property rights in a particular territory would constitute unlawful discrimination.

(96) It is appropriate to provide that, as one of the means by which the provider may make the information which he is obliged to supply easily accessible to the recipient, he supply his electronic address, including that of his website. Furthermore, the obligation to make available certain information in the provider's information documents which present his services in detail should not cover commercial communications of a general nature, such as advertising, but rather documents giving a detailed description of the services proposed, including documents on a website.

(97) It is necessary to provide in this Directive for certain rules on high quality of services, ensuring in particular information and transparency requirements. These rules should apply both in cases of cross border provision of services between Member States and in cases of services provided in a Member State by a provider established there, without imposing unnecessary burdens on SMEs. They should not in any way prevent Member States from applying, in conformity with this Directive and other Community law, additional or different quality requirements.

(98) Any operator providing services involving a direct and particular health, safety or financial risk for the recipient or a third person should, in principle, be covered by appropriate professional liability insurance, or by another form of guarantee which is equivalent or comparable, which means, in particular, that such an operator should as a general rule have adequate insurance cover for services

provided in one or more Member States other than the Member State of establishment.
(99) The insurance or guarantee should be appropriate to the nature and extent of the risk. Therefore it should be necessary for the provider to have cross–border cover only if that provider actually provides services in other Member States. Member States should not lay down more detailed rules concerning the insurance cover and fix for example minimum thresholds for the insured sum or limits on exclusions from the insurance cover. Providers and insurance companies should maintain the necessary flexibility to negotiate insurance policies precisely targeted to the nature and extent of the risk. Furthermore, it is not necessary for an obligation of appropriate insurance to be laid down by law. It should be sufficient if an insurance obligation is part of the ethical rules laid down by professional bodies. Finally, there should be no obligation for insurance companies to provide insurance cover.
(100) It is necessary to put an end to total prohibitions on commercial communications by the regulated professions, not by removing bans on the content of a commercial communication but rather by removing those bans which, in a general way and for a given profession, forbid one or more forms of commercial communication, such as a ban on all advertising in one or more given media. As regards the content and methods of commercial communication, it is necessary to encourage professionals to draw up, in accordance with Community law, codes of conduct at Community level.
(101) It is necessary and in the interest of recipients, in particular consumers, to ensure that it is possible for providers to offer multidisciplinary services and that restrictions in this regard be limited to what is necessary to ensure the impartiality, independence and integrity of the regulated professions. This does not affect restrictions or prohibitions on carrying out particular activities which aim at ensuring independence in cases in which a Member State entrusts a provider with a particular task, notably in the area of urban development, nor should it affect the application of competition rules.
(102) In order to increase transparency and promote assessments based on comparable criteria with regard to the quality of the services offered and supplied to recipients, it is important that information on the meaning of quality labels and other distinctive marks relating to these services be easily accessible. That obligation of transparency is particularly important in areas such as tourism, especially the hotel business, in which the use of a system of classification is widespread. Moreover, it is appropriate to examine the extent to which European standardisation could facilitate compatibility and quality of services. European standards are drawn up by the European standards–setting bodies, the European Committee for Standardisation (CEN), the European Committee for Electrotechnical Standardisation (CENELEC) and the European Telecommunications Standards Institute (ETSI). Where appropriate, the Commission may, in accordance with the procedures laid down in Directive 98/34/EC of the European Parliament and of the Council of 22 June 1998 laying down a procedure for the provision of information in the field of technical standards and regulations and of rules on Information Society services, issue a mandate for the drawing up of specific European standards.
(103) In order to solve potential problems with compliance with judicial decisions, it is appropriate to provide that Member States recognise equivalent guarantees lodged with institutions or bodies such as banks, insurance providers or other financial services providers established in another Member State.
(104) The development of a network of Member States' consumer protection authorities, which is the subject of Regulation (EC) No 2006/2004, complements the cooperation provided for in this Directive. The application of consumer protection legislation in cross–border cases, in particular with regard to new marketing and selling practices, as well as the need to remove certain specific obstacles to cooperation in this field, necessitates a greater degree of cooperation between Member States. In particular, it is necessary in this area to ensure that Member States require the cessation of illegal practices by operators in their territory who target consumers in another Member State.
(105) Administrative cooperation is essential to make the internal market in services function properly. Lack of cooperation between Member States results in proliferation of rules applicable to providers or duplication of controls for cross–border activities, and can also be used by rogue traders to avoid supervision or to circumvent applicable national rules on services. It is, therefore, essential to provide for clear, legally binding obligations for Member States to cooperate effectively.
(106) For the purposes of the Chapter on administrative cooperation, 'supervision' should cover activities such as monitoring and fact finding, problem solving, enforcement and imposition of sanctions and subsequent follow–up activities.
(107) In normal circumstances mutual assistance should take place directly between competent authorities. The liaison points designated by Member States should be required to facilitate this process only in the event of difficulties being encountered, for instance if assistance is required to identify the relevant competent authority.
(108) Certain obligations of mutual assistance should apply to all matters covered by this Directive, including those relating to cases where a provider establishes in another Member State. Other obli-

gations of mutual assistance should apply only in cases of cross–border provision of services, where the provision on the freedom to provide services applies. A further set of obligations should apply in all cases of cross–border provision of services, including areas not covered by the provision on the freedom to provide services. Cross–border provision of services should include cases where services are provided at a distance and where the recipient travels to the Member State of establishment of the provider in order to receive services.

(109) In cases where a provider moves temporarily to a Member State other than the Member State of establishment, it is necessary to provide for mutual assistance between those two Member States so that the former can carry out checks, inspections and enquiries at the request of the Member State of establishment or carry out such checks on its own initiative if these are merely factual checks.

(110) It should not be possible for Member States to circumvent the rules laid down in this Directive, including the provision on the freedom to provide services, by conducting checks, inspections or investigations which are discriminatory or disproportionate.

(111) The provisions of this Directive concerning exchange of information regarding the good repute of providers should not pre–empt initiatives in the area of police and judicial cooperation in criminal matters, in particular on the exchange of information between law enforcement authorities of the Member States and on criminal records.

(112) Cooperation between Member States requires a well–functioning electronic information system in order to allow competent authorities easily to identify their relevant interlocutors in other Member States and to communicate in an efficient way.

(113) It is necessary to provide that the Member States, in cooperation with the Commission, are to encourage interested parties to draw up codes of conduct at Community level, aimed, in particular, at promoting the quality of services and taking into account the specific nature of each profession. Those codes of conduct should comply with Community law, especially competition law. They should be compatible with legally binding rules governing professional ethics and conduct in the Member States.

(114) Member States should encourage the setting up of codes of conduct, in particular, by professional bodies, organisations and associations at Community level. These codes of conduct should include, as appropriate to the specific nature of each profession, rules for commercial communications relating to the regulated professions and rules of professional ethics and conduct of the regulated professions which aim, in particular, at ensuring independence, impartiality and professional secrecy. In addition, the conditions to which the activities of estate agents are subject should be included in such codes of conduct. Member States should take accompanying measures to encourage professional bodies, organisations and associations to implement at national level the codes of conduct adopted at Community level.

(115) Codes of conduct at Community level are intended to set minimum standards of conduct and are complementary to Member States' legal requirements. They do not preclude Member States, in accordance with Community law, from taking more stringent measures in law or national professional bodies from providing for greater protection in their national codes of conduct.

(116) Since the objectives of this Directive, namely the elimination of barriers to the freedom of establishment for providers in the Member States and to the free provision of services between Member States, cannot be sufficiently achieved by the Member States and can therefore, by reason of the scale of the action, be better achieved at Community level, the Community may adopt measures, in accordance with the principle of subsidiarity as set out in Article 5 of the Treaty. In accordance with the principle of proportionality, as set out in that Article, this Directive does not go beyond what is necessary in order to achieve those objectives.

(117) The measures necessary for the implementation of this Directive should be adopted in accordance with Council Decision 1999/468/EC of 28 June 1999 laying down the procedures for the exercise of implementing powers conferred on the Commission.

(118) In accordance with paragraph 34 of the Interinstitutional Agreement on better law–making, Member States are encouraged to draw up, for themselves and in the interest of the Community, their own tables, which will, as far as possible, illustrate the correlation between the Directive and the transposition measures, and to make them public,

HAVE ADOPTED THIS DIRECTIVE:

Chapter I. General Provisions

Article 1. Subject matter

(1) This Directive establishes general provisions facilitating the exercise of the freedom of establishment for service providers and the free movement of services, while maintaining a high quality of services.

(2) This Directive does not deal with the liberalisation of services of general economic interest, reserved to public or private entities, nor with the privatisation of public entities providing services.
(3) This Directive does not deal with the abolition of monopolies providing services nor with aids granted by Member States which are covered by Community rules on competition.
This Directive does not affect the freedom of Member States to define, in conformity with Community law, what they consider to be services of general economic interest, how those services should be organised and financed, in compliance with the State aid rules, and what specific obligations they should be subject to.
(4) This Directive does not affect measures taken at Community level or at national level, in conformity with Community law, to protect or promote cultural or linguistic diversity or media pluralism.
(5) This Directive does not affect Member States' rules of criminal law. However, Member States may not restrict the freedom to provide services by applying criminal law provisions which specifically regulate or affect access to or exercise of a service activity in circumvention of the rules laid down in this Directive.
(6) This Directive does not affect labour law, that is any legal or contractual provision concerning employment conditions, working conditions, including health and safety at work and the relationship between employers and workers, which Member States apply in accordance with national law which respects Community law. Equally, this Directive does not affect the social security legislation of the Member States.
(7) This Directive does not affect the exercise of fundamental rights as recognised in the Member States and by Community law. Nor does it affect the right to negotiate, conclude and enforce collective agreements and to take industrial action in accordance with national law and practices which respect Community law.

Article 2. Scope
(1) This Directive shall apply to services supplied by providers established in a Member State.
(2) This Directive shall not apply to the following activities:
(a) non–economic services of general interest;
(b) financial services, such as banking, credit, insurance and re–insurance, occupational or personal pensions, securities, investment funds, payment and investment advice, including the services listed in Annex I to Directive 2006/48/EC;
(c) electronic communications services and networks, and associated facilities and services, with respect to matters covered by Directives 2002/19/EC, 2002/20/EC, 2002/21/EC, 2002/22/EC and 2002/58/EC;
(d) services in the field of transport, including port services, falling within the scope of Title V of the Treaty;
(e) services of temporary work agencies;
(f) healthcare services whether or not they are provided via healthcare facilities, and regardless of the ways in which they are organised and financed at national level or whether they are public or private;
(g) audiovisual services, including cinematographic services, whatever their mode of production, distribution and transmission, and radio broadcasting;
(h) gambling activities which involve wagering a stake with pecuniary value in games of chance, including lotteries, gambling in casinos and betting transactions;
(i) activities which are connected with the exercise of official authority as set out in Article 45 of the Treaty;
(j) social services relating to social housing, childcare and support of families and persons permanently or temporarily in need which are provided by the State, by providers mandated by the State or by charities recognised as such by the State;
(k) private security services;
(l) services provided by notaries and bailiffs, who are appointed by an official act of government.
(3) This Directive shall not apply to the field of taxation.

Article 3. Relationship with other provisions of Community law
(1) If the provisions of this Directive conflict with a provision of another Community act governing specific aspects of access to or exercise of a service activity in specific sectors or for specific professions, the provision of the other Community act shall prevail and shall apply to those specific sectors or professions. These include:
(a) Directive 96/71/EC;
(b) Regulation (EEC) No 1408/71;
(c) Council Directive 89/552/EEC of 3 October 1989 on the coordination of certain provisions laid

down by law, regulation or administrative action in Member States concerning the pursuit of television broadcasting activities;
(d) Directive 2005/36/EC.
(2) This Directive does not concern rules of private international law, in particular rules governing the law applicable to contractual and non contractual obligations, including those which guarantee that consumers benefit from the protection granted to them by the consumer protection rules laid down in the consumer legislation in force in their Member State.
(3) Member States shall apply the provisions of this Directive in compliance with the rules of the Treaty on the right of establishment and the free movement of services.

Article 4. Definitions

For the purposes of this Directive, the following definitions shall apply:
1) 'service' means any self–employed economic activity, normally provided for remuneration, as referred to in Article 50 of the Treaty;
2) 'provider' means any natural person who is a national of a Member State, or any legal person as referred to in Article 48 of the Treaty and established in a Member State, who offers or provides a service;
3) 'recipient' means any natural person who is a national of a Member State or who benefits from rights conferred upon him by Community acts, or any legal person as referred to in Article 48 of the Treaty and established in a Member State, who, for professional or non–professional purposes, uses, or wishes to use, a service;
4) 'Member State of establishment' means the Member State in whose territory the provider of the service concerned is established;
5) 'establishment' means the actual pursuit of an economic activity, as referred to in Article 43 of the Treaty, by the provider for an indefinite period and through a stable infrastructure from where the business of providing services is actually carried out;
6) 'authorisation scheme' means any procedure under which a provider or recipient is in effect required to take steps in order to obtain from a competent authority a formal decision, or an implied decision, concerning access to a service activity or the exercise thereof;
7) 'requirement' means any obligation, prohibition, condition or limit provided for in the laws, regulations or administrative provisions of the Member States or in consequence of case–law, administrative practice, the rules of professional bodies, or the collective rules of professional associations or other professional organisations, adopted in the exercise of their legal autonomy; rules laid down in collective agreements negotiated by the social partners shall not as such be seen as requirements within the meaning of this Directive;
8) 'overriding reasons relating to the public interest' means reasons recognised as such in the case law of the Court of Justice, including the following grounds: public policy; public security; public safety; public health; preserving the financial equilibrium of the social security system; the protection of consumers, recipients of services and workers; fairness of trade transactions; combating fraud; the protection of the environment and the urban environment; the health of animals; intellectual property; the conservation of the national historic and artistic heritage; social policy objectives and cultural policy objectives;
9) 'competent authority' means any body or authority which has a supervisory or regulatory role in a Member State in relation to service activities, including, in particular, administrative authorities, including courts acting as such, professional bodies, and those professional associations or other professional organisations which, in the exercise of their legal autonomy, regulate in a collective manner access to service activities or the exercise thereof;
10) 'Member State where the service is provided' means the Member State where the service is supplied by a provider established in another Member State;
11) 'regulated profession' means a professional activity or a group of professional activities as referred to in Article 3(1)(a) of Directive 2005/36/EC;
12) 'commercial communication' means any form of communication designed to promote, directly or indirectly, the goods, services or image of an undertaking, organisation or person engaged in commercial, industrial or craft activity or practising a regulated profession. The following do not in themselves constitute commercial communications:
(a) information enabling direct access to the activity of the undertaking, organisation or person, including in particular a domain name or an electronic–mailing address;
(b) communications relating to the goods, services or image of the undertaking, organisation or person, compiled in an independent manner, particularly when provided for no financial consideration.

Chapter II. Administrative Simplification

Article 5. Simplification of procedures

(1) Member States shall examine the procedures and formalities applicable to access to a service activity and to the exercise thereof. Where procedures and formalities examined under this paragraph are not sufficiently simple, Member States shall simplify them.

(2) The Commission may introduce harmonised forms at Community level, in accordance with the procedure referred to in Article 40(2). These forms shall be equivalent to certificates, attestations and any other documents required of a provider.

(3) Where Member States require a provider or recipient to supply a certificate, attestation or any other document proving that a requirement has been satisfied, they shall accept any document from another Member State which serves an equivalent purpose or from which it is clear that the requirement in question has been satisfied. They may not require a document from another Member State to be produced in its original form, or as a certified copy or as a certified translation, save in the cases provided for in other Community instruments or where such a requirement is justified by an overriding reason relating to the public interest, including public order and security.

The first subparagraph shall not affect the right of Member States to require non–certified translations of documents in one of their official languages.

(4) Paragraph 3 shall not apply to the documents referred to in Article 7(2) and 50 of Directive 2005/36/EC, in Articles 45(3), 46, 49 and 50 of Directive 2004/18/EC of the European Parliament and of the Council of 31 March 2004 on the coordination of procedures for the award of public works contracts, public supply contracts and public service contracts, in Article 3(2) of Directive 98/5/EC of the European Parliament and of the Council of 16 February 1998 to facilitate practice of the profession of lawyer on a permanent basis in a Member State other than that in which the qualification was obtained, in the First Council Directive 68/151/EEC of 9 March 1968 on coordination of safeguards which, for the protection of the interests of members and others, are required by Member States of companies within the meaning of the second paragraph of Article 58 of the Treaty, with a view to making such safeguards equivalent throughout the Community and in the Eleventh Council Directive 89/666/EEC of 21 December 1989 concerning disclosure requirements in respect of branches opened in a Member State by certain types of company governed by the law of another State.

Article 6. Points of single contact

(1) Member States shall ensure that it is possible for providers to complete the following procedures and formalities through points of single contact:

(a) all procedures and formalities needed for access to his service activities, in particular, all declarations, notifications or applications necessary for authorisation from the competent authorities, including applications for inclusion in a register, a roll or a database, or for registration with a professional body or association;

(b) any applications for authorisation needed to exercise his service activities.

(2) The establishment of points of single contact shall be without prejudice to the allocation of functions and powers among the authorities within national systems.

Article 7. Right to information

(1) Member States shall ensure that the following information is easily accessible to providers and recipients through the points of single contact:

(a) requirements applicable to providers established in their territory, in particular those requirements concerning the procedures and formalities to be completed in order to access and to exercise service activities;

(b) the contact details of the competent authorities enabling the latter to be contacted directly, including the details of those authorities responsible for matters concerning the exercise of service activities;

(c) the means of, and conditions for, accessing public registers and databases on providers and services;

(d) the means of redress which are generally available in the event of dispute between the competent authorities and the provider or the recipient, or between a provider and a recipient or between providers;

(e) the contact details of the associations or organisations, other than the competent authorities, from which providers or recipients may obtain practical assistance.

(2) Member States shall ensure that it is possible for providers and recipients to receive, at their request, assistance from the competent authorities, consisting in information on the way in which

the requirements referred to in point (a) of paragraph 1 are generally interpreted and applied. Where appropriate, such advice shall include a simple step–by–step guide. The information shall be provided in plain and intelligible language.

(3) Member States shall ensure that the information and assistance referred to in paragraphs 1 and 2 are provided in a clear and unambiguous manner, that they are easily accessible at a distance and by electronic means and that they are kept up to date.

(4) Member States shall ensure that the points of single contact and the competent authorities respond as quickly as possible to any request for information or assistance as referred to in paragraphs 1 and 2 and, in cases where the request is faulty or unfounded, inform the applicant accordingly without delay.

(5) Member States and the Commission shall take accompanying measures in order to encourage points of single contact to make the information provided for in this Article available in other Community languages. This does not interfere with Member States' legislation on the use of languages.

(6) The obligation for competent authorities to assist providers and recipients does not require those authorities to provide legal advice in individual cases but concerns only general information on the way in which requirements are usually interpreted or applied.

Article 8. Procedures by electronic means

(1) Member States shall ensure that all procedures and formalities relating to access to a service activity and to the exercise thereof may be easily completed, at a distance and by electronic means, through the relevant point of single contact and with the relevant competent authorities.

(2) Paragraph 1 shall not apply to the inspection of premises on which the service is provided or of equipment used by the provider or to physical examination of the capability or of the personal integrity of the provider or of his responsible staff.

(3) The Commission shall, in accordance with the procedure referred to in Article 40(2), adopt detailed rules for the implementation of paragraph 1 of this Article with a view to facilitating the interoperability of information systems and use of procedures by electronic means between Member States, taking into account common standards developed at Community level.

Chapter III. Freedom of Establishment for Providers

Section 1. Authorisations

Article 9. Authorisation schemes

(1) Member States shall not make access to a service activity or the exercise thereof subject to an authorisation scheme unless the following conditions are satisfied:

(a) the authorisation scheme does not discriminate against the provider in question;

(b) the need for an authorisation scheme is justified by an overriding reason relating to the public interest;

(c) the objective pursued cannot be attained by means of a less restrictive measure, in particular because an **a posteriori** inspection would take place too late to be genuinely effective.

(2) In the report referred to in Article 39(1), Member States shall identify their authorisation schemes and give reasons showing their compatibility with paragraph 1 of this Article.

(3) This section shall not apply to those aspects of authorisation schemes which are governed directly or indirectly by other Community instruments.

Article 10. Condiations for the granting of authorisation

(1) Authorisation schemes shall be based on criteria which preclude the competent authorities from exercising their power of assessment in an arbitrary manner.

(2) The criteria referred to in paragraph 1 shall be:

(a) non–discriminatory;

(b) justified by an overriding reason relating to the public interest;

(c) proportionate to that public interest objective;

(d) clear and unambiguous;

(e) objective;

(f) made public in advance;

(g) transparent and accessible.

(3) The conditions for granting authorisation for a new establishment shall not duplicate requirements and controls which are equivalent or essentially comparable as regards their purpose to which the provider is already subject in another Member State or in the same Member State. The liaison points referred to in Article 28(2) and the provider shall assist the competent authority by providing any

necessary information regarding those requirements.

(4) The authorisation shall enable the provider to have access to the service activity, or to exercise that activity, throughout the national territory, including by means of setting up agencies, subsidiaries, branches or offices, except where an authorisation for each individual establishment or a limitation of the authorisation to a certain part of the territory is justified by an overriding reason relating to the public interest.

(5) The authorisation shall be granted as soon as it is established, in the light of an appropriate examination, that the conditions for authorisation have been met.

(6) Except in the case of the granting of an authorisation, any decision from the competent authorities, including refusal or withdrawal of an authorisation, shall be fully reasoned and shall be open to challenge before the courts or other instances of appeal.

(7) This Article shall not call into question the allocation of the competences, at local or regional level, of the Member States' authorities granting authorisations.

Article 11. Duration of authorisation

(1) An authorisation granted to a provider shall not be for a limited period, except where:

(a) the authorisation is being automatically renewed or is subject only to the continued fulfilment of requirements;

(b) the number of available authorisations is limited by an overriding reason relating to the public interest;

or

(c) a limited authorisation period can be justified by an overriding reason relating to the public interest.

(2) Paragraph 1 shall not concern the maximum period before the end of which the provider must actually commence his activity after receiving authorisation.

(3) Member States shall require a provider to inform the relevant point of single contact provided for in Article 6 of the following changes:

(a) the creation of subsidiaries whose activities fall within the scope of the authorisation scheme;

(b) changes in his situation which result in the conditions for authorisation no longer being met.

(4) This Article shall be without prejudice to the Member States' ability to revoke authorisations, when the conditions for authorisation are no longer met.

Article 12. Selection from among several candidates

(1) Where the number of authorisations available for a given activity is limited because of the scarcity of available natural resources or technical capacity, Member States shall apply a selection procedure to potential candidates which provides full guarantees of impartiality and transparency, including, in particular, adequate publicity about the launch, conduct and completion of the procedure.

(2) In the cases referred to in paragraph 1, authorisation shall be granted for an appropriate limited period and may not be open to automatic renewal nor confer any other advantage on the provider whose authorisation has just expired or on any person having any particular links with that provider.

(3) Subject to paragraph 1 and to Articles 9 and 10, Member States may take into account, in establishing the rules for the selection procedure, considerations of public health, social policy objectives, the health and safety of employees or self–employed persons, the protection of the environment, the preservation of cultural heritage and other overriding reasons relating to the public interest, in conformity with Community law.

Article 13. Authorisation procedures

(1) Authorisation procedures and formalities shall be clear, made public in advance and be such as to provide the applicants with a guarantee that their application will be dealt with objectively and impartially.

(2) Authorisation procedures and formalities shall not be dissuasive and shall not unduly complicate or delay the provision of the service. They shall be easily accessible and any charges which the applicants may incur from their application shall be reasonable and proportionate to the cost of the authorisation procedures in question and shall not exceed the cost of the procedures.

(3) Authorisation procedures and formalities shall provide applicants with a guarantee that their application will be processed as quickly as possible and, in any event, within a reasonable period which is fixed and made public in advance. The period shall run only from the time when all documentation has been submitted. When justified by the complexity of the issue, the time period may be extended once, by the competent authority, for a limited time. The extension and its duration shall be duly motivated and shall be notified to the applicant before the original period has expired.

(4) Failing a response within the time period set or extended in accordance with paragraph 3,

authorisation shall be deemed to have been granted. Different arrangements may nevertheless be put in place, where justified by overriding reasons relating to the public interest, including a legitimate interest of third parties.

(5) All applications for authorisation shall be acknowledged as quickly as possible. The acknowledgement must specify the following:

(a) the period referred to in paragraph 3;

(b) the available means of redress;

(c) where applicable, a statement that in the absence of a response within the period specified, the authorisation shall be deemed to have been granted.

(6) In the case of an incomplete application, the applicant shall be informed as quickly as possible of the need to supply any additional documentation, as well as of any possible effects on the period referred to in paragraph 3.

(7) When a request is rejected because it fails to comply with the required procedures or formalities, the applicant shall be informed of the rejection as quickly as possible.

Section 2. Requirements Prohibited or Subject to Evaluation

Article 14. Prohibited requirements

Member States shall not make access to, or the exercise of, a service activity in their territory subject to compliance with any of the following:

1) discriminatory requirements based directly or indirectly on nationality or, in the case of companies, the location of the registered office, including in particular:

(a) nationality requirements for the provider, his staff, persons holding the share capital or members of the provider's management or supervisory bodies;

(b) a requirement that the provider, his staff, persons holding the share capital or members of the provider's management or supervisory bodies be resident within the territory;

2) a prohibition on having an establishment in more than one Member State or on being entered in the registers or enrolled with professional bodies or associations of more than one Member State;

3) restrictions on the freedom of a provider to choose between a principal or a secondary establishment, in particular an obligation on the provider to have its principal establishment in their territory, or restrictions on the freedom to choose between establishment in the form of an agency, branch or subsidiary;

4) conditions of reciprocity with the Member State in which the provider already has an establishment, save in the case of conditions of reciprocity provided for in Community instruments concerning energy;

5) the case–by–case application of an economic test making the granting of authorisation subject to proof of the existence of an economic need or market demand, an assessment of the potential or current economic effects of the activity or an assessment of the appropriateness of the activity in relation to the economic planning objectives set by the competent authority; this prohibition shall not concern planning requirements which do not pursue economic aims but serve overriding reasons relating to the public interest;

6) the direct or indirect involvement of competing operators, including within consultative bodies, in the granting of authorisations or in the adoption of other decisions of the competent authorities, with the exception of professional bodies and associations or other organisations acting as the competent authority; this prohibition shall not concern the consultation of organisations, such as chambers of commerce or social partners, on matters other than individual applications for authorisation, or a consultation of the public at large;

7) an obligation to provide or participate in a financial guarantee or to take out insurance from a provider or body established in their territory. This shall not affect the possibility for Member States to require insurance or financial guarantees as such, nor shall it affect requirements relating to the participation in a collective compensation fund, for instance for members of professional bodies or organisations;

8) an obligation to have been pre–registered, for a given period, in the registers held in their territory or to have previously exercised the activity for a given period in their territory.

Article 15. Requirements to be evaluated

(1) Member States shall examine whether, under their legal system, any of the requirements listed in paragraph 2 are imposed and shall ensure that any such requirements are compatible with the conditions laid down in paragraph 3. Member States shall adapt their laws, regulations or administrative provisions so as to make them compatible with those conditions.

(2) Member States shall examine whether their legal system makes access to a service activity or the

exercise of it subject to compliance with any of the following non–discriminatory requirements:
(a) quantitative or territorial restrictions, in particular in the form of limits fixed according to population or of a minimum geographical distance between providers;
(b) an obligation on a provider to take a specific legal form;
(c) requirements which relate to the shareholding of a company;
(d) requirements, other than those concerning matters covered by Directive 2005/36/EC or provided for in other Community instruments, which reserve access to the service activity in question to particular providers by virtue of the specific nature of the activity;
(e) a ban on having more than one establishment in the territory of the same State;
(f) requirements fixing a minimum number of employees;
(g) fixed minimum and/or maximum tariffs with which the provider must comply;
(h) an obligation on the provider to supply other specific services jointly with his service.
(3) Member States shall verify that the requirements referred to in paragraph 2 satisfy the following conditions:
(a) non–discrimination: requirements must be neither directly nor indirectly discriminatory according to nationality nor, with regard to companies, according to the location of the registered office;
(b) necessity: requirements must be justified by an overriding reason relating to the public interest;
(c) proportionality: requirements must be suitable for securing the attainment of the objective pursued; they must not go beyond what is necessary to attain that objective and it must not be possible to replace those requirements with other, less restrictive measures which attain the same result.
(4) Paragraphs 1, 2 and 3 shall apply to legislation in the field of services of general economic interest only insofar as the application of these paragraphs does not obstruct the performance, in law or in fact, of the particular task assigned to them.
(5) In the mutual evaluation report provided for in Article 39(1), Member States shall specify the following:
(a) the requirements that they intend to maintain and the reasons why they consider that those requirements comply with the conditions set out in paragraph 3;
(b) the requirements which have been abolished or made less stringent.
(6) From 28 December 2006 Member States shall not introduce any new requirement of a kind listed in paragraph 2, unless that requirement satisfies the conditions laid down in paragraph 3.
(7) Member States shall notify the Commission of any new laws, regulations or administrative provisions which set requirements as referred to in paragraph 6, together with the reasons for those requirements. The Commission shall communicate the provisions concerned to the other Member States. Such notification shall not prevent Member States from adopting the provisions in question. Within a period of 3 months from the date of receipt of the notification, the Commission shall examine the compatibility of any new requirements with Community law and, where appropriate, shall adopt a decision requesting the Member State in question to refrain from adopting them or to abolish them.
The notification of a draft national law in accordance with Directive 98/34/EC shall fulfil the obligation of notification provided for in this Directive.

Chapter IV. Free Movement of Services

Section 1. Freedom to Provide Services and Related Derogations

Article 16. Freedom to provide services

(1) Member States shall respect the right of providers to provide services in a Member State other than that in which they are established.
The Member State in which the service is provided shall ensure free access to and free exercise of a service activity within its territory.
Member States shall not make access to or exercise of a service activity in their territory subject to compliance with any requirements which do not respect the following principles:
(a) non–discrimination: the requirement may be neither directly nor indirectly discriminatory with regard to nationality or, in the case of legal persons, with regard to the Member State in which they are established;
(b) necessity: the requirement must be justified for reasons of public policy, public security, public health or the protection of the environment;
(c) proportionality: the requirement must be suitable for attaining the objective pursued, and must not go beyond what is necessary to attain that objective.
(2) Member States may not restrict the freedom to provide services in the case of a provider established in another Member State by imposing any of the following requirements:

(a) an obligation on the provider to have an establishment in their territory;
(b) an obligation on the provider to obtain an authorisation from their competent authorities including entry in a register or registration with a professional body or association in their territory, except where provided for in this Directive or other instruments of Community law;
(c) a ban on the provider setting up a certain form or type of infrastructure in their territory, including an office or chambers, which the provider needs in order to supply the services in question;
(d) the application of specific contractual arrangements between the provider and the recipient which prevent or restrict service provision by the self–employed;
(e) an obligation on the provider to possess an identity document issued by its competent authorities specific to the exercise of a service activity;
(f) requirements, except for those necessary for health and safety at work, which affect the use of equipment and material which are an integral part of the service provided;
(g) restrictions on the freedom to provide the services referred to in Article 19.
(3) The Member State to which the provider moves shall not be prevented from imposing requirements with regard to the provision of a service activity, where they are justified for reasons of public policy, public security, public health or the protection of the environment and in accordance with paragraph 1. Nor shall that Member State be prevented from applying, in accordance with Community law, its rules on employment conditions, including those laid down in collective agreements.
(4) By 28 December 2011 the Commission shall, after consultation of the Member States and the social partners at Community level, submit to the European Parliament and the Council a report on the application of this Article, in which it shall consider the need to propose harmonisation measures regarding service activities covered by this Directive.

Article 17. Additional derogations from the freedom to provide services

Article 16 shall not apply to:
1) services of general economic interest which are provided in another Member State, inter alia:
(a) in the postal sector, services covered by Directive 97/67/EC of the European Parliament and of the Council of 15 December 1997 on common rules for the development of the internal market of Community postal services and the improvement of quality of service;
(b) in the electricity sector, services covered by Directive 2003/54/EC of the European Parliament and of the Council of 26 June 2003 concerning common rules for the internal market in electricity;
(c) in the gas sector, services covered by Directive 2003/55/EC of the European Parliament and of the Council of 26 June 2003 concerning common rules for the internal market in natural gas;
(d) water distribution and supply services and waste water services;
(e) treatment of waste;
2) matters covered by Directive 96/71/EC;
3) matters covered by Directive 95/46/EC of the European Parliament and of the Council of 24 October 1995 on the protection of individuals with regard to the processing of personal data and on the free movement of such data;
4) matters covered by Council Directive 77/249/EEC of 22 March 1977 to facilitate the effective exercise by lawyers of freedom to provide services;
5) the activity of judicial recovery of debts;
6) matters covered by Title II of Directive 2005/36/EC, as well as requirements in the Member State where the service is provided which reserve an activity to a particular profession;
7) matters covered by Regulation (EEC) No 1408/71;
8) as regards administrative formalities concerning the free movement of persons and their residence, matters covered by the provisions of Directive 2004/38/EC that lay down administrative formalities of the competent authorities of the Member State where the service is provided with which beneficiaries must comply;
9) as regards third country nationals who move to another Member State in the context of the provision of a service, the possibility for Member States to require visa or residence permits for third country nationals who are not covered by the mutual recognition regime provided for in Article 21 of the Convention implementing the Schengen Agreement of 14 June 1985 on the gradual abolition of checks at the common borders or the possibility to oblige third country nationals to report to the competent authorities of the Member State in which the service is provided on or after their entry;
10) as regards the shipment of waste, matters covered by Council Regulation (EEC) No 259/93 of 1 February 1993 on the supervision and control of shipments of waste within, into and out of the European Community;
11) copyright, neighbouring rights and rights covered by Council Directive 87/54/EEC of 16 December 1986 on the legal protection of topographies of semiconductor products and by Directive 96/9/EC

of the European Parliament and of the Council of 11 March 1996 on the legal protection of databases, as well as industrial property rights;
12) acts requiring by law the involvement of a notary;
13) matters covered by Directive 2006/43/EC of the European Parliament and of the Council of 17 May 2006 on statutory audit of annual accounts and consolidated accounts;
14) the registration of vehicles leased in another Member State;
15) provisions regarding contractual and non–contractual obligations, including the form of contracts, determined pursuant to the rules of private international law.

Article 18. Case–by–case derogations

(1) By way of derogation from Article 16, and in exceptional circumstances only, a Member State may, in respect of a provider established in another Member State, take measures relating to the safety of services.
(2) The measures provided for in paragraph 1 may be taken only if the mutual assistance procedure laid down in Article 35 is complied with and the following conditions are fulfilled:
(a) the national provisions in accordance with which the measure is taken have not been subject to Community harmonisation in the field of the safety of services;
(b) the measures provide for a higher level of protection of the recipient than would be the case in a measure taken by the Member State of establishment in accordance with its national provisions;
(c) the Member State of establishment has not taken any measures or has taken measures which are insufficient as compared with those referred to in Article 35(2);
(d) the measures are proportionate.
(3) Paragraphs 1 and 2 shall be without prejudice to provisions, laid down in Community instruments, which guarantee the freedom to provide services or which allow derogations therefrom.

Section 2. Rights of Recipients of Services

Article 19. Prohibited restrictions

Member States may not impose on a recipient requirements which restrict the use of a service supplied by a provider established in another Member State, in particular the following requirements:
(a) an obligation to obtain authorisation from or to make a declaration to their competent authorities;
(b) discriminatory limits on the grant of financial assistance by reason of the fact that the provider is established in another Member State or by reason of the location of the place at which the service is provided.

Article 20. Non–discrimination

(1) Member States shall ensure that the recipient is not made subject to discriminatory requirements based on his nationality or place of residence.
(2) Member States shall ensure that the general conditions of access to a service, which are made available to the public at large by the provider, do not contain discriminatory provisions relating to the nationality or place of residence of the recipient, but without precluding the possibility of providing for differences in the conditions of access where those differences are directly justified by objective criteria.

Article 21. Assistance for recipients

(1) Member States shall ensure that recipients can obtain, in their Member State of residence, the following information:
(a) general information on the requirements applicable in other Member States relating to access to, and exercise of, service activities, in particular those relating to consumer protection;
(b) general information on the means of redress available in the case of a dispute between a provider and a recipient;
(c) the contact details of associations or organisations, including the centres of the European Consumer Centres Network, from which providers or recipients may obtain practical assistance.
Where appropriate, advice from the competent authorities shall include a simple step–by–step guide. Information and assistance shall be provided in a clear and unambiguous manner, shall be easily accessible at a distance, including by electronic means, and shall be kept up to date.
(2) Member States may confer responsibility for the task referred to in paragraph 1 on points of single contact or on any other body, such as the centres of the European Consumer Centres Network, consumer associations or Euro Info Centres.
Member States shall communicate to the Commission the names and contact details of the designated bodies. The Commission shall transmit them to all Member States.
(3) In fulfilment of the requirements set out in paragraphs 1 and 2, the body approached by the

PART III   EUROPEAN UNION

recipient shall, if necessary, contact the relevant body for the Member State concerned. The latter shall send the information requested as soon as possible to the requesting body which shall forward the information to the recipient. Member States shall ensure that those bodies give each other mutual assistance and shall put in place all possible measures for effective cooperation. Together with the Commission, Member States shall put in place practical arrangements necessary for the implementation of paragraph 1.

(4) The Commission shall, in accordance with the procedure referred to in Article 40(2), adopt measures for the implementation of paragraphs 1, 2 and 3 of this Article, specifying the technical mechanisms for the exchange of information between the bodies of the various Member States and, in particular, the interoperability of information systems, taking into account common standards.

Chapter V. Quality of Services

Article 22. Information on providers and their services

(1) Member States shall ensure that providers make the following information available to the recipient:

(a) the name of the provider, his legal status and form, the geographic address at which he is established and details enabling him to be contacted rapidly and communicated with directly and, as the case may be, by electronic means;

(b) where the provider is registered in a trade or other similar public register, the name of that register and the provider's registration number, or equivalent means of identification in that register;

(c) where the activity is subject to an authorisation scheme, the particulars of the relevant competent authority or the single point of contact;

(d) where the provider exercises an activity which is subject to VAT, the identification number referred to in Article 22(1) of Sixth Council Directive 77/388/EEC of 17 May 1977 on the harmonisation of the laws of the Member States relating to turnover taxes – Common system of value added tax: uniform basis of assessment;

(e) in the case of the regulated professions, any professional body or similar institution with which the provider is registered, the professional title and the Member State in which that title has been granted;

(f) the general conditions and clauses, if any, used by the provider;

(g) the existence of contractual clauses, if any, used by the provider concerning the law applicable to the contract and/or the competent courts;

(h) the existence of an after–sales guarantee, if any, not imposed by law;

(i) the price of the service, where a price is pre–determined by the provider for a given type of service;

(j) the main features of the service, if not already apparent from the context;

(k) the insurance or guarantees referred to in Article 23(1), and in particular the contact details of the insurer or guarantor and the territorial coverage.

(2) Member States shall ensure that the information referred to in paragraph 1, according to the provider's preference:

(a) is supplied by the provider on his own initiative;

(b) is easily accessible to the recipient at the place where the service is provided or the contract concluded;

(c) can be easily accessed by the recipient electronically by means of an address supplied by the provider;

(d) appears in any information documents supplied to the recipient by the provider which set out a detailed description of the service he provides.

(3) Member States shall ensure that, at the recipient's request, providers supply the following additional information:

(a) where the price is not pre–determined by the provider for a given type of service, the price of the service or, if an exact price cannot be given, the method for calculating the price so that it can be checked by the recipient, or a sufficiently detailed estimate;

(b) as regards the regulated professions, a reference to the professional rules applicable in the Member State of establishment and how to access them;

(c) information on their multidisciplinary activities and partnerships which are directly linked to the service in question and on the measures taken to avoid conflicts of interest. That information shall be included in any information document in which providers give a detailed description of their services;

(d) any codes of conduct to which the provider is subject and the address at which these codes may be consulted by electronic means, specifying the language version available;

(e) where a provider is subject to a code of conduct, or member of a trade association or professional body which provides for recourse to a non–judicial means of dispute settlement, information in this respect. The provider shall specify how to access detailed information on the characteristics of, and conditions for, the use of non–judicial means of dispute settlement.

(4) Member States shall ensure that the information which a provider must supply in accordance with this Chapter is made available or communicated in a clear and unambiguous manner, and in good time before conclusion of the contract or, where there is no written contract, before the service is provided.

(5) The information requirements laid down in this Chapter are in addition to requirements already provided for in Community law and do not prevent Member States from imposing additional information requirements applicable to providers established in their territory.

(6) The Commission may, in accordance with the procedure referred to in Article 40(2), specify the content of the information provided for in paragraphs 1 and 3 of this Article according to the specific nature of certain activities and may specify the practical means of implementing paragraph 2 of this Article.

Article 23. Professional liability insurance and guarantees

(1) Member States may ensure that providers whose services present a direct and particular risk to the health or safety of the recipient or a third person, or to the financial security of the recipient, subscribe to professional liability insurance appropriate to the nature and extent of the risk, or provide a guarantee or similar arrangement which is equivalent or essentially comparable as regards its purpose.

(2) When a provider establishes himself in their territory, Member States may not require professional liability insurance or a guarantee from the provider where he is already covered by a guarantee which is equivalent, or essentially comparable as regards its purpose and the cover it provides in terms of the insured risk, the insured sum or a ceiling for the guarantee and possible exclusions from the cover, in another Member State in which the provider is already established. Where equivalence is only partial, Member States may require a supplementary guarantee to cover those aspects not already covered.

When a Member State requires a provider established in its territory to subscribe to professional liability insurance or to provide another guarantee, that Member State shall accept as sufficient evidence attestations of such insurance cover issued by credit institutions and insurers established in other Member States.

(3) Paragraphs 1 and 2 shall not affect professional insurance or guarantee arrangements provided for in other Community instruments.

(4) For the implementation of paragraph 1, the Commission may, in accordance with the regulatory procedure referred to in Article 40(2), establish a list of services which exhibit the characteristics referred to in paragraph 1 of this Article. The Commission may also, in accordance with the procedure referred to in Article 40(3), adopt measures designed to amend non–essential elements of this Directive by supplementing it by establishing common criteria for defining, for the purposes of the insurance or guarantees referred to in paragraph 1 of this Article, what is appropriate to the nature and extent of the risk.

(5) For the purpose of this Article
– 'direct and particular risk' means a risk arising directly from the provision of the service,
– 'health and safety' means, in relation to a recipient or a third person, the prevention of death or serious personal injury,
– 'financial security' means, in relation to a recipient, the prevention of substantial losses of money or of value of property,
– 'professional liability insurance' means insurance taken out by a provider in respect of potential liabilities to recipients and, where applicable, third parties arising out of the provision of the service.

Article 24. Commercial communications by the regulated professions

(1) Member States shall remove all total prohibitions on commercial communications by the regulated professions.

(2) Member States shall ensure that commercial communications by the regulated professions comply with professional rules, in conformity with Community law, which relate, in particular, to the independence, dignity and integrity of the profession, as well as to professional secrecy, in a manner consistent with the specific nature of each profession. Professional rules on commercial communications shall be non–discriminatory, justified by an overriding reason relating to the public interest and proportionate.

Article 25. Multidisciplinary activities

(1) Member States shall ensure that providers are not made subject to requirements which oblige them to exercise a given specific activity exclusively or which restrict the exercise jointly or in partnership of different activities.

However, the following providers may be made subject to such requirements:

(a) the regulated professions, in so far as is justified in order to guarantee compliance with the rules governing professional ethics and conduct, which vary according to the specific nature of each profession, and is necessary in order to ensure their independence and impartiality;

(b) providers of certification, accreditation, technical monitoring, test or trial services, in so far as is justified in order to ensure their independence and impartiality.

(2) Where multidisciplinary activities between providers referred to in points (a) and (b) of paragraph 1 are authorised, Member States shall ensure the following:

(a) that conflicts of interest and incompatibilities between certain activities are prevented;

(b) that the independence and impartiality required for certain activities is secured;

(c) that the rules governing professional ethics and conduct for different activities are compatible with one another, especially as regards matters of professional secrecy.

(3) In the report referred to in Article 39(1), Member States shall indicate which providers are subject to the requirements laid down in paragraph 1 of this Article, the content of those requirements and the reasons for which they consider them to be justified.

Article 26. Policy on quality of services

(1) Member States shall, in cooperation with the Commission, take accompanying measures to encourage providers to take action on a voluntary basis in order to ensure the quality of service provision, in particular through use of one of the following methods:

(a) certification or assessment of their activities by independent or accredited bodies;

(b) drawing up their own quality charter or participation in quality charters or labels drawn up by professional bodies at Community level.

(2) Member States shall ensure that information on the significance of certain labels and the criteria for applying labels and other quality marks relating to services can be easily accessed by providers and recipients.

(3) Member States shall, in cooperation with the Commission, take accompanying measures to encourage professional bodies, as well as chambers of commerce and craft associationsand consumer associations, in their territory to cooperate at Community level in order to promote the quality of service provision, especially by making it easier to assess the competence of a provider.

(4) Member States shall, in cooperation with the Commission, take accompanying measures to encourage the development of independent assessments, notably by consumer associations, in relation to the quality and defects of service provision, and, in particular, the development at Community level of comparative trials or testing and the communication of the results.

(5) Member States, in cooperation with the Commission, shall encourage the development of voluntary European standards with the aim of facilitating compatibility between services supplied by providers in different Member States, information to the recipient and the quality of service provision.

Article 27. Settlement of disputes

(1) Member States shall take the general measures necessary to ensure that providers supply contact details, in particular a postal address, fax number or e–mail addressand telephone number to which all recipients, including those resident in another Member State, can send a complaint or a request for information about the service provided. Providers shall supply their legal address if this is not their usual address for correspondence.

Member States shall take the general measures necessary to ensure that providers respond to the complaints referred to in the first subparagraph in the shortest possible time and make their best efforts to find a satisfactory solution.

(2) Member States shall take the general measures necessary to ensure that providers are obliged to demonstrate compliance with the obligations laid down in this Directive as to the provision of information and to demonstrate that the information is accurate.

(3) Where a financial guarantee is required for compliance with a judicial decision, Member States shall recognise equivalent guarantees lodged with a credit institution or insurer established in another Member State. Such credit institutions must be authorised in a Member State in accordance with Directive 2006/48/EC and such insurers in accordance, as appropriate, with First Council Directive 73/239/EEC of 24 July 1973 on the coordination of laws, regulations and administrative provisions relating to the taking–up and pursuit of the business of direct insurance other than life assurance and Directive 2002/83/EC of the European Parliament and of the Council of 5 November 2002 concerning life assurance.

(4) Member States shall take the general measures necessary to ensure that providers who are subject to a code of conduct, or are members of a trade association or professional body, which provides for recourse to a non–judicial means of dispute settlement inform the recipient thereof and mention that fact in any document which presents their services in detail, specifying how to access detailed information on the characteristics of, and conditions for, the use of such a mechanism.

Chapter VI. Administrative Cooperation

Article 28. Mutual assistance – general obligations

(1) Member States shall give each other mutual assistance, and shall put in place measures for effective cooperation with one another, in order to ensure the supervision of providers and the services they provide.
(2) For the purposes of this Chapter, Member States shall designate one or more liaison points, the contact details of which shall be communicated to the other Member States and the Commission. The Commission shall publish and regularly update the list of liaison points.
(3) Information requests and requests to carry out any checks, inspections and investigations under this Chapter shall be duly motivated, in particular by specifying the reason for the request. Information exchanged shall be used only in respect of the matter for which it was requested.
(4) In the event of receiving a request for assistance from competent authorities in another Member State, Member States shall ensure that providers established in their territory supply their competent authorities with all the information necessary for supervising their activities in compliance with their national laws.
(5) In the event of difficulty in meeting a request for information or in carrying out checks, inspections or investigations, the Member State in question shall rapidly inform the requesting Member State with a view to finding a solution.
(6) Member States shall supply the information requested by other Member States or the Commission by electronic means and within the shortest possible period of time.
(7) Member States shall ensure that registers in which providers have been entered, and which may be consulted by the competent authorities in their territory, may also be consulted, in accordance with the same conditions, by the equivalent competent authorities of the other Member States.
(8) Member States shall communicate to the Commission information on cases where other Member States do not fulfil their obligation of mutual assistance. Where necessary, the Commission shall take appropriate steps, including proceedings provided for in Article 226 of the Treaty, in order to ensure that the Member States concerned comply with their obligation of mutual assistance. The Commission shall periodically inform Member States about the functioning of the mutual assistance provisions.

Article 29. Mutual assistance – general obligations for the Member State of establishment

(1) With respect to providers providing services in another Member State, the Member State of establishment shall supply information on providers established in its territory when requested to do so by another Member State and, in particular, confirmation that a provider is established in its territory and, to its knowledge, is not exercising his activities in an unlawful manner.
(2) The Member State of establishment shall undertake the checks, inspections and investigations requested by another Member State and shall inform the latter of the results and, as the case may be, of the measures taken. In so doing, the competent authorities shall act to the extent permitted by the powers vested in them in their Member State. The competent authorities can decide on the most appropriate measures to be taken in each individual case in order to meet the request by another Member State.
(3) Upon gaining actual knowledge of any conduct or specific acts by a provider established in its territory which provides services in other Member States, that, to its knowledge, could cause serious damage to the health or safety of persons or to the environment, the Member State of establishment shall inform all other Member States and the Commission within the shortest possible period of time.

Article 30. Supervision by the Member State of establishment in the event of the temporary movement of a provider to another Member State

(1) With respect to cases not covered by Article 31(1), the Member State of establishment shall ensure that compliance with its requirements is supervised in conformity with the powers of supervision provided for in its national law, in particular through supervisory measures at the place of establishment of the provider.
(2) The Member State of establishment shall not refrain from taking supervisory or enforcement measures in its territory on the grounds that the service has been provided or caused damage in another Member State.

(3) The obligation laid down in paragraph 1 shall not entail a duty on the part of the Member State of establishment to carry out factual checks and controls in the territory of the Member State where the service is provided. Such checks and controls shall be carried out by the authorities of the Member State where the provider is temporarily operating at the request of the authorities of the Member State of establishment, in accordance with Article 31.

Article 31. Supervision by the Member State where the service is provided in the event of the temporary movement of the provider

(1) With respect to national requirements which may be imposed pursuant to Articles 16 or 17, the Member State where the service is provided is responsible for the supervision of the activity of the provider in its territory. In conformity with Community law, the Member State where the service is provided:
(a) shall take all measures necessary to ensure the provider complies with those requirements as regards the access to and the exercise of the activity;
(b) shall carry out the checks, inspections and investigations necessary to supervise the service provided.
(2) With respect to requirements other than those referred to in paragraph 1, where a provider moves temporarily to another Member State in order to provide a service without being established there, the competent authorities of that Member State shall participate in the supervision of the provider in accordance with paragraphs 3 and 4.
(3) At the request of the Member State of establishment, the competent authorities of the Member State where the service is provided shall carry out any checks, inspections and investigations necessary for ensuring the effective supervision by the Member State of establishment. In so doing, the competent authorities shall act to the extent permitted by the powers vested in them in their Member State. The competent authorities may decide on the most appropriate measures to be taken in each individual case in order to meet the request by the Member State of establishment.
(4) On their own initiative, the competent authorities of the Member State where the service is provided may conduct checks, inspections and investigations on the spot, provided that those checks, inspections or investigations are not discriminatory, are not motivated by the fact that the provider is established in another Member State and are proportionate.

Article 32. Alert mechanism

(1) Where a Member State becomes aware of serious specific acts or circumstances relating to a service activity that could cause serious damage to the health or safety of persons or to the environment in its territory or in the territory of other Member States, that Member State shall inform the Member State of establishment, the other Member States concerned and the Commission within the shortest possible period of time.
(2) The Commission shall promote and take part in the operation of a European network of Member States' authorities in order to implement paragraph 1.
(3) The Commission shall adopt and regularly update, in accordance with the procedure referred to in Article 40(2), detailed rules concerning the management of the network referred to in paragraph 2 of this Article.

Article 33. Information on the good repute of providers

(1) Member States shall, at the request of a competent authority in another Member State, supply information, in conformity with their national law, on disciplinary or administrative actions or criminal sanctions and decisions concerning insolvency or bankruptcy involving fraud taken by their competent authorities in respect of the provider which are directly relevant to the provider's competence or professional reliability. The Member State which supplies the information shall inform the provider thereof.
A request made pursuant to the first subparagraph must be duly substantiated, in particular as regards the reasons for the request for information.
(2) Sanctions and actions referred to in paragraph 1 shall only be communicated if a final decision has been taken. With regard to other enforceable decisions referred to in paragraph 1, the Member State which supplies the information shall specify whether a particular decision is final or whether an appeal has been lodged in respect of it, in which case the Member State in question should provide an indication of the date when the decision on appeal is expected.
Moreover, that Member State shall specify the provisions of national law pursuant to which the provider was found guilty or penalised.
(3) Implementation of paragraphs 1 and 2 must comply with rules on the provision of personal data and with rights guaranteed to persons found guilty or penalised in the Member States concerned,

including by professional bodies. Any information in question which is public shall be accessible to consumers.

Article 34. Accompanying measures

(1) The Commission, in cooperation with Member States, shall establish an electronic system for the exchange of information between Member States, taking into account existing information systems.
(2) Member States shall, with the assistance of the Commission, take accompanying measures to facilitate the exchange of officials in charge of the implementation of mutual assistance and training of such officials, including language and computer training.
(3) The Commission shall assess the need to establish a multi–annual programme in order to organise relevant exchanges of officials and training.

Article 35. Mutual assistance in the event of case–by–case derogations

(1) Where a Member State intends to take a measure pursuant to Article 18, the procedure laid down in paragraphs 2 to 6 of this Article shall apply without prejudice to court proceedings, including preliminary proceedings and acts carried out in the framework of a criminal investigation.
(2) The Member State referred to in paragraph 1 shall ask the Member State of establishment to take measures with regard to the provider, supplying all relevant information on the service in question and the circumstances of the case.
The Member State of establishment shall check, within the shortest possible period of time, whether the provider is operating lawfully and verify the facts underlying the request. It shall inform the requesting Member State within the shortest possible period of time of the measures taken or envisaged or, as the case may be, the reasons why it has not taken any measures.
(3) Following communication by the Member State of establishment as provided for in the second subparagraph of paragraph 2, the requesting Member State shall notify the Commission and the Member State of establishment of its intention to take measures, stating the following:
(a) the reasons why it believes the measures taken or envisaged by the Member State of establishment are inadequate;
(b) the reasons why it believes the measures it intends to take fulfil the conditions laid down in Article 18.
(4) The measures may not be taken until fifteen working days after the date of notification provided for in paragraph 3.
(5) Without prejudice to the possibility for the requesting Member State to take the measures in question upon expiry of the period specified in paragraph 4, the Commission shall, within the shortest possible period of time, examine the compatibility with Community law of the measures notified. Where the Commission concludes that the measure is incompatible with Community law, it shall adopt a decision asking the Member State concerned to refrain from taking the proposed measures or to put an end to the measures in question as a matter of urgency.
(6) In the case of urgency, a Member State which intends to take a measure may derogate from paragraphs 2, 3 and 4. In such cases, the measures shall be notified within the shortest possible period of time to the Commission and the Member State of establishment, stating the reasons for which the Member State considers that there is urgency.

Article 36. Implementing measures

In accordance with the procedure referred to in Article 40(3), the Commission shall adopt the implementing measures designed to amend non–essential elements of this Chapter by supplementing it by specifying the time–limits provided for in Articles 28 and 35. The Commission shall also adopt, in accordance with the procedure referred to in Article 40(2), the practical arrangements for the exchange of information by electronic means between Member States, and in particular the interoperability provisions for information systems.

Chapter VII. Convergence Programme

Article 37. Codes of conduct at Community level

(1) Member States shall, in cooperation with the Commission, take accompanying measures to encourage the drawing up at Community level, particularly by professional bodies, organisations and associations, of codes of conduct aimed at facilitating the provision of services or the establishment of a provider in another Member State, in conformity with Community law.
(2) Member States shall ensure that the codes of conduct referred to in paragraph 1 are accessible at a distance, by electronic means.

Article 38. Additional harmonisation

The Commission shall assess, by 28 December 2010 the possibility of presenting proposals for harmonisation instruments on the following subjects:
(a) access to the activity of judicial recovery of debts;
(b) private security services and transport of cash and valuables.

Article 39. Mutual evaluation

(1) By 28 December 2009 at the latest, Member States shall present a report to the Commission, containing the information specified in the following provisions:
(a) Article 9(2), on authorisation schemes;
(b) Article 15(5), on requirements to be evaluated;
(c) Article 25(3), on multidisciplinary activities.
(2) The Commission shall forward the reports provided for in paragraph 1 to the Member States, which shall submit their observations on each of the reports within six months of receipt. Within the same period, the Commission shall consult interested parties on those reports.
(3) The Commission shall present the reports and the Member States' observations to the Committee referred to in Article 40(1), which may make observations.
(4) In the light of the observations provided for in paragraphs 2 and 3, the Commission shall, by 28 December 2010 at the latest, present a summary report to the European Parliament and to the Council, accompanied where appropriate by proposals for additional initiatives.
(5) By 28 December 2009 at the latest, Member States shall present a report to the Commission on the national requirements whose application could fall under the third subparagraph of Article 16(1) and the first sentence of Article 16(3), providing reasons why they consider that the application of those requirements fulfil the criteria referred to in the third subparagraph of Article 16(1) and the first sentence of Article 16(3).
Thereafter, Member States shall transmit to the Commission any changes in their requirements, including new requirements, as referred to above, together with the reasons for them.
The Commission shall communicate the transmitted requirements to other Member States. Such transmission shall not prevent the adoption by Member States of the provisions in question. The Commission shall on an annual basis thereafter provide analyses and orientations on the application of these provisions in the context of this Directive.

Article 40. Committee procedure

(1) The Commission shall be assisted by a Committee.
(2) Where reference is made to this paragraph, Articles 5 and 7 of Decision 1999/468/EC shall apply, having regard to the provisions of Article 8 thereof. The period laid down in Article 5(6) of Decision 1999/468/EC shall be set at three months.
(3) Where reference is made to this paragraph, Article 5a(1) to (4), and Article 7 of Decision 1999/468/EC shall apply, having regard to the provisions of Article 8 thereof.

Article 41. Review clause

The Commission, by 28 December 2011 and every three years thereafter, shall present to the European Parliament and to the Council a comprehensive report on the application of this Directive. This report shall, in accordance with Article 16(4), address in particular the application of Article 16. It shall also consider the need for additional measures for matters excluded from the scope of application of this Directive. It shall be accompanied, where appropriate, by proposals for amendment of this Directive with a view to completing the Internal Market for services.

Article 42. Amendment of Directive 98/27/EC

In the Annex to Directive 98/27/EC of the European Parliament and of the Council of 19 May 1998 on injunctions for the protection of consumers' interests, the following point shall be added:

13. Directive 2006/123/EC of the European Parliament and of the Council of 12 December 2006 on services in the internal market.

Article 43. Protection of personal data

The implementation and application of this Directive and, in particular, the provisions on supervision shall respect the rules on the protection of personal data as provided for in Directives 95/46/EC and 2002/58/EC.

Chapter VIII. Final Provisions

Article 44. Transposition

(1) Member States shall bring into force the laws, regulations and administrative provisions necessary

to comply with this Directive before 28 December 2009.

They shall forthwith communicate to the Commission the text of those measures.

When Member States adopt these measures, they shall contain a reference to this Directive or shall be accompanied by such a reference on the occasion of their official publication. The methods of making such reference shall be laid down by Member States.

(2) Member States shall communicate to the Commission the text of the main provisions of national law which they adopt in the field covered by this Directive.

Article 45. Entry into force

This Directive shall enter into force on the day following that of its publication in the *Official Journal of the European Union*.

Article 46. Addressees

This Directive is addressed to the Member States.

PART III EUROPEAN UNION

Regulation (EU) No 492/2011 of the European Parliament and of the Council of 5 April 2011 on freedom of movement for workers within the Union

THE EUROPEAN PARLIAMENT AND THE COUNCIL OF THE EUROPEAN UNION,
Having regard to the Treaty on the Functioning of the European Union, and in particular Article 46 thereof,
Having regard to the proposal from the European Commission,
After transmission of the draft legislative act to the national parliaments,
Having regard to the opinion of the European Economic and Social Committee,
Acting in accordance with the ordinary legislative procedure,
Whereas:
(1) Regulation (EEC) No 1612/68 of the Council of 15 October 1968 on freedom of movement for workers within the Community has been substantially amended several times. In the interests of clarity and rationality the said Regulation should be codified.
(2) Freedom of movement for workers should be secured within the Union. The attainment of this objective entails the abolition of any discrimination based on nationality between workers of the Member States as regards employment, remuneration and other conditions of work and employment, as well as the right of such workers to move freely within the Union in order to pursue activities as employed persons subject to any limitations justified on grounds of public policy, public security or public health.
(3) Provisions should be laid down to enable the objectives laid down in Articles 45 and 46 of the Treaty on the Functioning of the European Union in the field of freedom of movement to be achieved.
(4) Freedom of movement constitutes a fundamental right of workers and their families. Mobility of labour within the Union must be one of the means by which workers are guaranteed the possibility of improving their living and working conditions and promoting their social advancement, while helping to satisfy the requirements of the economies of the Member States. The right of all workers in the Member States to pursue the activity of their choice within the Union should be affirmed.
(5) Such right should be enjoyed without discrimination by permanent, seasonal and frontier workers and by those who pursue their activities for the purpose of providing services.
(6) The right of freedom of movement, in order that it may be exercised, by objective standards, in freedom and dignity, requires that equality of treatment be ensured in fact and in law in respect of all matters relating to the actual pursuit of activities as employed persons and to eligibility for housing, and also that obstacles to the mobility of workers be eliminated, in particular as regards the conditions for the integration of the worker's family into the host country.
(7) The principle of non–discrimination between workers in the Union means that all nationals of Member States have the same priority as regards employment as is enjoyed by national workers.
(8) The machinery for vacancy clearance, in particular by means of direct cooperation between the central employment services and also between the regional services, as well as by coordination of the exchange of information, ensures in a general way a clearer picture of the labour market. Workers wishing to move should also be regularly informed of living and working conditions.
(9) Close links exist between freedom of movement for workers, employment and vocational training, particularly where the latter aims at putting workers in a position to take up concrete offers of employment from other regions of the Union. Such links make it necessary that the problems arising in this connection should no longer be studied in isolation but viewed as interdependent, account also being taken of the problems of employment at the regional level. It is therefore necessary to direct the efforts of Member States toward coordinating their employment policies,
HAVE ADOPTED THIS REGULATION:

Chapter I. Employment, Equal Treatment and Workers' Families

Section 1. Eligibility for Employment

Article 1. (1) Any national of a Member State shall, irrespective of his place of residence, have the right to take up an activity as an employed person, and to pursue such activity, within the territory of another Member State in accordance with the provisions laid down by law, regulation or administrative action governing the employment of nationals of that State.
(2) He shall, in particular, have the right to take up available employment in the territory of another Member State with the same priority as nationals of that State.

Article 2. Any national of a Member State and any employer pursuing an activity in the territory of a Member State may exchange their applications for and offers of employment, and may conclude and perform contracts of employment in accordance with the provisions in force laid down by law, regulation or administrative action, without any discrimination resulting therefrom.

Article 3. (1) Under this Regulation, provisions laid down by law, regulation or administrative action or administrative practices of a Member State shall not apply:
(a) where they limit application for and offers of employment, or the right of foreign nationals to take up and pursue employment or subject these to conditions not applicable in respect of their own nationals; or
(b) where, though applicable irrespective of nationality, their exclusive or principal aim or effect is to keep nationals of other Member States away from the employment offered.
The first subparagraph shall not apply to conditions relating to linguistic knowledge required by reason of the nature of the post to be filled.
(2) There shall be included in particular among the provisions or practices of a Member State referred to in the first subparagraph of paragraph 1 those which:
(a) prescribe a special recruitment procedure for foreign nationals;
(b) limit or restrict the advertising of vacancies in the press or through any other medium or subject it to conditions other than those applicable in respect of employers pursuing their activities in the territory of that Member State;
(c) subject eligibility for employment to conditions of registration with employment offices or impede recruitment of individual workers, where persons who do not reside in the territory of that State are concerned.

Article 4. (1) Provisions laid down by law, regulation or administrative action of the Member States which restrict by number or percentage the employment of foreign nationals in any undertaking, branch of activity or region, or at a national level, shall not apply to nationals of the other Member States.
(2) When in a Member State the granting of any benefit to undertakings is subject to a minimum percentage of national workers being employed, nationals of the other Member States shall be counted as national workers, subject to Directive 2005/36/EC of the European Parliament and of the Council of 7 September 2005 on the recognition of professional qualifications.

Article 5. A national of a Member State who seeks employment in the territory of another Member State shall receive the same assistance there as that afforded by the employment offices in that State to their own nationals seeking employment.

Article 6. (1) The engagement and recruitment of a national of one Member State for a post in another Member State shall not depend on medical, vocational or other criteria which are discriminatory on grounds of nationality by comparison with those applied to nationals of the other Member State who wish to pursue the same activity.
(2) A national who holds an offer in his name from an employer in a Member State other than that of which he is a national may have to undergo a vocational test, if the employer expressly requests this when making his offer of employment.

Section 2. Employment and Equality of Treatment

Article 7. (1) A worker who is a national of a Member State may not, in the territory of another Member State, be treated differently from national workers by reason of his nationality in respect of any conditions of employment and work, in particular as regards remuneration, dismissal, and, should he become unemployed, reinstatement or re–employment.
(2) He shall enjoy the same social and tax advantages as national workers.
(3) He shall also, by virtue of the same right and under the same conditions as national workers, have access to training in vocational schools and retraining centres.
(4) Any clause of a collective or individual agreement or of any other collective regulation concerning eligibility for employment, remuneration and other conditions of work or dismissal shall be null and void in so far as it lays down or authorises discriminatory conditions in respect of workers who are nationals of the other Member States.

Article 8. A worker who is a national of a Member State and who is employed in the territory of another Member State shall enjoy equality of treatment as regards membership of trade unions and the exercise of rights attaching thereto, including the right to vote and to be eligible for the administration or management posts of a trade union. He may be excluded from taking part in the management of bodies governed by public law and from holding an office governed by public law. Furthermore, he shall have the right of eligibility for workers' representative bodies in the undertaking.

PART III   EUROPEAN UNION

The first paragraph of this Article shall not affect laws or regulations in certain Member States which grant more extensive rights to workers coming from the other Member States.

Article 9. (1) A worker who is a national of a Member State and who is employed in the territory of another Member State shall enjoy all the rights and benefits accorded to national workers in matters of housing, including ownership of the housing he needs.
(2) A worker referred to in paragraph 1 may, with the same right as nationals, put his name down on the housing lists in the region in which he is employed, where such lists exist, and shall enjoy the resultant benefits and priorities.
If his family has remained in the country whence he came, they shall be considered for this purpose as residing in the said region, where national workers benefit from a similar presumption.

Section 3. Workers' Families

Article 10. The children of a national of a Member State who is or has been employed in the territory of another Member State shall be admitted to that State's general educational, apprenticeship and vocational training courses under the same conditions as the nationals of that State, if such children are residing in its territory.
Member States shall encourage all efforts to enable such children to attend these courses under the best possible conditions.

Chapter II. Clearance of Vacancies and Applications for Employment

Section 1. Cooperation between the Member States and with the Commission

Article 11.(1) The Member States or the Commission shall instigate or together undertake any study of employment or unemployment which they consider necessary for freedom of movement for workers within the Union.
The central employment services of the Member States shall cooperate closely with each other and with the Commission with a view to acting jointly as regards the clearing of vacancies and applications for employment within the Union and the resultant placing of workers in employment.
(2) To this end the Member States shall designate specialist services which shall be entrusted with organising work in the fields referred to in the second subparagraph of paragraph 1 and cooperating with each other and with the departments of the Commission.
The Member States shall notify the Commission of any change in the designation of such services and the Commission shall publish details thereof for information in the *Official Journal of the European Union*.

Article 12. (1) The Member States shall send to the Commission information on problems arising in connection with the freedom of movement and employment of workers and particulars of the state and development of employment.
(2) The Commission, taking the utmost account of the opinion of the Technical Committee referred to in Article 29 ('the Technical Committee'), shall determine the manner in which the information referred to in paragraph 1 of this Article is to be drawn up.
(3) In accordance with the procedure laid down by the Commission taking the utmost account of the opinion of the Technical Committee, the specialist service of each Member State shall send to the specialist services of the other Member States and to the European Coordination Office referred to in Article 18 such information concerning living and working conditions and the state of the labour market as is likely to be of guidance to workers from the other Member States. Such information shall be brought up to date regularly.
The specialist services of the other Member States shall ensure that wide publicity is given to such information, in particular by circulating it among the appropriate employment services and by all suitable means of communication for informing the workers concerned.

Section 2. Machinery for Vacancy Clearance

Article 13. (1) The specialist service of each Member State shall regularly send to the specialist services of the other Member States and to the European Coordination Office referred to in Article 18:
(a) details of vacancies which could be filled by nationals of other Member States;
(b) details of vacancies addressed to third countries;
(c) details of applications for employment by those who have formally expressed a wish to work in another Member State;
(d) information, by region and by branch of activity, on applicants who have declared themselves actually willing to accept employment in another country.

The specialist service of each Member State shall forward this information to the appropriate employment services and agencies as soon as possible.

(2) The details of vacancies and applications referred to in paragraph 1 shall be circulated according to a uniform system to be established by the European Coordination Office referred to in Article 18 in collaboration with the Technical Committee.

This system may be adapted if necessary.

Article 14. (1) Any vacancy within the meaning of Article 13 communicated to the employment services of a Member State shall be notified to and processed by the competent employment services of the other Member States concerned.

Such services shall forward to the services of the first Member State the details of suitable applications.

(2) The applications for employment referred to in point (c) of the first subparagraph of Article 13(1) shall be responded to by the relevant services of the Member States within a reasonable period, not exceeding 1 month.

(3) The employment services shall grant workers who are nationals of the Member States the same priority as the relevant measures grant to nationals vis-à-vis workers from third countries.

Article 15. (1) The provisions of Article 14 shall be implemented by the specialist services. However, in so far as they have been authorised by the central services and in so far as the organisation of the employment services of a Member State and the placing techniques employed make it possible:
(a) the regional employment services of the Member States shall:
(i) on the basis of the information referred to in Article 13, on which appropriate action will be taken, directly bring together and clear vacancies and applications for employment;
(ii) establish direct relations for clearance:
– of vacancies offered to a named worker,
– of individual applications for employment sent either to a specific employment service or to an employer pursuing his activity within the area covered by such a service,
– where the clearing operations concern seasonal workers who must be recruited as quickly as possible;
(b) the services territorially responsible for the border regions of two or more Member States shall regularly exchange data relating to vacancies and applications for employment in their area and, acting in accordance with their arrangements with the other employment services of their countries, shall directly bring together and clear vacancies and applications for employment.

If necessary, the services territorially responsible for border regions shall also set up cooperation and service structures to provide:
– users with as much practical information as possible on the various aspects of mobility, and
– management and labour, social services (in particular public, private or those of public interest) and all institutions concerned, with a framework of coordinated measures relating to mobility,
(c) official employment services which specialise in certain occupations or specific categories of persons shall cooperate directly with each other.

(2) The Member States concerned shall forward to the Commission the list, drawn up by common accord, of services referred to in paragraph 1 and the Commission shall publish such list for information, and any amendment thereto, in the *Official Journal of the European Union*.

Article 16. Adoption of recruiting procedures as applied by the implementing bodies provided for under agreements concluded between two or more Member States shall not be obligatory.

Section 3. Measures for Controlling the Balance of the Labour Market

Article 17. (1) On the basis of a report from the Commission drawn up from information supplied by the Member States, the latter and the Commission shall at least once a year analyse jointly the results of Union arrangements regarding vacancies and applications.

(2) The Member States shall examine with the Commission all the possibilities of giving priority to nationals of Member States when filling employment vacancies in order to achieve a balance between vacancies and applications for employment within the Union. They shall adopt all measures necessary for this purpose.

(3) Every 2 years the Commission shall submit a report to the European Parliament, the Council and the European Economic and Social Committee on the implementation of Chapter II, summarising the information required and the data obtained from the studies and research carried out and highlighting any useful points with regard to developments on the Union's labour market.

PART III EUROPEAN UNION

Section 4. European Coordination Office

Article 18. The European Office for Coordinating the Clearance of Vacancies and Applications for Employment ('the European Coordination Office'), established within the Commission, shall have the general task of promoting vacancy clearance at Union level. It shall be responsible in particular for all the technical duties in this field which, under the provisions of this Regulation, are assigned to the Commission, and especially for assisting the national employment services.
It shall summarise the information referred to in Articles 12 and 13 and the data arising out of the studies and research carried out pursuant to Article 11, so as to bring to light any useful facts about foreseeable developments on the Union labour market; such facts shall be communicated to the specialist services of the Member States and to the Advisory Committee referred to in Article 21 and the Technical Committee.

Article 19. (1) The European Coordination Office shall be responsible, in particular, for:
(a) coordinating the practical measures necessary for vacancy clearance at Union level and for analysing the resulting movements of workers;
(b) contributing to such objectives by implementing, in cooperation with the Technical Committee, joint methods of action at administrative and technical levels;
(c) carrying out, where a special need arises, and in agreement with the specialist services, the bringing together of vacancies and applications for employment for clearance by those specialist services.
(2) It shall communicate to the specialist services vacancies and applications for employment sent directly to the Commission, and shall be informed of the action taken thereon.

Article 20. The Commission may, in agreement with the competent authority of each Member State, and in accordance with the conditions and procedures which it shall determine on the basis of the opinion of the Technical Committee, organise visits and assignments for officials of other Member States, and also advanced programmes for specialist personnel.

Chapter III. Committees for Ensuring Close Cooperation between the Member States in Matters Concerning the Freedom of Movement of Workers and their Employment

Section 1. The Advisory Committee

Article 21. The Advisory Committee shall be responsible for assisting the Commission in the examination of any questions arising from the application of the Treaty on the Functioning of the European Union and measures taken in pursuance thereof, in matters concerning the freedom of movement of workers and their employment.

Article 22. The Advisory Committee shall be responsible in particular for:
(a) examining problems concerning freedom of movement and employment within the framework of national manpower policies, with a view to coordinating the employment policies of the Member States at Union level, thus contributing to the development of the economies and to an improved balance of the labour market;
(b) making a general study of the effects of implementing this Regulation and any supplementary measures;
(c) submitting to the Commission any reasoned proposals for revising this Regulation;
(d) delivering, either at the request of the Commission or on its own initiative, reasoned opinions on general questions or on questions of principle, in particular on exchange of information concerning developments in the labour market, on the movement of workers between Member States, on programmes or measures to develop vocational guidance and vocational training which are likely to increase the possibilities of freedom of movement and employment, and on all forms of assistance to workers and their families, including social assistance and the housing of workers.

Article 23. (1) The Advisory Committee shall be composed of six members for each Member State, two of whom shall represent the Government, two the trade unions and two the employers' associations.
(2) For each of the categories referred to in paragraph 1, one alternate member shall be appointed by each Member State.
(3) The term of office of the members and their alternates shall be 2 years. Their appointments shall be renewable.
On expiry of their term of office, the members and their alternates shall remain in office until replaced or until their appointments are renewed.

Article 24. The members of the Advisory Committee and their alternates shall be appointed by the Council, which shall endeavour, when selecting representatives of trade unions and employers' associations, to achieve adequate representation on the Committee of the various economic sectors concerned.

The list of members and their alternates shall be published by the Council for information in the *Official Journal of the European Union*.

Article 25. The Advisory Committee shall be chaired by a member of the Commission or his representative. The Chairman shall not vote. The Committee shall meet at least twice a year. It shall be convened by its Chairman, either on his own initiative, or at the request of at least one third of the members.

Secretarial services shall be provided for the Committee by the Commission.

Article 26. The Chairman may invite individuals or representatives of bodies with wide experience in the field of employment or movement of workers to take part in meetings as observers or as experts. The Chairman may be assisted by expert advisers.

Article 27. (1) An opinion delivered by the Advisory Committee shall not be valid unless two thirds of the members are present.

(2) Opinions shall state the reasons on which they are based; they shall be delivered by an absolute majority of the votes validly cast; they shall be accompanied by a written statement of the views expressed by the minority, when the latter so requests.

Article 28. The Advisory Committee shall establish its working methods by rules of procedure which shall enter into force after the Council, having received an opinion from the Commission, has given its approval. The entry into force of any amendment that the Committee decides to make thereto shall be subject to the same procedure.

Section 2. The Technical Committee

Article 29. The Technical Committee shall be responsible for assisting the Commission in the preparation, promotion and follow–up of all technical work and measures for giving effect to this Regulation and any supplementary measures.

Article 30. The Technical Committee shall be responsible in particular for:
(a) promoting and advancing cooperation between the public authorities concerned in the Member States on all technical questions relating to freedom of movement of workers and their employment;
(b) formulating procedures for the organisation of the joint activities of the public authorities concerned;
(c) facilitating the gathering of information likely to be of use to the Commission and the undertaking of the studies and research provided for in this Regulation, and encouraging exchange of information and experience between the administrative bodies concerned;
(d) investigating at a technical level the harmonisation of the criteria by which Member States assess the state of their labour markets.

Article 31. (1) The Technical Committee shall be composed of representatives of the Governments of the Member States. Each Government shall appoint as member of the Technical Committee one of the members who represent it on the Advisory Committee.

(2) Each Government shall appoint an alternate from among its other representatives — members or alternates — on the Advisory Committee.

Article 32. The Technical Committee shall be chaired by a member of the Commission or his representative. The Chairman shall not vote. The Chairman and the members of the Committee may be assisted by expert advisers.

Secretarial services shall be provided for the Committee by the Commission.

Article 33. The proposals and opinions formulated by the Technical Committee shall be submitted to the Commission, and the Advisory Committee shall be informed thereof. Any such proposals and opinions shall be accompanied by a written statement of the views expressed by the various members of the Technical Committee, when the latter so request.

Article 34. The Technical Committee shall establish its working methods by rules of procedure which shall enter into force after the Council, having received an opinion from the Commission, has given its approval. The entry into force of any amendment which the Committee decides to make thereto shall be subject to the same procedure.

PART III EUROPEAN UNION

Chapter IV. Final Provisions

Article 35. The rules of procedure of the Advisory Committee and of the Technical Committee in force on 8 November 1968 shall continue to apply.

Article 36. (1) This Regulation shall not affect the provisions of the Treaty establishing the European Atomic Energy Community which deal with eligibility for skilled employment in the field of nuclear energy, nor any measures taken in pursuance of that Treaty.
Nevertheless, this Regulation shall apply to the category of workers referred to in the first subparagraph and to members of their families in so far as their legal position is not governed by the above–mentioned Treaty or measures.
(2) This Regulation shall not affect measures taken in accordance with Article 48 of the Treaty on the Functioning of the European Union.
(3) This Regulation shall not affect the obligations of Member States arising out of special relations or future agreements with certain non–European countries or territories, based on institutional ties existing on 8 November 1968, or agreements in existence on 8 November 1968 with certain non–European countries or territories, based on institutional ties between them.
Workers from such countries or territories who, in accordance with this provision, are pursuing activities as employed persons in the territory of one of those Member States may not invoke the benefit of the provisions of this Regulation in the territory of the other Member States.

Article 37. Member States shall, for information purposes, communicate to the Commission the texts of agreements, conventions or arrangements concluded between them in the manpower field between the date of their being signed and that of their entry into force.

Article 38. The Commission shall adopt measures pursuant to this Regulation for its implementation. To this end it shall act in close cooperation with the central public authorities of the Member States.

Article 39. The administrative expenditure of the Advisory Committee and of the Technical Committee shall be included in the general budget of the European Union in the section relating to the Commission.

Article 40. This Regulation shall apply to the Member States and to their nationals, without prejudice to Articles 2 and 3.

Article 41. Regulation (EEC) No 1612/68 is hereby repealed.
References to the repealed Regulation shall be construed as references to this Regulation and shall be read in accordance with the correlation table in Annex II.

Article 42. This Regulation shall enter into force on the 20th day following its publication in the *Official Journal of the European Union*.
This Regulation shall be binding in its entirety and directly applicable in all Member States.

Commission Regulation (EU) No 1407/2013 of 18 December 2013 on the application of Articles 107 and 108 of the Treaty on the Functioning of the European Union to de minimis **aid**

THE EUROPEAN COMMISSION,
Having regard to the Treaty on the Functioning of the European Union, and in particular Article 108(4) thereof,
Having regard to Council Regulation (EC) No 994/98 of 7 May 1998 on the application of Articles 107 and 108 of the Treaty on the Functioning of the European Union to certain categories of horizontal State aid,
Having published a draft of this Regulation,
After consulting the Advisory Committee on State Aid,
Whereas:

(1) State funding meeting the criteria in Article 107(1) of the Treaty constitutes State aid and requires notification to the Commission by virtue of Article 108(3) of the Treaty. However, under Article 109 of the Treaty, the Council may determine categories of aid that are exempted from this notification requirement. In accordance with Article 108(4) of the Treaty the Commission may adopt regulations relating to those categories of State aid. By virtue of Regulation (EC) No 994/98 the Council decided, in accordance with Article 109 of the Treaty, that de minimis aid could constitute one such category. On that basis, de minimis aid, being aid granted to a single undertaking over a given period of time that does not exceed a certain fixed amount, is deemed not to meet all the criteria laid down in Article 107(1) of the Treaty and is therefore not subject to the notification procedure.

(2) The Commission has, in numerous decisions, clarified the notion of aid within the meaning of Article 107(1) of the Treaty. The Commission has also stated its policy with regard to a de minimis ceiling below which Article 107(1) of the Treaty can be considered not to apply, initially in its notice on the de minimis rule for State aid and subsequently in Commission Regulations (EC) No 69/2001 and (EC) No 1998/2006. In the light of the experience gained in applying Regulation (EC) No 1998/2006, it is appropriate to revise some of the conditions laid down in that Regulation and to replace it.

(3) It is appropriate to maintain the ceiling of EUR 200 000 as the amount of de minimis aid that a single undertaking may receive per Member State over any period of three years. That ceiling remains necessary to ensure that any measure falling under this Regulation can be deemed not to have any effect on trade between Member States and not to distort or threaten to distort competition.

(4) For the purposes of the rules on competition laid down in the Treaty an undertaking is any entity engaged in an economic activity, regardless of its legal status and the way in which it is financed. The Court of Justice of the European Union has ruled that all entities which are controlled (on a legal or on a de facto basis) by the same entity should be considered as a single undertaking. For the sake of legal certainty and to reduce the administrative burden, this Regulation should provide an exhaustive list of clear criteria for determining when two or more enterprises within the same Member State are to be considered as a single undertaking. The Commission has selected from the well-established criteria for defining 'linked enterprises' in the definition of small or medium–sized enterprises (SMEs) in Commission Recommendation 2003/361/EC and in Annex I to Commission Regulation (EC) No 800/2008 those criteria that are appropriate for the purposes of this Regulation. The criteria are already familiar to public authorities and should be applicable, given the scope of this Regulation, to both SMEs and large undertakings. Those criteria should ensure that a group of linked enterprises is considered as one single undertaking for the application of the de minimis rule, but that enterprises which have no relationship with each other except for the fact that each of them has a direct link to the same public body or bodies are not treated as being linked to each other. The specific situation of enterprises controlled by the same public body or bodies, which may have an independent power of decision, is therefore taken into account.

(5) In order to take account of the small average size of undertakings active in the road freight transport sector, it is appropriate to maintain the ceiling of EUR 100 000 for undertakings performing road freight transport for hire or reward. The provision of an integrated service where the actual transportation is only one element, such as removal services, postal or courier services or waste collection or processing services, should not be considered a transport service. In view of the overcapacity in the road freight transport sector and the objectives of transport policy as regards road congestion and freight transport, aid for the acquisition of road freight transport vehicles by undertakings performing road freight transport for hire or reward should be excluded from the scope of application of this Regulation. In view of the development of the road passenger transport sector, it is no longer appropriate to apply a lower ceiling to this sector.

(6) In view of the special rules which apply in the sectors of primary production of agricultural prod-

ucts, fishery and aquaculture and of the risk that amounts of aid below the ceiling laid down in this Regulation could nonetheless fulfil the criteria in Article 107(1) of the Treaty, this Regulation should not apply to those sectors.

(7) Considering the similarities between the processing and marketing of agricultural products and of non–agricultural products, this Regulation should apply to the processing and marketing of agricultural products, provided that certain conditions are met. Neither on–farm activities necessary for preparing a product for the first sale, such as harvesting, cutting and threshing of cereals, or packing of eggs, nor the first sale to resellers or processors should be considered as processing or marketing in this respect.

(8) The Court of Justice of the European Union has established that, once the Union has legislated for the establishment of a common organisation of the market in a given sector of agriculture, Member States are under an obligation to refrain from taking any measure which might undermine or create exceptions to it. For that reason, this Regulation should not apply to aid the amount of which is fixed on the basis of the price or quantity of products purchased or put on the market. Nor should it apply to support which is linked to an obligation to share the aid with primary producers.

(9) This Regulation should not apply to export aid or aid contingent upon the use of domestic over imported products. In particular, it should not apply to aid financing the establishment and operation of a distribution network in other Member States or in third countries. Aid towards the costs of participating in trade fairs, or of studies or consultancy services needed for the launch of a new or existing product on a new market in another Member State or a third country does not normally constitute export aid.

(10) The period of three years to be taken into account for the purposes of this Regulation should be assessed on a rolling basis so that, for each new grant of de minimis aid, the total amount of de minimis aid granted in the fiscal year concerned and during the previous two fiscal years needs to be taken into account.

(11) Where an undertaking is active in sectors excluded from the scope of this Regulation and is also active in other sectors or has other activities, this Regulation should apply to those other sectors or activities provided that the Member State concerned ensures, by appropriate means such as separation of activities or distinction of costs, that the activities in the excluded sectors do not benefit from the de minimis aid. The same principle should apply where an undertaking is active in sectors to which lower de minimis ceilings apply. If it cannot be ensured that the activities in sectors to which lower de minimis ceilings apply benefit from de minimis aid only up to those lower ceilings, the lowest ceiling should apply to all activities of the undertaking.

(12) This Regulation should lay down rules to ensure that it is not possible to circumvent maximum aid intensities laid down in specific regulations or Commission decisions. It should also provide for clear rules on cumulation that are easy to apply.

(13) This Regulation does not exclude the possibility that a measure might be considered not to be State aid within the meaning of Article 107(1) of the Treaty on grounds other than those set out in this Regulation, for instance because the measure complies with the market economy operator principle or because the measure does not involve a transfer of State resources. In particular, Union funding centrally managed by the Commission which is not directly or indirectly under the control of the Member State does not constitute State aid and should not be taken into account in determining whether the relevant ceiling is complied with.

(14) For the purposes of transparency, equal treatment and effective monitoring, this Regulation should apply only to de minimis aid for which it is possible to calculate precisely the gross grant equivalent ex ante without any need to undertake a risk assessment ('transparent aid'). Such a precise calculation can, for instance, be made for grants, interest rate subsidies, capped tax exemptions or other instruments that provide for a cap ensuring that the relevant ceiling is not exceeded. Providing for a cap means that as long as the precise amount of aid is not or not yet known, the Member State has to assume that the amount equals the cap in order to ensure that several aid measures together do not exceed the ceiling set out in this Regulation and to apply the rules on cumulation.

(15) For the purposes of transparency, equal treatment and the correct application of the de minimis ceiling, all Member States should apply the same method of calculation. In order to facilitate such calculation, aid amounts not taking the form of a cash grant should be converted into their gross grant equivalent. Calculation of the gross grant equivalent of transparent types of aid other than grants and of aid payable in several instalments requires the use of market interest rates prevailing at the time such aid is granted. With a view to uniform, transparent and simple application of the State aid rules, the market rates applicable for the purposes of this Regulation should be the reference rates, as set out in the Communication from the Commission on the revision of the method for setting the reference and discount rates.

(16) Aid comprised in loans, including de minimis risk finance aid taking the form of loans, should be considered transparent de minimis aid if the gross grant equivalent has been calculated on the basis of market interest rates prevailing at the time the aid is granted. In order to simplify the treatment of small loans of short duration, this Regulation should provide for a clear rule that is easy to apply and takes into account both the amount of the loan and its duration. Based on the Commission's experience, loans that are secured by collateral covering at least 50 % of the loan and that do not exceed either EUR 1 000 000 and a duration of five years or EUR 500 000 and a duration of 10 years can be considered as having a gross grant equivalent not exceeding the de minimis ceiling. Given the difficulties linked to determining the gross grant equivalent of aid granted to undertakings that may not be able to repay the loan, this rule should not apply to such undertakings.

(17) Aid comprised in capital injections should not be considered as transparent de minimis aid, unless the total amount of the public injection does not exceed the de minimis ceiling. Aid comprised in risk finance measures taking the form of equity or quasi–equity investments, as referred to in the risk finance guidelines, should not be considered as transparent de minimis aid unless the measure concerned provides capital not exceeding the de minimis ceiling.

(18) Aid comprised in guarantees, including de minimis risk finance aid taking the form of guarantees, should be considered as transparent if the gross grant equivalent has been calculated on the basis of safe–harbour premiums laid down in a Commission notice for the type of undertaking concerned. In order to simplify the treatment of guarantees of short duration securing up to 80 % of a relatively small loan, this Regulation should provide for a clear rule that is easy to apply and takes into account both the amount of the underlying loan and the duration of the guarantee. This rule should not apply to guarantees on underlying transactions not constituting a loan, such as guarantees on equity transactions. Where the guarantee does not exceed 80 % of the underlying loan, the amount guaranteed does not exceed EUR 1 500 000 and the duration of the guarantee does not exceed five years the guarantee can be considered as having a gross grant equivalent not exceeding the de minimis ceiling. The same applies where the guarantee does not exceed 80 % of the underlying loan, the amount guaranteed does not exceed EUR 750 000 and the duration of the guarantee does not exceed 10 years. In addition, Member States can use a methodology to calculate the gross grant equivalent of guarantees which has been notified to the Commission under another Commission Regulation in the State aid area applicable at that time and which has been accepted by the Commission as being in line with the Guarantee Notice, or any successor notice, provided that the accepted methodology explicitly addresses the type of guarantee and the type of underlying transaction at stake in the context of the application of this Regulation. Given the difficulties linked to determining the gross grant equivalent of aid granted to undertakings that may not be able to repay the loan, this rule should not apply to such undertakings.

(19) Where a de minimis aid scheme is implemented through financial intermediaries, it should be ensured that the latter do not receive any State aid. This can be done, for example, by requiring financial intermediaries that benefit from a State guarantee to pay a market–conform premium or to fully pass on any advantage to the final beneficiaries, or by respecting the de minimis ceiling and other conditions of this Regulation also at the level of the intermediaries.

(20) Upon notification by a Member State, the Commission may examine whether a measure which does not consist of a grant, loan, guarantee, capital injection or risk finance measure taking the form of an equity or quasi–equity investment leads to a gross grant equivalent that does not exceed the de minimis ceiling and could therefore fall within the scope of this Regulation.

(21) The Commission has a duty to ensure that State aid rules are complied with and in accordance with the cooperation principle laid down in Article 4(3) of the Treaty on European Union, Member States should facilitate the fulfilment of this task by establishing the necessary tools in order to ensure that the total amount of de minimis aid granted to a single undertaking under the de minimis rule does not exceed the overall permissible ceiling. To that end, when granting de minimis aid, Member States should inform the undertaking concerned of the amount of de minimis aid granted and of its de minimis character and should make express reference to this Regulation. Member States should be required to monitor aid granted to ensure the relevant ceilings are not exceeded and the cumulation rules are complied with. To comply with that obligation, before granting such aid, the Member State concerned should obtain from the undertaking a declaration about other de minimis aid covered by this Regulation or by other de minimis regulations received during the fiscal year concerned and the previous two fiscal years. Alternatively it should be possible for Member States to set up a central register with complete information on de minimis aid granted and check that any new grant of aid does not exceed the relevant ceiling.

(22) Before granting any new de minimis aid each Member State should verify that the de minimis ceiling will not be exceeded in that Member State by the new de minimis aid and that the other condi-

tions of this Regulation are complied with.

(23) Having regard to the Commission's experience and in particular the frequency with which it is generally necessary to revise State aid policy, the period of application of this Regulation should be limited. If this Regulation expires without being extended, Member States should have an adjustment period of six months with regard to de minimis aid covered by this Regulation,

HAS ADOPTED THIS REGULATION:

Article 1. Scope

(1) This Regulation applies to aid granted to undertakings in all sectors, with the exception of:
(a) aid granted to undertakings active in the fishery and aquaculture sector, as covered by Council Regulation (EC) No 104/2000;
(b) aid granted to undertakings active in the primary production of agricultural products;
(c) aid granted to undertakings active in the sector of processing and marketing of agricultural products, in the following cases:
(i) where the amount of the aid is fixed on the basis of the price or quantity of such products purchased from primary producers or put on the market by the undertakings concerned;
(ii) where the aid is conditional on being partly or entirely passed on to primary producers;
(d) aid to export–related activities towards third countries or Member States, namely aid directly linked to the quantities exported, to the establishment and operation of a distribution network or to other current expenditure linked to the export activity;
(e) aid contingent upon the use of domestic over imported goods.

(2) Where an undertaking is active in the sectors referred to in points (a), (b) or (c) of paragraph 1 and is also active in one or more of the sectors or has other activities falling within the scope of this Regulation, this Regulation shall apply to aid granted in respect of the latter sectors or activities, provided that the Member State concerned ensures, by appropriate means such as separation of activities or distinction of costs, that the activities in the sectors excluded from the scope of this Regulation do not benefit from the *de minimis* aid granted in accordance with this Regulation.

Article 2. Definitions

(1) For the purposes of this Regulation the following definitions shall apply:
(a) 'agricultural products' means products listed in Annex I to the Treaty, with the exception of fishery and aquaculture products covered by Regulation (EC) No 104/2000;
(b) 'processing of agricultural products' means any operation on an agricultural product resulting in a product which is also an agricultural product, except on–farm activities necessary for preparing an animal or plant product for the first sale;
(c) 'marketing of agricultural products' means holding or display with a view to sale, offering for sale, delivery or any other manner of placing on the market, except the first sale by a primary producer to resellers or processors and any activity preparing a product for such first sale; a sale by a primary producer to final consumers shall be considered as marketing if it takes place in separate premises reserved for that purpose.

(2) 'Single undertaking' includes, for the purposes of this Regulation, all enterprises having at least one of the following relationships with each other:
(a) one enterprise has a majority of the shareholders' or members' voting rights in another enterprise;
(b) one enterprise has the right to appoint or remove a majority of the members of the administrative, management or supervisory body of another enterprise;
(c) one enterprise has the right to exercise a dominant influence over another enterprise pursuant to a contract entered into with that enterprise or to a provision in its memorandum or articles of association;
(d) one enterprise, which is a shareholder in or member of another enterprise, controls alone, pursuant to an agreement with other shareholders in or members of that enterprise, a majority of shareholders' or members' voting rights in that enterprise.

Enterprises having any of the relationships referred to in points (a) to (d) of the first subparagraph through one or more other enterprises shall also be considered to be a single undertaking.

Article 3. De minimis aid

(1) Aid measures shall be deemed not to meet all the criteria in Article 107(1) of the Treaty, and shall therefore be exempt from the notification requirement in Article 108(3) of the Treaty, if they fulfil the conditions laid down in this Regulation.

(2) The total amount of *de minimis* aid granted per Member State to a single undertaking shall not exceed EUR 200 000 over any period of three fiscal years.

The total amount of *de minimis* aid granted per Member State to a single undertaking performing road freight transport for hire or reward shall not exceed EUR 100 000 over any period of three fiscal years. This *de minimis* aid shall not be used for the acquisition of road freight transport vehicles.

(3) If an undertaking performs road freight transport for hire or reward and also carries out other activities to which the ceiling of EUR 200 000 applies, the ceiling of EUR 200 000 shall apply to the undertaking, provided that the Member State concerned ensures, by appropriate means such as separation of activities or distinction of costs, that the benefit to the road freight transport activity does not exceed EUR 100 000 and that no *de minimis* aid is used for the acquisition of road freight transport vehicles.

(4) De minimis aid shall be deemed granted at the moment the legal right to receive the aid is conferred on the undertaking under the applicable national legal regime irrespective of the date of payment of the *de minimis* aid to the undertaking.

(5) The ceilings laid down in paragraph 2 shall apply irrespective of the form of the *de minimis* aid or the objective pursued and regardless of whether the aid granted by the Member State is financed entirely or partly by resources of Union origin. The period of three fiscal years shall be determined by reference to the fiscal years used by the undertaking in the Member State concerned.

(6) For the purposes of the ceilings laid down in paragraph 2, aid shall be expressed as a cash grant. All figures used shall be gross, that is, before any deduction of tax or other charge. Where aid is granted in a form other than a grant, the aid amount shall be the gross grant equivalent of the aid. Aid payable in several instalments shall be discounted to its value at the moment it is granted. The interest rate to be used for discounting purposes shall be the discount rate applicable at the time the aid is granted.

(7) Where the relevant ceiling laid down in paragraph 2 would be exceeded by the grant of new *de minimis* aid, none of that new aid may benefit from this Regulation.

(8) In the case of mergers or acquisitions, all prior *de minimis* aid granted to any of the merging undertakings shall be taken into account in determining whether any new *de minimis* aid to the new or the acquiring undertaking exceeds the relevant ceiling. De minimis aid lawfully granted before the merger or acquisition shall remain lawful.

(9) If one undertaking splits into two or more separate undertakings, *de minimis* aid granted prior to the split shall be allocated to the undertaking that benefited from it, which is in principle the undertaking taking over the activities for which the *de minimis* aid was used. If such an allocation is not possible, the *de minimis* aid shall be allocated proportionately on the basis of the book value of the equity capital of the new undertakings at the effective date of the split.

Article 4. Calculation of gross grant equivalent

(1) This Regulation shall apply only to aid in respect of which it is possible to calculate precisely the gross grant equivalent of the aid *ex ante* without any need to undertake a risk assessment ('transparent aid').

(2) Aid comprised in grants or interest rate subsidies shall be considered as transparent *de minimis* aid.

(3) Aid comprised in loans shall be considered as transparent *de minimis* aid if:

(a) the beneficiary is not subject to collective insolvency proceedings nor fulfils the criteria under its domestic law for being placed in collective insolvency proceedings at the request of its creditors. In case of large undertakings, the beneficiary shall be in a situation comparable to a credit rating of at least B–; and

(b) the loan is secured by collateral covering at least 50 % of the loan and the loan amounts to either EUR 1 000 000 (or EUR 500 000 for undertakings performing road freight transport) over five years or EUR 500 000 (or EUR 250 000 for undertakings performing road freight transport) over 10 years; if a loan is for less than those amounts and/or is granted for a period of less than five or 10 years respectively, the gross grant equivalent of that loan shall be calculated as a corresponding proportion of the relevant ceiling laid down in Article 3(2); or

(c) the gross grant equivalent has been calculated on the basis of the reference rate applicable at the time of the grant.

(4) Aid comprised in capital injections shall only be considered as transparent *de minimis* aid if the total amount of the public injection does not exceed the *de minimis* ceiling.

(5) Aid comprised in risk finance measures taking the form of equity or quasi–equity investments shall only be considered as transparent *de minimis* aid if the capital provided to a single undertaking does not exceed the *de minimis* ceiling.

(6) Aid comprised in guarantees shall be treated as transparent *de minimis* aid if:

(a) the beneficiary is not subject to collective insolvency proceedings nor fulfils the criteria under its domestic law for being placed in collective insolvency proceedings at the request of its creditors. In case of large undertakings, the beneficiary shall be in a situation comparable to a credit rating of at least B–; and

(b) the guarantee does not exceed 80 % of the underlying loan and either the amount guaranteed is EUR 1 500 000 (or EUR 750 000 for undertakings performing road freight transport) and the duration of the guarantee is five years or the amount guaranteed is EUR 750 000 (or EUR 375 000 for undertakings performing road freight transport) and the duration of the guarantee is 10 years; if the amount guaranteed is lower than these amounts and/or the guarantee is for a period of less than five or 10 years respectively, the gross grant equivalent of that guarantee shall be calculated as a corresponding proportion of the relevant ceiling laid down in Article 3(2); or

(c) the gross grant equivalent has been calculated on the basis of safe–harbour premiums laid down in a Commission notice; or

(d) before implementation,

(i) the methodology used to calculate the gross grant equivalent of the guarantee has been notified to the Commission under another Commission Regulation in the State aid area applicable at that time and accepted by the Commission as being in line with the Guarantee Notice, or any successor Notice; and

(ii) that methodology explicitly addresses the type of guarantee and the type of underlying transaction at stake in the context of the application of this Regulation.

(7) Aid comprised in other instruments shall be considered as transparent *de minimis* aid if the instrument provides for a cap ensuring that the relevant ceiling is not exceeded.

Article 5. Cumulation

(1) De minimis aid granted in accordance with this Regulation may be cumulated with *de minimis* aid granted in accordance with Commission Regulation (EU) No 360/2012 up to the ceiling laid down in that Regulation. It may be cumulated with *de minimis* aid granted in accordance with other *de minimis* regulations up to the relevant ceiling laid down in Article 3(2) of this Regulation.

(2) De minimis aid shall not be cumulated with State aid in relation to the same eligible costs or with State aid for the same risk finance measure, if such cumulation would exceed the highest relevant aid intensity or aid amount fixed in the specific circumstances of each case by a block exemption regulation or a decision adopted by the Commission. De minimis aid which is not granted for or attributable to specific eligible costs may be cumulated with other State aid granted under a block exemption regulation or a decision adopted by the Commission.

Article 6. Monitoring

(1) Where a Member State intends to grant *de minimis* aid in accordance with this Regulation to an undertaking, it shall inform that undertaking in writing of the prospective amount of the aid expressed as a gross grant equivalent and of its *de minimis* character, making express reference to this Regulation and citing its title and publication reference in the *Official Journal of the European Union*. Where *de minimis* aid is granted in accordance with this Regulation to different undertakings on the basis of a scheme and different amounts of individual aid are granted to those undertakings under that scheme, the Member State concerned may choose to fulfil that obligation by informing the undertakings of a fixed sum corresponding to the maximum aid amount to be granted under that scheme. In such case, the fixed sum shall be used for determining whether the relevant ceiling laid down in Article 3(2) is reached. Before granting the aid, the Member State shall obtain a declaration from the undertaking concerned, in written or electronic form, about any other *de minimis* aid received to which this Regulation or other *de minimis* regulations apply during the previous two fiscal years and the current fiscal year.

(2) Where a Member State has set up a central register of *de minimis* aid containing complete information on all *de minimis* aid granted by any authority within that Member State, paragraph 1 shall cease to apply from the moment the register covers a period of three fiscal years.

(3) A Member State shall grant new *de minimis* aid in accordance with this Regulation only after having checked that this will not raise the total amount of *de minimis* aid granted to the undertaking concerned to a level above the relevant ceiling laid down in Article 3(2) and that all the conditions laid down in this Regulation are complied with.

(4) Member States shall record and compile all the information regarding the application of this Regulation. Such records shall contain all information necessary to demonstrate that the conditions of this Regulation have been complied with. Records regarding individual *de minimis* aid shall be maintained for 10 fiscal years from the date on which the aid was granted. Records regarding a *de minimis* aid scheme shall be maintained for 10 fiscal years from the date on which the last individual aid was granted under such a scheme.

(5) On written request, the Member State concerned shall provide the Commission, within a period

of 20 working days or such longer period as may be fixed in the request, with all the information that the Commission considers necessary for assessing whether the conditions of this Regulation have been complied with, and in particular the total amount of *de minimis* aid within the meaning of this Regulation and of other *de minimis* regulations received by any undertaking.

Article 7. Transitional provisions

(1) This Regulation shall apply to aid granted before its entry into force if the aid fulfils all the conditions laid down in this Regulation. Any aid which does not fulfil those conditions will be assessed by the Commission in accordance with the relevant frameworks, guidelines, communications and notices.

(2) Any individual *de minimis* aid which was granted between 2 February 2001 and 30 June 2007 and fulfils the conditions of Regulation (EC) No 69/2001 shall be deemed not to meet all the criteria in Article 107(1) of the Treaty and shall therefore be exempt from the notification requirement in Article 108(3) of the Treaty.

(3) Any individual *de minimis* aid granted between 1 January 2007 and 30 June 2014 and which fulfils the conditions of Regulation (EC) No 1998/2006 shall be deemed not to meet all the criteria in Article 107(1) of the Treaty and shall therefore be exempt from the notification requirement in Article 108(3) of the Treaty.

(4) At the end of the period of validity of this Regulation, any *de minimis* aid scheme which fulfils the conditions of this Regulation shall remain covered by this Regulation for a further period of six months.

Article 8. Entry into force and period of application

This Regulation shall enter into force on 1 January 2014.
It shall apply until 31 December 2020.
This Regulation shall be binding in its entirety and directly applicable in all Member States.

PART III   EUROPEAN UNION

Commission Regulation (EU) No 651/2014 of 17 June 2014 declaring certain categories of aid compatible with the internal market in application of Articles 107 and 108 of the Treaty

THE EUROPEAN COMMISSION,
Having regard to the Treaty on the Functioning of the European Union, and in particular Article 108(4) thereof,
Having regard to Council Regulation (EC) No 994/98 of 7 May 1998 on the application of Articles 92 and 93 of the Treaty establishing the European Community to certain categories of horizontal State aid, and in particular Article 1(1)(a) and (b) thereof,
After consulting the Advisory Committee on State Aid,
Whereas:
(1) State funding meeting the criteria in Article 107(1) of the Treaty constitutes State aid and requires notification to the Commission by virtue of Article 108(3) of the Treaty. However, according to Article 109 of the Treaty, the Council may determine categories of aid that are exempted from this notification requirement. In accordance with Article 108(4) of the Treaty the Commission may adopt regulations relating to those categories of State aid. Council Regulation (EC) No 994/98 empowers the Commission to declare, in accordance with Article 109 of the Treaty, that the following categories may, under certain conditions, be exempted from the notification requirement: aid to small and medium–sized enterprises (SMEs), aid in favour of research and development, aid in favour of environmental protection, employment and training aid and aid that complies with the map approved by the Commission for each Member State for the grant of regional aid. On that basis, the Commission adopted Commission Regulation (EC) No 800/2008. Regulation (EC) No 800/2008 originally applied until 31 December 2013 but was subsequently prolonged by Commission Regulation (EU) No 1224/2013 of 29 November 2013 amending Regulation (EC) No 800/2008 as regards its period of application and now expires on 30 June 2014. On 22 July 2013 Regulation (EC) No 994/98 was amended by Council Regulation (EU) No 733/2013 of 22 July 2013 amending Regulation (EC) No 994/98 on the application of Articles 92 and 93 of the Treaty establishing the European Community to certain categories of horizontal State aid to empower the Commission to extend the block exemption to new categories of aid, in respect of which clear compatibility conditions can be defined. Such new categories of block exempted aid include: aid to make good the damage caused by certain natural disasters, social aid for transport for residents of remote regions, aid for broadband infrastructures, aid for innovation, aid for culture and heritage conservation, aid for sport and multifunctional recreational infrastructures. Provided that sufficient case experience is further developed allowing the design of operational exemption criteria ensuring the ex–ante compatibility of other categories of aid, the Commission intends to review the scope of this Regulation with a view to including certain types of aid in those areas. In particular, the Commission envisages developing criteria for port and airport infrastructure by December 2015.
(2) With its Communication on EU State Aid Modernisation (SAM), the Commission launched a wider review of the State aid rules. The main objectives of this modernisation are (i) to achieve sustainable, smart and inclusive growth in a competitive internal market, while contributing to Member State efforts towards a more efficient use of public finances, (ii) to focus Commission ex ante scrutiny of aid measures on cases with the biggest impact on the internal market, while strengthening Member State cooperation in State aid enforcement, and (iii) to streamline the rules and provide for faster, better informed and more robust decisions based on a clear economic rationale, a common approach and clear obligations. The review of Regulation (EC) No 800/2008 constitutes a central element of SAM.
(3) This Regulation should allow for better prioritisation of State aid enforcement activities, greater simplification and should enhance transparency, effective evaluation and the control of compliance with the State aid rules at national and Union levels, while preserving the institutional competences of the Commission and the Member States. In accordance with the principle of proportionality this Regulation does not go beyond what is necessary in order to achieve those objectives.
(4) The Commission's experience in applying Regulation (EC) No 800/2008 has allowed it to better define the conditions under which certain categories of aid can be considered compatible with the internal market and to extend the scope of block exemptions. It also revealed the necessity to strengthen transparency, monitoring and proper evaluation of very large schemes in light of their effect on competition in the internal market.
(5) The general conditions for the application of this Regulation should be defined on the basis of a set of common principles that ensure the aid serves a purpose of common interest, has a clear incentive effect, is appropriate and proportionate, is granted in full transparency and subject to a control mechanism and regular evaluation, and does not adversely affect trading conditions to an extent that

is contrary to the common interest.

(6) Aid that fulfils all the conditions laid down in this Regulation both general and specific to the relevant categories of aid should be exempted from the notification obligation laid down in Article 108(3) of the Treaty.

(7) State aid within the meaning of Article 107(1) of the Treaty not covered by this Regulation remains subject to the notification requirement of Article 108(3) of the Treaty. This Regulation is without prejudice to the possibility for Member States to notify aid the objectives of which correspond to objectives covered by this Regulation.

(8) In view of the greater potential impact of large schemes on trade and competition, aid schemes with an average annual State aid budget exceeding a threshold based on an absolute value should in principle be subject to State aid evaluation. The evaluation should aim at verifying whether the assumptions and conditions underlying the compatibility of the scheme have been achieved, as well as the effectiveness of the aid measure in the light of its general and specific objectives and should provide indications on the impact of the scheme on competition and trade. In order to ensure equal treatment, State aid evaluation should be carried out on the basis of an evaluation plan approved by the Commission. While such plan should normally be drawn up at the moment of the design of the scheme and approved in time for the scheme to enter into force, this may not be possible in all cases. Therefore, in order not to delay their entry into force, this Regulation will apply to such schemes for a maximum period of six months. The Commission may decide to extend this period, upon approval of the evaluation plan. To this end, the evaluation plan should be notified to the Commission within 20 working days following the entry into force of the scheme. The Commission can also exceptionally decide that an evaluation is not necessary given the specificities of the case. The Commission should receive from the Member State the necessary information to be able to carry out the assessment of the evaluation plan and request additional information without undue delay allowing the Member State to complete the missing elements for the Commission to take a decision. In view of the novelty of this process, the Commission will provide, in a separate document, a detailed guidance on the procedure applicable during the 6 months period for the approval of the evaluation plan and the relevant templates through which the evaluation plans will have to be submitted. Alterations of schemes subject to evaluation, other than modifications which cannot affect the compatibility of the aid scheme under this Regulation or cannot significantly affect the content of the approved evaluation plan, should be assessed taking account of the outcome of such evaluation and should be excluded from the scope of this Regulation. The alterations such as purely formal modifications, administrative modifications or alterations carried out within the framework of the EU co–financed measures should not, in principle, be considered as significantly affecting the content of the approved evaluation plan.

(9) This Regulation should not apply to aid contingent upon the use of domestic over imported products or aid to export–related activities. In particular, it should not apply to aid financing the establishment and operation of a distribution network in other countries. Aid towards the cost of participating in trade fairs or of studies or consultancy services needed for the launch of a new or existing product on a new market in another Member State or third country does not normally constitute aid to export–related activities.

(10) This Regulation should apply in principle across most sectors of the economy. However, in some sectors, such as the fisheries and aquaculture sector and primary agricultural production, the scope should be limited in the light of the special rules applicable.

(11) This Regulation should apply to the processing and marketing of agricultural products, provided that certain conditions are met. For the purposes of this Regulation neither on–farm activities necessary for preparing a product for the first sale, nor the first sale by a primary producer to resellers or processors or any activity preparing a product for a first sale should be considered processing or marketing.

(12) This Regulation should not apply to aid to facilitate the closure of uncompetitive coal mines, which is dealt with by the Council Decision of 10 December 2010 on State aid to facilitate the closure of uncompetitive coal mines. This Regulation should apply to other types of aid in the coal sector, with the exception of regional aid.

(13) The Commission should ensure that authorised aid does not adversely affect trading conditions to an extent that is contrary to the common interest. Therefore, aid in favour of a beneficiary which is subject to an outstanding recovery order following a previous Commission decision declaring an aid illegal and incompatible with the internal market should be excluded from the scope of this Regulation, with the exception of aid schemes to make good the damage caused by certain natural disasters.

(14) Aid granted to undertakings in difficulty should be excluded from the scope of this Regulation, since such aid should be assessed under the Community guidelines on State aid for rescuing and restructuring firms in difficulty of 1 October 2004 as prolonged by Commission communication

concerning the prolongation of the application of the Community guidelines on State aid for rescuing and restructuring firms in difficulty of 1 October 2004 or their successor Guidelines, in order to avoid their circumvention, with the exception of aid schemes to make good the damage caused by certain natural disasters. In order to provide legal certainty, it is appropriate to establish clear criteria that do not require an assessment of all the particularities of the situation of an undertaking to determine whether an undertaking is considered to be in difficulty for the purposes of this Regulation.

(15) State aid enforcement is highly dependent on the cooperation of Member States. Therefore, Member States should take all necessary measures to ensure compliance with this Regulation, including compliance of individual aid granted under block–exempted schemes.

(16) Due to the high risk of adversely affecting trading conditions, large amounts of aid granted either individually or cumulatively should be assessed by the Commission upon notification. Thresholds should therefore be set for each category of aid falling within the scope of this Regulation at a level which takes into account the category of aid concerned and its likely effect on trading conditions. Any aid granted above those thresholds should remain subject to the notification requirement of Article 108(3) of the Treaty. The thresholds set out in this Regulation should not be circumvented by artificially splitting up aid schemes or aid projects into several aid schemes or projects with similar characteristics, objectives or beneficiaries.

(17) For the purpose of transparency, equal treatment and effective monitoring, this Regulation should only apply to aid in respect of which it is possible to calculate precisely the gross grant equivalent ex ante without the need to undertake a risk assessment ('transparent aid'). For certain specific aid instruments, such as loans, guarantees, tax measures, risk finance measures and, in particular, repayable advances, this Regulation should define the conditions under which they can be considered transparent. Capital injections should not be considered transparent aid, without prejudice to specific conditions concerning risk finance and start–up aid. Aid comprised in guarantees should be considered as transparent if the gross grant equivalent has been calculated on the basis of safe–harbour premiums laid down for the respective type of undertaking. In the case of small and medium–sized enterprises (SMEs), the Commission Notice on the application of Articles 87 and 88 of the EC Treaty to State aid in the form of guarantees indicates levels of annual premium above which a State guarantee would be deemed not to constitute aid.

(18) In order to ensure that the aid is necessary and acts as an incentive to further develop activities or projects, this Regulation should not apply to aid for activities in which the beneficiary would in any case engage even in the absence of the aid. Aid should only be exempted from notification under this Regulation if the work on the aided project or activity starts after the beneficiary has submitted a written application for the aid.

(19) As regards any ad hoc aid covered by this Regulation granted to a beneficiary who is a large enterprise, the Member State should ensure that, in addition to complying with the conditions relating to incentive effect which apply to beneficiaries who are SMEs, the beneficiary has analysed, in an internal document, the viability of the aided project or activity with aid and without aid. The Member State should verify that this internal document confirms a material increase in the scope of the project/activity, a material increase in the total amount spent by the beneficiary on the subsidised project or activity or a material increase in the speed of completion of the project/activity concerned. Regional aid should be considered to have an incentive effect if the investment project would not have been carried out in the assisted region concerned in the absence of the aid.

(20) Automatic aid schemes in the form of tax advantages should continue to be subject to a specific condition concerning the incentive effect, due to the fact that this kind of aid is granted under different procedures than other categories of aid. Such schemes should already have been adopted before work on the aided project or activity started. However, this condition should not apply in the case of fiscal successor schemes provided the activity was already covered by the previous fiscal schemes in the form of tax advantages. For the assessment of the incentive effect of such schemes, the crucial moment is the moment when the tax measure was set out for the first time in the original scheme, which is then replaced by the successor scheme.

(21) As regards regional operating aid, regional urban development aid, aid for access to finance for SMEs, aid for the recruitment of disadvantaged workers, aid for employment of workers with disabilities and aid compensating for the additional costs of employing workers with disabilities, aid in the form of reductions in environmental taxes, aid to make good the damage caused by certain natural disasters, social aid for transport for residents of remote regions and aid for culture and heritage conservation, the requirement regarding the existence of an incentive effect does not apply or should be presumed as having been complied with, if the specific conditions set out for those categories of aid in this Regulation are fulfilled.

(22) With a view to ensuring that aid is proportionate and limited to the amount necessary, maximum

aid amounts should, whenever possible, be defined in terms of aid intensities in relation to a set of eligible costs. Where the maximum aid intensity cannot be set, because eligible costs cannot be identified or in order to provide simpler instruments for small amounts, maximum aid amounts defined in nominal terms should be set out in order to ensure proportionality of aid measures. The aid intensity and the maximum aid amounts should be fixed, in the light of the Commission's experience, at a level that minimises distortions of competition in the aided sector while appropriately addressing the market failure or cohesion issue. For regional investment aid, the aid intensity should comply with the allowable aid intensities under the regional aid maps.

(23) For the calculation of aid intensity, only eligible costs should be included. The Regulation shall not exempt aid which exceeds the relevant aid intensity as a result of including ineligible costs. The identification of eligible costs should be supported by clear, specific and up–to date documentary evidence. All figures used should be taken before any deduction of tax or other charges. Aid payable in several instalments should be discounted to its value at the moment it is granted. The eligible costs should also be discounted to their value at the moment of granting. The interest rate to be used for discounting purposes and for calculating the amount of aid in the case of aid which does not take the form of a grant should be respectively the discount rate and the reference rate applicable at the time of the grant, as laid down in the Commission Communication on the revision of the method for setting the reference and discount rates. Where aid is granted by means of tax advantages, aid tranches should be discounted on the basis of the discount rates applicable on the various dates when the tax advantages become effective. The use of aid in the form of repayable advances should be promoted, since such risk–sharing instruments are conducive to strengthened incentive effect of aid. It is therefore appropriate to establish that where aid is granted in the form of repayable advances the applicable aid intensities laid down in this Regulation may be increased, with the exception of regional aid since the latter may only be exempted if it complies with approved maps.

(24) In the case of tax advantages on future taxes, the applicable discount rate and the exact amount of the aid tranches may not be known in advance. In such cases, Member States should set in advance a cap on the discounted value of the aid respecting the applicable aid intensity. Subsequently, when the amount of the aid tranche at a given date becomes known, discounting can take place on the basis of the discount rate applicable at that time. The discounted value of each aid tranche should be deducted from the overall amount of the cap (capped amount).

(25) To determine whether the notification thresholds and the maximum aid intensities laid down in this Regulation are respected, the total amount of State aid measures for the aided activity or project should be taken into account. Moreover, this Regulation should specify the circumstances under which different categories of aid may be cumulated. Aid exempted by this Regulation and any other compatible aid exempted under other Regulation or approved by the Commission may be cumulated as long as those measures concern different identifiable eligible costs. Where different sources of aid are related to the same — partly or fully overlapping — identifiable eligible costs, cumulation should be allowed up to the highest aid intensity or aid amount applicable to that aid under this Regulation. This Regulation should also set out special rules for cumulation of aid measures with and without identifiable eligible costs, for cumulation with de minimis aid and for cumulation with aid in favour of workers with disabilities. De minimis aid is often not granted for or attributable to specific identifiable eligible costs. In such a case it should be possible to freely cumulate de minimis aid with State aid exempted under this Regulation. Where, however, de minimis aid is granted for the same identifiable eligible costs as State aid exempted under this Regulation, cumulation should only be allowed up to the maximum aid intensity as set out in Chapter III of this Regulation.

(26) Union funding centrally managed by the institutions, agencies, joint undertakings or other bodies of the Union, that is not directly or indirectly under the control of Member States, does not constitute State aid. Where such Union funding is combined with State aid, only the latter should be considered for determining whether notification thresholds and maximum aid intensities are respected, provided the total amount of public funding granted in relation to the same eligible costs does not exceed the most favourable funding rate laid down in the applicable rules of Union law.

(27) Given that State aid within the meaning of Article 107(1) of the Treaty is, in principle, prohibited, it is important for all parties to be able to check whether an aid is granted in compliance with the applicable rules. Transparency of State aid is, therefore, essential for the correct application of Treaty rules and leads to better compliance, greater accountability, peer review and ultimately more effective public spending. To ensure transparency, Member States should be required to establish comprehensive State aid websites, at regional or national level, setting out summary information about each aid measure exempted under this Regulation. That obligation should be a condition for the compatibility of the individual aid with the internal market. Following the standard practice regarding the publication of information in Directive 2013/37/EU of the European Parliament and of

the Council of 26 June 2013 amending Directive 2003/98/EC on the re–use of public sector information, a standard format should be used which allows the information to be searched, downloaded and easily published on the internet. The links to the State aid websites of all the Member States should be published on the Commission's website. In accordance with Article 3 of Regulation (EC) No 994/98, as amended by Regulation (EU) No 733/2013, summary information on each aid measure exempted under this Regulation should be published on the website of the Commission.

(28) To ensure effective monitoring of aid measures in accordance with Regulation (EC) No 994/98, as amended by Regulation (EU) No 733/2013, it is appropriate to establish requirements regarding the reporting by the Member States of aid measures which have been exempted pursuant to this Regulation and the application of this Regulation. Moreover, it is appropriate to establish rules concerning the records that Member States should keep regarding the aid exempted by this Regulation, in light of the limitation period established in Article 15 of Council Regulation (EC) No 659/1999 of 22 March 1999 laying down detailed rules for the application of Article 93 of the EC Treaty.

(29) To reinforce the effectiveness of compatibility conditions set out in this Regulation, it should be possible for the Commission to withdraw the benefit of the block exemption for the future aid measures in the event of failure to comply with these requirements. The Commission should be able to restrict the withdrawal of the benefit of the block exemption to certain types of aid, certain beneficiaries or aid measures adopted by certain authorities, where non–compliance with this Regulation affects only a limited group of measures or certain authorities. Such a targeted withdrawal should provide a proportionate remedy directly linked to the identified non–compliance with this Regulation. In case of failure to meet compatibility conditions set out in Chapters I and III, aid granted is not covered by this Regulation and, as a consequence, constitutes unlawful aid, which the Commission will examine in the framework of the relevant procedure as set out in Regulation No (EC) No 659/1999. In case of failure to fulfil the requirements of Chapter II, the withdrawal of the benefit of the block exemption in respect of the future aid measures does not affect the fact that the past measures complying with this Regulation were block exempted.

(30) To eliminate differences that might give rise to distortions of competition and to facilitate coordination between different Union and national initiatives concerning SMEs, as well as for reasons of administrative clarity and legal certainty, the definition of SME used for the purpose of this Regulation should be based on the definition in Commission Recommendation 2003/361/EC of 6 May 2003 concerning the definition of micro, small and medium sized enterprises.

(31) By addressing the handicaps of disadvantaged regions, regional aid promotes the economic, social and territorial cohesion of Member States and the Union as a whole. Regional aid is designed to assist the development of the most disadvantaged areas by supporting investment and job creation in a sustainable context. In areas fulfilling the conditions of Article 107(3)(a) of the Treaty, regional aid may be granted to promote the setting–up of new establishments, the extension of the capacity of an existing establishment, the diversification of the output of an establishment or a fundamental change in the overall production process of an existing establishment. Considering that large enterprises are less affected by regional handicaps than SMEs when investing in an area fulfilling the conditions of Article 107(3)(c) of the Treaty, regional aid to large enterprises should be exempted from the notification requirement only for initial investments in favour of new economic activity in those areas.

(32) Where a regional aid scheme is targeted at a limited number of sectors of the economy, the objective and likely effects of the scheme may be sectorial rather than horizontal. Therefore, sectorial schemes cannot be exempted from the notification requirement. However, the Commission, upon notification, can assess their possible positive effects under the applicable guidelines or frameworks or decisions. In particular, this is the case for aid schemes covering economic activities in the coal sector, the shipbuilding sector, the transport sector. Furthermore, due to particular characteristics of the steel and synthetic fibres sectors, it is considered that the negative effects of regional aid in those sectors cannot be outweighed by the positive cohesion effects; for those reasons, regional aid cannot be granted in these sectors. Finally, the tourism and broadband sectors play an important role in national economies and, in general, have a particularly positive effect on regional development. Regional aid schemes aimed at tourism activities and broadband should therefore be exempted from the notification requirement. Processing and marketing of agricultural products are also strongly linked with local and regional economies and should benefit from the block exemption.

(33) Energy generation, distribution and infrastructure are subject to sector–specific internal market legislation, which is reflected in the criteria for ensuring that aid in these areas is compatible with the internal market and consistent with the Union's environmental and energy policies. Regional aid granted under Section 1 of this Regulation pursues economic development and cohesion objectives, and is therefore subject to very different compatibility conditions. The provisions of this Regulation

on regional aid should therefore not apply to measures concerning energy generation, distribution and infrastructure.

(34) Investments enabling undertakings to go beyond Union standards or increase the level of environmental protection in the absence of Union standards, investments for early adaptation to future Union standards, investments for energy efficiency measures, including energy efficiency projects in buildings, investments for remediation of contaminated sites and aid for environmental studies do not directly influence the functioning of energy markets. At the same time, such investments may contribute to both regional policy objectives and to the energy and environmental objectives of the European Union. In such cases, the provisions of this Regulation relating to both regional aid and aid for environmental protection may be applicable, depending on the main objective pursued by the measure concerned.

(35) In order not to favour capital investment over investment in labour costs, it should be possible to measure regional investment aid on the basis of either the costs of the investment or the wage costs of employment directly created by an investment project.

(36) Regional investment aid should not be exempted from notification when it is granted to a beneficiary that has closed down the same or a similar activity in the European Economic Area in the two years preceding its application for regional investment aid or, at the time of the aid application, has concrete plans to close down such an activity within a period of up to two years after the initial investment for which aid is requested is completed in the area concerned.

(37) The Commission has gained sufficient experience in the application of Article 107(3)(a) and (c) of the Treaty as regards regional operating aid to compensate for the additional transport costs of goods produced in the outermost regions or in sparsely populated areas, and of goods further processed in those areas, as well as the additional production and operating costs (other than additional transport costs) incurred by beneficiaries established in the outermost regions. Since there is a risk of over–compensation for transport costs resulting from additional support under the POSEI programmes in the agriculture sector and since it cannot be excluded that some agricultural products are not produced in an alternative location, the agriculture sector should be excluded from regional operating aid to compensate the additional transport costs of goods produced in the outermost regions or in sparsely populated areas under this Regulation. Regional operating aid to compensate for additional costs in the outermost regions, other than additional transport costs, should only be considered compatible with the internal market and exempted from the notification requirement of Article 108(3) of the Treaty in so far as the level of that aid is limited to either 15 % of the gross value added annually created by the beneficiary in the outermost region concerned or 25 % of the annual labor costs incurred by the beneficiary in the outermost region concerned, or 10 % of the annual turnover of the beneficiary in the outermost region concerned. Where the aid does not exceed the amount resulting from one of those alternative methods to determine the additional operating costs (other than transport costs), it can be considered as justified in terms of contributing to regional development and proportionate to the handicaps that undertakings face in the outermost regions.

(38) By addressing the high concentration of economic, environmental and social problems of urban areas located in assisted areas identified in a regional aid map, urban development aid contributes to the economic, social and territorial cohesion of the Member States and the Union as a whole. The market failures to be addressed by urban development aid refer to the urban development funding environment, the lack of an integrated urban development approach, a funding deficit necessitating greater leverage of scarce public resources and the need for a more commercial approach to the regeneration of urban areas. Urban development aid to support the development of participative, integrated and sustainable strategies to tackle the additional problems identified in the assisted areas should therefore be covered by the block exemption.

(39) Investments corresponding to the Europe 2020 priorities in green technologies and the shift towards a low carbon economy, undertaken in assisted areas as identified in the relevant regional aid map, should be eligible for higher aid amounts by means of a regional bonus.

(40) SMEs play a decisive role in job creation and, more generally, act as a factor of social stability and economic development. However, their development may be hampered by market failures, leading to these SMEs suffering from the following typical handicaps. SMEs often have difficulties in obtaining capital or loans, given the risk–averse nature of certain financial markets and the limited collateral that they may be able to offer. Their limited resources may also restrict their access to information, notably regarding new technology and potential markets. To facilitate the development of the economic activities of SMEs, this Regulation should therefore exempt certain categories of aid when they are granted in favour of SMEs. Those categories should include, in particular SME investment aid and SME participation in fairs.

(41) SMEs participating in the European Territorial Cooperation (ETC) projects covered by Regula-

tion (EU) No 1299/2013 of the European Parliament and of the Council of 17 December 2013 on specific provisions for the support from the European Regional Development Fund to the European territorial cooperation goal often find difficulties in financing additional costs stemming from the cooperation between partners located in different regions and in different Member States or third countries. Given the importance of the ETC for the cohesion policy providing a framework for the implementation of joint actions and policy exchanges between national, regional and local actors from different Member States or third countries, this Regulation should address certain difficulties faced by ETC projects in order to facilitate their compliance with State aid rules. The ETC–specific issues that this Regulation should address relate to the applicable regional aid intensity for ETC projects, SMEs' cooperation costs linked to ETC projects and to obligations concerning publication and information, reporting and keeping records for monitoring purposes.

(42) Having regard to the specific handicaps and differences between SMEs, different basic aid intensities and different bonuses may apply.

(43) On the basis of the experience gained in applying the Community guidelines on State aid to promote risk capital investments in SMEs, there are a number of specific risk capital market failures in the Union in respect of certain types of investments at the different stages of the undertakings' development. Those market failures result from an imperfect matching of supply and demand for risk capital. As a result, the level of risk capital provided in the market may be too restricted and undertakings do not obtain funding despite having a valuable business model and growth prospects. The main source of market failure relevant to risk capital markets, which particularly affects access to capital by SMEs and which may justify public intervention, relates to imperfect or asymmetric information. It not only affects the provision of risk capital, but also hampers access to debt finance for certain SMEs. Consequently, risk finance measures which seek to attract private capital for risk finance provision to unlisted SMEs affected by the funding gap and which ensure profit–driven financing decisions and commercial management of financial intermediaries should be exempted from the notification requirement under certain conditions.

(44) Start–up aid for small enterprises, aid to alternative trading platforms specialised in SMEs and aid for costs related to the scouting of SMEs should also be exempted from the notification requirement under certain conditions.

(45) Aid for research and development and innovation aid can contribute to sustainable economic growth, strengthen competitiveness and boost employment. Experience with the application of Regulation (EC) No 800/2008 and the Community framework for State aid for research and development and innovation shows that market failures may prevent the market from reaching optimal output and lead to inefficiencies related to externalities, public goods/knowledge spill–overs, imperfect and asymmetric information, and coordination and network failures.

(46) SMEs, may experience difficulties in gaining access to new technological developments, knowledge transfer or highly qualified personnel. Aid for research and development projects, aid for feasibility studies and innovation aid for SMEs, including aid to cover the costs of industrial property rights, may remedy those problems and should therefore be exempted from the notification requirement under certain conditions.

(47) As regards project aid for research and development, the aided part of the research project should completely fall within the categories of fundamental research, industrial research or experimental development. When a project encompasses different tasks, each task should be qualified as falling under one of those categories or as not falling under any of those categories. That qualification need not necessarily be chronological, moving sequentially over time from fundamental research to activities closer to the market. Accordingly, a task which is carried out at a late project stage may be qualified as industrial research. Similarly, an activity carried out at an earlier stage may constitute experimental development. The aided part of the project may also include feasibility studies preparatory to research activities.

(48) High–quality research infrastructures are increasingly necessary for ground–breaking research and innovation because they attract global talent and are essential in supporting new information and communication technologies and key enabling technologies. Public research infrastructures should continue to partner with industry research. Access to publicly funded research infrastructures should be granted on a transparent and non–discriminatory basis and on market terms. If those conditions are not respected, the aid measure should not be exempted from the notification requirement. Multiple parties may own, operate and use a given research infrastructure, and public entities and undertakings may use the infrastructure collaboratively.

(49) Research infrastructures may perform both economic and non–economic activities. In order to avoid granting State aid to economic activities through public funding of non–economic activities, the costs and financing of economic and non–economic activities should be clearly separated. Where

an infrastructure is used for both economic and non–economic activities, the funding through State resources of the costs linked to the non–economic activities of the infrastructure does not constitute State aid. Public funding falls under State aid rules only insofar as it covers costs linked to the economic activities. Only the latter should be taken into account with a view to ensuring compliance with the notification thresholds and maximum aid intensities. If the infrastructure is used almost exclusively for a non–economic activity, its funding may fall outside State aid rules in its entirety, provided that the economic use remains purely ancillary, that is to say, an activity which is directly related to and necessary for the operation of the infrastructure or intrinsically linked to its main non–economic use, and is limited in scope. This should be considered to be the case when the economic activities consume the same inputs (such as material, equipment, labour and fixed capital) as the non–economic activities and the capacity allocated each year to such economic activity does not exceed 20 % of the research infrastructure's overall annual capacity.

(50) Aid for innovation clusters aims at tackling market failures linked with coordination problems hampering the development of clusters, or limiting the interactions and knowledge flows within clusters. State aid can either support investment in open and shared infrastructures for innovation clusters, or support the operation of clusters, so that collaboration, networking and learning is enhanced. Operating aid for innovation clusters should, however, only be allowed on a temporary basis for a limited period not exceeding 10 years. The ratio of the total amount of aid granted to the total eligible costs should not exceed 50 % during the period over which the aid is granted,

(51) Process and organisational innovation may suffer from market failures in the form of imperfect information and positive externalities, which should be addressed by specific measures. Aid for this type of innovation is mainly relevant for SMEs, as they face constraints that may hamper their capability to improve their production or delivery methods or to significantly enhance their business practices, workplace organisation and external relations. In order to stimulate large enterprises to collaborate with SMEs in process and organisational innovation activities, aid measures which support the costs of large enterprises for such activities should also benefit from the block exemption regulation under certain conditions.

(52) The promotion of training and the recruitment/employment of disadvantaged workers and of workers with disabilities constitutes a central objective of the economic and social policies of the Union and its Member States.

(53) Training usually generates positive externalities for society as a whole, since it increases the pool of skilled workers from which other firms may draw, improves the competitiveness of the Union industry and plays an important role in the Union employment strategy. Aid to promote training should therefore be exempted from the notification requirement under certain conditions. In the light of the particular handicaps which SMEs face and the higher relative costs that they must bear when they invest in training, the intensities of aid exempted by this Regulation should be increased for SMEs. Furthermore, the intensities of aid exempted by this Regulation should be increased if the training is given to disadvantaged workers or to workers with disabilities. The characteristics of training in the maritime transport sector justify a specific approach for that sector.

(54) Certain categories of disadvantaged workers and workers with disabilities still experience particular difficulties in entering and remaining in the labour market. For this reason, public authorities may apply measures providing incentives to undertakings to increase the levels of employment of these categories of workers, in particular of young people. As employment costs form part of the normal operating costs of any undertaking aid for the employment of disadvantaged workers and of workers with disabilities should have a positive effect on employment levels of those categories of workers and should not merely enable undertakings to reduce costs which they would otherwise have to bear. Consequently, such aid should be exempted from the notification requirement when it is likely to assist those categories of workers in entering or re–entering and remaining in the job market. As set out in the Communication from the Commission to The European Parliament, the Council, the European Economic And Social Committee and the Committee Of The Regions — European Disability Strategy 2010–2020: A Renewed Commitment to a Barrier–Free Europe the core elements of the EU disability strategy, combine anti–discrimination, equal opportunities and active inclusion measures and reflect the United Nations Convention on the Rights of Persons with Disabilities to which the EU and the majority of the Member States are a party. This Regulation should refer to aid for workers with disabilities in the sense of Article 1 of the Convention.

(55) As stated in the Communication from the Commission — Europe 2020: A strategy for smart, sustainable and inclusive growth, Sustainable growth for a resource efficient, greener and more competitive economy is one of the main pillars of the Europe 2020 objective of the smart, sustainable and inclusive growth strategy. Sustainable development is based, amongst other things, on a high level of protection and improvement of the quality of the environment. The area of environmental protection

is confronted with market failures so that, under normal market conditions, undertakings may not necessarily have an incentive to reduce the pollution caused by them since any such reduction may increase their costs without corresponding benefits. When undertakings are not obliged to internalise the costs of pollution, society as a whole bears these costs.

(56) Introducing mandatory environmental standards can address such market failure. A higher level of environmental protection can be achieved by investments that go beyond mandatory Union standards. In order to incentivise undertakings to improve the level of environmental protection beyond these mandatory Union standards, State aid in this area should be covered by the block exemption. In order not to dissuade Member States from setting mandatory national standards which are more stringent than the corresponding Union standards, such State aid should be exempt, irrespective of the presence of mandatory national standards that are more stringent than the Union standard.

(57) In principle aid should not be granted where investments bring undertakings into compliance with Union standards already adopted and not yet in force. However, State aid may result in undertakings improving their environmental behaviour if such State aid incentivises undertakings to adapt early to future Union standards before such standards enter into force and as long as such standards do not apply retroactively. Aid to undertakings to adapt to future Union standards, may result in a high level of environmental protection being achieved sooner and such aid should therefore be exempted.

(58) As part of the Europe 2020 strategy, the Union has set itself the objective of achieving a 20 % increase in energy efficiency by 2020 and has, in particular, adopted Directive 2012/27/EU of the European Parliament and of the Council of 25 October 2012 on energy efficiency, amending Directives 2009/125/EC and 2010/30/EU and repealing Directives 2004/8/EC and 2006/32/EC which establishes a common framework to promote energy efficiency within the Union pursuing the overall objective of saving at least 20 % of the Union's primary energy consumption. In order to facilitate the achievement of those targets, measures supporting energy efficiency, high–efficiency cogeneration as well as energy efficient district heating and cooling should be covered by the block exemption.

(59) Measures increasing the energy efficiency of buildings correspond to Europe 2020 priorities concerning a shift towards a low carbon economy. Due to the lack of an integrated approach for energy efficiency in buildings, such investments may often face a funding deficit necessitating greater leverage of scarce public resources. Therefore the Member States should have the possibility to support energy efficiency investments in buildings by granting aid in the form of direct grants to the building owners or tenants in line with the general provisions on energy efficiency measures but also in the form of loans and guarantees via financial intermediaries chosen under a transparent selection mechanism under the specific provisions for energy efficiency projects in buildings.

(60) To achieve the Union's renewable energy targets set out in Directive 2009/28/EC of the European Parliament and of the Council of 23 April 2009 on the promotion of the use of energy from renewable sources and amending and subsequently repealing Directives 2001/77/EC and 2003/30/EC and to the extent that additional support is needed on top of a regulatory framework such as the Union emission trading scheme in Directive 2003/87/EC of the European Parliament and of the Council of 13 October 2003 establishing a scheme for greenhouse gas emission allowance trading within the Community and amending Council Directive 96/61/EC, aid granted to investments supporting energy from renewable sources should be covered by the block exemption.

(61) In view of the limited distortions of trade and competition, the block exemption should also cover operating aid for small scale installations producing renewable energy, subject to well–defined conditions. Operating aid to larger scale installations should be covered by the block exemption where distortions of competition are limited. Therefore, such operating aid can be block exempted when granted to new and innovative technologies if the aid is granted on the basis of a competitive bidding process open to at least one such technology using a mechanism which exposes renewable energy producers to market prices. The total aid granted on this basis cannot be granted for more than 5 % of the planned new electricity capacity from renewable energy sources. Aid granted through bidding processes open to all renewable energy technologies should be fully covered by the block exemption. Operating aid schemes should in principle be opened to other EEA countries and contracting parties of the Energy Community to limit the overall distortive effects. Member States are encouraged to consider having a cooperation mechanism in place before allowing cross border support. In the absence of a cooperation mechanism, production from installations in other countries will not count towards their national renewable energy target. In view of these constraints, Member States should be allowed sufficient lead time in order to design appropriate support schemes that are open to other countries. Therefore, such opening is not a condition for exemption from notification, to the extent it is not required under the Treaty.

(62) With regard to aid for the production of hydropower, its impact can be twofold. On the one hand,

it has a positive impact in terms of low greenhouse gas emissions and on the other hand it might also have a negative impact on water systems and biodiversity. Therefore, when granting aid to hydropower Member States should comply with Directive 2000/60/EC of the European Parliament and of the Council of 23 October 2000 establishing a framework for Community action in the field of water policy and in particular Article 4(7) which lays down criteria in relation to allowing new modifications of bodies of water.

(63) Aid should only be granted to sustainable forms of renewable energy. Aid to biofuels should only be covered by this Regulation in so far as it is granted for sustainable biofuels in accordance with the Directive 2009/28/EC of the European Parliament and the Council. However, aid for food based biofuels should be excluded from aid under this Regulation to incentivise the shift towards the production of more advanced forms of biofuels. Aid to biofuels that are subject to a supply or blending obligation should be excluded from the scope of the block exemption as the above legal obligation may provide sufficient incentive for investments in these types of renewable energy.

(64) Aid in the form of tax reductions pursuant to Council Directive 2003/96/EC of 27 October 2003 restructuring the Community framework for the taxation of energy products and electricity favouring environmental protection covered by this Regulation can indirectly benefit the environment. However, environmental taxes should reflect the social cost of emissions while reductions from taxes may adversely impact on this objective. It therefore seems appropriate to limit their duration to the period of application of this Regulation. After this period, Member States should re–evaluate the appropriateness of the tax reductions concerned. In order to minimise the distortion of competition, the aid should be granted in the same way for all competitors found to be in a similar factual situation. To better preserve the price signal for undertakings which the environmental tax aims to give, Member States should have the option to design the tax reduction scheme based on a fixed annual compensation amount (tax refund) disbursement mechanism.

(65) In the light of the 'polluter pays principle', the costs of measures to deal with pollution should be borne by the polluter who causes the pollution. Aid for the remediation of contaminated sites is justified in cases where the person liable under the applicable law for the contamination cannot be identified. However, the conditions on environmental liability with regard to the prevention and remediation of environmental damage as defined in the Directive 2004/35/EC of the European Parliament and of the Council of 21 April 2004 on environmental liability with regard to the prevention and remedying of environmental damage as amended by Directive 2006/21/EC of the European Parliament and of the Council of 15 March 2006 on the management of waste from extractive industries and amending Directive 2004/35/EC and Directive 2009/31/EC of the European Parliament and of the Council of 23 April 2009 on the geological storage of carbon dioxide and amending Council Directive 85/337/EEC, European Parliament and Council Directives 2000/60/EC, 2001/80/EC, 2004/35/EC, 2006/12/EC, 2008/1/EC and Regulation (EC) No 1013/2006 should apply. Therefore, to facilitate the correction of existing environmental damage, this type of aid should be covered by the block exemption under certain conditions.

(66) In line with the waste hierarchy established in the European Union's Waste Framework Directive, the Seventh Environment Action Programme identifies waste re–use and recycling as key priorities of the European Union environmental policy. State aid for these activities can contribute to environmental protection provided that Article 4(1) of Directive 2008/98/EC of the European Parliament and of the Council of 19 November 2008 on waste and repealing certain Directives (Waste Framework Directive) are respected. Moreover, such aid should not indirectly relieve the polluters of a burden they should bear under Union law, or of a burden that should be considered a normal company cost. Therefore, aid benefitting such activities should be covered by the block exemption including when it concerns waste of other undertakings and where the materials treated would otherwise be disposed of, or be treated in a less environmentally friendly manner.

(67) A modern energy infrastructure is crucial both for an integrated energy market and to enable the Union to meet its climate and energy goals. In particular, infrastructure construction and upgrade in assisted regions contribute to the economic, social and territorial cohesion of Member States and the Union as a whole by supporting investment and job creation and the functioning of energy markets in the most disadvantaged areas. In order to limit any undue distortive effects of such aid, only aid to infrastructures subject to and in accordance with the internal energy market legislation should be block exempted.

(68) Environmental studies can help to identify the investments necessary to achieve a higher level of environmental protection. State aid to support the carrying out of environmental studies which aim to support investments in environmental protection as covered by this Regulation should therefore be covered by the block exemption. As energy audits are mandatory for large enterprises, they should not benefit from State aid.

(69) In accordance with Article 107(2)(b) of the Treaty, aid to make good the damage caused by natural disasters is compatible with the internal market. In order to provide legal certainty it is necessary to define the type of events that may constitute a natural disaster exempted by this Regulation. For the purposes of this Regulation, earthquakes, landslides, floods, in particular floods brought about by waters overflowing river banks or lake shores, avalanches, tornadoes, hurricanes, volcanic eruptions and wildfires of natural origin should be considered events constituting a natural disaster. Damage caused by adverse weather conditions such as frost, hail, ice, rain or drought, which occur on a more regular basis, should not be considered a natural disaster within the meaning of Article 107(2)(b) of the Treaty. In order to ensure that aid granted to make good the damage caused by natural disasters is indeed covered by the exemption, this Regulation should lay down conditions following established practice the fulfilment of which will ensure that aid schemes to make good the damage caused by natural disasters can benefit from block exemption. Those conditions should relate, in particular, to the formal recognition by the competent Member States' authorities of the character of the event as a natural disaster and to a direct causal link between the natural disaster and the damages suffered by the beneficiary undertaking, which may include undertakings in difficulty, and should ensure that overcompensation is avoided. The compensation should not exceed what is necessary to enable the beneficiary to return to the situation prevailing before the disaster occurred.

(70) Aid has a social character for air and maritime passenger transport where it addresses the problem of steady connectivity for residents of remote regions by reducing certain transport ticket costs for them. This may be the case for outermost regions, Malta, Cyprus, Ceuta and Melilla, other islands which are part of the territory of a Member State and sparsely populated areas. Where a remote region is linked to the European Economic Area by several transport routes, including indirect routes, aid should be possible for all those routes and for transport by all carriers operating on these routes. Aid should be granted without discrimination as to the identity of the carrier or type of service and may include regular, charter and low–cost services.

(71) Broadband connectivity is of strategic importance for the achievement of the Europe 2020 objective of smart, sustainable and inclusive growth and innovation and for social and territorial cohesion. Investment aid for broadband infrastructure aims at fostering the deployment of such infrastructure and related civil engineering works in areas where no comparable infrastructure exists nor is likely to be deployed by market operators in the near future. In the light of the Commission's experience, such investment aid does not give rise to undue distortions of trade and competition, provided that certain conditions are met. Such conditions should aim, in particular, at limiting distortions of competition by subjecting aid to technology–neutral competitive selection and by ensuring wholesale access to the subsidised networks, taking into account the aid received by the network operator. Although under certain conditions virtual unbundling may be considered equivalent to physical unbundling, until more experience is acquired, there is a need to assess on a case by case basis whether a particular non–physical or virtual wholesale access product should be considered equivalent to local loop unbundling of a copper or fibre network. For this reason, and until such experience in individual State aid cases or in the ex ante regulatory context can be taken into account in a future review, physical unbundling should be required for the purposes of benefiting from the present block exemption regulation. Where future costs and revenue developments are uncertain and there is a strong asymmetry of information, Member States should also adopt financing models that include monitoring and claw–back elements to allow a balanced sharing of unanticipated gains. To avoid a disproportionate burden on small, local projects, such models should be put in place only for projects exceeding a minimum threshold.

(72) In the culture and heritage conservation sector, a number of measures taken by Member States may not constitute aid because they do not fulfil all the criteria of Article 107(1) of the Treaty, for example because the activity is not economic or because trade between Member States is not affected. To the extent that such measures are covered by Article 107(1) of the Treaty, cultural institutions and projects do not typically give rise to any significant distortion of competition, and case practice has shown that such aid has limited effects on trade. Article 167 of the Treaty recognises the importance of promoting culture for the Union and its Member States and provides that the Union should take cultural aspects into account in its action under other provisions of the Treaty, in particular in order to respect and to promote the diversity of its cultures. As natural heritage is often crucial to shaping of artistic and cultural heritage, heritage conservation in the sense of this Regulation should be understood to cover also natural heritage linked to cultural heritage or formally recognised by the competent public authorities of a Member State. Because of the dual nature of culture, being on the one hand an economic good that offers important opportunities for the creation of wealth and employment, and, on the other, a vehicle of identities, values and meanings that mirror and shape our societies, State aid rules should acknowledge the specificities of culture

and the economic activities related to it. A list of eligible cultural purposes and activities should be established and eligible costs should be specified. The block exemption should cover both investment and operating aid below determined thresholds provided that overcompensation is excluded. In general, activities which, although they may present a cultural aspect, have a predominantly commercial character because of the higher potential for competition distortions, such as press and magazines (written or electronic), should not be covered. Furthermore, the list of eligible cultural purposes and activities should not include commercial activities such as fashion, design or video games.

(73) Audiovisual works play an important role in shaping European identities and reflect the different traditions of Member States and regions. While there is strong competition between films produced outside the Union, there is limited circulation of European films outside their country of origin due to the fragmentation into national or regional markets. The sector is characterised by high investment costs, a perceived lack of profitability due to limited audiences and difficulties to generate additional private funding. Due to these factors the Commission has developed specific criteria to assess the necessity, proportionality and adequacy of aid to script–writing, development, production, distribution and promotion of audiovisual works. New criteria were determined in the Communication from the Commission on State aid for films and other audiovisual works and should be reflected in block exemption rules for aid schemes for audiovisual works. Higher aid intensities are justified for cross–border productions and co–productions which are more likely to be distributed in several Member States.

(74) Investment aid measures for sport infrastructures should be covered by the block exemption if they fulfil the conditions laid down in this Regulation, to the extent they constitute State aid. In the sport sector a number of measures taken by Member States may not constitute State aid because the beneficiary does not carry out an economic activity or because there is no effect on trade between Member States. This could be, under certain circumstances, the case for aid measures which have a purely local character or which are taken in the field of amateur sport. Article 165 of the Treaty recognises the importance of promoting European sporting issues, while taking account of the specific nature of sport, its structures based on voluntary activity and its social and educational function. Aid to infrastructures which serve more than one purpose of recreation and are thus multifunctional should also be covered by the block exemption. However, aid to multifunctional tourism infrastructures such as leisure parks and hotel facilities should only be exempted if it is part of a regional aid scheme aimed at tourism activities in an assisted region which have a particular positive effect on regional development. The compatibility conditions regarding aid for sport or multifunctional infrastructures should ensure, in particular, open and non–discriminatory access to the infrastructures and a fair process of assignment of concessions to a third party in accordance with the relevant provisions of Union law and the case law of the Union to construct, upgrade and/or operate the infrastructure. If sport infrastructure is used by professional sport clubs, pricing conditions for the use of the infrastructure by those clubs should be made publicly available to ensure transparency and equal treatment of users. The exclusion of overcompensation should be ensured.

(75) As emphasized by the conclusions of the European Council of the 17 June 2010 endorsing the Europe 2020 Strategy, efforts should seek to address the main bottlenecks constraining growth at EU level, including those related to the functioning of the internal market and infrastructure. The availability of local infrastructures is an important prerequisite for development of business and consumer environment and for modernising and developing the industrial base in order to ensure the full functioning of the internal market as referred to in the Council Recommendation on broad guidelines for economic policies of the Member States and of the Union, which form part of the Europe 2020 integrated guidelines.Such infrastructures, made available to interested parties on an open, transparent and non–discriminatory basis, enable the creation of an environment conducive to private investment and growth, thus contributing positively to objectives of common interest, and in particular to the Europe 2020 priorities and objectives, while the risks of distortions remain limited. A number of measures taken by Member States with regard to local infrastructures do not constitute aid because they do not fulfil all the criteria of Article 107(1) of the Treaty, for example because the beneficiary does not carry out an economic activity, because there is no effect on trade between Member States, or because the measure consists of compensation for a service of general economic interest which fulfils all the criteria of the Altmark case–law. However, where the financing of such local infrastructures does constitute State aid within the meaning of Article 107(1) of the Treaty, such aid should be exempted from the notification requirement when only small amounts of aid are granted.

(76) Since aid for other types of infrastructures may be subject to specific and well–designed criteria which ensure its compatibility with the internal market, the provisions of this Regulation regarding aid for local infrastructures should not apply to aid to the following types of infrastructures: research infrastructures, innovation clusters, energy efficient district heating and cooling, energy infrastruc-

tures, waste recycling and re–use, broadband infrastructures, culture and heritage conservation, sport and multifunctional recreational infrastructures, airports and ports.

(77) In the light of the Commission's experience in this area, State aid policy should periodically be revised. The period of application of this Regulation should therefore be limited. It is appropriate to lay down transitional provisions, including the rules applicable to exempted aid schemes at the end of the period of application of this Regulation. Such rules should give Member States time to adapt to any future regime. The adjustment period should not, however, apply to regional aid schemes, including regional urban development aid schemes, the exemption of which must expire on the date on which the approved regional aid maps expire, and to certain risk finance aid schemes,

HAS ADOPTED THIS REGULATION:

Chapter I. Common Provisions

Article 1. Scope

(1) This Regulation shall apply to the following categories of aid:
(a) regional aid;
(b) aid to SMEs in the form of investment aid, operating aid and SMEs' access to finance;
(c) aid for environmental protection;
(d) aid for research and development and innovation;
(e) training aid;
(f) recruitment and employment aid for disadvantaged workers and workers with disabilities;
(g) aid to make good the damage caused by certain natural disasters;
(h) social aid for transport for residents of remote regions;
(i) aid for broadband infrastructures;
(j) aid for culture and heritage conservation;
(k) aid for sport and multifunctional recreational infrastructures; and
(l) aid for local infrastructures.

(2) This Regulation shall not apply to:
(a) schemes under Sections 1 (with the exception of Article 15), 2, 3, 4, 7 (with the exception of Article 44), and 10 of Chapter III of this Regulation, if the average annual State aid budget exceeds EUR 150 million, from six months after their entry into force. The Commission may decide that this Regulation shall continue to apply for a longer period to any of these aid schemes after having assessed the relevant evaluation plan notified by the Member State to the Commission, within 20 working days from the scheme's entry into force;
(b) any alterations of schemes referred to in Article 1(2)(a), other than modifications which cannot affect the compatibility of the aid scheme under this Regulation or cannot significantly affect the content of the approved evaluation plan;
(c) aid to export–related activities towards third countries or Member States, namely aid directly linked to the quantities exported, to the establishment and operation of a distribution network or to other current costs linked to the export activity;
(d) aid contingent upon the use of domestic over imported goods.

(3) This Regulation shall not apply to:
(a) aid granted in the fishery and aquaculture sector, as covered by Regulation (EU) No 1379/2013 of the European Parliament and of the Council of 11 December 2013 on the common organisation of the markets in fishery and aquaculture products, amending Council Regulations (EC) No 1184/2006 and (EC) No 1224/2009 and repealing council Regulation (EC) No 104/2000,with the exception of training aid, aid for SMEs' access to finance, aid in the field of research and development, innovation aid for SMEs and aid for disadvantaged workers and workers with disabilities;
(b) aid granted in the primary agricultural production sector, with the exception of compensation for additional costs other than transport costs in outermost regions as provided for in Article 15(2)(b), aid for consultancy in favour of SMEs, risk finance aid, aid for research and development, innovation aid for SMEs, environmental aid, training aid and aid for disadvantaged workers and workers with disabilities;
(c) aid granted in the sector of processing and marketing of agricultural products, in the following cases:
(i) where the amount of the aid is fixed on the basis of the price or quantity of such products purchased from primary producers or put on the market by the undertakings concerned; or
(ii) where the aid is conditional on being partly or entirely passed on to primary producers;
(d) aid to facilitate the closure of uncompetitive coal mines, as covered by Council Decision No 2010/787;
(e) the categories of regional aid excluded in Article 13.

Where an undertaking is active in the excluded sectors as referred to in points (a), (b) or (c) of the first subparagraph and in sectors which fall within the scope of this Regulation, this Regulation applies to aid granted in respect of the latter sectors or activities, provided that Member States ensure by appropriate means, such as separation of activities or distinction of costs, that the activities in the excluded sectors do not benefit from the aid granted in accordance with this Regulation.

(4) This Regulation shall not apply to:

(a) aid schemes which do not explicitly exclude the payment of individual aid in favour of an undertaking which is subject to an outstanding recovery order following a previous Commission decision declaring an aid illegal and incompatible with the internal market, with the exception of aid schemes to make good the damage caused by certain natural disasters;

(b) ad hoc aid in favour of an undertaking as referred to in point (a);

(c) aid to undertakings in difficulty, with the exception of aid schemes to make good the damage caused by certain natural disasters.

(5) This Regulation shall not apply to State aid measures, which entail, by themselves, by the conditions attached to them or by their financing method a non–severable violation of Union law, in particular:

(a) aid measures where the grant of aid is subject to the obligation for the beneficiary to have its headquarters in the relevant Member State or to be predominantly established in that Member State; However, the requirement to have an establishment or branch in the aid granting Member State at the moment of payment of the aid is allowed.

(b) aid measures where the grant of aid is subject to the obligation for the beneficiary to use nationally produced goods or national services;

(c) aid measures restricting the possibility for the beneficiaries to exploit the research, development and innovation results in other Member States.

Article 2. Definitions

For the purposes of this Regulation the following definitions shall apply:

(1) 'aid' means any measure fulfilling all the criteria laid down in Article 107(1) of the Treaty;

(2) 'small and medium–sized enterprises' or 'SMEs' means undertakings fulfilling the criteria laid down in Annex I;

(3) 'worker with disabilities' means any person who:

(a) is recognised as worker with disabilities under national law; or

(b) has long–term physical, mental, intellectual or sensory impairment(s) which, in interaction with various barriers, may hinder their full and effective participation in a work environment on an equal basis with other workers;

(4) 'disadvantaged worker' means any person who:

(a) has not been in regular paid employment for the previous 6 months; or

(b) is between 15 and 24 years of age; or

(c) has not attained an upper secondary educational or vocational qualification (International Standard Classification of Education 3) or is within two years after completing full–time education and who has not previously obtained his or her first regular paid employment; or

(d) is over the age of 50 years; or

(e) lives as a single adult with one or more dependents; or

(f) works in a sector or profession in a Member State where the gender imbalance is at least 25 % higher than the average gender imbalance across all economic sectors in that Member State, and belongs to that underrepresented gender group; or

(g) is a member of an ethnic minority within a Member State and who requires development of his or her linguistic, vocational training or work experience profile to enhance prospects of gaining access to stable employment;

(5) 'transport' means transport of passengers by aircraft, maritime transport, road, rail, or by inland waterway or freight transport services for hire or reward;

(6) 'transport costs' means the costs of transport for hire or reward actually paid by the beneficiaries per journey, comprising:

(a) freight charges, handling costs and temporary stocking costs, in so far as these costs relate to the journey;

(b) insurance costs applied to the cargo;

(c) taxes, duties or levies applied to the cargo and, if applicable, to the deadweight, both at point of origin and point of destination; and

(d) safety and security control costs, surcharges for increased fuel costs;

(7) 'remote regions' means outermost regions, Malta, Cyprus, Ceuta and Melilla, islands which are

part of the territory of a Member State and sparsely populated areas;

(8) 'marketing of agricultural products' means holding or display with a view to sale, offering for sale, delivery or any other manner of placing on the market, except the first sale by a primary producer to resellers or processors and any activity preparing a product for such first sale; a sale by a primary producer to final consumers shall be considered to be marketing if it takes place in separate premises reserved for that purpose;

(9) 'primary agricultural production' means production of products of the soil and of stock farming, listed in Annex I to the Treaty, without performing any further operation changing the nature of such products;

(10) 'processing of agricultural products' means any operation on an agricultural product resulting in a product which is also an agricultural product, except on–farm activities necessary for preparing an animal or plant product for the first sale;

(11) 'agricultural product' means the products listed in Annex I to the Treaty, except fishery and aquaculture products listed in Annex I to Regulation (EU) No 1379/2013 of the European Parliament and of the Council of 11 December 2013;

(12) 'outermost regions' means regions as defined in Article 349 of the Treaty. In accordance with European Council Decision 2010/718/EU, from 1 January 2012, Saint–Barthélemy ceased to be an outermost region. In accordance with European Council Decision 2012/419/EU on 1 January 2014, Mayotte became an outermost region;

(13) 'coal' means high–grade, medium–grade and low–grade category A and B coal within the meaning of the international codification system for coal established by the United Nations Economic Commission for Europe and clarified in the Council decision of 10 December 2010 on State aid to facilitate the closure of uncompetitive coal mines;

(14) 'individual aid' means:

(i) ad hoc aid; and

(ii) awards of aid to individual beneficiaries on the basis of an aid scheme;

(15) 'aid scheme' means any act on the basis of which, without further implementing measures being required, individual aid awards may be made to undertakings defined within the act in a general and abstract manner and any act on the basis of which aid which is not linked to a specific project may be granted to one or several undertakings for an indefinite period of time and/or for an indefinite amount;

(16) 'evaluation plan' means a document containing at least the following minimum elements: the objectives of the aid scheme to be evaluated, the evaluation questions, the result indicators, the envisaged methodology to conduct the evaluation, the data collection requirements, the proposed timing of the evaluation including the date of submission of the final evaluation report, the description of the independent body conducting the evaluation or the criteria that will be used for its selection and the modalities for ensuring the publicity of the evaluation;

(17) 'ad hoc aid' means aid not granted on the basis of an aid scheme;

(18) 'undertaking in difficulty' means an undertaking in respect of which at least one of the following circumstances occurs:

(a) In the case of a limited liability company (other than an SME that has been in existence for less than three years or, for the purposes of eligibility for risk finance aid, an SME within 7 years from its first commercial sale that qualifies for risk finance investments following due diligence by the selected financial intermediary), where more than half of its subscribed share capital has disappeared as a result of accumulated losses. This is the case when deduction of accumulated losses from reserves (and all other elements generally considered as part of the own funds of the company) leads to a negative cumulative amount that exceeds half of the subscribed share capital. For the purposes of this provision, 'limited liability company' refers in particular to the types of company mentioned in Annex I of Directive 2013/34/EU and 'share capital' includes, where relevant, any share premium.

(b) In the case of a company where at least some members have unlimited liability for the debt of the company (other than an SME that has been in existence for less than three years or, for the purposes of eligibility for risk finance aid, an SME within 7 years from its first commercial sale that qualifies for risk finance investments following due diligence by the selected financial intermediary), where more than half of its capital as shown in the company accounts has disappeared as a result of accumulated losses. For the purposes of this provision, 'a company where at least some members have unlimited liability for the debt of the company' refers in particular to the types of company mentioned in Annex II of Directive 2013/34/EU.

(c) Where the undertaking is subject to collective insolvency proceedings or fulfils the criteria under its domestic law for being placed in collective insolvency proceedings at the request of its creditors.

(d) Where the undertaking has received rescue aid and has not yet reimbursed the loan or terminated

the guarantee, or has received restructuring aid and is still subject to a restructuring plan.
(e) In the case of an undertaking that is not an SME, where, for the past two years:
(1) the undertaking's book debt to equity ratio has been greater than 7,5 and
(2) the undertaking's EBITDA interest coverage ratio has been below 1,0.
(19) 'territorial spending obligations': mean the obligations imposed by the authority granting the aid on beneficiaries to spend a minimum amount and/or conduct a minimum level of production activity in a particular territory;
(20) 'adjusted aid amount' means the maximum permissible aid amount for a large investment project, calculated according to the following formula:
maximum aid amount = $R \times (A + 0{,}50 \times B + 0 \times C)$
where: R is the maximum aid intensity applicable in the area concerned established in an approved regional map and which is in force on the date of granting the aid, excluding the increased aid intensity for SMEs; A is the initial EUR 50 million of eligible costs, B is the part of eligible costs between EUR 50 million and EUR 100 million and C is the part of eligible costs above EUR 100 million
(21) 'repayable advance' means a loan for a project which is paid in one or more instalments and the conditions for the reimbursement of which depend on the outcome of the project;
(22) 'gross grant equivalent' means the amount of the aid if it had been provided in the form of a grant to the beneficiary, before any deduction of tax or other charge;
(23) 'start of works' means the earlier of either the start of construction works relating to the investment, or the first legally binding commitment to order equipment or any other commitment that makes the investment irreversible. Buying land and preparatory works such as obtaining permits and conducting feasibility studies are not considered start of works. For take–overs, 'start of works' means the moment of acquiring the assets directly linked to the acquired establishment;
(24) 'large enterprises' means undertakings not fulfilling the criteria laid down in Annex I;
(25) 'fiscal successor scheme' means a scheme in the form of tax advantages which constitutes an amended version of a previously existing scheme in the form of tax advantages and which replaces it.
(26) 'aid intensity' means the gross aid amount expressed as a percentage of the eligible costs, before any deduction of tax or other charge;
(27) 'assisted areas' means areas designated in an approved regional aid map for the period 1.7.2014 – 31.12.2020 in application of Articles 107(3)(a) and (c) of the Treaty;
(28) 'date of granting of the aid' means the date when the legal right to receive the aid is conferred on the beneficiary under the applicable national legal regime;
(29) 'tangible assets' means assets consisting of land, buildings and plant, machinery and equipment;
(30) 'intangible assets' means assets that do not have a physical or financial embodiment such as patents, licences, know–how or other intellectual property;
(31) 'wage cost' means the total amount actually payable by the beneficiary of the aid in respect of the employment concerned, comprising over a defined period of time the gross wage before tax and compulsory contributions such as social security, child care and parent care costs;
(32) 'net increase in the number of employees' means a net increase in the number of employees in the establishment concerned compared with the average over a given period in time, and that any posts lost during that period must therefore be deducted and that the number of persons employed full–time, part–time and seasonal has to be considered with their annual labour unit fractions;
(33) 'dedicated infrastructure' means infrastructure that is built for ex–ante identifiable undertaking(s) and tailored to their needs.
(34) 'financial intermediary' means any financial institution regardless of its form and ownership, including fund–of–funds, private equity investment funds, public investment funds, banks, micro–finance institutions and guarantee societies;
(35) 'journey' means the movement of goods from the point of origin to the point of destination, including any intermediary sections or stages within or outside the Member State concerned, made using one or more means of transport;
(36) 'fair rate of return (FRR)' means the expected rate of return equivalent to a risk–adjusted discount rate which reflects the level of risk of a project and the nature and level of capital the private investors plan to invest;
(37) 'total financing' means the overall investment amount made into an eligible undertaking or project under Section 3 or under Articles 16 or 39 of this Regulation to the exclusion of entirely private investments provided on market terms and outside the scope of the relevant State aid measure;
(38) 'competitive bidding process' means a non–discriminatory bidding process that provides for the participation of a sufficient number of undertakings and where the aid is granted on the basis of either the initial bid submitted by the bidder or a clearing price. In addition, the budget or volume related to the bidding process is a binding constraint leading to a situation where not all bidders can receive aid;

(39) 'operating profit' means the difference between the discounted revenues and the discounted operating costs over the relevant lifetime of the investment, where this difference is positive. The operating costs include costs such as personnel costs, materials, contracted services, communications, energy, maintenance, rent, administration, but exclude, for the purpose of this Regulation, depreciation charges and the costs of financing if these have been covered by investment aid.

Definitions applying to regional aid

(40) Definitions applying to aid for broadband infrastructures (Section 10) are applicable to the relevant regional aid provisions.

(41) 'regional investment aid' means regional aid granted for an initial investment or an initial investment in favour of a new economic activity;

(42) 'regional operating aid' means aid to reduce an undertaking's current expenditure that is not related to an initial investment. This includes cost categories such as personnel costs, materials, contracted services, communications, energy, maintenance, rent, administration, etc., but excludes depreciation charges and the costs of financing if these have been included in the eligible costs when granting investment aid;

(43) 'steel sector' means all activities related to the production of one or more of the following products:

(a) pig iron and ferro–alloys:
pig iron for steelmaking, foundry and other pig iron, spiegeleisen and high–carbon ferro–manganese, not including other ferro–alloys;

(b) crude and semi–finished products of iron, ordinary steel or special steel:
liquid steel whether or not cast into ingots, including ingots for forging semi– finished products: blooms, billets and slabs; sheet bars and tinplate bars; hot–rolled wide coils, with the exception of production of liquid steel for castings from small and medium–sized foundries;

(c) hot finished products of iron, ordinary steel or special steel:
rails, sleepers, fishplates, soleplates, joists, heavy sections of 80 mm and over, sheet piling, bars and sections of less than 80 mm and flats of less than 150 mm, wire rod, tube rounds and squares, hot–rolled hoop and strip (including tube strip), hot–rolled sheet (coated or uncoated), plates and sheets of 3 mm thickness and over, universal plates of 150 mm and over, with the exception of wire and wire products, bright bars and iron castings;

(d) cold finished products:
tinplate, terneplate, blackplate, galvanised sheets, other coated sheets, cold–rolled sheets, electrical sheets and strip for tinplate, cold–rolled plate, in coil and in strip;

(e) tubes:
all seamless steel tubes, welded steel tubes with a diameter of over 406.4 mm;

(44) 'synthetic fibres sector' means:

(a) extrusion/texturisation of all generic types of fibre and yarn based on polyester, polyamide, acrylic or polypropylene, irrespective of their end–uses; or

(b) polymerisation (including polycondensation) where it is integrated with extrusion in terms of the machinery used; or

(c) any ancillary process linked to the contemporaneous installation of extrusion/texturisation capacity by the prospective beneficiary or by another company in the group to which it belongs and which, in the specific business activity concerned, is normally integrated with such capacity in terms of the machinery used;

(45) 'transport sector' means the transport of passengers by aircraft, maritime transport, road or rail and by inland waterway or freight transport services for hire or reward; more specifically, the 'transport sector' means the following activities in terms of NACE Rev. 2:

(a) NACE 49: Land transport and transport via pipelines, excluding NACE 49.32 Taxi operation, 49.42 Removal services, 49.5 Transport via pipeline;

(b) NACE 50: Water transport;

(c) NACE 51: Air transport, excluding NACE 51.22 Space transport.

(46) 'scheme targeted at a limited number of specific sectors of economic activity' means a scheme which covers activities falling within the scope of less than five classes (four–digit numerical code) of the NACE Rev. 2 statistical classification.

(47) 'tourism activity' means the following activities in terms of NACE Rev. 2:

(a) NACE 55: Accommodation;

(b) NACE 56: Food and beverage service activities;

(c) NACE 79: Travel agency, tour operator reservation service and related activities;

(d) NACE 90: Creative, arts and entertainment activities;

(e) NACE 91: Libraries, archives, museums and other cultural activities;
(f) NACE 93: Sports activities and amusement and recreation activities;
(48) 'sparsely populated areas' means those areas which are recognized by the Commission as such in the individual decisions on regional aid maps for the period 1.7.2014–31.12.2020;
(49) 'initial investment' means:
(a) an investment in tangible and intangible assets related to the setting–up of a new establishment, extension of the capacity of an existing establishment, diversification of the output of an establishment into products not previously produced in the establishment or a fundamental change in the overall production process of an existing establishment; or
(b) an acquisition of assets belonging to an establishment that has closed or would have closed had it not been purchased, and is bought by an investor unrelated to the seller and excludes sole acquisition of the shares of an undertaking;
(50) 'the same or a similar activity' means an activity falling under the same class (four–digit numerical code) of the NACE Rev. 2 statistical classification of economic activities as laid down in Regulation (EC) No 1893/2006 of the European Parliament and of the Council of 20 December 2006 establishing the statistical classification of economic activities NACE Revision 2 and amending Council Regulation (EEC) No 3037/90 as well as certain EC Regulations on specific statistical domains;
(51) 'initial investment in favour of new economic activity' means:
(a) an investment in tangible and intangible assets related to the setting up of a new establishment, or to the diversification of the activity of an establishment, under the condition that the new activity is not the same or a similar activity to the activity previously performed in the establishment;
(b) the acquisition of the assets belonging to an establishment that has closed or would have closed had it not been purchased, and is bought by an investor unrelated to the seller, under the condition that the new activity to be performed using the acquired assets is not the same or a similar activity to the activity performed in the establishment prior to the acquisition;
(52) 'large investment project' means an initial investment with eligible costs exceeding EUR 50 million, calculated at prices and exchange rates on the date of granting the aid;
(53) 'point of destination' means the place where the goods are unloaded;
(54) 'point of origin' means the place where the goods are loaded for transport;
(55) 'areas eligible for operating aid', means an outermost region referred to in Article 349 of the Treaty or a sparsely populated area, as determined in the approved regional aid map for the Member State concerned for the period 1.7.2014–31.12.2020;
(56) 'means of transport' means rail transport, road freight transport, inland waterway transport, maritime transport, air transport, and intermodal transport;
(57) 'urban development fund' ('UDF') means a specialised investment vehicle set up for the purpose of investing in urban development projects under an urban development aid measure. UDFs are managed by an urban development fund manager;
(58) 'urban development fund manager' means a professional management company with legal personality, selecting and making investments in eligible urban development projects;
(59) 'urban development project' ('UDP') means an investment project that has the potential to support the implementation of interventions envisaged by an integrated approach to sustainable urban development and contribute to achieving of the objectives defined therein, including projects with an internal rate of return which may not be sufficient to attract financing on a purely commercial basis. An urban development project may be organised as a separate block of finance within the legal structures of the beneficiary private investor or as a separate legal entity, e.g. a special purpose vehicle;
(60) 'integrated sustainable urban development strategy' means a strategy officially proposed and certified by a relevant local authority or public sector agency, defined for a specific urban geographic area and period, that set out integrated actions to tackle the economic, environmental, climate, demographic and social challenges affecting urban areas;
(61) 'in–kind contribution' means the contribution of land or real estate where the land or real estate forms part of the urban development project;

Definitions for Aid to SMEs

(62) 'employment directly created by an investment project' means employment concerning the activity to which the investment relates, including employment created following an increase in the utilisation rate of the capacity created by the investment;
(63) 'organisational cooperation' means the development of joint business strategies or management structures, the provision of common services or services to facilitate cooperation, coordinated activities such as research or marketing, the support of networks and clusters, the improvement of

accessibility and communication, the use of joint instruments to encourage entrepreneurship and trade with SMEs;
(64) 'advisory services linked to cooperation' means consulting, assistance and training for the exchange of knowledge and experiences and for improvement of cooperation;
(65) 'support services linked to cooperation' means the provision of office space, websites, data banks, libraries, market research, handbooks, working and model documents;

Definitions for Aid for access to finance for SMEs
(66) 'quasi–equity investment' means a type of financing that ranks between equity and debt, having a higher risk than senior debt and a lower risk than common equity and whose return for the holder is predominantly based on the profits or losses of the underlying target undertaking and which are unsecured in the event of default. Quasi–equity investments can be structured as debt, unsecured and subordinated, including mezzanine debt, and in some cases convertible into equity, or as preferred equity;
(67) 'guarantee' in the context of sections 1, 3 and 7 of the Regulation means a written commitment to assume responsibility for all or part of a third party's newly originated loan transactions such as debt or lease instruments, as well as quasi–equity instruments.;
(68) 'guarantee rate' means the percentage of loss coverage by a public investor of each and every transaction eligible under the relevant State aid measure;
(69) 'exit' means the liquidation of holdings by a financial intermediary or investor, including trade sale, write–offs, repayment of shares/loans, sale to another financial intermediary or another investor, sale to a financial institution and sale by public offering, including an initial public offering (IPO);
(70) 'financial endowment' means a repayable public investment made to a financial intermediary for the purposes of making investments under a risk finance measure, and where all the proceeds shall be returned to the public investor;
(71) 'risk finance investment' means equity and quasi–equity investments, loans including leases, guarantees, or a mix thereof to eligible undertakings for the purposes of making new investments;
(72) 'independent private investor' means a private investor who is not a shareholder of the eligible undertaking in which it invests, including business angels and financial institutions, irrespective of their ownership, to the extent that they bear the full risk in respect of their investment. Upon the creation of a new company, private investors, including the founders, are considered to be independent from that company;
(73) 'natural person' for the purpose of Articles 21 and 23 means a person other than a legal entity who is not an undertaking for the purposes of Article 107(1) of the Treaty;
(74) 'equity investment' means the provision of capital to an undertaking, invested directly or indirectly in return for the ownership of a corresponding share of that undertaking;
(75) 'first commercial sale' means the first sale by a company on a product or service market, excluding limited sales to test the market;
(76) 'unlisted SME' means an SME which is not listed on the official list of a stock exchange, except for alternative trading platforms.
(77) 'follow–on investment' means additional risk finance investment in a company subsequent to one or more previous risk finance investment rounds;
(78) 'replacement capital' means the purchase of existing shares in a company from an earlier investor or shareholder;
(79) 'entrusted entity' means the European Investment Bank and the European Investment Fund, an international financial institution in which a Member State is a shareholder, or a financial institution established in a Member State aiming at the achievement of public interest under the control of a public authority, a public law body, or a private law body with a public service mission: the entrusted entity can be selected or directly appointed in accordance with the provisions of Directive 2004/18/EC on the coordination of procedures for the award of public works contracts, public supply contracts and public service contracts, or any subsequent legislation replacing that Directive in full or in part;
(80) 'innovative enterprise' means an enterprise:
(a) that can demonstrate, by means of an evaluation carried out by an external expert that it will in the foreseeable future develop products, services or processes which are new or substantially improved compared to the state of the art in its industry, and which carry a risk of technological or industrial failure, or
(b) the research and development costs of which represent at least 10 % of its total operating costs in at least one of the three years preceding the granting of the aid or, in the case of a start–up enterprise without any financial history, in the audit of its current fiscal period, as certified by an external auditor;

(81) 'alternative trading platform' means a multilateral trading facility as defined in Article 4(1) (15) of Directive 2004/39/EC where the majority of the financial instruments admitted to trading are issued by SMEs;
(82) 'loan' means an agreement which obliges the lender to make available to the borrower an agreed amount of money for an agreed period of time and under which the borrower is obliged to repay the amount within the agreed period. It may take the form of a loan, or another funding instrument, including a lease, which provides the lender with a predominant component of minimum yield. The refinancing of existing loans shall not be an eligible loan.

Definitions for Aid for research and development and innovation
(83) 'research and knowledge–dissemination organisation' means an entity (such as universities or research institutes, technology transfer agencies, innovation intermediaries, research–oriented physical or virtual collaborative entities), irrespective of its legal status (organised under public or private law) or way of financing, whose primary goal is to independently conduct fundamental research, industrial research or experimental development or to widely disseminate the results of such activities by way of teaching, publication or knowledge transfer. Where such entity also pursues economic activities the financing, the costs and the revenues of those economic activities must be accounted for separately. Undertakings that can exert a decisive influence upon such an entity, in the quality of, for example, shareholders or members, may not enjoy preferential access to the results generated by it;
(84) 'fundamental research' means experimental or theoretical work undertaken primarily to acquire new knowledge of the underlying foundations of phenomena and observable facts, without any direct commercial application or use in view;
(85) 'industrial research' means the planned research or critical investigation aimed at the acquisition of new knowledge and skills for developing new products, processes or services or for bringing about a significant improvement in existing products, processes or services. It comprises the creation of components parts of complex systems, and may include the construction of prototypes in a laboratory environment or in an environment with simulated interfaces to existing systems as well as of pilot lines, when necessary for the industrial research and notably for generic technology validation;
(86) 'experimental development' means acquiring, combining, shaping and using existing scientific, technological, business and other relevant knowledge and skills with the aim of developing new or improved products, processes or services. This may also include, for example, activities aiming at the conceptual definition, planning and documentation of new products, processes or services;
Experimental development may comprise prototyping, demonstrating, piloting, testing and validation of new or improved products, processes or services in environments representative of real life operating conditions where the primary objective is to make further technical improvements on products, processes or services that are not substantially set. This may include the development of a commercially usable prototype or pilot which is necessarily the final commercial product and which is too expensive to produce for it to be used only for demonstration and validation purposes.
Experimental development does not include routine or periodic changes made to existing products, production lines, manufacturing processes, services and other operations in progress, even if those changes may represent improvements;
(87) 'feasibility study' means the evaluation and analysis of the potential of a project, which aims at supporting the process of decision–making by objectively and rationally uncovering its strengths and weaknesses, opportunities and threats, as well as identifying the resources required to carry it through and ultimately its prospects for success;
(88) 'personnel costs' means the costs of researchers, technicians and other supporting staff to the extent employed on the relevant project or activity;
(89) 'arm's length' means that the conditions of the transaction between the contracting parties do not differ from those which would be stipulated between independent enterprises and contain no element of collusion. Any transaction that results from an open, transparent and non–discriminatory procedure is considered as meeting the arm's length principle;
(90) 'effective collaboration' means collaboration between at least two independent parties to exchange knowledge or technology, or to achieve a common objective based on the division of labour where the parties jointly define the scope of the collaborative project, contribute to its implementation and share its risks, as well as its results. One or several parties may bear the full costs of the project and thus relieve other parties of its financial risks. Contract research and provision of research services are not considered forms of collaboration.
(91) 'research infrastructure' means facilities, resources and related services that are used by the scientific community to conduct research in their respective fields and covers scientific equipment or sets of instruments, knowledge–based resources such as collections, archives or structured scientific

information, enabling information and communication technology–based infrastructures such as grid, computing, software and communication, or any other entity of a unique nature essential to conduct research. Such infrastructures may be 'single–sited' or 'distributed' (an organised network of resources) in accordance with Article 2(a) of Council Regulation (EC) No 723/2009 of 25 June 2009 on the Community legal framework for a European Research Infrastructure Consortium (ERIC);

(92) 'innovation clusters' means structures or organised groups of independent parties (such as innovative start–ups, small, medium and large enterprises, as well as research and knowledge dissemination organisations, non–for–profit organisations and other related economic actors) designed to stimulate innovative activity through promotion, sharing of facilities and exchange of knowledge and expertise and by contributing effectively to knowledge transfer, networking, information dissemination and collaboration among the undertakings and other organisations in the cluster;

(93) 'highly qualified personnel' means staff having a tertiary education degree and at least 5 years of relevant professional experience which may also include doctoral training;

(94) 'innovation advisory services' means consultancy, assistance and training in the fields of knowledge transfer, acquisition, protection and exploitation of intangible assets, use of standards and regulations embedding them;

(95) 'innovation support services' means the provision of office space, data banks, libraries, market research, laboratories, quality labelling, testing and certification for the purpose of developing more effective products, processes or services;

(96) 'organisational innovation' means the implementation of a new organisational method in an undertaking's business practices, workplace organisation or external relations, excluding changes that are based on organisational methods already in use in the undertaking, changes in management strategy, mergers and acquisitions, ceasing to use a process, simple capital replacement or extension, changes resulting purely from changes in factor prices, customisation, localisation, regular, seasonal and other cyclical changes and trading of new or significantly improved products;

(97) 'process innovation' means the implementation of a new or significantly improved production or delivery method (including significant changes in techniques, equipment or software), excluding minor changes or improvements, increases in production or service capabilities through the addition of manufacturing or logistical systems which are very similar to those already in use, ceasing to use a process, simple capital replacement or extension, changes resulting purely from changes in factor prices, customisation, localisation, regular, seasonal and other cyclical changes and trading of new or significantly improved products;

(98) 'secondment' means temporary employment of staff by a beneficiary with the right for the staff to return to the previous employer;

Definitions for aid for disadvantaged workers and for workers with disabilities

(99) 'severely disadvantaged worker' means any person who:
(a) has not been in regular paid employment for at least 24 months; or
(b) has not been in regular paid employment for at least 12 months and belongs to one of the categories (b) to (g) mentioned under the definition of 'disadvantaged worker'.

(100) 'sheltered employment' means employment in an undertaking where at least 30 % of workers are workers with disabilities;

Definitions applying to aid for environmental protection

(101) 'environmental protection' means any action designed to remedy or prevent damage to physical surroundings or natural resources by a beneficiary's own activities, to reduce risk of such damage or to lead to a more efficient use of natural resources, including energy–saving measures and the use of renewable sources of energy;

(102) 'Union standard' means:
(a) a mandatory Union standard setting the levels to be attained in environmental terms by individual undertakings; or
(b) the obligation under Directive 2010/75/EU of the European Parliament and of the Council to use the best available techniques (BAT) and ensure that emission levels of pollutants are not higher than they would be when applying BAT; for the cases where emission levels associated with the BAT have been defined in implementing acts adopted under Directive 2010/75/EU, those levels will be applicable for the purpose of this Regulation; where those levels are expressed as a range, the limit where the BAT is first achieved will be applicable;

(103) 'energy efficiency' means an amount of saved energy determined by measuring and/or estimating consumption before and after implementation of an energy–efficiency improvement measure, whilst ensuring normalisation for external conditions that affect energy consumption;

(104) 'energy efficiency project' means an investment project that increases the energy efficiency of a building;

COMMISSION REGULATION 651/2014

(105) 'energy efficiency fund (EEF)' means a specialised investment vehicle set up for the purpose of investing in energy efficiency projects aimed at improving the energy efficiency of buildings in both the domestic and non–domestic sectors. EEFs are managed by an energy efficiency fund manager;
(106) 'energy efficiency fund manager' means a professional management company with a legal personality, selecting and making investments in eligible energy efficiency projects;
(107) 'high–efficiency cogeneration' means cogeneration which satisfies the definition of high efficiency cogeneration as set out in Article 2(34) of Directive 2012/27/EU of the European Parliament and of the Council of 25 October 2012 on energy efficiency, amending Directives 2009/125/EC and 2010/30/EU and repealing Directives 2004/8/EC and 2006/32/EC;
(108) 'cogeneration' or combined heat and power (CHP) means the simultaneous generation in one process of thermal energy and electrical and/or mechanical energy;
(109) 'energy from renewable energy sources' means energy produced by plants using only renewable energy sources, as well as the share in terms of calorific value of energy produced from renewable energy sources in hybrid plants which also use conventional energy sources. It includes renewable electricity used for filling storage systems, but excludes electricity produced as a result of storage systems;
(110) 'renewable energy sources' means the following renewable non–fossil energy sources: wind, solar, aerothermal, geothermal, hydrothermal and ocean energy, hydropower, biomass, landfill gas, sewage treatment plant gas and biogases;
(111) 'biofuel' means liquid or gaseous fuel for transport produced from biomass;
(112) 'sustainable biofuel' means a biofuel fulfilling the sustainability criteria set out in Article 17 of Directive 2009/28/EC;
(113) 'food based biofuel' means a biofuel produced from cereal and other starch rich crops, sugars and oil crops as defined in the Commission's Proposal for a Directive of the European Parliament and of the Council amending Directive 98/70/EC relating to the quality of petrol and diesel fuels and amending Directive 2009/28/EC on the promotion of the use of energy from renewable sources;
(114) 'new and innovative technology' means a new and unproven technology compared to the state of the art in the industry, which carries a risk of technological or industrial failure and is not an optimisation or scaling up of an existing technology;
(115) 'balancing responsibilities' means responsibility for imbalances (deviations between generation, consumption and commercial transactions) of a market participant or its chosen representative, referred to as the 'Balance Responsible Party', within a given period of time, referred to as the 'Imbalance Settlement Period';
(116) 'standard balancing responsibilities' means non–discriminatory balancing responsibilities across technologies which do not exempt any generator from those responsibilities;
(117) 'biomass' means the biodegradable fraction of products, waste and residues from agriculture (including vegetal and animal substances), forestry and related industries including fisheries and aquaculture, as well as biogases and the biodegradable fraction of industrial and municipal waste;
(118) 'total levelized costs of producing energy' is a calculation of the cost of generating electricity at the point of connection to a load or electricity grid. It includes the initial capital, discount rate, as well as the costs of continuous operation, fuel, and maintenance;
(119) 'environmental tax' means a tax with a specific tax base that has a clear negative effect on the environment or which seeks to tax certain activities, goods or services so that the environmental costs may be included in their price and/or so that producers and consumers are oriented towards activities which better respect the environment;
(120) 'Union minimum tax level' means the minimum level of taxation provided for in the Union legislation; for energy products and electricity it means the minimum level of taxation laid down in Annex I to Council Directive 2003/96/EC of 27 October 2003 restructuring the Community framework for the taxation of energy products and electricity;
(121) 'contaminated site' means a site where there is a confirmed presence, caused by man, of hazardous substances of such a level that they pose a significant risk to human health or the environment taking into account current and approved future use of the land;
(122) 'polluter pays principle' or 'PPP' means that the costs of measures to deal with pollution should be borne by the polluter who causes the pollution;
(123) 'pollution' means the damage caused by a polluter directly or indirectly damaging the environment, or by creating conditions leading to such damage to physical surroundings or natural resources;
(124) 'energy efficient district heating and cooling' means a district heating and cooling system which satisfies the definition of efficient district heating and cooling system set out in Article 2(41) and (42) of Directive 2012/27/EU. The definition includes the heating/cooling production plants and the network (including related facilities) necessary to distribute the heat/cooling from the production units to the customer premises;

PART III   EUROPEAN UNION

(125) 'polluter' means someone who directly or indirectly damages the environment or who creates conditions leading to such damage.

(126) 're–use' means any operation by which products or components that are not waste are used again for the same purpose for which they were conceived;

(127) 'preparing for re–use' means checking, cleaning or repairing recovery operations, by which products or components of products that have become waste are prepared so that they can be re–used without any other pre–processing;

(128) 'recycling' means any recovery operation by which waste materials are reprocessed into products, materials or substances whether for the original or other purposes. It includes the reprocessing of organic material but does not include energy recovery and the reprocessing into materials that are to be used as fuels or for backfilling operations;

(129) 'state of the art' means a process in which the re–use of a waste product to manufacture an end product is economically profitable normal practice. Where appropriate, the concept of state of the art must be interpreted from a Union technological and internal market perspective;

(130) 'energy infrastructure' means any physical equipment or facility which is located within the Union or linking the Union to one or more third countries and falling under the following categories:
(a) concerning electricity:
(i) infrastructure for transmission, as defined in Article 2(3) by Directive 2009/72/EC of 13 July 2009 concerning common rules for internal market in electricity;
(ii) infrastructure for distribution, as defined in Article 2(5) by Directive 2009/72/EC;
(iii) electricity storage, defined as facilities used for storing electricity on a permanent or temporary basis in above–ground or underground infrastructure or geological sites, provided they are directly connected to high–voltage transmission lines designed for a voltage of 110 kV or more;
(iv) any equipment or installation essential for the systems defined in points (i) to (iii) to operate safely, securely and efficiently, including protection, monitoring and control systems at all voltage levels and substations; and
(v) smart grids, defined as any equipment, line, cable or installation, both at transmission and low and medium voltage distribution level, aiming at two–way digital communication, real–time or close to real–time, interactive and intelligent monitoring and management of electricity generation, transmission, distribution and consumption within an electricity network in view of developing a network efficiently integrating the behaviour and actions of all users connected to it – generators, consumers and those that do both — in order to ensure an economically efficient, sustainable electricity system with low losses and high quality and security of supply and safety;
(b) concerning gas:
(i) transmission and distribution pipelines for the transport of natural gas and bio gas that form part of a network, excluding high–pressure pipelines used for upstream distribution of natural gas;
(ii) underground storage facilities connected to the high–pressure gas pipelines mentioned in point (i);
(iii) reception, storage and regasification or decompression facilities for liquefied natural gas ('LNG') or compressed natural gas ('CNG'); and
(iv) any equipment or installation essential for the system to operate safely, securely and efficiently or to enable bi–directional capacity, including compressor stations;
(c) concerning oil:
(i) pipelines used to transport crude oil;
(ii) pumping stations and storage facilities necessary for the operation of crude oil pipelines; and
(iii) any equipment or installation essential for the system in question to operate properly, securely and efficiently, including protection, monitoring and control systems and reverse–flow devices;
(d) concerning CO2: networks of pipelines, including associated booster stations, for the transport of CO2 to storage sites, with the aim to inject the CO2 in suitable underground geological formations for permanent storage;

(131) 'internal energy market legislation' includes Directive 2009/72/EC of the European Parliament and of the Council of 13 July 2009 concerning common rules for the internal market in electricity, Directive 2009/73/EC of the European Parliament and of the Council of 13 July 2009 concerning common rules for the internal market in natural gas, Regulation (EC) No 713/2009 of the European Parliament and of the Council of 13 July 2009 establishing an Agency for the Cooperation of Energy Regulators; Regulation (EC) No 714/2009 of the European Parliament and of the Council of 13 July 2009 on conditions for access to the network for cross–border exchanges and Regulation (EC) No 715/2009 of the European Parliament and of the Council of 13 July 2009 on conditions for access to the natural gas transmission networks or any subsequent legislation replacing these acts in full or in part;

Definitions applying to social aid for transport for residents of remote regions
(132) 'normal residence' means the place where a natural person lives for at least 185 days, in each calendar year, because of personal and occupational ties; in the case of a person whose occupational ties are in a different place from his/her personal ties and who lives in two or more Member States, the place of normal residence is regarded as the place of his/her personal ties provided that he/she returns there regularly; where a person is living in a Member State in order to carry out a task of a set duration, the place of residence is still regarded as being the place of his/her personal ties, irrespective of whether he/she returns there during the course of this activity; attendance at a university or school in another Member State does not constitute a transfer of normal residence; alternatively, 'normal residence' shall have the meaning attributed to it in Member States' national law.

Definitions for aid for broadband infrastructures
(133) 'basic broadband''Basic broadband networks' means networks with basic functionalities which are based on technology platforms such as asymmetric digital subscriber lines (up to ADSL2+ networks), non–enhanced cable (e.g. DOCSIS 2.0), mobile networks of third generation (UMTS) and satellite systems;
(134) 'broadband–related civil engineering works' means the civil engineering works which are necessary for the deployment of a broadband network, such as digging up a road in order to enable the placement of (broadband) ducts.
(135) 'ducts' means underground pipes or conduits used to house (fibre, copper or coax) cables of a broadband network.
(136) 'physical unbundling' grants access to the end–consumer access line and allows competitors' own transmission systems to directly transmit over it.
(137) 'passive broadband infrastructure' means a broadband network without any active component. It typically comprises civil engineering infrastructure, ducts and dark fibre and street cabinets.
(138) 'next generation access (NGA) networks' means advanced networks which have at least the following characteristics: (a) deliver services reliably at a very high speed per subscriber through optical (or equivalent technology) backhaul sufficiently close to user premises to guarantee the actual delivery of the very high speed; (b) support a variety of advanced digital services including converged all–IP services, and (c) have substantially higher upload speeds (compared to basic broadband networks). At the current stage of market and technological development, NGA networks are: (a) fibre–based access networks (FTTx), (b) advanced upgraded cable networks and (c) certain advanced wireless access networks capable of delivering reliable high–speeds per subscriber.
(139) 'wholesale access' means access which enables an operator to utilise the facilities of another operator. The widest possible access to be provided over the relevant network shall include, on the basis of the current technological developments, at least the following access products. For FTTH/FTTB networks: ducts access, access to dark fibre, unbundled access to the local loop, and bitstream access. For cable networks: duct access and bit–stream access. For FTTC networks: duct access, sub–loop unbundling and bit–stream access. For passive network infrastructure: duct access, access to dark fibre and/or unbundled access to the local loop. For ADSL–based broadband networks: unbundled access to the local loop, bit–stream access. For mobile or wireless networks: bit–stream, sharing of physical masts and access to the backhaul networks. For satellite platforms: bit–stream access.

Definitions for aid for culture and heritage conservation
(140) 'difficult audiovisual works': means the works identified as such by Member States on the basis of pre–defined criteria when setting up schemes or granting the aid and may include films whose sole original version is in a language of a Member State with a limited territory, population or language area, short films, films by first–time and second–time directors, documentaries, or low budget or otherwise commercially difficult works.
(141) Development Assistance Committee (DAC) List of the OECD: means all countries and territories that are eligible to receive official development assistance and included in the list compiled by the Organisation for Economic Cooperation and Development (OECD);
(142) 'reasonable profit' shall be determined with respect to the typical profit for the sector concerned. In any event, a rate of return on capital that does not exceed the relevant swap rate plus a premium of 100 basis points will be considered to be reasonable.

Definitions for aid for sport and multifunctional recreational infrastructures
(143) 'professional sport' means the practice of sport in the nature of gainful employment or remunerated service, irrespective of whether or not a formal labour contract has been established between the professional sportsperson and the relevant sport organisation, where the compensation exceeds the cost of participation and constitutes a significant part of the income for the sportsperson. Travel

PART III   EUROPEAN UNION

and accommodation expenses to participate to the sport event shall not be considered as compensation for the purposes of this Regulation.

Article 3. Conditions for exemption

Aid schemes, individual aid granted under aid schemes and ad hoc aid shall be compatible with the internal market within the meaning of Article 107(2) or (3) of the Treaty and shall be exempted from the notification requirement of Article 108(3) of the Treaty provided that such aid fulfils all the conditions laid down in Chapter I of this Regulation, as well as the specific conditions for the relevant category of aid laid down in Chapter III of this Regulation.

Article 4. Notification thresholds

(1) This Regulation shall not apply to aid which exceeds the following thresholds:
(a) for regional investment aid: the 'adjusted aid amount' of aid, as calculated in accordance with the mechanism defined in Article 2, point 20 for an investment with eligible costs of EUR 100 million;
(b) for regional urban development aid, EUR 20 million as laid down in Article 16(3);
(c) for investment aid to SMEs: EUR 7,5 million per undertaking per investment project;
(d) for aid for consultancy in favour of SMEs: EUR 2 million per undertaking, per project;
(e) for aid to SMEs for participation in fairs: EUR 2 million per undertaking, per year;
(f) for aid to SMEs for cooperation costs incurred by participating in European Territorial Cooperation projects: EUR 2 million per undertaking, per project;
(g) for risk finance aid: EUR 15 million per eligible undertaking as laid down in Article 21(9);
(h) for aid for start–ups: the amounts laid down per undertaking in Article 22(3), (4) and (5);
(i) for aid for research and development:
(i) if the project is predominantly fundamental research: EUR 40 million per undertaking, per project; that is the case where more than half of the eligible costs of the project are incurred through activities which fall within the category of fundamental research;
(ii) if the project is predominantly industrial research: EUR 20 million per undertaking, per project; that is the case where more than half of the eligible costs of the project are incurred through activities which fall within the category of industrial research or within the categories of industrial research and fundamental research taken together;
(iii) if the project is predominantly experimental development: EUR 15 million per undertaking, per project; that is the case where more than half of the eligible costs of the project are incurred through activities which fall within the category of experimental development;
(iv) if the project is a Eureka project or is implemented by a Joint Undertaking established on the basis of Article 185 or of Article 187 of the Treaty, the amounts referred to in points (i) to (iii) are doubled.
(v) if the aid for research and development projects is granted in the form of repayable advances which, in the absence of an accepted methodology to calculate their gross grant equivalent, are expressed as a percentage of the eligible costs and the measure provides that in case of a successful outcome of the project, as defined on the basis of a reasonable and prudent hypothesis, the advances will be repaid with an interest rate at least equal to the discount rate applicable at the time of grant, the amounts referred to in points (i) to (iv) are increased by 50 %;
(vi) aid for feasibility studies in preparation for research activities: EUR 7,5 million per study;
(j) for investment aid for research infrastructures: EUR 20 million per infrastructure;
(k) for aid for innovation clusters: EUR 7,5 million per cluster;
(l) innovation aid for SMEs: EUR 5 million per undertaking, per project;
(m) for aid for process and organisational innovation: EUR 7,5 million per undertaking, per project;
(n) for training aid: EUR 2 million per training project;
(o) for aid for the recruitment of disadvantaged workers: EUR 5 million per undertaking, per year;
(p) for aid for the employment of workers with disabilities in the form of wage subsidies: EUR 10 million per undertaking, per year;
(q) for aid for compensating the additional costs of employing workers with disabilities: EUR 10 million per undertaking, per year;
(r) for aid for compensating the costs of assistance provided to disadvantaged workers: EUR 5 million per undertaking, per year;
(s) for investment aid for environmental protection, excluding investment aid for the remediation of contaminated sites and aid for the distribution network part of the energy efficient district heating and cooling installation: EUR 15 million per undertaking per investment project;
(t) for investment aid for energy efficiency projects: EUR 10 million as laid down in Article 39(5);
(u) for investment aid for remediation of contaminated sites: EUR 20 million per undertaking per investment project;

(v) for operating aid for the production of electricity from renewable sources and operating aid for the promotion of energy from renewable sources in small scale installations: EUR 15 million per undertaking per project. When the aid is granted on the basis of a competitive bidding process under Article 42: EUR 150 million per year taking into account the combined budget of all schemes falling under Article 42;
(w) for investment aid for the district heating or cooling distribution network: EUR 20 million per undertaking per investment project;
(x) for investment aid for energy infrastructure: EUR 50 million per undertaking, per investment project;
(y) for aid for broadband infrastructures: EUR 70 million total costs per project;
(z) for investment aid for culture and heritage conservation: EUR 100 million per project; operating aid for culture and heritage conservation: EUR 50 million per undertaking per year;
(aa) for aid schemes for audiovisual works: EUR 50 million per scheme per year;
(bb) for investment aid for sports and multifunctional infrastructures: EUR 15 million or the total costs exceeding EUR 50 million per project; operating aid for sport infrastructure: EUR 2 million per infrastructure per year; and
(cc) for investment aid for local infrastructures: EUR 10 million or the total costs exceeding EUR 20 million for the same infrastructure.
(2) The thresholds set out or referred to in paragraph 1 shall not be circumvented by artificially splitting up the aid schemes or aid projects.

Article 5. Transparency of aid
(1) This Regulation shall apply only to aid in respect of which it is possible to calculate precisely the gross grant equivalent of the aid *ex ante* without any need to undertake a risk assessment ('transparent aid').
(2) The following categories of aid shall be considered to be transparent:
(a) aid comprised in grants and interest rate subsidies;
(b) aid comprised in loans, where the gross grant equivalent has been calculated on the basis of the reference rate prevailing at the time of the grant;
(c) aid comprised in guarantees:
(i) where the gross grant equivalent has been calculated on the basis of safe–harbour premiums laid down in a Commission notice; or
(ii) where before the implementation of the measure, the methodology to calculate the gross grant equivalent of the guarantee has been accepted on the basis of the Commission Notice on the application of Articles 87 and 88 of the EC Treaty to State aid in the form of guarantees, or any successor notice, following notification of that methodology to the Commission under any regulation adopted by the Commission in the State aid area applicable at the time, and the approved methodology explicitly addresses the type of guarantee and the type of underlying transaction at stake in the context of the application of this Regulation;
(d) aid in the form of tax advantages, where the measure provides for a cap ensuring that the applicable threshold is not exceeded;
(e) aid for regional urban development if the conditions laid down in Article 16 are fulfilled;
(f) aid comprised in risk finance measures if the conditions laid down in Article 21 are fulfilled;
(g) aid for start–ups if the conditions laid down in Article 22 are fulfilled;
(h) aid for energy efficiency projects if the conditions laid down in Article 39 are fulfilled;
(i) aid in the form of premiums in addition to the market price if the conditions laid down in Article 42 are fulfilled;
(j) aid in the form of repayable advances, if the total nominal amount of the repayable advance does not exceed the thresholds applicable under this Regulation or if, before implementation of the measure, the methodology to calculate the gross grant equivalent of the repayable advance has been accepted following its notification to the Commission.

Article 6. Incentive effect
(1) This Regulation shall apply only to aid which has an incentive effect.
(2) Aid shall be considered to have an incentive effect if the beneficiary has submitted a written application for the aid to the Member State concerned before work on the project or activity starts. The application for the aid shall contain at least the following information:
(a) undertaking's name and size;
(b) description of the project, including its start and end dates;
(c) location of the project;
(d) list of project costs;

(e) type of aid (grant, loan, guarantee, repayable advance, equity injection or other) and amount of public funding needed for the project;

(3) Ad hoc aid granted to large enterprises shall be considered to have an incentive effect if, in addition to ensuring that the condition laid down in paragraph 2 is fulfilled, the Member State has verified, before granting the aid concerned, that documentation prepared by the beneficiary establishes that the aid will result in one or more of the following:

(a) in the case of regional investment aid: that a project is carried out, which would not have been carried out in the area concerned or would not have been sufficiently profitable for the beneficiary in the area concerned in the absence of the aid.

(b) in all other cases, that there is:

– a material increase in the scope of the project/activity due to the aid, or

– a material increase in the total amount spent by the beneficiary on the project/activity due to the aid, or

– a material increase in the speed of completion of the project/activity concerned;

(4) By way of derogation from paragraphs 2 and 3, measures in the form of tax advantages shall be deemed to have an incentive effect if the following conditions are fulfilled:

(a) the measure establishes a right to aid in accordance with objective criteria and without further exercise of discretion by the Member State; and

(b) the measure has been adopted and is in force before work on the aided project or activity has started, except in the case of fiscal successor schemes, where the activity was already covered by the previous schemes in the form of tax advantages.

(5) By way of derogation from paragraphs 2, 3 and 4, the following categories of aid are not required to have or shall be deemed to have an incentive effect:

(a) regional operating aid, if the conditions laid down in Article 15 are fulfilled,

(b) aid for access to finance for SMEs, if the relevant conditions laid down in Articles 21 and 22 are fulfilled,

(c) aid for the recruitment of disadvantaged workers in the form of wage subsidies and aid for the employment of workers with disabilities in the form of wage subsidies, if the relevant conditions laid down in Articles 32 and 33 respectively are fulfilled,

(d) aid compensating for the additional costs of employing workers with disabilities, if the conditions laid down in Article 34 are fulfilled;

(e) aid in the form of reductions in environmental taxes under Directive 2003/96/EC, if the conditions laid down in Article 44 of this Regulation are fulfilled;

(f) aid to make good the damage caused by certain natural disasters, if the conditions laid down in Article 50 are fulfilled;

(g) social aid for transport for residents of remote regions, if the conditions laid down in Article 51 are fulfilled;

(h) aid for culture and heritage conservation, if the conditions laid down in Article 53 are fulfilled.

Article 7. Aid intensity and eligible costs

(1) For the purposes of calculating aid intensity and eligible costs, all figures used shall be taken before any deduction of tax or other charge. The eligible costs shall be supported by documentary evidence which shall be clear, specific and contemporary.

(2) Where aid is granted in a form other than a grant, the aid amount shall be the gross grant equivalent of the aid.

(3) Aid payable in several instalments shall be discounted to its value at the moment it is granted. The eligible costs shall be discounted to their value at the moment the aid is granted. The interest rate to be used for discounting purposes shall be the discount rate applicable at the moment the aid is granted.

(4) Where aid is granted by means of tax advantages, discounting of aid tranches shall take place on the basis of the discount rates applicable at the various times the tax advantage takes effect.

(5) Where aid is granted in the form of repayable advances which, in the absence of an accepted methodology to calculate their gross grant equivalent, are expressed as a percentage of the eligible costs and the measure provides that in case of a successful outcome of the project, as defined on the basis of a reasonable and prudent hypothesis, the advances will be repaid with an interest rate at least equal to the discount rate applicable at the moment the aid is granted, the maximum aid intensities laid down in Chapter III may be increased by 10 percentage points.

(6) Where regional aid is granted in the form of repayable advances, the maximum aid intensities established in a regional aid map in force at the moment the aid is granted may not be increased.

Article 8. Cumulation

(1) In determining whether the notification thresholds in Article 4 and the maximum aid intensities in Chapter III are respected, the total amount of State aid for the aided activity or project or undertaking shall be taken into account.

(2) Where Union funding centrally managed by the institutions, agencies, joint undertakings or other bodies of the Union that is not directly or indirectly under the control of the Member State is combined with State aid, only the latter shall be considered for determining whether notification thresholds and maximum aid intensities or maximum aid amounts are respected, provided that the total amount of public funding granted in relation to the same eligible costs does not exceed the most favourable funding rate laid down in the applicable rules of Union law.

(3) Aid with identifiable eligible costs exempted by this Regulation may be cumulated with:

(a) any other State aid, as long as those measures concern different identifiable eligible costs,

(b) any other State aid, in relation to the same eligible costs, partly or fully overlapping, only if such cumulation does not result in exceeding the highest aid intensity or aid amount applicable to this aid under this Regulation.

(4) Aid without identifiable eligible costs exempted under Articles 21, 22 and 23 of this Regulation may be cumulated with any other State aid with identifiable eligible costs. Aid without identifiable eligible costs may be cumulated with any other State aid without identifiable eligible costs, up to the highest relevant total financing threshold fixed in the specific circumstances of each case by this or another block exemption regulation or decision adopted by the Commission.

(5) State aid exempted under this Regulation shall not be cumulated with any *de minimis* aid in respect of the same eligible costs if such cumulation would result in an aid intensity exceeding those laid down in Chapter III of this Regulation.

(6) By way of derogation from paragraph 3(b), aid in favour of workers with disabilities, as provided for in Articles 33 and 34 may be cumulated with other aid exempted under this Regulation in relation to the same eligible costs above the highest applicable threshold under this Regulation, provided that such cumulation does not result in an aid intensity exceeding 100 % of the relevant costs over any period for which the workers concerned are employed.

Article 9. Publication and information

(1) The Member State concerned shall ensure the publication on a comprehensive State aid website, at national or regional level of:

(a) the summary information referred to in Article 11 in the standardised format laid down in Annex II or a link providing access to it;

(b) the full text of each aid measure, as referred to in Article 11 or a link providing access to the full text;

(c) the information referred to in Annex III on each individual aid award exceeding EUR 500 000. As regards aid granted to European Territorial Cooperation projects, the information referred to in this paragraph shall be placed on the website of the Member State in which the Managing Authority concerned, as defined in Article 21 of Regulation (EC) No 1299/2013 of the European Parliament and of the Council, is located. Alternatively, the participating Member States may also decide that each of them shall provide the information relating to the aid measures within their territory on the respective websites.

(2) For schemes in the form of tax advantages, and for schemes covered by Article 16 and 21 the conditions set out in paragraph 1(c) of this Article shall be considered fulfilled if Member States publish the required information on individual aid amounts in the following ranges (in EUR million):

0,5–1;
1–2;
2–5;
5–10;
10–30; and
30 and more.

(3) For schemes under Article 51 of this Regulation, the publication obligations laid down in this article shall not apply to final consumers.

(4) The information referred to in paragraph 1(c) of this Article shall be organised and accessible in a standardised manner, as described in Annex III, and shall allow for effective search and download functions. The information referred to in paragraph 1 shall be published within 6 months from the date the aid was granted, or for aid in the form of tax advantage, within 1 year from the date the tax declaration is due, and shall be available for at least 10 years from the date on which the aid was granted.

(5) The Commission shall publish on its website:

PART III   EUROPEAN UNION

(a) the links to the State aid websites referred to in paragraph 1 of this Article;
(b) the summary information referred to in Article 11.
(6) Member States shall comply with the provisions of this Article at the latest within two years after the entry into force of this Regulation.

Chapter II. Monitoring

Article 10. Withdrawal of the benefit of the block exemption
Where a Member State grants aid allegedly exempted from the notification requirement under this Regulation without fulfilling the conditions set out in Chapters I to III, the Commission may, after having provided the Member State concerned with the possibility to make its views known, adopt a decision stating that all or some of the future aid measures adopted by the Member State concerned which would otherwise fulfil the requirements of this Regulation, are to be notified to the Commission in accordance with Article 108(3) of the Treaty. The measures to be notified may be limited to the measures granting certain types of aid or in favour of certain beneficiaries or aid measures adopted by certain authorities of the Member State concerned.

Article 11. Reporting
Member States, or in the case of aid granted to European Territorial Cooperation projects, alternatively the Member State in which the Managing Authority, as defined in Article 21 of Regulation (EC) No 1299/2013 of the European Parliament and of the Council, is located, shall transmit to the Commission:
(a) via the Commission's electronic notification system, the summary information about each aid measure exempted under this Regulation in the standardised format laid down in Annex II, together with a link providing access to the full text of the aid measure, including its amendments, within 20 working days following its entry into force;
(b) an annual report, as referred to in the Commission Regulation (EC) No 794/2004 of 21 April 2004 implementing Council Regulation (EC) No 659/1999 of 22 March 1999 laying down detailed rules for the application of Article 93 of the EC Treaty as amended, in electronic form, on the application of this Regulation, containing the information indicated in the Implementing Regulation, in respect of each whole year or each part of the year during which this Regulation applies.

Article 12. Monitoring
In order to enable the Commission to monitor the aid exempted from notification by this Regulation, Member States, or alternatively, in the case of aid granted to European Territorial Cooperation projects, the Member State in which the Managing Authority is located, shall maintain detailed records with the information and supporting documentation necessary to establish that all the conditions laid down in this Regulation are fulfilled. Such records shall be kept for 10 years from the date on which the ad hoc aid was granted or the last aid was granted under the scheme. The Member State concerned shall provide the Commission within a period of 20 working days or such longer period as may be fixed in the request, with all the information and supporting documentation which the Commission considers necessary to monitor the application of this Regulation.

Chapter III. Specific Provisions for Different Categories of Aid

Section 1. Regional Aid

Subsection A. Regional Investment and Operating Aid

Article 13. Scope of regional aid
This Section shall not apply to:
(a) aid which favours activities in the steel sector, the coal sector, the shipbuilding sector, the synthetic fibers sector, the transport sector as well as the related infrastructure, energy generation, distribution and infrastructure;
(b) regional aid in the form of schemes which are targeted at a limited number of specific sectors of economic activity; schemes aimed at tourism activities, broadband infrastructures or processing and marketing of agricultural products are not considered to be targeted at specific sectors of economic activity;
(c) regional aid in the form of schemes which compensate the transport costs of goods produced in the outermost regions or in sparsely populated areas and granted in favour of:
(i) activities in the production, processing and marketing of products listed in Annex I to the Treaty; or
(ii) activities classified in Regulation (EC) No 1893/2006 of the European Parliament and of the

Council of 20 December 2006 establishing statistical classification of economic activities NACE Revision 2 and amending Council Regulation (EEC) No 3037/90 as well as certain EC Regulations on specific statistical domains (53) as agriculture, forestry and fishing under section A of the NACE Rev. 2 statistical classification of economic activities, mining and quarrying under section B of the NACE Rev. 2 and electricity, gas, steam and air conditioning supply under section D of the NACE Rev. 2; or

(iii) transport of goods by pipeline;

(d) individual regional investment aid to a beneficiary that has closed down the same or a similar activity in the European Economic Area in the two years preceding its application for regional investment aid or which, at the time of the aid application, has concrete plans to close down such an activity within a period of up to two years after the initial investment for which aid is requested is completed in the area concerned;

(e) regional operating aid granted to undertakings whose principal activities fall under Section K 'Financial and insurance activities' of the NACE Rev. 2 or to undertakings that perform intra–group activities whose principal activities fall under classes 70.10 'Activities of head offices' or 70.22 'Business and other management consultancy activities' of NACE Rev. 2.

Article 14. Regional investment aid

(1) Regional investment aid measures shall be compatible with the internal market within the meaning of Article 107(3) of the Treaty and shall be exempted from the notification requirement of Article 108(3) of the Treaty, provided that the conditions laid down in this Article and in Chapter I are fulfilled.

(2) The aid shall be granted in assisted areas.

(3) In assisted areas fulfilling the conditions of Article 107(3)(a) of the Treaty, the aid may be granted for an initial investment regardless of the size of the beneficiary. In assisted areas fulfilling the conditions of Article 107(3)(c) of the Treaty, the aid may be granted to SMEs for any form of initial investment. Aid to large enterprises shall only be granted for an initial investment in favour of new economic activity in the area concerned.

(4) The eligible costs shall be as follows:

(a) investment costs in tangible and intangible assets;

(b) the estimated wage costs arising from job creation as a result of an initial investment, calculated over a period of two years; or

(c) a combination of points (a) and (b) not exceeding the amount of (a) or (b), whichever is higher.

(5) The investment shall be maintained in the recipient area for at least five years, or at least three years in the case of SMEs, after completion of the investment. This shall not prevent the replacement of plant or equipment that has become outdated or broken within this period, provided that the economic activity is retained in the area concerned for the relevant minimum period.

(6) The assets acquired shall be new except for SMEs and for the acquisition of an establishment. Costs related to the lease of tangible assets may be taken into account under the following conditions:

(a) for land and buildings, the lease must continue for at least five years after the expected date of completion of the investment project for large undertakings or three years in the case of SMEs;

(b) for plant or machinery, the lease must take the form of financial leasing and must contain an obligation for the beneficiary of the aid to purchase the asset upon expiry of the term of the lease.

In the case of acquisition of the assets of an establishment within the meaning of Article 2 point 49, only the costs of buying the assets from third parties unrelated to the buyer shall be taken into consideration. The transaction shall take place under market conditions. If aid has already been granted for the acquisition of assets prior to their purchase, the costs of those assets shall be deducted from the eligible costs related to the acquisition of an establishment. Where a member of the family of the original owner, or an employee, takes over a small enterprise, the condition that the assets be bought from third parties unrelated to the buyer shall be waived. The acquisition of shares does not constitute initial investment.

(7) For aid granted for a fundamental change in the production process, the eligible costs must exceed the depreciation of the assets linked to the activity to be modernised in the course of the preceding three fiscal years. For aid granted for a diversification of an existing establishment, the eligible costs must exceed by at least 200 % the book value of the assets that are reused, as registered in the fiscal year preceding the start of works.

(8) Intangible assets are eligible for the calculation of investment costs if they fulfil the following conditions:

(a) they must be used exclusively in the establishment receiving the aid;

(b) they must be amortisable;

(c) they must be purchased under market conditions from third parties unrelated to the buyer; and
(d) they must be included in the assets of the undertaking receiving the aid and must remain associated with the project for which the aid is granted for at least five years or three years in the case of SMEs.
For large undertakings, costs of intangible assets are eligible only up to a limit of 50 % of the total eligible investment costs for the initial investment.
(9) Where eligible costs are calculated by reference to the estimated wage costs as referred to in paragraph 4(b), the following conditions shall be fulfilled:
(a) the investment project shall lead to a net increase in the number of employees in the establishment concerned, compared with the average over the previous 12 months, meaning that any job lost shall be deducted from the apparent created number of jobs during that period;
(b) each post shall be filled within three years of completion of works; and
(c) each job created through the investment shall be maintained in the area concerned for a period of at least five years from the date the post was first filled, or three years in the case of SMEs.
(10) Regional aid for broadband network development shall fulfil the following conditions:
(a) aid shall be granted only in areas where there is no network of the same category (either basic broadband or NGA) and where no such network is likely to be developed on commercial terms within three years from the decision to grant the aid; and
(b) the subsidised network operator must offer active and passive wholesale access under fair and non–discriminatory conditions including physical unbundling in the case of NGA networks; and
(c) aid shall be allocated on the basis of a competitive selection process.
(11) Regional aid for research infrastructures shall be granted only if the aid is made conditional on giving transparent and non–discriminatory access to the aided infrastructure.
(12) The aid intensity in gross grant equivalent shall not exceed the maximum aid intensity established in the regional aid map which is in force at the time the aid is granted in the area concerned. Where the aid intensity is calculated on the basis of paragraph 4(c), the maximum aid intensity shall not exceed the most favourable amount resulting from the application of that intensity on the basis of investment costs or wage costs. For large investment projects the aid amount shall not exceed the adjusted aid amount calculated in accordance with the mechanism defined in Article 2, point 20;
(13) Any initial investment started by the same beneficiary (at group level) within a period of three years from the date of start of works on another aided investment in the same level 3 region of the Nomenclature of Territorial Units for Statistics shall be considered to be part of a single investment project. Where such single investment project is a large investment project, the total aid amount for the single investment project shall not exceed the adjusted aid amount for large investment projects.
(14) The aid beneficiary must provide a financial contribution of at least 25 % of the eligible costs, either through its own resources or by external financing, in a form, which is free of any public support. In the outermost regions an investment made by an SME may receive an aid with a maximum aid intensity above 75 %, in such situations the remainder shall be provided by way of a financial contribution from the aid beneficiary.
(15) For an initial investment linked to European territorial cooperation projects covered by Regulation (EU) No 1299/2013, the aid intensity of the area in which the initial investment is located shall apply to all beneficiaries participating in the project. If the initial investment is located in two or more assisted areas, the maximum aid intensity shall be the one applicable in the assisted area where the highest amount of eligible costs is incurred. In assisted areas eligible for aid under Article 107(3)(c) of the Treaty, this provision shall apply to large undertakings only if the initial investment concerns a new economic activity.

Article 15. Regional operating aid

(1) Regional operating aid schemes in outermost regions and sparsely populated areas as designated by the Member States within their regional aid map approved by the Commission in accordance with paragraph 161 of the Guidelines on regional State aid for 2014–2020 shall be compatible with the internal market within the meaning of Article 107(3) of the Treaty and shall be exempted from the notification requirement of Article 108(3) of the Treaty, provided that the conditions laid down in this Article and in Chapter I are fulfilled.
(2) The regional operating aid schemes shall compensate for:
(a) the additional transport costs of goods which have been produced in areas eligible for operating aid, as well as additional transport costs of goods that are further processed in these areas, under the following conditions:
(i) the beneficiaries have their production activity in those areas;
(ii) the aid is objectively quantifiable in advance on the basis of a fixed sum or per tonne/kilometre

ratio or any other relevant unit;
(iii) these additional transport costs are calculated on the basis of the journey of the goods inside the national border of the Member State concerned using the means of transport which results in the lowest costs for the beneficiary. Only for outermost regions, additional transport costs of goods that are further processed in these areas may include the costs of transporting goods from any place of their production to these areas.
(b) the additional operating costs other than transport costs, incurred in outermost regions as a direct effect of one or several of the permanent handicaps referred to in Article 349 of the Treaty, under the following conditions:
(i) the beneficiaries have their economic activity in an outermost region;
(ii) the annual aid amount per beneficiary under all operating aid schemes does not exceed:
– 15 % of the gross value added annually created by the beneficiary in the outermost region concerned; or
– 25 % of the annual labour costs incurred by the beneficiary in the outermost region concerned; or
– 10 % of the annual turnover of the beneficiary realised in the outermost region concerned.
(3) The aid intensity shall not exceed 100 % of the eligible additional costs as determined in this Article.

Subsection B. Urban Development Aid

Article 16. Regional urban development aid

(1) Regional urban development aid shall be compatible with the internal market within the meaning of Article 107(3) of the Treaty and shall be exempted from the notification requirement of Article 108(3) of the Treaty, provided that the conditions laid down in this Article and in Chapter I are fulfilled.
(2) Urban development projects shall fulfil the following criteria:
(a) they are implemented via urban development funds in assisted areas;
(b) they are co–financed by the European Structural and Investment Funds;
(c) they support the implementation of an 'integrated sustainable urban development strategy';
(3) The total investment in an urban development project under any urban development aid measure shall not exceed EUR 20 million.
(4) The eligible costs shall be the overall costs of the urban development project to the extent that they comply with Articles 65 and 37 of Regulation (EU) No 1303/2013 of the European Parliament and of the Council.
(5) Aid granted by an urban development fund to the eligible urban development projects may take the form of equity, quasi–equity, loans, guarantees, or a mix thereof.
(6) The urban development aid shall leverage additional investment from private investors at the level of the urban development funds or the urban development projects, so as to achieve an aggregate amount reaching minimum 30 % of the total financing provided to an urban development project.
(7) Private and public investors may provide cash or an in–kind contribution or a combination of those for the implementation of an urban development project. An in–kind contribution shall be taken into account at its market value, as certified by an independent qualified expert or duly authorised official body.
(8) The urban development measures shall fulfil the following conditions:
(a) urban development fund managers shall be selected through an open, transparent and non–discriminatory call in accordance with the applicable Union and national laws. In particular, there shall be no discrimination between urban development fund managers on the basis of their place of establishment or incorporation in any Member State. Urban development fund managers may be required to fulfil predefined criteria objectively justified by the nature of the investments;
(b) the independent private investors shall be selected through an open, transparent and non–discriminatory call in accordance with applicable Union and national laws aimed at establishing the appropriate risk–reward sharing arrangements whereby, for investments other than guarantees, asymmetric profit–sharing shall be given preference over downside protection. If the private investors are not selected by such a call, the fair rate of return to the private investors shall be established by an independent expert selected via an open, transparent and non–discriminatory call;
(c) in the case of asymmetric loss–sharing between public and private investors, the first loss assumed by the public investor shall be capped at 25 % of the total investment;
(d) in the case of guarantees to private investors in urban development projects, the guarantee rate shall be limited to 80 % and total losses assumed by a Member State shall be capped at 25 % of the underlying guaranteed portfolio;
(e) the investors shall be allowed to be represented in the governance bodies of the urban develop-

ment fund, such as the supervisory board or the advisory committee;
(f) the urban development fund shall be established according to the applicable laws. The Member State shall provide for a due diligence process in order to ensure a commercially sound investment strategy for the purpose of implementing the urban development aid measure.
(9) Urban development funds shall be managed on a commercial basis and shall ensure profit–driven financing decisions. This is considered to be the case when the managers of the urban development fund fulfill the following conditions:
(a) the managers of urban development funds shall be obliged by law or contract to act with the diligence of a professional manager in good faith and avoiding conflicts of interest; best practices and regulatory supervision shall apply;
(b) the remuneration of the managers of urban development funds shall conform to market practices. This requirement is considered to be met where a manager is selected through an open, transparent and non–discriminatory call, based on objective criteria linked to experience, expertise and operational and financial capacity;
(c) the managers of urban development funds shall receive a remuneration linked to performance, or shall share part of the investment risks by co–investing own resources so as to ensure that their interests are permanently aligned with the interests of the public investors;
(d) the managers of urban development funds shall set out an investment strategy, criteria and the proposed timing of investments in urban development projects, establishing the *ex ante* financial viability and their expected impact on urban development;
(e) a clear and realistic exit strategy shall exist for each equity and quasi–equity investment.
(10) Where an urban development fund provides loans or guarantees to urban development projects, the following conditions shall be fulfilled:
(a) in the case of loans, the nominal amount of the loan is taken into account in calculating the maximum investment amount for the purposes of paragraph 3 of this Article;
(b) in the case of guarantees, the nominal amount of the underlying loan is taken into account in calculating the maximum investment amount for the purposes of paragraph 3 of this Article.
(11) The Member State may assign the implementation of the urban development aid measure to an entrusted entity.

Section 2. Aid to SMEs

Article 17. Investment aid to SMEs
(1) Investment aid to SMEs operating inside or outside the territory of the Union shall be compatible with the internal market within the meaning of Article 107(3) of the Treaty and shall be exempted from the notification requirement of Article 108(3) of the Treaty, provided that the conditions laid down in this Article and in Chapter I are fulfilled.
(2) The eligible costs shall be either or both of the following:
(a) the costs of investment in tangible and intangible assets;
(b) the estimated wage costs of employment directly created by the investment project, calculated over a period of two years.
(3) In order to be considered an eligible cost for the purposes of this Article, an investment shall consist of the following:
(a) an investment in tangible and/or intangible assets relating to the setting–up of a new establishment, the extension of an existing establishment, diversification of the output of an establishment into new additional products or a fundamental change in the overall production process of an existing establishment; or
(b) the acquisition of the assets belonging to an establishment, where the following conditions are fulfilled:
– the establishment has closed or would have closed had it not been purchased;
– the assets are purchased from third parties unrelated to the buyer;
– the transaction takes place under market conditions.
Where a member of the family of the original owner, or an employee, takes over a small enterprise, the condition that the assets shall be bought from third parties unrelated to the buyer shall be waived. The sole acquisition of the shares of an undertaking shall not constitute investment.
(4) Intangible assets shall fulfil all of the following conditions:
(a) they shall be used exclusively in the establishment receiving the aid;
(b) they shall be regarded as amortizable assets;
(c) they shall be purchased under market conditions from third parties unrelated to the buyer;
(d) they shall be included in the assets of the undertaking for at least three years;
(5) Employment directly created by an investment project shall fulfil the following conditions:

(a) it shall be created within three years of completion of the investment;
(b) there shall be a net increase in the number of employees in the establishment concerned, compared with the average over the previous 12 months;
(c) it shall be maintained during a minimum period of three years from the date the post was first filled.
(6) The aid intensity shall not exceed:
(a) 20 % of the eligible costs in the case of small enterprises;
(b) 10 % of the eligible costs in the case of medium–sized enterprises.

Article 18. Aid for consultancy in favour of SMEs
(1) Aid for consultancy in favour of SMEs shall be compatible with the internal market within the meaning of Article 107(3) of the Treaty and shall be exempted from the notification requirement of Article 108(3) of the Treaty, provided that the conditions laid down in this Article and in Chapter I are fulfilled.
(2) The aid intensity shall not exceed 50 % of the eligible costs.
(3) The eligible costs shall be the costs of consultancy services provided by external consultants.
(4) The services concerned shall not be a continuous or periodic activity nor relate to the undertaking's usual operating costs, such as routine tax consultancy services, regular legal services or advertising.

Article 19. Aid to SMEs for participation in fairs
(1) Aid to SMEs for participation in fairs shall be compatible with the internal market within the meaning of Article 107(3) of the Treaty and shall be exempted from the notification requirement of Article 108(3) of the Treaty, provided that the conditions laid down in this Article and in Chapter I are fulfilled.
(2) The eligible costs shall be the costs incurred for renting, setting up and running the stand for the participation of an undertaking in any particular fair or exhibition.
(3) The aid intensity shall not exceed 50 % of the eligible costs.

Article 20. Aid for cooperation costs incurred by SMEs participating in European Territorial Cooperation projects
(1) Aid for cooperation costs incurred by SMEs participating in the European Territorial Cooperation projects covered by Regulation (EC) No 1299/2013 of the European Parliament and of the Council shall be compatible with the internal market within the meaning of Article 107(3) of the Treaty and shall be exempted from the notification requirement of Article 108(3) of the Treaty, provided the conditions laid down in this Article and in Chapter I are fulfilled.
(2) The eligible costs shall be the following:
(a) costs for organisational cooperation including the cost of staff and offices to the extent that it is linked to the cooperation project;
(b) costs of advisory and support services linked to cooperation and delivered by external consultants and service providers;
(c) travel expenses, costs of equipment and investment expenditure directly related to the project and depreciation of tools and equipment used directly for the project.
(3) The services referred to in paragraph 2(b) shall not be a continuous or periodic activity nor relate to the undertaking's usual operating costs, such as routine tax consultancy services, regular legal services or routine advertising.
(4) The aid intensity shall not exceed 50 % of the eligible costs.

Section 3. Aid for Access to Finance for SMEs

Article 21. Risk finance aid
(1) Risk finance aid schemes in favour of SMEs shall be compatible with the internal market within the meaning of Article 107(3) of the Treaty and shall be exempted from the notification requirement of Article 108(3) of the Treaty, provided the conditions laid down in this Article and in Chapter I are fulfilled.
(2) At the level of financial intermediaries, risk finance aid to independent private investors may take one of the following forms:
(a) equity or quasi–equity, or financial endowment to provide risk finance investments directly or indirectly to eligible undertakings;
(b) loans to provide risk finance investments directly or indirectly to eligible undertakings;
(c) guarantees to cover losses from risk finance investments directly or indirectly to eligible undertakings.

(3) At the level of independent private investors, risk finance aid may take the forms mentioned in paragraph 2 of this Article, or be in the form of tax incentives to private investors who are natural persons providing risk finance directly or indirectly to eligible undertakings.
(4) At the level of eligible undertakings, risk finance aid may take the form of equity, quasi–equity investments, loans, guarantees, or a mix thereof.
(5) Eligible undertakings shall be undertakings which at the time of the initial risk finance investment are unlisted SMEs and fulfil at least one of the following conditions:
(a) they have not been operating in any market;
(b) they have been operating in any market for less than 7 years following their first commercial sale;
(c) they require an initial risk finance investment which, based on a business plan prepared in view of entering a new product or geographical market, is higher than 50 % of their average annual turnover in the preceding 5 years.
(6) The risk finance aid may also cover follow–on investments made in eligible undertakings, including after the 7 year period mentioned in paragraph 5(b), if the following cumulative conditions are fulfilled:
(a) the total amount of risk finance mentioned in paragraph 9 is not exceeded;
(b) the possibility of follow–on investments was foreseen in the original business plan;
(c) the undertaking receiving follow–on investments has not become linked, within the meaning of Article 3(3) of Annex I with another undertaking other than the financial intermediary or the independent private investor providing risk finance under the measure, unless the new entity fulfils the conditions of the SME definition.
(7) For equity and quasi–equity investments in eligible undertakings, a risk finance measure may provide support for replacement capital only if the latter is combined with new capital representing at least 50 % of each investment round into the eligible undertakings.
(8) For equity and quasi–equity investments as referred to in paragraph 2(a), no more than 30 % of the financial intermediary's aggregate capital contributions and uncalled committed capital may be used for liquidity management purposes.
(9) The total amount of risk finance referred to in paragraph 4 shall not exceed EUR 15 million per eligible undertaking under any risk finance measure.
(10) For risk finance measures providing equity, quasi–equity or loan investments to eligible undertakings, the risk finance measure shall leverage additional finance from independent private investors at the level of the financial intermediaries or the eligible undertakings, so as to achieve an aggregate private participation rate reaching the following minimum thresholds:
(a) 10 % of the risk finance provided to the eligible undertakings prior to their first commercial sale on any market;
(b) 40 % of the risk finance provided to the eligible undertakings referred to in paragraph 5(b) of this Article;
(c) 60 % of the risk finance for investment provided to eligible undertakings mentioned in paragraph 5(c) and for follow–on investments in eligible undertakings after the 7–year period mentioned in paragraph 5(b).
(11) Where a risk finance measure is implemented through a financial intermediary targeting eligible undertakings at different development stages as referred to in paragraph 10 and does not provide for private capital participation at the level of the eligible undertakings the financial intermediary shall achieve a private participation rate that represents at least the weighted average based on the volume of the individual investments in the underlying portfolio and resulting from the application of the minimum participation rates to such investments as referred to in paragraph 10.
(12) A risk finance measure shall not discriminate between financial intermediaries on the basis of their place of establishment or incorporation in any Member State. Financial intermediaries may be required to fulfil predefined criteria objectively justified by the nature of the investments.
(13) A risk finance measure shall fulfil the following conditions:
(a) it shall be implemented via one or more financial intermediaries, except for tax incentives to private investors in respect of their direct investments into eligible undertakings;
(b) financial intermediaries, as well as investors or fund managers shall be selected through an open, transparent and non–discriminatory call which is made in accordance with applicable Union and national laws and aimed at establishing appropriate risk–reward sharing arrangements whereby, for investments other than guarantees, asymmetric profit sharing shall be given preference over downside protection;
(c) in the case of asymmetric loss–sharing between public and private investors, the first loss assumed by the public investor shall be capped at 25 % of the total investment;
(d) in the case of guarantees falling under point 2(c), the guarantee rate shall be limited to 80 %

and total losses assumed by a Member State shall be capped at a maximum of 25 % of the underlying guaranteed portfolio. Only guarantees covering expected losses of the underlying guaranteed portfolio can be provided for free. If a guarantee also comprises coverage of unexpected losses, the financial intermediary shall pay, for the part of the guarantee covering unexpected losses, a market–conform guarantee premium.

(14) Risk finance measures shall ensure profit–driven financing decisions. This is considered to be the case where all of the following conditions are fulfilled:

(a) financial intermediaries shall be established according to the applicable laws.

(b) the Member State, or the entity entrusted with the implementation of the measure, shall provide for a due diligence process in order to ensure a commercially sound investment strategy for the purpose of implementing the risk finance measure, including an appropriate risk diversification policy aimed at achieving economic viability and efficient scale in terms of size and territorial scope of the relevant portfolio of investments;

(c) risk finance provided to the eligible undertakings shall be based on a viable business plan, containing details of product, sales and profitability development, establishing ex–ante financial viability;

(d) a clear and realistic exit strategy shall exist for each equity and quasi–equity investment.

(15) Financial intermediaries shall be managed on a commercial basis. This requirement is considered to be fulfilled where the financial intermediary and, depending on the type of risk finance measure, the fund manager, fulfil the following conditions:

(a) they shall be obliged by law or contract to act with the diligence of a professional manager in good faith and avoiding conflicts of interest; best practices and regulatory supervision shall apply;

(b) their remuneration shall conform to market practices. This requirement is presumed to be met where the manager or the financial intermediary is selected through an open, transparent and non–discriminatory selection call, based on objective criteria linked to experience, expertise and operational and financial capacity;

(c) they shall receive a remuneration linked to performance, or shall share part of the investment risks by co–investing own resources so as to ensure that their interests are permanently aligned with the interests of the public investor;

(d) they shall set out an investment strategy, criteria and the proposed timing of investments;

(e) investors shall be allowed to be represented in the governance bodies of the investment fund, such as the supervisory board or the advisory committee.

(16) A risk finance measure providing guarantees or loans to eligible undertakings, shall fulfil the following conditions:

(a) as a result of the measure, the financial intermediary shall undertake investments that would not have been carried out or would have been carried out in a restricted or different manner without the aid. The financial intermediary shall be able to demonstrate that it operates a mechanism that ensures that all the advantages are passed on to the largest extent to the final beneficiaries in the form of higher volumes of financing, riskier portfolios, lower collateral requirements, lower guarantee premiums or lower interest rates;

(b) in the case of loans, the nominal amount of the loan is taken into account in calculating the maximum investment amount for the purposes of paragraph 9;

(c) in the case of guarantees, the nominal amount of the underlying loan is taken into account in calculating the maximum investment amount for the purposes of paragraph 9. The guarantee shall not exceed 80 % of the underlying loan.

(17) A Member State may assign the implementation of a risk finance measure to an entrusted entity.

(18) Risk finance aid for SMEs that do not fulfil the conditions laid down in paragraph 5 shall be compatible with the internal market within the meaning of Article 107(3) of the Treaty and shall be exempted from the notification requirement of Article 108(3) of the Treaty, provided that

(a) at the level of the SMEs, the aid fulfils the conditions laid down in Regulation (EU) No 1407/2013; and

(b) all the conditions laid down in the present Article, with the exception of those set out in paragraphs 5, 6, 9, 10, and 11, are fulfilled; and

(c) for risk finance measures providing equity, quasi–equity or loan investments to eligible undertakings, the measure shall leverage additional financing from independent private investors at the level of the financial intermediaries or the SMEs, so as to achieve an aggregate private participation rate reaching at least 60 % of the risk finance provided to the SMEs.

Article 22. Aid for start–ups

(1) Start–up aid schemes shall be compatible with the internal market within the meaning of Article 107(3) of the Treaty and shall be exempted from the notification requirement of Article 108(3) of the

Treaty, provided the conditions laid down in this Article and in Chapter I are fulfilled.

(2) Eligible undertakings shall be unlisted small enterprises up to five years following their registration, which have not yet distributed profits and have not been formed through a merger. For eligible undertakings that are not subject to registration the five years eligibility period may be considered to start from the moment when the enterprise either starts its economic activity or is liable to tax for its economic activity.

(3) Start–up aid shall take the form of:

(a) loans with interest rates which are not conform with market conditions, with a duration of 10 years and up to a maximum nominal amount of EUR 1 million, or EUR 1,5 million for undertakings established in assisted areas fulfilling the conditions of Article 107(3)(c) of the Treaty, or EUR 2 million for undertakings established in assisted areas fulfilling the conditions of Article 107(3)(a) of the Treaty. For loans with a duration comprised between 5 and 10 years the maximum amounts may be adjusted by multiplying the amounts above by the ratio between 10 years and the actual duration of the loan. For loans with a duration of less than 5 years, the maximum amount shall be the same as for loans with a duration of 5 years;

(b) guarantees with premiums which are not conform with market conditions, with a duration of 10 years and up to maximum EUR 1,5 million of amount guaranteed, or EUR 2,25 million for undertakings established in assisted areas fulfilling the conditions of Article 107(3)(c) of the Treaty, or EUR 3 million for undertakings established in assisted areas fulfilling the conditions of Article 107(3)(a) of the Treaty. For guarantees with a duration comprised between 5 and 10 years the maximum amount guaranteed amounts may be adjusted by multiplying the amounts above by the ratio between 10 years and the actual duration of the guarantee. For guarantees with a duration of less than 5 years, the maximum amount guaranteed shall be the same as for guarantees with a duration of 5 years. The guarantee shall not exceed 80 % of the underlying loan.

(c) grants, including equity or quasi equity investment, interests rate and guarantee premium reductions up to EUR 0,4 million gross grant equivalent or EUR 0,6 million for undertakings established in assisted areas fulfilling the conditions of Article 107(3)(c) of the Treaty, or EUR 0,8 million for undertakings established in assisted areas fulfilling the conditions of Article 107(3)(a) of the Treaty.

(4) A beneficiary can receive support through a mix of the aid instruments referred to in paragraph 3 of this Article, provided that the proportion of the amount granted through one aid instrument, calculated on the basis of the maximum aid amount allowed for that instrument, is taken into account in order to determine the residual proportion of the maximum aid amount allowed for the other instruments forming part of such a mixed instrument.

(5) For small and innovative enterprises, the maximum amounts set out in paragraph 3 may be doubled.

Article 23. Aid to Alternative Trading Platforms Specialised in SMEs

(1) Aid in favour of alternative trading platforms specialised in SMEs shall be compatible with the internal market within the meaning of Article 107(3) of the Treaty and shall be exempted from the notification requirement of Article 108(3) of the Treaty, provided the conditions laid down in this Article and in Chapter I are fulfilled.

(2) Where the platform operator is a small enterprise, the aid measure may take the form of start–up aid to the platform operator, in which case the conditions laid down in Article 22 shall apply.

The aid measure may take the form of tax incentives to independent private investors that are natural persons in respect of their risk finance investments made through an alternative trading platform into undertakings eligible under the conditions laid down in Article 21.

Article 24. Aid for scouting costs

(1) Aid for scouting costs shall be compatible with the internal market within the meaning of Article 107(3) of the Treaty and shall be exempted from the notification requirement of Article 108(3) of the Treaty, provided the conditions laid down in this Article and in Chapter I are fulfilled.

(2) The eligible costs shall be the costs for initial screening and formal due diligence undertaken by managers of financial intermediaries or investors to identify eligible undertakings pursuant to Articles 21 and 22.

(3) The aid intensity shall not exceed 50 % of the eligible costs.

Section 4. Aid for Research and Development and Innovation

Article 25. Aid for research and development projects

(1) Aid for research and development projects shall be compatible with the internal market within the meaning of Article 107(3) of the Treaty and shall be exempted from the notification requirement of Article 108(3) of the Treaty provided that the conditions laid down in this Article and in Chapter I are fulfilled.

(2) The aided part of the research and development project shall completely fall within one or more of the following categories:
(a) fundamental research;
(b) industrial research;
(c) experimental development;
(d) feasibility studies.
(3) The eligible costs of research and development projects shall be allocated to a specific category of research and development and shall be the following:
(a) personnel costs: researchers, technicians and other supporting staff to the extent employed on the project;
(b) costs of instruments and equipment to the extent and for the period used for the project. Where such instruments and equipment are not used for their full life for the project, only the depreciation costs corresponding to the life of the project, as calculated on the basis of generally accepted accounting principles are considered as eligible.
(c) Costs for of buildings and land, to the extent and for the duration period used for the project. With regard to buildings, only the depreciation costs corresponding to the life of the project, as calculated on the basis of generally accepted accounting principles are considered as eligible. For land, costs of commercial transfer or actually incurred capital costs are eligible.
(d) costs of contractual research, knowledge and patents bought or licensed from outside sources at arm's length conditions, as well as costs of consultancy and equivalent services used exclusively for the project;
(e) additional overheads and other operating expenses, including costs of materials, supplies and similar products, incurred directly as a result of the project;
(4) The eligible costs for feasibility studies shall be the costs of the study.
(5) The aid intensity for each beneficiary shall not exceed:
(a) 100 % of the eligible costs for fundamental research;
(b) 50 % of the eligible costs for industrial research;
(c) 25 % of the eligible costs for experimental development;
(d) 50 % of the eligible costs for feasibility studies.
(6) The aid intensities for industrial research and experimental development may be increased up to a maximum aid intensity of 80 % of the eligible costs as follows:
(a) by 10 percentage points for medium–sized enterprises and by 20 percentage points for small enterprises;
(b) by 15 percentage points if one of the following conditions is fulfilled:
(i) the project involves effective collaboration:
– between undertakings among which at least one is an SME, or is carried out in at least two Member States, or in a Member State and in a Contracting Party of the EEA Agreement, and no single undertaking bears more than 70 % of the eligible costs, or
– between an undertaking and one or more research and knowledge–dissemination organisations, where the latter bear at least 10 % of the eligible costs and have the right to publish their own research results;
(ii) the results of the project are widely disseminated through conferences, publication, open access repositories, or free or open source software.
(7) The aid intensities for feasibility studies may be increased by 10 percentage points for medium–sized enterprises and by 20 percentage points for small enterprises;

Article 26. Investment aid for research infrastructures

(1) Aid for the construction or upgrade of research infrastructures that perform economic activities shall be compatible with the internal market within the meaning of Article 107(3) of the Treaty and shall be exempted from the notification requirement of Article 108(3) of the Treaty, provided that the conditions laid down in this Article and in Chapter I are fulfilled.
(2) Where a research infrastructure pursues both economic and non–economic activities, the financing, costs and revenues of each type of activity shall be accounted for separately on the basis of consistently applied and objectively justifiable cost accounting principles.
(3) The price charged for the operation or use of the infrastructure shall correspond to a market price.
(4) Access to the infrastructure shall be open to several users and be granted on a transparent and non–discriminatory basis. Undertakings which have financed at least 10 % of the investment costs of the infrastructure may be granted preferential access under more favourable conditions. In order to avoid overcompensation, such access shall be proportional to the undertaking's contribution to the investment costs and these conditions shall be made publicly available.

(5) The eligible costs shall be the investment costs in intangible and tangible assets.
(6) The aid intensity shall not exceed 50 % of the eligible costs.
(7) Where a research infrastructure receives public funding for both economic and non–economic activities, Member States shall put in place a monitoring and claw–back mechanism in order to ensure that the applicable aid intensity is not exceeded as a result of an increase in the share of economic activities compared to the situation envisaged at the time of awarding the aid.

Article 27. Aid for innovation clusters
(1) Aid for innovation clusters shall be compatible with the internal market within the meaning of Article 107(3) of the Treaty and shall be exempted from the notification requirement of Article 108(3) of the Treaty, provided that the conditions laid down in this Article and in Chapter I are fulfilled.
(2) Aid for innovation clusters shall be granted exclusively to the legal entity operating the innovation cluster (cluster organisation).
(3) Access to the cluster's premises, facilities and activities shall be open to several users and be granted on a transparent and non–discriminatory basis. Undertakings which have financed at least 10 % of the investment costs of the innovation cluster may be granted preferential access under more favourable conditions. In order to avoid overcompensation, such access shall be proportional to the undertaking's contribution to the investment costs and these conditions shall be made publicly available.
(4) The fees charged for using the cluster's facilities and for participating in the cluster's activities shall correspond to the market price or reflect their costs.
(5) Investment aid may be granted for the construction or upgrade of innovation clusters. The eligible costs shall be the investment costs in intangible and tangible assets.
(6) The aid intensity of investment aid for innovation clusters shall not exceed 50 % of the eligible costs. The aid intensity may be increased by 15 percentage points for innovation clusters located in assisted areas fulfilling the conditions of Article 107(3)(a) of the Treaty and by 5 percentage points for innovation clusters located in assisted areas fulfilling the conditions of Article 107(3)(c) of the Treaty
(7) Operating aid may be granted for the operation of innovation clusters. It shall not exceed 10 years.
(8) The eligible costs of operating aid for innovation clusters shall be the personnel and administrative costs (including overhead costs) relating to:
(a) animation of the cluster to facilitate collaboration, information sharing and the provision or channelling of specialised and customised business support services;
(b) marketing of the cluster to increase participation of new undertakings or organisations and to increase visibility;
(c) management of the cluster's facilities; organisation of training programmes, workshops and conferences to support knowledge sharing and networking and transnational cooperation.
(9) The aid intensity of operating aid shall not exceed 50 % of the total eligible costs during the period over which the aid is granted.

Article 28. Innovation aid for SMEs
(1) Innovation aid for SMEs shall be compatible with the internal market within the meaning of Article 107(3) of the Treaty and shall be exempted from the notification requirement of Article 108(3) of the Treaty, provided the conditions laid down in this Article and in Chapter I are fulfilled:
(2) The eligible costs shall be the following:
(a) costs for obtaining, validating and defending patents and other intangible assets;
(b) costs for secondment of highly qualified personnel from a research and knowledge–dissemination organization or a large enterprise, working on research, development and innovation activities in a newly created function within the beneficiary and not replacing other personnel;
(c) costs for innovation advisory and support services;
(3) The aid intensity shall not exceed 50 % of the eligible costs.
(4) In the particular case of aid for innovation advisory and support services the aid intensity can be increased up to 100 % of the eligible costs provided that the total amount of aid for innovation advisory and support services does not exceed EUR 200 000 per undertaking within any three year period.

Article 29. Aid for process and organisational innovation
(1) Aid for process and organisational innovation shall be compatible with the internal market within the meaning of Article 107(3) of the Treaty and shall be exempted from the notification requirement of Article 108(3) of the Treaty, provided the conditions laid down in this Article and in Chapter I are fulfilled.

(2) Aid to large undertakings shall only be compatible if they effectively collaborate with SMEs in the aided activity and the collaborating SMEs incur at least 30 % of the total eligible costs.
(3) The eligible costs shall be the following:
(a) personnel costs;
(b) costs of instruments, equipment, buildings and land to the extent and for the period used for the project;
(c) costs of contractual research, knowledge and patents bought or licensed from outside sources at arm's length conditions;
(d) additional overheads and other operating costs, including costs of materials, supplies and similar products, incurred directly as a result of the project.
(4) The aid intensity shall not exceed 15 % of the eligible costs for large undertakings and 50 % of the eligible costs for SMEs.

Article 30. Aid for research and development in the fishery and aquaculture sector
(1) Aid for research and development in the fishery and aquaculture sector shall be compatible with the internal market within the meaning of Article 107(3) of the Treaty and shall be exempted from the notification requirement of Article 108(3) of the Treaty, provided that the conditions laid down in this Article and in Chapter I are fulfilled.
(2) The aided project shall be of interest to all undertakings in the particular sector or sub–sector concerned.
(3) Prior to the date of the start of the aided project the following information shall be published on the internet:
(a) that the aided project will be carried out;
(b) the goals of the aided project;
(c) the approximate date for the publication of the results expected from the aided project and its place of publication on the internet;
(d) a reference that the results of the aided project will be available to all undertakings active in the particular sector or sub–sector concerned at no cost.
(4) The results of the aided project shall be made available on internet from the end date of the aided project or the date on which any information concerning those results is given to members of any particular organisation, whatever comes first. The results shall remain available on internet for a period of at least 5 years starting from the end date of the aided project.
(5) Aid shall be granted directly to the research and knowledge–dissemination organisation and shall not involve the direct granting of non–research related aid to an undertaking producing, processing or marketing fishery or aquaculture products.
(6) The eligible costs shall be those provided in Article 25(3).
(7) The aid intensity shall not exceed 100 % of the eligible costs.

Section 5. Training Aid

Article 31. Training aid
(1) Training aid shall be compatible with the internal market within the meaning of Article 107(3) of the Treaty and shall be exempted from the notification requirement of Article 108(3) of the Treaty, provided that the conditions laid down in this Article and in Chapter I are fulfilled.
(2) Aid shall not be granted for training which undertakings carry out to comply with national mandatory standards on training.
(3) The eligible costs shall be the following:
(a) trainers' personnel costs, for the hours during which the trainers participate in the training;
(b) trainers' and trainees' operating costs directly relating to the training project such as travel expenses, materials and supplies directly related to the project, depreciation of tools and equipment, to the extent that they are used exclusively for the training project. Accommodation costs are excluded except for the minimum necessary accommodation costs for trainees' who are workers with disabilities;
(c) costs of advisory services linked to the training project;
(d) trainees' personnel costs and general indirect costs (administrative costs, rent, overheads) for the hours during which the trainees participate in the training.
(4) The aid intensity shall not exceed 50 % of the eligible costs. It may be increased, up to a maximum aid intensity of 70 % of the eligible costs, as follows:
(a) by 10 percentage points if the training is given to workers with disabilities or disadvantaged workers;
(b) by 10 percentage points if the aid is granted to medium–sized enterprises and by 20 percentage

points if the aid is granted to small enterprises.
(5) Where the aid is granted in the maritime transport sector, the aid intensity may be increased to 100 % of the eligible costs provided that the following conditions are met:
(a) the trainees are not active members of the crew but are supernumerary on board; and
(b) the training is carried out on board of ships entered in Union registers.

Section 6. Aid for Disadvantaged Workers fnd for Workers with Disabilities

Article 32. Aid for the recruitment of disadvantaged workers in the form of wage subsidies
(1) Aid schemes for the recruitment of disadvantaged workers shall be compatible with the internal market within the meaning of Article 107(3) of the Treaty and shall be exempted from the notification requirement of Article 108(3) of the Treaty, provided the conditions laid down in this Article and in Chapter I are fulfilled.
(2) Eligible costs shall be the wage costs over a maximum period of 12 months following recruitment of a disadvantaged worker. Where the worker concerned is a severely disadvantaged worker, eligible costs shall be the wage costs over a maximum period of 24 months following recruitment.
(3) Where the recruitment does not represent a net increase, compared with the average over the previous 12 months, in the number of employees in the undertaking concerned, the post or posts shall have fallen vacant following voluntary departure, disability, retirement on grounds of age, voluntary reduction of working time or lawful dismissal for misconduct and not as a result of redundancy.
(4) Except in the case of lawful dismissal for misconduct, the disadvantaged workers shall be entitled to continuous employment for a minimum period consistent with the national legislation concerned or any collective agreements governing employment contracts.
(5) If the period of employment is shorter than 12 months, or 24 months in the case of severely disadvantaged workers, the aid shall be reduced pro rata accordingly.
(6) The aid intensity shall not exceed 50 % of the eligible costs.

Article 33. Aid for the employment of workers with disabilities in the form of wage subsidies
(1) Aid for the employment of workers with disabilities shall be compatible with the internal market within the meaning of Article 107(3) of the Treaty and shall be exempted from the notification requirement of Article 108(3) of the Treaty, provided the conditions laid down in this Article and in Chapter I are fulfilled.
(2) Eligible costs shall be the wage costs over any given period during which the worker with disabilities is employed.
(3) Where the recruitment does not represent a net increase, compared with the average over the previous 12 months, in the number of employees in the undertaking concerned, the post or posts shall have fallen vacant following voluntary departure, disabilities, retirement on grounds of age, voluntary reduction of working time or lawful dismissal for misconduct and not as a result of redundancy.
(4) Except in the case of lawful dismissal for misconduct, the workers with disabilities shall be entitled to continuous employment for a minimum period consistent with the national legislation concerned or any collective agreements which are legally binding for the undertaking and governing employment contracts.
(5) The aid intensity shall not exceed 75 % of the eligible costs.

Article 34. Aid for compensating the additional costs of employing workers with disabilities
(1) Aid for compensating the additional costs of employing workers with disabilities shall be compatible with the internal market within the meaning of Article 107(3) of the Treaty and shall be exempted from the notification requirement of Article 108(3) of the Treaty, provided the conditions laid down in this Article and in Chapter I are fulfilled.
(2) The eligible costs shall be the following:
(a) costs of adapting the premises;
(b) costs of employing staff solely for time spent on the assistance of the workers with disabilities and of training such staff to assist workers with disabilities;
(c) costs of adapting or acquiring equipment, or acquiring and validating software for use by workers with disabilities, including adapted or assistive technology facilities, which are additional to those which the beneficiary would have incurred had it employed workers who are not workers with disabilities;
(d) costs directly linked to transport of workers with disabilities to the working place and for work related activities;
(e) wage costs for the hours spent by a worker with disabilities on rehabilitation;
(f) where the beneficiary provides sheltered employment, the costs of constructing, installing or modernising the production units of the undertaking concerned, and any costs of administration and

transport, provided that such costs result directly from the employment of workers with disabilities.
(3) The aid intensity shall not exceed 100 % of the eligible costs.

Article 35. Aid for compensating the costs of assistance provided to disadvantaged workers

(1) Aid for compensating the costs of assistance provided to disadvantaged workers shall be compatible with the internal market within the meaning of Article 107(3) of the Treaty and shall be exempt from the notification requirement of Article 108(3) of the Treaty, provided the conditions laid down in this Article and in Chapter I are fulfilled.
(2) The eligible costs shall be the costs of:
(a) employing staff solely for time spent on the assistance of the disadvantaged workers over a maximum period of 12 months following recruitment of a disadvantaged worker or over a maximum period of 24 months following recruitment of a severely disadvantaged worker;
(b) of training such staff to assist disadvantaged workers.
(3) The assistance provided shall consist of measures to support the disadvantaged worker's autonomy and adaptation to the work environment, in accompanying the worker in social and administrative procedures, facilitation of communication with the entrepreneur and managing conflicts.
(4) The aid intensity shall not exceed 50 % of the eligible costs.

Section 7. Aid for Environmental Protection

Article 36. Investment aid enabling undertakings to go beyond Union standards for environmental protection or to increase the level of environmental protection in the absence of Union standards

(1) Investment aid enabling undertakings to go beyond Union standards for environmental protection or to increase the level of environmental protection in the absence of Union standards shall be compatible with the internal market within the meaning of Article 107(3) of the Treaty and shall be exempted from the notification requirement of Article 108(3) of the Treaty, provided that the conditions laid down in this Article and in Chapter I are fulfilled.
(2) The investment shall fulfil one of the following conditions:
(a) it shall enable the beneficiary to increase the level of environmental protection resulting from its activities by going beyond the applicable Union standards, irrespective of the presence of mandatory national standards that are more stringent than the Union standards;
(b) it shall enable the beneficiary to increase the level of environmental protection resulting from its activities in the absence of Union standards.
(3) Aid shall not be granted where investments are undertaken to ensure that undertakings comply with Union standards already adopted and not yet in force.
(4) By way of derogation from paragraph 3, aid may be granted for
(a) the acquisition of new transport vehicles for road, railway, inland waterway and maritime transport complying with adopted Union standards, provided that the acquisition occurs before those standards enter into force and that, once mandatory, they do not apply to vehicles already purchased before that date.
(b) retrofitting of existing transport vehicles for road, railway, inland waterway and maritime transport, provided that the Union standards were not yet in force at the date of entry into operation of those vehicles and that, once mandatory, they do not apply retroactively to those vehicles.
(5) The eligible costs shall be the extra investment costs necessary to go beyond the applicable Union standards or to increase the level of environmental protection in the absence of Union standards. They shall be determined as follows:
(a) where the costs of investing in environmental protection can be identified in the total investment cost as a separate investment, this environmental protection–related cost shall constitute the eligible costs;
(b) in all other cases, the costs of investing in environmental protection are identified by reference to a similar, less environmentally friendly investment that would have been credibly carried out without the aid. The difference between the costs of both investments identifies the environmental protection–related cost and constitutes the eligible costs.
The costs not directly linked to the achievement of a higher level of environmental protection shall not be eligible.
(6) The aid intensity shall not exceed 40 % of the eligible costs.
(7) The aid intensity may be increased by 10 percentage points for aid granted to medium sized undertakings and by 20 percentage points for aid granted to small undertakings.
(8) The aid intensity may be increased by 15 percentage points for investments located in assisted areas fulfilling the conditions of Article 107(3)(a) of the Treaty and by 5 percentage points for investments located in assisted areas fulfilling the conditions of Article 107(3)(c) of the Treaty.

PART III   EUROPEAN UNION

Article 37. Investment aid for early adaptation to future Union standards

(1) Aid encouraging undertakings to comply with new Union standards which increase the level of environmental protection and are not yet in force shall be compatible with the internal market within the meaning of Article 107(3) of the Treaty and shall be exempted from the notification requirement of Article 108(3) of the Treaty, provided that the conditions laid down in this Article and in Chapter I are fulfilled.

(2) The Union standards shall have been adopted and the investment shall be implemented and finalised at least one year before the date of entry into force of the standard concerned.

(3) The eligible costs shall be the extra investment costs necessary to go beyond the applicable Union standards. They shall be determined as follows:

(a) where the costs of investing in environmental protection can be identified in the total investment cost as a separate investment, this environmental protection–related cost shall constitute the eligible costs;

(b) in all other cases, the costs of investing in environmental protection are identified by reference to a similar, less environmentally friendly investment that would have been credibly carried out without the aid. The difference between the costs of both investments identifies the environmental protection–related cost and constitutes the eligible costs.

The costs not directly linked to the achievement of a higher level of environmental protection shall not be eligible.

(4) The aid intensity shall not exceed the following:

(a) 20 % of the eligible costs for small undertakings, 15 % of the eligible costs for medium–sized undertakings and 10 % of the eligible costs for large undertakings if the implementation and finalisation of the investment take place more than three years before the date of entry into force of the new Union standard;

(b) 15 % of the eligible costs for small undertakings, 10 % of the eligible costs for medium–sized undertakings and 5 % of the eligible costs for large undertakings if the implementation and finalisation of the investment take place between one and three years before the date of entry into force of the new Union standard.

(5) The aid intensity may be increased by 15 percentage points for investments located in assisted areas fulfilling the conditions of Article 107(3)(a) of the Treaty and by 5 percentage points for investments located in assisted areas fulfilling the conditions of Article 107(3)(c) of the Treaty.

Article 38. Investment aid for energy efficiency measures

(1) Investment aid enabling undertakings to achieve energy efficiency shall be compatible with the internal market within the meaning of Article 107(3) of the Treaty and shall be exempted from the notification requirement of Article 108(3) of the Treaty, provided that the conditions laid down in this Article and in Chapter I are fulfilled.

(2) Aid shall not be granted under this Article where improvements are undertaken to ensure that undertakings comply with Union standards already adopted, even if they are not yet in force.

(3) The eligible costs shall be the extra investment costs necessary to achieve the higher level of energy efficiency. They shall be determined as follows:

(a) where the costs of investing in energy efficiency can be identified in the total investment cost as a separate investment, this energy efficiency–related cost shall constitute the eligible costs;

(b) in all other cases, the costs of investing in energy efficiency are identified by reference to a similar, less energy efficient investment that would have been credibly carried out without the aid. The difference between the costs of both investments identifies the energy efficiency–related cost and constitutes the eligible costs.

The costs not directly linked to the achievement of a higher level of energy efficiency shall not be eligible.

(4) The aid intensity shall not exceed 30 % of the eligible costs.

(5) The aid intensity may be increased by 20 percentage points for aid granted to small undertakings and by 10 percentage points for aid granted to medium–sized undertakings.

(6) The aid intensity may be increased by 15 percentage points for investments located in assisted areas fulfilling the conditions of Article 107(3)(a) of the Treaty and by 5 percentage points for investments located in assisted areas fulfilling the conditions of Article 107(3)(c) of the Treaty.

Article 39. Investment aid for energy efficiency projects in buildings

(1) Investment aid for energy efficiency projects in buildings shall be compatible with the internal market within the meaning of Article 107(3) of the Treaty and shall be exempted from the notification requirement of Article 108(3) of the Treaty, provided that the conditions laid down in this Article and in Chapter I are fulfilled.

(2) Eligible for aid under the present Article are energy efficiency projects relating to buildings.
(3) The eligible costs shall be the overall costs of the energy efficiency project.
(4) The aid shall be granted in the form of an endowment, equity, a guarantee or loan to an energy efficiency fund or other financial intermediary, which shall fully pass it on to the final beneficiaries being the building owners or tenants.
(5) The aid granted by the energy efficiency fund or other financial intermediary to the eligible energy efficiency projects may take the form of loans or guarantees. The nominal value of the loan or the amount guaranteed shall not exceed EUR 10 million per project at the level of the final beneficiaries. The guarantee should not exceed 80 % of the underlying loan.
(6) The repayment by the building owners to the energy efficiency fund or other financial intermediary shall not be less than the nominal value of the loan.
(7) The energy efficiency aid shall leverage additional investment from private investors reaching at minimum 30 % of the total financing provided to an energy efficiency project. When the aid is provided by an energy efficiency fund, the leverage of private investment can be done at the level of the energy efficiency fund and/or at the level of the energy efficiency projects, so as to achieve an aggregate minimum 30 % of the total financing provided to an energy efficiency project.
(8) Member States can set up energy efficiency funds and/or can use financial intermediaries when providing energy efficiency aid. The following conditions must then be fulfilled:
(a) Financial intermediary managers, as well as energy efficiency fund managers shall be selected through an open, transparent and non–discriminatory call in accordance with applicable Union and national laws. In particular, there shall be no discrimination on the basis of their place of establishment or incorporation in any Member State. Financial intermediaries and energy efficiency fund managers may be required to fulfil predefined criteria objectively justified by the nature of the investments;
(b) The independent private investors shall be selected through an open, transparent and non–discriminatory call in accordance with applicable Union and national laws aimed at establishing the appropriate risk–reward sharing arrangements whereby, for investments other than guarantees, asymmetric profit–sharing shall be given preference over downside protection. If the private investors are not selected by such a call, the fair rate of return to the private investors shall be established by an independent expert selected via an open, transparent and non–discriminatory call;
(c) In the case of asymmetric loss–sharing between public and private investors, the first loss assumed by the public investor shall be capped at 25 % of the total investment;
(d) In the case of guarantees, the guarantee rate shall be limited to 80 % and total losses assumed by a Member State shall be capped at 25 % of the underlying guaranteed portfolio. Only guarantees covering the expected losses of the underlying guaranteed portfolio can be provided for free. If a guarantee also comprises coverage of unexpected losses, the financial intermediary shall pay, for the part of the guarantee covering unexpected losses, a market–conform guarantee premium;
(e) The investors shall be allowed to be represented in the governance bodies of the energy efficiency fund or financial intermediary, such as the supervisory board or the advisory committee;
(f) The energy efficiency fund or financial intermediary shall be established according to the applicable laws and the Member State shall provide for a due diligence process in order to ensure a commercially sound investment strategy for the purpose of implementing the energy efficiency aid measure.
(9) Financial intermediaries, including energy efficiency funds shall be managed on a commercial basis and shall ensure profit–driven financing decisions. This is considered to be the case when the financial intermediary and, as the case may be, the managers of the energy efficiency fund fulfil the following conditions:
(a) they are obliged by law or contract to act with the diligence of a professional manager in good faith and avoiding conflicts of interest; best practices and regulatory supervision shall apply;
(b) their remuneration conforms with market practices. This requirement is considered to be met where the manager is selected through an open, transparent and non–discriminatory call, based on objective criteria linked to experience, expertise and operational and financial capacity;
(c) they shall receive a remuneration linked to performance, or shall share part of the investment risks by co–investing own resources so as to ensure that their interests are permanently aligned with the interests of the public investor;
(d) they shall set out an investment strategy, criteria and the proposed timing of investments in energy efficiency projects, establishing the ex–ante financial viability and their expected impact on energy efficiency.
(e) a clear and realistic exit strategy shall exist for the public funds invested in the energy efficiency fund or granted to the financial intermediary, allowing the market to finance energy efficiency projects when the market is ready to do so.

(10) Energy efficiency improvements undertaken to ensure that the beneficiary complies with Union standards which have already been adopted shall not be exempted from the notification requirement under this Article.

Article 40. Investment aid for high–efficiency cogeneration
(1) Investment aid for high–efficiency cogeneration shall be compatible with the internal market within the meaning of Article 107(3) of the Treaty and shall be exempted from the notification requirement of Article 108(3) of the Treaty, provided that the conditions laid down in this Article and in Chapter I are fulfilled.
(2) The investment aid shall be granted in respect of newly installed or refurbished capacities only.
(3) The new cogeneration unit shall provide overall primary energy savings compared to separate production of heat and electricity as provided for by Directive 2012/27/EU of the European Parliament and of the Council of 25 October 2012 on energy efficiency, amending Directives 2009/125/EC and 2010/30/EU and repealing Directives 2004/8/EC and 2006/32/EC. The improvement of an existing cogeneration unit or conversion of an existing power generation unit into a cogeneration unit shall result in primary energy savings compared to the original situation.
(4) The eligible costs shall be the extra investment costs for the equipment needed for the installation to operate as a high–efficiency cogeneration installation, compared to conventional electricity or heating installations of the same capacity or the extra investment cost to upgrade to a higher efficiency when an existing installation already meets the high–efficiency threshold.
(5) The aid intensity shall not exceed 45 % of the eligible costs. The aid intensity may be increased by 20 percentage points for aid granted to small undertakings and by 10 percentage points for aid granted to medium–sized undertakings.
(6) The aid intensity may be increased by 15 percentage points for investments located in assisted areas fulfilling the conditions of Article 107(3)(a) of the Treaty and by 5 percentage points for investments located in assisted areas fulfilling the conditions of Article 107(3)(c) of the Treaty.

Article 41. Investment aid for the promotion of energy from renewable sources
(1) Investment aid for the promotion of energy from renewable energy sources shall be compatible with the internal market within the meaning of Article 107(3) of the Treaty and shall be exempted from the notification requirement of Article 108(3) of the Treaty, provided that the conditions laid down in this Article and in Chapter I are fulfilled.
(2) Investment aid for the production of biofuels shall be exempted from the notification requirement only to the extent that the aided investments are used for the production of sustainable biofuels other than food–based biofuels. However, investment aid to convert existing food–based biofuel plants into advanced biofuel plants shall be exempted under this Article, provided that the food–based production would be reduced commensurate to the new capacity.
(3) Aid shall not be granted for biofuels which are subject to a supply or blending obligation.
(4) Aid shall not be granted for hydropower installations that do not comply with Directive 2000/60/EC of the European Parliament.
(5) The investment aid shall be granted to new installations only. No aid shall be granted or paid out after the installation started operations and aid shall be independent from the output.
(6) The eligible costs shall be the extra investment costs necessary to promote the production of energy from renewable sources. They shall be determined as follows:
(a) where the costs of investing in the production of energy from renewable sources can be identified in the total investment cost as a separate investment, for instance as a readily identifiable add–on component to a pre–existing facility, this renewable energy–related cost shall constitute the eligible costs;
(b) where the costs of investing in the production of energy from renewable sources can be identified by reference to a similar, less environmentally friendly investment that would have been credibly carried out without the aid, this difference between the costs of both investments identifies the renewable energy–related cost and constitutes the eligible costs;
(c) for certain small installations where a less environmentally friendly investment cannot be established as plants of a limited size do not exist, the total investment costs to achieve a higher level of environmental protection shall constitute the eligible costs.
The costs not directly linked to the achievement of a higher level of environmental protection shall not be eligible.
(7) The aid intensity shall not exceed:
(a) 45 % of the eligible costs if the eligible costs are calculated on the basis of point (6)(a) or point (6)(b);
(b) 30 % of the eligible cost if the eligible costs are calculated on the basis of point point (6)(c).

(8) The aid intensity may be increased by 20 percentage points for aid granted to small undertakings and by 10 percentage points for aid granted to medium–sized undertakings.
(9) The aid intensity may be increased by 15 percentage points for investments located in assisted areas fulfilling the conditions of Article 107(3)(a) of the Treaty and by 5 percentage points for investments located in assisted areas fulfilling the conditions of Article 107(3)(c) of the Treaty.
(10) Where aid is granted in a competitive bidding process on the basis of clear, transparent and non–discriminatory criteria, the aid intensity may reach 100 % of the eligible costs. Such a bidding process shall be non–discriminatory and provide for the participation of all interested undertakings. The budget related to the bidding process shall be a binding constraint in the sense that not all participants can receive aid and the aid shall be granted on the basis of the initial bid submitted by the bidder, therefore excluding subsequent negotiations.

Article 42. Operating aid for the promotion of electricity from renewable sources

(1) Operating aid for the promotion of electricity from renewable energy sources shall be compatible with the internal market within the meaning of Article 107(3) of the Treaty and shall be exempted from the notification requirement of Article 108(3) of the Treaty, provided that the conditions laid down in this Article and in Chapter I are fulfilled.
(2) Aid shall be granted in a competitive bidding process on the basis of clear, transparent and non–discriminatory criteria which shall be open to all generators producing electricity from renewable energy sources on a non–discriminatory basis.
(3) The bidding process can be limited to specific technologies where a process open to all generators would lead to a suboptimal result which cannot be addressed in the process design in view of in particular:
(i) the longer–term potential of a given new and innovative technology; or
(ii) the need to achieve diversification; or
(iii) network constraints and grid stability; or
(iv) system (integration) costs; or
(v) the need to avoid distortions on the raw material markets from biomass support
Member States shall carry out a detailed assessment of the applicability of such conditions and report it to the Commission according to the modalities described in Article 11 (a).
(4) Aid shall be granted to new and innovative renewable energy technologies in a competitive bidding process open to at least one such technology on the basis of clear, transparent and non–discriminatory criteria. Such aid shall not be granted for more than 5 % of the planned new electricity capacity from renewable energy sources per year in total.
(5) Aid shall be granted as a premium in addition to the market price whereby the generators sell their electricity directly in the market.
(6) Aid beneficiaries shall be subject to standard balancing responsibilities. Beneficiaries may outsource balancing responsibilities to other undertakings on their behalf, such as aggregators.
(7) Aid shall not be granted when prices are negative.
(8) Aid may be granted in the absence of a competitive bidding process as described in paragraph 2 to installations with an installed electricity capacity of less than 1 MW for the production of electricity from all renewable sources except for wind energy, where aid may be granted in the absence of a competitive bidding process as described in paragraph 2 to installations with an installed electricity capacity of less than 6 MW or to installations with less than 6 generation units. Without prejudice to paragraph 9, when aid is granted in the absence of a competitive bidding process, the conditions under paragraphs 5, 6 and 7 shall be respected. In addition, when aid is granted in the absence of a competitive bidding process, the conditions under Article 43 paragraphs 5, 6 and 7 shall be applicable.
(9) The conditions under paragraphs 5, 6 and 7 shall not apply to operating aid granted to installations with an installed electricity capacity of less than 500 kW for the production of electricity from all renewable sources except for wind energy, where these conditions shall not apply to operating aid granted to installations with an installed electricity capacity of less than 3 MW or to installations with less than 3 generation units.
(10) For the purpose of calculating the above maximum capacities referred to in paragraphs 8 and 9, installations with a common connection point to the electricity grid shall be considered as one installation.
(11) Aid shall only be granted until the plant generating the electricity from renewable sources has been fully depreciated according to generally accepted accounting principles. Any investment aid previously received must be deducted from the operating aid.

Article 43. Operating aid for the promotion of energy from renewable sources in small scale installations

(1) Operating aid for the promotion of energy from renewable energy sources in small scale installations shall be compatible with the internal market within the meaning of Article 107(3) of the Treaty and shall be exempted from the notification requirement of Article 108(3) of the Treaty, provided that the conditions laid down in this Article and in Chapter I are fulfilled.
(2) Aid shall only be granted to installations with an installed capacity of less than 500 kW for the production of energy from all renewable sources except for wind energy, for which aid shall be granted to installations with an installed capacity of less than 3 MW or with less than 3 generation units and for biofuels, for which aid shall be granted to installations with an installed capacity of less than 50 000 tonnes/year. For the purpose of calculating those maximum capacities, small scale installations with a common connection point to the electricity grid shall be considered as one installation.
(3) Aid shall only be granted to installations producing sustainable biofuels other than food–based biofuels. However, operating aid to plants producing food–based biofuels that have started operation before 31 December 2013 and are not yet fully depreciated shall be exempted under this Article but in any event no later than 2020.
(4) Aid shall not be granted for biofuels which are subject to a supply or blending obligation.
(5) The aid per unit of energy shall not exceed the difference between the total levelized costs of producing energy from the renewable source in question and the market price of the form of energy concerned. The levelized costs shall be updated regularly and at least every year.
(6) The maximum rate of return used in the levelized cost calculation shall not exceed the relevant swap rate plus a premium of 100 basis points. The relevant swap rate shall be the swap rate of the currency in which the aid is granted for a maturity that reflects the depreciation period of the installations supported.
(7) Aid shall only be granted until the installation has been fully depreciated according to generally accepted accounting principles. Any investment aid granted to an installation shall be deducted from the operating aid.

Article 44. Aid in the form of reductions in environmental taxes under Directive 2003/96/EC
(1) Aid schemes in the form of reductions in environmental taxes fulfilling the conditions of Council Directive 2003/96/EC of 27 October 2003 restructuring the Community framework for the taxation of energy products and electricity shall be compatible with the internal market within the meaning of Article 107(3) of the Treaty and shall be exempted from the notification requirement of Article 108(3) of the Treaty, provided that the conditions laid down in this Article and in Chapter I are fulfilled.
(2) The beneficiaries of the tax reduction shall be selected on the basis of transparent and objective criteria and shall pay at least the respective minimum level of taxation set by Directive 2003/96/EC.
(3) Aid schemes in the form of tax reductions shall be based on a reduction of the applicable environmental tax rate or on the payment of a fixed compensation amount or on a combination of these mechanisms.
(4) Aid shall not be granted for biofuels which are subject to a supply or blending obligation.

Article 45. Investment aid for remediation of contaminated sites
(1) Investment aid to undertakings repairing environmental damage by remediating contaminated sites shall be compatible with the internal market within the meaning of Article 107(3) of the Treaty and shall be exempted from the notification requirement of Article 108(3) of the Treaty, provided that the conditions laid down in this Article and in Chapter I are fulfilled.
(2) The investment shall lead to the repair of the environmental damage, including damage to the quality of the soil or of surface water or groundwater.
(3) Where the legal or physical person liable for the environmental damage under the law applicable in each Member State without prejudice to the Union rules in this matter — in particular Directive 2004/35/EC of the European Parliament and of the Council of 21 April 2004 on environmental liability with regard to the prevention and remedying of environmental damage as amended by Directive 2006/21/EC of the European Parliament and of the Council of 15 March 2006 on the management of waste from extractive industries, Directive 2009/31/EC of the European Parliament and of the Council of 23 April 2009 on the geological storage of carbon dioxide and amending Council Directive 85/337/EEC, European Parliament and Council Directives 2000/60/EC, 2001/80/EC, 2004/35/EC, 2006/12/EC, 2008/1/EC and Regulation (EC) No 1013/2006 and Directive 2013/30/EU of the European Parliament and of the Council of 12 June 2013 on safety of offshore oil and gas operations and amending Directive 2004/35/EC – is identified, that person must finance the remediation in accordance with the 'polluter pays' principle, and no State aid shall be granted. Where the person liable under the applicable law is not identified or cannot be made to bear the costs, the person responsible for the remediation or decontamination work may receive State aid.
(4) The eligible costs shall be the costs incurred for the remediation work, less the increase in the

value of the land. All expenditure incurred by an undertaking in remediating its site, whether or not such expenditure can be shown as a fixed asset on its balance sheet, may be considered as eligible investment in the case of the remediation of contaminated sites.
(5) Evaluations of the increase in value of the land resulting from remediation shall be carried out by an independent expert.
(6) The aid intensity shall not exceed 100 % of the eligible costs.

Article 46. Investment aid for energy efficient district heating and cooling
(1) Investment aid for the installation of energy efficient district heating and cooling system shall be compatible with the internal market within the meaning of Article 107(3) of the Treaty and shall be exempted from the notification requirement of Article 108(3) of the Treaty, provided that the conditions laid down in this Article and in Chapter I are fulfilled.
(2) The eligible costs for the production plant shall be the extra costs needed for the construction, expansion and refurbishment of one or more generation units to operate as an energy efficient district heating and cooling system compared to a conventional production plant. The investment shall be an integral part of the energy efficient district heating and cooling system.
(3) The aid intensity for the production plant shall not exceed 45 % of the eligible costs. The aid intensity may be increased by 20 percentage points for aid granted to small undertakings and by 10 percentage points for aid granted to medium–sized undertakings.
(4) The aid intensity for the production plant may be increased by 15 percentage points for investments located in assisted areas fulfilling the conditions of Article 107(3)(a) of the Treaty and by 5 percentage points for investments located in assisted areas fulfilling the conditions of Article 107(3)(c) of the Treaty.
(5) The eligible costs for the distribution network shall be the investment costs.
(6) The aid amount for the distribution network shall not exceed the difference between the eligible costs and the operating profit. The operating profit shall be deducted from the eligible costs *ex ante* or through a claw–back mechanism.

Article 47. Investment aid for waste recycling and re–utilisation
(1) Investment aid for waste recycling and re–utilisation shall be compatible with the internal market within the meaning of Article 107(3) of the Treaty and shall be exempted from the notification requirement of Article 108(3) of the Treaty, provided that the conditions laid down in this Article and in Chapter I are fulfilled.
(2) The investment aid shall be granted for the recycling and re–utilisation of waste generated by other undertakings.
(3) The recycled or re–used materials treated would otherwise be disposed of, or be treated in a less environmentally friendly manner. Aid to waste recovery operations other than recycling shall not be block exempted under this Article.
(4) The aid shall not indirectly relieve the polluters from a burden that should be borne by them under Union law, or from a burden that should be considered a normal company cost.
(5) The investment shall not merely increase demand for the materials to be recycled without increasing collection of those materials.
(6) The investment shall go beyond the state of the art.
(7) The eligible costs shall be the extra investment costs necessary to realise an investment leading to better or more efficient recycling or re–use activities compared to a conventional process of re–use and recycling activities with the same capacity that would be constructed in the absence the aid.
(8) The aid intensity shall not exceed 35 % of the eligible costs. The aid intensity may be increased by 20 percentage points for aid granted to small undertakings and by 10 percentage points for aid granted to medium–sized undertakings.
(9) The aid intensity may be increased by 15 percentage points for investments located in assisted areas fulfilling the conditions of Article 107(3)(a) of the Treaty and by 5 percentage points for investments located in assisted areas fulfilling the conditions of Article 107(3)(c) of the Treaty.
(10) Aid for investments relating to the recycling and re–utilisation of the beneficiary's own waste shall not be exempt from the notification requirement under this Article.

Article 48. Investment aid for energy infrastructure
(1) Investment aid for the construction or upgrade of energy infrastructure shall be compatible with the internal market within the meaning of Article 107(3) of the Treaty and shall be exempted from the notification requirement of Article 108(3) of the Treaty, provided that the conditions laid down in this Article and in Chapter I are fulfilled.
(2) Aid shall be granted for energy infrastructure located in assisted areas.

(3) The energy infrastructure shall be subject to full tariff and access regulation according to internal energy market legislation.
(4) The eligible costs shall be the investment costs.
(5) The aid amount shall not exceed the difference between the eligible costs and the operating profit of the investment. The operating profit shall be deducted from the eligible costs *ex ante* or through a claw–back mechanism.
(6) Aid for investments in electricity and gas storage projects and oil infrastructure shall not be exempt from the notification requirement under this Article.

Article 49. Aid for environmental studies

(1) Aid for studies, including energy audits, directly linked to investments referred to in this Section shall be compatible with the internal market within the meaning of Article 107(3) of the Treaty and shall be exempted from the notification requirement of Article 108(3) of the Treaty, provided that the conditions laid down in this Article and in Chapter I are fulfilled.
(2) The eligible costs shall be the costs of the studies referred to in paragraph 1.
(3) The aid intensity shall not exceed 50 % of the eligible costs.
(4) The aid intensity may be increased by 20 percentage points for studies undertaken on behalf of small enterprises and by 10 percentage points for studies undertaken on behalf of medium size enterprises.
(5) Aid shall not be granted to large undertakings for energy audits carried out under Article 8(4) of the Directive 2012/27/EU, unless the energy audit is carried out in addition to the mandatory energy audit under that Directive.

Section 8. Aid to Make Good the Damage Caused by Certain Natural Disasters

Article 50. Aid schemes to make good the damage caused by certain natural disasters

(1) Aid schemes to make good the damage caused by earthquakes, avalanches, landslides, floods, tornadoes, hurricanes, volcanic eruptions and wild fires of natural origin shall be compatible with the internal market within the meaning of Article 107(2)(b) of the Treaty and shall be exempted from the notification requirement of Article 108(3) of the Treaty, provided that the conditions laid down in this Article and in Chapter I are fulfilled.
(2) Aid shall be granted subject to the following conditions:
(a) the competent public authorities of a Member State have formally recognised the character of the event as a natural disaster; and
(b) there is a direct causal link between the natural disaster and the damages suffered by the affected undertaking.
(3) Aid schemes related to a specific natural disaster shall be introduced within three years following the occurrence of the event. Aid on the basis of such schemes shall be granted within four years following the occurrence.
(4) The costs arising from the damage incurred as a direct consequence of the natural disaster, as assessed by an independent expert recognised by the competent national authority or by an insurance undertaking shall be eligible costs. Such damage may include material damage to assets such as buildings, equipment, machinery or stocks and loss of income due to the full or partial suspension of activity for a period not exceeding six months from the occurrence of the disaster. The calculation of the material damage shall be based on the repair cost or economic value of the affected asset before the disaster. It shall not exceed the repair cost or the decrease in fair market value caused by the disaster, that is to say the difference between the property's value immediately before and immediately after the occurrence of the disaster. Loss of income shall be calculated on the basis of financial data of the affected undertaking (earnings before interest and taxes (EBIT), depreciation and labour costs related only to the establishment affected by the natural disaster) by comparing the financial data for the six months after the occurrence of the disaster with the average of three years chosen among the five years preceding the occurrence of the disaster (by excluding the two years giving the best and the worst financial result) and calculated for the same six months period of the year. The damage shall be calculated at the level of the individual beneficiary.
(5) The aid and any other payments received to compensate for the damage, including payments under insurance policies, shall not exceed 100 % of the eligible costs.

Section 9. Social Aid for Transport for Residents of Remote Regions

Article 51. Social aid for transport for residents of remote regions

(1) Aid for air and maritime passenger transport shall be compatible with the internal market pursuant to Article 107(2)(a) of the Treaty and shall be exempted from the notification requirement of Article

108(3) of the Treaty, provided that the conditions laid down in this Article and in Chapter I are fulfilled.
(2) The entire aid shall be for the benefit of final consumers who have their normal residence in remote regions.
(3) The aid shall be granted for passenger transport on a route linking an airport or port in a remote region with another airport or port within the European Economic Area.
(4) The aid shall be granted without discrimination as to the identity of the carrier or type of service and without limitation as to the precise route to or from the remote region.
(5) The eligible costs shall be the price of a return ticket from or to the remote region, including all taxes and charges invoiced by the carrier to the consumer.
(6) The aid intensity shall not exceed 100 % of the eligible costs.

Section 10. Aid for Broadband Infrastructures

Article 52. Aid for broadband infrastructures
(1) Investment aid for broadband network development shall be compatible with the internal market pursuant to Article 107(3) of the Treaty and shall be exempted from the notification requirement of Article 108(3) of the Treaty, provided that the conditions laid down in this Article and in Chapter I are fulfilled.
(2) The eligible costs shall be the following:
(a) investment costs for the deployment of a passive broadband infrastructure;
(b) investment costs of broadband–related civil engineering works;
(c) investment costs for the deployment of basic broadband networks; and
(d) investment costs for the deployment of next generation access (NGA) networks.
(3) The investment shall be located in areas where there is no infrastructure of the same category (either basic broadband or NGA network) and where no such infrastructure is likely to be developed on commercial terms within three years from the moment of publication of the planned aid measure, which shall also be verified through an open public consultation.
(4) The aid shall be allocated on the basis of an open, transparent and non–discriminatory competitive selection process respecting the principle of technology neutrality.
(5) The network operator shall offer the widest possible active and passive wholesale access, according to Article 2, point 139 of this Regulation, under fair and non–discriminatory conditions, including physical unbundling in the case of NGA networks. Such wholesale access shall be granted for at least seven years and the right of access to ducts or poles shall not be limited in time. In the case of aid for the construction of ducts, the ducts shall be large enough to cater for several cable networks and different network topologies.
(6) The wholesale access price shall be based on the pricing principles set by the national regulatory authority and on benchmarks that prevail in other comparable, more competitive areas of the Member State or the Union taking into account the aid received by the network operator. The national regulatory authority shall be consulted on access conditions, including pricing, and in the event of dispute between access seekers and the subsidised infrastructure operator.
(7) Member States shall put in place a monitoring and claw–back mechanism if the amount of aid granted to the project exceeds EUR 10 million.

Section 11. Aid for Culture and Heritage Conservation

Article 53. Aid for culture and heritage conservation
(1) Aid for culture and heritage conservation shall be compatible with the internal market within the meaning of Article 107(3) of the Treaty and shall be exempted from the notification requirement of Article 108(3) of the Treaty, provided the conditions laid down in this Article and in Chapter I are fulfilled.
(2) The aid shall be granted for the following cultural purposes and activities:
(a) museums, archives, libraries, artistic and cultural centres or spaces, theatres, opera houses, concert halls, other live performance organisations, film heritage institutions and other similar artistic and cultural infrastructures, organisations and institutions;
(b) tangible heritage including all forms of movable or immovable cultural heritage and archaeological sites, monuments, historical sites and buildings; natural heritage linked to cultural heritage or if formally recognized as cultural or natural heritage by the competent public authorities of a Member State;
(c) intangible heritage in any form, including folklorist customs and crafts;
(d) art or cultural events and performances, festivals, exhibitions and other similar cultural activities;
(e) cultural and artistic education activities as well as promotion of the understanding of the impor-

tance of protection and promotion of the diversity of cultural expressions through educational and greater public awareness programs, including with the use of new technologies;
(f) writing, editing, production, distribution, digitisation and publishing of music and literature, including translations.
(3) The aid may take the form of:
(a) investment aid, including aid for the construction or upgrade of culture infrastructure;
(b) operating aid.
(4) For investment aid, the eligible costs shall be the investment costs in tangible and intangible assets, including:
(a) costs for the construction, upgrade, acquisition, conservation or improvement of infrastructure, if at least 80 % of either the time or the space capacity per year is used for cultural purposes;
(b) costs for the acquisition, including leasing, transfer of possession or physical relocation of cultural heritage;
(c) costs for safeguarding, preservation, restoration and rehabilitation of tangible and intangible cultural heritage, including extra costs for storage under appropriate conditions, special tools, materials and costs for documentation, research, digitalisation and publication;
(d) costs for improving the accessibility of cultural heritage to the public, including costs for digitisation and other new technologies, costs to improve accessibility for persons with special needs (in particular, ramps and lifts for disabled persons, braille indications and hands–on exhibits in museums) and for promoting cultural diversity with respect to presentations, programmes and visitors;
(e) costs for cultural projects and activities, cooperation and exchange programmes and grants including costs for selection procedures, costs for promotion and costs incurred directly as a result of the project;
(5) For operating aid, the eligible costs shall be the following:
(a) the cultural institution's or heritage site's costs linked to continuous or periodic activities including exhibitions, performances and events and similar cultural activities that occur in the ordinary course of business;
(b) costs of cultural and artistic education activities as well as promotion of the understanding of the importance of protection and promotion of the diversity of cultural expressions through educational and greater public awareness programs, including with the use of new technologies;
(c) costs of the improvement of public access to the cultural institution or heritage sites and activities including costs of digitisation and of use of new technologies as well as costs of improving accessibility for persons with disabilities;
(d) operating costs directly relating to the cultural project or activity, such as rent or lease of real estate and cultural venues, travel expenses, materials and supplies directly related to the cultural project or activity, architectural structures for exhibitions and stage sets, loan, lease and depreciation of tools, software and equipment, costs for access rights to copyright works and other related intellectual property rights protected contents, costs for promotion and costs incurred directly as a result of the project or activity; depreciation charges and the costs of financing are only eligible if they have not been covered by investment aid;
(e) costs for personnel working for the cultural institution or heritage site or for a project;
(f) costs for advisory and support services provided by outside consultants and service providers, incurred directly as a result of the project.
(6) For investment aid, the aid amount shall not exceed the difference between the eligible costs and the operating profit of the investment. The operating profit shall be deducted from the eligible costs *ex ante*, on the basis of reasonable projections, or through a claw–back mechanism. The operator of the infrastructure is allowed to keep a reasonable profit over the relevant period.
(7) For operating aid, the aid amount shall not exceed what is necessary to cover the operating losses and a reasonable profit over the relevant period. This shall be ensured *ex ante*, on the basis of reasonable projections, or through a claw–back mechanism.
(8) For aid not exceeding EUR 1 million, the maximum amount of aid may be set, alternatively to the method referred to in paragraphs 6 and 7, at 80 % of eligible costs.
(9) For publishing of music and literature as defined in paragraph 2(f), the maximum aid amount shall not exceed either the difference between the eligible costs and the project's discounted revenues or 70 % of the eligible costs. The revenues shall be deducted from the eligible costs *ex ante* or through a clawback mechanism. The eligible costs shall be the costs for publishing of music and literature, including the authors' fees (copyright costs), translators' fees, editors' fees, other editorial costs (proofreading, correcting, reviewing), layout and pre–press costs and printing or e–publication costs.
(10) Aid to press and magazines, whether they are published in print or electronically, shall not be eligible under this Article.

Article 54. Aid schemes for audiovisual works

(1) Aid schemes to support the script–writing, development, production, distribution and promotion of audiovisual works shall be compatible with the internal market pursuant to Article 107(3) of the Treaty and shall be exempted from the notification requirement of Article 108(3) of the Treaty, provided the conditions laid down in this Article and in Chapter I are fulfilled.

(2) Aid shall support a cultural product. To avoid manifest errors in the qualification of a product as cultural, each Member State shall establish effective processes, such as selection of proposals by one or more persons entrusted with the selection or verification against a predetermined list of cultural criteria.

(3) Aid may take the form of:
(a) aid to the production of audiovisual works;
(b) pre–production aid; and
(c) distribution aid.

(4) Where a Member States makes the aid subject to territorial spending obligations, aid schemes for the production of audiovisual works may either:
(a) require that up to 160 % of the aid granted to the production of a given audiovisual work is spent in the territory of the Member State granting the aid; or
(b) calculate the aid granted to the production of a given audiovisual work as a percentage of the expenditure on production activities in the granting Member State, typically in case of aid schemes in the form of tax incentives.

In both cases, if a Member States requires a minimum level of production activity in the territory concerned for projects to be eligible for aid, that level shall not exceed 50 % of the overall production budget. In addition, the maximum expenditure subject to territorial spending obligations shall in no case exceed 80 % of the overall production budget.

(5) The eligible costs shall be the following:
(a) for production aid: the overall costs of production of audiovisual works including costs to improve accessibility for persons with disabilities.
(b) for pre–production aid: the costs of script–writing and the development of audiovisual works.
(c) for distribution aid: the costs of distribution and promotion of audiovisual works.

(6) The aid intensity for the production of audiovisual works shall not exceed 50 % of the eligible costs.

(7) The aid intensity may be increased as follows:
(a) to 60 % of the eligible costs for cross–border productions funded by more than one Member State and involving producers from more than one Member State;
(b) to 100 % of the eligible costs for difficult audiovisual works and co–productions involving countries from the Development Assistance Committee (DAC) List of the OECD.

(8) The aid intensity for pre–production shall not exceed 100 % of the eligible costs. If the resulting script or project is made into an audiovisual work such as a film, the pre–production costs shall be incorporated in the overall budget and taken into account when calculating the aid intensity. The aid intensity for distribution shall be the same as the aid intensity for production.

(9) Aid shall not be reserved for specific production activities or individual parts of the production value chain. Aid for film studio infrastructures shall not be eligible under this Article.

(10) Aid shall not be reserved exclusively for nationals and beneficiaries shall not be required to have the status of undertaking established under national commercial law.

Section 12. Aid for Sport and Multifunctional Recreational Infrastructures

Article 55. Aid for sport and multifunctional recreational infrastructures

(1) Aid for sport and multifunctional recreational infrastructures shall be compatible with the internal market within the meaning of Article 107(3) of the Treaty and shall be exempted from the notification requirement of Article 108(3) of the Treaty, provided that the conditions laid down in this Article and in Chapter I are fulfilled.

(2) Sport infrastructure shall not be used exclusively by a single professional sport user. Use of the sport infrastructure by other professional or non–professional sport users shall annually account for at least 20 % of time capacity. If the infrastructure is used by several users simultaneously, corresponding fractions of time capacity usage shall be calculated.

(3) Multifunctional recreational infrastructure shall consist of recreational facilities with a multi–functional character offering, in particular, cultural and recreational services with the exception of leisure parks and hotel facilities.

(4) Access to the sport or multifunctional recreational infrastructures shall be open to several users and be granted on a transparent and non–discriminatory basis. Undertakings which have financed at

least 30 % of the investment costs of the infrastructure may be granted preferential access under more favourable conditions, provided those conditions are made publicly available.
(5) If sport infrastructure is used by professional sport clubs, Member States shall ensure that the pricing conditions for its use are made publicly available.
(6) Any concession or other entrustment to a third party to construct, upgrade and/or operate the sport or multifunctional recreational infrastructure shall be assigned on a open, transparent and non–discriminatory basis, having due regard to the applicable procurement rules.
(7) The aid may take the form of:
(a) investment aid, including aid for the construction or upgrade of sport and multifunctional recreational infrastructure;
(b) operating aid for sport infrastructure;
(8) For investment aid for sport and multifunctional recreational infrastructure the eligible costs shall be the investment costs in tangible and intangible assets.
(9) For operating aid for sport infrastructure the eligible costs shall be the operating costs of the provision of services by the infrastructure. Those operating costs include costs such as personnel costs, materials, contracted services, communications, energy, maintenance, rent, administration, etc., but exclude depreciation charges and the costs of financing if these have been covered by investment aid.
(10) For investment aid for sport and multifunctional recreational infrastructure, the aid amount shall not exceed the difference between the eligible costs and the operating profit of the investment. The operating profit shall be deducted from the eligible costs *ex ante*, on the basis of reasonable projections, or through a claw–back mechanism.
(11) For operating aid for sport infrastructure, the aid amount shall not exceed the operating losses over the relevant period. This shall be ensured *ex ante*, on the basis of reasonable projections, or through a claw–back mechanism.
(12) For aid not exceeding EUR 1 million, the maximum amount of aid may be set, alternatively to the method referred to in paragraphs 10 and 11, at 80 % of eligible costs.

Section 13. Aid for Local Infrastructures

Article 56. Investment aid for local infrastructures
(1) Financing for the construction or upgrade of local infrastructures which concerns infrastructure that contribute at a local level to improving the business and consumer environment and modernising and developing the industrial base shall be compatible with the internal market within the meaning of Article 107(3) of the Treaty and shall be exempt from the notification requirement of Article 108(3) of the Treaty, provided that the conditions laid down in this Article and in Chapter I are fulfilled.
(2) This Article shall not apply to aid for infrastructures that is covered by other sections of Chapter III of this Regulation with the exception of Section 1 — Regional aid. This Article shall also not apply to airport infrastructure and port infrastructure.
(3) The infrastructure shall be made available to interested users on an open, transparent and non–discriminatory basis. The price charged for the use or the sale of the infrastructure shall correspond to market price.
(4) Any concession or other entrustment to a third party to operate the infrastructure shall be assigned on an open, transparent and non–discriminatory basis, having due regard to the applicable procurement rules.
(5) The eligible costs shall be the investment costs in tangible and intangible assets.
(6) The aid amount shall not exceed the difference between the eligible costs and the operating profit of the investment. The operating profit shall be deducted from the eligible costs *ex ante*, on the basis of reasonable projections, or through a claw–back mechanism.
(7) Dedicated infrastructure shall not be exempted under this Article.

Chapter IV. Final Provisions

Article 57. Repeal
Regulation (EC) No 800/2008 shall be repealed.

Article 58. Transitional provisions
(1) This Regulation shall apply to individual aid granted before its entry into force, if the aid fulfils all the conditions laid down in this Regulation, with the exception of Article 9.
(2) Any aid not exempted from the notification requirement of Article 108(3) of the Treaty by virtue of this Regulation or other regulations adopted pursuant to Article 1 of Regulation (EC) No 994/98 previously in force shall be assessed by the Commission in accordance with the relevant frameworks, guidelines, communications and notices.

(3) Any individual aid granted before 1 January 2015 by virtue of any regulation adopted pursuant to Article 1 of Regulation (EC) No 994/98 in force at the time of granting the aid shall be compatible with the internal market and exempted from the notification requirement of Article 108(3) of the Treaty with the exclusion of regional aid. Risk capital aid schemes in favour of SMEs set up before 1 July 2014 and exempted from the notification requirement of Article 108(3) of the Treaty under Regulation (EC) No 800/2008, shall remain exempted and compatible with the internal market until the termination of the funding agreement, provided the commitment of the public funding into the supported private equity investment fund, on the basis of such agreement, was made before 1 January 2015 and the other conditions for exemption remain fulfilled.

(4) At the end of the period of validity of this Regulation, any aid schemes exempted under this Regulation shall remain exempted during an adjustment period of six months, with the exception of regional aid schemes. The exemption of regional aid schemes shall expire on the date of expiry of the approved regional aid maps. The exemption of risk finance aid exempted pursuant to Article 21(2)(a) shall expire at the end of the period foreseen in the funding agreement, provided the commitment of public funding to the supported private equity investment fund was made on the basis of such agreement within 6 months from the end of the period of validity of this Regulation and all other conditions for exemption remain fulfilled.

Article 59. This Regulation shall enter into force on 1 July 2014.

It shall apply until 31 December 2020.

This Regulation shall be binding in its entirety and directly applicable in all Member States.

PART III EUROPEAN UNION

Commission Decision (EU) 2015/1584 of 1 October 2014 on State aid SA.23098 (C 37/07) (ex NN 36/07) implemented by Italy in favour of Società di Gestione dell'Aeroporto di Alghero So.Ge.A.AL S.p.A. and various air carriers operating at Alghero airport

THE EUROPEAN COMMISSION,
Having regard to the Treaty on the Functioning of the European Union, and in particular the first subparagraph of Article 108(2) thereof,
Having regard to the Agreement on the European Economic Area, and in particular Article 62(1)(a) thereof,
Having called on interested parties to submit their comments pursuant to the provisions cited above and having regard to their comments,
Whereas:
[The remainder of the preamble is omitted.]
HAS ADOPTED THIS DECISION:

Article 1. (1) The direct grants for infrastructure, fittings and works and equipment which Italy granted to Alghero airport constitute State aid within the meaning of Article 107(1) of the Treaty. The State aid was granted by Italy in violation of Article 108(3) of the Treaty.
(2) The State aid referred to in paragraph 1 is compatible with the internal market within the meaning of Article 107(3)(c) of the Treaty.

Article 2. (1) The capital injections which Italy implemented for Alghero airport constitute State aid within the meaning of Article 107(1) of the Treaty. The State aid was granted by Italy in violation of Article 108(3) of the Treaty.
(2) The State aid referred to in paragraph 1 is compatible with the internal market within the meaning of Article 107(3)(c) of the Treaty.

Article 3. The measures which Italy implemented for Ryanair, Air One/Alitalia, Volare, bmibaby, Air Vallée and Air Italy do not constitute State aid within the meaning of Article 107(1) of the Treaty.

Article 4. (1) The measures which Italy implemented for Meridiana and Germanwings constitute State aid within the meaning of Article 107(1) of the Treaty. The State aid was granted by Italy in violation of Article 108(3) of the Treaty.
(2) The State aid referred to in paragraph 1 is incompatible with the internal market.

Article 5. (1) Italy shall recover the incompatible State aid referred to in Article 4 from the beneficiaries.
(2) The sums to be recovered shall bear interest from the date on which they were deemed to be put at the disposal of the beneficiaries until their actual recovery.
(3) The interest shall be calculated on a compound basis in accordance with Chapter V of Regulation (EC) No 794/2004.
(4) Italy shall cancel all outstanding payments of the aid referred to in Article 4 with effect from the date of adoption of this Decision.

Article 6. (1) Recovery of the aid referred to in Article 5 shall be immediate and effective.
(2) Italy shall ensure that this Decision is implemented within four months following the date of its notification.

Article 7. (1) Within two months following notification of this Decision, Italy shall submit the following information:
(a) the total amount of aid received by the beneficiaries;
(b) the total amount (principal and recovery interests) to be recovered from each beneficiary;
(c) a detailed description of the measures already taken and planned to comply with this Decision;
(d) documents demonstrating that the beneficiaries have been ordered to repay the aid.
(2) Italy shall keep the Commission informed of the progress of the national measures taken to implement this Decision until recovery of the aid referred to in Article 4 has been completed. It shall immediately submit, on simple request by the Commission, information on the measures already taken and planned to comply with this Decision. It shall also provide detailed information concerning the amounts of aid and recovery interest already recovered from the beneficiaries.

Article 8. This Decision is addressed to the Italian Republic.

COUNCIL REGULATION NO. 17

Regulation No 17: First Regulation implementing Articles 85 and 86 of the Treaty, OJ P 13, 21.2.1962, p. 204

THE COUNCIL OF THE EUROPEAN ECONOMIC COMMUNITY,
Having regard to the Treaty establishing the European Economic Community, and in particular Article 87 thereof;
Having regard to the proposal from the Commission;
Having regard to the Opinion of the Economic and Social Committee;
Having regard to the Opinion of the European Parliament;
Whereas, in order to establish a system ensuring that competition shall not be distorted in the common market, it is necessary to provide for balanced application of Articles 85 and 86 in a uniform manner in the Member States;
Whereas in establishing the rules for applying Article 85 (3) account must be taken of the need to ensure effective supervision and to simplify administration to the greatest possible extent;
Whereas it is accordingly necessary to make it obligatory, as a general principle, for undertakings which seek application of Article 85 (3) to notify to the Commission their agreements, decisions and concerted practices;
Whereas, on the one hand, such agreements, decisions and concerted practices are probably very numerous and cannot therefore all be examined at the same time and, on the other hand, some of them have special features which may make them less prejudicial to the development of the common market;
Whereas there is consequently a need to make more flexible arrangements for the time being in respect of certain categories of agreement, decision and concerted practice without prejudging their validity under Article 85;
Whereas it may be in the interest of undertakings to know whether any agreements, decisions or practices to which they are party, or propose to become party, may lead to action on the part of the Commission pursuant to Article 85 (1) or Article 86;
Whereas, in order to secure uniform application of Articles 85 and 86 in the common market, rules must be made under which the Commission, acting in close and constant liaison with the competent authorities of the Member States, may take the requisite measures for applying those Articles;
Whereas for this purpose the Commission must have the co-operation of the competent authorities of the Member States and be empowered, throughout the common market, to require such information to be supplied and to undertake such investigations as are necessary to bring to light any agreement, decision or concerted practice prohibited by Article 85 (1) or any abuse of a dominant position prohibited by Article 86:
Whereas, in order to carry out its duty of ensuring that the provisions of the Treaty are applied, the Commission must be empowered to address to undertakings or associations of undertakings recommendations and decisions for the purpose of bringing to an end infringements of Articles 85 and 86;
Whereas compliance with Articles 85 and 86 and the fulfilment of obligations imposed on undertakings and associations of undertakings under this Regulation must be enforceable by means of fines and periodic penalty payments;
Whereas undertakings concerned must be accorded the right to be heard by the Commission, third parties whose interests may be affected by a decision must be given the opportunity of submitting their comments beforehand, and it must be ensured that wide publicity is given to decisions taken;
Whereas all decisions taken by the Commission under this Regulation are subject to review by the Court of Justice under the conditions specified in the Treaty; whereas it is moreover desirable to confer upon the Court of Justice, pursuant to Article 172, unlimited jurisdiction in respect of decisions under which the Commission imposes fines or periodic penalty payments;
Whereas this Regulation may enter into force without prejudice to any other provisions that may hereafter be adopted pursuant to Article 87;
HAS ADOPTED THIS REGULATION:

Article 1. Basic provision
Without prejudice to Articles 6, 7 and 23 of this Regulation, agreements, decisions and concerted practices of the kind described in Article 85 (1) of the Treaty and the abuse of a dominant position in the market, within the meaning of Article 86 of the Treaty, shall be prohibited, no prior decision to that effect being required.

Article 2. Negative clearance
Upon application by the undertakings or associations of undertakings concerned, the Commission may certify that, on the basis of the facts in its possession, there are no grounds under Article 85 (1) or Article 86 of the Treaty for action on its part in respect of an agreement, decision or practice.

Article 3. Termination of infringements

(1) Where the Commission, upon application or upon its own initiative, finds that there is infringement of Article 85 or Article 86 of the Treaty, it may by decision require the undertakings or associations of undertakings concerned to bring such infringement to an end.
(2) Those entitled to make application are: (a) Member States;
(b) natural or legal persons who claim a legitimate interest.
(3) Without prejudice to the other provisions of this Regulation, the Commission may, before taking a decision under paragraph 1, address to the undertakings or associations of undertakings concerned recommendations for termination of the infringement.

Article 4. Notification of new agreements, decisions and practices

(1) Agreements, decisions and concerted practices of the kind described in Article 85 (1) of the Treaty which come into existence after the entry into force of this Regulation and in respect of which the parties seek application of Article 85 (3) must be notified to the Commission. Until they have been notified, no decision in application of Article 85 (3) may be taken.
(2) Paragraph 1 shall not apply to agreements, decisions or concerted practices where: (1) the only parties thereto are undertakings from one Member State and the agreements, decisions or practices do not relate either to imports or to exports between Member States;
(2) not more than two undertakings are party thereto, and the agreements only: (a) restrict the freedom of one party to the contract in determining the prices or conditions of business upon which the goods which he has obtained from the other party to the contract may be resold; or
(b) impose restrictions on the exercise of the rights of the assignee or user of industrial property rights-in particular patents, utility models, designs or trade marks-or of the person entitled under a contract to the assignment, or grant, of the right to use a method of manufacture or knowledge relating to the use and to the application of industrial processes;
(3) they have as their sole object: (a) the development or uniform application of standards or types; or
(b) joint research for improvement of techniques, provided the results are accessible to all parties thereto and may be used by each of them.
These agreements, decisions and practices may be notified to the Commission.

Article 5. Notification of existing agreements, decisions and practices

(1) Agreements, decisions and concerted practices of the kind described in Article 85 (1) of the Treaty which are in existence at the date of entry into force of this Regulation and in respect of which the parties seek application of Article 85 (3) shall be notified to the Commission before 1 August 1962.
(2) Paragraph 1 shall not apply to agreements, decisions or concerted practices falling within Article 4 (2); these may be notified to the Commission.

Article 6. Decisions pursuant to Article 85 (3)

(1) Whenever the Commission takes a decision pursuant to Article 85 (3) of the Treaty, it shall specify therein the date from which the decision shall take effect. Such date shall not be earlier than the date of notification.
(2) The second sentence of paragraph 1 shall not apply to agreements, decisions or concerted practices falling within Article 4 (2) and Article 5 (2), nor to those falling within Article 5 (1) which have been notified within the time limit specified in Article 5 (1).

Article 7. Special provisions for existing agreements, decisions and practices

(1) Where agreements, decisions and concerted practices in existence at the date of entry into force of this Regulation and notified before 1 August 1962 do not satisfy the requirements of Article 85 (3) of the Treaty and the undertakings or associations of undertakings concerned cease to give effect to them or modify them in such manner that they no longer fall within the prohibition contained in Article 85 (1) or that they satisfy the requirements of Article 85 (3), the prohibition contained in Article 85 (1) shall apply only for a period fixed by the Commission. A decision by the Commission pursuant to the foregoing sentence shall not apply as against undertakings and associations of undertakings which did not expressly consent to the notification.
(2) Paragraph 1 shall apply to agreements, decisions and concerted practices falling within Article 4 (2) which are in existence at the date of entry into force of this Regulation if they are notified before 1 January 1964.

Article 8. Duration and revocation of decisions under Article 85 (3)

(1) A decision in application of Article 85 (3) of the Treaty shall be issued for a specified period and conditions and obligations may be attached thereto.
(2) A decision may on application be renewed if the requirements of Article 85 (3) of the Treaty

continue to be satisfied.
(3) The Commission may revoke or amend its decision or prohibit specified acts by the parties: (a) where there has been a change in any of the facts which were basic to the making of the decision;
(b) where the parties commit a breach of any obligation attached to the decision;
(c) where the decision is based on incorrect information or was induced by deceit;
(d) where the parties abuse the exemption from the provisions of Article 85 (1) of the Treaty granted to them by the decision.
In cases to which subparagraphs (b), (c) or (d) apply, the decision may be revoked with retroactive effect.

Article 9. Powers
(1) Subject to review of its decision by the Court of Justice, the Commission shall have sole power to declare Article 85 (1) inapplicable pursuant to Article 85 (3) of the Treaty.
(2) The Commission shall have power to apply Article 85 (1) and Article 86 of the Treaty; this power may be exercised notwithstanding that the time limits specified in Article 5 (1) and in Article 7 (2) relating to notification have not expired.
(3) As long as the Commission has not initiated any procedure under Articles 2, 3 or 6, the authorities of the Member States shall remain competent to apply Article 85 (1) and Article 86 in accordance with Article 88 of the Treaty; they shall remain competent in this respect notwithstanding that the time limits specified in Article 5 (1) and in Article 7 (2) relating to notification have not expired.

Article 10. Liaison with the authorities of the Member States
(1) The Commission shall forthwith transmit to the competent authorities of the Member States a copy of the applications and notifications together with copies of the most important documents lodged with the Commission for the purpose of establishing the existence of infringements of Articles 85 or 86 of the Treaty or of obtaining negative clearance or a decision in application of Article 85 (3).
(2) The Commission shall carry out the procedure set out in paragraph 1 in close and constant liaison with the competent authorities of the Member States; such authorities shall have the right to express their views upon that procedure.
(3) An Advisory Committee on Restrictive Practices and Monopolies shall be consulted prior to the taking of any decision following upon a procedure under paragraph 1, and of any decision concerning the renewal, amendment or revocation of a decision pursuant to Article 85 (3) of the Treaty.
(4) The Advisory Committee shall be composed of officials competent in the matter of restrictive practices and monopolies. Each Member State shall appoint an official to represent it who, if prevented from attending, may be replaced by another official.
(5) The consultation shall take place at a joint meeting convened by the Commission; such meeting shall be held not earlier than fourteen days after dispatch of the notice convening it. The notice shall, in respect of each case to be examined, be accompanied by a summary of the case together with an indication of the most important documents, and a preliminary draft decision.
(6) The Advisory Committee may deliver an opinion notwithstanding that some of its members or their alternates are not present. A report of the outcome of the consultative proceedings shall be annexed to the draft decision. It shall not be made public.

Article 11. Requests for information
(1) In carrying out the duties assigned to it by Article 89 and by provisions adopted under Article 87 of the Treaty, the Commission may obtain all necessary information from the Governments and competent authorities of the Member States and from undertakings and associations of undertakings.
(2) When sending a request for information to an undertaking or association of undertakings, the Commission shall at the same time forward a copy of the request to the competent authority of the Member State in whose territory the seat of the undertaking or association of undertakings is situated.
(3) In its request the Commission shall state the legal basis and the purpose of the request and also the penalties provided for in Article 15 (1) (b) for supplying incorrect information.
(4) The owners of the undertakings or their representatives and, in the case of legal persons, companies or firms, or of associations having no legal personality, the persons authorised to represent them by law or by their constitution shall supply the information requested.
(5) Where an undertaking or association of undertakings does not supply the information requested within the time limit fixed by the Commission, or supplies incomplete information, the Commission shall by decision require the information to be supplied. The decision shall specify what information is required, fix an appropriate time limit within which it is to be supplied and indicate the penalties provided for in Article 15 (1) (b) and Article 16 (1) (c) and the right to have the decision reviewed by the Court of Justice.

PART III EUROPEAN UNION

(6) The Commission shall at the same time forward a copy of its decision to the competent authority of the Member State in whose territory the seat of the undertaking or association of undertakings is situated.

Article 12. Inquiry into sectors of the economy
(1) If in any sector of the economy the trend of trade between Member States, price movements, inflexibility of prices or other circumstances suggest that in the economic sector concerned competition is being restricted or distorted within the common market, the Commission may decide to conduct a general inquiry into that economic sector and in the course thereof may request undertakings in the sector concerned to supply the information necessary for giving effect to the principles formulated in Articles 85 and 86 of the Treaty and for carrying out the duties entrusted to the Commission.
(2) The Commission may in particular request every undertaking or association of undertakings in the economic sector concerned to communicate to it all agreements, decisions and concerted practices which are exempt from notification by virtue of Article 4 (2) and Article 5 (2).
(3) When making inquiries pursuant to paragraph 2, the Commission shall also request undertakings or groups of undertakings whose size suggests that they occupy a dominant position within the common market or a substantial part thereof to supply to the Commission such particulars of the structure of the undertakings and of their behaviour as are requisite to an appraisal of their position in the light of Article 86 of the Treaty.
(4) Article 10 (3) to (6) and Articles 11, 13 and 14 shall apply correspondingly.

Article 13. Investigations by the authorities of the Member States
(1) At the request of the Commission, the competent authorities of the Member States shall undertake the investigations which the Commission considers to be necessary under Article 14 (1), or which it has ordered by decision pursuant to Article 14 (3). The officials of the competent authorities of the Member States responsible for conducting these investigations shall exercise their powers upon production of an authorisation in writing issued by the competent authority of the Member State in whose territory the investigation is to be made. Such authorisation shall specify the subject matter and purpose of the investigation.
(2) If so requested by the Commission or by the competent authority of the Member State in whose territory the investigation is to be made, the officials of the Commission may assist the officials of such authorities in carrying out their duties.

Article 14. Investigating powers of the Commission
(1) In carrying out the duties assigned to it by Article 89 and by provisions adopted under Article 87 of the Treaty, the Commission may undertake all necessary investigations into undertakings and associations of undertakings. To this end the officials authorised by the Commission are empowered:
(a) to examine the books and other business records;
(b) to take copies of or extracts from the books and business records;
(c) to ask for oral explanations on the spot;
(d) to enter any premises; land and means of transport of undertakings.
(2) The officials of the Commission authorised for the purpose of these investigations shall exercise their powers upon production of an authorisation in writing specifying the subject matter and purpose of the investigation and the penalties provided for in Article 15 (1) (c) in cases where production of the required books or other business records is incomplete. In good time before the investigation, the Commission shall inform the competent authority of the Member State in whose territory the same is to be made of the investigation and of the identity of the authorised officials.
(3) Undertakings and associations of undertakings shall submit to investigations ordered by decision of the Commission. The decision shall specify the subject matter and purpose of the investigation, appoint the date on which it is to begin and indicate the penalties provided for in Article 15 (1) (c) and Article 16 (1) (d) and the right to have the decision reviewed by the Court of Justice.
(4) The Commission shall take decisions referred to in paragraph 3 after consultation with the competent authority of the Member State in whose territory the investigation is to be made.
(5) Officials of the competent authority of the Member State in whose territory the investigation is to be made may, at the request of such authority or of the Commission, assist the officials of the Commission in carrying out their duties.
(6) Where an undertaking opposes an investigation ordered pursuant to this Article, the Member State concerned shall afford the necessary assistance to the officials authorised by the Commission to enable them to make their investigation. Member States shall, after consultation with the Commission, take the necessary measures to this end before 1 October 1962.

Article 15. Fines

(1) The Commission may by decision impose on undertakings or associations of undertakings fines of from 100 to 5000 units of account where, intentionally or negligently: (a) they supply incorrect or misleading information in an application pursuant to Article 2 or in a notification pursuant to Articles 4 or 5; or
(b) they supply incorrect information in response to a request made pursuant to Article 11 (3) or (5) or to Article 12, or do not supply information within the time limit fixed by a decision taken under Article 11 (5); or
(c) they produce the required books or other business records in incomplete form during investigations under Article 13 or 14, or refuse to submit to an investigation ordered by decision issued in implementation of Article 14 (3).
(2) The Commission may by decision impose on undertakings or associations of undertakings fines of from 1000 to 1 000 000 units of account, or a sum in excess thereof but not exceeding 10 % of the turnover in the preceding business year of each of the undertakings participating in the infringement where, either intentionally or negligently: (a) they infringe Article 85 (1) or Article 86 of the Treaty; or
(b) they commit a breach of any obligation imposed pursuant to Article 8 (1).
In fixing the amount of the fine, regard shall be had both to the gravity and to the duration of the infringement.
(3) Article 10 (3) to (6) shall apply.
(4) Decisions taken pursuant to paragraphs 1 and 2 shall not be of a criminal law nature.
(5) The fines provided for in paragraph 2 (a) shall not be imposed in respect of acts taking place: (a) after notification to the Commission and before its decision in application of Article 85 (3) of the Treaty, provided they fall within the limits of the activity described in the notification;
(b) before notification and in the course of agreements, decisions or concerted practices in existence at the date of entry into force of this Regulation, provided that notification was effected within the time limits specified in Article 5 (1) and Article 7 (2).
(6) Paragraph 5 shall not have effect where the Commission has informed the undertakings concerned that after preliminary examination it is of opinion that Article 85 (1) of the Treaty applies and that application of Article 85 (3) is not justified.

Article 16. Periodic penalty payments

(1) The Commission may by decision impose on undertakings or associations of undertakings periodic penalty payments of from 50 to 1000 units of account per day, calculated from the date appointed by the decision, in order to compel them: (a) to put an end to an infringement of Article 85 or 86 of the Treaty, in accordance with a decision taken pursuant to Article 3 of this Regulation;
(b) to refrain from any act prohibited under Article 8 (3);
(c) to supply complete and correct information which it has requested by decision taken pursuant to Article 11 (5);
(d) to submit to an investigation which it has ordered by decision taken pursuant to Article 14 (3).
(2) Where the undertakings or associations of undertakings have satisfied the obligation which it was the purpose of the periodic penalty payment to enforce, the Commission may fix the total amount of the periodic penalty payment at a lower figure than that which would arise under the original decision.
(3) Article 10 (3) to (6) shall apply.

Article 17. Review by the Court of Justice

The Court of Justice shall have unlimited jurisdiction within the meaning of Article 172 of the Treaty to review decisions whereby the Commission has fixed a fine or periodic penalty payment; it may cancel, reduce or increase the fine or periodic penalty payment imposed.

Article 18. Unit of account

For the purposes of applying Articles 15 to 17 the unit of account shall be that adopted in drawing up the budget of the Community in accordance with Articles 207 and 209 of the Treaty.

Article 19. Hearing of the parties and of third persons

(1) Before taking decisions as provided for in Articles 2, 3, 6, 7, 8, 15 and 16, the Commission shall give the undertakings or associations of undertakings concerned the opportunity of being heard on the matters to which the Commission has taken objection.
(2) If the Commission or the competent authorities of the Member States consider it necessary, they may also hear other natural or legal persons. Applications to be heard on the part of such persons shall, where they show a sufficient interest, be granted.
(3) Where the Commission intends to give negative clearance pursuant to Article 2 or take a decision

in application of Article 85 (3) of the Treaty, it shall publish a summary of the relevant application or notification and invite all interested third parties to submit their observations within a time limit which it shall fix being not less than one month. Publication shall have regard to the legitimate interest of undertakings in the protection of their business secrets.

Article 20. Professional secrecy

(1) Information acquired as a result of the application of Articles 11, 12, 13 and 14 shall be used only for the purpose of the relevant request or investigation.

(2) Without prejudice to the provisions of Articles 19 and 21, the Commission and the competent authorities of the Member States, their officials and other servants shall not disclose information acquired by them as a result of the application of this Regulation and of the kind covered by the obligation of professional secrecy.

(3) The provisions of paragraphs 1 and 2 shall not prevent publication of general information or surveys which do not contain information of undertakings.

Article 21. Publication of decisions

(1) The Commission shall publish the decisions which it takes pursuant to Articles 2, 3, 6, 7 and 8.

(2) The publication shall state the names of the parties and the main content of the decision; it shall have regard to the legitimate interest of undertakings in the protection of their business secrets.

Article 22. Special provisions

(1) The Commission shall submit to the Council proposals for making certain categories of agreement, decision and concerted practice falling within Article 4 (2) or Article 5 (2) compulsorily notifiable under Article 4 or 5.

(2) Within one year from the date of entry into force of this Regulation, the Council shall examine, on a proposal from the Commission, what special provisions might be made for exempting from the provisions of this Regulation agreements, decisions and concerted practices falling within Article 4 (2) or Article 5 (2).

Article 23. Transitional provisions applicable to decisions of authorities of the Member States

(1) Agreements, decisions and concerted practices of the kind described in Article 85 (1) of the Treaty to which, before the entry into force of this Regulation, the competent authority of a Member State has declared Article 85 (1) to be inapplicable pursuant to Article 85 (3) shall not be subject to compulsory notification under Article 5. The decision of the competent authority of the Member State shall be deemed to be a decision within the meaning of Article 6; it shall cease to be valid upon expiration of the period fixed by such authority but in any event not more than three years after the entry into force of this Regulation. Article 8 (3) shall apply.

(2) Applications for renewal of decisions of the kind described in paragraph 1 shall be decided upon by the Commission in accordance with Article 8 (2).

Article 24. Implementing provisions

The Commission shall have power to adopt implementing provisions concerning the form, content and other details of applications pursuant to Articles 2 and 3 and of notifications pursuant to Articles 4 and 5, and concerning hearings pursuant to Article 19 (1) and (2).

This Regulation shall be binding in its entirety and directly applicable in all Member States.

COMMISSION NOTICE DE MINIMIS

Commission Notice 'De Minimis'(2014/C 291/01)
Communication from the Commission; Notice on agreements of minor importance which do not appreciably restrict competition under Article 101(1) of the Treaty on the Functioning of the European Union

I.

(1) Article 101(1) of the Treaty on the Functioning of the European Union prohibits agreements between undertakings which may affect trade between Member States and which have as their object or effect the prevention, restriction or distortion of competition within the internal market. The Court of Justice of the European Union has clarified that that provision is not applicable where the impact of the agreement on trade between Member States or on competition is not appreciable.

(2) The Court of Justice has also clarified that an agreement which may affect trade between Member States and which has as its object the prevention, restriction or distortion of competition within the internal market constitutes, by its nature and independently of any concrete effects that it may have, an appreciable restriction of competition. This Notice therefore does not cover agreements which have as their object the prevention, restriction or distortion of competition within the internal market.

(3) In this Notice the Commission indicates, with the help of market share thresholds, the circumstances in which it considers that agreements which may have as their effect the prevention, restriction or distortion of competition within the internal market do not constitute an appreciable restriction of competition under Article 101 of the Treaty. This negative definition of appreciability does not imply that agreements between undertakings which exceed the thresholds set out in this Notice constitute an appreciable restriction of competition. Such agreements may still have only a negligible effect on competition and may therefore not be prohibited by Article 101(1) of the Treaty.

(4) Agreements may also fall outside Article 101(1) of the Treaty because they are not capable of appreciably affecting trade between Member States. This Notice does not indicate what constitutes an appreciable effect on trade between Member States. Guidance to that effect is to be found in the Commission's Notice on effect on trade, in which the Commission quantifies, with the help of the combination of a 5 % market share threshold and a EUR 40 million turnover threshold, which agreements are in principle not capable of appreciably affecting trade between Member States. Such agreements normally fall outside Article 101(1) of the Treaty even if they have as their object the prevention, restriction or distortion of competition.

(5) In cases covered by this Notice, the Commission will not institute proceedings either upon a complaint or on its own initiative. In addition, where the Commission has instituted proceedings but undertakings can demonstrate that they have assumed in good faith that the market shares mentioned in points 8, 9, 10 and 11 were not exceeded, the Commission will not impose fines. Although not binding on them, this Notice is also intended to give guidance to the courts and competition authorities of the Member States in their application of Article 101 of the Treaty.

(6) The principles set out in this Notice also apply to decisions by associations of undertakings and to concerted practices.

(7) This Notice is without prejudice to any interpretation of Article 101 of the Treaty which may be given by the Court of Justice of the European Union.

II.

(8) The Commission holds the view that agreements between undertakings which may affect trade between Member States and which may have as their effect the prevention, restriction or distortion of competition within the internal market, do not appreciably restrict competition within the meaning of Article 101(1) of the Treaty:

(a) if the aggregate market share held by the parties to the agreement does not exceed 10 % on any of the relevant markets affected by the agreement, where the agreement is made between undertakings which are actual or potential competitors on any of those markets (agreements between competitors); or

(b) if the market share held by each of the parties to the agreement does not exceed 15 % on any of the relevant markets affected by the agreement, where the agreement is made between undertakings which are not actual or potential competitors on any of those markets (agreements between non-competitors).

(9) In cases where it is difficult to classify the agreement as either an agreement between competitors or an agreement between non-competitors the 10 % threshold is applicable.

(10) Where, in a relevant market, competition is restricted by the cumulative effect of agreements for the sale of goods or services entered into by different suppliers or distributors (cumulative foreclosure effect of parallel networks of agreements having similar effects on the market), the market share

PART III   EUROPEAN UNION

thresholds set out in point 8 and 9 are reduced to 5 %, both for agreements between competitors and for agreements between non-competitors. Individual suppliers or distributors with a market share not exceeding 5 %, are in general not considered to contribute significantly to a cumulative foreclosure effect. A cumulative foreclosure effect is unlikely to exist if less than 30 % of the relevant market is covered by parallel (networks of) agreements having similar effects.

(11) The Commission also holds the view that agreements do not appreciably restrict competition if the market shares of the parties to the agreement do not exceed the thresholds of respectively 10 %, 15 % and 5 % set out in points 8, 9 and 10 during two successive calendar years by more than 2 percentage points.

(12) In order to calculate the market share, it is necessary to determine the relevant market. This consists of the relevant product market and the relevant geographic market. When defining the relevant market, reference should be had to the Notice on the definition of the relevant market. The market shares are to be calculated on the basis of sales value data or, where appropriate, purchase value data. If value data are not available, estimates based on other reliable market information, including volume data, may be used.

(13) In view of the clarification of the Court of Justice referred to in point 2, this Notice does not cover agreements which have as their object the prevention, restriction or distortion of competition within the internal market. The Commission will thus not apply the safe harbour created by the market share thresholds set out in points 8, 9, 10 and 11 to such agreements. For instance, as regards agreements between competitors, the Commission will not apply the principles set out in this Notice to, in particular, agreements containing restrictions which, directly or indirectly, have as their object: a) the fixing of prices when selling products to third parties; b) the limitation of output or sales; or c) the allocation of markets or customers. Likewise, the Commission will not apply the safe harbour created by those market share thresholds to agreements containing any of the restrictions that are listed as hardcore restrictions in any current or future Commission block exemption regulation, which are considered by the Commission to generally constitute restrictions by object.

(14) The safe harbour created by the market share thresholds set out in points 8, 9, 10 and 11 is particularly relevant for categories of agreements not covered by any Commission block exemption regulation. The safe harbour is also relevant for agreements covered by a Commission block exemption regulation to the extent that those agreements contain a so-called excluded restriction, that is a restriction not listed as a hardcore restriction but nonetheless not covered by the Commission block exemption regulation.

(15) For the purpose of this Notice, the terms 'undertaking', 'party to the agreement', 'distributor' and 'supplier' include their respective connected undertakings.

(16) For the purpose of the Notice 'connected undertakings' are:

(a) undertakings in which a party to the agreement, directly or indirectly:

i. has the power to exercise more than half the voting rights, or

ii. has the power to appoint more than half the members of the supervisory board, board of management or bodies legally representing the undertaking, or

iii. has the right to manage the undertaking's affairs;

(b) undertakings which directly or indirectly have, over a party to the agreement, the rights or powers listed in (a);

(c) undertakings in which an undertaking referred to in (b) has, directly or indirectly, the rights or powers listed in (a);

(d) undertakings in which a party to the agreement together with one or more of the undertakings referred to in (a), (b) or (c), or in which two or more of the latter undertakings, jointly have the rights or powers listed in (a);

(e) undertakings in which the rights or the powers listed in (a) are jointly held by:

i. parties to the agreement or their respective connected undertakings referred to in (a) to (d), or

ii. one or more of the parties to the agreement or one or more of their connected undertakings referred to in (a) to (d) and one or more third parties.

(17) For the purposes of point (e) in point 16, the market share held by these jointly held undertakings is apportioned equally to each undertaking having the rights or the powers listed in point (a) in point 16.

Commission Notice on the definition of relevant market for the purposes of Community competition law (97/C 372/03)

I. Introduction

(1) The purpose of this notice is to provide guidance as to how the Commission applies the concept of relevant product and geographic market in its ongoing enforcement of Community competition law, in particular the application of Council Regulation No 17 and (EEC) No 4064/89, their equivalents in other sectoral applications such as transport, coal and steel, and agriculture, and the relevant provisions of the EEA Agreement. Throughout this notice, references to Articles 85 and 86 of the Treaty and to merger control are to be understood as referring to the equivalent provisions in the EEA Agreement and the ECSC Treaty.
(2) Market definition is a tool to identify and define the boundaries of competition between firms. It serves to establish the framework within which competition policy is applied by the Commission. The main purpose of market definition is to identify in a systematic way the competitive constraints that the undertakings involved face. The objective of defining a market in both its product and geographic dimension is to identify those actual competitors of the undertakings involved that are capable of constraining those undertakings' behaviour and of preventing them from behaving independently of effective competitive pressure. It is from this perspective that the market definition makes it possible inter alia to calculate market shares that would convey meaningful information regarding market power for the purposes of assessing dominance or for the purposes of applying Article 85.
(3) It follows from point 2 that the concept of 'relevant market' is different from other definitions of market often used in other contexts. For instance, companies often use the term 'market' to refer to the area where it sells its products or to refer broadly to the industry or sector where it belongs.
(4) The definition of the relevant market in both its product and its geographic dimensions often has a decisive influence on the assessment of a competition case. By rendering public the procedures which the Commission follows when considering market definition and by indicating the criteria and evidence on which it relies to reach a decision, the Commission expects to increase the transparency of its policy and decision-making in the area of competition policy.
(5) Increased transparency will also result in companies and their advisers being able to better anticipate the possibility that the Commission may raise competition concerns in an individual case. Companies could, therefore, take such a possibility into account in their own internal decision-making when contemplating, for instance, acquisitions, the creation of joint ventures, or the establishment of certain agreements. It is also intended that companies should be in a better position to understand what sort of information the Commission considers relevant for the purposes of market definition.
(6) The Commission's interpretation of 'relevant market' is without prejudice to the interpretation which may be given by the Court of Justice or the Court of First Instance of the European Communities.

II. Definition of Relevant Market

Definition of relevant product market and relevant geographic market
(7) The Regulations based on Article 85 and 86 of the Treaty, in particular in section 6 of Form A/B with respect to Regulation No 17, as well as in section 6 of Form CO with respect to Regulation (EEC) No 4064/89 on the control of concentrations having a Community dimension have laid down the following definitions, 'Relevant product markets' are defined as follows:
'A relevant product market comprises all those products and/or services which are regarded as interchangeable or substitutable by the consumer, by reason of the products' characteristics, their prices and their intended use'.
(8) 'Relevant geographic markets' are defined as follows:
'The relevant geographic market comprises the area in which the undertakings concerned are involved in the supply and demand of products or services, in which the conditions of competition are sufficiently homogeneous and which can be distinguished from neighbouring areas because the conditions of competition are appreciably different in those area'.
(9) The relevant market within which to assess a given competition issue is therefore established by the combination of the product and geographic markets. The Commission interprets the definitions in paragraphs 7 an 8 (which reflect the case-law of the Court of Justice and the Court of First Instance as well as its own decision-making practice) according to the orientations defined in this notice.

Concept of relevant market and objectives of Community competition policy
(10) The concept of relevant market is closely related to the objectives pursued under Community

competition policy. For example, under the Community's merger control, the objective in controlling structural changes in the supply of a product/service is to prevent the creation or reinforcement of a dominant position as a result of which effective competition would be significantly impeded in a substantial part of the common market. Under the Community's competition rules, a dominant position is such that a firm or group of firms would be in a position to behave to an appreciable extent independently of its competitors, customers and ultimately of its consumers. Such a position would usually arise when a firm or group of firms accounted for a large share of the supply in any given market, provided that other factors analysed in the assessment (such as entry barriers, customers' capacity to react, etc.) point in the same direction.

(11) The same approach is followed by the Commission in its application of Article 86 of the Treaty to firms that enjoy a single or collective dominant position. Within the meaning of Regulation No 17, the Commission has the power to investigate and bring to an end abuses of such a dominant position, which must also be defined by reference to the relevant market. Markets may also need to be defined in the application of Article 85 of the Treaty, in particular, in determining whether an appreciable restriction of competition exists or in establishing if the condition pursuant to Article 85 (3) (b) for an exemption from the application of Article 85 (1) is met.

(12) The criteria for defining the relevant market are applied generally for the analysis of certain types of behaviour in the market and for the analysis of structural changes in the supply of products. This methodology, though, might lead to different results depending on the nature of the competition issue being examined. For instance, the scope of the geographic market might be different when analysing a concentration, where the analysis is essentially prospective, from an analysis of past behaviour. The different time horizon considered in each case might lead to the result that different geographic markets are defined for the same products depending on whether the Commission is examining a change in the structure of supply, such as a concentration or a cooperative joint venture, or examining issues relating to certain past behaviour.

Basic principles for market definition
Competitive constraints
(13) Firms are subject to three main sources or competitive constraints: demand substitutability, supply substitutability and potential competition. From an economic point of view, for the definition of the relevant market, demand substitution constitutes the most immediate and effective disciplinary force on the suppliers of a given product, in particular in relation to their pricing decisions. A firm or a group of firms cannot have a significant impact on the prevailing conditions of sale, such as prices, if its customers are in a position to switch easily to available substitute products or to suppliers located elsewhere. Basically, the exercise of market definition consists in identifying the effective alternative sources of supply for the customers of the undertakings involved, in terms both of products/services and of geographic location of suppliers.

(14) The competitive constraints arising from supply side substitutability other then those described in paragraphs 20 to 23 and from potential competition are in general less immediate and in any case require an analysis of additional factors. As a result such constraints are taken into account at the assessment stage of competition analysis.

Demand substitution
(15) The assessment of demand substitution entails a determination of the range of products which are viewed as substitutes by the consumer. One way of making this determination can be viewed as a speculative experiment, postulating a hypothetical small, lasting change in relative prices and evaluating the likely reactions of customers to that increase. The exercise of market definition focuses on prices for operational and practical purposes, and more precisely on demand substitution arising from small, permanent changes in relative prices. This concept can provide clear indications as to the evidence that is relevant in defining markets.

(16) Conceptually, this approach means that, starting from the type of products that the undertakings involved sell and the area in which they sell them, additional products and areas will be included in, or excluded from, the market definition depending on whether competition from these other products and areas affect or restrain sufficiently the pricing of the parties' products in the short term.

(17) The question to be answered is whether the parties' customers would switch to readily available substitutes or to suppliers located elsewhere in response to a hypothetical small (in the range 5 % to 10 %) but permanent relative price increase in the products and areas being considered. If substitution were enough to make the price increase unprofitable because of the resulting loss of sales, additional substitutes and areas are included in the relevant market. This would be done until the set of products and geographical areas is such that small, permanent increases in relative prices would be profitable. The equivalent analysis is applicable in cases concerning the concentraiton of buying power, where

the starting point would then be the supplier and the price test serves to identify the alternative distribution channels or outlets for the supplier's products. In the application of these principles, careful account should be taken of certain particular situations as described within paragraphs 56 and 58.

(18) A practical example of this test can be provided by its application to a merger of, for instance, soft-drink bottlers. An issue to examine in such a case would be to decide whether different flavours of soft drinks belong to the same market. In practice, the question to address would be whether consumers of flavour A would switch to other flavours when confronted with a permanent price increase of 5 % to 10 % for flavour A. If a sufficient number of consumers would switch to, say, flavour B, to such an extent that the price increase for flavour A would not be profitable owing to the resulting loss of sales, then the market would comprise at least flavours A and B. The process would have to be extended in addition to other available flavours until a set of products is identified for which a price rise would not induce a sufficient substitution in demand.

(19) Generally, and in particular for the analysis of merger cases, the price to take into account will be the prevailing market price. This may not be the case where the prevailing price has been determined in the absence of sufficient competition. In particular for the investigation of abuses of dominant positions, the fact that the prevailing price might already have been substantially increased will be taken into account.

Supply substitution

(20) Supply-side substitutability may also be taken into account when defining markets in those situaitons in which its effects are equivalent to those of demand substitution in terms of effectiveness and immediacy. This means that suppliers are able to switch production to the relevant products and market them in the short term without incurring significant additional costs or risks in response to small and permanent changes in relative prices. When these conditions are met, the additional production that is put on the market will have a disciplinary effect on the competitive behaviour of the companies involved. Such an impact in terms of effectiveness and immediacy is equivalent to the demand substitution effect.

(21) These situations typically arise when companies market a wide range of qualities or grades of one product; even if, for a given final customer or group of consumers, the different qualities are not substitutable, the different qualities will be grouped into one product market, provided that most of the suppliers are able to offer and sell the various qualities immediately and without the significant increases in costs described above. In such cases, the relevant product market will encompass all products that are substitutable in demand and supply, and the current sales of those products will be aggregated so as to give the total value or volume of the market. The same reasoning may lead to group different geographic areas.

(22) A practical example of the approach to supply-side substitutability when defining product markets is to be found in the case of paper. Paer is usually supplied in a range of different qualities, from standard writing paper to high quality papers to be used, for instance, to publish art books. From a demand point of view, different qualities of paper cannot be used for any given use, i.e. an art book or a high quality publication cannot be based on lower quality papers. However, paper plants are prepared to manufacture the different qualities, and production can be adjusted with negligible costs and in a short time-frame. In the absence of particular difficulties in distribution, paper manufacturers are able therefore, to compete for orders of the various qualities, in particular if orders are placed with sufficient lead time to allow for modification of production plans. Under such circumstances, the Commission would not define a separate market for each quality of paper and its respective use. The various qualities of paper are included in the relevant market, and their sales added up to estimate total market galue and volume.

(23) When supply-side substitutability would entail the need to adjust significantly existing tangible and intangible assets, additional investments, strategic decisions or time delays, it will not be considered at the stage of market definition. Examples where supply-side substitution did not induce the Commission to enlarge the market are offered in the area of consumer products, in particular for branded beverages. Although bottling plants may in principle bottle different beverages, there are costs and lead times involved (in terms of advertising, product testing and distribution) before the products can actually be sold. In these cases, the effects of supply-side substitutability and other forms of potential competition would then be examined at a later stage.

Potential competition

(24) The third source of competitive constraint, potential competition, is not taken into account when defining markets, since the conditions under which potential competition will actually represent an effective competitive constraint depend on the analysis of specific factors and circumstances related to the conditions of entry. If required, this analysis is only carried out at a subsequent stage, in general once the position of the companies involved in the relevant market has already been ascertained, and when such position gives rise to concerns from a competition point of view.

PART III   EUROPEAN UNION

III. Evidence Relied on to Define Relevant Markets

The process of defining the relevant market in practice
Product dimension

(25) There is a range of evidence permitting an assessment of the extent to which substitution would take place. In individual cases, certain types of evidence will be determinant, depending very much on the characteristics and specificity of the industry and products or services that are being examined. The same type of evidence may be of no importance in other cases. In most cases, a decision will have to be based on the consideration of a number of criteria and different items of evidence. The Commission follows an open approach to empirical evidence, aimed at making an effective use of all available information which may be relevant in individual cases. The Commission does not follow a rigid hierarchy of different sources of information or types of evidence.

(26) The process of defining relevant markets may be summarized as follows: on the basis of the preliminary information available or information submitted by the undertakings involved, the Commission will usually be in a position to broadly establish the possible relevant markets within which, for instance, a concentration or a restriction of competition has to be assessed. In general, and for all practical purposes when handling individual cases, the question will usually be to decide on a few alternative possible relevant markets. For instance, with respect to the product market, the issue will often be to establish whether product A and product B belong or do not belong to the same product market. it is often the case that the inclusion of product B would be enough to remove any competition concerns.

(27) In such situations it is not necessary to consider whether the market includes additional products, or to reach a definitive conclusion on the precise product market. If under the conceivable alternative market definitions the operation in question does not raise competition concerns, the question of market definition will be left open, reducing thereby the burden on companies to supply information.

Geographic dimension

(28) The Commission's approach to geographic market definition might be summarized as follows: it will take a preliminary view of the scope of the geographic market on the basis of broad indications as to the distribution of market shares between the parties and their competitors, as well as a preliminary analysis of pricing and price differences at national and Community or EEA level. This initial view is used basically as a working hypothesis to focus the Commission's enquiries for the purposes of arriving at a precise geographic market definition.

(29) The reasons behind any particular configuration of prices and market shares need to be explored. Companies might enjoy high market shares in their domestic markets just because of the weight of the past, and conversely, a homogeneous presence of companies throughout the EEA might be consistent with national or regional geographic markets. The initial working hypothesis will therefore be checked against an analysis of demand characteristics (importance of national or local preferences, current patterns of purchases of customers, product differentiation/brands, other) in order to establish whether companies in different areas do indeed constitute a real alternative source of supply for consumers. The theoretical experiment is again based on substitution arising from changes in relative prices, and the question to answer is again whether the customers of the parties would switch their orders to companies located elsewhere in the short term and at a negligible cost.

(30) If necessary, a further check on supply factors will be carried out to ensure that those companies located in differing areas do not face impediments in developing their sales on competitive terms throughout the whole geographic market. This analysis will include an examination of requirements for a local presence in order to sell in that area the conditions of access to distribution channels, costs associated with setting up a distribution network, and the presence or absence of regulatory barriers arising from public procurement, price regulations, quotas and tariffs limiting trade or production, technical standards, monopolies, freedom of establishment, requirements for administrative authorizations, packaging regulations, etc. In short, the Commission will identify possible obstacles and barriers isolating companies located in a given area from the competitive pressure of companies located outside that area, so as to determine the precise degree of market interpenetration at national, European or global level.

(31) The actual pattern and evolution of trade flows offers useful supplementary indications as to the economic importance of each demand or supply factor mentioned above, and the extent to which they may or may not constitute actual barriers creating different geographic markets. The analysis of trade flows will generally address the question of transport costs and the extent to which these may hinder trade between different areas, having regard to plant location, costs of production and relative price levels.

Market integration in the Community

(32) Finally, the Commission also takes into account the continuing process of market integration, in particular in the Community, when defining geographic markets, especially in the area of concentrations and structural joint ventures. The measures adopted and implemented in the internal market programme to remove barriers to trade and further integrate the Community markets cannot be ignored when assessing the effects on competition of a concentration or a structural joint venture. A situation where national markets have been artificially isolated from each other because of the existence of legislative barriers that have now been removed will generally lead to a cautious assessment of past evidence regarding prices, market shares or trade patterns. A process of market integration that would, in the short term, lead to wider geographic markets may therefore be taken into consideration when defining the geographic market for the purposes of assessing concentrations and joint ventures.

The process of gathering evidence

(33) When a precise market definition is deemed necessary, the Commission will often contact the main customers and the main companies in the industry to enquire into their views about the boundaries of product and geographic markets and to obtain the necessary factual evidence to reach a conclusion. The Commission might also contact the relevant professional associations, and companies active in upstream markets, so as to be able to define, in so far as necessary, separate product and geographic markets, for different levels of production or distribution of the products/services in question. It might also request additional information to the undertakings involved.

(34) Where appropriate, the Commission will address written requests for information to the market players mentioned above. These requests will usually include questions relating to the perceptions of companies about reactions to hypothetical price increases and their views of the boundaries of the relevant market. They will also ask for provision of the factual information the Commission deems necessary to reach a conclusion on the extent of the relevant market. The Commission might also discuss with marketing directors or other officers of those companies to gain a better understanding on how negotiations between suppliers and customers take place and better understand issues relating to the definition of the relevant market. Where appropriate, they might also carry out visits or inspections to the premises of the parties, their customers and/or their competitors, in order to better understand how products are manufactured and sold.

(35) The type of evidence relevant to reach a conclusion as to the product market can be categorized as follows:

Evidence to define markets — product dimension

(36) An analysis of the product characteristics and its intended use allows the Commission, as a first step, to limit the field of investigation of possible substitutes. However, product characteristics and intended use are insufficient to show whether two products are demand substitutes. Functional inter-changeability or similarity in characteristics may not, in themselves, provide sufficient criteria, because the responsiveness of customers to relative price changes may be determinded by other considerations as well. For example, there may be different competitive contraints in the original equipment market for car components and in spare parts, thereby leading to a separate delineation of two relevant markets. Conversely, differences in product characteristics are not in themselves sufficient to exclude demand substitutability, since this will depend to a large extent on how customers value different characteristics.

(37) The type of evidence the Commission considers relevant to assess whether two products are demand substitutes can be categorized as follows:

(38) *Evidence of substitution in the recent past*. In certain cases, it is possible to analyse evidence relating to recent past events or shocks in the market that offer actual examples of substituion between two products. When available, this sort of information will normally be fundamental for market definition. If there have been changes in relative prices in the past (all else being equal), the reactions in terms of quantities demanded will be determinant in establishing substitutability. Launches of new products in the past can also offer useful information, when it is possible to precisely analyse which products have lost sales to the new product.

(39) There are a number of *quantitative tests* that have specifically been designed for the purpose of delineating markets. These tests consist of various econometric and statistical approaches estimates of elasticities and cross-price elasticities for the demand of a product, tests based on similarity of price movements over time, the analysis of causality between price series and similarity of price levels and/or their convergence. The Commission takes into account the available quantitative evidence capable of withstanding rigorous scrutiny for the purposes of establishing patterns of substitution in the past.

(40) Views of *customers and competitors*. The Commission often contacts the main customers and competitors of the companies involved in its enquiries, to gather their views on the boundaries of the product market as well as most of the factual information it requires to reach a conclusion on the scope of the market. Reasoned answers of customers and competitors as to what would happen if

relative prices for the candidate products were to increase in the candidate geographic area by a small amount (for instance of 5 % to 10 %) are taken into account when they are sufficiently backed by factual evidence.

(41) *Consumer preferences*. In the case of consumer goods, it may be difficult for the Commission to gather the direct views of end consumers about substitute products. *Marketing studies* that companies have commissioned in the past and that are used by companies in their own decision-making as to pricing of their products and/or marketing actions may provide useful information for the Commission's delineation of the relevant market. Consumer surveys on usage patterns and attitudes, data from consumer's purchasing patterns, the views expressed by retailers and more generally, market research studies submitted by the parties and their competitors are taken into account to establish whether an economically significant proportion of consumers consider two products as substitutable, also taking into account the importance of brands for the products in question. The methodology followed in consumer surveys carried out *ad hoc* by the undertakings involved or their competitors for the purposes of a merger procedure or a procedure pursuant to Regulation No 17 will usually be scrutinized with utmost care. Unlike pre-existing studies, they have not been prepared in the normal course of business for the adoption of business decisions.

(42) *Barriers and costs associated with switching demand to potential substitutes*. There are a number of barriers and costs that might prevent the Commission from considering two *prima facie* demand substitutes as belonging to one single product market. It is not possible to provide an exhaustive list of all the possible barriers to substitution and of switching costs. These barriers or obstacles might have a wide range of origins, and in its decisions, the Commission has been confronted with regulatory barriers or other forms of State intervention, constraints arising in downstream markets, need to incur specific capital investment or loss in current output in order to switch to alternative inputs, the location of customers, specific investment in production process, learning and human capital investment, retooling costs or other investments, uncertainty about quality and reputation of unknown suppliers, and others.

(43) *Different categories of customers and price discrimination*. The extent of the product market might be narrowed in the presence of distinct groups of customers. A distinct group of customers for the relevant product may constitute a narrower, distinct market when such ha group could be subject to price discrimination. This will usually be the case when two conditions are met: (a) it is possible to identify clearly which group an individual customer belongs to at the moment of selling the relevant products to him, and (b) trade among customers or arbitrage by third parties should not be feasible.

Evidence for defining markets — geographic dimension

(44) The type of evidence the Commission considers relevant to reach a conclusion as to the geographic market can be categorized as follows:

(45) *Past evidence of diversion of orders to other areas*. In certain cases, evidence on changes in prices between different areas and consequent reactions by customers might be available. Generally, the same quantitative tests used for product market definition might as well be used in geographic market definition, bearing in mind that international comparisons of prices might be more complex due to a number of factors such as exchange rate movements, taxation and product differentiation.

(46) *Basic demand characteristics*. The nature of demand for the relevant product may in itself determine the scope of the geographical market. Factors such as national preferences or preferences for national brands, language, culture and life style, and the need for a local presence have a strong potential to limit the geographic scope of competition.

(47) *Views of customers and competitors*. Where appropriate, the Commission will contact the main customers and competitors of the parties in its enquiries, to gather their views on the boundaries of the geographic market as well as most of the factual information it requires to reach a conclusion on the scope of the market when they are sufficiently backed by factual evidence.

(48) *Current geographic pattern of purchases*. An examination of the customers' current geographic pattern of purchases provides useful evidence as to the possible scope of the geographic market. When customers purchase from companies located anywhere in the Community or the EEA on similar terms, or they procure their supplies through effective tendering procedures in which companies from anywhere in the Community or the EEA submit bids, usually the geographic market will be considered to be Community-wide.

(49) *Trade flows/pattern of shipments*. When the number of customers is so large that it is not possible to obtain through them a clear picture of geographic purchasing patterns, information on trade flows might be used alternatively, provided that the trade statistics are available with a sufficient degree of detail for the relevant products. Trade flows, and above all, the rationale behind trade flows provide useful insights and information for the purpose of establishing the scope of the geographic

market but are not in themselves conclusive.

(50) *Barriers and switching costs associated to divert orders to companies located in other areas.* The absence of trans-border purchases or trade flows, for instance, does not necessarily mean that the market is at most national in scope. Still, barriers isolating the national market have to identified before it is concluded that the relevant geographic market in such a case is national. Perhaps the clearest obstacle for a customer to divert its orders to other areas is the impact of transport costs and transport restrictions arising from legislation or from the nature of the relevant products. The impact of transport costs will usually limit the scope of the geographic market for bulky, low-value products, bearing in mind that a transport disadvantage might also be compensated by a comparative advantage in other costs (labour costs or raw materials). Access to distribution in a given area, regulatory barriers still existing in certain sectors, quotas and custom tariffs might also constitute barriers isolating a geographic area from the competitive pressure of companies located outside that area. Significant switching costs in procuring supplies from companies located in other countries constitute additional sources of such barriers.

(51) On the basis of the evidence gathered, the Commission will then define a geographic market that could range from a local dimension to a global one, and there are examples of both local and global markets in past decisions of the Commission.

(52) The paragraphs above describe the different factors which might be relevant to define markets. This does not imply that in each individual case it will be necessary to obtain evidence and assess each of these factors. Often in practice the evidence provided by a susbset of these factors will be sufficient to reach a conclusion, as shown in the past decisional practice of the Commission.

IV. Calculation of Market Share

(53) The definition of the relevant market in both its product and geograhic dimensions allows the identification the suppliers and the customers/consumers active on that market. On that basis, a total market size and market shares for each supplier can be calculated on the basis of their sales of the relevant products in the relevant area. In practice, the total market size and market shares are often available from market sources, i.e. companies' estimates, studies commissioned from industry consultants and/or trade associations. When this is not the case, or when available estimates are not reliable, the Commission will usually ask each supplier in the relevant market to provide its own sales in order to calculate total market size and market shares.

(54) If sales are usually the reference to calculate market shares, there are nevertheless other indications that, depending on the specific products or industry in question, can offer useful information such as, in particular, capacity, the number of players in bidding markets, units of fleet as in aerospace, or the reserves held in the case of sectors such as mining.

(55) As a rule of thumb, both volume sales and value sales provide useful information. In cases of differentiated products, sales in value and their associated market share will usually be considered to better reflect the relative position and strength of each supplier.

V. Additional Considerations

(56) There are certain areas where the application of the principles above has to be undertaken with care. This is the case when considering primary and secondary markets, in particular, when the behaviour of undertakings at a point in time has to be analysed pursuant to Article 86. The method of defining markets in these cases is the same, i.e. assessing the responses of customers based on their purchasing decisions to relative price changes, but taking into account as well, constraints on substitution imposed by conditions in the connected markets. A narrow definition of market for secondary products, for instance, spare parts, may result when compatibility with the primary product is important. Problems of finding compatible secondary products together with the existence of high prices and a long lifetime of the primary products may render relative price increases of secondary products profitable. A different market definition may result if significant substitution between secondary products is possible or if the characteristics of the primary products make quick and direct consumer responses to relative price increases of the secondary products feasible.

(57) In certain cases, the existence of chains of substitution might lead to the definition of a relevant market where products or areas at the extreme of the market are not directly substitutable. An example might be provided by the geographic dimension of a product with significant transport costs. In such cases, deliveries from a given plant are limited to a certain area around each plant by the impact of transport costs. In principle, such an area could constitute the relevant geographic market. However, if the distribution of plants is such that there are considerable overlaps between the areas around different plants, it is possible that the pricing of those products will be constrained by a chain substitution effect, and lead to the definition of a broader geographic market. The same reasoning may apply if product B is a demand substitute for products A and C. Even if products A and C are not

direct demand substitutes, they might be found to be in the same relevant product market since their respective pricing might be constrained by substitution to B.

(58) From a practical perspective, the concept of chains of substitution has to be corroborated by actual evidence, for instance related to price interdependence at the extremes of the chains of substitution, in order to lead to an extension of the relevant market in an individual case. Price levels at the extremes of the chains would have to be of the same magnitude as well.

Council Regulation (EC) No 1/2003 of 16 December 2002 on the implementation of the rules on competition laid down in Articles 81 and 82 of the Treaty

THE COUNCIL OF THE EUROPEAN UNION,
Having regard to the Treaty establishing the European Community, and in particular Article 83 thereof,
Having regard to the proposal from the Commission,
Having regard to the opinion of the European Parliament,
Having regard to the opinion of the European Economic and Social Committee,
Whereas:
(1) In order to establish a system which ensures that competition in the common market is not distorted, Articles 81 and 82 of the Treaty must be applied effectively and uniformly in the Community. Council Regulation No 17 of 6 February 1962, First Regulation implementing Articles 81 and 82(4) of the Treaty, has allowed a Community competition policy to develop that has helped to disseminate a competition culture within the Community. In the light of experience, however, that Regulation should now be replaced by legislation designed to meet the challenges of an integrated market and a future enlargement of the Community.
(2) In particular, there is a need to rethink the arrangements for applying the exception from the prohibition on agreements, which restrict competition, laid down in Article 81(3) of the Treaty. Under Article 83(2)(b) of the Treaty, account must be taken in this regard of the need to ensure effective supervision, on the one hand, and to simplify administration to the greatest possible extent, on the other.
(3) The centralised scheme set up by Regulation No 17 no longer secures a balance between those two objectives. It hampers application of the Community competition rules by the courts and competition authorities of the Member States, and the system of notification it involves prevents the Commission from concentrating its resources on curbing the most serious infringements. It also imposes considerable costs on undertakings.
(4) The present system should therefore be replaced by a directly applicable exception system in which the competition authorities and courts of the Member States have the power to apply not only Article 81(1) and Article 82 of the Treaty, which have direct applicability by virtue of the case-law of the Court of Justice of the European Communities, but also Article 81(3) of the Treaty.
(5) In order to ensure an effective enforcement of the Community competition rules and at the same time the respect of fundamental rights of defence, this Regulation should regulate the burden of proof under Articles 81 and 82 of the Treaty. It should be for the party or the authority alleging an infringement of Article 81(1) and Article 82 of the Treaty to prove the existence thereof to the required legal standard. It should be for the undertaking or association of undertakings invoking the benefit of a defence against a finding of an infringement to demonstrate to the required legal standard that the conditions for applying such defence are satisfied. This Regulation affects neither national rules on the standard of proof nor obligations of competition authorities and courts of the Member States to ascertain the relevant facts of a case, provided that such rules and obligations are compatible with general principles of Community law.
(6) In order to ensure that the Community competition rules are applied effectively, the competition authorities of the Member States should be associated more closely with their application. To this end, they should be empowered to apply Community law.
(7) National courts have an essential part to play in applying the Community competition rules. When deciding disputes between private individuals, they protect the subjective rights under Community law, for example by awarding damages to the victims of infringements. The role of the national courts here complements that of the competition authorities of the Member States. They should therefore be allowed to apply Articles 81 and 82 of the Treaty in full.
(8) In order to ensure the effective enforcement of the Community competition rules and the proper functioning of the cooperation mechanisms contained in this Regulation, it is necessary to oblige the competition authorities and courts of the Member States to also apply Articles 81 and 82 of the Treaty where they apply national competition law to agreements and practices which may affect trade between Member States. In order to create a level playing field for agreements, decisions by associations of undertakings and concerted practices within the internal market, it is also necessary to determine pursuant to Article 83(2)(e) of the Treaty the relationship between national laws and Community competition law. To that effect it is necessary to provide that the application of national competition laws to agreements, decisions or concerted practices within the meaning of Article 81(1) of the Treaty may not lead to the prohibition of such agreements, decisions and concerted practices if they are not also prohibited under Community competition law. The notions of agreements, deci-

sions and concerted practices are autonomous concepts of Community competition law covering the coordination of behaviour of undertakings on the market as interpreted by the Community Courts. Member States should not under this Regulation be precluded from adopting and applying on their territory stricter national competition laws which prohibit or impose sanctions on unilateral conduct engaged in by undertakings. These stricter national laws may include provisions which prohibit or impose sanctions on abusive behaviour toward economically dependent undertakings. Furthermore, this Regulation does not apply to national laws which impose criminal sanctions on natural persons except to the extent that such sanctions are the means whereby competition rules applying to undertakings are enforced.

(9) Articles 81 and 82 of the Treaty have as their objective the protection of competition on the market. This Regulation, which is adopted for the implementation of these Treaty provisions, does not preclude Member States from implementing on their territory national legislation, which protects other legitimate interests provided that such legislation is compatible with general principles and other provisions of Community law. In so far as such national legislation pursues predominantly an objective different from that of protecting competition on the market, the competition authorities and courts of the Member States may apply such legislation on their territory. Accordingly, Member States may under this Regulation implement on their territory national legislation that prohibits or imposes sanctions on acts of unfair trading practice, be they unilateral or contractual. Such legislation pursues a specific objective, irrespective of the actual or presumed effects of such acts on competition on the market. This is particularly the case of legislation which prohibits undertakings from imposing on their trading partners, obtaining or attempting to obtain from them terms and conditions that are unjustified, disproportionate or without consideration.

(10) Regulations such as 19/65/EEC, (EEC) No 2821/71, (EEC) No 3976/87, (EEC) No 1534/91, or (EEC) No 479/92 empower the Commission to apply Article 81(3) of the Treaty by Regulation to certain categories of agreements, decisions by associations of undertakings and concerted practices. In the areas defined by such Regulations, the Commission has adopted and may continue to adopt so called "block" exemption Regulations by which it declares Article 81(1) of the Treaty inapplicable to categories of agreements, decisions and concerted practices. Where agreements, decisions and concerted practices to which such Regulations apply nonetheless have effects that are incompatible with Article 81(3) of the Treaty, the Commission and the competition authorities of the Member States should have the power to withdraw in a particular case the benefit of the block exemption Regulation.

(11) For it to ensure that the provisions of the Treaty are applied, the Commission should be able to address decisions to undertakings or associations of undertakings for the purpose of bringing to an end infringements of Articles 81 and 82 of the Treaty. Provided there is a legitimate interest in doing so, the Commission should also be able to adopt decisions which find that an infringement has been committed in the past even if it does not impose a fine. This Regulation should also make explicit provision for the Commission's power to adopt decisions ordering interim measures, which has been acknowledged by the Court of Justice.

(12) This Regulation should make explicit provision for the Commission's power to impose any remedy, whether behavioural or structural, which is necessary to bring the infringement effectively to an end, having regard to the principle of proportionality. Structural remedies should only be imposed either where there is no equally effective behavioural remedy or where any equally effective behavioural remedy would be more burdensome for the undertaking concerned than the structural remedy. Changes to the structure of an undertaking as it existed before the infringement was committed would only be proportionate where there is a substantial risk of a lasting or repeated infringement that derives from the very structure of the undertaking.

(13) Where, in the course of proceedings which might lead to an agreement or practice being prohibited, undertakings offer the Commission commitments such as to meet its concerns, the Commission should be able to adopt decisions which make those commitments binding on the undertakings concerned. Commitment decisions should find that there are no longer grounds for action by the Commission without concluding whether or not there has been or still is an infringement. Commitment decisions are without prejudice to the powers of competition authorities and courts of the Member States to make such a finding and decide upon the case. Commitment decisions are not appropriate in cases where the Commission intends to impose a fine.

(14) In exceptional cases where the public interest of the Community so requires, it may also be expedient for the Commission to adopt a decision of a declaratory nature finding that the prohibition in Article 81 or Article 82 of the Treaty does not apply, with a view to clarifying the law and ensuring its consistent application throughout the Community, in particular with regard to new types of agreements or practices that have not been settled in the existing case-law and administrative practice.

(15) The Commission and the competition authorities of the Member States should form together a

network of public authorities applying the Community competition rules in close cooperation. For that purpose it is necessary to set up arrangements for information and consultation. Further modalities for the cooperation within the network will be laid down and revised by the Commission, in close cooperation with the Member States.

(16) Notwithstanding any national provision to the contrary, the exchange of information and the use of such information in evidence should be allowed between the members of the network even where the information is confidential. This information may be used for the application of Articles 81 and 82 of the Treaty as well as for the parallel application of national competition law, provided that the latter application relates to the same case and does not lead to a different outcome. When the information exchanged is used by the receiving authority to impose sanctions on undertakings, there should be no other limit to the use of the information than the obligation to use it for the purpose for which it was collected given the fact that the sanctions imposed on undertakings are of the same type in all systems. The rights of defence enjoyed by undertakings in the various systems can be considered as sufficiently equivalent. However, as regards natural persons, they may be subject to substantially different types of sanctions across the various systems. Where that is the case, it is necessary to ensure that information can only be used if it has been collected in a way which respects the same level of protection of the rights of defence of natural persons as provided for under the national rules of the receiving authority.

(17) If the competition rules are to be applied consistently and, at the same time, the network is to be managed in the best possible way, it is essential to retain the rule that the competition authorities of the Member States are automatically relieved of their competence if the Commission initiates its own proceedings. Where a competition authority of a Member State is already acting on a case and the Commission intends to initiate proceedings, it should endeavour to do so as soon as possible. Before initiating proceedings, the Commission should consult the national authority concerned.

(18) To ensure that cases are dealt with by the most appropriate authorities within the network, a general provision should be laid down allowing a competition authority to suspend or close a case on the ground that another authority is dealing with it or has already dealt with it, the objective being that each case should be handled by a single authority. This provision should not prevent the Commission from rejecting a complaint for lack of Community interest, as the case-law of the Court of Justice has acknowledged it may do, even if no other competition authority has indicated its intention of dealing with the case.

(19) The Advisory Committee on Restrictive Practices and Dominant Positions set up by Regulation No 17 has functioned in a very satisfactory manner. It will fit well into the new system of decentralised application. It is necessary, therefore, to build upon the rules laid down by Regulation No 17, while improving the effectiveness of the organisational arrangements. To this end, it would be expedient to allow opinions to be delivered by written procedure. The Advisory Committee should also be able to act as a forum for discussing cases that are being handled by the competition authorities of the Member States, so as to help safeguard the consistent application of the Community competition rules.

(20) The Advisory Committee should be composed of representatives of the competition authorities of the Member States. For meetings in which general issues are being discussed, Member States should be able to appoint an additional representative. This is without prejudice to members of the Committee being assisted by other experts from the Member States.

(21) Consistency in the application of the competition rules also requires that arrangements be established for cooperation between the courts of the Member States and the Commission. This is relevant for all courts of the Member States that apply Articles 81 and 82 of the Treaty, whether applying these rules in lawsuits between private parties, acting as public enforcers or as review courts. In particular, national courts should be able to ask the Commission for information or for its opinion on points concerning the application of Community competition law. The Commission and the competition authorities of the Member States should also be able to submit written or oral observations to courts called upon to apply Article 81 or Article 82 of the Treaty. These observations should be submitted within the framework of national procedural rules and practices including those safeguarding the rights of the parties. Steps should therefore be taken to ensure that the Commission and the competition authorities of the Member States are kept sufficiently well informed of proceedings before national courts.

(22) In order to ensure compliance with the principles of legal certainty and the uniform application of the Community competition rules in a system of parallel powers, conflicting decisions must be avoided. It is therefore necessary to clarify, in accordance with the case-law of the Court of Justice, the effects of Commission decisions and proceedings on courts and competition authorities of the Member States. Commitment decisions adopted by the Commission do not affect the power of the

courts and the competition authorities of the Member States to apply Articles 81 and 82 of the Treaty.
(23) The Commission should be empowered throughout the Community to require such information to be supplied as is necessary to detect any agreement, decision or concerted practice prohibited by Article 81 of the Treaty or any abuse of a dominant position prohibited by Article 82 of the Treaty. When complying with a decision of the Commission, undertakings cannot be forced to admit that they have committed an infringement, but they are in any event obliged to answer factual questions and to provide documents, even if this information may be used to establish against them or against another undertaking the existence of an infringement.
(24) The Commission should also be empowered to undertake such inspections as are necessary to detect any agreement, decision or concerted practice prohibited by Article 81 of the Treaty or any abuse of a dominant position prohibited by Article 82 of the Treaty. The competition authorities of the Member States should cooperate actively in the exercise of these powers.
(25) The detection of infringements of the competition rules is growing ever more difficult, and, in order to protect competition effectively, the Commission's powers of investigation need to be supplemented. The Commission should in particular be empowered to interview any persons who may be in possession of useful information and to record the statements made. In the course of an inspection, officials authorised by the Commission should be empowered to affix seals for the period of time necessary for the inspection. Seals should normally not be affixed for more than 72 hours. Officials authorised by the Commission should also be empowered to ask for any information relevant to the subject matter and purpose of the inspection.
(26) Experience has shown that there are cases where business records are kept in the homes of directors or other people working for an undertaking. In order to safeguard the effectiveness of inspections, therefore, officials and other persons authorised by the Commission should be empowered to enter any premises where business records may be kept, including private homes. However, the exercise of this latter power should be subject to the authorisation of the judicial authority.
(27) Without prejudice to the case-law of the Court of Justice, it is useful to set out the scope of the control that the national judicial authority may carry out when it authorises, as foreseen by national law including as a precautionary measure, assistance from law enforcement authorities in order to overcome possible opposition on the part of the undertaking or the execution of the decision to carry out inspections in non-business premises. It results from the case-law that the national judicial authority may in particular ask the Commission for further information which it needs to carry out its control and in the absence of which it could refuse the authorisation. The case-law also confirms the competence of the national courts to control the application of national rules governing the implementation of coercive measures.
(28) In order to help the competition authorities of the Member States to apply Articles 81 and 82 of the Treaty effectively, it is expedient to enable them to assist one another by carrying out inspections and other fact-finding measures.
(29) Compliance with Articles 81 and 82 of the Treaty and the fulfilment of the obligations imposed on undertakings and associations of undertakings under this Regulation should be enforceable by means of fines and periodic penalty payments. To that end, appropriate levels of fine should also be laid down for infringements of the procedural rules.
(30) In order to ensure effective recovery of fines imposed on associations of undertakings for infringements that they have committed, it is necessary to lay down the conditions on which the Commission may require payment of the fine from the members of the association where the association is not solvent. In doing so, the Commission should have regard to the relative size of the undertakings belonging to the association and in particular to the situation of small and medium-sized enterprises. Payment of the fine by one or several members of an association is without prejudice to rules of national law that provide for recovery of the amount paid from other members of the association.
(31) The rules on periods of limitation for the imposition of fines and periodic penalty payments were laid down in Council Regulation (EEC) No 2988/74, which also concerns penalties in the field of transport. In a system of parallel powers, the acts, which may interrupt a limitation period, should include procedural steps taken independently by the competition authority of a Member State. To clarify the legal framework, Regulation (EEC) No 2988/74 should therefore be amended to prevent it applying to matters covered by this Regulation, and this Regulation should include provisions on periods of limitation.
(32) The undertakings concerned should be accorded the right to be heard by the Commission, third parties whose interests may be affected by a decision should be given the opportunity of submitting their observations beforehand, and the decisions taken should be widely publicised. While ensuring the rights of defence of the undertakings concerned, in particular, the right of access to the file, it is essential that business secrets be protected. The confidentiality of information exchanged in the

network should likewise be safeguarded.
(33) Since all decisions taken by the Commission under this Regulation are subject to review by the Court of Justice in accordance with the Treaty, the Court of Justice should, in accordance with Article 229 thereof be given unlimited jurisdiction in respect of decisions by which the Commission imposes fines or periodic penalty payments.
(34) The principles laid down in Articles 81 and 82 of the Treaty, as they have been applied by Regulation No 17, have given a central role to the Community bodies. This central role should be retained, whilst associating the Member States more closely with the application of the Community competition rules. In accordance with the principles of subsidiarity and proportionality as set out in Article 5 of the Treaty, this Regulation does not go beyond what is necessary in order to achieve its objective, which is to allow the Community competition rules to be applied effectively.
(35) In order to attain a proper enforcement of Community competition law, Member States should designate and empower authorities to apply Articles 81 and 82 of the Treaty as public enforcers. They should be able to designate administrative as well as judicial authorities to carry out the various functions conferred upon competition authorities in this Regulation. This Regulation recognises the wide variation which exists in the public enforcement systems of Member States. The effects of Article 11(6) of this Regulation should apply to all competition authorities. As an exception to this general rule, where a prosecuting authority brings a case before a separate judicial authority, Article 11(6) should apply to the prosecuting authority subject to the conditions in Article 35(4) of this Regulation. Where these conditions are not fulfilled, the general rule should apply. In any case, Article 11(6) should not apply to courts insofar as they are acting as review courts.
(36) As the case-law has made it clear that the competition rules apply to transport, that sector should be made subject to the procedural provisions of this Regulation. Council Regulation No 141 of 26 November 1962 exempting transport from the application of Regulation No 17 should therefore be repealed and Regulations (EEC) No 1017/68, (EEC) No 4056/86 and (EEC) No 3975/87 should be amended in order to delete the specific procedural provisions they contain.
(37) This Regulation respects the fundamental rights and observes the principles recognised in particular by the Charter of Fundamental Rights of the European Union. Accordingly, this Regulation should be interpreted and applied with respect to those rights and principles.
(38) Legal certainty for undertakings operating under the Community competition rules contributes to the promotion of innovation and investment. Where cases give rise to genuine uncertainty because they present novel or unresolved questions for the application of these rules, individual undertakings may wish to seek informal guidance from the Commission. This Regulation is without prejudice to the ability of the Commission to issue such informal guidance,
HAS ADOPTED THIS REGULATION:

Chapter I. Principles

Article 1. Application of Articles 81 and 82 of the Treaty
(1) Agreements, decisions and concerted practices caught by Article 81(1) of the Treaty which do not satisfy the conditions of Article 81(3) of the Treaty shall be prohibited, no prior decision to that effect being required.
(2) Agreements, decisions and concerted practices caught by Article 81(1) of the Treaty which satisfy the conditions of Article 81(3) of the Treaty shall not be prohibited, no prior decision to that effect being required.
(3) The abuse of a dominant position referred to in Article 82 of the Treaty shall be prohibited, no prior decision to that effect being required.

Article 2. Burden of proof
In any national or Community proceedings for the application of Articles 81 and 82 of the Treaty, the burden of proving an infringement of Article 81(1) or of Article 82 of the Treaty shall rest on the party or the authority alleging the infringement. The undertaking or association of undertakings claiming the benefit of Article 81(3) of the Treaty shall bear the burden of proving that the conditions of that paragraph are fulfilled.

Article 3. Relationship between Articles 81 and 82 of the Treaty and national competition laws
(1) Where the competition authorities of the Member States or national courts apply national competition law to agreements, decisions by associations of undertakings or concerted practices within the meaning of Article 81(1) of the Treaty which may affect trade between Member States within the meaning of that provision, they shall also apply Article 81 of the Treaty to such agreements, decisions or concerted practices. Where the competition authorities of the Member States or national courts apply national competition law to any abuse prohibited by Article 82 of the Treaty, they shall also apply Article 82 of the Treaty.

(2) The application of national competition law may not lead to the prohibition of agreements, decisions by associations of undertakings or concerted practices which may affect trade between Member States but which do not restrict competition within the meaning of Article 81(1) of the Treaty, or which fulfil the conditions of Article 81(3) of the Treaty or which are covered by a Regulation for the application of Article 81(3) of the Treaty. Member States shall not under this Regulation be precluded from adopting and applying on their territory stricter national laws which prohibit or sanction unilateral conduct engaged in by undertakings.

(3) Without prejudice to general principles and other provisions of Community law, paragraphs 1 and 2 do not apply when the competition authorities and the courts of the Member States apply national merger control laws nor do they preclude the application of provisions of national law that predominantly pursue an objective different from that pursued by Articles 81 and 82 of the Treaty.

Chapter II. Powers

Article 4. Powers of the Commission

For the purpose of applying Articles 81 and 82 of the Treaty, the Commission shall have the powers provided for by this Regulation.

Article 5. Powers of the competition authorities of the Member States

The competition authorities of the Member States shall have the power to apply Articles 81 and 82 of the Treaty in individual cases. For this purpose, acting on their own initiative or on a complaint, they may take the following decisions:
- requiring that an infringement be brought to an end,
- ordering interim measures,
- accepting commitments,
- imposing fines, periodic penalty payments or any other penalty provided for in their national law.

Where on the basis of the information in their possession the conditions for prohibition are not met they may likewise decide that there are no grounds for action on their part.

Article 6. Powers of the national courts

National courts shall have the power to apply Articles 81 and 82 of the Treaty.

Chapter III. Commission Decisions

Article 7. Finding and termination of infringement

(1) Where the Commission, acting on a complaint or on its own initiative, finds that there is an infringement of Article 81 or of Article 82 of the Treaty, it may by decision require the undertakings and associations of undertakings concerned to bring such infringement to an end. For this purpose, it may impose on them any behavioural or structural remedies which are proportionate to the infringement committed and necessary to bring the infringement effectively to an end. Structural remedies can only be imposed either where there is no equally effective behavioural remedy or where any equally effective behavioural remedy would be more burdensome for the undertaking concerned than the structural remedy. If the Commission has a legitimate interest in doing so, it may also find that an infringement has been committed in the past.

(2) Those entitled to lodge a complaint for the purposes of paragraph 1 are natural or legal persons who can show a legitimate interest and Member States.

Article 8. Interim measures

(1) In cases of urgency due to the risk of serious and irreparable damage to competition, the Commission, acting on its own initiative may by decision, on the basis of a prima facie finding of infringement, order interim measures.

(2) A decision under paragraph 1 shall apply for a specified period of time and may be renewed in so far this is necessary and appropriate.

Article 9. Commitments

(1) Where the Commission intends to adopt a decision requiring that an infringement be brought to an end and the undertakings concerned offer commitments to meet the concerns expressed to them by the Commission in its preliminary assessment, the Commission may by decision make those commitments binding on the undertakings. Such a decision may be adopted for a specified period and shall conclude that there are no longer grounds for action by the Commission.

(2) The Commission may, upon request or on its own initiative, reopen the proceedings:
(a) where there has been a material change in any of the facts on which the decision was based;
(b) where the undertakings concerned act contrary to their commitments; or

(c) where the decision was based on incomplete, incorrect or misleading information provided by the parties.

Article 10. Finding of inapplicability

Where the Community public interest relating to the application of Articles 81 and 82 of the Treaty so requires, the Commission, acting on its own initiative, may by decision find that Article 81 of the Treaty is not applicable to an agreement, a decision by an association of undertakings or a concerted practice, either because the conditions of Article 81(1) of the Treaty are not fulfilled, or because the conditions of Article 81(3) of the Treaty are satisfied.

The Commission may likewise make such a finding with reference to Article 82 of the Treaty.

Chapter IV. Cooperation

Article 11. Cooperation between the Commission and the competition authorities of the Member States

(1) The Commission and the competition authorities of the Member States shall apply the Community competition rules in close cooperation.

(2) The Commission shall transmit to the competition authorities of the Member States copies of the most important documents it has collected with a view to applying Articles 7, 8, 9, 10 and Article 29(1). At the request of the competition authority of a Member State, the Commission shall provide it with a copy of other existing documents necessary for the assessment of the case.

(3) The competition authorities of the Member States shall, when acting under Article 81 or Article 82 of the Treaty, inform the Commission in writing before or without delay after commencing the first formal investigative measure. This information may also be made available to the competition authorities of the other Member States.

(4) No later than 30 days before the adoption of a decision requiring that an infringement be brought to an end, accepting commitments or withdrawing the benefit of a block exemption Regulation, the competition authorities of the Member States shall inform the Commission. To that effect, they shall provide the Commission with a summary of the case, the envisaged decision or, in the absence thereof, any other document indicating the proposed course of action. This information may also be made available to the competition authorities of the other Member States. At the request of the Commission, the acting competition authority shall make available to the Commission other documents it holds which are necessary for the assessment of the case. The information supplied to the Commission may be made available to the competition authorities of the other Member States. National competition authorities may also exchange between themselves information necessary for the assessment of a case that they are dealing with under Article 81 or Article 82 of the Treaty.

(5) The competition authorities of the Member States may consult the Commission on any case involving the application of Community law.

(6) The initiation by the Commission of proceedings for the adoption of a decision under Chapter III shall relieve the competition authorities of the Member States of their competence to apply Articles 81 and 82 of the Treaty. If a competition authority of a Member State is already acting on a case, the Commission shall only initiate proceedings after consulting with that national competition authority.

Article 12. Exchange of information

(1) For the purpose of applying Articles 81 and 82 of the Treaty the Commission and the competition authorities of the Member States shall have the power to provide one another with and use in evidence any matter of fact or of law, including confidential information.

(2) Information exchanged shall only be used in evidence for the purpose of applying Article 81 or Article 82 of the Treaty and in respect of the subject-matter for which it was collected by the transmitting authority. However, where national competition law is applied in the same case and in parallel to Community competition law and does not lead to a different outcome, information exchanged under this Article may also be used for the application of national competition law.

(3) Information exchanged pursuant to paragraph 1 can only be used in evidence to impose sanctions on natural persons where:
- the law of the transmitting authority foresees sanctions of a similar kind in relation to an infringement of Article 81 or Article 82 of the Treaty or, in the absence thereof,
- the information has been collected in a way which respects the same level of protection of the rights of defence of natural persons as provided for under the national rules of the receiving authority. However, in this case, the information exchanged cannot be used by the receiving authority to impose custodial sanctions.

Article 13. Suspension or termination of proceedings

(1) Where competition authorities of two or more Member States have received a complaint or are acting on their own initiative under Article 81 or Article 82 of the Treaty against the same agreement, decision of an association or practice, the fact that one authority is dealing with the case shall be sufficient grounds for the others to suspend the proceedings before them or to reject the complaint. The Commission may likewise reject a complaint on the ground that a competition authority of a Member State is dealing with the case.
(2) Where a competition authority of a Member State or the Commission has received a complaint against an agreement, decision of an association or practice which has already been dealt with by another competition authority, it may reject it.

Article 14. Advisory Committee
(1) The Commission shall consult an Advisory Committee on Restrictive Practices and Dominant Positions prior to the taking of any decision under Articles 7, 8, 9, 10, 23, Article 24(2) and Article 29(1).
(2) For the discussion of individual cases, the Advisory Committee shall be composed of representatives of the competition authorities of the Member States. For meetings in which issues other than individual cases are being discussed, an additional Member State representative competent in competition matters may be appointed. Representatives may, if unable to attend, be replaced by other representatives.
(3) The consultation may take place at a meeting convened and chaired by the Commission, held not earlier than 14 days after dispatch of the notice convening it, together with a summary of the case, an indication of the most important documents and a preliminary draft decision. In respect of decisions pursuant to Article 8, the meeting may be held seven days after the dispatch of the operative part of a draft decision. Where the Commission dispatches a notice convening the meeting which gives a shorter period of notice than those specified above, the meeting may take place on the proposed date in the absence of an objection by any Member State. The Advisory Committee shall deliver a written opinion on the Commission's preliminary draft decision. It may deliver an opinion even if some members are absent and are not represented. At the request of one or several members, the positions stated in the opinion shall be reasoned.
(4) Consultation may also take place by written procedure. However, if any Member State so requests, the Commission shall convene a meeting. In case of written procedure, the Commission shall determine a time-limit of not less than 14 days within which the Member States are to put forward their observations for circulation to all other Member States. In case of decisions to be taken pursuant to Article 8, the time-limit of 14 days is replaced by seven days. Where the Commission determines a time-limit for the written procedure which is shorter than those specified above, the proposed time-limit shall be applicable in the absence of an objection by any Member State.
(5) The Commission shall take the utmost account of the opinion delivered by the Advisory Committee. It shall inform the Committee of the manner in which its opinion has been taken into account.
(6) Where the Advisory Committee delivers a written opinion, this opinion shall be appended to the draft decision. If the Advisory Committee recommends publication of the opinion, the Commission shall carry out such publication taking into account the legitimate interest of undertakings in the protection of their business secrets.
(7) At the request of a competition authority of a Member State, the Commission shall include on the agenda of the Advisory Committee cases that are being dealt with by a competition authority of a Member State under Article 81 or Article 82 of the Treaty. The Commission may also do so on its own initiative. In either case, the Commission shall inform the competition authority concerned.
A request may in particular be made by a competition authority of a Member State in respect of a case where the Commission intends to initiate proceedings with the effect of Article 11(6).
The Advisory Committee shall not issue opinions on cases dealt with by competition authorities of the Member States. The Advisory Committee may also discuss general issues of Community competition law.

Article 15. Cooperation with national courts
(1) In proceedings for the application of Article 81 or Article 82 of the Treaty, courts of the Member States may ask the Commission to transmit to them information in its possession or its opinion on questions concerning the application of the Community competition rules.
(2) Member States shall forward to the Commission a copy of any written judgment of national courts deciding on the application of Article 81 or Article 82 of the Treaty. Such copy shall be forwarded without delay after the full written judgment is notified to the parties.
(3) Competition authorities of the Member States, acting on their own initiative, may submit written observations to the national courts of their Member State on issues relating to the application of

Article 81 or Article 82 of the Treaty. With the permission of the court in question, they may also submit oral observations to the national courts of their Member State. Where the coherent application of Article 81 or Article 82 of the Treaty so requires, the Commission, acting on its own initiative, may submit written observations to courts of the Member States. With the permission of the court in question, it may also make oral observations.

For the purpose of the preparation of their observations only, the competition authorities of the Member States and the Commission may request the relevant court of the Member State to transmit or ensure the transmission to them of any documents necessary for the assessment of the case.

(4) This Article is without prejudice to wider powers to make observations before courts conferred on competition authorities of the Member States under the law of their Member State.

Article 16. Uniform application of Community competition law

(1) When national courts rule on agreements, decisions or practices under Article 81 or Article 82 of the Treaty which are already the subject of a Commission decision, they cannot take decisions running counter to the decision adopted by the Commission. They must also avoid giving decisions which would conflict with a decision contemplated by the Commission in proceedings it has initiated. To that effect, the national court may assess whether it is necessary to stay its proceedings. This obligation is without prejudice to the rights and obligations under Article 234 of the Treaty.

(2) When competition authorities of the Member States rule on agreements, decisions or practices under Article 81 or Article 82 of the Treaty which are already the subject of a Commission decision, they cannot take decisions which would run counter to the decision adopted by the Commission.

Chapter V. Powers of Investigation

Article 17. Investigations into sectors of the economy and into types of agreements

(1) Where the trend of trade between Member States, the rigidity of prices or other circumstances suggest that competition may be restricted or distorted within the common market, the Commission may conduct its inquiry into a particular sector of the economy or into a particular type of agreements across various sectors. In the course of that inquiry, the Commission may request the undertakings or associations of undertakings concerned to supply the information necessary for giving effect to Articles 81 and 82 of the Treaty and may carry out any inspections necessary for that purpose.

The Commission may in particular request the undertakings or associations of undertakings concerned to communicate to it all agreements, decisions and concerted practices.

The Commission may publish a report on the results of its inquiry into particular sectors of the economy or particular types of agreements across various sectors and invite comments from interested parties.

(2) Articles 14, 18, 19, 20, 22, 23 and 24 shall apply *mutatis mutandis*.

Article 18. Requests for information

(1) In order to carry out the duties assigned to it by this Regulation, the Commission may, by simple request or by decision, require undertakings and associations of undertakings to provide all necessary information.

(2) When sending a simple request for information to an undertaking or association of undertakings, the Commission shall state the legal basis and the purpose of the request, specify what information is required and fix the time-limit within which the information is to be provided, and the penalties provided for in Article 23 for supplying incorrect or misleading information.

(3) Where the Commission requires undertakings and associations of undertakings to supply information by decision, it shall state the legal basis and the purpose of the request, specify what information is required and fix the time-limit within which it is to be provided. It shall also indicate the penalties provided for in Article 23 and indicate or impose the penalties provided for in Article 24. It shall further indicate the right to have the decision reviewed by the Court of Justice.

(4) The owners of the undertakings or their representatives and, in the case of legal persons, companies or firms, or associations having no legal personality, the persons authorised to represent them by law or by their constitution shall supply the information requested on behalf of the undertaking or the association of undertakings concerned. Lawyers duly authorised to act may supply the information on behalf of their clients. The latter shall remain fully responsible if the information supplied is incomplete, incorrect or misleading.

(5) The Commission shall without delay forward a copy of the simple request or of the decision to the competition authority of the Member State in whose territory the seat of the undertaking or association of undertakings is situated and the competition authority of the Member State whose territory is affected.

(6) At the request of the Commission the governments and competition authorities of the Member

States shall provide the Commission with all necessary information to carry out the duties assigned to it by this Regulation.

Article 19. Power to take statements

(1) In order to carry out the duties assigned to it by this Regulation, the Commission may interview any natural or legal person who consents to be interviewed for the purpose of collecting information relating to the subject-matter of an investigation.

(2) Where an interview pursuant to paragraph 1 is conducted in the premises of an undertaking, the Commission shall inform the competition authority of the Member State in whose territory the interview takes place. If so requested by the competition authority of that Member State, its officials may assist the officials and other accompanying persons authorised by the Commission to conduct the interview.

Article 20. The Commission's powers of inspection

(1) In order to carry out the duties assigned to it by this Regulation, the Commission may conduct all necessary inspections of undertakings and associations of undertakings.

(2) The officials and other accompanying persons authorised by the Commission to conduct an inspection are empowered:

(a) to enter any premises, land and means of transport of undertakings and associations of undertakings;

(b) to examine the books and other records related to the business, irrespective of the medium on which they are stored;

(c) to take or obtain in any form copies of or extracts from such books or records;

(d) to seal any business premises and books or records for the period and to the extent necessary for the inspection;

(e) to ask any representative or member of staff of the undertaking or association of undertakings for explanations on facts or documents relating to the subject-matter and purpose of the inspection and to record the answers.

(3) The officials and other accompanying persons authorised by the Commission to conduct an inspection shall exercise their powers upon production of a written authorisation specifying the subject matter and purpose of the inspection and the penalties provided for in Article 23 in case the production of the required books or other records related to the business is incomplete or where the answers to questions asked under paragraph 2 of the present Article are incorrect or misleading. In good time before the inspection, the Commission shall give notice of the inspection to the competition authority of the Member State in whose territory it is to be conducted.

(4) Undertakings and associations of undertakings are required to submit to inspections ordered by decision of the Commission. The decision shall specify the subject matter and purpose of the inspection, appoint the date on which it is to begin and indicate the penalties provided for in Articles 23 and 24 and the right to have the decision reviewed by the Court of Justice. The Commission shall take such decisions after consulting the competition authority of the Member State in whose territory the inspection is to be conducted.

(5) Officials of as well as those authorised or appointed by the competition authority of the Member State in whose territory the inspection is to be conducted shall, at the request of that authority or of the Commission, actively assist the officials and other accompanying persons authorised by the Commission. To this end, they shall enjoy the powers specified in paragraph 2.

(6) Where the officials and other accompanying persons authorised by the Commission find that an undertaking opposes an inspection ordered pursuant to this Article, the Member State concerned shall afford them the necessary assistance, requesting where appropriate the assistance of the police or of an equivalent enforcement authority, so as to enable them to conduct their inspection.

(7) If the assistance provided for in paragraph 6 requires authorisation from a judicial authority according to national rules, such authorisation shall be applied for. Such authorisation may also be applied for as a precautionary measure.

(8) Where authorisation as referred to in paragraph 7 is applied for, the national judicial authority shall control that the Commission decision is authentic and that the coercive measures envisaged are neither arbitrary nor excessive having regard to the subject matter of the inspection. In its control of the proportionality of the coercive measures, the national judicial authority may ask the Commission, directly or through the Member State competition authority, for detailed explanations in particular on the grounds the Commission has for suspecting infringement of Articles 81 and 82 of the Treaty, as well as on the seriousness of the suspected infringement and on the nature of the involvement of the undertaking concerned. However, the national judicial authority may not call into question the necessity for the inspection nor demand that it be provided with the information in the Commission's file. The lawfulness of the Commission decision shall be subject to review only by the Court of Justice.

Article 21. Inspection of other premises

(1) If a reasonable suspicion exists that books or other records related to the business and to the subject-matter of the inspection, which may be relevant to prove a serious violation of Article 81 or Article 82 of the Treaty, are being kept in any other premises, land and means of transport, including the homes of directors, managers and other members of staff of the undertakings and associations of undertakings concerned, the Commission can by decision order an inspection to be conducted in such other premises, land and means of transport.

(2) The decision shall specify the subject matter and purpose of the inspection, appoint the date on which it is to begin and indicate the right to have the decision reviewed by the Court of Justice. It shall in particular state the reasons that have led the Commission to conclude that a suspicion in the sense of paragraph 1 exists. The Commission shall take such decisions after consulting the competition authority of the Member State in whose territory the inspection is to be conducted.

(3) A decision adopted pursuant to paragraph 1 cannot be executed without prior authorisation from the national judicial authority of the Member State concerned. The national judicial authority shall control that the Commission decision is authentic and that the coercive measures envisaged are neither arbitrary nor excessive having regard in particular to the seriousness of the suspected infringement, to the importance of the evidence sought, to the involvement of the undertaking concerned and to the reasonable likelihood that business books and records relating to the subject matter of the inspection are kept in the premises for which the authorisation is requested. The national judicial authority may ask the Commission, directly or through the Member State competition authority, for detailed explanations on those elements which are necessary to allow its control of the proportionality of the coercive measures envisaged.

However, the national judicial authority may not call into question the necessity for the inspection nor demand that it be provided with information in the Commission's file. The lawfulness of the Commission decision shall be subject to review only by the Court of Justice.

(4) The officials and other accompanying persons authorised by the Commission to conduct an inspection ordered in accordance with paragraph 1 of this Article shall have the powers set out in Article 20(2)(a), (b) and (c). Article 20(5) and (6) shall apply *mutatis mutandis*.

Article 22. Investigations by competition authorities of Member States

(1) The competition authority of a Member State may in its own territory carry out any inspection or other fact-finding measure under its national law on behalf and for the account of the competition authority of another Member State in order to establish whether there has been an infringement of Article 81 or Article 82 of the Treaty. Any exchange and use of the information collected shall be carried out in accordance with Article 12.

(2) At the request of the Commission, the competition authorities of the Member States shall undertake the inspections which the Commission considers to be necessary under Article 20(1) or which it has ordered by decision pursuant to Article 20(4). The officials of the competition authorities of the Member States who are responsible for conducting these inspections as well as those authorised or appointed by them shall exercise their powers in accordance with their national law.

If so requested by the Commission or by the competition authority of the Member State in whose territory the inspection is to be conducted, officials and other accompanying persons authorised by the Commission may assist the officials of the authority concerned.

Chapter VI. Penalties

Article 23. Fines

(1) The Commission may by decision impose on undertakings and associations of undertakings fines not exceeding 1 % of the total turnover in the preceding business year where, intentionally or negligently:

(a) they supply incorrect or misleading information in response to a request made pursuant to Article 17 or Article 18(2);

(b) in response to a request made by decision adopted pursuant to Article 17 or Article 18(3), they supply incorrect, incomplete or misleading information or do not supply information within the required time-limit;

(c) they produce the required books or other records related to the business in incomplete form during inspections under Article 20 or refuse to submit to inspections ordered by a decision adopted pursuant to Article 20(4);

(d) in response to a question asked in accordance with Article 20(2)(e),
- they give an incorrect or misleading answer,
- they fail to rectify within a time-limit set by the Commission an incorrect, incomplete or misleading

PART III EUROPEAN UNION

answer given by a member of staff, or
- they fail or refuse to provide a complete answer on facts relating to the subject-matter and purpose of an inspection ordered by a decision adopted pursuant to Article 20(4);
(e) seals affixed in accordance with Article 20(2)(d) by officials or other accompanying persons authorised by the Commission have been broken.
(2) The Commission may by decision impose fines on undertakings and associations of undertakings where, either intentionally or negligently:
(a) they infringe Article 81 or Article 82 of the Treaty; or
(b) they contravene a decision ordering interim measures under Article 8; or
(c) they fail to comply with a commitment made binding by a decision pursuant to Article 9.
For each undertaking and association of undertakings participating in the infringement, the fine shall not exceed 10 % of its total turnover in the preceding business year.
Where the infringement of an association relates to the activities of its members, the fine shall not exceed 10 % of the sum of the total turnover of each member active on the market affected by the infringement of the association.
(3) In fixing the amount of the fine, regard shall be had both to the gravity and to the duration of the infringement.
(4) When a fine is imposed on an association of undertakings taking account of the turnover of its members and the association is not solvent, the association is obliged to call for contributions from its members to cover the amount of the fine.
Where such contributions have not been made to the association within a time-limit fixed by the Commission, the Commission may require payment of the fine directly by any of the undertakings whose representatives were members of the decision-making bodies concerned of the association.
After the Commission has required payment under the second subparagraph, where necessary to ensure full payment of the fine, the Commission may require payment of the balance by any of the members of the association which were active on the market on which the infringement occurred.
However, the Commission shall not require payment under the second or the third subparagraph from undertakings which show that they have not implemented the infringing decision of the association and either were not aware of its existence or have actively distanced themselves from it before the Commission started investigating the case.
The financial liability of each undertaking in respect of the payment of the fine shall not exceed 10 % of its total turnover in the preceding business year.
(5) Decisions taken pursuant to paragraphs 1 and 2 shall not be of a criminal law nature.

Article 24. Periodic penalty payments

(1) The Commission may, by decision, impose on undertakings or associations of undertakings periodic penalty payments not exceeding 5 % of the average daily turnover in the preceding business year per day and calculated from the date appointed by the decision, in order to compel them:
(a) to put an end to an infringement of Article 81 or Article 82 of the Treaty, in accordance with a decision taken pursuant to Article 7;
(b) to comply with a decision ordering interim measures taken pursuant to Article 8;
(c) to comply with a commitment made binding by a decision pursuant to Article 9;
(d) to supply complete and correct information which it has requested by decision taken pursuant to Article 17 or Article 18(3);
(e) to submit to an inspection which it has ordered by decision taken pursuant to Article 20(4).
(2) Where the undertakings or associations of undertakings have satisfied the obligation which the periodic penalty payment was intended to enforce, the Commission may fix the definitive amount of the periodic penalty payment at a figure lower than that which would arise under the original decision. Article 23(4) shall apply correspondingly.

Chapter VII. Limitation Periods

Article 25. Limitation periods for the imposition of penalties

(1) The powers conferred on the Commission by Articles 23 and 24 shall be subject to the following limitation periods:
(a) three years in the case of infringements of provisions concerning requests for information or the conduct of inspections;
(b) five years in the case of all other infringements.
(2) Time shall begin to run on the day on which the infringement is committed. However, in the case of continuing or repeated infringements, time shall begin to run on the day on which the infringement ceases.

(3) Any action taken by the Commission or by the competition authority of a Member State for the purpose of the investigation or proceedings in respect of an infringement shall interrupt the limitation period for the imposition of fines or periodic penalty payments. The limitation period shall be interrupted with effect from the date on which the action is notified to at least one undertaking or association of undertakings which has participated in the infringement. Actions which interrupt the running of the period shall include in particular the following:
(a) written requests for information by the Commission or by the competition authority of a Member State;
(b) written authorisations to conduct inspections issued to its officials by the Commission or by the competition authority of a Member State;
(c) the initiation of proceedings by the Commission or by the competition authority of a Member State;
(d) notification of the statement of objections of the Commission or of the competition authority of a Member State.
(4) The interruption of the limitation period shall apply for all the undertakings or associations of undertakings which have participated in the infringement.
(5) Each interruption shall start time running afresh. However, the limitation period shall expire at the latest on the day on which a period equal to twice the limitation period has elapsed without the Commission having imposed a fine or a periodic penalty payment. That period shall be extended by the time during which limitation is suspended pursuant to paragraph 6.
(6) The limitation period for the imposition of fines or periodic penalty payments shall be suspended for as long as the decision of the Commission is the subject of proceedings pending before the Court of Justice.

Article 26. Limitation period for the enforcement of penalties

(1) The power of the Commission to enforce decisions taken pursuant to Articles 23 and 24 shall be subject to a limitation period of five years.
(2) Time shall begin to run on the day on which the decision becomes final.
(3) The limitation period for the enforcement of penalties shall be interrupted:
(a) by notification of a decision varying the original amount of the fine or periodic penalty payment or refusing an application for variation;
(b) by any action of the Commission or of a Member State, acting at the request of the Commission, designed to enforce payment of the fine or periodic penalty payment.
(4) Each interruption shall start time running afresh.
(5) The limitation period for the enforcement of penalties shall be suspended for so long as:
(a) time to pay is allowed;
(b) enforcement of payment is suspended pursuant to a decision of the Court of Justice.

Chapter VIII. Hearings and Professional Secrecy

Article 27. Hearing of the parties, complainants and others

(1) Before taking decisions as provided for in Articles 7, 8, 23 and Article 24(2), the Commission shall give the undertakings or associations of undertakings which are the subject of the proceedings conducted by the Commission the opportunity of being heard on the matters to which the Commission has taken objection. The Commission shall base its decisions only on objections on which the parties concerned have been able to comment. Complainants shall be associated closely with the proceedings.
(2) The rights of defence of the parties concerned shall be fully respected in the proceedings. They shall be entitled to have access to the Commission's file, subject to the legitimate interest of undertakings in the protection of their business secrets. The right of access to the file shall not extend to confidential information and internal documents of the Commission or the competition authorities of the Member States. In particular, the right of access shall not extend to correspondence between the Commission and the competition authorities of the Member States, or between the latter, including documents drawn up pursuant to Articles 11 and 14. Nothing in this paragraph shall prevent the Commission from disclosing and using information necessary to prove an infringement.
(3) If the Commission considers it necessary, it may also hear other natural or legal persons. Applications to be heard on the part of such persons shall, where they show a sufficient interest, be granted. The competition authorities of the Member States may also ask the Commission to hear other natural or legal persons.
(4) Where the Commission intends to adopt a decision pursuant to Article 9 or Article 10, it shall publish a concise summary of the case and the main content of the commitments or of the proposed

course of action. Interested third parties may submit their observations within a time limit which is fixed by the Commission in its publication and which may not be less than one month. Publication shall have regard to the legitimate interest of undertakings in the protection of their business secrets.

Article 28. Professional secrecy
(1) Without prejudice to Articles 12 and 15, information collected pursuant to Articles 17 to 22 shall be used only for the purpose for which it was acquired.
(2) Without prejudice to the exchange and to the use of information foreseen in Articles 11, 12, 14, 15 and 27, the Commission and the competition authorities of the Member States, their officials, servants and other persons working under the supervision of these authorities as well as officials and civil servants of other authorities of the Member States shall not disclose information acquired or exchanged by them pursuant to this Regulation and of the kind covered by the obligation of professional secrecy. This obligation also applies to all representatives and experts of Member States attending meetings of the Advisory Committee pursuant to Article 14.

Chapter IX. Exemption Regulations

Article 29. Withdrawal in individual cases
(1) Where the Commission, empowered by a Council Regulation, such as Regulations 19/65/EEC, (EEC) No 2821/71, (EEC) No 3976/87, (EEC) No 1534/91 or (EEC) No 479/92, to apply Article 81(3) of the Treaty by regulation, has declared Article 81(1) of the Treaty inapplicable to certain categories of agreements, decisions by associations of undertakings or concerted practices, it may, acting on its own initiative or on a complaint, withdraw the benefit of such an exemption Regulation when it finds that in any particular case an agreement, decision or concerted practice to which the exemption Regulation applies has certain effects which are incompatible with Article 81(3) of the Treaty.
(2) Where, in any particular case, agreements, decisions by associations of undertakings or concerted practices to which a Commission Regulation referred to in paragraph 1 applies have effects which are incompatible with Article 81(3) of the Treaty in the territory of a Member State, or in a part thereof, which has all the characteristics of a distinct geographic market, the competition authority of that Member State may withdraw the benefit of the Regulation in question in respect of that territory.

Chapter X. General Provisions

Article 30. Publication of decisions
(1) The Commission shall publish the decisions, which it takes pursuant to Articles 7 to 10, 23 and 24.
(2) The publication shall state the names of the parties and the main content of the decision, including any penalties imposed. It shall have regard to the legitimate interest of undertakings in the protection of their business secrets.

Article 31. Review by the Court of Justice
The Court of Justice shall have unlimited jurisdiction to review decisions whereby the Commission has fixed a fine or periodic penalty payment. It may cancel, reduce or increase the fine or periodic penalty payment imposed.

Article 32. Exclusions
This Regulation shall not apply to:
(a) international tramp vessel services as defined in Article 1(3)(a) of Regulation (EEC) No 4056/86;
(b) a maritime transport service that takes place exclusively between ports in one and the same Member State as foreseen in Article 1(2) of Regulation (EEC) No 4056/86;
(c) air transport between Community airports and third countries.

Article 33. Implementing provisions
(1) The Commission shall be authorised to take such measures as may be appropriate in order to apply this Regulation. The measures may concern, inter alia:
(a) the form, content and other details of complaints lodged pursuant to Article 7 and the procedure for rejecting complaints;
(b) the practical arrangements for the exchange of information and consultations provided for in Article 11;
(c) the practical arrangements for the hearings provided for in Article 27.
(2) Before the adoption of any measures pursuant to paragraph 1, the Commission shall publish a draft thereof and invite all interested parties to submit their comments within the time-limit it lays down, which may not be less than one month. Before publishing a draft measure and before adopting

it, the Commission shall consult the Advisory Committee on Restrictive Practices and Dominant Positions.

Chapter XI. Transitional, Amending and Final Provisions

Article 34. Transitional provisions

(1) Applications made to the Commission under Article 2 of Regulation No 17, notifications made under Articles 4 and 5 of that Regulation and the corresponding applications and notifications made under Regulations (EEC) No 1017/68, (EEC) No 4056/86 and (EEC) No 3975/87 shall lapse as from the date of application of this Regulation.

(2) Procedural steps taken under Regulation No 17 and Regulations (EEC) No 1017/68, (EEC) No 4056/86 and (EEC) No 3975/87 shall continue to have effect for the purposes of applying this Regulation.

Article 35. Designation of competition authorities of Member States

(1) The Member States shall designate the competition authority or authorities responsible for the application of Articles 81 and 82 of the Treaty in such a way that the provisions of this regulation are effectively complied with. The measures necessary to empower those authorities to apply those Articles shall be taken before 1 May 2004. The authorities designated may include courts.

(2) When enforcement of Community competition law is entrusted to national administrative and judicial authorities, the Member States may allocate different powers and functions to those different national authorities, whether administrative or judicial.

(3) The effects of Article 11(6) apply to the authorities designated by the Member States including courts that exercise functions regarding the preparation and the adoption of the types of decisions foreseen in Article 5. The effects of Article 11(6) do not extend to courts insofar as they act as review courts in respect of the types of decisions foreseen in Article 5.

(4) Notwithstanding paragraph 3, in the Member States where, for the adoption of certain types of decisions foreseen in Article 5, an authority brings an action before a judicial authority that is separate and different from the prosecuting authority and provided that the terms of this paragraph are complied with, the effects of Article 11(6) shall be limited to the authority prosecuting the case which shall withdraw its claim before the judicial authority when the Commission opens proceedings and this withdrawal shall bring the national proceedings effectively to an end.

Article 36. Amendment of Regulation (EEC) No 1017/68

Regulation (EEC) No 1017/68 is amended as follows:

(1) Article 2 is repealed;

(2) in Article 3(1), the words "The prohibition laid down in Article 2" are replaced by the words "The prohibition in Article 81(1) of the Treaty";

(3) Article 4 is amended as follows:

(a) In paragraph 1, the words "The agreements, decisions and concerted practices referred to in Article 2" are replaced by the words "Agreements, decisions and concerted practices pursuant to Article 81(1) of the Treaty";

(b) Paragraph 2 is replaced by the following:

"2. If the implementation of any agreement, decision or concerted practice covered by paragraph 1 has, in a given case, effects which are incompatible with the requirements of Article 81(3) of the Treaty, undertakings or associations of undertakings may be required to make such effects cease."

(4) Articles 5 to 29 are repealed with the exception of Article 13(3) which continues to apply to decisions adopted pursuant to Article 5 of Regulation (EEC) No 1017/68 prior to the date of application of this Regulation until the date of expiration of those decisions;

(5) in Article 30, paragraphs 2, 3 and 4 are deleted.

Article 37. Amendment of Regulation (EEC) No 2988/74

In Regulation (EEC) No 2988/74, the following Article is inserted:
"Article 7a
Exclusion
This Regulation shall not apply to measures taken under Council Regulation (EC) No 1/2003 of 16 December 2002 on the implementation of the rules on competition laid down in Articles 81 and 82 of the Treaty."

Article 38. Amendment of Regulation (EEC) No 4056/86

Regulation (EEC) No 4056/86 is amended as follows:

(1) Article 7 is amended as follows:

PART III   EUROPEAN UNION

(a) Paragraph 1 is replaced by the following:
"1. Breach of an obligation
Where the persons concerned are in breach of an obligation which, pursuant to Article 5, attaches to the exemption provided for in Article 3, the Commission may, in order to put an end to such breach and under the conditions laid down in Council Regulation (EC) No 1/2003 of 16 December 2002 on the implementation of the rules on competition laid down in Articles 81 and 82 of the Treaty adopt a decision that either prohibits them from carrying out or requires them to perform certain specific acts, or withdraws the benefit of the block exemption which they enjoyed."
(b) Paragraph 2 is amended as follows:
(i) In point (a), the words "under the conditions laid down in Section II" are replaced by the words "under the conditions laid down in Regulation (EC) No 1/2003";
(ii) The second sentence of the second subparagraph of point (c)(i) is replaced by the following:
"At the same time it shall decide, in accordance with Article 9 of Regulation (EC) No 1/2003, whether to accept commitments offered by the undertakings concerned with a view, inter alia, to obtaining access to the market for non-conference lines."
(2) Article 8 is amended as follows:
(a) Paragraph 1 is deleted.
(b) In paragraph 2 the words "pursuant to Article 10" are replaced by the words "pursuant to Regulation (EC) No 1/2003".
(c) Paragraph 3 is deleted;
(3) Article 9 is amended as follows:
(a) In paragraph 1, the words "Advisory Committee referred to in Article 15" are replaced by the words "Advisory Committee referred to in Article 14 of Regulation (EC) No 1/2003";
(b) In paragraph 2, the words "Advisory Committee as referred to in Article 15" are replaced by the words "Advisory Committee referred to in Article 14 of Regulation (EC) No 1/2003";
(4) Articles 10 to 25 are repealed with the exception of Article 13(3) which continues to apply to decisions adopted pursuant to Article 81(3) of the Treaty prior to the date of application of this Regulation until the date of expiration of those decisions;
(5) in Article 26, the words "the form, content and other details of complaints pursuant to Article 10, applications pursuant to Article 12 and the hearings provided for in Article 23(1) and (2)" are deleted.

Article 39. Amendment of Regulation (EEC) No 3975/87

Articles 3 to 19 of Regulation (EEC) No 3975/87 are repealed with the exception of Article 6(3) which continues to apply to decisions adopted pursuant to Article 81(3) of the Treaty prior to the date of application of this Regulation until the date of expiration of those decisions.

Article 40. Amendment of Regulations No 19/65/EEC, (EEC) No 2821/71 and (EEC) No 1534/91

Article 7 of Regulation No 19/65/EEC, Article 7 of Regulation (EEC) No 2821/71 and Article 7 of Regulation (EEC) No 1534/91 are repealed.

Article 41. Amendment of Regulation (EEC) No 3976/87

Regulation (EEC) No 3976/87 is amended as follows:
(1) Article 6 is replaced by the following:
"Article 6
The Commission shall consult the Advisory Committee referred to in Article 14 of Council Regulation (EC) No 1/2003 of 16 December 2002 on the implementation of the rules on competition laid down in Articles 81 and 82 of the Treaty before publishing a draft Regulation and before adopting a Regulation."
(2) Article 7 is repealed.

Article 42. Amendment of Regulation (EEC) No 479/92

Regulation (EEC) No 479/92 is amended as follows:
(1) Article 5 is replaced by the following:
"Article 5
Before publishing the draft Regulation and before adopting the Regulation, the Commission shall consult the Advisory Committee referred to in Article 14 of Council Regulation (EC) No 1/2003 of 16 December 2002 on the implementation of the rules on competition laid down in Articles 81 and 82 of the Treaty."
(2) Article 6 is repealed.

Article 43. Repeal of Regulations No 17 and No 141

(1) Regulation No 17 is repealed with the exception of Article 8(3) which continues to apply to deci-

sions adopted pursuant to Article 81(3) of the Treaty prior to the date of application of this Regulation until the date of expiration of those decisions.
(2) Regulation No 141 is repealed.
(3) References to the repealed Regulations shall be construed as references to this Regulation.

Article 44. Report on the application of the present Regulation
Five years from the date of application of this Regulation, the Commission shall report to the European Parliament and the Council on the functioning of this Regulation, in particular on the application of Article 11(6) and Article 17.
On the basis of this report, the Commission shall assess whether it is appropriate to propose to the Council a revision of this Regulation.

Article 45. Entry into force
This Regulation shall enter into force on the 20th day following that of its publication in the Official Journal of the European Communities.
It shall apply from 1 May 2004.
This Regulation shall be binding in its entirety and directly applicable in all Member States.

PART III   EUROPEAN UNION

Council Regulation (EC) No 139/2004 of 20 January 2004 on the control of concentrations between undertakings (the EC Merger Regulation)

THE COUNCIL OF THE EUROPEAN UNION,
Having regard to the Treaty establishing the European Community, and in particular Articles 83 and 308 thereof,
Having regard to the proposal from the Commission,
Having regard to the opinion of the European Parliament,
Having regard to the opinion of the European Economic and Social Committee,
Whereas:
(1) Council Regulation (EEC) No 4064/89 of 21 December 1989 on the control of concentrations between undertakings has been substantially amended. Since further amendments are to be made, it should be recast in the interest of clarity.
(2) For the achievement of the aims of the Treaty, Article 3(1)(g) gives the Community the objective of instituting a system ensuring that competition in the internal market is not distorted. Article 4(1) of the Treaty provides that the activities of the Member States and the Community are to be conducted in accordance with the principle of an open market economy with free competition. These principles are essential for the further development of the internal market.
(3) The completion of the internal market and of economic and monetary union, the enlargement of the European Union and the lowering of international barriers to trade and investment will continue to result in major corporate reorganisations, particularly in the form of concentrations.
(4) Such reorganisations are to be welcomed to the extent that they are in line with the requirements of dynamic competition and capable of increasing the competitiveness of European industry, improving the conditions of growth and raising the standard of living in the Community.
(5) However, it should be ensured that the process of reorganisation does not result in lasting damage to competition; Community law must therefore include provisions governing those concentrations which may significantly impede effective competition in the common market or in a substantial part of it.
(6) A specific legal instrument is therefore necessary to permit effective control of all concentrations in terms of their effect on the structure of competition in the Community and to be the only instrument applicable to such concentrations. Regulation (EEC) No 4064/89 has allowed a Community policy to develop in this field. In the light of experience, however, that Regulation should now be recast into legislation designed to meet the challenges of a more integrated market and the future enlargement of the European Union. In accordance with the principles of subsidiarity and of proportionality as set out in Article 5 of the Treaty, this Regulation does not go beyond what is necessary in order to achieve the objective of ensuring that competition in the common market is not distorted, in accordance with the principle of an open market economy with free competition.
(7) Articles 81 and 82, while applicable, according to the case-law of the Court of Justice, to certain concentrations, are not sufficient to control all operations which may prove to be incompatible with the system of undistorted competition envisaged in the Treaty. This Regulation should therefore be based not only on Article 83 but, principally, on Article 308 of the Treaty, under which the Community may give itself the additional powers of action necessary for the attainment of its objectives, and also powers of action with regard to concentrations on the markets for agricultural products listed in Annex I to the Treaty.
(8) The provisions to be adopted in this Regulation should apply to significant structural changes, the impact of which on the market goes beyond the national borders of any one Member State. Such concentrations should, as a general rule, be reviewed exclusively at Community level, in application of a "one-stop shop" system and in compliance with the principle of subsidiarity. Concentrations not covered by this Regulation come, in principle, within the jurisdiction of the Member States.
(9) The scope of application of this Regulation should be defined according to the geographical area of activity of the undertakings concerned and be limited by quantitative thresholds in order to cover those concentrations which have a Community dimension. The Commission should report to the Council on the implementation of the applicable thresholds and criteria so that the Council, acting in accordance with Article 202 of the Treaty, is in a position to review them regularly, as well as the rules regarding pre-notification referral, in the light of the experience gained; this requires statistical data to be provided by the Member States to the Commission to enable it to prepare such reports and possible proposals for amendments. The Commission's reports and proposals should be based on relevant information regularly provided by the Member States.
(10) A concentration with a Community dimension should be deemed to exist where the aggregate turnover of the undertakings concerned exceeds given thresholds; that is the case irrespective of

COUNCIL REGULATION 139/2004

whether or not the undertakings effecting the concentration have their seat or their principal fields of activity in the Community, provided they have substantial operations there.

(11) The rules governing the referral of concentrations from the Commission to Member States and from Member States to the Commission should operate as an effective corrective mechanism in the light of the principle of subsidiarity; these rules protect the competition interests of the Member States in an adequate manner and take due account of legal certainty and the "one-stop shop" principle.

(12) Concentrations may qualify for examination under a number of national merger control systems if they fall below the turnover thresholds referred to in this Regulation. Multiple notification of the same transaction increases legal uncertainty, effort and cost for undertakings and may lead to conflicting assessments. The system whereby concentrations may be referred to the Commission by the Member States concerned should therefore be further developed.

(13) The Commission should act in close and constant liaison with the competent authorities of the Member States from which it obtains comments and information.

(14) The Commission and the competent authorities of the Member States should together form a network of public authorities, applying their respective competences in close cooperation, using efficient arrangements for information-sharing and consultation, with a view to ensuring that a case is dealt with by the most appropriate authority, in the light of the principle of subsidiarity and with a view to ensuring that multiple notifications of a given concentration are avoided to the greatest extent possible. Referrals of concentrations from the Commission to Member States and from Member States to the Commission should be made in an efficient manner avoiding, to the greatest extent possible, situations where a concentration is subject to a referral both before and after its notification.

(15) The Commission should be able to refer to a Member State notified concentrations with a Community dimension which threaten significantly to affect competition in a market within that Member State presenting all the characteristics of a distinct market. Where the concentration affects competition on such a market, which does not constitute a substantial part of the common market, the Commission should be obliged, upon request, to refer the whole or part of the case to the Member State concerned. A Member State should be able to refer to the Commission a concentration which does not have a Community dimension but which affects trade between Member States and threatens to significantly affect competition within its territory. Other Member States which are also competent to review the concentration should be able to join the request. In such a situation, in order to ensure the efficiency and predictability of the system, national time limits should be suspended until a decision has been reached as to the referral of the case. The Commission should have the power to examine and deal with a concentration on behalf of a requesting Member State or requesting Member States.

(16) The undertakings concerned should be granted the possibility of requesting referrals to or from the Commission before a concentration is notified so as to further improve the efficiency of the system for the control of concentrations within the Community. In such situations, the Commission and national competition authorities should decide within short, clearly defined time limits whether a referral to or from the Commission ought to be made, thereby ensuring the efficiency of the system. Upon request by the undertakings concerned, the Commission should be able to refer to a Member State a concentration with a Community dimension which may significantly affect competition in a market within that Member State presenting all the characteristics of a distinct market; the undertakings concerned should not, however, be required to demonstrate that the effects of the concentration would be detrimental to competition. A concentration should not be referred from the Commission to a Member State which has expressed its disagreement to such a referral. Before notification to national authorities, the undertakings concerned should also be able to request that a concentration without a Community dimension which is capable of being reviewed under the national competition laws of at least three Member States be referred to the Commission. Such requests for pre-notification referrals to the Commission would be particularly pertinent in situations where the concentration would affect competition beyond the territory of one Member State. Where a concentration capable of being reviewed under the competition laws of three or more Member States is referred to the Commission prior to any national notification, and no Member State competent to review the case expresses its disagreement, the Commission should acquire exclusive competence to review the concentration and such a concentration should be deemed to have a Community dimension. Such pre-notification referrals from Member States to the Commission should not, however, be made where at least one Member State competent to review the case has expressed its disagreement with such a referral.

(17) The Commission should be given exclusive competence to apply this Regulation, subject to review by the Court of Justice.

(18) The Member States should not be permitted to apply their national legislation on competition

to concentrations with a Community dimension, unless this Regulation makes provision therefor. The relevant powers of national authorities should be limited to cases where, failing intervention by the Commission, effective competition is likely to be significantly impeded within the territory of a Member State and where the competition interests of that Member State cannot be sufficiently protected otherwise by this Regulation. The Member States concerned must act promptly in such cases; this Regulation cannot, because of the diversity of national law, fix a single time limit for the adoption of final decisions under national law.

(19) Furthermore, the exclusive application of this Regulation to concentrations with a Community dimension is without prejudice to Article 296 of the Treaty, and does not prevent the Member States from taking appropriate measures to protect legitimate interests other than those pursued by this Regulation, provided that such measures are compatible with the general principles and other provisions of Community law.

(20) It is expedient to define the concept of concentration in such a manner as to cover operations bringing about a lasting change in the control of the undertakings concerned and therefore in the structure of the market. It is therefore appropriate to include, within the scope of this Regulation, all joint ventures performing on a lasting basis all the functions of an autonomous economic entity. It is moreover appropriate to treat as a single concentration transactions that are closely connected in that they are linked by condition or take the form of a series of transactions in securities taking place within a reasonably short period of time.

(21) This Regulation should also apply where the undertakings concerned accept restrictions directly related to, and necessary for, the implementation of the concentration. Commission decisions declaring concentrations compatible with the common market in application of this Regulation should automatically cover such restrictions, without the Commission having to assess such restrictions in individual cases. At the request of the undertakings concerned, however, the Commission should, in cases presenting novel or unresolved questions giving rise to genuine uncertainty, expressly assess whether or not any restriction is directly related to, and necessary for, the implementation of the concentration. A case presents a novel or unresolved question giving rise to genuine uncertainty if the question is not covered by the relevant Commission notice in force or a published Commission decision.

(22) The arrangements to be introduced for the control of concentrations should, without prejudice to Article 86(2) of the Treaty, respect the principle of non-discrimination between the public and the private sectors. In the public sector, calculation of the turnover of an undertaking concerned in a concentration needs, therefore, to take account of undertakings making up an economic unit with an independent power of decision, irrespective of the way in which their capital is held or of the rules of administrative supervision applicable to them.

(23) It is necessary to establish whether or not concentrations with a Community dimension are compatible with the common market in terms of the need to maintain and develop effective competition in the common market. In so doing, the Commission must place its appraisal within the general framework of the achievement of the fundamental objectives referred to in Article 2 of the Treaty establishing the European Community and Article 2 of the Treaty on European Union.

(24) In order to ensure a system of undistorted competition in the common market, in furtherance of a policy conducted in accordance with the principle of an open market economy with free competition, this Regulation must permit effective control of all concentrations from the point of view of their effect on competition in the Community. Accordingly, Regulation (EEC) No 4064/89 established the principle that a concentration with a Community dimension which creates or strengthens a dominant position as a result of which effective competition in the common market or in a substantial part of it would be significantly impeded should be declared incompatible with the common market.

(25) In view of the consequences that concentrations in oligopolistic market structures may have, it is all the more necessary to maintain effective competition in such markets. Many oligopolistic markets exhibit a healthy degree of competition. However, under certain circumstances, concentrations involving the elimination of important competitive constraints that the merging parties had exerted upon each other, as well as a reduction of competitive pressure on the remaining competitors, may, even in the absence of a likelihood of coordination between the members of the oligopoly, result in a significant impediment to effective competition. The Community courts have, however, not to date expressly interpreted Regulation (EEC) No 4064/89 as requiring concentrations giving rise to such non-coordinated effects to be declared incompatible with the common market. Therefore, in the interests of legal certainty, it should be made clear that this Regulation permits effective control of all such concentrations by providing that any concentration which would significantly impede effective competition, in the common market or in a substantial part of it, should be declared incompatible with the common market. The notion of "significant impediment to effective competition" in Article

2(2) and (3) should be interpreted as extending, beyond the concept of dominance, only to the anticompetitive effects of a concentration resulting from the non-coordinated behaviour of undertakings which would not have a dominant position on the market concerned.

(26) A significant impediment to effective competition generally results from the creation or strengthening of a dominant position. With a view to preserving the guidance that may be drawn from past judgments of the European courts and Commission decisions pursuant to Regulation (EEC) No 4064/89, while at the same time maintaining consistency with the standards of competitive harm which have been applied by the Commission and the Community courts regarding the compatibility of a concentration with the common market, this Regulation should accordingly establish the principle that a concentration with a Community dimension which would significantly impede effective competition, in the common market or in a substantial part thereof, in particular as a result of the creation or strengthening of a dominant position, is to be declared incompatible with the common market.

(27) In addition, the criteria of Article 81(1) and (3) of the Treaty should be applied to joint ventures performing, on a lasting basis, all the functions of autonomous economic entities, to the extent that their creation has as its consequence an appreciable restriction of competition between undertakings that remain independent.

(28) In order to clarify and explain the Commission's appraisal of concentrations under this Regulation, it is appropriate for the Commission to publish guidance which should provide a sound economic framework for the assessment of concentrations with a view to determining whether or not they may be declared compatible with the common market.

(29) In order to determine the impact of a concentration on competition in the common market, it is appropriate to take account of any substantiated and likely efficiencies put forward by the undertakings concerned. It is possible that the efficiencies brought about by the concentration counteract the effects on competition, and in particular the potential harm to consumers, that it might otherwise have and that, as a consequence, the concentration would not significantly impede effective competition, in the common market or in a substantial part of it, in particular as a result of the creation or strengthening of a dominant position. The Commission should publish guidance on the conditions under which it may take efficiencies into account in the assessment of a concentration.

(30) Where the undertakings concerned modify a notified concentration, in particular by offering commitments with a view to rendering the concentration compatible with the common market, the Commission should be able to declare the concentration, as modified, compatible with the common market. Such commitments should be proportionate to the competition problem and entirely eliminate it. It is also appropriate to accept commitments before the initiation of proceedings where the competition problem is readily identifiable and can easily be remedied. It should be expressly provided that the Commission may attach to its decision conditions and obligations in order to ensure that the undertakings concerned comply with their commitments in a timely and effective manner so as to render the concentration compatible with the common market. Transparency and effective consultation of Member States as well as of interested third parties should be ensured throughout the procedure.

(31) The Commission should have at its disposal appropriate instruments to ensure the enforcement of commitments and to deal with situations where they are not fulfilled. In cases of failure to fulfil a condition attached to the decision declaring a concentration compatible with the common market, the situation rendering the concentration compatible with the common market does not materialise and the concentration, as implemented, is therefore not authorised by the Commission. As a consequence, if the concentration is implemented, it should be treated in the same way as a non-notified concentration implemented without authorisation. Furthermore, where the Commission has already found that, in the absence of the condition, the concentration would be incompatible with the common market, it should have the power to directly order the dissolution of the concentration, so as to restore the situation prevailing prior to the implementation of the concentration. Where an obligation attached to a decision declaring the concentration compatible with the common market is not fulfilled, the Commission should be able to revoke its decision. Moreover, the Commission should be able to impose appropriate financial sanctions where conditions or obligations are not fulfilled.

(32) Concentrations which, by reason of the limited market share of the undertakings concerned, are not liable to impede effective competition may be presumed to be compatible with the common market. Without prejudice to Articles 81 and 82 of the Treaty, an indication to this effect exists, in particular, where the market share of the undertakings concerned does not exceed 25 % either in the common market or in a substantial part of it.

(33) The Commission should have the task of taking all the decisions necessary to establish whether or not concentrations with a Community dimension are compatible with the common market, as well

as decisions designed to restore the situation prevailing prior to the implementation of a concentration which has been declared incompatible with the common market.

(34) To ensure effective control, undertakings should be obliged to give prior notification of concentrations with a Community dimension following the conclusion of the agreement, the announcement of the public bid or the acquisition of a controlling interest. Notification should also be possible where the undertakings concerned satisfy the Commission of their intention to enter into an agreement for a proposed concentration and demonstrate to the Commission that their plan for that proposed concentration is sufficiently concrete, for example on the basis of an agreement in principle, a memorandum of understanding, or a letter of intent signed by all undertakings concerned, or, in the case of a public bid, where they have publicly announced an intention to make such a bid, provided that the intended agreement or bid would result in a concentration with a Community dimension. The implementation of concentrations should be suspended until a final decision of the Commission has been taken. However, it should be possible to derogate from this suspension at the request of the undertakings concerned, where appropriate. In deciding whether or not to grant a derogation, the Commission should take account of all pertinent factors, such as the nature and gravity of damage to the undertakings concerned or to third parties, and the threat to competition posed by the concentration. In the interest of legal certainty, the validity of transactions must nevertheless be protected as much as necessary.

(35) A period within which the Commission must initiate proceedings in respect of a notified concentration and a period within which it must take a final decision on the compatibility or incompatibility with the common market of that concentration should be laid down. These periods should be extended whenever the undertakings concerned offer commitments with a view to rendering the concentration compatible with the common market, in order to allow for sufficient time for the analysis and market testing of such commitment offers and for the consultation of Member States as well as interested third parties. A limited extension of the period within which the Commission must take a final decision should also be possible in order to allow sufficient time for the investigation of the case and the verification of the facts and arguments submitted to the Commission.

(36) The Community respects the fundamental rights and observes the principles recognised in particular by the Charter of Fundamental Rights of the European Union. Accordingly, this Regulation should be interpreted and applied with respect to those rights and principles.

(37) The undertakings concerned must be afforded the right to be heard by the Commission when proceedings have been initiated; the members of the management and supervisory bodies and the recognised representatives of the employees of the undertakings concerned, and interested third parties, must also be given the opportunity to be heard.

(38) In order properly to appraise concentrations, the Commission should have the right to request all necessary information and to conduct all necessary inspections throughout the Community. To that end, and with a view to protecting competition effectively, the Commission's powers of investigation need to be expanded. The Commission should, in particular, have the right to interview any persons who may be in possession of useful information and to record the statements made.

(39) In the course of an inspection, officials authorised by the Commission should have the right to ask for any information relevant to the subject matter and purpose of the inspection; they should also have the right to affix seals during inspections, particularly in circumstances where there are reasonable grounds to suspect that a concentration has been implemented without being notified; that incorrect, incomplete or misleading information has been supplied to the Commission; or that the undertakings or persons concerned have failed to comply with a condition or obligation imposed by decision of the Commission. In any event, seals should only be used in exceptional circumstances, for the period of time strictly necessary for the inspection, normally not for more than 48 hours.

(40) Without prejudice to the case-law of the Court of Justice, it is also useful to set out the scope of the control that the national judicial authority may exercise when it authorises, as provided by national law and as a precautionary measure, assistance from law enforcement authorities in order to overcome possible opposition on the part of the undertaking against an inspection, including the affixing of seals, ordered by Commission decision. It results from the case-law that the national judicial authority may in particular ask of the Commission further information which it needs to carry out its control and in the absence of which it could refuse the authorisation. The case-law also confirms the competence of the national courts to control the application of national rules governing the implementation of coercive measures. The competent authorities of the Member States should cooperate actively in the exercise of the Commission's investigative powers.

(41) When complying with decisions of the Commission, the undertakings and persons concerned cannot be forced to admit that they have committed infringements, but they are in any event obliged to answer factual questions and to provide documents, even if this information may be used to estab-

lish against themselves or against others the existence of such infringements.
(42) For the sake of transparency, all decisions of the Commission which are not of a merely procedural nature should be widely publicised. While ensuring preservation of the rights of defence of the undertakings concerned, in particular the right of access to the file, it is essential that business secrets be protected. The confidentiality of information exchanged in the network and with the competent authorities of third countries should likewise be safeguarded.
(43) Compliance with this Regulation should be enforceable, as appropriate, by means of fines and periodic penalty payments. The Court of Justice should be given unlimited jurisdiction in that regard pursuant to Article 229 of the Treaty.
(44) The conditions in which concentrations, involving undertakings having their seat or their principal fields of activity in the Community, are carried out in third countries should be observed, and provision should be made for the possibility of the Council giving the Commission an appropriate mandate for negotiation with a view to obtaining non-discriminatory treatment for such undertakings.
(45) This Regulation in no way detracts from the collective rights of employees, as recognised in the undertakings concerned, notably with regard to any obligation to inform or consult their recognised representatives under Community and national law.
(46) The Commission should be able to lay down detailed rules concerning the implementation of this Regulation in accordance with the procedures for the exercise of implementing powers conferred on the Commission. For the adoption of such implementing provisions, the Commission should be assisted by an Advisory Committee composed of the representatives of the Member States as specified in Article 23,
HAS ADOPTED THIS REGULATION:

Article 1. Scope
(1) Without prejudice to Article 4(5) and Article 22, this Regulation shall apply to all concentrations with a Community dimension as defined in this Article.
(2) A concentration has a Community dimension where:
(a) the combined aggregate worldwide turnover of all the undertakings concerned is more than EUR 5000 million; and
(b) the aggregate Community-wide turnover of each of at least two of the undertakings concerned is more than EUR 250 million,
unless each of the undertakings concerned achieves more than two-thirds of its aggregate Community-wide turnover within one and the same Member State.
(3) A concentration that does not meet the thresholds laid down in paragraph 2 has a Community dimension where:
(a) the combined aggregate worldwide turnover of all the undertakings concerned is more than EUR 2500 million;
(b) in each of at least three Member States, the combined aggregate turnover of all the undertakings concerned is more than EUR 100 million;
(c) in each of at least three Member States included for the purpose of point (b), the aggregate turnover of each of at least two of the undertakings concerned is more than EUR 25 million; and
(d) the aggregate Community-wide turnover of each of at least two of the undertakings concerned is more than EUR 100 million,
unless each of the undertakings concerned achieves more than two-thirds of its aggregate Community-wide turnover within one and the same Member State.
(4) On the basis of statistical data that may be regularly provided by the Member States, the Commission shall report to the Council on the operation of the thresholds and criteria set out in paragraphs 2 and 3 by 1 July 2009 and may present proposals pursuant to paragraph 5.
(5) Following the report referred to in paragraph 4 and on a proposal from the Commission, the Council, acting by a qualified majority, may revise the thresholds and criteria mentioned in paragraph 3.

Article 2. Appraisal of concentrations
(1) Concentrations within the scope of this Regulation shall be appraised in accordance with the objectives of this Regulation and the following provisions with a view to establishing whether or not they are compatible with the common market.
In making this appraisal, the Commission shall take into account:
(a) the need to maintain and develop effective competition within the common market in view of, among other things, the structure of all the markets concerned and the actual or potential competition from undertakings located either within or outwith the Community;

(b) the market position of the undertakings concerned and their economic and financial power, the alternatives available to suppliers and users, their access to supplies or markets, any legal or other barriers to entry, supply and demand trends for the relevant goods and services, the interests of the intermediate and ultimate consumers, and the development of technical and economic progress provided that it is to consumers' advantage and does not form an obstacle to competition.

(2) A concentration which would not significantly impede effective competition in the common market or in a substantial part of it, in particular as a result of the creation or strengthening of a dominant position, shall be declared compatible with the common market.

(3) A concentration which would significantly impede effective competition, in the common market or in a substantial part of it, in particular as a result of the creation or strengthening of a dominant position, shall be declared incompatible with the common market.

(4) To the extent that the creation of a joint venture constituting a concentration pursuant to Article 3 has as its object or effect the coordination of the competitive behaviour of undertakings that remain independent, such coordination shall be appraised in accordance with the criteria of Article 81(1) and (3) of the Treaty, with a view to establishing whether or not the operation is compatible with the common market.

(5) In making this appraisal, the Commission shall take into account in particular:
- whether two or more parent companies retain, to a significant extent, activities in the same market as the joint venture or in a market which is downstream or upstream from that of the joint venture or in a neighbouring market closely related to this market,
- whether the coordination which is the direct consequence of the creation of the joint venture affords the undertakings concerned the possibility of eliminating competition in respect of a substantial part of the products or services in question.

Article 3. Definition of concentration

(1) A concentration shall be deemed to arise where a change of control on a lasting basis results from:
(a) the merger of two or more previously independent undertakings or parts of undertakings, or
(b) the acquisition, by one or more persons already controlling at least one undertaking, or by one or more undertakings, whether by purchase of securities or assets, by contract or by any other means, of direct or indirect control of the whole or parts of one or more other undertakings.

(2) Control shall be constituted by rights, contracts or any other means which, either separately or in combination and having regard to the considerations of fact or law involved, confer the possibility of exercising decisive influence on an undertaking, in particular by:
(a) ownership or the right to use all or part of the assets of an undertaking;
(b) rights or contracts which confer decisive influence on the composition, voting or decisions of the organs of an undertaking.

(3) Control is acquired by persons or undertakings which:
(a) are holders of the rights or entitled to rights under the contracts concerned; or
(b) while not being holders of such rights or entitled to rights under such contracts, have the power to exercise the rights deriving therefrom.

(4) The creation of a joint venture performing on a lasting basis all the functions of an autonomous economic entity shall constitute a concentration within the meaning of paragraph 1(b).

(5) A concentration shall not be deemed to arise where:
(a) credit institutions or other financial institutions or insurance companies, the normal activities of which include transactions and dealing in securities for their own account or for the account of others, hold on a temporary basis securities which they have acquired in an undertaking with a view to reselling them, provided that they do not exercise voting rights in respect of those securities with a view to determining the competitive behaviour of that undertaking or provided that they exercise such voting rights only with a view to preparing the disposal of all or part of that undertaking or of its assets or the disposal of those securities and that any such disposal takes place within one year of the date of acquisition; that period may be extended by the Commission on request where such institutions or companies can show that the disposal was not reasonably possible within the period set;
(b) control is acquired by an office-holder according to the law of a Member State relating to liquidation, winding up, insolvency, cessation of payments, compositions or analogous proceedings;
(c) the operations referred to in paragraph 1(b) are carried out by the financial holding companies referred to in Article 5(3) of Fourth Council Directive 78/660/EEC of 25 July 1978 based on Article 54(3)(g) of the Treaty on the annual accounts of certain types of companies provided however that the voting rights in respect of the holding are exercised, in particular in relation to the appointment of members of the management and supervisory bodies of the undertakings in which they have holdings, only to maintain the full value of those investments and not to determine directly or indirectly the competitive conduct of those undertakings.

Article 4. Prior notification of concentrations and pre-notification referral at the request of the notifying parties

(1) Concentrations with a Community dimension defined in this Regulation shall be notified to the Commission prior to their implementation and following the conclusion of the agreement, the announcement of the public bid, or the acquisition of a controlling interest.

Notification may also be made where the undertakings concerned demonstrate to the Commission a good faith intention to conclude an agreement or, in the case of a public bid, where they have publicly announced an intention to make such a bid, provided that the intended agreement or bid would result in a concentration with a Community dimension.

For the purposes of this Regulation, the term "notified concentration" shall also cover intended concentrations notified pursuant to the second subparagraph. For the purposes of paragraphs 4 and 5 of this Article, the term "concentration" includes intended concentrations within the meaning of the second subparagraph.

(2) A concentration which consists of a merger within the meaning of Article 3(1)(a) or in the acquisition of joint control within the meaning of Article 3(1)(b) shall be notified jointly by the parties to the merger or by those acquiring joint control as the case may be. In all other cases, the notification shall be effected by the person or undertaking acquiring control of the whole or parts of one or more undertakings.

(3) Where the Commission finds that a notified concentration falls within the scope of this Regulation, it shall publish the fact of the notification, at the same time indicating the names of the undertakings concerned, their country of origin, the nature of the concentration and the economic sectors involved. The Commission shall take account of the legitimate interest of undertakings in the protection of their business secrets.

(4) Prior to the notification of a concentration within the meaning of paragraph 1, the persons or undertakings referred to in paragraph 2 may inform the Commission, by means of a reasoned submission, that the concentration may significantly affect competition in a market within a Member State which presents all the characteristics of a distinct market and should therefore be examined, in whole or in part, by that Member State.

The Commission shall transmit this submission to all Member States without delay. The Member State referred to in the reasoned submission shall, within 15 working days of receiving the submission, express its agreement or disagreement as regards the request to refer the case. Where that Member State takes no such decision within this period, it shall be deemed to have agreed.

Unless that Member State disagrees, the Commission, where it considers that such a distinct market exists, and that competition in that market may be significantly affected by the concentration, may decide to refer the whole or part of the case to the competent authorities of that Member State with a view to the application of that State's national competition law.

The decision whether or not to refer the case in accordance with the third subparagraph shall be taken within 25 working days starting from the receipt of the reasoned submission by the Commission. The Commission shall inform the other Member States and the persons or undertakings concerned of its decision. If the Commission does not take a decision within this period, it shall be deemed to have adopted a decision to refer the case in accordance with the submission made by the persons or undertakings concerned.

If the Commission decides, or is deemed to have decided, pursuant to the third and fourth subparagraphs, to refer the whole of the case, no notification shall be made pursuant to paragraph 1 and national competition law shall apply. Article 9(6) to (9) shall apply *mutatis mutandis*.

(5) With regard to a concentration as defined in Article 3 which does not have a Community dimension within the meaning of Article 1 and which is capable of being reviewed under the national competition laws of at least three Member States, the persons or undertakings referred to in paragraph 2 may, before any notification to the competent authorities, inform the Commission by means of a reasoned submission that the concentration should be examined by the Commission.

The Commission shall transmit this submission to all Member States without delay.

Any Member State competent to examine the concentration under its national competition law may, within 15 working days of receiving the reasoned submission, express its disagreement as regards the request to refer the case.

Where at least one such Member State has expressed its disagreement in accordance with the third subparagraph within the period of 15 working days, the case shall not be referred. The Commission shall, without delay, inform all Member States and the persons or undertakings concerned of any such expression of disagreement.

Where no Member State has expressed its disagreement in accordance with the third subparagraph within the period of 15 working days, the concentration shall be deemed to have a Community

dimension and shall be notified to the Commission in accordance with paragraphs 1 and 2. In such situations, no Member State shall apply its national competition law to the concentration.
(6) The Commission shall report to the Council on the operation of paragraphs 4 and 5 by 1 July 2009. Following this report and on a proposal from the Commission, the Council, acting by a qualified majority, may revise paragraphs 4 and 5.

Article 5. Calculation of turnover

(1) Aggregate turnover within the meaning of this Regulation shall comprise the amounts derived by the undertakings concerned in the preceding financial year from the sale of products and the provision of services falling within the undertakings' ordinary activities after deduction of sales rebates and of value added tax and other taxes directly related to turnover. The aggregate turnover of an undertaking concerned shall not include the sale of products or the provision of services between any of the undertakings referred to in paragraph 4.
Turnover, in the Community or in a Member State, shall comprise products sold and services provided to undertakings or consumers, in the Community or in that Member State as the case may be.
(2) By way of derogation from paragraph 1, where the concentration consists of the acquisition of parts, whether or not constituted as legal entities, of one or more undertakings, only the turnover relating to the parts which are the subject of the concentration shall be taken into account with regard to the seller or sellers.
However, two or more transactions within the meaning of the first subparagraph which take place within a two-year period between the same persons or undertakings shall be treated as one and the same concentration arising on the date of the last transaction.
(3) In place of turnover the following shall be used:
(a) for credit institutions and other financial institutions, the sum of the following income items as defined in Council Directive 86/635/EEC, after deduction of value added tax and other taxes directly related to those items, where appropriate:
(i) interest income and similar income;
(ii) income from securities:
- income from shares and other variable yield securities,
- income from participating interests,
- income from shares in affiliated undertakings;
(iii) commissions receivable;
(iv) net profit on financial operations;
(v) other operating income.
The turnover of a credit or financial institution in the Community or in a Member State shall comprise the income items, as defined above, which are received by the branch or division of that institution established in the Community or in the Member State in question, as the case may be;
(b) for insurance undertakings, the value of gross premiums written which shall comprise all amounts received and receivable in respect of insurance contracts issued by or on behalf of the insurance undertakings, including also outgoing reinsurance premiums, and after deduction of taxes and parafiscal contributions or levies charged by reference to the amounts of individual premiums or the total volume of premiums; as regards Article 1(2)(b) and (3)(b), (c) and (d) and the final part of Article 1(2) and (3), gross premiums received from Community residents and from residents of one Member State respectively shall be taken into account.
(4) Without prejudice to paragraph 2, the aggregate turnover of an undertaking concerned within the meaning of this Regulation shall be calculated by adding together the respective turnovers of the following:
(a) the undertaking concerned;
(b) those undertakings in which the undertaking concerned, directly or indirectly:
(i) owns more than half the capital or business assets, or
(ii) has the power to exercise more than half the voting rights, or
(iii) has the power to appoint more than half the members of the supervisory board, the administrative board or bodies legally representing the undertakings, or
(iv) has the right to manage the undertakings' affairs;
(c) those undertakings which have in the undertaking concerned the rights or powers listed in (b);
(d) those undertakings in which an undertaking as referred to in (c) has the rights or powers listed in (b);
(e) those undertakings in which two or more undertakings as referred to in (a) to (d) jointly have the rights or powers listed in (b).
(5) Where undertakings concerned by the concentration jointly have the rights or powers listed in

paragraph 4(b), in calculating the aggregate turnover of the undertakings concerned for the purposes of this Regulation:
(a) no account shall be taken of the turnover resulting from the sale of products or the provision of services between the joint undertaking and each of the undertakings concerned or any other undertaking connected with any one of them, as set out in paragraph 4(b) to (e);
(b) account shall be taken of the turnover resulting from the sale of products and the provision of services between the joint undertaking and any third undertakings. This turnover shall be apportioned equally amongst the undertakings concerned.

Article 6. Examination of the notification and initiation of proceedings
(1) The Commission shall examine the notification as soon as it is received.
(a) Where it concludes that the concentration notified does not fall within the scope of this Regulation, it shall record that finding by means of a decision.
(b) Where it finds that the concentration notified, although falling within the scope of this Regulation, does not raise serious doubts as to its compatibility with the common market, it shall decide not to oppose it and shall declare that it is compatible with the common market.
A decision declaring a concentration compatible shall be deemed to cover restrictions directly related and necessary to the implementation of the concentration.
(c) Without prejudice to paragraph 2, where the Commission finds that the concentration notified falls within the scope of this Regulation and raises serious doubts as to its compatibility with the common market, it shall decide to initiate proceedings. Without prejudice to Article 9, such proceedings shall be closed by means of a decision as provided for in Article 8(1) to (4), unless the undertakings concerned have demonstrated to the satisfaction of the Commission that they have abandoned the concentration.
(2) Where the Commission finds that, following modification by the undertakings concerned, a notified concentration no longer raises serious doubts within the meaning of paragraph 1(c), it shall declare the concentration compatible with the common market pursuant to paragraph 1(b).
The Commission may attach to its decision under paragraph 1(b) conditions and obligations intended to ensure that the undertakings concerned comply with the commitments they have entered into vis-à-vis the Commission with a view to rendering the concentration compatible with the common market.
(3) The Commission may revoke the decision it took pursuant to paragraph 1(a) or (b) where:
(a) the decision is based on incorrect information for which one of the undertakings is responsible or where it has been obtained by deceit,
or
(b) the undertakings concerned commit a breach of an obligation attached to the decision.
(4) In the cases referred to in paragraph 3, the Commission may take a decision under paragraph 1, without being bound by the time limits referred to in Article 10(1).
(5) The Commission shall notify its decision to the undertakings concerned and the competent authorities of the Member States without delay.

Article 7. Suspension of concentrations
(1) A concentration with a Community dimension as defined in Article 1, or which is to be examined by the Commission pursuant to Article 4(5), shall not be implemented either before its notification or until it has been declared compatible with the common market pursuant to a decision under Articles 6(1)(b), 8(1) or 8(2), or on the basis of a presumption according to Article 10(6).
(2) Paragraph 1 shall not prevent the implementation of a public bid or of a series of transactions in securities including those convertible into other securities admitted to trading on a market such as a stock exchange, by which control within the meaning of Article 3 is acquired from various sellers, provided that:
(a) the concentration is notified to the Commission pursuant to Article 4 without delay; and
(b) the acquirer does not exercise the voting rights attached to the securities in question or does so only to maintain the full value of its investments based on a derogation granted by the Commission under paragraph 3.
(3) The Commission may, on request, grant a derogation from the obligations imposed in paragraphs 1 or 2. The request to grant a derogation must be reasoned. In deciding on the request, the Commission shall take into account inter alia the effects of the suspension on one or more undertakings concerned by the concentration or on a third party and the threat to competition posed by the concentration. Such a derogation may be made subject to conditions and obligations in order to ensure conditions of effective competition. A derogation may be applied for and granted at any time, be it before notification or after the transaction.
(4) The validity of any transaction carried out in contravention of paragraph 1 shall be dependent on a

decision pursuant to Article 6(1)(b) or Article 8(1), (2) or (3) or on a presumption pursuant to Article 10(6).
This Article shall, however, have no effect on the validity of transactions in securities including those convertible into other securities admitted to trading on a market such as a stock exchange, unless the buyer and seller knew or ought to have known that the transaction was carried out in contravention of paragraph 1.

Article 8. Powers of decision of the Commission

(1) Where the Commission finds that a notified concentration fulfils the criterion laid down in Article 2(2) and, in the cases referred to in Article 2(4), the criteria laid down in Article 81(3) of the Treaty, it shall issue a decision declaring the concentration compatible with the common market.
A decision declaring a concentration compatible shall be deemed to cover restrictions directly related and necessary to the implementation of the concentration.
(2) Where the Commission finds that, following modification by the undertakings concerned, a notified concentration fulfils the criterion laid down in Article 2(2) and, in the cases referred to in Article 2(4), the criteria laid down in Article 81(3) of the Treaty, it shall issue a decision declaring the concentration compatible with the common market.
The Commission may attach to its decision conditions and obligations intended to ensure that the undertakings concerned comply with the commitments they have entered into vis-à-vis the Commission with a view to rendering the concentration compatible with the common market.
A decision declaring a concentration compatible shall be deemed to cover restrictions directly related and necessary to the implementation of the concentration.
(3) Where the Commission finds that a concentration fulfils the criterion defined in Article 2(3) or, in the cases referred to in Article 2(4), does not fulfil the criteria laid down in Article 81(3) of the Treaty, it shall issue a decision declaring that the concentration is incompatible with the common market.
(4) Where the Commission finds that a concentration:
(a) has already been implemented and that concentration has been declared incompatible with the common market, or
(b) has been implemented in contravention of a condition attached to a decision taken under paragraph 2, which has found that, in the absence of the condition, the concentration would fulfil the criterion laid down in Article 2(3) or, in the cases referred to in Article 2(4), would not fulfil the criteria laid down in Article 81(3) of the Treaty,
the Commission may:
- require the undertakings concerned to dissolve the concentration, in particular through the dissolution of the merger or the disposal of all the shares or assets acquired, so as to restore the situation prevailing prior to the implementation of the concentration; in circumstances where restoration of the situation prevailing before the implementation of the concentration is not possible through dissolution of the concentration, the Commission may take any other measure appropriate to achieve such restoration as far as possible,
- order any other appropriate measure to ensure that the undertakings concerned dissolve the concentration or take other restorative measures as required in its decision.
In cases falling within point (a) of the first subparagraph, the measures referred to in that subparagraph may be imposed either in a decision pursuant to paragraph 3 or by separate decision.
(5) The Commission may take interim measures appropriate to restore or maintain conditions of effective competition where a concentration:
(a) has been implemented in contravention of Article 7, and a decision as to the compatibility of the concentration with the common market has not yet been taken;
(b) has been implemented in contravention of a condition attached to a decision under Article 6(1)(b) or paragraph 2 of this Article;
(c) has already been implemented and is declared incompatible with the common market.
(6) The Commission may revoke the decision it has taken pursuant to paragraphs 1 or 2 where:
(a) the declaration of compatibility is based on incorrect information for which one of the undertakings is responsible or where it has been obtained by deceit; or
(b) the undertakings concerned commit a breach of an obligation attached to the decision.
(7) The Commission may take a decision pursuant to paragraphs 1 to 3 without being bound by the time limits referred to in Article 10(3), in cases where:
(a) it finds that a concentration has been implemented
(i) in contravention of a condition attached to a decision under Article 6(1)(b), or
(ii) in contravention of a condition attached to a decision taken under paragraph 2 and in accordance with Article 10(2), which has found that, in the absence of the condition, the concentration would

COUNCIL REGULATION 139/2004

raise serious doubts as to its compatibility with the common market; or
(b) a decision has been revoked pursuant to paragraph 6.
(8) The Commission shall notify its decision to the undertakings concerned and the competent authorities of the Member States without delay.

Article 9. Referral to the competent authorities of the Member States
(1) The Commission may, by means of a decision notified without delay to the undertakings concerned and the competent authorities of the other Member States, refer a notified concentration to the competent authorities of the Member State concerned in the following circumstances.
(2) Within 15 working days of the date of receipt of the copy of the notification, a Member State, on its own initiative or upon the invitation of the Commission, may inform the Commission, which shall inform the undertakings concerned, that:
(a) a concentration threatens to affect significantly competition in a market within that Member State, which presents all the characteristics of a distinct market, or
(b) a concentration affects competition in a market within that Member State, which presents all the characteristics of a distinct market and which does not constitute a substantial part of the common market.
(3) If the Commission considers that, having regard to the market for the products or services in question and the geographical reference market within the meaning of paragraph 7, there is such a distinct market and that such a threat exists, either:
(a) it shall itself deal with the case in accordance with this Regulation; or
(b) it shall refer the whole or part of the case to the competent authorities of the Member State concerned with a view to the application of that State's national competition law.
If, however, the Commission considers that such a distinct market or threat does not exist, it shall adopt a decision to that effect which it shall address to the Member State concerned, and shall itself deal with the case in accordance with this Regulation.
In cases where a Member State informs the Commission pursuant to paragraph 2(b) that a concentration affects competition in a distinct market within its territory that does not form a substantial part of the common market, the Commission shall refer the whole or part of the case relating to the distinct market concerned, if it considers that such a distinct market is affected.
(4) A decision to refer or not to refer pursuant to paragraph 3 shall be taken:
(a) as a general rule within the period provided for in Article 10(1), second subparagraph, where the Commission, pursuant to Article 6(1)(b), has not initiated proceedings; or
(b) within 65 working days at most of the notification of the concentration concerned where the Commission has initiated proceedings under Article 6(1)(c), without taking the preparatory steps in order to adopt the necessary measures under Article 8(2), (3) or (4) to maintain or restore effective competition on the market concerned.
(5) If within the 65 working days referred to in paragraph 4(b) the Commission, despite a reminder from the Member State concerned, has not taken a decision on referral in accordance with paragraph 3 nor has taken the preparatory steps referred to in paragraph 4(b), it shall be deemed to have taken a decision to refer the case to the Member State concerned in accordance with paragraph 3(b).
(6) The competent authority of the Member State concerned shall decide upon the case without undue delay.
Within 45 working days after the Commission's referral, the competent authority of the Member State concerned shall inform the undertakings concerned of the result of the preliminary competition assessment and what further action, if any, it proposes to take. The Member State concerned may exceptionally suspend this time limit where necessary information has not been provided to it by the undertakings concerned as provided for by its national competition law.
Where a notification is requested under national law, the period of 45 working days shall begin on the working day following that of the receipt of a complete notification by the competent authority of that Member State.
(7) The geographical reference market shall consist of the area in which the undertakings concerned are involved in the supply and demand of products or services, in which the conditions of competition are sufficiently homogeneous and which can be distinguished from neighbouring areas because, in particular, conditions of competition are appreciably different in those areas. This assessment should take account in particular of the nature and characteristics of the products or services concerned, of the existence of entry barriers or of consumer preferences, of appreciable differences of the undertakings' market shares between the area concerned and neighbouring areas or of substantial price differences.
(8) In applying the provisions of this Article, the Member State concerned may take only the mea-

sures strictly necessary to safeguard or restore effective competition on the market concerned.
(9) In accordance with the relevant provisions of the Treaty, any Member State may appeal to the Court of Justice, and in particular request the application of Article 243 of the Treaty, for the purpose of applying its national competition law.

Article 10. Time limits for initiating proceedings and for decisions
(1) Without prejudice to Article 6(4), the decisions referred to in Article 6(1) shall be taken within 25 working days at most. That period shall begin on the working day following that of the receipt of a notification or, if the information to be supplied with the notification is incomplete, on the working day following that of the receipt of the complete information.
That period shall be increased to 35 working days where the Commission receives a request from a Member State in accordance with Article 9(2)or where, the undertakings concerned offer commitments pursuant to Article 6(2) with a view to rendering the concentration compatible with the common market.
(2) Decisions pursuant to Article 8(1) or (2) concerning notified concentrations shall be taken as soon as it appears that the serious doubts referred to in Article 6(1)(c) have been removed, particularly as a result of modifications made by the undertakings concerned, and at the latest by the time limit laid down in paragraph 3.
(3) Without prejudice to Article 8(7), decisions pursuant to Article 8(1) to (3) concerning notified concentrations shall be taken within not more than 90 working days of the date on which the proceedings are initiated. That period shall be increased to 105 working days where the undertakings concerned offer commitments pursuant to Article 8(2), second subparagraph, with a view to rendering the concentration compatible with the common market, unless these commitments have been offered less than 55 working days after the initiation of proceedings.
The periods set by the first subparagraph shall likewise be extended if the notifying parties make a request to that effect not later than 15 working days after the initiation of proceedings pursuant to Article 6(1)(c). The notifying parties may make only one such request. Likewise, at any time following the initiation of proceedings, the periods set by the first subparagraph may be extended by the Commission with the agreement of the notifying parties. The total duration of any extension or extensions effected pursuant to this subparagraph shall not exceed 20 working days.
(4) The periods set by paragraphs 1 and 3 shall exceptionally be suspended where, owing to circumstances for which one of the undertakings involved in the concentration is responsible, the Commission has had to request information by decision pursuant to Article 11 or to order an inspection by decision pursuant to Article 13.
The first subparagraph shall also apply to the period referred to in Article 9(4)(b).
(5) Where the Court of Justice gives a judgment which annuls the whole or part of a Commission decision which is subject to a time limit set by this Article, the concentration shall be re-examined by the Commission with a view to adopting a decision pursuant to Article 6(1).
The concentration shall be re-examined in the light of current market conditions.
The notifying parties shall submit a new notification or supplement the original notification, without delay, where the original notification becomes incomplete by reason of intervening changes in market conditions or in the information provided. Where there are no such changes, the parties shall certify this fact without delay.
The periods laid down in paragraph 1 shall start on the working day following that of the receipt of complete information in a new notification, a supplemented notification, or a certification within the meaning of the third subparagraph.
The second and third subparagraphs shall also apply in the cases referred to in Article 6(4) and Article 8(7).
(6) Where the Commission has not taken a decision in accordance with Article 6(1)(b), (c), 8(1), (2) or (3) within the time limits set in paragraphs 1 and 3 respectively, the concentration shall be deemed to have been declared compatible with the common market, without prejudice to Article 9.

Article 11. Requests for information
(1) In order to carry out the duties assigned to it by this Regulation, the Commission may, by simple request or by decision, require the persons referred to in Article 3(1)(b), as well as undertakings and associations of undertakings, to provide all necessary information.
(2) When sending a simple request for information to a person, an undertaking or an association of undertakings, the Commission shall state the legal basis and the purpose of the request, specify what information is required and fix the time limit within which the information is to be provided, as well as the penalties provided for in Article 14 for supplying incorrect or misleading information.
(3) Where the Commission requires a person, an undertaking or an association of undertakings to

supply information by decision, it shall state the legal basis and the purpose of the request, specify what information is required and fix the time limit within which it is to be provided. It shall also indicate the penalties provided for in Article 14 and indicate or impose the penalties provided for in Article 15. It shall further indicate the right to have the decision reviewed by the Court of Justice.
(4) The owners of the undertakings or their representatives and, in the case of legal persons, companies or firms, or associations having no legal personality, the persons authorised to represent them by law or by their constitution, shall supply the information requested on behalf of the undertaking concerned. Persons duly authorised to act may supply the information on behalf of their clients. The latter shall remain fully responsible if the information supplied is incomplete, incorrect or misleading.
(5) The Commission shall without delay forward a copy of any decision taken pursuant to paragraph 3 to the competent authorities of the Member State in whose territory the residence of the person or the seat of the undertaking or association of undertakings is situated, and to the competent authority of the Member State whose territory is affected. At the specific request of the competent authority of a Member State, the Commission shall also forward to that authority copies of simple requests for information relating to a notified concentration.
(6) At the request of the Commission, the governments and competent authorities of the Member States shall provide the Commission with all necessary information to carry out the duties assigned to it by this Regulation.
(7) In order to carry out the duties assigned to it by this Regulation, the Commission may interview any natural or legal person who consents to be interviewed for the purpose of collecting information relating to the subject matter of an investigation. At the beginning of the interview, which may be conducted by telephone or other electronic means, the Commission shall state the legal basis and the purpose of the interview.
Where an interview is not conducted on the premises of the Commission or by telephone or other electronic means, the Commission shall inform in advance the competent authority of the Member State in whose territory the interview takes place. If the competent authority of that Member State so requests, officials of that authority may assist the officials and other persons authorised by the Commission to conduct the interview.

Article 12. Inspections by the authorities of the Member States
(1) At the request of the Commission, the competent authorities of the Member States shall undertake the inspections which the Commission considers to be necessary under Article 13(1), or which it has ordered by decision pursuant to Article 13(4). The officials of the competent authorities of the Member States who are responsible for conducting these inspections as well as those authorised or appointed by them shall exercise their powers in accordance with their national law.
(2) If so requested by the Commission or by the competent authority of the Member State within whose territory the inspection is to be conducted, officials and other accompanying persons authorised by the Commission may assist the officials of the authority concerned.

Article 13. The Commission's powers of inspection
(1) In order to carry out the duties assigned to it by this Regulation, the Commission may conduct all necessary inspections of undertakings and associations of undertakings.
(2) The officials and other accompanying persons authorised by the Commission to conduct an inspection shall have the power:
(a) to enter any premises, land and means of transport of undertakings and associations of undertakings;
(b) to examine the books and other records related to the business, irrespective of the medium on which they are stored;
(c) to take or obtain in any form copies of or extracts from such books or records;
(d) to seal any business premises and books or records for the period and to the extent necessary for the inspection;
(e) to ask any representative or member of staff of the undertaking or association of undertakings for explanations on facts or documents relating to the subject matter and purpose of the inspection and to record the answers.
(3) Officials and other accompanying persons authorised by the Commission to conduct an inspection shall exercise their powers upon production of a written authorisation specifying the subject matter and purpose of the inspection and the penalties provided for in Article 14, in the production of the required books or other records related to the business which is incomplete or where answers to questions asked under paragraph 2 of this Article are incorrect or misleading. In good time before the inspection, the Commission shall give notice of the inspection to the competent authority of the Member State in whose territory the inspection is to be conducted.

(4) Undertakings and associations of undertakings are required to submit to inspections ordered by decision of the Commission. The decision shall specify the subject matter and purpose of the inspection, appoint the date on which it is to begin and indicate the penalties provided for in Articles 14 and 15 and the right to have the decision reviewed by the Court of Justice. The Commission shall take such decisions after consulting the competent authority of the Member State in whose territory the inspection is to be conducted.

(5) Officials of, and those authorised or appointed by, the competent authority of the Member State in whose territory the inspection is to be conducted shall, at the request of that authority or of the Commission, actively assist the officials and other accompanying persons authorised by the Commission. To this end, they shall enjoy the powers specified in paragraph 2.

(6) Where the officials and other accompanying persons authorised by the Commission find that an undertaking opposes an inspection, including the sealing of business premises, books or records, ordered pursuant to this Article, the Member State concerned shall afford them the necessary assistance, requesting where appropriate the assistance of the police or of an equivalent enforcement authority, so as to enable them to conduct their inspection.

(7) If the assistance provided for in paragraph 6 requires authorisation from a judicial authority according to national rules, such authorisation shall be applied for. Such authorisation may also be applied for as a precautionary measure.

(8) Where authorisation as referred to in paragraph 7 is applied for, the national judicial authority shall ensure that the Commission decision is authentic and that the coercive measures envisaged are neither arbitrary nor excessive having regard to the subject matter of the inspection. In its control of proportionality of the coercive measures, the national judicial authority may ask the Commission, directly or through the competent authority of that Member State, for detailed explanations relating to the subject matter of the inspection. However, the national judicial authority may not call into question the necessity for the inspection nor demand that it be provided with the information in the Commission's file. The lawfulness of the Commission's decision shall be subject to review only by the Court of Justice.

Article 14. Fines

(1) The Commission may by decision impose on the persons referred to in Article 3(1)b, undertakings or associations of undertakings, fines not exceeding 1 % of the aggregate turnover of the undertaking or association of undertakings concerned within the meaning of Article 5 where, intentionally or negligently:

(a) they supply incorrect or misleading information in a submission, certification, notification or supplement thereto, pursuant to Article 4, Article 10(5) or Article 22(3);

(b) they supply incorrect or misleading information in response to a request made pursuant to Article 11(2);

(c) in response to a request made by decision adopted pursuant to Article 11(3), they supply incorrect, incomplete or misleading information or do not supply information within the required time limit;

(d) they produce the required books or other records related to the business in incomplete form during inspections under Article 13, or refuse to submit to an inspection ordered by decision taken pursuant to Article 13(4);

(e) in response to a question asked in accordance with Article 13(2)(e),
- they give an incorrect or misleading answer,
- they fail to rectify within a time limit set by the Commission an incorrect, incomplete or misleading answer given by a member of staff, or
- they fail or refuse to provide a complete answer on facts relating to the subject matter and purpose of an inspection ordered by a decision adopted pursuant to Article 13(4);

(f) seals affixed by officials or other accompanying persons authorised by the Commission in accordance with Article 13(2)(d) have been broken.

(2) The Commission may by decision impose fines not exceeding 10 % of the aggregate turnover of the undertaking concerned within the meaning of Article 5 on the persons referred to in Article 3(1)b or the undertakings concerned where, either intentionally or negligently, they:

(a) fail to notify a concentration in accordance with Articles 4 or 22(3) prior to its implementation, unless they are expressly authorised to do so by Article 7(2) or by a decision taken pursuant to Article 7(3);

(b) implement a concentration in breach of Article 7;

(c) implement a concentration declared incompatible with the common market by decision pursuant to Article 8(3) or do not comply with any measure ordered by decision pursuant to Article 8(4) or (5);

(d) fail to comply with a condition or an obligation imposed by decision pursuant to Articles 6(1)(b),

Article 7(3) or Article 8(2), second subparagraph.
(3) In fixing the amount of the fine, regard shall be had to the nature, gravity and duration of the infringement.
(4) Decisions taken pursuant to paragraphs 1, 2 and 3 shall not be of a criminal law nature.

Article 15. Periodic penalty payments
(1) The Commission may by decision impose on the persons referred to in Article 3(1)b, undertakings or associations of undertakings, periodic penalty payments not exceeding 5 % of the average daily aggregate turnover of the undertaking or association of undertakings concerned within the meaning of Article 5 for each working day of delay, calculated from the date set in the decision, in order to compel them:
(a) to supply complete and correct information which it has requested by decision taken pursuant to Article 11(3);
(b) to submit to an inspection which it has ordered by decision taken pursuant to Article 13(4);
(c) to comply with an obligation imposed by decision pursuant to Article 6(1)(b), Article 7(3) or Article 8(2), second subparagraph; or;
(d) to comply with any measures ordered by decision pursuant to Article 8(4) or (5).
(2) Where the persons referred to in Article 3(1)(b), undertakings or associations of undertakings have satisfied the obligation which the periodic penalty payment was intended to enforce, the Commission may fix the definitive amount of the periodic penalty payments at a figure lower than that which would arise under the original decision.

Article 16. Review by the Court of Justice
The Court of Justice shall have unlimited jurisdiction within the meaning of Article 229 of the Treaty to review decisions whereby the Commission has fixed a fine or periodic penalty payments; it may cancel, reduce or increase the fine or periodic penalty payment imposed.

Article 17. Professional secrecy
(1) Information acquired as a result of the application of this Regulation shall be used only for the purposes of the relevant request, investigation or hearing.
(2) Without prejudice to Article 4(3), Articles 18 and 20, the Commission and the competent authorities of the Member States, their officials and other servants and other persons working under the supervision of these authorities as well as officials and civil servants of other authorities of the Member States shall not disclose information they have acquired through the application of this Regulation of the kind covered by the obligation of professional secrecy.
(3) Paragraphs 1 and 2 shall not prevent publication of general information or of surveys which do not contain information relating to particular undertakings or associations of undertakings.

Article 18. Hearing of the parties and of third persons
(1) Before taking any decision provided for in Article 6(3), Article 7(3), Article 8(2) to (6), and Articles 14 and 15, the Commission shall give the persons, undertakings and associations of undertakings concerned the opportunity, at every stage of the procedure up to the consultation of the Advisory Committee, of making known their views on the objections against them.
(2) By way of derogation from paragraph 1, a decision pursuant to Articles 7(3) and 8(5) may be taken provisionally, without the persons, undertakings or associations of undertakings concerned being given the opportunity to make known their views beforehand, provided that the Commission gives them that opportunity as soon as possible after having taken its decision.
(3) The Commission shall base its decision only on objections on which the parties have been able to submit their observations. The rights of the defence shall be fully respected in the proceedings. Access to the file shall be open at least to the parties directly involved, subject to the legitimate interest of undertakings in the protection of their business secrets.
(4) In so far as the Commission or the competent authorities of the Member States deem it necessary, they may also hear other natural or legal persons. Natural or legal persons showing a sufficient interest and especially members of the administrative or management bodies of the undertakings concerned or the recognised representatives of their employees shall be entitled, upon application, to be heard.

Article 19. Liaison with the authorities of the Member States
(1) The Commission shall transmit to the competent authorities of the Member States copies of notifications within three working days and, as soon as possible, copies of the most important documents lodged with or issued by the Commission pursuant to this Regulation. Such documents shall include commitments offered by the undertakings concerned vis-à-vis the Commission with a view

to rendering the concentration compatible with the common market pursuant to Article 6(2) or Article 8(2), second subparagraph.

(2) The Commission shall carry out the procedures set out in this Regulation in close and constant liaison with the competent authorities of the Member States, which may express their views upon those procedures. For the purposes of Article 9 it shall obtain information from the competent authority of the Member State as referred to in paragraph 2 of that Article and give it the opportunity to make known its views at every stage of the procedure up to the adoption of a decision pursuant to paragraph 3 of that Article; to that end it shall give it access to the file.

(3) An Advisory Committee on concentrations shall be consulted before any decision is taken pursuant to Article 8(1) to (6), Articles 14 or 15 with the exception of provisional decisions taken in accordance with Article 18(2).

(4) The Advisory Committee shall consist of representatives of the competent authorities of the Member States. Each Member State shall appoint one or two representatives; if unable to attend, they may be replaced by other representatives. At least one of the representatives of a Member State shall be competent in matters of restrictive practices and dominant positions.

(5) Consultation shall take place at a joint meeting convened at the invitation of and chaired by the Commission. A summary of the case, together with an indication of the most important documents and a preliminary draft of the decision to be taken for each case considered, shall be sent with the invitation. The meeting shall take place not less than 10 working days after the invitation has been sent. The Commission may in exceptional cases shorten that period as appropriate in order to avoid serious harm to one or more of the undertakings concerned by a concentration.

(6) The Advisory Committee shall deliver an opinion on the Commission's draft decision, if necessary by taking a vote. The Advisory Committee may deliver an opinion even if some members are absent and unrepresented. The opinion shall be delivered in writing and appended to the draft decision. The Commission shall take the utmost account of the opinion delivered by the Committee. It shall inform the Committee of the manner in which its opinion has been taken into account.

(7) The Commission shall communicate the opinion of the Advisory Committee, together with the decision, to the addressees of the decision. It shall make the opinion public together with the decision, having regard to the legitimate interest of undertakings in the protection of their business secrets.

Article 20. Publication of decisions

(1) The Commission shall publish the decisions which it takes pursuant to Article 8(1) to (6), Articles 14 and 15 with the exception of provisional decisions taken in accordance with Article 18(2) together with the opinion of the Advisory Committee in the *Official Journal of the European Union*.

(2) The publication shall state the names of the parties and the main content of the decision; it shall have regard to the legitimate interest of undertakings in the protection of their business secrets.

Article 21. Application of the Regulation and jurisdiction

(1) This Regulation alone shall apply to concentrations as defined in Article 3, and Council Regulations (EC) No 1/2003, (EEC) No 1017/68, (EEC) No 4056/86 and (EEC) No 3975/87 shall not apply, except in relation to joint ventures that do not have a Community dimension and which have as their object or effect the coordination of the competitive behaviour of undertakings that remain independent.

(2) Subject to review by the Court of Justice, the Commission shall have sole jurisdiction to take the decisions provided for in this Regulation.

(3) No Member State shall apply its national legislation on competition to any concentration that has a Community dimension.

The first subparagraph shall be without prejudice to any Member State's power to carry out any enquiries necessary for the application of Articles 4(4), 9(2) or after referral, pursuant to Article 9(3), first subparagraph, indent (b), or Article 9(5), to take the measures strictly necessary for the application of Article 9(8).

(4) Notwithstanding paragraphs 2 and 3, Member States may take appropriate measures to protect legitimate interests other than those taken into consideration by this Regulation and compatible with the general principles and other provisions of Community law.

Public security, plurality of the media and prudential rules shall be regarded as legitimate interests within the meaning of the first subparagraph.

Any other public interest must be communicated to the Commission by the Member State concerned and shall be recognised by the Commission after an assessment of its compatibility with the general principles and other provisions of Community law before the measures referred to above may be taken. The Commission shall inform the Member State concerned of its decision within 25 working days of that communication.

Article 22. Referral to the Commission

(1) One or more Member States may request the Commission to examine any concentration as defined in Article 3 that does not have a Community dimension within the meaning of Article 1 but affects trade between Member States and threatens to significantly affect competition within the territory of the Member State or States making the request.
Such a request shall be made at most within 15 working days of the date on which the concentration was notified, or if no notification is required, otherwise made known to the Member State concerned.
(2) The Commission shall inform the competent authorities of the Member States and the undertakings concerned of any request received pursuant to paragraph 1 without delay.
Any other Member State shall have the right to join the initial request within a period of 15 working days of being informed by the Commission of the initial request.
All national time limits relating to the concentration shall be suspended until, in accordance with the procedure set out in this Article, it has been decided where the concentration shall be examined. As soon as a Member State has informed the Commission and the undertakings concerned that it does not wish to join the request, the suspension of its national time limits shall end.
(3) The Commission may, at the latest 10 working days after the expiry of the period set in paragraph 2, decide to examine, the concentration where it considers that it affects trade between Member States and threatens to significantly affect competition within the territory of the Member State or States making the request. If the Commission does not take a decision within this period, it shall be deemed to have adopted a decision to examine the concentration in accordance with the request.
The Commission shall inform all Member States and the undertakings concerned of its decision. It may request the submission of a notification pursuant to Article 4.
The Member State or States having made the request shall no longer apply their national legislation on competition to the concentration.
(4) Article 2, Article 4(2) to (3), Articles 5, 6, and 8 to 21 shall apply where the Commission examines a concentration pursuant to paragraph 3. Article 7 shall apply to the extent that the concentration has not been implemented on the date on which the Commission informs the undertakings concerned that a request has been made.
Where a notification pursuant to Article 4 is not required, the period set in Article 10(1) within which proceedings may be initiated shall begin on the working day following that on which the Commission informs the undertakings concerned that it has decided to examine the concentration pursuant to paragraph 3.
(5) The Commission may inform one or several Member States that it considers a concentration fulfils the criteria in paragraph 1. In such cases, the Commission may invite that Member State or those Member States to make a request pursuant to paragraph 1.

Article 23. Implementing provisions

(1) The Commission shall have the power to lay down in accordance with the procedure referred to in paragraph 2:
(a) implementing provisions concerning the form, content and other details of notifications and submissions pursuant to Article 4;
(b) implementing provisions concerning time limits pursuant to Article 4(4), (5) Articles 7, 9, 10 and 22;
(c) the procedure and time limits for the submission and implementation of commitments pursuant to Article 6(2) and Article 8(2);
(d) implementing provisions concerning hearings pursuant to Article 18.
(2) The Commission shall be assisted by an Advisory Committee, composed of representatives of the Member States.
(a) Before publishing draft implementing provisions and before adopting such provisions, the Commission shall consult the Advisory Committee.
(b) Consultation shall take place at a meeting convened at the invitation of and chaired by the Commission. A draft of the implementing provisions to be taken shall be sent with the invitation. The meeting shall take place not less than 10 working days after the invitation has been sent.
(c) The Advisory Committee shall deliver an opinion on the draft implementing provisions, if necessary by taking a vote. The Commission shall take the utmost account of the opinion delivered by the Committee.

Article 24. Relations with third countries

(1) The Member States shall inform the Commission of any general difficulties encountered by their undertakings with concentrations as defined in Article 3 in a third country.
(2) Initially not more than one year after the entry into force of this Regulation and, thereafter

periodically, the Commission shall draw up a report examining the treatment accorded to undertakings having their seat or their principal fields of activity in the Community, in the terms referred to in paragraphs 3 and 4, as regards concentrations in third countries. The Commission shall submit those reports to the Council, together with any recommendations.

(3) Whenever it appears to the Commission, either on the basis of the reports referred to in paragraph 2 or on the basis of other information, that a third country does not grant undertakings having their seat or their principal fields of activity in the Community, treatment comparable to that granted by the Community to undertakings from that country, the Commission may submit proposals to the Council for an appropriate mandate for negotiation with a view to obtaining comparable treatment for undertakings having their seat or their principal fields of activity in the Community.

(4) Measures taken under this Article shall comply with the obligations of the Community or of the Member States, without prejudice to Article 307 of the Treaty, under international agreements, whether bilateral or multilateral.

Article 25. Repeal

(1) Without prejudice to Article 26(2), Regulations (EEC) No 4064/89 and (EC) No 1310/97 shall be repealed with effect from 1 May 2004.

(2) References to the repealed Regulations shall be construed as references to this Regulation and shall be read in accordance with the correlation table in the Annex.

Article 26. Entry into force and transitional provisions

(1) This Regulation shall enter into force on the 20th day following that of its publication in the *Official Journal of the European Union*.
It shall apply from 1 May 2004.

(2) Regulation (EEC) No 4064/89 shall continue to apply to any concentration which was the subject of an agreement or announcement or where control was acquired within the meaning of Article 4(1) of that Regulation before the date of application of this Regulation, subject, in particular, to the provisions governing applicability set out in Article 25(2) and (3) of Regulation (EEC) No 4064/89 and Article 2 of Regulation (EEC) No 1310/97.

(3) As regards concentrations to which this Regulation applies by virtue of accession, the date of accession shall be substituted for the date of application of this Regulation.

This Regulation shall be binding in its entirety and directly applicable in all Member States.

Commission Regulation (EC) No 773/2004 of 7 April 2004 relating to the conduct of proceedings by the Commission pursuant to Articles 81 and 82 of the EC Treaty

THE COMMISSION OF THE EUROPEAN COMMUNITIES,
Having regard to the Treaty establishing the European Community,
Having regard to the Agreement on the European Economic Area,
Having regard to Council Regulation (EC) No 1/2003 of 16 December 2002 on the implementation of the rules on competition laid down in Articles 81 and 82 of the Treaty, and in particular Article 33 thereof,
After consulting the Advisory Committee on Restrictive Practices and Dominant Positions,
Whereas:
(1) Regulation (EC) No 1/2003 empowers the Commission to regulate certain aspects of proceedings for the application of Articles 81 and 82 of the Treaty. It is necessary to lay down rules concerning the initiation of proceedings by the Commission as well as the handling of complaints and the hearing of the parties concerned.
(2) According to Regulation (EC) No 1/2003, national courts are under an obligation to avoid taking decisions which could run counter to decisions envisaged by the Commission in the same case. According to Article 11(6) of that Regulation, national competition authorities are relieved from their competence once the Commission has initiated proceedings for the adoption of a decision under Chapter III of Regulation (EC) No 1/2003. In this context, it is important that courts and competition authorities of the Member States are aware of the initiation of proceedings by the Commission. The Commission should therefore be able to make public its decisions to initiate proceedings.
(3) Before taking oral statements from natural or legal persons who consent to be interviewed, the Commission should inform those persons of the legal basis of the interview and its voluntary nature. The persons interviewed should also be informed of the purpose of the interview and of any record which may be made. In order to enhance the accuracy of the statements, the persons interviewed should also be given an opportunity to correct the statements recorded. Where information gathered from oral statements is exchanged pursuant to Article 12 of Regulation (EC) No 1/2003, that information should only be used in evidence to impose sanctions on natural persons where the conditions set out in that Article are fulfilled.
(4) Pursuant to Article 23(1)(d) of Regulation (EC) No 1/2003 fines may be imposed on undertakings and associations of undertakings where they fail to rectify within the time limit fixed by the Commission an incorrect, incomplete or misleading answer given by a member of their staff to questions in the course of inspections. It is therefore necessary to provide the undertaking concerned with a record of any explanations given and to establish a procedure enabling it to add any rectification, amendment or supplement to the explanations given by the member of staff who is not or was not authorised to provide explanations on behalf of the undertaking. The explanations given by a member of staff should remain in the Commission file as recorded during the inspection.
(5) Complaints are an essential source of information for detecting infringements of competition rules. It is important to define clear and efficient procedures for handling complaints lodged with the Commission.
(6) In order to be admissible for the purposes of Article 7 of Regulation (EC) No 1/2003, a complaint must contain certain specified information.
(7) In order to assist complainants in submitting the necessary facts to the Commission, a form should be drawn up. The submission of the information listed in that form should be a condition for a complaint to be treated as a complaint as referred to in Article 7 of Regulation (EC) No 1/2003.
(8) Natural or legal persons having chosen to lodge a complaint should be given the possibility to be associated closely with the proceedings initiated by the Commission with a view to finding an infringement. However, they should not have access to business secrets or other confidential information belonging to other parties involved in the proceedings.
(9) Complainants should be granted the opportunity of expressing their views if the Commission considers that there are insufficient grounds for acting on the complaint. Where the Commission rejects a complaint on the grounds that a competition authority of a Member State is dealing with it or has already done so, it should inform the complainant of the identity of that authority.
(10) In order to respect the rights of defence of undertakings, the Commission should give the parties concerned the right to be heard before it takes a decision.
(11) Provision should also be made for the hearing of persons who have not submitted a complaint as referred to in Article 7 of Regulation (EC) No 1/2003 and who are not parties to whom a statement of objections has been addressed but who can nevertheless show a sufficient interest. Consumer associations that apply to be heard should generally be regarded as having a sufficient interest, where

the proceedings concern products or services used by the end-consumer or products or services that constitute a direct input into such products or services. Where it considers this to be useful for the proceedings, the Commission should also be able to invite other persons to express their views in writing and to attend the oral hearing of the parties to whom a statement of objections has been addressed. Where appropriate, it should also be able to invite such persons to express their views at that oral hearing.

(12) To improve the effectiveness of oral hearings, the Hearing Officer should have the power to allow the parties concerned, complainants, other persons invited to the hearing, the Commission services and the authorities of the Member States to ask questions during the hearing.

(13) When granting access to the file, the Commission should ensure the protection of business secrets and other confidential information. The category of "other confidential information" includes information other than business secrets, which may be considered as confidential, insofar as its disclosure would significantly harm an undertaking or person. The Commission should be able to request undertakings or associations of undertakings that submit or have submitted documents or statements to identify confidential information.

(14) Where business secrets or other confidential information are necessary to prove an infringement, the Commission should assess for each individual document whether the need to disclose is greater than the harm which might result from disclosure.

(15) In the interest of legal certainty, a minimum time-limit for the various submissions provided for in this Regulation should be laid down.

(16) This Regulation replaces Commission Regulation (EC) No 2842/98 of 22 December 1998 on the hearing of parties in certain proceedings under Articles 85 and 86 of the EC Treaty, which should therefore be repealed.

(17) This Regulation aligns the procedural rules in the transport sector with the general rules of procedure in all sectors. Commission Regulation (EC) No 2843/98 of 22 December 1998 on the form, content and other details of applications and notifications provided for in Council Regulations (EEC) No 1017/68, (EEC) No 4056/86 and (EEC) No 3975/87 applying the rules on competition to the transport sector should therefore be repealed.

(18) Regulation (EC) No 1/2003 abolishes the notification and authorisation system. Commission Regulation (EC) No 3385/94 of 21 December 1994 on the form, content and other details of applications and notifications provided for in Council Regulation No 17 should therefore be repealed,

HAS ADOPTED THIS REGULATION:

Chapter I. Scope

Article 1. Subject-matter and scope

This regulation applies to proceedings conducted by the Commission for the application of Articles 81 and 82 of the Treaty.

Chapter II. Initiation of Proceedings

Article 2. Initiation of proceedings

(1) The Commission may decide to initiate proceedings with a view to adopting a decision pursuant to Chapter III of Regulation (EC) No 1/2003 at any point in time, but no later than the date on which it issues a preliminary assessment as referred to in Article 9(1) of that Regulation or a statement of objections or the date on which a notice pursuant to Article 27(4) of that Regulation is published, whichever is the earlier.

(2) The Commission may make public the initiation of proceedings, in any appropriate way. Before doing so, it shall inform the parties concerned.

(3) The Commission may exercise its powers of investigation pursuant to Chapter V of Regulation (EC) No 1/2003 before initiating proceedings.

(4) The Commission may reject a complaint pursuant to Article 7 of Regulation (EC) No 1/2003 without initiating proceedings.

Chapter III. Investigations by the Commission

Article 3. Power to take statements

(1) Where the Commission interviews a person with his consent in accordance with Article 19 of Regulation (EC) No 1/2003, it shall, at the beginning of the interview, state the legal basis and the purpose of the interview, and recall its voluntary nature. It shall also inform the person interviewed of its intention to make a record of the interview.

(2) The interview may be conducted by any means including by telephone or electronic means.

(3) The Commission may record the statements made by the persons interviewed in any form. A copy of any recording shall be made available to the person interviewed for approval. Where necessary, the Commission shall set a time-limit within which the person interviewed may communicate to it any correction to be made to the statement.

Article 4. Oral questions during inspections
(1) When, pursuant to Article 20(2)(e) of Regulation (EC) No 1/2003, officials or other accompanying persons authorised by the Commission ask representatives or members of staff of an undertaking or of an association of undertakings for explanations, the explanations given may be recorded in any form.
(2) A copy of any recording made pursuant to paragraph 1 shall be made available to the undertaking or association of undertakings concerned after the inspection.
(3) In cases where a member of staff of an undertaking or of an association of undertakings who is not or was not authorised by the undertaking or by the association of undertakings to provide explanations on behalf of the undertaking or association of undertakings has been asked for explanations, the Commission shall set a time-limit within which the undertaking or the association of undertakings may communicate to the Commission any rectification, amendment or supplement to the explanations given by such member of staff. The rectification, amendment or supplement shall be added to the explanations as recorded pursuant to paragraph 1.

Chapter IV. Handling of Complaints

Article 5. Admissibility of complaints
(1) Natural and legal persons shall show a legitimate interest in order to be entitled to lodge a complaint for the purposes of Article 7 of Regulation (EC) No 1/2003.
Such complaints shall contain the information required by Form C, as set out in the Annex. The Commission may dispense with this obligation as regards part of the information, including documents, required by Form C.
(2) Three paper copies as well as, if possible, an electronic copy of the complaint shall be submitted to the Commission. The complainant shall also submit a non-confidential version of the complaint, if confidentiality is claimed for any part of the complaint.
(3) Complaints shall be submitted in one of the official languages of the Community.

Article 6. Participation of complainants in proceedings
(1) Where the Commission issues a statement of objections relating to a matter in respect of which it has received a complaint, it shall provide the complainant with a copy of the non-confidential version of the statement of objections and set a time-limit within which the complainant may make known its views in writing.
(2) The Commission may, where appropriate, afford complainants the opportunity of expressing their views at the oral hearing of the parties to which a statement of objections has been issued, if complainants so request in their written comments.

Article 7. Rejection of complaints
(1) Where the Commission considers that on the basis of the information in its possession there are insufficient grounds for acting on a complaint, it shall inform the complainant of its reasons and set a time-limit within which the complainant may make known its views in writing. The Commission shall not be obliged to take into account any further written submission received after the expiry of that time-limit.
(2) If the complainant makes known its views within the time-limit set by the Commission and the written submissions made by the complainant do not lead to a different assessment of the complaint, the Commission shall reject the complaint by decision.
(3) If the complainant fails to make known its views within the time-limit set by the Commission, the complaint shall be deemed to have been withdrawn.

Article 8. Access to information
(1) Where the Commission has informed the complainant of its intention to reject a complaint pursuant to Article 7(1) the complainant may request access to the documents on which the Commission bases its provisional assessment. For this purpose, the complainant may however not have access to business secrets and other confidential information belonging to other parties involved in the proceedings.
(2) The documents to which the complainant has had access in the context of proceedings conducted by the Commission under Articles 81 and 82 of the Treaty may only be used by the complainant for the purposes of judicial or administrative proceedings for the application of those Treaty provisions.

Article 9. Rejections of complaints pursuant to Article 13 of Regulation (EC) No 1/2003

Where the Commission rejects a complaint pursuant to Article 13 of Regulation (EC) No 1/2003, it shall inform the complainant without delay of the national competition authority which is dealing or has already dealt with the case.

Chapter V. Exercise of the Right to be Heard

Article 10. Statement of objections and reply

(1) The Commission shall inform the parties concerned in writing of the objections raised against them. The statement of objections shall be notified to each of them.

(2) The Commission shall, when notifying the statement of objections to the parties concerned, set a time-limit within which these parties may inform it in writing of their views. The Commission shall not be obliged to take into account written submissions received after the expiry of that time-limit.

(3) The parties may, in their written submissions, set out all facts known to them which are relevant to their defence against the objections raised by the Commission. They shall attach any relevant documents as proof of the facts set out. They shall provide a paper original as well as an electronic copy or, where they do not provide an electronic copy, 28 paper copies of their submission and of the documents attached to it. They may propose that the Commission hear persons who may corroborate the facts set out in their submission.

Article 11. Right to be heard

(1) The Commission shall give the parties to whom it has addressed a statement of objections the opportunity to be heard before consulting the Advisory Committee referred to in Article 14(1) of Regulation (EC) No 1/2003.

(2) The Commission shall, in its decisions, deal only with objections in respect of which the parties referred to in paragraph 1 have been able to comment.

Article 12. Right to an oral hearing

The Commission shall give the parties to whom it has addressed a statement of objections the opportunity to develop their arguments at an oral hearing, if they so request in their written submissions.

Article 13. Hearing of other persons

(1) If natural or legal persons other than those referred to in Articles 5 and 11 apply to be heard and show a sufficient interest, the Commission shall inform them in writing of the nature and subject matter of the procedure and shall set a time-limit within which they may make known their views in writing.

(2) The Commission may, where appropriate, invite persons referred to in paragraph 1 to develop their arguments at the oral hearing of the parties to whom a statement of objections has been addressed, if the persons referred to in paragraph 1 so request in their written comments.

(3) The Commission may invite any other person to express its views in writing and to attend the oral hearing of the parties to whom a statement of objections has been addressed. The Commission may also invite such persons to express their views at that oral hearing.

Article 14. Conduct of oral hearings

(1) Hearings shall be conducted by a Hearing Officer in full independence.

(2) The Commission shall invite the persons to be heard to attend the oral hearing on such date as it shall determine.

(3) The Commission shall invite the competition authorities of the Member States to take part in the oral hearing. It may likewise invite officials and civil servants of other authorities of the Member States.

(4) Persons invited to attend shall either appear in person or be represented by legal representatives or by representatives authorised by their constitution as appropriate. Undertakings and associations of undertakings may also be represented by a duly authorised agent appointed from among their permanent staff.

(5) Persons heard by the Commission may be assisted by their lawyers or other qualified persons admitted by the Hearing Officer.

(6) Oral hearings shall not be public. Each person may be heard separately or in the presence of other persons invited to attend, having regard to the legitimate interest of the undertakings in the protection of their business secrets and other confidential information.

(7) The Hearing Officer may allow the parties to whom a statement of objections has been addressed, the complainants, other persons invited to the hearing, the Commission services and the authorities of the Member States to ask questions during the hearing.

(8) The statements made by each person heard shall be recorded. Upon request, the recording of the hearing shall be made available to the persons who attended the hearing. Regard shall be had to the legitimate interest of the parties in the protection of their business secrets and other confidential information.

Chapter VI. Access to the File and Treatment of Confidential Information

Article 15. Access to the file and use of documents

(1) If so requested, the Commission shall grant access to the file to the parties to whom it has addressed a statement of objections. Access shall be granted after the notification of the statement of objections.

(2) The right of access to the file shall not extend to business secrets, other confidential information and internal documents of the Commission or of the competition authorities of the Member States. The right of access to the file shall also not extend to correspondence between the Commission and the competition authorities of the Member States or between the latter where such correspondence is contained in the file of the Commission.

(3) Nothing in this Regulation prevents the Commission from disclosing and using information necessary to prove an infringement of Articles 81 or 82 of the Treaty.

(4) Documents obtained through access to the file pursuant to this Article shall only be used for the purposes of judicial or administrative proceedings for the application of Articles 81 and 82 of the Treaty.

Article 16. Identification and protection of confidential information

(1) Information, including documents, shall not be communicated or made accessible by the Commission in so far as it contains business secrets or other confidential information of any person.

(2) Any person which makes known its views pursuant to Article 6(1), Article 7(1), Article 10(2) and Article 13(1) and (3) or subsequently submits further information to the Commission in the course of the same procedure, shall clearly identify any material which it considers to be confidential, giving reasons, and provide a separate non-confidential version by the date set by the Commission for making its views known.

(3) Without prejudice to paragraph 2 of this Article, the Commission may require undertakings and associations of undertakings which produce documents or statements pursuant to Regulation (EC) No 1/2003 to identify the documents or parts of documents which they consider to contain business secrets or other confidential information belonging to them and to identify the undertakings with regard to which such documents are to be considered confidential. The Commission may likewise require undertakings or associations of undertakings to identify any part of a statement of objections, a case summary drawn up pursuant to Article 27(4) of Regulation (EC) No 1/2003 or a decision adopted by the Commission which in their view contains business secrets.

The Commission may set a time-limit within which the undertakings and associations of undertakings are to:

(a) substantiate their claim for confidentiality with regard to each individual document or part of document, statement or part of statement;

(b) provide the Commission with a non-confidential version of the documents or statements, in which the confidential passages are deleted;

(c) provide a concise description of each piece of deleted information.

(4) If undertakings or associations of undertakings fail to comply with paragraphs 2 and 3, the Commission may assume that the documents or statements concerned do not contain confidential information.

Chapter VII. General and Final Provisions

Article 17. Time-limits

(1) In setting the time-limits provided for in Article 3(3), Article 4(3), Article 6(1), Article 7(1), Article 10(2) and Article 16(3), the Commission shall have regard both to the time required for preparation of the submission and to the urgency of the case.

(2) The time-limits referred to in Article 6(1), Article 7(1) and Article 10(2) shall be at least four weeks. However, for proceedings initiated with a view to adopting interim measures pursuant to Article 8 of Regulation (EC) No 1/2003, the time-limit may be shortened to one week.

(3) The time-limits referred to in Article 3(3), Article 4(3) and Article 16(3) shall be at least two weeks.

(4) Where appropriate and upon reasoned request made before the expiry of the original time-limit, time-limits may be extended.

PART III   EUROPEAN UNION

Article 18. Repeals
Regulations (EC) No 2842/98, (EC) No 2843/98 and (EC) No 3385/94 are repealed.
References to the repealed regulations shall be construed as references to this regulation.

Article 19. Transitional provisions
Procedural steps taken under Regulations (EC) No 2842/98 and (EC) No 2843/98 shall continue to have effect for the purpose of applying this Regulation.

Article 20. Entry into force
This Regulation shall enter into force on 1 May 2004.
This Regulation shall be binding in its entirety and directly applicable in all Member States.

COMMISSION REGULATION 330/2010

Commission Regulation (EU) No 330/2010 of 20 April 2010 on the application of Article 101(3) of the Treaty on the Functioning of the European Union to categories of vertical agreements and concerted practices

THE EUROPEAN COMMISSION,
Having regard to the Treaty on the Functioning of the European Union,
Having regard to Regulation No 19/65/EEC of the Council of 2 March 1965 on the application of Article 85(3) of the Treaty to certain categories of agreements and concerted practices, and in particular Article 1 thereof,
Having published a draft of this Regulation,
After consulting the Advisory Committee on Restrictive Practices and Dominant Positions,
Whereas:
(1) Regulation No 19/65/EEC empowers the Commission to apply Article 101(3) of the Treaty on the Functioning of the European Union by regulation to certain categories of vertical agreements and corresponding concerted practices falling within Article 101(1) of the Treaty.
(2) Commission Regulation (EC) No 2790/1999 of 22 December 1999 on the application of Article 81(3) of the Treaty to categories of vertical agreements and concerted practices defines a category of vertical agreements which the Commission regarded as normally satisfying the conditions laid down in Article 101(3) of the Treaty. In view of the overall positive experience with the application of that Regulation, which expires on 31 May 2010, and taking into account further experience acquired since its adoption, it is appropriate to adopt a new block exemption regulation.
(3) The category of agreements which can be regarded as normally satisfying the conditions laid down in Article 101(3) of the Treaty includes vertical agreements for the purchase or sale of goods or services where those agreements are concluded between non-competing undertakings, between certain competitors or by certain associations of retailers of goods. It also includes vertical agreements containing ancillary provisions on the assignment or use of intellectual property rights. The term 'vertical agreements' should include the corresponding concerted practices.
(4) For the application of Article 101(3) of the Treaty by regulation, it is not necessary to define those vertical agreements which are capable of falling within Article 101(1) of the Treaty. In the individual assessment of agreements under Article 101(1) of the Treaty, account has to be taken of several factors, and in particular the market structure on the supply and purchase side.
(5) The benefit of the block exemption established by this Regulation should be limited to vertical agreements for which it can be assumed with sufficient certainty that they satisfy the conditions of Article 101(3) of the Treaty.
(6) Certain types of vertical agreements can improve economic efficiency within a chain of production or distribution by facilitating better coordination between the participating undertakings. In particular, they can lead to a reduction in the transaction and distribution costs of the parties and to an optimisation of their sales and investment levels.
(7) The likelihood that such efficiency-enhancing effects will outweigh any anti-competitive effects due to restrictions contained in vertical agreements depends on the degree of market power of the parties to the agreement and, therefore, on the extent to which those undertakings face competition from other suppliers of goods or services regarded by their customers as interchangeable or substitutable for one another, by reason of the products' characteristics, their prices and their intended use.
(8) It can be presumed that, where the market share held by each of the undertakings party to the agreement on the relevant market does not exceed 30 %, vertical agreements which do not contain certain types of severe restrictions of competition generally lead to an improvement in production or distribution and allow consumers a fair share of the resulting benefits.
(9) Above the market share threshold of 30 %, there can be no presumption that vertical agreements falling within the scope of Article 101(1) of the Treaty will usually give rise to objective advantages of such a character and size as to compensate for the disadvantages which they create for competition. At the same time, there is no presumption that those vertical agreements are either caught by Article 101(1) of the Treaty or that they fail to satisfy the conditions of Article 101(3) of the Treaty.
(10) This Regulation should not exempt vertical agreements containing restrictions which are likely to restrict competition and harm consumers or which are not indispensable to the attainment of the efficiency-enhancing effects. In particular, vertical agreements containing certain types of severe restrictions of competition such as minimum and fixed resale-prices, as well as certain types of territorial protection, should be excluded from the benefit of the block exemption established by this Regulation irrespective of the market share of the undertakings concerned.
(11) In order to ensure access to or to prevent collusion on the relevant market, certain conditions should be attached to the block exemption. To this end, the exemption of non-compete obligations

should be limited to obligations which do not exceed a defined duration. For the same reasons, any direct or indirect obligation causing the members of a selective distribution system not to sell the brands of particular competing suppliers should be excluded from the benefit of this Regulation.
(12) The market-share limitation, the non-exemption of certain vertical agreements and the conditions provided for in this Regulation normally ensure that the agreements to which the block exemption applies do not enable the participating undertakings to eliminate competition in respect of a substantial part of the products in question.
(13) The Commission may withdraw the benefit of this Regulation, pursuant to Article 29(1) of Council Regulation (EC) No 1/2003 of 16 December 2002 on the implementation of the rules on competition laid down in Articles 81 and 82 of the Treaty, where it finds in a particular case that an agreement to which the exemption provided for in this Regulation applies nevertheless has effects which are incompatible with Article 101(3) of the Treaty.
(14) The competition authority of a Member State may withdraw the benefit of this Regulation pursuant to Article 29(2) of Regulation (EC) No 1/2003 in respect of the territory of that Member State, or a part thereof where, in a particular case, an agreement to which the exemption provided for in this Regulation applies nevertheless has effects which are incompatible with Article 101(3) of the Treaty in the territory of that Member State, or in a part thereof, and where such territory has all the characteristics of a distinct geographic market.
(15) In determining whether the benefit of this Regulation should be withdrawn pursuant to Article 29 of Regulation (EC) No 1/2003, the anti-competitive effects that may derive from the existence of parallel networks of vertical agreements that have similar effects which significantly restrict access to a relevant market or competition therein are of particular importance. Such cumulative effects may for example arise in the case of selective distribution or non compete obligations.
(16) In order to strengthen supervision of parallel networks of vertical agreements which have similar anti-competitive effects and which cover more than 50 % of a given market, the Commission may by regulation declare this Regulation inapplicable to vertical agreements containing specific restraints relating to the market concerned, thereby restoring the full application of Article 101 of the Treaty to such agreements,
HAS ADOPTED THIS REGULATION:

Article 1. Definitions

(1) For the purposes of this Regulation, the following definitions shall apply:

(a) 'vertical agreement' means an agreement or concerted practice entered into between two or more undertakings each of which operates, for the purposes of the agreement or the concerted practice, at a different level of the production or distribution chain, and relating to the conditions under which the parties may purchase, sell or resell certain goods or services;

(b) 'vertical restraint' means a restriction of competition in a vertical agreement falling within the scope of Article 101(1) of the Treaty;

(c) 'competing undertaking' means an actual or potential competitor; 'actual competitor' means an undertaking that is active on the same relevant market; 'potential competitor' means an undertaking that, in the absence of the vertical agreement, would, on realistic grounds and not just as a mere theoretical possibility, in case of a small but permanent increase in relative prices be likely to undertake, within a short period of time, the necessary additional investments or other necessary switching costs to enter the relevant market;

(d) 'non-compete obligation' means any direct or indirect obligation causing the buyer not to manufacture, purchase, sell or resell goods or services which compete with the contract goods or services, or any direct or indirect obligation on the buyer to purchase from the supplier or from another undertaking designated by the supplier more than 80 % of the buyer's total purchases of the contract goods or services and their substitutes on the relevant market, calculated on the basis of the value or, where such is standard industry practice, the volume of its purchases in the preceding calendar year;

(e) 'selective distribution system' means a distribution system where the supplier undertakes to sell the contract goods or services, either directly or indirectly, only to distributors selected on the basis of specified criteria and where these distributors undertake not to sell such goods or services to unauthorised distributors within the territory reserved by the supplier to operate that system;

(f) 'intellectual property rights' includes industrial property rights, know how, copyright and neighbouring rights;

(g) 'know-how' means a package of non-patented practical information, resulting from experience and testing by the supplier, which is secret, substantial and identified: in this context, 'secret' means that the know-how is not generally known or easily accessible; 'substantial' means that the know-how is significant and useful to the buyer for the use, sale or resale of the contract goods or services;

'identified' means that the know-how is described in a sufficiently comprehensive manner so as to make it possible to verify that it fulfils the criteria of secrecy and substantiality;
(h) 'buyer' includes an undertaking which, under an agreement falling within Article 101(1) of the Treaty, sells goods or services on behalf of another undertaking;
(i) 'customer of the buyer' means an undertaking not party to the agreement which purchases the contract goods or services from a buyer which is party to the agreement.
(2) For the purposes of this Regulation, the terms 'undertaking', 'supplier' and 'buyer' shall include their respective connected undertakings.
'Connected undertakings' means:
(a) undertakings in which a party to the agreement, directly or indirectly:
(i) has the power to exercise more than half the voting rights, or
(ii) has the power to appoint more than half the members of the supervisory board, board of management or bodies legally representing the undertaking, or
(iii) has the right to manage the undertaking's affairs;
(b) undertakings which directly or indirectly have, over a party to the agreement, the rights or powers listed in point (a);
(c) undertakings in which an undertaking referred to in point (b) has, directly or indirectly, the rights or powers listed in point (a);
(d) undertakings in which a party to the agreement together with one or more of the undertakings referred to in points (a), (b) or (c), or in which two or more of the latter undertakings, jointly have the rights or powers listed in point (a);
(e) undertakings in which the rights or the powers listed in point (a) are jointly held by:
(i) parties to the agreement or their respective connected undertakings referred to in points (a) to (d), or
(ii) one or more of the parties to the agreement or one or more of their connected undertakings referred to in points (a) to (d) and one or more third parties.

Article 2. Exemption

(1) Pursuant to Article 101(3) of the Treaty and subject to the provisions of this Regulation, it is hereby declared that Article 101(1) of the Treaty shall not apply to vertical agreements.
This exemption shall apply to the extent that such agreements contain vertical restraints.
(2) The exemption provided for in paragraph 1 shall apply to vertical agreements entered into between an association of undertakings and its members, or between such an association and its suppliers, only if all its members are retailers of goods and if no individual member of the association, together with its connected undertakings, has a total annual turnover exceeding EUR 50 million. Vertical agreements entered into by such associations shall be covered by this Regulation without prejudice to the application of Article 101 of the Treaty to horizontal agreements concluded between the members of the association or decisions adopted by the association.
(3) The exemption provided for in paragraph 1 shall apply to vertical agreements containing provisions which relate to the assignment to the buyer or use by the buyer of intellectual property rights, provided that those provisions do not constitute the primary object of such agreements and are directly related to the use, sale or resale of goods or services by the buyer or its customers. The exemption applies on condition that, in relation to the contract goods or services, those provisions do not contain restrictions of competition having the same object as vertical restraints which are not exempted under this Regulation.
(4) The exemption provided for in paragraph 1 shall not apply to vertical agreements entered into between competing undertakings. However, it shall apply where competing undertakings enter into a non-reciprocal vertical agreement and:
(a) the supplier is a manufacturer and a distributor of goods, while the buyer is a distributor and not a competing undertaking at the manufacturing level; or
(b) the supplier is a provider of services at several levels of trade, while the buyer provides its goods or services at the retail level and is not a competing undertaking at the level of trade where it purchases the contract services.
(5) This Regulation shall not apply to vertical agreements the subject matter of which falls within the scope of any other block exemption regulation, unless otherwise provided for in such a regulation.

Article 3. Market share threshold

(1) The exemption provided for in Article 2 shall apply on condition that the market share held by the supplier does not exceed 30 % of the relevant market on which it sells the contract goods or services and the market share held by the buyer does not exceed 30 % of the relevant market on which it purchases the contract goods or services.

(2) For the purposes of paragraph 1, where in a multi party agreement an undertaking buys the contract goods or services from one undertaking party to the agreement and sells the contract goods or services to another undertaking party to the agreement, the market share of the first undertaking must respect the market share threshold provided for in that paragraph both as a buyer and a supplier in order for the exemption provided for in Article 2 to apply.

Article 4. Restrictions that remove the benefit of the block exemption – hardcore restrictions

The exemption provided for in Article 2 shall not apply to vertical agreements which, directly or indirectly, in isolation or in combination with other factors under the control of the parties, have as their object:

(a) the restriction of the buyer's ability to determine its sale price, without prejudice to the possibility of the supplier to impose a maximum sale price or recommend a sale price, provided that they do not amount to a fixed or minimum sale price as a result of pressure from, or incentives offered by, any of the parties;

(b) the restriction of the territory into which, or of the customers to whom, a buyer party to the agreement, without prejudice to a restriction on its place of establishment, may sell the contract goods or services, except:

(i) the restriction of active sales into the exclusive territory or to an exclusive customer group reserved to the supplier or allocated by the supplier to another buyer, where such a restriction does not limit sales by the customers of the buyer,

(ii) the restriction of sales to end users by a buyer operating at the wholesale level of trade,

(iii) the restriction of sales by the members of a selective distribution system to unauthorised distributors within the territory reserved by the supplier to operate that system, and

(iv) the restriction of the buyer's ability to sell components, supplied for the purposes of incorporation, to customers who would use them to manufacture the same type of goods as those produced by the supplier;

(c) the restriction of active or passive sales to end users by members of a selective distribution system operating at the retail level of trade, without prejudice to the possibility of prohibiting a member of the system from operating out of an unauthorised place of establishment;

(d) the restriction of cross-supplies between distributors within a selective distribution system, including between distributors operating at different level of trade;

(e) the restriction, agreed between a supplier of components and a buyer who incorporates those components, of the supplier's ability to sell the components as spare parts to end-users or to repairers or other service providers not entrusted by the buyer with the repair or servicing of its goods.

Article 5. Excluded restrictions

(1) The exemption provided for in Article 2 shall not apply to the following obligations contained in vertical agreements:

(a) any direct or indirect non-compete obligation, the duration of which is indefinite or exceeds five years;

(b) any direct or indirect obligation causing the buyer, after termination of the agreement, not to manufacture, purchase, sell or resell goods or services;

(c) any direct or indirect obligation causing the members of a selective distribution system not to sell the brands of particular competing suppliers.

For the purposes of point (a) of the first subparagraph, a non-compete obligation which is tacitly renewable beyond a period of five years shall be deemed to have been concluded for an indefinite duration.

(2) By way of derogation from paragraph 1(a), the time limitation of five years shall not apply where the contract goods or services are sold by the buyer from premises and land owned by the supplier or leased by the supplier from third parties not connected with the buyer, provided that the duration of the non-compete obligation does not exceed the period of occupancy of the premises and land by the buyer.

(3) By way of derogation from paragraph 1(b), the exemption provided for in Article 2 shall apply to any direct or indirect obligation causing the buyer, after termination of the agreement, not to manufacture, purchase, sell or resell goods or services where the following conditions are fulfilled:

(a) the obligation relates to goods or services which compete with the contract goods or services;

(b) the obligation is limited to the premises and land from which the buyer has operated during the contract period;

(c) the obligation is indispensable to protect know-how transferred by the supplier to the buyer;

(d) the duration of the obligation is limited to a period of one year after termination of the agreement.

Paragraph 1(b) is without prejudice to the possibility of imposing a restriction which is unlimited in time on the use and disclosure of know-how which has not entered the public domain.

COMMISSION REGULATION 330/2010

Article 6. Non-application of this Regulation
Pursuant to Article 1a of Regulation No 19/65/EEC, the Commission may by regulation declare that, where parallel networks of similar vertical restraints cover more than 50 % of a relevant market, this Regulation shall not apply to vertical agreements containing specific restraints relating to that market.

Article 7. Application of the market share threshold
For the purposes of applying the market share thresholds provided for in Article 3 the following rules shall apply:
(a) the market share of the supplier shall be calculated on the basis of market sales value data and the market share of the buyer shall be calculated on the basis of market purchase value data. If market sales value or market purchase value data are not available, estimates based on other reliable market information, including market sales and purchase volumes, may be used to establish the market share of the undertaking concerned;
(b) the market shares shall be calculated on the basis of data relating to the preceding calendar year;
(c) the market share of the supplier shall include any goods or services supplied to vertically integrated distributors for the purposes of sale;
(d) if a market share is initially not more than 30 % but subsequently rises above that level without exceeding 35 %, the exemption provided for in Article 2 shall continue to apply for a period of two consecutive calendar years following the year in which the 30 % market share threshold was first exceeded;
(e) if a market share is initially not more than 30 % but subsequently rises above 35 %, the exemption provided for in Article 2 shall continue to apply for one calendar year following the year in which the level of 35 % was first exceeded;
(f) the benefit of points (d) and (e) may not be combined so as to exceed a period of two calendar years;
(g) the market share held by the undertakings referred to in point (e) of the second subparagraph of Article 1(2) shall be apportioned equally to each undertaking having the rights or the powers listed in point (a) of the second subparagraph of Article 1(2).

Article 8. Application of the turnover threshold
(1) For the purpose of calculating total annual turnover within the meaning of Article 2(2), the turnover achieved during the previous financial year by the relevant party to the vertical agreement and the turnover achieved by its connected undertakings in respect of all goods and services, excluding all taxes and other duties, shall be added together. For this purpose, no account shall be taken of dealings between the party to the vertical agreement and its connected undertakings or between its connected undertakings.
(2) The exemption provided for in Article 2 shall remain applicable where, for any period of two consecutive financial years, the total annual turnover threshold is exceeded by no more than 10 %.

Article 9. Transitional period
The prohibition laid down in Article 101(1) of the Treaty shall not apply during the period from 1 June 2010 to 31 May 2011 in respect of agreements already in force on 31 May 2010 which do not satisfy the conditions for exemption provided for in this Regulation but which, on 31 May 2010, satisfied the conditions for exemption provided for in Regulation (EC) No 2790/1999.

Article 10. Period of validity
This Regulation shall enter into force on 1 June 2010.
It shall expire on 31 May 2022.
This Regulation shall be binding in its entirety and directly applicable in all Member States.

PART III EUROPEAN UNION

Commission notice – Guidelines on the effect on trade concept contained in Articles 81 and 82 of the Treaty (OJ C 101, 27.4.2004).

Summary

Articles 101 and 102 of the Treaty on the Functioning of the European Union (TFEU) (ex-Articles 81 and 82 of the Treaty Establishing the European Community (TEC)) are applicable to horizontal and vertical agreements and practices on the part of undertakings which may affect trade between European Union (EU) countries.

The present guidelines spell out a rule indicating when agreements are in general unlikely to be capable of appreciably affecting trade between EU countries. They are not intended to be exhaustive. The aim is to set out the methodology for the application of the effect on trade concept and to provide guidance on its application in frequently occurring situations. Although not binding on them, these guidelines also intend to give guidance to the courts and authorities of the EU countries in their application of the effect on trade concept contained in Articles 101 and 102 TFEU.

The effect on trade criterion confines the scope of application of Articles 101 and 102 TFEU to agreements and practices that are capable of having a minimum level of cross-border effects within the EU.

In the case of Article 101 TFEU, it is the agreement that must be capable of affecting trade between EU countries. If the agreement as a whole is capable of affecting trade between EU countries, there is EU law jurisdiction in respect of the entire agreement, including any parts of the agreement that individually do not affect trade between EU countries. In cases where the contractual relations between the same parties cover several activities, these activities must, in order to form part of the same agreement, be directly linked and form an integral part of the same overall business arrangement. If not, each activity constitutes a separate agreement.

In the case of Article 102 TFEU, it is the abuse that must affect trade between EU countries. This does not imply, however, that each element of the behaviour must be assessed in isolation. Conduct that forms part of an overall strategy pursued by the dominant undertaking must be assessed in terms of its overall impact. Where a dominant undertaking adopts various practices in pursuit of the same aim, for instance practices that aim at eliminating or foreclosing competitors, in order for Article 102 TFEU to be applicable to all the practices forming part of this overall strategy, it is sufficient that at least one of these practices is capable of affecting trade between EU countries.

Analysis of the concept of affecting trade requires that three aspects in particular be addressed:

- *the concept of "trade between EU countries"*: the concept of "trade" is not limited to traditional exchanges of goods and services across borders. It is a wider concept, covering all cross-border economic activity including establishment. This interpretation is consistent with the fundamental objective of the Treaty to promote free movement of goods, services, persons and capital. The requirement that there must be an effect on trade "between EU countries" implies that there must be an impact on cross-border economic activity involving at least two EU countries;

- *the notion "may affect"*: the function of the notion "may affect" is to define the nature of the required impact on trade between EU countries. According to the standard test developed by the Court of Justice, the notion "may affect" implies that it must be possible to foresee with a sufficient degree of probability on the basis of a set of objective factors of law or fact that the agreement or practice may have an influence, direct or indirect, actual or potential, on the pattern of trade between EU countries. In cases where the agreement or practice is liable to affect the competitive structure inside the EU, EU law jurisdiction is established;

- *the concept of "appreciability"*: the effect on trade criterion incorporates a quantitative element, limiting EU law jurisdiction to agreements and practices that are capable of having effects of a certain magnitude. Appreciability can be appraised in particular by reference to the position and the importance of the relevant undertakings on the market for the products concerned. The assessment of appreciability depends on the circumstances of each individual case, in particular the nature of the agreement and practice, the nature of the products covered and the market position of the undertakings concerned. In its notice on agreements of minor importance, the Commission states that agreements between small and medium-sized enterprises rarely affect trade between EU countries to a significant degree. The Commission holds the view that in principle agreements are not capable of appreciably affecting trade between EU countries when the following cumulative conditions are met: The threshold of EUR 40 million is calculated on the basis of total EU sales excluding tax during the previous financial year by the undertakings concerned, of the products covered by the agreement (the contract products). Sales between entities that form part of the same undertaking are excluded. In order to apply the market share threshold, it is necessary to determine the relevant market.

COMMISSION NOTICE GUIDELINES ON THE EFFECTS OF TRADE

The Commission will apply the negative presumption to the application of the concept of affecting trade to all agreements, including agreements that by their very nature are capable of affecting trade between EU countries as well as agreements that involve trade with undertakings located in non-EU countries. Outside the scope of negative presumption, the Commission will take account of qualitative elements relating to the nature of the agreement or practice and the nature of the products that they concern.

The positive presumption relating to appreciability in the case of agreements also takes into account whether and how agreements and practices cover several EU countries, whether they are confined to a single EU country or to part of a single EU country. Agreements and practices involving non-EU countries are also dealt with. In the case of agreements and practices whose object is not to restrict competition inside the EU, it is normally necessary to proceed with a more detailed analysis of whether or not cross-border economic activity inside the EU, and thus patterns of trade between EU countries, are capable of being affected.

PART III EUROPEAN UNION

Commission Notice on Immunity from fines and reduction of fines in cartel cases (2006/C 298/11)

I. Introduction

(1) This notice sets out the framework for rewarding cooperation in the Commission investigation by undertakings which are or have been party to secret cartels affecting the Community. Cartels are agreements and/or concerted practices between two or more competitors aimed at coordinating their competitive behaviour on the market and/or influencing the relevant parameters of competition through practices such as the fixing of purchase or selling prices or other trading conditions, the allocation of production or sales quotas, the sharing of markets including bid-rigging, restrictions of imports or exports and/or anti-competitive actions against other competitors. Such practices are among the most serious violations of Article 81 EC.

(2) By artificially limiting the competition that would normally prevail between them, undertakings avoid exactly those pressures that lead them to innovate, both in terms of product development and the introduction of more efficient production methods. Such practices also lead to more expensive raw materials and components for the Community companies that purchase from such producers. They ultimately result in artificial prices and reduced choice for the consumer. In the long term, they lead to a loss of competitiveness and reduced employment opportunities.

(3) By their very nature, secret cartels are often difficult to detect and investigate without the cooperation of undertakings or individuals implicated in them. Therefore, the Commission considers that it is in the Community interest to reward undertakings involved in this type of illegal practices which are willing to put an end to their participation and co-operate in the Commission's investigation, independently of the rest of the undertakings involved in the cartel. The interests of consumers and citizens in ensuring that secret cartels are detected and punished outweigh the interest in fining those undertakings that enable the Commission to detect and prohibit such practices.

(4) The Commission considers that the collaboration of an undertaking in the detection of the existence of a cartel has an intrinsic value. A decisive contribution to the opening of an investigation or to the finding of an infringement may justify the granting of immunity from any fine to the undertaking in question, on condition that certain additional requirements are fulfilled.

(5) Moreover, co-operation by one or more undertakings may justify a reduction of a fine by the Commission. Any reduction of a fine must reflect an undertaking's actual contribution, in terms of quality and timing, to the Commission's establishment of the infringement. Reductions are to be limited to those undertakings that provide the Commission with evidence that adds significant value to that already in the Commission's possession.

(6) In addition to submitting pre-existing documents, undertakings may provide the Commission with voluntary presentations of their knowledge of a cartel and their role therein prepared specially to be submitted under this leniency programme. These initiatives have proved to be useful for the effective investigation and termination of cartel infringements and they should not be discouraged by discovery orders issued in civil litigation. Potential leniency applicants might be dissuaded from cooperating with the Commission under this Notice if this could impair their position in civil proceedings, as compared to companies who do not cooperate. Such undesirable effect would significantly harm the public interest in ensuring effective public enforcement of Article 81 EC in cartel cases and thus its subsequent or parallel effective private enforcement.

(7) The supervisory task conferred on the Commission by the Treaty in competition matters does not only include the duty to investigate and punish individual infringements, but also encompasses the duty to pursue a general policy. The protection of corporate statements in the public interest is not a bar to their disclosure to other addressees of the statement of objections in order to safeguard their rights of defence in the procedure before the Commission, to the extent that it is technically possible to combine both interests by rendering corporate statements accessible only at the Commission premises and normally on a single occasion following the formal notification of the objections. Moreover, the Commission will process personal data in the context of this notice in conformity with its obligations under Regulation (EC) No 45/2001.

II. Immunity from Fines

A. Requirements to qualify for immunity from fines

(8) The Commission will grant immunity from any fine which would otherwise have been imposed to an undertaking disclosing its participation in an alleged cartel affecting the Community if that undertaking is the first to submit information and evidence which in the Commission's view will enable it to:

COMMISSION NOTICE IMMUNITY FROM FINES IN CARTEL CASES

(a) carry out a targeted inspection in connection with the alleged cartel; or
(b) find an infringement of Article 81 EC in connection with the alleged cartel.
(9) For the Commission to be able to carry out a targeted inspection within the meaning of point (8) (a), the undertaking must provide the Commission with the information and evidence listed below, to the extent that this, in the Commission's view, would not jeopardize the inspections:
(a) A corporate statement which includes, in so far as it is known to the applicant at the time of the submission:
- A detailed description of the alleged cartel arrangement, including for instance its aims, activities and functioning; the product or service concerned, the geographic scope, the duration of and the estimated market volumes affected by the alleged cartel; the specific dates, locations, content of and participants in alleged cartel contacts, and all relevant explanations in connection with the pieces of evidence provided in support of the application.
- The name and address of the legal entity submitting the immunity application as well as the names and addresses of all the other undertakings that participate(d) in the alleged cartel;
- The names, positions, office locations and, where necessary, home addresses of all individuals who, to the applicant's knowledge, are or have been involved in the alleged cartel, including those individuals which have been involved on the applicant's behalf;
- Information on which other competition authorities, inside or outside the EU, have been approached or are intended to be approached in relation to the alleged cartel; and
(b) Other evidence relating to the alleged cartel in possession of the applicant or available to it at the time of the submission, including in particular any evidence contemporaneous to the infringement.
(10) Immunity pursuant to point (8)(a) will not be granted if, at the time of the submission, the Commission had already sufficient evidence to adopt a decision to carry out an inspection in connection with the alleged cartel or had already carried out such an inspection.
(11) Immunity pursuant to point (8)(b) will only be granted on the cumulative conditions that the Commission did not have, at the time of the submission, sufficient evidence to find an infringement of Article 81 EC in connection with the alleged cartel and that no undertaking had been granted conditional immunity from fines under point (8)(a) in connection with the alleged cartel. In order to qualify, an undertaking must be the first to provide contemporaneous, incriminating evidence of the alleged cartel as well as a corporate statement containing the kind of information specified in point (9)(a), which would enable the Commission to find an infringement of Article 81 EC.
(12) In addition to the conditions set out in points (8)(a), (9) and (10) or in points (8)(b) and 11, all the following conditions must be met in any case to qualify for any immunity from a fine:
(a) The undertaking cooperates genuinely, fully, on a continuous basis and expeditiously from the time it submits its application throughout the Commission's administrative procedure. This includes:
- providing the Commission promptly with all relevant information and evidence relating to the alleged cartel that comes into its possession or is available to it;
- remaining at the Commission's disposal to answer promptly to any request that may contribute to the establishment of the facts;
- making current (and, if possible, former) employees and directors available for interviews with the Commission;
- not destroying, falsifying or concealing relevant information or evidence relating to the alleged cartel; and
- not disclosing the fact or any of the content of its application before the Commission has issued a statement of objections in the case, unless otherwise agreed;
(b) The undertaking ended its involvement in the alleged cartel immediately following its application, except for what would, in the Commission's view, be reasonably necessary to preserve the integrity of the inspections;
(c) When contemplating making its application to the Commission, the undertaking must not have destroyed, falsified or concealed evidence of the alleged cartel nor disclosed the fact or any of the content of its contemplated application, except to other competition authorities.
(13) An undertaking which took steps to coerce other undertakings to join the cartel or to remain in it is not eligible for immunity from fines. It may still qualify for a reduction of fines if it fulfils the relevant requirements and meets all the conditions therefor.

B. Procedure

(14) An undertaking wishing to apply for immunity from fines should contact the Commission's Directorate General for Competition. The undertaking may either initially apply for a marker or immediately proceed to make a formal application to the Commission for immunity from fines in order to meet the conditions in points (8)(a) or (8)(b), as appropriate. The Commission may disregard

PART III EUROPEAN UNION

any application for immunity from fines on the ground that it has been submitted after the statement of objections has been issued.

(15) The Commission services may grant a marker protecting an immunity applicant's place in the queue for a period to be specified on a case-by-case basis in order to allow for the gathering of the necessary information and evidence. To be eligible to secure a marker, the applicant must provide the Commission with information concerning its name and address, the parties to the alleged cartel, the affected product(s) and territory(-ies), the estimated duration of the alleged cartel and the nature of the alleged cartel conduct. The applicant should also inform the Commission on other past or possible future leniency applications to other authorities in relation to the alleged cartel and justify its request for a marker. Where a marker is granted, the Commission services determine the period within which the applicant has to perfect the marker by submitting the information and evidence required to meet the relevant threshold for immunity. Undertakings which have been granted a marker cannot perfect it by making a formal application in hypothetical terms. If the applicant perfects the marker within the period set by the Commission services, the information and evidence provided will be deemed to have been submitted on the date when the marker was granted.

(16) An undertaking making a formal immunity application to the Commission must:
(a) provide the Commission with all information and evidence relating to the alleged cartel available to it, as specified in points (8) and (9), including corporate statements; or
(b) initially present this information and evidence in hypothetical terms, in which case the undertaking must present a detailed descriptive list of the evidence it proposes to disclose at a later agreed date. This list should accurately reflect the nature and content of the evidence, whilst safeguarding the hypothetical nature of its disclosure. Copies of documents, from which sensitive parts have been removed, may be used to illustrate the nature and content of the evidence. The name of the applying undertaking and of other undertakings involved in the alleged cartel need not be disclosed until the evidence described in its application is submitted. However, the product or service concerned by the alleged cartel, the geographic scope of the alleged cartel and the estimated duration must be clearly identified.

(17) If requested, the Directorate General for Competition will provide an acknowledgement of receipt of the undertaking's application for immunity from fines, confirming the date and, where appropriate, time of the application.

(18) Once the Commission has received the information and evidence submitted by the undertaking under point (16)(a) and has verified that it meets the conditions set out in points (8)(a) or (8)(b), as appropriate, it will grant the undertaking conditional immunity from fines in writing.

(19) If the undertaking has presented information and evidence in hypothetical terms, the Commission will verify that the nature and content of the evidence described in the detailed list referred to in point (16)(b) will meet the conditions set out in points (8)(a) or (8)(b), as appropriate, and inform the undertaking accordingly. Following the disclosure of the evidence no later than on the date agreed and having verified that it corresponds to the description made in the list, the Commission will grant the undertaking conditional immunity from fines in writing.

(20) If it becomes apparent that immunity is not available or that the undertaking failed to meet the conditions set out in points (8)(a) or (8)(b), as appropriate, the Commission will inform the undertaking in writing. In such case, the undertaking may withdraw the evidence disclosed for the purposes of its immunity application or request the Commission to consider it under section III of this notice. This does not prevent the Commission from using its normal powers of investigation in order to obtain the information.

(21) The Commission will not consider other applications for immunity from fines before it has taken a position on an existing application in relation to the same alleged infringement, irrespective of whether the immunity application is presented formally or by requesting a marker.

(22) If at the end of the administrative procedure, the undertaking has met the conditions set out in point (12), the Commission will grant it immunity from fines in the relevant decision. If at the end of the administrative procedure, the undertaking has not met the conditions set out in point (12), the undertaking will not benefit from any favorable treatment under this Notice. If the Commission, after having granted conditional immunity ultimately finds that the immunity applicant has acted as a coercer, it will withhold immunity.

III. Reduction of a Fine

A. Requirements to qualify for reduction of a fine

(23) Undertakings disclosing their participation in an alleged cartel affecting the Community that do not meet the conditions under section II above may be eligible to benefit from a reduction of any fine that would otherwise have been imposed.

(24) In order to qualify, an undertaking must provide the Commission with evidence of the alleged infringement which represents significant added value with respect to the evidence already in the Commission's possession and must meet the cumulative conditions set out in points (12)(a) to (12)(c) above.

(25) The concept of 'added value' refers to the extent to which the evidence provided strengthens, by its very nature and/or its level of detail, the Commission's ability to prove the alleged cartel. In this assessment, the Commission will generally consider written evidence originating from the period of time to which the facts pertain to have a greater value than evidence subsequently established. Incriminating evidence directly relevant to the facts in question will generally be considered to have a greater value than that with only indirect relevance. Similarly, the degree of corroboration from other sources required for the evidence submitted to be relied upon against other undertakings involved in the case will have an impact on the value of that evidence, so that compelling evidence will be attributed a greater value than evidence such as statements which require corroboration if contested.

(26) The Commission will determine in any final decision adopted at the end of the administrative procedure the level of reduction an undertaking will benefit from, relative to the fine which would otherwise be imposed. For the:
- first undertaking to provide significant added value: a reduction of 30-50 %,
- second undertaking to provide significant added value: a reduction of 20-30 %,
- subsequent undertakings that provide significant added value: a reduction of up to 20 %.

In order to determine the level of reduction within each of these bands, the Commission will take into account the time at which the evidence fulfilling the condition in point (24) was submitted and the extent to which it represents added value.

If the applicant for a reduction of a fine is the first to submit compelling evidence in the sense of point (25) which the Commission uses to establish additional facts increasing the gravity or the duration of the infringement, the Commission will not take such additional facts into account when setting any fine to be imposed on the undertaking which provided this evidence.

B. Procedure

(27) An undertaking wishing to benefit from a reduction of a fine must make a formal application to the Commission and it must present it with sufficient evidence of the alleged cartel to qualify for a reduction of a fine in accordance with point (24) of this Notice. Any voluntary submission of evidence to the Commission which the undertaking that submits it wishes to be considered for the beneficial treatment of section III of this Notice must be clearly identified at the time of its submission as being part of a formal application for a reduction of a fine.

(28) If requested, the Directorate General for Competition will provide an acknowledgement of receipt of the undertaking's application for a reduction of a fine and of any subsequent submissions of evidence, confirming the date and, where appropriate, time of each submission. The Commission will not take any position on an application for a reduction of a fine before it has taken a position on any existing applications for conditional immunity from fines in relation to the same alleged cartel.

(29) If the Commission comes to the preliminary conclusion that the evidence submitted by the undertaking constitutes significant added value within the meaning of points (24) and (25), and that the undertaking has met the conditions of points (12) and (27), it will inform the undertaking in writing, no later than the date on which a statement of objections is notified, of its intention to apply a reduction of a fine within a specified band as provided in point (26). The Commission will also, within the same time frame, inform the undertaking in writing if it comes to the preliminary conclusion that the undertaking does not qualify for a reduction of a fine. The Commission may disregard any application for a reduction of fines on the grounds that it has been submitted after the statement of objections has been issued.

(30) The Commission will evaluate the final position of each undertaking which filed an application for a reduction of a fine at the end of the administrative procedure in any decision adopted. The Commission will determine in any such final decision:
(a) whether the evidence provided by an undertaking represented significant added value with respect to the evidence in the Commission's possession at that same time;
(b) whether the conditions set out in points (12)(a) to (12)(c) above have been met;
(c) the exact level of reduction an undertaking will benefit from within the bands specified in point (26).

If the Commission finds that the undertaking has not met the conditions set out in point (12), the undertaking will not benefit from any favourable treatment under this Notice.

IV. Corporate Statements Made to Qualify under this Notice

(31) A corporate statement is a voluntary presentation by or on behalf of an undertaking to the

Commission of the undertaking's knowledge of a cartel and its role therein prepared specially to be submitted under this Notice. Any statement made vis-à-vis the Commission in relation to this notice, forms part of the Commission's file and can thus be used in evidence.

(32) Upon the applicant's request, the Commission may accept that corporate statements be provided orally unless the applicant has already disclosed the content of the corporate statement to third parties. Oral corporate statements will be recorded and transcribed at the Commission's premises. In accordance with Article 19 of Council Regulation (EC) No 1/2003 and Articles 3 and 17 of Commission Regulation (EC) No 773/2004, undertakings making oral corporate statements will be granted the opportunity to check the technical accuracy of the recording, which will be available at the Commission's premises and to correct the substance of their oral statements within a given time limit. Undertakings may waive these rights within the said time-limit, in which case the recording will from that moment on be deemed to have been approved. Following the explicit or implicit approval of the oral statement or the submission of any corrections to it, the undertaking shall listen to the recordings at the Commission's premises and check the accuracy of the transcript within a given time limit. Non-compliance with the last requirement may lead to the loss of any beneficial treatment under this Notice.

(33) Access to corporate statements is only granted to the addressees of a statement of objections, provided that they commit, — together with the legal counsels getting access on their behalf -, not to make any copy by mechanical or electronic means of any information in the corporate statement to which access is being granted and to ensure that the information to be obtained from the corporate statement will solely be used for the purposes mentioned below. Other parties such as complainants will not be granted access to corporate statements. The Commission considers that this specific protection of a corporate statement is not justified as from the moment when the applicant discloses to third parties the content thereof.

(34) In accordance with the Commission Notice on rules for access to the Commission file, access to the file is only granted to the addressees of a statement of objections on the condition that the information thereby obtained may only be used for the purposes of judicial or administrative proceedings for the application of the Union competition rules. Any failure during the proceedings to comply with the provisions of Regulation (EC) No 773/2004 on the use of information obtained through access to the file may be regarded as lack of cooperation within the meaning of points (12) and (27) of this Notice. Under certain circumstances it is subject to penalties to be laid down under national law. Moreover, if any such use is made after the Commission has already adopted a prohibition decision in the proceedings, the Commission may, in addition to applicable penalties under national law, in any legal proceedings before the Union Courts, ask the Court to increase the fine in respect of the responsible undertaking. Should any of the above limitations to the use of information be breached, at any point in time, with the involvement of an outside counsel, the Commission may report the incident to the bar of that counsel, with a view to disciplinary action.

(35) Corporate statements made under the present Notice will only be transmitted to the competition authorities of the Member States pursuant to Article 12 of Regulation No 1/2003, provided that the conditions set out in the Network Notice are met and provided that the level of protection against disclosure awarded by the receiving competition authority is equivalent to the one conferred by the Commission.

(35a) In line with paragraph 26a of the Commission Notice on the co-operation between the Commission and the courts of the EU Member States in the application of Articles 101 and 102 of the Treaty, the Commission will not at any time transmit leniency corporate statements to national courts for use in actions for damages for breaches of those Treaty provisions. This paragraph is without prejudice to the situation referred to in Article 6(7) of Directive 2014/104/EU.

V. General Considerations

(36) The Commission will not take a position on whether or not to grant conditional immunity, or otherwise on whether or not to reward any application, if it becomes apparent that the application concerns infringements covered by the five years limitation period for the imposition of penalties stipulated in Article 25(1)(b) of Regulation 1/2003, as such applications would be devoid of purpose.

(37) From the date of its publication in the Official Journal, this notice replaces the 2002 Commission notice on immunity from fines and reduction of fines in cartel cases for all cases in which no undertaking has contacted the Commission in order to take advantage of the favourable treatment set out in that notice. However, points (31) to (35) of the current notice will be applied from the moment of its publication to all pending and new applications for immunity from fines or reduction of fines.

(38) The Commission is aware that this notice will create legitimate expectations on which undertakings may rely when disclosing the existence of a cartel to the Commission.

(39) In line with the Commission's practice, the fact that an undertaking cooperated with the Commission during its administrative procedure will be indicated in any decision, so as to explain the reason for the immunity or reduction of the fine. The fact that immunity or reduction in respect of fines is granted cannot protect an undertaking from the civil law consequences of its participation in an infringement of Article 81 EC.

(40) The Commission considers that normally public disclosure of documents and written or recorded statements received in the context of this notice would undermine certain public or private interests, for example the protection of the purpose of inspections and investigations, within the meaning of Article 4 of Regulation (EC) No 1049/2001, even after the decision has been taken.